# Place-of-Service Codes for Professional Claim

Listed below are place-of-service codes and descriptions. These codes should be used on professio... service(s) were rendered. Check with individual payers (eg, Medicare, Medicaid, other private in... regarding these codes. If you would like to comment on a code(s) or description(s), please send y...

| Place of Service Code(s) | Place of Service Name | Place of Service Description |
|---|---|---|
| 01 | Pharmacy | A facility or location where drugs and other medically related items and services are sold, dispensed, or otherwise provided directly to patients. (Effective 10/1/05) |
| 02 | Unassigned | N/A |
| 03 | School | A facility whose primary purpose is education. |
| 04 | Homeless Shelter | A facility or location whose primary purpose is to provide temporary housing to homeless individuals (eg, emergency shelters, individual or family shelters). |
| 05 | Indian Health Service Free-Standing Facility | A facility or location, owned and operated by the Indian Health Service, which provides diagnostic, therapeutic (surgical and non-surgical), and rehabilitation services to American Indians and Alaska Natives who do not require hospitalization. |
| 06 | Indian Health Service Provider-Based Facility | A facility or location, owned and operated by the Indian Health Service, which provides diagnostic, therapeutic (surgical and non-surgical), and rehabilitation services rendered by, or under the supervision of, physicians to American Indians and Alaska Natives admitted as inpatients or outpatients. |
| 07 | Tribal 638 Free-Standing Facility | A facility or location owned and operated by a federally recognized American Indian or Alaska Native tribe or tribal organization under a 638 agreement which provides diagnostic, therapeutic (surgical and non-surgical), and rehabilitation services to tribal members who do not require hospitalization. |
| 08 | Tribal 638 Provider-Based Facility | A facility or location owned and operated by a federally recognized American Indian or Alaska Native tribe or tribal organization under a 638 agreement which provides diagnostic, therapeutic (surgical and non-surgical), and rehabilitation services to tribal members admitted as inpatients or outpatients. |
| 09 | Prison-Correctional Facility | A prison, jail, reformatory, work farm, detention center, or any other similar facility maintained by either Federal, State, or local authorities for the purpose of confinement or rehabilitation of adult or juvenile criminal offenders. |
| 10 | Unassigned | N/A |
| 11 | Office | Location, other than a hospital, skilled nursing facility (SNF), military treatment facility, community health center, State or local public health clinic, or intermediate care facility (ICF), where the health professional routinely provides health examinations, diagnosis, and treatment of illness or injury on an ambulatory basis. |
| 12 | Home | Location, other than a hospital or other facility, where the patient receives care in a private residence. |
| 13 | Assisted Living Facility | Congregate residential facility with self-contained living units providing assessment of each resident's needs and on-site support 24 hours a day, 7 days a week, with the capacity to deliver or arrange for services including some health care and other services. |
| 14 | Group Home | A residence, with shared living areas, where clients receive supervision and other services such as social and/or behavioral services, custodial service, and minimal services (eg, medication administration). (Effective 10/1/03) |
| 15 | Mobile Unit | A facility/unit that moves from place-to-place equipped to provide preventive, screening, diagnostic, and/or treatment services. |
| 16 | Temporary Lodging | A short term accommodation such as a hotel, camp ground, hostel, cruise ship or resort where the patient receives care, and which is not identified by any other POS code. |
| 17 | Walk-in Retail Health Clinic | A walk-in health clinic, other than an office, urgent care facility, pharmacy, or independent clinic, which is not described by any other Place of Service code, that is located within a retail operation and provides on an ambulatory basis, preventive and primary care services. (Effective 5/1/10) |
| 18 | Place of Employment—Worksite | A location, not described by any other POS code, owned or operated by a public or private entity where the patient is employed, and where a health professional provides on-going or episodic occupational medical, therapeutic or rehabilitative services to the individual. (This code is available for use effective January 1, 2013 but no later than May 1, 2013) |
| 19 | Unassigned | N/A |
| 20 | Urgent Care Facility | Location, distinct from a hospital emergency department, an office, or a clinic, whose purpose is to diagnose and treat illness or injury for unscheduled, ambulatory patients seeking immediate medical attention. (Effective 1/1/03) |
| 21 | Inpatient Hospital | A facility, other than psychiatric, which primarily provides diagnostic, therapeutic (both surgical and non-surgical), and rehabilitation services by, or under, the supervision of physicians to patients admitted for a variety of medical conditions. |
| 22 | Outpatient Hospital | A portion of a hospital which provides diagnostic, therapeutic (both surgical and non-surgical), and rehabilitation services to sick or injured persons who do not require hospitalization or institutionalization. |
| 23 | Emergency Room—Hospital | A portion of a hospital where emergency diagnosis and treatment of illness or injury is provided. |
| 24 | Ambulatory Surgical Center | A free-standing facility, other than a physician's office, where surgical and diagnostic services are provided on an ambulatory basis. |
| 25 | Birthing Center | A facility, other than a hospital's maternity facilities or a physician's office, which provides a setting for labor, delivery, and immediate postpartum care as well as immediate care of newborn infants. |
| 26 | Military Treatment Facility | A medical facility operated by one or more of the Uniformed Services. Military treatment facility (MTF) also refers to certain former U.S. Public Health Service (USPHS) facilities now designated as Uniformed Service Treatment Facilities (USTF). |
| 27-30 | Unassigned | N/A |

| 31 | Skilled Nursing Facility | A facility that primarily provides inpatient skilled nursing care and related services to patients who require medical, nursing, or rehabilitative services but does not provide the level of care or treatment available in a hospital. |
|----|--------------------------|-----|
| 32 | Nursing Facility | A facility that primarily provides to residents skilled nursing care and related services for the rehabilitation of injured, disabled, or sick persons, or, on a regular basis, health-related care services above the level of custodial care to other than mentally retarded individuals. |
| 33 | Custodial Care Facility | A facility that provides room, board, and other personal assistance services, generally on a long-term basis, and which does not include a medical component. |
| 34 | Hospice | A facility, other than a patient's home, in which palliative and supportive care for terminally ill patients and their families are provided. |
| 35-40 | Unassigned | N/A |
| 41 | Ambulance—Land | A land vehicle specifically designed, equipped and staffed for lifesaving and transporting the sick or injured. |
| 42 | Ambulance—Air or Water | An air or water vehicle specifically designed, equipped, and staffed for lifesaving and transporting the sick or injured. |
| 43-48 | Unassigned | N/A |
| 49 | Independent Clinic | A location, not part of a hospital and not described by any other Place of Service code, that is organized and operated to provide preventive, diagnostic, therapeutic, rehabilitative, or palliative services to outpatients only. (Effective 10/1/03) |
| 50 | Federally Qualified Health Center | A facility located in a medically underserved area that provides Medicare beneficiaries preventive primary medical care under the general direction of a physician. |
| 51 | Inpatient Psychiatric Facility | A facility that provides inpatient psychiatric services for the diagnosis and treatment of mental illness on a 24-hour basis, by or under the supervision of a physician. |
| 52 | Psychiatric Facility— Partial Hospitalization | A facility for the diagnosis and treatment of mental illness that provides a planned therapeutic program for patients who do not require full time hospitalization, but who need broader programs than are possible from outpatient visits to a hospital-based or hospital-affiliated facility. |
| 53 | Community Mental Health Center | A facility that provides the following services: outpatient services, including specialized outpatient services for children, the elderly, individuals who are chronically ill, and residents of the CMHC's community mental health area who have been discharged from inpatient treatment at a mental health facility; 24 hour a day emergency care services; day treatment, other partial hospitalization services, or psychosocial rehabilitation services; screening for patients being considered for admission to State mental health facilities to determine the appropriateness of such admission; and consultation and education services. |
| 54 | Intermediate Care Facility/Mentally Retarded | A facility that primarily provides health-related care and services above the level of custodial care to mentally retarded individuals but does not provide the level of care or treatment available in a hospital or SNF. |
| 55 | Residential Substance Abuse Treatment Facility | A facility which provides treatment for substance (alcohol and drug) abuse to live-in residents who do not require acute medical care. Services include individual and group therapy and counseling, family counseling, laboratory tests, drugs and supplies, psychological testing, and room and board. |
| 56 | Psychiatric Residential Treatment Center | A facility or distinct part of a facility for psychiatric care which provides a total 24-hour therapeutically planned and professionally staffed group living and learning environment. |
| 57 | Non-residential Substance Abuse Treatment Facility | A location that provides treatment for substance (alcohol and drug) abuse on an ambulatory basis. Services include individual and group therapy and counseling, family counseling, laboratory tests, drugs and supplies, and psychological testing. (Effective 10/1/03) |
| 58-59 | Unassigned | N/A |
| 60 | Mass Immunization Center | A location where providers administer pneumococcal pneumonia and influenza virus vaccinations and submit these services as electronic media claims, paper claims, or using the roster billing method. This generally takes place in a mass immunization setting, such as, a public health center, pharmacy, or mall but may include a physician office setting. |
| 61 | Comprehensive Inpatient Rehabilitation Facility | A facility that provides comprehensive rehabilitation services under the supervision of a physician to inpatients with physical disabilities. Services include physical therapy, occupational therapy, speech pathology, social or psychological services, and orthotics and prosthetics services. |
| 62 | Comprehensive Outpatient Rehabilitation Facility | A facility that provides comprehensive rehabilitation services under the supervision of a physician to outpatients with physical disabilities. Services include physical therapy, occupational therapy, and speech pathology services. |
| 63-64 | Unassigned | N/A |
| 65 | End-Stage Renal Disease Treatment Facility | A facility other than a hospital, which provides dialysis treatment, maintenance, and/or training to patients or caregivers on an ambulatory or home-care basis. |
| 66-70 | Unassigned | N/A |
| 71 | Public Health Clinic | A facility maintained by either State or local health departments that provides ambulatory primary medical care under the general direction of a physician. |
| 72 | Rural Health Clinic | A certified facility which is located in a rural medically underserved area that provides ambulatory primary medical care under the general direction of a physician. |
| 73-80 | Unassigned | N/A |
| 81 | Independent Laboratory | A laboratory certified to perform diagnostic and/or clinical tests independent of an institution or a physician's office. |
| 82-98 | Unassigned | N/A |
| 99 | Other Place of Service | Other place of service not identified above. |

current procedural terminology

# *cpt*® 2014

# Standard Edition

Michelle Abraham, MHA, CCS-P
Jay T. Ahlman
Angela J. Boudreau
Judy Connelly
Lia Levreau-Davis, CCP
Biljana Dimovski, BA, CDC
Desiree D. Evans, AAS

Rejina L. Glenn
DeHandro Hayden, BS
Nadia Khalid, BS, RHIA, RMM
Elizabeth Lumakovska, MPA, RHIT
Janette Meggs, RHIA
Marie L. Mindeman, BA, RHIT
Karen E. O'Hara, BS, CCS-P

Mary R. O'Heron, RHIA
Danielle Pavloski, BS, RHIT, CCS-P
Desiree Rozell, MPA
Lianne Stancik, RHIT
Asif A. Syed, MD, MPH
Ada Walker, CCA
Arletrice Watkins, MHA, RHIA

AMA
AMERICAN MEDICAL
ASSOCIATION

Standard ISBN: 978-1-60359-845-3
ISSN: 0276-8283

# Foreword

*Current Procedural Terminology* (CPT®), Fourth Edition, is a listing of descriptive terms and identifying codes for reporting medical services and procedures performed by physicians. The purpose of the terminology is to provide a uniform language that will accurately describe medical, surgical, and diagnostic services, and will thereby provide an effective means for reliable nationwide communication among physicians, patients, and third parties. *CPT 2014* is the most recent revision of a work that first appeared in 1966.

CPT descriptive terms and identifying codes currently serve a wide variety of important functions in the field of medical nomenclature. The CPT code set is useful for administrative management purposes such as claims processing and for the development of guidelines for medical care review. The uniform language is also applicable to medical education and outcomes, health services, and quality research by providing a useful basis for local, regional, and national utilization comparisons. The CPT code set is the most widely accepted nomenclature for the reporting of physician procedures and services under government and private health insurance programs. In 2000, the CPT code set was designated by the Department of Health and Human Services as the national coding standard for physician and other health care professional services and procedures under the Health Insurance Portability and Accountability Act (HIPAA). This means that for all financial and administrative health care transactions sent electronically, the CPT code set will need to be used.

The changes that appear in this revision have been prepared by the CPT Editorial Panel with the assistance of physicians representing all specialties of medicine, and with important contributions from many third-party payers and governmental agencies.

The American Medical Association trusts that this revision will continue the usefulness of its predecessors in identifying, describing, and coding medical, surgical, and diagnostic services.

# Acknowledgments

Publication of the annual CPT codebook represents many challenges and opportunities. From reconciling the many differences of opinion about the best way to describe a procedure, to the last details on placement of a semicolon, many individuals and organizations devote their energies and expertise to the preparation of this revision.

The editorial staff wishes to express sincere thanks to the many national medical specialty societies, health insurance organizations and agencies, and individual physicians and other health professionals who have made contributions.

Thanks are due to Robert A. Musacchio, PhD, Sr VP, American Medical Association; Claudia Bonnell, Blue Cross and Blue Shield Association; Nelly Leon-Chisen, American Hospital Association; Sue Bowman, RHIA, American Health Information Management Association; and Raemarie Jiminez, CPC, American Academy of Professional Coders, for their invaluable assistance in enhancing the CPT code set.

For their assistance in development of the CPT Category II codes:

Ronald A. Gabel, MD
Darryl T. Gray, MD, ScD
Sam J. W. Romeo, MD, MBA

We recognize the following people for efforts in working with the Physician Consortium for Performance Improvement® (PCPI™) and other quality measurement organizations:

Mark Antman, DDS, MBA
Katherine Ast, MSW, LCSW
Kendra Hanley, MS
Karen S. Kmetik, PhD
Marjorie C. Rallins, DPM
Kimberly Smuk, BS, RHIA
Beth Tapper, MA
Samantha Tierney, MPH

# AMA CPT Editorial Panel

*Chair*
Peter A. Hollmann, MD*

*Vice-Chair*
Kenneth P. Brin, MD, PhD, FACC*

Albert E. Bothe, Jr, MD, FACS
Boyd R. Buser, DO, FACOFP
Leslie F. Davidson, PhD, OTR/L
Frank J. Dubeck, Jr, MD, FACP*
Richard Duszak, Jr, MD, FACR*
David A. Ellington, MD
Ronald A. Gabel, MD
Edith Hambrick, MD, JD
M. Bradford Henley, MD, MBA
Christopher L. Jagmin, MD
Katharine Krol, MD
Victor L. Lewis, MD
Julia M. Pillsbury, DO, FAAO, FACOP
Antonio E. Puente, PhD
Mark S. Synovec, MD*

*Secretary*
Marie L. Mindeman, BA, RHIT

*Member of the CPT Executive Committee
†New Panel Member
‡New Advisors

# AMA CPT Advisory Committee

*American Academy of Allergy, Asthma and Immunology*
Donald W. Aaronson, MD, JD, MPH

*American Academy of Child & Adolescent Psychiatry*
David I. Berland, MD
Benjamin N. Shain, MD, PhD

*American Academy of Dermatology*
Alexander Miller, MD
Ann F. Haas, MD‡

*American Academy of Disability Evaluating Physicians*
Douglas W. Martin, MD, FAADEP, FACOEM
James B. Talmage, MD‡

*American Academy of Family Physicians*
Robert J. Carr, Jr, MD
Gretchen M. Dickson, MD, MBA

*American Academy of Neurology*
Marc R. Nuwer, MD, PhD, FAAN, FACP
Bruce H. Cohen, MD, FAAN

*American Academy of Ophthalmology*
Michael X. Repka, MD, MBA

*American Academy of Orthopaedic Surgeons*
Richard J. Friedman, MD, FACSC
M. Bradford Henley, MD, MBA‡

*American Academy of Otolaryngic Allergy*
Paul T. Fass, MD, FACS
Bryan D. Leatherman, MD

*American Academy of Otolaryngology Head and Neck Surgery*
Bradley F. Marple, MD, FAAOA
Brendan C. Stack, Jr, MD, FACS, FACE
Lawrence M. Simon, MD, FAAP‡

*American Academy of Pain Medicine*
Eduardo M. Fraifeld, MD

*American Academy of Pediatrics*
Richard A. Molteni, MD
Joel F. Bradley, Jr, MD, FAAP‡
Sanjeev Y. Tuli, MD, MEd, FAAP

*American Academy of Physical Medicine and Rehabilitation*
Francis P. Lagattuta, MD
Jeffrey S. Brault, DO

*American Academy of Sleep Medicine*
Amy J. Aronsky, DO, FAASM, FCCP, CBSM
William C. Sherrill, Jr, MD

*American Association for Clinical Chemistry*
Robert L. Murray, JD, PhD
Shannon Haymond, PhD, DABCC‡

*American Association for Thoracic Surgery*
Kirk R. Kanter, MD
Stephen J. Lahey, MD

*American Association of Clinical Endocrinologists*
Eric A. Orzeck, MD, FACP, FACE

*American Association of Neurological Surgeons*
R. Patrick Jacob, MD
Henry H. Woo, MD, FAANS‡

*American Association of Neuromuscular and Electrodiagnostic Medicine*
Andrea J. Boon, MD

*American Clinical Neurophysiology Society*
Marc R. Nuwer, MD, PhD, FAAN, FACP
Ronald G. Emerson, MD‡

*American College of Allergy, Asthma and Immunology*
Gary N. Gross, MD

*American College of Cardiology*
Robert N. Piana, MD, FACC
Patricio A. Frais, MD, FACC

*American College of Chest Physicians*
Steve G. Peters, MD
Michael E. Nelson, MD, FCCP

*American College of Emergency Physicians*
Kenneth L. DeHart, MD, FACEP
Jacob Mark J. Meredith, III, MD, MMM, FACEP‡

*American College of Gastroenterology*
Daniel C. DeMarco, MD, FACG

*American College of Medical Genetics and Genomics*
David B. Flannery, MD

*American College of Medical Quality*
Joel Grossman, MD

*American College of Mohs Surgery*
David B. Pharis, MD, PC

*American College of Nuclear Medicine*
Scott C. Bartley, MD

*American College of Occupational and Environmental Medicine*
Lee S. Glass, MD, JD

*American College of Physicians*
R. Scott Hanson, MD, MPH
Jeannine Z. Engel, MD, FACP

*American College of Radiation Oncology*
Andy W. Su, MD
Paul E. Wallner, DO, FACR, FAOCR, FASTRO, FACRO

*American College of Radiology*
Daniel Picus, MD, FACR, RCC
Timothy A. Crummy, MD, RCC‡

*American College of Rheumatology*
Gerald M. Eisenberg, MD, FACP, FACR
Robert J. Lloyd, MD, FACR

*American College of Surgeons*
Linda M. Barney, MD, FACS
Mark T. Savarise, MD, FACS

*American Congress of Obstetricians and Gynecologists*
Jordan G. Pritzker, MD, MBA, FACOG
Jon K. Hathaway, MD, PhD

*American Dental Association*
Anthony M. Spina, DDS, MD
Joshua E. Everts, DDS, MD‡

*American Gastroenterological Association*
Joel V. Brill, MD, AGAF, FASGE, FACG, CHCQM

*American Geriatric Society*
Robert A. Zorowitz, MD, MBA, FACP, AGSF, CMD

*American Institute of Ultrasound in Medicine*
Harvey L. Nisenbaum, MD

*American Medical Directors Association*
Dennis L. Stone, MD, MBA

*American Orthopaedic Association*
Blair C. Filler, MD

*American Osteopathic Association*
Judith A. O'Connell, DO, FAAO
Robert B. Goldberg, DO

*American Psychiatric Association*
David K. Nace, MD
Jeremy S. Musher, MD, DFAPA

*American Roentgen Ray Society*
Mark D. Alson, MD, FACR, RCC

*American Society for Aesthetic Plastic Surgery, Inc.*
Paul R. Weiss, MD

*American Society for Clinical Pathology*
Lee H. Hilborne, MD, MPH, FASCP

*American Society for Dermatologic Surgery*
Murad Alam, MD
Jeremy S. Bordeaux, MD, MPH

*American Society for Gastrointestinal Endoscopy*
Glenn D. Littenberg, MD, FACP
Christopher Y. Kim, MD, MBA, FACG, FASGE, AGAF, FACP

*American Society for Radiation Oncology*
David C. Beyer, MD, FACR, FACRO, FASTRO

*American Society for Reproductive Medicine*
John T. Queenan, Jr, MD, FACOG
Drew V. Moffitt, MD‡

*American Society for Surgery of the Hand*
Daniel J. Nagle, MD
Leo S. Benson, MD‡

*American Society of Anesthesiologists*
Peter A. Goldzweig, DO
Kevin E. Vorenkamp, MD‡

*American Society of Cataract and Refractive Surgery*
Stephen S. Lane, MD

*American Society of Clinical Oncology*
Christian A. Thomas, MD‡

*American Society of Colon and Rectal Surgeons*
James I. Merlino, MD
Stephen M. Sentovich, MD, MBA, FCS, FASCRS‡
William J. Harb, MD, FACS‡

*American Society of Cytopathology*
Carol A. Filomena, MD

*American Society of General Surgeons*
Charles Drueck, III, MD, FACS

*American Society of Hematology*
Samuel M. Silver, MD, PhD, FACP, FAHA
Robert Weinstein, MD‡

*American Society of Neuroradiology*
Raymond K. Tu, MD
Jacqueline A. Bello, MD, FACR

*American Society of Ophthalmic Plastic and Reconstructive Surgery*
L. Neal Freeman, MD, MBA, CCS-P, FACS

*American Society of Plastic Surgeons*
Raymond V. Janevicius, MD
Deborah S. Bash, MD

*American Thoracic Society*
Stephen P. Hoffmann, MD

*American Urological Association*
Jeffrey A. Dann, MD, MBA
Ronald P. Kaufman, Jr, MD, FACS

*Association of University Radiologists*
Robert K. Zeman, MD, FACR

*College of American Pathologists*
Michael D. McEachin, MD

*Congress of Neurological Surgeons*
Joseph S. Cheng, MD

*Heart Rhythm Society*
Amit J. Shanker, MD
Oussama M. Wazni, MD‡

*Infectious Disease Society of America*
Steven K. Schmitt, MD

*International Spinal Intervention Society*
Scott I. Horn, DO
Claire Tibiletti, MD

*North American Spine Society*
William Mitchell, MD
David R. O'Brien, Jr, MD

*Radiological Society of North America*
Timothy A. Crummy, MD

*Renal Physicians Association*
Chester A. Amedia, Jr, MD, FACP
Richard J. Hamburger, MD
Timothy A. Pflederer, MD‡

*Society for Investigative Dermatology*
Stephen P. Stone, MD

*Society for Vascular Surgery*
Sean P. Roddy, MD, FACS

*Society of American Gastrointestinal Endoscopic Surgeons*
Michael B. Edye, MD
John S. Roth, MD, FACS‡
Kevin E. Wasco, MD, FACS‡

*Society of Cardiovascular Angiography and Interventions*
Arthur C. Lee, MD, FSCAI‡

*Society of Critical Care Medicine*
George A. Sample, MD, FCCP

*Society of Interventional Radiology*
Donald F. Denny, Jr, MD
Timothy L. Swan, MD

*Society of Nuclear Medicine and Molecular Imaging*
Gary L. Dillehay, MD, FACNP, FACR

*Society of Thoracic Surgeons*
Francis C. Nichols, III, MD
Jeffrey P. Jacobs, MD, FACS, FACC, FCCP

*The Endocrine Society*
Richard A. Guthrie, MD
Allan R. Glass, MD‡

*The Triological Society*
Richard W. Waguespack, MD, FACS

*United States and Canadian Academy of Pathology*
David S. Wilkinson, MD, PhD

# AMA Health Care Professionals Advisory Committee (HCPAC)

Peter A. Hollmann, MD*, Co-Chair
*AMA CPT Editorial Panel*
Antonio E. Puente, PhD, Co-Chair
*AMA CPT Editorial Panel*

*Academy of Nutrition and Dietetics*
Keith-Thomas Ayoob, EdD, RN, FADA, CSP
Jessie M. Pavlianc, MS, RD, CSR, LD‡

*American Academy of Audiology*
Brad A. Stach, PhD
Paul M. Pessis, AuD

*American Academy of Physician Assistants*
Patrick J. Cafferty, MPAS, PA-C‡

*American Association of Naturopathic Physicians*
Wendell B. Milliman, ND
Eva Miller, ND

*American Association for Respiratory Care*
Susan Rinaldo-Gallo, MEd, RRT, FAARC

*American Chiropractic Association*
Craig S. Little, DC, FACO
Leo Bronston DC, MappSC‡

*American Massage Therapy Association*
Susan B. Rosen, LPM

*American Nurses Association*
Julie E. Chicoine, JD, RN, CPC

*American Occupational Therapy Association*
Mary Jo McGuire, MS, OTR/L, FAOTA‡
Deborah Y. Slater, MS, OT/L, FAOTA‡

*American Optometric Association*
Douglas C. Morrow, OD
Rebecca H. Wartman, OD

*American Physical Therapy Association*
Helene M. Fearon, PT
Kathleen M. Picard, PT‡

*American Podiatric Medical Association*
Phillip E. Ward, DPM
Ira H. Kraus, DPM

*American Psychological Association*
Neil H. Pliskin, PhD

*American Speech Hearing Association*
R. Wayne Holland, EdD, CCC-SLP
Stuart G. Trembath, MA, CCC-A

*National Athletic Trainers' Association*
Karen D. Fennell, MS, ATC, LAT
Clark E. Simpson, MBA, MEd, ATC‡

*National Association of Social Workers*
Mirean F. Coleman, LICSW

*National Society of Genetic Counselors*
Leslie H. Cohen, MS, CGC

*Pharmacist Services Technical Advisory Coalition*
Daniel E. Buffington, PharmD, MBA

# Contents

# Contents

# Introduction

▶*Current Procedural Terminology* (CPT®), Fourth Edition, is a set of codes, descriptions, and guidelines intended to describe procedures and services performed by physicians and other health care professionals, or entities. Each procedure or service is identified with a five-digit code. The use of CPT codes simplifies the reporting of procedures and services. In the CPT code set, the term "procedure" is used to describe services, including diagnostic tests.

Inclusion of a descriptor and its associated five-digit code number in the CPT Category I code set is based on whether the procedure or service is consistent with contemporary medical practice and is performed by many practitioners in clinical practice in multiple locations. Inclusion in the CPT code set does not represent endorsement by the American Medical Association (AMA) of any particular diagnostic or therapeutic procedure or service. Inclusion or exclusion of a procedure or service does not imply any health insurance coverage or reimbursement policy.◀

The CPT code set is published annually in the late summer or early fall as both electronic data files and books. The release of CPT data files on the Internet typically precedes the book by several weeks. In any case, January 1 is the effective date for use of the update of the CPT code set. The interval between the release of the update and the effective date is considered the implementation period and is intended to allow physicians and other providers, payers, and vendors to incorporate CPT changes into their systems. The exceptions to this schedule of release and effective dates are CPT Category III and vaccine product codes, which are released twice a year on January 1 or July 1 with effective dates for use six months later, and CPT Category II codes. Changes to the CPT code set are meant to be applied prospectively from the effective date.

The main body of the Category I section is listed in six sections. Each section is divided into subsections with anatomic, procedural, condition, or descriptor subheadings. The procedures and services with their identifying codes are presented in numeric order with one exception—the entire **Evaluation and Management** section (99201-99499) appears at the beginning of the listed procedures. These items are used by most physicians in reporting a significant portion of their services.

## Section Numbers and Their Sequences

Evaluation and Management . . . . . . . . . . . . . 99201-99499
Anesthesiology . . . . . . . . . . . . . 00100-01999, 99100-99140
Surgery . . . . . . . . . . . . . . . . . . . . . . . . . . . . . 10021-69990
Radiology (Including Nuclear Medicine
     and Diagnostic Ultrasound) . . . . . . . . 70010-79999
Pathology and Laboratory . . . . . . . . . . . . . . 80047-89398
Medicine (except
     Anesthesiology) . . . . . . . 90281-99199, 99500-99607

The first and last code numbers and the subsection name of the items appear at the top margin of most pages (eg,

"11010-11306 Surgery/Integumentary System"). The continuous pagination of the CPT codebook is found on the lower margin of each page along with explanation of any code symbols that are found on that page.

## Instructions for Use of the CPT Codebook

Select the name of the procedure or service that accurately identifies the service performed. Do not select a CPT code that merely approximates the service provided. If no such specific code exists, then report the service using the appropriate unlisted procedure or service code. In surgery, it may be an operation; in medicine, a diagnostic or therapeutic procedure; in radiology, a radiograph. Other additional procedures performed or pertinent special services are also listed. When necessary, any modifying or extenuating circumstances are added. Any service or procedure should be adequately documented in the medical record.

▶It is equally important to recognize that as techniques in medicine and surgery have evolved, new types of services, including minimally invasive surgery, as well as endovascular, percutaneous, and endoscopic interventions have challenged the traditional distinction of Surgery vs Medicine. Thus, the listing of a service or procedure in a specific section of this book should not be interpreted as strictly classifying the service or procedure as "surgery" or "not surgery" for insurance or other purposes. The placement of a given service in a specific section of the book may reflect historical or other considerations (eg, placement of the percutaneous peripheral vascular endovascular interventions in the Surgery/Cardiovascular System section, while the percutaneous coronary interventions appear in the Medicine/Cardiovascular section).

When advanced practice nurses and physician assistants are working with physicians, they are considered as working in the exact same specialty and exact same subspecialties as the physician. A "physician or other qualified health care professional" is an individual who is qualified by education, training, licensure/regulation (when applicable), and facility privileging (when applicable) who performs a professional service within his/her scope of practice and independently reports that professional service. These professionals are distinct from "clinical staff." A clinical staff member is a person who works under the supervision of a physician or other qualified health care professional and who is allowed by law, regulation, and facility policy to perform or assist in the performance of a specified professional service, but who does not individually report that professional service. Other policies may also affect who may report specific services.◀

Throughout the CPT code set the use of terms such as "physician," "qualified health care professional," or "individual" is not intended to indicate that other entities may not report the service. In selected instances, specific instructions may define a service as limited to professionals or limited to other entities (eg, hospital or home health agency).

Instructions, typically included as parenthetical notes with selected codes, indicate that a code should not be reported with another code or codes. These instructions are intended to prevent errors of significant probability and are not all inclusive. For example, the code with such instructions may be a component of another code and therefore it would be incorrect to report both codes even when the component service is performed. These instructions are not intended as a listing of all possible code combinations that should not be reported, nor do they indicate all possible code combinations that are appropriately reported. When reporting codes for services provided, it is important to assure the accuracy and quality of coding through verification of the intent of the code by use of the related guidelines, parenthetical instructions, and coding resources, including *CPT Assistant* and other publications resulting from collaborative efforts of the American Medical Association with the medical specialty societies (ie, *Clinical Examples in Radiology*).

## Format of the Terminology

The CPT code set has been developed as stand-alone descriptions of medical procedures. However, some of the procedures in the CPT codebook are not printed in their entirety but refer back to a common portion of the procedure listed in a preceding entry. This is evident when an entry is followed by one or more indentations. This is done in an effort to conserve space.

### Example

**25100**    Arthrotomy, wrist joint; with biopsy

**25105**        with synovectomy

Note that the common part of code 25100 (the part before the semicolon) should also be considered part of code 25105. Therefore, the full procedure represented by code 25105 should read:

**25105**    Arthrotomy, wrist joint; with synovectomy

## Requests to Update the CPT Nomenclature

▶The effectiveness of the CPT nomenclature depends on constant updating to reflect changes in medical practice. This can only be accomplished through the interest and timely suggestions of practicing physicians and other quali-fied health care professionals, specialty/professional societies, state medical associations, organizations, agencies, individual users of the CPT code set, and other stakeholders. Accordingly, the AMA welcomes correspondence, inquiries, and suggestions concerning CPT coding and nomenclature for old and new procedures and services, as well as any mat-ters relating to the CPT code set.

For information on submission of an application to add, delete, or revise codes contained in the CPT code set, please see www.ama-assn.org/go/cpt-processfaq or contact:◀

CPT Editorial Research & Development
American Medical Association
330 North Wabash Avenue
Suite 39300
Chicago IL 60611-5885

▶Code change applications are available at the AMA's CPT Web site: www.ama-assn.org/go/cpt-application.

All proposed changes to the CPT code set will be considered by the CPT Editorial Panel, in consultation with medical specialty societies as represented by the CPT Advisory Committee, other health care professional societies as repre-sented by the Health Care Professionals Advisory Committee (HCPAC), and other interested parties.◀

## Application Submission Requirements

▶All complete CPT code change applications are reviewed and evaluated by the CPT staff, the CPT/HCPAC Advisory Committee, and the CPT Editorial Panel. Strict confor-mance with the following is required for review of a code change application:

- Submission of a complete application, including all neces-sary supporting documents

- Adherence to all posted deadlines

- Cooperation with requests from the CPT staff and/or Editorial Panel members for clarification and information; *and*

- Compliance with CPT Lobbying Policy◀

## General Criteria for Category I and Category III Codes

▶All Category I or Category III code change applications must satisfy each of the following criteria:

- The proposed descriptor is unique, well-defined, and describes a procedure or service that is clearly identified and distinguished from existing procedures and services already in the CPT code set.

- The descriptor structure, guidelines, and instructions are consistent with the current CPT Editorial Panel standards for maintenance of the code set.

- The proposed descriptor for the procedure or service is neither a fragmentation of an existing procedure or service nor currently reportable as a complete service by one or more existing codes (with the exclusion of unlisted codes). However, procedures and services frequently performed together may require new or revised codes.

- The structure and content of the proposed code descriptor accurately reflects the procedure or service as typically per-formed. If always or frequently performed with one or more other procedures or services, the descriptor structure and content will reflect the typical combination or com-plete procedure or service.

- The descriptor for the procedure or service is not proposed as a means to report extraordinary circumstances related to the performance of a procedure or service already described in the CPT code set; *and*

- The procedure or service satisfies the category-specific cri-teria set forth below.◀

## Category-Specific Requirements

### Category I Criteria

▶A proposal for a new or revised Category I code must satisfy all of the following criteria:

- All devices and drugs necessary for performance of the procedure or service have received FDA clearance or approval when such is required for performance of the procedure or service.

- The procedure or service is performed by many physicians or other qualified health care professionals across the United States.

- The procedure or service is performed with frequency consistent with the intended clinical use (ie, a service for a common condition should have high volume, whereas a service commonly performed for a rare condition may have low volume).

- The procedure or service is consistent with current medical practice.

- The clinical efficacy of the procedure or service is documented in literature that meets the requirements set forth in the CPT code change application.◀

### Category III Criteria

▶The following **criteria** are used by the CPT/HCPAC Advisory Committee and the CPT Editorial Panel for evaluating Category III code **applications**:

- The procedure or service is currently or recently performed in humans; **and**

At least one of the following additional criteria has been met:

- The application is supported by at least one CPT or HCPAC advisor representing practitioners who would use this procedure or service; **or**

- The actual or potential clinical efficacy of the specific procedure or service is supported by peer reviewed literature, which is available in English for examination by the CPT Editorial Panel; **or**

- There is (a) at least one Institutional Review Board–approved protocol of a study of the procedure or service being performed; (b) a description of a current and ongoing United States trial outlining the efficacy of the procedure or service; or (c) other evidence of evolving clinical utilization.◀

## Guidelines

Specific guidelines are presented at the beginning of each of the sections. These guidelines define items that are necessary to appropriately interpret and report the procedures and services contained in that section. For example, in the **Medicine** section, specific instructions are provided for handling unlisted services or procedures, special reports, and supplies and materials provided. Guidelines also provide explanations regarding terms that apply only to a particular section. For instance, **Radiology Guidelines** provide a definition of the unique term, "radiological supervision and interpretation." While in **Anesthesia**, a discussion of reporting time is included.

## Add-on Codes

Some of the listed procedures are commonly carried out in addition to the primary procedure performed. These additional or supplemental procedures are designated as add-on codes with the ✚ symbol and they are listed in **Appendix D** of the CPT codebook. Add-on codes in CPT 2014 can be readily identified by specific descriptor nomenclature that includes phrases such as "each additional" or "(List separately in addition to primary procedure)."

The add-on code concept in *CPT 2014* applies only to add-on procedures or services performed by the same physician. Add-on codes describe additional intra-service work associated with the primary procedure, eg, additional digit(s), lesion(s), neurorrhaphy(s), vertebral segment(s), tendon(s), joint(s).

Add-on codes are always performed in addition to the primary service or procedure and must never be reported as a stand-alone code. All add-on codes found in the CPT codebook are exempt from the multiple procedure concept (see the modifier 51 definition in **Appendix A**).

## Modifiers

A modifier provides the means to report or indicate that a service or procedure that has been performed has been altered by some specific circumstance but not changed in its definition or code. Modifiers also enable health care professionals to effectively respond to payment policy requirements established by other entities. The judicious application of modifiers obviates the necessity for separate procedure listings that may describe the modifying circumstance. Modifiers may be used to indicate to the recipient of a report that:

- A service or procedure had both a professional and technical component.

- A service or procedure was performed by more than one physician or other health care professional and/or in more than one location.

- A service or procedure was increased or reduced.

- Only part of a service was performed.

- An adjunctive service was performed.

- A bilateral procedure was performed.

- A service or procedure was provided more than once.

- Unusual events occurred.

*Example*

A physician providing diagnostic or therapeutic radiology services, ultrasound, or nuclear medicine services in a hospital would add modifier 26 to report the professional component.

73090 with modifier 26 = Professional component only for an X-ray of the forearm

*Example*

Two surgeons may be required to manage a specific surgical problem. When two surgeons work together as primary surgeons performing distinct part(s) of a procedure, each surgeon should report his/her distinct operative work by adding modifier 62 to the procedure code and any associated code(s)

for that procedure as long as both surgeons continue to work together as primary surgeons. Each surgeon should report the co-surgery once using the same procedure code. Modifier 62 would be applicable. For instance, a neurological surgeon and an otolaryngologist are working as co-surgeons in performing transphenoidal excision of a pituitary neoplasm.

The first surgeon would report:

61548 62 = Hypophysectomy or excision of pituitary tumor, transnasal or transseptal approach, nonstereotactic + two surgeons modifier

**and** the second surgeon would report:

61548 62 = Hypophysectomy or excision of pituitary tumor, transnasal or transseptal approach, nonstereotactic + two surgeons modifier

If additional procedure(s) (including add-on procedure[s]) are performed during the same surgical session, separate code(s) may also be reported with modifier 62 added. It should be noted that if a co-surgeon acts as an assistant in the performance of additional procedure(s) during the same surgical session, those services may be reported using separate procedure code(s) with modifier 80 or modifier 82 added, as appropriate. A complete listing of modifiers is found in **Appendix A.**

## Place of Service and Facility Reporting

Some codes have specified places of service (eg, evaluation and management codes are specific to a setting). Other services and procedures may have instructions specific to the place of service (eg, therapeutic, prophylactic, and diagnostic injections and infusions). The CPT code set is designated for reporting physician and qualified health care professional services. It is also the designated code set for reporting services provided by organizations or facilities (eg, hospitals) in specific circumstances. Throughout the CPT code set, the use of terms such as "physician," "qualified health care professional," or "individual" is not intended to indicate that other entities may not report the service. In selected instances, specific instructions may define a service as limited to professionals or limited to other entities (eg, hospital or home health agency). The CPT code set uses the term "facility" to describe such providers and the term "nonfacility" to describe services settings or circumstances in which no facility reporting may occur. Services provided in the home by an agency are facility services. Services provided in the home by a physician or qualified health care professional who is not a representative of the agency are nonfacility services.

## Unlisted Procedure or Service

It is recognized that there may be services or procedures performed by physicians or other qualified health care professionals that are not found in the CPT code set. Therefore, a number of specific code numbers have been designated for reporting unlisted procedures. When an unlisted procedure number is used, the service or procedure should be described (see specific section guidelines). Each of these unlisted procedural code numbers (with the appropriate accompanying topical entry) relates to a specific section of the book and is presented in the guidelines of that section.

In some cases alternative coding and procedural nomenclature as contained in other code sets may allow appropriate reporting of a more specific code. CPT references to use an unlisted procedure code do not preclude the reporting of an appropriate code that may be found in other code sets.

## Results, Testing, Interpretation, and Report

Results are the technical component of a service. Testing leads to results; results lead to interpretation. Reports are the work product of the interpretation of test results. Certain procedures or services described in CPT involve a technical component (eg, tests) which produce "results" (eg, data, images, slides). For clinical use, some of these results require interpretation. Some CPT descriptors specifically require interpretation and reporting to report that code.

## Special Report

A service that is rarely provided, unusual, variable, or new may require a special report. Pertinent information should include an adequate definition or description of the nature, extent, and need for the procedure and the time, effort, and equipment necessary to provide the service.

## Time

The CPT code set contains many codes with a time basis for code selection. The following standards shall apply to time measurement, unless there are code or code-range–specific instructions in guidelines, parenthetical instructions, or code descriptors to the contrary. Time is the face-to-face time with the patient. Phrases such as "interpretation and report" in the code descriptor are not intended to indicate in all cases that report writing is part of the reported time. A unit of time is attained when the mid-point is passed. For example, an hour is attained when 31 minutes have elapsed (more than midway between zero and sixty minutes). A second hour is attained when a total of 91 minutes have elapsed. When codes are ranked in sequential typical times and the actual time is between two typical times, the code with the typical time closest to the actual time is used. See also the **Evaluation and Management (E/M) Services Guidelines**. When another service is performed concurrently with a time-based service, the time associated with the concurrent service should not be included in the time used for reporting the time-based service. Some services measured in units other than days extend across calendar dates. When this occurs a continuous service does not reset and create a first hour. However, any disruption in the service does create a new initial service. For example, if intravenous hydration (96360, 96361) is given from 11 PM to 2 AM, 96360 would be reported once and 96361 twice. For facility reporting on a single date of service or for continuous services that last beyond midnight (ie, over a range of dates), report the total units of time provided continuously.

## Code Symbols

A summary listing of additions, deletions, and revisions applicable to the CPT codebook is found in **Appendix B.** New procedure numbers added to the CPT codebook are identified throughout the text with the symbol ● placed before the code number. In instances where a code revision has resulted in a substantially altered procedure descriptor, the symbol ▲ is placed before the code number. The symbols ► ◄ are used to indicate new and revised text other than the procedure descriptors. These symbols indicate CPT Editorial Panel actions. The symbol ○ is used to indicate reinstated/recycled code. The AMA reserves the right to correct typographical errors and make stylistic improvements.

CPT add-on codes are annotated by the symbol ✚ and are listed in **Appendix D.** The symbol ⊘ is used to identify codes that are exempt from the use of modifier 51 but have not been designated as CPT add-on procedures or services. A list of codes exempt from modifier 51 usage is included in **Appendix E.** The symbol ⊙ is used to identify codes that include moderate sedation (see **Appendix G**). The symbol ✗ is used to identify codes for vaccines that are pending FDA approval (see **Appendix K**). The symbol # is used to identify codes that are listed out of numerical sequence (see **Appendix N**).

Resequenced codes that are not placed numerically are identified with the # symbol, and a reference placed numerically (eg, Code is out of numerical sequence. See…) as a navigational alert to direct the user to the location of the out-of-sequence code (see **Appendix N**). Resequencing is utilized to allow placement of related concepts in appropriate locations within the families of codes regardless of the availability of numbers for sequential numerical placement.

## Alphabetical Reference Index

This codebook features an expanded alphabetical index that includes listings by procedure and anatomic site. Procedures and services commonly known by their eponyms or other designations are also included.

## CPT 2014 in Electronic Formats

CPT 2014 procedure codes and descriptions are also available as data file on CD-ROM or as downloadable data file. The CPT data file is available in ASCII and EBCDIC formats and provides a convenient way to import the 2014 CPT codes and descriptions into existing documentation or into any billing and claims reporting software that accepts a text (.TXT) file format. The data file contains the complete official AMA CPT guidelines, descriptor package, and new descriptors for consumers and clinicians. For more information call 800 621-8335 or visit **amastore.com**.

Subscriptions to *CPT Assistant* and *Clinical Examples in Radiology* can be purchased from AMA's Unified Service Center at 800 621-8335. Individual back issues are available for purchase by calling 800 621-8335 or at **amastore.com**.

*CPT Assistant* and *Clinical Examples in Radiology* are now online! Based on the best-selling hard copy newsletters, *CPT Assistant Online* and *Clinical Examples in Radiology Online* put the content medical coding professionals rely on daily in a more user-friendly format. Benefits exclusive to the online versions include:

- Monthly (*CPT Assistant*) and quarterly (*Clinical Examples in Radiology*) updates! The home screen notifies you when a new issue is available and you can review the latest issue in its entirety.

- Unlimited access to every archived issue and article dating back to when the newsletter first published.

- A historical CPT code list that references when a code was added, deleted, and/or revised since 1990.

- Simple search capabilities, including intuitive menus and a cumulative index of article titles.

- Anatomical illustrations, charts, and graphs for quick reference.

For more information call 800 621-8335 or visit **amacodingonline.com**.

Current and past editions *of CPT Changes: An Insider's View* can be purchased by calling the AMA's Unified Service Center at 800 621-8335 or visiting **amastore.com**.

In addition, *CPT Changes: An Insider's View* is now available online. Instantly access current CPT code changes and historical changes dating back to 2000. This invaluable online library provides you with an easy and efficient way to search every edition of *CPT Changes: An Insider's View* for the official interpretation and rationale behind every code and guideline change. For more information call 800 621-8335 or visit **amacodingonline.com**.

# Illustrated Anatomical and Procedural Review

It is essential that coders have a thorough understanding of medical terminology and anatomy to code accurately. The following section reviewing the basics of vocabulary and anatomy can be used as a quick reference to help you with your coding. It is not intended as a replacement for up-to-date medical dictionaries and anatomy texts, which are essential tools for accurate coding.

## Prefixes, Suffixes, and Roots

Although medical terminology may seem complex, many medical terms can be broken into component parts, which makes them easier to understand. Many of these terms are derived from Latin or Greek words, but some include the names of physicians.

Prefixes are word parts that appear at the beginning of a word and modify its meaning; suffixes are found at the end of words. By learning what various prefixes and suffixes mean, it is possible to decipher the meaning of a word quickly. The following lists are a quick reference for some common prefixes and suffixes.

## Numbers

| Prefix | Meaning | Example |
| --- | --- | --- |
| mono-, uni- | one | monocyte, unilateral |
| bi- | two | bilateral |
| tri- | three | triad |
| quadr- | four | quadriplegia |
| hex-, sex- | six | hexose |
| diplo- | double | diplopia |

## Surgical Procedures

| Suffix | Meaning | Example |
| --- | --- | --- |
| -centesis | puncture a cavity to remove fluid | amniocentesis |
| -ectomy | surgical removal (excision) | appendectomy |
| -ostomy | a new permanent opening | colostomy |
| -otomy | cutting into (incision) | tracheotomy |
| -orrhaphy | surgical repair/suture | herniorrhaphy |
| -opexy | surgical fixation | nephropexy |
| -oplasty | surgical repair | rhinoplasty |
| -otripsy | crushing, destroying | lithotripsy |

## Conditions

| Prefix | Meaning | Example |
| --- | --- | --- |
| ambi- | both | ambidextrous |
| aniso- | unequal | anisocoria |
| dys- | bad, painful, difficult | dysphoria |
| eu- | good, normal | euthanasia |
| hetero- | different | heterogeneous |
| homo- | same | homogeneous |
| hyper- | excessive, above | hypergastric |
| hypo- | deficient, below | hypogastric |
| iso- | equal, same | isotonic |
| mal- | bad, poor | malaise |
| megalo- | large | megalocardia |

| Suffix | Meaning | Example |
| --- | --- | --- |
| -algia | pain | neuralgia |
| -asthenia | weakness | myasthenia |
| -emia | blood | anemia |
| -iasis | condition of | amebiasis |
| -itis | inflammation | appendicitis |
| -lysis | destruction, break down | hemolysis |
| -lytic | destroy, break down | hemolytic |
| -oid | like | lipoid |
| -oma | tumor | carcinoma |
| -opathy | disease of | arthropathy |
| -orrhagia | hemorrhage | menorrhagia |
| -orrhea | flow or discharge | amenorrhea |
| -osis | abnormal condition of | tuberculosis |
| -paresis | weakness | hemiparesis |
| -plasia | growth | hyperplasia |
| -plegia | paralysis | paraplegia |
| -pnea | breathing | apnea |

## Directions and Positions

| Prefix | Meaning | Example |
|--------|---------|---------|
| ab- | away from | abduction |
| ad- | toward | adduction |
| ecto, exo- | outside | ectopic, exocrine |
| endo- | within | endoscope |
| epi- | upon | epigastric |
| infra- | below, under | infrastructure |
| ipsi- | same | ipsilateral |
| meso- | middle | mesopexy |
| meta- | after, beyond, transformation | metastasis |
| peri- | surrounding | pericardium |
| retro- | behind, back | retroversion |
| trans- | across, through | transvaginal |

| Word | Meaning |
|------|---------|
| anterior or ventral | at or near the front surface of the body |
| posterior or dorsal | at or near the back surface of the body |
| superior | above |
| inferior | below |
| lateral | side |
| distal | farthest from center |
| proximal | nearest to center |
| medial | middle |
| supine | face up or palm up |
| prone | face down or palm down |
| sagittal | vertical body plane, divides the body into equal right and left sides |
| transverse | horizontal body plane, divides the body into top and bottom sections |
| coronal | vertical body plane, divides the body into front and back sections |

## Additional References

For best coding results, you will need to use other reference materials in addition to your coding books. These references include a medical dictionary and one or more anatomy books that can be purchased from the American Medical Association by calling (800) 621-8335.

## Medical Dictionaries

*Stedman's CPT® Dictionary,* 2nd ed.
Chicago, IL: American Medical Association, 2009.
OP300609

*Merriam-Webster's Medical Desk Dictionary.*
Springfield, MA: Merriam Webster.
OP941493

*Stedman's Medical Dictionary.* 27th ed.
Baltimore, MD: Williams & Wilkins; 2000.
OP982900

## Anatomy References

Kirschner, CG. *Netter's Atlas of Human Anatomy for CPT® Coding,* 2nd ed.
Chicago, IL: American Medical Association; 2005.
OP490609

Kirschner, CG. *Netter's Atlas of Human Anatomy for CPT® and ICD-9-CM Coding Series: Musculoskeletal.*
Chicago, IL: American Medical Association
OP492206

Netter, FH. *Atlas of Human Anatomy.* 3rd ed.
East Hanover, NJ: Novartis; 2003.
OP936798

## List of Illustrations

To further aid coders in properly assigning CPT codes, the codebook contains a number of anatomical illustrations.

## Anatomical Illustrations

On the following pages (xix-xxvii), there are 31 anatomical illustrations:

| Figure | Illustration Title |
|--------|-------------------|
| Figure 1A | Body Planes—3/4 View |
| Figure 1B | Body Aspects—Side View |
| Figure 1C | Body Planes—Front View |
| Figure 2 | Structure of Skin |
| Figure 3 | Skeletal System |
| Figure 4 | Skull |
| Figure 5A | Muscular System—Front |
| Figure 5B | Muscular System—Back |
| Figure 6A | Thoracic Vertebra—Superior View |
| Figure 6B | Lumbar Vertebra—Superior View |
| Figure 6C | Lumbar Vertebrae—Lateral View |
| Figure 7 | Bones, Muscles, and Tendons of Hand |
| Figure 8 | Bones and Muscles of Foot |
| Figure 9 | Paranasal Sinuses |
| Figure 10 | Respiratory System |
| Figure 11 | Aortic Anatomy |
| Figure 12 | Cardiac Anatomy |
| Figure 13A | Circulatory System—Arteries |
| Figure 13B | Circulatory System—Veins |
| Figure 14 | Brachial Artery |
| Figure 15 | Lymphatic System |
| Figure 16 | Digestive System |
| Figure 17 | Urinary System |
| Figure 18A | Male Genital System |
| Figure 18B | Female Genital System |
| Figure 19 | Nervous System |
| Figure 20A | Brain Anatomy |
| Figure 20B | Sagittal Section of Brain and Brain Stem |
| Figure 21 | Eye Anatomy |
| Figure 22 | Ear Anatomy |
| Figure 23 | Endocrine System |

## Figure 1A
## **Body Planes — 3/4 View**

Coronal (frontal) plane

Sagittal plane (at the body's median)

Horizontal or transverse plane

## Figure 1B
## **Body Aspects — Side View**

Superior (cranial) aspect

Posterior aspect

Anterior aspect

Dorsal surface of hand

Palmar surface of hand

Dorsal surface of foot

Plantar surface of foot

Inferior aspect

## Figure 1C
## **Body Planes — Front View**

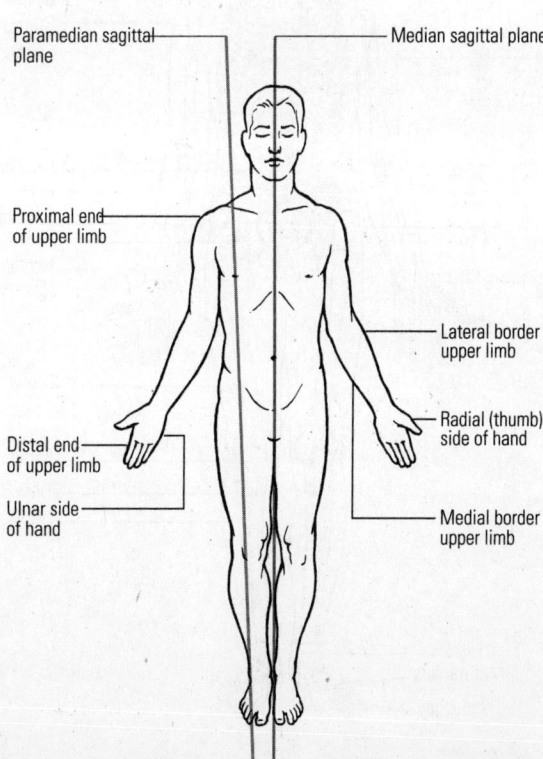

Paramedian sagittal plane

Median sagittal plane

Proximal end of upper limb

Lateral border upper limb

Radial (thumb) side of hand

Distal end of upper limb

Ulnar side of hand

Medial border upper limb

## Figure 2
## **Structure of Skin**

Hair shaft

Hair root

Epidermis

Dermis

Sebaceous gland

Nerve endings

Hair bulb

Sweat gland

Subcutaneous tissue

Cutaneous nerve

Blood vessels

## Figure 3
## **Skeletal System**

Skull

Maxilla
Mandible
Cervical vertebra
First rib
Scapula
Sternum

Clavicle

Humerus

Radius
Ulna

Carpals

Metacarpals
Phalanges

Lumbar vertebra
Ilium
Sacrum
Pubis
Ischium

Femur

Patella
Tibia
Fibula

Tarsals
Metatarsals
Phalanges

## Figure 4
## **Skull**

Parietal bone

Temporal bone
Sphenoid bone

Zygomatic bone

Maxilla

Frontal bone

Nasal bone

Mandible

Frontal bone

Nasal bone
Zygomatic bone
Maxilla bone

Mandible

Parietal bone

Occipital bone

Temporal bone

Temporomandibular joint

## Figure 5A
## Muscular System — Front

Sternocleidomastoid m.
Omohyoid m.
Sternohyoid m.
Trapezius m.
Deltoid m.
Pectoralis major m.
Latissimus dorsi m.
Serratas anterior m.
Oblique external m.
Rectus abdominus m.

Biceps m.
Brachialus m.
Brachioradialus m.
Pronator teres m.
Flexor carpi radialus m.
Palmaris longus m.
Flexor digitorum superficialis m.
Flexor carpi ulnaris m.

Pectineus m.
Adductor longus m.
Adductor magnus m.
Gracilis m.
Sartorius m.
Rectus femoris m.
Vastus medialis m.  } Quadriceps
Vastus lateralis m.

Peroneus longus m.
Tibialis anterior m.
Gastrocnemius m.
Extensor digitorum longus m.
Soleus m.

## Figure 5B
## Muscular System — Back

Trapezius m.
Deltoid m.
Infraspinatus m.
Teres minor m.
Teres major m.
Triceps m.
Latissimus dorsi m.
Anconeus m.
Extensor carpi radialis longus m.
Flexor carpi ulnaris m.
Extensor carpi radialis brevis m.
Extensor digitorum m.
Extensor carpi ulnaris m.
Abductor pollicis longus m.
Extensor pollicis brevis m.

Gluteus medius m.
Gluteus maximus m.
Adductor magnus m.
Biceps femoris m.
Semitendinosus m.
Gracilis m.
Semimembranosus m.
Vastus lateralis m.
Sartorius m.

Gastrocnemius m.

Peroneus longus m.
Flexor hallicis longus m.

## Figure 6A
## Thoracic Vertebra — Superior View

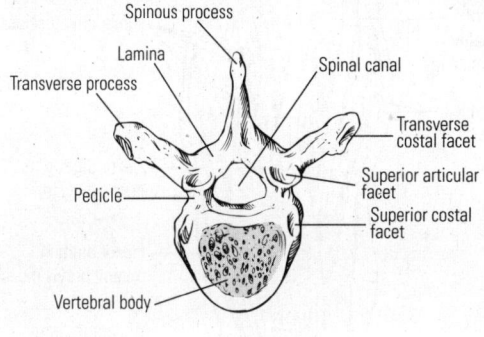

Spinous process
Lamina
Transverse process
Spinal canal
Transverse costal facet
Superior articular facet
Pedicle
Superior costal facet
Vertebral body

## Figure 6B
## Lumbar Vertebra — Superior View

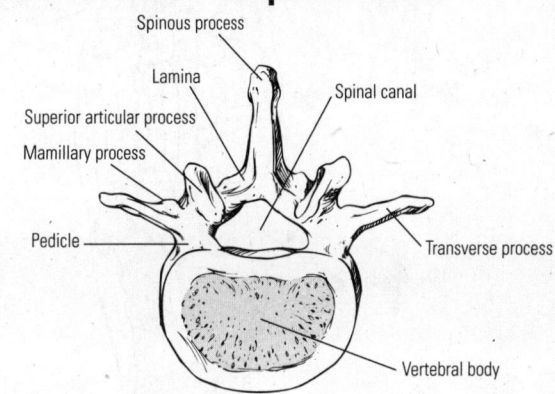

Spinous process
Lamina
Superior articular process
Mamillary process
Spinal canal
Pedicle
Transverse process
Vertebral body

## Figure 6C
## Lumbar Vertebrae — Lateral View

Pedicle
Superior articular process
Vertebral body
Transverse process
Spinous process
Inferior articular process
Intervertebral discs
Inferior vertebral notch
Intervertebral foramen
Superior vertebral notch
L1
L2
L3
L4
L5

## Figure 7
## Bones, Muscles, and Tendons of Hand

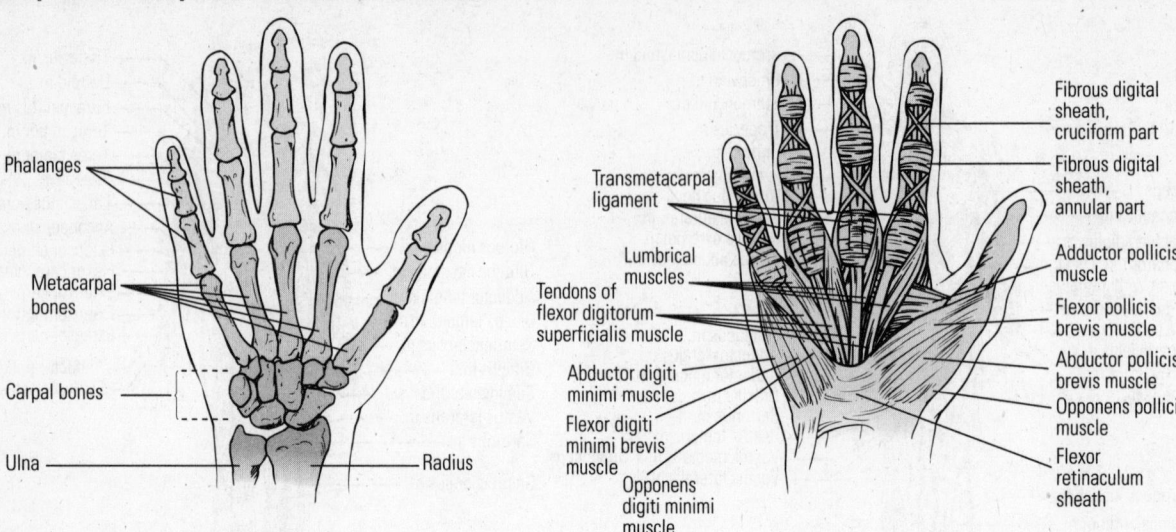

## Figure 8
## Bones and Muscles of Foot

## Figure 9
## Paranasal Sinuses

Figure 10
# Respiratory System

- Nasal cavity
- Larynx
- Right bronchus
- Right lung
- Nasopharynx
- Oropharynx
- Epiglottis
- Esophagus
- Trachea
- Left bronchus
- Left lung

Figure 11
# Aortic Anatomy

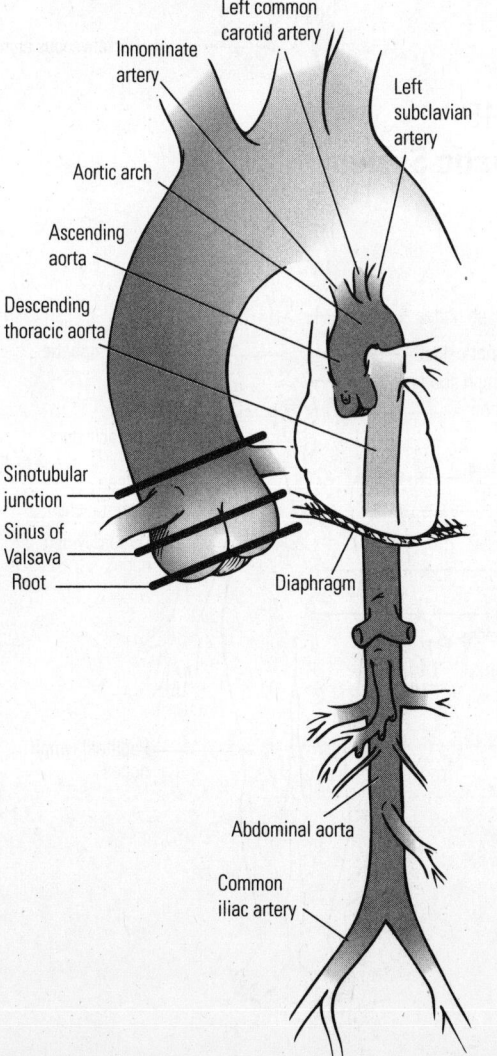

- Left common carotid artery
- Innominate artery
- Left subclavian artery
- Aortic arch
- Ascending aorta
- Descending thoracic aorta
- Sinotubular junction
- Sinus of Valsava
- Root
- Diaphragm
- Abdominal aorta
- Common iliac artery

Figure 12
# Cardiac Anatomy

- Superior vena cava
- Right pulmonary artery
- Pulmonary valve
- Location of sinoatrial node
- Location of atrioventricular node
- Right atrium
- Tricuspid valve
- Right ventricle
- Inferior vena cava
- Aorta
- Pulmonary artery
- Left atrium
- Aortic valve
- Mitral valve
- Left ventricle
- Ventricular septum
- Descending thoracic aorta

## Figure 13A
## Circulatory System—Arteries

Superficial temporal a.
Posterior auricular a.
Common carotid a.
Subclavian a.
Brachiocephalic trunk
Axillary a.
Deep brachial a.
Brachial a.
Aorta
Radial a.
Interosseous a.
Ulnar a.
Deep palmar arch
Superficial palmar arch
Descending genicular a.

External carotid a.
Internal carotid a.
Vertebral a.
Aorta and arch
Pulmonary a.
Cardiac a.
Thoracic aorta
Celiac trunk
Superior mesenteric a.
Renal a.
Gonadal a.
Inferior mesenteric a.
Common iliac a.
External iliac a.
Internal iliac a.
Deep femoral a.
Femoral a.
Popliteal a.
Anterior tibial a.
Peroneal a.
Posterior tibial a.

## Figure 13B
## Circulatory System—Veins

Superficial temporal v.
External jugular v.
Subclavian v.
Brachiocephalic v.
Axillary v.
Brachial v.
Cepalic v.
Basilic v.
Median cubital v.
Medial antebrachial v.
Superficial venous palmar arch
Small saphenous v.

Facial v.
Internal jugular v.
Superior vena cava
Hepatic v.
Renal v.
Gonadal v.
Inferior vena cava
Common iliac v.
Internal iliac v.
External iliac v.
Deep femoral v.
Femoral v.
Great saphenous v.
Popliteal v.
Anterior tibial v.
Posterior tibial v.
Dorsal venous arch

## Figure 14
## Brachial Artery

Brachiocephalic vein
Subclavian vein
Superior vena cava
Upper arm cephalic vein
Brachial artery
Brachial vein
Basilic vein
Radial artery
Lower arm cephalic vein
Ulnar artery

## Figure 15
## Lymphatic System

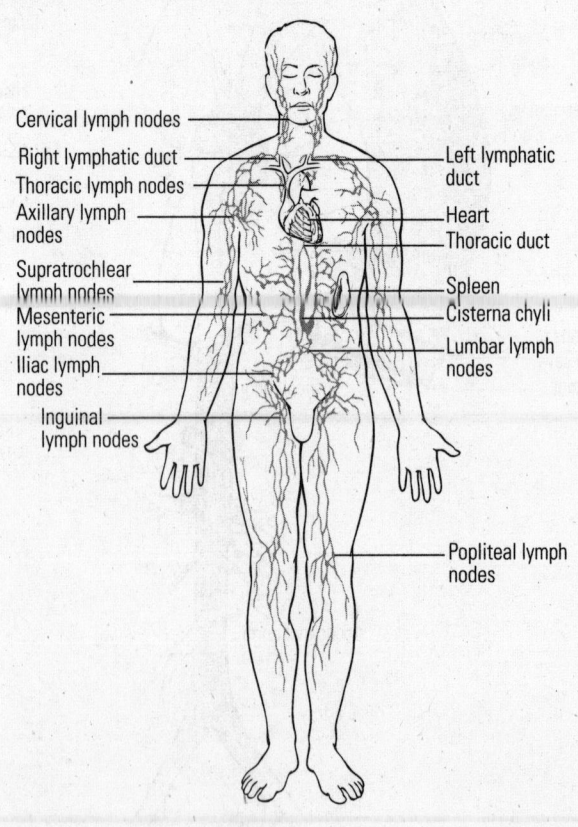

Cervical lymph nodes
Right lymphatic duct
Thoracic lymph nodes
Axillary lymph nodes
Supratrochlear lymph nodes
Mesenteric lymph nodes
Iliac lymph nodes
Inguinal lymph nodes

Left lymphatic duct
Heart
Thoracic duct
Spleen
Cisterna chyli
Lumbar lymph nodes
Popliteal lymph nodes

Figure 16
**Digestive System**

Oral cavity
Tongue
Oropharynx
Esophagus
Liver
Stomach
Gall bladder
Pancreas
Duodenum
Transverse colon
Ascending colon
Jejunum
Ileum
Cecum
Appendix
Sigmoid colon
Rectum
Anal canal and anus

Figure 17
**Urinary System**

Right kidney
Left kidney
Ureters
Urinary bladder
Urethra (empties through penis or in front of vagina)

Figure 18A
**Male Genital System**

Deferent duct
Urinary bladder and cavity
Seminal vesicle
Corpus cavernosa
Ejaculatory duct
Corpus spongiosum
Prostate gland
Penis
Spermatic cord and deferent duct
Glans penis
Prepuce
Epididymus
Testes
Scrotum

Figure 18B
**Female Genital System**

Uterine tube
Fundus of uterus
Ampulla
Infundibulum with fimbriae
Ligament of ovary
Ovary
Body of uterus and uterine cavity
Cervix and cervical canal
Vagina

## Figure 19
## Nervous System

Brain
Cerebellum
Spinal cord
Brachial plexus
Musculocutaneous n.
Radial nerve
Intercostal nerves (with ribs)
Subcostal nerve (12th thoracic)
Median nerve
Iliohypogastric nerve
Ilioinguinal nerve
Deep branch of radial nerve
Lat. femoral cutaneous nerve
Genitofemoral nerve
Superficial branch of radial nerve
Obturator nerve
Ulnar nerve
Lumbar plexus
Sacral plexus
Femoral nerve
Pudendal nerve
Sciatic nerve
Muscular branches of femoral nerve
Saphenous nerve
Tibial nerve
Common peroneal nerve
Deep peroneal nerve
Superficial peroneal nerve

## Figure 20A
## Brain Anatomy

Longitudinal fissure
Frontal lobes
Parietal lobes
Occipital lobes
Frontal lobe
Parietal lobe
Occipital lobe
Temporal lobe
Cerebellum

## Figure 20B
## Sagittal Section of Brain and Brain Stem

Cerebrum
Corpus collosum
Ventricles
Thalamus
Hypothalamus
Midbrain
Pituitary gland
Cerebellum
Pons
Brain stem
Medulla

Figure 21
**Eye Anatomy**

Figure 22
**Ear Anatomy**

Figure 23
**Endocrine System**

# Evaluation and Management (E/M) Services Guidelines

In addition to the information presented in the Introduction, several other items unique to this section are defined or identified here.

## Classification of Evaluation and Management (E/M) Services

The E/M section is divided into broad categories such as office visits, hospital visits, and consultations. Most of the categories are further divided into two or more subcategories of E/M services. For example, there are two subcategories of office visits (new patient and established patient) and there are two subcategories of hospital visits (initial and subsequent). The subcategories of E/M services are further classified into levels of E/M services that are identified by specific codes. This classification is important because the nature of work varies by type of service, place of service, and the patient's status.

The basic format of the levels of E/M services is the same for most categories. First, a unique code number is listed. Second, the place and/or type of service is specified, eg, office consultation. Third, the content of the service is defined, eg, comprehensive history and comprehensive examination. (See "Levels of E/M Services," page 3, for details on the content of E/M services.) Fourth, the nature of the presenting problem(s) usually associated with a given level is described. Fifth, the time typically required to provide the service is specified. (A detailed discussion of time is provided on page 4.)

## Definitions of Commonly Used Terms

Certain key words and phrases are used throughout the E/M section. The following definitions are intended to reduce the potential for differing interpretations and to increase the consistency of reporting by physicians in differing specialties. E/M services may also be reported by other qualified health care professionals who are authorized to perform such services within the scope of their practice.

## New and Established Patient

Solely for the purposes of distinguishing between new and established patients, **professional services** are those face-to-face services rendered by physicians and other qualified health care professionals who may report evaluation and management services reported by a specific CPT code(s). A new patient is one who has not received any professional services from the physician/qualified health care professional or another physician/qualified health care professional of the **exact** same specialty **and subspecialty** who belongs to the same group practice, within the past three years.

An established patient is one who has received professional services from the physician/qualified health care professional or another physician/qualified health care professional of the **exact** same specialty **and subspecialty** who belongs to the same group practice, within the past three years. See Decision Tree.

In the instance where a physician/qualified health care professional is on call for or covering for another physician/qualified health care professional, the patient's encounter will be classified as it would have been by the physician/qualified health care professional who is not available. When advanced practice nurses and physician assistants are working with physicians they are considered as working in the exact same specialty and exact same subspecialties as the physician.

No distinction is made between new and established patients in the emergency department. E/M services in the emergency department category may be reported for any new or established patient who presents for treatment in the emergency department.

The decision tree on page 2 is provided to aid in determining whether to report the E/M service provided as a new or an established patient encounter.

## Chief Complaint

A chief complaint is a concise statement describing the symptom, problem, condition, diagnosis, or other factor that is the reason for the encounter, usually stated in the patient's words.

## Concurrent Care and Transfer of Care

Concurrent care is the provision of similar services (eg, hospital visits) to the same patient by more than one physician or other qualified health care professional on the same day. When concurrent care is provided, no special reporting is required. Transfer of care is the process whereby a physician or other qualified health care professional who is providing management for some or all of a patient's problems relinquishes this responsibility to another physician or other qualified health care professional who explicitly agrees to accept this responsibility and who, from the initial encounter, is not providing consultative services. The physician or other qualified health care professional transferring care is then no longer providing care for these problems though he or she may continue providing care for other conditions when appropriate. Consultation codes should not be reported by the physician or other qualified health care professional who has agreed to accept transfer of care before an initial evaluation but are appropriate to report if the decision to accept transfer of care cannot be made until after the initial consultation evaluation, regardless of site of service.

---

**Decision Tree for New vs Established Patients**

# Decision Tree for New vs Established Patients

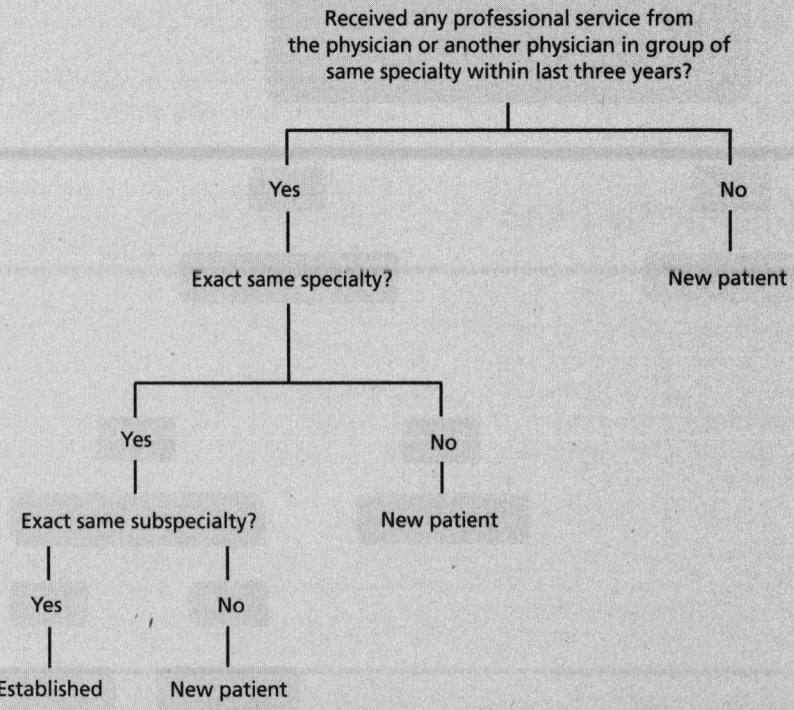

---

## Counseling

Counseling is a discussion with a patient and/or family concerning one or more of the following areas:

■ Diagnostic results, impressions, and/or recommended diagnostic studies

■ Prognosis

■ Risks and benefits of management (treatment) options

■ Instructions for management (treatment) and/or follow-up

■ Importance of compliance with chosen management (treatment) options

■ Risk factor reduction

■ Patient and family education

(For psychotherapy, see 90832-90834, 90836-90840)

## Family History

A review of medical events in the patient's family that includes significant information about:

■ The health status or cause of death of parents, siblings, and children

■ Specific diseases related to problems identified in the Chief Complaint or History of the Present Illness, and/or System Review

■ Diseases of family members that may be hereditary or place the patient at risk

## History of Present Illness

A chronological description of the development of the patient's present illness from the first sign and/or symptom to the present. This includes a description of location, quality, severity, timing, context, modifying factors, and associated signs and symptoms significantly related to the presenting problem(s).

## Levels of E/M Services

Within each category or subcategory of E/M service, there are three to five levels of E/M services available for reporting purposes. Levels of E/M services are **not** interchangeable among the different categories or subcategories of service. For example, the first level of E/M services in the subcategory of office visit, new patient, does not have the same definition as the first level of E/M services in the subcategory of office visit, established patient.

The levels of E/M services include examinations, evaluations, treatments, conferences with or concerning patients, preventive pediatric and adult health supervision, and similar medical services, such as the determination of the need and/or location for appropriate care. Medical screening includes the history, examination, and medical decision-making required to determine the need and/or location for appropriate care and treatment of the patient (eg, office and other outpatient setting, emergency department, nursing facility). The levels of

E/M services encompass the wide variations in skill, effort, time, responsibility, and medical knowledge required for the prevention or diagnosis and treatment of illness or injury and the promotion of optimal health. Each level of E/M services may be used by all physicians or other qualified health care professionals.

The descriptors for the levels of E/M services recognize seven components, six of which are used in defining the levels of E/M services. These components are:

■ History

■ Examination

■ Medical decision making

■ Counseling

■ Coordination of care

■ Nature of presenting problem

■ Time

The first three of these components (history, examination, and medical decision making) are considered the **key** components in selecting a level of E/M services. (See "Determine the Extent of History Obtained," page 6.)

The next three components (counseling, coordination of care, and the nature of the presenting problem) are considered **contributory** factors in the majority of encounters. Although the first two of these contributory factors are important E/M services, it is not required that these services be provided at every patient encounter.

Coordination of care with other physicians, other health care professionals, or agencies without a patient encounter on that day is reported using the case management codes.

The final component, time, is discussed in detail on page 4.

Any specifically identifiable procedure (ie, identified with a specific CPT code) performed on or subsequent to the date of initial or subsequent E/M services should be reported separately.

The actual performance and/or interpretation of diagnostic tests/studies ordered during a patient encounter are not included in the levels of E/M services. Physician performance of diagnostic tests/studies for which specific CPT codes are available may be reported separately, in addition to the appropriate E/M code. The physician's interpretation of the results of diagnostic tests/ studies (ie, professional component) with preparation of a separate distinctly identifiable signed written report may also be reported separately, using the appropriate CPT code with modifier 26 appended.

The physician or other health care professional may need to indicate that on the day a procedure or service identified by a CPT code was performed, the patient's condition required a significant separately identifiable E/M service above and beyond other services provided or beyond the usual preservice and postservice care associated with the procedure that was performed. The E/M service may be caused or prompted by the symptoms or condition for which the procedure and/or service was provided. This circumstance may be reported by adding modifier 25 to the appropriate level of E/M service. As such, different diagnoses are not required for reporting of the procedure and the E/M services on the same date.

## Nature of Presenting Problem

A presenting problem is a disease, condition, illness, injury, symptom, sign, finding, complaint, or other reason for encounter, with or without a diagnosis being established at the time of the encounter. The E/M codes recognize five types of presenting problems that are defined as follows:

*Minimal:* A problem that may not require the presence of the physician or other qualified health care professional, but service is provided under the physician's or other qualified health care professional's supervision.

*Self-limited or minor:* A problem that runs a definite and prescribed course, is transient in nature, and is not likely to permanently alter health status OR has a good prognosis with management/compliance.

*Low severity:* A problem where the risk of morbidity without treatment is low; there is little to no risk of mortality without treatment; full recovery without functional impairment is expected.

*Moderate severity:* A problem where the risk of morbidity without treatment is moderate; there is moderate risk of mortality without treatment; uncertain prognosis OR increased probability of prolonged functional impairment.

*High severity:* A problem where the risk of morbidity without treatment is high to extreme; there is a moderate to high risk of mortality without treatment OR high probability of severe, prolonged functional impairment.

## Past History

A review of the patient's past experiences with illnesses, injuries, and treatments that includes significant information about:

- Prior major illnesses and injuries
- Prior operations
- Prior hospitalizations
- Current medications
- Allergies (eg, drug, food)
- Age appropriate immunization status
- Age appropriate feeding/dietary status

## Social History

An age appropriate review of past and current activities that includes significant information about:

- Marital status and/or living arrangements
- Current employment
- Occupational history
- Use of drugs, alcohol, and tobacco
- Level of education
- Sexual history
- Other relevant social factors

## System Review (Review of Systems)

An inventory of body systems obtained through a series of questions seeking to identify signs and/or symptoms that the patient may be experiencing or has experienced. For the purposes of the CPT codebook the following elements of a system review have been identified:

- Constitutional symptoms (fever, weight loss, etc)
- Eyes
- Ears, nose, mouth, throat
- Cardiovascular
- Respiratory
- Gastrointestinal
- Genitourinary
- Musculoskeletal
- Integumentary (skin and/or breast)
- Neurological
- Psychiatric
- Endocrine
- Hematologic/lymphatic
- Allergic/immunologic

The review of systems helps define the problem, clarify the differential diagnosis, identify needed testing, or serves as baseline data on other systems that might be affected by any possible management options.

## Time

The inclusion of time in the definitions of levels of E/M services has been implicit in prior editions of the CPT codebook. The inclusion of time as an explicit factor beginning in *CPT 1992* is done to assist in selecting the most appropriate level of E/M services. It should be recognized that the specific times expressed in the visit code descriptors are averages and, therefore, represent a range of times that may be higher or lower depending on actual clinical circumstances.

Time is **not** a descriptive component for the emergency department levels of E/M services because emergency department services are typically provided on a variable intensity basis, often involving multiple encounters with several patients over an extended period of time.

Therefore, it is often difficult to provide accurate estimates of the time spent face-to-face with the patient.

Studies to establish levels of E/M services employed surveys of practicing physicians to obtain data on the amount of time and work associated with typical E/M services. Since "work" is not easily quantifiable, the codes must rely on other objective, verifiable measures that correlate with physicians' estimates of their "work." It has been demonstrated that estimations of **intraservice** time (as explained on the next page), both within and across specialties, is a variable that is predictive of the "work" of E/M services. This same research has shown there is a strong relationship between intraservice time and total time for E/M services. Intraservice time, rather than total time, was chosen for inclusion with the codes because of its relative ease of measurement and because of its direct correlation with measurements of the total amount of time and work associated with typical E/M services.

Intraservice times are defined as **face-to-face** time for office and other outpatient visits and as **unit/floor** time for hospital and other inpatient visits. This distinction is necessary because most of the work of typical office visits takes place during the face-to-face time with the patient, while most of the work of typical hospital visits takes place during the time spent on the patient's floor or unit. When prolonged time occurs in either the office or the inpatient areas, the appropriate add-on code should be reported.

*Face-to-face time (office and other outpatient visits and office consultations):* For coding purposes, face-to-face time for these services is defined as only that time spent face-to-face with the patient and/or family. This includes the time spent performing such tasks as obtaining a history, examination, and counseling the patient.

Time is also spent doing work before or after the face-to-face time with the patient, performing such tasks as reviewing records and tests, arranging for further services, and communicating further with other professionals and the patient through written reports and telephone contact.

This **non-face-to-face** time for office services—also called pre- and postencounter time—is not included in the time component described in the E/M codes. However, the pre- and post-non-face-to-face work associated with an encounter was included in calculating the total work of typical services in physician surveys.

Thus, the face-to-face time associated with the services described by any E/M code is a valid proxy for the total work done before, during, and after the visit.

*Unit/floor time (hospital observation services, inpatient hospital care, initial inpatient hospital consultations, nursing facility):* For reporting purposes, intraservice time for these services is defined as unit/floor time, which includes the time present on the patient's hospital unit and at the bedside rendering services for that patient. This includes the time to establish and/or

review the patient's chart, examine the patient, write notes, and communicate with other professionals and the patient's family.

In the hospital, pre- and post-time includes time spent off the patient's floor performing such tasks as reviewing pathology and radiology findings in another part of the hospital.

This pre- and postvisit time is not included in the time component described in these codes. However, the pre- and postwork performed during the time spent off the floor or unit was included in calculating the total work of typical services in physician surveys.

Thus, the unit/floor time associated with the services described by any code is a valid proxy for the total work done before, during, and after the visit.

## Unlisted Service

An E/M service may be provided that is not listed in this section of the CPT codebook. When reporting such a service, the appropriate unlisted code may be used to indicate the service, identifying it by "Special Report," as discussed in the following paragraph. The "Unlisted Services" and accompanying codes for the E/M section are as follows:

99429    **Unlisted preventive** medicine service

99499    **Unlisted evaluation and management** service

## Special Report

An unlisted service or one that is unusual, variable, or new may require a special report demonstrating the medical appropriateness of the service. Pertinent information should include an adequate definition or description of the nature, extent, and need for the procedure and the time, effort, and equipment necessary to provide the service. Additional items that may be included are complexity of symptoms, final diagnosis, pertinent physical findings, diagnostic and therapeutic procedures, concurrent problems, and follow-up care.

## Clinical Examples

Clinical examples of the codes for E/M services are provided to assist in understanding the meaning of the descriptors and selecting the correct code. The clinical examples are listed in Appendix C. Each example was developed by the specialties shown.

The same problem, when seen by different specialties, may involve different amounts of work. Therefore, the appropriate level of encounter should be reported using the descriptors rather than the examples.

# Instructions for Selecting a Level of E/M Service

## Review the Reporting Instructions for the Selected Category or Subcategory

Most of the categories and many of the subcategories of service have special guidelines or instructions unique to that category or subcategory. Where these are indicated, eg, "Inpatient Hospital Care," special instructions will be presented preceding the levels of E/M services.

## Review the Level of E/M Service Descriptors and Examples in the Selected Category or Subcategory

The descriptors for the levels of E/M services recognize seven components, six of which are used in defining the levels of E/M services. These components are:

- History
- Examination
- Medical decision making
- Counseling
- Coordination of care
- Nature of presenting problem
- Time

The first three of these components (ie, history, examination, and medical decision making) should be considered the **key** components in selecting the level of E/M services. An exception to this rule is in the case of visits that consist predominantly of counseling or coordination of care (see numbered paragraph 3, page 7).

The nature of the presenting problem and time are provided in some levels to assist the physician in determining the appropriate level of E/M service.

## Determine the Extent of History Obtained

The extent of the history is dependent upon clinical judgment and on the nature of the presenting problem(s). The levels of E/M services recognize four types of history that are defined as follows:

*Problem focused:* Chief complaint; brief history of present illness or problem.

*Expanded problem focused:* Chief complaint; brief history of present illness; problem pertinent system review.

*Detailed:* Chief complaint; extended history of present illness; problem pertinent system review extended to include a review of a limited number of additional systems; **pertinent** past, family, and/or social history **directly related to the patient's problems.**

*Comprehensive:* Chief complaint; extended history of present illness; review of systems that is directly related to the problem(s) identified in the history of the present illness plus a review of all additional body systems; **complete** past, family, and social history.

The comprehensive history obtained as part of the preventive medicine E/M service is not problem-oriented and does not involve a chief complaint or present illness. It does, however, include a comprehensive system review and comprehensive or interval past, family, and social history as well as a comprehensive assessment/history of pertinent risk factors.

## Determine the Extent of Examination Performed

The extent of the examination performed is dependent on clinical judgment and on the nature of the presenting problem(s). The levels of E/M services recognize four types of examination that are defined as follows:

*Problem focused:* A limited examination of the affected body area or organ system.

*Expanded problem focused:* A limited examination of the affected body area or organ system and other symptomatic or related organ system(s).

*Detailed:* An extended examination of the affected body area(s) and other symptomatic or related organ system(s).

*Comprehensive:* A general multisystem examination or a complete examination of a single organ system. **Note:** The comprehensive examination performed as part of the preventive medicine E/M service is multisystem but its extent is based on age and risk factors identified.

For the purposes of these CPT definitions, the following body areas are recognized:

- Head, including the face
- Neck
- Chest, including breasts and axilla
- Abdomen
- Genitalia, groin, buttocks
- Back
- Each extremity

For the purposes of these CPT definitions, the following organ systems are recognized:

- Eyes
- Ears, nose, mouth, and throat
- Cardiovascular
- Respiratory
- Gastrointestinal
- Genitourinary
- Musculoskeletal
- Skin
- Neurologic
- Psychiatric
- Hematologic/lymphatic/immunologic

## Determine the Complexity of Medical Decision Making

Medical decision making refers to the complexity of establishing a diagnosis and/or selecting a management option as measured by:

- The number of possible diagnoses and/or the number of management options that must be considered
- The amount and/or complexity of medical records, diagnostic tests, and/or other information that must be obtained, reviewed, and analyzed
- The risk of significant complications, morbidity, and/or mortality, as well as comorbidities, associated with the patient's presenting problem(s), the diagnostic procedure(s), and/or the possible management options

Four types of medical decision making are recognized: straightforward, low complexity, moderate complexity, and high complexity. To qualify for a given type of decision making, two of the three elements in Table 1 must be met or exceeded.

Comorbidities/underlying diseases, in and of themselves, are not considered in selecting a level of E/M services *unless* their presence significantly increases the complexity of the medical decision making.

## Select the Appropriate Level of E/M Services Based on the Following

1. For the following categories/subcategories, **all of the key components,** ie, history, examination, and medical decision making, must meet or exceed the stated requirements to qualify for a particular level of E/M service: office, new patient; hospital observation services; initial hospital care; office consultations; initial inpatient consultations; emergency department services; initial nursing facility care; domiciliary care, new patient; and home, new patient.

2. For the following categories/subcategories, **two of the three key components** (ie, history, examination, and medical decision making) must meet or exceed the stated requirements to qualify for a particular level of E/M services: office, established patient; subsequent hospital care; subsequent nursing facility care; domiciliary care, established patient; and home, established patient.

3. When counseling and/or coordination of care dominates (more than 50%) the encounter with the patient and/or family (face-to-face time in the office or other outpatient setting or floor/unit time in the hospital or nursing facility), then **time** shall be considered the key or controlling factor to qualify for a particular level of E/M services. This includes time spent with parties who have assumed responsibility for the care of the patient or decision making whether or not they are family members (eg, foster parents, person acting in loco parentis, legal guardian). The extent of counseling and/or coordination of care must be documented in the medical record

Table 1
## Complexity of Medical Decision Making

| Number of Diagnoses or Management Options | Amount and/or Complexity of Data to be Reviewed | Risk of Complications and/or Morbidity or Mortality | Type of Decision Making |
|---|---|---|---|
| minimal | minimal or none | minimal | **straightforward** |
| limited | limited | low | **low complexity** |
| multiple | moderate | moderate | **moderate complexity** |
| extensive | extensive | high | **high complexity** |

# Evaluation and Management

## Office or Other Outpatient Services

The following codes are used to report evaluation and management services provided in the office or in an outpatient or other ambulatory facility. A patient is considered an outpatient until inpatient admission to a health care facility occurs.

To report services provided to a patient who is admitted to a hospital or nursing facility in the course of an encounter in the office or other ambulatory facility, see the notes for initial hospital inpatient care (page 11) or initial nursing facility care (page 19).

For services provided in the emergency department, see 99281-99285.

For observation care, see 99217-99226.

For observation or inpatient care services (including admission and discharge services), see 99234-99236.

### New Patient

**99201** **Office or other outpatient visit** for the evaluation and management of a new patient, which requires these 3 key components:

- **A problem focused history;**
- **A problem focused examination;**
- **Straightforward medical decision making.**

Counseling and/or coordination of care with other physicians, other qualified health care professionals, or agencies are provided consistent with the nature of the problem(s) and the patient's and/or family's needs.

Usually, the presenting problem(s) are self limited or minor. Typically, 10 minutes are spent face-to-face with the patient and/or family.

**99202** **Office or other outpatient visit** for the evaluation and management of a new patient, which requires these 3 key components:

- **An expanded problem focused history;**
- **An expanded problem focused examination;**
- **Straightforward medical decision making.**

Counseling and/or coordination of care with other physicians, other qualified health care professionals, or agencies are provided consistent with the nature of the problem(s) and the patient's and/or family's needs.

Usually, the presenting problem(s) are of low to moderate severity. Typically, 20 minutes are spent face-to-face with the patient and/or family.

**99203** **Office or other outpatient visit** for the evaluation and management of a new patient, which requires these 3 key components:

- **A detailed history;**
- **A detailed examination;**
- **Medical decision making of low complexity.**

Counseling and/or coordination of care with other physicians, other qualified health care professionals, or agencies are provided consistent with the nature of the problem(s) and the patient's and/or family's needs.

Usually, the presenting problem(s) are of moderate severity. Typically, 30 minutes are spent face-to-face with the patient and/or family.

**99204** **Office or other outpatient visit** for the evaluation and management of a new patient, which requires these 3 key components:

- **A comprehensive history;**
- **A comprehensive examination;**
- **Medical decision making of moderate complexity.**

Counseling and/or coordination of care with other physicians, other qualified health care professionals, or agencies are provided consistent with the nature of the problem(s) and the patient's and/or family's needs.

Usually, the presenting problem(s) are of moderate to high severity. Typically, 45 minutes are spent face-to-face with the patient and/or family.

**99205** **Office or other outpatient visit** for the evaluation and management of a new patient, which requires these 3 key components:

- **A comprehensive history;**
- **A comprehensive examination;**
- **Medical decision making of high complexity.**

Counseling and/or coordination of care with other physicians, other qualified health care professionals, or agencies are provided consistent with the nature of the problem(s) and the patient's and/or family's needs.

Usually, the presenting problem(s) are of moderate to high severity. Typically, 60 minutes are spent face-to-face with the patient and/or family.

### Established Patient

**99211** **Office or other outpatient visit** for the evaluation and management of an established patient, that may not require the presence of a physician or other qualified health care professional. Usually, the presenting problem(s) are minimal. Typically, 5 minutes are spent performing or supervising these services.

**99212**    **Office or other outpatient visit** for the evaluation and management of an established patient, which requires at least 2 of these 3 key components:

- **A problem focused history;**
- **A problem focused examination;**
- **Straightforward medical decision making.**

Counseling and/or coordination of care with other physicians, other qualified health care professionals, or agencies are provided consistent with the nature of the problem(s) and the patient's and/or family's needs.

Usually, the presenting problem(s) are self limited or minor. Typically, 10 minutes are spent face-to-face with the patient and/or family.

**99213**    **Office or other outpatient visit** for the evaluation and management of an established patient, which requires at least 2 of these 3 key components:

- **An expanded problem focused history;**
- **An expanded problem focused examination;**
- **Medical decision making of low complexity.**

Counseling and coordination of care with other physicians, other qualified health care professionals, or agencies are provided consistent with the nature of the problem(s) and the patient's and/or family's needs.

Usually, the presenting problem(s) are of low to moderate severity. Typically, 15 minutes are spent face-to-face with the patient and/or family.

**99214**    **Office or other outpatient visit** for the evaluation and management of an established patient, which requires at least 2 of these 3 key components:

- **A detailed history;**
- **A detailed examination;**
- **Medical decision making of moderate complexity.**

Counseling and/or coordination of care with other physicians, other qualified health care professionals, or agencies are provided consistent with the nature of the problem(s) and the patient's and/or family's needs.

Usually, the presenting problem(s) are of moderate to high severity. Typically, 25 minutes are spent face-to-face with the patient and/or family.

**99215**    **Office or other outpatient visit** for the evaluation and management of an established patient, which requires at least 2 of these 3 key components:

- **A comprehensive history;**
- **A comprehensive examination;**
- **Medical decision making of high complexity.**

Counseling and/or coordination of care with other physicians, other qualified health care professionals, or agencies are provided consistent with the nature of the problem(s) and the patient's and/or family's needs.

Usually, the presenting problem(s) are of moderate to high severity. Typically, 40 minutes are spent face-to-face with the patient and/or family.

# Hospital Observation Services

The following codes are used to report evaluation and management services provided to patients designated/admitted as "observation status" in a hospital. It is not necessary that the patient be located in an observation area designated by the hospital.

If such an area does exist in a hospital (as a separate unit in the hospital, in the emergency department, etc.), these codes are to be utilized if the patient is placed in such an area.

For definitions of key components and commonly used terms, please see **Evaluation and Management Services Guidelines.**

## Observation Care Discharge Services

Observation care discharge of a patient from "observation status" includes final examination of the patient, discussion of the hospital stay, instructions for continuing care, and preparation of discharge records. For observation or inpatient hospital care including the admission and discharge of the patient on the same date, see codes 99234-99236 as appropriate.

**99217**    **Observation care discharge** day management (This code is to be utilized to report all services provided to a patient on discharge from "observation status" if the discharge is on other than the initial date of "observation status." To report services to a patient designated as "observation status" or "inpatient status" and discharged on the same date, use the codes for Observation or Inpatient Care Services [including Admission and Discharge Services, 99234-99236 as appropriate.])

## Initial Observation Care

### New or Established Patient

The following codes are used to report the encounter(s) by the supervising physician or other qualified health care professional with the patient when designated as "observation status." This refers to the initiation of observation status, supervision of the care plan for observation and performance of periodic reassessments. For observation encounters by other physicians, see office or other outpatient consultation codes (99241-99245) or subsequent observation care codes (99224-99226) as appropriate.

To report services provided to a patient who is admitted to the hospital after receiving hospital observation care services on the same date, see the notes for initial hospital

Evaluation/Management

Evaluation/Management

inpatient care (page 11). For observation care services on other than the initial or discharge date, see subsequent observation services codes (99224-99226). For a patient admitted to the hospital on a date subsequent to the date of observation status, the hospital admission would be reported with the appropriate initial hospital care code (99221-99223). For a patient admitted and discharged from observation or inpatient status on the same date, the services should be reported with codes 99234-99236 as appropriate. Do not report observation discharge (99217) in conjunction with a hospital admission (99221-99223).

When "observation status" is initiated in the course of an encounter in another site of service (eg, hospital emergency department, office, nursing facility) all evaluation and management services provided by the supervising physician or other qualified health care professional in conjunction with initiating "observation status" are considered part of the initial observation care when performed on the same date. The observation care level of service reported by the supervising physician or other qualified health care professional should include the services related to initiating "observation status" provided in the other sites of service as well as in the observation setting.

Evaluation and management services including new or established patient office or other outpatient services (99201-99215), emergency department services (99281-99285), nursing facility services (99304-99318), domiciliary, rest home, or custodial care services (99324-99337), home services (99341-99350), and preventive medicine services (99381-99429) on the same date related to the admission to "observation status" should not be reported separately.

These codes may not be utilized for post-operative recovery if the procedure is considered part of the surgical "package." These codes apply to all evaluation and management services that are provided on the same date of initiating "observation status."

**99218** **Initial observation care,** per day, for the evaluation and management of a patient which requires these 3 key components:

- **A detailed or comprehensive history;**
- **A detailed or comprehensive examination; and**
- **Medical decision making that is straightforward or of low complexity.**

Counseling and/or coordination of care with other physicians, other qualified health care professionals, or agencies are provided consistent with the nature of the problem(s) and the patient's and/or family's needs.

Usually, the problem(s) requiring admission to "observation status" are of low severity. Typically, 30 minutes are spent at the bedside and on the patient's hospital floor or unit.

**99219** **Initial observation care,** per day, for the evaluation and management of a patient, which requires these 3 key components:

- **A comprehensive history;**
- **A comprehensive examination; and**
- **Medical decision making of moderate complexity.**

Counseling and/or coordination of care with other physicians, other qualified health care professionals, or agencies are provided consistent with the nature of the problem(s) and the patient's and/or family's needs.

Usually, the problem(s) requiring admission to "observation status" are of moderate severity. Typically, 50 minutes are spent at the bedside and on the patient's hospital floor or unit.

**99220** **Initial observation care,** per day, for the evaluation and management of a patient, which requires these 3 key components:

- **A comprehensive history;**
- **A comprehensive examination; and**
- **Medical decision making of high complexity.**

Counseling and/or coordination of care with other physicians, other qualified health care professionals, or agencies are provided consistent with the nature of the problem(s) and the patient's and/or family's needs.

Usually, the problem(s) requiring admission to "observation status" are of high severity. Typically, 70 minutes are spent at the bedside and on the patient's hospital floor or unit.

## Subsequent Observation Care

All levels of subsequent observation care include reviewing the medical record and reviewing the results of diagnostic studies and changes in the patient's status (ie, changes in history, physical condition, and response to management) since the last assessment.

**# 99224** **Subsequent observation care,** per day, for the evaluation and management of a patient, which requires at least 2 of these 3 key components:

- **Problem focused interval history;**
- **Problem focused examination;**
- **Medical decision making that is straightforward or of low complexity.**

Counseling and/or coordination of care with other physicians, other qualified health care professionals, or agencies are provided consistent with the nature of the problem(s) and the patient's and/or family's needs.

Usually, the patient is stable, recovering, or improving. Typically, 15 minutes are spent at the bedside and on the patient's hospital floor or unit.

**# 99225    Subsequent observation care,** per day, for the evaluation and management of a patient, which requires at least 2 of these 3 key components:

- **An expanded problem focused interval history;**
- **An expanded problem focused examination;**
- **Medical decision making of moderate complexity.**

Counseling and/or coordination of care with other physicians, other qualified health care professionals, or agencies are provided consistent with the nature of the problem(s) and the patient's and/or family's needs.

Usually, the patient is responding inadequately to therapy or has developed a minor complication. Typically, 25 minutes are spent at the bedside and on the patient's hospital floor or unit.

**# 99226    Subsequent observation care,** per day, for the evaluation and management of a patient, which requires at least 2 of these 3 key components:

- **A detailed interval history;**
- **A detailed examination;**
- **Medical decision making of high complexity.**

Counseling and/or coordination of care with other physicians, other qualified health care professionals, or agencies are provided consistent with the nature of the problem(s) and the patient's and/or family's needs.

Usually, the patient is unstable or has developed a significant complication or a significant new problem. Typically, 35 minutes are spent at the bedside and on the patient's hospital floor or unit.

# Hospital Inpatient Services

The following codes are used to report evaluation and management services provided to hospital inpatients. Hospital inpatient services include those services provided to patients in a "partial hospital" setting. These codes are to be used to report these partial hospitalization services. See also psychiatry notes in the full text of the CPT code set.

For definitions of key components and commonly used terms, please see **Evaluation and Management Services Guidelines.** For Hospital Observation Services, see 99218-99220, 99224-99226. For a patient admitted and discharged from observation or inpatient status on the same date, the services should be reported with codes 99234-99236 as appropriate.

## Initial Hospital Care

### New or Established Patient

The following codes are used to report the first hospital inpatient encounter with the patient by the admitting physician.

For initial inpatient encounters by physicians other than the admitting physician, see initial inpatient consultation codes (99251-99255) or subsequent hospital care codes (99231-99233) as appropriate.

For admission services for the neonate (28 days of age or younger) requiring intensive observation, frequent interventions, and other intensive care services, see 99477.

When the patient is admitted to the hospital as an inpatient in the course of an encounter in another site of service (eg, hospital emergency department, observation status in a hospital, office, nursing facility) all evaluation and management services provided by that physician in conjunction with that admission are considered part of the initial hospital care when performed on the same date as the admission. The inpatient care level of service reported by the admitting physician should include the services related to the admission he/she provided in the other sites of service as well as in the inpatient setting.

Evaluation and management services including new or established patient office or other outpatient services (99201-99215), emergency department services (99281-99285), nursing facility services (99304-99318), domiciliary, rest home, or custodial care services (99324-99337), home services (99341-99350), and preventive medicine services (99381-99397) on the same date related to the admission to "observation status" should **not** be reported separately. For a patient admitted and discharged from observation or inpatient status on the same date, the services should be reported with codes 99234-99236 as appropriate.

**99221    Initial hospital care,** per day, for the evaluation and management of a patient, which requires these 3 key components:

- **A detailed or comprehensive history;**
- **A detailed or comprehensive examination; and**
- **Medical decision making that is straightforward or of low complexity.**

Counseling and/or coordination of care with other physicians, other qualified health care professionals, or agencies are provided consistent with the nature of the problem(s) and the patient's and/or family's needs.

Usually, the problem(s) requiring admission are of low severity. Typically, 30 minutes are spent at the bedside and on the patient's hospital floor or unit.

**99222    Initial hospital care,** per day, for the evaluation and management of a patient, which requires these 3 key components:

- **A comprehensive history;**
- **A comprehensive examination; and**
- **Medical decision making of moderate complexity.**

Counseling and/or coordination of care with other physicians, other qualified health care professionals, or agencies are provided consistent with the nature of the problem(s) and the patient's and/or family's needs.

Usually, the problem(s) requiring admission are of moderate severity. Typically, 50 minutes are spent at the bedside and on the patient's hospital floor or unit.

**99223**  **Initial hospital care,** per day, for the evaluation and management of a patient, which requires these 3 key components:

- **A comprehensive history;**
- **A comprehensive examination; and**
- **Medical decision making of high complexity.**

Counseling and/or coordination of care with other physicians, other qualified health care professionals, or agencies are provided consistent with the nature of the problem(s) and the patient's and/or family's needs.

Usually, the problem(s) requiring admission are of high severity. Typically, 70 minutes are spent at the bedside and on the patient's hospital floor or unit.

**99224**  Code is out of numerical sequence. See 99224-99226

**99225**  Code is out of numerical sequence. See 99224-99226

**99226**  Code is out of numerical sequence. See 99224-99226

## Subsequent Hospital Care

All levels of subsequent hospital care include reviewing the medical record and reviewing the results of diagnostic studies and changes in the patient's status (ie, changes in history, physical condition and response to management) since the last assessment.

**99231**  **Subsequent hospital care,** per day, for the evaluation and management of a patient, which requires at least 2 of these 3 key components:

- **A problem focused interval history;**
- **A problem focused examination;**
- **Medical decision making that is straightforward or of low complexity.**

Counseling and/or coordination of care with other physicians, other qualified health care professionals, or agencies are provided consistent with the nature of the problem(s) and the patient's and/or family's needs.

Usually, the patient is stable, recovering or improving. Typically, 15 minutes are spent at the bedside and on the patient's hospital floor or unit.

**99232**  **Subsequent hospital care,** per day, for the evaluation and management of a patient, which requires at least 2 of these 3 key components:

- **An expanded problem focused interval history;**
- **An expanded problem focused examination;**
- **Medical decision making of moderate complexity.**

Counseling and/or coordination of care with other physicians, other qualified health care professionals, or agencies are provided consistent with the nature of the problem(s) and the patient's and/or family's needs.

Usually, the patient is responding inadequately to therapy or has developed a minor complication. Typically, 25 minutes are spent at the bedside and on the patient's hospital floor or unit.

**99233**  **Subsequent hospital care,** per day, for the evaluation and management of a patient, which requires at least 2 of these 3 key components:

- **A detailed interval history;**
- **A detailed examination;**
- **Medical decision making of high complexity.**

Counseling and/or coordination of care with other physicians, other qualified health care professionals, or agencies are provided consistent with the nature of the problem(s) and the patient's and/or family's needs.

Usually, the patient is unstable or has developed a significant complication or a significant new problem. Typically, 35 minutes are spent at the bedside and on the patient's hospital floor or unit.

## Observation or Inpatient Care Services (Including Admission and Discharge Services)

The following codes are used to report observation or inpatient hospital care services provided to patients admitted and discharged on the same date of service. When a patient is admitted to the hospital from observation status on the same date, only the initial hospital care code should be reported. The initial hospital care code reported by the admitting physician or other qualified health care professional should include the services related to the observation status services he/she provided on the same date of inpatient admission.

When "observation status" is initiated in the course of an encounter in another site of service (eg, hospital emergency department, office, nursing facility) all evaluation and management services provided by the supervising physician or other qualified health care professional in conjunction with initiating "observation status" are considered part of the initial observation care when performed on the same date. The observation care level of service should include the services related to initiating "observation status" provided in the other sites of service as well as in the observation setting when provided by the same individual.

For patients admitted to observation or inpatient care and discharged on a different date, see codes 99218-99220, 99224-99226, 99217, or 99221-99223, 99238 and 99239.

**99234**   **Observation or inpatient hospital care,** for the evaluation and management of a patient including admission and discharge on the same date, which requires these 3 key components:

- **A detailed or comprehensive history;**
- **A detailed or comprehensive examination; and**
- **Medical decision making that is straightforward or of low complexity.**

Counseling and/or coordination of care with other physicians, other qualified health care professionals, or agencies are provided consistent with the nature of the problem(s) and the patient's and/or family's needs.

Usually the presenting problem(s) requiring admission are of low severity. Typically, 40 minutes are spent at the bedside and on the patient's hospital floor or unit.

**99235**   **Observation or inpatient hospital care,** for the evaluation and management of a patient including admission and discharge on the same date, which requires these 3 key components:

- **A comprehensive history;**
- **A comprehensive examination; and**
- **Medical decision making of moderate complexity.**

Counseling and/or coordination of care with other physicians, other qualified health care professionals, or agencies are provided consistent with the nature of the problem(s) and the patient's and/or family's needs.

Usually the presenting problem(s) requiring admission are of moderate severity. Typically, 50 minutes are spent at the bedside and on the patient's hospital floor or unit.

**99236**   **Observation or inpatient hospital care,** for the evaluation and management of a patient including admission and discharge on the same date, which requires these 3 key components:

- **A comprehensive history;**
- **A comprehensive examination; and**
- **Medical decision making of high complexity.**

Counseling and/or coordination of care with other physicians, other qualified health care professionals, or agencies are provided consistent with the nature of the problem(s) and the patient's and/or family's needs.

Usually the presenting problem(s) requiring admission are of high severity. Typically, 55 minutes are spent at the bedside and on the patient's hospital floor or unit.

## Hospital Discharge Services

The hospital discharge day management codes are to be used to report the total duration of time spent by a physician for final hospital discharge of a patient. The codes include, as appropriate, final examination of the patient, discussion of the hospital stay, even if the time spent by the physician on that date is not continuous, instructions for continuing care to all relevant caregivers,

and preparation of discharge records, prescriptions and referral forms. For a patient admitted and discharged from observation or inpatient status on the same date, the services should be reported with codes 99234-99236 as appropriate.

**99238**   **Hospital discharge day management**; 30 minutes or less

**99239**     more than 30 minutes

▶(These codes are to be utilized to report all services provided to a patient on the date of discharge, if other than the initial date of inpatient status. To report services to a patient who is admitted as an inpatient and discharged on the same date, see codes 99234-99236 for observation or inpatient hospital care including the admission and discharge of the patient on the same date. To report concurrent care services provided by an individual other than the physician or qualified health care professional performing the discharge day management service, use subsequent hospital care codes [99231-99233] on the day of discharge.)◀

(For Observation Care Discharge, use 99217)

(For observation or inpatient hospital care including the admission and discharge of the patient on the same date, see 99234-99236)

(For Nursing Facility Care Discharge, see 99315, 99316)

(For discharge services provided to newborns admitted and discharged on the same date, use 99463)

# Consultations

A consultation is a type of evaluation and management service provided at the request of another physician or appropriate source to either recommend care for a specific condition or problem or to determine whether to accept responsibility for ongoing management of the patient's entire care or for the care of a specific condition or problem.

A physician consultant may initiate diagnostic and/or therapeutic services at the same or subsequent visit.

A "consultation" initiated by a patient and/or family, and not requested by a physician or other appropriate source (eg, physician assistant, nurse practitioner, doctor of chiropractic, physical therapist, occupational therapist, speech-language pathologist, psychologist, social worker, lawyer, or insurance company), is not reported using the consultation codes but may be reported using the office visit, home service, or domiciliary/rest home care codes as appropriate.

The written or verbal request for consult may be made by a physician or other appropriate source and documented in the patient's medical record by either the consulting or requesting physician or appropriate source. The consultant's opinion and any services that were ordered or performed must also be documented in the patient's medical record and communicated by written report to the requesting physician or other appropriate source.

If a consultation is mandated (eg, by a third-party payer) modifier 32 should also be reported.

Any specifically identifiable procedure (ie, identified with a specific CPT code) performed on or subsequent to the date of the initial consultation should be reported separately.

If subsequent to the completion of a consultation the consultant assumes responsibility for management of a portion or all of the patient's condition(s), the appropriate **Evaluation and Management** services code for the site of service should be reported. In the hospital or nursing facility setting, the consultant should use the appropriate inpatient consultation code for the initial encounter and then subsequent hospital or nursing facility care codes. In the office setting, the consultant should use the appropriate office or other outpatient consultation codes and then the established patient office or other outpatient services codes.

To report services provided to a patient who is admitted to a hospital or nursing facility in the course of an encounter in the office or other ambulatory facility, see the notes for Initial Hospital Inpatient Care (page 11) or Initial Nursing Facility Care (page 19).

For definitions of key components and commonly used terms, please see **Evaluation and Management Services Guidelines.**

# Office or Other Outpatient Consultations

## New or Established Patient

The following codes are used to report consultations provided in the office or in an outpatient or other ambulatory facility, including hospital observation services, home services, domiciliary, rest home, or emergency department (see the preceding consultation definition above). Follow-up visits in the consultant's office or other outpatient facility that are initiated by the consultant or patient are reported using the appropriate codes for established patients, office visits (99211-99215), domiciliary, rest home (99334-99337), or home (99347-99350). If an additional request for an opinion or advice regarding the same or a new problem is received from another physician or other appropriate source and documented in the medical record, the office consultation codes may be used again. Services that constitute transfer of care (ie, are provided for the management of the patient's entire care or for the care of a specific condition or problem) are reported with the appropriate new or established patient codes for office or other outpatient visits, domiciliary, rest home services, or home services.

**99241** **Office consultation** for a new or established patient, which requires these 3 key components:

- **A problem focused history;**
- **A problem focused examination; and**
- **Straightforward medical decision making.**

Counseling and/or coordination of care with other physicians, other qualified health care professionals, or agencies are provided consistent with the nature of the problem(s) and the patient's and/or family's needs.

Usually, the presenting problem(s) are self limited or minor. Typically, 15 minutes are spent face-to-face with the patient and/or family.

**99242** **Office consultation** for a new or established patient, which requires these 3 key components:

- **An expanded problem focused history;**
- **An expanded problem focused examination; and**
- **Straightforward medical decision making.**

Counseling and/or coordination of care with other physicians, other qualified health care professionals, or agencies are provided consistent with the nature of the problem(s) and the patient's and/or family's needs.

Usually, the presenting problem(s) are of low severity. Typically, 30 minutes are spent face-to-face with the patient and/or family.

**99243** **Office consultation** for a new or established patient, which requires these 3 key components:

- **A detailed history;**
- **A detailed examination; and**
- **Medical decision making of low complexity.**

Counseling and/or coordination of care with other physicians, other qualified health care professionals, or agencies are provided consistent with the nature of the problem(s) and the patient's and/or family's needs.

Usually, the presenting problem(s) are of moderate severity. Typically, 40 minutes are spent face-to-face with the patient and/or family.

**99244** **Office consultation** for a new or established patient, which requires these 3 key components:

- **A comprehensive history;**
- **A comprehensive examination; and**
- **Medical decision making of moderate complexity.**

Counseling and/or coordination of care with other physicians, other qualified health care professionals, or agencies are provided consistent with the nature of the problem(s) and the patient's and/or family's needs.

Usually, the presenting problem(s) are of moderate to high severity. Typically, 60 minutes are spent face-to-face with the patient and/or family.

**99245** **Office consultation** for a new or established patient, which requires these 3 key components:

- **A comprehensive history;**
- **A comprehensive examination; and**
- **Medical decision making of high complexity.**

Counseling and/or coordination of care with other physicians, other qualified health care professionals, or agencies are provided consistent with the nature of the problem(s) and the patient's and/or family's needs.

Usually, the presenting problem(s) are of moderate to high severity. Typically, 80 minutes are spent face-to-face with the patient and/or family.

# Inpatient Consultations

## New or Established Patient

The following codes are used to report physician or other qualified health care professional consultations provided to hospital inpatients, residents of nursing facilities, or patients in a partial hospital setting. Only one consultation should be reported by a consultant per admission. Subsequent services during the same admission are reported using subsequent hospital care codes (99231-99233) or subsequent nursing facility care codes (99307-99310), including services to complete the initial consultation, monitor progress, revise recommendations, or address a new problem. Use subsequent hospital care codes (99231-99233) or subsequent nursing facility care codes (99307-99310) to report transfer of care services (see page 2, Concurrent Care and Transfer of Care definitions).

When an inpatient consultation is performed on a date that a patient is admitted to a hospital or nursing facility, all evaluation and management services provided by the consultant related to the admission are reported with the inpatient consultation service code (99251-99255). If a patient is admitted after an outpatient consultation (office, emergency department, etc), and the patient is not seen on the unit on the date of admission, only report the outpatient consultation code (99241-99245). If the patient is seen by the consultant on the unit on the date of admission, report all evaluation and management services provided by the consultant related to the admission with either the inpatient consultation code (99251-99255) or with the initial inpatient admission service code (99221-99223). Do not report both an outpatient consultation (99241-99245) and inpatient consultation (99251-99255) for services related to the same inpatient stay. When transfer of care services are provided on a date subsequent to the outpatient consultation, use the subsequent hospital care codes (99231-99233) or subsequent nursing facility care codes (99307-99310).

**99251**　　**Inpatient consultation** for a new or established patient, which requires these 3 key components:

- **A problem focused history;**
- **A problem focused examination; and**
- **Straightforward medical decision making.**

Counseling and/or coordination of care with other physicians, other qualified health care professionals, or agencies are provided consistent with the nature of the problem(s) and the patient's and/or family's needs.

Usually, the presenting problem(s) are self limited or minor. Typically, 20 minutes are spent at the bedside and on the patient's hospital floor or unit.

**99252**　　**Inpatient consultation** for a new or established patient, which requires these 3 key components:

- **An expanded problem focused history;**
- **An expanded problem focused examination; and**
- **Straightforward medical decision making.**

Counseling and/or coordination of care with other physicians, other qualified health care professionals, or agencies are provided consistent with the nature of the problem(s) and the patient's and/or family's needs.

Usually, the presenting problem(s) are of low severity. Typically, 40 minutes are spent at the bedside and on the patient's hospital floor or unit.

**99253**　　**Inpatient consultation** for a new or established patient, which requires these 3 key components:

- **A detailed history;**
- **A detailed examination; and**
- **Medical decision making of low complexity.**

Counseling and/or coordination of care with other physicians, other qualified health care professionals, or agencies are provided consistent with the nature of the problem(s) and the patient's and/or family's needs.

Usually, the presenting problem(s) are of moderate severity. Typically, 55 minutes are spent at the bedside and on the patient's hospital floor or unit.

**99254**　　**Inpatient consultation** for a new or established patient, which requires these 3 key components:

- **A comprehensive history;**
- **A comprehensive examination; and**
- **Medical decision making of moderate complexity.**

Counseling and/or coordination of care with other physicians, other qualified health care professionals, or agencies are provided consistent with the nature of the problem(s) and the patient's and/or family's needs.

Usually, the presenting problem(s) are of moderate to high severity. Typically, 80 minutes are spent at the bedside and on the patient's hospital floor or unit.

**99255**　　**Inpatient consultation** for a new or established patient, which requires these 3 key components:

- **A comprehensive history;**
- **A comprehensive examination; and**
- **Medical decision making of high complexity.**

Counseling and/or coordination of care with other physicians, other qualified health care professionals, or agencies are provided consistent with the nature of the problem(s) and the patient's and/or family's needs.

Usually, the presenting problem(s) are of moderate to high severity. Typically, 110 minutes are spent at the bedside and on the patient's hospital floor or unit.

# Emergency Department Services

## New or Established Patient

The following codes are used to report evaluation and management services provided in the emergency department. No distinction is made between new and established patients in the emergency department.

An emergency department is defined as an organized hospital-based facility for the provision of unscheduled episodic services to patients who present for immediate medical attention. The facility must be available 24 hours a day.

For critical care services provided in the emergency department, see Critical Care notes and 99291, 99292.

For evaluation and management services provided to a patient in an observation area of a hospital, see 99217-99220.

For observation or inpatient care services (including admission and discharge services), see 99234-99236.

99281    **Emergency department visit** for the evaluation and management of a patient, which requires these 3 key components:

- **A problem focused history;**
- **A problem focused examination; and**
- **Straightforward medical decision making.**

Counseling and/or coordination of care with other physicians, other qualified health care professionals, or agencies are provided consistent with the nature of the problem(s) and the patient's and/or family's needs.

Usually, the presenting problem(s) are self limited or minor.

99282    **Emergency department visit** for the evaluation and management of a patient, which requires these 3 key components:

- **An expanded problem focused history;**
- **An expanded problem focused examination; and**
- **Medical decision making of low complexity.**

Counseling and/or coordination of care with other physicians, other qualified health care professionals, or agencies are provided consistent with the nature of the problem(s) and the patient's and/or family's needs.

Usually, the presenting problem(s) are of low to moderate severity.

99283    **Emergency department visit** for the evaluation and management of a patient, which requires these 3 key components:

- **An expanded problem focused history;**
- **An expanded problem focused examination; and**
- **Medical decision making of moderate complexity.**

Counseling and/or coordination of care with other physicians, other qualified health care professionals, or agencies are provided consistent with the nature of the problem(s) and the patient's and/or family's needs.

Usually, the presenting problem(s) are of moderate severity.

99284    **Emergency department visit** for the evaluation and management of a patient, which requires these 3 key components:

- **A detailed history;**
- **A detailed examination; and**
- **Medical decision making of moderate complexity.**

Counseling and/or coordination of care with other physicians, other qualified health care professionals, or agencies are provided consistent with the nature of the problem(s) and the patient's and/or family's needs.

Usually, the presenting problem(s) are of high severity, and require urgent evaluation by the physician physicians, or other qualified health care professionals but do not pose an immediate significant threat to life or physiologic function.

99285    **Emergency department visit** for the evaluation and management of a patient, which requires these 3 key components within the constraints imposed by the urgency of the patient's clinical condition and/or mental status:

- **A comprehensive history;**
- **A comprehensive examination; and**
- **Medical decision making of high complexity.**

Counseling and/or coordination of care with other physicians, other qualified health care professionals, or agencies are provided consistent with the nature of the problem(s) and the patient's and/or family's needs.

Usually, the presenting problem(s) are of high severity and pose an immediate significant threat to life or physiologic function.

## Other Emergency Services

In directed emergency care, advanced life support, the physician or other qualified health care professional is located in a hospital emergency or critical care department, and is in two-way voice communication with ambulance or rescue personnel outside the hospital. Direction of the performance of necessary medical procedures includes but is not limited to: telemetry of cardiac rhythm; cardiac and/or pulmonary resuscitation; endotracheal or esophageal obturator airway intubation; administration of intravenous fluids and/or administration of intramuscular, intratracheal or subcutaneous drugs; and/or electrical conversion of arrhythmia.

**99288**   **Physician or other qualified health care professional direction of** emergency medical systems (EMS) emergency care, advanced life support

(99289 has been deleted. To report, use 99466)

(99290 has been deleted. To report, use 99467)

# Critical Care Services

Critical care is the direct delivery by a physician(s) or other qualified health care professional of medical care for a critically ill or critically injured patient. A critical illness or injury acutely impairs one or more vital organ systems such that there is a high probability of imminent or life threatening deterioration in the patient's condition. Critical care involves high complexity decision making to assess, manipulate, and support vital system function(s) to treat single or multiple vital organ system failure and/ or to prevent further life threatening deterioration of the patient's condition. Examples of vital organ system failure include, but are not limited to: central nervous system failure, circulatory failure, shock, renal, hepatic, metabolic, and/or respiratory failure. Although critical care typically requires interpretation of multiple physiologic parameters and/or application of advanced technology(s), critical care may be provided in life threatening situations when these elements are not present. Critical care may be provided on multiple days, even if no changes are made in the treatment rendered to the patient, provided that the patient's condition continues to require the level of attention described above.

Providing medical care to a critically ill, injured, or post-operative patient qualifies as a critical care service only if both the illness or injury and the treatment being provided meet the above requirements. Critical care is usually, but not always, given in a critical care area, such as the coronary care unit, intensive care unit, pediatric intensive care unit, respiratory care unit, or the emergency care facility.

Inpatient critical care services provided to infants 29 days through 71 months of age are reported with pediatric critical care codes 99471-99476. The pediatric critical care codes are reported as long as the infant/young child qualifies for critical care services during the hospital stay through 71 months of age. Inpatient critical care services provided to neonates (28 days of age or younger) are reported with the neonatal critical care codes 99468 and 99469. The neonatal critical care codes are reported as long as the neonate qualifies for critical care services during the hospital stay through the 28th postnatal day. The reporting of the pediatric and neonatal critical care services is not based on time or the type of unit (eg, pediatric or neonatal critical care unit) and it is not dependent upon the type of physician or other qualified health care professional delivering the care. To report critical care services provided in the outpatient setting (eg, emergency department or office), for neonates and pediatric patients up through 71 months of age, see the critical care codes 99291, 99292. If the same individual provides critical care services for a neonatal or pediatric patient in both the outpatient and inpatient settings on the same day, report only the appropriate neonatal or pediatric critical care code 99468-99472 for all critical care services provided on that day. Also report 99291-99292 for neonatal or pediatric critical care services provided by the individual providing critical care at one facility but transferring the patient to another facility. Critical care services provided by a second individual of a different specialty not reporting a per day neonatal or pediatric critical care code can be reported with codes 99291, 99292. For additional instructions on reporting these services, see the Neonatal and Pediatric Critical Care section and codes 99468-99476.

Services for a patient who is not critically ill but happens to be in a critical care unit are reported using other appropriate E/M codes.

Critical care and other E/M services may be provided to the same patient on the same date by the same individual.

For reporting by professionals, the following services are included in critical care when performed during the critical period by the physician(s) providing critical care: the interpretation of cardiac output measurements (93561, 93562), chest X-rays (71010, 71015, 71020), pulse oximetry (94760, 94761, 94762), blood gases, and information data stored in computers (eg, ECGs, blood pressures, hematologic data [99090]); gastric intubation (43752, 43753); temporary transcutaneous pacing (92953); ventilatory management (94002-94004, 94660, 94662); and vascular access procedures (36000, 36410, 36415, 36591, 36600). Any services performed that are not included in this listing should be reported separately. Facilities may report the above services separately.

Codes 99291, 99292 should be reported for the attendance during the transport of critically ill or critically injured patients older than 24 months of age to or from a facility or hospital. For transport services of critically ill or critically injured pediatric patients 24 months of age or younger, see 99466, 99467.

Codes 99291, 99292 are used to report the total duration of time spent in provision of critical care services to a critically ill or critically injured patient, even if the time spent providing care on that date is not continuous. For any given period of time spent providing critical care services, the individual must devote his or her full attention to the patient and, therefore, cannot provide services to any other patient during the same period of time.

Time spent with the individual patient should be recorded in the patient's record. The time that can be reported as critical care is the time spent engaged in work directly related to the individual patient's care whether that time was spent at the immediate bedside or elsewhere on the floor or unit. For example, time spent on the unit or at the nursing station on the floor reviewing test results or imaging studies, discussing the critically ill patient's care with other medical staff or documenting critical care services in the medical record would be reported as critical care, even though it does not occur at the bedside. Also, when the patient is unable or lacks capacity to participate in discussions, time spent on the floor or unit with family members or surrogate decision makers obtaining a medical history, reviewing the patient's condition or prognosis, or discussing treatment or limitation(s) of treatment may be reported as critical care, provided that the conversation bears directly on the management of the patient.

Time spent in activities that occur outside of the unit or off the floor (eg, telephone calls whether taken at home, in the office, or elsewhere in the hospital) may not be reported as critical care since the individual is not immediately available to the patient. Time spent in activities that do not directly contribute to the treatment of the patient may not be reported as critical care, even if they are performed in the critical care unit (eg, participation in administrative meetings or telephone calls to discuss other patients). Time spent performing separately reportable procedures or services should not be included in the time reported as critical care time. No individual may report remote real-time interactive video-conferenced critical care services (0188T, 0189T) for the period in which any other physician or qualified health care professional reports codes 99291, 99292.

Code 99291 is used to report the first 30-74 minutes of critical care on a given date. It should be used only once per date even if the time spent by the individual is not continuous on that date. Critical care of less than 30 minutes total duration on a given date should be reported with the appropriate E/M code.

Code 99292 is used to report additional block(s) of time, of up to 30 minutes each beyond the first 74 minutes. (See the following table.)

The following examples illustrate the correct reporting of critical care services:

**Total Duration of Critical Care Codes**

| | |
|---|---|
| less than 30 minutes | appropriate E/M codes |
| 30-74 minutes (30 minutes - 1 hr. 14 min.) | 99291 X 1 |
| 75-104 minutes (1 hr. 15 min. - 1 hr. 44 min.) | 99291 X 1 AND 99292 X 1 |
| 105-134 minutes (1 hr. 45 min. - 2 hr. 14 min.) | 99291 X 1 AND 99292 X 2 |
| 135-164 minutes (2 hr. 15 min. - 2 hr. 44 min.) | 99291 X 1 AND 99292 X 3 |
| 165-194 minutes (2 hr. 45 min. - 3 hr. 14 min.) | 99291 X 1 AND 99292 X 4 |
| 195 minutes or longer (3 hr. 15 min. - etc.) | 99291 and 99292 as appropriate (see illustrated reporting examples above) |

**99291** **Critical care, evaluation and management** of the critically ill or critically injured patient; first 30-74 minutes

+ **99292** each additional 30 minutes (List separately in addition to code for primary service)

(Use 99292 in conjunction with 99291)

(99293 has been deleted. To report, use 99471)

(99294 has been deleted. To report, use 99472)

(99295 has been deleted. To report, use 99468)

(99296 has been deleted. To report, use 99469)

(99298 has been deleted. To report, use 99478)

(99299 has been deleted. To report, use 99479)

(99300 has been deleted. To report, use 99480)

# Nursing Facility Services

The following codes are used to report evaluation and management services to patients in nursing facilities (formerly called skilled nursing facilities [SNFs], intermediate care facilities [ICFs], or long-term care facilities [LTCFs]).

These codes should also be used to report evaluation and management services provided to a patient in a psychiatric residential treatment center (a facility or a distinct part of a facility for psychiatric care, which provides a 24-hour therapeutically planned and professionally staffed group living and learning environment). If procedures such as medical psychotherapy are provided in addition to evaluation and management services, these should be reported in addition to the evaluation and management services provided.

Nursing facilities that provide convalescent, rehabilitative, or long term care are required to conduct comprehensive, accurate, standardized, and reproducible assessments of each resident's functional capacity using a Resident Assessment Instrument (RAI). All RAIs include the Minimum Data Set (MDS), Resident Assessment Protocols (RAPs), and utilization guidelines. The MDS is the primary screening and assessment tool; the RAPs trigger the identification of potential problems and provide guidelines for follow-up assessments.

Physicians have a central role in assuring that all residents receive thorough assessments and that medical plans of care are instituted or revised to enhance or maintain the residents' physical and psychosocial functioning. This role includes providing input in the development of the MDS and a multi-disciplinary plan of care, as required by regulations pertaining to the care of nursing facility residents.

Two major subcategories of nursing facility services are recognized: Initial Nursing Facility Care and Subsequent Nursing Facility Care. Both subcategories apply to new or established patients.

For definitions of key components and commonly used terms, please see **Evaluation and Management Services Guidelines.**

> (For care plan oversight services provided to nursing facility residents, see 99379-99380)

# Initial Nursing Facility Care

## New or Established Patient

When the patient is admitted to the nursing facility in the course of an encounter in another site of service (eg, hospital emergency department, office), all evaluation and management services provided by that physician in conjunction with that admission are considered part of the initial nursing facility care when performed on the same date as the admission or readmission. The nursing facility care level of service reported by the admitting physician should include the services related to the admission he/she provided in the other sites of service as well as in the nursing facility setting.

Hospital discharge or observation discharge services performed on the same date of nursing facility admission or readmission may be reported separately. For a patient discharged from inpatient status on the same date of nursing facility admission or readmission, the hospital discharge services should be reported with codes 99238, 99239 as appropriate. For a patient discharged from observation status on the same date of nursing facility admission or readmission, the observation care discharge services should be reported with code 99217. For a patient admitted and discharged from observation or

inpatient status on the same date, see codes 99234-99236.

> (For nursing facility care discharge, see 99315, 99316)

**99304**    Initial nursing facility care, per day, for the evaluation and management of a patient, which requires these 3 key components:

- **A detailed or comprehensive history;**
- **A detailed or comprehensive examination; and**
- **Medical decision making that is straightforward or of low complexity.**

Counseling and/or coordination of care with other physicians, other qualified health care professionals, or agencies are provided consistent with the nature of the problem(s) and the patient's and/or family's needs.

Usually, the problem(s) requiring admission are of low severity. Typically, 25 minutes are spent at the bedside and on the patient's facility floor or unit.

**99305**    Initial nursing facility care, per day, for the evaluation and management of a patient, which requires these 3 key components:

- **A comprehensive history;**
- **A comprehensive examination; and**
- **Medical decision making of moderate complexity.**

Counseling and/or coordination of care with other physicians, other qualified health care professionals, or agencies are provided consistent with the nature of the problem(s) and the patient's and/or family's needs.

Usually, the problem(s) requiring admission are of moderate severity. Typically, 35 minutes are spent at the bedside and on the patient's facility floor or unit.

**99306**    Initial nursing facility care, per day, for the evaluation and management of a patient, which requires these 3 key components:

- **A comprehensive history;**
- **A comprehensive examination; and**
- **Medical decision making of high complexity.**

Counseling and/or coordination of care with other physicians, other qualified health care professionals, or agencies are provided consistent with the nature of the problem(s) and the patient's and/or family's needs.

Usually, the problem(s) requiring admission are of high severity. Typically, 45 minutes are spent at the bedside and on the patient's facility floor or unit.

## Subsequent Nursing Facility Care

All levels of subsequent nursing facility care include reviewing the medical record and reviewing the results of diagnostic studies and changes in the patient's status (ie, changes in history, physical condition, and response to management) since the last assessment by the physician or other qualified health are professional.

Evaluation/Management

**Evaluation/Management**

**99307** Subsequent nursing facility care, per day, for the evaluation and management of a patient, which requires at least 2 of these 3 key components:

- **A problem focused interval history;**
- **A problem focused examination;**
- **Straightforward medical decision making.**

Counseling and/or coordination of care with other physicians, other qualified health care professionals, or agencies are provided consistent with the nature of the problem(s) and the patient's and/or family's needs.

Usually, the patient is stable, recovering, or improving. Typically, 10 minutes are spent at the bedside and on the patient's facility floor or unit.

**99308** Subsequent nursing facility care, per day, for the evaluation and management of a patient, which requires at least 2 of these 3 key components:

- **An expanded problem focused interval history;**
- **An expanded problem focused examination;**
- **Medical decision making of low complexity.**

Counseling and/or coordination of care with other physicians, other qualified health care professionals, or agencies are provided consistent with the nature of the problem(s) and the patient's and/or family's needs.

Usually, the patient is responding inadequately to therapy or has developed a minor complication. Typically, 15 minutes are spent at the bedside and on the patient's facility floor or unit.

**99309** Subsequent nursing facility care, per day, for the evaluation and management of a patient, which requires at least 2 of these 3 key components:

- **A detailed interval history;**
- **A detailed examination;**
- **Medical decision making of moderate complexity.**

Counseling and/or coordination of care with other physicians, other qualified health care professionals, or agencies are provided consistent with the nature of the problem(s) and the patient's and/or family's needs.

Usually, the patient has developed a significant complication or a significant new problem. Typically, 25 minutes are spent at the bedside and on the patient's facility floor or unit.

**99310** Subsequent nursing facility care, per day, for the evaluation and management of a patient, which requires at least 2 of these 3 key components:

- **A comprehensive interval history;**
- **A comprehensive examination;**
- **Medical decision making of high complexity.**

Counseling and/or coordination of care with other physicians, other qualified health care professionals, or agencies are provided consistent with the nature of the problem(s) and the patient's and/or family's needs.

The patient may be unstable or may have developed a significant new problem requiring immediate physician attention. Typically, 35 minutes are spent at the bedside and on the patient's facility floor or unit.

## Nursing Facility Discharge Services

The nursing facility discharge day management codes are to be used to report the total duration of time spent by a physician or other qualified health care professional for the final nursing facility discharge of a patient. The codes include, as appropriate, final examination of the patient, discussion of the nursing facility stay, even if the time spent on that date is not continuous. Instructions are given for continuing care to all relevant caregivers, and preparation of discharge records, prescriptions and referral forms.

**99315** Nursing facility discharge day management; 30 minutes or less

**99316** more than 30 minutes

## Other Nursing Facility Services

**99318** Evaluation and management of a patient involving an annual nursing facility assessment, which requires these 3 key components:

- **A detailed interval history;**
- **A comprehensive examination; and**
- **Medical decision making that is of low to moderate complexity.**

Counseling and/or coordination of care with other physicians, other qualified health care professionals, or agencies are provided consistent with the nature of the problem(s) and the patient's and/or family's needs.

Usually, the patient is stable, recovering, or improving. Typically, 30 minutes are spent at the bedside and on the patient's facility floor or unit.

(Do not report 99318 on the same date of service as nursing facility services codes 99304-99316)

## Domiciliary, Rest Home (eg, Boarding Home), or Custodial Care Services

The following codes are used to report evaluation and management services in a facility which provides room, board and other personal assistance services, generally on a long-term basis. They also are used to report evaluation and management services in an assisted living facility.

The facility's services do not include a medical component.

For definitions of key components and commonly used terms, please see **Evaluation and Management Services Guidelines.**

(For care plan oversight services provided to a patient in a domiciliary facility under the care of a home health agency, see 99374, 99375, and for hospice agency, see 99377, 99378. For care plan oversight provided to a patient under hospice or home health agency care, see 99339, 99340)

## New Patient

**99324**    Domiciliary or rest home visit for the evaluation and management of a new patient, which requires these 3 key components:

- **A problem focused history;**
- **A problem focused examination; and**
- **Straightforward medical decision making.**

Counseling and/or coordination of care with other physicians, other qualified health care professionals, or agencies are provided consistent with the nature of the problem(s) and the patient's and/or family's needs.

Usually, the presenting problem(s) are of low severity. Typically, 20 minutes are spent with the patient and/or family or caregiver.

**99325**    Domiciliary or rest home visit for the evaluation and management of a new patient, which requires these 3 key components:

- **An expanded problem focused history;**
- **An expanded problem focused examination; and**
- **Medical decision making of low complexity.**

Counseling and/or coordination of care with other physicians, other qualified health care professionals, or agencies are provided consistent with the nature of the problem(s) and the patient's and/or family's needs.

Usually, the presenting problem(s) are of moderate severity. Typically, 30 minutes are spent with the patient and/or family or caregiver.

**99326**    Domiciliary or rest home visit for the evaluation and management of a new patient, which requires these 3 key components:

- **A detailed history;**
- **A detailed examination; and**
- **Medical decision making of moderate complexity.**

Counseling and/or coordination of care with other physicians, other qualified health care professionals, or agencies are provided consistent with the nature of the problem(s) and the patient's and/or family's needs.

Usually, the presenting problem(s) are of moderate to high severity. Typically, 45 minutes are spent with the patient and/or family or caregiver.

**99327**    Domiciliary or rest home visit for the evaluation and management of a new patient, which requires these 3 key components:

- **A comprehensive history;**
- **A comprehensive examination; and**
- **Medical decision making of moderate complexity.**

Counseling and/or coordination of care with other physicians, other qualified health care professionals, or agencies are provided consistent with the nature of the problem(s) and the patient's and/or family's needs.

Usually, the presenting problem(s) are of high severity. Typically, 60 minutes are spent with the patient and/or family or caregiver.

**99328**    Domiciliary or rest home visit for the evaluation and management of a new patient, which requires these 3 key components:

- **A comprehensive history;**
- **A comprehensive examination; and**
- **Medical decision making of high complexity.**

Counseling and/or coordination of care with other physicians, other qualified health care professionals, or agencies are provided consistent with the nature of the problem(s) and the patient's and/or family's needs.

Usually, the patient is unstable or has developed a significant new problem requiring immediate physician attention. Typically, 75 minutes are spent with the patient and/or family or caregiver.

## Established Patient

**99334**    Domiciliary or rest home visit for the evaluation and management of an established patient, which requires at least 2 of these 3 key components:

- **A problem focused interval history;**
- **A problem focused examination;**
- **Straightforward medical decision making.**

Counseling and/or coordination of care with other physicians, other qualified health care professionals, or agencies are provided consistent with the nature of the problem(s) and the patient's and/or family's needs.

Usually, the presenting problem(s) are self-limited or minor. Typically, 15 minutes are spent with the patient and/or family or caregiver.

**99335**    Domiciliary or rest home visit for the evaluation and management of an established patient, which requires at least 2 of these 3 key components:

- **An expanded problem focused interval history;**
- **An expanded problem focused examination;**
- **Medical decision making of low complexity.**

Evaluation/Management

Counseling and/or coordination of care with other physicians, other qualified health care professionals, or agencies are provided consistent with the nature of the problem(s) and the patient's and/or family's needs.

Usually, the presenting problem(s) are of low to moderate severity. Typically, 25 minutes are spent with the patient and/or family or caregiver.

**99336** Domiciliary or rest home visit for the evaluation and management of an established patient, which requires at least 2 of these 3 key components:

- **A detailed interval history;**
- **A detailed examination;**
- **Medical decision making of moderate complexity.**

Counseling and/or coordination of care with other physicians, other qualified health care professionals, or agencies are provided consistent with the nature of the problem(s) and the patient's and/or family's needs.

Usually, the presenting problem(s) are of moderate to high severity. Typically, 40 minutes are spent with the patient and/or family or caregiver.

**99337** Domiciliary or rest home visit for the evaluation and management of an established patient, which requires at least 2 of these 3 key components:

- **A comprehensive interval history;**
- **A comprehensive examination;**
- **Medical decision making of moderate to high complexity.**

Counseling and/or coordination of care with other physicians, other qualified health care professionals, or agencies are provided consistent with the nature of the problem(s) and the patient's and/or family's needs.

Usually, the presenting problem(s) are of moderate to high severity. The patient may be unstable or may have developed a significant new problem requiring immediate physician attention. Typically, 60 minutes are spent with the patient and/or family or caregiver.

# Domiciliary, Rest Home (eg, Assisted Living Facility), or Home Care Plan Oversight Services

(For instructions on the use of 99339, 99340, see introductory notes for 99374-99380)

(For care plan oversight services for patients under the care of a home health agency, hospice, or nursing facility, see 99374-99380)

(Do not report 99339, 99340 for time reported with 98966-98969, 99441-99444)

**99339** Individual physician supervision of a patient (patient not present) in home, domiciliary or rest home (eg, assisted living facility) requiring complex and multidisciplinary care modalities involving regular physician development and/or revision of care plans, review of subsequent reports of patient status, review of related laboratory and other studies, communication (including telephone calls) for purposes of assessment or care decisions with health care professional(s), family member(s), surrogate decision maker(s) (eg, legal guardian) and/or key caregiver(s) involved in patient's care, integration of new information into the medical treatment plan and/or adjustment of medical therapy, within a calendar month; 15-29 minutes

**99340**          30 minutes or more

(Do not report 99339, 99340 for patients under the care of a home health agency, enrolled in a hospice program, or for nursing facility residents)

(Do not report 99339, 99340 during the same month with 99487-99489)

(Do not report 99339, 99340 when performed during the service time of codes 99495 or 99496)

# Home Services

The following codes are used to report evaluation and management services provided in a private residence.

For definitions of key components and commonly used terms, please see **Evaluation and Management Services Guidelines.**

(For care plan oversight services provided to a patient in the home under the care of a home health agency, see 99374, 99375, and for hospice agency, see 99377, 99378. For care plan oversight provided to a patient under hospice or home health agency care, see 99339, 99340)

## New Patient

**99341** **Home visit** for the evaluation and management of a new patient, which requires these 3 key components:

- **A problem focused history;**
- **A problem focused examination; and**
- **Straightforward medical decision making.**

Counseling and/or coordination of care with other physicians, other qualified health care professionals, or agencies are provided consistent with the nature of the problem(s) and the patient's and/or family's needs.

Usually, the presenting problem(s) are of low severity. Typically, 20 minutes are spent face-to-face with the patient and/or family.

**99342** **Home visit** for the evaluation and management of a new patient, which requires these 3 key components:

- **An expanded problem focused history;**
- **An expanded problem focused examination; and**
- **Medical decision making of low complexity.**

Counseling and/or coordination of care with other physicians, other qualified health care professionals, or agencies are provided consistent with the nature of the problem(s) and the patient's and/or family's needs.

Usually, the presenting problem(s) are of moderate severity. Typically, 30 minutes are spent face-to-face with the patient and/or family.

**99343** **Home visit** for the evaluation and management of a new patient, which requires these 3 key components:

- **A detailed history;**
- **A detailed examination; and**
- **Medical decision making of moderate complexity.**

Counseling and/or coordination of care with other physicians, other qualified health care professionals, or agencies are provided consistent with the nature of the problem(s) and the patient's and/or family's needs.

Usually, the presenting problem(s) are of moderate to high severity. Typically, 45 minutes are spent face-to-face with the patient and/or family.

**99344** **Home visit** for the evaluation and management of a new patient, which requires these 3 key components:

- **A comprehensive history;**
- **A comprehensive examination; and**
- **Medical decision making of moderate complexity.**

Counseling and/or coordination of care with other physicians, other qualified health care professionals, or agencies are provided consistent with the nature of the problem(s) and the patient's and/or family's needs.

Usually, the presenting problem(s) are of high severity. Typically, 60 minutes are spent face-to-face with the patient and/or family.

**99345** **Home visit** for the evaluation and management of a new patient, which requires these 3 key components:

- **A comprehensive history;**
- **A comprehensive examination; and**
- **Medical decision making of high complexity.**

Counseling and/or coordination of care with other physicians, other qualified health care professionals, or agencies are provided consistent with the nature of the problem(s) and the patient's and/or family's needs.

Usually, the patient is unstable or has developed a significant new problem requiring immediate physician attention. Typically, 75 minutes are spent face-to-face with the patient and/or family.

## Established Patient

**99347** **Home visit** for the evaluation and management of an established patient, which requires at least 2 of these 3 key components:

- **A problem focused interval history;**

- **A problem focused examination;**
- **Straightforward medical decision making.**

Counseling and/or coordination of care with other physicians, other qualified health care professionals, or agencies are provided consistent with the nature of the problem(s) and the patient's and/or family's needs.

Usually, the presenting problem(s) are self limited or minor. Typically, 15 minutes are spent face-to-face with the patient and/or family.

**99348** **Home visit** for the evaluation and management of an established patient, which requires at least 2 of these 3 key components:

- **An expanded problem focused interval history;**
- **An expanded problem focused examination;**
- **Medical decision making of low complexity.**

Counseling and/or coordination of care with other physicians, other qualified health care professionals, or agencies are provided consistent with the nature of the problem(s) and the patient's and/or family's needs.

Usually, the presenting problem(s) are of low to moderate severity. Typically, 25 minutes are spent face-to-face with the patient and/or family.

**99349** **Home visit** for the evaluation and management of an established patient, which requires at least 2 of these 3 key components:

- **A detailed interval history;**
- **A detailed examination;**
- **Medical decision making of moderate complexity.**

Counseling and/or coordination of care with other physicians, other qualified health care professionals, or agencies are provided consistent with the nature of the problem(s) and the patient's and/or family's needs.

Usually, the presenting problem(s) are moderate to high severity. Typically, 40 minutes are spent face-to-face with the patient and/or family.

**99350** **Home visit** for the evaluation and management of an established patient, which requires at least 2 of these 3 key components:

- **A comprehensive interval history;**
- **A comprehensive examination;**
- **Medical decision making of moderate to high complexity.**

Counseling and/or coordination of care with other physicians, other qualified health care professionals, or agencies are provided consistent with the nature of the problem(s) and the patient's and/or family's needs.

Usually, the presenting problem(s) are of moderate to high severity. The patient may be unstable or may have developed a significant new problem requiring immediate physician attention. Typically, 60 minutes are spent face-to-face with the patient and/or family.

# Prolonged Services

## Prolonged Service With Direct Patient Contact

Codes 99354-99357 are used when a physician or other qualified health care professional provides prolonged service involving direct patient contact that is provided beyond the usual service in either the inpatient or outpatient setting. Direct patient contact is face-to-face and includes additional non-face-to-face services on the patient's floor or unit in the hospital or nursing facility during the same session. This service is reported in addition to the designated evaluation and management services at any level and any other services provided at the same session as evaluation and management services. Appropriate codes should be selected for supplies provided or procedures performed in the care of the patient during this period.

Codes 99354-99355 are used to report the total duration of face-to-face time spent by a physician or other qualified health care professional on a given date providing prolonged service in the office or other outpatient setting, even if the time spent by the physician or other qualified health care professional on that date is not continuous. Codes 99356-99357 are used to report the total duration of time spent by a physician or other qualified health care professional at the bedside and on the patient's floor or unit in the hospital or nursing facility on a given date providing prolonged service to a patient, even if the time spent by the physician or other qualified health care professional on that date is not continuous.

Code 99354 or 99356 is used to report the first hour of prolonged service on a given date, depending on the place of service.

Either code should be used only once per date, even if the time spent by the physician or other qualified health care professional is not continuous on that date. Prolonged service of less than 30 minutes total duration on a given date is not separately reported because the work involved is included in the total work of the evaluation and management codes.

Code 99355 or 99357 is used to report each additional 30 minutes beyond the first hour, depending on the place of service. Either code may also be used to report the final 15-30 minutes of prolonged service on a given date. Prolonged service of less than 15 minutes beyond the first hour or less than 15 minutes beyond the final 30 minutes is not reported separately.

The use of the time based add-on codes requires that the primary evaluation and management service have a typical or specified time published in the CPT codebook.

The following examples illustrate the correct reporting of prolonged physician or other qualified health care

professional service with direct patient contact in the office setting:

| Total Duration of Prolonged Services | Code(s) |
|---|---|
| less than 30 minutes | Not reported separately |
| 30-74 minutes (30 minutes - 1 hr. 14 min.) | 99354 X 1 |
| 75-104 minutes (1 hr. 15 min. - 1 hr. 44 min.) | 99354 X 1 AND 99355 X 1 |
| 105 or more (1 hr. 45 min. or more) | 99354 X 1 AND 99355 X 2 or more for each additional 30 minutes. |

+ **99354**  Prolonged service in the office or other outpatient setting requiring direct patient contact beyond the usual service; first hour (List separately in addition to code for office or other outpatient **Evaluation and Management** service)

(Use 99354 in conjunction with 90837, 99201-99215, 99241-99245, 99324-99337, 99341-99350)

+ **99355**  each additional 30 minutes (List separately in addition to code for prolonged service)

(Use 99355 in conjunction with 99354)

+ **99356**  Prolonged service in the inpatient or observation setting, requiring unit/floor time beyond the usual service; first hour (List separately in addition to code for inpatient **Evaluation and Management** service)

(Use 99356 in conjunction with 90837, 99218-99220, 99221-99223, 99224-99226, 99231-99233, 99234-99236, 99251-99255, 99304-99310)

+ **99357**  each additional 30 minutes (List separately in addition to code for prolonged service)

(Use 99357 in conjunction with 99356)

## Prolonged Service Without Direct Patient Contact

Codes 99358 and 99359 are used when a prolonged service is provided that is neither face-to-face time in the office or outpatient setting, nor additional unit/floor time in the hospital or nursing facility setting during the same session of an evaluation and management service and is beyond the usual physician or other qualified health care professional service time.

This service is to be reported in relation to other physician or other qualified health care professional services, including evaluation and management services at any level. This prolonged service may be reported on a different date than the primary service to which it is related. For example, extensive record review may relate to a previous evaluation and management service performed earlier and commences upon receipt of past records. However, it must relate to a service or patient

Evaluation/Management

where (face-to-face) patient care has occurred or will occur and relate to ongoing patient management. A typical time for the primary service need not be established within the CPT code set.

Codes 99358 and 99359 are used to report the total duration of non-face-to-face time spent by a physician or other qualified health care professional on a given date providing prolonged service, even if the time spent by the physician or other qualified health care professional on that date is not continuous. Code 99358 is used to report the first hour of prolonged service on a given date regardless of the place of service. It should be used only once per date.

Prolonged service of less than 30 minutes total duration on a given date is not separately reported.

Code 99359 is used to report each additional 30 minutes beyond the first hour regardless of the place of service. It may also be used to report the final 15 to 30 minutes of prolonged service on a given date.

Prolonged service of less than 15 minutes beyond the first hour or less than 15 minutes beyond the final 30 minutes is not reported separately.

Do not report 99358, 99359 for time spent in care plan oversight services (99339, 99340, 99374-99380), anticoagulant management (99363, 99364), medical team conferences (99366-99368), on-line medical evaluations (99444), or other non-face-to-face services that have more specific codes and no upper time limit in the CPT code set. Codes 99358, 99359 may be reported when related to other non-face-to-face services codes that have a published maximum time (eg, telephone services).

**99358**    **Prolonged evaluation and management service** before and/or after direct patient care; first hour

+ **99359**        each additional 30 minutes (List separately in addition to code for prolonged service)

(Use 99359 in conjunction with 99358)

(Do not report 99358, 99359 during the same month with 99487-99489)

(Do not report 99358, 99359 when performed during the service time of codes 99495 or 99496)

## Standby Services

Code 99360 is used to report physician or other qualified health care professional standby services that are requested by another individual and that involve prolonged attendance without direct (face-to-face) patient contact. Care or services may not be provided to other patients during this period. This code is not used to report time spent proctoring another individual. It is also not used if the period of standby ends with the performance of a procedure, subject to a surgical package by the individual who was on standby.

Code 99360 is used to report the total duration of time spent on a given date on standby. Standby service of less than 30 minutes total duration on a given date is not reported separately.

Second and subsequent periods of standby beyond the first 30 minutes may be reported only if a full 30 minutes of standby was provided for each unit of service reported.

**99360**    **Standby service,** requiring prolonged attendance, each 30 minutes (eg, operative standby, standby for frozen section, for cesarean/high risk delivery, for monitoring EEG)

(For hospital mandated on call services, see 99026, 99027)

(99360 may be reported in addition to 99460, 99465 as appropriate)

(Do not report 99360 in conjunction with 99464)

# Case Management Services

Case management is a process in which a physician or another qualified health care professional is responsible for direct care of a patient and, additionally, for coordinating, managing access to, initiating, and/or supervising other health care services needed by the patient.

## Anticoagulant Management

Anticoagulant services are intended to describe the outpatient management of warfarin therapy, including ordering, review, and interpretation of International Normalized Ratio (INR) testing, communication with patient, and dosage adjustments as appropriate.

When reporting these services, the work of anticoagulant management may not be used as a basis for reporting an evaluation and management (E/M) service or care plan oversight time during the reporting period. Do not report these services with 98966-98969, 99441-99444 when telephone or on-line services address anticoagulation with warfarin management. If a significant, separately identifiable E/M service is performed, report the appropriate E/M service code using modifier 25.

These services are outpatient services only. When anticoagulation therapy is initiated or continued in the inpatient or observation setting, a new period begins after discharge and is reported with 99364. Do not report 99363-99364 with 99217-99239, 99291-99292, 99304-99318, 99471-99480 or other code(s) for physician review, interpretation, and patient management of home INR testing for a patient with mechanical heart valve(s).

Any period less than 60 continuous outpatient days is not reported. If less than the specified minimum number of services per period are performed, do not report the anticoagulant management services (99363-99364).

**99363** Anticoagulant management for an outpatient taking warfarin, physician review and interpretation of International Normalized Ratio (INR) testing, patient instructions, dosage adjustment (as needed), and ordering of additional tests; initial 90 days of therapy (must include a minimum of 8 INR measurements)

**99364** each subsequent 90 days of therapy (must include a minimum of 3 INR measurements)

(Do not report 99363, 99364 during the same month with 99487-99489)

(Do not report 99363, 99364 when performed during the service time of codes 99495 or 99496)

# Medical Team Conferences

Medical team conferences include face-to-face participation by a minimum of three qualified health care professionals from different specialties or disciplines (each of whom provide direct care to the patient), with or without the presence of the patient, family member(s), community agencies, surrogate decision maker(s) (eg, legal guardian), and/or caregiver(s). The participants are actively involved in the development, revision, coordination, and implementation of health care services needed by the patient. Reporting participants shall have performed face-to-face evaluations or treatments of the patient, independent of any team conference, within the previous 60 days.

Physicians or other qualified health care professionals who may report evaluation and management services should report their time spent in a team conference with the patient and/or family present using evaluation and management (E/M) codes (and time as the key controlling factor for code selection when counseling and/or coordination of care dominates the service). These introductory guidelines do not apply to services reported using E/M codes (see E/M services guidelines). However, the individual must be directly involved with the patient, providing face-to-face services outside of the conference visit with other physicians, and qualified health care professionals, or agencies.

Reporting participants shall document their participation in the team conference as well as their contributed information and subsequent treatment recommendations.

No more than one individual from the same specialty may report 99366-99368 at the same encounter.

Individuals should not report 99366-99368 when their participation in the medical team conference is part of a facility or organizational service contractually provided by the organization or facility.

The team conference starts at the beginning of the review of an individual patient and ends at the conclusion of the review. Time related to record keeping and report generation is not reported. The reporting participant shall be present for all time reported. The time reported is not limited to the time that the participant is communicating to the other team members or patient and/or family. Time reported for medical team conferences may not be used in the determination of time for other services such as care plan oversight (99374-99380), home, domiciliary, or rest home care plan oversight (99339-99340), prolonged services (99354-99359), psychotherapy, or any E/M service. For team conferences where the patient is present for any part of the duration of the conference, nonphysician qualified health care professionals (eg, speech-language pathologists, physical therapists, occupational therapists, social workers, dietitians) report the team conference face-to-face code 99366.

## Medical Team Conference, Direct (Face-to-Face) Contact With Patient and/or Family

**99366** **Medical team conference** with interdisciplinary team of health care professionals, face-to-face with patient and/or family, 30 minutes or more, participation by nonphysician qualified health care professional

(Team conference services of less than 30 minutes duration are not reported separately)

(For team conference services by a physician with patient and/or family present, see Evaluation and Management services)

(Do not report 99366 during the same month with 99487-99489)

(Do not report 99366 when performed during the service time of codes 99495 or 99496)

## Medical Team Conference, Without Direct (Face-to-Face) Contact With Patient and/or Family

**99367** **Medical team conference** with interdisciplinary team of health care professionals, patient and/or family not present, 30 minutes or more; participation by physician

**99368** participation by nonphysician qualified health care professional

(Team conference services of less than 30 minutes duration are not reported separately)

(Do not report 99367, 99368 during the same month with 99487-99489)

(Do not report 99367, 99368 when performed during the service time of codes 99495 or 99496)

# Care Plan Oversight Services

Care plan oversight services are reported separately from codes for office/outpatient, hospital, home, nursing facility or domiciliary, or non-face-to-face services. The complexity and approximate time of the care plan oversight services provided within a 30-day period determine code selection. Only one individual may report services for a given period of time, to reflect the sole or predominant supervisory role with a particular patient. These codes should not be reported for supervision of patients in nursing facilities or under the care of home health agencies unless they require recurrent supervision of therapy.

The work involved in providing very low intensity or infrequent supervision services is included in the pre- and post-encounter work for home, office/outpatient and nursing facility or domiciliary visit codes.

> (For care plan oversight services of patients in the home, domiciliary, or rest home [eg, assisted living facility], see 99339, 99340, and for hospice agency, see 99377, 99378)

> (Do not report 99374-99380 for time reported with 98966-98969, 99441-99444)

> (Do not report 99374-99378 during the same month with 99487-99489)

> (Do not report 99374-99380 when performed during the service time of codes 99495 or 99496)

**99374**  **Supervision** of a patient under care of home health agency (patient not present) in home, domiciliary or equivalent environment (eg, Alzheimer's facility) requiring complex and multidisciplinary care modalities involving regular development and/or revision of care plans by that individual, review of subsequent reports of patient status, review of related laboratory and other studies, communication (including telephone calls) for purposes of assessment or care decisions with health care professional(s), family member(s), surrogate decision maker(s) (eg, legal guardian) and/or key caregiver(s) involved in patient's care, integration of new information into the medical treatment plan and/or adjustment of medical therapy, within a calendar month; 15-29 minutes

**99375**      30 minutes or more

**99377**  **Supervision** of a hospice patient (patient not present) requiring complex and multidisciplinary care modalities involving regular development and/or revision of care plans by that individual, review of subsequent reports of patient status, review of related laboratory and other studies, communication (including telephone calls) for purposes of assessment or care decisions with health care professional(s), family member(s), surrogate decision maker(s) (eg, legal guardian) and/or key caregiver(s) involved in patient's care, integration of new information into the medical treatment plan and/or adjustment of medical therapy, within a calendar month; 15-29 minutes

**99378**      30 minutes or more

**99379**  **Supervision** of a nursing facility patient (patient not present) requiring complex and multidisciplinary care modalities involving regular development and/or revision of care plans by that individual, review of subsequent reports of patient status, review of related laboratory and other studies, communication (including telephone calls) for purposes of assessment or care decisions with health care professional(s), family member(s), surrogate decision maker(s) (eg, legal guardian) and/or key caregiver(s) involved in patient's care, integration of new information into the medical treatment plan and/or adjustment of medical therapy, within a calendar month; 15-29 minutes

**99380**      30 minutes or more

# Preventive Medicine Services

The following codes are used to report the preventive medicine evaluation and management of infants, children, adolescents, and adults.

The extent and focus of the services will largely depend on the age of the patient.

If an abnormality is encountered or a preexisting problem is addressed in the process of performing this preventive medicine evaluation and management service, and if the problem or abnormality is significant enough to require additional work to perform the key components of a problem-oriented E/M service, then the appropriate Office/Outpatient code 99201-99215 should also be reported. Modifier 25 should be added to the Office/Outpatient code to indicate that a significant, separately identifiable evaluation and management service was provided on the same day as the preventive medicine service. The appropriate preventive medicine service is additionally reported.

An insignificant or trivial problem/abnormality that is encountered in the process of performing the preventive medicine evaluation and management service and which does not require additional work and the performance of the key components of a problem-oriented E/M service should not be reported.

The "comprehensive" nature of the Preventive Medicine Services codes 99381-99397 reflects an age and gender appropriate history/exam and is **not** synonymous with the "comprehensive" examination required in Evaluation and Management codes 99201-99350.

Codes 99381-99397 include counseling/anticipatory guidance/risk factor reduction interventions which are provided at the time of the initial or periodic comprehensive preventive medicine examination. (Refer to codes 99401-99412 for reporting those counseling/anticipatory guidance/risk factor reduction interventions that are provided at an encounter separate from the preventive medicine examination.)

Vaccine/toxoid products, immunization administrations, ancillary studies involving laboratory, radiology, other

Evaluation/Management

procedures, or screening tests (eg, vision, hearing, developmental) identified with a specific CPT code are reported separately. For immunization administration and vaccine risk/benefit counseling, see 90460, 90461, 90471-90474. For vaccine/toxoid products, see 90476-90749.

## New Patient

**99381** **Initial comprehensive preventive medicine** evaluation and management of an individual including an age and gender appropriate history, examination, counseling/anticipatory guidance/risk factor reduction interventions, and the ordering of laboratory/diagnostic procedures, new patient; infant (age younger than 1 year)

**99382** early childhood (age 1 through 4 years)

**99383** late childhood (age 5 through 11 years)

**99384** adolescent (age 12 through 17 years)

**99385** 18-39 years

**99386** 40-64 years

**99387** 65 years and older

## Established Patient

**99391** **Periodic comprehensive preventive medicine** reevaluation and management of an individual including an age and gender appropriate history, examination, counseling/anticipatory guidance/risk factor reduction interventions, and the ordering of laboratory/diagnostic procedures, established patient; infant (age younger than 1 year)

**99392** early childhood (age 1 through 4 years)

**99393** late childhood (age 5 through 11 years)

**99394** adolescent (age 12 through 17 years)

**99395** 18-39 years

**99396** 40-64 years

**99397** 65 years and older

## Counseling Risk Factor Reduction and Behavior Change Intervention

## New or Established Patient

These codes are used to report services provided face-to-face by a physician or other qualified health care professional for the purpose of promoting health and preventing illness or injury. They are distinct from evaluation and management (E/M) services that may be reported separately when performed. Risk factor reduction services are used for persons without a specific illness for which the counseling might otherwise be used as part of treatment.

Preventive medicine counseling and risk factor reduction interventions will vary with age and should address such issues as family problems, diet and exercise, substance use, sexual practices, injury prevention, dental health, and diagnostic and laboratory test results available at the time of the encounter.

Behavior change interventions are for persons who have a behavior that is often considered an illness itself, such as tobacco use and addiction, substance abuse/misuse, or obesity. Behavior change services may be reported when performed as part of the treatment of condition(s) related to or potentially exacerbated by the behavior or when performed to change the harmful behavior that has not yet resulted in illness. Any E/M services reported on the same day must be distinct, and time spent providing these services may not be used as a basis for the E/M code selection. Behavior change services involve specific validated interventions of assessing readiness for change and barriers to change, advising a change in behavior, assisting by providing specific suggested actions and motivational counseling, and arranging for services and follow-up.

For counseling groups of patients with symptoms or established illness, use 99078.

Health and Behavior Assessment/Intervention services (96150-96155) should not be reported on the same day as codes 99401-99412.

## Preventive Medicine, Individual Counseling

**99401** **Preventive medicine counseling** and/or risk factor reduction intervention(s) provided to an individual (separate procedure); approximately 15 minutes

**99402** approximately 30 minutes

**99403** approximately 45 minutes

**99404** approximately 60 minutes

## Behavior Change Interventions, Individual

**99406** Smoking and tobacco use cessation counseling visit; intermediate, greater than 3 minutes up to 10 minutes

**99407** intensive, greater than 10 minutes

(Do not report 99407 in conjunction with 99406)

**99408** Alcohol and/or substance (other than tobacco) abuse structured screening (eg, AUDIT, DAST), and brief intervention (SBI) services; 15 to 30 minutes

(Do not report services of less than 15 minutes with 99408)

**99409** greater than 30 minutes

(Do not report 99409 in conjunction with 99408)

(Do not report 99408, 99409 in conjunction with 99420)

⊙=Moderate sedation ✚=Add-on code ✗=FDA approval pending #=Resequenced code ○=Recycled/reinstated code

(Use 99408, 99409 only for initial screening and brief intervention)

### Preventive Medicine, Group Counseling

99411    **Preventive medicine counseling** and/or risk factor reduction intervention(s) provided to individuals in a group setting (separate procedure); approximately 30 minutes

99412       approximately 60 minutes

## Other Preventive Medicine Services

99420    **Administration and interpretation** of health risk assessment instrument (eg, health hazard appraisal)

99429    **Unlisted preventive** medicine service

(99431 has been deleted. To report, use 99460)

(99432 has been deleted. To report, use 99461)

(99433 has been deleted. To report, use 99462)

(99435 has been deleted. To report, use 99463)

(99436 has been deleted. To report, use 99464)

(99440 has been deleted. To report, use 99465)

# Non-Face-to-Face Services

## Telephone Services

Telephone services are non-face-to-face evaluation and management (E/M) services provided to a patient using the telephone by a physician or other qualified health care professional, who may report evaluation and management services. These codes are used to report episodes of patient care initiated by an established patient or guardian of an established patient. If the telephone service ends with a decision to see the patient within 24 hours or next available urgent visit appointment, the code is not reported; rather the encounter is considered part of the preservice work of the subsequent E/M service, procedure, and visit. Likewise if the telephone call refers to an E/M service performed and reported by that individual within the previous seven days (either requested or unsolicited patient follow-up) or within the postoperative period of the previously completed procedure, then the service(s) are considered part of that previous E/M service or procedure. (Do not report 99441-99443 if reporting 99441-99444 performed in the previous seven days.)

(For telephone services provided by a qualified nonphysician who may not report evaluation and management services [eg, speech-language pathologists, physical therapists, occupational therapists, social workers, dietitians], see 98966-98968)

99441    Telephone evaluation and management service by a physician or other qualified health care professional who may report evaluation and management services provided to an established patient, parent, or guardian not originating from a related E/M service provided within the previous 7 days nor leading to an E/M service or procedure within the next 24 hours or soonest available appointment; 5-10 minutes of medical discussion

99442       11-20 minutes of medical discussion

99443       21-30 minutes of medical discussion

(Do not report 99441-99443 when using 99339-99340, 99374-99380 for the same call[s])

(Do not report 99441-99443 for anticoagulation management when reporting 99363, 99364)

(Do not report 99441-99443 during the same month with 99487-99489)

(Do not report 99441-99443 when performed during the service time of codes 99495 or 99496)

## On-Line Medical Evaluation

An on-line electronic medical evaluation is a non-face-to-face evaluation and management (E/M) service by a physician to a patient using Internet resources in response to a patient's on-line inquiry. Reportable services involve the physician's personal timely response to the patient's inquiry and must involve permanent storage (electronic or hard copy) of the encounter. This service is reported only once for the same episode of care during a seven-day period, although multiple physicians could report their exchange with the same patient. If the on-line medical evaluation refers to an E/M service previously performed and reported by the physician within the previous seven days (either physician requested or unsolicited patient follow-up) or within the postoperative period of the previously completed procedure, then the service(s) are considered covered by the previous E/M service or procedure. A reportable service encompasses the sum of communication (eg, related telephone calls, prescription provision, laboratory orders) pertaining to the on-line patient encounter.

(For an on-line medical evaluation provided by a qualified nonphysician health care professional, use 98969)

99444    Online evaluation and management service provided by a physician or other qualified health care professional who may report evaluation and management services provided to an established patient or guardian, not originating from a related E/M service provided within the previous 7 days, using the Internet or similar electronic communications network

(Do not report 99444 when using 99339, 99340, 99374-99380 for the same communication[s])

(Do not report 99444 for anticoagulation management when reporting 99363, 99364)

(Do not report 99444 during the same month with 99487-99489)

(Do not report 99444 when performed during the service time of codes 99495 or 99496)

## ►Interprofessional Telephone/Internet Consultations◄

►The consultant should use the following codes to report interprofessional telephone/Internet consultations. An interprofessional telephone/Internet consultation is an assessment and management service in which a patient's treating (eg, attending or primary) physician or other qualified health care professional requests the opinion and/or treatment advice of a physician with specific specialty expertise (the consultant) to assist the treating physician or other qualified health care professional in the diagnosis and/or management of the patient's problem without the need for the patient's face-to-face contact with the consultant.

These services are typically provided in complex and/or urgent situations where a timely face-to-face service with the consultant may not be feasible (eg, geographic distance). These codes should not be reported by a consultant who has agreed to accept transfer of care before the telephone/Internet assessment, but are appropriate to report if the decision to accept transfer of care cannot be made until after the initial interprofessional telephone/Internet consultation.

The patient for whom the interprofessional telephone/Internet consultation is requested may be either a new patient to the consultant or an established patient with a new problem or an exacerbation of an existing problem. However, the consultant should not have seen the patient in a face-to-face encounter within the last 14 days. When the telephone/Internet consultation leads to an immediate transfer of care or other face-to-face service (eg, a surgery, a hospital visit, or a scheduled office evaluation of the patient) within the next 14 days or next available appointment date of the consultant, these codes are not reported.

Review of pertinent medical records, laboratory studies, imaging studies, medication profile, pathology specimens, etc may be required and transmitted electronically by fax or by mail immediately before the telephone/Internet consultation or following the consultation.

The review of this data is included in the telephone/Internet consultation service and should not be reported separately. The majority of the service time reported (greater than 50%) must be devoted to the medical consultative verbal/Internet discussion. This service should not be reported more than once within a seven-day interval.

If more than one telephone/Internet contact(s) is required to complete the consultation request (eg, discussion of test results), the entirety of the service and the cumulative discussion and information review time should be reported with a single code.

The written or verbal request for telephone/Internet advice by the treating/requesting physician or other qualified health care professional should be documented in the patient's medical record, including the reason for the request, and concludes with a verbal opinion report and written report from the consultant to the treating/requesting physician or other qualified health care professional.

Telephone/Internet consultations of less than five minutes should not be reported. Consultant communications with the patient and/or family may be reported using 99441, 99442, 99443, 99444, 98966, 98967, 98968, 98969 and the time related to these services is not used in reporting 99446, 99447, 99448, 99449.

When the sole purpose of the telephone/Internet communication is to arrange a transfer of care or other face-to-face service, these codes are not reported.

The treating/requesting physician or other qualified health care professional may report the prolonged service codes 99354, 99355, 99356, 99357 for the time spent on the interprofessional telephone/Internet discussion with the consultant (eg, specialist) if the time **exceeds 30 minutes** beyond the typical time of the appropriate E/M service performed and the patient is present (on-site) and accessible to the treating/requesting physician or other qualified health care professional. If the interprofessional telephone/Internet assessment and management service occurs when the patient is not present or on-site, and the discussion time **exceeds 30 minutes** beyond the typical time of the appropriate E/M service performed, then the non-face-to-face prolonged service codes 99358, 99359 may be reported by the treating/requesting physician or other qualified health care professional.◄

►(For telephone services provided by a physician to a patient, see 99441, 99442, 99443)◄

►(For telephone services provided by a qualified health care professional to a patient, see 98966, 98967, 98968)◄

►(For an on-line medical evaluation provided by a physician to a patient, use 99444)◄

►(For an on-line assessment and management service provided by a qualified health care professional to a patient, use 98969)◄

● **99446** Interprofessional telephone/Internet assessment and management service provided by a consultative physician including a verbal and written report to the patient's treating/requesting physician or other qualified health care professional; 5-10 minutes of medical consultative discussion and review

● **99447** 11-20 minutes of medical consultative discussion and review

● 99448    21-30 minutes of medical consultative discussion and review

● 99449    31 minutes or more of medical consultative discussion and review

# Special Evaluation and Management Services

The following codes are used to report evaluations performed to establish baseline information prior to life or disability insurance certificates being issued. This service is performed in the office or other setting, and applies to both new and established patients. When using these codes, no active management of the problem(s) is undertaken during the encounter.

If other evaluation and management services and/or procedures are performed on the same date, the appropriate E/M or procedure code(s) should be reported in addition to these codes.

## Basic Life and/or Disability Evaluation Services

99450    **Basic life** and/or disability examination that includes:

- **Measurement of height, weight, and blood pressure;**

- **Completion of a medical history following a life insurance pro forma;**

- **Collection of blood sample and/or urinalysis complying with "chain of custody" protocols; and**

- **Completion of necessary documentation/ certificates.**

## Work Related or Medical Disability Evaluation Services

99455    **Work related** or medical disability examination by the treating physician that includes:

- **Completion of a medical history commensurate with the patient's condition;**

- **Performance of an examination commensurate with the patient's condition;**

- **Formulation of a diagnosis, assessment of capabilities and stability, and calculation of impairment;**

- **Development of future medical treatment plan; and**

- **Completion of necessary documentation/ certificates and report.**

99456    **Work related** or medical disability examination by other than the treating physician that includes:

- **Completion of a medical history commensurate with the patient's condition;**

- **Performance of an examination commensurate with the patient's condition;**

- **Formulation of a diagnosis, assessment of capabilities and stability, and calculation of impairment;**

- **Development of future medical treatment plan; and**

- **Completion of necessary documentation/ certificates and report.**

(Do not report 99455, 99456 in conjunction with 99080 for the completion of Workman's Compensation forms)

# Newborn Care Services

The following codes are used to report the services provided to newborns (birth through the first 28 days) in several different settings. Use of the normal newborn codes is limited to the initial care of the newborn in the first days after birth prior to home discharge.

Evaluation and Management (E/M) services for the newborn include maternal and/or fetal and newborn history, newborn physical examination(s), ordering of diagnostic tests and treatments, meetings with the family, and documentation in the medical record.

When delivery room attendance services (99464) or delivery room resuscitation services (99465) are required, report these in addition to normal newborn services Evaluation and Management codes.

For E/M services provided to newborns who are other than normal, see codes for hospital inpatient services (99221-99233) and neonatal intensive and critical care services (99466-99469, 99477-99480). When normal newborn services are provided by the same individual on the same date that the newborn later becomes ill and receives additional intensive or critical care services, report the appropriate E/M code with modifier 25 for these services in addition to the normal newborn code.

Procedures (eg, 54150, newborn circumcision) are not included with the normal newborn codes, and when performed, should be reported in addition to the newborn services.

When newborns are seen in follow-up after the date of discharge in the office or outpatient setting, see 99201-99215, 99381, 99391 as appropriate.

99460    Initial hospital or birthing center care, per day, for evaluation and management of normal newborn infant

99461    Initial care, per day, for evaluation and management of normal newborn infant seen in other than hospital or birthing center

Evaluation/Management

**99462**  Subsequent hospital care, per day, for evaluation and management of normal newborn

**99463**  Initial hospital or birthing center care, per day, for evaluation and management of normal newborn infant admitted and discharged on the same date

(For newborn hospital discharge services provided on a date subsequent to the admission date, see 99238, 99239)

## Delivery/Birthing Room Attendance and Resuscitation Services

**99464**  Attendance at delivery (when requested by the delivering physician or other qualified health care professional) and initial stabilization of newborn

(99464 may be reported in conjunction with 99460, 99468, 99477)

(Do not report 99464 in conjunction with 99465)

**99465**  Delivery/birthing room resuscitation, provision of positive pressure ventilation and/or chest compressions in the presence of acute inadequate ventilation and/or cardiac output

(99465 may be reported in conjunction with 99460, 99468, 99477)

(Do not report 99465 in conjunction with 99464)

(Procedures that are performed as a necessary part of the resuscitation [eg, intubation, vascular lines] are reported separately in addition to 99465. In order to report these procedures, they must be performed as a necessary component of the resuscitation and not as a convenience before admission to the neonatal intensive care unit)

## Inpatient Neonatal Intensive Care Services and Pediatric and Neonatal Critical Care Services

## Pediatric Critical Care Patient Transport

Codes 99466, 99467 are used to report the physical attendance and direct face-to-face care by a physician during the interfacility transport of a critically ill or critically injured pediatric patient 24 months of age or younger. Codes 99485, 99486 are used to report the control physician's non-face-to-face supervision of interfacility transport of a critically ill or critically injured pediatric patient 24 months of age or younger. These codes are not reported together for the same patient by the same physician. For the purpose of reporting 99466 and 99467, face-to-face care begins when the physician assumes primary responsibility of the pediatric patient at

the referring facility, and ends when the receiving facility accepts responsibility for the pediatric patient's care. Only the time the physician spends in direct face-to-face contact with the patient during the transport should be reported. Pediatric patient transport services involving less than 30 minutes of face-to-face physician care should not be reported using 99466, 99467. Procedure(s) or service(s) performed by other members of the transporting team may not be reported by the supervising physician.

Codes 99485, 99486 are used to report control physician's non-face-to-face supervision of interfacility pediatric critical care transport, which includes all two-way communication between the control physician and the specialized transport team prior to transport, at the referring facility and during transport of the patient back to the receiving facility. The "control" physician is the physician directing transport services. These codes do not include pretransport communication between the control physician and the referring facility before or following patient transport. These codes are only reported for patients 24 months of age or younger who are critically ill or critically injured. The control physician provides treatment advice to a specialized transport team who are present and delivering the hands-on patient care. The control physician does not report any services provided by the specialized transport team. The control physician's non-face-to-face time begins with the first contact by the control physician with the specialized transport team and ends when the patient's care is handed over to the receiving facility team. Refer to 99466 and 99467 for face-to-face transport care of the critically ill/injured patient. Time spent with the individual patient's transport team and reviewing data submissions should be recorded. Code 99485 is used to report the first 16-45 minutes of direction on a given date and should only be used once even if time spent by the physician is discontinuous. Do not report services of 15 minutes or less or any time when another physician is reporting 99466, 99467. Do not report 99485 or 99486 in conjunction with 99466, 99467 when performed by the same physician.

For the definition of the critically injured pediatric patient, see the **Neonatal and Pediatric Critical Care Services** section.

The non-face-to-face direction of emergency care to a patient's transporting staff by a physician located in a hospital or other facility by two-way communication is not considered direct face-to-face care and should not be reported with 99466, 99467. Physician-directed non-face-to-face emergency care through outside voice communication to transporting staff personnel is reported with 99288 or 99485, 99486 based upon the age and clinical condition of the patient.

Emergency department services (99281-99285), initial hospital care (99221-99223), critical care (99291, 99292), initial date neonatal intensive (99477) or critical care (99468) are only reported after the patient has been admitted to the emergency department, the inpatient floor, or the critical care unit of the receiving facility. If inpatient critical care services are reported in the referring facility prior to transfer to the receiving hospital, use the critical care codes (99291, 99292).

▶The following services are included when performed during the pediatric patient transport by the physician providing critical care and may not be reported separately: routine monitoring evaluations (eg, heart rate, respiratory rate, blood pressure, and pulse oximetry), the interpretation of cardiac output measurements (93562), chest X-rays (71010, 71015, 71020), pulse oximetry (94760, 94761, 94762), blood gases and information data stored in computers (eg, ECGs, blood pressures, hematologic data) (99090), gastric intubation (43752, 43753), temporary transcutaneous pacing (92953), ventilatory management (94002, 94003, 94660, 94662), and vascular access procedures (36000, 36400, 36405, 36406, 36415, 36591, 36600). Any services performed which are not listed above should be reported separately.◀

Services provided by the specialized transport team during non-face-to-face transport supervision are not reported by the control physician.

Code 99466 is used to report the first 30 to 74 minutes of direct face-to-face time with the transport pediatric patient and should be reported only once on a given date. Code 99467 is used to report each additional 30 minutes provided on a given date. Face-to-face services of less than 30 minutes should not be reported with these codes.

▶Code 99485 is used to report the first 30 minutes of non-face-to-face supervision of an interfacility transport of a critically ill or critically injured pediatric patient and should be reported only once per date of service. Only the communication time spent by the supervising physician with the specialty transport team members during an interfacility transport should be reported. Code 99486 is used to report each additional 30 minutes beyond the initial 30 minutes. Non-face-to-face interfacility transport of 15 minutes or less is not reported.◀

> ▶(For total body and selective head cooling of neonates, see 99481, 99482)◀

**99466**    **Critical care** face-to-face services, during an interfacility transport of critically ill or critically injured pediatric patient, 24 months of age or younger; first 30-74 minutes of hands-on care during transport

**+ 99467**    each additional 30 minutes (List separately in addition to code for primary service)

(Use 99467 in conjunction with 99466)

(Critical care of less than 30 minutes total duration should be reported with the appropriate E/M code)

**# 99485**    Supervision by a control physician of interfacility transport care of the critically ill or critically injured pediatric patient, 24 months of age or younger, includes two-way communication with transport team before transport, at the referring facility and during the transport, including data interpretation and report; first 30 minutes

**#+ 99486**    each additional 30 minutes (List separately in addition to code for primary procedure)

(Use 99486 in conjunction with 99485)

(For physician direction of emergency medical systems supervision for a pediatric patient older than 24 months of age, or at any age if not critically ill or injured, use 99288)

(Do not report 99485, 99486 with any other services reported by the control physician for the same period)

(Do not report 99485, 99486 in conjunction with 99466, 99467 when performed by the same physician)

## Inpatient Neonatal and Pediatric Critical Care

The same definitions for critical care services apply for the adult, child, and neonate.

Codes 99468, 99469 are used to report the services of directing the inpatient care of a critically ill neonate or infant 28 days of age or younger. They represent care starting with the date of admission (99468) to a critical care unit and subsequent day(s) (99469) that the neonate remains critical. These codes may be reported only by a single individual and only once per day, per patient, per hospital stay in a given facility. If readmitted to the neonatal critical care unit during the same day, report the subsequent day(s) code 99469 for the first day of readmission to critical care, and 99469 for each day of critical care following readmission.

The initial day neonatal critical care code (99468) can be used in addition to 99464 or 99465 as appropriate, when the physician or other qualified health care professional is present for the delivery (99464) or resuscitation (99465) is required. Other procedures performed as a necessary part of the resuscitation (eg, endotracheal intubation [31500]) are also reported separately when performed as part of the pre-admission delivery room care. In order to report these procedures separately, they must be performed as a necessary component of the resuscitation and not simply as a convenience before admission to the neonatal intensive care unit.

Codes 99471-99476 are used to report direction of the inpatient care of a critically ill infant or young child from 29 days of postnatal age through less than 6 years of age. They represent care starting with the date of admission (99471, 99475) to all subsequent day(s) (99472, 99476) the infant or child remains critical. These codes may be reported only by a single individual and only once per day, per patient in a given setting. Services for the critically ill or critically injured child 6 years of age or older would be reported with the time based critical care codes (99291, 99292). Report 99471, 99475 only once per hospital stay in a given facility. If readmitted to the pediatric critical care unit during the same stay, report 99472 or 99476 for the first day of readmission to critical care and 99472 for each day of critical care following readmission.

The pediatric and neonatal critical care codes include those procedures listed for the critical care codes (99291, 99292). In addition, the following procedures are also included (and are not separately reported by professionals, but may be reported by facilities) in the pediatric and neonatal critical care service codes (99468-99472, 99475, 99476) and the intensive care services codes (99477-99480).

Any services performed that are not included in these listings may be reported separately. Facilities may report the included services separately.

Invasive or non-invasive electronic monitoring of vital signs

Vascular access procedures

   Peripheral vessel catheterization (36000)

   Other arterial catheters (36140, 36620)

   Umbilical venous catheters (36510)

   Central vessel catheterization (36555)

   Vascular access procedures (36400, 36405, 36406)

   Vascular punctures (36420, 36600)

   Umbilical arterial catheters (36660)

Airway and ventilation management

   Endotracheal intubation (31500)

   Ventilatory management (94002-94004)

   Bedside pulmonary function testing (94375)

   Surfactant administration (94610)

   Continuous positive airway pressure (CPAP) (94660)

Monitoring or interpretation of blood gases or oxygen saturation (94760-94762)

Car Seat Evaluation (94780-94781)

Transfusion of blood components (36430, 36440)

Oral or nasogastric tube placement (43752)

Suprapubic bladder aspiration (51100)

Bladder catheterization (51701, 51702)

Lumbar puncture (62270)

Any services performed which are not listed above may be reported separately.

When a neonate or infant is not critically ill but requires intensive observation, frequent interventions, and other intensive care services, the Continuing Intensive Care Services codes (99477-99480) should be used to report these services.

To report critical care services provided in the outpatient setting (eg, emergency department or office) for neonates and pediatric patients of any age, see the Critical Care codes 99291, 99292. If the same individual provides critical care services for a neonatal or pediatric patient less than 6 years of age in both the outpatient and inpatient settings on the same day, report only the appropriate Neonatal or Pediatric Critical Care codes 99468-99476 for all critical care services provided on that day. Critical care services provided by a second individual of a different specialty not reporting a per-day neonatal or pediatric critical care code can be reported with 99291, 99292.

When critical care services are provided to neonates or pediatric patients less than 6 years of age at two separate institutions by an individual from a different group on the same date of service, the individual from the referring institution should report their critical care services with the time-based critical care codes (99291, 99292) and the receiving institution should report the appropriate initial day of care code 99468, 99471, 99475 for the same date of service.

Critical care services to a pediatric patient 6 years of age or older are reported with the time based critical care codes 99291, 99292.

When the critically ill neonate or pediatric patient improves and is transferred to a lower level of care to another individual in another group within the same facility, the transferring individual does not report a per day critical care service. Subsequent hospital care (99231-99233) or time-based critical care services (99291-99292) is reported, as appropriate based upon the condition of the neonate or child. The receiving individual reports subsequent intensive care (99478-99480) or subsequent hospital care (99231-99233) services, as appropriate based upon the condition of the neonate or child.

When the neonate or infant becomes critically ill on a day when initial or subsequent intensive care services (99477-99480), hospital services (99221-99233), or normal newborn services (99460, 99461, 99462) have been performed by one individual and is transferred to a critical care level of care provided by a different individual in a different group, the transferring individual reports either the time-based critical care services performed (99291, 99292) for the time spent providing critical care to the patient, the intensive care service (99477-99480), hospital care services (99221-99233), or normal newborn service (99460, 99461, 99462) performed, but only one service. The receiving individual reports initial or subsequent inpatient neonatal or pediatric critical care (99468-99476), as appropriate based upon the patient's age and whether this is the first or subsequent admission to the critical care unit for the hospital stay.

When a newborn becomes critically ill on the same day they have already received normal newborn care (99460, 99461, 99462), and the same individual or group assumes critical care, report initial critical care service (99468) with modifier 25 in addition to the normal newborn code.

When a neonate, infant, or child requires initial critical care services on the same day the patient already has received hospital care or intensive care services by the same individual or group, only the initial critical care service code (99468, 99471, 99475) is reported,

Time-based critical care services (99291, 99292) are not reportable by the same individual or different individual within the same group when neonatal or pediatric critical care services (99468-99476) are reported for the same patient on the same day.

No individual may report remote real-time videoconferenced critical care (0188T, 0189T) when neonatal or pediatric intensive or critical care services (99468-99476) are reported.

**99468** **Initial inpatient neonatal critical care,** per day, for the evaluation and management of a critically ill neonate, 28 days of age or younger

**99469** **Subsequent inpatient neonatal critical care,** per day, for the evaluation and management of a critically ill neonate, 28 days of age or younger

**99471** **Initial inpatient pediatric critical care,** per day, for the evaluation and management of a critically ill infant or young child, 29 days through 24 months of age

**99472** **Subsequent inpatient pediatric critical care,** per day, for the evaluation and management of a critically ill infant or young child, 29 days through 24 months of age

**99475** **Initial inpatient pediatric critical care,** per day, for the evaluation and management of a critically ill infant or young child, 2 through 5 years of age

**99476** **Subsequent inpatient pediatric critical care,** per day, for the evaluation and management of a critically ill infant or young child, 2 through 5 years of age

#+● **99481** Total body systemic hypothermia in a critically ill neonate per day (List separately in addition to code for primary procedure)

  ►(Use 99481 in conjunction with 99291, 99292, 99468, 99469)◄

#+● **99482** Selective head hypothermia in a critically ill neonate per day (List separately in addition to code for primary procedure)

  ►(Use 99482 in conjunction with 99291, 99292, 99468, 99469)◄

  ►(Services by the professional during either cooling approach include radiographic confirmation of core temperature probe, assessment of continuous amplitude EEG monitoring, and interpretation of cooling-related laboratory evaluations)◄

  ►(Do not report 99481, 99482 in conjunction with 99221, 99222, 99223, 99231, 99232, 99233, 99477, 99478, 99479, 99480)◄

## Initial and Continuing Intensive Care Services

Code 99477 represents the initial day of inpatient care for the child who is not critically ill but requires intensive observation, frequent interventions, and other intensive care services. Codes 99478-99480 are used to report the subsequent day services of directing the continuing intensive care of the low birth weight (LBW 1500-2500 grams) present body weight infant, very low birth weight (VLBW less than 1500 grams) present body weight infant, or normal (2501-5000 grams) present body weight newborn who does not meet the definition of critically ill but continues to require intensive observation, frequent interventions, and other intensive care services. These services are for infants and neonates who are not critically ill but continue to require intensive cardiac and respiratory monitoring, continuous and/or frequent vital sign monitoring, heat maintenance, enteral and/or parenteral nutritional adjustments, laboratory and oxygen monitoring, and constant observation by the health care team under direct supervision of the physician or other qualified health care professional. Codes 99477-99480 may be reported by a single individual and only once per day, per patient in a given facility. If readmitted to the intensive care unit during the same hospital stay, report 99478-99480 for the first day of intensive care and for each successive day that the child requires intensive care services.

These codes include the same procedures that are outlined in the **Neonatal and Pediatric Critical Care Services** section and these services should not be separately reported.

The initial day neonatal intensive care code (99477) can be used in addition to 99464 or 99465 as appropriate, when the physician or other qualified health care professional is present for the delivery (99464) or resuscitation (99465) is required. In this situation, report 99477 with modifier 25. Other procedures performed as a necessary part of the resuscitation (eg, endotracheal intubation [31500]) are also reported separately when performed as part of the pre-admission delivery room care. In order to report these procedures separately, they must be performed as a necessary component of the resuscitation and not simply as a convenience before admission to the neonatal intensive care unit.

The same procedures are included as bundled services with the neonatal intensive care codes as those listed for the neonatal (99468, 99469) and pediatric (99471-99476) critical care codes.

When the neonate or infant improves after the initial day and no longer requires intensive care services and is transferred to a lower level of care, the transferring individual does not report a per day intensive care service. Subsequent hospital care (99231-99233) or subsequent normal newborn care (99460, 99462) is reported as appropriate based upon the condition of the neonate or infant. If the transfer to a lower level of care occurs on the same day as initial intensive care services were provided by the transferring individual, 99477 may be reported.

When the neonate or infant is transferred after the initial day within the same facility to the care of another individual in a different group, both individuals report subsequent hospital care (99231-99233) services. The receiving individual reports subsequent hospital care (99231-99233) or subsequent normal newborn care (99462).

When the neonate or infant becomes critically ill on a day when initial or subsequent intensive care services (99477-99480) have been reported by one individual and is transferred to a critical care level of care provided by a different individual from a different group, the transferring individual reports either the time-based critical care services performed (99291, 99292) for the time spent providing critical care to the patient or the initial or subsequent intensive care (99477-99480) service, but not both. The receiving individual reports initial or subsequent inpatient neonatal or pediatric critical care (99468-99476) based upon the patient's age and whether this is the first or subsequent admission to critical care for the same hospital stay.

When the neonate or infant becomes critically ill on a day when initial or subsequent intensive care services (99477-99480) have been performed by the same individual or group, report only initial or subsequent inpatient neonatal or pediatric critical care (99468-99476) based upon the patient's age and whether this is the first or subsequent admission to critical care for the same hospital stay.

For the subsequent care of the sick neonate younger than 28 days of age but more than 5000 grams who does not require intensive or critical care services, use codes 99231-99233.

**99477**    **Initial hospital care,** per day, for the evaluation and management of the neonate, 28 days of age or younger, who requires intensive observation, frequent interventions, and other intensive care services

(For the initiation of inpatient care of the normal newborn, use 99460)

(For the initiation of care of the critically ill neonate, use 99468)

(For initiation of inpatient hospital care of the ill neonate not requiring intensive observation, frequent interventions, and other intensive care services, see 99221-99223)

**99478**    **Subsequent intensive care,** per day, for the evaluation and management of the recovering very low birth weight infant (present body weight less than 1500 grams)

**99479**    **Subsequent intensive care,** per day, for the evaluation and management of the recovering low birth weight infant (present body weight of 1500-2500 grams)

**99480**    **Subsequent intensive care,** per day, for the evaluation and management of the recovering infant (present body weight of 2501-5000 grams)

**99481**    Code is out of numerical sequence. See 99468-99482

**99482**    Code is out of numerical sequence. See 99468-99482

**99485**    Code is out of numerical sequence. See 99466-99486

**99486**    Code is out of numerical sequence. See 99466-99486

# Complex Chronic Care Coordination Services

▶Complex chronic care coordination services are patient centered management and support services provided by physicians, other qualified health care professionals, and clinical staff to an individual who resides at home or in a domiciliary, rest home, or assisted living facility. These services typically involve clinical staff developing, substantially revising, and implementing a care plan under direction of the physician or other qualified health care professional. Substantial revision to a care plan typically occurs when the patient's clinical condition changes sufficiently (eg, identification of a new problem requiring additional interventions, introduction of new interventions because existing interventions are deemed ineffective, exacerbation of an existing problem requiring new interventions) to require more intensive staff monitoring, changes in the treatment regimen, and additional time to educate the patient and/or caregiver about the patient's condition and/or change in treatment plan and prognosis. These services address the coordination of care by multiple professionals, disciplines, and/or community service agencies. The reporting individual provides or oversees the management and/or coordination of services, as needed, for all medical conditions, psychosocial needs, and instrumental and basic activities of daily living (IADL/ADL).

Patients who require complex chronic care coordination services may be identified by practice-specific or other published algorithms that recognize multiple illnesses, multiple medication use, inability to perform activities of daily living, requirement for a caregiver, and/or repeat admissions or emergency department visits. Typical adult patients take or receive three or more prescription medications and may also be receiving other types of therapeutic interventions (eg, physical therapy, occupational therapy) and have two or more chronic continuous or episodic health conditions expected to last at least 12 months, or until the death of the patient, that place the patient at significant risk of death, acute exacerbation/decompensation, or functional decline. Typical pediatric patients receive three or more therapeutic interventions (eg, medications, nutritional support, respiratory therapy) and have two or more chronic continuous or episodic health conditions expected to last at least 12 months, or until the death of the patient, that place the patient at significant risk of death, acute exacerbation/decompensation, or functional decline. Because of the complex nature of their diseases and morbidities, these patients commonly require the coordination of a number of specialties and services. In some cases, due to inability to perform IADL/ADL and/ or cognitive impairment the patient is unable to adhere to the treatment plan without substantial assistance from a caregiver. For example, patients may have medical and psychiatric behavioral co-morbidities (eg, dementia and chronic obstructive pulmonary disease or substance abuse and diabetes) that complicate their care. Social support requirements or access to care difficulties may cause a need for these services. Medical, functional, and/or psychosocial problems that require medical decision making of moderate or high complexity and extensive clinical staff support are required. Medical decision making as defined in the Evaluation and Management (E/M) guidelines is not only applied to the face-to-face services, but is determined by the nature of the problems addressed by the reporting individual during the month. A plan of care must be documented and shared with the patient and/or caregiver.

A care plan is based on a physical, mental, cognitive, social, functional, and environmental (re)assessment and an inventory of resources and supports. It is a comprehensive plan of care for all health problems. It typically includes, but is not limited to, the following elements: problem list, expected outcome and prognosis, measurable treatment goals, symptom management, planned interventions, medication management, community/social services ordered, how the services of agencies and specialists unconnected to the practice will be directed/coordinated, identification of the individuals responsible for each intervention, requirements for periodic review, and, when applicable, revision of the care plan.

Codes 99487-99489 are reported only **once** per calendar month and include all non-face-to-face complex chronic care coordination services and none or 1 face-to-face office or other outpatient, home, or domiciliary visit. Physicians or other qualified health care professionals may not report care coordination services if the care plan is unchanged or requires minimal change (eg, only a medication is changed or an adjustment in a treatment modality is ordered). Codes 99487-99489 may only be reported by the single physician or other qualified health care professional who assumes the care coordination role with a particular patient for the calendar month.◄

Code selection is as follows:

Code 99487 is reported when, during the calendar month, there is no face-to-face visit with the physician or other qualified health care professional and at least 31 minutes of clinical staff time is spent in care coordination activities. 99488 is reported when, during the calendar month, there is a face-to-face visit with the physician or other qualified health care professional and at least 31 minutes of clinical staff time is spent in care coordination activities.

►The face-to-face and non-face-to-face time spent by the clinical staff in communicating with the patient and/or family, caregivers, other professionals and agencies; revising, documenting and implementing the care plan; or teaching self management is used in determining the complex chronic care coordination clinical staff time for the month. Only the time of the clinical staff of the reporting professional is counted. Only count the time of one clinical staff member when two or more clinical staff members are meeting about the patient. **Note:** Do not count any clinical staff time on the date of the first visit or on a day when the physician or qualified health care professional reports an E/M service (office or other outpatient services 99211-99215, domiciliary, rest home services 99334-99337, home services 99347-99350).

Care coordination activities performed by clinical staff typically include:

- communication and engagement with patient, family members, guardian or caretaker, surrogate decision makers, and/or other professionals regarding aspects of care;

- communication with home health agencies and other community services utilized by the patient;

- collection of health outcomes data and registry documentation;

- patient and/or family/caretaker education to support self-management, independent living, and activities of daily living;

- assessment and support for treatment regimen adherence and medication management;

- identification of available community and health resources;

---

▲=Revised code   ●=New code   ► ◄=Contains new or revised text   ⊘=Modifier 51 exempt

**Evaluation/Management**

- facilitating access to care and services needed by the patient and/or family;

- development, communication, and maintenance of a comprehensive care plan.

The care coordination office/practice must have the following capabilities:

- provide 24/7 access to physicians or other qualified health care professionals or clinical staff;

- use a standardized methodology to identify patients who require chronic complex care coordination services;

- have an internal care coordination process/function whereby a patient identified as meeting the requirements for these services starts receiving them in a timely manner;

- use a form and format in the medical record that is standardized within the practice;

- be able to engage and educate patients and caregivers as well as coordinate care among all service professionals, as appropriate for each patient.

If a face-to-face visit was provided during the month by the physician or other qualified health care professional, report 99488. Additional E/M services beyond the first visit may be reported separately by the same physician or other qualified health care professional during the same calendar month. Complex care coordination services include care plan oversight services (99339, 99340, 99374-99380), prolonged services without direct patient contact (99358, 99359), anticoagulant management (99363, 99364), medical team conferences (99366-99368), education and training (98960-98962, 99071, 99078), telephone services (98966-98968, 99441-99443), on-line medical evaluation (98969, 99444), preparation of special reports (99080), analysis of data (99090, 99091), transitional care management services (99495, 99496), medication therapy management services (99605-99607) and, if performed, these services may not be reported separately during the month for which 99487-99489 are reported. All other services may be reported. Do not report 99487-99489 if reporting ESRD services (90951-90970) during the same month. If the complex chronic care coordination services are performed within the postoperative period of a reported surgery, the same individual may not report 99487-99489.◄

Complex chronic care coordination can be reported in any calendar month during which the clinical staff time requirements are met. If care coordination resumes after a discharge during a new month, start a new period or report transitional care management services (99495, 99496) as appropriate. If discharge occurs in the same month, continue the reporting period or report Transitional Care Management Services. Do not report 99487-99489 for any post-discharge complex chronic care coordination services for any days within 30 days of discharge, if reporting 99495, 99496.

| Total Duration of Staff Care Coordination Services | Code(s) |
|---|---|
| Less than 30 minutes | Not reported separately |
| 31 to 74 minutes (31 minutes - 1 hr. 14 min.) | 99487 or 99488 x 1 |
| 75 - 104 minutes (1 hr. 15 min. - 1 hr. 44 min.) | 99487 or 99488 x 1 and 99489 x 1 |
| 105 minutes or more (1 hr. 45 min. or more) | 99487 or 99488 x 1 and 99489 x 2 or more for each additional 30 minutes |

**99487** Complex chronic care coordination services; first hour of clinical staff time directed by a physician or other qualified health care professional with no face-to-face visit, per calendar month

**99488** first hour of clinical staff time directed by a physician or other qualified health care professional with one face-to-face visit, per calendar month

**+ 99489** each additional 30 minutes of clinical staff time directed by a physician or other qualified health care professional, per calendar month (List separately in addition to code for primary procedure)

(Report 99489 in conjunction with 99487, 99488)

►(Do not report 99487-99489 during the same month with 90951-90970, 98960-98962, 98966-98969, 99071, 99078, 99080, 99090, 99091, 99339, 99340, 99358, 99359, 99363, 99364, 99366-99368, 99374-99380, 99441-99444, 99495, 99496, 99605-99607)◄

# Transitional Care Management Services

►Codes 99495 and 99496 are used to report transitional care management services (TCM). These services are for a new or established patient whose medical and/or psychosocial problems require moderate or high complexity medical decision making during transitions in care from an inpatient hospital setting (including acute hospital, rehabilitation hospital, long-term acute care hospital), partial hospital, observation status in a hospital, or skilled nursing facility/nursing facility to the patient's community setting (home, domiciliary, rest home, or assisted living). TCM commences upon the date of discharge and continues for the next 29 days.◄

TCM is comprised of one face-to-face visit within the specified timeframes, in combination with non- face-to-face services that may be performed by the physician or other qualified health care professional and/or licensed clinical staff under his/her direction.

Non-face-to-face services provided by clinical staff, under the direction of the physician or other qualified health care professional, may include:

- communication (with patient, family members, guardian or caretaker, surrogate decision makers, and/or other professionals) regarding aspects of care,

- communication with home health agencies and other community services utilized by the patient,

- patient and/or family/caretaker education to support self-management, independent living, and activities of daily living,

- assessment and support for treatment regimen adherence and medication management,

- identification of available community and health resources,

- facilitating access to care and services needed by the patient and/or family

Non-face-to-face services provided by the physician or other qualified health care provider may include:

- obtaining and reviewing the discharge information (eg, discharge summary, as available, or continuity of care documents);

- reviewing need for or follow-up on pending diagnostic tests and treatments;

- interaction with other qualified health care professionals who will assume or reassume care of the patient's system-specific problems;

- education of patient, family, guardian, and/or caregiver;

- establishment or reestablishment of referrals and arranging for needed community resources;

- assistance in scheduling any required follow-up with community providers and services.

▶TCM requires a face-to-face visit, initial patient contact, and medication reconciliation within specified time frames. The first face-to-face visit is part of the TCM service and not reported separately. Additional E/M services provided on subsequent dates after the first face-to-face visit may be reported separately. TCM requires an interactive contact with the patient or caregiver, as appropriate, within two business days of discharge. The contact may be direct (face-to-face), telephonic, or by electronic means. Medication reconciliation and management must occur no later than the date of the face-to-face visit.◀

These services address any needed coordination of care performed by multiple disciplines and community service agencies. The reporting individual provides or oversees the management and/or coordination of services, as needed, for all medical conditions, psychosocial needs and activity of daily living support by providing first contact and continuous access.

Medical decision making and the date of the first face-to-face visit are used to select and report the appropriate TCM code. For 99496, the face-to-face visit must occur within 7 calendar days of the date discharge and medical decision making must be of high complexity. For 99495, the face-to-face visit must occur within 14 calendar days of the date of discharge and medical decision making must be of at least moderate complexity.

| Type of Medical Decision Making | Face-to-face visit within 7 days | Face to face visit within 8 to 14 days |
|---|---|---|
| Moderate Complexity | 99495 | 99495 |
| High Complexity | 99496 | 99495 |

Medical decision making is defined by the E/M Services Guidelines. The medical decision making over the service period reported is used to define the medical decision making of TCM. Documentation includes the timing of the initial post discharge communication with the patient or caregivers, date of the face-to-face visit, and the complexity of medical decision making.

▶Only one individual may report these services and only once per patient within 30 days of discharge. Another TCM may not be reported by the same individual or group for any subsequent discharge(s) within the 30 days. The same individual may report hospital or observation discharge services and TCM. However, the discharge service may not constitute the required face-to-face visit. The same individual should not report TCM services provided in the postoperative period of a service that the individual reported.◀

A physician or other qualified health care professional who reports codes 99495, 99496 may not report care plan oversight services (99339, 99340, 99374-99380), prolonged services without direct patient contact (99358, 99359), anticoagulant management (99363, 99364), medical team conferences (99366-99368), education and training (98960-98962, 99071, 99078), telephone services (98966-98968, 99441-99443), end stage renal disease services (90951-90970), online medical evaluation services (98969, 99444), preparation of special reports (99080), analysis of data (99090, 99091), complex chronic care coordination services (99487-99489), medication therapy management services (99605-99607), during the time period covered by the transitional care management services codes.

**99495**    **Transitional Care Management Services** with the following required elements:

- Communication (direct contact, telephone, electronic) with the patient and/or caregiver within 2 business days of discharge

- Medical decision making of at least moderate complexity during the service period

- Face-to-face visit, within 14 calendar days of discharge

**99496**    **Transitional Care Management Services** with the following required elements:

- Communication (direct contact, telephone, electronic) with the patient and/or caregiver within 2 business days of discharge

- Medical decision making of high complexity during the service period

- Face-to-face visit, within 7 calendar days of discharge

(Do not report 90951-90970, 98960-98962, 98966-98969, 99071, 99078, 99080, 99090, 99091, 99339, 99340, 99358, 99359, 99363, 99364, 99366-99368, 99374-99380, 99441-99444, 99487-99489, 99605-99607 when performed during the service time of codes 99495 or 99496)

# Other Evaluation and Management Services

**99499**    **Unlisted evaluation and management** service

# Anesthesia Guidelines

Services involving administration of anesthesia are reported by the use of the anesthesia five-digit procedure code (00100-01999) plus modifier codes (defined under "Anesthesia Modifiers" later in these Guidelines).

The reporting of anesthesia services is appropriate by or under the responsible supervision of a physician. These services may include but are not limited to general, regional, supplementation of local anesthesia, or other supportive services in order to afford the patient the anesthesia care deemed optimal by the anesthesiologist during any procedure. These services include the usual preoperative and postoperative visits, the anesthesia care during the procedure, the administration of fluids and/or blood and the usual monitoring services (eg, ECG, temperature, blood pressure, oximetry, capnography, and mass spectrometry). Unusual forms of monitoring (eg, intra-arterial, central venous, and Swan-Ganz) are not included.

Items used by all physicians in reporting their services are presented in the **Introduction.** Some of the commonalities are repeated in this section for the convenience of those physicians referring to this section on **Anesthesia.** Other definitions and items unique to anesthesia are also listed.

To report moderate (conscious) sedation provided by a physician also performing the service for which conscious sedation is being provided, see codes 99143-99145.

For the procedures listed in Appendix G, when a second physician other than the health care professional performing the diagnostic or therapeutic services provides moderate (conscious) sedation in the facility setting (eg, hospital, outpatient hospital/ambulatory surgery center, skilled nursing facility), the second physician reports the associated moderate sedation procedure/service 99148-99150; when these services are performed by the second physician in the nonfacility setting (eg, physician office, freestanding imaging center), codes 99148-99150 would not be reported. Moderate sedation does not include minimal sedation (anxiolysis), deep sedation, or monitored anesthesia care (00100-01999).

To report regional or general anesthesia p rovided by a physician also performing the services for which the anesthesia is being provided, see modifier 47 in Appendix A.

## Time Reporting

Time for anesthesia procedures may be reported as is customary in the local area. Anesthesia time begins when the anesthesiologist begins to prepare the patient for the induction of anesthesia in the operating room (or in an equivalent area) and ends when the anesthesiologist is no longer in personal attendance, that is, when the patient may be safely placed under postoperative supervision.

## Anesthesia Services

Services rendered in the office, home, or hospital; consultation; and other medical services are listed in the **Evaluation and Management Services** section (99201-99499 series) on page 8. "Special Services and Reporting" (99000-99091 series) are listed in the **Medicine** section.

## Supplied Materials

Supplies and materials provided (eg, sterile trays, drugs) over and above those usually included with the office visit or other services rendered may be listed separately. Drugs, tray supplies, and materials provided should be listed and identified with 99070 or the appropriate supply code.

## Separate or Multiple Procedures

When multiple surgical procedures are performed during a single anesthetic administration, the anesthesia code representing the most complex procedure is reported. The time reported is the combined total for all procedures.

## Special Report

A service that is rarely provided, unusual, variable, or new may require a special report. Pertinent information should include an adequate definition or description of the nature, extent, and need for the procedure and the time, effort, and equipment necessary to provide the service.

**Anesthesia**

# Anesthesia Modifiers

All anesthesia services are reported by use of the anesthesia five-digit procedure code (00100-01999) plus the addition of a physical status modifier. The use of other optional modifiers may be appropriate.

## Physical Status Modifiers

Physical Status modifiers are represented by the initial letter 'P' followed by a single digit from 1 to 6 as defined in the following list:

**P1:** A normal healthy patient

**P2:** A patient with mild systemic disease

**P3:** A patient with severe systemic disease

**P4:** A patient with severe systemic disease that is a constant threat to life

**P5:** A moribund patient who is not expected to survive without the operation

**P6:** A declared brain-dead patient whose organs are being removed for donor purposes

These six levels are consistent with the American Society of Anesthesiologists (ASA) ranking of patient physical status. Physical status is included in the CPT codebook to distinguish among various levels of complexity of the anesthesia service provided.

Example: 00100-P1

# Qualifying Circumstances

More than one qualifying circumstance may be selected.

Many anesthesia services are provided under particularly difficult circumstances, depending on factors such as extraordinary condition of patient, notable operative conditions, and/or unusual risk factors. This section includes a list of important qualifying circumstances that significantly affect the character of the anesthesia service provided. These procedures would not be reported alone but would be reported as additional procedure numbers qualifying an anesthesia procedure or service.

**+ 99100**    Anesthesia for patient of extreme age, younger than 1 year and older than 70 (List separately in addition to code for primary anesthesia procedure)

(For procedure performed on infants younger than 1 year of age at time of surgery, see 00326, 00561, 00834, 00836)

**+ 99116**    Anesthesia complicated by utilization of total body hypothermia (List separately in addition to code for primary anesthesia procedure)

**+ 99135**    Anesthesia complicated by utilization of controlled hypotension (List separately in addition to code for primary anesthesia procedure)

**+ 99140**    Anesthesia complicated by emergency conditions (specify) (List separately in addition to code for primary anesthesia procedure)

(An emergency is defined as existing when delay in treatment of the patient would lead to a significant increase in the threat to life or body part)

# Anesthesia

## Head

**00100**    Anesthesia for procedures on salivary glands, including biopsy

**00102**    Anesthesia for procedures involving plastic repair of cleft lip

**00103**    Anesthesia for reconstructive procedures of eyelid (eg, blepharoplasty, ptosis surgery)

**00104**    Anesthesia for electroconvulsive therapy

**00120**    Anesthesia for procedures on external, middle, and inner ear including biopsy; not otherwise specified

**00124**        otoscopy

**00126**        tympanotomy

**00140**    Anesthesia for procedures on eye; not otherwise specified

**00142**        lens surgery

**00144**        corneal transplant

**00145**        vitreoretinal surgery

**00147**        iridectomy

**00148**        ophthalmoscopy

**00160**    Anesthesia for procedures on nose and accessory sinuses; not otherwise specified

**00162**        radical surgery

**00164**        biopsy, soft tissue

**00170**    Anesthesia for intraoral procedures, including biopsy; not otherwise specified

**00172**        repair of cleft palate

**00174**        excision of retropharyngeal tumor

**00176**        radical surgery

**00190**    Anesthesia for procedures on facial bones or skull; not otherwise specified

**00192**        radical surgery (including prognathism)

**00210**    Anesthesia for intracranial procedures; not otherwise specified

**00211**        craniotomy or craniectomy for evacuation of hematoma

**00212**        subdural taps

**00214**        burr holes, including ventriculography

**00215**        cranioplasty or elevation of depressed skull fracture, extradural (simple or compound)

**00216**        vascular procedures

**00218**        procedures in sitting position

**00220**        cerebrospinal fluid shunting procedures

**00222**        electrocoagulation of intracranial nerve

## Neck

**00300**    Anesthesia for all procedures on the integumentary system, muscles and nerves of head, neck, and posterior trunk, not otherwise specified

**00320**    Anesthesia for all procedures on esophagus, thyroid, larynx, trachea and lymphatic system of neck; not otherwise specified, age 1 year or older

**00322**        needle biopsy of thyroid

(For procedures on cervical spine and cord, see 00600, 00604, 00670)

**00326**    Anesthesia for all procedures on the larynx and trachea in children younger than 1 year of age

(Do not report 00326 in conjunction with 99100)

**00350**    Anesthesia for procedures on major vessels of neck; not otherwise specified

**00352**        simple ligation

(For arteriography, use 01916)

## Thorax (Chest Wall and Shoulder Girdle)

**00400**    Anesthesia for procedures on the integumentary system on the extremities, anterior trunk and perineum; not otherwise specified

**00402**        reconstructive procedures on breast (eg, reduction or augmentation mammoplasty, muscle flaps)

**00404**        radical or modified radical procedures on breast

**00406**        radical or modified radical procedures on breast with internal mammary node dissection

**00410**        electrical conversion of arrhythmias

**00450**    Anesthesia for procedures on clavicle and scapula; not otherwise specified

**00452**        radical surgery

**00454**        biopsy of clavicle

**00470**    Anesthesia for partial rib resection; not otherwise specified

**00472**        thoracoplasty (any type)

**00474**        radical procedures (eg, pectus excavatum)

**Anesthesia**

# Intrathoracic

**00500**   Anesthesia for all procedures on esophagus

**00520**   Anesthesia for closed chest procedures; (including bronchoscopy) not otherwise specified

**00522**      needle biopsy of pleura

**00524**      pneumocentesis

**00528**      mediastinoscopy and diagnostic thoracoscopy not utilizing 1 lung ventilation

(For tracheobronchial reconstruction, use 00539)

**00529**      mediastinoscopy and diagnostic thoracoscopy utilizing 1 lung ventilation

**00530**   Anesthesia for permanent transvenous pacemaker insertion

**00532**   Anesthesia for access to central venous circulation

**00534**   Anesthesia for transvenous insertion or replacement of pacing cardioverter-defibrillator

(For transthoracic approach, use 00560)

**00537**   Anesthesia for cardiac electrophysiologic procedures including radiofrequency ablation

**00539**   Anesthesia for tracheobronchial reconstruction

**00540**   Anesthesia for thoracotomy procedures involving lungs, pleura, diaphragm, and mediastinum (including surgical thoracoscopy); not otherwise specified

**00541**      utilizing 1 lung ventilation

(For thoracic spine and cord anesthesia procedures via an anterior transthoracic approach, see 00625-00626)

**00542**      decortication

**00546**      pulmonary resection with thoracoplasty

**00548**      intrathoracic procedures on the trachea and bronchi

**00550**   Anesthesia for sternal debridement

**00560**   Anesthesia for procedures on heart, pericardial sac, and great vessels of chest; without pump oxygenator

**00561**      with pump oxygenator, younger than 1 year of age

(Do not report 00561 in conjunction with 99100, 99116, and 99135)

**00562**      with pump oxygenator, age 1 year or older, for all non-coronary bypass procedures (eg, valve procedures) or for re-operation for coronary bypass more than 1 month after original operation

**00563**      with pump oxygenator with hypothermic circulatory arrest

**00566**   Anesthesia for direct coronary artery bypass grafting; without pump oxygenator

**00567**      with pump oxygenator

**00580**   Anesthesia for heart transplant or heart/lung transplant

# Spine and Spinal Cord

**00600**   Anesthesia for procedures on cervical spine and cord; not otherwise specified

(For percutaneous image-guided spine and spinal cord anesthesia procedures, see 01935, 01936)

**00604**      procedures with patient in the sitting position

**00620**   Anesthesia for procedures on thoracic spine and cord; not otherwise specified

**00622**      thoracolumbar sympathectomy

**00625**   Anesthesia for procedures on the thoracic spine and cord, via an anterior transthoracic approach; not utilizing 1 lung ventilation

**00626**      utilizing 1 lung ventilation

(For anesthesia for thoracotomy procedures other than spinal, see 00540-00541)

**00630**   Anesthesia for procedures in lumbar region; not otherwise specified

**00632**      lumbar sympathectomy

**00634**      chemonucleolysis

**00635**      diagnostic or therapeutic lumbar puncture

**00640**   Anesthesia for manipulation of the spine or for closed procedures on the cervical, thoracic or lumbar spine

**00670**   Anesthesia for extensive spine and spinal cord procedures (eg, spinal instrumentation or vascular procedures)

# Upper Abdomen

**00700**   Anesthesia for procedures on upper anterior abdominal wall; not otherwise specified

**00702**      percutaneous liver biopsy

**00730**   Anesthesia for procedures on upper posterior abdominal wall

**00740**   Anesthesia for upper gastrointestinal endoscopic procedures, endoscope introduced proximal to duodenum

**00750**   Anesthesia for hernia repairs in upper abdomen; not otherwise specified

**00752**      lumbar and ventral (incisional) hernias and/or wound dehiscence

**00754**      omphalocele

**00756**      transabdominal repair of diaphragmatic hernia

**00770**   Anesthesia for all procedures on major abdominal blood vessels

**00790**   Anesthesia for intraperitoneal procedures in upper abdomen including laparoscopy; not otherwise specified

**00792**      partial hepatectomy or management of liver hemorrhage (excluding liver biopsy)

**00794**    pancreatectomy, partial or total (eg, Whipple procedure)

**00796**    liver transplant (recipient)

(For harvesting of liver, use 01990)

**00797**    gastric restrictive procedure for morbid obesity

# Lower Abdomen

**00800**    Anesthesia for procedures on lower anterior abdominal wall; not otherwise specified

**00802**    panniculectomy

**00810**    Anesthesia for lower intestinal endoscopic procedures, endoscope introduced distal to duodenum

**00820**    Anesthesia for procedures on lower posterior abdominal wall

**00830**    Anesthesia for hernia repairs in lower abdomen; not otherwise specified

**00832**    ventral and incisional hernias

(For hernia repairs in the infant 1 year of age or younger, see 00834, 00836)

**00834**    Anesthesia for hernia repairs in the lower abdomen not otherwise specified, younger than 1 year of age

(Do not report 00834 in conjunction with 99100)

**00836**    Anesthesia for hernia repairs in the lower abdomen not otherwise specified, infants younger than 37 weeks gestational age at birth and younger than 50 weeks gestational age at time of surgery

(Do not report 00836 in conjunction with 99100)

**00840**    Anesthesia for intraperitoneal procedures in lower abdomen including laparoscopy; not otherwise specified

**00842**    amniocentesis

**00844**    abdominoperineal resection

**00846**    radical hysterectomy

**00848**    pelvic exenteration

**00851**    tubal ligation/transection

**00860**    Anesthesia for extraperitoneal procedures in lower abdomen, including urinary tract; not otherwise specified

**00862**    renal procedures, including upper one-third of ureter, or donor nephrectomy

**00864**    total cystectomy

**00865**    radical prostatectomy (suprapubic, retropubic)

**00866**    adrenalectomy

**00868**    renal transplant (recipient)

(For donor nephrectomy, use 00862)

(For harvesting kidney from brain-dead patient, use 01990)

**00870**    cystolithotomy

**00872**    Anesthesia for lithotripsy, extracorporeal shock wave; with water bath

**00873**    without water bath

**00880**    Anesthesia for procedures on major lower abdominal vessels; not otherwise specified

**00882**    inferior vena cava ligation

# Perineum

(For perineal procedures on integumentary system, muscles and nerves, see 00300, 00400)

**00902**    Anesthesia for; anorectal procedure

**00904**    radical perineal procedure

**00906**    vulvectomy

**00908**    perineal prostatectomy

**00910**    Anesthesia for transurethral procedures (including urethrocystoscopy); not otherwise specified

**00912**    transurethral resection of bladder tumor(s)

**00914**    transurethral resection of prostate

**00916**    post-transurethral resection bleeding

**00918**    with fragmentation, manipulation and/or removal of ureteral calculus

**00920**    Anesthesia for procedures on male genitalia (including open urethral procedures); not otherwise specified

**00921**    vasectomy, unilateral or bilateral

**00922**    seminal vesicles

**00924**    undescended testis, unilateral or bilateral

**00926**    radical orchiectomy, inguinal

**00928**    radical orchiectomy, abdominal

**00930**    orchiopexy, unilateral or bilateral

**00932**    complete amputation of penis

**00934**    radical amputation of penis with bilateral inguinal lymphadenectomy

**00936**    radical amputation of penis with bilateral inguinal and iliac lymphadenectomy

**00938**    insertion of penile prosthesis (perineal approach)

**00940**    Anesthesia for vaginal procedures (including biopsy of labia, vagina, cervix or endometrium); not otherwise specified

**00942**    colpotomy, vaginectomy, colporrhaphy, and open urethral procedures

**00944**    vaginal hysterectomy

**00948**    cervical cerclage

**00950**    culdoscopy

---

▲=Revised code    ●=New code    ▶◀=Contains new or revised text    ⊘=Modifier 51 exempt

**Anesthesia**

00952    hysteroscopy and/or hysterosalpingography

## Pelvis (Except Hip)

01112    Anesthesia for bone marrow aspiration and/or biopsy, anterior or posterior iliac crest

01120    Anesthesia for procedures on bony pelvis

01130    Anesthesia for body cast application or revision

01140    Anesthesia for interpelviabdominal (hindquarter) amputation

01150    Anesthesia for radical procedures for tumor of pelvis, except hindquarter amputation

01160    Anesthesia for closed procedures involving symphysis pubis or sacroiliac joint

01170    Anesthesia for open procedures involving symphysis pubis or sacroiliac joint

01173    Anesthesia for open repair of fracture disruption of pelvis or column fracture involving acetabulum

01180    Anesthesia for obturator neurectomy; extrapelvic

01190        intrapelvic

## Upper Leg (Except Knee)

01200    Anesthesia for all closed procedures involving hip joint

01202    Anesthesia for arthroscopic procedures of hip joint

01210    Anesthesia for open procedures involving hip joint; not otherwise specified

01212        hip disarticulation

01214        total hip arthroplasty

01215        revision of total hip arthroplasty

01220    Anesthesia for all closed procedures involving upper two-thirds of femur

01230    Anesthesia for open procedures involving upper two-thirds of femur; not otherwise specified

01232        amputation

01234        radical resection

01250    Anesthesia for all procedures on nerves, muscles, tendons, fascia, and bursae of upper leg

01260    Anesthesia for all procedures involving veins of upper leg, including exploration

01270    Anesthesia for procedures involving arteries of upper leg, including bypass graft; not otherwise specified

01272        femoral artery ligation

01274        femoral artery embolectomy

## Knee and Popliteal Area

01320    Anesthesia for all procedures on nerves, muscles, tendons, fascia, and bursae of knee and/or popliteal area

01340    Anesthesia for all closed procedures on lower one-third of femur

01360    Anesthesia for all open procedures on lower one-third of femur

01380    Anesthesia for all closed procedures on knee joint

01382    Anesthesia for diagnostic arthroscopic procedures of knee joint

01390    Anesthesia for all closed procedures on upper ends of tibia, fibula, and/or patella

01392    Anesthesia for all open procedures on upper ends of tibia, fibula, and/or patella

01400    Anesthesia for open or surgical arthroscopic procedures on knee joint; not otherwise specified

01402        total knee arthroplasty

01404        disarticulation at knee

01420    Anesthesia for all cast applications, removal, or repair involving knee joint

01430    Anesthesia for procedures on veins of knee and popliteal area; not otherwise specified

01432        arteriovenous fistula

01440    Anesthesia for procedures on arteries of knee and popliteal area; not otherwise specified

01442        popliteal thromboendarterectomy, with or without patch graft

01444        popliteal excision and graft or repair for occlusion or aneurysm

## Lower Leg (Below Knee, Includes Ankle and Foot)

01462    Anesthesia for all closed procedures on lower leg, ankle, and foot

01464    Anesthesia for arthroscopic procedures of ankle and/or foot

01470    Anesthesia for procedures on nerves, muscles, tendons, and fascia of lower leg, ankle, and foot; not otherwise specified

01472        repair of ruptured Achilles tendon, with or without graft

01474        gastrocnemius recession (eg, Strayer procedure)

01480    Anesthesia for open procedures on bones of lower leg, ankle, and foot; not otherwise specified

01482        radical resection (including below knee amputation)

01484        osteotomy or osteoplasty of tibia and/or fibula

**01486**      total ankle replacement

**01490**   Anesthesia for lower leg cast application, removal, or repair

**01500**   Anesthesia for procedures on arteries of lower leg, including bypass graft; not otherwise specified

**01502**      embolectomy, direct or with catheter

**01520**   Anesthesia for procedures on veins of lower leg; not otherwise specified

**01522**      venous thrombectomy, direct or with catheter

# Shoulder and Axilla

Includes humeral head and neck, sternoclavicular joint, acromioclavicular joint, and shoulder joint.

**01610**   Anesthesia for all procedures on nerves, muscles, tendons, fascia, and bursae of shoulder and axilla

**01620**   Anesthesia for all closed procedures on humeral head and neck, sternoclavicular joint, acromioclavicular joint, and shoulder joint

**01622**   Anesthesia for diagnostic arthroscopic procedures of shoulder joint

**01630**   Anesthesia for open or surgical arthroscopic procedures on humeral head and neck, sternoclavicular joint, acromioclavicular joint, and shoulder joint; not otherwise specified

         (01632 has been deleted. To report, see 01630, 01638)

**01634**      shoulder disarticulation

**01636**      interthoracoscapular (forequarter) amputation

**01638**      total shoulder replacement

**01650**   Anesthesia for procedures on arteries of shoulder and axilla; not otherwise specified

**01652**      axillary-brachial aneurysm

**01654**      bypass graft

**01656**      axillary-femoral bypass graft

**01670**   Anesthesia for all procedures on veins of shoulder and axilla

**01680**   Anesthesia for shoulder cast application, removal or repair; not otherwise specified

**01682**      shoulder spica

# Upper Arm and Elbow

**01710**   Anesthesia for procedures on nerves, muscles, tendons, fascia, and bursae of upper arm and elbow; not otherwise specified

**01712**      tenotomy, elbow to shoulder, open

**01714**      tenoplasty, elbow to shoulder

**01716**      tenodesis, rupture of long tendon of biceps

**01730**   Anesthesia for all closed procedures on humerus and elbow

**01732**   Anesthesia for diagnostic arthroscopic procedures of elbow joint

**01740**   Anesthesia for open or surgical arthroscopic procedures of the elbow; not otherwise specified

**01742**      osteotomy of humerus

**01744**      repair of nonunion or malunion of humerus

**01756**      radical procedures

**01758**      excision of cyst or tumor of humerus

**01760**      total elbow replacement

**01770**   Anesthesia for procedures on arteries of upper arm and elbow; not otherwise specified

**01772**      embolectomy

**01780**   Anesthesia for procedures on veins of upper arm and elbow; not otherwise specified

**01782**      phleborrhaphy

# Forearm, Wrist, and Hand

**01810**   Anesthesia for all procedures on nerves, muscles, tendons, fascia, and bursae of forearm, wrist, and hand

**01820**   Anesthesia for all closed procedures on radius, ulna, wrist, or hand bones

**01829**   Anesthesia for diagnostic arthroscopic procedures on the wrist

**01830**   Anesthesia for open or surgical arthroscopic/endoscopic procedures on distal radius, distal ulna, wrist, or hand joints; not otherwise specified

**01832**      total wrist replacement

**01840**   Anesthesia for procedures on arteries of forearm, wrist, and hand; not otherwise specified

**01842**      embolectomy

**01844**   Anesthesia for vascular shunt, or shunt revision, any type (eg, dialysis)

**01850**   Anesthesia for procedures on veins of forearm, wrist, and hand; not otherwise specified

**01852**      phleborrhaphy

**01860**   Anesthesia for forearm, wrist, or hand cast application, removal, or repair

# Radiological Procedures

**01916**   Anesthesia for diagnostic arteriography/venography

         (Do not report 01916 in conjunction with therapeutic codes 01924-01926, 01930-01933)

**Anesthesia**

**01920**  Anesthesia for cardiac catheterization including coronary angiography and ventriculography (not to include Swan-Ganz catheter)

**01922**  Anesthesia for non-invasive imaging or radiation therapy

**01924**  Anesthesia for therapeutic interventional radiological procedures involving the arterial system; not otherwise specified

**01925**      carotid or coronary

**01926**      intracranial, intracardiac, or aortic

**01930**  Anesthesia for therapeutic interventional radiological procedures involving the venous/lymphatic system (not to include access to the central circulation); not otherwise specified

**01931**      intrahepatic or portal circulation (eg, transvenous intrahepatic portosystemic shunt[s] [TIPS])

**01932**      intrathoracic or jugular

**01933**      intracranial

**01935**  Anesthesia for percutaneous image guided procedures on the spine and spinal cord; diagnostic

**01936**      therapeutic

# Burn Excisions or Debridement

**01951**  Anesthesia for second- and third-degree burn excision or debridement with or without skin grafting, any site, for total body surface area (TBSA) treated during anesthesia and surgery; less than 4% total body surface area

**01952**      between 4% and 9% of total body surface area

+ **01953**      each additional 9% total body surface area or part thereof (List separately in addition to code for primary procedure)

(Use 01953 in conjunction with 01952)

# Obstetric

**01958**  Anesthesia for external cephalic version procedure

**01960**  Anesthesia for vaginal delivery only

**01961**  Anesthesia for cesarean delivery only

**01962**  Anesthesia for urgent hysterectomy following delivery

**01963**  Anesthesia for cesarean hysterectomy without any labor analgesia/anesthesia care

**01965**  Anesthesia for incomplete or missed abortion procedures

**01966**  Anesthesia for induced abortion procedures

**01967**  Neuraxial labor analgesia/anesthesia for planned vaginal delivery (this includes any repeat subarachnoid needle placement and drug injection and/or any necessary replacement of an epidural catheter during labor)

+ **01968**  Anesthesia for cesarean delivery following neuraxial labor analgesia/anesthesia (List separately in addition to code for primary procedure performed)

(Use 01968 in conjunction with 01967)

+ **01969**  Anesthesia for cesarean hysterectomy following neuraxial labor analgesia/anesthesia (List separately in addition to code for primary procedure performed)

(Use 01969 in conjunction with 01967)

# Other Procedures

**01990**  Physiological support for harvesting of organ(s) from brain-dead patient

**01991**  Anesthesia for diagnostic or therapeutic nerve blocks and injections (when block or injection is performed by a different physician or other qualified health care professional); other than the prone position

**01992**      prone position

(Do not report 01991 or 01992 in conjunction with 99143-99150)

(When regional intravenous administration of local anesthetic agent or other medication in the upper or lower extremity is used as the anesthetic for a surgical procedure, report the appropriate anesthesia code. To report a Bier block for pain management, use 64999)

(For intra-arterial or intravenous therapy for pain management, see 96373, 96374)

**01996**  Daily hospital management of epidural or subarachnoid continuous drug administration

(Report code 01996 for daily hospital management of continuous epidural or subarachnoid drug administration performed after insertion of an epidural or subarachnoid catheter)

**01999**  Unlisted anesthesia procedure(s)

# Surgery Guidelines

Guidelines to direct general reporting of services are presented in the **Introduction.** Some of the commonalities are repeated here for the convenience of those referring to this section on **Surgery.** Other definitions and items unique to Surgery are also listed.

## Services

Services rendered in the office, home, or hospital, consultations, and other medical services are listed in the **Evaluation and Management Services** section (99201-99499) beginning on page 8. "Special Services and Reports" (99000-99091) are listed in the **Medicine** section.

## CPT Surgical Package Definition

By their very nature, the services to any patient are variable. The CPT codes that represent a readily identifiable surgical procedure thereby include, on a procedure-by-procedure basis, a variety of services. In defining the specific services "included" in a given CPT surgical code, the following services are always included in addition to the operation per se:

- Local infiltration, metacarpal/metatarsal/digital block or topical anesthesia

- Subsequent to the decision for surgery, one related Evaluation and Management (E/M) encounter on the date immediately prior to or on the date of procedure (including history and physical)

- Immediate postoperative care, including dictating operative notes, talking with the family and other physicians or other qualified health care professionals

- Writing orders

- Evaluating the patient in the postanesthesia recovery area

- Typical postoperative follow-up care

## Follow-Up Care for Diagnostic Procedures

Follow-up care for diagnostic procedures (eg, endoscopy, arthroscopy, injection procedures for radiography) includes only that care related to recovery from the diagnostic procedure itself. Care of the condition for which the diagnostic procedure was performed or of other concomitant conditions is not included and may be listed separately.

## Follow-Up Care for Therapeutic Surgical Procedures

Follow-up care for therapeutic surgical procedures includes only that care which is usually a part of the surgical service. Complications, exacerbations, recurrence, or the presence of other diseases or injuries requiring additional services should be separately reported.

## Supplied Materials

Supplies and materials (eg, sterile trays/drugs), over and above those usually included with the procedure(s) rendered are reported separately. List drugs, trays, supplies, and materials provided. Identify as 99070 or specific supply code.

## Reporting More Than One Procedure/Service

When more than one procedure/service is performed on the same date, same session or during a post-operative period (subject to the "surgical package" concept), several CPT modifiers may apply (see Appendix A for definition).

## Separate Procedure

Some of the procedures or services listed in the CPT codebook that are commonly carried out as an integral component of a total service or procedure have been identified by the inclusion of the term "separate procedure." The codes designated as "separate procedure" should not be reported in addition to the code for the total procedure or service of which it is considered an integral component.

However, when a procedure or service that is designated as a "separate procedure" is carried out independently or considered to be unrelated or distinct from other procedures/services provided at that time, it may be reported by itself, or in addition to other procedures/services by appending modifier 59 to the specific "separate procedure" code to indicate that the procedure is not considered to be a component of another procedure, but is a distinct, independent procedure. This may represent a different session, different procedure or surgery, different site or organ system, separate incision/excision, separate lesion, or separate injury (or area of injury in extensive injuries).

# Unlisted Service or Procedure

A service or procedure may be provided that is not listed in this edition of the CPT codebook. When reporting such a service, the appropriate "Unlisted Procedure" code may be used to indicate the service, identifying it by "Special Report" as discussed in the section below. The "Unlisted Procedures" and accompanying codes for **Surgery** are as follows:

| | |
|---|---|
| 15999 | Unlisted procedure, excision pressure ulcer |
| 17999 | Unlisted procedure, skin, mucous membrane and subcutaneous tissue |
| 19499 | Unlisted procedure, breast |
| 20999 | Unlisted procedure, musculoskeletal system, general |
| 21089 | Unlisted maxillofacial prosthetic procedure |
| 21299 | Unlisted craniofacial and maxillofacial procedure |
| 21499 | Unlisted musculoskeletal procedure, head |
| 21899 | Unlisted procedure, neck or thorax |
| 22899 | Unlisted procedure, spine |
| 22999 | Unlisted procedure, abdomen, musculoskeletal system |
| 23929 | Unlisted procedure, shoulder |
| 24999 | Unlisted procedure, humerus or elbow |
| 25999 | Unlisted procedure, forearm or wrist |
| 26989 | Unlisted procedure, hands or fingers |
| 27299 | Unlisted procedure, pelvis or hip joint |
| 27599 | Unlisted procedure, femur or knee |
| 27899 | Unlisted procedure, leg or ankle |
| 28899 | Unlisted procedure, foot or toes |
| 29799 | Unlisted procedure, casting or strapping |
| 29999 | Unlisted procedure, arthroscopy |
| 30999 | Unlisted procedure, nose |
| 31299 | Unlisted procedure, accessory sinuses |
| 31599 | Unlisted procedure, larynx |
| 31899 | Unlisted procedure, trachea, bronchi |
| 32999 | Unlisted procedure, lungs and pleura |
| 33999 | Unlisted procedure, cardiac surgery |
| 36299 | Unlisted procedure, vascular injection |
| 37501 | Unlisted vascular endoscopy procedure |

| | |
|---|---|
| 37799 | Unlisted procedure, vascular surgery |
| 38129 | Unlisted laparoscopy procedure, spleen |
| 38589 | Unlisted laparoscopy procedure, lymphatic system |
| 38999 | Unlisted procedure, hemic or lymphatic system |
| 39499 | Unlisted procedure, mediastinum |
| 39599 | Unlisted procedure, diaphragm |
| 40799 | Unlisted procedure, lips |
| 40899 | Unlisted procedure, vestibule of mouth |
| 41599 | Unlisted procedure, tongue, floor of mouth |
| 41899 | Unlisted procedure, dentoalveolar structures |
| 42299 | Unlisted procedure, palate, uvula |
| 42699 | Unlisted procedure, salivary glands or ducts |
| 42999 | Unlisted procedure, pharynx, adenoids, or tonsils |
| 43289 | Unlisted laparoscopy procedure, esophagus |
| 43499 | Unlisted procedure, esophagus |
| 43659 | Unlisted laparoscopy procedure, stomach |
| 43999 | Unlisted procedure, stomach |
| 44238 | Unlisted laparoscopy procedure, intestine (except rectum) |
| 44799 | Unlisted procedure, intestine |
| 44899 | Unlisted procedure, Meckel's diverticulum and the mesentery |
| 44979 | Unlisted laparoscopy procedure, appendix |
| 45499 | Unlisted laparoscopy procedure, rectum |
| 45999 | Unlisted procedure, rectum |
| 46999 | Unlisted procedure, anus |
| 47379 | Unlisted laparoscopic procedure, liver |
| 47399 | Unlisted procedure, liver |
| 47579 | Unlisted laparoscopy procedure, biliary tract |
| 47999 | Unlisted procedure, biliary tract |
| 48999 | Unlisted procedure, pancreas |
| 49329 | Unlisted laparoscopy procedure, abdomen, peritoneum and omentum |
| 49659 | Unlisted laparoscopy procedure, hernioplasty, herniorrhaphy, herniotomy |
| 49999 | Unlisted procedure, abdomen, peritoneum and omentum |
| 50549 | Unlisted laparoscopy procedure, renal |
| 50949 | Unlisted laparoscopy procedure, ureter |
| 51999 | Unlisted laparoscopy procedure, bladder |
| 53899 | Unlisted procedure, urinary system |
| 54699 | Unlisted laparoscopy procedure, testis |
| 55559 | Unlisted laparoscopy procedure, spermatic cord |
| 55899 | Unlisted procedure, male genital system |

**58578** Unlisted laparoscopy procedure, uterus

**58579** Unlisted hysteroscopy procedure, uterus

**58679** Unlisted laparoscopy procedure, oviduct, ovary

**58999** Unlisted procedure, female genital system (nonobstetrical)

**59897** Unlisted fetal invasive procedure, including ultrasound guidance, when performed

**59898** Unlisted laparoscopy procedure, maternity care and delivery

**59899** Unlisted procedure, maternity care and delivery

**60659** Unlisted laparoscopy procedure, endocrine system

**60699** Unlisted procedure, endocrine system

**64999** Unlisted procedure, nervous system

**66999** Unlisted procedure, anterior segment of eye

**67299** Unlisted procedure, posterior segment

**67399** Unlisted procedure, ocular muscle

**67599** Unlisted procedure, orbit

**67999** Unlisted procedure, eyelids

**68399** Unlisted procedure, conjunctiva

**68899** Unlisted procedure, lacrimal system

**69399** Unlisted procedure, external ear

**69799** Unlisted procedure, middle ear

**69949** Unlisted procedure, inner ear

**69979** Unlisted procedure, temporal bone, middle fossa approach

# Special Report

A service that is rarely provided, unusual, variable, or new may require a special report. Pertinent information should include an adequate definition or description of the nature, extent, and need for the procedure, and the time, effort, and equipment necessary to provide the service.

# Surgical Destruction

Surgical destruction is a part of a surgical procedure and different methods of destruction are not ordinarily listed separately unless the technique substantially alters the standard management of a problem or condition. Exceptions under special circumstances are provided for by separate code numbers.

Surgery

# Surgery

## General

▶(For percutaneous image-guided fluid collection drainage by catheter of soft tissue [eg, extremity, abdominal wall, neck], use 10030)◀

**10021**  Fine needle aspiration; without imaging guidance

**10022**      with imaging guidance

▶(For placement of percutaneous localization device[s] [eg, clip, metallic pellet, during breast biopsy], see 19081-19086)◀

(For radiological supervision and interpretation, see 76942, 77002, 77012, 77021)

▶(For percutaneous needle biopsy other than fine needle aspiration, see 19081-19086 for breast, 20206 for muscle, 32400 for pleura, 32405 for lung or mediastinum, 42400 for salivary gland, 47000 for liver, 48102 for pancreas, 49180 for abdominal or retroperitoneal mass, 50200 for kidney, 54500 for testis, 54800 for epididymis, 60100 for thyroid, 62267 for nucleus pulposus, intervertebral disc, or paravertebral tissue, 62269 for spinal cord)◀

(For evaluation of fine needle aspirate, see 88172, 88173)

## Integumentary System

### Skin, Subcutaneous, and Accessory Structures

#### ▶Introduction and Removal◀

⊙● **10030**  Image-guided fluid collection drainage by catheter (eg, abscess, hematoma, seroma, lymphocele, cyst), soft tissue (eg, extremity, abdominal wall, neck), percutaneous

▶(Report 10030 for each individual collection drained with a separate catheter)◀

▶(Do not report 10030 in conjunction with 75989, 76942, 77002, 77003, 77012, 77021)◀

▶(For image-guided fluid collection drainage, percutaneous or transvaginal/transrectal of visceral, peritoneal, or retroperitoneal collections, see 49405-49407)◀

## Incision and Drainage

(For excision, see 11400, et seq)

**10040**  Acne surgery (eg, marsupialization, opening or removal of multiple milia, comedones, cysts, pustules)

**10060**  Incision and drainage of abscess (eg, carbuncle, suppurative hidradenitis, cutaneous or subcutaneous abscess, cyst, furuncle, or paronychia); simple or single

**10061**      complicated or multiple

**10080**  Incision and drainage of pilonidal cyst; simple

**10081**      complicated

(For excision of pilonidal cyst, see 11770-11772)

**10120**  Incision and removal of foreign body, subcutaneous tissues; simple

**10121**      complicated

(To report wound exploration due to penetrating trauma without laparotomy or thoracotomy, see 20100-20103, as appropriate)

(To report debridement associated with open fracture(s) and/or dislocation(s), use 11010-11012, as appropriate)

**10140**  Incision and drainage of hematoma, seroma or fluid collection

(If imaging guidance is performed, see 76942, 77012, 77021)

**10160**  Puncture aspiration of abscess, hematoma, bulla, or cyst

(If imaging guidance is performed, see 76942, 77012, 77021)

**10180**  Incision and drainage, complex, postoperative wound infection

(For secondary closure of surgical wound, see 12020, 12021, 13160)

## Debridement

Wound debridements (11042-11047) are reported by depth of tissue that is removed and by surface area of the wound. These services may be reported for injuries, infections, wounds and chronic ulcers. When performing debridement of a single wound, report depth using the deepest level of tissue removed. In multiple wounds, sum the surface area of those wounds that are at the same depth, but do not combine sums from different depths. For example: When bone is debrided from a 4 sq cm heel ulcer and from a 10 sq cm ischial ulcer, report the work with a single code, 11044. When subcutaneous tissue is debrided from a 16 sq cm dehisced abdominal wound and a 10 sq cm thigh wound, report the work with 11042 for the first 20 sq cm and 11045 for the second 6 sq cm.

If all four wounds were debrided on the same day, use modifier 59 with either 11042, or 11044 as appropriate.

(For dermabrasions, see 15780-15783)

(For nail debridement, see 11720-11721)

(For burn(s), see 16000-16035)

(For pressure ulcers, see 15920-15999)

**11000**   Debridement of extensive eczematous or infected skin; up to 10% of body surface

(For abdominal wall or genitalia debridement for necrotizing soft tissue infection, see 11004-11006)

**+ 11001**   each additional 10% of the body surface, or part thereof (List separately in addition to code for primary procedure)

(Use 11001 in conjunction with 11000)

**11004**   Debridement of skin, subcutaneous tissue, muscle and fascia for necrotizing soft tissue infection; external genitalia and perineum

**11005**   abdominal wall, with or without fascial closure

**11006**   external genitalia, perineum and abdominal wall, with or without fascial closure

(If orchiectomy is performed, use 54520)

(If testicular transplantation is performed, use 54680)

**+ 11008**   Removal of prosthetic material or mesh, abdominal wall for infection (eg, for chronic or recurrent mesh infection or necrotizing soft tissue infection) (List separately in addition to code for primary procedure)

(Use 11008 in conjunction with 10180, 11004-11006)

(Do not report 11008 in conjunction with 11000-11001, 11010-11044)

(Report skin grafts or flaps separately when performed for closure at the same session as 11004-11008)

(When insertion of mesh is used for closure, use 49568)

**11010**   Debridement including removal of foreign material at the site of an open fracture and/or an open dislocation (eg, excisional debridement); skin and subcutaneous tissues

**11011**   skin, subcutaneous tissue, muscle fascia, and muscle

**11012**   skin, subcutaneous tissue, muscle fascia, muscle, and bone

(11040, 11041 have been deleted)

(For debridement of skin, ie, epidermis and/or dermis only, see 97597, 97598)

(For active wound care management, see 97597, 97598)

(For debridement of burn wounds, see 16020-16030)

**11042**   Debridement, subcutaneous tissue (includes epidermis and dermis, if performed); first 20 sq cm or less

(For debridement of skin [ie, epidermis and/or dermis only], see 97597, 97598)

**#+ 11045**   each additional 20 sq cm, or part thereof (List separately in addition to code for primary procedure)

(Use 11045 in conjunction with 11042)

**11043**   Debridement, muscle and/or fascia (includes epidermis, dermis, and subcutaneous tissue, if performed); first 20 sq cm or less

**#+ 11046**   each additional 20 sq cm, or part thereof (List separately in addition to code for primary procedure)

(Use 11046 in conjunction with 11043)

**11044**   Debridement, bone (includes epidermis, dermis, subcutaneous tissue, muscle and/or fascia, if performed); first 20 sq cm or less

**11045**   Code is out of numerical sequence. See 11000-11047

**11046**   Code is out of numerical sequence. See 11000-11047

**+ 11047**   each additional 20 sq cm, or part thereof (List separately in addition to code for primary procedure)

(Do not report 11042-11047 in conjunction with 97597-97602 for the same wound)

(Use 11047 in conjunction with 11044)

## Paring or Cutting

(To report destruction, see 17000-17004)

**11055**   Paring or cutting of benign hyperkeratotic lesion (eg, corn or callus); single lesion

**11056**   2 to 4 lesions

**11057**   more than 4 lesions

## Biopsy

During certain surgical procedures in the integumentary system, such as excision, destruction, or shave removals, the removed tissue is often submitted for pathologic examination. The obtaining of tissue for pathology during the course of these procedures is a routine component of such procedures. This obtaining of tissue is not considered a separate biopsy procedure and is not separately reported. The use of a biopsy procedure code (eg, 11100, 11101) indicates that the procedure to obtain tissue for pathologic examination was performed independently, or was unrelated or distinct from other procedures/services provided at that time. Such biopsies are not considered components of other procedures when performed on different lesions or different sites on the same date, and are to be reported separately.

(For biopsy of conjunctiva, use 68100; eyelid, use 67810)

**11100**   Biopsy of skin, subcutaneous tissue and/or mucous membrane (including simple closure), unless otherwise listed; single lesion

**+ 11101**   each separate/additional lesion (List separately in addition to code for primary procedure)

(Use 11101 in conjunction with 11100)

Integumentary

## Removal of Skin Tags

Removal by scissoring or any sharp method, ligature strangulation, electrosurgical destruction or combination of treatment modalities, including chemical destruction or electrocauterization of wound, with or without local anesthesia.

**11200** Removal of skin tags, multiple fibrocutaneous tags, any area; up to and including 15 lesions

**+ 11201** each additional 10 lesions, or part thereof (List separately in addition to code for primary procedure)

(Use 11201 in conjunction with 11200)

## Shaving of Epidermal or Dermal Lesions

Shaving is the sharp removal by transverse incision or horizontal slicing to remove epidermal and dermal lesions without a full-thickness dermal excision. This includes local anesthesia, chemical or electrocauterization of the wound. The wound does not require suture closure.

**11300** Shaving of epidermal or dermal lesion, single lesion, trunk, arms or legs; lesion diameter 0.5 cm or less

**11301** lesion diameter 0.6 to 1.0 cm

**11302** lesion diameter 1.1 to 2.0 cm

**11303** lesion diameter over 2.0 cm

**11305** Shaving of epidermal or dermal lesion, single lesion, scalp, neck, hands, feet, genitalia; lesion diameter 0.5 cm or less

**11306** lesion diameter 0.6 to 1.0 cm

**11307** lesion diameter 1.1 to 2.0 cm

**11308** lesion diameter over 2.0 cm

**11310** Shaving of epidermal or dermal lesion, single lesion, face, ears, eyelids, nose, lips, mucous membrane; lesion diameter 0.5 cm or less

**11311** lesion diameter 0.6 to 1.0 cm

**11312** lesion diameter 1.1 to 2.0 cm

**11313** lesion diameter over 2.0 cm

## Excision—Benign Lesions

Excision (including simple closure) of benign lesions of skin (eg, neoplasm, cicatricial, fibrous, inflammatory, congenital, cystic lesions), includes local anesthesia. See appropriate size and area below. For shave removal, see 11300 et seq, and for electrosurgical and other methods see 17000 et seq.

Excision is defined as full-thickness (through the dermis) removal of a lesion, including margins, and includes simple (non-layered) closure when performed. Report separately each benign lesion excised. Code selection is determined by measuring the greatest clinical diameter of the apparent lesion plus that margin required for complete excision (lesion diameter plus the most narrow margins required equals the excised diameter). The margins refer to the most narrow margin required to adequately excise the lesion, based on individual judgment. The measurement of lesion plus margin is made prior to excision. The excised diameter is the same whether the surgical defect is repaired in a linear fashion, or reconstructed (eg, with a skin graft).

The closure of defects created by incision, excision, or trauma may require intermediate or complex closure. Repair by intermediate or complex closure should be reported separately. For excision of benign lesions requiring more than simple closure, ie, requiring intermediate or complex closure, report 11400-11446 in addition to appropriate intermediate (12031-12057) or complex closure (13100-13153) codes. For reconstructive closure, see 15002-15261, 15570-15770. For excision performed in conjunction with adjacent tissue transfer, report only the adjacent tissue transfer code (14000-14302). Excision of lesion (11400-11446) is not separately reportable with adjacent tissue transfer. See page 56 for the definition of *intermediate* or *complex* closure.

**11400** Excision, benign lesion including margins, except skin tag (unless listed elsewhere), trunk, arms or legs; excised diameter 0.5 cm or less

**11401** excised diameter 0.6 to 1.0 cm

**11402** excised diameter 1.1 to 2.0 cm

**11403** excised diameter 2.1 to 3.0 cm

**11404** excised diameter 3.1 to 4.0 cm

**11406** excised diameter over 4.0 cm

(For unusual or complicated excision, add modifier 22)

**11420** Excision, benign lesion including margins, except skin tag (unless listed elsewhere), scalp, neck, hands, feet, genitalia; excised diameter 0.5 cm or less

**11421** excised diameter 0.6 to 1.0 cm

**11422** excised diameter 1.1 to 2.0 cm

**11423** excised diameter 2.1 to 3.0 cm

**11424** excised diameter 3.1 to 4.0 cm

**11426** excised diameter over 4.0 cm

(For unusual or complicated excision, add modifier 22)

**11440** Excision, other benign lesion including margins, except skin tag (unless listed elsewhere), face, ears, eyelids, nose, lips, mucous membrane; excised diameter 0.5 cm or less

**11441** excised diameter 0.6 to 1.0 cm

**11442** excised diameter 1.1 to 2.0 cm

**11443** excised diameter 2.1 to 3.0 cm

**11444** excised diameter 3.1 to 4.0 cm

**11446**        excised diameter over 4.0 cm

(For unusual or complicated excision, add modifier 22)

(For eyelids involving more than skin, see also 67800 et seq)

**11450**   Excision of skin and subcutaneous tissue for hidradenitis, axillary; with simple or intermediate repair

**11451**        with complex repair

**11462**   Excision of skin and subcutaneous tissue for hidradenitis, inguinal; with simple or intermediate repair

**11463**        with complex repair

**11470**   Excision of skin and subcutaneous tissue for hidradenitis, perianal, perineal, or umbilical; with simple or intermediate repair

**11471**        with complex repair

(When skin graft or flap is used for closure, use appropriate procedure code in addition)

(For bilateral procedure, add modifier 50)

## Excision—Malignant Lesions

Excision (including simple closure) of malignant lesions of skin (eg, basal cell carcinoma, squamous cell carcinoma, melanoma) includes local anesthesia. (See appropriate size and body area below.) For destruction of malignant lesions of skin, see destruction codes 17260-17286.

Excision is defined as full-thickness (through the dermis) removal of a lesion including margins, and includes simple (non-layered) closure when performed. Report separately each malignant lesion excised. Code selection is determined by measuring the greatest clinical diameter of the apparent lesion plus that margin required for complete excision (lesion diameter plus the most narrow margins required equals the excised diameter). The margins refer to the most narrow margin required to adequately excise the lesion, based on the physician's judgment. The measurement of lesion plus margin is made prior to excision. The excised diameter is the same whether the surgical defect is repaired in a linear fashion, or reconstructed (eg, with a skin graft).

The closure of defects created by incision, excision, or trauma may require intermediate or complex closure. Repair by intermediate or complex closure should be reported separately. For excision of malignant lesions requiring more than simple closure, ie, requiring intermediate or complex closure, report 11600-11646 in addition to appropriate intermediate (12031-12057) or complex closure (13100-13153) codes. For reconstructive closure, see 15002-15261, 15570-15770. For excision performed in conjunction with adjacent tissue transfer, report only the adjacent tissue transfer code (14000-14302). Excision of lesion (11600-11646) is not separately reportable with adjacent tissue transfer. See

page 56 for the definition of *intermediate* or *complex* closure.

When frozen section pathology shows the margins of excision were not adequate, an additional excision may be necessary for complete tumor removal. Use only one code to report the additional excision and re-excision(s) based on the final widest excised diameter required for complete tumor removal at the same operative session. To report a re-excision procedure performed to widen margins at a subsequent operative session, see codes 11600-11646, as appropriate. Append modifier 58 if the re-excision procedure is performed during the postoperative period of the primary excision procedure.

**11600**   Excision, malignant lesion including margins, trunk, arms, or legs; excised diameter 0.5 cm or less

**11601**        excised diameter 0.6 to 1.0 cm

**11602**        excised diameter 1.1 to 2.0 cm

**11603**        excised diameter 2.1 to 3.0 cm

**11604**        excised diameter 3.1 to 4.0 cm

**11606**        excised diameter over 4.0 cm

**11620**   Excision, malignant lesion including margins, scalp, neck, hands, feet, genitalia; excised diameter 0.5 cm or less

**11621**        excised diameter 0.6 to 1.0 cm

**11622**        excised diameter 1.1 to 2.0 cm

**11623**        excised diameter 2.1 to 3.0 cm

**11624**        excised diameter 3.1 to 4.0 cm

**11626**        excised diameter over 4.0 cm

**11640**   Excision, malignant lesion including margins, face, ears, eyelids, nose, lips; excised diameter 0.5 cm or less

**11641**        excised diameter 0.6 to 1.0 cm

**11642**        excised diameter 1.1 to 2.0 cm

**11643**        excised diameter 2.1 to 3.0 cm

**11644**        excised diameter 3.1 to 4.0 cm

**11646**        excised diameter over 4.0 cm

(For eyelids involving more than skin, see also 67800 et seq)

## Nails

(For drainage of paronychia or onychia, see 10060, 10061)

**11719**   Trimming of nondystrophic nails, any number

**11720**   Debridement of nail(s) by any method(s); 1 to 5

**11721**        6 or more

**11730**   Avulsion of nail plate, partial or complete, simple; single

**+ 11732**        each additional nail plate (List separately in addition to code for primary procedure)

(Use 11732 in conjunction with 11730)

| | |
|---|---|
| **11740** | Evacuation of subungual hematoma |
| **11750** | Excision of nail and nail matrix, partial or complete (eg, ingrown or deformed nail), for permanent removal; |
| **11752** | with amputation of tuft of distal phalanx |

(For skin graft, if used, use 15050)

| | |
|---|---|
| **11755** | Biopsy of nail unit (eg, plate, bed, matrix, hyponychium, proximal and lateral nail folds) (separate procedure) |
| **11760** | Repair of nail bed |
| **11762** | Reconstruction of nail bed with graft |
| **11765** | Wedge excision of skin of nail fold (eg, for ingrown toenail) |

## Pilonidal Cyst

| | |
|---|---|
| **11770** | Excision of pilonidal cyst or sinus; simple |
| **11771** | extensive |
| **11772** | complicated |

(For incision of pilonidal cyst, see 10080, 10081)

## Introduction

| | |
|---|---|
| **11900** | Injection, intralesional; up to and including 7 lesions |
| **11901** | more than 7 lesions |

(11900, 11901 are not to be used for preoperative local anesthetic injection)

(For veins, see 36470, 36471)

(For intralesional chemotherapy administration, see 96405, 96406)

| | |
|---|---|
| **11920** | Tattooing, intradermal introduction of insoluble opaque pigments to correct color defects of skin, including micropigmentation; 6.0 sq cm or less |
| **11921** | 6.1 to 20.0 sq cm |
| **✛ 11922** | each additional 20.0 sq cm, or part thereof (List separately in addition to code for primary procedure) |

(Use 11922 in conjunction with 11921)

| | |
|---|---|
| **11950** | Subcutaneous injection of filling material (eg, collagen); 1 cc or less |
| **11951** | 1.1 to 5.0 cc |
| **11952** | 5.1 to 10.0 cc |
| **11954** | over 10.0 cc |
| **11960** | Insertion of tissue expander(s) for other than breast, including subsequent expansion |

(For breast reconstruction with tissue expander(s), use 19357)

| | |
|---|---|
| **11970** | Replacement of tissue expander with permanent prosthesis |

| | |
|---|---|
| **11971** | Removal of tissue expander(s) without insertion of prosthesis |

(11975 has been deleted. To report insertion of non-biodegradable drug delivery implant for contraception, use 11981)

| | |
|---|---|
| **11976** | Removal, implantable contraceptive capsules |

(11977 has been deleted. To report removal of implantable contraceptive capsules with subsequent insertion of non-biodegradable drug delivery implant, use 11976 and 11981)

| | |
|---|---|
| **11980** | Subcutaneous hormone pellet implantation (implantation of estradiol and/or testosterone pellets beneath the skin) |
| **11981** | Insertion, non-biodegradable drug delivery implant |
| **11982** | Removal, non-biodegradable drug delivery implant |
| **11983** | Removal with reinsertion, non-biodegradable drug delivery implant |

## Repair (Closure)

Use the codes in this section to designate wound closure utilizing sutures, staples, or tissue adhesives (eg, 2-cyanoacrylate), either singly or in combination with each other, or in combination with adhesive strips. Wound closure utilizing adhesive strips as the sole repair material should be coded using the appropriate E/M code.

**Definitions**

The repair of wounds may be classified as Simple, Intermediate, or Complex.

*Simple repair* is used when the wound is superficial; eg, involving primarily epidermis or dermis, or subcutaneous tissues without significant involvement of deeper structures, and requires simple one layer closure. This includes local anesthesia and chemical or electrocauterization of wounds not closed.

*Intermediate repair* includes the repair of wounds that, in addition to the above, require layered closure of one or more of the deeper layers of subcutaneous tissue and superficial (non-muscle) fascia, in addition to the skin (epidermal and dermal) closure. Single-layer closure of heavily contaminated wounds that have required extensive cleaning or removal of particulate matter also constitutes intermediate repair.

*Complex repair* includes the repair of wounds requiring more than layered closure, viz., scar revision, debridement (eg, traumatic lacerations or avulsions), extensive undermining, stents or retention sutures. Necessary preparation includes creation of a limited defect for repairs or the debridement of complicated lacerations or avulsions. Complex repair does not include excision of benign (11400-11446) or malignant (11600-11646) lesions, excisional preparation of a wound bed (15002-15005) or debridement of an open fracture or open dislocation.

Instructions for listing services at time of wound repair:

1. The repaired wound(s) should be measured and recorded in centimeters, whether curved, angular, or stellate.

2. When multiple wounds are repaired, add together the lengths of those in the same classification (see above) and from all anatomic sites that are grouped together into the same code descriptor. For example, add together the lengths of intermediate repairs to the trunk and extremities. Do not add lengths of repairs from different groupings of anatomic sites (eg, face and extremities). Also, do not add together lengths of different classifications (eg, intermediate and complex repairs).

When more than one classification of wounds is repaired, list the more complicated as the primary procedure and the less complicated as the secondary procedure, using modifier 59.

3. Decontamination and/or debridement: Debridement is considered a separate procedure only when gross contamination requires prolonged cleansing, when appreciable amounts of devitalized or contaminated tissue are removed, or when debridement is carried out separately without immediate primary closure.

> (For extensive debridement of soft tissue and/or bone, not associated with open fracture(s) and/or dislocation(s) resulting from penetrating and/or blunt trauma, see 11042-11047.)

> (For extensive debridement of subcutaneous tissue, muscle fascia, muscle, and/or bone associated with open fracture(s) and/or dislocation(s), see 11010-11012.)

4. Involvement of nerves, blood vessels and tendons: Report under appropriate system (Nervous, Cardiovascular, Musculoskeletal) for repair of these structures. The repair of these associated wounds is included in the primary procedure unless it qualifies as a complex repair, in which case modifier 59 applies.

Simple ligation of vessels in an open wound is considered as part of any wound closure.

Simple "exploration" of nerves, blood vessels or tendons exposed in an open wound is also considered part of the essential treatment of the wound and is not a separate procedure unless appreciable dissection is required. If the wound requires enlargement, extension of dissection (to determine penetration), debridement, removal of foreign body(s), ligation or coagulation of minor subcutaneous and/or muscular blood vessel(s) of the subcutaneous tissue, muscle fascia, and/or muscle, not requiring thoracotomy or laparotomy, use codes 20100-20103, as appropriate.

## Repair—Simple

Sum of lengths of repairs for each group of anatomic sites.

| | |
|---|---|
| **12001** | Simple repair of superficial wounds of scalp, neck, axillae, external genitalia, trunk and/or extremities (including hands and feet); 2.5 cm or less |
| **12002** | 2.6 cm to 7.5 cm |
| **12004** | 7.6 cm to 12.5 cm |
| **12005** | 12.6 cm to 20.0 cm |
| **12006** | 20.1 cm to 30.0 cm |
| **12007** | over 30.0 cm |
| **12011** | Simple repair of superficial wounds of face, ears, eyelids, nose, lips and/or mucous membranes; 2.5 cm or less |
| **12013** | 2.6 cm to 5.0 cm |
| **12014** | 5.1 cm to 7.5 cm |
| **12015** | 7.6 cm to 12.5 cm |
| **12016** | 12.6 cm to 20.0 cm |
| **12017** | 20.1 cm to 30.0 cm |
| **12018** | over 30.0 cm |
| **12020** | Treatment of superficial wound dehiscence; simple closure |
| **12021** | with packing |

(For extensive or complicated secondary wound closure, use 13160)

## Repair—Intermediate

Sum of lengths of repairs for each group of anatomic sites.

| | |
|---|---|
| **12031** | Repair, intermediate, wounds of scalp, axillae, trunk and/or extremities (excluding hands and feet); 2.5 cm or less |
| **12032** | 2.6 cm to 7.5 cm |
| **12034** | 7.6 cm to 12.5 cm |
| **12035** | 12.6 cm to 20.0 cm |
| **12036** | 20.1 cm to 30.0 cm |
| **12037** | over 30.0 cm |
| **12041** | Repair, intermediate, wounds of neck, hands, feet and/or external genitalia; 2.5 cm or less |
| **12042** | 2.6 cm to 7.5 cm |
| **12044** | 7.6 cm to 12.5 cm |
| **12045** | 12.6 cm to 20.0 cm |
| **12046** | 20.1 cm to 30.0 cm |
| **12047** | over 30.0 cm |

**Integumentary**

**12051** Repair, intermediate, wounds of face, ears, eyelids, nose, lips and/or mucous membranes; 2.5 cm or less

**12052** 2.6 cm to 5.0 cm

**12053** 5.1 cm to 7.5 cm

**12054** 7.6 cm to 12.5 cm

**12055** 12.6 cm to 20.0 cm

**12056** 20.1 cm to 30.0 cm

**12057** over 30.0 cm

## Repair—Complex

Reconstructive procedures, complicated wound closure.

Sum of lengths of repairs for each group of anatomic sites.

(For full thickness repair of lip or eyelid, see respective anatomical subsections)

**13100** Repair, complex, trunk; 1.1 cm to 2.5 cm

(For 1.0 cm or less, see simple or intermediate repairs)

**13101** 2.6 cm to 7.5 cm

**+ 13102** each additional 5 cm or less (List separately in addition to code for primary procedure)

(Use 13102 in conjunction with 13101)

**13120** Repair, complex, scalp, arms, and/or legs; 1.1 cm to 2.5 cm

(For 1.0 cm or less, see simple or intermediate repairs)

**13121** 2.6 cm to 7.5 cm

**+ 13122** each additional 5 cm or less (List separately in addition to code for primary procedure)

(Use 13122 in conjunction with 13121)

**13131** Repair, complex, forehead, cheeks, chin, mouth, neck, axillae, genitalia, hands and/or feet; 1.1 cm to 2.5 cm

(For 1.0 cm or less, see simple or intermediate repairs)

**13132** 2.6 cm to 7.5 cm

**+ 13133** each additional 5 cm or less (List separately in addition to code for primary procedure)

(Use 13133 in conjunction with 13132)

►(13150 has been deleted)◄

►(For 1.0 cm or less, see simple or intermediate repairs)◄

**▲ 13151** Repair, complex, eyelids, nose, ears and/or lips; 1.1 cm to 2.5 cm

**▲ 13152** 2.6 cm to 7.5 cm

**+▲ 13153** each additional 5 cm or less (List separately in addition to code for primary procedure)

(Use 13153 in conjunction with 13152)

**13160** Secondary closure of surgical wound or dehiscence, extensive or complicated

(For packing or simple secondary wound closure, see 12020, 12021)

## Adjacent Tissue Transfer or Rearrangement

For full thickness repair of lip or eyelid, see respective anatomical subsections.

Codes 14000-14302 are used for excision (including lesion) and/or repair by adjacent tissue transfer or rearrangement (eg, Z-plasty, W-plasty, V-Y plasty, rotation flap, random island flap, advancement flap). When applied in repairing lacerations, the procedures listed must be performed by the surgeon to accomplish the repair. They do not apply to direct closure or rearrangement of traumatic wounds incidentally resulting in these configurations. Undermining alone of adjacent tissues to achieve closure, without additional incisions, does not constitute adjacent tissue transfer, see complex repair codes 13100-13160. The excision of a benign lesion (11400-11446) or a malignant lesion (11600-11646) is not separately reportable with codes 14000-14302.

Skin graft necessary to close secondary defect is considered an additional procedure. For purposes of code selection, the term "defect" includes the primary and secondary defects. The primary defect resulting from the excision and the secondary defect resulting from flap design to perform the reconstruction are measured together to determine the code.

**14000** Adjacent tissue transfer or rearrangement, trunk; defect 10 sq cm or less

**14001** defect 10.1 sq cm to 30.0 sq cm

**14020** Adjacent tissue transfer or rearrangement, scalp, arms and/or legs; defect 10 sq cm or less

**14021** defect 10.1 sq cm to 30.0 sq cm

**14040** Adjacent tissue transfer or rearrangement, forehead, cheeks, chin, mouth, neck, axillae, genitalia, hands and/or feet; defect 10 sq cm or less

**14041** defect 10.1 sq cm to 30.0 sq cm

**14060** Adjacent tissue transfer or rearrangement, eyelids, nose, ears and/or lips; defect 10 sq cm or less

**14061** defect 10.1 sq cm to 30.0 sq cm

(For eyelid, full thickness, see 67961 et seq)

(14300 has been deleted. To report, see 14301, 14302)

**14301** Adjacent tissue transfer or rearrangement, any area; defect 30.1 sq cm to 60.0 sq cm

**+ 14302** each additional 30.0 sq cm, or part thereof (List separately in addition to code for primary procedure)

(Use 14302 in conjunction with 14301)

**14350**    Filleted finger or toe flap, including preparation of recipient site

## Skin Replacement Surgery

Skin replacement surgery consists of **surgical preparation** and topical placement of an **autograft** (including tissue cultured autograft) or **skin substitute graft** (ie, homograft, allograft, xenograft). The graft is anchored using the individual's choice of fixation. When services are performed in the office, routine dressing supplies are not reported separately.

The following definition should be applied to those codes that reference "100 sq cm or 1% of body area of infants and children" when determining the involvement of body size: The measurement of 100 sq cm is applicable to adults and children 10 years of age and older; and percentages of body surface area apply to infants and children younger than 10 years of age. The measurements apply to the size of the recipient area.

Procedures involving wrist and/or ankle are reported with codes that include arm or leg in the descriptor.

When a primary procedure requires a skin substitute or skin autograft for definitive skin closure (eg, orbitectomy, radical mastectomy, deep tumor removal), use 15100-15278 in conjunction with primary procedure.

For biological implant for soft tissue reinforcement, use 15777 in conjunction with primary procedure.

The supply of skin substitute graft(s) should be reported separately in conjunction with 15271-15278.

### Definitions

Surgical preparation codes 15002-15005 for skin replacement surgery describe the initial services related to preparing a clean and viable wound surface for placement of an autograft, flap, skin substitute graft or for negative pressure wound therapy. In some cases, closure may be possible using adjacent tissue transfer (14000-14061) or complex repair (13100-13153). In all cases, appreciable nonviable tissue is removed to treat a burn, traumatic wound or a necrotizing infection. The clean wound bed may also be created by incisional release of a scar contracture resulting in a surface defect from separation of tissues. The intent is to heal the wound by primary intention, or by the use of negative pressure wound therapy. Patient conditions may require the closure or application of graft, flap, or skin substitute to be delayed, but in all cases the intent is to include these treatments or negative pressure wound therapy to heal the wound. Do not report 15002-15005 for removal of nonviable tissue/debris in a chronic wound (eg, venous or diabetic) when the wound is left to heal by secondary intention. See active wound management codes (97597, 97598) and debridement codes (11042-11047) for this service. For necrotizing soft tissue infections in specific anatomic locations, see 11004-11008.

Select the appropriate code from 15002-15005 based upon location and size of the resultant defect. For multiple wounds, sum the surface area of all wounds from all anatomic sites that are grouped together into the same code descriptor. For example, sum the surface area of all wounds on the trunk and arms. Do not sum wounds from different groupings of anatomic sites (eg, face and arms). Use 15002 or 15004, as appropriate, for excisions and incisional releases resulting in wounds up to and including 100 sq cm of surface area. Use 15003 or 15005 for each additional 100 sq cm or part thereof. For example: Surgical preparation of a 20 sq cm wound on the right hand and a 15 sq cm wound on the left hand would be reported with a single code, 15004. Surgical preparation of a 75 sq cm wound on the right thigh and a 75 sq cm wound on the left thigh would be reported with 15002 for the first 100 sq cm and 15003 for the second 50 sq cm. If all four wounds required surgical preparation on the same day, use modifier 59 with 15002, and 15004.

**Autografts/tissue cultured autografts** include the harvest and/or application of an autologous skin graft. Repair of donor site requiring skin graft or local flaps is reported separately. Removal of current graft and/or simple cleansing of the wound is included, when performed. Do not report 97602. Debridement is considered a separate procedure only when gross contamination requires prolonged cleansing, when appreciable amounts of devitalized or contaminated tissue are removed, or when debridement is carried out separately without immediate primary closure.

Select the appropriate code from 15040-15261 based upon type of autograft and location and size of the defect. The measurements apply to the size of the recipient area. For multiple wounds, sum the surface area of all wounds from all anatomic sites that are grouped together into the same code descriptor. For example, sum the surface area of all wounds on the trunk and arms. Do not sum wounds from different groupings of anatomic sites (eg, face and arms).

**Skin substitute grafts** include non-autologous human skin (dermal or epidermal, cellular and acellular) grafts (eg, homograft, allograft), non-human skin substitute grafts (ie, xenograft), and biological products that form a sheet scaffolding for skin growth. These codes are not to be reported for application of non-graft wound dressings (eg, gel, ointment, foam, liquid) or injected skin substitutes. Removal of current graft and/or simple cleansing of the wound is included, when performed. Do not report 97602. Debridement is considered a separate procedure only when gross contamination requires prolonged cleansing, when appreciable amounts of devitalized or contaminated tissue are removed, or when debridement is carried out separately without immediate primary closure.

Select the appropriate code from 15271-15278 based upon location and size of the defect. For multiple wounds, sum the surface area of all wounds from all

*Integumentary*

anatomic sites that are grouped together into the same code descriptor. For example, sum the surface area of all wounds on the trunk and arms. Do not sum wounds from different groupings of anatomic sites (eg, face and arms).

## Surgical Preparation

**15002** Surgical preparation or creation of recipient site by excision of open wounds, burn eschar, or scar (including subcutaneous tissues), or incisional release of scar contracture, trunk, arms, legs; first 100 sq cm or 1% of body area of infants and children

(For linear scar revision, see 13100-13153)

**+ 15003** each additional 100 sq cm, or part thereof, or each additional 1% of body area of infants and children (List separately in addition to code for primary procedure)

(Use 15003 in conjunction with 15002)

**15004** Surgical preparation or creation of recipient site by excision of open wounds, burn eschar, or scar (including subcutaneous tissues), or incisional release of scar contracture, face, scalp, eyelids, mouth, neck, ears, orbits, genitalia, hands, feet and/or multiple digits; first 100 sq cm or 1% of body area of infants and children

**+ 15005** each additional 100 sq cm, or part thereof, or each additional 1% of body area of infants and children (List separately in addition to code for primary procedure)

(Use 15005 in conjunction with 15004)

## *Autografts/Tissue Cultured Autograft*

**15040** Harvest of skin for tissue cultured skin autograft, 100 sq cm or less

**15050** Pinch graft, single or multiple, to cover small ulcer, tip of digit, or other minimal open area (except on face), up to defect size 2 cm diameter

**15100** Split-thickness autograft, trunk, arms, legs; first 100 sq cm or less, or 1% of body area of infants and children (except 15050)

**+ 15101** each additional 100 sq cm, or each additional 1% of body area of infants and children, or part thereof (List separately in addition to code for primary procedure)

(Use 15101 in conjunction with 15100)

**15110** Epidermal autograft, trunk, arms, legs; first 100 sq cm or less, or 1% of body area of infants and children

**+ 15111** each additional 100 sq cm, or each additional 1% of body area of infants and children, or part thereof (List separately in addition to code for primary procedure)

(Use 15111 in conjunction with 15110)

**15115** Epidermal autograft, face, scalp, eyelids, mouth, neck, ears, orbits, genitalia, hands, feet, and/or multiple digits; first 100 sq cm or less, or 1% of body area of infants and children

**+ 15116** each additional 100 sq cm, or each additional 1% of body area of infants and children, or part thereof (List separately in addition to code for primary procedure)

(Use 15116 in conjunction with 15115)

**15120** Split-thickness autograft, face, scalp, eyelids, mouth, neck, ears, orbits, genitalia, hands, feet, and/or multiple digits; first 100 sq cm or less, or 1% of body area of infants and children (except 15050)

**+ 15121** each additional 100 sq cm, or each additional 1% of body area of infants and children, or part thereof (List separately in addition to code for primary procedure)

(Use 15121 in conjunction with 15120)

(For eyelids, see also 67961-67975)

**15130** Dermal autograft, trunk, arms, legs; first 100 sq cm or less, or 1% of body area of infants and children

**+ 15131** each additional 100 sq cm, or each additional 1% of body area of infants and children, or part thereof (List separately in addition to code for primary procedure)

(Use 15131 in conjunction with 15130)

**15135** Dermal autograft, face, scalp, eyelids, mouth, neck, ears, orbits, genitalia, hands, feet, and/or multiple digits; first 100 sq cm or less, or 1% of body area of infants and children

**+ 15136** each additional 100 sq cm, or each additional 1% of body area of infants and children, or part thereof (List separately in addition to code for primary procedure)

(Use 15136 in conjunction with 15135)

**15150** Tissue cultured skin autograft, trunk, arms, legs; first 25 sq cm or less

**+ 15151** additional 1 sq cm to 75 sq cm (List separately in addition to code for primary procedure)

(Do not report 15151 more than once per session)

(Use 15151 in conjunction with 15150)

**+ 15152** each additional 100 sq cm, or each additional 1% of body area of infants and children, or part thereof (List separately in addition to code for primary procedure)

(Use 15152 in conjunction with 15151)

**15155** Tissue cultured skin autograft, face, scalp, eyelids, mouth, neck, ears, orbits, genitalia, hands, feet, and/or multiple digits; first 25 sq cm or less

**+ 15156** additional 1 sq cm to 75 sq cm (List separately in addition to code for primary procedure)

(Do not report 15156 more than once per session)

(Use 15156 in conjunction with 15155)

**+ 15157**     each additional 100 sq cm, or each additional 1% of body area of infants and children, or part thereof (List separately in addition to code for primary procedure)

(Use 15157 in conjunction with 15156)

(15170-15176 have been deleted. To report, see 15271-15278)

**15200**     Full thickness graft, free, including direct closure of donor site, trunk; 20 sq cm or less

**+ 15201**     each additional 20 sq cm, or part thereof (List separately in addition to code for primary procedure)

(Use 15201 in conjunction with 15200)

**15220**     Full thickness graft, free, including direct closure of donor site, scalp, arms, and/or legs; 20 sq cm or less

**+ 15221**     each additional 20 sq cm, or part thereof (List separately in addition to code for primary procedure)

(Use 15221 in conjunction with 15220)

**15240**     Full thickness graft, free, including direct closure of donor site, forehead, cheeks, chin, mouth, neck, axillae, genitalia, hands, and/or feet; 20 sq cm or less

(For finger tip graft, use 15050)

(For repair of syndactyly, fingers, see 26560-26562)

**+ 15241**     each additional 20 sq cm, or part thereof (List separately in addition to code for primary procedure)

(Use 15241 in conjunction with 15240)

**15260**     Full thickness graft, free, including direct closure of donor site, nose, ears, eyelids, and/or lips; 20 sq cm or less

**+ 15261**     each additional 20 sq cm, or part thereof (List separately in addition to code for primary procedure)

(Use 15261 in conjunction with 15260)

(For eyelids, see also 67961-67975)

(Repair of donor site requiring skin graft or local flaps is considered a separate procedure)

## Skin Substitute Grafts

The supply of skin substitute graft(s) should be reported separately in conjunction with 15271-15278. For biologic implant for soft tissue reinforcement, use 15777 in conjunction with code for primary procedure.

**15271**     Application of skin substitute graft to trunk, arms, legs, total wound surface area up to 100 sq cm; first 25 sq cm or less wound surface area

**+ 15272**     each additional 25 sq cm wound surface area, or part thereof (List separately in addition to code for primary procedure)

(Use 15272 in conjunction with 15271)

(For total wound surface area greater than or equal to 100 sq cm, see 15273, 15274)

(Do not report 15271, 15272 in conjunction with 15273, 15274)

**15273**     Application of skin substitute graft to trunk, arms, legs, total wound surface area greater than or equal to 100 sq cm; first 100 sq cm wound surface area, or 1% of body area of infants and children

**+ 15274**     each additional 100 sq cm wound surface area, or part thereof, or each additional 1% of body area of infants and children, or part thereof (List separately in addition to code for primary procedure)

(Use 15274 in conjunction with 15273)

(For total wound surface area up to 100 sq cm, see 15271, 15272)

**15275**     Application of skin substitute graft to face, scalp, eyelids, mouth, neck, ears, orbits, genitalia, hands, feet, and/or multiple digits, total wound surface area up to 100 sq cm; first 25 sq cm or less wound surface area

**+ 15276**     each additional 25 sq cm wound surface area, or part thereof (List separately in addition to code for primary procedure)

(Use 15276 in conjunction with 15275)

(For total wound surface area greater than or equal to 100 sq cm, see 15277, 15278)

(Do not report 15275, 15276 in conjunction with 15277, 15278)

**15277**     Application of skin substitute graft to face, scalp, eyelids, mouth, neck, ears, orbits, genitalia, hands, feet, and/or multiple digits, total wound surface area greater than or equal to 100 sq cm; first 100 sq cm wound surface area, or 1% of body area of infants and children

**+ 15278**     each additional 100 sq cm wound surface area, or part thereof, or each additional 1% of body area of infants and children, or part thereof (List separately in addition to code for primary procedure)

(Use 15278 in conjunction with 15277)

(For total wound surface area up to 100 sq cm, see 15275, 15276)

(Do not report 15271-15278 in conjunction with 97602)

(15300, 15301 have been deleted. To report, see 15271-15274)

(15320, 15321 have been deleted. To report, see 15275-15278)

(15330, 15331 have been deleted. To report, see 15271-15274)

(15335, 15336 have been deleted. To report, see 15275-15278)

(15340, 15341 have been deleted. To report, see 15271-15278)

(15360, 15361 have been deleted. To report, see 15271-15274)

(15365, 15366 have been deleted. To report, see 15275-15278)

(15400, 15401 have been deleted. To report, see 15271-15274)

(15420, 15421 have been deleted. To report, see 15275-15278)

(15430, 15431 have been deleted. To report, see 15271-15278)

## Flaps (Skin and/or Deep Tissues)

The regions listed refer to the recipient area (not the donor site) when a flap is being attached in a transfer or to a final site.

The regions listed refer to a donor site when a tube is formed for later transfer or when a "delay" of flap occurs prior to the transfer. Codes 15732-15738 are described by donor site of the muscle, myocutaneous, or fasciocutaneous flap.

Codes 15570-15738 do not include extensive immobilization (eg, large plaster casts and other immobilizing devices are considered additional separate procedures).

A repair of a donor site requiring a skin graft or local flaps is considered an additional separate procedure.

> (For microvascular flaps, see 15756-15758)
>
> (For flaps without inclusion of a vascular pedicle, see 15570-15576)
>
> (For adjacent tissue transfer flaps, see 14000-14302)

**15570**    Formation of direct or tubed pedicle, with or without transfer; trunk

**15572**        scalp, arms, or legs

**15574**        forehead, cheeks, chin, mouth, neck, axillae, genitalia, hands or feet

**15576**        eyelids, nose, ears, lips, or intraoral

**15600**    Delay of flap or sectioning of flap (division and inset); at trunk

**15610**        at scalp, arms, or legs

**15620**        at forehead, cheeks, chin, neck, axillae, genitalia, hands, or feet

**15630**        at eyelids, nose, ears, or lips

**15650**    Transfer, intermediate, of any pedicle flap (eg, abdomen to wrist, Walking tube), any location

> (For eyelids, nose, ears, or lips, see also anatomical area)
>
> (For revision, defatting or rearranging of transferred pedicle flap or skin graft, see 13100-14302)

**15731**    Forehead flap with preservation of vascular pedicle (eg, axial pattern flap, paramedian forehead flap)

> (For muscle, myocutaneous, or fasciocutaneous flap of the head or neck, use 15732)

**15732**    Muscle, myocutaneous, or fasciocutaneous flap; head and neck (eg, temporalis, masseter muscle, sternocleidomastoid, levator scapulae)

> (For forehead flap with preservation of vascular pedicle, use 15731)

**15734**        trunk

**15736**        upper extremity

**15738**        lower extremity

## Other Flaps and Grafts

Code 15740 describes a cutaneous flap, transposed into a nearby but not immediately adjacent defect, with a pedicle that incorporates an anatomically named axial vessel into its design. The flap is typically transferred through a tunnel underneath the skin and sutured into its new position. The donor site is closed directly.

Neurovascular pedicle procedures are reported with 15750. This code includes not only skin but also a functional motor or sensory nerve(s). The flap serves to reinnervate a damaged portion of the body dependent on touch or movement (eg, thumb).

Repair of donor site requiring skin graft or local flaps should be reported as an additional procedure.

For random island flaps, V-Y subcutaneous flaps, advancement flaps, and other flaps from adjacent areas without clearly defined anatomically named axial vessels, see 14000-14302.

**15740**    Flap; island pedicle requiring identification and dissection of an anatomically named axial vessel

**15750**        neurovascular pedicle

**15756**    Free muscle or myocutaneous flap with microvascular anastomosis

> (Do not report code 69990 in addition to code 15756)

**15757**    Free skin flap with microvascular anastomosis

> (Do not report code 69990 in addition to code 15757)

**15758**    Free fascial flap with microvascular anastomosis

> (Do not report code 69990 in addition to code 15758)

**15760**    Graft; composite (eg, full thickness of external ear or nasal ala), including primary closure, donor area

**15770**        derma-fat-fascia

**15775**    Punch graft for hair transplant; 1 to 15 punch grafts

**15776**        more than 15 punch grafts

> (For strip transplant, use 15220)

**+▲ 15777**    Implantation of biologic implant (eg, acellular dermal matrix) for soft tissue reinforcement (ie, breast, trunk) (List separately in addition to code for primary procedure)

> ►(For implantation of biologic implants for soft tissue reinforcement in tissues other than breast and trunk, use 17999)◄

(For bilateral breast procedure, report 15777 with modifier 50)

(For implantation of mesh or other prosthesis for open incisional or ventral hernia repair, use 49568 in conjunction with 49560-49566)

(For insertion of mesh or other prosthesis for closure of a necrotizing soft tissue infection wound, use 49568 in conjunction with 11004-11006)

(For topical application of skin substitute graft to a wound surface, see 15271-15278)

(For repair of anorectal fistula with plug (eg, porcine small intestine submucosa [SIS]), use 46707)

(For insertion of mesh or other prosthesis for repair of pelvic floor defect, use 57267)

(The supply of biologic implant should be reported separately in conjunction with 15777)

## Other Procedures

15780　Dermabrasion; total face (eg, for acne scarring, fine wrinkling, rhytids, general keratosis)

15781　　segmental, face

15782　　regional, other than face

15783　　superficial, any site (eg, tattoo removal)

15786　Abrasion; single lesion (eg, keratosis, scar)

+ 15787　　each additional 4 lesions or less (List separately in addition to code for primary procedure)

(Use 15787 in conjunction with 15786)

15788　Chemical peel, facial; epidermal

15789　　dermal

15792　Chemical peel, nonfacial; epidermal

15793　　dermal

15819　Cervicoplasty

15820　Blepharoplasty, lower eyelid;

15821　　with extensive herniated fat pad

15822　Blepharoplasty, upper eyelid;

15823　　with excessive skin weighting down lid

(For bilateral blepharoplasty, add modifier 50)

15824　Rhytidectomy; forehead

(For repair of brow ptosis, use 67900)

15825　　neck with platysmal tightening (platysmal flap, P-flap)

15826　　glabellar frown lines

15828　　cheek, chin, and neck

15829　　superficial musculoaponeurotic system (SMAS) flap

(For bilateral rhytidectomy, add modifier 50)

15830　Excision, excessive skin and subcutaneous tissue (includes lipectomy); abdomen, infraumbilical panniculectomy

(Do not report 15830 in conjunction with 12031-12037, 13100-13102, 14000, 14001, 14302)

15832　　thigh

15833　　leg

15834　　hip

15835　　buttock

15836　　arm

15837　　forearm or hand

15838　　submental fat pad

15839　　other area

(For bilateral procedure, add modifier 50)

15840　Graft for facial nerve paralysis; free fascia graft (including obtaining fascia)

(For bilateral procedure, add modifier 50)

15841　　free muscle graft (including obtaining graft)

15842　　free muscle flap by microsurgical technique

(Do not report code 69990 in addition to code 15842)

15845　　regional muscle transfer

(For intravenous fluorescein examination of blood flow in graft or flap, use 15860)

(For nerve transfers, decompression, or repair, see 64831-64876, 64905, 64907, 69720, 69725, 69740, 69745, 69955)

+ 15847　Excision, excessive skin and subcutaneous tissue (includes lipectomy), abdomen (eg, abdominoplasty) (includes umbilical transposition and fascial plication) (List separately in addition to code for primary procedure)

(Use 15847 in conjunction with 15830)

(For abdominal wall hernia repair, see 49491-49587)

(To report other abdominoplasty, use 17999)

15850　Removal of sutures under anesthesia (other than local), same surgeon

15851　Removal of sutures under anesthesia (other than local), other surgeon

15852　Dressing change (for other than burns) under anesthesia (other than local)

15860　Intravenous injection of agent (eg, fluorescein) to test vascular flow in flap or graft

15876　Suction assisted lipectomy; head and neck

15877　　trunk

15878　　upper extremity

15879　　lower extremity

---

▲=Revised code　●=New code　▶◀=Contains new or revised text　⊘=Modifier 51 exempt

## Pressure Ulcers (Decubitus Ulcers)

**15920** Excision, coccygeal pressure ulcer, with coccygectomy; with primary suture

**15922**      with flap closure

**15931** Excision, sacral pressure ulcer, with primary suture;

**15933**      with ostectomy

**15934** Excision, sacral pressure ulcer, with skin flap closure;

**15935**      with ostectomy

**15936** Excision, sacral pressure ulcer, in preparation for muscle or myocutaneous flap or skin graft closure;

**15937**      with ostectomy

(For repair of defect using muscle or myocutaneous flap, use code(s) 15734 and/or 15738 in addition to 15936, 15937. For repair of defect using split skin graft, use codes 15100 and/or 15101 in addition to 15936, 15937)

**15940** Excision, ischial pressure ulcer, with primary suture;

**15941**      with ostectomy (ischiectomy)

**15944** Excision, ischial pressure ulcer, with skin flap closure;

**15945**      with ostectomy

**15946** Excision, ischial pressure ulcer, with ostectomy, in preparation for muscle or myocutaneous flap or skin graft closure

(For repair of defect using muscle or myocutaneous flap, use code(s) 15734 and/or 15738 in addition to 15946. For repair of defect using split skin graft, use codes 15100 and/or 15101 in addition to 15946)

**15950** Excision, trochanteric pressure ulcer, with primary suture;

**15951**      with ostectomy

**15952** Excision, trochanteric pressure ulcer, with skin flap closure;

**15953**      with ostectomy

**15956** Excision, trochanteric pressure ulcer, in preparation for muscle or myocutaneous flap or skin graft closure;

**15958**      with ostectomy

(For repair of defect using muscle or myocutaneous flap, use code(s) 15734 and/or 15738 in addition to 15956, 15958. For repair of defect using split skin graft, use codes 15100 and/or 15101 in addition to 15956, 15958)

**15999** Unlisted procedure, excision pressure ulcer

(For free skin graft to close ulcer or donor site, see 15002 et seq)

## Burns, Local Treatment

Procedures 16000-16036 refer to local treatment of burned surface only. Codes 16020-16030 include the application of materials (eg, dressings) not described in codes 15100-15278.

List percentage of body surface involved and depth of burn.

For necessary related medical services (eg, hospital visits, detention) in management of burned patients, see appropriate services in **Evaluation and Management** and **Medicine** sections.

For the application of skin grafts or skin substitutes, see codes 15100-15777.

**16000** Initial treatment, first degree burn, when no more than local treatment is required

**16020** Dressings and/or debridement of partial-thickness burns, initial or subsequent; small (less than 5% total body surface area)

**16025**      medium (eg, whole face or whole extremity, or 5% to 10% total body surface area)

**16030**      large (eg, more than 1 extremity, or greater than 10% total body surface area)

**16035** Escharotomy; initial incision

**+ 16036**      each additional incision (List separately in addition to code for primary procedure)

(Use 16036 in conjunction with 16035)

(For debridement, curettement of burn wound, see 16020-16030)

## Destruction

*Destruction* means the ablation of benign, premalignant or malignant tissues by any method, with or without curettement, including local anesthesia, and not usually requiring closure.

Any method includes electrosurgery, cryosurgery, laser and chemical treatment. Lesions include condylomata, papillomata, molluscum contagiosum, herpetic lesions, warts (ie, common, plantar, flat), milia, or other benign, premalignant (eg, actinic keratoses), or malignant lesions.

(For destruction of lesion(s) in specific anatomic sites, see 40820, 46900-46917, 46924, 54050-54057, 54065, 56501, 56515, 57061, 57065, 67850, 68135)

(For laser treatment for inflammatory skin disease, see 96920-96922)

(For paring or cutting of benign hyperkeratotic lesions (eg, corns or calluses), see 11055-11057)

(For sharp removal or electrosurgical destruction of skin tags and fibrocutaneous tags, see 11200, 11201)

(For cryotherapy of acne, use 17340)

(For initiation or follow-up care of topical chemotherapy (eg, 5-FU or similar agents), see appropriate office visits)

(For shaving of epidermal or dermal lesions, see 11300-11313)

## Destruction, Benign or Premalignant Lesions

**17000**   Destruction (eg, laser surgery, electrosurgery, cryosurgery, chemosurgery, surgical curettement), premalignant lesions (eg, actinic keratoses); first lesion

**✚ 17003**   second through 14 lesions, each (List separately in addition to code for first lesion)

(Use 17003 in conjunction with 17000)

(For destruction of common or plantar warts, see 17110, 17111)

**⃠ 17004**   Destruction (eg, laser surgery, electrosurgery, cryosurgery, chemosurgery, surgical curettement), premalignant lesions (eg, actinic keratoses), 15 or more lesions

(Do not report 17004 in conjunction with 17000-17003)

**17106**   Destruction of cutaneous vascular proliferative lesions (eg, laser technique); less than 10 sq cm

**17107**   10.0 to 50.0 sq cm

**17108**   over 50.0 sq cm

**17110**   Destruction (eg, laser surgery, electrosurgery, cryosurgery, chemosurgery, surgical curettement), of benign lesions other than skin tags or cutaneous vascular proliferative lesions; up to 14 lesions

**17111**   15 or more lesions

**17250**   Chemical cauterization of granulation tissue (proud flesh, sinus or fistula)

(17250 is not to be used with removal or excision codes for the same lesion)

## Destruction, Malignant Lesions, Any Method

**17260**   Destruction, malignant lesion (eg, laser surgery, electrosurgery, cryosurgery, chemosurgery, surgical curettement), trunk, arms or legs; lesion diameter 0.5 cm or less

**17261**   lesion diameter 0.6 to 1.0 cm

**17262**   lesion diameter 1.1 to 2.0 cm

**17263**   lesion diameter 2.1 to 3.0 cm

**17264**   lesion diameter 3.1 to 4.0 cm

**17266**   lesion diameter over 4.0 cm

**17270**   Destruction, malignant lesion (eg, laser surgery, electrosurgery, cryosurgery, chemosurgery, surgical curettement), scalp, neck, hands, feet, genitalia; lesion diameter 0.5 cm or less

**17271**   lesion diameter 0.6 to 1.0 cm

**17272**   lesion diameter 1.1 to 2.0 cm

**17273**   lesion diameter 2.1 to 3.0 cm

**17274**   lesion diameter 3.1 to 4.0 cm

**17276**   lesion diameter over 4.0 cm

**17280**   Destruction, malignant lesion (eg, laser surgery, electrosurgery, cryosurgery, chemosurgery, surgical curettement), face, ears, eyelids, nose, lips, mucous membrane; lesion diameter 0.5 cm or less

**17281**   lesion diameter 0.6 to 1.0 cm

**17282**   lesion diameter 1.1 to 2.0 cm

**17283**   lesion diameter 2.1 to 3.0 cm

**17284**   lesion diameter 3.1 to 4.0 cm

**17286**   lesion diameter over 4.0 cm

## Mohs Micrographic Surgery

Mohs micrographic surgery is a technique for the removal of complex or ill-defined skin cancer with histologic examination of 100% of the surgical margins. It requires the integration of an individual functioning in two separate and distinct capacities: surgeon and pathologist. If either of these responsibilities is delegated to another physician or other qualified health care professional who reports the services separately, these codes should not be reported. The Mohs surgeon removes the tumor tissue and maps and divides the tumor specimen into pieces, and each piece is embedded into an individual tissue block for histopathologic examination. Thus a tissue block in Mohs surgery is defined as an individual tissue piece embedded in a mounting medium for sectioning.

If repair is performed, use separate repair, flap, or graft codes. If a biopsy of a suspected skin cancer is performed on the same day as Mohs surgery because there was no prior pathology confirmation of a diagnosis, then report diagnostic skin biopsy (11100, 11101) and frozen section pathology (88331) with modifier 59 to distinguish from the subsequent definitive surgical procedure of Mohs surgery.

▶(If additional special pathology procedures, stains or immunostains are required, see 88311-88314, 88342, 88343)◀

(Do not report 88314 in conjunction with 17311-17315 for routine frozen section stain (eg, hematoxylin and eosin, toluidine blue) performed during Mohs surgery. When a nonroutine histochemical stain on frozen tissue is utilized, report 88314 with modifier 59)

(Do not report 88302-88309 on the same specimen as part of the Mohs surgery)

**17311**   Mohs micrographic technique, including removal of all gross tumor, surgical excision of tissue specimens, mapping, color coding of specimens, microscopic examination of specimens by the surgeon, and histopathologic preparation including routine stain(s) (eg, hematoxylin and eosin, toluidine blue), head, neck, hands, feet, genitalia, or any location with surgery directly involving muscle, cartilage, bone, tendon, major nerves, or vessels; first stage, up to 5 tissue blocks

**Integumentary**

**Integumentary**

+ **17312**   each additional stage after the first stage, up to 5 tissue blocks (List separately in addition to code for primary procedure)

(Use 17312 in conjunction with 17311)

**17313**   Mohs micrographic technique, including removal of all gross tumor, surgical excision of tissue specimens, mapping, color coding of specimens, microscopic examination of specimens by the surgeon, and histopathologic preparation including routine stain(s) (eg, hematoxylin and eosin, toluidine blue), of the trunk, arms, or legs; first stage, up to 5 tissue blocks

+ **17314**   each additional stage after the first stage, up to 5 tissue blocks (List separately in addition to code for primary procedure)

(Use 17314 in conjunction with 17313)

+ **17315**   Mohs micrographic technique, including removal of all gross tumor, surgical excision of tissue specimens, mapping, color coding of specimens, microscopic examination of specimens by the surgeon, and histopathologic preparation including routine stain(s) (eg, hematoxylin and eosin, toluidine blue), each additional block after the first 5 tissue blocks, any stage (List separately in addition to code for primary procedure)

(Use 17315 in conjunction with 17311-17314)

## Other Procedures

**17340**   Cryotherapy ($CO_2$ slush, liquid N2) for acne

**17360**   Chemical exfoliation for acne (eg, acne paste, acid)

**17380**   Electrolysis epilation, each 30 minutes

(For actinotherapy, use 96900)

**17999**   Unlisted procedure, skin, mucous membrane and subcutaneous tissue

# Breast

## Incision

**19000**   Puncture aspiration of cyst of breast;

+ **19001**   each additional cyst (List separately in addition to code for primary procedure)

(Use 19001 in conjunction with 19000)

▶(If imaging guidance is performed, see 76942, 77021)◀

**19020**   Mastotomy with exploration or drainage of abscess, deep

**19030**   Injection procedure only for mammary ductogram or galactogram

(For radiological supervision and interpretation, see 77053, 77054)

## Excision

Excisional breast surgery includes certain biopsy procedures, the removal of cysts or other benign or malignant tumors or lesions, and the surgical treatment of breast and chest wall malignancies. Biopsy procedures may be percutaneous or open, and they involve the removal of differing amounts of tissue for diagnosis.

▶Breast biopsies, without image guidance are reported with 19100 and 19101. Image-guided breast biopsies, including the placement of localization devices when performed, are reported using codes 19081-19086. The image-guided placement of localization devices without biopsy are reported with 19281-19288. When more than one biopsy or localization device placement is performed using the same imaging modality, use an add-on code. If additional biopsies are performed using different imaging modalities, report another primary code for each additional modality. When an open incisional biopsy is performed after image-guided placement of a localization device, 19101 is reported and the appropriate image-guided localization device placement code is reported. The open excision of breast lesions (eg, lesions of the breast ducts, cysts, benign or malignant tumors), without specific attention to adequate surgical margins, with or without the preoperative placement of radiological markers, is reported using codes 19110-19126. Partial mastectomy procedures (eg, lumpectomy, tylectomy, quadrantectomy, or segmentectomy) describe open excisions of breast tissue with specific attention to adequate surgical margins.◀

Partial mastectomy procedures are reported using codes 19301 or 19302 as appropriate. Documentation for partial mastectomy procedures includes attention to the removal of adequate surgical margins surrounding the breast mass or lesion.

Total mastectomy procedures include simple mastectomy, complete mastectomy, subcutaneous mastectomy, modified radical mastectomy, radical mastectomy, and more extended procedures (eg, Urban type operation). Total mastectomy procedures are reported using codes 19303-19307 as appropriate.

Excisions or resections of chest wall tumors including ribs, with or without reconstruction, with or without mediastinal lymphadenectomy, are reported using codes 19260, 19271, or 19272. Codes 19260-19272 are not restricted to breast tumors and are used to report resections of chest wall tumors originating from any chest wall component. (For excision of lung or pleura, see 32310 et seq)

(To report bilateral procedure, report modifier 50 with the procedure code)

● **19081**   Biopsy, breast, with placement of breast localization device(s) (eg, clip, metallic pellet), when performed, and imaging of the biopsy specimen, when performed, percutaneous; first lesion, including stereotactic guidance

**+● 19082**    each additional lesion, including stereotactic guidance (List separately in addition to code for primary procedure)

►(Use 19082 in conjunction with 19081)◄

**● 19083**    Biopsy, breast, with placement of breast localization device(s) (eg, clip, metallic pellet), when performed, and imaging of the biopsy specimen, when performed, percutaneous; first lesion, including ultrasound guidance

**+● 19084**    each additional lesion, including ultrasound guidance (List separately in addition to code for primary procedure)

►(Use 19084 in conjunction with 19083)◄

**● 19085**    Biopsy, breast, with placement of breast localization device(s) (eg, clip, metallic pellet), when performed, and imaging of the biopsy specimen, when performed, percutaneous; first lesion, including magnetic resonance guidance

**+● 19086**    each additional lesion, including magnetic resonance guidance (List separately in addition to code for primary procedure)

►(Use 19086 in conjunction with 19085)◄

►(Do not report 19081-19086 in conjunction with 19281-19288, 76098, 76942, 77002, 77021 for same lesion)◄

**19100**    Biopsy of breast; percutaneous, needle core, not using imaging guidance (separate procedure)

(For fine needle aspiration, use 10021)

**19101**    open, incisional

►(For placement of percutaneous localization clip with imaging guidance, see 19281-19288)◄

►(19102, 19103 have been deleted. To report, see 19081-19086)◄

**19105**    Ablation, cryosurgical, of fibroadenoma, including ultrasound guidance, each fibroadenoma

(Do not report 19105 in conjunction with 76940, 76942)

(For adjacent lesions treated with 1 cryoprobe insertion, report once)

**19110**    Nipple exploration, with or without excision of a solitary lactiferous duct or a papilloma lactiferous duct

**19112**    Excision of lactiferous duct fistula

**19120**    Excision of cyst, fibroadenoma, or other benign or malignant tumor, aberrant breast tissue, duct lesion, nipple or areolar lesion (except 19300), open, male or female, 1 or more lesions

**19125**    Excision of breast lesion identified by preoperative placement of radiological marker, open; single lesion

**+ 19126**    each additional lesion separately identified by a preoperative radiological marker (List separately in addition to code for primary procedure)

(Use 19126 in conjunction with 19125)

**19260**    Excision of chest wall tumor including ribs

**19271**    Excision of chest wall tumor involving ribs, with plastic reconstruction; without mediastinal lymphadenectomy

**19272**    with mediastinal lymphadenectomy

(Do not report 19260, 19271, 19272 in conjunction with 32100, 32503, 32504, 32551, 32554, 32555)

## Introduction

►Breast biopsies without image guidance are reported with 19100 and 19101. Image-guided breast biopsies, including the placement of localization devices when performed, are reported using 19081-19086. The image-guided placement of localization devices without image-guided biopsy are reported with 19281-19288. When more than one biopsy or localization device placement is performed using the same imaging modality, use an add-on code. If additional biopsies are performed using different imaging modalities, report another primary code for each additional modality. When an open incisional biopsy is performed after image-guided placement of a localization device, 19101 is reported and the appropriate image-guided localization device placement code is reported.◄

**● 19281**    Placement of breast localization device(s) (eg, clip, metallic pellet, wire/needle, radioactive seeds), percutaneous; first lesion, including mammographic guidance

**+● 19282**    each additional lesion, including mammographic guidance (List separately in addition to code for primary procedure)

►(Use 19282 in conjunction with 19281)◄

**● 19283**    Placement of breast localization device(s) (eg, clip, metallic pellet, wire/needle, radioactive seeds), percutaneous; first lesion, including stereotactic guidance

**+● 19284**    each additional lesion, including stereotactic guidance (List separately in addition to code for primary procedure)

►(Use 19284 in conjunction with 19283)◄

**● 19285**    Placement of breast localization device(s) (eg, clip, metallic pellet, wire/needle, radioactive seeds), percutaneous; first lesion, including ultrasound guidance

**+● 19286**    each additional lesion, including ultrasound guidance (List separately in addition to code for primary procedure)

►(Use 19286 in conjunction with 19285)◄

**● 19287**    Placement of breast localization device(s) (eg clip, metallic pellet, wire/needle, radioactive seeds), percutaneous; first lesion, including magnetic resonance guidance

*Integumentary*

**Integumentary**

**+● 19288**     each additional lesion, including magnetic resonance guidance (List separately in addition to code for primary procedure)

▶(Use 19288 in conjunction with 19287)◀

▶(Do not report 19281-19288 in conjunction with 19081-19086, 76942, 77002, 77021 for same lesion)◀

▶(For surgical specimen radiography, use 76098)◀

▶(19290, 19291 have been deleted)◀

▶(To report image-guided placement of breast localization devices during image-guided biopsy, see 19081-19086. To report image-guided placement of breast localization devices without image-guided biopsy, see 19281-19288)◀

▶(19295 has been deleted)◀

**19296**     Placement of radiotherapy afterloading expandable catheter (single or multichannel) into the breast for interstitial radioelement application following partial mastectomy, includes imaging guidance; on date separate from partial mastectomy

**+ 19297**     concurrent with partial mastectomy (List separately in addition to code for primary procedure)

(Use 19297 in conjunction with 19301 or 19302)

**⊙ 19298**     Placement of radiotherapy afterloading brachytherapy catheters (multiple tube and button type) into the breast for interstitial radioelement application following (at the time of or subsequent to) partial mastectomy, includes imaging guidance

## Mastectomy Procedures

**19300**     Mastectomy for gynecomastia

**19301**     Mastectomy, partial (eg, lumpectomy, tylectomy, quadrantectomy, segmentectomy);

**19302**         with axillary lymphadenectomy

(For placement of radiotherapy afterloading balloon/brachytherapy catheters, see 19290-19298)

**19303**     Mastectomy, simple, complete

(For immediate or delayed insertion of implant, see 19340, 19342)

(For gynecomastia, use 19300)

**19304**     Mastectomy, subcutaneous

(For immediate or delayed insertion of implant, see 19340, 19342)

**19305**     Mastectomy, radical, including pectoral muscles, axillary lymph nodes

(For immediate or delayed insertion of implant, see 19340, 19342)

**19306**     Mastectomy, radical, including pectoral muscles, axillary and internal mammary lymph nodes (Urban type operation)

(For immediate or delayed insertion of implant, see 19340, 19342)

**19307**     Mastectomy, modified radical, including axillary lymph nodes, with or without pectoralis minor muscle, but excluding pectoralis major muscle

(For immediate or delayed insertion of implant, see 19340, 19342)

## Repair and/or Reconstruction

(To report bilateral procedure, report modifier 50 with the procedure code)

(For biologic implant for soft tissue reinforcement, use 15777 in conjunction with primary procedure)

**19316**     Mastopexy

**19318**     Reduction mammaplasty

**19324**     Mammaplasty, augmentation; without prosthetic implant

**19325**         with prosthetic implant

(For flap or graft, use also appropriate number)

**19328**     Removal of intact mammary implant

**19330**     Removal of mammary implant material

**19340**     Immediate insertion of breast prosthesis following mastopexy, mastectomy or in reconstruction

**19342**     Delayed insertion of breast prosthesis following mastopexy, mastectomy or in reconstruction

(For supply of implant, use 99070)

(For preparation of custom breast implant, use 19396)

**19350**     Nipple/areola reconstruction

**19355**     Correction of inverted nipples

**19357**     Breast reconstruction, immediate or delayed, with tissue expander, including subsequent expansion

**19361**     Breast reconstruction with latissimus dorsi flap, without prosthetic implant

(For insertion of prosthesis, use also 19340)

**19364**     Breast reconstruction with free flap

(Do not report code 69990 in addition to code 19364)

(19364 includes harvesting of the flap, microvascular transfer, closure of the donor site, and inset shaping the flap into a breast)

**19366**     Breast reconstruction with other technique

(For operating microscope, use 69990)

(For insertion of prosthesis, use also 19340 or 19342)

**19367**   Breast reconstruction with transverse rectus abdominis myocutaneous flap (TRAM), single pedicle, including closure of donor site;

**19368**       with microvascular anastomosis (supercharging)

        (Do not report code 69990 in addition to code 19368)

**19369**   Breast reconstruction with transverse rectus abdominis myocutaneous flap (TRAM), double pedicle, including closure of donor site

**19370**   Open periprosthetic capsulotomy, breast

**19371**   Periprosthetic capsulectomy, breast

**19380**   Revision of reconstructed breast

**19396**   Preparation of moulage for custom breast implant

## Other Procedures

**19499**   Unlisted procedure, breast

# Musculoskeletal System

Cast and strapping procedures appear at the end of this section.

The services listed below include the application and removal of the first cast or traction device only. Subsequent replacement of cast and/or traction device may require an additional listing.

**Definitions**

The terms "closed treatment," "open treatment," and "percutaneous skeletal fixation" have been carefully chosen to accurately reflect current orthopaedic procedural treatments.

*Closed treatment* specifically means that the fracture site is not surgically opened (exposed to the external environment and directly visualized). This terminology is used to describe procedures that treat fractures by three methods: (1) without manipulation; (2) with manipulation; or (3) with or without traction.

*Open treatment* is used when the fractured bone is either: (1) surgically opened (exposed to the external environment) and the fracture (bone ends) visualized and internal fixation may be used; or (2) the fractured bone is opened remote from the fracture site in order to insert an intramedullary nail across the fracture site (the fracture site is not opened and visualized).

*Percutaneous skeletal fixation* describes fracture treatment which is neither open nor closed. In this procedure, the fracture fragments are not visualized, but fixation (eg, pins) is placed across the fracture site, usually under X-ray imaging.

The type of fracture (eg, open, compound, closed) does not have any coding correlation with the type of treatment (eg, closed, open, or percutaneous) provided.

The codes for treatment of fractures and joint injuries (dislocations) are categorized by the type of manipulation (reduction) and stabilization (fixation or immobilization). These codes can apply to either open (compound) or closed fractures or joint injuries.

Skeletal traction is the application of a force (distracting or traction force) to a limb segment through a wire, pin, screw, or clamp that is attached (eg, penetrates) to bone.

Skin traction is the application of a force (longitudinal) to a limb using felt or strapping applied directly to skin only.

External fixation is the usage of skeletal pins plus an attaching mechanism/device used for temporary or definitive treatment of acute or chronic bony deformity.

Codes for obtaining autogenous bone grafts, cartilage, tendon, fascia lata grafts or other tissues through separate incisions are to be used only when the graft is not already listed as part of the basic procedure.

Re-reduction of a fracture and/or dislocation performed by the primary physician or other qualified health care professional may be identified by the addition of modifier 76 to the usual procedure number to indicate "Repeat Procedure or Service by Same Physician or Other Qualified Health Care Professional." (See Appendix A guidelines.)

Codes for external fixation are to be used only when external fixation is not already listed as part of the basic procedure.

All codes for suction irrigation have been deleted. To report, list only the primary surgical procedure performed (eg, sequestrectomy, deep incision).

*Manipulation* is used throughout the musculoskeletal fracture and dislocation subsections to specifically mean the attempted reduction or restoration of a fracture or joint dislocation to its normal anatomic alignment by the application of manually applied forces.

▶*Excision of subcutaneous soft connective tissue tumors* (including simple or intermediate repair) involves the simple or marginal resection of tumors confined to subcutaneous tissue below the skin but above the deep fascia. These tumors are usually benign and are resected without removing a significant amount of surrounding normal tissue. Code selection is based on the location and size of the tumor. Code selection is determined by measuring the greatest diameter of the tumor plus that margin required for complete excision of the tumor. The margins refer to the most narrow margin required to adequately excise the tumor, based on the physician's judgment. The measurement of the tumor plus margin is made at the time of the excision. Appreciable vessel exploration and/or neuroplasty should be reported separately. Extensive undermining or other techniques to close a defect created by skin excision may require a complex repair which should be reported separately. Dissection or elevation of tissue planes to permit resection of the tumor is included in the excision. For excision of benign lesions of cutaneous origin (eg, sebaceous cyst), see 11400-11446.◀

*Excision of fascial or subfascial soft tissue tumors* (including simple or intermediate repair) involves the resection of tumors confined to the tissue within or below the deep fascia, but not involving the bone. These tumors are usually benign, are often intramuscular, and are resected without removing a significant amount of surrounding normal tissue. Code selection is based on size and location of the tumor. Code selection is determined by measuring the greatest diameter of the tumor plus that margin required for complete excision of the tumor. The margins refer to the most narrow margin required to adequately excise the tumor, based on individual judgment. The measurement of the tumor plus margin is made at the time of the excision. Appreciable vessel exploration and/or neuroplasty should be reported separately. Extensive undermining or other techniques to close a defect created by skin excision may require a complex repair which should be reported separately.

Dissection or elevation of tissue planes to permit resection of the tumor is included in the excision.

Digital (ie, fingers and toes) subfascial tumors are defined as those tumors involving the tendons, tendon sheaths, or joints of the digit. Tumors which simply abut but do not breach the tendon, tendon sheath, or joint capsule are considered subcutaneous soft tissue tumors.

▶*Radical resection of soft connective tissue tumors* (including simple or intermediate repair) involves the resection of the tumor with wide margins of normal tissue. Appreciable vessel exploration and/or neuroplasty repair or reconstruction (eg, adjacent tissue transfer[s], flap[s]) should be reported separately. Extensive undermining or other techniques to close a defect created by skin excision may require a complex repair which should be reported separately. Dissection or elevation of tissue planes to permit resection of the tumor is included in the excision. Although these tumors may be confined to a specific layer (eg, subcutaneous, subfascial), radical resection may involve removal of tissue from one or more layers. Radical resection of soft tissue tumors is most commonly used for malignant connective tissue tumors or very aggressive benign connective tissue tumors. Code selection is based on size and location of the tumor. Code selection is determined by measuring the greatest diameter of the tumor plus that margin required for complete excision of the tumor. The margins refer to the most narrow margin required to adequately excise the tumor, based on individual judgment. The measurement of the tumor plus margin is made at the time of the excision. For radical resection of tumor(s) of cutaneous origin (eg, melanoma), see 11600-11646.◀

*Radical resection of bone tumors* (including simple or intermediate repair) involves the resection of the tumor with wide margins of normal tissue. Appreciable vessel exploration and/or neuroplasty and complex bone repair or reconstruction (eg, adjacent tissue transfer[s], flap[s]) should be reported separately. Extensive undermining or other techniques to close a defect created by skin excision may require a complex repair which should be reported separately. Dissection or elevation of tissue planes to permit resection of the tumor is included in the excision. It may require removal of the entire bone if tumor growth is extensive (eg, clavicle). Radical resection of bone tumors is usually performed for malignant tumors or very aggressive benign tumors. If surrounding soft tissue is removed during these procedures, the radical resection of soft tissue tumor codes should not be reported separately. Code selection is based solely on the location of the tumor, **not** on the size of the tumor or whether the tumor is benign or malignant, primary or metastatic.

# General

## Incision

(20000 has been deleted)

(For incision and drainage procedures, cutaneous/subcutaneous, see 10060, 10061)

**20005**　Incision and drainage of soft tissue abscess, subfascial (ie, involves the soft tissue below the deep fascia)

## Wound Exploration—Trauma (eg, Penetrating Gunshot, Stab Wound)

20100-20103 relate to wound(s) resulting from penetrating trauma. These codes describe surgical exploration and enlargement of the wound, extension of dissection (to determine penetration), debridement, removal of foreign body(s), ligation or coagulation of minor subcutaneous and/or muscular blood vessel(s), of the subcutaneous tissue, muscle fascia, and/or muscle, not requiring thoracotomy or laparotomy. If a repair is done to major structure(s) or major blood vessel(s) requiring thoracotomy or laparotomy, then those specific code(s) would supersede the use of codes 20100-20103. To report simple, intermediate, or complex repair of wound(s) that do not require enlargement of the wound, extension of dissection, etc, as stated above, use specific Repair code(s) in the **Integumentary System** section.

**20100**　Exploration of penetrating wound (separate procedure); neck

**20101**　　chest

**20102**　　abdomen/flank/back

**20103**　　extremity

## Excision

**20150**　Excision of epiphyseal bar, with or without autogenous soft tissue graft obtained through same fascial incision

(For aspiration of bone marrow, use 38220)

**20200**　Biopsy, muscle; superficial

**20205**　　deep

**20206**　Biopsy, muscle, percutaneous needle

(If imaging guidance is performed, see 76942, 77012, 77021)

(For fine needle aspiration, use 10021 or 10022)

(For evaluation of fine needle aspirate, see 88172-88173)

(For excision of muscle tumor, deep, see specific anatomic section)

**20220**　Biopsy, bone, trocar, or needle; superficial (eg, ilium, sternum, spinous process, ribs)

**Musculoskeletal**

**Musculoskeletal**

20225    deep (eg, vertebral body, femur)

(For bone marrow biopsy, use 38221)

(For radiologic supervision and interpretation, see 77002, 77012, 77021)

20240    Biopsy, bone, open; superficial (eg, ilium, sternum, spinous process, ribs, trochanter of femur)

20245    deep (eg, humerus, ischium, femur)

20250    Biopsy, vertebral body, open; thoracic

20251    lumbar or cervical

(For sequestrectomy, osteomyelitis or drainage of bone abscess, see anatomical area)

## Introduction or Removal

(For injection procedure for arthrography, see anatomical area)

20500    Injection of sinus tract; therapeutic (separate procedure)

20501    diagnostic (sinogram)

(For radiological supervision and interpretation, use 76080)

(For contrast injection[s] and radiological assessment of gastrostomy, duodenostomy, jejunostomy, gastro-jejunostomy, or cecostomy [or other colonic] tube including fluoroscopic imaging guidance, use 49465)

20520    Removal of foreign body in muscle or tendon sheath; simple

20525    deep or complicated

20526    Injection, therapeutic (eg, local anesthetic, corticosteroid), carpal tunnel

20527    Injection, enzyme (eg, collagenase), palmar fascial cord (ie, Dupuytren's contracture)

(For manipulation of palmar fascial cord (ie, Dupuytren's cord) post enzyme injection (eg, collagenase), use 26341)

20550    Injection(s); single tendon sheath, or ligament, aponeurosis (eg, plantar "fascia")

(For injection of Morton's neuroma, see 64455, 64632)

20551    single tendon origin/insertion

(Do not report 20550, 20551 in conjunction with 0232T)

(For injection(s) of platelet rich plasma, use 0232T)

20552    Injection(s); single or multiple trigger point(s), 1 or 2 muscle(s)

20553    single or multiple trigger point(s), 3 or more muscle(s)

(If imaging guidance is performed, see 76942, 77002, 77021)

20555    Placement of needles or catheters into muscle and/or soft tissue for subsequent interstitial radioelement application (at the time of or subsequent to the procedure)

(For placement of devices into the breast for interstitial radioelement application, see 19296-19298)

(For placement of needles, catheters, or devices into muscle or soft tissue of the head and neck, for interstitial radioelement application, use 41019)

(For placement of needles or catheters for interstitial radioelement application into prostate, use 55875)

(For placement of needles or catheters into the pelvic organs or genitalia [except prostate] for interstitial radioelement application, use 55920)

(For interstitial radioelement application, see 77776-77778, 77785-77787)

(For imaging guidance, see 76942, 77002, 77012, 77021)

20600    Arthrocentesis, aspiration and/or injection; small joint or bursa (eg, fingers, toes)

20605    intermediate joint or bursa (eg, temporomandibular, acromioclavicular, wrist, elbow or ankle, olecranon bursa)

20610    major joint or bursa (eg, shoulder, hip, knee joint, subacromial bursa)

(If imaging guidance is performed, see 76942, 77002, 77012, 77021)

20612    Aspiration and/or injection of ganglion cyst(s) any location

(To report multiple ganglion cyst aspirations/injections, use 20612 and append modifier 59)

20615    Aspiration and injection for treatment of bone cyst

20650    Insertion of wire or pin with application of skeletal traction, including removal (separate procedure)

20660    Application of cranial tongs, caliper, or stereotactic frame, including removal (separate procedure)

20661    Application of halo, including removal; cranial

20662    pelvic

20663    femoral

20664    Application of halo, including removal, cranial, 6 or more pins placed, for thin skull osteology (eg, pediatric patients, hydrocephalus, osteogenesis imperfecta)

20665    Removal of tongs or halo applied by another individual

20670    Removal of implant; superficial (eg, buried wire, pin or rod) (separate procedure)

20680    deep (eg, buried wire, pin, screw, metal band, nail, rod or plate)

20690    Application of a uniplane (pins or wires in 1 plane), unilateral, external fixation system

20692    Application of a multiplane (pins or wires in more than 1 plane), unilateral, external fixation system (eg, Ilizarov, Monticelli type)

**20693** Adjustment or revision of external fixation system requiring anesthesia (eg, new pin[s] or wire[s] and/or new ring[s] or bar[s])

**20694** Removal, under anesthesia, of external fixation system

**20696** Application of multiplane (pins or wires in more than 1 plane), unilateral, external fixation with stereotactic computer-assisted adjustment (eg, spatial frame), including imaging; initial and subsequent alignment(s), assessment(s), and computation(s) of adjustment schedule(s)

(Do not report 20696 in conjunction with 20692, 20697)

⊘ **20697** exchange (ie, removal and replacement) of strut, each

(Do not report 20697 in conjunction with 20692, 20696)

# Replantation

**20802** Replantation, arm (includes surgical neck of humerus through elbow joint), complete amputation

(To report replantation of incomplete arm amputation, see specific code[s] for repair of bone[s], ligament[s], tendon[s], nerve[s], or blood vessel[s] with modifier 52)

**20805** Replantation, forearm (includes radius and ulna to radial carpal joint), complete amputation

(To report replantation of incomplete forearm amputation, see specific code[s] for repair of bone[s], ligament[s], tendon[s], nerve[s], or blood vessel[s] with modifier 52)

**20808** Replantation, hand (includes hand through metacarpophalangeal joints), complete amputation

(To report replantation of incomplete hand amputation, see specific code[s] for repair of bone[s], ligament[s], tendon[s], nerve[s], or blood vessel[s] with modifier 52)

**20816** Replantation, digit, excluding thumb (includes metacarpophalangeal joint to insertion of flexor sublimis tendon), complete amputation

(To report replantation of incomplete digit amputation, excluding thumb, see specific code[s] for repair of bone[s], ligament[s], tendon[s], nerve[s], or blood vessel[s] with modifier 52)

**20822** Replantation, digit, excluding thumb (includes distal tip to sublimis tendon insertion), complete amputation

(To report replantation of incomplete digit amputation, excluding thumb, see specific code[s] for repair of bone[s], ligament[s], tendon[s], nerve[s], or blood vessel[s] with modifier 52)

**20824** Replantation, thumb (includes carpometacarpal joint to MP joint), complete amputation

(To report replantation of incomplete thumb amputation, see specific code[s] for repair of bone[s], ligament[s], tendon[s], nerve[s], or blood vessel[s] with modifier 52)

**20827** Replantation, thumb (includes distal tip to MP joint), complete amputation

(To report replantation of incomplete thumb amputation, see specific code[s] for repair of bone[s], ligament[s], tendon[s], nerve[s], or blood vessel[s] with modifier 52)

(To report replantation of complete leg amputation, see specific code[s] for repair of bone[s], ligament[s], tendon[s], nerve[s], or blood vessel[s] with modifier 52)

(To report replantation of incomplete leg amputation, see specific code[s] for repair of bone[s], ligament[s], tendon[s], nerve[s], or blood vessel[s] with modifier 52)

**20838** Replantation, foot, complete amputation

(To report replantation of incomplete foot amputation, see specific code[s] for repair of bone[s], ligament[s], tendon[s], nerve[s], or blood vessel[s] with modifier 52)

# Grafts (or Implants)

Codes for obtaining autogenous bone, cartilage, tendon, fascia lata grafts, or other tissues through separate skin/fascial incisions should be reported separately unless the code descriptor references the harvesting of the graft or implant (eg, includes obtaining graft).

Do not append modifier 62 to bone graft codes 20900-20938.

(For spinal surgery bone graft[s] see codes 20930-20938)

**20900** Bone graft, any donor area; minor or small (eg, dowel or button)

**20902** major or large

**20910** Cartilage graft; costochondral

**20912** nasal septum

(For ear cartilage, use 21235)

**20920** Fascia lata graft; by stripper

**20922** by incision and area exposure, complex or sheet

**20924** Tendon graft, from a distance (eg, palmaris, toe extensor, plantaris)

**20926** Tissue grafts, other (eg, paratenon, fat, dermis)

(For injection[s] of platelet rich plasma, use 0232T)

+ **20930** Allograft, morselized, or placement of osteopromotive material, for spine surgery only (List separately in addition to code for primary procedure)

(Use 20930 in conjunction with 22319, 22532, 22533, 22548-22558, 22590-22612, 22630, 22633, 22634, 22800-22812)

+ **20931** Allograft, structural, for spine surgery only (List separately in addition to code for primary procedure)

(Use 20931 in conjunction with 22319, 22532-22533, 22548-22558, 22590-22612, 22630, 22633, 22634, 22800-22812)

**Musculoskeletal**

**+ 20936**   Autograft for spine surgery only (includes harvesting the graft); local (eg, ribs, spinous process, or laminar fragments) obtained from same incision (List separately in addition to code for primary procedure)

(Use 20936 in conjunction with 22319, 22532, 22533, 22548-22558, 22590-22612, 22630, 22633, 22634, 22800-22812)

**+ 20937**   morselized (through separate skin or fascial incision) (List separately in addition to code for primary procedure)

(Use 20937 in conjunction with 22319, 22532, 22533, 22548-22558, 22590-22612, 22630, 22633, 22634, 22800-22812)

**+ 20938**   structural, bicortical or tricortical (through separate skin or fascial incision) (List separately in addition to code for primary procedure)

(Use 20938 in conjunction with 22319, 22532, 22533, 22548-22558, 22590-22612, 22630, 22633, 22634, 22800-22812)

(For needle aspiration of bone marrow for the purpose of bone grafting, use 38220. Do not report 38220-38230 for bone marrow aspiration for platelet rich stem cell injection. For bone marrow aspiration for platelet rich stem cell injection, use 0232T)

## Other Procedures

**20950**   Monitoring of interstitial fluid pressure (includes insertion of device, eg, wick catheter technique, needle manometer technique) in detection of muscle compartment syndrome

**20955**   Bone graft with microvascular anastomosis; fibula

**20956**   iliac crest

**20957**   metatarsal

**20962**   other than fibula, iliac crest, or metatarsal

(Do not report code 69990 in addition to codes 20955-20962)

**20969**   Free osteocutaneous flap with microvascular anastomosis; other than iliac crest, metatarsal, or great toe

**20970**   iliac crest

**20972**   metatarsal

**20973**   great toe with web space

(Do not report code 69990 in addition to codes 20969-20973)

(For great toe, wrap-around procedure, use 26551)

**⊘ 20974**   Electrical stimulation to aid bone healing; noninvasive (nonoperative)

**⊘ 20975**   invasive (operative)

**20979**   Low intensity ultrasound stimulation to aid bone healing, noninvasive (nonoperative)

**⊙ 20982**   Ablation, bone tumor(s) (eg, osteoid osteoma, metastasis) radiofrequency, percutaneous, including computed tomographic guidance

(Do not report 20982 in conjunction with 77013)

**+ 20985**   Computer-assisted surgical navigational procedure for musculoskeletal procedures, image-less (List separately in addition to code for primary procedure)

(Do not report 20985 in conjunction with 61781-61783)

(20986, 20987 have been deleted)

(For computer-assisted navigational procedures with image guidance based on pre-operative and intraoperatively obtained images, see 0054T, 0055T)

**20999**   Unlisted procedure, musculoskeletal system, general

# Head

Skull, facial bones, and temporomandibular joint.

## Incision

(For incision and drainage of superficial abscess and hematoma, see 10060, 10061)

(For incision and drainage of soft tissue abscess, use 20005)

(For removal of embedded foreign body from dentoalveolar structure, see 41805, 41806)

**21010**   Arthrotomy, temporomandibular joint

(To report bilateral procedure, report 21010 with modifier 50)

## Excision

**21011**   Excision, tumor, soft tissue of face or scalp, subcutaneous; less than 2 cm

**21012**   2 cm or greater

►(For excision of benign lesions of cutaneous origin [eg, sebaceous cyst], see 11420-11426)◄

**21013**   Excision, tumor, soft tissue of face and scalp, subfascial (eg, subgaleal, intramuscular); less than 2 cm

**21014**   2 cm or greater

**▲ 21015**   Radical resection of tumor (eg, sarcoma), soft tissue of face or scalp; less than 2 cm

(To report excision of skull tumor for osteomyelitis, use 61501)

**▲ 21016**   2 cm or greater

►(For radical resection of tumor[s] of cutaneous origin [eg, melanoma], see 11620-11646)◄

**21025**   Excision of bone (eg, for osteomyelitis or bone abscess); mandible

**21026**   facial bone(s)

Musculoskeletal

**21029** Removal by contouring of benign tumor of facial bone (eg, fibrous dysplasia)

**21030** Excision of benign tumor or cyst of maxilla or zygoma by enucleation and curettage

**21031** Excision of torus mandibularis

**21032** Excision of maxillary torus palatinus

**21034** Excision of malignant tumor of maxilla or zygoma

**21040** Excision of benign tumor or cyst of mandible, by enucleation and/or curettage

(For enucleation and/or curettage of benign cysts or tumors of mandible not requiring osteotomy, use 21040)

(For excision of benign tumor or cyst of mandible requiring osteotomy, see 21046-21047)

**21044** Excision of malignant tumor of mandible;

**21045** radical resection

(For bone graft, use 21215)

**21046** Excision of benign tumor or cyst of mandible; requiring intra-oral osteotomy (eg, locally aggressive or destructive lesion[s])

**21047** requiring extra-oral osteotomy and partial mandibulectomy (eg, locally aggressive or destructive lesion[s])

**21048** Excision of benign tumor or cyst of maxilla; requiring intra-oral osteotomy (eg, locally aggressive or destructive lesion[s])

**21049** requiring extra-oral osteotomy and partial maxillectomy (eg, locally aggressive or destructive lesion[s])

**21050** Condylectomy, temporomandibular joint (separate procedure)

(For bilateral procedures, report 21050 with modifier 50)

**21060** Meniscectomy, partial or complete, temporomandibular joint (separate procedure)

(For bilateral procedures, report 21060 with modifier 50)

**21070** Coronoidectomy (separate procedure)

(For bilateral procedures, report 21070 with modifier 50)

## Manipulation

**21073** Manipulation of temporomandibular joint(s) (TMJ), therapeutic, requiring an anesthesia service (ie, general or monitored anesthesia care)

(For TMJ manipulation without an anesthesia service [ie, general or monitored anesthesia care], see 97140, 98925-98929, 98943)

(For closed treatment of temporomandibular dislocation, see 21480, 21485)

## Head Prosthesis

Codes 21076-21089 describe professional services for the rehabilitation of patients with oral, facial, or other anatomical deficiencies by means of prostheses such as an artificial eye, ear, or nose or intraoral obturator to close a cleft. Codes 21076-21089 should only be used when the physician or other qualified health care professional actually designs and prepares the prosthesis (ie, not prepared by an outside laboratory).

(For application or removal of caliper or tongs, see 20660, 20665)

**21076** Impression and custom preparation; surgical obturator prosthesis

**21077** orbital prosthesis

**21079** interim obturator prosthesis

**21080** definitive obturator prosthesis

**21081** mandibular resection prosthesis

**21082** palatal augmentation prosthesis

**21083** palatal lift prosthesis

**21084** speech aid prosthesis

**21085** oral surgical splint

**21086** auricular prosthesis

**21087** nasal prosthesis

**21088** facial prosthesis

## Other Procedures

**21089** Unlisted maxillofacial prosthetic procedure

## Introduction or Removal

**21100** Application of halo type appliance for maxillofacial fixation, includes removal (separate procedure)

**21110** Application of interdental fixation device for conditions other than fracture or dislocation, includes removal

(For removal of interdental fixation by another individual, see 20670-20680)

**21116** Injection procedure for temporomandibular joint arthrography

(For radiological supervision and interpretation, use 70332. Do not report 77002 in conjunction with 70332)

## Repair, Revision, and/or Reconstruction

(For cranioplasty, see 21179, 21180 and 62116, 62120, 62140-62147)

**21120** Genioplasty; augmentation (autograft, allograft, prosthetic material)

**21121** sliding osteotomy, single piece

**Musculoskeletal**

**21122**       sliding osteotomies, 2 or more osteotomies (eg, wedge excision or bone wedge reversal for asymmetrical chin)

**21123**       sliding, augmentation with interpositional bone grafts (includes obtaining autografts)

**21125** Augmentation, mandibular body or angle; prosthetic material

**21127**       with bone graft, onlay or interpositional (includes obtaining autograft)

**21137** Reduction forehead; contouring only

**21138**       contouring and application of prosthetic material or bone graft (includes obtaining autograft)

**21139**       contouring and setback of anterior frontal sinus wall

**21141** Reconstruction midface, LeFort I; single piece, segment movement in any direction (eg, for Long Face Syndrome), without bone graft

**21142**       2 pieces, segment movement in any direction, without bone graft

**21143**       3 or more pieces, segment movement in any direction, without bone graft

**21145**       single piece, segment movement in any direction, requiring bone grafts (includes obtaining autografts)

**21146**       2 pieces, segment movement in any direction, requiring bone grafts (includes obtaining autografts) (eg, ungrafted unilateral alveolar cleft)

**21147**       3 or more pieces, segment movement in any direction, requiring bone grafts (includes obtaining autografts) (eg, ungrafted bilateral alveolar cleft or multiple osteotomies)

**21150** Reconstruction midface, LeFort II; anterior intrusion (eg, Treacher-Collins Syndrome)

**21151**       any direction, requiring bone grafts (includes obtaining autografts)

**21154** Reconstruction midface, LeFort III (extracranial), any type, requiring bone grafts (includes obtaining autografts); without LeFort I

**21155**       with LeFort I

**21159** Reconstruction midface, LeFort III (extra and intracranial) with forehead advancement (eg, mono bloc), requiring bone grafts (includes obtaining autografts); without LeFort I

**21160**       with LeFort I

**21172** Reconstruction superior-lateral orbital rim and lower forehead, advancement or alteration, with or without grafts (includes obtaining autografts)

(For frontal or parietal craniotomy performed for craniosynostosis, use 61556)

**21175** Reconstruction, bifrontal, superior-lateral orbital rims and lower forehead, advancement or alteration (eg, plagiocephaly, trigonocephaly, brachycephaly), with or without grafts (includes obtaining autografts)

(For bifrontal craniotomy performed for craniosynostosis, use 61557)

**21179** Reconstruction, entire or majority of forehead and/or supraorbital rims; with grafts (allograft or prosthetic material)

**21180**       with autograft (includes obtaining grafts)

(For extensive craniectomy for multiple suture craniosynostosis, use only 61558 or 61559)

**21181** Reconstruction by contouring of benign tumor of cranial bones (eg, fibrous dysplasia), extracranial

**21182** Reconstruction of orbital walls, rims, forehead, nasoethmoid complex following intra- and extracranial excision of benign tumor of cranial bone (eg, fibrous dysplasia), with multiple autografts (includes obtaining grafts); total area of bone grafting less than 40 sq cm

**21183**       total area of bone grafting greater than 40 sq cm but less than 80 sq cm

**21184**       total area of bone grafting greater than 80 sq cm

(For excision of benign tumor of cranial bones, see 61563, 61564)

**21188** Reconstruction midface, osteotomies (other than LeFort type) and bone grafts (includes obtaining autografts)

**21193** Reconstruction of mandibular rami, horizontal, vertical, C, or L osteotomy; without bone graft

**21194**       with bone graft (includes obtaining graft)

**21195** Reconstruction of mandibular rami and/or body, sagittal split; without internal rigid fixation

**21196**       with internal rigid fixation

**21198** Osteotomy, mandible, segmental;

**21199**       with genioglossus advancement

(To report total osteotomy of the maxilla, see 21141-21160)

**21206** Osteotomy, maxilla, segmental (eg, Wassmund or Schuchard)

**21208** Osteoplasty, facial bones; augmentation (autograft, allograft, or prosthetic implant)

**21209**       reduction

**21210** Graft, bone; nasal, maxillary or malar areas (includes obtaining graft)

(For cleft palate repair, see 42200-42225)

**21215**       mandible (includes obtaining graft)

**21230** Graft; rib cartilage, autogenous, to face, chin, nose or ear (includes obtaining graft)

| | |
|---|---|
| 21235 | ear cartilage, autogenous, to nose or ear (includes obtaining graft) |

(To report graft augmentation of facial bones, use 21208)

| | |
|---|---|
| 21240 | Arthroplasty, temporomandibular joint, with or without autograft (includes obtaining graft) |
| 21242 | Arthroplasty, temporomandibular joint, with allograft |
| 21243 | Arthroplasty, temporomandibular joint, with prosthetic joint replacement |
| 21244 | Reconstruction of mandible, extraoral, with transosteal bone plate (eg, mandibular staple bone plate) |
| 21245 | Reconstruction of mandible or maxilla, subperiosteal implant; partial |
| 21246 | complete |
| 21247 | Reconstruction of mandibular condyle with bone and cartilage autografts (includes obtaining grafts) (eg, for hemifacial microsomia) |
| 21248 | Reconstruction of mandible or maxilla, endosteal implant (eg, blade, cylinder); partial |
| 21249 | complete |

(To report midface reconstruction, see 21141-21160)

| | |
|---|---|
| 21255 | Reconstruction of zygomatic arch and glenoid fossa with bone and cartilage (includes obtaining autografts) |
| 21256 | Reconstruction of orbit with osteotomies (extracranial) and with bone grafts (includes obtaining autografts) (eg, micro-ophthalmia) |
| 21260 | Periorbital osteotomies for orbital hypertelorism, with bone grafts; extracranial approach |
| 21261 | combined intra- and extracranial approach |
| 21263 | with forehead advancement |
| 21267 | Orbital repositioning, periorbital osteotomies, unilateral, with bone grafts; extracranial approach |
| 21268 | combined intra- and extracranial approach |
| 21270 | Malar augmentation, prosthetic material |

(For malar augmentation with bone graft, use 21210)

| | |
|---|---|
| 21275 | Secondary revision of orbitocraniofacial reconstruction |
| 21280 | Medial canthopexy (separate procedure) |

(For medial canthoplasty, use 67950)

| | |
|---|---|
| 21282 | Lateral canthopexy |
| 21295 | Reduction of masseter muscle and bone (eg, for treatment of benign masseteric hypertrophy); extraoral approach |
| 21296 | intraoral approach |

## Other Procedures

| | |
|---|---|
| 21299 | Unlisted craniofacial and maxillofacial procedure |

## Fracture and/or Dislocation

(For operative repair of skull fracture, see 62000-62010)

(To report closed treatment of skull fracture, use the appropriate Evaluation and Management code)

| | |
|---|---|
| 21310 | Closed treatment of nasal bone fracture without manipulation |
| 21315 | Closed treatment of nasal bone fracture; without stabilization |
| 21320 | with stabilization |
| 21325 | Open treatment of nasal fracture; uncomplicated |
| 21330 | complicated, with internal and/or external skeletal fixation |
| 21335 | with concomitant open treatment of fractured septum |
| 21336 | Open treatment of nasal septal fracture, with or without stabilization |
| 21337 | Closed treatment of nasal septal fracture, with or without stabilization |
| 21338 | Open treatment of nasoethmoid fracture; without external fixation |
| 21339 | with external fixation |
| 21340 | Percutaneous treatment of nasoethmoid complex fracture, with splint, wire or headcap fixation, including repair of canthal ligaments and/or the nasolacrimal apparatus |
| 21343 | Open treatment of depressed frontal sinus fracture |
| 21344 | Open treatment of complicated (eg, comminuted or involving posterior wall) frontal sinus fracture, via coronal or multiple approaches |
| 21345 | Closed treatment of nasomaxillary complex fracture (LeFort II type), with interdental wire fixation or fixation of denture or splint |
| 21346 | Open treatment of nasomaxillary complex fracture (LeFort II type); with wiring and/or local fixation |
| 21347 | requiring multiple open approaches |
| 21348 | with bone grafting (includes obtaining graft) |
| 21355 | Percutaneous treatment of fracture of malar area, including zygomatic arch and malar tripod, with manipulation |
| 21356 | Open treatment of depressed zygomatic arch fracture (eg, Gillies approach) |
| 21360 | Open treatment of depressed malar fracture, including zygomatic arch and malar tripod |
| 21365 | Open treatment of complicated (eg, comminuted or involving cranial nerve foramina) fracture(s) of malar area, including zygomatic arch and malar tripod; with internal fixation and multiple surgical approaches |
| 21366 | with bone grafting (includes obtaining graft) |
| 21385 | Open treatment of orbital floor blowout fracture; transantral approach (Caldwell-Luc type operation) |

Musculoskeletal

**Musculoskeletal**

| | |
|---|---|
| **21386** | periorbital approach |
| **21387** | combined approach |
| **21390** | periorbital approach, with alloplastic or other implant |
| **21395** | periorbital approach with bone graft (includes obtaining graft) |
| **21400** | Closed treatment of fracture of orbit, except blowout; without manipulation |
| **21401** | with manipulation |
| **21406** | Open treatment of fracture of orbit, except blowout; without implant |
| **21407** | with implant |
| **21408** | with bone grafting (includes obtaining graft) |
| **21421** | Closed treatment of palatal or maxillary fracture (LeFort I type), with interdental wire fixation or fixation of denture or splint |
| **21422** | Open treatment of palatal or maxillary fracture (LeFort I type); |
| **21423** | complicated (comminuted or involving cranial nerve foramina), multiple approaches |
| **21431** | Closed treatment of craniofacial separation (LeFort III type) using interdental wire fixation of denture or splint |
| **21432** | Open treatment of craniofacial separation (LeFort III type); with wiring and/or internal fixation |
| **21433** | complicated (eg, comminuted or involving cranial nerve foramina), multiple surgical approaches |
| **21435** | complicated, utilizing internal and/or external fixation techniques (eg, head cap, halo device, and/or intermaxillary fixation) |
| | (For removal of internal or external fixation device, use 20670) |
| **21436** | complicated, multiple surgical approaches, internal fixation, with bone grafting (includes obtaining graft) |
| **21440** | Closed treatment of mandibular or maxillary alveolar ridge fracture (separate procedure) |
| **21445** | Open treatment of mandibular or maxillary alveolar ridge fracture (separate procedure) |
| **21450** | Closed treatment of mandibular fracture; without manipulation |
| **21451** | with manipulation |
| **21452** | Percutaneous treatment of mandibular fracture, with external fixation |
| **21453** | Closed treatment of mandibular fracture with interdental fixation |
| **21454** | Open treatment of mandibular fracture with external fixation |
| **21461** | Open treatment of mandibular fracture; without interdental fixation |

| | |
|---|---|
| **21462** | with interdental fixation |
| **21465** | Open treatment of mandibular condylar fracture |
| **21470** | Open treatment of complicated mandibular fracture by multiple surgical approaches including internal fixation, interdental fixation, and/or wiring of dentures or splints |
| **21480** | Closed treatment of temporomandibular dislocation; initial or subsequent |
| **21485** | complicated (eg, recurrent requiring intermaxillary fixation or splinting), initial or subsequent |
| **21490** | Open treatment of temporomandibular dislocation |
| | (For interdental wire fixation, use 21497) |
| **21495** | Open treatment of hyoid fracture |
| | (For laryngoplasty with open reduction of fracture, use 31584) |
| | (To report treatment of closed fracture of larynx, use the applicable Evaluation and Management codes) |
| **21497** | Interdental wiring, for condition other than fracture |

## Other Procedures

| | |
|---|---|
| **21499** | Unlisted musculoskeletal procedure, head |
| | (For unlisted craniofacial or maxillofacial procedure, use 21299) |

# Neck (Soft Tissues) and Thorax

(For cervical spine and back, see 21920 et seq)

(For injection of fracture site or trigger point, use 20550)

## Incision

(For incision and drainage of abscess or hematoma, superficial, see 10060, 10140)

| | |
|---|---|
| **21501** | Incision and drainage, deep abscess or hematoma, soft tissues of neck or thorax; |
| | (For posterior spine subfascial incision and drainage, see 22010-22015) |
| **21502** | with partial rib ostectomy |
| **21510** | Incision, deep, with opening of bone cortex (eg, for osteomyelitis or bone abscess), thorax |

## Excision

(For bone biopsy, see 20220-20251)

| | |
|---|---|
| **21550** | Biopsy, soft tissue of neck or thorax |
| | (For needle biopsy of soft tissue, use 20206) |
| **21552** | Code is out of numerical sequence. See 21550-21632 |
| **21554** | Code is out of numerical sequence. See 21550-21632 |
| **21555** | Excision, tumor, soft tissue of neck or anterior thorax, subcutaneous; less than 3 cm |

**# 21552**          3 cm or greater

▶(For excision of benign lesions of cutaneous origin [eg, sebaceous cyst], see 11420-11426)◀

**21556**    Excision, tumor, soft tissue of neck or anterior thorax, subfascial (eg, intramuscular); less than 5 cm

**# 21554**          5 cm or greater

**▲ 21557**    Radical resection of tumor (eg, sarcoma), soft tissue of neck or anterior thorax; less than 5 cm

**▲ 21558**          5 cm or greater

▶(For radical resection of tumor[s] of cutaneous origin [eg, melanoma], see 11600-11620)◀

**21600**    Excision of rib, partial

(For radical resection of chest wall and rib cage for tumor, use 19260)

(For radical debridement of chest wall and rib cage for injury, see 11044, 11047)

**21610**    Costotransversectomy (separate procedure)

**21615**    Excision first and/or cervical rib;

**21616**        with sympathectomy

**21620**    Ostectomy of sternum, partial

**21627**    Sternal debridement

(For debridement and closure, use 21750)

**21630**    Radical resection of sternum;

**21632**        with mediastinal lymphadenectomy

## Repair, Revision, and/or Reconstruction

(For superficial wound, see **Integumentary System** section under Repair—Simple)

**21685**    Hyoid myotomy and suspension

**21700**    Division of scalenus anticus; without resection of cervical rib

**21705**        with resection of cervical rib

**21720**    Division of sternocleidomastoid for torticollis, open operation; without cast application

(For transection of spinal accessory and cervical nerves, see 63191, 64722)

**21725**        with cast application

**21740**    Reconstructive repair of pectus excavatum or carinatum; open

**21742**        minimally invasive approach (Nuss procedure), without thoracoscopy

**21743**        minimally invasive approach (Nuss procedure), with thoracoscopy

**21750**    Closure of median sternotomy separation with or without debridement (separate procedure)

## Fracture and/or Dislocation

**21800**    Closed treatment of rib fracture, uncomplicated, each

**21805**    Open treatment of rib fracture without fixation, each

**21810**    Treatment of rib fracture requiring external fixation (flail chest)

**21820**    Closed treatment of sternum fracture

**21825**    Open treatment of sternum fracture with or without skeletal fixation

(For sternoclavicular dislocation, see 23520-23532)

## Other Procedures

**21899**    Unlisted procedure, neck or thorax

# Back and Flank

## Excision

**21920**    Biopsy, soft tissue of back or flank; superficial

**21925**        deep

(For needle biopsy of soft tissue, use 20206)

**21930**    Excision, tumor, soft tissue of back or flank, subcutaneous; less than 3 cm

**21931**        3 cm or greater

▶(For excision of benign lesions of cutaneous origin [eg, sebaceous cyst], see 11400-11406)◀

**21932**    Excision, tumor, soft tissue of back or flank, subfascial (eg, intramuscular); less than 5 cm

**21933**        5 cm or greater

**▲ 21935**    Radical resection of tumor (eg, sarcoma), soft tissue of back or flank; less than 5 cm

**▲ 21936**        5 cm or greater

▶(For radical resection of tumor[s] of cutaneous origin [eg, melanoma], see 11600-11606)◀

# Spine (Vertebral Column)

Cervical, thoracic, and lumbar spine.

Within the spine section, bone grafting procedures are reported separately and in addition to arthrodesis. For bone grafts in other Musculoskeletal sections, see specific code(s) descriptor(s) and/or accompanying guidelines.

To report bone grafts performed after arthrodesis, see 20930-20938. Do not append modifier 62 to bone graft codes 20900-20938.

*Example:*

Posterior arthrodesis of L5-S1 for degenerative disc disease utilizing morselized autogenous iliac bone graft harvested through a separate fascial incision.

Report as 22612 and 20937.

Musculoskeletal

Within the spine section, instrumentation is reported separately and in addition to arthrodesis. To report instrumentation procedures performed with definitive vertebral procedure(s), see 22840-22855. Instrumentation procedure codes 22840-22848 and 22851 are reported in addition to the definitive procedure(s). Modifier 62 may not be appended to the definitive or add-on spinal instrumentation procedure code(s) 22840-22848 and 22850-22852.

*Example:*

Posterior arthrodesis of L4-S1, utilizing morselized autogenous iliac bone graft harvested through separate fascial incision, and pedicle screw fixation.

Report as 22612, 22614, 22842, and 20937.

Vertebral procedures are sometimes followed by arthrodesis and in addition may include bone grafts and instrumentation.

When arthrodesis is performed in addition to another procedure, the arthrodesis should be reported in addition to the original procedure with modifier 51 (multiple procedures). Examples are after osteotomy, fracture care, vertebral corpectomy, and laminectomy. Bone grafts and instrumentation are never performed without arthrodesis.

*Example:*

Treatment of a burst fracture of L2 by corpectomy followed by arthrodesis of L1-L3, utilizing anterior instrumentation L1-L3 and structural allograft.

Report as 63090, 22558-51, 22585, 22845, and 20931.

When two surgeons work together as primary surgeons performing distinct part(s) of a single reportable procedure, each surgeon should report his/her distinct operative work by appending modifier 62 to the single definitive procedure code. If additional procedure(s) (including add-on procedure[s]) are performed during the same surgical session, separate code(s) may be reported by each co-surgeon, with modifier 62 appended (see Appendix A).

*Example:*

A 42-year-old male with a history of posttraumatic degenerative disc disease at L3-4 and L4-5 (internal disc disruption) underwent surgical repair. Surgeon A performed an anterior exposure of the spine with mobilization of the great vessels. Surgeon B performed anterior (minimal) discectomy and fusion at L3-4 and L4-5 using anterior interbody technique.

Report surgeon A: 22558 append modifier 62, 22585 append modifier 62

Report surgeon B: 22558 append modifier 62, 22585 append modifier 62, 20931

(Do not append modifier 62 to bone graft code 20931)

(For injection procedure for myelography, use 62284)

(For injection procedure for discography, see 62290, 62291)

(For injection procedure, chemonucleolysis, single or multiple levels, use 62292)

(For injection procedure for facet joints, see 64490-64495, 64633-64636)

(For needle or trocar biopsy, see 20220-20225)

## Incision

**22010**  Incision and drainage, open, of deep abscess (subfascial), posterior spine; cervical, thoracic, or cervicothoracic

**22015**  lumbar, sacral, or lumbosacral

(Do not report 22015 in conjunction with 22010)

(Do not report 22015 in conjunction with instrumentation removal, 10180, 22850, 22852)

(For incision and drainage of abscess or hematoma, superficial, see 10060, 10140)

## Excision

For the following codes, when two surgeons work together as primary surgeons performing distinct part(s) of partial vertebral body excision, each surgeon should report his/her distinct operative work by appending modifier 62 to the procedure code. In this situation, modifier 62 may be appended to the procedure code(s) 22100-22102, 22110-22114 and, as appropriate, to the associated additional vertebral segment add-on code(s) 22103, 22116 as long as both surgeons continue to work together as primary surgeons.

(For bone biopsy, see 20220-20251)

(To report soft tissue biopsy of back or flank, see 21920-21925)

(For needle biopsy of soft tissue, use 20206)

(To report excision of soft tissue tumor of back or flank, use 21930)

**22100**  Partial excision of posterior vertebral component (eg, spinous process, lamina or facet) for intrinsic bony lesion, single vertebral segment; cervical

**22101**  thoracic

**22102**  lumbar

(For insertion of posterior spinous process distraction devices, see 0171T, 0172T)

**+ 22103**  each additional segment (List separately in addition to code for primary procedure)

(Use 22103 in conjunction with 22100, 22101, 22102)

**22110**  Partial excision of vertebral body, for intrinsic bony lesion, without decompression of spinal cord or nerve root(s), single vertebral segment; cervical

**22112**  thoracic

**22114**      lumbar

**+ 22116**      each additional vertebral segment (List separately in addition to code for primary procedure)

(Use 22116 in conjunction with 22110, 22112, 22114)

(For complete or near complete resection of vertebral body, see vertebral corpectomy, 63081-63091)

(For spinal reconstruction with bone graft [autograft, allograft] and/or methylmethacrylate of cervical vertebral body, use 63081 and 22554 and 20931 or 20938)

(For spinal reconstruction with bone graft [autograft, allograft] and/or methylmethacrylate of thoracic vertebral body, use 63085 or 63087 and 22556 and 20931 or 20938)

(For spinal reconstruction with bone graft [autograft, allograft] and/or methylmethacrylate of lumbar vertebral body, use 63087 or 63090 and 22558 and 20931 or 20938)

(For spinal reconstruction following vertebral body resection, use 63082 or 63086 or 63088 or 63091, and 22585)

(For harvest of bone autograft for vertebral reconstruction, see 20931 or 20938)

(For cervical spinal reconstruction with prosthetic replacement of resected vertebral bodies, see codes 63081 and 22554 and 20931 or 20938 and 22851)

(For thoracic spinal reconstruction with prosthetic replacement of resected vertebral bodies, see codes 63085 or 63087 and 22556 and 20931 or 20938 and 22851)

(For lumbar spinal reconstruction with prosthetic replacement of resected vertebral bodies, see codes 63087 or 63090 and 22558, and 20931 or 20938 and 22851)

(For osteotomy of spine, see 22210-22226)

## Osteotomy

To report arthrodesis, see codes 22590-22632. (Report in addition to code[s] for the definitive procedure with modifier 51.)

To report instrumentation procedures, see 22840-22855. (Report in addition to code[s] for the definitive procedure[s].) Do not append modifier 62 to spinal instrumentation codes 22840-22848 and 22850-22852.

To report bone graft procedures, see 20930-20938. (Report in addition to code[s] for the definitive procedure[s].) Do not append modifier 62 to bone graft codes 20900-20938.

For the following codes, when two surgeons work together as primary surgeons performing distinct part(s) of an anterior spine osteotomy, each surgeon should report his/her distinct operative work by appending modifier 62 to the procedure code. In this situation, modifier 62 may be appended to the procedure code(s) 22210-22214, 22220-22224 and, as appropriate, to

associated additional segment add-on code(s) 22216, 22226 as long as both surgeons continue to work together as primary surgeons.

Spinal osteotomy procedures are reported when a portion(s) of the vertebral segment(s) is cut and removed in preparation for re-aligning the spine as part of a spinal deformity correction. For excision of an intrinsic lesion of the vertebra without deformity correction, see 22100-22116. For decompression of the spinal cord and/or nerve roots, see 63001-63308.

The three columns are defined as anterior (anterior two-thirds of the vertebral body), middle (posterior third of the vertebral body and the pedicle), and posterior (articular facets, lamina, and spinous process).

**22206**      Osteotomy of spine, posterior or posterolateral approach, 3 columns, 1 vertebral segment (eg, pedicle/vertebral body subtraction); thoracic

(Do not report 22206 in conjunction with 22207)

**22207**      lumbar

(Do not report 22207 in conjunction with 22206)

**+ 22208**      each additional vertebral segment (List separately in addition to code for primary procedure)

(Use 22208 in conjunction with 22206, 22207)

(Do not report 22206, 22207, 22208 in conjunction with 22210-22226, 22830, 63001-63048, 63055-63066, 63075-63091, 63101-63103, when performed at the same level)

**22210**      Osteotomy of spine, posterior or posterolateral approach, 1 vertebral segment; cervical

**22212**      thoracic

**22214**      lumbar

**+ 22216**      each additional vertebral segment (List separately in addition to primary procedure)

(Use 22216 in conjunction with 22210, 22212, 22214)

**22220**      Osteotomy of spine, including discectomy, anterior approach, single vertebral segment; cervical

**22222**      thoracic

**22224**      lumbar

**+ 22226**      each additional vertebral segment (List separately in addition to code for primary procedure)

(Use 22226 in conjunction with 22220, 22222, 22224)

(For vertebral corpectomy, see 63081-63091)

## Fracture and/or Dislocation

To report arthrodesis, see codes 22590-22632. (Report in addition to code[s] for the definitive procedure with modifier 51.)

To report instrumentation procedures, see 22840-22855. (Report in addition to code[s] for the definitive

Musculoskeletal

**Musculoskeletal**

procedure[s].) Do not append modifier 62 to spinal instrumentation codes 22840-22848 and 22850-22852.

To report bone graft procedures, see 20930-20938. (Report in addition to code[s] for the definitive procedure[s].) Do not append modifier 62 to bone graft codes 20900-20938.

For the following codes, when two surgeons work together as primary surgeons performing distinct part(s) of open fracture and/or dislocation procedure(s), each surgeon should report his/her distinct operative work by appending modifier 62 to the procedure code. In this situation, modifier 62 may be appended to the procedure code(s) 22318-22327 and, as appropriate, the associated additional fracture vertebrae or dislocated segment add-on code 22328 as long as both surgeons continue to work together as primary surgeons.

**22305**  Closed treatment of vertebral process fracture(s)

**22310**  Closed treatment of vertebral body fracture(s), without manipulation, requiring and including casting or bracing

**22315**  Closed treatment of vertebral fracture(s) and/or dislocation(s) requiring casting or bracing, with and including casting and/or bracing by manipulation or traction

(For spinal subluxation, use 97140)

**22318**  Open treatment and/or reduction of odontoid fracture(s) and or dislocation(s) (including os odontoideum), anterior approach, including placement of internal fixation; without grafting

**22319**    with grafting

**22325**  Open treatment and/or reduction of vertebral fracture(s) and/or dislocation(s), posterior approach, 1 fractured vertebra or dislocated segment; lumbar

**22326**    cervical

**22327**    thoracic

**+ 22328**    each additional fractured vertebra or dislocated segment (List separately in addition to code for primary procedure)

(Use 22328 in conjunction with 22325-22327)

(For treatment of vertebral fracture by the anterior approach, see corpectomy 63081-63091, and appropriate arthrodesis, bone graft and instrument codes)

(For decompression of spine following fracture, see 63001-63091; for arthrodesis of spine following fracture, see 22548-22632)

## Manipulation

(For spinal manipulation without anesthesia, use 97140)

**22505**  Manipulation of spine requiring anesthesia, any region

## Vertebral Body, Embolization or Injection

⊙ **22520**  Percutaneous vertebroplasty (bone biopsy included when performed), 1 vertebral body, unilateral or bilateral injection; thoracic

⊙ **22521**    lumbar

⊙**+ 22522**    each additional thoracic or lumbar vertebral body (List separately in addition to code for primary procedure)

(Do not report 22520-22522 in conjunction with 20225, 22310-22315, 22325, 22327 when performed at the same level as 22520-22522)

(Use 22522 in conjunction with 22520, 22521 as appropriate)

(For radiological supervision and interpretation, see 72291, 72292)

**22523**  Percutaneous vertebral augmentation, including cavity creation (fracture reduction and bone biopsy included when performed) using mechanical device, 1 vertebral body, unilateral or bilateral cannulation (eg, kyphoplasty); thoracic

**22524**    lumbar

**+ 22525**    each additional thoracic or lumbar vertebral body (List separately in addition to code for primary procedure)

(Do not report 22523-22525 in conjunction with 20225, 22310-22315, 22325, 22327 when performed at the same level as 22523-22525)

(Use 22525 in conjunction with 22523, 22524)

(For radiological supervision and interpretation, see 72291, 72292)

⊙ **22526**  Percutaneous intradiscal electrothermal annuloplasty, unilateral or bilateral including fluoroscopic guidance; single level

⊙**+ 22527**    1 or more additional levels (List separately in addition to code for primary procedure)

(Use 22527 in conjunction with 22526)

(Do not report codes 22526, 22527 in conjunction with 77002, 77003)

(For percutaneous intradiscal annuloplasty using method other than electrothermal, use 22899)

## Arthrodesis

Arthrodesis may be performed in the absence of other procedures and therefore when it is combined with another definitive procedure (eg, osteotomy, fracture care, vertebral corpectomy or laminectomy), modifier 51 is appropriate. However, arthrodesis codes 22585, 22614, and 22632 are considered add-on procedure codes and should not be used with modifier 51.

To report instrumentation procedures, see 22840-22855. (Codes 22840-22848, 22851 are reported in conjunction with code[s] for the definitive procedure[s]. When instrumentation reinsertion or removal is reported in conjunction with other definitive procedures including arthrodesis, decompression, and exploration of fusion, append modifier 51 to 22849, 22850, 22852, and 22855.) To report exploration of fusion, use 22830. (When exploration is reported in conjunction with other definitive procedures, including arthrodesis and decompression, append modifier 51 to 22830.) Do not append modifier 62 to spinal instrumentation codes 22840-22848 and 22850-22852.

To report bone graft procedures, see 20930-20938. (Report in addition to code[s] for the definitive procedure[s].) Do not append modifier 62 to bone graft codes 20900-20938.

### Lateral Extracavitary Approach Technique

**22532**   Arthrodesis, lateral extracavitary technique, including minimal discectomy to prepare interspace (other than for decompression); thoracic

**22533**      lumbar

**+ 22534**      thoracic or lumbar, each additional vertebral segment (List separately in addition to code for primary procedure)

(Use 22534 in conjunction with 22532 and 22533)

### Anterior or Anterolateral Approach Technique

Procedure codes 22554-22558 are for SINGLE interspace; for additional interspaces, use 22585. A vertebral interspace is the non-bony compartment between two adjacent vertebral bodies, which contains the intervertebral disc, and includes the nucleus pulposus, annulus fibrosus, and two cartilagenous endplates.

For the following codes, when two surgeons work together as primary surgeons performing distinct part(s) of an anterior interbody arthrodesis, each surgeon should report his/her distinct operative work by appending modifier 62 to the procedure code. In this situation, modifier 62 may be appended to the procedure code(s) 22548-22558 and, as appropriate, to the associated additional interspace add-on code 22585 as long as both surgeons continue to work together as primary surgeons.

**22548**   Arthrodesis, anterior transoral or extraoral technique, clivus-C1-C2 (atlas-axis), with or without excision of odontoid process

(For intervertebral disc excision by laminotomy or laminectomy, see 63020-63042)

**22551**   Arthrodesis, anterior interbody, including disc space preparation, discectomy, osteophytectomy and decompression of spinal cord and/or nerve roots; cervical below C2

**+ 22552**      cervical below C2, each additional interspace (List separately in addition to code for separate procedure)

(Use 22552 in conjunction with 22551)

**22554**   Arthrodesis, anterior interbody technique, including minimal discectomy to prepare interspace (other than for decompression); cervical below C2

(Do not report 22554 in conjunction with 63075, even if performed by a separate individual. To report anterior cervical discectomy and interbody fusion at the same level during the same session, use 22551)

**22556**      thoracic

**22558**      lumbar

(For arthrodesis using pre-sacral interbody technique, see 22586, 0195T)

**+ 22585**      each additional interspace (List separately in addition to code for primary procedure)

(Use 22585 in conjunction with 22554, 22556, 22558)

(Do not report 22585 in conjunction with 63075, even if performed by a separate individual. To report anterior cervical discectomy and interbody fusion at the same level during the same session, use 22552)

**22586**   Arthrodesis, pre-sacral interbody technique, including disc space preparation, discectomy, with posterior instrumentation, with image guidance, includes bone graft when performed, L5-S1 interspace

(Do not report 22586 in conjunction with 20930-20938, 22840, 22848, 72275, 77002, 77003, 77011, 77012)

### Posterior, Posterolateral or Lateral Transverse Process Technique

To report instrumentation procedures, see 22840-22855. (Report in addition to code[s] for the definitive procedure[s].) Do not append modifier 62 to spinal instrumentation codes 22840-22848 and 22850-22852.

To report bone graft procedures, see 20930-20938. (Report in addition to code[s] for the definitive procedure[s].) Do not append modifier 62 to bone graft codes 20900-20938.

A vertebral segment describes the basic constituent part into which the spine may be divided. It represents a single complete vertebral bone with its associated articular processes and laminae. A vertebral interspace is the non-bony compartment between two adjacent vertebral bodies which contains the intervertebral disc, and includes the nucleus pulposus, annulus fibrosus, and two cartilagenous endplates.

**22590**   Arthrodesis, posterior technique, craniocervical (occiput-C2)

**22595**   Arthrodesis, posterior technique, atlas-axis (C1-C2)

**22600**   Arthrodesis, posterior or posterolateral technique, single level; cervical below C2 segment

**22610**      thoracic (with lateral transverse technique, when performed)

Musculoskeletal

**22612**   lumbar (with lateral transverse technique, when performed)

(Do not report 22612 in conjunction with 22630 for the same interspace and segment, use 22633)

**+ 22614**   each additional vertebral segment (List separately in addition to code for primary procedure)

(Use 22614 in conjunction with 22600, 22610, 22612, 22630 or 22633 when performed at a different level. When performing a posterior or posterolateral technique for fusion/arthrodesis at an additional level, use 22614. When performing a posterior interbody fusion arthrodesis at an additional level, use 22632. When performing a combined posterior or posterolateral technique with posterior interbody arthrodesis at an additional level, use 22634)

(For facet joint fusion, see 0219T-0222T)

(For placement of a posterior intrafacet implant, see 0219T-0222T)

**22630**   Arthrodesis, posterior interbody technique, including laminectomy and/or discectomy to prepare interspace (other than for decompression), single interspace; lumbar

(Do not report 22630 in conjunction with 22612 for the same interspace and segment, use 22633)

**+ 22632**   each additional interspace (List separately in addition to code for primary procedure)

(Use 22632 in conjunction with 22612, 22630, or 22633 when performed at a different level. When performing a posterior interbody fusion arthrodesis at an additional level, use 22632. When performing a posterior or posterolateral technique for fusion/arthrodesis at an additional level, use 22614. When performing a combined posterior or posterolateral technique with posterior interbody arthrodesis at an additional level, use 22634)

**22633**   Arthrodesis, combined posterior or posterolateral technique with posterior interbody technique including laminectomy and/or discectomy sufficient to prepare interspace (other than for decompression), single interspace and segment; lumbar

(Do not report with 22612 or 22630 at the same level)

**+ 22634**   each additional interspace and segment (List separately in addition to code for primary procedure)

(Use 22634 in conjunction with 22633)

### Spine Deformity (eg, Scoliosis, Kyphosis)

To report instrumentation procedures, see 22840-22855. (Report in addition to code[s] for the definitive procedure[s].) Do not append modifier 62 to spinal instrumentation codes 22840-22848 and 22850-22852.

To report bone graft procedures, see 20930-20938. (Report in addition to code[s] for the definitive procedure[s].) Do not append modifier 62 to bone graft codes 20900-20938.

A vertebral segment describes the basic constituent part into which the spine may be divided. It represents a single complete vertebral bone with its associated articular processes and laminae.

For the following codes, when two surgeons work together as primary surgeons performing distinct part(s) of an arthrodesis for spinal deformity, each surgeon should report his/her distinct operative work by appending modifier 62 to the procedure code. In this situation, modifier 62 may be appended to procedure code(s) 22800-22819 as long as both surgeons continue to work together as primary surgeons.

**22800**   Arthrodesis, posterior, for spinal deformity, with or without cast; up to 6 vertebral segments

**22802**   7 to 12 vertebral segments

**22804**   13 or more vertebral segments

**22808**   Arthrodesis, anterior, for spinal deformity, with or without cast; 2 to 3 vertebral segments

**22810**   4 to 7 vertebral segments

**22812**   8 or more vertebral segments

**22818**   Kyphectomy, circumferential exposure of spine and resection of vertebral segment(s) (including body and posterior elements); single or 2 segments

**22819**   3 or more segments

(To report arthrodesis, see 22800-22804 and add modifier 51)

### Exploration

To report instrumentation procedures, see 22840-22855. (Codes 22840-22848 and 22851 are reported in conjunction with code[s] for the definitive procedure[s]. When instrumentation reinsertion or removal is reported in conjunction with other definitive procedures including arthrodesis, decompression, and exploration of fusion, append modifier 51 to 22849, 22850, 22852 and 22855.) Code 22849 should not be reported with 22850, 22852, and 22855 at the same spinal levels. To report exploration of fusion, see 22830. (When exploration is reported in conjunction with other definitive procedures, including arthrodesis and decompression, append modifier 51 to 22830.)

(To report bone graft procedures, see 20930-20938)

**22830**   Exploration of spinal fusion

### Spinal Instrumentation

Segmental instrumentation is defined as fixation at each end of the construct and at least one additional interposed bony attachment.

Non-segmental instrumentation is defined as fixation at each end of the construct and may span several vertebral segments without attachment to the intervening segments.

Insertion of spinal instrumentation is reported separately and in addition to arthrodesis. Instrumentation procedure codes 22840-22848 and 22851 are reported in addition to the definitive procedure(s). Do not append modifier 62 to spinal instrumentation codes 22840-22848 and 22850-22852.

To report bone graft procedures, see 20930-20938. (Report in addition to code[s] for definitive procedure[s].) Do not append modifier 62 to bone graft codes 20900-20938.

A vertebral segment describes the basic constituent part into which the spine may be divided. It represents a single complete vertebral bone with its associated articular processes and laminae. A vertebral interspace is the non-bony compartment between two adjacent vertebral bodies, which contains the intervertebral disc, and includes the nucleus pulposus, annulus fibrosus, and two cartilagenous endplates.

Codes 22849, 22850, 22852, and 22855 are subject to modifier 51 if reported with other definitive procedure(s), including arthrodesis, decompression, and exploration of fusion. Code 22849 should not be reported in conjunction with 22850, 22852, and 22855 at the same spinal levels. Only the appropriate insertion code (22840-22848) should be reported when previously placed spinal instrumentation is being removed or revised during the same session where new instrumentation is inserted at levels including all or part of the previously instrumented segments. Do not report the reinsertion (22849) or removal (22850, 22852, 22855) procedures in addition to the insertion of the new instrumentation (22840-22848).

+ **22840**   Posterior non-segmental instrumentation (eg, Harrington rod technique, pedicle fixation across 1 interspace, atlantoaxial transarticular screw fixation, sublaminar wiring at C1, facet screw fixation) (List separately in addition to code for primary procedure)

(Use 22840 in conjunction with 22100-22102, 22110-22114, 22206, 22207, 22210-22214, 22220-22224, 22305-22327, 22532, 22533, 22548-22558, 22590-22612, 22630, 22633, 22634, 22800-22812, 63001-63030, 63040-63042, 63045-63047, 63050-63056, 63064, 63075, 63077, 63081, 63085, 63087, 63090, 63101, 63102, 63170-63290, 63300-63307)

(For insertion of posterior spinous process distraction devices, see 0171T, 0172T)

+ **22841**   Internal spinal fixation by wiring of spinous processes (List separately in addition to code for primary procedure)

(Use 22841 in conjunction with 22100-22102, 22110-22114, 22206, 22207, 22210-22214, 22220-22224, 22305-22327, 22532, 22533, 22548-22558, 22590-22612, 22630, 22633, 22634, 22800-22812, 63001-63030, 63040-63042, 63045-63047, 63050-63056, 63064, 63075, 63077, 63081, 63085, 63087, 63090, 63101, 63102, 63170-63290, 63300-63307)

+ **22842**   Posterior segmental instrumentation (eg, pedicle fixation, dual rods with multiple hooks and sublaminar wires); 3 to 6 vertebral segments (List separately in addition to code for primary procedure)

(Use 22842 in conjunction with 22100-22102, 22110-22114, 22206, 22207, 22210-22214, 22220-22224, 22305-22327, 22532, 22533, 22548-22558, 22590-22612, 22630, 22633, 22634, 22800-22812, 63001-63030, 63040-63042, 63045-63047, 63050-63056, 63064, 63075, 63077, 63081, 63085, 63087, 63090, 63101, 63102, 63170-63290, 63300-63307)

+ **22843**   7 to 12 vertebral segments (List separately in addition to code for primary procedure)

(Use 22843 in conjunction with 22100-22102, 22110-22114, 22206, 22207, 22210-22214, 22220-22224, 22305-22327, 22532, 22533, 22548-22558, 22590-22612, 22630, 22633, 22634, 22800-22812, 63001-63030, 63040-63042, 63045-63047, 63050-63056, 63064, 63075, 63077, 63081, 63085, 63087, 63090, 63101, 63102, 63170-63290, 63300-63307)

+ **22844**   13 or more vertebral segments (List separately in addition to code for primary procedure)

(Use 22844 in conjunction with 22100-22102, 22110-22114, 22206, 22207, 22210-22214, 22220-22224, 22305-22327, 22532, 22533, 22548-22558, 22590-22612, 22630, 22633, 22634, 22800-22812, 63001-63030, 63040-63042, 63045-63047, 63050-63056, 63064, 63075, 63077, 63081, 63085, 63087, 63090, 63101, 63102, 63170-63290, 63300-63307)

+ **22845**   Anterior instrumentation; 2 to 3 vertebral segments (List separately in addition to code for primary procedure)

(Use 22845 in conjunction with 22100-22102, 22110-22114, 22206, 22207, 22210-22214, 22220-22224, 22305-22327, 22532, 22533, 22548-22558, 22590-22612, 22630, 22633, 22634, 22800-22812, 63001-63030, 63040-63042, 63045-63047, 63050-63056, 63064, 63075, 63077, 63081, 63085, 63087, 63090, 63101, 63102, 63170-63290, 63300-63307)

+ **22846**   4 to 7 vertebral segments (List separately in addition to code for primary procedure)

(Use 22846 in conjunction with 22100-22102, 22110-22114, 22206, 22207, 22210-22214, 22220-22224, 22305-22327, 22532, 22533, 22548-22558, 22590-22612, 22630, 22633, 22634, 22800-22812, 63001-63030, 63040-63042, 63045-63047, 63050-63056, 63064, 63075, 63077, 63081, 63085, 63087, 63090, 63101, 63102, 63170-63290, 63300-63307)

+ **22847**   8 or more vertebral segments (List separately in addition to code for primary procedure)

(Use 22847 in conjunction with 22100-22102, 22110-22114, 22206, 22207, 22210-22214, 22220-22224, 22305-22327, 22532, 22533, 22548-22558, 22590-22612, 22630, 22633, 22634, 22800-22812, 63001-63030, 63040-63042, 63045-63047, 63050-63056, 63064, 63075, 63077, 63081, 63085, 63087, 63090, 63101, 63102, 63170-63290, 63300-63307)

**Musculoskeletal**

+ **22848**   Pelvic fixation (attachment of caudal end of instrumentation to pelvic bony structures) other than sacrum (List separately in addition to code for primary procedure)

(Use 22848 in conjunction with 22100-22102, 22110-22114, 22206, 22207, 22210-22214, 22220-22224, 22305-22327, 22532, 22533, 22548-22558, 22590-22612, 22630, 22633, 22634, 22800-22812, 63001-63030, 63040-63042, 63045-63047, 63050-63056, 63064, 63075, 63077, 63081, 63085, 63087, 63090, 63101, 63102, 63170-63290, 63300-63307)

**22849**   Reinsertion of spinal fixation device

**22850**   Removal of posterior nonsegmental instrumentation (eg, Harrington rod)

+ **22851**   Application of intervertebral biomechanical device(s) (eg, synthetic cage(s), methylmethacrylate) to vertebral defect or interspace (List separately in addition to code for primary procedure)

(Use 22851 in conjunction with 22100-22102, 22110-22114, 22206, 22207, 22210-22214, 22220-22224, 22305-22327, 22532, 22533, 22548-22558, 22590-22612, 22630, 22633, 22634, 22800-22812, 63001-63030, 63040-63042, 63045-63047, 63050-63056, 63064, 63075, 63077, 63081, 63085, 63087, 63090, 63101, 63102, 63170-63290, 63300-63307)

(For application of an intervertebral bone device/graft, see 20930-20938)

(For insertion of posterior spinous process distraction devices, see 0171T, 0172T)

**22852**   Removal of posterior segmental instrumentation

**22855**   Removal of anterior instrumentation

**22856**   Total disc arthroplasty (artificial disc), anterior approach, including discectomy with end plate preparation (includes osteophytectomy for nerve root or spinal cord decompression and microdissection), single interspace, cervical

(Do not report 22856 in conjunction with 22554, 22845, 22851, 63075 when performed at the same level)

(Do not report 22856 in conjunction with 69990)

(For additional interspace cervical total disc arthroplasty, use 0092T)

**22857**   Total disc arthroplasty (artificial disc), anterior approach, including discectomy to prepare interspace (other than for decompression), single interspace, lumbar

(Do not report 22857 in conjunction with 22558, 22845, 22851, 49010 when performed at the same level)

(For additional interspace, use Category III code 0163T)

**22861**   Revision including replacement of total disc arthroplasty (artificial disc), anterior approach, single interspace; cervical

(Do not report 22861 in conjunction with 22845, 22851, 22864, 63075 when performed at the same level)

(Do not report 22861 in conjunction with 69990)

(For additional interspace revision of cervical total disc arthroplasty, use 0098T)

**22862**   lumbar

(Do not report 22862 in conjunction with 22558, 22845, 22851, 22865, 49010 when performed at the same level)

(For additional interspace, use Category III code 0165T)

**22864**   Removal of total disc arthroplasty (artificial disc), anterior approach, single interspace; cervical

(Do not report 22864 in conjunction with 22861, 69990)

(For additional interspace removal of cervical total disc arthroplasty, use 0095T)

**22865**   lumbar

(Do not report 22865 in conjunction with 49010)

(For additional interspace, see Category III code 0164T)

(22856-22865 include fluoroscopy when performed)

(For decompression, see 63001-63048)

## Other Procedures

**22899**   Unlisted procedure, spine

# Abdomen

## Excision

**22900**   Excision, tumor, soft tissue of abdominal wall, subfascial (eg, intramuscular); less than 5 cm

**22901**      5 cm or greater

**22902**   Excision, tumor, soft tissue of abdominal wall, subcutaneous; less than 3 cm

**22903**      3 cm or greater

▶(For excision of benign lesions of cutaneous origin [eg, sebaceous cyst], see 11400-11406)◀

▲ **22904**   Radical resection of tumor (eg, sarcoma), soft tissue of abdominal wall; less than 5 cm

▲ **22905**      5 cm or greater

▶(For radical resection of tumor[s] of cutaneous origin [eg, melanoma], see 11600-11606)◀

## Other Procedures

**22999**   Unlisted procedure, abdomen, musculoskeletal system

# Shoulder

The area known as the shoulder is made up of the clavicle, scapula, humerus head and neck, sterno-clavicular joint, acromioclavicular joint, and shoulder joint.

# Incision

**23000**   Removal of subdeltoid calcareous deposits, open

(For arthroscopic removal of bursal deposits, use 29999)

**23020**   Capsular contracture release (eg, Sever type procedure)

(For incision and drainage procedures, superficial, see 10040-10160)

**23030**   Incision and drainage, shoulder area; deep abscess or hematoma

**23031**        infected bursa

**23035**   Incision, bone cortex (eg, osteomyelitis or bone abscess), shoulder area

**23040**   Arthrotomy, glenohumeral joint, including exploration, drainage, or removal of foreign body

**23044**   Arthrotomy, acromioclavicular, sternoclavicular joint, including exploration, drainage, or removal of foreign body

# Excision

**23065**   Biopsy, soft tissue of shoulder area; superficial

**23066**        deep

(For needle biopsy of soft tissue, use 20206)

**23071**   Code is out of numerical sequence. See 23065-23220

**23073**   Code is out of numerical sequence. See 23065-23220

**23075**   Excision, tumor, soft tissue of shoulder area, subcutaneous; less than 3 cm

\# **23071**        3 cm or greater

►(For excision of benign lesions of cutaneous origin [eg, sebaceous cyst], see 11400-11406)◄

**23076**   Excision, tumor, soft tissue of shoulder area, subfascial (eg, intramuscular); less than 5 cm

\# **23073**        5 cm or greater

▲ **23077**   Radical resection of tumor (eg, sarcoma), soft tissue of shoulder area; less than 5 cm

▲ **23078**        5 cm or greater

►(For radical resection of tumor[s] of cutaneous origin [eg, melanoma], see 11600-11606)◄

**23100**   Arthrotomy, glenohumeral joint, including biopsy

**23101**   Arthrotomy, acromioclavicular joint or sternoclavicular joint, including biopsy and/or excision of torn cartilage

**23105**   Arthrotomy; glenohumeral joint, with synovectomy, with or without biopsy

**23106**        sternoclavicular joint, with synovectomy, with or without biopsy

**23107**   Arthrotomy, glenohumeral joint, with joint exploration, with or without removal of loose or foreign body

**23120**   Claviculectomy; partial

(For arthroscopic procedure, use 29824)

**23125**        total

**23130**   Acromioplasty or acromionectomy, partial, with or without coracoacromial ligament release

**23140**   Excision or curettage of bone cyst or benign tumor of clavicle or scapula;

**23145**        with autograft (includes obtaining graft)

**23146**        with allograft

**23150**   Excision or curettage of bone cyst or benign tumor of proximal humerus;

**23155**        with autograft (includes obtaining graft)

**23156**        with allograft

**23170**   Sequestrectomy (eg, for osteomyelitis or bone abscess), clavicle

**23172**   Sequestrectomy (eg, for osteomyelitis or bone abscess), scapula

**23174**   Sequestrectomy (eg, for osteomyelitis or bone abscess), humeral head to surgical neck

**23180**   Partial excision (craterization, saucerization, or diaphysectomy) bone (eg, osteomyelitis), clavicle

**23182**   Partial excision (craterization, saucerization, or diaphysectomy) bone (eg, osteomyelitis), scapula

**23184**   Partial excision (craterization, saucerization, or diaphysectomy) bone (eg, osteomyelitis), proximal humerus

**23190**   Ostectomy of scapula, partial (eg, superior medial angle)

**23195**   Resection, humeral head

(For replacement with implant, use 23470)

**23200**   Radical resection of tumor; clavicle

**23210**        scapula

**23220**   Radical resection of tumor, proximal humerus

(23221, 23222 have been deleted)

# Introduction or Removal

(For arthrocentesis or needling of bursa, use 20610)

(For K-wire or pin insertion or removal, see 20650, 20670, 20680)

**23330**   Removal of foreign body, shoulder; subcutaneous

►(23331, 23332 have been deleted)◄

►(To report removal of foreign body, see 23330, 23333)◄

● **23333**        deep (subfascial or intramuscular)

● **23334**   Removal of prosthesis, includes debridement and synovectomy when performed; humeral **or** glenoid component

---

▲=Revised code   ●=New code   ►◄=Contains new or revised text   ⊘=Modifier 51 exempt                American Medical Association   **87**

**Musculoskeletal**

**Musculoskeletal**

● **23335**    humeral **and** glenoid components (eg, total shoulder)

▶(Do not report 23334, 23335 in conjunction with 23473, 23474 if a prosthesis [ie, humeral and/or glenoid component(s)] is being removed and replaced in the same shoulder during the same surgical session)◀

▶(To report removal of hardware, other than humeral and/or glenoid prosthesis, use 20680)◀

**23350**    Injection procedure for shoulder arthrography or enhanced CT/MRI shoulder arthrography

(For radiographic arthrography, radiological supervision and interpretation, use 73040. Fluoroscopy [77002] is inclusive of radiographic arthrography)

(When fluoroscopic guided injection is performed for enhanced CT arthrography, use 23350, 77002, and 73201 or 73202)

(When fluoroscopic guided injection is performed for enhanced MR arthrography, use 23350, 77002, and 73222 or 73223)

(For enhanced CT or enhanced MRI arthrography, use 77002 and either 73201, 73202, 73222, or 73223)

(To report biopsy of the shoulder and joint, see 29805-29826)

## Repair, Revision, and/or Reconstruction

**23395**    Muscle transfer, any type, shoulder or upper arm; single

**23397**        multiple

**23400**    Scapulopexy (eg, Sprengels deformity or for paralysis)

**23405**    Tenotomy, shoulder area; single tendon

**23406**        multiple tendons through same incision

**23410**    Repair of ruptured musculotendinous cuff (eg, rotator cuff) open; acute

**23412**        chronic

(For arthroscopic procedure, use 29827)

**23415**    Coracoacromial ligament release, with or without acromioplasty

(For arthroscopic procedure, use 29826)

**23420**    Reconstruction of complete shoulder (rotator) cuff avulsion, chronic (includes acromioplasty)

**23430**    Tenodesis of long tendon of biceps

(For arthroscopic biceps tenodesis, use 29828)

**23440**    Resection or transplantation of long tendon of biceps

**23450**    Capsulorrhaphy, anterior; Putti-Platt procedure or Magnuson type operation

(To report arthroscopic thermal capsulorrhaphy, use 29999)

**23455**        with labral repair (eg, Bankart procedure)

(For arthroscopic procedure, use 29806)

**23460**    Capsulorrhaphy, anterior, any type; with bone block

**23462**        with coracoid process transfer

(To report open thermal capsulorrhaphy, use 23929)

**23465**    Capsulorrhaphy, glenohumeral joint, posterior, with or without bone block

(For sternoclavicular and acromioclavicular reconstruction, see 23530, 23550)

**23466**    Capsulorrhaphy, glenohumeral joint, any type multi-directional instability

**23470**    Arthroplasty, glenohumeral joint; hemiarthroplasty

**23472**        total shoulder (glenoid and proximal humeral replacement (eg, total shoulder))

▶(For removal of total shoulder implants, see 23334, 23335)◀

(For osteotomy, proximal humerus, use 24400)

**23473**    Revision of total shoulder arthroplasty, including allograft when performed; humeral **or** glenoid component

**23474**        humeral **and** glenoid component

▶(Do not report 23473, 23474 in conjunction with 23334, 23335 if a prosthesis [ie, humeral and/or glenoid component(s)] is being removed and replaced in the same shoulder during the same surgical session)◀

**23480**    Osteotomy, clavicle, with or without internal fixation;

**23485**        with bone graft for nonunion or malunion (includes obtaining graft and/or necessary fixation)

**23490**    Prophylactic treatment (nailing, pinning, plating or wiring) with or without methylmethacrylate; clavicle

**23491**        proximal humerus

## Fracture and/or Dislocation

**23500**    Closed treatment of clavicular fracture; without manipulation

**23505**        with manipulation

**23515**    Open treatment of clavicular fracture, includes internal fixation, when performed

**23520**    Closed treatment of sternoclavicular dislocation; without manipulation

**23525**        with manipulation

**23530**    Open treatment of sternoclavicular dislocation, acute or chronic;

**23532**        with fascial graft (includes obtaining graft)

**23540**    Closed treatment of acromioclavicular dislocation; without manipulation

**23545**        with manipulation

**23550**    Open treatment of acromioclavicular dislocation, acute or chronic;

**23552**        with fascial graft (includes obtaining graft)

**23570**   Closed treatment of scapular fracture; without manipulation

**23575**     with manipulation, with or without skeletal traction (with or without shoulder joint involvement)

**23585**   Open treatment of scapular fracture (body, glenoid or acromion) includes internal fixation, when performed

**23600**   Closed treatment of proximal humeral (surgical or anatomical neck) fracture; without manipulation

**23605**     with manipulation, with or without skeletal traction

**23615**   Open treatment of proximal humeral (surgical or anatomical neck) fracture, includes internal fixation, when performed, includes repair of tuberosity(s), when performed;

**23616**     with proximal humeral prosthetic replacement

**23620**   Closed treatment of greater humeral tuberosity fracture; without manipulation

**23625**     with manipulation

**23630**   Open treatment of greater humeral tuberosity fracture, includes internal fixation, when performed

**23650**   Closed treatment of shoulder dislocation, with manipulation; without anesthesia

**23655**     requiring anesthesia

**23660**   Open treatment of acute shoulder dislocation

(Repairs for recurrent dislocations, see 23450-23466)

**23665**   Closed treatment of shoulder dislocation, with fracture of greater humeral tuberosity, with manipulation

**23670**   Open treatment of shoulder dislocation, with fracture of greater humeral tuberosity, includes internal fixation, when performed

**23675**   Closed treatment of shoulder dislocation, with surgical or anatomical neck fracture, with manipulation

**23680**   Open treatment of shoulder dislocation, with surgical or anatomical neck fracture, includes internal fixation, when performed

## Manipulation

**23700**   Manipulation under anesthesia, shoulder joint, including application of fixation apparatus (dislocation excluded)

## Arthrodesis

**23800**   Arthrodesis, glenohumeral joint;

**23802**     with autogenous graft (includes obtaining graft)

## Amputation

**23900**   Interthoracoscapular amputation (forequarter)

**23920**   Disarticulation of shoulder;

**23921**     secondary closure or scar revision

## Other Procedures

**23929**   Unlisted procedure, shoulder

# Humerus (Upper Arm) and Elbow

The elbow area includes the head and neck of the radius and olecranon process.

## Incision

(For incision and drainage procedures, superficial, see 10040-10160)

**23930**   Incision and drainage, upper arm or elbow area; deep abscess or hematoma

**23931**     bursa

**23935**   Incision, deep, with opening of bone cortex (eg, for osteomyelitis or bone abscess), humerus or elbow

**24000**   Arthrotomy, elbow, including exploration, drainage, or removal of foreign body

**24006**   Arthrotomy of the elbow, with capsular excision for capsular release (separate procedure)

## Excision

**24065**   Biopsy, soft tissue of upper arm or elbow area; superficial

**24066**     deep (subfascial or intramuscular)

(For needle biopsy of soft tissue, use 20206)

**24071**   Code is out of numerical sequence. See 24065-24155

**24073**   Code is out of numerical sequence. See 24065-24155

**24075**   Excision, tumor, soft tissue of upper arm or elbow area, subcutaneous; less than 3 cm

# **24071**     3 cm or greater

►(For excision of benign lesions of cutaneous origin [eg, sebaceous cyst], see 11400-11406)◄

**24076**   Excision, tumor, soft tissue of upper arm or elbow area, subfascial (eg, intramuscular); less than 5 cm

# **24073**     5 cm or greater

▲ **24077**   Radical resection of tumor (eg, sarcoma), soft tissue of upper arm or elbow area; less than 5 cm

▲ **24079**     5 cm or greater

►(For radical resection of tumor[s] of cutaneous origin [eg, melanoma], see 11600-11606)◄

**24100**   Arthrotomy, elbow; with synovial biopsy only

**24101**     with joint exploration, with or without biopsy, with or without removal of loose or foreign body

**24102**     with synovectomy

**24105**   Excision, olecranon bursa

**24110**   Excision or curettage of bone cyst or benign tumor, humerus;

Musculoskeletal

24115     with autograft (includes obtaining graft)

24116     with allograft

24120     Excision or curettage of bone cyst or benign tumor of head or neck of radius or olecranon process;

24125     with autograft (includes obtaining graft)

24126     with allograft

24130     Excision, radial head

(For replacement with implant, use 24366)

24134     Sequestrectomy (eg, for osteomyelitis or bone abscess), shaft or distal humerus

24136     Sequestrectomy (eg, for osteomyelitis or bone abscess), radial head or neck

24138     Sequestrectomy (eg, for osteomyelitis or bone abscess), olecranon process

24140     Partial excision (craterization, saucerization, or diaphysectomy) bone (eg, osteomyelitis), humerus

24145     Partial excision (craterization, saucerization, or diaphysectomy) bone (eg, osteomyelitis), radial head or neck

24147     Partial excision (craterization, saucerization, or diaphysectomy) bone (eg, osteomyelitis), olecranon process

24149     Radical resection of capsule, soft tissue, and heterotopic bone, elbow, with contracture release (separate procedure)

(For capsular and soft tissue release only, use 24006)

24150     Radical resection of tumor, shaft or distal humerus

(24151 has been deleted)

24152     Radical resection of tumor, radial head or neck

(24153 has been deleted)

24155     Resection of elbow joint (arthrectomy)

## Introduction or Removal

(For K-wire or pin insertion or removal, see 20650, 20670, 20680)

(For arthrocentesis or needling of bursa or joint, use 20605)

▲ 24160     Removal of prosthesis, includes debridement and synovectomy when performed; humeral **and** ulnar components

▶(To report removal of foreign body, elbow, see 24200, 24201)◀

▶(To report removal of hardware from the distal humerus or proximal ulna, other than humeral and ulnar prosthesis, use 20680)◀

▶(Do not report 24160 in conjunction with 24370 or 24371 if a prosthesis [ie, humeral and/or ulnar component(s)] is being removed and replaced in the same elbow during the same surgical session)◀

▲ 24164     radial head

▶(To report removal of foreign body, elbow, see 24200, 24201)◀

▶(To report removal of hardware from proximal radius, other than radial head prosthesis, use 20680)◀

24200     Removal of foreign body, upper arm or elbow area; subcutaneous

24201     deep (subfascial or intramuscular)

24220     Injection procedure for elbow arthrography

(For radiological supervision and interpretation, use 73085. Do not report 77002 in conjunction with 73085)

(For injection for tennis elbow, use 20550)

## Repair, Revision, and/or Reconstruction

24300     Manipulation, elbow, under anesthesia

(For application of external fixation, see 20690 or 20692)

24301     Muscle or tendon transfer, any type, upper arm or elbow, single (excluding 24320-24331)

24305     Tendon lengthening, upper arm or elbow, each tendon

24310     Tenotomy, open, elbow to shoulder, each tendon

24320     Tenoplasty, with muscle transfer, with or without free graft, elbow to shoulder, single (Seddon-Brookes type procedure)

24330     Flexor-plasty, elbow (eg, Steindler type advancement);

24331     with extensor advancement

24332     Tenolysis, triceps

24340     Tenodesis of biceps tendon at elbow (separate procedure)

24341     Repair, tendon or muscle, upper arm or elbow, each tendon or muscle, primary or secondary (excludes rotator cuff)

24342     Reinsertion of ruptured biceps or triceps tendon, distal, with or without tendon graft

24343     Repair lateral collateral ligament, elbow, with local tissue

24344     Reconstruction lateral collateral ligament, elbow, with tendon graft (includes harvesting of graft)

24345     Repair medial collateral ligament, elbow, with local tissue

24346     Reconstruction medial collateral ligament, elbow, with tendon graft (includes harvesting of graft)

24357     Tenotomy, elbow, lateral or medial (eg, epicondylitis, tennis elbow, golfer's elbow); percutaneous

24358     debridement, soft tissue and/or bone, open

24359     debridement, soft tissue and/or bone, open with tendon repair or reattachment

(Do not report 24357-24359 in conjunction with 29837, 29838)

Musculoskeletal

**24360**   Arthroplasty, elbow; with membrane (eg, fascial)

**24361**       with distal humeral prosthetic replacement

**24362**       with implant and fascia lata ligament reconstruction

**24363**       with distal humerus and proximal ulnar prosthetic replacement (eg, total elbow)

          (For revision of total elbow implant, see 24370, 24371)

**24365**   Arthroplasty, radial head;

**24366**       with implant

**24370**   Revision of total elbow arthroplasty, including allograft when performed; humeral **or** ulnar component

**24371**       humeral **and** ulnar component

          (Do not report 24370, 24371 in conjunction with 24160 if a prosthesis [ie, humeral and/or ulnar component(s)] is being removed and replaced in the same elbow)

**24400**   Osteotomy, humerus, with or without internal fixation

**24410**   Multiple osteotomies with realignment on intramedullary rod, humeral shaft (Sofield type procedure)

**24420**   Osteoplasty, humerus (eg, shortening or lengthening) (excluding 64876)

**24430**   Repair of nonunion or malunion, humerus; without graft (eg, compression technique)

**24435**       with iliac or other autograft (includes obtaining graft)

          (For proximal radius and/or ulna, see 25400-25420)

**24470**   Hemiepiphyseal arrest (eg, cubitus varus or valgus, distal humerus)

**24495**   Decompression fasciotomy, forearm, with brachial artery exploration

**24498**   Prophylactic treatment (nailing, pinning, plating or wiring), with or without methylmethacrylate, humeral shaft

## Fracture and/or Dislocation

**24500**   Closed treatment of humeral shaft fracture; without manipulation

**24505**       with manipulation, with or without skeletal traction

**24515**   Open treatment of humeral shaft fracture with plate/screws, with or without cerclage

**24516**   Treatment of humeral shaft fracture, with insertion of intramedullary implant, with or without cerclage and/or locking screws

**24530**   Closed treatment of supracondylar or transcondylar humeral fracture, with or without intercondylar extension; without manipulation

**24535**       with manipulation, with or without skin or skeletal traction

**24538**   Percutaneous skeletal fixation of supracondylar or transcondylar humeral fracture, with or without intercondylar extension

**24545**   Open treatment of humeral supracondylar or transcondylar fracture, includes internal fixation, when performed; without intercondylar extension

**24546**       with intercondylar extension

**24560**   Closed treatment of humeral epicondylar fracture, medial or lateral; without manipulation

**24565**       with manipulation

**24566**   Percutaneous skeletal fixation of humeral epicondylar fracture, medial or lateral, with manipulation

**24575**   Open treatment of humeral epicondylar fracture, medial or lateral, includes internal fixation, when performed

**24576**   Closed treatment of humeral condylar fracture, medial or lateral; without manipulation

**24577**       with manipulation

**24579**   Open treatment of humeral condylar fracture, medial or lateral, includes internal fixation, when performed

          (To report closed treatment of fractures without manipulation, see 24530, 24560, 24576, 24650, 24670)

          (To report closed treatment of fractures with manipulation, see 24535, 24565, 24577, 24675)

**24582**   Percutaneous skeletal fixation of humeral condylar fracture, medial or lateral, with manipulation

**24586**   Open treatment of periarticular fracture and/or dislocation of the elbow (fracture distal humerus and proximal ulna and/or proximal radius);

**24587**       with implant arthroplasty

          (See also 24361)

**24600**   Treatment of closed elbow dislocation; without anesthesia

**24605**       requiring anesthesia

**24615**   Open treatment of acute or chronic elbow dislocation

**24620**   Closed treatment of Monteggia type of fracture dislocation at elbow (fracture proximal end of ulna with dislocation of radial head), with manipulation

**24635**   Open treatment of Monteggia type of fracture dislocation at elbow (fracture proximal end of ulna with dislocation of radial head), includes internal fixation, when performed

**24640**   Closed treatment of radial head subluxation in child, nursemaid elbow, with manipulation

**24650**   Closed treatment of radial head or neck fracture; without manipulation

**24655**       with manipulation

**24665**   Open treatment of radial head or neck fracture, includes internal fixation or radial head excision, when performed;

**24666**       with radial head prosthetic replacement

**24670**   Closed treatment of ulnar fracture, proximal end (eg, olecranon or coronoid process[es]); without manipulation

Musculoskeletal

**Musculoskeletal**

| 24675 | with manipulation |
|---|---|
| 24685 | Open treatment of ulnar fracture, proximal end (eg, olecranon or coronoid process[es]), includes internal fixation, when performed |
| | (Do not report 24685 in conjunction with 24100-24102) |

## Arthrodesis

| 24800 | Arthrodesis, elbow joint; local |
|---|---|
| 24802 | with autogenous graft (includes obtaining graft) |

## Amputation

| 24900 | Amputation, arm through humerus; with primary closure |
|---|---|
| 24920 | open, circular (guillotine) |
| 24925 | secondary closure or scar revision |
| 24930 | re-amputation |
| 24931 | with implant |
| 24935 | Stump elongation, upper extremity |
| 24940 | Cineplasty, upper extremity, complete procedure |

## Other Procedures

| 24999 | Unlisted procedure, humerus or elbow |
|---|---|

# Forearm and Wrist

Radius, ulna, carpal bones, and joints.

## Incision

| 25000 | Incision, extensor tendon sheath, wrist (eg, deQuervains disease) |
|---|---|
| | (For decompression median nerve or for carpal tunnel syndrome, use 64721) |
| 25001 | Incision, flexor tendon sheath, wrist (eg, flexor carpi radialis) |
| 25020 | Decompression fasciotomy, forearm and/or wrist, flexor OR extensor compartment; without debridement of nonviable muscle and/or nerve |
| 25023 | with debridement of nonviable muscle and/or nerve |
| | (For decompression fasciotomy with brachial artery exploration, use 24495) |
| | (For incision and drainage procedures, superficial, see 10060-10160) |
| | (For debridement, see also 11000-11044) |
| 25024 | Decompression fasciotomy, forearm and/or wrist, flexor AND extensor compartment; without debridement of nonviable muscle and/or nerve |
| 25025 | with debridement of nonviable muscle and/or nerve |

| 25028 | Incision and drainage, forearm and/or wrist; deep abscess or hematoma |
|---|---|
| 25031 | bursa |
| 25035 | Incision, deep, bone cortex, forearm and/or wrist (eg, osteomyelitis or bone abscess) |
| 25040 | Arthrotomy, radiocarpal or midcarpal joint, with exploration, drainage, or removal of foreign body |

## Excision

| 25065 | Biopsy, soft tissue of forearm and/or wrist; superficial |
|---|---|
| 25066 | deep (subfascial or intramuscular) |
| | (For needle biopsy of soft tissue, use 20206) |
| 25071 | Code is out of numerical sequence. See 25065-25240 |
| 25073 | Code is out of numerical sequence. See 25065-25240 |
| 25075 | Excision, tumor, soft tissue of forearm and/or wrist area, subcutaneous; less than 3 cm |
| # 25071 | 3 cm or greater |
| | ▶(For excision of benign lesions of cutaneous origin [eg, sebaceous cyst], see 11400-11406)◀ |
| 25076 | Excision, tumor, soft tissue of forearm and/or wrist area, subfascial (eg, intramuscular); less than 3 cm |
| # 25073 | 3 cm or greater |
| ▲ 25077 | Radical resection of tumor (eg, sarcoma), soft tissue of forearm and/or wrist area; less than 3 cm |
| ▲ 25078 | 3 cm or greater |
| | ▶(For radical resection of tumor[s] of cutaneous origin [eg, melanoma], see 11600-11606)◀ |
| 25085 | Capsulotomy, wrist (eg, contracture) |
| 25100 | Arthrotomy, wrist joint; with biopsy |
| 25101 | with joint exploration, with or without biopsy, with or without removal of loose or foreign body |
| 25105 | with synovectomy |
| 25107 | Arthrotomy, distal radioulnar joint including repair of triangular cartilage, complex |
| 25109 | Excision of tendon, forearm and/or wrist, flexor or extensor, each |
| 25110 | Excision, lesion of tendon sheath, forearm and/or wrist |
| 25111 | Excision of ganglion, wrist (dorsal or volar); primary |
| 25112 | recurrent |
| | (For hand or finger, use 26160) |
| 25115 | Radical excision of bursa, synovia of wrist, or forearm tendon sheaths (eg, tenosynovitis, fungus, Tbc, or other granulomas, rheumatoid arthritis); flexors |
| 25116 | extensors, with or without transposition of dorsal retinaculum |
| | (For finger synovectomies, use 26145) |

⊙=Moderate sedation   ✚=Add-on code   ✒=FDA approval pending   #=Resequenced code   ○=Recycled/reinstated code

| | |
|---|---|
| **25118** | Synovectomy, extensor tendon sheath, wrist, single compartment; |
| **25119** | with resection of distal ulna |
| **25120** | Excision or curettage of bone cyst or benign tumor of radius or ulna (excluding head or neck of radius and olecranon process); |
| | (For head or neck of radius or olecranon process, see 24120-24126) |
| **25125** | with autograft (includes obtaining graft) |
| **25126** | with allograft |
| **25130** | Excision or curettage of bone cyst or benign tumor of carpal bones; |
| **25135** | with autograft (includes obtaining graft) |
| **25136** | with allograft |
| **25145** | Sequestrectomy (eg, for osteomyelitis or bone abscess), forearm and/or wrist |
| **25150** | Partial excision (craterization, saucerization, or diaphysectomy) of bone (eg, for osteomyelitis); ulna |
| **25151** | radius |
| | (For head or neck of radius or olecranon process, see 24145, 24147) |
| **25170** | Radical resection of tumor, radius or ulna |
| **25210** | Carpectomy; 1 bone |
| | (For carpectomy with implant, see 25441-25445) |
| **25215** | all bones of proximal row |
| **25230** | Radial styloidectomy (separate procedure) |
| **25240** | Excision distal ulna partial or complete (eg, Darrach type or matched resection) |
| | (For implant replacement, distal ulna, use 25442) |
| | (For obtaining fascia for interposition, see 20920, 20922) |

## Introduction or Removal

| | |
|---|---|
| | (For K-wire, pin or rod insertion or removal, see 20650, 20670, 20680) |
| **25246** | Injection procedure for wrist arthrography |
| | (For radiological supervision and interpretation, use 73115. Do not report 77002 in conjunction with 73115) |
| | (For foreign body removal, superficial use 20520) |
| **25248** | Exploration with removal of deep foreign body, forearm or wrist |
| **25250** | Removal of wrist prosthesis; (separate procedure) |
| **25251** | complicated, including total wrist |
| **25259** | Manipulation, wrist, under anesthesia |
| | (For application of external fixation, see 20690 or 20692) |

## Repair, Revision, and/or Reconstruction

| | |
|---|---|
| **25260** | Repair, tendon or muscle, flexor, forearm and/or wrist; primary, single, each tendon or muscle |
| **25263** | secondary, single, each tendon or muscle |
| **25265** | secondary, with free graft (includes obtaining graft), each tendon or muscle |
| **25270** | Repair, tendon or muscle, extensor, forearm and/or wrist; primary, single, each tendon or muscle |
| **25272** | secondary, single, each tendon or muscle |
| **25274** | secondary, with free graft (includes obtaining graft), each tendon or muscle |
| **25275** | Repair, tendon sheath, extensor, forearm and/or wrist, with free graft (includes obtaining graft) (eg, for extensor carpi ulnaris subluxation) |
| **25280** | Lengthening or shortening of flexor or extensor tendon, forearm and/or wrist, single, each tendon |
| **25290** | Tenotomy, open, flexor or extensor tendon, forearm and/or wrist, single, each tendon |
| **25295** | Tenolysis, flexor or extensor tendon, forearm and/or wrist, single, each tendon |
| **25300** | Tenodesis at wrist; flexors of fingers |
| **25301** | extensors of fingers |
| **25310** | Tendon transplantation or transfer, flexor or extensor, forearm and/or wrist, single; each tendon |
| **25312** | with tendon graft(s) (includes obtaining graft), each tendon |
| **25315** | Flexor origin slide (eg, for cerebral palsy, Volkmann contracture), forearm and/or wrist; |
| **25316** | with tendon(s) transfer |
| **25320** | Capsulorrhaphy or reconstruction, wrist, open (eg, capsulodesis, ligament repair, tendon transfer or graft) (includes synovectomy, capsulotomy and open reduction) for carpal instability |
| **25332** | Arthroplasty, wrist, with or without interposition, with or without external or internal fixation |
| | (For obtaining fascia for interposition, see 20920, 20922) |
| | (For prosthetic replacement arthroplasty, see 25441-25446) |
| **25335** | Centralization of wrist on ulna (eg, radial club hand) |
| **25337** | Reconstruction for stabilization of unstable distal ulna or distal radioulnar joint, secondary by soft tissue stabilization (eg, tendon transfer, tendon graft or weave, or tenodesis) with or without open reduction of distal radioulnar joint |
| | (For harvesting of fascia lata graft, see 20920, 20922) |
| **25350** | Osteotomy, radius; distal third |
| **25355** | middle or proximal third |
| **25360** | Osteotomy; ulna |

---

*Musculoskeletal*

**Musculoskeletal**

| | |
|---|---|
| **25365** | radius AND ulna |
| **25370** | Multiple osteotomies, with realignment on intramedullary rod (Sofield type procedure); radius OR ulna |
| **25375** | radius AND ulna |
| **25390** | Osteoplasty, radius OR ulna; shortening |
| **25391** | lengthening with autograft |
| **25392** | Osteoplasty, radius AND ulna; shortening (excluding 64876) |
| **25393** | lengthening with autograft |
| **25394** | Osteoplasty, carpal bone, shortening |
| **25400** | Repair of nonunion or malunion, radius OR ulna; without graft (eg, compression technique) |
| **25405** | with autograft (includes obtaining graft) |
| **25415** | Repair of nonunion or malunion, radius AND ulna; without graft (eg, compression technique) |
| **25420** | with autograft (includes obtaining graft) |
| **25425** | Repair of defect with autograft; radius OR ulna |
| **25426** | radius AND ulna |
| **25430** | Insertion of vascular pedicle into carpal bone (eg, Hori procedure) |
| **25431** | Repair of nonunion of carpal bone (excluding carpal scaphoid (navicular)) (includes obtaining graft and necessary fixation), each bone |
| **25440** | Repair of nonunion, scaphoid carpal (navicular) bone, with or without radial styloidectomy (includes obtaining graft and necessary fixation) |
| **25441** | Arthroplasty with prosthetic replacement; distal radius |
| **25442** | distal ulna |
| **25443** | scaphoid carpal (navicular) |
| **25444** | lunate |
| **25445** | trapezium |
| **25446** | distal radius and partial or entire carpus (total wrist) |
| **25447** | Arthroplasty, interposition, intercarpal or carpometacarpal joints |
| | (For wrist arthroplasty, use 25332) |
| **25449** | Revision of arthroplasty, including removal of implant, wrist joint |
| **25450** | Epiphyseal arrest by epiphysiodesis or stapling; distal radius OR ulna |
| **25455** | distal radius AND ulna |
| **25490** | Prophylactic treatment (nailing, pinning, plating or wiring) with or without methylmethacrylate; radius |
| **25491** | ulna |
| **25492** | radius AND ulna |

## Fracture and/or Dislocation

| | |
|---|---|
| | (For application of external fixation in addition to internal fixation, use 20690 and the appropriate internal fixation code) |
| **25500** | Closed treatment of radial shaft fracture; without manipulation |
| **25505** | with manipulation |
| **25515** | Open treatment of radial shaft fracture, includes internal fixation, when performed |
| **25520** | Closed treatment of radial shaft fracture and closed treatment of dislocation of distal radioulnar joint (Galeazzi fracture/dislocation) |
| **25525** | Open treatment of radial shaft fracture, includes internal fixation, when performed, and closed treatment of distal radioulnar joint dislocation (Galeazzi fracture/dislocation), includes percutaneous skeletal fixation, when performed |
| **25526** | Open treatment of radial shaft fracture, includes internal fixation, when performed, and open treatment of distal radioulnar joint dislocation (Galeazzi fracture/dislocation), includes internal fixation, when performed, includes repair of triangular fibrocartilage complex |
| **25530** | Closed treatment of ulnar shaft fracture; without manipulation |
| **25535** | with manipulation |
| **25545** | Open treatment of ulnar shaft fracture, includes internal fixation, when performed |
| **25560** | Closed treatment of radial and ulnar shaft fractures; without manipulation |
| **25565** | with manipulation |
| **25574** | Open treatment of radial AND ulnar shaft fractures, with internal fixation, when performed; of radius OR ulna |
| **25575** | of radius AND ulna |
| **25600** | Closed treatment of distal radial fracture (eg, Colles or Smith type) or epiphyseal separation, includes closed treatment of fracture of ulnar styloid, when performed; without manipulation |
| **25605** | with manipulation |
| | (Do not report 25600, 25605 in conjunction with 25650) |
| **25606** | Percutaneous skeletal fixation of distal radial fracture or epiphyseal separation |
| | (Do not report 25606 in conjunction with 25650) |
| | (For percutaneous treatment of ulnar styloid fracture, use 25651) |
| | (For open treatment of ulnar styloid fracture, use 25652) |
| **25607** | Open treatment of distal radial extra-articular fracture or epiphyseal separation, with internal fixation |
| | (Do not report 25607 in conjunction with 25650) |

(For percutaneous treatment of ulnar styloid fracture, use 25651)

(For open treatment of ulnar styloid fracture, use 25652)

**25608**  Open treatment of distal radial intra-articular fracture or epiphyseal separation; with internal fixation of 2 fragments

(Do not report 25608 in conjunction with 25609)

**25609**    with internal fixation of 3 or more fragments

(Do not report 25608, 25609 in conjunction with 25650)

(For percutaneous treatment of ulnar styloid fracture, use 25651)

(For open treatment of ulnar styloid fracture, use 25652)

**25622**  Closed treatment of carpal scaphoid (navicular) fracture; without manipulation

**25624**    with manipulation

**25628**  Open treatment of carpal scaphoid (navicular) fracture, includes internal fixation, when performed

**25630**  Closed treatment of carpal bone fracture (excluding carpal scaphoid [navicular]); without manipulation, each bone

**25635**    with manipulation, each bone

**25645**  Open treatment of carpal bone fracture (other than carpal scaphoid [navicular]), each bone

**25650**  Closed treatment of ulnar styloid fracture

(Do not report 25650 in conjunction with 25600, 25605, 25607-25609)

**25651**  Percutaneous skeletal fixation of ulnar styloid fracture

**25652**  Open treatment of ulnar styloid fracture

**25660**  Closed treatment of radiocarpal or intercarpal dislocation, 1 or more bones, with manipulation

**25670**  Open treatment of radiocarpal or intercarpal dislocation, 1 or more bones

**25671**  Percutaneous skeletal fixation of distal radioulnar dislocation

**25675**  Closed treatment of distal radioulnar dislocation with manipulation

**25676**  Open treatment of distal radioulnar dislocation, acute or chronic

**25680**  Closed treatment of trans-scaphoperilunar type of fracture dislocation, with manipulation

**25685**  Open treatment of trans-scaphoperilunar type of fracture dislocation

**25690**  Closed treatment of lunate dislocation, with manipulation

**25695**  Open treatment of lunate dislocation

## Arthrodesis

**25800**  Arthrodesis, wrist; complete, without bone graft (includes radiocarpal and/or intercarpal and/or carpometacarpal joints)

**25805**    with sliding graft

**25810**    with iliac or other autograft (includes obtaining graft)

**25820**  Arthrodesis, wrist; limited, without bone graft (eg, intercarpal or radiocarpal)

**25825**    with autograft (includes obtaining graft)

**25830**  Arthrodesis, distal radioulnar joint with segmental resection of ulna, with or without bone graft (eg, Sauve-Kapandji procedure)

## Amputation

**25900**  Amputation, forearm, through radius and ulna;

**25905**    open, circular (guillotine)

**25907**    secondary closure or scar revision

**25909**    re-amputation

**25915**  Krukenberg procedure

**25920**  Disarticulation through wrist;

**25922**    secondary closure or scar revision

**25924**    re-amputation

**25927**  Transmetacarpal amputation;

**25929**    secondary closure or scar revision

**25931**    re-amputation

## Other Procedures

**25999**  Unlisted procedure, forearm or wrist

# Hand and Fingers

## Incision

**26010**  Drainage of finger abscess; simple

**26011**    complicated (eg, felon)

**26020**  Drainage of tendon sheath, digit and/or palm, each

**26025**  Drainage of palmar bursa; single, bursa

**26030**    multiple bursa

**26034**  Incision, bone cortex, hand or finger (eg, osteomyelitis or bone abscess)

**26035**  Decompression fingers and/or hand, injection injury (eg, grease gun)

**26037**  Decompressive fasciotomy, hand (excludes 26035)

(For injection injury, use 26035)

Musculoskeletal

**Musculoskeletal**

**26040**   Fasciotomy, palmar (eg, Dupuytren's contracture); percutaneous

**26045**       open, partial

(For palmar fasciotomy by enzyme injection (eg, collagenase), see 20527, 26341)

(For fasciectomy, see 26121-26125)

**26055**   Tendon sheath incision (eg, for trigger finger)

**26060**   Tenotomy, percutaneous, single, each digit

**26070**   Arthrotomy, with exploration, drainage, or removal of loose or foreign body; carpometacarpal joint

**26075**       metacarpophalangeal joint, each

**26080**       interphalangeal joint, each

## Excision

**26100**   Arthrotomy with biopsy; carpometacarpal joint, each

**26105**       metacarpophalangeal joint, each

**26110**       interphalangeal joint, each

**26111**   Code is out of numerical sequence. See 26100-26262

**26113**   Code is out of numerical sequence. See 26100-26262

**26115**   Excision, tumor or vascular malformation, soft tissue of hand or finger, subcutaneous; less than 1.5 cm

**# 26111**       1.5 cm or greater

▶(For excision of benign lesions of cutaneous origin [eg, sebaceous cyst], see 11420-11426)◀

**26116**   Excision, tumor, soft tissue, or vascular malformation, of hand or finger, subfascial (eg, intramuscular); less than 1.5 cm

**# 26113**       1.5 cm or greater

**▲ 26117**   Radical resection of tumor (eg, sarcoma), soft tissue of hand or finger; less than 3 cm

**▲ 26118**       3 cm or greater

▶(For radical resection of tumor[s] of cutaneous origin [eg, melanoma], see 11620-11626)◀

**26121**   Fasciectomy, palm only, with or without Z-plasty, other local tissue rearrangement, or skin grafting (includes obtaining graft)

**26123**   Fasciectomy, partial palmar with release of single digit including proximal interphalangeal joint, with or without Z-plasty, other local tissue rearrangement, or skin grafting (includes obtaining graft);

**+ 26125**       each additional digit (List separately in addition to code for primary procedure)

(Use 26125 in conjunction with 26123)

(For palmar fasciotomy by enzyme injection (eg, collagenase), see 20527, 26341)

(For fasciotomy, see 26040, 26045)

**26130**   Synovectomy, carpometacarpal joint

**26135**   Synovectomy, metacarpophalangeal joint including intrinsic release and extensor hood reconstruction, each digit

**26140**   Synovectomy, proximal interphalangeal joint, including extensor reconstruction, each interphalangeal joint

**26145**   Synovectomy, tendon sheath, radical (tenosynovectomy), flexor tendon, palm and/or finger, each tendon

(For tendon sheath synovectomies at wrist, see 25115, 25116)

**26160**   Excision of lesion of tendon sheath or joint capsule (eg, cyst, mucous cyst, or ganglion), hand or finger

(For wrist ganglion, see 25111, 25112)

(For trigger digit, use 26055)

**26170**   Excision of tendon, palm, flexor or extensor, single, each tendon

(Do not report 26170 in conjunction with 26390, 26415)

**26180**   Excision of tendon, finger, flexor or extensor, each tendon

(Do not report 26180 in conjunction with 26390, 26415)

**26185**   Sesamoidectomy, thumb or finger (separate procedure)

**26200**   Excision or curettage of bone cyst or benign tumor of metacarpal;

**26205**       with autograft (includes obtaining graft)

**26210**   Excision or curettage of bone cyst or benign tumor of proximal, middle, or distal phalanx of finger;

**26215**       with autograft (includes obtaining graft)

**26230**   Partial excision (craterization, saucerization, or diaphysectomy) bone (eg, osteomyelitis); metacarpal

**26235**       proximal or middle phalanx of finger

**26236**       distal phalanx of finger

**26250**   Radical resection of tumor, metacarpal

(26255 has been deleted)

**26260**   Radical resection of tumor, proximal or middle phalanx of finger

(26261 has been deleted)

**26262**   Radical resection of tumor, distal phalanx of finger

## Introduction or Removal

**26320**   Removal of implant from finger or hand

(For removal of foreign body in hand or finger, see 20520, 20525)

## Repair, Revision, and/or Reconstruction

**26340**   Manipulation, finger joint, under anesthesia, each joint

(For application of external fixation, see 20690 or 20692)

---

**26341**    Manipulation, palmar fascial cord (ie, Dupuytren's cord), post enzyme injection (eg, collagenase), single cord

(For enzyme injection (eg, collagenase), palmar fascial cord (eg, Dupuytren's contracture), use 20527)

(Report custom orthotic fabrication/application separately)

**26350**    Repair or advancement, flexor tendon, not in zone 2 digital flexor tendon sheath (eg, no man's land); primary or secondary without free graft, each tendon

**26352**        secondary with free graft (includes obtaining graft), each tendon

**26356**    Repair or advancement, flexor tendon, in zone 2 digital flexor tendon sheath (eg, no man's land); primary, without free graft, each tendon

**26357**        secondary, without free graft, each tendon

**26358**        secondary, with free graft (includes obtaining graft), each tendon

**26370**    Repair or advancement of profundus tendon, with intact superficialis tendon; primary, each tendon

**26372**        secondary with free graft (includes obtaining graft), each tendon

**26373**        secondary without free graft, each tendon

**26390**    Excision flexor tendon, with implantation of synthetic rod for delayed tendon graft, hand or finger, each rod

**26392**    Removal of synthetic rod and insertion of flexor tendon graft, hand or finger (includes obtaining graft), each rod

**26410**    Repair, extensor tendon, hand, primary or secondary; without free graft, each tendon

**26412**        with free graft (includes obtaining graft), each tendon

**26415**    Excision of extensor tendon, with implantation of synthetic rod for delayed tendon graft, hand or finger, each rod

**26416**    Removal of synthetic rod and insertion of extensor tendon graft (includes obtaining graft), hand or finger, each rod

**26418**    Repair, extensor tendon, finger, primary or secondary; without free graft, each tendon

**26420**        with free graft (includes obtaining graft) each tendon

**26426**    Repair of extensor tendon, central slip, secondary (eg, boutonniere deformity); using local tissue(s), including lateral band(s), each finger

**26428**        with free graft (includes obtaining graft), each finger

**26432**    Closed treatment of distal extensor tendon insertion, with or without percutaneous pinning (eg, mallet finger)

**26433**    Repair of extensor tendon, distal insertion, primary or secondary; without graft (eg, mallet finger)

**26434**        with free graft (includes obtaining graft)

(For tenovaginotomy for trigger finger, use 26055)

**26437**    Realignment of extensor tendon, hand, each tendon

**26440**    Tenolysis, flexor tendon; palm OR finger, each tendon

**26442**        palm AND finger, each tendon

**26445**    Tenolysis, extensor tendon, hand OR finger, each tendon

**26449**    Tenolysis, complex, extensor tendon, finger, including forearm, each tendon

**26450**    Tenotomy, flexor, palm, open, each tendon

**26455**    Tenotomy, flexor, finger, open, each tendon

**26460**    Tenotomy, extensor, hand or finger, open, each tendon

**26471**    Tenodesis; of proximal interphalangeal joint, each joint

**26474**        of distal joint, each joint

**26476**    Lengthening of tendon, extensor, hand or finger, each tendon

**26477**    Shortening of tendon, extensor, hand or finger, each tendon

**26478**    Lengthening of tendon, flexor, hand or finger, each tendon

**26479**    Shortening of tendon, flexor, hand or finger, each tendon

**26480**    Transfer or transplant of tendon, carpometacarpal area or dorsum of hand; without free graft, each tendon

**26483**        with free tendon graft (includes obtaining graft), each tendon

**26485**    Transfer or transplant of tendon, palmar; without free tendon graft, each tendon

**26489**        with free tendon graft (includes obtaining graft), each tendon

**26490**    Opponensplasty; superficialis tendon transfer type, each tendon

**26492**        tendon transfer with graft (includes obtaining graft), each tendon

**26494**        hypothenar muscle transfer

**26496**        other methods

(For thumb fusion in opposition, use 26820)

**26497**    Transfer of tendon to restore intrinsic function; ring and small finger

**26498**        all 4 fingers

**26499**    Correction claw finger, other methods

**26500**    Reconstruction of tendon pulley, each tendon; with local tissues (separate procedure)

**26502**        with tendon or fascial graft (includes obtaining graft) (separate procedure)

**26508**    Release of thenar muscle(s) (eg, thumb contracture)

**26510**    Cross intrinsic transfer, each tendon

**26516**    Capsulodesis, metacarpophalangeal joint; single digit

**26517**        2 digits

**26518**        3 or 4 digits

**Musculoskeletal**

---

▲=Revised code    ●=New code    ▶◀=Contains new or revised text    ⊘=Modifier 51 exempt

**26520** Capsulectomy or capsulotomy; metacarpophalangeal joint, each joint

**26525** interphalangeal joint, each joint

(To report carpometacarpal joint arthroplasty, use 25447)

**26530** Arthroplasty, metacarpophalangeal joint; each joint

**26531** with prosthetic implant, each joint

**26535** Arthroplasty, interphalangeal joint; each joint

**26536** with prosthetic implant, each joint

**26540** Repair of collateral ligament, metacarpophalangeal or interphalangeal joint

**26541** Reconstruction, collateral ligament, metacarpophalangeal joint, single; with tendon or fascial graft (includes obtaining graft)

**26542** with local tissue (eg, adductor advancement)

**26545** Reconstruction, collateral ligament, interphalangeal joint, single, including graft, each joint

**26546** Repair non-union, metacarpal or phalanx (includes obtaining bone graft with or without external or internal fixation)

**26548** Repair and reconstruction, finger, volar plate, interphalangeal joint

**26550** Pollicization of a digit

**26551** Transfer, toe-to-hand with microvascular anastomosis; great toe wrap-around with bone graft

(For great toe with web space, use 20973)

**26553** other than great toe, single

**26554** other than great toe, double

(Do not report code 69990 in addition to codes 26551-26554)

**26555** Transfer, finger to another position without microvascular anastomosis

**26556** Transfer, free toe joint, with microvascular anastomosis

(Do not report code 69990 in addition to code 26556)

(To report great toe-to-hand transfer, use 20973)

**26560** Repair of syndactyly (web finger) each web space; with skin flaps

**26561** with skin flaps and grafts

**26562** complex (eg, involving bone, nails)

**26565** Osteotomy; metacarpal, each

**26567** phalanx of finger, each

**26568** Osteoplasty, lengthening, metacarpal or phalanx

**26580** Repair cleft hand

**26587** Reconstruction of polydactylous digit, soft tissue and bone

(For excision of polydactylous digit, soft tissue only, use 11200)

**26590** Repair macrodactylia, each digit

**26591** Repair, intrinsic muscles of hand, each muscle

**26593** Release, intrinsic muscles of hand, each muscle

**26596** Excision of constricting ring of finger, with multiple Z-plasties

(To report release of scar contracture or graft repairs see 11042, 14040-14041, or 15120, 15240)

## Fracture and/or Dislocation

**26600** Closed treatment of metacarpal fracture, single; without manipulation, each bone

**26605** with manipulation, each bone

**26607** Closed treatment of metacarpal fracture, with manipulation, with external fixation, each bone

**26608** Percutaneous skeletal fixation of metacarpal fracture, each bone

**26615** Open treatment of metacarpal fracture, single, includes internal fixation, when performed, each bone

**26641** Closed treatment of carpometacarpal dislocation, thumb, with manipulation

**26645** Closed treatment of carpometacarpal fracture dislocation, thumb (Bennett fracture), with manipulation

**26650** Percutaneous skeletal fixation of carpometacarpal fracture dislocation, thumb (Bennett fracture), with manipulation

**26665** Open treatment of carpometacarpal fracture dislocation, thumb (Bennett fracture), includes internal fixation, when performed

**26670** Closed treatment of carpometacarpal dislocation, other than thumb, with manipulation, each joint; without anesthesia

**26675** requiring anesthesia

**26676** Percutaneous skeletal fixation of carpometacarpal dislocation, other than thumb, with manipulation, each joint

**26685** Open treatment of carpometacarpal dislocation, other than thumb; includes internal fixation, when performed, each joint

**26686** complex, multiple, or delayed reduction

**26700** Closed treatment of metacarpophalangeal dislocation, single, with manipulation; without anesthesia

**26705** requiring anesthesia

**26706** Percutaneous skeletal fixation of metacarpophalangeal dislocation, single, with manipulation

**26715** Open treatment of metacarpophalangeal dislocation, single, includes internal fixation, when performed

**26720** Closed treatment of phalangeal shaft fracture, proximal or middle phalanx, finger or thumb, without manipulation, each

⊙=Moderate sedation ✚=Add-on code ✗=FDA approval pending #=Resequenced code ○=Recycled/reinstated code

**Musculoskeletal**

26725    with manipulation, with or without skin or skeletal traction, each

26727    Percutaneous skeletal fixation of unstable phalangeal shaft fracture, proximal or middle phalanx, finger or thumb, with manipulation, each

26735    Open treatment of phalangeal shaft fracture, proximal or middle phalanx, finger or thumb, includes internal fixation, when performed, each

26740    Closed treatment of articular fracture, involving metacarpophalangeal or interphalangeal joint; without manipulation, each

26742    with manipulation, each

26746    Open treatment of articular fracture, involving metacarpophalangeal or interphalangeal joint, includes internal fixation, when performed, each

26750    Closed treatment of distal phalangeal fracture, finger or thumb; without manipulation, each

26755    with manipulation, each

26756    Percutaneous skeletal fixation of distal phalangeal fracture, finger or thumb, each

26765    Open treatment of distal phalangeal fracture, finger or thumb, includes internal fixation, when performed, each

26770    Closed treatment of interphalangeal joint dislocation, single, with manipulation; without anesthesia

26775    requiring anesthesia

26776    Percutaneous skeletal fixation of interphalangeal joint dislocation, single, with manipulation

26785    Open treatment of interphalangeal joint dislocation, includes internal fixation, when performed, single

## Arthrodesis

26820    Fusion in opposition, thumb, with autogenous graft (includes obtaining graft)

26841    Arthrodesis, carpometacarpal joint, thumb, with or without internal fixation;

26842    with autograft (includes obtaining graft)

26843    Arthrodesis, carpometacarpal joint, digit, other than thumb, each;

26844    with autograft (includes obtaining graft)

26850    Arthrodesis, metacarpophalangeal joint, with or without internal fixation;

26852    with autograft (includes obtaining graft)

26860    Arthrodesis, interphalangeal joint, with or without internal fixation;

+ 26861    each additional interphalangeal joint (List separately in addition to code for primary procedure)

(Use 26861 in conjunction with 26860)

26862    with autograft (includes obtaining graft)

+ 26863    with autograft (includes obtaining graft), each additional joint (List separately in addition to code for primary procedure)

(Use 26863 in conjunction with 26862)

## Amputation

(For hand through metacarpal bones, use 25927)

26910    Amputation, metacarpal, with finger or thumb (ray amputation), single, with or without interosseous transfer

(For repositioning, see 26550, 26555)

26951    Amputation, finger or thumb, primary or secondary, any joint or phalanx, single, including neurectomies; with direct closure

26952    with local advancement flaps (V-Y, hood)

(For repair of soft tissue defect requiring split or full thickness graft or other pedicle flaps, see 15050-15758)

## Other Procedures

26989    Unlisted procedure, hands or fingers

# Pelvis and Hip Joint

Including head and neck of femur.

## Incision

(For incision and drainage procedures, superficial, see 10040-10160)

26990    Incision and drainage, pelvis or hip joint area; deep abscess or hematoma

26991    infected bursa

26992    Incision, bone cortex, pelvis and/or hip joint (eg, osteomyelitis or bone abscess)

27000    Tenotomy, adductor of hip, percutaneous (separate procedure)

27001    Tenotomy, adductor of hip, open

(To report bilateral procedure, report 27001 with modifier 50)

27003    Tenotomy, adductor, subcutaneous, open, with obturator neurectomy

(To report bilateral procedure, report 27003 with modifier 50)

27005    Tenotomy, hip flexor(s), open (separate procedure)

27006    Tenotomy, abductors and/or extensor(s) of hip, open (separate procedure)

27025    Fasciotomy, hip or thigh, any type

(To report bilateral procedure, report 27025 with modifier 50)

**Musculoskeletal**

**27027**   Decompression fasciotomy(ies), pelvic (buttock) compartment(s) (eg, gluteus medius-minimus, gluteus maximus, iliopsoas, and/or tensor fascia lata muscle), unilateral

(To report bilateral procedure, report 27027 with modifier 50)

**27030**   Arthrotomy, hip, with drainage (eg, infection)

**27033**   Arthrotomy, hip, including exploration or removal of loose or foreign body

**27035**   Denervation, hip joint, intrapelvic or extrapelvic intra-articular branches of sciatic, femoral, or obturator nerves

(For obturator neurectomy, see 64763, 64766)

**27036**   Capsulectomy or capsulotomy, hip, with or without excision of heterotopic bone, with release of hip flexor muscles (ie, gluteus medius, gluteus minimus, tensor fascia latae, rectus femoris, sartorius, iliopsoas)

## Excision

**27040**   Biopsy, soft tissue of pelvis and hip area; superficial

**27041**       deep, subfascial or intramuscular

**27043**   Code is out of numerical sequence. See 27040-27080

**27045**   Code is out of numerical sequence. See 27040-27080

(For needle biopsy of soft tissue, use 20206)

**27047**   Excision, tumor, soft tissue of pelvis and hip area, subcutaneous; less than 3 cm

**# 27043**       3 cm or greater

►(For excision of benign lesions of cutaneous origin [eg, sebaceous cyst], see 11400-11406)◄

**27048**   Excision, tumor, soft tissue of pelvis and hip area, subfascial (eg, intramuscular); less than 5 cm

**# 27045**       5 cm or greater

**▲ 27049**   Radical resection of tumor (eg, sarcoma), soft tissue of pelvis and hip area; less than 5 cm

**#▲ 27059**       5 cm or greater

►(For radical resection of tumor[s] of cutaneous origin [eg, melanoma], see 11000-11006)◄

**27050**   Arthrotomy, with biopsy; sacroiliac joint

**27052**       hip joint

**27054**   Arthrotomy with synovectomy, hip joint

**27057**   Decompression fasciotomy(ies), pelvic (buttock) compartment(s) (eg, gluteus medius-minimus, gluteus maximus, iliopsoas, and/or tensor fascia lata muscle) with debridement of nonviable muscle, unilateral

(To report bilateral procedure, report 27057 with modifier 50)

**27059**   Code is out of numerical sequence. See 27040-27080

**27060**   Excision; ischial bursa

**27062**       trochanteric bursa or calcification

(For arthrocentesis or needling of bursa, use 20610)

**27065**   Excision of bone cyst or benign tumor, wing of ilium, symphysis pubis, or greater trochanter of femur; superficial, includes autograft, when performed

**27066**       deep (subfascial), includes autograft, when performed

**27067**       with autograft requiring separate incision

**27070**   Partial excision, wing of ilium, symphysis pubis, or greater trochanter of femur, (craterization, saucerization) (eg, osteomyelitis or bone abscess); superficial

**27071**       deep (subfascial or intramuscular)

**27075**   Radical resection of tumor; wing of ilium, 1 pubic or ischial ramus or symphysis pubis

**27076**       ilium, including acetabulum, both pubic rami, or ischium and acetabulum

**27077**       innominate bone, total

**27078**       ischial tuberosity and greater trochanter of femur

(27079 has been deleted)

**27080**   Coccygectomy, primary

(For pressure (decubitus) ulcer, see 15920, 15922 and 15931-15958)

## Introduction or Removal

**27086**   Removal of foreign body, pelvis or hip; subcutaneous tissue

**27087**       deep (subfascial or intramuscular)

**27090**   Removal of hip prosthesis; (separate procedure)

**27091**       complicated, including total hip prosthesis, methylmethacrylate with or without insertion of spacer

**27093**   Injection procedure for hip arthrography; without anesthesia

(For radiological supervision and interpretation, use 73525. Do not report 77002 in conjunction with 73525)

**27095**       with anesthesia

(For radiological supervision and interpretation, use 73525. Do not report 77002 in conjunction with 73525)

**27096**   Injection procedure for sacroiliac joint, anesthetic/steroid, with image guidance (fluoroscopy or CT) including arthrography when performed

(27096 is to be used only with CT or fluoroscopic imaging confirmation of intra-articular needle positioning)

(If CT or fluoroscopy imaging is not performed, use 20552)

(Code 27096 is a unilateral procedure. For bilateral procedure, use modifier 50)

## Repair, Revision, and/or Reconstruction

**27097**   Release or recession, hamstring, proximal

**27098**   Transfer, adductor to ischium

**27100**   Transfer external oblique muscle to greater trochanter including fascial or tendon extension (graft)

**27105**   Transfer paraspinal muscle to hip (includes fascial or tendon extension graft)

**27110**   Transfer iliopsoas; to greater trochanter of femur

**27111**        to femoral neck

**27120**   Acetabuloplasty; (eg, Whitman, Colonna, Haygroves, or cup type)

**27122**        resection, femoral head (eg, Girdlestone procedure)

**27125**   Hemiarthroplasty, hip, partial (eg, femoral stem prosthesis, bipolar arthroplasty)

> (For prosthetic replacement following fracture of the hip, use 27236)

**27130**   Arthroplasty, acetabular and proximal femoral prosthetic replacement (total hip arthroplasty), with or without autograft or allograft

**27132**   Conversion of previous hip surgery to total hip arthroplasty, with or without autograft or allograft

**27134**   Revision of total hip arthroplasty; both components, with or without autograft or allograft

**27137**        acetabular component only, with or without autograft or allograft

**27138**        femoral component only, with or without allograft

**27140**   Osteotomy and transfer of greater trochanter of femur (separate procedure)

**27146**   Osteotomy, iliac, acetabular or innominate bone;

**27147**        with open reduction of hip

**27151**        with femoral osteotomy

**27156**        with femoral osteotomy and with open reduction of hip

**27158**   Osteotomy, pelvis, bilateral (eg, congenital malformation)

**27161**   Osteotomy, femoral neck (separate procedure)

**27165**   Osteotomy, intertrochanteric or subtrochanteric including internal or external fixation and/or cast

**27170**   Bone graft, femoral head, neck, intertrochanteric or subtrochanteric area (includes obtaining bone graft)

**27175**   Treatment of slipped femoral epiphysis; by traction, without reduction

**27176**        by single or multiple pinning, in situ

**27177**   Open treatment of slipped femoral epiphysis; single or multiple pinning or bone graft (includes obtaining graft)

**27178**        closed manipulation with single or multiple pinning

**27179**        osteoplasty of femoral neck (Heyman type procedure)

**27181**        osteotomy and internal fixation

**27185**   Epiphyseal arrest by epiphysiodesis or stapling, greater trochanter of femur

**27187**   Prophylactic treatment (nailing, pinning, plating or wiring) with or without methylmethacrylate, femoral neck and proximal femur

## Fracture and/or Dislocation

**27193**   Closed treatment of pelvic ring fracture, dislocation, diastasis or subluxation; without manipulation

**27194**        with manipulation, requiring more than local anesthesia

**27200**   Closed treatment of coccygeal fracture

**27202**   Open treatment of coccygeal fracture

**27215**   Open treatment of iliac spine(s), tuberosity avulsion, or iliac wing fracture(s), unilateral, for pelvic bone fracture patterns that do not disrupt the pelvic ring, includes internal fixation, when performed

> (To report bilateral procedure, report 27215 with modifier 50)

**27216**   Percutaneous skeletal fixation of posterior pelvic bone fracture and/or dislocation, for fracture patterns that disrupt the pelvic ring, unilateral (includes ipsilateral ilium, sacroiliac joint and/or sacrum)

> (To report bilateral procedure, report 27216 with modifier 50)

> ▶(For percutaneous/minimally invasive stabilization for arthrodesis of the sacroiliac joint without fracture and/or dislocation, use 0334T)◀

**27217**   Open treatment of anterior pelvic bone fracture and/or dislocation for fracture patterns that disrupt the pelvic ring, unilateral, includes internal fixation, when performed (includes pubic symphysis and/or ipsilateral superior/inferior rami)

> (To report bilateral procedure, report 27217 with modifier 50)

**27218**   Open treatment of posterior pelvic bone fracture and/or dislocation, for fracture patterns that disrupt the pelvic ring, unilateral, includes internal fixation, when performed (includes ipsilateral ilium, sacroiliac joint and/or sacrum)

> (To report bilateral procedure, report 27218 with modifier 50)

> ▶(For percutaneous/minimally invasive stabilization for arthrodesis of the sacroiliac joint without fracture and/or dislocation, use 0334T)◀

**27220**   Closed treatment of acetabulum (hip socket) fracture(s); without manipulation

**27222**        with manipulation, with or without skeletal traction

**27226**   Open treatment of posterior or anterior acetabular wall fracture, with internal fixation

**Musculoskeletal**

**Musculoskeletal**

**27227**   Open treatment of acetabular fracture(s) involving anterior or posterior (one) column, or a fracture running transversely across the acetabulum, with internal fixation

**27228**   Open treatment of acetabular fracture(s) involving anterior and posterior (two) columns, includes T-fracture and both column fracture with complete articular detachment, or single column or transverse fracture with associated acetabular wall fracture, with internal fixation

**27230**   Closed treatment of femoral fracture, proximal end, neck; without manipulation

**27232**        with manipulation, with or without skeletal traction

**27235**   Percutaneous skeletal fixation of femoral fracture, proximal end, neck

**27236**   Open treatment of femoral fracture, proximal end, neck, internal fixation or prosthetic replacement

**27238**   Closed treatment of intertrochanteric, peritrochanteric, or subtrochanteric femoral fracture; without manipulation

**27240**        with manipulation, with or without skin or skeletal traction

**27244**   Treatment of intertrochanteric, peritrochanteric, or subtrochanteric femoral fracture; with plate/screw type implant, with or without cerclage

**27245**        with intramedullary implant, with or without interlocking screws and/or cerclage

**27246**   Closed treatment of greater trochanteric fracture, without manipulation

**27248**   Open treatment of greater trochanteric fracture, includes internal fixation, when performed

**27250**   Closed treatment of hip dislocation, traumatic; without anesthesia

**27252**        requiring anesthesia

**27253**   Open treatment of hip dislocation, traumatic, without internal fixation

**27254**   Open treatment of hip dislocation, traumatic, with acetabular wall and femoral head fracture, with or without internal or external fixation

(For treatment of acetabular fracture with fixation, see 27226, 27227)

**27256**   Treatment of spontaneous hip dislocation (developmental, including congenital or pathological), by abduction, splint or traction; without anesthesia, without manipulation

**27257**        with manipulation, requiring anesthesia

**27258**   Open treatment of spontaneous hip dislocation (developmental, including congenital or pathological), replacement of femoral head in acetabulum (including tenotomy, etc);

**27259**        with femoral shaft shortening

**27265**   Closed treatment of post hip arthroplasty dislocation; without anesthesia

**27266**        requiring regional or general anesthesia

**27267**   Closed treatment of femoral fracture, proximal end, head; without manipulation

**27268**        with manipulation

**27269**   Open treatment of femoral fracture, proximal end, head, includes internal fixation, when performed

(Do not report 27269 in conjunction with 27033, 27253)

## Manipulation

**27275**   Manipulation, hip joint, requiring general anesthesia

## Arthrodesis

**27280**   Arthrodesis, sacroiliac joint (including obtaining graft)

(To report bilateral procedure, report 27280 with modifier 50)

▶(For percutaneous/minimally invasive stabilization for arthrodesis of the sacroiliac joint, use 0334T)◀

**27282**   Arthrodesis, symphysis pubis (including obtaining graft)

**27284**   Arthrodesis, hip joint (including obtaining graft);

**27286**        with subtrochanteric osteotomy

## Amputation

**27290**   Interpelviabdominal amputation (hindquarter amputation)

**27295**   Disarticulation of hip

## Other Procedures

**27299**   Unlisted procedure, pelvis or hip joint

# Femur (Thigh Region) and Knee Joint

Including tibial plateaus.

## Incision

(For incision and drainage of abscess or hematoma, superficial, see 10040-10160)

**27301**   Incision and drainage, deep abscess, bursa, or hematoma, thigh or knee region

**27303**   Incision, deep, with opening of bone cortex, femur or knee (eg, osteomyelitis or bone abscess)

**27305**   Fasciotomy, iliotibial (tenotomy), open

(For combined Ober-Yount fasciotomy, use 27025)

**27306**   Tenotomy, percutaneous, adductor or hamstring; single tendon (separate procedure)

**27307**        multiple tendons

**27310**   Arthrotomy, knee, with exploration, drainage, or removal of foreign body (eg, infection)

## Excision

**27323**    Biopsy, soft tissue of thigh or knee area; superficial

**27324**        deep (subfascial or intramuscular)

         (For needle biopsy of soft tissue, use 20206)

**27325**    Neurectomy, hamstring muscle

**27326**    Neurectomy, popliteal (gastrocnemius)

**27327**    Excision, tumor, soft tissue of thigh or knee area, subcutaneous; less than 3 cm

**# 27337**        3 cm or greater

         ▶(For excision of benign lesions of cutaneous origin [eg, sebaceous cyst], see 11400-11406)◀

**27328**    Excision, tumor, soft tissue of thigh or knee area, subfascial (eg, intramuscular); less than 5 cm

**# 27339**        5 cm or greater

**27329**    Code is out of numerical sequence. See 27323-27365

**27330**    Arthrotomy, knee; with synovial biopsy only

**27331**        including joint exploration, biopsy, or removal of loose or foreign bodies

**27332**    Arthrotomy, with excision of semilunar cartilage (meniscectomy) knee; medial OR lateral

**27333**        medial AND lateral

**27334**    Arthrotomy, with synovectomy, knee; anterior OR posterior

**27335**        anterior AND posterior including popliteal area

**27337**    Code is out of numerical sequence. See 27323-27365

**27339**    Code is out of numerical sequence. See 27323-27365

**27340**    Excision, prepatellar bursa

**27345**    Excision of synovial cyst of popliteal space (eg, Baker's cyst)

**27347**    Excision of lesion of meniscus or capsule (eg, cyst, ganglion), knee

**27350**    Patellectomy or hemipatellectomy

**27355**    Excision or curettage of bone cyst or benign tumor of femur;

**27356**        with allograft

**27357**        with autograft (includes obtaining graft)

**+ 27358**        with internal fixation (List in addition to code for primary procedure)

         (Use 27358 in conjunction with 27355, 27356, or 27357)

**27360**    Partial excision (craterization, saucerization, or diaphysectomy) bone, femur, proximal tibia and/or fibula (eg, osteomyelitis or bone abscess)

**#▲ 27329**    Radical resection of tumor (eg, sarcoma), soft tissue of thigh or knee area; less than 5 cm

**▲ 27364**        5 cm or greater

         ▶(For radical resection of tumor[s] of cutaneous origin [eg, melanoma], see 11600-11606)◀

**27365**    Radical resection of tumor, femur or knee

         (For radical resection of tumor, soft tissue of thigh or knee area, see 27329, 27364)

## Introduction or Removal

**27370**    Injection procedure for knee arthrography

         (For radiological supervision and interpretation, use 73580. Do not report 77002 in conjunction with 73580)

**27372**    Removal of foreign body, deep, thigh region or knee area

         (For removal of knee prosthesis including "total knee," use 27488)

         (For surgical arthroscopic knee procedures, see 29870-29887)

## Repair, Revision, and/or Reconstruction

**27380**    Suture of infrapatellar tendon; primary

**27381**        secondary reconstruction, including fascial or tendon graft

**27385**    Suture of quadriceps or hamstring muscle rupture; primary

**27386**        secondary reconstruction, including fascial or tendon graft

**27390**    Tenotomy, open, hamstring, knee to hip; single tendon

**27391**        multiple tendons, 1 leg

**27392**        multiple tendons, bilateral

**27393**    Lengthening of hamstring tendon; single tendon

**27394**        multiple tendons, 1 leg

**27395**        multiple tendons, bilateral

**27396**    Transplant or transfer (with muscle redirection or rerouting), thigh (eg, extensor to flexor); single tendon

**27397**        multiple tendons

**27400**    Transfer, tendon or muscle, hamstrings to femur (eg, Egger's type procedure)

**27403**    Arthrotomy with meniscus repair, knee

         (For arthroscopic repair, use 29882)

**27405**    Repair, primary, torn ligament and/or capsule, knee; collateral

**27407**        cruciate

         (For cruciate ligament reconstruction, use 27427)

**27409**        collateral and cruciate ligaments

         (For ligament reconstruction, see 27427-27429)

Musculoskeletal

**Musculoskeletal**

**27412** Autologous chondrocyte implantation, knee

(Do not report 27412 in conjunction with 20926, 27331, 27570)

(For harvesting of chondrocytes, use 29870)

**27415** Osteochondral allograft, knee, open

(For arthroscopic implant of osteochondral allograft, use 29867)

(Do not report 27415 in conjunction with 27416)

**27416** Osteochondral autograft(s), knee, open (eg, mosaicplasty) (includes harvesting of autograft[s])

(Do not report 27416 in conjunction with 27415, 29870, 29871, 29875, 29884 when performed at the same session and/or 29874, 29877, 29879, 29885-29887 when performed in the same compartment)

(For arthroscopic osteochondral autograft of knee, use 29866)

**27418** Anterior tibial tubercleplasty (eg, Maquet type procedure)

**27420** Reconstruction of dislocating patella; (eg, Hauser type procedure)

**27422** with extensor realignment and/or muscle advancement or release (eg, Campbell, Goldwaite type procedure)

**27424** with patellectomy

**27425** Lateral retinacular release, open

(For arthroscopic lateral release, use 29873)

**27427** Ligamentous reconstruction (augmentation), knee; extra-articular

**27428** intra-articular (open)

**27429** intra-articular (open) and extra-articular

(For primary repair of ligament(s) performed in conjunction with reconstruction, report 27405, 27407 or 27409 in conjunction with 27427, 27428 or 27429)

**27430** Quadricepsplasty (eg, Bennett or Thompson type)

**27435** Capsulotomy, posterior capsular release, knee

**27437** Arthroplasty, patella; without prosthesis

**27438** with prosthesis

**27440** Arthroplasty, knee, tibial plateau;

**27441** with debridement and partial synovectomy

**27442** Arthroplasty, femoral condyles or tibial plateau(s), knee;

**27443** with debridement and partial synovectomy

**27445** Arthroplasty, knee, hinge prosthesis (eg, Walldius type)

**27446** Arthroplasty, knee, condyle and plateau; medial OR lateral compartment

**27447** medial AND lateral compartments with or without patella resurfacing (total knee arthroplasty)

(For revision of total knee arthroplasty, use 27487)

(For removal of total knee prosthesis, use 27488)

**27448** Osteotomy, femur, shaft or supracondylar; without fixation

(To report bilateral procedure, report 27448 with modifier 50)

**27450** with fixation

(To report bilateral procedure, report 27450 with modifier 50)

**27454** Osteotomy, multiple, with realignment on intramedullary rod, femoral shaft (eg, Sofield type procedure)

**27455** Osteotomy, proximal tibia, including fibular excision or osteotomy (includes correction of genu varus [bowleg] or genu valgus [knock-knee]); before epiphyseal closure

(To report bilateral procedure, report 27455 with modifier 50)

**27457** after epiphyseal closure

(To report bilateral procedure, report 27457 with modifier 50)

**27465** Osteoplasty, femur; shortening (excluding 64876)

**27466** lengthening

**27468** combined, lengthening and shortening with femoral segment transfer

**27470** Repair, nonunion or malunion, femur, distal to head and neck; without graft (eg, compression technique)

**27472** with iliac or other autogenous bone graft (includes obtaining graft)

**27475** Arrest, epiphyseal, any method (eg, epiphysiodesis); distal femur

**27477** tibia and fibula, proximal

**27479** combined distal femur, proximal tibia and fibula

**27485** Arrest, hemiepiphyseal, distal femur or proximal tibia or fibula (eg, genu varus or valgus)

**27486** Revision of total knee arthroplasty, with or without allograft; 1 component

**27487** femoral and entire tibial component

**27488** Removal of prosthesis, including total knee prosthesis, methylmethacrylate with or without insertion of spacer, knee

**27495** Prophylactic treatment (nailing, pinning, plating, or wiring) with or without methylmethacrylate, femur

**27496** Decompression fasciotomy, thigh and/or knee, 1 compartment (flexor or extensor or adductor);

**27497** with debridement of nonviable muscle and/or nerve

**27498** Decompression fasciotomy, thigh and/or knee, multiple compartments;

**27499** with debridement of nonviable muscle and/or nerve

## Fracture and/or Dislocation

(For arthroscopic treatment of intercondylar spine[s] and tuberosity fracture[s] of the knee, see 29850, 29851)

(For arthroscopic treatment of tibial fracture, see 29855, 29856)

**27500**  Closed treatment of femoral shaft fracture, without manipulation

**27501**  Closed treatment of supracondylar or transcondylar femoral fracture with or without intercondylar extension, without manipulation

**27502**  Closed treatment of femoral shaft fracture, with manipulation, with or without skin or skeletal traction

**27503**  Closed treatment of supracondylar or transcondylar femoral fracture with or without intercondylar extension, with manipulation, with or without skin or skeletal traction

**27506**  Open treatment of femoral shaft fracture, with or without external fixation, with insertion of intramedullary implant, with or without cerclage and/or locking screws

**27507**  Open treatment of femoral shaft fracture with plate/screws, with or without cerclage

**27508**  Closed treatment of femoral fracture, distal end, medial or lateral condyle, without manipulation

**27509**  Percutaneous skeletal fixation of femoral fracture, distal end, medial or lateral condyle, or supracondylar or transcondylar, with or without intercondylar extension, or distal femoral epiphyseal separation

**27510**  Closed treatment of femoral fracture, distal end, medial or lateral condyle, with manipulation

**27511**  Open treatment of femoral supracondylar or transcondylar fracture without intercondylar extension, includes internal fixation, when performed

**27513**  Open treatment of femoral supracondylar or transcondylar fracture with intercondylar extension, includes internal fixation, when performed

**27514**  Open treatment of femoral fracture, distal end, medial or lateral condyle, includes internal fixation, when performed

**27516**  Closed treatment of distal femoral epiphyseal separation; without manipulation

**27517**     with manipulation, with or without skin or skeletal traction

**27519**  Open treatment of distal femoral epiphyseal separation, includes internal fixation, when performed

**27520**  Closed treatment of patellar fracture, without manipulation

**27524**  Open treatment of patellar fracture, with internal fixation and/or partial or complete patellectomy and soft tissue repair

**27530**  Closed treatment of tibial fracture, proximal (plateau); without manipulation

**27532**     with or without manipulation, with skeletal traction

(For arthroscopic treatment, see 29855, 29856)

**27535**  Open treatment of tibial fracture, proximal (plateau); unicondylar, includes internal fixation, when performed

**27536**     bicondylar, with or without internal fixation

(For arthroscopic treatment, see 29855, 29856)

**27538**  Closed treatment of intercondylar spine(s) and/or tuberosity fracture(s) of knee, with or without manipulation

(For arthroscopic treatment, see 29850, 29851)

**27540**  Open treatment of intercondylar spine(s) and/or tuberosity fracture(s) of the knee, includes internal fixation, when performed

**27550**  Closed treatment of knee dislocation; without anesthesia

**27552**     requiring anesthesia

**27556**  Open treatment of knee dislocation, includes internal fixation, when performed; without primary ligamentous repair or augmentation/reconstruction

**27557**     with primary ligamentous repair

**27558**     with primary ligamentous repair, with augmentation/reconstruction

**27560**  Closed treatment of patellar dislocation; without anesthesia

(For recurrent dislocation, see 27420-27424)

**27562**     requiring anesthesia

**27566**  Open treatment of patellar dislocation, with or without partial or total patellectomy

## Manipulation

**27570**  Manipulation of knee joint under general anesthesia (includes application of traction or other fixation devices)

## Arthrodesis

**27580**  Arthrodesis, knee, any technique

## Amputation

**27590**  Amputation, thigh, through femur, any level;

**27591**     immediate fitting technique including first cast

**27592**     open, circular (guillotine)

**27594**     secondary closure or scar revision

**27596**     re-amputation

**27598**  Disarticulation at knee

## Other Procedures

**27599**  Unlisted procedure, femur or knee

Musculoskeletal

# Leg (Tibia and Fibula) and Ankle Joint

## Incision

**27600**    Decompression fasciotomy, leg; anterior and/or lateral compartments only

**27601**        posterior compartment(s) only

**27602**        anterior and/or lateral, and posterior compartment(s)

(For incision and drainage procedures, superficial, see 10040-10160)

(For decompression fasciotomy with debridement, see 27892-27894)

**27603**    Incision and drainage, leg or ankle; deep abscess or hematoma

**27604**        infected bursa

**27605**    Tenotomy, percutaneous, Achilles tendon (separate procedure); local anesthesia

**27606**        general anesthesia

**27607**    Incision (eg, osteomyelitis or bone abscess), leg or ankle

**27610**    Arthrotomy, ankle, including exploration, drainage, or removal of foreign body

**27612**    Arthrotomy, posterior capsular release, ankle, with or without Achilles tendon lengthening

(See also 27685)

## Excision

**27613**    Biopsy, soft tissue of leg or ankle area; superficial

**27614**        deep (subfascial or intramuscular)

(For needle biopsy of soft tissue, use 20206)

▲ **27615**    Radical resection of tumor (eg, sarcoma), soft tissue of leg or ankle area; less than 5 cm

▲ **27616**        5 cm or greater

►(For radical resection of tumor[s] of cutaneous origin [eg, melanoma], see 11600-11606)◄

**27618**    Excision, tumor, soft tissue of leg or ankle area, subcutaneous; less than 3 cm

# **27632**        3 cm or greater

►(For excision of benign lesions of cutaneous origin [eg, sebaceous cyst], see 11400-11406)◄

**27619**    Excision, tumor, soft tissue of leg or ankle area, subfascial (eg, intramuscular); less than 5 cm

# **27634**        5 cm or greater

**27620**    Arthrotomy, ankle, with joint exploration, with or without biopsy, with or without removal of loose or foreign body

**27625**    Arthrotomy, with synovectomy, ankle;

**27626**        including tenosynovectomy

**27630**    Excision of lesion of tendon sheath or capsule (eg, cyst or ganglion), leg and/or ankle

**27632**    Code is out of numerical sequence. See 27613-27647

**27634**    Code is out of numerical sequence. See 27613-27647

**27635**    Excision or curettage of bone cyst or benign tumor, tibia or fibula;

**27637**        with autograft (includes obtaining graft)

**27638**        with allograft

**27640**    Partial excision (craterization, saucerization, or diaphysectomy), bone (eg, osteomyelitis); tibia

(For exostosis excision, use 27635)

**27641**        fibula

(For exostosis excision, use 27635)

**27645**    Radical resection of tumor; tibia

**27646**        fibula

**27647**        talus or calcaneus

## Introduction or Removal

**27648**    Injection procedure for ankle arthrography

(For radiological supervision and interpretation, use 73615. Do not report 77002 in conjunction with 73615)

(For ankle arthroscopy, see 29894-29898)

## Repair, Revision, and/or Reconstruction

**27650**    Repair, primary, open or percutaneous, ruptured Achilles tendon;

**27652**        with graft (includes obtaining graft)

**27654**    Repair, secondary, Achilles tendon, with or without graft

**27656**    Repair, fascial defect of leg

**27658**    Repair, flexor tendon, leg; primary, without graft, each tendon

**27659**        secondary, with or without graft, each tendon

**27664**    Repair, extensor tendon, leg; primary, without graft, each tendon

**27665**        secondary, with or without graft, each tendon

**27675**    Repair, dislocating peroneal tendons; without fibular osteotomy

**27676**        with fibular osteotomy

**27680**    Tenolysis, flexor or extensor tendon, leg and/or ankle; single, each tendon

**27681**        multiple tendons (through separate incision[s])

**27685**    Lengthening or shortening of tendon, leg or ankle; single tendon (separate procedure)

**27686**        multiple tendons (through same incision), each

---

27687    Gastrocnemius recession (eg, Strayer procedure)

(Toe extensors are considered as a group to be a single tendon when transplanted into midfoot)

27690    Transfer or transplant of single tendon (with muscle redirection or rerouting); superficial (eg, anterior tibial extensors into midfoot)

27691        deep (eg, anterior tibial or posterior tibial through interosseous space, flexor digitorum longus, flexor hallucis longus, or peroneal tendon to midfoot or hindfoot)

+ 27692        each additional tendon (List separately in addition to code for primary procedure)

(Use 27692 in conjunction with 27690, 27691)

27695    Repair, primary, disrupted ligament, ankle; collateral

27696        both collateral ligaments

27698    Repair, secondary, disrupted ligament, ankle, collateral (eg, Watson-Jones procedure)

27700    Arthroplasty, ankle;

27702        with implant (total ankle)

27703        revision, total ankle

27704    Removal of ankle implant

27705    Osteotomy; tibia

27707        fibula

27709        tibia and fibula

27712        multiple, with realignment on intramedullary rod (eg, Sofield type procedure)

(For osteotomy to correct genu varus [bowleg] or genu valgus [knock-knee], see 27455-27457)

27715    Osteoplasty, tibia and fibula, lengthening or shortening

27720    Repair of nonunion or malunion, tibia; without graft, (eg, compression technique)

27722        with sliding graft

27724        with iliac or other autograft (includes obtaining graft)

27725        by synostosis, with fibula, any method

27726    Repair of fibula nonunion and/or malunion with internal fixation

(Do not report 27726 in conjunction with 27707)

27727    Repair of congenital pseudarthrosis, tibia

27730    Arrest, epiphyseal (epiphysiodesis), open; distal tibia

27732        distal fibula

27734        distal tibia and fibula

27740    Arrest, epiphyseal (epiphysiodesis), any method, combined, proximal and distal tibia and fibula;

27742        and distal femur

(For epiphyseal arrest of proximal tibia and fibula, use 27477)

27745    Prophylactic treatment (nailing, pinning, plating or wiring) with or without methylmethacrylate, tibia

## Fracture and/or Dislocation

27750    Closed treatment of tibial shaft fracture (with or without fibular fracture); without manipulation

27752        with manipulation, with or without skeletal traction

27756    Percutaneous skeletal fixation of tibial shaft fracture (with or without fibular fracture) (eg, pins or screws)

27758    Open treatment of tibial shaft fracture (with or without fibular fracture), with plate/screws, with or without cerclage

27759    Treatment of tibial shaft fracture (with or without fibular fracture) by intramedullary implant, with or without interlocking screws and/or cerclage

27760    Closed treatment of medial malleolus fracture; without manipulation

27762        with manipulation, with or without skin or skeletal traction

27766    Open treatment of medial malleolus fracture, includes internal fixation, when performed

27767    Closed treatment of posterior malleolus fracture; without manipulation

27768        with manipulation

27769    Open treatment of posterior malleolus fracture, includes internal fixation, when performed

(Do not report 27767-27769 in conjunction with 27808-27823)

27780    Closed treatment of proximal fibula or shaft fracture; without manipulation

27781        with manipulation

27784    Open treatment of proximal fibula or shaft fracture, includes internal fixation, when performed

27786    Closed treatment of distal fibular fracture (lateral malleolus); without manipulation

27788        with manipulation

27792    Open treatment of distal fibular fracture (lateral malleolus), includes internal fixation, when performed

(For treatment of tibia and fibula shaft fractures, see 27750-27759)

27808    Closed treatment of bimalleolar ankle fracture (eg, lateral and medial malleoli, or lateral and posterior malleoli or medial and posterior malleoli); without manipulation

27810        with manipulation

27814    Open treatment of bimalleolar ankle fracture (eg, lateral and medial malleoli, or lateral and posterior malleoli, or medial and posterior malleoli), includes internal fixation, when performed

**Musculoskeletal**

**Musculoskeletal**

**27816** Closed treatment of trimalleolar ankle fracture; without manipulation

**27818**  with manipulation

**27822** Open treatment of trimalleolar ankle fracture, includes internal fixation, when performed, medial and/or lateral malleolus; without fixation of posterior lip

**27823**  with fixation of posterior lip

**27824** Closed treatment of fracture of weight bearing articular portion of distal tibia (eg, pilon or tibial plafond), with or without anesthesia; without manipulation

**27825**  with skeletal traction and/or requiring manipulation

**27826** Open treatment of fracture of weight bearing articular surface/portion of distal tibia (eg, pilon or tibial plafond), with internal fixation, when performed; of fibula only

**27827**  of tibia only

**27828**  of both tibia and fibula

**27829** Open treatment of distal tibiofibular joint (syndesmosis) disruption, includes internal fixation, when performed

**27830** Closed treatment of proximal tibiofibular joint dislocation; without anesthesia

**27831**  requiring anesthesia

**27832** Open treatment of proximal tibiofibular joint dislocation, includes internal fixation, when performed, or with excision of proximal fibula

**27840** Closed treatment of ankle dislocation; without anesthesia

**27842**  requiring anesthesia, with or without percutaneous skeletal fixation

**27846** Open treatment of ankle dislocation, with or without percutaneous skeletal fixation; without repair or internal fixation

**27848**  with repair or internal or external fixation

(For surgical or diagnostic arthroscopic procedures, see 29894-29898)

## Manipulation

**27860** Manipulation of ankle under general anesthesia (includes application of traction or other fixation apparatus)

## Arthrodesis

**27870** Arthrodesis, ankle, open

(For arthroscopic ankle arthrodesis, use 29899)

**27871** Arthrodesis, tibiofibular joint, proximal or distal

## Amputation

**27880** Amputation, leg, through tibia and fibula;

**27881**  with immediate fitting technique including application of first cast

**27882**  open, circular (guillotine)

**27884**  secondary closure or scar revision

**27886**  re-amputation

**27888** Amputation, ankle, through malleoli of tibia and fibula (eg, Syme, Pirogoff type procedures), with plastic closure and resection of nerves

**27889** Ankle disarticulation

## Other Procedures

**27892** Decompression fasciotomy, leg; anterior and/or lateral compartments only, with debridement of nonviable muscle and/or nerve

(For decompression fasciotomy of the leg without debridement, use 27600)

**27893**  posterior compartment(s) only, with debridement of nonviable muscle and/or nerve

(For decompression fasciotomy of the leg without debridement, use 27601)

**27894**  anterior and/or lateral, and posterior compartment(s), with debridement of nonviable muscle and/or nerve

(For decompression fasciotomy of the leg without debridement, use 27602)

**27899** Unlisted procedure, leg or ankle

# Foot and Toes

## Incision

(For incision and drainage procedures, superficial, see 10040-10160)

**28001** Incision and drainage, bursa, foot

**28002** Incision and drainage below fascia, with or without tendon sheath involvement, foot; single bursal space

**28003**  multiple areas

**28005** Incision, bone cortex (eg, osteomyelitis or bone abscess), foot

**28008** Fasciotomy, foot and/or toe

(See also 28060, 28062, 28250)

**28010** Tenotomy, percutaneous, toe; single tendon

**28011**  multiple tendons

(For open tenotomy, see 28230-28234)

**28020** Arthrotomy, including exploration, drainage, or removal of loose or foreign body; intertarsal or tarsometatarsal joint

**28022**  metatarsophalangeal joint

**28024**  interphalangeal joint

**28035** Release, tarsal tunnel (posterior tibial nerve decompression)

(For other nerve entrapments, see 64704, 64722)

## Excision

28039    Code is out of numerical sequence. See 28043-28175

28041    Code is out of numerical sequence. See 28043-28175

28043    Excision, tumor, soft tissue of foot or toe, subcutaneous; less than 1.5 cm

\# 28039        1.5 cm or greater

►(For excision of benign lesions of cutaneous origin [eg, sebaceous cyst], see 11420-11426)◄

28045    Excision, tumor, soft tissue of foot or toe, subfascial (eg, intramuscular); less than 1.5 cm

\# 28041        1.5 cm or greater

▲ 28046    Radical resection of tumor (eg, sarcoma), soft tissue of foot or toe; less than 3 cm

▲ 28047        3 cm or greater

►(For radical resection of tumor[s] of cutaneous origin [eg, melanoma], see 11620-11626)◄

28050    Arthrotomy with biopsy; intertarsal or tarsometatarsal joint

28052        metatarsophalangeal joint

28054        interphalangeal joint

28055    Neurectomy, intrinsic musculature of foot

28060    Fasciectomy, plantar fascia; partial (separate procedure)

28062        radical (separate procedure)

(For plantar fasciotomy, see 28008, 28250)

28070    Synovectomy; intertarsal or tarsometatarsal joint, each

28072        metatarsophalangeal joint, each

28080    Excision, interdigital (Morton) neuroma, single, each

28086    Synovectomy, tendon sheath, foot; flexor

28088        extensor

28090    Excision of lesion, tendon, tendon sheath, or capsule (including synovectomy) (eg, cyst or ganglion); foot

28092        toe(s), each

28100    Excision or curettage of bone cyst or benign tumor, talus or calcaneus;

28102        with iliac or other autograft (includes obtaining graft)

28103        with allograft

28104    Excision or curettage of bone cyst or benign tumor, tarsal or metatarsal, except talus or calcaneus;

28106        with iliac or other autograft (includes obtaining graft)

28107        with allograft

28108    Excision or curettage of bone cyst or benign tumor, phalanges of foot

(For ostectomy, partial (eg, hallux valgus, Silver type procedure), use 28290)

28110    Ostectomy, partial excision, fifth metatarsal head (bunionette) (separate procedure)

28111    Ostectomy, complete excision; first metatarsal head

28112        other metatarsal head (second, third or fourth)

28113        fifth metatarsal head

28114        all metatarsal heads, with partial proximal phalangectomy, excluding first metatarsal (eg, Clayton type procedure)

28116    Ostectomy, excision of tarsal coalition

28118    Ostectomy, calcaneus;

28119        for spur, with or without plantar fascial release

28120    Partial excision (craterization, saucerization, sequestrectomy, or diaphysectomy) bone (eg, osteomyelitis or bossing); talus or calcaneus

28122        tarsal or metatarsal bone, except talus or calcaneus

(For partial excision of talus or calcaneus, use 28120)

(For cheilectomy for hallux rigidus, use 28289)

28124        phalanx of toe

28126    Resection, partial or complete, phalangeal base, each toe

28130    Talectomy (astragalectomy)

(For calcanectomy, use 28118)

28140    Metatarsectomy

28150    Phalangectomy, toe, each toe

28153    Resection, condyle(s), distal end of phalanx, each toe

28160    Hemiphalangectomy or interphalangeal joint excision, toe, proximal end of phalanx, each

28171    Radical resection of tumor; tarsal (except talus or calcaneus)

28173        metatarsal

28175        phalanx of toe

(For talus or calcaneus, use 27647)

## Introduction or Removal

28190    Removal of foreign body, foot; subcutaneous

28192        deep

28193        complicated

## Repair, Revision, and/or Reconstruction

28200    Repair, tendon, flexor, foot; primary or secondary, without free graft, each tendon

28202        secondary with free graft, each tendon (includes obtaining graft)

28208    Repair, tendon, extensor, foot; primary or secondary, each tendon

Musculoskeletal

**28210**        secondary with free graft, each tendon (includes obtaining graft)

**28220**   Tenolysis, flexor, foot; single tendon

**28222**        multiple tendons

**28225**   Tenolysis, extensor, foot; single tendon

**28226**        multiple tendons

**28230**   Tenotomy, open, tendon flexor; foot, single or multiple tendon(s) (separate procedure)

**28232**        toe, single tendon (separate procedure)

**28234**   Tenotomy, open, extensor, foot or toe, each tendon

(For tendon transfer to midfoot or hindfoot, see 27690, 27691)

**28238**   Reconstruction (advancement), posterior tibial tendon with excision of accessory tarsal navicular bone (eg, Kidner type procedure)

(For subcutaneous tenotomy, see 28010, 28011)

(For transfer or transplant of tendon with muscle redirection or rerouting, see 27690-27692)

(For extensor hallucis longus transfer with great toe IP fusion (Jones procedure), use 28760)

**28240**   Tenotomy, lengthening, or release, abductor hallucis muscle

**28250**   Division of plantar fascia and muscle (eg, Steindler stripping) (separate procedure)

**28260**   Capsulotomy, midfoot; medial release only (separate procedure)

**28261**        with tendon lengthening

**28262**        extensive, including posterior talotibial capsulotomy and tendon(s) lengthening (eg, resistant clubfoot deformity)

**28264**   Capsulotomy, midtarsal (eg, Heyman type procedure)

**28270**   Capsulotomy; metatarsophalangeal joint, with or without tenorrhaphy, each joint (separate procedure)

**28272**        interphalangeal joint, each joint (separate procedure)

**28280**   Syndactylization, toes (eg, webbing or Kelikian type procedure)

**28285**   Correction, hammertoe (eg, interphalangeal fusion, partial or total phalangectomy)

**28286**   Correction, cock-up fifth toe, with plastic skin closure (eg, Ruiz-Mora type procedure)

**28288**   Ostectomy, partial, exostectomy or condylectomy, metatarsal head, each metatarsal head

**28289**   Hallux rigidus correction with cheilectomy, debridement and capsular release of the first metatarsophalangeal joint

**28290**   Correction, hallux valgus (bunion), with or without sesamoidectomy; simple exostectomy (eg, Silver type procedure)

**28292**   Keller, McBride, or Mayo type procedure

**28293**   resection of joint with implant

**28294**   with tendon transplants (eg, Joplin type procedure)

**28296**   with metatarsal osteotomy (eg, Mitchell, Chevron, or concentric type procedures)

**28297**   Lapidus-type procedure

**28298**   by phalanx osteotomy

**28299**   by double osteotomy

**28300**   Osteotomy; calcaneus (eg, Dwyer or Chambers type procedure), with or without internal fixation

**28302**        talus

**28304**   Osteotomy, tarsal bones, other than calcaneus or talus;

**28305**        with autograft (includes obtaining graft) (eg, Fowler type)

**28306**   Osteotomy, with or without lengthening, shortening or angular correction, metatarsal; first metatarsal

**28307**        first metatarsal with autograft (other than first toe)

**28308**        other than first metatarsal, each

**28309**        multiple (eg, Swanson type cavus foot procedure)

**28310**   Osteotomy, shortening, angular or rotational correction; proximal phalanx, first toe (separate procedure)

**28312**        other phalanges, any toe

**28313**   Reconstruction, angular deformity of toe, soft tissue procedures only (eg, overlapping second toe, fifth toe, curly toes)

**28315**   Sesamoidectomy, first toe (separate procedure)

**28320**   Repair, nonunion or malunion; tarsal bones

**28322**        metatarsal, with or without bone graft (includes obtaining graft)

**28340**   Reconstruction, toe, macrodactyly; soft tissue resection

**28341**        requiring bone resection

**28344**   Reconstruction, toe(s); polydactyly

**28345**        syndactyly, with or without skin graft(s), each web

**28360**   Reconstruction, cleft foot

## Fracture and/or Dislocation

**28400**   Closed treatment of calcaneal fracture; without manipulation

**28405**        with manipulation

**28406**   Percutaneous skeletal fixation of calcaneal fracture, with manipulation

**28415**   Open treatment of calcaneal fracture, includes internal fixation, when performed;

**28420**        with primary iliac or other autogenous bone graft (includes obtaining graft)

**28430**   Closed treatment of talus fracture; without manipulation

**28435**        with manipulation

**28436**   Percutaneous skeletal fixation of talus fracture, with manipulation

**28445**   Open treatment of talus fracture, includes internal fixation, when performed

**28446**   Open osteochondral autograft, talus (includes obtaining graft[s])

(Do not report 28446 in conjunction with 27705, 27707)

(For arthroscopic osteochondral talus graft, use 29892)

(For open osteochondral allograft or repairs with industrial grafts, use 28899)

**28450**   Treatment of tarsal bone fracture (except talus and calcaneus); without manipulation, each

**28455**        with manipulation, each

**28456**   Percutaneous skeletal fixation of tarsal bone fracture (except talus and calcaneus), with manipulation, each

**28465**   Open treatment of tarsal bone fracture (except talus and calcaneus), includes internal fixation, when performed, each

**28470**   Closed treatment of metatarsal fracture; without manipulation, each

**28475**        with manipulation, each

**28476**   Percutaneous skeletal fixation of metatarsal fracture, with manipulation, each

**28485**   Open treatment of metatarsal fracture, includes internal fixation, when performed, each

**28490**   Closed treatment of fracture great toe, phalanx or phalanges; without manipulation

**28495**        with manipulation

**28496**   Percutaneous skeletal fixation of fracture great toe, phalanx or phalanges, with manipulation

**28505**   Open treatment of fracture, great toe, phalanx or phalanges, includes internal fixation, when performed

**28510**   Closed treatment of fracture, phalanx or phalanges, other than great toe; without manipulation, each

**28515**        with manipulation, each

**28525**   Open treatment of fracture, phalanx or phalanges, other than great toe, includes internal fixation, when performed, each

**28530**   Closed treatment of sesamoid fracture

**28531**   Open treatment of sesamoid fracture, with or without internal fixation

**28540**   Closed treatment of tarsal bone dislocation, other than talotarsal; without anesthesia

**28545**        requiring anesthesia

**28546**   Percutaneous skeletal fixation of tarsal bone dislocation, other than talotarsal, with manipulation

**28555**   Open treatment of tarsal bone dislocation, includes internal fixation, when performed

**28570**   Closed treatment of talotarsal joint dislocation; without anesthesia

**28575**        requiring anesthesia

**28576**   Percutaneous skeletal fixation of talotarsal joint dislocation, with manipulation

**28585**   Open treatment of talotarsal joint dislocation, includes internal fixation, when performed

**28600**   Closed treatment of tarsometatarsal joint dislocation; without anesthesia

**28605**        requiring anesthesia

**28606**   Percutaneous skeletal fixation of tarsometatarsal joint dislocation, with manipulation

**28615**   Open treatment of tarsometatarsal joint dislocation, includes internal fixation, when performed

**28630**   Closed treatment of metatarsophalangeal joint dislocation; without anesthesia

**28635**        requiring anesthesia

**28636**   Percutaneous skeletal fixation of metatarsophalangeal joint dislocation, with manipulation

**28645**   Open treatment of metatarsophalangeal joint dislocation, includes internal fixation, when performed

**28660**   Closed treatment of interphalangeal joint dislocation; without anesthesia

**28665**        requiring anesthesia

**28666**   Percutaneous skeletal fixation of interphalangeal joint dislocation, with manipulation

**28675**   Open treatment of interphalangeal joint dislocation, includes internal fixation, when performed

## Arthrodesis

**28705**   Arthrodesis; pantalar

**28715**        triple

**28725**        subtalar

**28730**   Arthrodesis, midtarsal or tarsometatarsal, multiple or transverse;

**28735**        with osteotomy (eg, flatfoot correction)

**28737**   Arthrodesis, with tendon lengthening and advancement, midtarsal, tarsal navicular-cuneiform (eg, Miller type procedure)

**28740**   Arthrodesis, midtarsal or tarsometatarsal, single joint

**28750**   Arthrodesis, great toe; metatarsophalangeal joint

**28755**        interphalangeal joint

**Musculoskeletal**

**Musculoskeletal**

28760  Arthrodesis, with extensor hallucis longus transfer to first metatarsal neck, great toe, interphalangeal joint (eg, Jones type procedure)

(For hammertoe operation or interphalangeal fusion, use 28285)

## Amputation

28800  Amputation, foot; midtarsal (eg, Chopart type procedure)

28805      transmetatarsal

28810  Amputation, metatarsal, with toe, single

28820  Amputation, toe; metatarsophalangeal joint

28825      interphalangeal joint

(For amputation of tuft of distal phalanx, use 11752)

## Other Procedures

28890  Extracorporeal shock wave, high energy, performed by a physician or other qualified health care professional, requiring anesthesia other than local, including ultrasound guidance, involving the plantar fascia

(For extracorporeal shock wave therapy involving musculoskeletal system not otherwise specified, see 0019T, 0101T, 0102T)

(For extracorporeal shock wave therapy involving integumentary system not otherwise specified, see 0299T, 0300T)

(Do not report 28890 in conjunction with 0299T, 0300T when treating the same area)

28899  Unlisted procedure, foot or toes

## Application of Casts and Strapping

The listed procedures apply when the cast application or strapping is a replacement procedure used during or after the period of follow-up care, or when the cast application or strapping is an initial service performed without a restorative treatment or procedure(s) to stabilize or protect a fracture, injury, or dislocation and/or to afford comfort to a patient. Restorative treatment or procedure(s) rendered by another individual following the application of the initial cast/splint/strap may be reported with a treatment of fracture and/or dislocation code.

An individual who applies the initial cast, strap, or splint and also assumes all of the subsequent fracture, dislocation, or injury care cannot use the application of casts and strapping codes as an initial service, since the first cast/splint or strap application is included in the treatment of fracture and/or dislocation codes. (See notes under Musculoskeletal System, page 70.) A temporary cast/splint/strap is not considered to be part of the preoperative care, and the use of the modifier 56 is not applicable. Additional evaluation and management services are reportable only if significant identifiable further services are provided at the time of the cast application or strapping.

If cast application or strapping is provided as an initial service (eg, casting of a sprained ankle or knee) in which no other procedure or treatment (eg, surgical repair, reduction of a fracture, or joint dislocation) is performed or is expected to be performed by an individual rendering the initial care only, use the casting, strapping, and/or supply code (99070) in addition to an evaluation and management code as appropriate.

Listed procedures include removal of cast or strapping.

(For orthotics management and training, see 97760-97762)

## Body and Upper Extremity

### Casts

29000  Application of halo type body cast (see 20661-20663 for insertion)

29010  Application of Risser jacket, localizer, body; only

29015      including head

29020  Application of turnbuckle jacket, body; only

29025      including head

29035  Application of body cast, shoulder to hips;

29040      including head, Minerva type

29044      including 1 thigh

29046      including both thighs

29049  Application, cast; figure-of-eight

29055      shoulder spica

29058      plaster Velpeau

29065      shoulder to hand (long arm)

29075      elbow to finger (short arm)

29085      hand and lower forearm (gauntlet)

29086      finger (eg, contracture)

### Splints

29105  Application of long arm splint (shoulder to hand)

29125  Application of short arm splint (forearm to hand); static

29126      dynamic

29130  Application of finger splint; static

29131      dynamic

### Strapping—Any Age

29200  Strapping; thorax

(29220 has been deleted)

(To report low back strapping, use 29799)

29240      shoulder (eg, Velpeau)

| 29260 | elbow or wrist |
|---|---|
| 29280 | hand or finger |

## Lower Extremity

### Casts

| 29305 | Application of hip spica cast; 1 leg |
|---|---|
| 29325 | 1 and one-half spica or both legs |

(For hip spica (body) cast, including thighs only, use 29046)

| 29345 | Application of long leg cast (thigh to toes); |
|---|---|
| 29355 | walker or ambulatory type |
| 29358 | Application of long leg cast brace |
| 29365 | Application of cylinder cast (thigh to ankle) |
| 29405 | Application of short leg cast (below knee to toes); |
| 29425 | walking or ambulatory type |
| 29435 | Application of patellar tendon bearing (PTB) cast |
| 29440 | Adding walker to previously applied cast |
| 29445 | Application of rigid total contact leg cast |
| 29450 | Application of clubfoot cast with molding or manipulation, long or short leg |

(To report bilateral procedure, use 29450 with modifier 50)

### Splints

| 29505 | Application of long leg splint (thigh to ankle or toes) |
|---|---|
| 29515 | Application of short leg splint (calf to foot) |

### Strapping—Any Age

| 29520 | Strapping; hip |
|---|---|
| 29530 | knee |
| 29540 | ankle and/or foot |

(Do not report 29540 in conjunction with 29581, 29582)

| 29550 | toes |
|---|---|
| 29580 | Unna boot |

(Do not report 29580 in conjunction with 29581, 29582)

| 29581 | Application of multi-layer compression system; leg (below knee), including ankle and foot |
|---|---|

►(Do not report 29581 in conjunction with 29540, 29580, 29582, 36475, 36476, 36478, 36479)◄

| 29582 | thigh and leg, including ankle and foot, when performed |
|---|---|

►(Do not report 29582 in conjunction with 29540, 29580, 29581, 36475, 36476, 36478, 36479)◄

| 29583 | upper arm and forearm |
|---|---|

(Do not report 29583 in conjunction with 29584)

| 29584 | upper arm, forearm, hand, and fingers |
|---|---|

(Do not report 29584 in conjunction with 29583)

(29590 has been deleted)

## Removal or Repair

Codes for cast removals should be employed only for casts applied by another individual.

| 29700 | Removal or bivalving; gauntlet, boot or body cast |
|---|---|
| 29705 | full arm or full leg cast |
| 29710 | shoulder or hip spica, Minerva, or Risser jacket, etc. |
| 29715 | turnbuckle jacket |
| 29720 | Repair of spica, body cast or jacket |
| 29730 | Windowing of cast |
| 29740 | Wedging of cast (except clubfoot casts) |
| 29750 | Wedging of clubfoot cast |

(To report bilateral procedure, use 29750 with modifier 50)

## Other Procedures

| 29799 | Unlisted procedure, casting or strapping |
|---|---|

## Endoscopy/Arthroscopy

Surgical endoscopy/arthroscopy always includes a diagnostic endoscopy/arthroscopy.

When arthroscopy is performed in conjunction with arthrotomy, add modifier 51.

| 29800 | Arthroscopy, temporomandibular joint, diagnostic, with or without synovial biopsy (separate procedure) |
|---|---|
| 29804 | Arthroscopy, temporomandibular joint, surgical |

(For open procedure, use 21010)

| 29805 | Arthroscopy, shoulder, diagnostic, with or without synovial biopsy (separate procedure) |
|---|---|

(For open procedure, see 23065-23066, 23100-23101)

| 29806 | Arthroscopy, shoulder, surgical; capsulorrhaphy |
|---|---|

(For open procedure, see 23450-23466)

(To report thermal capsulorrhaphy, use 29999)

| 29807 | repair of SLAP lesion |
|---|---|
| 29819 | with removal of loose body or foreign body |

(For open procedure, see 23040-23044, 23107)

| 29820 | synovectomy, partial |
|---|---|

(For open procedure, see 23105)

**Musculoskeletal**

**Musculoskeletal**

**29821**  synovectomy, complete

(For open procedure, see 23105)

**29822**  debridement, limited

(For open procedure, see specific open shoulder procedure performed)

**29823**  debridement, extensive

(For open procedure, see specific open shoulder procedure performed)

**29824**  distal claviculectomy including distal articular surface (Mumford procedure)

(For open procedure, use 23120)

**29825**  with lysis and resection of adhesions, with or without manipulation

(For open procedure, see specific open shoulder procedure performed)

**+ 29826**  decompression of subacromial space with partial acromioplasty, with coracoacromial ligament (ie, arch) release, when performed (List separately in addition to code for primary procedure)

(For open procedure, use 23130 or 23415)

(Use 29826 in conjunction with 29806-29825, 29827, 29828)

**29827**  with rotator cuff repair

(For open or mini-open rotator cuff repair, use 23412)

(When arthroscopic distal clavicle resection is performed at the same setting, use 29824 and append modifier 51)

**29828**  biceps tenodesis

(Do not report 29828 in conjunction with 29805, 29820, 29822)

(For open biceps tenodesis, use 23430)

**29830**  Arthroscopy, elbow, diagnostic, with or without synovial biopsy (separate procedure)

**29834**  Arthroscopy, elbow, surgical; with removal of loose body or foreign body

**29835**  synovectomy, partial

**29836**  synovectomy, complete

**29837**  debridement, limited

**29838**  debridement, extensive

**29840**  Arthroscopy, wrist, diagnostic, with or without synovial biopsy (separate procedure)

**29843**  Arthroscopy, wrist, surgical; for infection, lavage and drainage

**29844**  synovectomy, partial

**29845**  synovectomy, complete

**29846**  excision and/or repair of triangular fibrocartilage and/or joint debridement

**29847**  internal fixation for fracture or instability

**29848**  Endoscopy, wrist, surgical, with release of transverse carpal ligament

(For open procedure, use 64721)

**29850**  Arthroscopically aided treatment of intercondylar spine(s) and/or tuberosity fracture(s) of the knee, with or without manipulation; without internal or external fixation (includes arthroscopy)

**29851**  with internal or external fixation (includes arthroscopy)

(For bone graft, use 20900, 20902)

**29855**  Arthroscopically aided treatment of tibial fracture, proximal (plateau); unicondylar, includes internal fixation, when performed (includes arthroscopy)

**29856**  bicondylar, includes internal fixation, when performed (includes arthroscopy)

(For bone graft, use 20900, 20902)

**29860**  Arthroscopy, hip, diagnostic with or without synovial biopsy (separate procedure)

**29861**  Arthroscopy, hip, surgical; with removal of loose body or foreign body

**29862**  with debridement/shaving of articular cartilage (chondroplasty), abrasion arthroplasty, and/or resection of labrum

**29863**  with synovectomy

**# 29914**  with femoroplasty (ie, treatment of cam lesion)

**# 29915**  with acetabuloplasty (ie, treatment of pincer lesion)

(Do not report 29914, 29915 in conjunction with 29862, 29863)

**# 29916**  with labral repair

(Do not report 29916 in conjunction with 29915, 29862, 29863)

**29866**  Arthroscopy, knee, surgical; osteochondral autograft(s) (eg, mosaicplasty) (includes harvesting of the autograft[s])

(Do not report 29866 in conjunction with 29870, 29871, 29875, 29884 when performed at the same session and/or 29874, 29877, 29879, 29885-29887 when performed in the same compartment)

(For open osteochondral autograft of knee, use 27416)

**29867**  osteochondral allograft (eg, mosaicplasty)

(Do not report 29867 in conjunction with 27570, 29870, 29871, 29875, 29884 when performed at the same session and/or 29874, 29877, 29879, 29885-29887 when performed in the same compartment)

(Do not report 29867 in conjunction with 27415)

**29868**  meniscal transplantation (includes arthrotomy for meniscal insertion), medial or lateral

(Do not report 29868 in conjunction with 29870, 29871, 29875, 29880, 29883, 29884 when performed at the same session or 29874, 29877, 29881, 29882 when performed in the same compartment)

⊙ =Moderate sedation  ✚ =Add-on code  ∕ =FDA approval pending  # =Resequenced code  ○ =Recycled/reinstated code

**29870**   Arthroscopy, knee, diagnostic, with or without synovial biopsy (separate procedure)

(For open autologous chondrocyte implantation of the knee, use 27412)

**29871**   Arthroscopy, knee, surgical; for infection, lavage and drainage

(For implantation of osteochondral graft for treatment of articular surface defect, see 27412, 27415, 29866, 29867)

**29873**       with lateral release

(For open lateral release, use 27425)

**29874**       for removal of loose body or foreign body (eg, osteochondritis dissecans fragmentation, chondral fragmentation)

**29875**       synovectomy, limited (eg, plica or shelf resection) (separate procedure)

**29876**       synovectomy, major, 2 or more compartments (eg, medial or lateral)

**29877**       debridement/shaving of articular cartilage (chondroplasty)

(When performed with arthroscopic meniscectomy, see 29880 or 29881)

**29879**       abrasion arthroplasty (includes chondroplasty where necessary) or multiple drilling or microfracture

**29880**       with meniscectomy (medial AND lateral, including any meniscal shaving) including debridement/shaving of articular cartilage (chondroplasty), same or separate compartment(s), when performed

**29881**       with meniscectomy (medial OR lateral, including any meniscal shaving) including debridement/shaving of articular cartilage (chondroplasty), same or separate compartment(s), when performed

**29882**       with meniscus repair (medial OR lateral)

**29883**       with meniscus repair (medial AND lateral)

(For meniscal transplantation, medial or lateral, knee, use 29868)

**29884**       with lysis of adhesions, with or without manipulation (separate procedure)

**29885**       drilling for osteochondritis dissecans with bone grafting, with or without internal fixation (including debridement of base of lesion)

**29886**       drilling for intact osteochondritis dissecans lesion

**29887**       drilling for intact osteochondritis dissecans lesion with internal fixation

**29888**   Arthroscopically aided anterior cruciate ligament repair/augmentation or reconstruction

**29889**   Arthroscopically aided posterior cruciate ligament repair/augmentation or reconstruction

(Procedures 29888 and 29889 should not be used with reconstruction procedures 27427-27429)

**29891**   Arthroscopy, ankle, surgical, excision of osteochondral defect of talus and/or tibia, including drilling of the defect

**29892**   Arthroscopically aided repair of large osteochondritis dissecans lesion, talar dome fracture, or tibial plafond fracture, with or without internal fixation (includes arthroscopy)

**29893**   Endoscopic plantar fasciotomy

**29894**   Arthroscopy, ankle (tibiotalar and fibulotalar joints), surgical; with removal of loose body or foreign body

**29895**       synovectomy, partial

**29897**       debridement, limited

**29898**       debridement, extensive

**29899**       with ankle arthrodesis

(For open ankle arthrodesis, use 27870)

**29900**   Arthroscopy, metacarpophalangeal joint, diagnostic, includes synovial biopsy

(Do not report 29900 with 29901, 29902)

**29901**   Arthroscopy, metacarpophalangeal joint, surgical; with debridement

**29902**       with reduction of displaced ulnar collateral ligament (eg, Stener lesion)

**29904**   Arthroscopy, subtalar joint, surgical; with removal of loose body or foreign body

**29905**       with synovectomy

**29906**       with debridement

**29907**       with subtalar arthrodesis

**29914**   Code 29914 is out of numerical sequence. See 29800-29999

**29915**   Code 29915 is out of numerical sequence. See 29800-29999

**29916**   Code 29916 is out of numerical sequence. See 29800-29999

**29999**   Unlisted procedure, arthroscopy

**Musculoskeletal**

# Respiratory System

## Nose

### Incision

**30000**   Drainage abscess or hematoma, nasal, internal approach

(For external approach, see 10060, 10140)

**30020**   Drainage abscess or hematoma, nasal septum

(For lateral rhinotomy, see specific application [eg, 30118, 30320])

### Excision

**30100**   Biopsy, intranasal

(For biopsy skin of nose, see 11100, 11101)

**30110**   Excision, nasal polyp(s), simple

(30110 would normally be completed in an office setting)

(To report bilateral procedure, use 30110 with modifier 50)

**30115**   Excision, nasal polyp(s), extensive

(30115 would normally require the facilities available in a hospital setting)

(To report bilateral procedure, use 30115 with modifier 50)

**30117**   Excision or destruction (eg, laser), intranasal lesion; internal approach

**30118**       external approach (lateral rhinotomy)

**30120**   Excision or surgical planing of skin of nose for rhinophyma

**30124**   Excision dermoid cyst, nose; simple, skin, subcutaneous

**30125**       complex, under bone or cartilage

**30130**   Excision inferior turbinate, partial or complete, any method

(For excision of superior or middle turbinate, use 30999)

**30140**   Submucous resection inferior turbinate, partial or complete, any method

(Do not report 30130 or 30140 in conjunction with 30801, 30802, 30930)

(For submucous resection of superior or middle turbinate, use 30999)

(For endoscopic resection of concha bullosa of middle turbinate, use 31240)

(For submucous resection of nasal septum, use 30520)

**30150**   Rhinectomy; partial

**30160**       total

▶(For closure and/or reconstruction, primary or delayed, see **Integumentary System,** 13151-13160, 14060-14302, 15120, 15121, 15260, 15261, 15760, 20900-20912)◀

### Introduction

**30200**   Injection into turbinate(s), therapeutic

**30210**   Displacement therapy (Proetz type)

**30220**   Insertion, nasal septal prosthesis (button)

### Removal of Foreign Body

**30300**   Removal foreign body, intranasal; office type procedure

**30310**       requiring general anesthesia

**30320**       by lateral rhinotomy

### Repair

(For obtaining tissues for graft, see 20900-20926, 21210)

**30400**   Rhinoplasty, primary; lateral and alar cartilages and/or elevation of nasal tip

▶(For columellar reconstruction, see 13151 et seq)◀

**30410**       complete, external parts including bony pyramid, lateral and alar cartilages, and/or elevation of nasal tip

**30420**       including major septal repair

**30430**   Rhinoplasty, secondary; minor revision (small amount of nasal tip work)

**30435**       intermediate revision (bony work with osteotomies)

**30450**       major revision (nasal tip work and osteotomies)

**30460**   Rhinoplasty for nasal deformity secondary to congenital cleft lip and/or palate, including columellar lengthening; tip only

**30462**       tip, septum, osteotomies

**30465**   Repair of nasal vestibular stenosis (eg, spreader grafting, lateral nasal wall reconstruction)

(30465 excludes obtaining graft. For graft procedure, see 20900-20926, 21210)

(30465 is used to report a bilateral procedure. For unilateral procedure, use modifier 52)

**30520**   Septoplasty or submucous resection, with or without cartilage scoring, contouring or replacement with graft

(For submucous resection of turbinates, use 30140)

**30540**   Repair choanal atresia; intranasal

**30545**       transpalatine

(Do not report modifier 63 in conjunction with 30540, 30545)

**30560**  Lysis intranasal synechia

**30580**  Repair fistula; oromaxillary (combine with 31030 if antrotomy is included)

**30600**      oronasal

**30620**  Septal or other intranasal dermatoplasty (does not include obtaining graft)

**30630**  Repair nasal septal perforations

## Destruction

**30801**  Ablation, soft tissue of inferior turbinates, unilateral or bilateral, any method (eg, electrocautery, radiofrequency ablation, or tissue volume reduction); superficial

(For ablation of superior or middle turbinates, use 30999)

**30802**      intramural (ie, submucosal)

(Do not report 30801 in conjunction with 30802)

(Do not report 30801, 30802, 30930 in conjunction with 30130 or 30140)

(For cautery performed for control of nasal hemorrhage, see 30901-30906)

## Other Procedures

**30901**  Control nasal hemorrhage, anterior, simple (limited cautery and/or packing) any method

(To report bilateral procedure, use 30901 with modifier 50)

**30903**  Control nasal hemorrhage, anterior, complex (extensive cautery and/or packing) any method

(To report bilateral procedure, use 30903 with modifier 50)

**30905**  Control nasal hemorrhage, posterior, with posterior nasal packs and/or cautery, any method; initial

**30906**      subsequent

**30915**  Ligation arteries; ethmoidal

**30920**      internal maxillary artery, transantral

(For ligation external carotid artery, use 37600)

**30930**  Fracture nasal inferior turbinate(s), therapeutic

(Do not report 30801, 30802, 30930 in conjunction with 30130 or 30140)

(For fracture of superior or middle turbinate[s], use 30999)

**30999**  Unlisted procedure, nose

## Accessory Sinuses

### Incision

**31000**  Lavage by cannulation; maxillary sinus (antrum puncture or natural ostium)

(To report bilateral procedure, use 31000 with modifier 50)

**31002**      sphenoid sinus

**31020**  Sinusotomy, maxillary (antrotomy); intranasal

(To report bilateral procedure, use 31020 with modifier 50)

**31030**      radical (Caldwell-Luc) without removal of antrochoanal polyps

(To report bilateral procedure, use 31030 with modifier 50)

**31032**      radical (Caldwell-Luc) with removal of antrochoanal polyps

(To report bilateral procedure, use 31032 with modifier 50)

**31040**  Pterygomaxillary fossa surgery, any approach

(For transantral ligation of internal maxillary artery, use 30920)

**31050**  Sinusotomy, sphenoid, with or without biopsy;

**31051**      with mucosal stripping or removal of polyp(s)

**31070**  Sinusotomy frontal; external, simple (trephine operation)

(For frontal intranasal sinusotomy, use 31276)

**31075**      transorbital, unilateral (for mucocele or osteoma, Lynch type)

**31080**      obliterative without osteoplastic flap, brow incision (includes ablation)

**31081**      obliterative, without osteoplastic flap, coronal incision (includes ablation)

**31084**      obliterative, with osteoplastic flap, brow incision

**31085**      obliterative, with osteoplastic flap, coronal incision

**31086**      nonobliterative, with osteoplastic flap, brow incision

**31087**      nonobliterative, with osteoplastic flap, coronal incision

**31090**  Sinusotomy, unilateral, 3 or more paranasal sinuses (frontal, maxillary, ethmoid, sphenoid)

### Excision

**31200**  Ethmoidectomy; intranasal, anterior

**31201**      intranasal, total

**31205**      extranasal, total

**Respiratory**

**31225**   Maxillectomy; without orbital exenteration

**31230**       with orbital exenteration (en bloc)

(For orbital exenteration only, see 65110 et seq)

(For skin grafts, see 15120 et seq)

## Endoscopy

A surgical sinus endoscopy includes a sinusotomy (when appropriate) and diagnostic endoscopy.

Codes 31295-31297 describe dilation of sinus ostia by displacement of tissue, any method, and include fluoroscopy if performed.

Codes 31233-31297 are used to report unilateral procedures unless otherwise specified.

Codes 31231-31235 for diagnostic evaluation refer to employing a nasal/sinus endoscope to inspect the interior of the nasal cavity and the middle and superior meatus, the turbinates, and the spheno-ethmoid recess. Any time a diagnostic evaluation is performed all these areas would be inspected and a separate code is not reported for each area.

**31231**   Nasal endoscopy, diagnostic, unilateral or bilateral (separate procedure)

**31233**   Nasal/sinus endoscopy, diagnostic with maxillary sinusoscopy (via inferior meatus or canine fossa puncture)

(Do not report 31233 in conjunction with 31295 when performed on the same sinus)

**31235**   Nasal/sinus endoscopy, diagnostic with sphenoid sinusoscopy (via puncture of sphenoidal face or cannulation of ostium)

(Do not report 31235 in conjunction with 31297 when performed on the same sinus)

**31237**   Nasal/sinus endoscopy, surgical; with biopsy, polypectomy or debridement (separate procedure)

**31238**       with control of nasal hemorrhage

**31239**       with dacryocystorhinostomy

**31240**       with concha bullosa resection

(For endoscopic osteomeatal complex [OMC] resection with antrostomy and/or anterior ethmoidectomy, with or without removal of polyp[s], use 31254 and 31256)

(For endoscopic osteomeatal complex [OMC] resection with antrostomy, removal of antral mucosal disease, and/or anterior ethmoidectomy, with or without removal of polyp[s], use 31254 and 31267)

(For endoscopic frontal sinus exploration, osteomeatal complex [OMC] resection and/or anterior ethmoidectomy, with or without removal of polyp[s], use 31254 and 31276)

(For endoscopic frontal sinus exploration, osteomeatal complex [OMC] resection, antrostomy, and/or anterior ethmoidectomy, with or without removal of polyp[s], use 31254, 31256, and 31276)

(For endoscopic nasal diagnostic endoscopy, see 31231-31235)

(For endoscopic osteomeatal complex [OMC] resection, frontal sinus exploration, antrostomy, removal of antral mucosal disease, and/or anterior ethmoidectomy, with or without removal of polyp[s], use 31254, 31267, and 31276)

**31254**   Nasal/sinus endoscopy, surgical; with ethmoidectomy, partial (anterior)

**31255**       with ethmoidectomy, total (anterior and posterior)

**31256**   Nasal/sinus endoscopy, surgical, with maxillary antrostomy;

(For endoscopic anterior and posterior ethmoidectomy [APE] and antrostomy, with or without removal of polyp[s], use 31255 and 31256)

(For endoscopic anterior and posterior ethmoidectomy [APE], antrostomy and removal of antral mucosal disease, with or without removal of polyp[s], use 31255 and 31267)

(For endoscopic anterior and posterior ethmoidectomy [APE], and frontal sinus exploration, with or without removal of polyp[s], use 31255 and 31276)

**31267**       with removal of tissue from maxillary sinus

(Do not report 31256, 31267 in conjunction with 31295 when performed on the same sinus)

(For endoscopic anterior and posterior ethmoidectomy [APE], and frontal sinus exploration and antrostomy, with or without removal of polyp[s], use 31255, 31256, and 31276)

(For endoscopic anterior and posterior ethmoidectomy [APE], frontal sinus exploration, antrostomy, and removal of antral mucosal disease, with or without removal of polyp[s], use 31255, 31267, and 31276)

**31276**   Nasal/sinus endoscopy, surgical with frontal sinus exploration, with or without removal of tissue from frontal sinus

(Do not report 31276 in conjunction with 31296 when performed on the same sinus)

(For endoscopic anterior and posterior ethmoidectomy and sphenoidotomy [APS], with or without removal of polyp[s], use 31255, 31287 or 31288)

(For endoscopic anterior and posterior ethmoidectomy and sphenoidotomy [APS], and antrostomy, with or without removal of polyp[s], use 31255, 31256, and 31287 or 31288)

(For endoscopic anterior and posterior ethmoidectomy and sphenoidotomy [APS], antrostomy and removal of antral mucosal disease, with or without removal of polyp[s], use 31255, 31267, and 31287 or 31288)

(For endoscopic anterior and posterior ethmoidectomy and sphenoidotomy [APS], and frontal sinus exploration with or without removal of polyp[s], use 31255, 31287 or 31288, and 31276)

(For endoscopic anterior and posterior ethmoidectomy and sphenoidotomy [APS], with or without removal of polyp[s], with frontal sinus exploration and antrostomy, use 31255, 31256, 31287 or 31288, and 31276)

(For unilateral endoscopy of 2 or more sinuses, see 31231-31235)

(For endoscopic anterior and posterior ethmoidectomy and sphenoidotomy [APS], frontal sinus exploration, antrostomy and removal of antral mucosal disease, with or without removal of polyp[s], see 31255, 31267, 31287 or 31288 and 31276)

**31287**   Nasal/sinus endoscopy, surgical, with sphenoidotomy;

**31288**       with removal of tissue from the sphenoid sinus

(Do not report 31287, 31288 in conjunction with 31297 when performed on the same sinus)

**31290**   Nasal/sinus endoscopy, surgical, with repair of cerebrospinal fluid leak; ethmoid region

**31291**       sphenoid region

**31292**   Nasal/sinus endoscopy, surgical; with medial or inferior orbital wall decompression

**31293**       with medial orbital wall and inferior orbital wall decompression

**31294**       with optic nerve decompression

**31295**   Nasal/sinus endoscopy, surgical; with dilation of maxillary sinus ostium (eg, balloon dilation), transnasal or via canine fossa

(Do not report 31295 in conjunction with 31233, 31256, 31267 when performed on the same sinus)

**31296**       with dilation of frontal sinus ostium (eg, balloon dilation)

(Do not report 31296 in conjunction with 31276 when performed on the same sinus)

**31297**       with dilation of sphenoid sinus ostium (eg, balloon dilation)

(Do not report 31297 in conjunction with 31235, 31287, 31288 when performed on the same sinus)

## Other Procedures

(For hypophysectomy, transantral or transeptal approach, use 61548)

(For transcranial hypophysectomy, use 61546)

**31299**   Unlisted procedure, accessory sinuses

# Larynx

## Excision

**31300**   Laryngotomy (thyrotomy, laryngofissure); with removal of tumor or laryngocele, cordectomy

**31320**       diagnostic

**31360**   Laryngectomy; total, without radical neck dissection

**31365**       total, with radical neck dissection

**31367**       subtotal supraglottic, without radical neck dissection

**31368**       subtotal supraglottic, with radical neck dissection

**31370**   Partial laryngectomy (hemilaryngectomy); horizontal

**31375**       laterovertical

**31380**       anterovertical

**31382**       antero-latero-vertical

**31390**   Pharyngolaryngectomy, with radical neck dissection; without reconstruction

**31395**       with reconstruction

**31400**   Arytenoidectomy or arytenoidopexy, external approach

(For endoscopic arytenoidectomy, use 31560)

**31420**   Epiglottidectomy

## Introduction

⊘ **31500**   Intubation, endotracheal, emergency procedure

**31502**   Tracheotomy tube change prior to establishment of fistula tract

## Endoscopy

▶For endoscopic procedures, report appropriate endoscopy of each anatomic site examined. Laryngoscopy includes examination of the tongue base, larynx, and hypopharynx. If using operating microscope, telescope, or both, use the applicable code only once per operative session.◀

**31505**   Laryngoscopy, indirect; diagnostic (separate procedure)

**31510**       with biopsy

**31511**       with removal of foreign body

**31512**       with removal of lesion

**31513**       with vocal cord injection

**31515**   Laryngoscopy direct, with or without tracheoscopy; for aspiration

**31520**       diagnostic, newborn

(Do not report modifier 63 in conjunction with 31520)

**31525**       diagnostic, except newborn

**Respiratory**

**Respiratory**

**31526**   diagnostic, with operating microscope or telescope

(Do not report code 69990 in addition to code 31526)

**31527**   with insertion of obturator

**31528**   with dilation, initial

**31529**   with dilation, subsequent

**31530**   Laryngoscopy, direct, operative, with foreign body removal;

**31531**   with operating microscope or telescope

(Do not report code 69990 in addition to code 31531)

**31535**   Laryngoscopy, direct, operative, with biopsy;

**31536**   with operating microscope or telescope

(Do not report code 69990 in addition to code 31536)

**31540**   Laryngoscopy, direct, operative, with excision of tumor and/or stripping of vocal cords or epiglottis;

**31541**   with operating microscope or telescope

(Do not report code 69990 in addition to code 31541)

**31545**   Laryngoscopy, direct, operative, with operating microscope or telescope, with submucosal removal of non-neoplastic lesion(s) of vocal cord; reconstruction with local tissue flap(s)

**31546**   reconstruction with graft(s) (includes obtaining autograft)

(Do not report 31546 in addition to 20926 for graft harvest)

(For reconstruction of vocal cord with allograft, use 31599)

(Do not report 31545 or 31546 in conjunction with 31540, 31541, 69990)

**31560**   Laryngoscopy, direct, operative, with arytenoidectomy;

**31561**   with operating microscope or telescope

(Do not report code 69990 in addition to code 31561)

**31570**   Laryngoscopy, direct, with injection into vocal cord(s), therapeutic;

**31571**   with operating microscope or telescope

(Do not report code 69990 in addition to code 31571)

**31575**   Laryngoscopy, flexible fiberoptic; diagnostic

**31576**   with biopsy

**31577**   with removal of foreign body

**31578**   with removal of lesion

(To report flexible fiberoptic endoscopic evaluation of swallowing, see 92612-92613)

(To report flexible fiberoptic endoscopic evaluation with sensory testing, see 92614-92615)

(To report flexible fiberoptic endoscopic evaluation of swallowing with sensory testing, see 92616-92617)

(For flexible fiberoptic laryngoscopy as part of flexible fiberoptic endoscopic evaluation of swallowing and/or laryngeal sensory testing by cine or video recording, see 92612-92617)

**31579**   Laryngoscopy, flexible or rigid fiberoptic, with stroboscopy

## Repair

**31580**   Laryngoplasty; for laryngeal web, 2-stage, with keel insertion and removal

**31582**   for laryngeal stenosis, with graft or core mold, including tracheotomy

**31584**   with open reduction of fracture

**31587**   Laryngoplasty, cricoid split

**31588**   Laryngoplasty, not otherwise specified (eg, for burns, reconstruction after partial laryngectomy)

**31590**   Laryngeal reinnervation by neuromuscular pedicle

## Destruction

**31595**   Section recurrent laryngeal nerve, therapeutic (separate procedure), unilateral

## Other Procedures

**31599**   Unlisted procedure, larynx

# Trachea and Bronchi

## Incision

**31600**   Tracheostomy, planned (separate procedure);

**31601**   younger than 2 years

**31603**   Tracheostomy, emergency procedure; transtracheal

**31605**   cricothyroid membrane

**31610**   Tracheostomy, fenestration procedure with skin flaps

(For endotracheal intubation, use 31500)

(For tracheal aspiration under direct vision, use 31515)

**31611**   Construction of tracheoesophageal fistula and subsequent insertion of an alaryngeal speech prosthesis (eg, voice button, Blom-Singer prosthesis)

**31612**   Tracheal puncture, percutaneous with transtracheal aspiration and/or injection

**31613**   Tracheostoma revision; simple, without flap rotation

**31614**   complex, with flap rotation

# Endoscopy

For endoscopy procedures, code appropriate endoscopy of each anatomic site examined. Surgical bronchoscopy always includes diagnostic bronchoscopy when performed by the same physician. Codes 31622-31651, 31660, 31661 include fluoroscopic guidance, when performed.

(For tracheoscopy, see laryngoscopy codes 31515-31578)

⊙ **31615**    Tracheobronchoscopy through established tracheostomy incision

⊙✛ **31620**    Endobronchial ultrasound (EBUS) during bronchoscopic diagnostic or therapeutic intervention(s) (List separately in addition to code for primary procedure[s])

(Use 31620 in conjunction with 31622-31646)

⊙ **31622**    Bronchoscopy, rigid or flexible, including fluoroscopic guidance, when performed; diagnostic, with cell washing, when performed (separate procedure)

⊙ **31623**      with brushing or protected brushings

⊙ **31624**      with bronchial alveolar lavage

⊙ **31625**      with bronchial or endobronchial biopsy(s), single or multiple sites

⊙ **31626**      with placement of fiducial markers, single or multiple

(Report supply of device separately)

⊙✛ **31627**      with computer-assisted, image-guided navigation (List separately in addition to code for primary procedure[s])

(31627 includes 3D reconstruction. Do not report 31627 in conjunction with 76376, 76377)

(Use 31627 in conjunction with 31615, 31622-31626, 31628-31631, 31635, 31636, 31638-31643)

⊙ **31628**      with transbronchial lung biopsy(s), single lobe

(31628 should be reported only once regardless of how many transbronchial lung biopsies are performed in a lobe)

(To report transbronchial lung biopsies performed on additional lobe, use 31632)

⊙ **31629**      with transbronchial needle aspiration biopsy(s), trachea, main stem and/or lobar bronchus(i)

(31629 should be reported only once for upper airway biopsies regardless of how many transbronchial needle aspiration biopsies are performed in the upper airway or in a lobe)

(To report transbronchial needle aspiration biopsies performed on additional lobe[s], use 31633)

**31630**      with tracheal/bronchial dilation or closed reduction of fracture

**31631**      with placement of tracheal stent(s) (includes tracheal/bronchial dilation as required)

(For placement of bronchial stent, see 31636, 31637)

(For revision of tracheal/bronchial stent, use 31638)

✛ **31632**      with transbronchial lung biopsy(s), each additional lobe (List separately in addition to code for primary procedure)

(Use 31632 in conjunction with 31628)

(31632 should be reported only once regardless of how many transbronchial lung biopsies are performed in a lobe)

✛ **31633**      with transbronchial needle aspiration biopsy(s), each additional lobe (List separately in addition to code for primary procedure)

(Use 31633 in conjunction with 31629)

(31633 should be reported only once regardless of how many transbronchial needle aspiration biopsies are performed in the trachea or the additional lobe)

⊙ **31634**      with balloon occlusion, with assessment of air leak, with administration of occlusive substance (eg, fibrin glue), if performed

(Do not report 31634 in conjunction with 31647, 31651 at the same session)

⊙ **31635**      with removal of foreign body

(For removal of implanted bronchial valves, see 31648-31649)

**31636**      with placement of bronchial stent(s) (includes tracheal/bronchial dilation as required), initial bronchus

✛ **31637**      each additional major bronchus stented (List separately in addition to code for primary procedure)

(Use 31637 in conjunction with 31636)

**31638**      with revision of tracheal or bronchial stent inserted at previous session (includes tracheal/bronchial dilation as required)

**31640**      with excision of tumor

**31641**      with destruction of tumor or relief of stenosis by any method other than excision (eg, laser therapy, cryotherapy)

(For bronchoscopic photodynamic therapy, report 31641 in addition to 96570, 96571 as appropriate)

**31643**      with placement of catheter(s) for intracavitary radioelement application

(For intracavitary radioelement application, see 77761-77763, 77785-77787)

⊙ **31645**      with therapeutic aspiration of tracheobronchial tree, initial (eg, drainage of lung abscess)

⊙ **31646**      with therapeutic aspiration of tracheobronchial tree, subsequent

(For catheter aspiration of tracheobronchial tree at bedside, use 31725)

⊙ **31647**      with balloon occlusion, when performed, assessment of air leak, airway sizing, and insertion of bronchial valve(s), initial lobe

**Respiratory**

#⊙✚ **31651**  with balloon occlusion, when performed, assessment of air leak, airway sizing, and insertion of bronchial valve(s), each additional lobe (List separately in addition to code for primary procedure[s])

(Use 31651 in conjunction with 31647)

⊙ **31648**  with removal of bronchial valve(s), initial lobe

(For removal and insertion of a bronchial valve at the same session, see 31647,31648, and 31651)

⊙✚ **31649**  with removal of bronchial valve(s), each additional lobe (List separately in addition to code for primary procedure)

(Use 31649 in conjunction with 31648)

**31651**  Code is out of numerical sequence. See 31615-31649

(31656 has been deleted. To report, use 31899)

## Bronchial Thermoplasty

⊙ **31660**  Bronchoscopy, rigid or flexible, including fluoroscopic guidance, when performed; with bronchial thermoplasty, 1 lobe

⊙ **31661**  with bronchial thermoplasty, 2 or more lobes

## Introduction

(For endotracheal intubation, use 31500)

(For tracheal aspiration under direct vision, see 31515)

(31715 has been deleted. To report, use 31899)

**31717**  Catheterization with bronchial brush biopsy

**31720**  Catheter aspiration (separate procedure); nasotracheal

⊙ **31725**  tracheobronchial with fiberscope, bedside

**31730**  Transtracheal (percutaneous) introduction of needle wire dilator/stent or indwelling tube for oxygen therapy

## Excision, Repair

**31750**  Tracheoplasty; cervical

**31755**  tracheopharyngeal fistulization, each stage

**31760**  intrathoracic

**31766**  Carinal reconstruction

**31770**  Bronchoplasty; graft repair

**31775**  excision stenosis and anastomosis

(For lobectomy and bronchoplasty, use 32501)

**31780**  Excision tracheal stenosis and anastomosis; cervical

**31781**  cervicothoracic

**31785**  Excision of tracheal tumor or carcinoma; cervical

**31786**  thoracic

**31800**  Suture of tracheal wound or injury; cervical

**31805**  intrathoracic

**31820**  Surgical closure tracheostomy or fistula; without plastic repair

**31825**  with plastic repair

(For repair tracheoesophageal fistula, see 43305, 43312)

**31830**  Revision of tracheostomy scar

## Other Procedures

**31899**  Unlisted procedure, trachea, bronchi

# Lungs and Pleura

Pleural cavity or lung biopsy procedures may be accomplished using a percutaneous, thoracoscopic (Video-Assisted Thoracoscopic Surgery [VATS]), or thoracotomy approach. They involve the removal of differing amounts of tissue for diagnosis. A biopsy may be performed using different techniques such as incision or wedge. Lung resection procedures include diagnostic and therapeutic procedures, including the removal of blebs, bullae, cysts, and benign or malignant tumors or lesions. These procedures may involve the removal of small portions of the lung or even an entire lung. Additionally, lung resection procedures may require the removal of adjacent structures. Both diagnostic lung biopsies and therapeutic lung resections can be performed utilizing a wedge technique. However, a diagnostic biopsy of a lung nodule using a wedge technique requires only that a tissue sample be obtained without particular attention to resection margins. A therapeutic wedge resection requires attention to margins and complete resection even when the wedge resection is ultimately followed by a more extensive resection. In the case of a wedge resection in which intraoperative pathology consultation determines that a more extensive resection is required in the same anatomic location, it becomes classified as a diagnostic wedge resection (32507, 32668). When no more extensive resection is required, the same procedure is a therapeutic wedge resection (32505, 32666).

Pleural or lung biopsies or diagnostic wedge resections should be reported using codes 32096, 32097, 32098, 32400, 32405, 32507, 32607, 32608, 32609, or 32668. The open or thoracoscopic (VATS) therapeutic resection of lung mass or nodules via a wedge resection is reported using codes 32505, 32506, 32666, and 32667. More extensive anatomic lung resection procedures, which can be performed with either thoracotomy or thoracoscopic (VATS) approaches, include: segmentectomy, lobectomy, bilobectomy, and pneumonectomy.

When diagnostic biopsy(ies) of the lung are performed, regardless of the approach (ie, open or thoracoscopic [VATS]) or technique (eg, incisional resection, cautery resection, or stapled wedge), and the specimen is sent for intraoperative pathology consultation, and during that same operative session the surgeon uses these results to determine the extent of the necessary surgical resection that includes the anatomical location biopsied, only the most extensive procedure performed (eg, segmentectomy, lobectomy, thoracoscopic [VATS] lobectomy) should be reported.

The therapeutic wedge resection codes (32505, 32506, 32666, or 32667) should not be reported in addition to the more extensive lung procedure (eg, lobectomy) unless the therapeutic wedge resection was performed on a different lobe or on the contralateral lung, whether or not an intraoperative pathology consultation is used to determine the extent of lung resection. When a diagnostic wedge resection is followed by a more extensive procedure in the same anatomical location, report add-on codes 32507 or 32668 with the more extensive procedure(s). When a therapeutic wedge resection (32505, 32506, 32666, or 32667) is performed in a different lobe than the more extensive lung resection (eg, lobectomy), report the therapeutic wedge resection with modifier 59.

## Incision

(32000 has been deleted. To report, use 32421)

(32002 has been deleted. To report, use 32422)

(32005 has been deleted. To report, use 32560)

(32019 has been deleted. To report, use 32550)

(32020 has been deleted. To report, use 32551)

**32035**    Thoracostomy; with rib resection for empyema

**32036**       with open flap drainage for empyema

(To report wound exploration due to penetrating trauma without thoracotomy, use 20101)

(32095 has been deleted. To report, see 32096, 32097, 32098 for thoracotomy with biopsy of the lung or pleura)

**32096**    Thoracotomy, with diagnostic biopsy(ies) of lung infiltrate(s) (eg, wedge, incisional), unilateral

(Do not report 32096 more than once per lung)

(Do not report 32096 in conjunction with 32440, 32442, 32445, 32488)

**32097**    Thoracotomy, with diagnostic biopsy(ies) of lung nodule(s) or mass(es) (eg, wedge, incisional), unilateral

(Do not report 32097 more than once per lung)

(Do not report 32097 in conjunction with 32440, 32442, 32445, 32488)

**32098**    Thoracotomy, with biopsy(ies) of pleura

**32100**    Thoracotomy; with exploration

(Do not report 32100 in conjunction with 19260, 19271, 19272, 32503, 32504)

**32110**       with control of traumatic hemorrhage and/or repair of lung tear

**32120**       for postoperative complications

**32124**       with open intrapleural pneumonolysis

**32140**       with cyst(s) removal, includes pleural procedure when performed

**32141**       with resection-plication of bullae, includes any pleural procedure when performed

(For lung volume reduction, use 32491)

**32150**       with removal of intrapleural foreign body or fibrin deposit

**32151**       with removal of intrapulmonary foreign body

**32160**       with cardiac massage

(For segmental or other resections of lung, see 32480-32504)

**32200**    Pneumonostomy, with open drainage of abscess or cyst

▶(32201 has been deleted)◀

▶(For percutaneous image-guided drainage of abscess or cyst of lungs or mediastinum by catheter placement, use 49405)◀

**32215**    Pleural scarification for repeat pneumothorax

**32220**    Decortication, pulmonary (separate procedure); total

**32225**       partial

## Excision/Resection

**32310**    Pleurectomy, parietal (separate procedure)

**32320**    Decortication and parietal pleurectomy

**32400**    Biopsy, pleura; percutaneous needle

(If imaging guidance is performed, see 76942, 77002, 77012, 77021)

(For fine needle aspiration, use 10021 or 10022)

(32402 has been deleted. To report open biopsy of pleura, use 32098)

⊙ **32405**    Biopsy, lung or mediastinum, percutaneous needle

(For open biopsy of lung, see 32096, 32097. For open biopsy of mediastinum, see 39000 or 39010. For thoracoscopic [VATS] biopsy of lung, pleura, pericardium, or mediastinal space structure, see 32604, 32606, 32607, 32608, 32609)

(For radiological supervision and interpretation, see 76942, 77002, 77012, 77021)

(For fine needle aspiration, use 10022)

## Removal

(32420 has been deleted. To report, use 32405)

(32421 and 32422 have been deleted. To report, see 32554, 32555)

**32440**    Removal of lung, pneumonectomy;

**Respiratory**

**32442**      with resection of segment of trachea followed by broncho-tracheal anastomosis (sleeve pneumonectomy)

**32445**      extrapleural

(For extrapleural pneumonectomy, with empyemectomy, use 32445 and 32540)

(If lung resection is performed with chest wall tumor resection, report the appropriate chest wall tumor resection 19260-19272, in addition to lung resection 32440-32445)

**32480**  Removal of lung, other than pneumonectomy; single lobe (lobectomy)

**32482**      2 lobes (bilobectomy)

**32484**      single segment (segmentectomy)

(For removal of lung with bronchoplasty, use 32501)

**32486**      with circumferential resection of segment of bronchus followed by broncho-bronchial anastomosis (sleeve lobectomy)

**32488**      with all remaining lung following previous removal of a portion of lung (completion pneumonectomy)

(For lobectomy or segmentectomy, with concomitant decortication, use 32320 and the appropriate removal of lung code)

**32491**      with resection-plication of emphysematous lung(s) (bullous or non-bullous) for lung volume reduction, sternal split or transthoracic approach, includes any pleural procedure, when performed

(32500 has been deleted. To report open wedge resection of lung, see 32505, 32506, 32507)

(If lung resection is performed with chest wall tumor resection, report the appropriate chest wall tumor resection 19260-19272, in addition to lung resection 32480, 32482, 32484, 32486, 32488, 32505, 32506, 32507)

**+ 32501**  Resection and repair of portion of bronchus (bronchoplasty) when performed at time of lobectomy or segmentectomy (List separately in addition to code for primary procedure)

(Use 32501 in conjunction with 32480, 32482, 32484)

(32501 is to be used when a portion of the bronchus to preserved lung is removed and requires plastic closure to preserve function of that preserved lung. It is not to be used for closure for the proximal end of a resected bronchus)

**32503**  Resection of apical lung tumor (eg, Pancoast tumor), including chest wall resection, rib(s) resection(s), neurovascular dissection, when performed; without chest wall reconstruction(s)

**32504**      with chest wall reconstruction

(Do not report 32503, 32504 in conjunction with 19260, 19271, 19272, 32100, 32551, 32554, 32555)

**32505**  Thoracotomy; with therapeutic wedge resection (eg, mass, nodule), initial

(Do not report 32505 in conjunction with 32440, 32442, 32445, 32488)

**+ 32506**      with therapeutic wedge resection (eg, mass or nodule), each additional resection, ipsilateral (List separately in addition to code for primary procedure)

(Report 32506 only in conjunction with 32505)

(If lung resection is performed with chest wall tumor resection, report the appropriate chest wall tumor resection 19260-19272, in addition to lung resection 32480, 32482, 32484, 32486, 32488, 32505, 32506, 32507)

**+ 32507**      with diagnostic wedge resection followed by anatomic lung resection (List separately in addition to code for primary procedure)

(Report 32507 in conjunction with 32440, 32442, 32445, 32480, 32482, 32484, 32486, 32488, 32503, 32504)

**32540**  Extrapleural enucleation of empyema (empyemectomy)

(For extrapleural enucleation of empyema [empyemectomy] with lobectomy, use 32540 and the appropriate removal of lung code)

## Introduction and Removal

⊙ **32550**  Insertion of indwelling tunneled pleural catheter with cuff

▶(Do not report 32550 in conjunction with 32554, 32555, 32556, 32557 when performed on the same side of the chest)◄

(If imaging guidance is performed, use 75989)

⊙ **32551**  Tube thoracostomy, includes connection to drainage system (eg, water seal), when performed, open (separate procedure)

**32552**  Removal of indwelling tunneled pleural catheter with cuff

⊙ **32553**  Placement of interstitial device(s) for radiation therapy guidance (eg, fiducial markers, dosimeter), percutaneous, intra-thoracic, single or multiple

(Report supply of device separately)

(For imaging guidance, see 76942, 77002, 77012, 77021)

(For percutaneous placement of interstitial device[s] for intra-abdominal, intrapelvic, and/or retroperitoneal radiation therapy guidance, use 49411)

**32554**  Thoracentesis, needle or catheter, aspiration of the pleural space; without imaging guidance

**32555**      with imaging guidance

**32556**  Pleural drainage, percutaneous, with insertion of indwelling catheter; without imaging guidance

**32557**        with imaging guidance

(For insertion of indwelling tunneled pleural catheter with cuff, use 32550)

(For open procedure, use 32551)

►(Do not report 32554-32557 in conjunction with 32550, 32551 when performed on the same side of the chest)◄

►(Do not report 32554-32557 in conjunction with 75989, 76942, 77002, 77012, 77021)◄

## Destruction

The instillation of a fibrinolytic agent may be performed multiple times per day over the course of several days. Code 32561 should be reported only once on the initial day treatment. Code 32562 should be reported only once on each subsequent day of treatment.

**32560**    Instillation, via chest tube/catheter, agent for pleurodesis (eg, talc for recurrent or persistent pneumothorax)

(For chest tube insertion, use 32551)

**32561**    Instillation(s), via chest tube/catheter, agent for fibrinolysis (eg, fibrinolytic agent for break up of multiloculated effusion); initial day

(For chest tube insertion, use 32551)

**32562**        subsequent day

(For chest tube insertion, use 32551)

## Thoracoscopy (Video-assisted thoracic surgery [VATS])

Surgical thoracoscopy (video-assisted thoracic surgery [VATS]) always includes diagnostic thoracoscopy.

**32601**    Thoracoscopy, diagnostic (separate procedure); lungs, pericardial sac, mediastinal or pleural space, without biopsy

(32602 has been deleted. To report lung or pleural space biopsy[ies], see 32607, 32608, 32609)

(32603 has been deleted. To report diagnostic thoracoscopy, pericardial sac, without biopsy, use 32601)

**32604**        pericardial sac, with biopsy

(32605 has been deleted. To report diagnostic thoracoscopy within the mediastinal space, use 32601)

(For open pericardial bipsy, use 39010)

**32606**        mediastinal space, with biopsy

**32607**    Thoracoscopy; with diagnostic biopsy(ies) of lung infiltrate(s) (eg, wedge, incisional), unilateral

(Do not report 32607 more than once per lung)

(Do not report 32607 in conjunction with 32440, 32442, 32445, 32488, 32671)

**32608**        with diagnostic biopsy(ies) of lung nodule(s) or mass(es) (eg, wedge, incisional), unilateral

(Do not report 32608 more than once per lung)

(Do not report 32608 in conjunction with 32440, 32442, 32445, 32488, 32671)

**32609**        with biopsy(ies) of pleura

**32650**    Thoracoscopy, surgical; with pleurodesis (eg, mechanical or chemical)

**32651**        with partial pulmonary decortication

**32652**        with total pulmonary decortication, including intrapleural pneumonolysis

**32653**        with removal of intrapleural foreign body or fibrin deposit

**32654**        with control of traumatic hemorrhage

**32655**        with resection-plication of bullae, includes any pleural procedure when performed

(For thoracoscopic [VATS] lung volume reduction surgery, use 32672)

**32656**        with parietal pleurectomy

(32657 has been deleted. To report thoracoscopic [VATS] wedge resection of lung, see 32666, 32667, 32668)

**32658**        with removal of clot or foreign body from pericardial sac

**32659**        with creation of pericardial window or partial resection of pericardial sac for drainage

(32660 has been deleted)

**32661**        with excision of pericardial cyst, tumor, or mass

**32662**        with excision of mediastinal cyst, tumor, or mass

**32663**        with lobectomy (single lobe)

(For thoracoscopic [VATS] segmentectomy, use 32669)

**32664**        with thoracic sympathectomy

**32665**        with esophagomyotomy (Heller type)

(For exploratory thoracoscopy, and exploratory thoracoscopy with biopsy, see 32601-32609)

**32666**        with therapeutic wedge resection (eg, mass, nodule), initial unilateral

(To report bilateral procedure, report 32666 with modifier 50)

(Do not report 32666 in conjunction with 32440, 32442, 32445, 32488, 32671)

**+ 32667**      with therapeutic wedge resection (eg, mass or nodule), each additional resection, ipsilateral (List separately in addition to code for primary procedure)

(Report 32667 only in conjunction with 32666)

(Do not report 32667 in conjunction with 32440, 32442, 32445, 32488, 32671)

Respiratory

**Respiratory**

+ **32668**    with diagnostic wedge resection followed by anatomic lung resection (List separately in addition to code for primary procedure)

(Report 32668 in conjunction with 32440, 32442, 32445, 32480, 32482, 32484, 32486, 32488, 32503, 32504, 32663, 32669, 32670, 32671)

**32669**    with removal of a single lung segment (segmentectomy)

**32670**    with removal of two lobes (bilobectomy)

**32671**    with removal of lung (pneumonectomy)

**32672**    with resection-plication for emphysematous lung (bullous or non-bullous) for lung volume reduction (LVRS), unilateral includes any pleural procedure, when performed

**32673**    with resection of thymus, unilateral or bilateral

(For open thymectomy see 60520, 60521, 60522)

(For open excision mediastinal cyst, see 39200; for open excision mediastinal tumor, use 39220)

(For exploratory thoracoscopy, and exploratory thoracoscopy with biopsy, see 32601-32609)

+ **32674**    with mediastinal and regional lymphadenectomy (List separately in addition to code for primary procedure)

(On the right, mediastinal lymph nodes include the paratracheal, subcarinal, paraesophageal, and inferior pulmonary ligament)

(On the left, mediastinal lymph nodes include the aortopulmonary window, subcarinal, paraesophageal, and inferior pulmonary ligament)

►(Report 32674 in conjunction with 19260, 31760, 31766, 31786, 32096- 32200, 32220-32320, 32440-32491, 32503-32505, 32601-32663, 32666, 32669-32673, 32815, 33025, 33030, 33050-33130, 39200-39220, 39560, 39561, 43101, 43112, 43117, 43118, 43122, 43123, 43351, 60270, 60505)◄

(To report mediastinal and regional lymphadenectomy via thoracotomy, use 38746)

## Stereotactic Radiation Therapy

Thoracic stereotactic body radiation therapy (SRS/SBRT) is a distinct procedure which may involve collaboration between a surgeon and radiation oncologist. The surgeon identifies and delineates the target for therapy. The radiation oncologist reports the appropriate code(s) for clinical treatment planning, physics and dosimetry, treatment delivery and management from the Radiation Oncology section (see 77295, 77331, 77370, 77373, 77435). The same physician should not report target delineation services with radiation treatment management codes (77427-77499).

Target delineation involves specific determination of tumor borders to identify tumor volume and relationship with adjacent structures (eg, chest wall, intraparenchymal vasculature and atelectatic lung) and previously placed fiducial markers, when present. Target delineation also includes availability to identify and validate the thoracic target prior to treatment delivery when a fiducial-less tracking system is utilized.

Do not report target delineation more than once per entire course of treatment when the treatment requires greater than one session.

**32701**    Thoracic target(s) delineation for stereotactic body radiation therapy (SRS/SBRT), (photon or particle beam), entire course of treatment

(Do not report 32701 in conjunction with 77261-77799)

(For placement of fiducial markers, see 31626, 32553)

## Repair

**32800**    Repair lung hernia through chest wall

**32810**    Closure of chest wall following open flap drainage for empyema (Clagett type procedure)

**32815**    Open closure of major bronchial fistula

**32820**    Major reconstruction, chest wall (posttraumatic)

## Lung Transplantation

Lung allotransplantation involves three distinct components of physician work:

1. *Cadaver donor pneumonectomy(s)*, which include(s) harvesting the allograft and cold preservation of the allograft (perfusing with cold preservation solution and cold maintenance) (use 32850).

2. *Backbench work*:

Preparation of a cadaver donor single lung allograft prior to transplantation, including dissection of the allograft from surrounding soft tissues to prepare the pulmonary venous/atrial cuff, pulmonary artery, and bronchus unilaterally (use 32855).

Preparation of a cadaver donor double lung allograft prior to transplantation, including dissection of the allograft from surrounding soft tissues to prepare the pulmonary venous/atrial cuff, pulmonary artery, and bronchus bilaterally (use 32856).

3. *Recipient lung allotransplantation*, which includes transplantation of a single or double lung allograft and care of the recipient (see 32851-32854).

**32850**    Donor pneumonectomy(s) (including cold preservation), from cadaver donor

32851   Lung transplant, single; without cardiopulmonary bypass

32852        with cardiopulmonary bypass

32853   Lung transplant, double (bilateral sequential or en bloc); without cardiopulmonary bypass

32854        with cardiopulmonary bypass

32855   Backbench standard preparation of cadaver donor lung allograft prior to transplantation, including dissection of allograft from surrounding soft tissues to prepare pulmonary venous/atrial cuff, pulmonary artery, and bronchus; unilateral

32856        bilateral

(For repair or resection procedures on the donor lung, see 32491, 32505, 32506, 32507, 35216, 35276)

## Surgical Collapse Therapy; Thoracoplasty

(See also 32503, 32504)

32900   Resection of ribs, extrapleural, all stages

32905   Thoracoplasty, Schede type or extrapleural (all stages);

32906        with closure of bronchopleural fistula

(For open closure of major bronchial fistula, use 32815)

(For resection of first rib for thoracic outlet compression, see 21615, 21616)

32940   Pneumonolysis, extraperiosteal, including filling or packing procedures

32960   Pneumothorax, therapeutic, intrapleural injection of air

## Other Procedures

32997   Total lung lavage (unilateral)

(For bronchoscopic bronchial alveolar lavage, use 31624)

32998   Ablation therapy for reduction or eradication of 1 or more pulmonary tumor(s) including pleura or chest wall when involved by tumor extension, percutaneous, radiofrequency, unilateral

(For imaging guidance and monitoring, see 76940, 77013, 77022)

32999   Unlisted procedure, lungs and pleura

**Respiratory**

# Cardiovascular System

Selective vascular catheterizations should be coded to include introduction and all lesser order selective catheterizations used in the approach (eg, the description for a selective right middle cerebral artery catheterization includes the introduction and placement catheterization of the right common and internal carotid arteries).

Additional second and/or third order arterial catheterizations within the same family of arteries supplied by a single first order artery should be expressed by 36218 or 36248. Additional first order or higher catheterizations in vascular families supplied by a first order vessel different from a previously selected and coded family should be separately coded using the conventions described above.

(For monitoring, operation of pump and other nonsurgical services, see 99190-99192, 99291, 99292, 99354-99360)

(For other medical or laboratory related services, see appropriate section)

(For radiological supervision and interpretation, see 75600-75978)

## Heart and Pericardium

### Pericardium

(For thoracoscopic (VATS) pericardial procedures, see 32601, 32604, 32658, 32659, 32661)

⊙ **33010** Pericardiocentesis; initial

(For radiological supervision and interpretation, use 76930)

⊙ **33011** subsequent

(For radiological supervision and interpretation, use 76930)

**33015** Tube pericardiotomy

**33020** Pericardiotomy for removal of clot or foreign body (primary procedure)

**33025** Creation of pericardial window or partial resection for drainage

(For thoracoscopic (VATS) pericardial window, use 32659)

**33030** Pericardiectomy, subtotal or complete; without cardiopulmonary bypass

**33031** with cardiopulmonary bypass

**33050** Resection of pericardial cyst or tumor

(For open pericardial biopsy, use 39010)

(For thoracoscopic (VATS) resection of pericardial cyst, tumor or mass, use 32661)

## Cardiac Tumor

**33120** Excision of intracardiac tumor, resection with cardiopulmonary bypass

**33130** Resection of external cardiac tumor

## Transmyocardial Revascularization

**33140** Transmyocardial laser revascularization, by thoracotomy; (separate procedure)

+ **33141** performed at the time of other open cardiac procedure(s) (List separately in addition to code for primary procedure)

(Use 33141 in conjunction with 33400-33496, 33510-33536, 33542)

## Pacemaker or Pacing Cardioverter-Defibrillator

A pacemaker system includes a pulse generator containing electronics, a battery, and one or more electrodes (leads). Pulse generators are placed in a subcutaneous "pocket" created in either a subclavicular site or underneath the abdominal muscles just below the ribcage. Electrodes may be inserted through a vein (transvenous) or they may be placed on the surface of the heart (epicardial). The epicardial location of electrodes requires a thoracotomy for electrode insertion.

A single chamber pacemaker system includes a pulse generator and one electrode inserted in either the atrium or ventricle. A dual chamber pacemaker system includes a pulse generator and one electrode inserted in the right atrium and one electrode inserted in the right ventricle. In certain circumstances, an additional electrode may be required to achieve pacing of the left ventricle (bi-ventricular pacing). In this event, transvenous (cardiac vein) placement of the electrode should be separately reported using code 33224 or 33225. Epicardial placement of the electrode should be separately reported using 33202-33203.

Like a pacemaker system, a pacing cardioverter-defibrillator (ICD) system includes a pulse generator and electrodes, although pacing cardioverter-defibrillators may require multiple leads, even when only a single chamber is being paced. A pacing cardioverter-defibrillator system may be inserted in a single chamber (pacing in the ventricle) or in dual chambers (pacing in atrium and ventricle). These devices use a combination of antitachycardia pacing, low-energy cardioversion or defibrillating shocks to treat ventricular tachycardia or ventricular fibrillation.

Pacing cardioverter-defibrillator pulse generators may be implanted in a subcutaneous infraclavicular pocket or in an abdominal pocket. Removal of a pacing cardioverter-defibrillator pulse generator requires opening of the existing subcutaneous pocket and disconnection of the pulse generator from its electrode(s). A thoracotomy (or laparotomy in the case of abdominally placed pulse generators) is not required to remove the pulse generator.

The electrodes (leads) of a pacing cardioverter-defibrillator system are positioned in the heart via the venous system (transvenously), in most circumstances. In certain circumstances, an additional electrode may be required to achieve pacing of the left ventricle (bi-ventricular pacing). In this event, transvenous (cardiac vein) placement of the electrode should be separately reported using code 33224 or 33225. Epicardial placement of the electrode should be separately reported using 33202-33203.

Electrode positioning on the epicardial surface of the heart requires a thoracotomy, or thoracoscopic placement of the leads. Removal of electrode(s) may first be attempted by transvenous extraction (33234, 33235, or 33244). However, if transvenous extraction is unsuccessful, a thoracotomy may be required to remove the electrodes (33238 or 33243). Use 33212, 33213, 33221, 33230, 33231, 33240 as appropriate in addition to the thoracotomy or endoscopic epicardial lead placement codes (33202 or 33203) to report the insertion of the generator if done by the same physician during the same session.

When the "battery" of a pacemaker or pacing cardioverter-defibrillator is changed, it is actually the pulse generator that is changed. Removal of pacemaker or pacing cardioverter-defibrillator pulse generator only is reported with 33233 or 33241. Removal of a pacemaker or pacing cardioverter-defibrillator pulse generator with insertion of a new pulse generator without any replacement or insertion of a lead(s) is reported with 33227- 33229 and 33262- 33264. Insertion of a new pulse generator, when existing leads are already in place and when no prior pulse generator is removed, is reported with 33212, 33213, 33221, 33230, 33231, 33240. When a pulse generator insertion involves the insertion or replacement of one or more lead(s), use the system codes 33206- 33208 for pacemaker or 33249 for pacing cardioverter-defibrillator. Removal of a pulse generator ( 33233 or 33241) or extraction of transvenous leads ( 33234, 33235 or 33244) should be reported separately. An exception involves a pacemaker upgrade from single to dual system which includes removal of pulse generator, replacement of new pulse generator, and insertion of new lead, reported with 33214.

►Revision of a skin pocket is included in 33206-33249, 33262-33264. When revision of a skin pocket involves incision and drainage of a hematoma or complex wound infection, see 10140, 10180, 11042, 11043, 11044, 11045, 11046, 11047 as appropriate.

Relocation of a skin pocket for a pacemaker (33222) or cardioverter-defibrillator (33223) is necessary for various clinical situations such as infection or erosion. Relocation of an existing pulse generator may be performed as a stand-alone procedure or at the time of a pulse generator or electrode insertion, replacement, or repositioning.

When skin pocket relocation is performed as part of an explant of an existing generator followed by replacement with a new generator, the pocket relocation is reported separately. Skin pocket relocation includes all work associated with the initial pocket (eg, opening the pocket, incision and drainage of hematoma or abscess if performed, and any closure performed) in addition to the creation of a new pocket for the new generator to be placed.◄

Repositioning of a pacemaker electrode, pacing cardioverter-defibrillator electrode(s), or a left ventricular pacing electrode is reported using 33215 or 33226, as appropriate.

The pacemaker and pacing cardioverter-defibrillator device evaluation codes 93279-93299 may not be reported in conjunction with pulse generator and lead insertion or revision codes 33206-33249. Defibrillator threshold testing (DFT) during pacing cardioverter-defibrillator insertion or replacement may be separately reported using 93640, 93641.

Radiological supervision and interpretation related to the pacemaker or pacing cardioverter-defibrillator procedure is included in 33206-33249. To report fluoroscopic guidance for diagnostic lead evaluation without lead insertion, replacement, or revision procedures, use 76000.

►A subcutaneous implantable defibrillator system is an implantable technology that uses a subcutaneous pulse generator attached to a single subcutaneous electrode to treat ventricular tachyarrhythmias. For these services see 0319T-0328T.◄

The following definitions apply to 33206-33249.

**Single lead:** a pacemaker or pacing cardioverter-defibrillator with pacing and sensing function in only one chamber of the heart.

**Dual lead:** a pacemaker or pacing cardioverter-defibrillator with pacing and sensing function in only two chambers of the heart.

**Multiple lead:** a pacemaker or pacing cardioverter-defibrillator with pacing and sensing function in three or more chambers of the heart.

| | |
|---|---|
| **33202** | Insertion of epicardial electrode(s); open incision (eg, thoracotomy, median sternotomy, subxiphoid approach) |
| **33203** | endoscopic approach (eg, thoracoscopy, pericardioscopy) |

(When epicardial lead placement is performed with insertion of the generator, report 33202, 33203 in conjunction with 33212, 33213, 33221, 33230, 33231, 33240)

| | |
|---|---|
| ⊙ **33206** | Insertion of new or replacement of permanent pacemaker with transvenous electrode(s); atrial |
| ⊙ **33207** | ventricular |

**Cardiovascular**

| Transvenous Procedure | System | |
|---|---|---|
| | **Pacemaker** | **Implantable Cardioverter-Defibrillator** |
| Insert transvenous single lead only without pulse generator | 33216 | 33216 |
| Insert transvenous dual leads without pulse generator | 33217 | 33217 |
| Insert transvenous multiple leads without pulse generator | 33217 + 33224 | 33217 + 33224 |
| Initial pulse generator insertion only with existing single lead | 33212 | 33240 |
| Initial pulse generator insertion only with existing dual leads | 33213 | 33230 |
| Initial pulse generator insertion only with existing multiple leads | 33221 | 33231 |
| Initial pulse generator insertion or replacement plus insertion of transvenous single lead | 33206 (atrial) or 33207 (ventricular) | 33249 |
| Initial pulse generator insertion or replacement plus insertion of transvenous dual leads | 33208 | 33249 |
| Initial pulse generator insertion or replacement plus insertion of transvenous multiple leads | 33208 + 33225 | 33249 + 33225 |
| Upgrade single chamber system to dual chamber system | 33214 (includes removal of existing pulse generator) | 33241 + 33249 |
| Removal pulse generator only (without replacement) | 33233 | 33241 |
| Removal pulse generator with replacement pulse generator only single lead system (transvenous) | 33227 | 33262 |
| Removal pulse generator with replacement pulse generator only dual lead system (transvenous) | 33228 | 33263 |
| Removal pulse generator with replacement pulse generator only multiple lead system (transvenous) | 33229 | 33264 |
| Removal transvenous electrode only single lead system | 33234 | 33244 |
| Removal transvenous electrode only dual lead system | 33235 | 33244 |
| Removal and replacement of pulse generator and transvenous electrodes | 33233 + (33234 or 33235) + (33206 or 33207 or 33208) and 33225, when appropriate | 33241 + 33244 + 33249 and 33225, when appropriate |
| Conversion of existing system to bi-ventricular system (addition of LV lead and removal of current pulse generator with insertion of new pulse generator with bi-ventricular pacing capabilities) | 33225 + 33228 or 33229 | 33225 + 33263 or 33264 |

⊙ **33208**    atrial and ventricular

(Codes 33206-33208 include subcutaneous insertion of the pulse generator and transvenous placement of electrode[s])

(For removal and replacement of pacemaker pulse generator and transvenous electrode(s), use 33233 in conjunction with either 33234 or 33235 and 33206-33208)

(Do not report 33206-33208 in conjunction with 33227-33229)

⊙ **33210**    Insertion or replacement of temporary transvenous single chamber cardiac electrode or pacemaker catheter (separate procedure)

⊙ **33211**    Insertion or replacement of temporary transvenous dual chamber pacing electrodes (separate procedure)

⊙ **33212**    Insertion of pacemaker pulse generator only; with existing single lead

⊙ **33213**        with existing dual leads

#⊙ **33221**        with existing multiple leads

(Do not report 33212, 33213, 33221 in conjunction with 33233 for removal and replacement of the pacemaker pulse generator. Use 33227-33229, as appropriate, when pulse generator replacement is indicated)

(When epicardial lead placement is performed with insertion of generator, report 33202, 33203 in conjunction with 33212, 33213, 33221)

⊙ **33214**  Upgrade of implanted pacemaker system, conversion of single chamber system to dual chamber system (includes removal of previously placed pulse generator, testing of existing lead, insertion of new lead, insertion of new pulse generator)

(Do not report 33214 in conjunction with 33227-33229)

**33215**  Repositioning of previously implanted transvenous pacemaker or pacing cardioverter-defibrillator (right atrial or right ventricular) electrode

⊙ **33216**  Insertion of a single transvenous electrode, permanent pacemaker or cardioverter-defibrillator

⊙ **33217**  Insertion of 2 transvenous electrodes, permanent pacemaker or cardioverter-defibrillator

(Do not report 33216-33217 in conjunction with 33214)

(For insertion or replacement of a cardiac venous system lead, see 33224, 33225)

⊙ **33218**  Repair of single transvenous electrode, permanent pacemaker or pacing cardioverter-defibrillator

(For repair of single permanent pacemaker or pacing cardioverter-defibrillator electrode with replacement of pulse generator, see 33227-33229 or 33262-33264 and 33218)

⊙ **33220**  Repair of 2 transvenous electrodes for permanent pacemaker or pacing cardioverter-defibrillator

(For repair of 2 transvenous electrodes for permanent pacemaker or pacing cardioverter-defibrillator with replacement of pulse generator, use 33220 in conjunction with 33228, 33229, 33263, 33264)

**33221**  Code is out of numerical sequence. See 33202-33249

⊙▲ **33222**  Relocation of skin pocket for pacemaker

►(Do not report 33222 in conjunction with 10140, 10180, 11042, 11043, 11044, 11045, 11046, 11047, 13100, 13101, 13102)◄

⊙▲ **33223**  Relocation of skin pocket for cardioverter-defibrillator

►(Do not report 33223 in conjunction with 10140, 10180, 11042, 11043, 11044, 11045, 11046, 11047, 13100, 13101, 13102)◄

**33224**  Insertion of pacing electrode, cardiac venous system, for left ventricular pacing, with attachment to previously placed pacemaker or pacing cardioverter-defibrillator pulse generator (including revision of pocket, removal, insertion, and/or replacement of existing generator)

(When epicardial electrode placement is performed, report 33224 in conjunction with 33202, 33203)

+ **33225**  Insertion of pacing electrode, cardiac venous system, for left ventricular pacing, at time of insertion of pacing cardioverter-defibrillator or pacemaker pulse generator (eg, for upgrade to dual chamber system) (List separately in addition to code for primary procedure)

►(Use 33225 in conjunction with 33206, 33207, 33208, 33212, 33213, 33214, 33216, 33217, 33221, 33223, 33228, 33229, 33230, 33231, 33233, 33234, 33235, 33240, 33249, 33263, 33264)◄

(Use 33225 in conjunction with 33222 only with pacemaker pulse generator pocket relocation and with 33223 only with pacing cardioverter-defibrillator [ICD] pocket relocation)

**33226**  Repositioning of previously implanted cardiac venous system (left ventricular) electrode (including removal, insertion and/or replacement of existing generator)

**33227**  Code is out of numerical sequence. See 33202-33249

**33228**  Code is out of numerical sequence. See 33202-33249

**33229**  Code is out of numerical sequence. See 33202-33249

**33230**  Code is out of numerical sequence. See 33202-33249

**33231**  Code is out of numerical sequence. See 33202-33249

⊙ **33233**  Removal of permanent pacemaker pulse generator only

#⊙ **33227**  Removal of permanent pacemaker pulse generator with replacement of pacemaker pulse generator; single lead system

#⊙ **33228**      dual lead system

#⊙ **33229**      multiple lead system

(Do not report 33227-33229 in conjunction with 33233)

(For removal and replacement of pacemaker pulse generator and transvenous electrode[s], use 33233 in conjunction with either 33234 or 33235 and 33206-33208)

⊙ **33234**  Removal of transvenous pacemaker electrode(s); single lead system, atrial or ventricular

⊙ **33235**      dual lead system

**33236**  Removal of permanent epicardial pacemaker and electrodes by thoracotomy; single lead system, atrial or ventricular

**33237**      dual lead system

**33238**  Removal of permanent transvenous electrode(s) by thoracotomy

⊙ **33240**  Insertion of pacing cardioverter-defibrillator pulse generator only; with existing single lead

(Use 33240, as appropriate, in addition to the epicardial lead placement codes to report the insertion of the generator when done by the same physician during the same session)

#⊙ **33230**      with existing dual leads

**Cardiovascular**

**Cardiovascular**

#⊙ **33231**        with existing multiple leads

(Do not report 33230, 33231, 33240 in conjunction with 33241 for removal and replacement of the pacing cardioverter-defibrillator pulse generator. Use 33262-33264, as appropriate, when pulse generator replacement is indicated)

(When epicardial lead placement is performed with insertion of generator, report 33202, 33203 in conjunction with 33230, 33231, 33240)

⊙ **33241**   Removal of pacing cardioverter-defibrillator pulse generator only

(For removal and replacement of a pacing cardioverter-defibrillator pulse generator and electrode(s), use 33241 in conjunction with either 33243 or 33244 and 33249)

#⊙ **33262**   Removal of pacing cardioverter-defibrillator pulse generator with replacement of pacing cardioverter-defibrillator pulse generator; single lead system

#⊙ **33263**        dual lead system

#⊙ **33264**        multiple lead system

(Do not report 33262-33264 in conjunction with 33241)

(For removal of electrode[s] by thoracotomy in conjunction with pulse generator removal or replacement, use 33243 in conjunction with 33241, 33262-33264)

(For removal of electrode[s] by transvenous extraction in conjunction with pulse generator removal or replacement, use 33244 in conjunction with 33241, 33262-33264)

(For repair of implantable cardioverter-defibrillator pulse generator and/or leads, see 33218, 33220)

**33243**   Removal of single or dual chamber pacing cardioverter-defibrillator electrode(s); by thoracotomy

⊙ **33244**        by transvenous extraction

⊙ **33249**   Insertion or replacement of permanent pacing cardioverter-defibrillator system with transvenous lead(s), single or dual chamber

(For removal and replacement of a pacing cardioverter-defibrillator system [pulse generator and electrodes], report 33241 in conjunction with either 33243 or 33244 and 33249)

(For insertion of implantable cardioverter-defibrillator lead(s), without thoracotomy, use 33216 or 33217)

# Electrophysiologic Operative Procedures

This family of codes describes the surgical treatment of supraventricular dysrhythmias. Tissue ablation, disruption, and reconstruction can be accomplished by many methods including surgical incision or through the use of a variety of energy sources (eg, radiofrequency, cryotherapy, microwave, ultrasound, laser). If excision or isolation of the left atrial appendage by any method, including stapling, oversewing, ligation, or plication, is performed in conjunction with any of the atrial tissue

ablation and reconstruction (maze) procedures (33254-33259, 33265-33266), it is considered part of the procedure. Codes 33254-33256 are only to be reported when there is no concurrently performed procedure that requires median sternotomy or cardiopulmonary bypass. The appropriate atrial tissue ablation add-on code, 33257, 33258, 33259 should be reported in addition to an open cardiac procedure requiring sternotomy or cardiopulmonary bypass if performed concurrently.

## Definitions

*Limited* operative ablation and reconstruction includes:

Surgical isolation of triggers of supraventricular dysrhythmias by operative ablation that isolates the pulmonary veins or other anatomically defined triggers in the left or right atrium.

*Extensive* operative ablation and reconstruction includes:

1. The services included in *"limited"*

2. Additional ablation of atrial tissue to eliminate sustained supraventricular dysrhythmias. This must include operative ablation that involves either the right atrium, the atrial septum, or left atrium in continuity with the atrioventricular annulus.

## Incision

**33250**   Operative ablation of supraventricular arrhythmogenic focus or pathway (eg, Wolff-Parkinson-White, atrioventricular node re-entry), tract(s) and/or focus (foci); without cardiopulmonary bypass

(For intraoperative pacing and mapping by a separate provider, use 93631)

**33251**        with cardiopulmonary bypass

**33254**   Operative tissue ablation and reconstruction of atria, limited (eg, modified maze procedure)

**33255**   Operative tissue ablation and reconstruction of atria, extensive (eg, maze procedure); without cardiopulmonary bypass

**33256**        with cardiopulmonary bypass

(Do not report 33254-33256 in conjunction with 32100, 32551, 33120, 33130, 33210, 33211, 33400-33507, 33510-33523, 33533-33548, 33600-33853, 33860-33864, 33910-33920)

+ **33257**   Operative tissue ablation and reconstruction of atria, performed at the time of other cardiac procedure(s), limited (eg, modified maze procedure) (List separately in addition to code for primary procedure)

(Use 33257 in conjunction with 33120-33130, 33250-33251, 33261, 33300-33335, 33400-33496, 33500-33507, 33510-33516, 33533-33548, 33600-33619, 33641-33697, 33702-33732, 33735-33767, 33770-33814, 33840-33877, 33910-33922, 33925-33926, 33935, 33945, 33975-33980)

**+ 33258**　Operative tissue ablation and reconstruction of atria, performed at the time of other cardiac procedure(s), extensive (eg, maze procedure), without cardiopulmonary bypass (List separately in addition to code for primary procedure)

(Use 33258 in conjunction with 33130, 33250, 33300, 33310, 33320, 33321, 33330, 33332, 33401, 33414-33417, 33420, 33470-33472, 33501-33503, 33510-33516, 33533-33536, 33690, 33735, 33737, 33800-33813, 33840-33852, 33915, 33925 when the procedure is performed without cardiopulmonary bypass)

**+ 33259**　Operative tissue ablation and reconstruction of atria, performed at the time of other cardiac procedure(s), extensive (eg, maze procedure), with cardiopulmonary bypass (List separately in addition to code for primary procedure)

(Use 33259 in conjunction with 33120, 33251, 33261, 33305, 33315, 33322, 33335, 33400, 33403-33413, 33422-33468, 33474-33478, 33496, 33500, 33504-33507, 33510-33516, 33533-33548, 33600-33688, 33692-33722, 33730, 33732, 33736, 33750-33767, 33770-33781, 33786-33788, 33814, 33853, 33860-33877, 33910, 33916-33922, 33926, 33935, 33945, 33975-33980 when the procedure is performed with cardiopulmonary bypass)

(Do not report 33257, 33258 and 33259 in conjunction with 32551, 33210, 33211, 33254-33256, 33265, 33266)

**33261**　Operative ablation of ventricular arrhythmogenic focus with cardiopulmonary bypass

**33262**　Code is out of numerical sequence. See 33202-33264

**33263**　Code is out of numerical sequence. See 33202-33264

**33264**　Code is out of numerical sequence. See 33202-33264

## Endoscopy

**33265**　Endoscopy, surgical; operative tissue ablation and reconstruction of atria, limited (eg, modified maze procedure), without cardiopulmonary bypass

**33266**　operative tissue ablation and reconstruction of atria, extensive (eg, maze procedure), without cardiopulmonary bypass

(Do not report 33265-33266 in conjunction with 32551, 33210, 33211)

## Patient-Activated Event Recorder

⊙▲ **33282**　Implantation of patient-activated cardiac event recorder

(Initial implantation includes programming. For subsequent electronic analysis and/or reprogramming, use 93285, 93291, 93298, 93299)

⊙▲ **33284**　Removal of an implantable, patient-activated cardiac event recorder

## Heart (Including Valves) and Great Vessels

Patients receiving major cardiac procedures may require simultaneous cardiopulmonary bypass insertion of cannulae into the venous and arterial vasculatures with support of circulation and oxygenation by a heart-lung machine. Most services are described by codes in dyad arrangements to allow distinct reporting of procedures with or without cardiopulmonary bypass. Cardiopulmonary bypass is distinct from support of cardiac output using devices (eg, ventricular assist or intra-aortic balloon). For cardiac assist services see 33960-33983, 33990-33992.

**33300**　Repair of cardiac wound; without bypass

**33305**　　with cardiopulmonary bypass

**33310**　Cardiotomy, exploratory (includes removal of foreign body, atrial or ventricular thrombus); without bypass

**33315**　　with cardiopulmonary bypass

(Do not report removal of thrombus [33310-33315] in conjunction with other cardiac procedures unless a separate incision in the heart is required to remove the atrial or ventricular thrombus)

(If removal of thrombus with cardiopulmonary bypass [33315] is reported in conjunction with 33120, 33130, 33420-33430, 33460-33468, 33496, 33542, 33545, 33641-33647, 33670, 33681, 33975-33980 which requires a separate heart incision, report 33315 with modifier 59)

**33320**　Suture repair of aorta or great vessels; without shunt or cardiopulmonary bypass

**33321**　　with shunt bypass

**33322**　　with cardiopulmonary bypass

**33330**　Insertion of graft, aorta or great vessels; without shunt, or cardiopulmonary bypass

**33332**　　with shunt bypass

**33335**　　with cardiopulmonary bypass

## Cardiac Valves

(For multiple valve procedures, see 33400-33478 and add modifier 51 to the secondary valve procedure code)

### Aortic Valve

►Codes 33361, 33362, 33363, 33364, 33365, 33366 are used to report transcatheter aortic valve replacement (TAVR)/transcatheter aortic valve implantation (TAVI). TAVR/TAVI requires two physician operators and all components of the procedure are reported using modifier 62.

Codes 33361, 33362, 33363, 33364, 33365, 33366 include the work, when performed, of percutaneous access, placing the access sheath, balloon aortic valvuloplasty, advancing the valve delivery system into

**Cardiovascular**

position, repositioning the valve as needed, deploying the valve, temporary pacemaker insertion for rapid pacing (33210), and closure of the arteriotomy when performed. Codes 33361, 33362, 33363, 33364, 33365, 33366 include open arterial or cardiac approach.◄

Angiography, radiological supervision, and interpretation performed to guide TAVR/TAVI (eg, guiding valve placement, documenting completion of the intervention, assessing the vascular access site for closure) are included in these codes.

►Diagnostic left heart catheterization codes (93452, 93453, 93458-93461) and the supravalvular aortography code (93567) should **not** be used with TAVR/TAVI services (33361, 33362, 33363, 33364, 33365, 33366) to report:◄

1. Contrast injections, angiography, roadmapping, and/or fluoroscopic guidance for the TAVR/TAVI,

2. Aorta/left ventricular outflow tract measurement for the TAVR/TAVI, or

► 3. Post-TAVR/TAVI aortic or left ventricular angiography, as this work is captured in the TAVR/TAVI services codes (33361, 33362, 33363, 33364, 33365, 33366).◄

Diagnostic coronary angiography performed at the time of TAVR/TAVI may be separately reportable if:

1. No prior catheter-based coronary angiography study is available and a full diagnostic study is performed, or

2. A prior study is available, but as documented in the medical record:

   a. The patient's condition with respect to the clinical indication has changed since the prior study, or

   b. There is inadequate visualization of the anatomy and/or pathology, or

   c. There is a clinical change during the procedure that requires new evaluation.

   d. For same session/same day diagnostic coronary angiography services, report the appropriate diagnostic cardiac catheterization code(s) appended with modifier 59 indicating separate and distinct procedural service from TAVR/TAVI.

Diagnostic coronary angiography performed at a separate session from an interventional procedure may be separately reportable.

►Other cardiac catheterization services may be reported separately when performed for diagnostic purposes not intrinsic to TAVR/TAVI.◄

Percutaneous coronary interventional procedures are reported separately, when performed.

When transcatheter ventricular support is required in conjunction with TAVR/TAVI, the appropriate code should be reported with the appropriate ventricular assist device (VAD) procedure code (33990-33993, 33975, 33976, 33999) or balloon pump insertion code (33967, 33970, 33973).

►The TAVR/TAVI cardiovascular access and delivery procedures are reported with 33361, 33362, 33363, 33364, 33365, 33366. When cardiopulmonary bypass is performed in conjunction with TAVR/TAVI, codes 33361, 33362, 33363, 33364, 33365, 33366 should be reported with the appropriate add-on code for percutaneous peripheral bypass (33367), open peripheral bypass (33368), or central bypass (33369).◄

| | |
|---|---|
| **33361** | Transcatheter aortic valve replacement (TAVR/TAVI) with prosthetic valve; percutaneous femoral artery approach |
| **33362** | open femoral artery approach |
| **33363** | open axillary artery approach |
| **33364** | open iliac artery approach |
| **33365** | transaortic approach (eg, median sternotomy, mediastinotomy) |
| ● **33366** | transapical exposure (eg, left thoracotomy) |
| + **33367** | cardiopulmonary bypass support with percutaneous peripheral arterial and venous cannulation (eg, femoral vessels) (List separately in addition to code for primary procedure) |

►(Use 33367 in conjunction with 33361, 33362, 33363, 33364, 33365, 33366)◄

(Do not report 33367 in conjunction with 33368, 33369)

| | |
|---|---|
| + **33368** | cardiopulmonary bypass support with open peripheral arterial and venous cannulation (eg, femoral, iliac, axillary vessels) (List separately in addition to code for primary procedure) |

►(Use 33368 in conjunction with 33361, 33362, 33363, 33364, 33365, 33366)◄

(Do not report 33368 in conjunction with 33367, 33369)

| | |
|---|---|
| + **33369** | cardiopulmonary bypass support with central arterial and venous cannulation (eg, aorta, right atrium, pulmonary artery) (List separately in addition to code for primary procedure) |

►(Use 33369 in conjunction with 33361, 33362, 33363, 33364, 33365, 33366)◄

(Do not report 33369 in conjunction with 33367, 33368)

| | |
|---|---|
| **33400** | Valvuloplasty, aortic valve; open, with cardiopulmonary bypass |
| **33401** | open, with inflow occlusion |
| **33403** | using transventricular dilation, with cardiopulmonary bypass |

(Do not report modifier 63 in conjunction with 33401, 33403)

33404    Construction of apical-aortic conduit

33405    Replacement, aortic valve, with cardiopulmonary bypass; with prosthetic valve other than homograft or stentless valve

33406       with allograft valve (freehand)

   (For aortic valve valvotomy, [commissurotomy] with inflow occlusion, use 33401)

   (For aortic valve valvotomy, [commissurotomy] with cardiopulmonary bypass, use 33403)

33410       with stentless tissue valve

33411    Replacement, aortic valve; with aortic annulus enlargement, noncoronary sinus

33412       with transventricular aortic annulus enlargement (Konno procedure)

33413       by translocation of autologous pulmonary valve with allograft replacement of pulmonary valve (Ross procedure)

33414    Repair of left ventricular outflow tract obstruction by patch enlargement of the outflow tract

33415    Resection or incision of subvalvular tissue for discrete subvalvular aortic stenosis

33416    Ventriculomyotomy (-myectomy) for idiopathic hypertrophic subaortic stenosis (eg, asymmetric septal hypertrophy)

   ►(For percutaneous transcatheter septal reduction therapy, use 93583)◄

33417    Aortoplasty (gusset) for supravalvular stenosis

## Mitral Valve

33420    Valvotomy, mitral valve; closed heart

33422       open heart, with cardiopulmonary bypass

33425    Valvuloplasty, mitral valve, with cardiopulmonary bypass;

33426       with prosthetic ring

33427       radical reconstruction, with or without ring

33430    Replacement, mitral valve, with cardiopulmonary bypass

## Tricuspid Valve

33460    Valvectomy, tricuspid valve, with cardiopulmonary bypass

33463    Valvuloplasty, tricuspid valve; without ring insertion

33464       with ring insertion

33465    Replacement, tricuspid valve, with cardiopulmonary bypass

33468    Tricuspid valve repositioning and plication for Ebstein anomaly

## Pulmonary Valve

33470    Valvotomy, pulmonary valve, closed heart; transventricular

   (Do not report modifier 63 in conjunction with 33470)

33471       via pulmonary artery

   (To report percutaneous valvuloplasty of pulmonary valve, use 92990)

33472    Valvotomy, pulmonary valve, open heart; with inflow occlusion

   (Do not report modifier 63 in conjunction with 33472)

33474       with cardiopulmonary bypass

33475    Replacement, pulmonary valve

33476    Right ventricular resection for infundibular stenosis, with or without commissurotomy

33478    Outflow tract augmentation (gusset), with or without commissurotomy or infundibular resection

   (Use 33478 in conjunction with 33768 when a cavopulmonary anastomosis to a second superior vena cava is performed)

## Other Valvular Procedures

33496    Repair of non-structural prosthetic valve dysfunction with cardiopulmonary bypass (separate procedure)

   (For reoperation, use 33530 in addition to 33496)

## Coronary Artery Anomalies

Basic procedures include endarterectomy or angioplasty.

33500    Repair of coronary arteriovenous or arteriocardiac chamber fistula; with cardiopulmonary bypass

33501       without cardiopulmonary bypass

33502    Repair of anomalous coronary artery from pulmonary artery origin; by ligation

33503       by graft, without cardiopulmonary bypass

   (Do not report modifier 63 in conjunction with 33502, 33503)

33504       by graft, with cardiopulmonary bypass

33505       with construction of intrapulmonary artery tunnel (Takeuchi procedure)

33506       by translocation from pulmonary artery to aorta

   (Do not report modifier 63 in conjunction with 33505, 33506)

33507    Repair of anomalous (eg, intramural) aortic origin of coronary artery by unroofing or translocation

**Cardiovascular**

## Endoscopy

Surgical vascular endoscopy always includes diagnostic endoscopy.

**+ 33508**    Endoscopy, surgical, including video-assisted harvest of vein(s) for coronary artery bypass procedure (List separately in addition to code for primary procedure)

(Use 33508 in conjunction with 33510-33523)

(For open harvest of upper extremity vein procedure, use 35500)

## Venous Grafting Only for Coronary Artery Bypass

The following codes are used to report coronary artery bypass procedures using venous grafts only. These codes should NOT be used to report the performance of coronary artery bypass procedures using arterial grafts and venous grafts during the same procedure. See 33517-33523 and 33533-33536 for reporting combined arterial-venous grafts.

Procurement of the saphenous vein graft is included in the description of the work for 33510-33516 and should not be reported as a separate service or co-surgery. To report harvesting of an upper extremity vein, use 35500 in addition to the bypass procedure. To report harvesting of a femoropopliteal vein segment, report 35572 in addition to the bypass procedure. When surgical assistant performs graft procurement, add modifier 80 to 33510-33516. For percutaneous ventricular assist device insertion, removal, repositioning, see 33990-33993.

**33510**    Coronary artery bypass, vein only; single coronary venous graft

**33511**        2 coronary venous grafts

**33512**        3 coronary venous grafts

**33513**        4 coronary venous grafts

**33514**        5 coronary venous grafts

**33516**        6 or more coronary venous grafts

## Combined Arterial-Venous Grafting for Coronary Bypass

The following codes are used to report coronary artery bypass procedures using venous grafts and arterial grafts during the same procedure. These codes may NOT be used alone.

To report combined arterial-venous grafts it is necessary to report two codes: (1) the appropriate combined arterial-venous graft code (33517-33523); and (2) the appropriate arterial graft code (33533-33536).

Procurement of the saphenous vein graft is included in the description of the work for 33517-33523 and should not be reported as a separate service or co-surgery. Procurement of the artery for grafting is included in the

description of the work for 33533-33536 and should not be reported as a separate service or co-surgery, except when an upper extremity artery (eg, radial artery) is procured. To report harvesting of an upper extremity artery, use 35600 in addition to the bypass procedure. To report harvesting of an upper extremity vein, use 35500 in addition to the bypass procedure. To report harvesting of a femoropopliteal vein segment, report 35572 in addition to the bypass procedure. When surgical assistant performs arterial and/or venous graft procurement, add modifier 80 to 33517-33523, 33533-33536, as appropriate. For percutaneous ventricular assist device insertion, removal, repositioning, see 33990-33993.

**+ 33517**    Coronary artery bypass, using venous graft(s) and arterial graft(s); single vein graft (List separately in addition to code for primary procedure)

(Use 33517 in conjunction with 33533-33536)

**+ 33518**        2 venous grafts (List separately in addition to code for primary procedure)

(Use 33518 in conjunction with 33533-33536)

**+ 33519**        3 venous grafts (List separately in addition to code for primary procedure)

(Use 33519 in conjunction with 33533-33536)

**+ 33521**        4 venous grafts (List separately in addition to code for primary procedure)

(Use 33521 in conjunction with 33533-33536)

**+ 33522**        5 venous grafts (List separately in addition to code for primary procedure)

(Use 33522 in conjunction with 33533-33536)

**+ 33523**        6 or more venous grafts (List separately in addition to code for primary procedure)

(Use 33523 in conjunction with 33533-33536)

**+ 33530**    Reoperation, coronary artery bypass procedure or valve procedure, more than 1 month after original operation (List separately in addition to code for primary procedure)

(Use 33530 in conjunction with 33400-33496; 33510-33536, 33863)

## Arterial Grafting for Coronary Artery Bypass

The following codes are used to report coronary artery bypass procedures using either arterial grafts only or a combination of arterial-venous grafts. The codes include the use of the internal mammary artery, gastroepiploic artery, epigastric artery, radial artery, and arterial conduits procured from other sites.

To report combined arterial-venous grafts it is necessary to report two codes: (1) the appropriate arterial graft code (33533-33536); and (2) the appropriate combined arterial-venous graft code (33517-33523).

Procurement of the artery for grafting is included in the description of the work for 33533-33536 and should not be reported as a separate service or co-surgery, except when an upper extremity artery (eg, radial artery) is procured. To report harvesting of an upper extremity artery, use 35600 in addition to the bypass procedure. To report harvesting of an upper extremity vein, use 35500 in addition to the bypass procedure. To report harvesting of a femoropopliteal vein segment, report 35572 in addition to the bypass procedure. When surgical assistant performs arterial and/or venous graft procurement, add modifier 80 to 33517-33523, 33533-33536, as appropriate. For percutaneous ventricular assist device insertion, removal, repositioning, see 33990-33993.

**33533**    Coronary artery bypass, using arterial graft(s); single arterial graft

**33534**        2 coronary arterial grafts

**33535**        3 coronary arterial grafts

**33536**        4 or more coronary arterial grafts

**33542**    Myocardial resection (eg, ventricular aneurysmectomy)

**33545**    Repair of postinfarction ventricular septal defect, with or without myocardial resection

**33548**    Surgical ventricular restoration procedure, includes prosthetic patch, when performed (eg, ventricular remodeling, SVR, SAVER, Dor procedures)

(Do not report 33548 in conjunction with 32551, 33210, 33211, 33310, 33315)

(For Batista procedure or pachopexy, use 33999)

## Coronary Endarterectomy

+ **33572**    Coronary endarterectomy, open, any method, of left anterior descending, circumflex, or right coronary artery performed in conjunction with coronary artery bypass graft procedure, each vessel (List separately in addition to primary procedure)

(Use 33572 in conjunction with 33510-33516, 33533-33536)

## Single Ventricle and Other Complex Cardiac Anomalies

**33600**    Closure of atrioventricular valve (mitral or tricuspid) by suture or patch

**33602**    Closure of semilunar valve (aortic or pulmonary) by suture or patch

**33606**    Anastomosis of pulmonary artery to aorta (Damus-Kaye-Stansel procedure)

**33608**    Repair of complex cardiac anomaly other than pulmonary atresia with ventricular septal defect by construction or replacement of conduit from right or left ventricle to pulmonary artery

(For repair of pulmonary artery arborization anomalies by unifocalization, see 33925-33926)

**33610**    Repair of complex cardiac anomalies (eg, single ventricle with subaortic obstruction) by surgical enlargement of ventricular septal defect

(Do not report modifier 63 in conjunction with 33610)

**33611**    Repair of double outlet right ventricle with intraventricular tunnel repair;

(Do not report modifier 63 in conjunction with 33611)

**33612**        with repair of right ventricular outflow tract obstruction

**33615**    Repair of complex cardiac anomalies (eg, tricuspid atresia) by closure of atrial septal defect and anastomosis of atria or vena cava to pulmonary artery (simple Fontan procedure)

**33617**    Repair of complex cardiac anomalies (eg, single ventricle) by modified Fontan procedure

(Use 33617 in conjunction with 33768 when a cavopulmonary anastomosis to a second superior vena cava is performed)

**33619**    Repair of single ventricle with aortic outflow obstruction and aortic arch hypoplasia (hypoplastic left heart syndrome) (eg, Norwood procedure)

(Do not report modifier 63 in conjunction with 33619)

**33620**    Application of right and left pulmonary artery bands (eg, hybrid approach stage 1)

(For banding of the main pulmonary artery related to septal defect, use 33690)

**33621**    Transthoracic insertion of catheter for stent placement with catheter removal and closure (eg, hybrid approach stage 1)

▶(For placement of stent, use 37236)◀

(Report both 33620, 33621 if performed in same session)

**33622**    Reconstruction of complex cardiac anomaly (eg, single ventricle or hypoplastic left heart) with palliation of single ventricle with aortic outflow obstruction and aortic arch hypoplasia, creation of cavopulmonary anastomosis, and removal of right and left pulmonary bands (eg, hybrid approach stage 2, Norwood, bidirectional Glenn, pulmonary artery debanding)

(Do not report 33622 in conjunction with 33619, 33767, 33822, 33840, 33845, 33851, 33853, 33917)

(For bilateral, bidirectional Glenn procedure, use 33622 in conjunction with 33768)

## Septal Defect

**33641**    Repair atrial septal defect, secundum, with cardiopulmonary bypass, with or without patch

**33645**    Direct or patch closure, sinus venosus, with or without anomalous pulmonary venous drainage

(Do not report 33645 in conjunction with 33724, 33726)

**Cardiovascular**

**Cardiovascular**

**33647**   Repair of atrial septal defect and ventricular septal defect, with direct or patch closure

(Do not report modifier 63 in conjunction with 33647)

(For repair of tricuspid atresia (eg, Fontan, Gago procedures), use 33615)

**33660**   Repair of incomplete or partial atrioventricular canal (ostium primum atrial septal defect), with or without atrioventricular valve repair

**33665**   Repair of intermediate or transitional atrioventricular canal, with or without atrioventricular valve repair

**33670**   Repair of complete atrioventricular canal, with or without prosthetic valve

(Do not report modifier 63 in conjunction with 33670)

**33675**   Closure of multiple ventricular septal defects;

**33676**      with pulmonary valvotomy or infundibular resection (acyanotic)

**33677**      with removal of pulmonary artery band, with or without gusset

(Do not report 33675-33677 in conjunction with 32100, 32551, 32554, 32555, 33210, 33681, 33684, 33688)

(For percutaneous closure, use 93581)

**33681**   Closure of single ventricular septal defect, with or without patch;

**33684**      with pulmonary valvotomy or infundibular resection (acyanotic)

**33688**      with removal of pulmonary artery band, with or without gusset

(For pulmonary vein repair requiring creation of atrial septal defect, use 33724)

**33690**   Banding of pulmonary artery

(For right and left pulmonary artery banding in a single ventricle [eg, hybrid approach stage 1], use 33620)

(Do not report modifier 63 in conjunction with 33690)

**33692**   Complete repair tetralogy of Fallot without pulmonary atresia;

**33694**      with transannular patch

(Do not report modifier 63 in conjunction with 33694)

(For ligation and takedown of a systemic-to-pulmonary artery shunt, performed in conjunction with a congenital heart procedure; see 33924)

**33697**   Complete repair tetralogy of Fallot with pulmonary atresia including construction of conduit from right ventricle to pulmonary artery and closure of ventricular septal defect

(For ligation and takedown of a systemic-to-pulmonary artery shunt, performed in conjunction with a congenital heart procedure; see 33924)

## Sinus of Valsalva

**33702**   Repair sinus of Valsalva fistula, with cardiopulmonary bypass;

**33710**      with repair of ventricular septal defect

**33720**   Repair sinus of Valsalva aneurysm, with cardiopulmonary bypass

**33722**   Closure of aortico-left ventricular tunnel

## Venous Anomalies

**33724**   Repair of isolated partial anomalous pulmonary venous return (eg, Scimitar Syndrome)

(Do not report 33724 in conjunction with 32551, 33210, 33211)

**33726**   Repair of pulmonary venous stenosis

(Do not report 33726 in conjunction with 32551, 33210, 33211)

**33730**   Complete repair of anomalous pulmonary venous return (supracardiac, intracardiac, or infracardiac types)

(Do not report modifier 63 in conjunction with 33730)

(For partial anomalous pulmonary venous return, use 33724; for repair of pulmonary venous stenosis, use 33726)

**33732**   Repair of cor triatriatum or supravalvular mitral ring by resection of left atrial membrane

(Do not report modifier 63 in conjunction with 33732)

## Shunting Procedures

**33735**   Atrial septectomy or septostomy; closed heart (Blalock-Hanlon type operation)

**33736**      open heart with cardiopulmonary bypass

(Do not report modifier 63 in conjunction with 33735, 33736)

**33737**      open heart, with inflow occlusion

(For transvenous method cardiac catheterization balloon atrial septectomy or septostomy (Rashkind type), use 92992)

(For blade method cardiac catheterization atrial septectomy or septostomy (Sang-Park septostomy), use 92993)

**33750**   Shunt; subclavian to pulmonary artery (Blalock-Taussig type operation)

**33755**      ascending aorta to pulmonary artery (Waterston type operation)

**33762**      descending aorta to pulmonary artery (Potts-Smith type operation)

(Do not report modifier 63 in conjunction with 33750, 33755, 33762)

**33764**      central, with prosthetic graft

33766     superior vena cava to pulmonary artery for flow to 1 lung (classical Glenn procedure)

33767     superior vena cava to pulmonary artery for flow to both lungs (bidirectional Glenn procedure)

+ 33768     Anastomosis, cavopulmonary, second superior vena cava (List separately in addition to primary procedure)

(Use 33768 in conjunction with 33478, 33617, 33622, 33767)

(Do not report 33768 in conjunction with 32551, 33210, 33211)

## Transposition of the Great Vessels

33770     Repair of transposition of the great arteries with ventricular septal defect and subpulmonary stenosis; without surgical enlargement of ventricular septal defect

33771     with surgical enlargement of ventricular septal defect

33774     Repair of transposition of the great arteries, atrial baffle procedure (eg, Mustard or Senning type) with cardiopulmonary bypass;

33775     with removal of pulmonary band

33776     with closure of ventricular septal defect

33777     with repair of subpulmonic obstruction

33778     Repair of transposition of the great arteries, aortic pulmonary artery reconstruction (eg, Jatene type);

(Do not report modifier 63 in conjunction with 33778)

33779     with removal of pulmonary band

33780     with closure of ventricular septal defect

33781     with repair of subpulmonic obstruction

33782     Aortic root translocation with ventricular septal defect and pulmonary stenosis repair (ie, Nikaidoh procedure); without coronary ostium reimplantation

(Do not report 33782 in conjunction with 33412, 33413, 33608, 33681, 33770, 33771, 33778, 33780, 33920)

33783     with reimplantation of 1 or both coronary ostia

## Truncus Arteriosus

33786     Total repair, truncus arteriosus (Rastelli type operation)

(Do not report modifier 63 in conjunction with 33786)

33788     Reimplantation of an anomalous pulmonary artery

(For pulmonary artery band, use 33690)

## Aortic Anomalies

33800     Aortic suspension (aortopexy) for tracheal decompression (eg, for tracheomalacia) (separate procedure)

33802     Division of aberrant vessel (vascular ring);

33803     with reanastomosis

33813     Obliteration of aortopulmonary septal defect; without cardiopulmonary bypass

33814     with cardiopulmonary bypass

33820     Repair of patent ductus arteriosus; by ligation

33822     by division, younger than 18 years

33824     by division, 18 years and older

►(For percutaneous transcatheter closure of patent ductus arteriosus, use 93582)◄

33840     Excision of coarctation of aorta, with or without associated patent ductus arteriosus; with direct anastomosis

33845     with graft

33851     repair using either left subclavian artery or prosthetic material as gusset for enlargement

33852     Repair of hypoplastic or interrupted aortic arch using autogenous or prosthetic material; without cardiopulmonary bypass

33853     with cardiopulmonary bypass

(For repair of hypoplastic left heart syndrome (eg, Norwood type), via excision of coarctation of aorta, use 33619)

## Thoracic Aortic Aneurysm

33860     Ascending aorta graft, with cardiopulmonary bypass, includes valve suspension, when performed

(33861 has been deleted. To report, use 33864)

33863     Ascending aorta graft, with cardiopulmonary bypass, with aortic root replacement using valved conduit and coronary reconstruction (eg, Bentall)

(Do not report 33863 in conjunction with 33405, 33406, 33410, 33411, 33412, 33413, 33860)

33864     Ascending aorta graft, with cardiopulmonary bypass with valve suspension, with coronary reconstruction and valve-sparing aortic root remodeling (eg, David Procedure, Yacoub Procedure)

(Do not report 33864 in conjunction with 33400, 33860-33863)

33870     Transverse arch graft, with cardiopulmonary bypass

33875     Descending thoracic aorta graft, with or without bypass

33877     Repair of thoracoabdominal aortic aneurysm with graft, with or without cardiopulmonary bypass

## Endovascular Repair of Descending Thoracic Aorta

Codes 33880-33891 represent a family of procedures to report placement of an endovascular graft for repair of the descending thoracic aorta. These codes include all device introduction, manipulation, positioning, and deployment. All balloon angioplasty and/or stent

**Cardiovascular**

**Cardiovascular**

deployment within the target treatment zone for the endoprosthesis, either before or after endograft deployment, are not separately reportable. Open arterial exposure and associated closure of the arteriotomy sites (eg, 34812, 34820, 34833, 34834), introduction of guidewires and catheters (eg, 36140, 36200-36218), and extensive repair or replacement of an artery (eg, 35226, 35286) should be additionally reported. Transposition of subclavian artery to carotid, and carotid-carotid bypass performed in conjunction with endovascular repair of the descending thoracic aorta (eg, 33889, 33891) should be separately reported. The primary codes, 33880 and 33881, include placement of all distal extensions, if required, in the distal thoracic aorta, while proximal extensions, if needed, are reported separately.

For fluoroscopic guidance in conjunction with endovascular repair of the thoracic aorta, see codes 75956-75959 as appropriate. Codes 75956 and 75957 include all angiography of the thoracic aorta and its branches for diagnostic imaging prior to deployment of the primary endovascular devices (including all routine components of modular devices), fluoroscopic guidance in the delivery of the endovascular components, and intraprocedural arterial angiography (eg, confirm position, detect endoleak, evaluate runoff). Code 75958 includes the analogous services for placement of each proximal thoracic endovascular extension. Code 75959 includes the analogous services for placement of a distal thoracic endovascular extension(s) placed during a procedure after the primary repair.

Other interventional procedures performed at the time of endovascular repair of the descending thoracic aorta should be additionally reported (eg, innominate, carotid, subclavian, visceral, or iliac artery transluminal angioplasty or stenting, arterial embolization, intravascular ultrasound) when performed before or after deployment of the aortic prostheses.

(For transcatheter placement of wireless physiologic sensor in aneurysmal sac, use 34806)

(For analysis, interpretation, and report of implanted wireless pressure sensor in aneurysmal sac, use 93982)

**33880** Endovascular repair of descending thoracic aorta (eg, aneurysm, pseudoaneurysm, dissection, penetrating ulcer, intramural hematoma, or traumatic disruption); involving coverage of left subclavian artery origin, initial endoprosthesis plus descending thoracic aortic extension(s), if required, to level of celiac artery origin

(For radiological supervision and interpretation, use 75956 in conjunction with 33880)

**33881** not involving coverage of left subclavian artery origin, initial endoprosthesis plus descending thoracic aortic extension(s), if required, to level of celiac artery origin

(For radiological supervision and interpretation, use 75957 in conjunction with 33881)

**33883** Placement of proximal extension prosthesis for endovascular repair of descending thoracic aorta (eg, aneurysm, pseudoaneurysm, dissection, penetrating ulcer, intramural hematoma, or traumatic disruption); initial extension

(For radiological supervision and interpretation, use 75958 in conjunction with 33883)

(Do not report 33881, 33883 when extension placement converts repair to cover left subclavian origin. Use only 33880)

**+ 33884** each additional proximal extension (List separately in addition to code for primary procedure)

(Use 33884 in conjunction with 33883)

(For radiological supervision and interpretation, use 75958 in conjunction with 33884)

**33886** Placement of distal extension prosthesis(s) delayed after endovascular repair of descending thoracic aorta

(Do not report 33886 in conjunction with 33880, 33881)

(Report 33886 once, regardless of number of modules deployed)

(For radiological supervision and interpretation, use 75959 in conjunction with 33886)

**33889** Open subclavian to carotid artery transposition performed in conjunction with endovascular repair of descending thoracic aorta, by neck incision, unilateral

(Do not report 33889 in conjunction with 35694)

**33891** Bypass graft, with other than vein, transcervical retropharyngeal carotid-carotid, performed in conjunction with endovascular repair of descending thoracic aorta, by neck incision

(Do not report 33891 in conjunction with 35509, 35601)

## Pulmonary Artery

**33910** Pulmonary artery embolectomy; with cardiopulmonary bypass

**33915** without cardiopulmonary bypass

**33916** Pulmonary endarterectomy, with or without embolectomy, with cardiopulmonary bypass

**33917** Repair of pulmonary artery stenosis by reconstruction with patch or graft

**33920** Repair of pulmonary atresia with ventricular septal defect, by construction or replacement of conduit from right or left ventricle to pulmonary artery

(For repair of other complex cardiac anomalies by construction or replacement of right or left ventricle to pulmonary artery conduit, use 33608)

**33922** Transection of pulmonary artery with cardiopulmonary bypass

(Do not report modifier 63 in conjunction with 33922)

**+ 33924**   Ligation and takedown of a systemic-to-pulmonary artery shunt, performed in conjunction with a congenital heart procedure (List separately in addition to code for primary procedure)

(Use 33924 in conjunction with 33470-33475, 33600-33619, 33684-33688, 33692-33697, 33735-33767, 33770-33781, 33786, 33920-33922)

**33925**   Repair of pulmonary artery arborization anomalies by unifocalization; without cardiopulmonary bypass

**33926**        with cardiopulmonary bypass

## Heart/Lung Transplantation

Heart with or without lung allotransplantation involves three distinct components of physician work:

1. *Cadaver donor cardiectomy with or without pneumonectomy,* which includes harvesting the allograft and cold preservation of the allograft (perfusing with cold preservation solution and cold maintenance) (see 33930, 33940).

2. *Backbench work:*

   Preparation of a cadaver donor heart and lung allograft prior to transplantation, including dissection of the allograft from surrounding soft tissues to prepare the aorta, superior vena cava, inferior vena cava, and trachea for implantation (use 33933).

   Preparation of a cadaver donor heart allograft prior to transplantation, including dissection of the allograft from surrounding soft tissues to prepare aorta, superior vena cava, inferior vena cava, pulmonary artery, and left atrium for implantation (use 33944).

3. *Recipient heart with or without lung allotransplantation,* which includes transplantation of allograft and care of the recipient (see 33935, 33945).

(For implantation of a total replacement heart system (artificial heart) with recipient cardiectomy or heart replacement system components, see Category III codes 0051T-0053T)

**33930**   Donor cardiectomy-pneumonectomy (including cold preservation)

**33933**   Backbench standard preparation of cadaver donor heart/lung allograft prior to transplantation, including dissection of allograft from surrounding soft tissues to prepare aorta, superior vena cava, inferior vena cava, and trachea for implantation

**33935**   Heart-lung transplant with recipient cardiectomy-pneumonectomy

**33940**   Donor cardiectomy (including cold preservation)

**33944**   Backbench standard preparation of cadaver donor heart allograft prior to transplantation, including dissection of allograft from surrounding soft tissues to prepare aorta, superior vena cava, inferior vena cava, pulmonary artery, and left atrium for implantation

(For repair or resection procedures on the donor heart, see 33300, 33310, 33320, 33400, 33463, 33464, 33510, 33641, 35216, 35276 or 35685)

**33945**   Heart transplant, with or without recipient cardiectomy

## Cardiac Assist

The insertion of a ventricular assist device (VAD) can be performed via percutaneous (33990, 33991) or transthoracic (33975, 33976, 33979) approach. The location of the ventricular assist device may be intracorporeal or extracorporeal.

For surgical insertion of cannula(s) for prolonged extracorporeal circulation for cardiopulmonary insufficiency (ECMO), use 36822.

Open arterial exposure when necessary to facilitate percutaneous ventricular assist device insertion (33990, 33991), may be reported separately (34812). Extensive repair or replacement of an artery may be additionally reported (eg, 35226 or 35286).

Removal of a ventricular assist device (33977, 33978, 33980, 33992) includes removal of the entire device, including the cannulas. Removal of a percutaneous ventricular assist device at the same session as insertion is not separately reportable. For removal of a percutaneous ventricular assist device at a separate and distinct session, but on the same day as insertion, report 33992 appended with modifier 59 indicating a distinct procedural service.

Repositioning of a percutaneous ventricular assist device at the same session as insertion is not separately reportable. Repositioning of percutaneous ventricular assist device not necessitating imaging guidance is not a reportable service. For repositioning of a percutaneous ventricular assist device necessitating imaging guidance at a separate and distinct session, but on the same day as insertion, report 33993 with modifier 59 indicating a distinct procedural service.

Replacement of a ventricular assist device pump (ie, 33981-33983) includes the removal of the pump and insertion of a new pump, connection, de-airing, and initiation of the new pump.

Replacement of the entire implantable ventricular assist device system, ie, pump(s) and cannulas, is reported using the insertion codes (ie, 33975, 33976, 33979). Removal (ie, 33977, 33978, 33980) of the ventricular assist device system being replaced is not separately reported. Replacement of a percutaneous ventricular assist device is reported using implantation codes (ie, 33990, 33991). Removal (ie, 33992) is not reported separately.

**33960**   Prolonged extracorporeal circulation for cardiopulmonary insufficiency; initial day

Cardiovascular

⊘ **33961**      each subsequent day

(Do not report modifier 63 in conjunction with 33960, 33961)

(For insertion of cannula for prolonged extracorporeal circulation, use 36822)

**33967**   Insertion of intra-aortic balloon assist device, percutaneous

**33968**   Removal of intra-aortic balloon assist device, percutaneous

**33970**   Insertion of intra-aortic balloon assist device through the femoral artery, open approach

**33971**   Removal of intra-aortic balloon assist device including repair of femoral artery, with or without graft

**33973**   Insertion of intra-aortic balloon assist device through the ascending aorta

**33974**   Removal of intra-aortic balloon assist device from the ascending aorta, including repair of the ascending aorta, with or without graft

**33975**   Insertion of ventricular assist device; extracorporeal, single ventricle

**33976**      extracorporeal, biventricular

**33977**   Removal of ventricular assist device; extracorporeal, single ventricle

**33978**      extracorporeal, biventricular

**33979**   Insertion of ventricular assist device, implantable intracorporeal, single ventricle

**33980**   Removal of ventricular assist device, implantable intracorporeal, single ventricle

**33981**   Replacement of extracorporeal ventricular assist device, single or biventricular, pump(s), single or each pump

**33982**   Replacement of ventricular assist device pump(s); implantable intracorporeal, single ventricle, without cardiopulmonary bypass

**33983**      implantable intracorporeal, single ventricle, with cardiopulmonary bypass

⊙ **33990**   Insertion of ventricular assist device, percutaneous including radiological supervision and interpretation; arterial access only

⊙ **33991**      both arterial and venous access, with transseptal puncture

⊙ **33992**   Removal of percutaneous ventricular assist device at separate and distinct session from insertion

⊙ **33993**   Repositioning of percutaneous ventricular assist device with imaging guidance at separate and distinct session from insertion

## Other Procedures

**33999**   Unlisted procedure, cardiac surgery

## Arteries and Veins

Primary vascular procedure listings include establishing both inflow and outflow by whatever procedures necessary. Also included is that portion of the operative arteriogram performed by the surgeon, as indicated. Sympathectomy, when done, is included in the listed aortic procedures. For unlisted vascular procedure, use 37799.

## Embolectomy/Thrombectomy

### Arterial, With or Without Catheter

**34001**   Embolectomy or thrombectomy, with or without catheter; carotid, subclavian or innominate artery, by neck incision

**34051**      innominate, subclavian artery, by thoracic incision

**34101**      axillary, brachial, innominate, subclavian artery, by arm incision

**34111**      radial or ulnar artery, by arm incision

**34151**      renal, celiac, mesentery, aortoiliac artery, by abdominal incision

**34201**      femoropopliteal, aortoiliac artery, by leg incision

**34203**      popliteal-tibio-peroneal artery, by leg incision

### Venous, Direct or With Catheter

**34401**   Thrombectomy, direct or with catheter; vena cava, iliac vein, by abdominal incision

**34421**      vena cava, iliac, femoropopliteal vein, by leg incision

**34451**      vena cava, iliac, femoropopliteal vein, by abdominal and leg incision

**34471**      subclavian vein, by neck incision

**34490**      axillary and subclavian vein, by arm incision

## Venous Reconstruction

**34501**   Valvuloplasty, femoral vein

**34502**   Reconstruction of vena cava, any method

**34510**   Venous valve transposition, any vein donor

**34520**   Cross-over vein graft to venous system

**34530**   Saphenopopliteal vein anastomosis

## Endovascular Repair of Abdominal Aortic Aneurysm

Codes 34800-34826 represent a family of component procedures to report placement of an endovascular graft for abdominal aortic aneurysm repair. These codes describe open femoral or iliac artery exposure, device manipulation and deployment, and closure of the arteriotomy sites. Balloon angioplasty and/or stent

Cardiovascular

deployment within the target treatment zone for the endoprosthesis, either before or after endograft deployment, are not separately reportable. Introduction of guidewires and catheters should be reported separately (eg, 36200, 36245-36248, 36140). Extensive repair or replacement of an artery should be additionally reported (eg, 35226 or 35286).

For fluoroscopic guidance in conjunction with endovascular aneurysm repair, see code 75952 or 75953, as appropriate. Code 75952 includes angiography of the aorta and its branches for diagnostic imaging prior to deployment of the endovascular device (including all routine components of modular devices), fluoroscopic guidance in the delivery of the endovascular components, and intraprocedural arterial angiography (eg, confirm position, detect endoleak, evaluate runoff). Code 75953 includes the analogous services for placement of additional extension prostheses (not for routine components of modular devices).

Other interventional procedures performed at the time of endovascular abdominal aortic aneurysm repair should be additionally reported (eg, renal transluminal angioplasty, arterial embolization, intravascular ultrasound, balloon angioplasty or stenting of native artery[s] outside the endoprosthesis target zone, when done before or after deployment of graft).

▶(For fenestrated endovascular repair of the visceral aorta, see 34841-34844. For fenestrated endovascular repair of the visceral aorta and concomitant infrarenal abdominal aorta, see 34845-34848)◀

(For transcatheter placement of wireless physiologic sensor in aneurysmal sac, use 34806)

(For analysis, interpretation and report of implanted wireless pressure sensor in aneurysmal sac, use 93982)

**34800**    Endovascular repair of infrarenal abdominal aortic aneurysm or dissection; using aorto-aortic tube prosthesis

**34802**      using modular bifurcated prosthesis (1 docking limb)

**34803**      using modular bifurcated prosthesis (2 docking limbs)

**34804**      using unibody bifurcated prosthesis

**34805**      using aorto-uniiliac or aorto-unifemoral prosthesis

(For radiological supervision and interpretation, use 75952 in conjunction with 34800-34805)

▶(Do not report 34800, 34802, 34803, 34804, 34805 in conjunction with 34841-34848)◀

**+ 34806**    Transcatheter placement of wireless physiologic sensor in aneurysmal sac during endovascular repair, including radiological supervision and interpretation, instrument calibration, and collection of pressure data (List separately in addition to code for primary procedure)

(Use 34806 in conjunction with 33880, 33881, 33886, 34800-34805, 34825, 34900)

(Do not report 34806 in conjunction with 93982)

**+ 34808**    Endovascular placement of iliac artery occlusion device (List separately in addition to code for primary procedure)

(Use 34808 in conjunction with 34800, 34805, 34813, 34825, 34826)

(For open arterial exposure, report 34812, 34820, 34833, 34834 as appropriate, in addition to 34800-34808)

**34812**    Open femoral artery exposure for delivery of endovascular prosthesis, by groin incision, unilateral

(For bilateral procedure, use modifier 50)

**+ 34813**    Placement of femoral-femoral prosthetic graft during endovascular aortic aneurysm repair (List separately in addition to code for primary procedure)

(Use 34813 in conjunction with 34812)

(For femoral artery grafting, see 35521, 35533, 35539, 35540, 35556, 35558, 35566, 35621, 35646, 35654-35661, 35666, 35700)

**34820**    Open iliac artery exposure for delivery of endovascular prosthesis or iliac occlusion during endovascular therapy, by abdominal or retroperitoneal incision, unilateral

(For bilateral procedure, use modifier 50)

**34825**    Placement of proximal or distal extension prosthesis for endovascular repair of infrarenal abdominal aortic or iliac aneurysm, false aneurysm, or dissection; initial vessel

**+ 34826**      each additional vessel (List separately in addition to code for primary procedure)

(Use 34826 in conjunction with 34825)

(Use 34825, 34826 in addition to 34800-34805, 34900 as appropriate)

(For radiological supervision and interpretation, use 75953)

**34830**    Open repair of infrarenal aortic aneurysm or dissection, plus repair of associated arterial trauma, following unsuccessful endovascular repair; tube prosthesis

**34831**      aorto-bi-iliac prosthesis

**34832**      aorto-bifemoral prosthesis

**34833**    Open iliac artery exposure with creation of conduit for delivery of aortic or iliac endovascular prosthesis, by abdominal or retroperitoneal incision, unilateral

(Do not report 34833 in addition to 34820)

(For bilateral procedure, use modifier 50)

**34834**    Open brachial artery exposure to assist in the deployment of aortic or iliac endovascular prosthesis by arm incision, unilateral

(For bilateral procedure, use modifier 50)

## ▶Fenestrated Endovascular Repair of the Visceral and Infrarenal Aorta◀

▶The upper abdominal aorta that contains the celiac, superior mesenteric, and renal arteries is termed the visceral aorta. For reporting purposes, the thoracic aorta extends from the aortic valve to the aortic segment just proximal to the celiac artery. Codes 34841-34848 are used to report placement of a fenestrated endovascular graft in the visceral aorta, either alone or in combination with the infrarenal aorta for aneurysm, pseudoaneurysm, dissection, penetrating ulcer, intramural hematoma, or traumatic disruption. The fenestrated main body endoprosthesis is deployed within the visceral aorta. Fenestrations within the fabric allow for selective catheterization of the visceral and/or renal arteries and subsequent placement of an endoprosthesis (ie, bare metal or covered stent) to maintain flow to the visceral artery.

Fenestrated aortic repair is reported based on the extent of aorta treated. Codes 34841-34844 describe repair using proximal endoprostheses that span from the visceral aortic component to one, two, three, or four visceral artery origins and distal extent limited to the infrarenal aorta. These devices do not extend into the common iliac arteries. Codes 34845-34848 are used to report deployment of a fenestrated endoprosthesis that spans from the visceral aorta (including one, two, three, or four visceral artery origins) through the infrarenal aorta into the common iliac arteries. The infrarenal component may be a bifurcated unibody device, a modular bifurcated docking system with docking limb(s), or an aorto-uniiliac or aorta-unifemoral device. Codes 34845-34848 include placement of unilateral or bilateral docking limbs (depending on the device). Any additional stent graft extensions that terminate in the common iliac arteries are included in the work described by 34845-34848. Codes 34825 and 34826 may not be separately reported for proximal abdominal aortic extension prosthesis(es) or for distal extension prosthesis(es) that terminate in the aorta or the common iliac arteries. However, codes 34825 and 34826 may be reported for distal extension prosthesis(es) that terminate in the internal iliac, external iliac, or common femoral artery(s).

Codes 34841-34844 and 34845-34848 define the total number of visceral and/or renal arteries (ie, celiac, superior mesenteric, and/or unilateral or bilateral renal artery[s]) requiring placement of an endoprosthesis (ie, bare metal or covered stent) through an aortic endograft fenestration.

Introduction of guide wires and catheters in the aorta and visceral and/or renal arteries is included in the work of 34841-34848 and is not separately reportable. However, catheterization of the hypogastric artery(s) and/or arterial families outside the treatment zone of the graft may be separately reported. Balloon angioplasty within the target treatment zone of the endograft, either before or after endograft deployment, is not separately reportable. Fluoroscopic guidance and radiological supervision and interpretation in conjunction with fenestrated endovascular aortic repair is not separately reportable and includes angiographic diagnostic imaging of the aorta and its branches prior to deployment of the fenestrated endovascular device, fluoroscopic guidance in the delivery of the fenestrated endovascular components, and intraprocedural arterial angiography (eg, confirm position, detect endoleak, evaluate runoff) done at the time of the endovascular aortic repair.

Exposure of the access vessels (eg, 34812) may be reported separately. Extensive repair of an artery (eg, 35226, 35286) may be reported separately. For concomitant endovascular treatment of the descending thoracic aorta, report 33880-33886 and 75956-75959 with 34841-34848. For isolated endovascular infrarenal abdominal aortic aneurysm repair that does not require placement of a fenestrated graft to preserve flow to the visceral branch(es), see 34800-34805.

Other interventional procedures performed at the time of fenestrated endovascular abdominal aortic aneurysm repair may be reported separately (eg, arterial embolization, intravascular ultrasound, balloon angioplasty or stenting of native artery[s] outside the endoprosthesis target zone, when done before or after deployment of endoprosthesis).◄

● **34841** Endovascular repair of visceral aorta (eg, aneurysm, pseudoaneurysm, dissection, penetrating ulcer, intramural hematoma, or traumatic disruption) by deployment of a fenestrated visceral aortic endograft and all associated radiological supervision and interpretation, including target zone angioplasty, when performed; including one visceral artery endoprosthesis (superior mesenteric, celiac or renal artery)

● **34842** including two visceral artery endoprostheses (superior mesenteric, celiac and/or renal artery[s])

● **34843** including three visceral artery endoprostheses (superior mesenteric, celiac and/or renal artery[s])

● **34844** including four or more visceral artery endoprostheses (superior mesenteric, celiac and/or renal artery[s])

►(Do not report 34841-34844 in conjunction with 34800, 34802, 34803, 34804, 34805, 34845-34848, 35081, 35102, 35452, 35472, 75952)◄

● **34845** Endovascular repair of visceral aorta and infrarenal abdominal aorta (eg, aneurysm, pseudoaneurysm, dissection, penetrating ulcer, intramural hematoma, or traumatic disruption) with a fenestrated visceral aortic endograft and concomitant unibody or modular infrarenal aortic endograft and all associated radiological supervision and interpretation, including target zone angioplasty, when performed; including one visceral artery endoprosthesis (superior mesenteric, celiac or renal artery)

● **34846** including two visceral artery endoprostheses (superior mesenteric, celiac and/or renal artery[s])

● **34847** including three visceral artery endoprostheses (superior mesenteric, celiac and/or renal artery[s])

● **34848** including four or more visceral artery endoprostheses (superior mesenteric, celiac and/or renal artery[s])

⊙=Moderate sedation ✦=Add-on code ✗=FDA approval pending #=Resequenced code ○=Recycled/reinstated code

►(Do not report 34845-34848 in conjunction with 34800, 34802, 34803, 34804, 34805, 34841-34844, 35081, 35102, 35452, 35472, 75952)◄

►(Do not report 34841-34848 in conjunction with 37236, 37237 for bare metal or covered stents placed into the visceral branches within the endoprosthesis target zone)◄

►(For placement of distal extension prosthesis[es] terminating in the internal iliac, external iliac, or common femoral artery[s], see 34825-34826, 75953, 0254T, 0255T)◄

►(Use 34845-34848 in conjunction with 37220-37223 only when 34845-34848 are performed outside the target treatment zone of the endoprosthesis)◄

## Endovascular Repair of Iliac Aneurysm

Code 34900 represents a procedure to report introduction, positioning, and deployment of an endovascular graft for treatment of aneurysm, pseudoaneurysm, or arteriovenous malformation or trauma of the iliac artery (common, hypogastric, external). All balloon angioplasty and/or stent deployments within the target treatment zone for the endoprosthesis, either before or after endograft deployment, are included in the work of 34900 and are not separately reportable. Open femoral or iliac artery exposure (eg, 34812, 34820), introduction of guidewires and catheters (eg, 36200, 36245-36248), and extensive repair or replacement of an artery (eg, 35206-35286) should be additionally reported.

For fluoroscopic guidance in conjunction with endovascular iliac aneurysm repair, see code 75954. Code 75954 includes angiography of the aorta and iliac arteries for diagnostic imaging prior to deployment of the endovascular device (including all routine components), fluoroscopic guidance in the delivery of the endovascular components, and intraprocedural arterial angiography to confirm appropriate position of the graft, detect endoleaks, and evaluate the status of the runoff vessels (eg, evaluation for dissection, stenosis, thrombosis, distal embolization, or iatrogenic injury).

Other interventional procedures performed at the time of endovascular iliac aneurysm repair should be additionally reported (eg, transluminal angioplasty outside the aneurysm target zone, arterial embolization, intravascular ultrasound).

**34900**    Endovascular repair of iliac artery (eg, aneurysm, pseudoaneurysm, arteriovenous malformation, trauma) using ilio-iliac tube endoprosthesis

(For endovascular repair of iliac artery bifurcation [eg, aneurysm, pseudoaneurysm, arteriovenous malformation, trauma] using bifurcated endoprosthesis, use 0254T)

(For radiological supervision and interpretation, use 75954)

(For placement of extension prosthesis during endovascular iliac artery repair, use 34825)

(For bilateral procedure, use modifier 50)

## Direct Repair of Aneurysm or Excision (Partial or Total) and Graft Insertion for Aneurysm, Pseudoaneurysm, Ruptured Aneurysm, and Associated Occlusive Disease

Procedures 35001-35152 include preparation of artery for anastomosis including endarterectomy.

(For direct repairs associated with occlusive disease only, see 35201-35286)

(For intracranial aneurysm, see 61700 et seq)

(For endovascular repair of abdominal aortic aneurysm, see 34800-34826)

(For endovascular repair of iliac artery aneurysm, see 34900)

(For thoracic aortic aneurysm, see 33860-33875)

(For endovascular repair of descending thoracic aorta, involving coverage of left subclavian artery origin, use 33880)

**35001**    Direct repair of aneurysm, pseudoaneurysm, or excision (partial or total) and graft insertion, with or without patch graft; for aneurysm and associated occlusive disease, carotid, subclavian artery, by neck incision

**35002**        for ruptured aneurysm, carotid, subclavian artery, by neck incision

**35005**        for aneurysm, pseudoaneurysm, and associated occlusive disease, vertebral artery

**35011**        for aneurysm and associated occlusive disease, axillary-brachial artery, by arm incision

**35013**        for ruptured aneurysm, axillary-brachial artery, by arm incision

**35021**        for aneurysm, pseudoaneurysm, and associated occlusive disease, innominate, subclavian artery, by thoracic incision

**35022**        for ruptured aneurysm, innominate, subclavian artery, by thoracic incision

**35045**        for aneurysm, pseudoaneurysm, and associated occlusive disease, radial or ulnar artery

**35081**        for aneurysm, pseudoaneurysm, and associated occlusive disease, abdominal aorta

**35082**        for ruptured aneurysm, abdominal aorta

**35091**        for aneurysm, pseudoaneurysm, and associated occlusive disease, abdominal aorta involving visceral vessels (mesenteric, celiac, renal)

**35092**        for ruptured aneurysm, abdominal aorta involving visceral vessels (mesenteric, celiac, renal)

**Cardiovascular**

| 35102 | for aneurysm, pseudoaneurysm, and associated occlusive disease, abdominal aorta involving iliac vessels (common, hypogastric, external) |
| 35103 | for ruptured aneurysm, abdominal aorta involving iliac vessels (common, hypogastric, external) |
| 35111 | for aneurysm, pseudoaneurysm, and associated occlusive disease, splenic artery |
| 35112 | for ruptured aneurysm, splenic artery |
| 35121 | for aneurysm, pseudoaneurysm, and associated occlusive disease, hepatic, celiac, renal, or mesenteric artery |
| 35122 | for ruptured aneurysm, hepatic, celiac, renal, or mesenteric artery |
| 35131 | for aneurysm, pseudoaneurysm, and associated occlusive disease, iliac artery (common, hypogastric, external) |
| 35132 | for ruptured aneurysm, iliac artery (common, hypogastric, external) |
| 35141 | for aneurysm, pseudoaneurysm, and associated occlusive disease, common femoral artery (profunda femoris, superficial femoral) |
| 35142 | for ruptured aneurysm, common femoral artery (profunda femoris, superficial femoral) |
| 35151 | for aneurysm, pseudoaneurysm, and associated occlusive disease, popliteal artery |
| 35152 | for ruptured aneurysm, popliteal artery |

## Repair Arteriovenous Fistula

| 35180 | Repair, congenital arteriovenous fistula; head and neck |
| 35182 | thorax and abdomen |
| 35184 | extremities |
| 35188 | Repair, acquired or traumatic arteriovenous fistula; head and neck |
| 35189 | thorax and abdomen |
| 35190 | extremities |

## Repair Blood Vessel Other Than for Fistula, With or Without Patch Angioplasty

(For AV fistula repair, see 35180-35190)

| 35201 | Repair blood vessel, direct; neck |
| 35206 | upper extremity |
| 35207 | hand, finger |
| 35211 | intrathoracic, with bypass |
| 35216 | intrathoracic, without bypass |
| 35221 | intra-abdominal |
| 35226 | lower extremity |
| 35231 | Repair blood vessel with vein graft; neck |

| 35236 | upper extremity |
| 35241 | intrathoracic, with bypass |
| 35246 | intrathoracic, without bypass |
| 35251 | intra-abdominal |
| 35256 | lower extremity |
| 35261 | Repair blood vessel with graft other than vein; neck |
| 35266 | upper extremity |
| 35271 | intrathoracic, with bypass |
| 35276 | intrathoracic, without bypass |
| 35281 | intra-abdominal |
| 35286 | lower extremity |

## Thromboendarterectomy

(For coronary artery, see 33510-33536 and 33572)

(35301-35372 include harvest of saphenous or upper extremity vein when performed)

| 35301 | Thromboendarterectomy, including patch graft, if performed; carotid, vertebral, subclavian, by neck incision |
| 35302 | superficial femoral artery |
| 35303 | popliteal artery |

(Do not report 35302, 35303 in conjunction with 35500, 37225, 37227)

| 35304 | tibioperoneal trunk artery |
| 35305 | tibial or peroneal artery, initial vessel |
| + 35306 | each additional tibial or peroneal artery (List separately in addition to code for primary procedure) |

(Use 35306 in conjunction with 35305)

(Do not report 35304, 35305, 35306 in conjunction with 35500, 37229, 37231, 37233, 37235)

| 35311 | subclavian, innominate, by thoracic incision |
| 35321 | axillary-brachial |
| 35331 | abdominal aorta |
| 35341 | mesenteric, celiac, or renal |
| 35351 | iliac |
| 35355 | iliofemoral |
| 35361 | combined aortoiliac |
| 35363 | combined aortoiliofemoral |
| 35371 | common femoral |
| 35372 | deep (profunda) femoral |
| + 35390 | Reoperation, carotid, thromboendarterectomy, more than 1 month after original operation (List separately in addition to code for primary procedure) |

(Use 35390 in conjunction with 35301)

## Angioscopy

+ **35400**    Angioscopy (non-coronary vessels or grafts) during therapeutic intervention (List separately in addition to code for primary procedure)

## Transluminal Angioplasty

If done as part of another operation, use modifier 51 or use modifier 52.

(For radiological supervision and interpretation, see 75962-75968 and 75978)

### Open

**35450**    Transluminal balloon angioplasty, open; renal or other visceral artery

**35452**        aortic

▶(Do not report 35452 in conjunction with 34841-34848)◀

(35454, 35456 have been deleted. To report, see 37220-37227)

**35458**        brachiocephalic trunk or branches, each vessel

▶(Do not report 35458 in conjunction with 37217 for ipsilateral services)◀

(35459 has been deleted. To report, see 37228-37235)

**35460**        venous

### Percutaneous

Codes for catheter placement and the radiologic supervision and interpretation should also be reported, in addition to the code(s) for the therapeutic aspect of the procedure.

(35470 has been deleted. To report, see 37228-37235)

⊙ **35471**    Transluminal balloon angioplasty, percutaneous; renal or visceral artery

⊙ **35472**        aortic

▶(Do not report 35472 in conjunction with 34841-34848)◀

(35473, 35474 have been deleted. To report, see 37220-37227)

⊙ **35475**        brachiocephalic trunk or branches, each vessel

⊙ **35476**        venous

(For radiological supervision and interpretation, use 75978)

(35480 has been deleted. To report, see 0234T, 0235T)

(35481 has been deleted. To report, use 0236T)

(35482 has been deleted. To report, use 0238T)

(35483 has been deleted. To report, see 37225, 37227)

(35484 has been deleted. To report, use 0237T)

(35485 has been deleted. To report, see 37229, 37231, 37233, 37235)

(35490 has been deleted. To report, see 0234T, 0235T)

(35491 has been deleted. To report, use 0236T)

(35492 has been deleted. To report, use 0238T)

(35493 has been deleted. To report, see 37225, 37227)

(35494 has been deleted. To report, use 0237T)

(35495 has been deleted. To report, see 37229, 37231, 37233, 37235)

## Bypass Graft

### Vein

Procurement of the saphenous vein graft is included in the description of the work for 35501-35587 and should not be reported as a separate service or co-surgery. To report harvesting of an upper extremity vein, use 35500 in addition to the bypass procedure. To report harvesting of a femoropopliteal vein segment, use 35572 in addition to the bypass procedure. To report harvesting and construction of an autogenous composite graft of two segments from two distant locations, report 35682 in addition to the bypass procedure, for autogenous composite of three or more segments from distant sites, report 35683.

+ **35500**    Harvest of upper extremity vein, 1 segment, for lower extremity or coronary artery bypass procedure (List separately in addition to code for primary procedure)

(Use 35500 in conjunction with 33510-33536, 35556, 35566, 35570, 35571, 35583-35587)

(For harvest of more than one vein segment, see 35682, 35683)

(For endoscopic procedure, use 33508)

**35501**    Bypass graft, with vein; common carotid-ipsilateral internal carotid

**35506**        carotid-subclavian or subclavian-carotid

**35508**        carotid-vertebral

**35509**        carotid-contralateral carotid

**35510**        carotid-brachial

**35511**        subclavian-subclavian

**35512**        subclavian-brachial

**35515**        subclavian-vertebral

**35516**        subclavian-axillary

**35518**        axillary-axillary

**Cardiovascular**

**Cardiovascular**

35521      axillary-femoral

(For bypass graft performed with synthetic graft, use 35621)

35522      axillary-brachial

35523      brachial-ulnar or -radial

(Do not report 35523 in conjunction with 35206, 35500, 35525, 36838)

(For bypass graft performed with synthetic conduit, use 37799)

35525      brachial-brachial

35526      aortosubclavian, aortoinnominate, or aortocarotid

(For bypass graft performed with synthetic graft, use 35626)

35531      aortoceliac or aortomesenteric

35533      axillary-femoral-femoral

(For bypass graft performed with synthetic graft, use 35654)

35535      hepatorenal

(Do not report 35535 in conjunction with 35221, 35251, 35281, 35500, 35536, 35560, 35631, 35636)

35536      splenorenal

35537      aortoiliac

(For bypass graft performed with synthetic graft, use 35637)

(Do not report 35537 in conjunction with 35538)

35538      aortobi-iliac

(For bypass graft performed with synthetic graft, use 35638)

(Do not report 35538 in conjunction with 35537)

35539      aortofemoral

(For bypass graft performed with synthetic graft, use 35647)

(Do not report 35539 in conjunction with 35540)

35540      aortobifemoral

(For bypass graft performed with synthetic graft, use 35646)

(Do not report 35540 in conjunction with 35539)

(35548 has been deleted. To report, see 35537, 35539, 35565)

(35549 has been deleted. To report, see 35537, 35538, 35539, 35540, 35565)

(35551 has been deleted. To report, see 35539, 35540, 35556, 35583)

35556      femoral-popliteal

35558      femoral-femoral

35560      aortorenal

35563      ilioiliac

35565      iliofemoral

35566      femoral-anterior tibial, posterior tibial, peroneal artery or other distal vessels

35570      tibial-tibial, peroneal-tibial, or tibial/peroneal trunk-tibial

(Do not report 35570 in conjunction with 35256, 35286)

35571      popliteal-tibial, -peroneal artery or other distal vessels

+ 35572      Harvest of femoropopliteal vein, 1 segment, for vascular reconstruction procedure (eg, aortic, vena caval, coronary, peripheral artery) (List separately in addition to code for primary procedure)

(Use 35572 in conjunction with 33510-33516, 33517-33523, 33533-33536, 34502, 34520, 35001, 35002, 35011-35022, 35102, 35103, 35121-35152, 35231-35256, 35501-35587, 35879-35907)

(For bilateral procedure, use modifier 50)

## In-Situ Vein

(To report aortobifemoral bypass using synthetic conduit, and femoral-popliteal bypass with vein conduit in-situ, use 35646 and 35583. To report aorto[uni]femoral bypass with synthetic conduit, and femoral-popliteal bypass with vein conduit in-situ, use 35647 and 35583. To report aortofemoral bypass using vein conduit, and femoral-popliteal bypass with vein conduit in-situ, use 35539 and 35583)

35583      In-situ vein bypass; femoral-popliteal

35585      femoral-anterior tibial, posterior tibial, or peroneal artery

35587      popliteal-tibial, peroneal

## Other Than Vein

(For arterial transposition and/or reimplantation, see 35691-35695)

+ 35600      Harvest of upper extremity artery, 1 segment, for coronary artery bypass procedure (List separately in addition to code for primary procedure)

(Use 35600 in conjunction with 33533–33536)

35601      Bypass graft, with other than vein; common carotid-ipsilateral internal carotid

35606      carotid-subclavian

(For open transcervical common carotid-common carotid bypass performed in conjunction with endovascular repair of descending thoracic aorta, use 33891)

(For open subclavian to carotid artery transposition performed in conjunction with endovascular thoracic aneurysm repair by neck incision, use 33889)

| 35612 | subclavian-subclavian |
| 35616 | subclavian-axillary |
| 35621 | axillary-femoral |
| 35623 | axillary-popliteal or -tibial |
| 35626 | aortosubclavian, aortoinnominate, or aortocarotid |
| 35631 | aortoceliac, aortomesenteric, aortorenal |
| 35632 | ilio-celiac |

(Do not report 35632 in conjunction with 35221, 35251, 35281, 35531, 35631)

| 35633 | ilio-mesenteric |

(Do not report 35633 in conjunction with 35221, 35251, 35281, 35531, 35631)

| 35634 | iliorenal |

(Do not report 35634 in conjunction with 35221, 35251, 35281, 35560, 35536, 35631)

| 35636 | splenorenal (splenic to renal arterial anastomosis) |
| 35637 | aortoiliac |

(Do not report 35637 in conjunction with 35638, 35646)

| 35638 | aortobi-iliac |

(Do not report 35638 in conjunction with 35637, 35646)

(For open placement of aortobi-iliac prosthesis following unsuccessful endovascular repair, use 34831)

| 35642 | carotid-vertebral |
| 35645 | subclavian-vertebral |
| 35646 | aortobifemoral |

(For bypass graft performed with vein graft, use 35540)

(For open placement of aortobifemoral prosthesis following unsuccessful endovascular repair, use 34832)

| 35647 | aortofemoral |

(For bypass graft performed with vein graft, use 35539)

| 35650 | axillary-axillary |

(35651 has been deleted. To report, see 35646, 35647, 35656)

| 35654 | axillary-femoral-femoral |
| 35656 | femoral-popliteal |
| 35661 | femoral-femoral |
| 35663 | ilioiliac |
| 35665 | iliofemoral |
| 35666 | femoral-anterior tibial, posterior tibial, or peroneal artery |
| 35671 | popliteal-tibial or -peroneal artery |

## Composite Grafts

Codes 35682-35683 are used to report harvest and anastomosis of multiple vein segments from distant sites for use as arterial bypass graft conduits. These codes are intended for use when the two or more vein segments are harvested from a limb other than that undergoing bypass.

+ **35681** Bypass graft; composite, prosthetic and vein (List separately in addition to code for primary procedure)

(Do not report 35681 in addition to 35682, 35683)

+ **35682** autogenous composite, 2 segments of veins from 2 locations (List separately in addition to code for primary procedure)

(Use 35682 in conjunction with 35556, 35566, 35570, 35571, 35583-35587)

(Do not report 35682 in addition to 35681, 35683)

+ **35683** autogenous composite, 3 or more segments of vein from 2 or more locations (List separately in addition to code for primary procedure)

(Use 35683 in conjunction with 35556, 35566, 35570, 35571, 35583-35587)

(Do not report 35683 in addition to 35681, 35682)

## Adjuvant Techniques

Adjuvant (additional) technique(s) may be required at the time a bypass graft is created to improve patency of the lower extremity autogenous or synthetic bypass graft (eg, femoral-popliteal, femoral-tibial, or popliteal-tibial arteries). Code 35685 should be reported in addition to the primary synthetic bypass graft procedure, when an interposition of venous tissue (vein patch or cuff) is placed at the anastomosis between the synthetic bypass conduit and the involved artery (includes harvest).

Code 35686 should be reported in addition to the primary bypass graft procedure, when autogenous vein is used to create a fistula between the tibial or peroneal artery and vein at or beyond the distal bypass anastomosis site of the involved artery.

(For composite graft(s), see 35681-35683)

+ **35685** Placement of vein patch or cuff at distal anastomosis of bypass graft, synthetic conduit (List separately in addition to code for primary procedure)

(Use 35685 in conjunction with 35656, 35666, or 35671)

+ **35686** Creation of distal arteriovenous fistula during lower extremity bypass surgery (non-hemodialysis) (List separately in addition to code for primary procedure)

(Use 35686 in conjunction with 35556, 35566, 35570, 35571, 35583-35587, 35623, 35656, 35666, 35671)

**Cardiovascular**

# Arterial Transposition

**35691**   Transposition and/or reimplantation; vertebral to carotid artery

**35693**       vertebral to subclavian artery

**35694**       subclavian to carotid artery

    (For open subclavian to carotid artery transposition performed in conjunction with endovascular repair of descending thoracic aorta, use 33889)

**35695**       carotid to subclavian artery

**+ 35697**   Reimplantation, visceral artery to infrarenal aortic prosthesis, each artery (List separately in addition to code for primary procedure)

    (Do not report 35697 in conjunction with 33877)

# Excision, Exploration, Repair, Revision

**+ 35700**   Reoperation, femoral-popliteal or femoral (popliteal)-anterior tibial, posterior tibial, peroneal artery, or other distal vessels, more than 1 month after original operation (List separately in addition to code for primary procedure)

    (Use 35700 in conjunction with 35556, 35566, 35570, 35571, 35583, 35585, 35587, 35656, 35666, 35671)

**35701**   Exploration (not followed by surgical repair), with or without lysis of artery; carotid artery

**35721**       femoral artery

**35741**       popliteal artery

**35761**       other vessels

**35800**   Exploration for postoperative hemorrhage, thrombosis or infection; neck

**35820**       chest

**35840**       abdomen

**35860**       extremity

**35870**   Repair of graft enteric fistula

**35875**   Thrombectomy of arterial or venous graft (other than hemodialysis graft or fistula);

**35876**       with revision of arterial or venous graft

    (For thrombectomy of hemodialysis graft or fistula, see 36831, 36833)

Codes 35879 and 35881 describe open revision of graft-threatening stenoses of lower extremity arterial bypass graft(s) (previously constructed with autogenous vein conduit) using vein patch angioplasty or segmental vein interposition techniques. For thrombectomy with revision of any non-coronary arterial or venous graft, including those of the lower extremity, (other than hemodialysis graft or fistula), use 35876. For direct repair (other than for fistula) of a lower extremity blood vessel (with or without patch angioplasty), use 35226. For repair (other than for fistula) of a lower extremity blood vessel using a vein graft, use 35256.

**35879**   Revision, lower extremity arterial bypass, without thrombectomy, open; with vein patch angioplasty

**35881**       with segmental vein interposition

    (For revision of femoral anastomosis of synthetic arterial bypass graft, see 35883, 35884)

    (For excision of infected graft, see 35901-35907 and appropriate revascularization code)

**35883**   Revision, femoral anastomosis of synthetic arterial bypass graft in groin, open; with nonautogenous patch graft (eg, Dacron, ePTFE, bovine pericardium)

    (For bilateral procedure, use modifier 50)

    (Do not report 35883 in conjunction with 35700, 35875, 35876, 35884)

**35884**       with autogenous vein patch graft

    (For bilateral procedure, use modifier 50)

    (Do not report 35884 in conjunction with 35700, 35875, 35876, 35883)

**35901**   Excision of infected graft; neck

**35903**       extremity

**35905**       thorax

**35907**       abdomen

# Vascular Injection Procedures

Listed services for injection procedures include necessary local anesthesia, introduction of needles or catheter, injection of contrast media with or without automatic power injection, and/or necessary pre- and postinjection care specifically related to the injection procedure.

Selective vascular catheterization should be coded to include introduction and all lesser order selective catheterization used in the approach (eg, the description for a selective right middle cerebral artery catheterization includes the introduction and placement catheterization of the right common and internal carotid arteries).

Additional second and/or third order arterial catheterization within the same family of arteries or veins supplied by a single first order vessel should be expressed by 36012, 36218, or 36248.

Additional first order or higher catheterization in vascular families supplied by a first order vessel different from a previously selected and coded family should be separately coded using the conventions described above.

    (For radiological supervision and interpretation, see **Radiology**)

    (For injection procedures in conjunction with cardiac catheterization, see 93452-93461, 93563-93568)

    (For chemotherapy of malignant disease, see 96401-96549)

Cardiovascular

### Intravenous

An intracatheter is a sheathed combination of needle and short catheter.

**36000**    Introduction of needle or intracatheter, vein

**36002**    Injection procedures (eg, thrombin) for percutaneous treatment of extremity pseudoaneurysm

(For imaging guidance, see 76942, 77002, 77012, 77021)

(For ultrasound guided compression repair of pseudoaneurysms, use 76936)

(Do not report 36002 for vascular sealant of an arteriotomy site)

**36005**    Injection procedure for extremity venography (including introduction of needle or intracatheter)

(For radiological supervision and interpretation, see 75820, 75822)

⊙ **36010**    Introduction of catheter, superior or inferior vena cava

**36011**    Selective catheter placement, venous system; first order branch (eg, renal vein, jugular vein)

**36012**        second order, or more selective, branch (eg, left adrenal vein, petrosal sinus)

**36013**    Introduction of catheter, right heart or main pulmonary artery

**36014**    Selective catheter placement, left or right pulmonary artery

**36015**    Selective catheter placement, segmental or subsegmental pulmonary artery

(For insertion of flow directed catheter (eg, Swan-Ganz), use 93503)

(For venous catheterization for selective organ blood sampling, use 36500)

### Intra-Arterial—Intra-Aortic

(For radiological supervision and interpretation, see **Radiology**)

**36100**    Introduction of needle or intracatheter, carotid or vertebral artery

(For bilateral procedure, report 36100 with modifier 50)

**36120**    Introduction of needle or intracatheter; retrograde brachial artery

⊙ **36140**        extremity artery

(For insertion of arteriovenous cannula, see 36810-36821)

(36145 has been deleted. To report see 36147, 36148)

***Diagnostic Studies of Arteriovenous (AV) Shunts for Dialysis:*** For diagnostic studies, the arteriovenous (AV) dialysis shunt (AV shunt) is defined as beginning with the arterial anastomosis and extending to the right atrium. This definition includes all upper and lower extremity AV shunts (arteriovenous fistulae [AVF] and arteriovenous

grafts [AVG]). Code 36147 includes the work of directly accessing and imaging the entire AV shunt. Antegrade and/or retrograde punctures of the AV shunt are typically used for imaging, and contrast may be injected directly through a needle or through a catheter placed into the AV shunt. Occasionally the catheter needs to be advanced further into the shunt to adequately visualize the arterial anastomosis or the central veins, and all manipulation of the catheter for diagnostic imaging of the AV shunt is included in 36147. Advancement of the catheter to the vena cava to adequately image that segment of the AV shunt is included in 36147 and is not separately reported. Advancement of the catheter tip through the arterial anastomosis to adequately visualize the anastomosis is also considered integral to the work of 36147 and is not separately reported.

Ultrasound guidance for puncture of the AV shunt is not included in 36147. Particularly in the case of new or failing AVF, ultrasound may be necessary to safely and effectively puncture the AV access for evaluation, and this may be reported separately with 76937 if all the appropriate elements for reporting 76937 are performed.

Evaluation of the peri-anastomotic portion of the inflow is considered an integral part of the dialysis fistulagram and is included in the work of 36147. The peri-anastomotic portion of the vessel at the arterial anastomosis includes the short segment of the artery immediately adjacent to the anastomosis, the anastomosis itself, and the portion of the vessel or graft immediately distal to the anastomosis.

The arterial inflow to the AV access is considered a separate vessel. If a more proximal inflow problem separate from the peri-anastomotic segment is suspected and additional catheter work and imaging must be done for adequate evaluation, this work is not included in 36147. If a catheter is selectively advanced from the AV shunt puncture into the inflow artery, an additional catheterization code may be reported. In the typical case of an upper extremity AV shunt, 36215 is used to report this work, and includes placement of the catheter retrograde into the inflow artery and into the aorta if necessary (ie, 36200 may not be also reported since that work is included in the work defined by 36215).

***Interventions for Arteriovenous (AV) Shunts Created for Dialysis (AV Grafts and AV Fistulae):*** For the purposes of coding interventional procedures in arteriovenous (AV) shunts created for dialysis (both arteriovenous fistulae [AVF] and arteriovenous grafts [AVG]), the AV shunt is artificially divided into two vessel segments. The first segment is peripheral and extends from the peri-arterial anastomosis through the axillary vein (or entire cephalic vein in the case of cephalic venous outflow). The second segment includes the veins central to the axillary and cephalic veins, including the subclavian and innominate veins through the vena cava. Interventions performed in a single segment, regardless of

**Cardiovascular**

the number of lesions treated, are coded as a single intervention.

The AV shunt is considered to be venous and most interventions are coded with the venous intervention codes (ie, angioplasty is reported with venous angioplasty codes 35476, 75978). Codes 35476 and 75978 would be reported once to describe all angioplasty work performed in one segment of the AV dialysis shunt, regardless of the number of distinct lesions treated within that segment, the number of times the balloon is inflated, or the number of balloon catheters required to open all lesions.

There is an exception to the use of venous interventional codes. When there is a stenosis at the arterial anastomosis, it typically extends across the anastomosis and involves the artery just proximal to and at the anastomosis as well as the outflow vessel or graft. This segment is called the peri-anastomotic (or juxta-anastomotic) region, and even though the stenosis can involve multiple vessels, it is typically a single lesion with a single etiology crossing the anastomosis, and treatment to open this lesion crosses from the artery into the vein or venous graft. An intervention treated in this peri-anastomotic segment is coded as an arterial intervention (35475, 75962). Since the entire segment of the AV shunt from the peri-arterial anastomosis through the axillary vein is considered a single vessel for coding of interventions, the arterial angioplasty codes include the work of opening the peri-anastomotic stenosis, as well as all other stenoses treated within this segment of the vessel. Codes 35475 and 75962 are reported once to describe all work done to angioplasty any lesion from the peri-arterial anastomosis through the axillary vein in procedures that involve angioplasty of the peri-arterial anastomosis of the AV shunt. In these special instances, venous angioplasty codes would not be reported additionally for this first or most peripheral shunt segment, even if balloon angioplasty is performed on segments of the AV dialysis shunt that are purely venous anatomy within this specific vessel segment.

It is never appropriate to report removal of the arterial plug during a declot/thrombectomy procedure as an arterial or venous angioplasty (35475, 35476). Removal of the arterial plug is included in the work of a fistula thrombectomy (36870), even if a balloon catheter is used to mechanically dislodge the resistant thrombus.

The central veins (eg, subclavian, innominate, and cava) are considered an additional, separate venous vessel segment for purposes of interventional coding for AV dialysis shunt interventions. If one or more central venous stenoses are treated with angioplasty, this is reported as a single venous angioplasty (35476, 75978), regardless of the number of discrete lesions treated within this segment, and also independent of the number of balloon inflations or number of balloon catheters or sizes required. This additional work should be clearly documented in the patient record and in the recorded images.

►The same rules used for angioplasty apply to stent placements for AV dialysis shunts with respect to the number of interventions reported for each patient. Either 37236 or 37238 is reported once to describe all work of stenting lesions within the defined AV dialysis shunt segment from the peri-arterial anastomosis through the axillary and cephalic veins, regardless of the number of stents placed or the number of discrete lesions treated within that vessel segment. Code 37238 is reported for placement of AV access stent unless the treated lesion includes the peri-anastomotic region. This peri-anastomotic region is considered an artery and therefore 37236 is reported instead of 37238. If additional stenting is required for central venous stenosis, this may be reported as an additional stent placement (37239), describing all the work of stent placement within the central venous segment.◄

The work of catheterizing all the veins in the dialysis AV shunt is included in 36147 (and, if appropriate, 36148). Selective catheterization of the inferior/superior vena cava and central veins cannot be separately reported when performed from a direct puncture of the AVF/AVG.

►However, if additional venous side branches off of the conduit, known as accessory veins, are separately catheterized for diagnosis or intervention such as embolization of a large competing accessory vein, this additional work may be separately reported using the appropriate selective venous catheterization codes (36011 and 36012). The embolization may be reported using 37241 once, irrespective of the number of branches embolized.◄

⊙ **36147**    Introduction of needle and/or catheter, arteriovenous shunt created for dialysis (graft/fistula); initial access with complete radiological evaluation of dialysis access, including fluoroscopy, image documentation and report (includes access of shunt, injection[s] of contrast, and all necessary imaging from the arterial anastomosis and adjacent artery through entire venous outflow including the inferior or superior vena cava)

(If 36147 indicates the need for a therapeutic intervention requiring a second catheterization of the shunt, use 36148)

(Do not report 36147 in conjunction with 75791)

⊙✚ **36148**    additional access for therapeutic intervention (List separately in addition to code for primary procedure)

(Use 36148 in conjunction with 36147)

**36160**    Introduction of needle or intracatheter, aortic, translumbar

***Diagnostic Studies of Cervicocerebral Arteries:*** Codes 36221-36228 describe non-selective and selective arterial catheter placement and diagnostic imaging of the aortic arch, carotid, and vertebral arteries. Codes 36221-36226 include the work of accessing the vessel, placement of catheter(s), contrast injection(s), fluoroscopy, radiological supervision and interpretation, and closure of the arteriotomy by pressure, or application of an arterial closure device. Codes 36221-36228 describe arterial contrast injections with arterial, capillary, and venous phase imaging, when performed.

Code 36227 is an add-on code to report unilateral selective arterial catheter placement and diagnostic imaging of the ipsilateral external carotid circulation and includes all the work of accessing the additional vessel, placement of catheter(s), contrast injection(s), fluoroscopy, radiological supervision and interpretation. Code 36227 is reported in conjunction with 36222, 36223, or 36224.

Code 36228 is an add-on code to report unilateral selective arterial catheter placement and diagnostic imaging of the initial and each additional intracranial branch of the internal carotid or vertebral arteries. Code 36228 is reported in conjunction with 36224 or 36226. This includes any additional second or third order catheter selective placement in the same primary branch of the internal carotid, vertebral, or basilar artery and includes all the work of accessing the additional vessel, placement of catheter(s), contrast injection(s), fluoroscopy, radiological supervision and interpretation. It is not reported more than twice per side regardless of the number of additional branches selectively catheterized.

Codes 36221-36226 are built on progressive hierarchies with more intensive services inclusive of less intensive services. The code inclusive of all of the services provided for that vessel should be reported (ie, use the code inclusive of the most intensive services provided). Only one code in the range 36222-36224 may be reported for each ipsilateral carotid territory. Only one code in the range 36225-36226 may be reported for each ipsilateral vertebral territory.

Code 36221 is reported for non-selective arterial catheter placement in the thoracic aorta and diagnostic imaging of the aortic arch and great vessel origins. Codes 36222-36228 are reported for unilateral artery catheterization. Do not report 36221 in conjunction with 36222-36226 as these selective codes include the work of 36221 when performed.

Do not report 36222, 36223, or 36224 together for ipsilateral angiography. Instead, select the code that represents the most comprehensive service using the following hierarchy of complexity (listed in descending order of complexity): 36224>36223>36222.

Do not report 36225 and 36226 together for ipsilateral angiography. Select the code that represents the more comprehensive service using the following hierarchy of complexity (listed in descending order of complexity): 36226>36225.

When bilateral carotid and/or vertebral arterial catheterization and imaging is performed, add modifier 50 to codes 36222-36228 if the same procedure is performed on both sides. For example, bilateral extracranial carotid angiography with selective

catheterization of each common carotid artery would be reported with 36222 and modifier 50. However, when different territory(ies) is studied in the same session on both sides of the body, modifiers may be required to report the imaging performed. Use modifier 59 to denote that different carotid and/or vertebral arteries are being studied. For example, when selective right internal carotid artery catheterization accompanied by right extracranial and intracranial carotid angiography is followed by selective left common carotid artery catheterization with left extracranial carotid angiography, use 36224 to report the right side and 36222-59 to report the left side.

Diagnostic angiography of the cervicocerebral vessels may be followed by an interventional procedure at the same session. Interventional procedures may be separately reportable using standard coding conventions.

Do not report 75774 as part of diagnostic angiography of the extracranial and intracranial cervicocerebral vessels. It may be appropriate to report 75774 for diagnostic angiography of upper extremities and other vascular beds performed in the same session.

Report 76376 or 76377 for 3D rendering when performed in conjunction with 36221-36228.

Report 76937 for ultrasound guidance for vascular access, when performed in conjunction with 36221-36228.

⊙ **36200**   Introduction of catheter, aorta

> (For non-selective angiography of the extracranial carotid and/or cerebral vessels and cervicocerebral arch, when performed, use 36221)

**36215**   Selective catheter placement, arterial system; each first order thoracic or brachiocephalic branch, within a vascular family

> (For catheter placement for coronary angiography, see 93454-93461)

**36216**      initial second order thoracic or brachiocephalic branch, within a vascular family

**36217**      initial third order or more selective thoracic or brachiocephalic branch, within a vascular family

+ **36218**      additional second order, third order, and beyond, thoracic or brachiocephalic branch, within a vascular family (List in addition to code for initial second or third order vessel as appropriate)

> (Use 36218 in conjunction with 36216, 36217)

> (For angiography, see 36147, 36222-36228, 75600-75774, 75791)

> (For angioplasty, see 35471, 35472, 35475)

> ▶(For transcatheter therapies, see 37200, 37202, 37211, 37213, 37214, 37236, 37237, 37238, 37239, 37241, 37242, 37243, 37244, 61624, 61626)◀

**Cardiovascular**

**Cardiovascular**

(When coronary artery, arterial conduit [eg, internal mammary, inferior epigastric or free radical artery] or venous bypass graft angiography is performed in conjunction with cardiac catheterization, see the appropriate cardiac catheterization, injection procedure, and imaging supervision code[s] [93455, 93457, 93459, 93461, 93530-93533, 93564] in the **Medicine** section. When internal mammary artery angiography only is performed without a concomitant cardiac catheterization, use 36216 or 36217 as appropriate)

⊙ **36221** Non-selective catheter placement, thoracic aorta, with angiography of the extracranial carotid, vertebral, and/or intracranial vessels, unilateral or bilateral, and all associated radiological supervision and interpretation, includes angiography of the cervicocerebral arch, when performed

(Do not report 36221 with 36222-36226)

⊙ **36222** Selective catheter placement, common carotid or innominate artery, unilateral, any approach, with angiography of the ipsilateral extracranial carotid circulation and all associated radiological supervision and interpretation, includes angiography of the cervicocerebral arch, when performed

⊙ **36223** Selective catheter placement, common carotid or innominate artery, unilateral, any approach, with angiography of the ipsilateral intracranial carotid circulation and all associated radiological supervision and interpretation, includes angiography of the extracranial carotid and cervicocerebral arch, when performed

⊙ **36224** Selective catheter placement, internal carotid artery, unilateral, with angiography of the ipsilateral intracranial carotid circulation and all associated radiological supervision and interpretation, includes angiography of the extracranial carotid and cervicocerebral arch, when performed

⊙ **36225** Selective catheter placement, subclavian or innominate artery, unilateral, with angiography of the ipsilateral vertebral circulation and all associated radiological supervision and interpretation, includes angiography of the cervicocerebral arch, when performed

⊙ **36226** Selective catheter placement, vertebral artery, unilateral, with angiography of the ipsilateral vertebral circulation and all associated radiological supervision and interpretation, includes angiography of the cervicocerebral arch, when performed

⊙➕ **36227** Selective catheter placement, external carotid artery, unilateral, with angiography of the ipsilateral external carotid circulation and all associated radiological supervision and interpretation (List separately in addition to code for primary procedure)

(Use 36227 in conjunction with 36222, 36223, or 36224)

▶(Do not report 36221-36227 in conjunction with 37217 for ipsilateral services)◀

⊙➕ **36228** Selective catheter placement, each intracranial branch of the internal carotid or vertebral arteries, unilateral, with angiography of the selected vessel circulation and all associated radiological supervision and interpretation (eg, middle cerebral artery, posterior inferior cerebellar artery) (List separately in addition to code for primary procedure)

(Use 36228 in conjunction with 36224 or 36226)

(Do not report 36228 more than twice per side)

⊙ **36245** Selective catheter placement, arterial system; each first order abdominal, pelvic, or lower extremity artery branch, within a vascular family

⊙ **36246** initial second order abdominal, pelvic, or lower extremity artery branch, within a vascular family

⊙ **36247** initial third order or more selective abdominal, pelvic, or lower extremity artery branch, within a vascular family

⊙➕ **36248** additional second order, third order, and beyond, abdominal, pelvic, or lower extremity artery branch, within a vascular family (List in addition to code for initial second or third order vessel as appropriate)

(Use 36248 in conjunction with 36246, 36247)

⊙ **36251** Selective catheter placement (first-order), main renal artery and any accessory renal artery(s) for renal angiography, including arterial puncture and catheter placement(s), fluoroscopy, contrast injection(s), image postprocessing, permanent recording of images, and radiological supervision and interpretation, including pressure gradient measurements when performed, and flush aortogram when performed; unilateral

⊙ **36252** bilateral

⊙ **36253** Superselective catheter placement (one or more second order or higher renal artery branches) renal artery and any accessory renal artery(s) for renal angiography, including arterial puncture, catheterization, fluoroscopy, contrast injection(s), image postprocessing, permanent recording of images, and radiological supervision and interpretation, including pressure gradient measurements when performed, and flush aortogram when performed; unilateral

(Do not report 36253 in conjunction with 36251 when performed for the same kidney)

⊙ **36254** bilateral

(Do not report 36254 in conjunction with 36252)

(Placement of closure device at the vascular access site is not separately reported with 36251-36254)

▶(Do not report 36251, 36252, 36253, 36254 in conjunction with 0338T, 0339T)◀

**36260** Insertion of implantable intra-arterial infusion pump (eg, for chemotherapy of liver)

**36261** Revision of implanted intra-arterial infusion pump

**36262** Removal of implanted intra-arterial infusion pump

**36299** Unlisted procedure, vascular injection

### Venous

Venipuncture, needle or catheter for diagnostic study or intravenous therapy, percutaneous. These codes are also used to report the therapy as specified. For collection of a specimen from an established catheter, use 36592. For collection of a specimen from a completely implantable venous access device, use 36591.

**36400** Venipuncture, younger than age 3 years, necessitating the skill of a physician or other qualified health care professional, not to be used for routine venipuncture; femoral or jugular vein

**36405** scalp vein

**36406** other vein

**36410** Venipuncture, age 3 years or older, necessitating the skill of a physician or other qualified health care professional (separate procedure), for diagnostic or therapeutic purposes (not to be used for routine venipuncture)

**36415** Collection of venous blood by venipuncture

(Do not report modifier 63 in conjunction with 36415)

**36416** Collection of capillary blood specimen (eg, finger, heel, ear stick)

**36420** Venipuncture, cutdown; younger than age 1 year

(Do not report modifier 63 in conjunction with 36420)

**36425** age 1 or over

►(Do not report 36425 in conjunction with 36475, 36476, 36478)◄

**36430** Transfusion, blood or blood components

**36440** Push transfusion, blood, 2 years or younger

**36450** Exchange transfusion, blood; newborn

(Do not report modifier 63 in conjunction with 36450)

**36455** other than newborn

**36460** Transfusion, intrauterine, fetal

(Do not report modifier 63 in conjunction with 36460)

(For radiological supervision and interpretation, use 76941)

**36468** Single or multiple injections of sclerosing solutions, spider veins (telangiectasia); limb or trunk

►(Do not report 36468 in conjunction with 37241 in the same surgical field)◄

**36469** face

**36470** Injection of sclerosing solution; single vein

**36471** multiple veins, same leg

►(For vascular embolization and occlusion procedures, use 37241)◄

►(Do not report 36470, 36471 in conjunction with 37241 in the same surgical field)◄

**36475** Endovenous ablation therapy of incompetent vein, extremity, inclusive of all imaging guidance and monitoring, percutaneous, radiofrequency; first vein treated

**+ 36476** second and subsequent veins treated in a single extremity, each through separate access sites (List separately in addition to code for primary procedure)

(Use 36476 in conjunction with 36475)

►(Do not report 36475, 36476 in conjunction with 29581, 29582, 36000, 36002, 36005, 36410, 36425, 36478, 36479, 37241-37244, 75894, 76000, 76001, 76937, 76942, 76998, 77022, 93970, 93971 in the same surgical field)◄

**36478** Endovenous ablation therapy of incompetent vein, extremity, inclusive of all imaging guidance and monitoring, percutaneous, laser; first vein treated

**+ 36479** second and subsequent veins treated in a single extremity, each through separate access sites (List separately in addition to code for primary procedure)

(Use 36479 in conjunction with 36478)

►(Do not report 36478, 36479 in conjunction with 29581, 29582, 36000, 36002, 36005, 36410, 36425, 36475, 36476, 37241, 75894, 76000, 76001, 76937, 76942, 76998, 77022, 93970, 93971 in the same surgical field)◄

⊙ **36481** Percutaneous portal vein catheterization by any method

(For radiological supervision and interpretation, see 75885, 75887)

**36500** Venous catheterization for selective organ blood sampling

(For catheterization in superior or inferior vena cava, use 36010)

(For radiological supervision and interpretation, use 75893)

**36510** Catheterization of umbilical vein for diagnosis or therapy, newborn

(Do not report modifier 63 in conjunction with 36510)

**36511** Therapeutic apheresis; for white blood cells

**36512** for red blood cells

**36513** for platelets

**36514** for plasma pheresis

**36515** with extracorporeal immunoadsorption and plasma reinfusion

**36516** with extracorporeal selective adsorption or selective filtration and plasma reinfusion

(For professional evaluation, use modifier 26)

**36522** Photopheresis, extracorporeal

**Cardiovascular**

## Central Venous Access Procedures

To qualify as a central venous access catheter or device, the tip of the catheter/device must terminate in the subclavian, brachiocephalic (innominate) or iliac veins, the superior or inferior vena cava, or the right atrium. The venous access device may be either centrally inserted (jugular, subclavian, femoral vein or inferior vena cava catheter entry site) or peripherally inserted (eg, basilic or cephalic vein). The device may be accessed for use either via exposed catheter (external to the skin), via a subcutaneous port or via a subcutaneous pump.

The procedures involving these types of devices fall into five categories:

1. *Insertion* (placement of catheter through a newly established venous access)

2. *Repair* (fixing device without replacement of either catheter or port/pump, other than pharmacologic or mechanical correction of intracatheter or pericatheter occlusion [see 36595 or 36596])

3. *Partial replacement* of only the catheter component associated with a port/pump device, but not entire device

4. *Complete replacement* of entire device via same venous access site (complete exchange)

5. *Removal* of entire device.

There is no coding distinction between venous access achieved percutaneously versus by cutdown or based on catheter size.

For the repair, partial (catheter only) replacement, complete replacement, or removal of both catheters (placed from separate venous access sites) of a multi-catheter device, with or without subcutaneous ports/pumps, use the appropriate code describing the service with a frequency of two.

If an existing central venous access device is removed and a new one placed via a separate venous access site, appropriate codes for both procedures (removal of old, if code exists, and insertion of new device) should be reported.

When imaging is used for these procedures, either for gaining access to the venous entry site or for manipulating the catheter into final central position, use 76937, 77001.

> (For refilling and maintenance of an implantable pump or reservoir for intravenous or intra-arterial drug delivery, use 96522)

## Insertion of Central Venous Access Device

⊙ **36555** Insertion of non-tunneled centrally inserted central venous catheter; younger than 5 years of age

(For peripherally inserted non-tunneled central venous catheter, younger than 5 years of age, use 36568)

**36556** age 5 years or older

(For peripherally inserted non-tunneled central venous catheter, age 5 years or older, use 36569)

⊙ **36557** Insertion of tunneled centrally inserted central venous catheter, without subcutaneous port or pump; younger than 5 years of age

⊙ **36558** age 5 years or older

(For peripherally inserted central venous catheter with port, 5 years or older, use 36571)

⊙ **36560** Insertion of tunneled centrally inserted central venous access device, with subcutaneous port; younger than 5 years of age

(For peripherally inserted central venous access device with subcutaneous port, younger than 5 years of age, use 36570)

⊙ **36561** age 5 years or older

(For peripherally inserted central venous catheter with subcutaneous port, 5 years or older, use 36571)

⊙ **36563** Insertion of tunneled centrally inserted central venous access device with subcutaneous pump

⊙ **36565** Insertion of tunneled centrally inserted central venous access device, requiring 2 catheters via 2 separate venous access sites; without subcutaneous port or pump (eg, Tesio type catheter)

⊙ **36566** with subcutaneous port(s)

⊙ **36568** Insertion of peripherally inserted central venous catheter (PICC), without subcutaneous port or pump; younger than 5 years of age

(For placement of centrally inserted non-tunneled central venous catheter, without subcutaneous port or pump, younger than 5 years of age, use 36555)

**36569** age 5 years or older

(For placement of centrally inserted non-tunneled central venous catheter, without subcutaneous port or pump, age 5 years or older, use 36556)

⊙ **36570** Insertion of peripherally inserted central venous access device, with subcutaneous port; younger than 5 years of age

(For insertion of tunneled centrally inserted central venous access device with subcutaneous port, younger than 5 years of age, use 36560)

⊙ **36571** age 5 years or older

(For insertion of tunneled centrally inserted central venous access device with subcutaneous port, age 5 years or older, use 36561)

# The Central Venous Access Procedures Table

| | Non-tunneled | Tunneled Without Port or Pump | Central Tunneled | Tunneled With Port | Tunneled With Pump | Peripheral | <5 years | ≥5 years | Any Age |
|---|---|---|---|---|---|---|---|---|---|
| **Insertion** | | | | | | | | | |
| **Catheter** | 36555 | | | | | | 36555 | | |
| | 36556 | | | | | | | 36556 | |
| | | 36557 | 36557 | | | | 36557 | | |
| | | 36558 | 36558 | | | | | 36558 | |
| | 36568 (w/o port or pump) | | | | | 36568 (w/o port or pump) | 36568 (w/o port or pump) | | |
| | 36569 (w/o port or pump) | | | | | 36569 (w/o port or pump) | | 36569 (w/o port or pump) | |
| **Device** | | | 36560 | 36560 | | | 36560 | | |
| | | | 36561 | 36561 | | | | 36561 | |
| | | | 36563 | | 36563 | | | | 36563 |
| | | 36565 | 36565 | | | | | | 36565 |
| | | | 36566 | 36566 | | | | | |
| | 36570 (w port) | | | 36570 (w port) | | 36570 (w port) | 36570 (w port) | | |
| | 36571 (w port) | | | 36571 (w port) | | 36571 (w port) | | 36571 (w port) | |
| **Repair** | | | | | | | | | |
| **Catheter** | 36575 (w/o port or pump) | 36575 (w/o port or pump) | 36575 (w/o port or pump) | | | 36575 (w/o port or pump) | | | 36575 |
| **Device** | 36576 (w port or pump) | | | | | 36576 (w port or pump) | | | 36576 |
| **Partial Replacement – Central Venous Access Device (Catheter only)** | | | | | | | | | |
| | | | 36578 | 36578 | 36578 | 36578 | | | 36578 |
| **Complete Replacement – Central Venous Access Device (Through Same Venous Access Site)** | | | | | | | | | |
| **Catheter** | 36580 (w/o port or pump) | | | | | | | | 36580 |
| | | 36581 | 36581 | | | | | | 36581 |
| | 36584 (w/o port or pump) | | | | | 36584 (w/o port or pump) | | | 36584 |
| **Device** | | | 36582 | 36582 | | | | | 36582 |
| | | | 36583 | | 36583 | | | | 36583 |
| | | | | 36585 (w port) | | 36585 (w port) | | | 36585 |
| **Removal** | | | | | | | | | |
| **Catheter** | | 36589 | | | | | | | 36589 |
| **Device** | | | 36590 | 36590 | 36590 | 36590 | | | 36590 |
| **Removal of Obstructive Material from Device** | | | | | | | | | |
| | 36595 (pericatheter) | 36595 (pericatheter) | 36595 (pericatheter) | 36595 (pericatheter) | 36595 (pericatheter) | 36595 (pericatheter) | | | 36595 (pericatheter) |
| | 36596 (intraluminal) | 36596 (intraluminal) | 36596 (intraluminal) | 36596 (intraluminal) | 36596 (intraluminal) | 36596 (intraluminal) | | | 36596 (intraluminal) |
| **Repositioning of Catheter** | | | | | | | | | |
| | 36597 | 36597 | 36597 | 36597 | 36597 | 36597 | 36597 | 36597 | 36597 |

**Cardiovascular**

▲=Revised code   ●=New code   ►◄=Contains new or revised text   ⊘=Modifier 51 exempt

### Repair of Central Venous Access Device

(For mechanical removal of pericatheter obstructive material, use 36595)

(For mechanical removal of intracatheter obstructive material, use 36596)

**36575**  Repair of tunneled or non-tunneled central venous access catheter, without subcutaneous port or pump, central or peripheral insertion site

⊙ **36576**  Repair of central venous access device, with subcutaneous port or pump, central or peripheral insertion site

### Partial Replacement of Central Venous Access Device (Catheter Only)

⊙ **36578**  Replacement, catheter only, of central venous access device, with subcutaneous port or pump, central or peripheral insertion site

(For complete replacement of entire device through same venous access, use 36582 or 36583)

### Complete Replacement of Central Venous Access Device Through Same Venous Access Site

**36580**  Replacement, complete, of a non-tunneled centrally inserted central venous catheter, without subcutaneous port or pump, through same venous access

⊙ **36581**  Replacement, complete, of a tunneled centrally inserted central venous catheter, without subcutaneous port or pump, through same venous access

⊙ **36582**  Replacement, complete, of a tunneled centrally inserted central venous access device, with subcutaneous port, through same venous access

⊙ **36583**  Replacement, complete, of a tunneled centrally inserted central venous access device, with subcutaneous pump, through same venous access

**36584**  Replacement, complete, of a peripherally inserted central venous catheter (PICC), without subcutaneous port or pump, through same venous access

⊙ **36585**  Replacement, complete, of a peripherally inserted central venous access device, with subcutaneous port, through same venous access

### Removal of Central Venous Access Device

**36589**  Removal of tunneled central venous catheter, without subcutaneous port or pump

⊙ **36590**  Removal of tunneled central venous access device, with subcutaneous port or pump, central or peripheral insertion

(Do not report 36589 or 36590 for removal of non-tunneled central venous catheters)

### Other Central Venous Access Procedures

**36591**  Collection of blood specimen from a completely implantable venous access device

(Do not report 36591 in conjunction with other services except a laboratory service)

(For collection of venous blood specimen by venipuncture, use 36415)

(For collection of capillary blood specimen, use 36416)

**36592**  Collection of blood specimen using established central or peripheral catheter, venous, not otherwise specified

(For blood collection from an established arterial catheter, use 37799)

(Do not report 36592 in conjunction with other services except a laboratory service)

**36593**  Declotting by thrombolytic agent of implanted vascular access device or catheter

**36595**  Mechanical removal of pericatheter obstructive material (eg, fibrin sheath) from central venous device via separate venous access

(Do not report 36595 in conjunction with 36593)

(For venous catheterization, see 36010-36012)

(For radiological supervision and interpretation, use 75901)

**36596**  Mechanical removal of intraluminal (intracatheter) obstructive material from central venous device through device lumen

(Do not report 36596 in conjunction with 36593)

(For venous catheterization, see 36010-36012)

(For radiological supervision and interpretation, use 75902)

**36597**  Repositioning of previously placed central venous catheter under fluoroscopic guidance

(For fluoroscopic guidance, use 76000)

**36598**  Contrast injection(s) for radiologic evaluation of existing central venous access device, including fluoroscopy, image documentation and report

(Do not report 36598 in conjunction with 76000)

(Do not report 36598 in conjunction with 36595, 36596)

(For complete diagnostic studies, see 75820, 75825, 75827)

## Arterial

**36600**  Arterial puncture, withdrawal of blood for diagnosis

⊘ **36620**  Arterial catheterization or cannulation for sampling, monitoring or transfusion (separate procedure); percutaneous

**36625**          cutdown

**36640**   Arterial catheterization for prolonged infusion therapy (chemotherapy), cutdown

(See also 96420-96425)

(For arterial catheterization for occlusion therapy, see 75894)

**36660**   Catheterization, umbilical artery, newborn, for diagnosis or therapy

(Do not report modifier 63 in conjunction with 36660)

## Intraosseous

**36680**   Placement of needle for intraosseous infusion

## Hemodialysis Access, Intervascular Cannulation for Extracorporeal Circulation, or Shunt Insertion

**36800**   Insertion of cannula for hemodialysis, other purpose (separate procedure); vein to vein

**36810**       arteriovenous, external (Scribner type)

**36815**       arteriovenous, external revision, or closure

**36818**   Arteriovenous anastomosis, open; by upper arm cephalic vein transposition

(Do not report 36818 in conjunction with 36819, 36820, 36821, 36830 during a unilateral upper extremity procedure. For bilateral upper extremity open arteriovenous anastomoses performed at the same operative session, use modifier 50 or 59 as appropriate)

**36819**       by upper arm basilic vein transposition

(Do not report 36819 in conjunction with 36818, 36820, 36821, 36830 during a unilateral upper extremity procedure. For bilateral upper extremity open arteriovenous anastomoses performed at the same operative session, use modifier 50 or 59 as appropriate)

**36820**       by forearm vein transposition

**36821**       direct, any site (eg, Cimino type) (separate procedure)

**36822**   Insertion of cannula(s) for prolonged extracorporeal circulation for cardiopulmonary insufficiency (ECMO) (separate procedure)

(For maintenance of prolonged extracorporeal circulation, see 33960, 33961)

**36823**   Insertion of arterial and venous cannula(s) for isolated extracorporeal circulation including regional chemotherapy perfusion to an extremity, with or without hyperthermia, with removal of cannula(s) and repair of arteriotomy and venotomy sites

(36823 includes chemotherapy perfusion supported by a membrane oxygenator/perfusion pump. Do not report 96409-96425 in conjunction with 36823)

**36825**   Creation of arteriovenous fistula by other than direct arteriovenous anastomosis (separate procedure); autogenous graft

(For direct arteriovenous anastomosis, use 36821)

**36830**       nonautogenous graft (eg, biological collagen, thermoplastic graft)

(For direct arteriovenous anastomosis, use 36821)

**36831**   Thrombectomy, open, arteriovenous fistula without revision, autogenous or nonautogenous dialysis graft (separate procedure)

**36832**   Revision, open, arteriovenous fistula; without thrombectomy, autogenous or nonautogenous dialysis graft (separate procedure)

**36833**       with thrombectomy, autogenous or nonautogenous dialysis graft (separate procedure)

(36834 has been deleted. To report an arteriovenous access fistula or graft revision, use 36832)

**36835**   Insertion of Thomas shunt (separate procedure)

**36838**   Distal revascularization and interval ligation (DRIL), upper extremity hemodialysis access (steal syndrome)

(Do not report 36838 in conjunction with 35512, 35522, 35523, 36832, 37607, 37618)

**36860**   External cannula declotting (separate procedure); without balloon catheter

**36861**       with balloon catheter

(If imaging guidance is performed, use 76000)

⊙ **36870**   Thrombectomy, percutaneous, arteriovenous fistula, autogenous or nonautogenous graft (includes mechanical thrombus extraction and intra-graft thrombolysis)

(Do not report 36870 in conjunction with 36593)

(For catheterization, see 36147, 36148)

(For radiological supervision and interpretation, see 36147, 75791)

## Portal Decompression Procedures

**37140**   Venous anastomosis, open; portocaval

(For peritoneal-venous shunt, use 49425)

**37145**       renoportal

**37160**       caval-mesenteric

**37180**       splenorenal, proximal

**37181**       splenorenal, distal (selective decompression of esophagogastric varices, any technique)

(For percutaneous procedure, use 37182)

---

**37182** Insertion of transvenous intrahepatic portosystemic shunt(s) (TIPS) (includes venous access, hepatic and portal vein catheterization, portography with hemodynamic evaluation, intrahepatic tract formation/dilatation, stent placement and all associated imaging guidance and documentation)

(Do not report 75885 or 75887 in conjunction with 37182)

(For open procedure, use 37140)

⊙ **37183** Revision of transvenous intrahepatic portosystemic shunt(s) (TIPS) (includes venous access, hepatic and portal vein catheterization, portography with hemodynamic evaluation, intrahepatic tract recanulization/dilatation, stent placement and all associated imaging guidance and documentation)

(Do not report 75885 or 75887 in conjunction with 37183)

(For repair of arteriovenous aneurysm, use 36832)

## Transcatheter Procedures

Codes for catheter placement and the radiologic supervision and interpretation should also be reported, in addition to the code(s) for the therapeutic aspect of the procedure.

### Mechanical Thrombectomy

Code(s) for catheter placement(s), diagnostic studies, and other percutaneous interventions (eg, transluminal balloon angioplasty, stent placement) provided are separately reportable.

Codes 37184-37188 specifically include intraprocedural fluoroscopic radiological supervision and interpretation services for guidance of the procedure.

Intraprocedural injection(s) of a thrombolytic agent is an included service and not separately reportable in conjunction with mechanical thrombectomy. However, subsequent or prior continuous infusion of a thrombolytic is not an included service and is separately reportable (see 37211-37214).

For coronary mechanical thrombectomy, use 92973.

For mechanical thrombectomy for dialysis fistula, use 36870.

### Transcatheter Thrombolytic Infusion

Codes 37211 or 37212 are used to report the initial day of transcatheter thrombolytic infusion(s) including follow-up arteriography/venography, and catheter position change or exchange, when performed. To report bilateral thrombolytic infusion through a separate access site(s), use modifier 50 in conjunction with 37211, 37212. Code 37213 is used to report continued transcatheter thrombolytic infusion(s) on subsequent day(s), other than initial day and final day of treatment. Code 37214 is used to report final day of transcatheter thrombolytic infusion(s). When initiation and completion of thrombolysis occur on the same day, report only 37211 or 37212.

Code(s) for catheter placement(s), diagnostic studies, and other percutaneous interventions (eg, transluminal balloon angioplasty, stent placement) provided may be separately reportable.

Codes 37211-37214 include fluoroscopic guidance and associated radiological supervision and interpretation.

Ongoing evaluation and management services on the day of the procedure related to thrombolysis are included in 37211-37214. If a significant, separately identifiable E/M service is performed by the same physician on the same day of the procedure, report the appropriate level of E/M service and append modifier 25.

Ultrasound guidance for vascular access is not included in 37211-37214. Code 76937 may be reported separately when performed if all the required elements are performed.

### Arterial Mechanical Thrombectomy

Arterial mechanical thrombectomy may be performed as a "primary" transcatheter procedure with pretreatment planning, performance of the procedure, and postprocedure evaluation focused on providing this service. Typically, the diagnosis of thrombus has been made prior to the procedure, and a mechanical thrombectomy is planned preoperatively. Primary mechanical thrombectomy is reported per vascular family using 37184 for the initial vessel treated and 37185 for second or all subsequent vessel(s) within the same vascular family. To report mechanical thrombectomy of an additional vascular family treated through a separate access site, use modifier 51 in conjunction with 37184-37185.

Primary mechanical thrombectomy may precede or follow another percutaneous intervention. Most commonly primary mechanical thrombectomy will precede another percutaneous intervention with the decision regarding the need for other services not made until after mechanical thrombectomy has been performed. Occasionally, the performance of primary mechanical thrombectomy may follow another percutaneous intervention.

Do **NOT** report 37184-37185 for mechanical thrombectomy performed for the retrieval of short segments of thrombus or embolus evident during other percutaneous interventional procedures. See 37186 for these procedures.

Arterial mechanical thrombectomy is considered a "secondary" transcatheter procedure for removal or retrieval of short segments of thrombus or embolus when performed either before or after another percutaneous intervention (eg, percutaneous transluminal balloon angioplasty, stent placement). Secondary mechanical thrombectomy is reported using 37186. Do **NOT** report 37186 in conjunction with 37184-37185.

*Venous Mechanical Thrombectomy*

Use 37187 to report the initial application of venous mechanical thrombectomy. To report bilateral venous mechanical thrombectomy performed through a separate access site(s), use modifier 50 in conjunction with 37187. For repeat treatment on a subsequent day during a course of thrombolytic therapy, use 37188.

## Arterial Mechanical Thrombectomy

⊙ **37184**    Primary percutaneous transluminal mechanical thrombectomy, noncoronary, arterial or arterial bypass graft, including fluoroscopic guidance and intraprocedural pharmacological thrombolytic injection(s); initial vessel

(Do not report 37184 in conjunction with 76000, 76001, 96374, 99143-99150)

⊙+ **37185**    second and all subsequent vessel(s) within the same vascular family (List separately in addition to code for primary mechanical thrombectomy procedure)

(Do not report 37185 in conjunction with 76000, 76001, 96375)

⊙+ **37186**    Secondary percutaneous transluminal thrombectomy (eg, nonprimary mechanical, snare basket, suction technique), noncoronary, arterial or arterial bypass graft, including fluoroscopic guidance and intraprocedural pharmacological thrombolytic injections, provided in conjunction with another percutaneous intervention other than primary mechanical thrombectomy (List separately in addition to code for primary procedure)

(Do not report 37186 in conjunction with 76000, 76001, 96375)

## Venous Mechanical Thrombectomy

⊙ **37187**    Percutaneous transluminal mechanical thrombectomy, vein(s), including intraprocedural pharmacological thrombolytic injections and fluoroscopic guidance

(Do not report 37187 in conjunction with 76000, 76001, 96375)

⊙ **37188**    Percutaneous transluminal mechanical thrombectomy, vein(s), including intraprocedural pharmacological thrombolytic injections and fluoroscopic guidance, repeat treatment on subsequent day during course of thrombolytic therapy

(Do not report 37188 in conjunction with 76000, 76001, 96375)

## Other Procedures

⊙ **37191**    Insertion of intravascular vena cava filter, endovascular approach including vascular access, vessel selection, and radiological supervision and interpretation, intraprocedural roadmapping, and imaging guidance (ultrasound and fluoroscopy), when performed

(For open surgical interruption of the inferior vena cava through a laparotomy or retroperitoneal exposure, use 37619)

⊙ **37192**    Repositioning of intravascular vena cava filter, endovascular approach including vascular access, vessel selection, and radiological supervision and interpretation, intraprocedural roadmapping, and imaging guidance (ultrasound and fluoroscopy), when performed

(Do not report 37192 in conjunction with 37191)

⊙ **37193**    Retrieval (removal) of intravascular vena cava filter, endovascular approach including vascular access, vessel selection, and radiological supervision and interpretation, intraprocedural roadmapping, and imaging guidance (ultrasound and fluoroscopy), when performed

(Do not report 37193 in conjunction with 37197)

**37195**    Thrombolysis, cerebral, by intravenous infusion

⊙ **37197**    Transcatheter retrieval, percutaneous, of intravascular foreign body (eg, fractured venous or arterial catheter), includes radiological supervision and interpretation, and imaging guidance (ultrasound or fluoroscopy), when performed

(For percutaneous retrieval of a vena cava filter, use 37193)

**37200**    Transcatheter biopsy

(For radiological supervision and interpretation, use 75970)

(37201 has been deleted. To report see 37211-37214)

#⊙ **37211**    Transcatheter therapy, arterial infusion for thrombolysis other than coronary, any method, including radiological supervision and interpretation, initial treatment day

#⊙ **37212**    Transcatheter therapy, venous infusion for thrombolysis, any method, including radiological supervision and interpretation, initial treatment day

#⊙ **37213**    Transcatheter therapy, arterial or venous infusion for thrombolysis other than coronary, any method, including radiological supervision and interpretation, continued treatment on subsequent day during course of thrombolytic therapy, including follow-up catheter contrast injection, position change, or exchange, when performed;

#⊙ **37214**    cessation of thrombolysis including removal of catheter and vessel closure by any method

(Report 37211-37214 once per date of treatment)

**Cardiovascular**

---

(For declotting by thrombolytic agent of implanted vascular access device or catheter, use 36593)

▶(Do not report 37211-37214 in conjunction with 75898)◀

**37202** Transcatheter therapy, infusion other than for thrombolysis, any type (eg, spasmolytic, vasoconstrictive)

(For thrombolysis of coronary vessels, see 92975, 92977)

(For radiological supervision and interpretation, use 75896)

(37203 has been deleted. To report, use 37197)

(For removal of a vena cava filter, use 37193)

▶(37204 has been deleted. To report, see 37241, 37242, 37243, 37244. For transcatheter occlusion or embolization in the central nervous system, use 61624. For transcatheter occlusion or embolization for non-central nervous system in the head and neck, use 61626)◀

▶(37205-37208 have been deleted. To report, see 37236-37239)◀

(37209 has been deleted. For exchange of a previously placed intravascular catheter during thrombolytic therapy, see 37211-37214)

▶(37210 has been deleted. To report, use 37243)◀

**37211** Code is out of numerical sequence. See 37191-37216

**37212** Code is out of numerical sequence. See 37191-37216

**37213** Code is out of numerical sequence. See 37191-37216

**37214** Code is out of numerical sequence. See 37191-37216

⊙ **37215** Transcatheter placement of intravascular stent(s), cervical carotid artery, percutaneous; with distal embolic protection

⊙ **37216** without distal embolic protection

(37215 and 37216 include all ipsilateral selective carotid catheterization, all diagnostic imaging for ipsilateral, cervical and cerebral carotid arteriography, and all related radiological supervision and interpretation. When ipsilateral carotid arteriogram (including imaging and selective catheterization) confirms the need for carotid stenting, 37215 and 37216 are inclusive of these services. If carotid stenting is not indicated, then the appropriate codes for carotid catheterization and imaging should be reported in lieu of 37215 and 37216)

(Do not report 37215, 37216 in conjunction with 36222-36224 for the treated carotid artery)

▶(For percutaneous transcatheter placement of extracranial vertebral or intrathoracic carotid artery stent[s], see Category III codes 0075T, 0076T)◀

● **37217** Transcatheter placement of an intravascular stent(s), intrathoracic common carotid artery or innominate artery by retrograde treatment, via open ipsilateral cervical carotid artery exposure, including angioplasty, when performed, and radiological supervision and interpretation

▶(37217 includes open vessel exposure and vascular access closure, all access and selective catheterization of the vessel, traversing the lesion, and any radiological supervision and interpretation directly related to the intervention when performed, standard closure of arteriotomy by suture, and imaging performed to document completion of the intervention in addition to the intervention[s] performed. Carotid artery revascularization services [eg, 33891, 35301, 35509, 35510, 35601, 35606] performed during the same session may be reported separately, when performed)◀

▶(Do not report 37217 in conjunction with 35201, 35458, 36221-36227, 75962 for ipsilateral services)◀

▶(For percutaneous transcatheter placement of intravascular cervical carotid artery stent[s], see 37215, 37216)◀

▶(For percutaneous transcatheter placement of intrathoracic carotid artery stent[s], see 0075T, 0076T)◀

▶(For transcatheter placement of intracranial stent[s], use 61635)◀

## Endovascular Revascularization (Open or Percutaneous, Transcatheter)

Codes 37220-37235 are to be used to describe lower extremity endovascular revascularization services performed for occlusive disease. These lower extremity codes are built on progressive hierarchies with more intensive services inclusive of lesser intensive services. The code inclusive of all of the services provided for that vessel should be reported (ie, use the code inclusive of the most intensive services provided). Only one code from this family (37220-37235) should be reported for each lower extremity vessel treated.

These lower extremity endovascular revascularization codes all include the work of accessing and selectively catheterizing the vessel, traversing the lesion, radiological supervision and interpretation directly related to the intervention(s) performed, embolic protection if used, closure of the arteriotomy by pressure and application of an arterial closure device or standard closure of the puncture by suture, and imaging performed to document completion of the intervention in addition to the intervention(s) performed. Extensive repair or replacement of an artery may be additionally reported (eg, 35226 or 35286). These codes describe endovascular procedures performed percutaneously and/or through an open surgical exposure. These codes include balloon angioplasty (eg, low-profile, cutting balloon, cryoplasty), atherectomy (eg, directional, rotational, laser), and stenting (eg, balloon-expandable, self-expanding, bare metal, covered, drug-eluting). Each code in this family (37220-37235) includes balloon angioplasty, when performed.

These codes describe revascularization therapies (ie, transluminal angioplasty, atherectomy, and stent placement) provided in three arterial vascular territories: iliac, femoral/popliteal, and tibial/peroneal.

When treating multiple vessels within a territory, report each additional vessel using an add-on code, as applicable. Select the base code that represents the most complex service using the following hierarchy of complexity (in descending order of complexity): atherectomy and stent> atherectomy>stent>angioplasty. When treating multiple lesions within the same vessel, report one service that reflects the combined procedures, whether done on one lesion or different lesions, using the same hierarchy.

1. *Iliac Vascular Territory*—The iliac territory is divided into 3 vessels: common iliac, internal iliac, and external iliac.

2. *Femoral/Popliteal Vascular Territory*—The entire femoral/popliteal territory in 1 lower extremity is considered a single vessel for CPT reporting specifically for the endovascular lower extremity revascularization codes 37224-37227.

3. *Tibial/Peroneal Territory*—The tibial/peroneal territory is divided into 3 vessels: anterior tibial, posterior tibial, and peroneal arteries.

There are specific coding guidelines for each of the 3 vascular territories.

1. *Iliac Vascular Territory*—A single primary code is used for the initial iliac artery treated in each leg (37220 or 37221). If other iliac vessels are also treated in that leg, these interventions are reported with the appropriate add-on code(s) (37222, 37223). Up to 2 add-on codes can be used in a unilateral iliac vascular territory since there are 3 vessels which could be treated. Add-on codes are used for different vessels, not distinct lesions within the same vessel.

2. *Femoral/Popliteal Territory*—A single interventional code is used no matter what combination of angioplasty/stent/atherectomy is applied to all segments, including the common, deep and superficial femoral arteries as well as the popliteal artery (37224, 37225, 37226, or 37227). There are no add-on codes for additional vessels treated within the femoral/ popliteal territory. Because only 1 service is reported when 2 lesions are treated in this territory, report the most complex service (eg, use 37227 if a stent is placed for 1 lesion and an atherectomy is performed on a second lesion)

3. *Tibial/Peroneal Territory*—A single primary code is used for the initial tibial/peroneal artery treated in each leg (37228, 37229, 37230, or 37231). If other tibial/ peroneal vessels are also treated in the same leg, these

interventions are reported with the appropriate add-on code(s) (37232-37235). Up to 2 add-on codes could be used to describe services provided in a single leg since there are 3 tibial/peroneal vessels which could be treated. Add-on codes are used for different vessels, not distinct lesions within the same vessel. The common tibio-peroneal trunk is considered part of the tibial/ peroneal territory, but is not considered a separate, fourth segment of vessel in the tibio-peroneal family for CPT reporting of endovascular lower extremity interventions. For instance, if lesions in the common tibio-peroneal trunk are treated in conjunction with lesions in the posterior tibial artery, a single code would be reported for treatment of this segment.

When treating multiple territories in the same leg, one primary lower extremity revascularization code is used for each territory treated. When second or third vessel(s) are treated in the iliac and/or tibial/peroneal territories, add-on code(s) are used to report the additional service(s). When more than one stent is placed in the same vessel, the code should be reported only once.

When multiple vessels in multiple territories in a single leg are treated at the same setting, the primary code for the treatment in the initial vessel in each vascular territory is reported. Add-on code(s) are reported when second and third iliac or tibial/peroneal arteries are treated in addition to the initial vessel in that vascular territory.

If a lesion extends across the margins of one vessel vascular territory into another, but can be opened with a single therapy, this intervention should be reported with a single code despite treating more than one vessel and/or vascular territory. For instance, if a stenosis extends from the common iliac artery into the proximal external iliac artery, and a single stent is placed to open the entire lesion, this therapy should be coded as a single stent placement in the iliac artery (37221). In this example, a code for an additional vessel treatment would not be used (do not report both 37221 and 37223).

For bifurcation lesions distal to the common iliac origins which require therapy of 2 distinct branches of the iliac or tibial/peroneal vascular territories, a primary code and an add-on code would be used to describe the intervention. In the femoral/popliteal territory, all branches are included in the primary code, so treatment of a bifurcation lesion would be reported as a single code.

When the same territor(ies) of both legs are treated in the same session, modifiers may be required to describe the interventions. Use modifier 59 to denote that different legs are being treated, even if the mode of therapy is different.

Mechanical thrombectomy and/or thrombolysis in the lower extremity vessels are sometimes necessary to aid in restoring flow to areas of occlusive disease, and are reported separately.

Cardiovascular

⊙ **37220** Revascularization, endovascular, open or percutaneous, iliac artery, unilateral, initial vessel; with transluminal angioplasty

⊙ **37221** with transluminal stent placement(s), includes angioplasty within the same vessel, when performed

▶(Use 37220, 37221 in conjunction with 34802-34805, 34825, 34826, 34845-34848, 34900, 0254T only when 37220 or 37221 are performed outside the target treatment zone of the endoprosthesis)◀

⊙✚ **37222** Revascularization, endovascular, open or percutaneous, iliac artery, each additional ipsilateral iliac vessel; with transluminal angioplasty (List separately in addition to code for primary procedure)

(Use 37222 in conjunction with 37220, 37221)

⊙✚ **37223** with transluminal stent placement(s), includes angioplasty within the same vessel, when performed (List separately in addition to code for primary procedure)

(Use 37223 in conjunction with 37221)

▶(Use 37222, 37223 in conjunction with 34802-34805, 34825, 34826, 34845-34848, 34900, 0254T only when 37222 or 37223 are performed outside the target treatment zone of the endoprosthesis)◀

⊙ **37224** Revascularization, endovascular, open or percutaneous, femoral, popliteal artery(s), unilateral; with transluminal angioplasty

⊙ **37225** with atherectomy, includes angioplasty within the same vessel, when performed

⊙ **37226** with transluminal stent placement(s), includes angioplasty within the same vessel, when performed

⊙ **37227** with transluminal stent placement(s) and atherectomy, includes angioplasty within the same vessel, when performed

⊙ **37228** Revascularization, endovascular, open or percutaneous, tibial, peroneal artery, unilateral, initial vessel; with transluminal angioplasty

⊙ **37229** with atherectomy, includes angioplasty within the same vessel, when performed

⊙ **37230** with transluminal stent placement(s), includes angioplasty within the same vessel, when performed

⊙ **37231** with transluminal stent placement(s) and atherectomy, includes angioplasty within the same vessel, when performed

⊙✚ **37232** Revascularization, endovascular, open or percutaneous, tibial/peroneal artery, unilateral, each additional vessel; with transluminal angioplasty (List separately in addition to code for primary procedure)

(Use 37232 in conjunction with 37228-37231)

⊙✚ **37233** with atherectomy, includes angioplasty within the same vessel, when performed (List separately in addition to code for primary procedure)

(Use 37233 in conjunction with 37229, 37231)

⊙✚ **37234** with transluminal stent placement(s), includes angioplasty within the same vessel, when performed (List separately in addition to code for primary procedure)

(Use 37234 in conjunction with 37229, 37230, 37231)

⊙✚ **37235** with transluminal stent placement(s) and atherectomy, includes angioplasty within the same vessel, when performed (List separately in addition to code for primary procedure)

(Use 37235 in conjunction with 37231)

▶Codes 37236-37239 are used to report endovascular revascularization for vessels other than lower extremity (ie, 37221, 37223, 37226, 37227, 37230, 37231, 37234, 37235), cervical carotid (ie, 37215, 37216), intracranial (ie, 61635), intracoronary (ie, 92928, 92929, 92933, 92934, 92937, 92938, 92941, 92943, 92944), extracranial vertebral or intrathoracic carotid (ie, 0075T, 0076T) performed percutaneously and/or through an open surgical exposure, or open retrograde intrathoracic common carotid or innominate (37217).

Codes 37236, 37237 describe transluminal intravascular stent insertion in an artery while 37238, 37239 describe transluminal intravascular stent insertion in a vein. Multiple stents placed in a single vessel may only be reported with a single code. If a lesion extends across the margins of one vessel into another, but can be treated with a single therapy, the intervention should be reported only once. When additional, different vessels are treated in the same session, report 37237 and/or 37239 as appropriate. Each code in this family (37236-37239) includes any and all balloon angioplasty(s) performed in the treated vessel, including any pre-dilation (whether performed as a primary or secondary angioplasty), post-dilation following stent placement, treatment of a lesion outside the stented segment but in the same vessel, or use of larger/smaller balloon to achieve therapeutic result. Angioplasty in a separate and distinct vessel may be reported separately. Non-selective and/or selective catheterization(s) (eg, 36005, 36010-36015, 36200, 36215-36218, 36245-36248) is reported separately.

Codes 37236-37239 include radiological supervision and interpretation directly related to the intervention(s) performed, closure of the arteriotomy by pressure, application of an arterial closure device or standard closure of the puncture by suture, and imaging performed to document completion of the intervention in addition to the intervention(s) performed. Extensive repair or replacement of an artery may be reported separately (eg, 35226 or 35286). Report 76937 for ultrasound guidance for vascular access, when performed in conjunction with 37236-37239. Intravascular ultrasound may be reported separately (ie, 37250, 37251). For mechanical thrombectomy and/or thrombolytic therapy, when performed, see 37184-37188, 37211-37214.

Intravascular stents, both covered and uncovered, are a class of devices that may be used as part of an embolization procedure. As such, there is the potential for overlap among codes used for placement of vascular stents and those used for embolization. When a stent is placed for the purpose of providing a latticework for deployment of embolization coils, such as for embolization of an aneurysm, the embolization code is reported and not the stent code. If a covered stent is deployed as the sole management of an aneurysm, pseudoaneurysm, or vascular extravasation, then the stent deployment code should be reported and not the embolization code.◄

⊙● **37236**  Transcatheter placement of an intravascular stent(s) (except lower extremity, cervical carotid, extracranial vertebral or intrathoracic carotid, intracranial, or coronary), open or percutaneous, including radiological supervision and interpretation and including all angioplasty within the same vessel, when performed; initial artery

⊙+● **37237**  each additional artery (List separately in addition to code for primary procedure)

►(Use 37237 in conjunction with 37236)◄

►(Do not report 37236, 37237 in conjunction with 34841-34848 for bare metal or covered stents placed into the visceral branches within the endoprosthesis target zone)◄

►(For stent placement(s) in iliac, femoral, popliteal, or tibial/peroneal artery(s), see 37221, 37223, 37226, 37227, 37230, 37231, 37234, 37235)◄

►(For transcatheter placement of intravascular cervical carotid artery stent(s), see 37215, 37216)◄

►(For transcatheter placement of intracranial stent(s), use 61635)◄

►(For transcatheter placement of intracoronary stent(s), see 92928, 92929, 92933, 92934, 92937, 92938, 92941, 92943, 92944)◄

►(For stenting of visceral arteries in conjunction with fenestrated endovascular repair, see 34841-34848)◄

►(For percutaneous transcatheter placement of extracranial vertebral artery or intrathoracic carotid artery stent(s), see Category III codes 0075T, 0076T)◄

►(For open retrograde transcatheter placement of intrathoracic common carotid/innominate artery stent(s), use 37217)◄

⊙● **37238**  Transcatheter placement of an intravascular stent(s), open or percutaneous, including radiological supervision and interpretation and including angioplasty within the same vessel, when performed; initial vein

⊙+● **37239**  each additional vein (List separately in addition to code for primary procedure)

►(Use 37239 in conjunction with 37238)◄

## ►Vascular Embolization and Occlusion◄

►Codes 37241-37244 are used to describe the work of vascular embolization and occlusion procedures, excluding the central nervous system and the head and neck, which are reported using 61624, 61626, 61710, and 75894, and excluding the ablation/sclerotherapy procedures for venous insufficiency/telangiectasia of the extremities/skin, which are reported using 36468, 36470, and 36471. Embolization and occlusion procedures are performed for a wide variety of clinical indications and in a range of vascular territories. Arteries, veins, and lymphatics may all be the target of embolization.

The embolization codes include all associated radiological supervision and interpretation, intra-procedural guidance and road mapping, and imaging necessary to document completion of the procedure. Code(s) for catheter placement(s) and diagnostic studies may be separately reportable using the appropriate diagnostic angiography codes with an appropriate modifier (eg, modifier 59). Please see the guidelines on the reporting of diagnostic angiography preceding 75600 in the **Vascular Procedures, Aorta and Arteries** section.

Code 37241 is used to report vascular embolization or occlusion procedures performed for venous conditions other than hemorrhage. Examples include embolization of venous malformations, capillary hemangiomas, varicoceles, and visceral varices. Embolization of side branch(es) of an outflow vein from a hemodialysis access would be reported using 37241.

Code 37242 is used to report vascular embolization or occlusion performed for arterial conditions other than hemorrhage or tumor such as arteriovenous malformations and arteriovenous fistulas whether congenital or acquired. Embolizations of aneurysms and pseudoaneurysms are also reported with 37242. Tumor embolization is reported with 37243. Note that injection to treat an extremity pseudoaneurysm is correctly reported with 36002. Sometimes, embolization and occlusion of an artery are performed prior to another planned interventional procedure; an example is embolization of the left gastric artery prior to planned implantation of a hepatic artery chemotherapy port. The artery embolization is reported with 37242.

Code 37243 is used to report embolization for the purpose of tissue ablation and organ infarction or ischemia. This can be performed in many clinical circumstances, including embolization of benign or malignant tumors of the liver, kidney, uterus, or other organs. When chemotherapy is given as part of an embolization procedure, additional codes (eg, 96420) may be separately reported. When a radioisotope (eg, Yttrium-90) is injected as part of an embolization, then additional codes (eg, 79445) may be separately reported. Uterine fibroid embolization is reported with 37243.

**Cardiovascular**

Code 37244 is used to report embolization for treatment of hemorrhage or vascular or lymphatic extravasation. Examples include embolization for management of gastrointestinal bleed, trauma-induced hemorrhage of the viscera or pelvis, embolization of the thoracic duct for chylous effusion and bronchial artery embolization for hemoptysis. Embolization of the uterine arteries for management of hemorrhage (eg, postpartum hemorrhage) is also reported with 37244.

Intravascular stents, both covered and uncovered, are a class of devices that may be used as part of an embolization procedure. As such, there is the potential for overlap among codes used for placement of vascular stents and those used for embolization. When a stent is placed for the purpose of providing a latticework for deployment of embolization coils, such as for embolization of an aneurysm, the embolization code is reported and not the stent code. If a stent is deployed as the sole management of an aneurysm, pseudoaneurysm, or vascular extravasation, then the stent deployment code should be reported and not the embolization code.

Only one embolization code should be reported for each surgical field (ie, the area immediately surrounding and directly involved in a treatment/procedure). For example, embolization of one or more venous side branches in a single arm for a patient with a dialysis arteriovenous fistula is reported with 37241 only once per session. Embolization procedures performed at a single setting and including multiple surgical fields (eg, a patient with multiple trauma and bleeding from the pelvis and the spleen) may be reported with multiple embolization codes with the appropriate modifier (eg, modifier 59).

There may be overlapping indications for an embolization procedure. The code for the immediate indication for the embolization should be used. For instance, if the immediate cause for embolization is bleeding in a patient with an aneurysm, report 37244.◄

⊙● **37241**   Vascular embolization or occlusion, inclusive of all radiological supervision and interpretation, intraprocedural roadmapping, and imaging guidance necessary to complete the intervention; venous, other than hemorrhage (eg, congenital or acquired venous malformations, venous and capillary hemangiomas, varices, varicoceles)

►(For sclerosis of veins or endovenous ablation of incompetent extremity veins, see 36468-36479)◄

►(Do not report 37241 in conjunction with 36468, 36470, 36471, 36475-36479, 75894, 75898 in the same surgical field)◄

⊙● **37242**   arterial, other than hemorrhage or tumor (eg, congenital or acquired arterial malformations, arteriovenous malformations, arteriovenous fistulas, aneurysms, pseudoaneurysms)

►(For percutaneous treatment of extremity pseudoaneurysm, use 36002)◄

⊙● **37243**   for tumors, organ ischemia, or infarction

⊙● **37244**   for arterial or venous hemorrhage or lymphatic extravasation

►(Do not report 37242-37244 in conjunction with 75894, 75898 in the same surgical field)◄

►(For embolization procedures of the central nervous system or head and neck, see 61624, 61626, 61710)◄

## Intravascular Ultrasound Services

Intravascular ultrasound services include all transducer manipulations and repositioning within the specific vessel being examined, both before and after therapeutic intervention (eg, stent placement).

Vascular access for intravascular ultrasound performed during a therapeutic intervention is not reported separately.

+ **37250**   Intravascular ultrasound (non-coronary vessel) during diagnostic evaluation and/or therapeutic intervention; initial vessel (List separately in addition to code for primary procedure)

+ **37251**   each additional vessel (List separately in addition to code for primary procedure)

(Use 37251 in conjunction with 37250)

(For catheterizations, see 36215-36248)

►(For transcatheter therapies, see 37200, 37202, 37236-37239, 37241-37244, 61624, 61626)◄

(For radiological supervision and interpretation see 75945, 75946)

## Endoscopy

Surgical vascular endoscopy always includes diagnostic endoscopy.

**37500**   Vascular endoscopy, surgical, with ligation of perforator veins, subfascial (SEPS)

(For open procedure, use 37760)

**37501**   Unlisted vascular endoscopy procedure

## Ligation

(For phleborraphy and arteriorraphy, see 35201-35286)

**37565**   Ligation, internal jugular vein

**37600**   Ligation; external carotid artery

**37605**   internal or common carotid artery

**37606**      internal or common carotid artery, with gradual occlusion, as with Selverstone or Crutchfield clamp

(For transcatheter permanent arterial occlusion or embolization, see 61624-61626)

(For endovascular temporary arterial balloon occlusion, use 61623)

(For ligation treatment of intracranial aneurysm, use 61703)

**37607**    Ligation or banding of angioaccess arteriovenous fistula

**37609**    Ligation or biopsy, temporal artery

**37615**    Ligation, major artery (eg, post-traumatic, rupture); neck

**37616**      chest

**37617**      abdomen

**37618**      extremity

**37619**    Ligation of inferior vena cava

(For endovascular delivery of an inferior vena cava filter, use 37191)

(37620 has been deleted. To report, see 37191 for endovascular placement of intravascular filter or 37619 for open surgical ligation of the inferior vena cava)

**37650**    Ligation of femoral vein

(For bilateral procedure, report 37650 with modifier 50)

**37660**    Ligation of common iliac vein

**37700**    Ligation and division of long saphenous vein at saphenofemoral junction, or distal interruptions

(Do not report 37700 in conjunction with 37718, 37722)

(For bilateral procedure, report 37700 with modifier 50)

**37718**    Ligation, division, and stripping, short saphenous vein

(For bilateral procedure, use modifier 50)

(Do not report 37718 in conjunction with 37735, 37780)

**37722**    Ligation, division, and stripping, long (greater) saphenous veins from saphenofemoral junction to knee or below

(For ligation and stripping of the short saphenous vein, use 37718)

(For bilateral procedure, report 37722 with modifier 50)

(Do not report 37722 in conjunction with 37700, 37735)

(For ligation, division, and stripping of the greater saphenous vein, use 37722. For ligation, division, and stripping of the short saphenous vein, use 37718)

**37735**    Ligation and division and complete stripping of long or short saphenous veins with radical excision of ulcer and skin graft and/or interruption of communicating veins of lower leg, with excision of deep fascia

(Do not report 37735 in conjunction with 37700, 37718, 37722, 37780)

(For bilateral procedure, report 37735 with modifier 50)

**37760**    Ligation of perforator veins, subfascial, radical (Linton type), including skin graft, when performed, open,1 leg

(For endoscopic procedure, use 37500)

**37761**    Ligation of perforator vein(s), subfascial, open, including ultrasound guidance, when performed, 1 leg

(For bilateral procedure, report 37761 with modifier 50)

(Do not report 37760, 37761 in conjunction with 76937, 76942, 76998, 93971)

(For endoscopic ligation of subfascial perforator veins, use 37500)

**37765**    Stab phlebectomy of varicose veins, 1 extremity; 10-20 stab incisions

(For less than 10 incisions, use 37799)

(For more than 20 incisions, use 37766)

**37766**      more than 20 incisions

**37780**    Ligation and division of short saphenous vein at saphenopopliteal junction (separate procedure)

(For bilateral procedure, report 37780 with modifier 50)

**37785**    Ligation, division, and/or excision of varicose vein cluster(s), 1 leg

(For bilateral procedure, report 37785 with modifier 50)

## Other Procedures

**37788**    Penile revascularization, artery, with or without vein graft

**37790**    Penile venous occlusive procedure

**37799**    Unlisted procedure, vascular surgery

# Hemic and Lymphatic Systems

## Spleen

### Excision

**38100**    Splenectomy; total (separate procedure)

**38101**      partial (separate procedure)

**+ 38102**      total, en bloc for extensive disease, in conjunction with other procedure (List in addition to code for primary procedure)

### Repair

**38115**    Repair of ruptured spleen (splenorrhaphy) with or without partial splenectomy

*Cardiovascular*

## Laparoscopy

Surgical laparoscopy always includes diagnostic laparoscopy. To report a diagnostic laparoscopy (peritoneoscopy) (separate procedure), use 49320.

**38120**   Laparoscopy, surgical, splenectomy

**38129**   Unlisted laparoscopy procedure, spleen

## Introduction

**38200**   Injection procedure for splenoportography

(For radiological supervision and interpretation, use 75810)

# General

## Bone Marrow or Stem Cell Services/ Procedures

Codes 38207-38215 describe various steps used to preserve, prepare and purify bone marrow/stem cells prior to transplantation or reinfusion. Each code may be reported only once per day regardless of the quantity of bone marrow/stem cells manipulated.

**38204**   Management of recipient hematopoietic progenitor cell donor search and cell acquisition

**38205**   Blood-derived hematopoietic progenitor cell harvesting for transplantation, per collection; allogeneic

**38206**         autologous

**38207**   Transplant preparation of hematopoietic progenitor cells; cryopreservation and storage

(For diagnostic cryopreservation and storage, use 88240)

**38208**         thawing of previously frozen harvest, without washing, per donor

(For diagnostic thawing and expansion of frozen cells, use 88241)

**38209**         thawing of previously frozen harvest, with washing, per donor

**38210**         specific cell depletion within harvest, T-cell depletion

**38211**         tumor cell depletion

**38212**         red blood cell removal

**38213**         platelet depletion

**38214**         plasma (volume) depletion

**38215**         cell concentration in plasma, mononuclear, or buffy coat layer

(Do not report 38207-38215 in conjunction with 88182, 88184-88189)

**38220**   Bone marrow; aspiration only

(For needle aspiration of bone marrow for the purpose of bone grafting, use 38220)

(Do not report 38220-38230 for bone marrow aspiration for platelet rich stem cell injection. For bone marrow aspiration for platelet rich stem cell injection, use 0232T)

**38221**         biopsy, needle or trocar

(For bone marrow biopsy interpretation, use 88305)

**38230**   Bone marrow harvesting for transplantation; allogeneic

**38232**         autologous

(For autologous and allogeneic blood-derived peripheral stem cell harvesting for transplantation, see 38205-38206)

(For bone marrow aspiration, use 38220)

## Transplantation and Post-Transplantation Cellular Infusions

Hematopoietic cell transplantation (HCT) refers to the infusion of hematopoietic progenitor cells (HPC) obtained from bone marrow, peripheral blood apheresis, and/or umbilical cord blood. These procedure codes (38240-38243) include physician monitoring of multiple physiologic parameters, physician verification of cell processing, evaluation of the patient during as well as immediately before and after the HPC/lymphocyte infusion, physician presence during the HPC/lymphocyte infusion with associated direct physician supervision of clinical staff, and management of uncomplicated adverse events (eg, nausea, urticaria) during the infusion, which is not separately reportable.

HCT may be autologous (when the HPC donor and recipient are the same person) or allogeneic (when the HPC donor and recipient are not the same person). Code 38241 is used to report any autologous transplant while 38240 is used to report an allogeneic transplant. In some cases allogeneic transplants involve more than one donor and cells from each donor are infused sequentially whereby one unit of 38240 is reported for each donor infused. Code 38242 is used to report a donor lymphocyte infusion. Code 38243 is used to report a HPC boost from the original allogeneic HPC donor. A lymphocyte infusion or HPC boost can occur days, months or even years after the initial hematopoietic cell transplant. The lymphocyte infusion is used to treat relapse, infection, or post-transplant lymphoproliferative syndrome. HPC boost represents an infusion of hematopoietic progenitor cells from the original donor that is being used to treat a relapse or post-transplant cytopenia(s). Codes 38240, 38242, and 38243 should not be reported together on the same date of service.

If a separately identifiable evaluation and management service is performed on the same date of service, the appropriate E/M service code, including office or other outpatient services, established (99211-99215), hospital observation services (99217-99220, 99224-99226), hospital inpatient services (99221-99223, 99231-99239), and inpatient neonatal and pediatric critical care (99471, 99472, 99475, 99476) may be reported, using modifier 25, in addition to 38240, 38242 or 38243. Post-transplant infusion management of adverse reactions is reported separately using the appropriate E/M, prolonged service or critical care code(s). In accordance with place of service and facility reporting guidelines, the fluid used to administer the cells and other infusions for incidental hydration (eg, 96360, 96361) are not separately reportable. Similarly, infusion(s) of any medication(s) concurrently with the transplant infusion are not separately reportable. However, hydration or administration of medications (eg, antibiotics, narcotics) unrelated to the transplant are separately reportable using modifier 59.

| | |
|---|---|
| 38240 | Hematopoietic progenitor cell (HPC); allogeneic transplantation per donor |
| 38241 | autologous transplantation |
| # 38243 | HPC boost |
| 38242 | Allogeneic lymphocyte infusions |

(For bone marrow aspiration, use 38220)

(For modification, treatment, and processing of hematopoietic progenitor cell specimens for transplantation, see 38210-38215)

(For cryopreservation, freezing, and storage of hematopoietic progenitor cells for transplantation, use 38207)

(For thawing and expansion of hematopoietic progenitor cells for transplantation, see 38208, 38209)

(For compatibility studies, see 81379-81383, 86812-86822)

| | |
|---|---|
| 38243 | Code is out of numerical sequence. See 38240-38242 |

## Lymph Nodes and Lymphatic Channels

### Incision

| | |
|---|---|
| 38300 | Drainage of lymph node abscess or lymphadenitis; simple |
| 38305 | extensive |
| 38308 | Lymphangiotomy or other operations on lymphatic channels |
| 38380 | Suture and/or ligation of thoracic duct; cervical approach |
| 38381 | thoracic approach |
| 38382 | abdominal approach |

### Excision

(For injection for sentinel node identification, use 38792)

| | |
|---|---|
| 38500 | Biopsy or excision of lymph node(s); open, superficial |

(Do not report 38500 with 38700-38780)

| | |
|---|---|
| 38505 | by needle, superficial (eg, cervical, inguinal, axillary) |

(If imaging guidance is performed, see 76942, 77012, 77021)

(For fine needle aspiration, use 10021 or 10022)

(For evaluation of fine needle aspirate, see 88172, 88173)

| | |
|---|---|
| 38510 | open, deep cervical node(s) |
| 38520 | open, deep cervical node(s) with excision scalene fat pad |
| 38525 | open, deep axillary node(s) |
| 38530 | open, internal mammary node(s) |

(Do not report 38530 with 38720-38746)

(For percutaneous needle biopsy, retroperitoneal lymph node or mass, use 49180. For fine needle aspiration, use 10022)

| | |
|---|---|
| 38542 | Dissection, deep jugular node(s) |

(For radical cervical neck dissection, use 38720)

| | |
|---|---|
| 38550 | Excision of cystic hygroma, axillary or cervical; without deep neurovascular dissection |
| 38555 | with deep neurovascular dissection |

### Limited Lymphadenectomy for Staging

| | |
|---|---|
| 38562 | Limited lymphadenectomy for staging (separate procedure); pelvic and para-aortic |

(When combined with prostatectomy, use 55812 or 55842)

(When combined with insertion of radioactive substance into prostate, use 55862)

| | |
|---|---|
| 38564 | retroperitoneal (aortic and/or splenic) |

### Laparoscopy

Surgical laparoscopy always includes diagnostic laparoscopy. To report a diagnostic laparoscopy (peritoneoscopy) (separate procedure), use 49320.

| | |
|---|---|
| 38570 | Laparoscopy, surgical; with retroperitoneal lymph node sampling (biopsy), single or multiple |
| 38571 | with bilateral total pelvic lymphadenectomy |
| 38572 | with bilateral total pelvic lymphadenectomy and peri-aortic lymph node sampling (biopsy), single or multiple |

(For drainage of lymphocele to peritoneal cavity, use 49323)

| | |
|---|---|
| 38589 | Unlisted laparoscopy procedure, lymphatic system |

**Cardiovascular**

## Radical Lymphadenectomy (Radical Resection of Lymph Nodes)

(For limited pelvic and retroperitoneal lymphadenectomies, see 38562, 38564)

**38700** Suprahyoid lymphadenectomy

(For bilateral procedure, report 38700 with modifier 50)

**38720** Cervical lymphadenectomy (complete)

(For bilateral procedure, report 38720 with modifier 50)

**38724** Cervical lymphadenectomy (modified radical neck dissection)

**38740** Axillary lymphadenectomy; superficial

**38745** complete

**+ 38746** Thoracic lymphadenectomy by thoracotomy, mediastinal and regional lymphadenectomy (List separately in addition to code for primary procedure)

(On the right, mediastinal lymph nodes include the paratracheal, subcarinal, paraesophageal, and inferior pulmonary ligament)

(On the left, mediastinal lymph nodes include the aortopulmonary window, subcarinal, paraesophageal, and inferior pulmonary ligament)

▶(Report 38746 in conjunction with 19260, 31760, 31766, 31786, 32096-32200, 32220-32320, 32440-32491, 32503-32505, 33025, 33030, 33050-33130, 39200-39220, 39560, 39561, 43101, 43112, 43117, 43118, 43122, 43123, 43351, 60270, 60505)◀

(To report mediastinal and regional lymphadenectomy via thoracoscopy [VATS], see 32674)

**+ 38747** Abdominal lymphadenectomy, regional, including celiac, gastric, portal, peripancreatic, with or without para-aortic and vena caval nodes (List separately in addition to code for primary procedure)

**38760** Inguinofemoral lymphadenectomy, superficial, including Cloquets node (separate procedure)

(For bilateral procedure, report 38760 with modifier 50)

**38765** Inguinofemoral lymphadenectomy, superficial, in continuity with pelvic lymphadenectomy, including external iliac, hypogastric, and obturator nodes (separate procedure)

(For bilateral procedure, report 38765 with modifier 50)

**38770** Pelvic lymphadenectomy, including external iliac, hypogastric, and obturator nodes (separate procedure)

(For bilateral procedure, report 38770 with modifier 50)

**38780** Retroperitoneal transabdominal lymphadenectomy, extensive, including pelvic, aortic, and renal nodes (separate procedure)

(For excision and repair of lymphedematous skin and subcutaneous tissue, see 15004-15005, 15570-15650)

## Introduction

**38790** Injection procedure; lymphangiography

(For bilateral procedure, report 38790 with modifier 50)

(For radiological supervision and interpretation, see 75801-75807)

**38792** radioactive tracer for identification of sentinel node

(For excision of sentinel node, see 38500-38542)

(For nuclear medicine lymphatics and lymph gland imaging, use 78195)

(For intraoperative identification (eg, mapping) of sentinel lymph node(s) including injection of non-radioactive dye, see 38900)

**38794** Cannulation, thoracic duct

## Other Procedures

**+ 38900** Intraoperative identification (eg, mapping) of sentinel lymph node(s) includes injection of non-radioactive dye, when performed (List separately in addition to code for primary procedure)

(Use 38900 in conjunction with 19302, 19307, 38500, 38510, 38520, 38525, 38530, 38542, 38740, 38745)

(For injection of radioactive tracer for identification of sentinel node, use 38792)

**38999** Unlisted procedure, hemic or lymphatic system

# Mediastinum and Diaphragm

## Mediastinum

### Incision

**39000** Mediastinotomy with exploration, drainage, removal of foreign body, or biopsy; cervical approach

**39010** transthoracic approach, including either transthoracic or median sternotomy

(For VATS pericardial biopsy, use 32604)

### Excision/Resection

**39200** Resection of mediastinal cyst

**39220** Resection of mediastinal tumor

(For substernal thyroidectomy, use 60270)

(For thymectomy, use 60520)

(For thoracoscopic [VATS] resection of mediastinal cyst, tumor, or mass, use 32662)

Cardiovascular

## Endoscopy

**39400**    Mediastinoscopy, includes biopsy(ies), when performed

## Other Procedures

**39499**    Unlisted procedure, mediastinum

# Diaphragm

## Repair

(For transabdominal repair of diaphragmatic [esophageal hiatal] hernia, use 43325)

(For laparoscopic repair of diaphragmatic [esophageal hiatal] hernias and fundoplication, see 43280, 43281, 43282)

**39501**    Repair, laceration of diaphragm, any approach

(39502 has been deleted. To report transabdominal paraesophageal hiatal hernia repair with fundoplasty, vagotomy, and/or pyloroplasty when performed, see 43332, 43333, 43335, 43337)

(For laparoscopic paraesophageal hernia repair, see 43281, 43282)

**39503**    Repair, neonatal diaphragmatic hernia, with or without chest tube insertion and with or without creation of ventral hernia

(Do not report modifier 63 in conjunction with 39503)

(39520 has been deleted. To report transthoracic diaphragmatic [esophageal hiatal] hernia repair, see 43334, 43335)

(For laparoscopic paraesophageal hernia repair, see 43281, 43282)

(39530 has been deleted. To report thoracoabdominal diaphragmatic [esophageal hiatal] hernia repair, see 43336, 43337)

(39531 has been deleted. To report thoracoabdominal diaphragmatic [esophageal hiatal] hernia repair, see 43336, 43337)

**39540**    Repair, diaphragmatic hernia (other than neonatal), traumatic; acute

**39541**        chronic

**39545**    Imbrication of diaphragm for eventration, transthoracic or transabdominal, paralytic or nonparalytic

**39560**    Resection, diaphragm; with simple repair (eg, primary suture)

**39561**        with complex repair (eg, prosthetic material, local muscle flap)

## Other Procedures

**39599**    Unlisted procedure, diaphragm

**Cardiovascular**

---

▲=Revised code    ●=New code    ▶◀=Contains new or revised text    ⊘=Modifier 51 exempt

# Digestive System

## Lips

(For procedures on skin of lips, see 10040 et seq)

### Excision

**40490**  Biopsy of lip

**40500**  Vermilionectomy (lip shave), with mucosal advancement

**40510**  Excision of lip; transverse wedge excision with primary closure

**40520**  V-excision with primary direct linear closure

(For excision of mucous lesions, see 40810-40816)

**40525**  full thickness, reconstruction with local flap (eg, Estlander or fan)

**40527**  full thickness, reconstruction with cross lip flap (Abbe-Estlander)

**40530**  Resection of lip, more than one-fourth, without reconstruction

(For reconstruction, see 13131 et seq)

### Repair (Cheiloplasty)

**40650**  Repair lip, full thickness; vermilion only

**40652**  up to half vertical height

**40654**  over one-half vertical height, or complex

**40700**  Plastic repair of cleft lip/nasal deformity; primary, partial or complete, unilateral

**40701**  primary bilateral, 1-stage procedure

**40702**  primary bilateral, 1 of 2 stages

**40720**  secondary, by recreation of defect and reclosure

(For bilateral procedure, report 40720 with modifier 50)

(To report rhinoplasty only for nasal deformity secondary to congenital cleft lip, see 30460, 30462)

(For repair of cleft lip, with cross lip pedicle flap (Abbe-Estlander type), use 40527)

**40761**  with cross lip pedicle flap (Abbe-Estlander type), including sectioning and inserting of pedicle

(For repair cleft palate, see 42200 et seq)

(For other reconstructive procedures, see 14060, 14061, 15120-15261, 15574, 15576, 15630)

### Other Procedures

**40799**  Unlisted procedure, lips

## Vestibule of Mouth

The vestibule is the part of the oral cavity outside the dentoalveolar structures; it includes the mucosal and submucosal tissue of lips and cheeks.

### Incision

**40800**  Drainage of abscess, cyst, hematoma, vestibule of mouth; simple

**40801**  complicated

**40804**  Removal of embedded foreign body, vestibule of mouth; simple

**40805**  complicated

**40806**  Incision of labial frenum (frenotomy)

### Excision, Destruction

**40808**  Biopsy, vestibule of mouth

**40810**  Excision of lesion of mucosa and submucosa, vestibule of mouth; without repair

**40812**  with simple repair

**40814**  with complex repair

**40816**  complex, with excision of underlying muscle

**40818**  Excision of mucosa of vestibule of mouth as donor graft

**40819**  Excision of frenum, labial or buccal (frenumectomy, frenulectomy, frenectomy)

**40820**  Destruction of lesion or scar of vestibule of mouth by physical methods (eg, laser, thermal, cryo, chemical)

### Repair

**40830**  Closure of laceration, vestibule of mouth; 2.5 cm or less

**40831**  over 2.5 cm or complex

**40840**  Vestibuloplasty; anterior

**40842**  posterior, unilateral

**40843**  posterior, bilateral

**40844**  entire arch

**40845**  complex (including ridge extension, muscle repositioning)

(For skin grafts, see 15002 et seq)

### Other Procedures

**40899**  Unlisted procedure, vestibule of mouth

⊙=Moderate sedation  ✚=Add-on code  ✔=FDA approval pending  #=Resequenced code  ○=Recycled/reinstated code

**Digestive**

# Tongue and Floor of Mouth

## Incision

**41000**    Intraoral incision and drainage of abscess, cyst, or hematoma of tongue or floor of mouth; lingual

**41005**    sublingual, superficial

**41006**    sublingual, deep, supramylohyoid

**41007**    submental space

**41008**    submandibular space

**41009**    masticator space

**41010**    Incision of lingual frenum (frenotomy)

**41015**    Extraoral incision and drainage of abscess, cyst, or hematoma of floor of mouth; sublingual

**41016**    submental

**41017**    submandibular

**41018**    masticator space

(For frenoplasty, use 41520)

**41019**    Placement of needles, catheters, or other device(s) into the head and/or neck region (percutaneous, transoral, or transnasal) for subsequent interstitial radioelement application

(For imaging guidance, see 76942, 77002, 77012, 77021)

(For stereotactic insertion of intracranial brachytherapy radiation sources, use 61770)

(For interstitial radioelement application, see 77776-77787)

## Excision

**41100**    Biopsy of tongue; anterior two-thirds

**41105**    posterior one-third

**41108**    Biopsy of floor of mouth

**41110**    Excision of lesion of tongue without closure

**41112**    Excision of lesion of tongue with closure; anterior two-thirds

**41113**    posterior one-third

**41114**    with local tongue flap

(Do not report 41114 in conjunction with 41112 or 41113)

**41115**    Excision of lingual frenum (frenectomy)

**41116**    Excision, lesion of floor of mouth

**41120**    Glossectomy; less than one-half tongue

**41130**    hemiglossectomy

**41135**    partial, with unilateral radical neck dissection

**41140**    complete or total, with or without tracheostomy, without radical neck dissection

**41145**    complete or total, with or without tracheostomy, with unilateral radical neck dissection

**41150**    composite procedure with resection floor of mouth and mandibular resection, without radical neck dissection

**41153**    composite procedure with resection floor of mouth, with suprahyoid neck dissection

**41155**    composite procedure with resection floor of mouth, mandibular resection, and radical neck dissection (Commando type)

## Repair

**41250**    Repair of laceration 2.5 cm or less; floor of mouth and/or anterior two-thirds of tongue

**41251**    posterior one-third of tongue

**41252**    Repair of laceration of tongue, floor of mouth, over 2.6 cm or complex

## Other Procedures

**41500**    Fixation of tongue, mechanical, other than suture (eg, K-wire)

**41510**    Suture of tongue to lip for micrognathia (Douglas type procedure)

**41512**    Tongue base suspension, permanent suture technique

(For fixation of tongue, mechanical, other than suture, use 41500)

(For suture of tongue to lip for micrognathia, use 41510)

**41520**    Frenoplasty (surgical revision of frenum, eg, with Z-plasty)

(For frenotomy, see 40806, 41010)

**41530**    Submucosal ablation of the tongue base, radiofrequency, 1 or more sites, per session

**41599**    Unlisted procedure, tongue, floor of mouth

# Dentoalveolar Structures

## Incision

**41800**    Drainage of abscess, cyst, hematoma from dentoalveolar structures

**41805**    Removal of embedded foreign body from dentoalveolar structures; soft tissues

**41806**    bone

## Excision, Destruction

**41820**    Gingivectomy, excision gingiva, each quadrant

**41821**    Operculectomy, excision pericoronal tissues

**41822**    Excision of fibrous tuberosities, dentoalveolar structures

**Digestive**

| | |
|---|---|
| 41823 | Excision of osseous tuberosities, dentoalveolar structures |
| 41825 | Excision of lesion or tumor (except listed above), dentoalveolar structures; without repair |
| 41826 | with simple repair |
| 41827 | with complex repair |

(For nonexcisional destruction, use 41850)

| | |
|---|---|
| 41828 | Excision of hyperplastic alveolar mucosa, each quadrant (specify) |
| 41830 | Alveolectomy, including curettage of osteitis or sequestrectomy |
| 41850 | Destruction of lesion (except excision), dentoalveolar structures |

## Other Procedures

| | |
|---|---|
| 41870 | Periodontal mucosal grafting |
| 41872 | Gingivoplasty, each quadrant (specify) |
| 41874 | Alveoloplasty, each quadrant (specify) |

(For closure of lacerations, see 40830, 40831)

(For segmental osteotomy, use 21206)

(For reduction of fractures, see 21421-21490)

| | |
|---|---|
| 41899 | Unlisted procedure, dentoalveolar structures |

# Palate and Uvula

## Incision

| | |
|---|---|
| 42000 | Drainage of abscess of palate, uvula |

## Excision, Destruction

| | |
|---|---|
| 42100 | Biopsy of palate, uvula |
| 42104 | Excision, lesion of palate, uvula; without closure |
| 42106 | with simple primary closure |
| 42107 | with local flap closure |

(For skin graft, see 14040-14302)

(For mucosal graft, use 40818)

| | |
|---|---|
| 42120 | Resection of palate or extensive resection of lesion |

(For reconstruction of palate with extraoral tissue, see 14040-14302, 15050, 15120, 15240, 15576)

| | |
|---|---|
| 42140 | Uvulectomy, excision of uvula |
| 42145 | Palatopharyngoplasty (eg, uvulopalatopharyngoplasty, uvulopharyngoplasty) |

(For removal of exostosis of the bony palate, see 21031, 21032)

| | |
|---|---|
| 42160 | Destruction of lesion, palate or uvula (thermal, cryo or chemical) |

## Repair

| | |
|---|---|
| 42180 | Repair, laceration of palate; up to 2 cm |
| 42182 | over 2 cm or complex |
| 42200 | Palatoplasty for cleft palate, soft and/or hard palate only |
| 42205 | Palatoplasty for cleft palate, with closure of alveolar ridge; soft tissue only |
| 42210 | with bone graft to alveolar ridge (includes obtaining graft) |
| 42215 | Palatoplasty for cleft palate; major revision |
| 42220 | secondary lengthening procedure |
| 42225 | attachment pharyngeal flap |
| 42226 | Lengthening of palate, and pharyngeal flap |
| 42227 | Lengthening of palate, with island flap |
| 42235 | Repair of anterior palate, including vomer flap |

(For repair of oronasal fistula, use 30600)

| | |
|---|---|
| 42260 | Repair of nasolabial fistula |

(For repair of cleft lip, see 40700 et seq)

| | |
|---|---|
| 42280 | Maxillary impression for palatal prosthesis |
| 42281 | Insertion of pin-retained palatal prosthesis |

## Other Procedures

| | |
|---|---|
| 42299 | Unlisted procedure, palate, uvula |

# Salivary Gland and Ducts

## Incision

| | |
|---|---|
| 42300 | Drainage of abscess; parotid, simple |
| 42305 | parotid, complicated |
| 42310 | Drainage of abscess; submaxillary or sublingual, intraoral |
| 42320 | submaxillary, external |
| 42330 | Sialolithotomy; submandibular (submaxillary), sublingual or parotid, uncomplicated, intraoral |
| 42335 | submandibular (submaxillary), complicated, intraoral |
| 42340 | parotid, extraoral or complicated intraoral |

## Excision

| | |
|---|---|
| 42400 | Biopsy of salivary gland; needle |

(For fine needle aspiration, see 10021, 10022)

(For evaluation of fine needle aspirate, see 88172, 88173)

(If imaging guidance is performed, see 76942, 77002, 77012, 77021)

| | |
|---|---|
| 42405 | incisional |

(If imaging guidance is performed, see 76942, 77002, 77012, 77021)

Digestive

| | | |
|---|---|---|
| 42408 | Excision of sublingual salivary cyst (ranula) | |

42409    Marsupialization of sublingual salivary cyst (ranula)

42410    Excision of parotid tumor or parotid gland; lateral lobe, without nerve dissection

42415        lateral lobe, with dissection and preservation of facial nerve

42420        total, with dissection and preservation of facial nerve

42425        total, en bloc removal with sacrifice of facial nerve

42426        total, with unilateral radical neck dissection

        (For suture or grafting of facial nerve, see 64864, 64865, 69740, 69745)

42440    Excision of submandibular (submaxillary) gland

42450    Excision of sublingual gland

## Repair

42500    Plastic repair of salivary duct, sialodochoplasty; primary or simple

42505        secondary or complicated

42507    Parotid duct diversion, bilateral (Wilke type procedure);

42508        with excision of 1 submandibular gland

42509        with excision of both submandibular glands

42510        with ligation of both submandibular (Wharton's) ducts

## Other Procedures

42550    Injection procedure for sialography

        (For radiological supervision and interpretation, use 70390)

42600    Closure salivary fistula

42650    Dilation salivary duct

42660    Dilation and catheterization of salivary duct, with or without injection

42665    Ligation salivary duct, intraoral

42699    Unlisted procedure, salivary glands or ducts

# Pharynx, Adenoids, and Tonsils

## Incision

42700    Incision and drainage abscess; peritonsillar

42720        retropharyngeal or parapharyngeal, intraoral approach

42725        retropharyngeal or parapharyngeal, external approach

## Excision, Destruction

42800    Biopsy; oropharynx

        ►(42802 has been deleted. To report biopsy of hypopharynx, see 31510, 31535, 31536, 31576)◄

42804        nasopharynx, visible lesion, simple

42806        nasopharynx, survey for unknown primary lesion

        (For laryngoscopic biopsy, see 31510, 31535, 31536)

42808    Excision or destruction of lesion of pharynx, any method

42809    Removal of foreign body from pharynx

42810    Excision branchial cleft cyst or vestige, confined to skin and subcutaneous tissues

42815    Excision branchial cleft cyst, vestige, or fistula, extending beneath subcutaneous tissues and/or into pharynx

42820    Tonsillectomy and adenoidectomy; younger than age 12

42821        age 12 or over

42825    Tonsillectomy, primary or secondary; younger than age 12

42826        age 12 or over

42830    Adenoidectomy, primary; younger than age 12

42831        age 12 or over

42835    Adenoidectomy, secondary; younger than age 12

42836        age 12 or over

42842    Radical resection of tonsil, tonsillar pillars, and/or retromolar trigone; without closure

42844        closure with local flap (eg, tongue, buccal)

42845        closure with other flap

        (For closure with other flap(s), use appropriate number for flap(s))

        (When combined with radical neck dissection, use also 38720)

42860    Excision of tonsil tags

42870    Excision or destruction lingual tonsil, any method (separate procedure)

        (For resection of the nasopharynx [eg, juvenile angiofibroma] by bicoronal and/or transzygomatic approach, see 61586 and 61600)

42890    Limited pharyngectomy

42892    Resection of lateral pharyngeal wall or pyriform sinus, direct closure by advancement of lateral and posterior pharyngeal walls

        (When combined with radical neck dissection, use also 38720)

42894    Resection of pharyngeal wall requiring closure with myocutaneous or fasciocutaneous flap or free muscle, skin, or fascial flap with microvascular anastomosis

        (When combined with radical neck dissection, use also 38720)

        (For limited pharyngectomy with radical neck dissection, use 38720 with 42890)

        (For flap used for reconstruction, see 15732, 15734, 15756, 15757, 15758)

**Digestive**

## Repair

**42900** Suture pharynx for wound or injury

**42950** Pharyngoplasty (plastic or reconstructive operation on pharynx)

(For pharyngeal flap, use 42225)

**42953** Pharyngoesophageal repair

(For closure with myocutaneous or other flap, use appropriate number in addition)

## Other Procedures

**42955** Pharyngostomy (fistulization of pharynx, external for feeding)

**42960** Control oropharyngeal hemorrhage, primary or secondary (eg, post-tonsillectomy); simple

**42961** complicated, requiring hospitalization

**42962** with secondary surgical intervention

**42970** Control of nasopharyngeal hemorrhage, primary or secondary (eg, postadenoidectomy); simple, with posterior nasal packs, with or without anterior packs and/or cautery

**42971** complicated, requiring hospitalization

**42972** with secondary surgical intervention

**42999** Unlisted procedure, pharynx, adenoids, or tonsils

# Esophagus

## Incision

(For esophageal intubation with laparotomy, use 43510)

**43020** Esophagotomy, cervical approach, with removal of foreign body

**43030** Cricopharyngeal myotomy

**43045** Esophagotomy, thoracic approach, with removal of foreign body

## Excision

(For gastrointestinal reconstruction for previous esophagectomy, see 43360, 43361)

**43100** Excision of lesion, esophagus, with primary repair; cervical approach

**43101** thoracic or abdominal approach

(For wide excision of malignant lesion of cervical esophagus, with total laryngectomy without radical neck dissection, see 43107, 43116, 43124, and 31360)

(For wide excision of malignant lesion of cervical esophagus, with total laryngectomy with radical neck dissection, see 43107, 43116, 43124, and 31365)

**43107** Total or near total esophagectomy, without thoracotomy; with pharyngogastrostomy or cervical esophagogastrostomy, with or without pyloroplasty (transhiatal)

**43108** with colon interposition or small intestine reconstruction, including intestine mobilization, preparation and anastomosis(es)

**43112** Total or near total esophagectomy, with thoracotomy; with pharyngogastrostomy or cervical esophagogastrostomy, with or without pyloroplasty

**43113** with colon interposition or small intestine reconstruction, including intestine mobilization, preparation, and anastomosis(es)

**43116** Partial esophagectomy, cervical, with free intestinal graft, including microvascular anastomosis, obtaining the graft and intestinal reconstruction

(Do not report 43116 in conjunction with 69990)

(Report 43116 with the modifier 52 appended if intestinal or free jejunal graft with microvascular anastomosis is performed by another physician)

(For free jejunal graft with microvascular anastomosis performed by another physician, use 43496)

**43117** Partial esophagectomy, distal two-thirds, with thoracotomy and separate abdominal incision, with or without proximal gastrectomy; with thoracic esophagogastrostomy, with or without pyloroplasty (Ivor Lewis)

**43118** with colon interposition or small intestine reconstruction, including intestine mobilization, preparation, and anastomosis(es)

(For total esophagectomy with gastropharyngostomy, see 43107, 43124)

(For esophagogastrectomy (lower third) and vagotomy, use 43122)

**43121** Partial esophagectomy, distal two-thirds, with thoracotomy only, with or without proximal gastrectomy, with thoracic esophagogastrostomy, with or without pyloroplasty

**43122** Partial esophagectomy, thoracoabdominal or abdominal approach, with or without proximal gastrectomy; with esophagogastrostomy, with or without pyloroplasty

**43123** with colon interposition or small intestine reconstruction, including intestine mobilization, preparation, and anastomosis(es)

**43124** Total or partial esophagectomy, without reconstruction (any approach), with cervical esophagostomy

**43130** Diverticulectomy of hypopharynx or esophagus, with or without myotomy; cervical approach

**43135** thoracic approach

# Endoscopy

For endoscopic procedures, code appropriate endoscopy of each anatomic site examined.

►When bleeding occurs as a result of an endoscopic procedure, control of bleeding is not reported separately during the same operative session.

Esophagoscopy includes examination from the cricopharyngeus muscle (upper esophageal sphincter) to and including the gastroesophageal junction. It may also include examination of the proximal region of the stomach via retroflexion when performed. Surgical endoscopy always includes diagnostic endoscopy.◄

## ►Esophagoscopy◄

● **43191**   Esophagoscopy, rigid, transoral; diagnostic, including collection of specimen(s) by brushing or washing when performed (separate procedure)

►(To report transnasal esophagoscopy, see 43197, 43198)◄

►(For diagnostic flexible transoral esophagoscopy, use 43200)◄

● **43192**   with directed submucosal injection(s), any substance

►(For flexible transoral esophagoscopy with directed submucosal injection(s), use 43201)◄

►(For flexible transoral esophagoscopy with injection sclerosis of esophageal varices, use 43204)◄

►(For rigid transoral esophagoscopy with injection sclerosis of esophageal varices, use 43499)◄

● **43193**   with biopsy, single or multiple

►(For flexible transoral esophagoscopy with collection of specimen or biopsy, see 43200, 43202)◄

● **43194**   with removal of foreign body

►(For radiological supervision and interpretation, use 74235)◄

►(For flexible transoral esophagoscopy with removal of foreign body, use 43215)◄

● **43195**   with balloon dilation (less than 30 mm diameter)

►(If imaging guidance is performed, use 74360)◄

►(For esophageal dilation with balloon 30 mm diameter or larger, see 43214, 43233)◄

►(For dilation without endoscopic visualization, see 43450, 43453)◄

►(For flexible transoral esophagoscopy with balloon dilation [less than 30 mm diameter], use 43220)◄

● **43196**   with insertion of guide wire followed by dilation over guide wire

►(For flexible transoral esophagoscopy with insertion of guide wire followed by dilation over guide wire, use 43226)◄

►(For radiological supervision and interpretation, use 74360)◄

● **43197**   Esophagoscopy, flexible, transnasal; diagnostic, includes collection of specimen(s) by brushing or washing when performed (separate procedure)

►(Do not report 43197 in conjunction with 31575, 43191, 43192, 43193, 43194, 43195, 43196, 43200-43232, 43235-43259, 92511)◄

►(For transoral esophagoscopy with biopsy or collection of specimen, see 43191, 43193, 43200, 43202)◄

►(Do not report 43197 in conjunction with 31231 unless separate type of endoscope [eg, rigid endoscope] is used)◄

● **43198**   with biopsy, single or multiple

►(For transoral esophagoscopy with biopsy or collection of specimen, see 43191, 43193, 43200, 43202)◄

►(Do not report 43198 in conjunction with 31575, 43191, 43192, 43193, 43194, 43195, 43196, 43200-43232, 43235-43259, 92511)◄

►(Do not report 43198 in conjunction with 31231 unless separate type of endoscope [eg, rigid endoscope] is used)◄

⊙▲ **43200**   Esophagoscopy, flexible, transoral; diagnostic, including collection of specimen(s) by brushing or washing, when performed (separate procedure)

►(For diagnostic rigid transoral esophagoscopy, use 43191)◄

►(For diagnostic flexible transnasal esophagoscopy, use 43197)◄

►(For diagnostic upper gastrointestinal endoscopy, use 43235)◄

⊙▲ **43201**   with directed submucosal injection(s), any substance

►(For rigid transoral esophagoscopy with directed submucosal injection[s], use 43192)◄

►(For flexible transoral esophagoscopy with injection sclerosis of esophageal varices, use 43204)◄

►(For rigid transoral esophagoscopy with injection sclerosis of esophageal varices, use 43499)◄

►(Do not report 43201 in conjunction with 43211, 43204, 43227)◄

⊙▲ **43202**   with biopsy, single or multiple

►(For rigid transoral esophagoscopy with biopsy, use 43193)◄

►(For flexible transnasal esophagoscopy with biopsy, use 43198)◄

►(For upper gastrointestinal endoscopy with biopsy or collection of specimen, see 43235, 43239)◄

⊙▲ **43204**   with injection sclerosis of esophageal varices

►(For rigid transoral esophagoscopy with injection sclerosis of esophageal varices, use 43499)◄

►(Do not report 43204 in conjunction with 43201, 43227)◄

**Digestive**

⊙▲ **43205**      with band ligation of esophageal varices

▶(Do not report 43205 in conjunction with 43211, 43227)◀

⊙▲ **43206**      with optical endomicroscopy

(Report supply of contrast agent separately)

(Do not report 43206 in conjunction with 88375)

**43211**      Code is out of numerical sequence. See 43191-43232

**43212**      Code is out of numerical sequence. See 43191-43232

**43213**      Code is out of numerical sequence. See 43191-43232

**43214**      Code is out of numerical sequence. See 43191-43232

⊙▲ **43215**      with removal of foreign body

(For radiological supervision and interpretation, use 74235)

▶(For rigid transoral esophagoscopy with removal of foreign body, use 43194)◀

▶(For upper gastrointestinal endoscopy with removal of foreign body, use 43247)◀

⊙▲ **43216**      with removal of tumor(s), polyp(s), or other lesion(s) by hot biopsy forceps or bipolar cautery

⊙▲ **43217**      with removal of tumor(s), polyp(s), or other lesion(s) by snare technique

▶(For upper gastrointestinal endoscopy with removal of tumor[s], polyp[s], or other lesion[s] by snare technique, use 43251)◀

▶(Do not report 43217 in conjunction with 43211)◀

#⊙● **43211**      with endoscopic mucosal resection

▶(Do not report 43211 in conjunction with 43201, 43205, 43217)◀

▶(Do not report 43211 in conjunction with 43202 when biopsy is performed on the same lesion)◀

▶(43219 has been deleted. To report, use 43212)◀

#⊙● **43212**      with placement of endoscopic stent (includes pre- and post-dilation and guide wire passage, when performed)

▶(Do not report 43212 in conjunction with 43220, 43226)◀

⊙▲ **43220**      with transendoscopic balloon dilation (less than 30 mm diameter)

▶(For rigid transoral esophagoscopy with balloon dilation [less than 30 mm diameter], use 43195)◀

(If imaging guidance is performed, use 74360)

▶(For esophageal dilation with balloon 30 mm diameter or larger, use 43214)◀

▶(For dilation without endoscopic visualization, see 43450, 43453)◀

▶(Do not report 43220 in conjunction with 43212, 43226, 43229)◀

#⊙● **43213**      with dilation of esophagus, by balloon or dilator, retrograde (includes fluoroscopic guidance, when performed)

▶(Do not report 43213 in conjunction with 74360, 76000, 76001)◀

#⊙● **43214**      with dilation of esophagus with balloon (30 mm diameter or larger) (includes fluoroscopic guidance, when performed)

▶(Do not report 43214 in conjunction with 74360, 76000, 76001)◀

⊙▲ **43226**      with insertion of guide wire followed by passage of dilator(s) over guide wire

(For radiological supervision and interpretation, use 74360)

▶(For rigid transoral esophagoscopy with insertion of guide wire followed by dilation over guide wire, use 43196)◀

▶(Do not report 43226 in conjunction with 43212, 43229)◀

⊙▲ **43227**      with control of bleeding, any method

▶(Do not report 43227 in conjunction with 43204, 43205)◀

▶(43228 has been deleted. To report, use 43229)◀

⊙● **43229**      with ablation of tumor(s), polyp(s), or other lesion(s) (includes pre- and post-dilation and guide wire passage, when performed)

▶(Do not report 43229 in conjunction with 43220, 43226)◀

▶(For esophagoscopic photodynamic therapy, report 43229 in conjunction with 96570, 96571 as appropriate)◀

⊙▲ **43231**      with endoscopic ultrasound examination

(Do not report 43231 in conjunction with 76975)

⊙▲ **43232**      with transendoscopic ultrasound-guided intramural or transmural fine needle aspiration/biopsy(s)

▶(Do not report 43232 in conjunction with 76942, 76975)◀

(For interpretation of specimen, see 88172-88173)

**43233**      Code is out of numerical sequence. See 43235-43273

▶(43234 has been deleted. To report esophagogastroscopy, see 43197, 43200, 43235)◀

## ▶Esophagogastroduodenoscopy◀

▶(For examination of the esophagus from the cricopharyngeus muscle [upper esophageal sphincter] to and including the gastroesophageal junction, including examination of the proximal region of the stomach via retroflexion when performed, see 43197, 43198, 43200, 43201, 43202, 43204, 43205, 43206, 43211, 43212, 43213, 43214, 43215, 43216, 43217, 43220, 43226, 43227, 43229, 43231, 43232)◀

►(Use 43233, 43235-43259,43266, 43270 for examination of a surgically altered stomach where the jejunum is examined distal to the anastomosis [eg, gastric bypass, gastroenterostomy {Billroth II}])◄

►To report esophagogastroscopy where the duodenum is deliberately not examined [eg, judged clinically not pertinent], or because significant situations preclude such exam [eg, significant gastric retention precludes safe exam of duodenum], append modifier 52 if repeat examination is not planned, or modifier 53 if repeat examination is planned.◄

⊙▲ 43235    Esophagogastroduodenoscopy, flexible, transoral; diagnostic, including collection of specimen(s) by brushing or washing, when performed (separate procedure)

⊙▲ 43236       with directed submucosal injection(s), any substance

(For injection sclerosis of esophageal and/or gastric varices, use 43243)

►(Do not report 43236 in conjunction with 43243, 43254,43255)◄

⊙▲ 43237       with endoscopic ultrasound examination limited to the esophagus, stomach or duodenum, and adjacent structures

(Do not report 43237 in conjunction with 76942, 76975)

⊙▲ 43238       with transendoscopic ultrasound-guided intramural or transmural fine needle aspiration/biopsy(s), esophagus (includes endoscopic ultrasound examination limited to the esophagus, stomach or duodenum, and adjacent structures)

►(Do not report 43238 in conjunction with 43237, 76942, 76975)◄

⊙▲ 43239       with biopsy, single or multiple

⊙▲ 43240       with transmural drainage of pseudocyst (includes placement of transmural drainage catheter[s]/stent[s], when performed, and endoscopic ultrasound, when performed)

►(Do not report 43240 in conjunction with 43242, 43259, 43266)◄

►(For endoscopic pancreatic necrosectomy, use 48999)◄

⊙▲ 43241       with insertion of intraluminal tube or catheter

►(Do not report 43241 in conjunction with 43266)◄

►(For naso- or oro-gastric tube placement requiring physician's or other qualified health care professional's skill and fluoroscopic guidance, use 43752)◄

►(For enteric tube placement, see 44500, 74340)◄

⊙▲ 43242       with transendoscopic ultrasound-guided intramural or transmural fine needle aspiration/biopsy(s) (includes endoscopic ultrasound examination of the esophagus, stomach, and either the duodenum or a surgically altered stomach where the jejunum is examined distal to the anastomosis)

►(Do not report 43242 in conjunction with 43240, 43259, 76942, 76975)◄

►(For transendoscopic ultrasound-guided transmural fine needle aspiration/biopsy limited to the esophagus, use 43238)◄

(For interpretation of specimen, see 88172-88173)

⊙▲ 43243       with injection sclerosis of esophageal/gastric varices

►(Do not report 43243 in conjunction with 43236, 43255)◄

⊙▲ 43244       with band ligation of esophageal/gastric varices

►(Do not report 43244 in conjunction with 43254, 43255)◄

⊙▲ 43245       with dilation of gastric/duodenal stricture(s) (eg, balloon, bougie)

►(Do not report 43245 in conjunction with 43266)◄

►(For radiological supervision and interpretation, use 74360)◄

⊙▲ 43246       with directed placement of percutaneous gastrostomy tube

(For nonendoscopic percutaneous placement of gastrostomy tube, see 49440)

⊙▲ 43247       with removal of foreign body

(For radiological supervision and interpretation, use 74235)

⊙▲ 43248       with insertion of guide wire followed by passage of dilator(s) through esophagus over guide wire

►(Do not report 43248 in conjunction with 43266, 43270)◄

►(If imaging guidance is performed, use 74360)◄

⊙▲ 43249       with transendoscopic balloon dilation of esophagus (less than 30 mm diameter)

►(Do not report 43249 in conjunction with 43266, 43270)◄

►(If imaging guidance is performed, use 74360)◄

#⊙● 43233       with dilation of esophagus with balloon (30 mm diameter or larger) (includes fluoroscopic guidance, when performed)

►(Do not report 43233 in conjunction with 74360, 76000, 76001)◄

⊙▲ 43250       with removal of tumor(s), polyp(s), or other lesion(s) by hot biopsy forceps or bipolar cautery

⊙▲ 43251       with removal of tumor(s), polyp(s), or other lesion(s) by snare technique

►(Do not report 43251 in conjunction with 43254)◄

►(For endoscopic mucosal resection, use 43254)◄

⊙▲ 43252       with optical endomicroscopy

(Report supply of contrast agent separately)

(Do not report 43252 in conjunction with 88375)

(For biopsy specimen pathology, use 88305)

**Digestive**

⊙● **43253** with transendoscopic ultrasound-guided transmural injection of diagnostic or therapeutic substance(s) (eg, anesthetic, neurolytic agent) or fiducial marker(s) (includes endoscopic ultrasound examination of the esophagus, stomach, and either the duodenum or a surgically altered stomach where the jejunum is examined distal to the anastomosis)

►(Do not report 43253 in conjunction with 43237, 43238, 43240, 43242, 43259, 76942, 76975)◄

►(For transendoscopic ultrasound-guided transmural fine needle aspiration/biopsy limited to the esophagus, use 43238)◄

►(For interpretation of specimen, see 88172, 88173)◄

⊙● **43254** with endoscopic mucosal resection

►(Do not report 43254 in conjunction with 43236, 43244, 43251)◄

►(Endoscopic mucosal resection includes biopsy of the same lesion, when performed)◄

⊙▲ **43255** with control of bleeding, any method

►(Do not report 43255 in conjunction with 43243, 43244)◄

►(43256 has been deleted. To report, use 43266)◄

#⊙● **43266** with placement of endoscopic stent (includes pre- and post-dilation and guide wire passage, when performed)

►(Do not report 43266 in conjunction with 43240, 43241, 43245, 43248, 43249)◄

⊙▲ **43257** with delivery of thermal energy to the muscle of lower esophageal sphincter and/or gastric cardia, for treatment of gastroesophageal reflux disease

►(43258 has been deleted. To report, use 43270)◄

#⊙● **43270** with ablation of tumor(s), polyp(s), or other lesion(s) (includes pre- and post-dilation and guide wire passage, when performed)

(For injection sclerosis of esophageal varices, use 43204, 43243)

►(Do not report 43270 in conjunction with 43248, 43249)◄

⊙▲ **43259** with endoscopic ultrasound examination, including the esophagus, stomach, and either the duodenum or a surgically altered stomach where the jejunum is examined distal to the anastomosis

►(Do not report 43259 in conjunction with 43240, 76975)◄

## ►Endoscopic Retrograde Cholangiopancreatography (ERCP)◄

►Report the appropriate code(s) for each service performed. Therapeutic ERCP (43261, 43262, 43263, 43264, 43265, 43274, 43275, 43276, 43277, 43278) includes diagnostic ERCP (43260). ERCP includes guide wire passage when performed. An ERCP is considered complete if one or more of the ductal system(s),

(pancreatic/biliary) is/are visualized. To report ERCP attempted but with unsuccessful cannulation of any ductal system, see 43235-43259.

Codes 43274, 43275, 43276, and 43277 describe ERCP with stent placement, removal or replacement (exchange) of stent(s), and balloon dilation within the pancreatico-biliary system. For reporting purposes, ducts that may be reported as stented or subject to stent replacement (exchange) or to balloon dilation include:

*Pancreas:* major and minor ducts

*Biliary tree:* common bile duct, right hepatic duct, left hepatic duct, cystic duct/gallbladder

ERCP with stent placement includes any balloon dilation performed in that duct. ERCP with more than one stent placement (eg, different ducts or side by side in the same duct) performed during the same day/session may be reported with 43274 more than once with modifier 59 appended to the subsequent procedure(s). For ERCP with more than one stent exchanged during the same day/session, 43276 may be reported for the initial stent exchange, and 43276 with modifier 59 for each additional stent exchange. ERCP with balloon dilation of more than one duct during the same day/session may be reported with modifier 59 appended to the subsequent procedure(s). Sphincteroplasty, which is balloon dilation of the ampulla (sphincter of Oddi), is reported with 43277, and includes sphincterotomy (43262) when performed.

To report ERCP via altered postoperative anatomy, see 43260, 43262, 43263, 43264, 43265, 43273, 43274, 43275, 43276, 43277, 43278, for Billroth II gastroenterostomy. See 47999 (Unlisted procedure, biliary tract) or 48999 (Unlisted procedure, pancreas) for ERCP via gastrostomy (laparoscopic or open) or via Roux-en-Y anatomy (eg, post-bariatric gastric bypass, post-total gastrectomy).

To report optical endomicroscopy of the biliary tract, use 47999. To report optical endomicroscopy of the pancreas, use 48999. Optical endomicroscopy may be reported not more than once per session.

Stone destruction includes any stone removal in the same ductal system (biliary/pancreatic). Code 43277 may be separately reported if sphincteroplasty or dilation of a ductal stricture is required before proceeding to remove stones/debris from the duct during the same session. Dilation that is incidental to the passage of an instrument to clear stones or debris is not separately reported.◄

►(Do not report 43277 for use of a balloon catheter to clear stones/debris from a duct. Any dilation of the duct that may occur during this maneuver is considered inherent to the work of 43264 and 43265)◄

►(For radiological supervision and interpretation, see 74328, 74329, 74330)◄

Digestive

⊙▲ **43260**    Endoscopic retrograde cholangiopancreatography (ERCP); diagnostic, including collection of specimen(s) by brushing or washing, when performed (separate procedure)

⊙ **43261**        with biopsy, single or multiple

⊙ **43262**        with sphincterotomy/papillotomy

▶(43262 may be reported when sphincterotomy is performed in addition to 43261, 43263, 43264, 43265, 43275, 43278)◀

▶(Do not report 43262 in conjunction with 43274 for stent placement or replacement [exchange] in the same location)◀

⊙▲ **43263**        with pressure measurement of sphincter of Oddi

▶(Do not report 43263 more than once per session)◀

⊙▲ **43264**        with removal of calculi/debris from biliary/pancreatic duct(s)

▶(Do not report 43264 if no calculi or debris are found, even if balloon catheter is deployed)◀

▶(Do not report 43264 in conjunction with 43265)◀

⊙▲ **43265**        with destruction of calculi, any method (eg, mechanical, electrohydraulic, lithotripsy)

▶(Do not report 43265 if no calculi or debris are found, even if balloon catheter is deployed)◀

▶(Do not report 43265 in conjunction with 43264)◀

**43266**    Code is out of numerical sequence. See 43235-43273

▶(43267 has been deleted. To report, use 43274)◀

▶(43268 has been deleted. To report, use 43274)◀

#⊙● **43274**        with placement of endoscopic stent into biliary or pancreatic duct, including pre- and post-dilation and guide wire passage, when performed, including sphincterotomy, when performed, each stent

▶(For stent placement in both the pancreatic duct and the common bile duct during the same operative session, placement of separate stents in both the right and left hepatic ducts, or placement of two side-by-side stents in the same duct, 43274 may be reported for each additional stent placed, using modifier 59 with the subsequent procedure[s])◀

▶(To report naso-biliary or naso-pancreatic drainage tube placement, use 43274)◀

▶(Do not report 43274 in conjunction with 43262, 43275, 43276, 43277 for stent placement or replacement [exchange] in the same duct)◀

▶(43269 has been deleted. To report, see 43275, 43276)◀

▶(43271 has been deleted. To report, use 43277)◀

▶(43272 has been deleted. To report, use 43278)◀

#⊙● **43275**        with removal of foreign body(s) or stent(s) from biliary/pancreatic duct(s)

▶(Do not report 43275 in conjunction with 43274, 43276)◀

▶(For removal of stent from biliary or pancreatic duct without ERCP, use 43247)◀

▶(Report 43275 once for removal of one or more stents or foreign bodies from biliary/pancreatic duct[s] during the same session)◀

#⊙● **43276**        with removal and exchange of stent(s), biliary or pancreatic duct, including pre- and post-dilation and guide wire passage, when performed, including sphincterotomy, when performed, each stent exchanged

▶(43276 includes removal and replacement [exchange] of one stent. For replacement [exchange] of additional stent[s] during the same session, report 43276 with modifier 59 for each additional replacement [exchange])◀

▶(Do not report 43276 in conjunction with 43275)◀

▶(Do not report 43276 in conjunction with 43274 for stent placement or exchange in the same duct)◀

#⊙● **43277**        with trans-endoscopic balloon dilation of biliary/pancreatic duct(s) or of ampulla (sphincteroplasty), including sphincterotomy, when performed, each duct

▶(Do not report 43277 for incidental dilation using balloon for stone/debris removal reported with 43264, 43265)◀

▶(If sphincterotomy without sphincteroplasty is performed on a separate pancreatic duct orifice during the same session [ie, pancreas divisum], report 43262 with modifier 59)◀

▶(Do not report 43277 in conjunction with 43274, 43276 for dilation and stent placement/replacement [exchange] in the same duct)◀

▶(For bilateral balloon dilation [both right and left hepatic ducts], 43277 may be reported twice with modifier 59 appended to the second procedure)◀

#⊙● **43278**        with ablation of tumor(s), polyp(s), or other lesion(s), including pre- and post-dilation and guide wire passage, when performed

▶(For ampullectomy, use 43254)◀

⊙+▲ **43273**    Endoscopic cannulation of papilla with direct visualization of pancreatic/common bile duct(s) (List separately in addition to code(s) for primary procedure)

▶(Report 43273 once per procedure)◀

▶(Use 43273 in conjunction with 43260, 43261, 43262, 43263, 43264, 43265, 43274, 43275, 43276, 43277, 43278)◀

**43274**    Code is out of numerical sequence. See 43260-43273

**43275**    Code is out of numerical sequence. See 43260-43273

**43276**    Code is out of numerical sequence. See 43260-43273

**43277**    Code is out of numerical sequence. See 43260-43273

**43278**    Code is out of numerical sequence. See 43260-43273

**Digestive**

---

▲=Revised code    ●=New code    ▶ ◀=Contains new or revised text    ⊘=Modifier 51 exempt

## Laparoscopy

Surgical laparoscopy always includes diagnostic laparoscopy. To report a diagnostic laparoscopy (peritoneoscopy) (separate procedure), use 49320.

**43279** Laparoscopy, surgical, esophagomyotomy (Heller type), with fundoplasty, when performed

(For open approach, see 43330, 43331)

(Do not report 43279 in conjunction with 43280)

**43280** Laparoscopy, surgical, esophagogastric fundoplasty (eg, Nissen, Toupet procedures)

(Do not report 43280 in conjunction with 43279)

(For open approach, see 43327, 43328)

**43281** Laparoscopy, surgical, repair of paraesophageal hernia, includes fundoplasty, when performed; without implantation of mesh

**43282** with implantation of mesh

(To report transabdominal paraesophageal hiatal hernia repair, see 43332, 43333. To report transthoracic diaphragmatic hernia repair, see 43334, 43335)

▶(Do not report 43213, 43214, 43220, 43233, 43249, 43281, 43282 in conjunction with 43280, 43450, 43453, 49568)◀

**+ 43283** Laparoscopy, surgical, esophageal lengthening procedure (eg, Collis gastroplasty or wedge gastroplasty) (List separately in addition to code for primary procedure)

(Use 43283 in conjunction with 43280, 43281, 43282)

**43289** Unlisted laparoscopy procedure, esophagus

## Repair

**43300** Esophagoplasty (plastic repair or reconstruction), cervical approach; without repair of tracheoesophageal fistula

**43305** with repair of tracheoesophageal fistula

**43310** Esophagoplasty (plastic repair or reconstruction), thoracic approach; without repair of tracheoesophageal fistula

**43312** with repair of tracheoesophageal fistula

**43313** Esophagoplasty for congenital defect (plastic repair or reconstruction), thoracic approach; without repair of congenital tracheoesophageal fistula

**43314** with repair of congenital tracheoesophageal fistula

(Do not report modifier 63 in conjunction with 43313, 43314)

**43320** Esophagogastrostomy (cardioplasty), with or without vagotomy and pyloroplasty, transabdominal or transthoracic approach

(43324 has been deleted. To report esophagogastric fundoplasty, see 43327, 43328)

(For laparoscopic procedure, use 43280)

**43325** Esophagogastric fundoplasty; with fundic patch (Thal-Nissen procedure)

(For cricopharyngeal myotomy, use 43030)

(43326 has been deleted. To report esophagogastric fundoplasty with gastroplasty, see 43327, 43328, 43332-43338)

**43327** Esophagogastric fundoplasty partial or complete; laparotomy

**43328** thoracotomy

**43330** Esophagomyotomy (Heller type); abdominal approach

(For laparoscopic esophagomyotomy procedure, use 43279)

**43331** thoracic approach

(For thoracoscopic esophagomyotomy, use 32665)

**43332** Repair, paraesophageal hiatal hernia (including fundoplication), via laparotomy, except neonatal; without implantation of mesh or other prosthesis

**43333** with implantation of mesh or other prosthesis

(For neonatal diaphragmatic hernia repair, use 39503)

**43334** Repair, paraesophageal hiatal hernia (including fundoplication), via thoracotomy, except neonatal; without implantation of mesh or other prosthesis

**43335** with implantation of mesh or other prosthesis

(For neonatal diaphragmatic hernia repair, use 39503)

**43336** Repair, paraesophageal hiatal hernia, (including fundoplication), via thoracoabdominal incision, except neonatal; without implantation of mesh or other prosthesis

**43337** with implantation of mesh or other prosthesis

(For neonatal diaphragmatic hernia repair, use 39503)

**+ 43338** Esophageal lengthening procedure (eg, Collis gastroplasty or wedge gastroplasty) (List separately in addition to code for primary procedure)

(Use 43338 in conjunction with 43280, 43327-43337)

**43340** Esophagojejunostomy (without total gastrectomy); abdominal approach

**43341** thoracic approach

**43350** Esophagostomy, fistulization of esophagus, external; abdominal approach

**43351** thoracic approach

**43352** cervical approach

**43360** Gastrointestinal reconstruction for previous esophagectomy, for obstructing esophageal lesion or fistula, or for previous esophageal exclusion; with stomach, with or without pyloroplasty

**43361** with colon interposition or small intestine reconstruction, including intestine mobilization, preparation, and anastomosis(es)

**43400**    Ligation, direct, esophageal varices

**43401**    Transection of esophagus with repair, for esophageal varices

**43405**    Ligation or stapling at gastroesophageal junction for pre-existing esophageal perforation

**43410**    Suture of esophageal wound or injury; cervical approach

**43415**       transthoracic or transabdominal approach

**43420**    Closure of esophagostomy or fistula; cervical approach

**43425**       transthoracic or transabdominal approach

(To report transabdominal paraesophageal hiatal hernia repair, see 43332, 43333. To report transthoracic diaphragmatic hernia repair, see 43334, 43335)

## Manipulation

(For associated esophagogram, use 74220)

**43450**    Dilation of esophagus, by unguided sound or bougie, single or multiple passes

(For radiological supervision and interpretation, use 74360)

⊙ **43453**    Dilation of esophagus, over guide wire

►(For dilation with endoscopic visualization, see 43195, 43226)◄

►(For dilation of esophagus, by balloon or dilator, see 43214, 43220, 43233, 43249)◄

(For radiological supervision and interpretation, use 74360)

►(43456 has been deleted. To report, use 43213)◄

►(43458 has been deleted. To report, see 43214, 43233)◄

►(For endoscopic dilation of esophagus with balloon less than 30 mm diameter, see 43195, 43220, 43249)◄

►(For endoscopic dilation of esophagus with balloon 30 mm diameter or larger, see 43214, 43233)◄

**43460**    Esophagogastric tamponade, with balloon (Sengstaken type)

(For removal of esophageal foreign body by balloon catheter, see 43215, 43247, 74235)

## Other Procedures

**43496**    Free jejunum transfer with microvascular anastomosis

(Do not report code 69990 in addition to code 43496)

**43499**    Unlisted procedure, esophagus

## Stomach

### Incision

**43500**    Gastrotomy; with exploration or foreign body removal

**43501**       with suture repair of bleeding ulcer

**43502**       with suture repair of pre-existing esophagogastric laceration (eg, Mallory-Weiss)

**43510**       with esophageal dilation and insertion of permanent intraluminal tube (eg, Celestin or Mousseaux-Barbin)

**43520**    Pyloromyotomy, cutting of pyloric muscle (Fredet-Ramstedt type operation)

(Do not report modifier 63 in conjunction with 43520)

### Excision

(43600 has been deleted)

**43605**    Biopsy of stomach, by laparotomy

**43610**    Excision, local; ulcer or benign tumor of stomach

**43611**       malignant tumor of stomach

**43620**    Gastrectomy, total; with esophagoenterostomy

**43621**       with Roux-en-Y reconstruction

**43622**       with formation of intestinal pouch, any type

**43631**    Gastrectomy, partial, distal; with gastroduodenostomy

**43632**       with gastrojejunostomy

**43633**       with Roux-en-Y reconstruction

**43634**       with formation of intestinal pouch

+ **43635**    Vagotomy when performed with partial distal gastrectomy (List separately in addition to code[s] for primary procedure)

(Use 43635 in conjunction with 43631, 43632, 43633, 43634)

**43640**    Vagotomy including pyloroplasty, with or without gastrostomy; truncal or selective

(For pyloroplasty, use 43800)

(For vagotomy, see 64752-64760)

**43641**       parietal cell (highly selective)

(For upper gastrointestinal endoscopy, see 43235-43259)

### Laparoscopy

Surgical laparoscopy always includes diagnostic laparoscopy. To report a diagnostic laparoscopy (peritoneoscopy) (separate procedure), use 49320.

(For upper gastrointestinal endoscopy including esophagus, stomach, and either the duodenum and/or jejunum, see 43235-43259)

**Digestive**

---

**43644** Laparoscopy, surgical, gastric restrictive procedure; with gastric bypass and Roux-en-Y gastroenterostomy (roux limb 150 cm or less)

(Do not report 43644 in conjunction with 43846, 49320)

(Esophagogastroduodenoscopy [EGD] performed for a separate condition should be reported with modifier 59)

(For greater than 150 cm, use 43645)

(For open procedure, use 43846)

**43645** with gastric bypass and small intestine reconstruction to limit absorption

(Do not report 43645 in conjunction with 49320, 43847)

**43647** Laparoscopy, surgical; implantation or replacement of gastric neurostimulator electrodes, antrum

**43648** revision or removal of gastric neurostimulator electrodes, antrum

(For open approach, see 43881, 43882)

(For insertion of gastric neurostimulator pulse generator, use 64590)

(For revision or removal of gastric neurostimulator pulse generator, use 64595)

(For electronic analysis and programming of gastric neurostimulator pulse generator, see 95980-95982)

(For laparoscopic implantation, revision, or removal of gastric neurostimulator electrodes, lesser curvature [morbid obesity],use 43659)

(For laparoscopic implantation, revision, replacement, or removal of vagus nerve blocking neurostimulator electrode array and/or pulse generator at the esophagogastric junction, see 0312T-0317T)

**43651** Laparoscopy, surgical; transection of vagus nerves, truncal

**43652** transection of vagus nerves, selective or highly selective

**43653** gastrostomy, without construction of gastric tube (eg, Stamm procedure) (separate procedure)

**43659** Unlisted laparoscopy procedure, stomach

## Introduction

**43752** Naso- or oro-gastric tube placement, requiring physician's skill and fluoroscopic guidance (includes fluoroscopy, image documentation and report)

(Do not report 43752 in conjunction with critical care codes 99291-99292, neonatal critical care codes 99468, 99469, pediatric critical care codes 99471, 99472 or low birth weight intensive care service codes 99478, 99479)

(For percutaneous placement of gastrostomy tube, use 49440)

(For enteric tube placement, see 44500, 74340)

**43753** Gastric intubation and aspiration(s) therapeutic, necessitating physician's skill (eg, for gastrointestinal hemorrhage), including lavage if performed

**43754** Gastric intubation and aspiration, diagnostic; single specimen (eg, acid analysis)

**43755** collection of multiple fractional specimens with gastric stimulation, single or double lumen tube (gastric secretory study) (eg, histamine, insulin, pentagastrin, calcium, secretin), includes drug administration

(For gastric acid analysis, use 82930)

(For naso- or oro-gastric tube placement by physician with fluoroscopic guidance, use 43752)

(Report the drug[s] or substance[s] administered. The fluid used to administer the drug[s] is not separately reported)

**43756** Duodenal intubation and aspiration, diagnostic, includes image guidance; single specimen (eg, bile study for crystals or afferent loop culture)

**43757** collection of multiple fractional specimens with pancreatic or gallbladder stimulation, single or double lumen tube, includes drug administration

(For appropriate chemical analysis procedures, see 89049-89240)

(Report the substances[s] or drug[s] administered. The fluid used to administer the drug[s] is not separately reported)

**43760** Change of gastrostomy tube, percutaneous, without imaging or endoscopic guidance

(To report fluoroscopically guided replacement of gastrostomy tube, use 49450)

(For endoscopic placement of gastrostomy tube, use 43246)

**43761** Repositioning of a naso- or oro-gastric feeding tube, through the duodenum for enteric nutrition

(Do not report 43761 in conjunction with 44500, 49446)

(If imaging guidance is performed, use 76000)

(For endoscopic conversion of a gastrostomy tube to jejunostomy tube, use 44373)

(For placement of a long gastrointestinal tube into the duodenum, use 44500)

## Bariatric Surgery

Bariatric surgical procedures may involve the stomach, duodenum, jejunum, and/or the ileum.

### Laparoscopy

Surgical laparoscopy always includes diagnostic laparoscopy. To report a diagnostic laparoscopy (separate procedure), use 49320.

⊙=Moderate sedation ✚=Add-on code ✔=FDA approval pending #=Resequenced code ○=Recycled/reinstated code

Typical postoperative follow-up care (see Surgery Guidelines, CPT Surgical Package Definition) after gastric restriction using the adjustable gastric restrictive device includes subsequent restrictive device adjustment(s) through the postoperative period for the typical patient. Adjustment consists of changing the gastric restrictive device component diameter by injection or aspiration of fluid through the subcutaneous port component.

**43770** Laparoscopy, surgical, gastric restrictive procedure; placement of adjustable gastric restrictive device (eg, gastric band and subcutaneous port components)

(For individual component placement, report 43770 with modifier 52)

**43771** revision of adjustable gastric restrictive device component only

**43772** removal of adjustable gastric restrictive device component only

**43773** removal and replacement of adjustable gastric restrictive device component only

(Do not report 43773 in conjunction with 43772)

**43774** removal of adjustable gastric restrictive device and subcutaneous port components

(For removal and replacement of both gastric band and subcutaneous port components, use 43659)

**43775** longitudinal gastrectomy (ie, sleeve gastrectomy)

(For open gastric restrictive procedure, without gastric bypass, for morbid obesity, other than vertical-banded gastroplasty, use 43843)

(For laparoscopic implantation, revision, replacement, removal or reprogramming of vagus nerve blocking neurostimulator electrode array and/or pulse generator at the esophagogastric junction, see 0312T-0317T)

## Other Procedures

**43800** Pyloroplasty

(For pyloroplasty and vagotomy, use 43640)

**43810** Gastroduodenostomy

**43820** Gastrojejunostomy; without vagotomy

**43825** with vagotomy, any type

**43830** Gastrostomy, open; without construction of gastric tube (eg, Stamm procedure) (separate procedure)

**43831** neonatal, for feeding

(For change of gastrostomy tube, use 43760)

(Do not report modifier 63 in conjunction with 43831)

**43832** with construction of gastric tube (eg, Janeway procedure)

(For percutaneous endoscopic gastrostomy, use 43246)

**43840** Gastrorrhaphy, suture of perforated duodenal or gastric ulcer, wound, or injury

**43842** Gastric restrictive procedure, without gastric bypass, for morbid obesity; vertical-banded gastroplasty

**43843** other than vertical-banded gastroplasty

(For laparoscopic longitudinal gastrectomy [ie, sleeve gastrectomy], use 43775)

**43845** Gastric restrictive procedure with partial gastrectomy, pylorus-preserving duodenoileostomy and ileoileostomy (50 to 100 cm common channel) to limit absorption (biliopancreatic diversion with duodenal switch)

(Do not report 43845 in conjunction with 43633, 43847, 44130, 49000)

**43846** Gastric restrictive procedure, with gastric bypass for morbid obesity; with short limb (150 cm or less) Roux-en-Y gastroenterostomy

(For greater than 150 cm, use 43847)

(For laparoscopic procedure, use 43644)

**43847** with small intestine reconstruction to limit absorption

**43848** Revision, open, of gastric restrictive procedure for morbid obesity, other than adjustable gastric restrictive device (separate procedure)

(For laparoscopic adjustable gastric restrictive procedures, see 43770-43774)

(For gastric restrictive port procedures, see 43886-43888)

**43850** Revision of gastroduodenal anastomosis (gastroduodenostomy) with reconstruction; without vagotomy

**43855** with vagotomy

**43860** Revision of gastrojejunal anastomosis (gastrojejunostomy) with reconstruction, with or without partial gastrectomy or intestine resection; without vagotomy

**43865** with vagotomy

**43870** Closure of gastrostomy, surgical

**43880** Closure of gastrocolic fistula

**43881** Implantation or replacement of gastric neurostimulator electrodes, antrum, open

**43882** Revision or removal of gastric neurostimulator electrodes, antrum, open

(For laparoscopic approach, see 43647, 43648)

(For insertion of gastric neurostimulator pulse generator, use 64590)

(For revision or removal of gastric neurostimulator pulse generator, use 64595)

(For electronic analysis and programming of gastric neurostimulator pulse generator, see 95980-95982)

(For open implantation, revision, or removal of gastric neurostimulator electrodes, lesser curvature [morbid obesity],use 43999)

(For laparoscopic implantation, revision, replacement, removal or reprogramming of vagus nerve blocking neurostimulator electrode array and/or pulse generator at the esophagogastric junction, see 0312T-0317T)

(For open implantation, revision, or removal of gastric lesser curvature or vagal trunk (EGJ) neurostimulator electrodes, [morbid obesity], use 43999)

**43886** Gastric restrictive procedure, open; revision of subcutaneous port component only

**43887** removal of subcutaneous port component only

**43888** removal and replacement of subcutaneous port component only

(Do not report 43888 in conjunction with 43774, 43887)

(For laparoscopic removal of both gastric restrictive device and subcutaneous port components, use 43774)

(For removal and replacement of both gastric restrictive device and subcutaneous port components, use 43659)

**43999** Unlisted procedure, stomach

# Intestines (Except Rectum)

## Incision

**44005** Enterolysis (freeing of intestinal adhesion) (separate procedure)

(Do not report 44005 in addition to 45136)

(For laparoscopic approach, use 44180)

**44010** Duodenotomy, for exploration, biopsy(s), or foreign body removal

**+ 44015** Tube or needle catheter jejunostomy for enteral alimentation, intraoperative, any method (List separately in addition to primary procedure)

**44020** Enterotomy, small intestine, other than duodenum; for exploration, biopsy(s), or foreign body removal

**44021** for decompression (eg, Baker tube)

**44025** Colotomy, for exploration, biopsy(s), or foreign body removal

(For exteriorization of intestine (Mikulicz resection with crushing of spur), see 44602-44605)

**44050** Reduction of volvulus, intussusception, internal hernia, by laparotomy

**44055** Correction of malrotation by lysis of duodenal bands and/or reduction of midgut volvulus (eg, Ladd procedure)

(Do not report modifier 63 in conjunction with 44055)

## Excision

Intestinal allotransplantation involves three distinct components of physician work:

1. *Cadaver donor enterectomy,* which includes harvesting the intestine graft and cold preservation of the graft (perfusing with cold preservation solution and cold maintenance) (use 44132). *Living donor enterectomy,* which includes harvesting the intestine graft, cold preservation of the graft (perfusing with cold preservation solution and cold maintenance), and care of the donor (use 44133).

2. *Backbench work:*

   Standard preparation of an intestine allograft prior to transplantation includes mobilization and fashioning of the superior mesenteric artery and vein(see 44715).

   Additional reconstruction of an intestine allograft prior to transplantation may include venous and/or arterial anastomosis(es) (see 44720-44721).

3. *Recipient intestinal allotransplantation with or without recipient enterectomy,* which includes transplantation of allograft and care of the recipient (see 44135, 44136).

**44100** Biopsy of intestine by capsule, tube, peroral (1 or more specimens)

**44110** Excision of 1 or more lesions of small or large intestine not requiring anastomosis, exteriorization, or fistulization; single enterotomy

**44111** multiple enterotomies

**44120** Enterectomy, resection of small intestine; single resection and anastomosis

(Do not report 44120 in addition to 45136)

**+ 44121** each additional resection and anastomosis (List separately in addition to code for primary procedure)

(Use 44121 in conjunction with 44120)

**44125** with enterostomy

**44126** Enterectomy, resection of small intestine for congenital atresia, single resection and anastomosis of proximal segment of intestine; without tapering

**44127** with tapering

**+ 44128** each additional resection and anastomosis (List separately in addition to code for primary procedure)

(Use 44128 in conjunction with 44126, 44127)

(Do not report modifier 63 in conjunction with 44126, 44127, 44128)

**44130** Enteroenterostomy, anastomosis of intestine, with or without cutaneous enterostomy (separate procedure)

**44132** Donor enterectomy (including cold preservation), open; from cadaver donor

44133          partial, from living donor

(For backbench intestinal graft preparation or reconstruction, see 44715, 44720, 44721)

44135    Intestinal allotransplantation; from cadaver donor

44136         from living donor

44137    Removal of transplanted intestinal allograft, complete

(For partial removal of transplant allograft, see 44120, 44121, 44140)

+ 44139    Mobilization (take-down) of splenic flexure performed in conjunction with partial colectomy (List separately in addition to primary procedure)

(Use 44139 in conjunction with 44140-44147)

44140    Colectomy, partial; with anastomosis

(For laparoscopic procedure, use 44204)

44141         with skin level cecostomy or colostomy

44143         with end colostomy and closure of distal segment (Hartmann type procedure)

(For laparoscopic procedure, use 44206)

44144         with resection, with colostomy or ileostomy and creation of mucofistula

44145         with coloproctostomy (low pelvic anastomosis)

(For laparoscopic procedure, use 44207)

44146         with coloproctostomy (low pelvic anastomosis), with colostomy

(For laparoscopic procedure, use 44208)

44147         abdominal and transanal approach

44150    Colectomy, total, abdominal, without proctectomy; with ileostomy or ileoproctostomy

(For laparoscopic procedure, use 44210)

44151         with continent ileostomy

44155    Colectomy, total, abdominal, with proctectomy; with ileostomy

(For laparoscopic procedure, use 44212)

44156         with continent ileostomy

44157         with ileoanal anastomosis, includes loop ileostomy, and rectal mucosectomy, when performed

44158         with ileoanal anastomosis, creation of ileal reservoir (S or J), includes loop ileostomy, and rectal mucosectomy, when performed

(For laparoscopic procedure, use 44211)

44160    Colectomy, partial, with removal of terminal ileum with ileocolostomy

(For laparoscopic procedure, use 44205)

## Laparoscopy

Surgical laparoscopy always includes diagnostic laparoscopy. To report a diagnostic laparoscopy (peritoneoscopy) (separate procedure), use 49320.

### Incision

44180    Laparoscopy, surgical, enterolysis (freeing of intestinal adhesion) (separate procedure)

(For laparoscopy with salpingolysis, ovariolysis, use 58660)

### Enterostomy—External Fistulization of Intestines

44186    Laparoscopy, surgical; jejunostomy (eg, for decompression or feeding)

44187         ileostomy or jejunostomy, non-tube

(For open procedure, use 44310)

44188    Laparoscopy, surgical, colostomy or skin level cecostomy

(For open procedure, use 44320)

(Do not report 44188 in conjunction with 44970)

### Excision

44202    Laparoscopy, surgical; enterectomy, resection of small intestine, single resection and anastomosis

+ 44203         each additional small intestine resection and anastomosis (List separately in addition to code for primary procedure)

(Use 44203 in conjunction with 44202)

(For open procedure, see 44120, 44121)

44204         colectomy, partial, with anastomosis

(For open procedure, use 44140)

44205         colectomy, partial, with removal of terminal ileum with ileocolostomy

(For open procedure, use 44160)

44206         colectomy, partial, with end colostomy and closure of distal segment (Hartmann type procedure)

(For open procedure, use 44143)

44207         colectomy, partial, with anastomosis, with coloproctostomy (low pelvic anastomosis)

(For open procedure, use 44145)

44208         colectomy, partial, with anastomosis, with coloproctostomy (low pelvic anastomosis) with colostomy

(For open procedure, use 44146)

**Digestive**

**44210**    colectomy, total, abdominal, without proctectomy, with ileostomy or ileoproctostomy

(For open procedure, use 44150)

**44211**    colectomy, total, abdominal, with proctectomy, with ileoanal anastomosis, creation of ileal reservoir (S or J), with loop ileostomy, includes rectal mucosectomy, when performed

(For open procedure, see 44157, 44158)

**44212**    colectomy, total, abdominal, with proctectomy, with ileostomy

(For open procedure, use 44155)

**+ 44213** Laparoscopy, surgical, mobilization (take-down) of splenic flexure performed in conjunction with partial colectomy (List separately in addition to primary procedure)

(Use 44213 in conjunction with 44204-44208)

(For open procedure, use 44139)

## Repair

**44227** Laparoscopy, surgical, closure of enterostomy, large or small intestine, with resection and anastomosis

(For open procedure, see 44625, 44626)

## Other Procedures

**44238** Unlisted laparoscopy procedure, intestine (except rectum)

## Enterostomy—External Fistulization of Intestines

**44300** Placement, enterostomy or cecostomy, tube open (eg, for feeding or decompression) (separate procedure)

(For percutaneous placement of duodenostomy, jejunostomy, gastro-jejunostomy or cecostomy [or other colonic] tube including fluoroscopic imaging guidance, see 49441-49442)

**44310** Ileostomy or jejunostomy, non-tube

(For laparoscopic procedure, use 44187)

(Do not report 44310 in conjunction with 44144, 44150-44151, 44155, 44156, 45113, 45119, 45136)

**44312** Revision of ileostomy; simple (release of superficial scar) (separate procedure)

**44314**    complicated (reconstruction in-depth) (separate procedure)

**44316** Continent ileostomy (Kock procedure) (separate procedure)

(For fiberoptic evaluation, use 44385)

**44320** Colostomy or skin level cecostomy;

(For laparoscopic procedure, use 44188)

(Do not report 44320 in conjunction with 44141, 44144, 44146, 44605, 45110, 45119, 45126, 45563, 45805, 45825, 50810, 51597, 57307, or 58240)

**44322**    with multiple biopsies (eg, for congenital megacolon) (separate procedure)

**44340** Revision of colostomy; simple (release of superficial scar) (separate procedure)

**44345**    complicated (reconstruction in-depth) (separate procedure)

**44346**    with repair of paracolostomy hernia (separate procedure)

## Endoscopy, Small Intestine and Stomal

Surgical endoscopy always includes diagnostic endoscopy.

▶(For upper gastrointestinal endoscopy, see 43235-43257, 43270)◀

⊙ **44360** Small intestinal endoscopy, enteroscopy beyond second portion of duodenum, not including ileum; diagnostic, with or without collection of specimen(s) by brushing or washing (separate procedure)

⊙ **44361**    with biopsy, single or multiple

⊙ **44363**    with removal of foreign body

⊙ **44364**    with removal of tumor(s), polyp(s), or other lesion(s) by snare technique

⊙ **44365**    with removal of tumor(s), polyp(s), or other lesion(s) by hot biopsy forceps or bipolar cautery

⊙ **44366**    with control of bleeding (eg, injection, bipolar cautery, unipolar cautery, laser, heater probe, stapler, plasma coagulator)

⊙ **44369**    with ablation of tumor(s), polyp(s), or other lesion(s) not amenable to removal by hot biopsy forceps, bipolar cautery or snare technique

⊙ **44370**    with transendoscopic stent placement (includes predilation)

⊙ **44372**    with placement of percutaneous jejunostomy tube

⊙ **44373**    with conversion of percutaneous gastrostomy tube to percutaneous jejunostomy tube

(For fiberoptic jejunostomy through stoma, use 43235)

⊙ **44376** Small intestinal endoscopy, enteroscopy beyond second portion of duodenum, including ileum; diagnostic, with or without collection of specimen(s) by brushing or washing (separate procedure)

⊙ **44377**    with biopsy, single or multiple

⊙ **44378**    with control of bleeding (eg, injection, bipolar cautery, unipolar cautery, laser, heater probe, stapler, plasma coagulator)

Digestive

⊙ **44379**   with transendoscopic stent placement (includes predilation)

⊙ **44380**   Ileoscopy, through stoma; diagnostic, with or without collection of specimen(s) by brushing or washing (separate procedure)

⊙ **44382**   with biopsy, single or multiple

⊙ **44383**   with transendoscopic stent placement (includes predilation)

⊙ **44385**   Endoscopic evaluation of small intestinal (abdominal or pelvic) pouch; diagnostic, with or without collection of specimen(s) by brushing or washing (separate procedure)

⊙ **44386**   with biopsy, single or multiple

⊙ **44388**   Colonoscopy through stoma; diagnostic, with or without collection of specimen(s) by brushing or washing (separate procedure)

⊙ **44389**   with biopsy, single or multiple

⊙ **44390**   with removal of foreign body

⊙ **44391**   with control of bleeding (eg, injection, bipolar cautery, unipolar cautery, laser, heater probe, stapler, plasma coagulator)

⊙ **44392**   with removal of tumor(s), polyp(s), or other lesion(s) by hot biopsy forceps or bipolar cautery

⊙ **44393**   with ablation of tumor(s), polyp(s), or other lesion(s) not amenable to removal by hot biopsy forceps, bipolar cautery or snare technique

⊙ **44394**   with removal of tumor(s), polyp(s), or other lesion(s) by snare technique

(For colonoscopy per rectum, see 45330-45385)

⊙ **44397**   with transendoscopic stent placement (includes predilation)

## Introduction

⊙⊘ **44500**   Introduction of long gastrointestinal tube (eg, Miller-Abbott) (separate procedure)

(For radiological supervision and interpretation, use 74340)

(For naso- or oro-gastric tube placement, use 43752)

## Repair

**44602**   Suture of small intestine (enterorrhaphy) for perforated ulcer, diverticulum, wound, injury or rupture; single perforation

**44603**   multiple perforations

**44604**   Suture of large intestine (colorrhaphy) for perforated ulcer, diverticulum, wound, injury or rupture (single or multiple perforations); without colostomy

**44605**   with colostomy

**44615**   Intestinal stricturoplasty (enterotomy and enterorrhaphy) with or without dilation, for intestinal obstruction

**44620**   Closure of enterostomy, large or small intestine;

**44625**   with resection and anastomosis other than colorectal

**44626**   with resection and colorectal anastomosis (eg, closure of Hartmann type procedure)

(For laparoscopic procedure, use 44227)

**44640**   Closure of intestinal cutaneous fistula

**44650**   Closure of enteroenteric or enterocolic fistula

**44660**   Closure of enterovesical fistula; without intestinal or bladder resection

**44661**   with intestine and/or bladder resection

(For closure of renocolic fistula, see 50525, 50526)

(For closure of gastrocolic fistula, use 43880)

(For closure of rectovesical fistula, see 45800, 45805)

**44680**   Intestinal plication (separate procedure)

## Other Procedures

**44700**   Exclusion of small intestine from pelvis by mesh or other prosthesis, or native tissue (eg, bladder or omentum)

(For therapeutic radiation clinical treatment, see **Radiation Oncology** section)

✛ **44701**   Intraoperative colonic lavage (List separately in addition to code for primary procedure)

(Use 44701 in conjunction with 44140, 44145, 44150, or 44604 as appropriate)

(Do not report 44701 in conjunction with 44300, 44950-44960)

**44705**   Preparation of fecal microbiota for instillation, including assessment of donor specimen

(Do not report 44705 in conjunction with 74283)

(For fecal instillation by oro-nasogastric tube or enema, use 44799)

**44715**   Backbench standard preparation of cadaver or living donor intestine allograft prior to transplantation, including mobilization and fashioning of the superior mesenteric artery and vein

**44720**   Backbench reconstruction of cadaver or living donor intestine allograft prior to transplantation; venous anastomosis, each

**44721**   arterial anastomosis, each

**44799**   Unlisted procedure, intestine

(For unlisted laparoscopic procedure, intestine except rectum, use 44238)

**Digestive**

# Meckel's Diverticulum and the Mesentery

## Excision

**44800**    Excision of Meckel's diverticulum (diverticulectomy) or omphalomesenteric duct

**44820**    Excision of lesion of mesentery (separate procedure)

(With intestine resection, see 44120 or 44140 et seq)

## Suture

**44850**    Suture of mesentery (separate procedure)

(For reduction and repair of internal hernia, use 44050)

## Other Procedures

**44899**    Unlisted procedure, Meckel's diverticulum and the mesentery

# Appendix

## Incision

**44900**    Incision and drainage of appendiceal abscess, open

▶(44901 has been deleted)◀

▶(For percutaneous image-guided drainage by catheter of appendiceal abscess, use 49406)◀

## Excision

**44950**    Appendectomy;

(Incidental appendectomy during intra-abdominal surgery does not usually warrant a separate identification. If necessary to report, add modifier 52)

+ **44955**    when done for indicated purpose at time of other major procedure (not as separate procedure) (List separately in addition to code for primary procedure)

**44900**    for ruptured appendix with abscess or generalized peritonitis

## Laparoscopy

Surgical laparoscopy always includes diagnostic laparoscopy. To report a diagnostic laparoscopy (peritoneoscopy) (separate procedure), use 49320.

**44970**    Laparoscopy, surgical, appendectomy

**44979**    Unlisted laparoscopy procedure, appendix

# Rectum

## Incision

**45000**    Transrectal drainage of pelvic abscess

▶(For transrectal image-guided fluid collection drainage by catheter of pelvic abscess, use 49407)◀

**45005**    Incision and drainage of submucosal abscess, rectum

**45020**    Incision and drainage of deep supralevator, pelvirectal, or retrorectal abscess

(See also 46050, 46060)

## Excision

**45100**    Biopsy of anorectal wall, anal approach (eg, congenital megacolon)

(For endoscopic biopsy, use 45305)

**45108**    Anorectal myomectomy

**45110**    Proctectomy; complete, combined abdominoperineal, with colostomy

(For laparoscopic procedure, use 45395)

**45111**    partial resection of rectum, transabdominal approach

**45112**    Proctectomy, combined abdominoperineal, pull-through procedure (eg, colo-anal anastomosis)

(For colo-anal anastomosis with colonic reservoir or pouch, use 45119)

**45113**    Proctectomy, partial, with rectal mucosectomy, ileoanal anastomosis, creation of ileal reservoir (S or J), with or without loop ileostomy

**45114**    Proctectomy, partial, with anastomosis; abdominal and transsacral approach

**45116**    transsacral approach only (Kraske type)

**45119**    Proctectomy, combined abdominoperineal pull-through procedure (eg, colo-anal anastomosis), with creation of colonic reservoir (eg, J-pouch), with diverting enterostomy when performed

(For laparoscopic procedure, use 45397)

**45120**    Proctectomy, complete (for congenital megacolon), abdominal and perineal approach; with pull-through procedure and anastomosis (eg, Swenson, Duhamel, or Soave type operation)

**45121**    with subtotal or total colectomy, with multiple biopsies

**45123**    Proctectomy, partial, without anastomosis, perineal approach

**45126**   Pelvic exenteration for colorectal malignancy, with proctectomy (with or without colostomy), with removal of bladder and ureteral transplantations, and/or hysterectomy, or cervicectomy, with or without removal of tube(s), with or without removal of ovary(s), or any combination thereof

**45130**   Excision of rectal procidentia, with anastomosis; perineal approach

**45135**        abdominal and perineal approach

**45136**   Excision of ileoanal reservoir with ileostomy

(Do not report 45136 in addition to 44005, 44120, 44310)

**45150**   Division of stricture of rectum

**45160**   Excision of rectal tumor by proctotomy, transsacral or transcoccygeal approach

(45170 has been deleted. To report excision of rectal tumor, transanal approach, see 45171, 45172)

**45171**   Excision of rectal tumor, transanal approach; not including muscularis propria (ie, partial thickness)

**45172**        including muscularis propria (ie, full thickness)

(For destruction of rectal tumor, transanal approach, use 45190)

(For transanal endoscopic microsurgical [ie, TEMS] excision of rectal tumor, including muscularis propria [ie, full thickness], use 0184T)

# Destruction

**45190**   Destruction of rectal tumor (eg, electrodesiccation, electrosurgery, laser ablation, laser resection, cryosurgery) transanal approach

(For excision of rectal tumor, transanal approach, see 45171, 45172)

(For transanal endoscopic microsurgical [ie, TEMS] excision of rectal tumor, including muscularis propria [ie, full thickness], use 0184T)

# Endoscopy

## Definitions

***Proctosigmoidoscopy*** is the examination of the rectum and sigmoid colon.

***Sigmoidoscopy*** is the examination of the entire rectum, sigmoid colon and may include examination of a portion of the descending colon.

***Colonoscopy*** is the examination of the entire colon, from the rectum to the cecum, and may include the examination of the terminal ileum.

When performing an endoscopy on a patient who is scheduled and prepared for a total colonoscopy, if the physician is unable to advance the colonoscope beyond the splenic flexure, due to unforeseen circumstances,

report the colonoscopy code with modifier 53 and appropriate documentation.

Surgical endoscopy always includes diagnostic endoscopy.

For computed tomographic colonography, see 74261-74263.

**45300**   Proctosigmoidoscopy, rigid; diagnostic, with or without collection of specimen(s) by brushing or washing (separate procedure)

⊙ **45303**        with dilation (eg, balloon, guide wire, bougie)

(For radiological supervision and interpretation, use 74360)

⊙ **45305**        with biopsy, single or multiple

⊙ **45307**        with removal of foreign body

⊙ **45308**        with removal of single tumor, polyp, or other lesion by hot biopsy forceps or bipolar cautery

⊙ **45309**        with removal of single tumor, polyp, or other lesion by snare technique

⊙ **45315**        with removal of multiple tumors, polyps, or other lesions by hot biopsy forceps, bipolar cautery or snare technique

⊙ **45317**        with control of bleeding (eg, injection, bipolar cautery, unipolar cautery, laser, heater probe, stapler, plasma coagulator)

⊙ **45320**        with ablation of tumor(s), polyp(s), or other lesion(s) not amenable to removal by hot biopsy forceps, bipolar cautery or snare technique (eg, laser)

⊙ **45321**        with decompression of volvulus

⊙ **45327**        with transendoscopic stent placement (includes predilation)

**45330**   Sigmoidoscopy, flexible; diagnostic, with or without collection of specimen(s) by brushing or washing (separate procedure)

**45331**        with biopsy, single or multiple

⊙ **45332**        with removal of foreign body

⊙ **45333**        with removal of tumor(s), polyp(s), or other lesion(s) by hot biopsy forceps or bipolar cautery

⊙ **45334**        with control of bleeding (eg, injection, bipolar cautery, unipolar cautery, laser, heater probe, stapler, plasma coagulator)

⊙ **45335**        with directed submucosal injection(s), any substance

⊙ **45337**        with decompression of volvulus, any method

⊙ **45338**        with removal of tumor(s), polyp(s), or other lesion(s) by snare technique

⊙ **45339**        with ablation of tumor(s), polyp(s), or other lesion(s) not amenable to removal by hot biopsy forceps, bipolar cautery or snare technique

⊙ **45340**        with dilation by balloon, 1 or more strictures

(Do not report 45340 in conjunction with 45345)

**Digestive**

⊙ **45341**   with endoscopic ultrasound examination

⊙ **45342**   with transendoscopic ultrasound guided intramural or transmural fine needle aspiration/biopsy(s)

(Do not report 45341, 45342 in conjunction with 76942, 76975)

(For interpretation of specimen, see 88172-88173)

(For transrectal ultrasound utilizing rigid probe device, use 76872)

⊙ **45345**   with transendoscopic stent placement (includes predilation)

⊙ **45355**   Colonoscopy, rigid or flexible, transabdominal via colotomy, single or multiple

(For fiberoptic colonoscopy beyond 25cm to splenic flexure, see 45330-45345)

⊙ **45378**   Colonoscopy, flexible, proximal to splenic flexure; diagnostic, with or without collection of specimen(s) by brushing or washing, with or without colon decompression (separate procedure)

⊙ **45379**   with removal of foreign body

⊙ **45380**   with biopsy, single or multiple

⊙ **45381**   with directed submucosal injection(s), any substance

⊙ **45382**   with control of bleeding (eg, injection, bipolar cautery, unipolar cautery, laser, heater probe, stapler, plasma coagulator)

⊙ **45383**   with ablation of tumor(s), polyp(s), or other lesion(s) not amenable to removal by hot biopsy forceps, bipolar cautery or snare technique

⊙ **45384**   with removal of tumor(s), polyp(s), or other lesion(s) by hot biopsy forceps or bipolar cautery

⊙ **45385**   with removal of tumor(s), polyp(s), or other lesion(s) by snare technique

(For small intestine and stomal endoscopy, see 44360-44393)

⊙ **45386**   with dilation by balloon, 1 or more strictures

(Do not report 45386 in conjunction with 45387)

⊙ **45387**   with transendoscopic stent placement (includes predilation)

⊙ **45391**   with endoscopic ultrasound examination

(Do not report 45391 in conjunction with 45330, 45341, 45342, 45378, 76872)

⊙ **45392**   with transendoscopic ultrasound guided intramural or transmural fine needle aspiration/biopsy(s)

(Do not report 45392 in conjunction with 45330, 45341, 45342, 45378, 76872)

## Laparoscopy

Surgical laparoscopy always includes diagnostic laparoscopy. To report a diagnostic laparoscopy (peritoneoscopy) (separate procedure), use 49320.

### Excision

**45395**   Laparoscopy, surgical; proctectomy, complete, combined abdominoperineal, with colostomy

(For open procedure, use 45110)

**45397**   proctectomy, combined abdominoperineal pull-through procedure (eg, colo-anal anastomosis), with creation of colonic reservoir (eg, J-pouch), with diverting enterostomy, when performed

(For open procedure, use 45119)

### Repair

**45400**   Laparoscopy, surgical; proctopexy (for prolapse)

(For open procedure, use 45540, 45541)

**45402**   proctopexy (for prolapse), with sigmoid resection

(For open procedure, use 45550)

**45499**   Unlisted laparoscopy procedure, rectum

## Repair

**45500**   Proctoplasty; for stenosis

**45505**   for prolapse of mucous membrane

**45520**   Perirectal injection of sclerosing solution for prolapse

**45540**   Proctopexy (eg, for prolapse); abdominal approach

(For laparoscopic procedure, use 45400)

**45541**   perineal approach

**45550**   with sigmoid resection, abdominal approach

(For laparoscopic procedure, use 45402)

**45560**   Repair of rectocele (separate procedure)

(For repair of rectocele with posterior colporrhaphy, use 57250)

**45562**   Exploration, repair, and presacral drainage for rectal injury;

**45563**   with colostomy

**45800**   Closure of rectovesical fistula;

**45805**   with colostomy

**45820**   Closure of rectourethral fistula;

**45825**   with colostomy

(For rectovaginal fistula closure, see 57300-57308)

## Manipulation

**45900**   Reduction of procidentia (separate procedure) under anesthesia

**45905**   Dilation of anal sphincter (separate procedure) under anesthesia other than local

**45910**   Dilation of rectal stricture (separate procedure) under anesthesia other than local

**45915**   Removal of fecal impaction or foreign body (separate procedure) under anesthesia

## Other Procedures

Surgical diagnostic anorectal exam (45990) includes the following elements: external perineal exam, digital rectal exam, pelvic exam (when performed), diagnostic anoscopy, and diagnostic rigid proctoscopy.

**45990**   Anorectal exam, surgical, requiring anesthesia (general, spinal, or epidural), diagnostic

(Do not report 45990 in conjunction with 45300-45327, 46600, 57410, 99170)

**45999**   Unlisted procedure, rectum

(For unlisted laparoscopic procedure, rectum, use 45499)

## Anus

For incision of thrombosed external hemorrhoid, use 46083. For ligation of internal hemorrhoid(s), see 46221, 46945, 46946. For excision of internal and/or external hemorrhoid(s), see 46250-46262, 46320. For injection of hemorrhoid(s), use 46500. For destruction of internal hemorrhoid(s) by thermal energy, use 46930. For destruction of hemorrhoid(s) by cryosurgery, use 46999. For hemorrhoidopexy, use 46947.

## Incision

(For subcutaneous fistulotomy, use 46270)

**46020**   Placement of seton

(Do not report 46020 in addition to 46060, 46280, 46600, 0249T)

**46030**   Removal of anal seton, other marker

**46040**   Incision and drainage of ischiorectal and/or perirectal abscess (separate procedure)

**46045**   Incision and drainage of intramural, intramuscular, or submucosal abscess, transanal, under anesthesia

**46050**   Incision and drainage, perianal abscess, superficial

(See also 45020, 46060)

**46060**   Incision and drainage of ischiorectal or intramural abscess, with fistulectomy or fistulotomy, submuscular, with or without placement of seton

(Do not report 46060 in addition to 46020)

(See also 45020)

**46070**   Incision, anal septum (infant)

(For anoplasty, see 46700-46705)

(Do not report modifier 63 in conjunction with 46070)

**46080**   Sphincterotomy, anal, division of sphincter (separate procedure)

**46083**   Incision of thrombosed hemorrhoid, external

## Excision

**46200**   Fissurectomy, including sphincterotomy, when performed

(46210, 46211 have been deleted. To report, use 46999)

**46220**   Code is out of numerical sequence. See 46200-46288

**46221**   Hemorrhoidectomy, internal, by rubber band ligation(s)

(For ligation, hemorrhoidal vascular bundle(s), including ultrasound guidance, use 0249T)

# **46945**   Hemorrhoidectomy, internal, by ligation other than rubber band; single hemorrhoid column/group

# **46946**       2 or more hemorrhoid columns/groups

(Do not report 46221, 46945, and 46946 in conjunction with 0249T)

# **46220**   Excision of single external papilla or tag, anus

**46230**   Excision of multiple external papillae or tags, anus

# **46320**   Excision of thrombosed hemorrhoid, external

**46250**   Hemorrhoidectomy, external, 2 or more columns/groups

(For hemorrhoidectomy, external, single column/group, use 46999)

**46255**   Hemorrhoidectomy, internal and external, single column/group;

**46257**       with fissurectomy

**46258**       with fistulectomy, including fissurectomy, when performed

**46260**   Hemorrhoidectomy, internal and external, 2 or more columns/groups;

**46261**       with fissurectomy

**46262**       with fistulectomy, including fissurectomy, when performed

(Do not report 46250-46262 in conjunction with 0249T)

**46270**   Surgical treatment of anal fistula (fistulectomy/fistulotomy); subcutaneous

**46275**       intersphincteric

**46280**       transsphincteric, suprasphincteric, extrasphincteric or multiple, including placement of seton, when performed

(Do not report 46280 in conjunction with 46020)

**46285**       second stage

**46288**   Closure of anal fistula with rectal advancement flap

**46320**   Code is out of numerical sequence. See 46200-46288

## Introduction

**46500**   Injection of sclerosing solution, hemorrhoids

**46505**   Chemodenervation of internal anal sphincter

▶(For chemodenervation of other muscles, see 64612, 64616, 64617, 64642, 64643, 64644, 64645, 64646, 64647. For destruction of nerve by neurolytic agent, use 64630)◀

(Report the specific service in conjunction with the specific substance(s) or drug(s) provided)

## Endoscopy

Surgical endoscopy always includes diagnostic endoscopy.

**46600**   Anoscopy; diagnostic, with or without collection of specimen(s) by brushing or washing (separate procedure)

(Do not report 46600 in conjunction with 46020, 0249T)

(For diagnostic high resolution anoscopy [HRA], use 0226T)

**46604**      with dilation (eg, balloon, guide wire, bougie)

**46606**      with biopsy, single or multiple

(For high resolution anoscopy [HRA] with biopsy, use 0227T)

**46608**      with removal of foreign body

**46610**      with removal of single tumor, polyp, or other lesion by hot biopsy forceps or bipolar cautery

**46611**      with removal of single tumor, polyp, or other lesion by snare technique

**46612**      with removal of multiple tumors, polyps, or other lesions by hot biopsy forceps, bipolar cautery or snare technique

**46614**      with control of bleeding (eg, injection, bipolar cautery, unipolar cautery, laser, heater probe, stapler, plasma coagulator)

**46615**      with ablation of tumor(s), polyp(s), or other lesion(s) not amenable to removal by hot biopsy forceps, bipolar cautery or snare technique

(For delivery of thermal energy to the muscle of the anal canal, use 0288T)

## Repair

**46700**   Anoplasty, plastic operation for stricture; adult

**46705**      infant

(Do not report modifier 63 in conjunction with 46705)

(For simple incision of anal septum, use 46070)

**46706**   Repair of anal fistula with fibrin glue

**46707**   Repair of anorectal fistula with plug (eg, porcine small intestine submucosa [SIS])

**46710**   Repair of ileoanal pouch fistula/sinus (eg, perineal or vaginal), pouch advancement; transperineal approach

**46712**      combined transperineal and transabdominal approach

**46715**   Repair of low imperforate anus; with anoperineal fistula (cut-back procedure)

**46716**      with transposition of anoperineal or anovestibular fistula

(Do not report modifier 63 in conjunction with 46715, 46716)

**46730**   Repair of high imperforate anus without fistula; perineal or sacroperineal approach

**46735**      combined transabdominal and sacroperineal approaches

(Do not report modifier 63 in conjunction with 46730, 46735)

**46740**   Repair of high imperforate anus with rectourethral or rectovaginal fistula; perineal or sacroperineal approach

**46742**      combined transabdominal and sacroperineal approaches

(Do not report modifier 63 in conjunction with 46740, 46742)

**46744**   Repair of cloacal anomaly by anorectovaginoplasty and urethroplasty, sacroperineal approach

(Do not report modifier 63 in conjunction with 46744)

**46746**   Repair of cloacal anomaly by anorectovaginoplasty and urethroplasty, combined abdominal and sacroperineal approach;

**46748**      with vaginal lengthening by intestinal graft or pedicle flaps

**46750**   Sphincteroplasty, anal, for incontinence or prolapse; adult

**46751**      child

**46753**   Graft (Thiersch operation) for rectal incontinence and/or prolapse

**46754**   Removal of Thiersch wire or suture, anal canal

**46760**   Sphincteroplasty, anal, for incontinence, adult; muscle transplant

**46761**      levator muscle imbrication (Park posterior anal repair)

**46762**      implantation artificial sphincter

# **46947**   Hemorrhoidopexy (eg, for prolapsing internal hemorrhoids) by stapling

## Destruction

**46900**   Destruction of lesion(s), anus (eg, condyloma, papilloma, molluscum contagiosum, herpetic vesicle), simple; chemical

**46910**      electrodesiccation

**46916**      cryosurgery

**46917**      laser surgery

| 46922 | surgical excision |
|---|---|
| 46924 | Destruction of lesion(s), anus (eg, condyloma, papilloma, molluscum contagiosum, herpetic vesicle), extensive (eg, laser surgery, electrosurgery, cryosurgery, chemosurgery) |
| 46930 | Destruction of internal hemorrhoid(s) by thermal energy (eg, infrared coagulation, cautery, radiofrequency) |

(46934-46936 have been deleted)

(46937, 46938 have been deleted. To report, use 45190)

| 46940 | Curettage or cautery of anal fissure, including dilation of anal sphincter (separate procedure); initial |
| 46942 | subsequent |
| 46945 | Code is out of numerical sequence. See 46200-46288 |
| 46946 | Code is out of numerical sequence. See 46200-46288 |
| 46947 | Code is out of numerical sequence. See 46700-46947 |

## Other Procedures

| 46999 | Unlisted procedure, anus |

# Liver

## Incision

| ⊙ 47000 | Biopsy of liver, needle; percutaneous |
|---|---|

(If imaging guidance is performed, see 76942, 77002, 77012, 77021)

| + 47001 | when done for indicated purpose at time of other major procedure (List separately in addition to code for primary procedure) |

(If imaging guidance is performed, see 76942, 77002)

(For fine needle aspiration in conjunction with 47000, 47001, see 10021, 10022)

(For evaluation of fine needle aspirate in conjunction with 47000, 47001, see 88172, 88173)

| 47010 | Hepatotomy, for open drainage of abscess or cyst, 1 or 2 stages |

►(47011 has been deleted)◄

►(For percutaneous image-guided fluid collection drainage by catheter of hepatic abscess or cyst, use 49405)◄

| 47015 | Laparotomy, with aspiration and/or injection of hepatic parasitic (eg, amoebic or echinococcal) cyst(s) or abscess(es) |

## Excision

| 47100 | Biopsy of liver, wedge |
|---|---|
| 47120 | Hepatectomy, resection of liver; partial lobectomy |
| 47122 | trisegmentectomy |
| 47125 | total left lobectomy |
| 47130 | total right lobectomy |

## Liver Transplantation

Liver allotransplantation involves three distinct components of physician work:

1. *Cadaver donor hepatectomy,* which includes harvesting the graft and cold preservation of the graft (perfusing with cold preservation solution and cold maintenance) (use 47133). *Living donor hepatectomy,* which includes harvesting the graft, cold preservation of the graft (perfusing with cold preservation solution and cold maintenance), and care of the donor (see 47140-47142).

2. *Backbench work:*

Standard preparation of the whole liver graft will include one of the following:

Preparation of whole liver graft (including cholecystectomy, if necessary, and dissection and removal of surrounding soft tissues to prepare vena cava, portal vein, hepatic artery, and common bile duct for implantation) (use 47143).

Preparation as described for whole liver graft, plus trisegment split into two partial grafts (use 47144).

Preparation as described for whole liver graft, plus lobe split into two partial grafts (use 47145).

Additional reconstruction of the liver graft may include venous and/or arterial anastomosis(es) (see 47146, 47147).

3. *Recipient liver allotransplantation,* which includes recipient hepatectomy (partial or whole), transplantation of the allograft (partial or whole), and care of the recipient (see 47135, 47136).

| 47133 | Donor hepatectomy (including cold preservation), from cadaver donor |
|---|---|
| 47135 | Liver allotransplantation; orthotopic, partial or whole, from cadaver or living donor, any age |
| 47136 | heterotopic, partial or whole, from cadaver or living donor, any age |
| 47140 | Donor hepatectomy (including cold preservation), from living donor; left lateral segment only (segments II and III) |
| 47141 | total left lobectomy (segments II, III and IV) |
| 47142 | total right lobectomy (segments V, VI, VII and VIII) |
| 47143 | Backbench standard preparation of cadaver donor whole liver graft prior to allotransplantation, including cholecystectomy, if necessary, and dissection and removal of surrounding soft tissues to prepare the vena cava, portal vein, hepatic artery, and common bile duct for implantation; without trisegment or lobe split |
| 47144 | with trisegment split of whole liver graft into 2 partial liver grafts (ie, left lateral segment [segments II and III] and right trisegment [segments I and IV through VIII]) |

**Digestive**

**47145** with lobe split of whole liver graft into 2 partial liver grafts (ie, left lobe [segments II, III, and IV] and right lobe [segments I and V through VIII])

**47146** Backbench reconstruction of cadaver or living donor liver graft prior to allotransplantation; venous anastomosis, each

**47147** arterial anastomosis, each

(Do not report 47143-47147 in conjunction with 47120-47125, 47600, 47610)

## Repair

**47300** Marsupialization of cyst or abscess of liver

**47350** Management of liver hemorrhage; simple suture of liver wound or injury

**47360** complex suture of liver wound or injury, with or without hepatic artery ligation

**47361** exploration of hepatic wound, extensive debridement, coagulation and/or suture, with or without packing of liver

**47362** re-exploration of hepatic wound for removal of packing

## Laparoscopy

Surgical laparoscopy always includes diagnostic laparoscopy. To report a diagnostic laparoscopy (peritoneoscopy) (separate procedure), use 49320.

**47370** Laparoscopy, surgical, ablation of 1 or more liver tumor(s); radiofrequency

(For imaging guidance, use 76940)

**47371** cryosurgical

(For imaging guidance, use 76940)

**47379** Unlisted laparoscopic procedure, liver

## Other Procedures

**47380** Ablation, open, of 1 or more liver tumor(s); radiofrequency

(For imaging guidance, use 76940)

**47381** cryosurgical

(For imaging guidance, use 76940)

⊙ **47382** Ablation, 1 or more liver tumor(s), percutaneous, radiofrequency

(For imaging guidance and monitoring, see 76940, 77013, 77022)

**47399** Unlisted procedure, liver

# Biliary Tract

## Incision

**47400** Hepaticotomy or hepaticostomy with exploration, drainage, or removal of calculus

**47420** Choledochotomy or choledochostomy with exploration, drainage, or removal of calculus, with or without cholecystotomy; without transduodenal sphincterotomy or sphincteroplasty

**47425** with transduodenal sphincterotomy or sphincteroplasty

**47460** Transduodenal sphincterotomy or sphincteroplasty, with or without transduodenal extraction of calculus (separate procedure)

**47480** Cholecystotomy or cholecystostomy, open, with exploration, drainage, or removal of calculus (separate procedure)

(For percutaneous cholecystostomy, use 47490)

## Introduction

**47490** Cholecystostomy, percutaneous, complete procedure, including imaging guidance, catheter placement, cholecystogram when performed, and radiological supervision and interpretation

(Do not report 47490 in conjunction with 47505, 74305, 75989, 76942, 77002, 77012, 77021)

**47500** Injection procedure for percutaneous transhepatic cholangiography

(For radiological supervision and interpretation, use 74320)

**47505** Injection procedure for cholangiography through an existing catheter (eg, percutaneous transhepatic or T-tube)

(For radiological supervision and interpretation, use 74305)

**47510** Introduction of percutaneous transhepatic catheter for biliary drainage

(For radiological supervision and interpretation, use 75980)

**47511** Introduction of percutaneous transhepatic stent for internal and external biliary drainage

(For radiological supervision and interpretation, use 75982)

⊙ **47525** Change of percutaneous biliary drainage catheter

(For radiological supervision and interpretation, use 75984)

**47530** Revision and/or reinsertion of transhepatic tube

(For radiological supervision and interpretation, use 75984)

Digestive

## Endoscopy

Surgical endoscopy always includes diagnostic endoscopy.

**+ 47550**     Biliary endoscopy, intraoperative (choledochoscopy) (List separately in addition to code for primary procedure)

**▲ 47552**     Biliary endoscopy, percutaneous via T-tube or other tract; diagnostic, with collection of specimen(s) by brushing and/or washing, when performed (separate procedure)

**47553**          with biopsy, single or multiple

**47554**          with removal of calculus/calculi

**47555**          with dilation of biliary duct stricture(s) without stent

**47556**          with dilation of biliary duct stricture(s) with stent

►(For ERCP, see 43260-43278, 74328, 74329, 74330, 74363, 75982)◄

(If imaging guidance is performed, see 74363, 75982)

## Laparoscopy

Surgical laparoscopy always includes diagnostic laparoscopy. To report a diagnostic laparoscopy (peritoneoscopy) (separate procedure), use 49320.

**47560**     Laparoscopy, surgical; with guided transhepatic cholangiography, without biopsy

**47561**          with guided transhepatic cholangiography with biopsy

**47562**          cholecystectomy

**47563**          cholecystectomy with cholangiography

**47564**          cholecystectomy with exploration of common duct

**47570**          cholecystoenterostomy

**47579**     Unlisted laparoscopy procedure, biliary tract

## Excision

**47600**     Cholecystectomy;

**47605**          with cholangiography

(For laparoscopic approach, see 47562-47564)

**47610**     Cholecystectomy with exploration of common duct;

(For cholecystectomy with exploration of common duct with biliary endoscopy, use 47610 with 47550)

**47612**          with choledochoenterostomy

**47620**          with transduodenal sphincterotomy or sphincteroplasty, with or without cholangiography

**47630**     Biliary duct stone extraction, percutaneous via T-tube tract, basket, or snare (eg, Burhenne technique)

(For radiological supervision and interpretation, use 74327)

**47700**     Exploration for congenital atresia of bile ducts, without repair, with or without liver biopsy, with or without cholangiography

(Do not report modifier 63 in conjunction with 47700)

**47701**     Portoenterostomy (eg, Kasai procedure)

(Do not report modifier 63 in conjunction with 47701)

**47711**     Excision of bile duct tumor, with or without primary repair of bile duct; extrahepatic

**47712**          intrahepatic

(For anastomosis, see 47760-47800)

**47715**     Excision of choledochal cyst

## Repair

**47720**     Cholecystoenterostomy; direct

(For laparoscopic approach, use 47570)

**47721**          with gastroenterostomy

**47740**          Roux-en-Y

**47741**          Roux-en-Y with gastroenterostomy

**47760**     Anastomosis, of extrahepatic biliary ducts and gastrointestinal tract

**47765**     Anastomosis, of intrahepatic ducts and gastrointestinal tract

**47780**     Anastomosis, Roux-en-Y, of extrahepatic biliary ducts and gastrointestinal tract

**47785**     Anastomosis, Roux-en-Y, of intrahepatic biliary ducts and gastrointestinal tract

**47800**     Reconstruction, plastic, of extrahepatic biliary ducts with end-to-end anastomosis

**47801**     Placement of choledochal stent

**47802**     U-tube hepaticoenterostomy

**47900**     Suture of extrahepatic biliary duct for pre-existing injury (separate procedure)

## Other Procedures

**47999**     Unlisted procedure, biliary tract

## Pancreas

►(For peroral pancreatic endoscopic procedures, see 43260-43265, 43274-43278)◄

## Incision

**48000**     Placement of drains, peripancreatic, for acute pancreatitis;

**48001**          with cholecystostomy, gastrostomy, and jejunostomy

**48020**     Removal of pancreatic calculus

**Digestive**

## Excision

**48100**  Biopsy of pancreas, open (eg, fine needle aspiration, needle core biopsy, wedge biopsy)

**48102**  Biopsy of pancreas, percutaneous needle

(For radiological supervision and interpretation, see 76942, 77002, 77012, 77021)

(For fine needle aspiration, use 10022)

(For evaluation of fine needle aspirate, see 88172, 88173)

**48105**  Resection or debridement of pancreas and peripancreatic tissue for acute necrotizing pancreatitis

**48120**  Excision of lesion of pancreas (eg, cyst, adenoma)

**48140**  Pancreatectomy, distal subtotal, with or without splenectomy; without pancreaticojejunostomy

**48145**  with pancreaticojejunostomy

**48146**  Pancreatectomy, distal, near-total with preservation of duodenum (Child-type procedure)

**48148**  Excision of ampulla of Vater

**48150**  Pancreatectomy, proximal subtotal with total duodenectomy, partial gastrectomy, choledochoenterostomy and gastrojejunostomy (Whipple-type procedure); with pancreatojejunostomy

**48152**  without pancreatojejunostomy

**48153**  Pancreatectomy, proximal subtotal with near-total duodenectomy, choledochoenterostomy and duodenojejunostomy (pylorus-sparing, Whipple-type procedure); with pancreatojejunostomy

**48154**  without pancreatojejunostomy

**48155**  Pancreatectomy, total

**48160**  Pancreatectomy, total or subtotal, with autologous transplantation of pancreas or pancreatic islet cells

## Introduction

**+ 48400**  Injection procedure for intraoperative pancreatography (List separately in addition to code for primary procedure)

(For radiological supervision and interpretation, see 74300-74305)

## Repair

**48500**  Marsupialization of pancreatic cyst

**48510**  External drainage, pseudocyst of pancreas, open

▶(48511 has been deleted)◀

▶(For percutaneous image-guided fluid collection drainage by catheter of pancreatic pseudocyst, use 49405)◀

**48520**  Internal anastomosis of pancreatic cyst to gastrointestinal tract; direct

**48540**  Roux-en-Y

**48545**  Pancreatorrhaphy for injury

**48547**  Duodenal exclusion with gastrojejunostomy for pancreatic injury

**48548**  Pancreaticojejunostomy, side-to-side anastomosis (Puestow-type operation)

## Pancreas Transplantation

Pancreas allotransplantation involves three distinct components of physician work:

1. *Cadaver donor pancreatectomy,* which includes harvesting the pancreas graft, with or without duodenal segment, and cold preservation of the graft (perfusing with cold preservation solution and cold maintenance) (use 48550).

2. *Backbench work:*

   Standard preparation of a cadaver donor pancreas allograft prior to transplantation includes dissection of the allograft from surrounding soft tissues, splenectomy, duodenotomy, ligation of bile duct, ligation of mesenteric vessels, and Y-graft arterial anastomoses from the iliac artery to the superior mesenteric artery and to the splenic artery (use 48551).

   Additional reconstruction of a cadaver donor pancreas allograft prior to transplantation may include venous anastomosis(es) (use 48552).

3. *Recipient pancreas allotransplantation,* which includes transplantation of allograft, and care of the recipient (use 48554).

**48550**  Donor pancreatectomy (including cold preservation), with or without duodenal segment for transplantation

**48551**  Backbench standard preparation of cadaver donor pancreas allograft prior to transplantation, including dissection of allograft from surrounding soft tissues, splenectomy, duodenotomy, ligation of bile duct, ligation of mesenteric vessels, and Y-graft arterial anastomoses from iliac artery to superior mesenteric artery and to splenic artery

**48552**  Backbench reconstruction of cadaver donor pancreas allograft prior to transplantation, venous anastomosis, each

(Do not report 48551 and 48552 in conjunction with 35531, 35563, 35685, 38100-38102, 44010, 44820, 44850, 47460, 47505-47525, 47550-47556, 48100-48120, 48545)

**48554**  Transplantation of pancreatic allograft

**48556**  Removal of transplanted pancreatic allograft

## Other Procedures

**48999**  Unlisted procedure, pancreas

Digestive

# Abdomen, Peritoneum, and Omentum

## Incision

**49000**   Exploratory laparotomy, exploratory celiotomy with or without biopsy(s) (separate procedure)

(To report wound exploration due to penetrating trauma without laparotomy, use 20102)

**49002**   Reopening of recent laparotomy

(To report re-exploration of hepatic wound for removal of packing, use 47362)

**49010**   Exploration, retroperitoneal area with or without biopsy(s) (separate procedure)

(To report wound exploration due to penetrating trauma without laparotomy, use 20102)

**49020**   Drainage of peritoneal abscess or localized peritonitis, exclusive of appendiceal abscess, open

(For appendiceal abscess, use 44900)

►(49021 has been deleted)◄

►(For percutaneous image-guided fluid collection drainage by catheter of peritoneal abscess or localized peritonitis, use 49406)◄

**49040**   Drainage of subdiaphragmatic or subphrenic abscess, open

►(49041 has been deleted)◄

►(For percutaneous drainage of subdiaphragmatic or subphrenic abscess, use 49406)◄

**49060**   Drainage of retroperitoneal abscess, open

►(49061 has been deleted)◄

►(For percutaneous drainage of retroperitoneal abscess, use 49406)◄

**49062**   Drainage of extraperitoneal lymphocele to peritoneal cavity, open

(49080, 49081 have been deleted. To report, see 49082-49084)

**49082**   Abdominal paracentesis (diagnostic or therapeutic); without imaging guidance

**49083**       with imaging guidance

(Do not report 49083 in conjunction with 76942, 77002, 77012, 77021)

**49084**   Peritoneal lavage, including imaging guidance, when performed

(Do not report 49084 in conjunction with 76942, 77002, 77012, 77021)

## Excision, Destruction

(For lysis of intestinal adhesions, use 44005)

**49180**   Biopsy, abdominal or retroperitoneal mass, percutaneous needle

(If imaging guidance is performed, see 76942, 77002, 77012, 77021)

(For fine needle aspiration, use 10021 or 10022)

(For evaluation of fine needle aspirate, see 88172, 88173)

**49203**   Excision or destruction, open, intra-abdominal tumors, cysts or endometriomas, 1 or more peritoneal, mesenteric, or retroperitoneal primary or secondary tumors; largest tumor 5 cm diameter or less

**49204**       largest tumor 5.1-10.0 cm diameter

**49205**       largest tumor greater than 10.0 cm diameter

(Do not report 49203-49205 in conjunction with 38770, 38780, 49000, 49010, 49215, 50010, 50205, 50225, 50236, 50250, 50290, 58900-58960)

(For partial or total nephrectomy, use 50220 or 50240 in conjunction with 49203-49205)

(For colectomy, use 44140 in conjunction with 49203-49205)

(For small bowel resection, use 44120 in conjunction with 49203-49205)

(For vena caval resection with reconstruction, use 49203-49205 in conjunction with 37799)

(For resection of recurrent ovarian, tubal, primary peritoneal, or uterine malignancy, see 58957, 58958)

(For cryoablation of renal tumors, see 50250, 50593)

**49215**   Excision of presacral or sacrococcygeal tumor

(Do not report modifier 63 in conjunction with 49215)

**49220**   Staging laparotomy for Hodgkins disease or lymphoma (includes splenectomy, needle or open biopsies of both liver lobes, possibly also removal of abdominal nodes, abdominal node and/or bone marrow biopsies, ovarian repositioning)

**49250**   Umbilectomy, omphalectomy, excision of umbilicus (separate procedure)

**49255**   Omentectomy, epiploectomy, resection of omentum (separate procedure)

## Laparoscopy

Surgical laparoscopy always includes diagnostic laparoscopy. To report a diagnostic laparoscopy (peritoneoscopy), (separate procedure), use 49320.

For laparoscopic fulguration or excision of lesions of the ovary, pelvic viscera, or peritoneal surface use 58662.

**49320**   Laparoscopy, abdomen, peritoneum, and omentum, diagnostic, with or without collection of specimen(s) by brushing or washing (separate procedure)

**Digestive**

---

**49321** Laparoscopy, surgical; with biopsy (single or multiple)

**49322** with aspiration of cavity or cyst (eg, ovarian cyst) (single or multiple)

**49323** with drainage of lymphocele to peritoneal cavity

►(For open drainage, use 49060)◄

**49324** with insertion of tunneled intraperitoneal catheter

(For subcutaneous extension of intraperitoneal catheter with remote chest exit site, use 49435 in conjunction with 49324)

(For open insertion of tunneled intraperitoneal catheter, use 49421)

**49325** with revision of previously placed intraperitoneal cannula or catheter, with removal of intraluminal obstructive material if performed

**+ 49326** with omentopexy (omental tacking procedure) (List separately in addition to code for primary procedure)

(Use 49326 in conjunction with 49324, 49325)

**+ 49327** with placement of interstitial device(s) for radiation therapy guidance (eg, fiducial markers, dosimeter), intra-abdominal, intrapelvic, and/or retroperitoneum, including imaging guidance, if performed, single or multiple (List separately in addition to code for primary procedure)

(Use 49327 in conjunction with laparoscopic abdominal, pelvic, or retroperitoneal procedure[s] performed concurrently)

(For placement of interstitial device[s] for intra-abdominal, intrapelvic, and/or retroperitoneal radiation therapy guidance concurrent with open procedure, use 49412)

(For percutaneous placement of interstitial device[s] for intra-abdominal, intrapelvic, and/or retroperitoneal radiation therapy guidance, use 49411)

**49329** Unlisted laparoscopy procedure, abdomen, peritoneum and omentum

## Introduction, Revision, Removal

**49400** Injection of air or contrast into peritoneal cavity (separate procedure)

(For radiological supervision and interpretation, use 74190)

**49402** Removal of peritoneal foreign body from peritoneal cavity

(For lysis of intestinal adhesions, use 44005)

►(For open or percutaneous peritoneal drainage or lavage, see 49406, 49020, 49040, 49082-49084, as appropriate)◄

►(For percutaneous insertion of a tunneled intraperitoneal catheter without subcutaneous port, use 49418)◄

⊙● **49405** Image-guided fluid collection drainage by catheter (eg, abscess, hematoma, seroma, lymphocele, cyst); visceral (eg, kidney, liver, spleen, lung/mediastinum), percutaneous

►(Do not report 49405 in conjunction with 75989, 76942, 77002, 77003, 77012, 77021)◄

►(For percutaneous cholecystostomy, use 47490)◄

►(For pneumonostomy, use 32200)◄

►(For thoracentesis, see 32554, 32555)◄

►(For pleural drainage, see 32556, 32557)◄

►(For open drainage, see 32200, 47010, 48510)◄

⊙● **49406** peritoneal or retroperitoneal, percutaneous

►(Do not report 49406 in conjunction with 75989, 76942, 77002, 77003, 77012, 77021)◄

►(For abdominal paracentesis [diagnostic or therapeutic], see 49082, 49083)◄

►(For open drainage, see 44900, 49020, 49040, 49060, 50020, 58805, 58822)◄

►(For peritoneal lavage or paracentesis, see 49082, 49083, 49084)◄

►(For percutaneous insertion of a tunneled intraperitoneal catheter without subcutaneous port, use 49418)◄

⊙● **49407** peritoneal or retroperitoneal, transvaginal or transrectal

►(Do not report 49407 in conjunction with 75989, 76942, 77002, 77003, 77012, 77021)◄

►(Report 49405, 49406, 49407 separately for each individual collection drained with a separate catheter)◄

►(For thoracentesis, see 32554, 32555)◄

►(For percutaneous pleural drainage, see 32556, 32557)◄

►(For open drainage, see 45000, 58800, 58820)◄

►(For percutaneous image-guided fluid collection drainage by catheter [eg, abscess, hematoma, seroma, lymphocele, cyst] for soft tissue [eg, extremity, abdominal wall, neck], use 10030)◄

►(For open or percutaneous peritoneal drainage or lavage, see 49020, 49040, 49082 as appropriate)◄

⊙ **49411** Placement of interstitial device(s) for radiation therapy guidance (eg, fiducial markers, dosimeter), percutaneous, intra-abdominal, intra-pelvic (except prostate), and/or retroperitoneum, single or multiple

(Report supply of device separately)

(For imaging guidance, see 76942, 77002, 77012, 77021)

(For percutaneous placement of interstitial device[s] for intra-thoracic radiation therapy guidance, use 32553)

**+ 49412** Placement of interstitial device(s) for radiation therapy guidance (eg, fiducial markers, dosimeter), open, intra-abdominal, intrapelvic, and/or retroperitoneum, including image guidance, if performed, single or multiple (List separately in addition to code for primary procedure)

(Use 49412 in conjunction with open abdominal, pelvic, or retroperitoneal procedure[s] performed concurrently)

(For placement of interstitial device[s] for intra-abdominal, intrapelvic, and/or retroperitoneal radiation therapy guidance concurrent with laparoscopic procedure, use 49327)

(For percutaneous placement of interstitial device[s] for intra-abdominal, intrapelvic, and/or retroperitoneal radiation therapy guidance, use 49411)

**⊙ 49418** Insertion of tunneled intraperitoneal catheter (eg, dialysis, intraperitoneal chemotherapy instillation, management of ascites), complete procedure, including imaging guidance, catheter placement, contrast injection when performed, and radiological supervision and interpretation, percutaneous

**49419** Insertion of tunneled intraperitoneal catheter, with subcutaneous port (ie, totally implantable)

(For removal, use 49422)

▶(49420 has been deleted. To report open placement of a tunneled intraperitoneal catheter for dialysis, use 49421. To report open or percutaneous peritoneal drainage or lavage, see 49406, 49020, 49040, 49082-49084, as appropriate. To report percutaneous insertion of a tunneled intraperitoneal catheter without subcutaneous port, use 49418)◀

**49421** Insertion of tunneled intraperitoneal catheter for dialysis, open

(For laparoscopic insertion of tunneled intraperitoneal catheter, use 49324)

(For subcutaneous extension of intraperitoneal catheter with remote chest exit site, use 49435 in conjunction with 49421)

**49422** Removal of tunneled intraperitoneal catheter

(For removal of a non-tunneled catheter, use appropriate E/M code)

**49423** Exchange of previously placed abscess or cyst drainage catheter under radiological guidance (separate procedure)

(For radiological supervision and interpretation, use 75984)

**49424** Contrast injection for assessment of abscess or cyst via previously placed drainage catheter or tube (separate procedure)

(For radiological supervision and interpretation, use 76080)

**49425** Insertion of peritoneal-venous shunt

**49426** Revision of peritoneal-venous shunt

(For shunt patency test, use 78291)

**49427** Injection procedure (eg, contrast media) for evaluation of previously placed peritoneal-venous shunt

(For radiological supervision and interpretation, see 75809, 78291)

**49428** Ligation of peritoneal-venous shunt

**49429** Removal of peritoneal-venous shunt

**+ 49435** Insertion of subcutaneous extension to intraperitoneal cannula or catheter with remote chest exit site (List separately in addition to code for primary procedure)

(Use 49435 in conjunction with 49324, 49421)

**49436** Delayed creation of exit site from embedded subcutaneous segment of intraperitoneal cannula or catheter

## Initial Placement

Do not additionally report 43752 for placement of a nasogastric (NG) or orogastric (OG) tube to insufflate the stomach prior to percutaneous gastrointestinal tube placement. NG or OG tube placement is considered part of the procedure in this family of codes.

**⊙ 49440** Insertion of gastrostomy tube, percutaneous, under fluoroscopic guidance including contrast injection(s), image documentation and report

(For conversion to a gastro-jejunostomy tube at the time of initial gastrostomy tube placement, use 49440 in conjunction with 49446)

**⊙ 49441** Insertion of duodenostomy or jejunostomy tube, percutaneous, under fluoroscopic guidance including contrast injection(s), image documentation and report

(For conversion of gastrostomy tube to gastro-jejunostomy tube, use 49446)

**⊙ 49442** Insertion of cecostomy or other colonic tube, percutaneous, under fluoroscopic guidance including contrast injection(s), image documentation and report

## Conversion

**⊙ 49446** Conversion of gastrostomy tube to gastro-jejunostomy tube, percutaneous, under fluoroscopic guidance including contrast injection(s), image documentation and report

(For conversion to a gastro-jejunostomy tube at the time of initial gastrostomy tube placement, use 49446 in conjunction with 49440)

## Replacement

If an existing gastrostomy, duodenostomy, jejunostomy, gastro-jejunostomy, or cecostomy (or other colonic) tube is removed and a new tube is placed via a separate

**Digestive**

percutaneous access site, the placement of the new tube is not considered a replacement and would be reported using the appropriate initial placement codes 49440-49442.

**49450** Replacement of gastrostomy or cecostomy (or other colonic) tube, percutaneous, under fluoroscopic guidance including contrast injection(s), image documentation and report

(To report a percutaneous change of a gastrostomy tube without imaging or endoscopic guidance, use 43760)

**49451** Replacement of duodenostomy or jejunostomy tube, percutaneous, under fluoroscopic guidance including contrast injection(s), image documentation and report

**49452** Replacement of gastro-jejunostomy tube, percutaneous, under fluoroscopic guidance including contrast injection(s), image documentation and report

## Mechanical Removal of Obstructive Material

**49460** Mechanical removal of obstructive material from gastrostomy, duodenostomy, jejunostomy, gastro-jejunostomy, or cecostomy (or other colonic) tube, any method, under fluoroscopic guidance including contrast injection(s), if performed, image documentation and report

(Do not report 49460 in conjunction with 49450-49452, 49465)

## Other

**49465** Contrast injection(s) for radiological evaluation of existing gastrostomy, duodenostomy, jejunostomy, gastro-jejunostomy, or cecostomy (or other colonic) tube, from a percutaneous approach including image documentation and report

(Do not report 49465 in conjunction with 49450-49460)

# Repair

## Hernioplasty, Herniorrhaphy, Herniotomy

The hernia repair codes in this section are categorized primarily by the type of hernia (inguinal, femoral, incisional, etc).

Some types of hernias are further categorized as "initial" or "recurrent" based on whether or not the hernia has required previous repair(s).

Additional variables accounted for by some of the codes include patient age and clinical presentation (reducible vs. incarcerated or strangulated).

With the exception of the incisional hernia repairs (see 49560-49566) the use of mesh or other prostheses is not separately reported.

The excision/repair of strangulated organs or structures such as testicle(s), intestine, ovaries are reported by using the appropriate code for the excision/repair (eg, 44120, 54520, and 58940) in addition to the appropriate code for the repair of the strangulated hernia.

(For reduction and repair of intra-abdominal hernia, use 44050)

(For debridement of abdominal wall, see 11042, 11043)

(Codes 49491-49651 are unilateral procedures. To report bilateral procedure, report modifier 50 with the appropriate procedure code)

**49491** Repair, initial inguinal hernia, preterm infant (younger than 37 weeks gestation at birth), performed from birth up to 50 weeks postconception age, with or without hydrocelectomy; reducible

**49492** incarcerated or strangulated

(Do not report modifier 63 in conjunction with 49491, 49492)

(Postconception age equals gestational age at birth plus age of infant in weeks at the time of the hernia repair. Initial inguinal hernia repairs that are performed on preterm infants who are older than 50 weeks postconception age and younger than age 6 months at the time of surgery, should be reported using codes 49495, 49496)

**49495** Repair, initial inguinal hernia, full term infant younger than age 6 months, or preterm infant older than 50 weeks postconception age and younger than age 6 months at the time of surgery, with or without hydrocelectomy; reducible

**49496** incarcerated or strangulated

(Do not report modifier 63 in conjunction with 49495, 49496)

(Postconception age equals gestational age at birth plus age in weeks at the time of the hernia repair. Initial inguinal hernia repairs that are performed on preterm infants who are younger than or up to 50 weeks postconception age but younger than 6 months of age since birth, should be reported using codes 49491, 49492. Inguinal hernia repairs on infants age 6 months to younger than 5 years should be reported using codes 49500-49501)

**49500** Repair initial inguinal hernia, age 6 months to younger than 5 years, with or without hydrocelectomy; reducible

**49501** incarcerated or strangulated

**49505** Repair initial inguinal hernia, age 5 years or older; reducible

**49507** incarcerated or strangulated

(For inguinal hernia repair, with simple orchiectomy, see 49505 or 49507 and 54520)

(For inguinal hernia repair, with excision of hydrocele or spermatocele, see 49505 or 49507 and 54840 or 55040)

49520 Repair recurrent inguinal hernia, any age; reducible

49521      incarcerated or strangulated

49525 Repair inguinal hernia, sliding, any age

(For incarcerated or strangulated inguinal hernia repair, see 49496, 49501, 49507, 49521)

49540 Repair lumbar hernia

49550 Repair initial femoral hernia, any age; reducible

49553      incarcerated or strangulated

49555 Repair recurrent femoral hernia; reducible

49557      incarcerated or strangulated

49560 Repair initial incisional or ventral hernia; reducible

49561      incarcerated or strangulated

49565 Repair recurrent incisional or ventral hernia; reducible

49566      incarcerated or strangulated

+ 49568 Implantation of mesh or other prosthesis for open incisional or ventral hernia repair or mesh for closure of debridement for necrotizing soft tissue infection (List separately in addition to code for the incisional or ventral hernia repair)

(Use 49568 in conjunction with 11004-11006, 49560-49566)

49570 Repair epigastric hernia (eg, preperitoneal fat); reducible (separate procedure)

49572      incarcerated or strangulated

49580 Repair umbilical hernia, younger than age 5 years; reducible

49582      incarcerated or strangulated

49585 Repair umbilical hernia, age 5 years or older; reducible

49587      incarcerated or strangulated

49590 Repair spigelian hernia

49600 Repair of small omphalocele, with primary closure

(Do not report modifier 63 in conjunction with 49600)

49605 Repair of large omphalocele or gastroschisis; with or without prosthesis

49606      with removal of prosthesis, final reduction and closure, in operating room

(Do not report modifier 63 in conjunction with 49605, 49606)

49610 Repair of omphalocele (Gross type operation); first stage

49611      second stage

(Do not report modifier 63 in conjunction with 49610, 49611)

(For diaphragmatic or hiatal hernia repair, see 39503, 43332)

(For surgical repair of omentum, use 49999)

## *Laparoscopy*

Surgical laparoscopy always includes diagnostic laparoscopy. To report a diagnostic laparoscopy (peritoneoscopy) (separate procedure), use 49320.

49650 Laparoscopy, surgical; repair initial inguinal hernia

49651      repair recurrent inguinal hernia

49652 Laparoscopy, surgical, repair, ventral, umbilical, spigelian or epigastric hernia (includes mesh insertion, when performed); reducible

(Do not report 49652 in conjunction with 44180, 49568)

49653      incarcerated or strangulated

(Do not report 49653 in conjunction with 44180, 49568)

49654 Laparoscopy, surgical, repair, incisional hernia (includes mesh insertion, when performed); reducible

(Do not report 49654 in conjunction with 44180, 49568)

49655      incarcerated or strangulated

(Do not report 49655 in conjunction with 44180, 49568)

49656 Laparoscopy, surgical, repair, recurrent incisional hernia (includes mesh insertion, when performed); reducible

(Do not report 49656 in conjunction with 44180, 49568)

49657      incarcerated or strangulated

(Do not report 49657 in conjunction with 44180, 49568)

49659 Unlisted laparoscopy procedure, hernioplasty, herniorrhaphy, herniotomy

## Suture

49900 Suture, secondary, of abdominal wall for evisceration or dehiscence

(For suture of ruptured diaphragm, see 39540, 39541)

(For debridement of abdominal wall, see 11042, 11043)

## Other Procedures

49904 Omental flap, extra-abdominal (eg, for reconstruction of sternal and chest wall defects)

(Code 49904 includes harvest and transfer. If a second surgeon harvests the omental flap, then the 2 surgeons should code 49904 as co-surgeons, using modifier 62)

+ 49905 Omental flap, intra-abdominal (List separately in addition to code for primary procedure)

(Do not report 49905 in conjunction with 44700)

49906 Free omental flap with microvascular anastomosis

(Do not report code 69990 in addition to 49906)

49999 Unlisted procedure, abdomen, peritoneum and omentum

**Digestive**

# Urinary System

(For provision of chemotherapeutic agents, report both the specific service in addition to code(s) for the specific substance(s) or drug(s) provided)

## Kidney

### Incision

(For retroperitoneal exploration, abscess, tumor, or cyst, see 49010, 49060, 49203-49205)

**50010** Renal exploration, not necessitating other specific procedures

(For laparoscopic ablation of renal mass lesion(s), use 50542)

**50020** Drainage of perirenal or renal abscess, open

▶(50021 has been deleted)◀

▶(For percutaneous image-guided fluid collection drainage by catheter of perirenal/renal abscess, use 49405)◀

**50040** Nephrostomy, nephrotomy with drainage

**50045** Nephrotomy, with exploration

(For renal endoscopy performed in conjunction with this procedure, see 50570-50580)

**50060** Nephrolithotomy; removal of calculus

**50065** secondary surgical operation for calculus

**50070** complicated by congenital kidney abnormality

**50075** removal of large staghorn calculus filling renal pelvis and calyces (including anatrophic pyelolithotomy)

**50080** Percutaneous nephrostolithotomy or pyelostolithotomy, with or without dilation, endoscopy, lithotripsy, stenting, or basket extraction; up to 2 cm

**50081** over 2 cm

(For establishment of nephrostomy without nephrostolithotomy, see 50040, 50395, 52334)

(For fluoroscopic guidance, see 76000, 76001)

**50100** Transection or repositioning of aberrant renal vessels (separate procedure)

**50120** Pyelotomy; with exploration

(For renal endoscopy performed in conjunction with this procedure, see 50570-50580)

**50125** with drainage, pyelostomy

**50130** with removal of calculus (pyelolithotomy, pelviolithotomy, including coagulum pyelolithotomy)

**50135** complicated (eg, secondary operation, congenital kidney abnormality)

(For supply of anticarcinogenic agents, use 99070 in addition to code for primary procedure)

### Excision

(For excision of retroperitoneal tumor or cyst, see 49203-49205)

(For laparoscopic ablation of renal mass lesion(s), use 50542)

⊙ **50200** Renal biopsy; percutaneous, by trocar or needle

(For radiological supervision and interpretation, see 76942, 77002, 77012, 77021)

(For fine needle aspiration, use 10022)

(For evaluation of fine needle aspirate, see 88172, 88173)

**50205** by surgical exposure of kidney

**50220** Nephrectomy, including partial ureterectomy, any open approach including rib resection;

**50225** complicated because of previous surgery on same kidney

**50230** radical, with regional lymphadenectomy and/or vena caval thrombectomy

(When vena caval resection with reconstruction is necessary, use 37799)

**50234** Nephrectomy with total ureterectomy and bladder cuff; through same incision

**50236** through separate incision

**50240** Nephrectomy, partial

(For laparoscopic partial nephrectomy, use 50543)

**50250** Ablation, open, 1 or more renal mass lesion(s), cryosurgical, including intraoperative ultrasound guidance and monitoring, if performed

(For laparoscopic ablation of renal mass lesions, use 50542)

(For percutaneous ablation of renal tumors, see 50592, 50593)

**50280** Excision or unroofing of cyst(s) of kidney

(For laparoscopic ablation of renal cysts, use 50541)

**50290** Excision of perinephric cyst

## Renal Transplantation

Renal *auto*transplantation includes reimplantation of the autograft as the primary procedure, along with secondary extra-corporeal procedure(s) (eg, partial nephrectomy, nephrolithotomy) reported with modifier 51 (see 50380 and applicable secondary procedure(s)).

Renal *allo*transplantation involves three distinct components of physician work:

1. ***Cadaver donor nephrectomy, unilateral or bilateral,*** which includes harvesting the graft(s) and cold preservation of the graft(s) (perfusing with cold preservation solution and cold maintenance) (use 50300). ***Living donor nephrectomy,*** which includes

Urinary

harvesting the graft, cold preservation of the graft (perfusing with cold preservation solution and cold maintenance), and care of the donor (see 50320, 50547).

2. ***Backbench work:***

Standard preparation of a cadaver donor renal allograft prior to transplantation including dissection and removal of perinephric fat, diaphragmatic and retroperitoneal attachments; excision of adrenal gland; and preparation of ureter(s), renal vein(s), and renal artery(s), ligating branches, as necessary (use 50323).

Standard preparation of a living donor renal allograft (open or laparoscopic) prior to transplantation including dissection and removal of perinephric fat and preparation of ureter(s), renal vein(s), and renal artery(s), ligating branches, as necessary (use 50325).

Additional reconstruction of a cadaver or living donor renal allograft prior to transplantation may include venous, arterial, and/or ureteral anastomosis(es) necessary for implantation (see 50327-50329).

3. ***Recipient renal allotransplantation,*** which includes transplantation of the allograft (with or without recipient nephrectomy) and care of the recipient (see 50360, 50365).

> (For dialysis, see 90935-90999)
>
> (For laparoscopic donor nephrectomy, use 50547)
>
> (For laparoscopic drainage of lymphocele to peritoneal cavity, use 49323)

**50300**    Donor nephrectomy (including cold preservation); from cadaver donor, unilateral or bilateral

**50320**        open, from living donor

**50323**    Backbench standard preparation of cadaver donor renal allograft prior to transplantation, including dissection and removal of perinephric fat, diaphragmatic and retroperitoneal attachments, excision of adrenal gland, and preparation of ureter(s), renal vein(s), and renal artery(s), ligating branches, as necessary

> (Do not report 50323 in conjunction with 60540, 60545)

**50325**    Backbench standard preparation of living donor renal allograft (open or laparoscopic) prior to transplantation, including dissection and removal of perinephric fat and preparation of ureter(s), renal vein(s), and renal artery(s), ligating branches, as necessary

**50327**    Backbench reconstruction of cadaver or living donor renal allograft prior to transplantation; venous anastomosis, each

**50328**        arterial anastomosis, each

**50329**        ureteral anastomosis, each

**50340**    Recipient nephrectomy (separate procedure)

> (For bilateral procedure, report 50340 with modifier 50)

**50360**    Renal allotransplantation, implantation of graft; without recipient nephrectomy

**50365**        with recipient nephrectomy

> (For bilateral procedure, report 50365 with modifier 50)

**50370**    Removal of transplanted renal allograft

**50380**    Renal autotransplantation, reimplantation of kidney

> (For renal autotransplantation extra-corporeal [bench] surgery, use autotransplantation as the primary procedure and report secondary procedure[s] [eg, partial nephrectomy, nephrolithotomy] with modifier 51)

## Introduction

### Renal Pelvis Catheter Procedures

#### *Internally Dwelling*

⊙ **50382**    Removal (via snare/capture) and replacement of internally dwelling ureteral stent via percutaneous approach, including radiological supervision and interpretation

> (For bilateral procedure, use modifier 50)
>
> (For removal and replacement of an internally dwelling ureteral stent via a transurethral approach, use 50385)

⊙ **50384**    Removal (via snare/capture) of internally dwelling ureteral stent via percutaneous approach, including radiological supervision and interpretation

> (For bilateral procedure, use modifier 50)
>
> (Do not report 50382, 50384 in conjunction with 50395)
>
> (For removal of an internally dwelling ureteral stent via a transurethral approach, use 50386)

⊙ **50385**    Removal (via snare/capture) and replacement of internally dwelling ureteral stent via transurethral approach, without use of cystoscopy, including radiological supervision and interpretation

⊙ **50386**    Removal (via snare/capture) of internally dwelling ureteral stent via transurethral approach, without use of cystoscopy, including radiological supervision and interpretation

#### *Externally Accessible*

⊙ **50387**    Removal and replacement of externally accessible transnephric ureteral stent (eg, external/internal stent) requiring fluoroscopic guidance, including radiological supervision and interpretation

> (For bilateral procedure, use modifier 50)
>
> (For removal and replacement of externally accessible ureteral stent via ureterostomy or ilieal conduit, use 50688)

**Urinary**

(For removal without replacement of an externally accessible ureteral stent not requiring fluoroscopic guidance, see Evaluation and Management services codes)

**50389** Removal of nephrostomy tube, requiring fluoroscopic guidance (eg, with concurrent indwelling ureteral stent)

(Removal of nephrostomy tube not requiring fluoroscopic guidance is considered inherent to E/M services. Report the appropriate level of E/M service provided)

## Other Introduction Procedures

**50390** Aspiration and/or injection of renal cyst or pelvis by needle, percutaneous

(For radiological supervision and interpretation, see 74425, 74470, 76942, 77002, 77012, 77021)

(For evaluation of fine needle aspirate, see 88172, 88173)

**50391** Instillation(s) of therapeutic agent into renal pelvis and/or ureter through established nephrostomy, pyelostomy or ureterostomy tube (eg, anticarcinogenic or antifungal agent)

**50392** Introduction of intracatheter or catheter into renal pelvis for drainage and/or injection, percutaneous

(For radiological supervision and interpretation, see 74475, 76942, 77012)

**50393** Introduction of ureteral catheter or stent into ureter through renal pelvis for drainage and/or injection, percutaneous

(For radiological supervision and interpretation, see 74480, 76942, 77002, 77012)

**50394** Injection procedure for pyelography (as nephrostogram, pyelostogram, antegrade pyeloureterograms) through nephrostomy or pyelostomy tube, or indwelling ureteral catheter

(For radiological supervision and interpretation, use 74425)

**50395** Introduction of guide into renal pelvis and/or ureter with dilation to establish nephrostomy tract, percutaneous

(For radiological supervision and interpretation, see 74475, 74480, 74485)

(For nephrostolithotomy, see 50080, 50081)

(For retrograde percutaneous nephrostomy, use 52334)

(For endoscopic surgery, see 50551-50561)

**50396** Manometric studies through nephrostomy or pyelostomy tube, or indwelling ureteral catheter

(For radiological supervision and interpretation, see 74425, 74475, 74480)

**50398** Change of nephrostomy or pyelostomy tube

(For radiological supervision and interpretation, use 75984)

## Repair

**50400** Pyeloplasty (Foley Y-pyeloplasty), plastic operation on renal pelvis, with or without plastic operation on ureter, nephropexy, nephrostomy, pyelostomy, or ureteral splinting; simple

**50405** complicated (congenital kidney abnormality, secondary pyeloplasty, solitary kidney, calycoplasty)

(For laparoscopic approach, use 50544)

**50500** Nephrorrhaphy, suture of kidney wound or injury

**50520** Closure of nephrocutaneous or pyelocutaneous fistula

**50525** Closure of nephrovisceral fistula (eg, renocolic), including visceral repair; abdominal approach

**50526** thoracic approach

**50540** Symphysiotomy for horseshoe kidney with or without pyeloplasty and/or other plastic procedure, unilateral or bilateral (1 operation)

## Laparoscopy

Surgical laparoscopy always includes diagnostic laparoscopy. To report a diagnostic laparoscopy (peritoneoscopy) (separate procedure), use 49320.

**50541** Laparoscopy, surgical; ablation of renal cysts

**50542** ablation of renal mass lesion(s), including intraoperative ultrasound guidance and monitoring, when performed

(For open procedure, use 50250)

(For percutaneous ablation of renal tumors, see 50592, 50593)

**50543** partial nephrectomy

(For open procedure, use 50240)

**50544** pyeloplasty

**50545** radical nephrectomy (includes removal of Gerota's fascia and surrounding fatty tissue, removal of regional lymph nodes, and adrenalectomy)

(For open procedure, use 50230)

**50546** nephrectomy, including partial ureterectomy

**50547** donor nephrectomy (including cold preservation), from living donor

(For open procedure, use 50320)

(For backbench renal allograft standard preparation prior to transplantation, use 50325)

(For backbench renal allograft reconstruction prior to transplantation, see 50327-50329)

**50548** nephrectomy with total ureterectomy

(For open procedure, see 50234, 50236)

Urinary

**50549**     Unlisted laparoscopy procedure, renal

(For laparoscopic drainage of lymphocele to peritoneal cavity, use 49323)

## Endoscopy

(For supplies and materials, use 99070)

**50551**     Renal endoscopy through established nephrostomy or pyelostomy, with or without irrigation, instillation, or ureteropyelography, exclusive of radiologic service;

**50553**          with ureteral catheterization, with or without dilation of ureter

**50555**          with biopsy

**50557**          with fulguration and/or incision, with or without biopsy

**50561**          with removal of foreign body or calculus

**50562**          with resection of tumor

(When procedures 50570-50580 provide a significant identifiable service, they may be added to 50045 and 50120)

**50570**     Renal endoscopy through nephrotomy or pyelotomy, with or without irrigation, instillation, or ureteropyelography, exclusive of radiologic service;

(For nephrotomy, use 50045)

(For pyelotomy, use 50120)

**50572**          with ureteral catheterization, with or without dilation of ureter

**50574**          with biopsy

**50575**          with endopyelotomy (includes cystoscopy, ureteroscopy, dilation of ureter and ureteral pelvic junction, incision of ureteral pelvic junction and insertion of endopyelotomy stent)

**50576**          with fulguration and/or incision, with or without biopsy

**50580**          with removal of foreign body or calculus

## Other Procedures

**50590**     Lithotripsy, extracorporeal shock wave

⊙ **50592**     Ablation, 1 or more renal tumor(s), percutaneous, unilateral, radiofrequency

(50592 is a unilateral procedure. For bilateral procedure, report 50592 with modifier 50)

(For imaging guidance and monitoring, see 76940, 77013, 77022)

⊙ **50593**     Ablation, renal tumor(s), unilateral, percutaneous, cryotherapy

(50593 is a unilateral procedure. For bilateral procedure, report 50593 with modifier 50)

(For imaging guidance and monitoring, see codes 76940, 77013, 77022)

# Ureter

## Incision

**50600**     Ureterotomy with exploration or drainage (separate procedure)

(For ureteral endoscopy performed in conjunction with this procedure, see 50970-50980)

**50605**     Ureterotomy for insertion of indwelling stent, all types

**50610**     Ureterolithotomy; upper one-third of ureter

**50620**          middle one-third of ureter

**50630**          lower one-third of ureter

(For laparoscopic approach, use 50945)

(For transvesical ureterolithotomy, use 51060)

(For cystotomy with stone basket extraction of ureteral calculus, use 51065)

▶(For endoscopic extraction or manipulation of ureteral calculus, see 50080, 50081, 50561, 50961, 50980, 52320-52330, 52352, 52353, 52356)◀

## Excision

(For ureterocele, see 51535, 52300)

**50650**     Ureterectomy, with bladder cuff (separate procedure)

**50660**     Ureterectomy, total, ectopic ureter, combination abdominal, vaginal and/or perineal approach

## Introduction

**50684**     Injection procedure for ureterography or ureteropyelography through ureterostomy or indwelling ureteral catheter

(For radiological supervision and interpretation, use 74425)

**50686**     Manometric studies through ureterostomy or indwelling ureteral catheter

**50688**     Change of ureterostomy tube or externally accessible ureteral stent via ileal conduit

(If imaging guidance is performed, use 75984)

**50690**     Injection procedure for visualization of ileal conduit and/or ureteropyelography, exclusive of radiologic service

(For radiological supervision and interpretation, use 74425)

**Urinary**

## Repair

**50700** Ureteroplasty, plastic operation on ureter (eg, stricture)

**50715** Ureterolysis, with or without repositioning of ureter for retroperitoneal fibrosis

(For bilateral procedure, report 50715 with modifier 50)

**50722** Ureterolysis for ovarian vein syndrome

**50725** Ureterolysis for retrocaval ureter, with reanastomosis of upper urinary tract or vena cava

**50727** Revision of urinary-cutaneous anastomosis (any type urostomy);

**50728** with repair of fascial defect and hernia

**50740** Ureteropyelostomy, anastomosis of ureter and renal pelvis

**50750** Ureterocalycostomy, anastomosis of ureter to renal calyx

**50760** Ureteroureterostomy

**50770** Transureteroureterostomy, anastomosis of ureter to contralateral ureter

(Codes 50780-50785 include minor procedures to prevent vesicoureteral reflux)

**50780** Ureteroneocystostomy; anastomosis of single ureter to bladder

(For bilateral procedure, report 50780 with modifier 50)

(When combined with cystourethroplasty or vesical neck revision, use 51820)

**50782** anastomosis of duplicated ureter to bladder

**50783** with extensive ureteral tailoring

**50785** with vesico-psoas hitch or bladder flap

(For bilateral procedure, report 50785 with modifier 50)

**50800** Ureteroenterostomy, direct anastomosis of ureter to intestine

(For bilateral procedure, report 50800 with modifier 50)

**50810** Ureterosigmoidostomy, with creation of sigmoid bladder and establishment of abdominal or perineal colostomy, including intestine anastomosis

**50815** Ureterocolon conduit, including intestine anastomosis

(For bilateral procedure, report 50815 with modifier 50)

**50820** Ureteroileal conduit (ileal bladder), including intestine anastomosis (Bricker operation)

(For bilateral procedure, report 50820 with modifier 50)

(For combination of 50800-50820 with cystectomy, see 51580-51595)

**50825** Continent diversion, including intestine anastomosis using any segment of small and/or large intestine (Kock pouch or Camey enterocystoplasty)

**50830** Urinary undiversion (eg, taking down of ureteroileal conduit, ureterosigmoidostomy or ureteroenterostomy with ureteroureterostomy or ureteroneocystostomy)

**50840** Replacement of all or part of ureter by intestine segment, including intestine anastomosis

(For bilateral procedure, report 50840 with modifier 50)

**50845** Cutaneous appendico-vesicostomy

**50860** Ureterostomy, transplantation of ureter to skin

(For bilateral procedure, report 50860 with modifier 50)

**50900** Ureterorrhaphy, suture of ureter (separate procedure)

**50920** Closure of ureterocutaneous fistula

**50930** Closure of ureterovisceral fistula (including visceral repair)

**50940** Deligation of ureter

(For ureteroplasty, ureterolysis, see 50700-50860)

## Laparoscopy

Surgical laparoscopy always includes diagnostic laparoscopy. To report a diagnostic laparoscopy (peritoneoscopy) (separate procedure), use 49320.

**50945** Laparoscopy, surgical; ureterolithotomy

**50947** ureteroneocystostomy with cystoscopy and ureteral stent placement

**50948** ureteroneocystostomy without cystoscopy and ureteral stent placement

(For open ureteroneocystostomy, see 50780-50785)

**50949** Unlisted laparoscopy procedure, ureter

## Endoscopy

**50951** Ureteral endoscopy through established ureterostomy, with or without irrigation, instillation, or ureteropyelography, exclusive of radiologic service;

**50953** with ureteral catheterization, with or without dilation of ureter

**50955** with biopsy

**50957** with fulguration and/or incision, with or without biopsy

**50961** with removal of foreign body or calculus

(When procedures 50970-50980 provide a significant identifiable service, they may be added to 50600)

**50970** Ureteral endoscopy through ureterotomy, with or without irrigation, instillation, or ureteropyelography, exclusive of radiologic service;

(For ureterotomy, use 50600)

**50972** with ureteral catheterization, with or without dilation of ureter

**50974** with biopsy

**50976** with fulguration and/or incision, with or without biopsy

**50980** with removal of foreign body or calculus

# Bladder

## Incision

**51020**  Cystotomy or cystostomy; with fulguration and/or insertion of radioactive material

**51030**      with cryosurgical destruction of intravesical lesion

**51040**  Cystostomy, cystotomy with drainage

**51045**  Cystotomy, with insertion of ureteral catheter or stent (separate procedure)

**51050**  Cystolithotomy, cystotomy with removal of calculus, without vesical neck resection

**51060**  Transvesical ureterolithotomy

**51065**  Cystotomy, with calculus basket extraction and/or ultrasonic or electrohydraulic fragmentation of ureteral calculus

**51080**  Drainage of perivesical or prevesical space abscess

▶(For percutaneous image-guided fluid collection drainage by catheter of perivesicular or prevesicular space abscess, use 49406)◀

## Removal

**51100**  Aspiration of bladder; by needle

**51101**      by trocar or intracatheter

**51102**      with insertion of suprapubic catheter

(For imaging guidance, see 76942, 77002, 77012)

## Excision

**51500**  Excision of urachal cyst or sinus, with or without umbilical hernia repair

**51520**  Cystotomy; for simple excision of vesical neck (separate procedure)

**51525**      for excision of bladder diverticulum, single or multiple (separate procedure)

**51530**      for excision of bladder tumor

(For transurethral resection, see 52234-52240, 52305)

**51535**  Cystotomy for excision, incision, or repair of ureterocele

(For bilateral procedure, report 51535 with modifier 50)

(For transurethral excision, use 52300)

**51550**  Cystectomy, partial; simple

**51555**      complicated (eg, postradiation, previous surgery, difficult location)

**51565**  Cystectomy, partial, with reimplantation of ureter(s) into bladder (ureteroneocystostomy)

**51570**  Cystectomy, complete; (separate procedure)

**51575**      with bilateral pelvic lymphadenectomy, including external iliac, hypogastric, and obturator nodes

**51580**  Cystectomy, complete, with ureterosigmoidostomy or ureterocutaneous transplantations;

**51585**      with bilateral pelvic lymphadenectomy, including external iliac, hypogastric, and obturator nodes

**51590**  Cystectomy, complete, with ureteroileal conduit or sigmoid bladder, including intestine anastomosis;

**51595**      with bilateral pelvic lymphadenectomy, including external iliac, hypogastric, and obturator nodes

**51596**  Cystectomy, complete, with continent diversion, any open technique, using any segment of small and/or large intestine to construct neobladder

**51597**  Pelvic exenteration, complete, for vesical, prostatic or urethral malignancy, with removal of bladder and ureteral transplantations, with or without hysterectomy and/or abdominoperineal resection of rectum and colon and colostomy, or any combination thereof

(For pelvic exenteration for gynecologic malignancy, use 58240)

## Introduction

**51600**  Injection procedure for cystography or voiding urethrocystography

(For radiological supervision and interpretation, see 74430, 74455)

**51605**  Injection procedure and placement of chain for contrast and/or chain urethrocystography

(For radiological supervision and interpretation, use 74430)

**51610**  Injection procedure for retrograde urethrocystography

(For radiological supervision and interpretation, use 74450)

**51700**  Bladder irrigation, simple, lavage and/or instillation

(Codes 51701-51702 are reported only when performed independently. Do not report 51701-51702 when catheter insertion is an inclusive component of another procedure.)

**51701**  Insertion of non-indwelling bladder catheter (eg, straight catheterization for residual urine)

**51702**  Insertion of temporary indwelling bladder catheter; simple (eg, Foley)

▶(Do not report 51702 in conjunction with 0071T, 0072T)◀

**51703**      complicated (eg, altered anatomy, fractured catheter/balloon)

**51705**  Change of cystostomy tube; simple

**51710**      complicated

(If imaging guidance is performed, use 75984)

**51715**  Endoscopic injection of implant material into the submucosal tissues of the urethra and/or bladder neck

**Urinary**

**51720** Bladder instillation of anticarcinogenic agent (including retention time)

## Urodynamics

The following section (51725-51798) lists procedures that may be used separately or in many and varied combinations.

When multiple procedures are performed in the same investigative session, modifier 51 should be employed.

All procedures in this section imply that these services are performed by, or are under the direct supervision of, a physician or other qualified health care professional and that all instruments, equipment, fluids, gases, probes, catheters, technician's fees, medications, gloves, trays, tubing, and other sterile supplies be provided by that individual. When the individual only interprets the results and/or operates the equipment, a professional component, modifier 26, should be used to identify these services.

**51725** Simple cystometrogram (CMG) (eg, spinal manometer)

**51726** Complex cystometrogram (ie, calibrated electronic equipment);

**51727** with urethral pressure profile studies (ie, urethral closure pressure profile), any technique

**51728** with voiding pressure studies (ie, bladder voiding pressure), any technique

**51729** with voiding pressure studies (ie, bladder voiding pressure) and urethral pressure profile studies (ie, urethral closure pressure profile), any technique

#+ **51797** Voiding pressure studies, intra-abdominal (ie, rectal, gastric, intraperitoneal) (List separately in addition to code for primary procedure)

(Use 51797 in conjunction with 51728, 51729)

**51736** Simple uroflowmetry (UFR) (eg, stop-watch flow rate, mechanical uroflowmeter)

**51741** Complex uroflowmetry (eg, calibrated electronic equipment)

(51772 has been deleted. To report urethral pressure profile studies, see 51727, 51729)

**51784** Electromyography studies (EMG) of anal or urethral sphincter, other than needle, any technique

**51785** Needle electromyography studies (EMG) of anal or urethral sphincter, any technique

**51792** Stimulus evoked response (eg, measurement of bulbocavernosus reflex latency time)

(51795 has been deleted. To report bladder voiding pressure studies, see 51728, 51729)

**51797** Code is out of numerical sequence. See 51725-51798

**51798** Measurement of post-voiding residual urine and/or bladder capacity by ultrasound, non-imaging

## Repair

**51800** Cystoplasty or cystourethroplasty, plastic operation on bladder and/or vesical neck (anterior Y-plasty, vesical fundus resection), any procedure, with or without wedge resection of posterior vesical neck

**51820** Cystourethroplasty with unilateral or bilateral ureteroneocystostomy

**51840** Anterior vesicourethropexy, or urethropexy (eg, Marshall-Marchetti-Krantz, Burch); simple

**51841** complicated (eg, secondary repair)

(For urethropexy (Pereyra type), use 57289)

**51845** Abdomino-vaginal vesical neck suspension, with or without endoscopic control (eg, Stamey, Raz, modified Pereyra)

**51860** Cystorrhaphy, suture of bladder wound, injury or rupture; simple

**51865** complicated

**51880** Closure of cystostomy (separate procedure)

**51900** Closure of vesicovaginal fistula, abdominal approach

(For vaginal approach, see 57320-57330)

**51920** Closure of vesicouterine fistula;

**51925** with hysterectomy

(For closure of vesicoenteric fistula, see 44660, 44661)

(For closure of rectovesical fistula, see 45800-45805)

**51940** Closure, exstrophy of bladder

(See also 54390)

**51960** Enterocystoplasty, including intestinal anastomosis

**51980** Cutaneous vesicostomy

## Laparoscopy

Surgical laparoscopy always includes diagnostic laparoscopy. To report a diagnostic laparoscopy (peritoneoscopy) (separate procedure), use 49320.

**51990** Laparoscopy, surgical; urethral suspension for stress incontinence

**51992** sling operation for stress incontinence (eg, fascia or synthetic)

(For open sling operation for stress incontinence, use 57288)

(For reversal or removal of sling operation for stress incontinence, use 57287)

**51999** Unlisted laparoscopy procedure, bladder

Urinary

# Endoscopy—Cystoscopy, Urethroscopy, Cystourethroscopy

Endoscopic descriptions are listed so that the main procedure can be identified without having to list all the minor related functions performed at the same time. For example: meatotomy, urethral calibration and/or dilation, urethroscopy, and cystoscopy prior to a transurethral resection of prostate; ureteral catheterization following extraction of ureteral calculus; internal urethrotomy and bladder neck fulguration when performing a cystourethroscopy for the female urethral syndrome. When the secondary procedure requires significant additional time and effort, it may be identified by the addition of modifier 22.

For example: urethrotomy performed for a documented pre-existing stricture or bladder neck contracture.

**52000**      Cystourethroscopy (separate procedure)

▶(Do not report 52000 in conjunction with 52001, 52320, 52325, 52327, 52330, 52332, 52334, 52341, 52342, 52343, 52356)◀

**52001**      Cystourethroscopy with irrigation and evacuation of multiple obstructing clots

(Do not report 52001 in conjunction with 52000)

**52005**      Cystourethroscopy, with ureteral catheterization, with or without irrigation, instillation, or ureteropyelography, exclusive of radiologic service;

**52007**           with brush biopsy of ureter and/or renal pelvis

**52010**      Cystourethroscopy, with ejaculatory duct catheterization, with or without irrigation, instillation, or duct radiography, exclusive of radiologic service

(For radiological supervision and interpretation, use 74440)

## Transurethral Surgery

### Urethra and Bladder

**52204**      Cystourethroscopy, with biopsy(s)

**52214**      Cystourethroscopy, with fulguration (including cryosurgery or laser surgery) of trigone, bladder neck, prostatic fossa, urethra, or periurethral glands

(For transurethral fulguration of prostate tissue performed within the postoperative period of 52601 or 52630 performed by the same physician, append modifier 78)

(For transurethral fulguration of prostate tissue performed within the postoperative period of a related procedure performed by the same physician, append modifier 78)

(For transurethral fulguration of prostate for postoperative bleeding performed by the same physician, append modifier 78)

**52224**      Cystourethroscopy, with fulguration (including cryosurgery or laser surgery) or treatment of MINOR (less than 0.5 cm) lesion(s) with or without biopsy

**52234**      Cystourethroscopy, with fulguration (including cryosurgery or laser surgery) and/or resection of; SMALL bladder tumor(s) (0.5 up to 2.0 cm)

**52235**           MEDIUM bladder tumor(s) (2.0 to 5.0 cm)

**52240**           LARGE bladder tumor(s)

**52250**      Cystourethroscopy with insertion of radioactive substance, with or without biopsy or fulguration

**52260**      Cystourethroscopy, with dilation of bladder for interstitial cystitis; general or conduction (spinal) anesthesia

**52265**           local anesthesia

**52270**      Cystourethroscopy, with internal urethrotomy; female

**52275**           male

**52276**      Cystourethroscopy with direct vision internal urethrotomy

**52277**      Cystourethroscopy, with resection of external sphincter (sphincterotomy)

**52281**      Cystourethroscopy, with calibration and/or dilation of urethral stricture or stenosis, with or without meatotomy, with or without injection procedure for cystography, male or female

**52282**      Cystourethroscopy, with insertion of permanent urethral stent

(For placement of temporary prostatic urethral stent, use 53855)

**52283**      Cystourethroscopy, with steroid injection into stricture

**52285**      Cystourethroscopy for treatment of the female urethral syndrome with any or all of the following: urethral meatotomy, urethral dilation, internal urethrotomy, lysis of urethrovaginal septal fibrosis, lateral incisions of the bladder neck, and fulguration of polyp(s) of urethra, bladder neck, and/or trigone

**52287**      Cystourethroscopy, with injection(s) for chemodenervation of the bladder

(The supply of the chemodenervation agent is reported separately)

**52290**      Cystourethroscopy; with ureteral meatotomy, unilateral or bilateral

**52300**           with resection or fulguration of orthotopic ureterocele(s), unilateral or bilateral

**52301**           with resection or fulguration of ectopic ureterocele(s), unilateral or bilateral

**52305**           with incision or resection of orifice of bladder diverticulum, single or multiple

**52310**      Cystourethroscopy, with removal of foreign body, calculus, or ureteral stent from urethra or bladder (separate procedure); simple

---

▲=Revised code   ●=New code   ▶◀=Contains new or revised text   ⊘=Modifier 51 exempt

**Urinary**

**52315**      complicated

**52317**   Litholapaxy: crushing or fragmentation of calculus by any means in bladder and removal of fragments; simple or small (less than 2.5 cm)

**52318**      complicated or large (over 2.5 cm)

## Ureter and Pelvis

Therapeutic cystourethroscopy always includes diagnostic cystourethroscopy. To report a diagnostic cystourethroscopy, use 52000. Therapeutic cystourethroscopy with ureteroscopy and/or pyeloscopy always includes diagnostic cystourethroscopy with ureteroscopy and/or pyeloscopy. To report a diagnostic cystourethroscopy with ureteroscopy and/or pyeloscopy, use 52351.

▶Do not report 52000 in conjunction with 52320-52343, 52356.◀

Do not report 52351 in conjunction with 52344-52346, 52352-52356.

The insertion and removal of a temporary ureteral catheter (52005) during diagnostic or therapeutic cystourethroscopy with ureteroscopy and/or pyeloscopy is included in 52320-52356 and should not be reported separately.

To report insertion of a self-retaining, indwelling stent performed during diagnostic or therapeutic cystourethroscopy with ureteroscopy and/or pyeloscopy, report 52332, in addition to primary procedure(s) performed (52320-52330, 52334-52352, 52354, 52355), and append modifier 51. Code 52332 is used to report a unilateral procedure unless otherwise specified.◀

For bilateral insertion of self-retaining, indwelling ureteral stents, use code 52332, and append modifier 50.

To report cystourethroscopic removal of a self-retaining, indwelling ureteral stent, see 52310, 52315, and append modifier 58, if appropriate.

**52320**   Cystourethroscopy (including ureteral catheterization); with removal of ureteral calculus

**52325**      with fragmentation of ureteral calculus (eg, ultrasonic or electro-hydraulic technique)

**52327**      with subureteric injection of implant material

**52330**      with manipulation, without removal of ureteral calculus

      ▶(Do not report 52320, 52325, 52327, 52330 in conjunction with 52000)◀

**52332**   Cystourethroscopy, with insertion of indwelling ureteral stent (eg, Gibbons or double-J type)

      ▶(Do not report 52332 in conjunction with 52000, 52353, 52356 when performed together on the same side)◀

**52334**   Cystourethroscopy with insertion of ureteral guide wire through kidney to establish a percutaneous nephrostomy, retrograde

(For percutaneous nephrostolithotomy, see 50080, 50081; for establishment of nephrostomy tract only, use 50395)

▶(For cystourethroscopy, with ureteroscopy and/or pyeloscopy, see 52351-52356)◀

(For cystourethroscopy with incision, fulguration, or resection of congenital posterior urethral valves or obstructive hypertrophic mucosal folds, use 52400)

▶(Do not report 52334 in conjunction with 52000, 52351)◀

**52341**   Cystourethroscopy; with treatment of ureteral stricture (eg, balloon dilation, laser, electrocautery, and incision)

**52342**      with treatment of ureteropelvic junction stricture (eg, balloon dilation, laser, electrocautery, and incision)

**52343**      with treatment of intra-renal stricture (eg, balloon dilation, laser, electrocautery, and incision)

      ▶(Do not report 52341, 52342, 52343 in conjunction with 52000, 52351)◀

**52344**   Cystourethroscopy with ureteroscopy; with treatment of ureteral stricture (eg, balloon dilation, laser, electrocautery, and incision)

**52345**      with treatment of ureteropelvic junction stricture (eg, balloon dilation, laser, electrocautery, and incision)

**52346**      with treatment of intra-renal stricture (eg, balloon dilation, laser, electrocautery, and incision)

(For transurethral resection or incision of ejaculatory ducts, use 52402)

▶(Do not report 52344, 52345, 52346 in conjunction with 52351)◀

**52351**   Cystourethroscopy, with ureteroscopy and/or pyeloscopy; diagnostic

(For radiological supervision and interpretation, use 74485)

▶(Do not report 52351 in conjunction with 52341, 52342, 52343, 52344, 52345, 52346, 52352-52356)◀

**52352**      with removal or manipulation of calculus (ureteral catheterization is included)

**52353**      with lithotripsy (ureteral catheterization is included)

▶(Do not report 52353 in conjunction with 52332, 52356 when performed together on the same side)◀

#● **52356**      with lithotripsy including insertion of indwelling ureteral stent (eg, Gibbons or double-J type)

▶(Do not report 52356 in conjunction with 52332, 52353 when performed together on the same side)◀

**52354**      with biopsy and/or fulguration of ureteral or renal pelvic lesion

**52355**      with resection of ureteral or renal pelvic tumor

**52356**   Code is out of numerical sequence. See 52320-52355

## Vesical Neck and Prostate

**52400**  Cystourethroscopy with incision, fulguration, or resection of congenital posterior urethral valves, or congenital obstructive hypertrophic mucosal folds

**52402**  Cystourethroscopy with transurethral resection or incision of ejaculatory ducts

**52450**  Transurethral incision of prostate

**52500**  Transurethral resection of bladder neck (separate procedure)

**52601**  Transurethral electrosurgical resection of prostate, including control of postoperative bleeding, complete (vasectomy, meatotomy, cystourethroscopy, urethral calibration and/or dilation, and internal urethrotomy are included)

(For other approaches, see 55801-55845)

(52606 has been deleted. For transurethral fulguration of prostate, use 52214)

(52612, 52614, 52620 have been deleted. For first stage transurethral partial resection of prostate, use 52601. For second stage partial resection of prostate, use 52601 with modifier 58. For transurethral resection of residual or regrowth of obstructive prostate tissue, use 52630)

**52630**  Transurethral resection; residual or regrowth of obstructive prostate tissue including control of postoperative bleeding, complete (vasectomy, meatotomy, cystourethroscopy, urethral calibration and/or dilation, and internal urethrotomy are included)

(For resection of residual prostate tissue performed within the postoperative period of a related procedure performed by the same physician, append modifier 78)

**52640**      of postoperative bladder neck contracture

**52647**  Laser coagulation of prostate, including control of postoperative bleeding, complete (vasectomy, meatotomy, cystourethroscopy, urethral calibration and/or dilation, and internal urethrotomy are included if performed)

**52648**  Laser vaporization of prostate, including control of postoperative bleeding, complete (vasectomy, meatotomy, cystourethroscopy, urethral calibration and/or dilation, internal urethrotomy and transurethral resection of prostate are included if performed)

**52649**  Laser enucleation of the prostate with morcellation, including control of postoperative bleeding, complete (vasectomy, meatotomy, cystourethroscopy, urethral calibration and/or dilation, internal urethrotomy and transurethral resection of prostate are included if performed)

(Do not report 52649 in conjunction with 52000, 52276, 52281, 52601, 52647, 52648, 53020, 55250)

**52700**  Transurethral drainage of prostatic abscess

(For litholapaxy, use 52317, 52318)

## Urethra

(For endoscopy, see cystoscopy, urethroscopy, cystourethroscopy, 52000-52700)

(For injection procedure for urethrocystography, see 51600-51610)

## Incision

**53000**  Urethrotomy or urethrostomy, external (separate procedure); pendulous urethra

**53010**      perineal urethra, external

**53020**  Meatotomy, cutting of meatus (separate procedure); except infant

**53025**      infant

(Do not report modifier 63 in conjunction with 53025)

**53040**  Drainage of deep periurethral abscess

(For subcutaneous abscess, see 10060, 10061)

**53060**  Drainage of Skene's gland abscess or cyst

**53080**  Drainage of perineal urinary extravasation; uncomplicated (separate procedure)

**53085**      complicated

## Excision

**53200**  Biopsy of urethra

**53210**  Urethrectomy, total, including cystostomy; female

**53215**      male

**53220**  Excision or fulguration of carcinoma of urethra

**53230**  Excision of urethral diverticulum (separate procedure); female

**53235**      male

**53240**  Marsupialization of urethral diverticulum, male or female

**53250**  Excision of bulbourethral gland (Cowper's gland)

**53260**  Excision or fulguration; urethral polyp(s), distal urethra

(For endoscopic approach, see 52214, 52224)

**53265**      urethral caruncle

**53270**      Skene's glands

**53275**      urethral prolapse

## Repair

(For hypospadias, see 54300-54352)

**53400**  Urethroplasty; first stage, for fistula, diverticulum, or stricture (eg, Johannsen type)

**53405**      second stage (formation of urethra), including urinary diversion

**Urinary**

**Urinary**

**53410**　Urethroplasty, 1-stage reconstruction of male anterior urethra

**53415**　Urethroplasty, transpubic or perineal, 1-stage, for reconstruction or repair of prostatic or membranous urethra

**53420**　Urethroplasty, 2-stage reconstruction or repair of prostatic or membranous urethra; first stage

**53425**　　　second stage

**53430**　Urethroplasty, reconstruction of female urethra

**53431**　Urethroplasty with tubularization of posterior urethra and/or lower bladder for incontinence (eg, Tenago, Leadbetter procedure)

**53440**　Sling operation for correction of male urinary incontinence (eg, fascia or synthetic)

**53442**　Removal or revision of sling for male urinary incontinence (eg, fascia or synthetic)

**53444**　Insertion of tandem cuff (dual cuff)

**53445**　Insertion of inflatable urethral/bladder neck sphincter, including placement of pump, reservoir, and cuff

**53446**　Removal of inflatable urethral/bladder neck sphincter, including pump, reservoir, and cuff

**53447**　Removal and replacement of inflatable urethral/bladder neck sphincter including pump, reservoir, and cuff at the same operative session

**53448**　Removal and replacement of inflatable urethral/bladder neck sphincter including pump, reservoir, and cuff through an infected field at the same operative session including irrigation and debridement of infected tissue

(Do not report 11042, 11043 in addition to 53448)

**53449**　Repair of inflatable urethral/bladder neck sphincter, including pump, reservoir, and cuff

**53450**　Urethromeatoplasty, with mucosal advancement

(For meatotomy, see 53020, 53025)

**53460**　Urethromeatoplasty, with partial excision of distal urethral segment (Richardson type procedure)

**53500**　Urethrolysis, transvaginal, secondary, open, including cystourothroscopy (eg, postsurgical obstruction, scarring)

(For urethrolysis by retropubic approach, use 53899)

(Do not report 53500 in conjunction with 52000)

**53502**　Urethrorrhaphy, suture of urethral wound or injury, female

**53505**　Urethrorrhaphy, suture of urethral wound or injury; penile

**53510**　　　perineal

**53515**　　　prostatomembranous

**53520**　Closure of urethrostomy or urethrocutaneous fistula, male (separate procedure)

(For closure of urethrovaginal fistula, use 57310)

(For closure of urethrorectal fistula, see 45820, 45825)

## Manipulation

(For radiological supervision and interpretation, use 74485)

**53600**　Dilation of urethral stricture by passage of sound or urethral dilator, male; initial

**53601**　　　subsequent

**53605**　Dilation of urethral stricture or vesical neck by passage of sound or urethral dilator, male, general or conduction (spinal) anesthesia

(For dilation of urethral stricture, male, performed under local anesthesia, see 53600, 53601, 53620, 53621)

**53620**　Dilation of urethral stricture by passage of filiform and follower, male; initial

**53621**　　　subsequent

**53660**　Dilation of female urethra including suppository and/or instillation; initial

**53661**　　　subsequent

**53665**　Dilation of female urethra, general or conduction (spinal) anesthesia

(For urethral catheterization, see 51701-51703)

(For dilation of urethra performed under local anesthesia, female, see 53660, 53661)

## Other Procedures

(For 2 or 3 glass urinalysis, use 81020)

**53850**　Transurethral destruction of prostate tissue; by microwave thermotherapy

**53852**　　　by radiofrequency thermotherapy

(53853 has been deleted. To report, use 55899)

**53855**　Insertion of a temporary prostatic urethral stent, including urethral measurement

(For insertion of permanent urethral stent, use 52282)

**53860**　Transurethral radiofrequency micro-remodeling of the female bladder neck and proximal urethra for stress urinary incontinence

**53899**　Unlisted procedure, urinary system

# Male Genital System

## Penis

### Incision

(For abdominal perineal gangrene debridement, see 11004-11006)

**54000**   Slitting of prepuce, dorsal or lateral (separate procedure); newborn

(Do not report modifier 63 in conjunction with 54000)

**54001**      except newborn

**54015**   Incision and drainage of penis, deep

(For skin and subcutaneous abscess, see 10060-10160)

### Destruction

**54050**   Destruction of lesion(s), penis (eg, condyloma, papilloma, molluscum contagiosum, herpetic vesicle), simple; chemical

**54055**      electrodesiccation

**54056**      cryosurgery

**54057**      laser surgery

**54060**      surgical excision

**54065**   Destruction of lesion(s), penis (eg, condyloma, papilloma, molluscum contagiosum, herpetic vesicle), extensive (eg, laser surgery, electrosurgery, cryosurgery, chemosurgery)

(For destruction or excision of other lesions, see **Integumentary System**)

### Excision

**54100**   Biopsy of penis; (separate procedure)

**54105**      deep structures

**54110**   Excision of penile plaque (Peyronie disease);

**54111**      with graft to 5 cm in length

**54112**      with graft greater than 5 cm in length

**54115**   Removal foreign body from deep penile tissue (eg, plastic implant)

**54120**   Amputation of penis; partial

**54125**      complete

**54130**   Amputation of penis, radical; with bilateral inguinofemoral lymphadenectomy

**54135**      in continuity with bilateral pelvic lymphadenectomy, including external iliac, hypogastric and obturator nodes

(For lymphadenectomy [separate procedure], see 38760-38770)

**54150**   Circumcision, using clamp or other device with regional dorsal penile or ring block

(Do not report modifier 63 in conjunction with 54150)

(Report 54150 with modifier 52 when performed without dorsal penile or ring block)

**54160**   Circumcision, surgical excision other than clamp, device, or dorsal slit; neonate (28 days of age or less)

(Do not report modifier 63 in conjunction with 54160)

**54161**      older than 28 days of age

**54162**   Lysis or excision of penile post-circumcision adhesions

**54163**   Repair incomplete circumcision

**54164**   Frenulotomy of penis

(Do not report 54164 with circumcision codes 54150-54161, 54162, 54163)

### Introduction

**54200**   Injection procedure for Peyronie disease;

**54205**      with surgical exposure of plaque

**54220**   Irrigation of corpora cavernosa for priapism

**54230**   Injection procedure for corpora cavernosography

(For radiological supervision and interpretation, use 74445)

**54231**   Dynamic cavernosometry, including intracavernosal injection of vasoactive drugs (eg, papaverine, phentolamine)

**54235**   Injection of corpora cavernosa with pharmacologic agent(s) (eg, papaverine, phentolamine)

**54240**   Penile plethysmography

**54250**   Nocturnal penile tumescence and/or rigidity test

### Repair

(For other urethroplasties, see 53400-53430)

(For penile revascularization, use 37788)

**54300**   Plastic operation of penis for straightening of chordee (eg, hypospadias), with or without mobilization of urethra

**54304**   Plastic operation on penis for correction of chordee or for first stage hypospadias repair with or without transplantation of prepuce and/or skin flaps

**54308**   Urethroplasty for second stage hypospadias repair (including urinary diversion); less than 3 cm

**54312**      greater than 3 cm

**54316**   Urethroplasty for second stage hypospadias repair (including urinary diversion) with free skin graft obtained from site other than genitalia

**54318**   Urethroplasty for third stage hypospadias repair to release penis from scrotum (eg, third stage Cecil repair)

**Male Genital**

**54322**  1-stage distal hypospadias repair (with or without chordee or circumcision); with simple meatal advancement (eg, Magpi, V-flap)

**54324**        with urethroplasty by local skin flaps (eg, flip-flap, prepucial flap)

**54326**        with urethroplasty by local skin flaps and mobilization of urethra

**54328**        with extensive dissection to correct chordee and urethroplasty with local skin flaps, skin graft patch, and/or island flap

        (For urethroplasty and straightening of chordee, use 54308)

**54332**  1-stage proximal penile or penoscrotal hypospadias repair requiring extensive dissection to correct chordee and urethroplasty by use of skin graft tube and/or island flap

**54336**  1-stage perineal hypospadias repair requiring extensive dissection to correct chordee and urethroplasty by use of skin graft tube and/or island flap

**54340**  Repair of hypospadias complications (ie, fistula, stricture, diverticula); by closure, incision, or excision, simple

**54344**        requiring mobilization of skin flaps and urethroplasty with flap or patch graft

**54348**        requiring extensive dissection and urethroplasty with flap, patch or tubed graft (includes urinary diversion)

**54352**  Repair of hypospadias cripple requiring extensive dissection and excision of previously constructed structures including re-release of chordee and reconstruction of urethra and penis by use of local skin as grafts and island flaps and skin brought in as flaps or grafts

**54360**  Plastic operation on penis to correct angulation

**54380**  Plastic operation on penis for epispadias distal to external sphincter;

**54385**        with incontinence

**54390**        with exstrophy of bladder

**54400**  Insertion of penile prosthesis; non-inflatable (semi-rigid)

**54401**        inflatable (self-contained)

        (For removal or replacement of penile prosthesis, see 54415, 54416)

**54405**  Insertion of multi-component, inflatable penile prosthesis, including placement of pump, cylinders, and reservoir

        (For reduced services, report 54405 with modifier 52)

**54406**  Removal of all components of a multi-component, inflatable penile prosthesis without replacement of prosthesis

        (For reduced services, report 54406 with modifier 52)

**54408**  Repair of component(s) of a multi-component, inflatable penile prosthesis

**54410**  Removal and replacement of all component(s) of a multi-component, inflatable penile prosthesis at the same operative session

**54411**  Removal and replacement of all components of a multi-component inflatable penile prosthesis through an infected field at the same operative session, including irrigation and debridement of infected tissue

        (For reduced services, report 54411 with modifier 52)

        (Do not report 11042, 11043 in addition to 54411)

**54415**  Removal of non-inflatable (semi-rigid) or inflatable (self-contained) penile prosthesis, without replacement of prosthesis

**54416**  Removal and replacement of non-inflatable (semi-rigid) or inflatable (self-contained) penile prosthesis at the same operative session

**54417**  Removal and replacement of non-inflatable (semi-rigid) or inflatable (self-contained) penile prosthesis through an infected field at the same operative session, including irrigation and debridement of infected tissue

        (Do not report 11042, 11043 in addition to 54417)

**54420**  Corpora cavernosa-saphenous vein shunt (priapism operation), unilateral or bilateral

**54430**  Corpora cavernosa-corpus spongiosum shunt (priapism operation), unilateral or bilateral

**54435**  Corpora cavernosa-glans penis fistulization (eg, biopsy needle, Winter procedure, rongeur, or punch) for priapism

**54440**  Plastic operation of penis for injury

## Manipulation

**54450**  Foreskin manipulation including lysis of preputial adhesions and stretching

# Testis

## Excision

        (For abdominal perineal gangrene debridement, see 11004-11006)

**54500**  Biopsy of testis, needle (separate procedure)

        (For fine needle aspiration, see 10021, 10022)

        (For evaluation of fine needle aspirate, see 88172, 88173)

**54505**  Biopsy of testis, incisional (separate procedure)

        (For bilateral procedure, report 54505 with modifier 50)

        (When combined with vasogram, seminal vesiculogram, or epididymogram, use 55300)

**54512**  Excision of extraparenchymal lesion of testis

**54520**  Orchiectomy, simple (including subcapsular), with or without testicular prosthesis, scrotal or inguinal approach

        (For bilateral procedure, report 54520 with modifier 50)

Male Genital

54522    Orchiectomy, partial

54530    Orchiectomy, radical, for tumor; inguinal approach

54535        with abdominal exploration

(For orchiectomy with repair of hernia, see 49505 or 49507 and 54520)

(For radical retroperitoneal lymphadenectomy, use 38780)

## Exploration

54550    Exploration for undescended testis (inguinal or scrotal area)

(For bilateral procedure, report 54550 with modifier 50)

54560    Exploration for undescended testis with abdominal exploration

(For bilateral procedure, report 54560 with modifier 50)

## Repair

54600    Reduction of torsion of testis, surgical, with or without fixation of contralateral testis

54620    Fixation of contralateral testis (separate procedure)

54640    Orchiopexy, inguinal approach, with or without hernia repair

(For bilateral procedure, report 54640 with modifier 50)

(For inguinal hernia repair performed in conjunction with inguinal orchiopexy, see 49495-49525)

54650    Orchiopexy, abdominal approach, for intra-abdominal testis (eg, Fowler-Stephens)

(For laparoscopic approach, use 54692)

54660    Insertion of testicular prosthesis (separate procedure)

(For bilateral procedure, report 54660 with modifier 50)

54670    Suture or repair of testicular injury

54680    Transplantation of testis(es) to thigh (because of scrotal destruction)

## Laparoscopy

Surgical laparoscopy always includes diagnostic laparoscopy. To report a diagnostic laparoscopy (peritoneoscopy) (separate procedure), use 49320.

54690    Laparoscopy, surgical; orchiectomy

54692        orchiopexy for intra-abdominal testis

54699    Unlisted laparoscopy procedure, testis

# Epididymis

## Incision

54700    Incision and drainage of epididymis, testis and/or scrotal space (eg, abscess or hematoma)

(For debridement of necrotizing soft tissue infection of external genitalia, see 11004-11006)

## Excision

54800    Biopsy of epididymis, needle

(For fine needle aspiration, see 10021, 10022)

(For evaluation of fine needle aspirate, see 88172, 88173)

54830    Excision of local lesion of epididymis

54840    Excision of spermatocele, with or without epididymectomy

54860    Epididymectomy; unilateral

54861        bilateral

## Exploration

54865    Exploration of epididymis, with or without biopsy

## Repair

54900    Epididymovasostomy, anastomosis of epididymis to vas deferens; unilateral

54901        bilateral

(For operating microscope, use 69990)

# Tunica Vaginalis

## Incision

55000    Puncture aspiration of hydrocele, tunica vaginalis, with or without injection of medication

## Excision

55040    Excision of hydrocele; unilateral

55041        bilateral

(With hernia repair, see 49495-49501)

## Repair

55060    Repair of tunica vaginalis hydrocele (Bottle type)

**Male Genital**

# Scrotum

## Incision

55100    Drainage of scrotal wall abscess

(See also 54700)

(For debridement of necrotizing soft tissue infection of external genitalia, see 11004-11006)

55110    Scrotal exploration

55120    Removal of foreign body in scrotum

## Excision

(For excision of local lesion of skin of scrotum, see **Integumentary System**)

55150    Resection of scrotum

## Repair

55175    Scrotoplasty; simple

55180        complicated

# Vas Deferens

## Incision

55200    Vasotomy, cannulization with or without incision of vas, unilateral or bilateral (separate procedure)

## Excision

55250    Vasectomy, unilateral or bilateral (separate procedure), including postoperative semen examination(s)

## Introduction

55300    Vasotomy for vasograms, seminal vesiculograms, or epididymograms, unilateral or bilateral

(For radiological supervision and interpretation, use 74440)

(When combined with biopsy of testis, see 54505 and use modifier 51)

## Repair

55400    Vasovasostomy, vasovasorrhaphy

(For bilateral procedure, report 55400 with modifier 50)

(For operating microscope, use 69990)

## Suture

55450    Ligation (percutaneous) of vas deferens, unilateral or bilateral (separate procedure)

# Spermatic Cord

## Excision

55500    Excision of hydrocele of spermatic cord, unilateral (separate procedure)

55520    Excision of lesion of spermatic cord (separate procedure)

55530    Excision of varicocele or ligation of spermatic veins for varicocele; (separate procedure)

55535        abdominal approach

55540        with hernia repair

## Laparoscopy

Surgical laparoscopy always includes diagnostic laparoscopy. To report a diagnostic laparoscopy (peritoneoscopy) (separate procedure), use 49320.

55550    Laparoscopy, surgical, with ligation of spermatic veins for varicocele

55559    Unlisted laparoscopy procedure, spermatic cord

# Seminal Vesicles

## Incision

55600    Vesiculotomy;

(For bilateral procedure, report 55600 with modifier 50)

55605        complicated

## Excision

55650    Vesiculectomy, any approach

(For bilateral procedure, report 55650 with modifier 50)

55680    Excision of Mullerian duct cyst

(For injection procedure, see 52010, 55300)

# Prostate

## Incision

55700    Biopsy, prostate; needle or punch, single or multiple, any approach

(If imaging guidance is performed, use 76942)

(For fine needle aspiration, see 10021, 10022)

(For evaluation of fine needle aspirate, see 88172, 88173)

(For transperineal stereotactic template guided saturation prostate biopsies, use 55706)

55705        incisional, any approach

Male Genital

**55706** Biopsies, prostate, needle, transperineal, stereotactic template guided saturation sampling, including imaging guidance

(Do not report 55706 in conjunction with 55700)

**55720** Prostatotomy, external drainage of prostatic abscess, any approach; simple

**55725** complicated

(For transurethral drainage, use 52700)

## Excision

(For transurethral removal of prostate, see 52601-52640)

(For transurethral destruction of prostate, see 53850-53852)

(For limited pelvic lymphadenectomy for staging [separate procedure], use 38562)

(For independent node dissection, see 38770-38780)

**55801** Prostatectomy, perineal, subtotal (including control of postoperative bleeding, vasectomy, meatotomy, urethral calibration and/or dilation, and internal urethrotomy)

**55810** Prostatectomy, perineal radical;

**55812** with lymph node biopsy(s) (limited pelvic lymphadenectomy)

**55815** with bilateral pelvic lymphadenectomy, including external iliac, hypogastric and obturator nodes

(If 55815 is carried out on separate days, use 38770 with modifier 50 and 55810)

**55821** Prostatectomy (including control of postoperative bleeding, vasectomy, meatotomy, urethral calibration and/or dilation, and internal urethrotomy); suprapubic, subtotal, 1 or 2 stages

**55831** retropubic, subtotal

**55840** Prostatectomy, retropubic radical, with or without nerve sparing;

**55842** with lymph node biopsy(s) (limited pelvic lymphadenectomy)

**55845** with bilateral pelvic lymphadenectomy, including external iliac, hypogastric, and obturator nodes

(If 55845 is carried out on separate days, use 38770 with modifier 50 and 55840)

(For laparoscopic retropubic radical prostatectomy, use 55866)

**55860** Exposure of prostate, any approach, for insertion of radioactive substance;

(For application of interstitial radioelement, see 77776-77778)

**55862** with lymph node biopsy(s) (limited pelvic lymphadenectomy)

**55865** with bilateral pelvic lymphadenectomy, including external iliac, hypogastric and obturator nodes

## Laparoscopy

Surgical laparoscopy always includes diagnostic laparoscopy. To report a diagnostic laparoscopy (peritoneoscopy) (separate procedure), use 49320.

**55866** Laparoscopy, surgical prostatectomy, retropubic radical, including nerve sparing, includes robotic assistance, when performed

(For open procedure, use 55840)

## Other Procedures

(For artificial insemination, see 58321, 58322)

**55870** Electroejaculation

**55873** Cryosurgical ablation of the prostate (includes ultrasonic guidance and monitoring)

**55875** Transperineal placement of needles or catheters into prostate for interstitial radioelement application, with or without cystoscopy

(For placement of needles or catheters into pelvic organs and/or genitalia [except prostate] for interstitial radioelement application, use 55920)

(For interstitial radioelement application, see 77776-77787)

(For ultrasonic guidance for interstitial radioelement application, use 76965)

**55876** Placement of interstitial device(s) for radiation therapy guidance (eg, fiducial markers, dosimeter), prostate (via needle, any approach), single or multiple

(Report supply of device separately)

(For imaging guidance, see 76942, 77002, 77012, 77021)

**55899** Unlisted procedure, male genital system

## Reproductive System Procedures

**55920** Placement of needles or catheters into pelvic organs and/or genitalia (except prostate) for subsequent interstitial radioelement application

(For placement of needles or catheters into prostate, use 55875)

(For insertion of uterine tandems and/or vaginal ovoids for clinical brachytherapy, use 57155)

(For insertion of Heyman capsules for clinical brachytherapy, use 58346)

## Intersex Surgery

**55970** Intersex surgery; male to female

**55980** female to male

**Male Genital**

---

# Female Genital System

(For pelvic laparotomy, use 49000)

(For excision or destruction of endometriomas, open method, see 49203-49205, 58957, 58958)

(For paracentesis, see 49082, 49083, 49084)

(For secondary closure of abdominal wall evisceration or disruption, use 49900)

(For fulguration or excision of lesions, laparoscopic approach, use 58662)

(For chemotherapy, see 96401-96549)

## Vulva, Perineum, and Introitus

### Definitions

The following definitions apply to the vulvectomy codes (56620-56640):

A *simple* procedure is the removal of skin and superficial subcutaneous tissues.

A *radical* procedure is the removal of skin and deep subcutaneous tissue.

A *partial* procedure is the removal of less than 80% of the vulvar area.

A *complete* procedure is the removal of greater than 80% of the vulvar area.

## Incision

(For incision and drainage of sebaceous cyst, furuncle, or abscess, see 10040, 10060, 10061)

**56405** Incision and drainage of vulva or perineal abscess

**56420** Incision and drainage of Bartholin's gland abscess

(For incision and drainage of Skene's gland abscess or cyst, use 53060)

**56440** Marsupialization of Bartholin's gland cyst

**56441** Lysis of labial adhesions

**56442** Hymenotomy, simple incision

## Destruction

**56501** Destruction of lesion(s), vulva; simple (eg, laser surgery, electrosurgery, cryosurgery, chemosurgery)

**56515** extensive (eg, laser surgery, electrosurgery, cryosurgery, chemosurgery)

(For destruction of Skene's gland cyst or abscess, use 53270)

(For cautery destruction of urethral caruncle, use 53265)

## Excision

**56605** Biopsy of vulva or perineum (separate procedure); 1 lesion

**+ 56606** each separate additional lesion (List separately in addition to code for primary procedure)

(Use 56606 in conjunction with 56605)

(For excision of local lesion, see 11420-11426, 11620-11626)

**56620** Vulvectomy simple; partial

**56625** complete

(For skin graft, see 15002 et seq)

**56630** Vulvectomy, radical, partial;

(For skin graft, if used, see 15004-15005, 15120, 15121, 15240, 15241)

**56631** with unilateral inguinofemoral lymphadenectomy

**56632** with bilateral inguinofemoral lymphadenectomy

**56633** Vulvectomy, radical, complete;

**56634** with unilateral inguinofemoral lymphadenectomy

**56637** with bilateral inguinofemoral lymphadenectomy

**56640** Vulvectomy, radical, complete, with inguinofemoral, iliac, and pelvic lymphadenectomy

(For bilateral procedure, report 56640 with modifier 50)

(For lymphadenectomy, see 38760-38780)

**56700** Partial hymenectomy or revision of hymenal ring

**56740** Excision of Bartholin's gland or cyst

(For excision of Skene's gland, use 53270)

(For excision of urethral caruncle, use 53265)

(For excision or fulguration of urethral carcinoma, use 53220)

(For excision or marsupialization of urethral diverticulum, see 53230, 53240)

## Repair

(For repair of urethra for mucosal prolapse, use 53275)

**56800** Plastic repair of introitus

**56805** Clitoroplasty for intersex state

**56810** Perineoplasty, repair of perineum, nonobstetrical (separate procedure)

(See also 56800)

(For repair of wounds to genitalia, see 12001-12007, 12041-12047, 13131-13133)

(For repair of recent injury of vagina and perineum, nonobstetrical, use 57210)

(For anal sphincteroplasty, see 46750, 46751)

(For episiorrhaphy, episioperineorrhaphy for recent injury of vulva and/or perineum, nonobstetrical, use 57210)

## Endoscopy

**56820**　　Colposcopy of the vulva;

**56821**　　　　with biopsy(s)

(For colposcopic examinations/procedures involving the vagina, see 57420, 57421; cervix, see 57452-57461)

## Vagina

### Incision

**57000**　　Colpotomy; with exploration

**57010**　　　　with drainage of pelvic abscess

**57020**　　Colpocentesis (separate procedure)

**57022**　　Incision and drainage of vaginal hematoma; obstetrical/postpartum

**57023**　　　　non-obstetrical (eg, post-trauma, spontaneous bleeding)

### Destruction

**57061**　　Destruction of vaginal lesion(s); simple (eg, laser surgery, electrosurgery, cryosurgery, chemosurgery)

**57065**　　　　extensive (eg, laser surgery, electrosurgery, cryosurgery, chemosurgery)

### Excision

**57100**　　Biopsy of vaginal mucosa; simple (separate procedure)

**57105**　　　　extensive, requiring suture (including cysts)

**57106**　　Vaginectomy, partial removal of vaginal wall;

**57107**　　　　with removal of paravaginal tissue (radical vaginectomy)

**57109**　　　　with removal of paravaginal tissue (radical vaginectomy) with bilateral total pelvic lymphadenectomy and para-aortic lymph node sampling (biopsy)

**57110**　　Vaginectomy, complete removal of vaginal wall;

**57111**　　　　with removal of paravaginal tissue (radical vaginectomy)

**57112**　　　　with removal of paravaginal tissue (radical vaginectomy) with bilateral total pelvic lymphadenectomy and para-aortic lymph node sampling (biopsy)

**57120**　　Colpocleisis (Le Fort type)

**57130**　　Excision of vaginal septum

**57135**　　Excision of vaginal cyst or tumor

## Introduction

**57150**　　Irrigation of vagina and/or application of medicament for treatment of bacterial, parasitic, or fungoid disease

⊙ **57155**　　Insertion of uterine tandem and/or vaginal ovoids for clinical brachytherapy

(For placement of needles or catheters into pelvic organs and/or genitalia [except prostate] for interstitial radioelement application, use 55920)

(For insertion of radioelement sources or ribbons, see 77761-77763, 77785-77787)

**57156**　　Insertion of a vaginal radiation afterloading apparatus for clinical brachytherapy

**57160**　　Fitting and insertion of pessary or other intravaginal support device

**57170**　　Diaphragm or cervical cap fitting with instructions

**57180**　　Introduction of any hemostatic agent or pack for spontaneous or traumatic nonobstetrical vaginal hemorrhage (separate procedure)

## Repair

(For urethral suspension, Marshall-Marchetti-Krantz type, abdominal approach, see 51840, 51841)

(For laparoscopic suspension, use 51990)

**57200**　　Colporrhaphy, suture of injury of vagina (nonobstetrical)

**57210**　　Colpoperineorrhaphy, suture of injury of vagina and/or perineum (nonobstetrical)

**57220**　　Plastic operation on urethral sphincter, vaginal approach (eg, Kelly urethral plication)

**57230**　　Plastic repair of urethrocele

**57240**　　Anterior colporrhaphy, repair of cystocele with or without repair of urethrocele

**57250**　　Posterior colporrhaphy, repair of rectocele with or without perineorrhaphy

(For repair of rectocele [separate procedure] without posterior colporrhaphy, use 45560)

**57260**　　Combined anteroposterior colporrhaphy;

**57265**　　　　with enterocele repair

+ **57267**　　Insertion of mesh or other prosthesis for repair of pelvic floor defect, each site (anterior, posterior compartment), vaginal approach (List separately in addition to code for primary procedure)

(Use 57267 in conjunction with 45560, 57240-57265, 57285)

**57268**　　Repair of enterocele, vaginal approach (separate procedure)

**57270**　　Repair of enterocele, abdominal approach (separate procedure)

**57280**　　Colpopexy, abdominal approach

**Female Genital**

---

▲=Revised code　　●=New code　　▶ ◀=Contains new or revised text　　⊘=Modifier 51 exempt

**57282**   Colpopexy, vaginal; extra-peritoneal approach (sacrospinous, iliococcygeus)

**57283**   intra-peritoneal approach (uterosacral, levator myorrhaphy)

(Do not report 57283 in conjunction with 57556, 58263, 58270, 58280, 58292, 58294)

**57284**   Paravaginal defect repair (including repair of cystocele, if performed); open abdominal approach

(Do not report 57284 in conjunction with 51840, 51841, 51990, 57240, 57260, 57265, 58152, 58267)

**57285**   vaginal approach

(Do not report 57285 in conjunction with 51990, 57240, 57260, 57265, 58267)

**57287**   Removal or revision of sling for stress incontinence (eg, fascia or synthetic)

**57288**   Sling operation for stress incontinence (eg, fascia or synthetic)

(For laparoscopic approach, use 51992)

**57289**   Pereyra procedure, including anterior colporrhaphy

**57291**   Construction of artificial vagina; without graft

**57292**   with graft

**57295**   Revision (including removal) of prosthetic vaginal graft; vaginal approach

**57296**   open abdominal approach

(For laparoscopic approach, use 57426)

**57300**   Closure of rectovaginal fistula; vaginal or transanal approach

**57305**   abdominal approach

**57307**   abdominal approach, with concomitant colostomy

**57308**   transperineal approach, with perineal body reconstruction, with or without levator plication

**57310**   Closure of urethrovaginal fistula;

**57311**   with bulbocavernosus transplant

**57320**   Closure of vesicovaginal fistula; vaginal approach

(For concomitant cystostomy, see 51020-51040, 51101, 51102)

**57330**   transvesical and vaginal approach

(For abdominal approach, use 51900)

**57335**   Vaginoplasty for intersex state

## Manipulation

**57400**   Dilation of vagina under anesthesia (other than local)

**57410**   Pelvic examination under anesthesia (other than local)

**57415**   Removal of impacted vaginal foreign body (separate procedure) under anesthesia (other than local)

(For removal without anesthesia of an impacted vaginal foreign body, use the appropriate E/M code)

## Endoscopy/Laparoscopy

**57420**   Colposcopy of the entire vagina, with cervix if present;

**57421**   with biopsy(s) of vagina/cervix

(For colposcopic visualization of cervix and adjacent upper vagina, use 57452)

(When reporting colposcopies of multiple sites, use modifier 51 as appropriate. For colposcopic examinations/procedures involving the vulva, see 56820, 56821; cervix, see 57452-57461)

(For endometrial sampling [biopsy] performed in conjunction with colposcopy, use 58110)

**57423**   Paravaginal defect repair (including repair of cystocele, if performed), laparoscopic approach

(Do not report 57423 in conjunction with 49320, 51840, 51841, 51990, 57240, 57260, 58152, 58267)

**57425**   Laparoscopy, surgical, colpopexy (suspension of vaginal apex)

**57426**   Revision (including removal) of prosthetic vaginal graft, laparoscopic approach

(For vaginal approach, see 57295. For open abdominal approach, see 57296)

## Cervix Uteri

(For cervicography, use Category III code 0003T)

## Endoscopy

(For colposcopic examinations/procedures involving the vulva, see 56820, 56821; vagina, see 57420, 57421)

**57452**   Colposcopy of the cervix including upper/adjacent vagina,

(Do not report 57452 in addition to 57454-57461)

**57454**   with biopsy(s) of the cervix and endocervical curettage

**57455**   with biopsy(s) of the cervix

**57456**   with endocervical curettage

**57460**   with loop electrode biopsy(s) of the cervix

**57461**   with loop electrode conization of the cervix

(Do not report 57461 in addition to 57456)

(For endometrial sampling [biopsy] performed in conjunction with colposcopy, use 58110)

**Female Genital**

# Excision

(For radical surgical procedures, see 58200-58240)

**57500**    Biopsy of cervix, single or multiple, or local excision of lesion, with or without fulguration (separate procedure)

**57505**    Endocervical curettage (not done as part of a dilation and curettage)

**57510**    Cautery of cervix; electro or thermal

**57511**        cryocautery, initial or repeat

**57513**        laser ablation

**57520**    Conization of cervix, with or without fulguration, with or without dilation and curettage, with or without repair; cold knife or laser

(See also 58120)

**57522**        loop electrode excision

**57530**    Trachelectomy (cervicectomy), amputation of cervix (separate procedure)

**57531**    Radical trachelectomy, with bilateral total pelvic lymphadenectomy and para-aortic lymph node sampling biopsy, with or without removal of tube(s), with or without removal of ovary(s)

(For radical abdominal hysterectomy, use 58210)

**57540**    Excision of cervical stump, abdominal approach;

**57545**        with pelvic floor repair

**57550**    Excision of cervical stump, vaginal approach;

**57555**        with anterior and/or posterior repair

**57556**        with repair of enterocele

(For insertion of intrauterine device, use 58300)

(For insertion of any hemostatic agent or pack for control of spontaneous non-obstetrical hemorrhage, see 57180)

**57558**    Dilation and curettage of cervical stump

# Repair

**57700**    Cerclage of uterine cervix, nonobstetrical

**57720**    Trachelorrhaphy, plastic repair of uterine cervix, vaginal approach

# Manipulation

**57800**    Dilation of cervical canal, instrumental (separate procedure)

# Corpus Uteri

## Excision

**58100**    Endometrial sampling (biopsy) with or without endocervical sampling (biopsy), without cervical dilation, any method (separate procedure)

(For endocervical curettage only, use 57505)

(For endometrial sampling [biopsy] performed in conjunction with colposcopy [57420, 57421, 57452-57461], use 58110)

**+ 58110**    Endometrial sampling (biopsy) performed in conjunction with colposcopy (List separately in addition to code for primary procedure)

(Use 58110 in conjunction with 57420, 57421, 57452-57461)

**58120**    Dilation and curettage, diagnostic and/or therapeutic (nonobstetrical)

(For postpartum hemorrhage, use 59160)

**58140**    Myomectomy, excision of fibroid tumor(s) of uterus, 1 to 4 intramural myoma(s) with total weight of 250 g or less and/or removal of surface myomas; abdominal approach

**58145**        vaginal approach

**58146**    Myomectomy, excision of fibroid tumor(s) of uterus, 5 or more intramural myomas and/or intramural myomas with total weight greater than 250 g, abdominal approach

(Do not report 58146 in addition to 58140-58145, 58150-58240)

## Hysterectomy Procedures

**58150**    Total abdominal hysterectomy (corpus and cervix), with or without removal of tube(s), with or without removal of ovary(s);

**58152**        with colpo-urethrocystopexy (eg, Marshall-Marchetti-Krantz, Burch)

(For urethrocystopexy without hysterectomy, see 51840, 51841)

**58180**    Supracervical abdominal hysterectomy (subtotal hysterectomy), with or without removal of tube(s), with or without removal of ovary(s)

**58200**    Total abdominal hysterectomy, including partial vaginectomy, with para-aortic and pelvic lymph node sampling, with or without removal of tube(s), with or without removal of ovary(s)

**58210**    Radical abdominal hysterectomy, with bilateral total pelvic lymphadenectomy and para-aortic lymph node sampling (biopsy), with or without removal of tube(s), with or without removal of ovary(s)

(For radical hysterectomy with ovarian transposition, use also 58825)

**58240**    Pelvic exenteration for gynecologic malignancy, with total abdominal hysterectomy or cervicectomy, with or without removal of tube(s), with or without removal of ovary(s), with removal of bladder and ureteral transplantations, and/or abdominoperineal resection of rectum and colon and colostomy, or any combination thereof

(For pelvic exenteration for lower urinary tract or male genital malignancy, use 51597)

**Female Genital**

**58260**   Vaginal hysterectomy, for uterus 250 g or less;

**58262**      with removal of tube(s), and/or ovary(s)

**58263**      with removal of tube(s), and/or ovary(s), with repair of enterocele

**58267**      with colpo-urethrocystopexy (Marshall-Marchetti-Krantz type, Pereyra type) with or without endoscopic control

**58270**      with repair of enterocele

(For repair of enterocele with removal of tubes and/or ovaries, use 58263)

**58275**   Vaginal hysterectomy, with total or partial vaginectomy;

**58280**      with repair of enterocele

**58285**   Vaginal hysterectomy, radical (Schauta type operation)

**58290**   Vaginal hysterectomy, for uterus greater than 250 g;

**58291**      with removal of tube(s) and/or ovary(s)

**58292**      with removal of tube(s) and/or ovary(s), with repair of enterocele

**58293**      with colpo-urethrocystopexy (Marshall-Marchetti-Krantz type, Pereyra type) with or without endoscopic control

**58294**      with repair of enterocele

## Introduction

(To report insertion of non-biodegradable drug delivery implant for contraception, use 11981. To report removal of implantable contraceptive capsules with subsequent insertion of non-biodegradable drug delivery implant, use 11976 and 11981)

**58300**   Insertion of intrauterine device (IUD)

**58301**   Removal of intrauterine device (IUD)

**58321**   Artificial insemination; intra-cervical

**58322**      intra-uterine

**58323**   Sperm washing for artificial insemination

**58340**   Catheterization and introduction of saline or contrast material for saline infusion sonohysterography (SIS) or hysterosalpingography

(For radiological supervision and interpretation of saline infusion sonohysterography, use 76831)

(For radiological supervision and interpretation of hysterosalpingography, use 74740)

**58345**   Transcervical introduction of fallopian tube catheter for diagnosis and/or re-establishing patency (any method), with or without hysterosalpingography

(For radiological supervision and interpretation, use 74742)

**58346**   Insertion of Heyman capsules for clinical brachytherapy

(For placement of needles or catheters into pelvic organs and/or genitalia [except prostate] for interstitial radioelement application, use 55920)

(For insertion of radioelement sources or ribbons, see 77761-77763, 77785-77787)

**58350**   Chromotubation of oviduct, including materials

(To report the supply of any materials, use 99070)

**58353**   Endometrial ablation, thermal, without hysteroscopic guidance

(For hysteroscopic procedure, use 58563)

**58356**   Endometrial cryoablation with ultrasonic guidance, including endometrial curettage, when performed

(Do not report 58356 in conjunction with 58100, 58120, 58340, 76700, 76856)

## Repair

**58400**   Uterine suspension, with or without shortening of round ligaments, with or without shortening of sacrouterine ligaments; (separate procedure)

**58410**      with presacral sympathectomy

(For anastomosis of tubes to uterus, use 58752)

**58520**   Hysterorrhaphy, repair of ruptured uterus (nonobstetrical)

**58540**   Hysteroplasty, repair of uterine anomaly (Strassman type)

(For closure of vesicouterine fistula, use 51920)

## Laparoscopy/Hysteroscopy

Surgical laparoscopy always includes diagnostic laparoscopy. To report a diagnostic laparoscopy (peritoneoscopy) (separate procedure), use 49320. To report a diagnostic hysteroscopy (separate procedure), use 58555.

**58541**   Laparoscopy, surgical, supracervical hysterectomy, for uterus 250 g or less;

**58542**      with removal of tube(s) and/or ovary(s)

(Do not report 58541, 58542 in conjunction with 49320, 57000, 57180, 57410, 58140-58146, 58545, 58546, 58561, 58661, 58670, 58671)

**58543**   Laparoscopy, surgical, supracervical hysterectomy, for uterus greater than 250 g;

**58544**      with removal of tube(s) and/or ovary(s)

(Do not report 58543-58544 in conjunction with 49320, 57000, 57180, 57410, 58140-58146, 58545, 58546, 58561, 58661, 58670, 58671)

**58545**   Laparoscopy, surgical, myomectomy, excision; 1 to 4 intramural myomas with total weight of 250 g or less and/or removal of surface myomas

**58546**      5 or more intramural myomas and/or intramural myomas with total weight greater than 250 g

**58548**      Laparoscopy, surgical, with radical hysterectomy, with bilateral total pelvic lymphadenectomy and para-aortic lymph node sampling (biopsy), with removal of tube(s) and ovary(s), if performed

     (Do not report 58548 in conjunction with 38570-38572, 58210, 58285, 58550-58554)

**58550**      Laparoscopy, surgical, with vaginal hysterectomy, for uterus 250 g or less;

**58552**      with removal of tube(s) and/or ovary(s)

     (Do not report 58550-58552 in conjunction with 49320, 57000, 57180, 57410, 58140-58146, 58545, 58546, 58561, 58661, 58670, 58671)

**58553**      Laparoscopy, surgical, with vaginal hysterectomy, for uterus greater than 250 g;

**58554**      with removal of tube(s) and/or ovary(s)

     (Do not report 58553-58554 in conjunction with 49320, 57000, 57180, 57410, 58140-58146, 58545, 58546, 58561, 58661, 58670, 58671)

**58555**      Hysteroscopy, diagnostic (separate procedure)

**58558**      Hysteroscopy, surgical; with sampling (biopsy) of endometrium and/or polypectomy, with or without D & C

**58559**      with lysis of intrauterine adhesions (any method)

**58560**      with division or resection of intrauterine septum (any method)

**58561**      with removal of leiomyomata

**58562**      with removal of impacted foreign body

**58563**      with endometrial ablation (eg, endometrial resection, electrosurgical ablation, thermoablation)

**58565**      with bilateral fallopian tube cannulation to induce occlusion by placement of permanent implants

     (Do not report 58565 in conjunction with 58555 or 57800)

     (For unilateral procedure, use modifier 52)

**58570**      Laparoscopy, surgical, with total hysterectomy, for uterus 250 g or less;

**58571**      with removal of tube(s) and/or ovary(s)

**58572**      Laparoscopy, surgical, with total hysterectomy, for uterus greater than 250 g;

**58573**      with removal of tube(s) and/or ovary(s)

     (Do not report 58570-58573 in conjunction with 49320, 57000, 57180, 57410, 58140-58146, 58150, 58545, 58546, 58561, 58661, 58670, 58671)

**58578**      Unlisted laparoscopy procedure, uterus

**58579**      Unlisted hysteroscopy procedure, uterus

## Oviduct/Ovary

### Incision

**58600**      Ligation or transection of fallopian tube(s), abdominal or vaginal approach, unilateral or bilateral

**58605**      Ligation or transection of fallopian tube(s), abdominal or vaginal approach, postpartum, unilateral or bilateral, during same hospitalization (separate procedure)

     (For laparoscopic procedures, use 58670, 58671)

**+ 58611**      Ligation or transection of fallopian tube(s) when done at the time of cesarean delivery or intra-abdominal surgery (not a separate procedure) (List separately in addition to code for primary procedure)

**58615**      Occlusion of fallopian tube(s) by device (eg, band, clip, Falope ring) vaginal or suprapubic approach

     (For laparoscopic approach, use 58671)

     (For lysis of adnexal adhesions, use 58740)

### Laparoscopy

Surgical laparoscopy always includes diagnostic laparoscopy. To report a diagnostic laparoscopy (peritoneoscopy) (separate procedure), use 49320.

**58660**      Laparoscopy, surgical; with lysis of adhesions (salpingolysis, ovariolysis) (separate procedure)

**58661**      with removal of adnexal structures (partial or total oophorectomy and/or salpingectomy)

**58662**      with fulguration or excision of lesions of the ovary, pelvic viscera, or peritoneal surface by any method

**58670**      with fulguration of oviducts (with or without transection)

**58671**      with occlusion of oviducts by device (eg, band, clip, or Falope ring)

**58672**      with fimbrioplasty

**58673**      with salpingostomy (salpingoneostomy)

     (Codes 58672 and 58673 are used to report unilateral procedures. For bilateral procedure, use modifier 50)

**58679**      Unlisted laparoscopy procedure, oviduct, ovary

     (For laparoscopic aspiration of ovarian cyst, use 49322)

     (For laparoscopic biopsy of the ovary or fallopian tube, use 49321)

### Excision

**58700**      Salpingectomy, complete or partial, unilateral or bilateral (separate procedure)

**58720**      Salpingo-oophorectomy, complete or partial, unilateral or bilateral (separate procedure)

**Female Genital**

## Repair

**58740** Lysis of adhesions (salpingolysis, ovariolysis)

(For laparoscopic approach, use 58660)

(For excision or destruction of endometriomas, open method, see 49203-49205, 58957, 58958)

(For fulguration or excision of lesions, laparoscopic approach, use 58662)

**58750** Tubotubal anastomosis

**58752** Tubouterine implantation

**58760** Fimbrioplasty

(For laparoscopic approach, use 58672)

**58770** Salpingostomy (salpingoneostomy)

(For laparoscopic approach, use 58673)

## Ovary

### Incision

**58800** Drainage of ovarian cyst(s), unilateral or bilateral (separate procedure); vaginal approach

**58805** abdominal approach

**58820** Drainage of ovarian abscess; vaginal approach, open

**58822** abdominal approach

►(58823 has been deleted)◄

►(For transrectal image-guided fluid collection drainage by catheter of pelvic abscess, use 49407)◄

**58825** Transposition, ovary(s)

### Excision

**58900** Biopsy of ovary, unilateral or bilateral (separate procedure)

(For laparoscopic biopsy of the ovary or fallopian tube, use 49321)

**58920** Wedge resection or bisection of ovary, unilateral or bilateral

**58925** Ovarian cystectomy, unilateral or bilateral

**58940** Oophorectomy, partial or total, unilateral or bilateral;

(For oophorectomy with concomitant debulking for ovarian malignancy, use 58952)

**58943** for ovarian, tubal or primary peritoneal malignancy, with para-aortic and pelvic lymph node biopsies, peritoneal washings, peritoneal biopsies, diaphragmatic assessments, with or without salpingectomy(s), with or without omentectomy

**58950** Resection (initial) of ovarian, tubal or primary peritoneal malignancy with bilateral salpingo-oophorectomy and omentectomy;

**58951** with total abdominal hysterectomy, pelvic and limited para-aortic lymphadenectomy

**58952** with radical dissection for debulking (ie, radical excision or destruction, intra-abdominal or retroperitoneal tumors)

(For resection of recurrent ovarian, tubal, primary peritoneal, or uterine malignancy, see 58957, 58958)

**58953** Bilateral salpingo-oophorectomy with omentectomy, total abdominal hysterectomy and radical dissection for debulking;

**58954** with pelvic lymphadenectomy and limited para-aortic lymphadenectomy

**58956** Bilateral salpingo-oophorectomy with total omentectomy, total abdominal hysterectomy for malignancy

(Do not report 58956 in conjunction with 49255, 58150, 58180, 58262, 58263, 58550, 58661, 58700, 58720, 58900, 58925, 58940, 58957, 58958)

**58957** Resection (tumor debulking) of recurrent ovarian, tubal, primary peritoneal, uterine malignancy (intra-abdominal, retroperitoneal tumors), with omentectomy, if performed;

**58958** with pelvic lymphadenectomy and limited para-aortic lymphadenectomy

(Do not report 58957, 58958 in conjunction with 38770, 38780, 44005, 49000, 49203-49215, 49255, 58900-58960)

**58960** Laparotomy, for staging or restaging of ovarian, tubal, or primary peritoneal malignancy (second look), with or without omentectomy, peritoneal washing, biopsy of abdominal and pelvic peritoneum, diaphragmatic assessment with pelvic and limited para-aortic lymphadenectomy

(Do not report 58960 in conjunction with 58957, 58958)

## In Vitro Fertilization

**58970** Follicle puncture for oocyte retrieval, any method

(For radiological supervision and interpretation, use 76948)

**58974** Embryo transfer, intrauterine

**58976** Gamete, zygote, or embryo intrafallopian transfer, any method

(For laparoscopic adnexal procedures, see 58660-58673)

## Other Procedures

**58999** Unlisted procedure, female genital system (nonobstetrical)

# Maternity Care and Delivery

The services normally provided in uncomplicated maternity cases include antepartum care, delivery, and postpartum care.

Antepartum care includes the initial and subsequent history, physical examinations, recording of weight, blood pressures, fetal heart tones, routine chemical urinalysis, and monthly visits up to 28 weeks gestation, biweekly visits to 36 weeks gestation, and weekly visits until delivery. Any other visits or services within this time period should be coded separately.

Postpartum care only services (59430) include office or other outpatient visits following vaginal or cesarean section delivery.

Delivery services include admission to the hospital, the admission history and physical examination, management of uncomplicated labor, vaginal delivery (with or without episiotomy, with or without forceps), or cesarean delivery. When reporting delivery only services (59409, 59514, 59612, 59620), report inpatient postdelivery management and discharge services using Evaluation and Management Services codes (99217-99239). Delivery and postpartum services (59410, 59515, 59614, 59622) include delivery services and all inpatient and outpatient postpartum services. Medical complications of pregnancy (eg, cardiac problems, neurological problems, diabetes, hypertension, toxemia, hyperemesis, preterm labor, premature rupture of membranes, trauma) and medical problems complicating labor and delivery management may require additional resources and may be reported separately.

For surgical complications of pregnancy (eg, appendectomy, hernia, ovarian cyst, Bartholin cyst), see services in the **Surgery** section.

If all or part of the antepartum and/or postpartum patient care is provided except delivery due to termination of pregnancy by abortion or referral to another physician or other qualified health care professional for delivery, see the antepartum and postpartum care codes 59425, 59426, and 59430.

(For circumcision of newborn, see 54150, 54160)

## Antepartum and Fetal Invasive Services

(For fetal intrauterine transfusion, use 36460)

(For unlisted fetal invasive procedure, use 59897)

**59000**  Amniocentesis; diagnostic

(For radiological supervision and interpretation, use 76946)

**59001**  therapeutic amniotic fluid reduction (includes ultrasound guidance)

**59012**  Cordocentesis (intrauterine), any method

(For radiological supervision and interpretation, use 76941)

**59015**  Chorionic villus sampling, any method

(For radiological supervision and interpretation, use 76945)

**59020**  Fetal contraction stress test

**59025**  Fetal non-stress test

**59030**  Fetal scalp blood sampling

(For repeat fetal scalp blood sampling, use 59030 and see modifiers 76 and 77)

**59050**  Fetal monitoring during labor by consulting physician (ie, non-attending physician) with written report; supervision and interpretation

**59051**      interpretation only

**59070**  Transabdominal amnioinfusion, including ultrasound guidance

**59072**  Fetal umbilical cord occlusion, including ultrasound guidance

**59074**  Fetal fluid drainage (eg, vesicocentesis, thoracocentesis, paracentesis), including ultrasound guidance

**59076**  Fetal shunt placement, including ultrasound guidance

## Excision

**59100**  Hysterotomy, abdominal (eg, for hydatidiform mole, abortion)

(When tubal ligation is performed at the same time as hysterotomy, use 58611 in addition to 59100)

**59120**  Surgical treatment of ectopic pregnancy; tubal or ovarian, requiring salpingectomy and/or oophorectomy, abdominal or vaginal approach

**59121**      tubal or ovarian, without salpingectomy and/or oophorectomy

**59130**      abdominal pregnancy

**59135**      interstitial, uterine pregnancy requiring total hysterectomy

**59136**      interstitial, uterine pregnancy with partial resection of uterus

**59140**      cervical, with evacuation

**59150**  Laparoscopic treatment of ectopic pregnancy; without salpingectomy and/or oophorectomy

**59151**      with salpingectomy and/or oophorectomy

**59160**  Curettage, postpartum

## Introduction

(For intrauterine fetal transfusion, use 36460)

(For introduction of hypertonic solution and/or prostaglandins to initiate labor, see 59850-59857)

**59200**  Insertion of cervical dilator (eg, laminaria, prostaglandin) (separate procedure)

**Female Genital**

## Repair

(For tracheloplasty, use 57700)

**59300** Episiotomy or vaginal repair, by other than attending

**59320** Cerclage of cervix, during pregnancy; vaginal

**59325** abdominal

**59350** Hysterorrhaphy of ruptured uterus

## Vaginal Delivery, Antepartum and Postpartum Care

**59400** Routine obstetric care including antepartum care, vaginal delivery (with or without episiotomy, and/or forceps) and postpartum care

**59409** Vaginal delivery only (with or without episiotomy and/or forceps);

**59410** including postpartum care

**59412** External cephalic version, with or without tocolysis

(Use 59412 in addition to code[s] for delivery)

**59414** Delivery of placenta (separate procedure)

(For antepartum care only, see 59425, 59426 or appropriate E/M code[s])

(For 1-3 antepartum care visits, see appropriate E/M code[s])

**59425** Antepartum care only; 4-6 visits

**59426** 7 or more visits

**59430** Postpartum care only (separate procedure)

## Cesarean Delivery

(For standby attendance for infant, use 99360)

(For low cervical cesarean section, see 59510, 59515, 59525)

**59510** Routine obstetric care including antepartum care, cesarean delivery, and postpartum care

**59514** Cesarean delivery only;

**59515** including postpartum care

(For classic cesarean section, see 59510, 59515, 59525)

**+ 59525** Subtotal or total hysterectomy after cesarean delivery (List separately in addition to code for primary procedure)

(Use 59525 in conjunction with 59510, 59514, 59515, 59618, 59620, 59622)

(For extraperitoneal cesarean section, or cesarean section with subtotal or total hysterectomy, see 59510, 59515, 59525)

## Delivery After Previous Cesarean Delivery

Patients who have had a previous cesarean delivery and now present with the expectation of a vaginal delivery are coded using codes 59610-59622. If the patient has a successful vaginal delivery after a previous cesarean delivery (VBAC), use codes 59610-59614. If the attempt is unsuccessful and another cesarean delivery is carried out, use codes 59618-59622. To report elective cesarean deliveries use code 59510, 59514 or 59515.

**59610** Routine obstetric care including antepartum care, vaginal delivery (with or without episiotomy, and/or forceps) and postpartum care, after previous cesarean delivery

**59612** Vaginal delivery only, after previous cesarean delivery (with or without episiotomy and/or forceps);

**59614** including postpartum care

**59618** Routine obstetric care including antepartum care, cesarean delivery, and postpartum care, following attempted vaginal delivery after previous cesarean delivery

**59620** Cesarean delivery only, following attempted vaginal delivery after previous cesarean delivery;

**59622** including postpartum care

## Abortion

(For medical treatment of spontaneous complete abortion, any trimester, use E/M codes 99201-99233)

(For surgical treatment of spontaneous abortion, use 59812)

**59812** Treatment of incomplete abortion, any trimester, completed surgically

**59820** Treatment of missed abortion, completed surgically; first trimester

**59821** second trimester

**59830** Treatment of septic abortion, completed surgically

**59840** Induced abortion, by dilation and curettage

**59841** Induced abortion, by dilation and evacuation

**59850** Induced abortion, by 1 or more intra-amniotic injections (amniocentesis-injections), including hospital admission and visits, delivery of fetus and secundines;

**59851** with dilation and curettage and/or evacuation

**59852** with hysterotomy (failed intra-amniotic injection)

(For insertion of cervical dilator, use 59200)

**59855** Induced abortion, by 1 or more vaginal suppositories (eg, prostaglandin) with or without cervical dilation (eg, laminaria), including hospital admission and visits, delivery of fetus and secundines;

**59856** with dilation and curettage and/or evacuation

**59857** with hysterotomy (failed medical evacuation)

⊙=Moderate sedation  ✦=Add-on code  ✗=FDA approval pending  #=Resequenced code  ○=Recycled/reinstated code

## Other Procedures

**59866**     Multifetal pregnancy reduction(s) (MPR)

**59870**     Uterine evacuation and curettage for hydatidiform mole

**59871**     Removal of cerclage suture under anesthesia (other than local)

**59897**     Unlisted fetal invasive procedure, including ultrasound guidance, when performed

**59898**     Unlisted laparoscopy procedure, maternity care and delivery

**59899**     Unlisted procedure, maternity care and delivery

# Endocrine System

(For pituitary and pineal surgery, see **Nervous System**)

## Thyroid Gland

### Incision

**60000**     Incision and drainage of thyroglossal duct cyst, infected

### Excision

**60100**     Biopsy thyroid, percutaneous core needle

           (If imaging guidance is performed, see 76942, 77002, 77012, 77021)

           (For fine needle aspiration, use 10021 or 10022)

           (For evaluation of fine needle aspirate, see 88172, 88173)

**60200**     Excision of cyst or adenoma of thyroid, or transection of isthmus

**60210**     Partial thyroid lobectomy, unilateral; with or without isthmusectomy

**60212**        with contralateral subtotal lobectomy, including isthmusectomy

**60220**     Total thyroid lobectomy, unilateral; with or without isthmusectomy

**60225**        with contralateral subtotal lobectomy, including isthmusectomy

**60240**     Thyroidectomy, total or complete

           (For thyroidectomy, subtotal or partial, use 60271)

**60252**     Thyroidectomy, total or subtotal for malignancy; with limited neck dissection

**60254**        with radical neck dissection

**60260**     Thyroidectomy, removal of all remaining thyroid tissue following previous removal of a portion of thyroid

           (For bilateral procedure, report 60260 with modifier 50)

**60270**     Thyroidectomy, including substernal thyroid; sternal split or transthoracic approach

**60271**        cervical approach

**60280**     Excision of thyroglossal duct cyst or sinus;

**60281**        recurrent

           (For thyroid ultrasonography, use 76536)

### Removal

**60300**     Aspiration and/or injection, thyroid cyst

           (For fine needle aspiration, see 10021, 10022)

           (If imaging guidance is performed, see 76942, 77012)

## Parathyroid, Thymus, Adrenal Glands, Pancreas, and Carotid Body

### Excision

(For pituitary and pineal surgery, see **Nervous System**)

**60500**     Parathyroidectomy or exploration of parathyroid(s);

**60502**        re-exploration

**60505**        with mediastinal exploration, sternal split or transthoracic approach

**+ 60512**     Parathyroid autotransplantation (List separately in addition to code for primary procedure)

           (Use 60512 in conjunction with 60500, 60502, 60505, 60212, 60225, 60240, 60252, 60254, 60260, 60270, 60271)

**60520**     Thymectomy, partial or total; transcervical approach (separate procedure)

**60521**        sternal split or transthoracic approach, without radical mediastinal dissection (separate procedure)

**60522**        sternal split or transthoracic approach, with radical mediastinal dissection (separate procedure)

           (For thoracoscopic [VATS] thymectomy, see 32673)

**60540**     Adrenalectomy, partial or complete, or exploration of adrenal gland with or without biopsy, transabdominal, lumbar or dorsal (separate procedure);

**60545**        with excision of adjacent retroperitoneal tumor

           (Do not report 60540, 60545 in conjunction with 50323)

           (For bilateral procedure, report 60540 with modifier 50)

           (For excision of remote or disseminated pheochromocytoma, see 49203-49205)

           (For laparoscopic approach, use 60650)

**60600**     Excision of carotid body tumor; without excision of carotid artery

**60605**        with excision of carotid artery

**Female Genital**

## Laparoscopy

Surgical laparoscopy always includes diagnostic
laparoscopy. To report a diagnostic laparoscopy
(peritoneoscopy) (separate procedure), use 49320.

**60650** Laparoscopy, surgical, with adrenalectomy, partial or
complete, or exploration of adrenal gland with or without
biopsy, transabdominal, lumbar or dorsal

**60659** Unlisted laparoscopy procedure, endocrine system

## Other Procedures

**60699** Unlisted procedure, endocrine system

⊙=Moderate sedation ✚=Add-on code ✗=FDA approval pending #=Resequenced code ○=Recycled/reinstated code

**Female Genital**

# Nervous System

## Skull, Meninges, and Brain

(For injection procedure for cerebral angiography, see 36100-36218)

(For injection procedure for ventriculography, see 61026, 61120)

(For injection procedure for pneumoencephalography, use 61055)

### Injection, Drainage, or Aspiration

**61000**   Subdural tap through fontanelle, or suture, infant, unilateral or bilateral; initial

**61001**   subsequent taps

**61020**   Ventricular puncture through previous burr hole, fontanelle, suture, or implanted ventricular catheter/reservoir; without injection

**61026**   with injection of medication or other substance for diagnosis or treatment

**61050**   Cisternal or lateral cervical (C1-C2) puncture; without injection (separate procedure)

**61055**   with injection of medication or other substance for diagnosis or treatment (eg, C1-C2)

(For radiological supervision and interpretation, see **Radiology**)

**61070**   Puncture of shunt tubing or reservoir for aspiration or injection procedure

(For radiological supervision and interpretation, use 75809)

### Twist Drill, Burr Hole(s), or Trephine

**61105**   Twist drill hole for subdural or ventricular puncture

⊘ **61107**   Twist drill hole(s) for subdural, intracerebral, or ventricular puncture; for implanting ventricular catheter, pressure recording device, or other intracerebral monitoring device

(For intracranial neuroendoscopic ventricular catheter placement, use 62160)

**61108**   for evacuation and/or drainage of subdural hematoma

**61120**   Burr hole(s) for ventricular puncture (including injection of gas, contrast media, dye, or radioactive material)

**61140**   Burr hole(s) or trephine; with biopsy of brain or intracranial lesion

**61150**   with drainage of brain abscess or cyst

**61151**   with subsequent tapping (aspiration) of intracranial abscess or cyst

**61154**   Burr hole(s) with evacuation and/or drainage of hematoma, extradural or subdural

(For bilateral procedure, report 61154 with modifier 50)

**61156**   Burr hole(s); with aspiration of hematoma or cyst, intracerebral

**61210**   for implanting ventricular catheter, reservoir, EEG electrode(s), pressure recording device, or other cerebral monitoring device (separate procedure)

(For intracranial neuroendoscopic ventricular catheter placement, use 62160)

**61215**   Insertion of subcutaneous reservoir, pump or continuous infusion system for connection to ventricular catheter

(For refilling and maintenance of an implantable infusion pump for spinal or brain drug therapy, use 95990)

(For chemotherapy, use 96450)

**61250**   Burr hole(s) or trephine, supratentorial, exploratory, not followed by other surgery

(For bilateral procedure, report 61250 with modifier 50)

**61253**   Burr hole(s) or trephine, infratentorial, unilateral or bilateral

(If burr hole[s] or trephine are followed by craniotomy at same operative session, use 61304-61321; do not use 61250 or 61253)

### Craniectomy or Craniotomy

**61304**   Craniectomy or craniotomy, exploratory; supratentorial

**61305**   infratentorial (posterior fossa)

**61312**   Craniectomy or craniotomy for evacuation of hematoma, supratentorial; extradural or subdural

**61313**   intracerebral

**61314**   Craniectomy or craniotomy for evacuation of hematoma, infratentorial; extradural or subdural

**61315**   intracerebellar

+ **61316**   Incision and subcutaneous placement of cranial bone graft (List separately in addition to code for primary procedure)

(Use 61316 in conjunction with 61304, 61312, 61313, 61322, 61323, 61340, 61570, 61571, 61680-61705)

**61320**   Craniectomy or craniotomy, drainage of intracranial abscess; supratentorial

**61321**   infratentorial

**61322**   Craniectomy or craniotomy, decompressive, with or without duraplasty, for treatment of intracranial hypertension, without evacuation of associated intraparenchymal hematoma; without lobectomy

(Do not report 61313 in addition to 61322)

(For subtemporal decompression, use 61340)

**Nervous**

---

**61323**    with lobectomy

(Do not report 61313 in addition to 61323)

(For subtemporal decompression, use 61340)

**61330**   Decompression of orbit only, transcranial approach

(For bilateral procedure, report 61330 with modifier 50)

**61332**   Exploration of orbit (transcranial approach); with biopsy

**61333**    with removal of lesion

**61334**    with removal of foreign body

**61340**   Subtemporal cranial decompression (pseudotumor cerebri, slit ventricle syndrome)

(For bilateral procedure, report 61340 with modifier 50)

(For decompressive craniotomy or craniectomy for intracranial hypertension, without hematoma evacuation, see 61322, 61323)

**61343**   Craniectomy, suboccipital with cervical laminectomy for decompression of medulla and spinal cord, with or without dural graft (eg, Arnold-Chiari malformation)

**61345**   Other cranial decompression, posterior fossa

(For orbital decompression by lateral wall approach, Kroenlein type, use 67445)

**61440**   Craniotomy for section of tentorium cerebelli (separate procedure)

**61450**   Craniectomy, subtemporal, for section, compression, or decompression of sensory root of gasserian ganglion

**61458**   Craniectomy, suboccipital; for exploration or decompression of cranial nerves

**61460**    for section of 1 or more cranial nerves

**61470**    for medullary tractotomy

**61480**    for mesencephalic tractotomy or pedunculotomy

**61490**   Craniotomy for lobotomy, including cingulotomy

(For bilateral procedure, report 61490 with modifier 50)

**61500**   Craniectomy; with excision of tumor or other bone lesion of skull

**61501**    for osteomyelitis

**61510**   Craniectomy, trephination, bone flap craniotomy; for excision of brain tumor, supratentorial, except meningioma

**61512**    for excision of meningioma, supratentorial

**61514**    for excision of brain abscess, supratentorial

**61516**    for excision or fenestration of cyst, supratentorial

(For excision of pituitary tumor or craniopharyngioma, see 61545, 61546, 61548)

**＋ 61517**   Implantation of brain intracavitary chemotherapy agent (List separately in addition to code for primary procedure)

(Use 61517 only in conjunction with 61510 or 61518)

(Do not report 61517 for brachytherapy insertion. For intracavitary insertion of radioelement sources or ribbons, see 77785-77787)

**61518**   Craniectomy for excision of brain tumor, infratentorial or posterior fossa; except meningioma, cerebellopontine angle tumor, or midline tumor at base of skull

**61519**    meningioma

**61520**    cerebellopontine angle tumor

**61521**    midline tumor at base of skull

**61522**   Craniectomy, infratentorial or posterior fossa; for excision of brain abscess

**61524**    for excision or fenestration of cyst

**61526**   Craniectomy, bone flap craniotomy, transtemporal (mastoid) for excision of cerebellopontine angle tumor;

**61530**    combined with middle/posterior fossa craniotomy/craniectomy

**61531**   Subdural implantation of strip electrodes through 1 or more burr or trephine hole(s) for long-term seizure monitoring

(For stereotactic implantation of electrodes, use 61760)

(For craniotomy for excision of intracranial arteriovenous malformation, see 61680-61692)

**61533**   Craniotomy with elevation of bone flap; for subdural implantation of an electrode array, for long-term seizure monitoring

(For continuous EEG monitoring, see 95950-95954)

**61534**    for excision of epileptogenic focus without electrocorticography during surgery

**61535**    for removal of epidural or subdural electrode array, without excision of cerebral tissue (separate procedure)

**61536**    for excision of cerebral epileptogenic focus, with electrocorticography during surgery (includes removal of electrode array)

**61537**    for lobectomy, temporal lobe, without electrocorticography during surgery

**61538**    for lobectomy, temporal lobe, with electrocorticography during surgery

**61539**    for lobectomy, other than temporal lobe, partial or total, with electrocorticography during surgery

**61540**    for lobectomy, other than temporal lobe, partial or total, without electrocorticography during surgery

**61541**    for transection of corpus callosum

**61542**    for total hemispherectomy

**61543**     for partial or subtotal (functional) hemispherectomy

**61544**     for excision or coagulation of choroid plexus

**61545**     for excision of craniopharyngioma

(For craniotomy for selective amygdalohippocampectomy, use 61566)

(For craniotomy for multiple subpial transections during surgery, use 61567)

**61546**   Craniotomy for hypophysectomy or excision of pituitary tumor, intracranial approach

**61548**   Hypophysectomy or excision of pituitary tumor, transnasal or transseptal approach, nonstereotactic

(Do not report code 69990 in addition to code 61548)

**61550**   Craniectomy for craniosynostosis; single cranial suture

**61552**     multiple cranial sutures

(For cranial reconstruction for orbital hypertelorism, see 21260-21263)

(For reconstruction, see 21172-21180)

**61556**   Craniotomy for craniosynostosis; frontal or parietal bone flap

**61557**     bifrontal bone flap

**61558**   Extensive craniectomy for multiple cranial suture craniosynostosis (eg, cloverleaf skull); not requiring bone grafts

**61559**     recontouring with multiple osteotomies and bone autografts (eg, barrel-stave procedure) (includes obtaining grafts)

(For reconstruction, see 21172-21180)

**61563**   Excision, intra and extracranial, benign tumor of cranial bone (eg, fibrous dysplasia); without optic nerve decompression

**61564**     with optic nerve decompression

(For reconstruction, see 21181-21183)

**61566**   Craniotomy with elevation of bone flap; for selective amygdalohippocampectomy

**61567**     for multiple subpial transections, with electrocorticography during surgery

**61570**   Craniectomy or craniotomy; with excision of foreign body from brain

**61571**     with treatment of penetrating wound of brain

(For sequestrectomy for osteomyelitis, use 61501)

**61575**   Transoral approach to skull base, brain stem or upper spinal cord for biopsy, decompression or excision of lesion;

**61576**     requiring splitting of tongue and/or mandible (including tracheostomy)

(For arthrodesis, use 22548)

## Surgery of Skull Base

The surgical management of lesions involving the skull base (base of anterior, middle, and posterior cranial fossae) often requires the skills of several surgeons of different surgical specialties working together or in tandem during the operative session. These operations are usually not staged because of the need for definitive closure of dura, subcutaneous tissues, and skin to avoid serious infections such as osteomyelitis and/or meningitis.

The procedures are categorized according to

(1) *approach procedure* necessary to obtain adequate exposure to the lesion (pathologic entity), (2) *definitive procedure(s)* necessary to biopsy, excise or otherwise treat the lesion, and (3) *repair/reconstruction* of the defect present following the definitive procedure(s).

The *approach procedure* is described according to anatomical area involved, ie, anterior cranial fossa, middle cranial fossa, posterior cranial fossa, and brain stem or upper spinal cord.

The *definitive procedure(s)* describes the repair, biopsy, resection, or excision of various lesions of the skull base and, when appropriate, primary closure of the dura, mucous membranes, and skin.

The *repair/reconstruction procedure(s)* is reported separately if extensive dural grafting, cranioplasty, local or regional myocutaneous pedicle flaps, or extensive skin grafts are required.

For primary closure, see the appropriate codes (ie, 15732, 15756-15758).

When one surgeon performs the approach procedure, another surgeon performs the definitive procedure, and another surgeon performs the repair/reconstruction procedure, each surgeon reports only the code for the specific procedure performed.

If one surgeon performs more than one procedure (ie, approach procedure and definitive procedure), then both codes are reported, adding modifier 51 to the secondary, additional procedure(s).

### Approach Procedures

#### Anterior Cranial Fossa

**61580**   Craniofacial approach to anterior cranial fossa; extradural, including lateral rhinotomy, ethmoidectomy, sphenoidectomy, without maxillectomy or orbital exenteration

**61581**     extradural, including lateral rhinotomy, orbital exenteration, ethmoidectomy, sphenoidectomy and/or maxillectomy

**61582**     extradural, including unilateral or bifrontal craniotomy, elevation of frontal lobe(s), osteotomy of base of anterior cranial fossa

**Nervous**

---

▲=Revised code     ●=New code     ▶◀=Contains new or revised text     ⊘=Modifier 51 exempt

**61583** intradural, including unilateral or bifrontal craniotomy, elevation or resection of frontal lobe, osteotomy of base of anterior cranial fossa

**61584** Orbitocranial approach to anterior cranial fossa, extradural, including supraorbital ridge osteotomy and elevation of frontal and/or temporal lobe(s); without orbital exenteration

**61585** with orbital exenteration

**61586** Bicoronal, transzygomatic and/or LeFort I osteotomy approach to anterior cranial fossa with or without internal fixation, without bone graft

### Middle Cranial Fossa

**61590** Infratemporal pre-auricular approach to middle cranial fossa (parapharyngeal space, infratemporal and midline skull base, nasopharynx), with or without disarticulation of the mandible, including parotidectomy, craniotomy, decompression and/or mobilization of the facial nerve and/or petrous carotid artery

**61591** Infratemporal post-auricular approach to middle cranial fossa (internal auditory meatus, petrous apex, tentorium, cavernous sinus, parasellar area, infratemporal fossa) including mastoidectomy, resection of sigmoid sinus, with or without decompression and/or mobilization of contents of auditory canal or petrous carotid artery

**61592** Orbitocranial zygomatic approach to middle cranial fossa (cavernous sinus and carotid artery, clivus, basilar artery or petrous apex) including osteotomy of zygoma, craniotomy, extra- or intradural elevation of temporal lobe

### Posterior Cranial Fossa

**61595** Transtemporal approach to posterior cranial fossa, jugular foramen or midline skull base, including mastoidectomy, decompression of sigmoid sinus and/or facial nerve, with or without mobilization

**61596** Transcochlear approach to posterior cranial fossa, jugular foramen or midline skull base, including labyrinthectomy, decompression, with or without mobilization of facial nerve and/or petrous carotid artery

**61597** Transcondylar (far lateral) approach to posterior cranial fossa, jugular foramen or midline skull base, including occipital condylectomy, mastoidectomy, resection of C1-C3 vertebral body(s), decompression of vertebral artery, with or without mobilization

**61598** Transpetrosal approach to posterior cranial fossa, clivus or foramen magnum, including ligation of superior petrosal sinus and/or sigmoid sinus

## Definitive Procedures

### Base of Anterior Cranial Fossa

**61600** Resection or excision of neoplastic, vascular or infectious lesion of base of anterior cranial fossa; extradural

**61601** intradural, including dural repair, with or without graft

### Base of Middle Cranial Fossa

**61605** Resection or excision of neoplastic, vascular or infectious lesion of infratemporal fossa, parapharyngeal space, petrous apex; extradural

**61606** intradural, including dural repair, with or without graft

**61607** Resection or excision of neoplastic, vascular or infectious lesion of parasellar area, cavernous sinus, clivus or midline skull base; extradural

**61608** intradural, including dural repair, with or without graft

Codes 61609-61612 are reported in addition to code(s) for primary procedure(s) 61605-61608. Report only one transection or ligation of carotid artery code per operative session.

**+ 61609** Transection or ligation, carotid artery in cavernous sinus; without repair (List separately in addition to code for primary procedure)

**+ 61610** with repair by anastomosis or graft (List separately in addition to code for primary procedure)

**+ 61611** Transection or ligation, carotid artery in petrous canal; without repair (List separately in addition to code for primary procedure)

**+ 61612** with repair by anastomosis or graft (List separately in addition to code for primary procedure)

**61613** Obliteration of carotid aneurysm, arteriovenous malformation, or carotid-cavernous fistula by dissection within cavernous sinus

### Base of Posterior Cranial Fossa

**61615** Resection or excision of neoplastic, vascular or infectious lesion of base of posterior cranial fossa, jugular foramen, foramen magnum, or C1-C3 vertebral bodies; extradural

**61616** intradural, including dural repair, with or without graft

## Repair and/or Reconstruction of Surgical Defects of Skull Base

**61618** Secondary repair of dura for cerebrospinal fluid leak, anterior, middle or posterior cranial fossa following surgery of the skull base; by free tissue graft (eg, pericranium, fascia, tensor fascia lata, adipose tissue, homologous or synthetic grafts)

Nervous

**61619**    by local or regionalized vascularized pedicle flap or myocutaneous flap (including galea, temporalis, frontalis or occipitalis muscle)

## Endovascular Therapy

**61623**    Endovascular temporary balloon arterial occlusion, head or neck (extracranial/intracranial) including selective catheterization of vessel to be occluded, positioning and inflation of occlusion balloon, concomitant neurological monitoring, and radiologic supervision and interpretation of all angiography required for balloon occlusion and to exclude vascular injury post occlusion

(If selective catheterization and angiography of arteries other than artery to be occluded is performed, use appropriate catheterization and radiologic supervision and interpretation codes)

(If complete diagnostic angiography of the artery to be occluded is performed immediately prior to temporary occlusion, use appropriate radiologic supervision and interpretation codes only)

**61624**    Transcatheter permanent occlusion or embolization (eg, for tumor destruction, to achieve hemostasis, to occlude a vascular malformation), percutaneous, any method; central nervous system (intracranial, spinal cord)

▶(For non-central nervous system and non-head or neck embolization, see 37241-37244)◀

(For radiological supervision and interpretation, use 75894)

**61626**    non-central nervous system, head or neck (extracranial, brachiocephalic branch)

▶(For non-central nervous system and non-head or neck embolization, see 37241-37244)◀

(For radiological supervision and interpretation, use 75894)

**61630**    Balloon angioplasty, intracranial (eg, atherosclerotic stenosis), percutaneous

**61635**    Transcatheter placement of intravascular stent(s), intracranial (eg, atherosclerotic stenosis), including balloon angioplasty, if performed

(61630 and 61635 include all selective vascular catheterization of the target vascular family, all diagnostic imaging for arteriography of the target vascular family, and all related radiological supervision and interpretation. When diagnostic arteriogram (including imaging and selective catheterization) confirms the need for angioplasty or stent placement, 61630 and 61635 are inclusive of these services. If angioplasty or stenting are not indicated, then the appropriate codes for selective catheterization and imaging should be reported in lieu of 61630 and 61635)

**61640**    Balloon dilatation of intracranial vasospasm, percutaneous; initial vessel

**+ 61641**    each additional vessel in same vascular family (List separately in addition to code for primary procedure)

**+ 61642**    each additional vessel in different vascular family (List separately in addition to code for primary procedure)

(Use 61641 and 61642 in conjunction with 61640)

(61640, 61641, 61642 include all selective vascular catheterization of the target vessel, contrast injection[s], vessel measurement, roadmapping, postdilatation angiography, and fluoroscopic guidance for the balloon dilatation)

## Surgery for Aneurysm, Arteriovenous Malformation, or Vascular Disease

Includes craniotomy when appropriate for procedure.

**61680**    Surgery of intracranial arteriovenous malformation; supratentorial, simple

**61682**        supratentorial, complex

**61684**        infratentorial, simple

**61686**        infratentorial, complex

**61690**        dural, simple

**61692**        dural, complex

**61697**    Surgery of complex intracranial aneurysm, intracranial approach; carotid circulation

**61698**        vertebrobasilar circulation

(61697, 61698 involve aneurysms that are larger than 15 mm or with calcification of the aneurysm neck, or with incorporation of normal vessels into the aneurysm neck, or a procedure requiring temporary vessel occlusion, trapping, or cardiopulmonary bypass to successfully treat the aneurysm)

**61700**    Surgery of simple intracranial aneurysm, intracranial approach; carotid circulation

**61702**        vertebrobasilar circulation

**61703**    Surgery of intracranial aneurysm, cervical approach by application of occluding clamp to cervical carotid artery (Selverstone-Crutchfield type)

(For cervical approach for direct ligation of carotid artery, see 37600-37606)

**61705**    Surgery of aneurysm, vascular malformation or carotid-cavernous fistula; by intracranial and cervical occlusion of carotid artery

**61708**        by intracranial electrothrombosis

(For ligation or gradual occlusion of internal/common carotid artery, see 37605, 37606)

**61710**        by intra-arterial embolization, injection procedure, or balloon catheter

**Nervous**

**61711** Anastomosis, arterial, extracranial-intracranial (eg, middle cerebral/cortical) arteries

(For carotid or vertebral thromboendarterectomy, use 35301)

(Use 69990 when the surgical microscope is employed for the microsurgical procedure. Do not use 69990 for visualization with magnifying loupes or corrected vision)

## Stereotaxis

**61720** Creation of lesion by stereotactic method, including burr hole(s) and localizing and recording techniques, single or multiple stages; globus pallidus or thalamus

**61735** subcortical structure(s) other than globus pallidus or thalamus

**61750** Stereotactic biopsy, aspiration, or excision, including burr hole(s), for intracranial lesion;

**61751** with computed tomography and/or magnetic resonance guidance

(For radiological supervision and interpretation of computerized tomography, see 70450, 70460, or 70470 as appropriate)

(For radiological supervision and interpretation of magnetic resonance imaging, see 70551, 70552, or 70553 as appropriate)

**61760** Stereotactic implantation of depth electrodes into the cerebrum for long-term seizure monitoring

**61770** Stereotactic localization, including burr hole(s), with insertion of catheter(s) or probe(s) for placement of radiation source

**+ 61781** Stereotactic computer-assisted (navigational) procedure; cranial, intradural (List separately in addition to code for primary procedure)

(Do not report 61781 in conjunction with 61720-61791, 61796-61799, 61863-61868, 62201, 77371-77373, 77432)

**+ 61782** cranial, extradural (List separately in addition to code for primary procedure)

(Do not report 61781, 61782 by the same individual during the same surgical session)

**+ 61783** spinal (List separately in addition to code for primary procedure)

(Do not report 61783 in conjunction with 63620, 63621)

**61790** Creation of lesion by stereotactic method, percutaneous, by neurolytic agent (eg, alcohol, thermal, electrical, radiofrequency); gasserian ganglion

**61791** trigeminal medullary tract

(61793 has been deleted. To report, see 61796-61800, 63620-63621)

## Stereotactic Radiosurgery (Cranial)

Cranial stereotactic radiosurgery is a distinct procedure that utilizes externally generated ionizing radiation to inactivate or eradicate defined target(s) in the head without the need to make an incision. The target is defined by and the treatment is delivered using high-resolution stereotactic imaging. Stereotactic radiosurgery codes and headframe application procedures are reported by the neurosurgeon. The radiation oncologist reports the appropriate code(s) for clinical treatment planning, physics and dosimetry, treatment delivery, and management from the **Radiation Oncology** section (77261-77790). Any necessary planning, dosimetry, targeting, positioning, or blocking by the neurosurgeon is included in the stereotactic radiation surgery services. The same individual should not report stereotactic radiosurgery services with radiation treatment management codes (77427-77435).

Cranial stereotactic radiosurgery is typically performed in a single planning and treatment session, using a rigidly attached stereotactic guiding device, other immobilization technology and/or a stereotactic image-guidance system, but can be performed with more than one planning session and in a limited number of treatment sessions, up to a maximum of five sessions. Do not report stereotactic radiosurgery more than once per lesion per course of treatment when the treatment requires more than one session.

Codes 61796 and 61797 involve stereotactic radiosurgery for simple cranial lesions. Simple cranial lesions are lesions less than 3.5 cm in maximum dimension that do not meet the definition of a complex lesion provided below. Report code 61796 when all lesions are simple.

Codes 61798 and 61799 involve stereotactic radiosurgery for complex cranial lesions and procedures that create therapeutic lesions (eg, thalamotomy or pallidotomy). All lesions 3.5 cm in maximum dimension or greater are complex. When performing therapeutic lesion creation procedures, report code 61798 only once regardless of the number of lesions created. Schwannomas, arterio-venous malformations, pituitary tumors, glomus tumors, pineal region tumors and cavernous sinus/parasellar/petroclival tumors are complex. Any lesion that is adjacent (5mm or less) to the optic nerve/optic chiasm/optic tract or within the brainstem is complex. If treating multiple lesions, and any single lesion treated is complex, use 61798.

Do not report codes 61796-61800 in conjunction with code 20660.

Codes 61796-61799 include computer-assisted planning. Do not report codes 61796-61799 in conjunction with 61781-61783.

(For intensity modulated beam delivery plan and treatment, see 77301, 77418. For stereotactic body radiation therapy, see 77373, 77435)

(61795 has been deleted. To report, see 61781, 61782, 61783)

**61796** Stereotactic radiosurgery (particle beam, gamma ray, or linear accelerator); 1 simple cranial lesion

(Do not report 61796 more than once per course of treatment)

(Do not report 61796 in conjunction with 61798)

**+ 61797** each additional cranial lesion, simple (List separately in addition to code for primary procedure)

(Use 61797 in conjunction with 61796, 61798)

(For each course of treatment, 61797 and 61799 may be reported no more than once per lesion. Do not report any combination of 61797 and 61799 more than 4 times for entire course of treatment regardless of number of lesions treated)

**61798** 1 complex cranial lesion

(Do not report 61798 more than once per course of treatment)

(Do not report 61798 in conjunction with 61796)

**+ 61799** each additional cranial lesion, complex (List separately in addition to code for primary procedure)

(Use 61799 in conjunction with 61798)

(For each course of treatment, 61797 and 61799 may be reported no more than once per lesion. Do not report any combination of 61797 and 61799 more than 4 times for entire course of treatment regardless of number of lesions treated)

**+ 61800** Application of stereotactic headframe for stereotactic radiosurgery (List separately in addition to code for primary procedure)

(Use 61800 in conjunction with 61796, 61798)

## Neurostimulators (Intracranial)

Codes 61850-61888 apply to both simple and complex neurostimulators. For initial or subsequent electronic analysis and programming of neurostimulator pulse generators, see codes 95970-95975.

Microelectrode recording, when performed by the operating surgeon in association with implantation of neurostimulator electrode arrays, is an inclusive service and should not be reported separately. If another individual participates in neurophysiological mapping during a deep brain stimulator implantation procedure, this service may be reported by the second individual with codes 95961-95962.

**61850** Twist drill or burr hole(s) for implantation of neurostimulator electrodes, cortical

**61860** Craniectomy or craniotomy for implantation of neurostimulator electrodes, cerebral, cortical

**61863** Twist drill, burr hole, craniotomy, or craniectomy with stereotactic implantation of neurostimulator electrode array in subcortical site (eg, thalamus, globus pallidus, subthalamic nucleus, periventricular, periaqueductal gray), without use of intraoperative microelectrode recording; first array

**+ 61864** each additional array (List separately in addition to primary procedure)

(Use 61864 in conjunction with 61863)

**61867** Twist drill, burr hole, craniotomy, or craniectomy with stereotactic implantation of neurostimulator electrode array in subcortical site (eg, thalamus, globus pallidus, subthalamic nucleus, periventricular, periaqueductal gray), with use of intraoperative microelectrode recording; first array

**+ 61868** each additional array (List separately in addition to primary procedure)

(Use 61868 in conjunction with 61867)

**61870** Craniectomy for implantation of neurostimulator electrodes, cerebellar; cortical

**61875** subcortical

**61880** Revision or removal of intracranial neurostimulator electrodes

**61885** Insertion or replacement of cranial neurostimulator pulse generator or receiver, direct or inductive coupling; with connection to a single electrode array

**61886** with connection to 2 or more electrode arrays

(For percutaneous placement of cranial nerve (eg, vagus, trigeminal) neurostimulator electrode(s), use 64553)

(For revision or removal of cranial nerve (eg, vagus, trigeminal) neurostimulator electrode array, use 64569)

**61888** Revision or removal of cranial neurostimulator pulse generator or receiver

(Do not report 61888 in conjunction with 61885 or 61886 for the same pulse generator)

## Repair

**62000** Elevation of depressed skull fracture; simple, extradural

**62005** compound or comminuted, extradural

**62010** with repair of dura and/or debridement of brain

**62100** Craniotomy for repair of dural/cerebrospinal fluid leak, including surgery for rhinorrhea/otorrhea

(For repair of spinal dural/CSF leak, see 63707, 63709)

**62115** Reduction of craniomegalic skull (eg, treated hydrocephalus); not requiring bone grafts or cranioplasty

**Nervous**

| | |
|---|---|
| **62116** | with simple cranioplasty |
| **62117** | requiring craniotomy and reconstruction with or without bone graft (includes obtaining grafts) |
| **62120** | Repair of encephalocele, skull vault, including cranioplasty |
| **62121** | Craniotomy for repair of encephalocele, skull base |
| **62140** | Cranioplasty for skull defect; up to 5 cm diameter |
| **62141** | larger than 5 cm diameter |
| **62142** | Removal of bone flap or prosthetic plate of skull |
| **62143** | Replacement of bone flap or prosthetic plate of skull |
| **62145** | Cranioplasty for skull defect with reparative brain surgery |
| **62146** | Cranioplasty with autograft (includes obtaining bone grafts); up to 5 cm diameter |
| **62147** | larger than 5 cm diameter |
| **+ 62148** | Incision and retrieval of subcutaneous cranial bone graft for cranioplasty (List separately in addition to code for primary procedure) |
| | (Use 62148 in conjunction with 62140-62147) |

## Neuroendoscopy

Surgical endoscopy always includes diagnostic endoscopy.

| | |
|---|---|
| **+ 62160** | Neuroendoscopy, intracranial, for placement or replacement of ventricular catheter and attachment to shunt system or external drainage (List separately in addition to code for primary procedure) |
| | (Use 62160 only in conjunction with 61107, 61210, 62220-62230, 62258) |
| **62161** | Neuroendoscopy, intracranial; with dissection of adhesions, fenestration of septum pellucidum or intraventricular cysts (including placement, replacement, or removal of ventricular catheter) |
| **62162** | with fenestration or excision of colloid cyst, including placement of external ventricular catheter for drainage |
| **62163** | with retrieval of foreign body |
| **62164** | with excision of brain tumor, including placement of external ventricular catheter for drainage |
| **62165** | with excision of pituitary tumor, transnasal or trans-sphenoidal approach |

## Cerebrospinal Fluid (CSF) Shunt

| | |
|---|---|
| **62180** | Ventriculocisternostomy (Torkildsen type operation) |
| **62190** | Creation of shunt; subarachnoid/subdural-atrial, -jugular, -auricular |
| **62192** | subarachnoid/subdural-peritoneal, -pleural, other terminus |

| | |
|---|---|
| **62194** | Replacement or irrigation, subarachnoid/subdural catheter |
| **62200** | Ventriculocisternostomy, third ventricle; |
| **62201** | stereotactic, neuroendoscopic method |
| | (For intracranial neuroendoscopic procedures, see 62161-62165) |
| **62220** | Creation of shunt; ventriculo-atrial, -jugular, -auricular |
| | (For intracranial neuroendoscopic ventricular catheter placement, use 62160) |
| **62223** | ventriculo-peritoneal, -pleural, other terminus |
| | (For intracranial neuroendoscopic ventricular catheter placement, use 62160) |
| **62225** | Replacement or irrigation, ventricular catheter |
| | (For intracranial neuroendoscopic ventricular catheter placement, use 62160) |
| **62230** | Replacement or revision of cerebrospinal fluid shunt, obstructed valve, or distal catheter in shunt system |
| | (For intracranial neuroendoscopic ventricular catheter placement, use 62160) |
| **62252** | Reprogramming of programmable cerebrospinal shunt |
| **62256** | Removal of complete cerebrospinal fluid shunt system; without replacement |
| **62258** | with replacement by similar or other shunt at same operation |
| | (For percutaneous irrigation or aspiration of shunt reservoir, use 61070) |
| | (For reprogramming of programmable CSF shunt, use 62252) |
| | (For intracranial neuroendoscopic ventricular catheter placement, use 62160) |

## Spine and Spinal Cord

(For application of caliper or tongs, use 20660)

(For treatment of fracture or dislocation of spine, see 22305-22327)

## Injection, Drainage, or Aspiration

Injection of contrast during fluoroscopic guidance and localization is an inclusive component of 62263, 62264, 62267, 62270-62273, 62280-62282, 62310-62319. Fluoroscopic guidance and localization is reported with 77003, unless a formal contrast study (myelography, epidurography, or arthrography) is performed, in which case the use of fluoroscopy is included in the supervision and interpretation codes.

For radiologic supervision and interpretation of epidurography, use 72275. Code 72275 is only to be used when an epidurogram is performed, images documented, and a formal radiologic report is issued.

Nervous

Code 62263 describes a catheter-based treatment involving targeted injection of various substances (eg, hypertonic saline, steroid, anesthetic) via an indwelling epidural catheter. Code 62263 includes percutaneous insertion and removal of an epidural catheter (remaining in place over a several-day period), for the administration of multiple injections of a neurolytic agent(s) performed during serial treatment sessions (ie, spanning two or more treatment days). If required, adhesions or scarring may also be lysed by mechanical means. Code 62263 is **not** reported for each adhesiolysis treatment, but should be reported **once** to describe the entire series of injections/infusions spanning two or more treatment days.

Code 62264 describes multiple adhesiolysis treatment sessions performed on the same day. Adhesions or scarring may be lysed by injections of neurolytic agent(s). If required, adhesions or scarring may also be lysed mechanically using a percutaneously-deployed catheter.

Codes 62263 and 62264 include the procedure of injections of contrast for epidurography (72275) and fluoroscopic guidance and localization (77003) during initial or subsequent sessions.

Fluoroscopy (for localization) may be used in the placement of injections reported with 62310-62319, but is not required. If used, fluoroscopy should be reported with 77003. For epidurography, use 72275.

The placement and use of a catheter to administer one or more epidural or subarachnoid injections on a single calendar day should be reported in the same manner as if a needle had been used, ie, as a single injection using either 62310 or 62311. Such injections should not be reported with 62318 or 62319.

Threading a catheter into the epidural space, injecting substances at one or more levels and then removing the catheter should be treated as a single injection (62310, 62311). If the catheter is left in place to deliver substance(s) over a prolonged period (ie, more than a single calendar day) either continuously or via intermittent bolus, use 62318, 62319 as appropriate.

When reporting 62310-62319, code choice is based on the region at which the needle or catheter entered the body (eg, lumbar). Codes 62310-62319 should be reported only once, when the substance injected spreads or catheter tip insertion moves into another spinal region (eg, 62311 is reported only once for injection or catheter insertion at L3-4 with spread of the substance or placement of the catheter tip to the thoracic region).

Percutaneous spinal procedures are done with indirect visualization (eg, image guidance or endoscopic approaches) and without direct visualization (including through a microscope). Endoscopic assistance during an open procedure with direct visualization is reported using excision codes (eg, 63020-63035).

(Report 01996 for daily hospital management of continuous epidural or subarachnoid drug administration performed in conjunction with 62318-62319)

**62263**  Percutaneous lysis of epidural adhesions using solution injection (eg, hypertonic saline, enzyme) or mechanical means (eg, catheter) including radiologic localization (includes contrast when administered), multiple adhesiolysis sessions; 2 or more days

(62263 includes codes 72275 and 77003)

**62264**  1 day

(Do not report 62264 with 62263)

(62264 includes codes 72275 and 77003)

**62267**  Percutaneous aspiration within the nucleus pulposus, intervertebral disc, or paravertebral tissue for diagnostic purposes

(For imaging, use 77003)

(Do not report 62267 in conjunction with 10022, 20225, 62287, 62290, 62291)

**62268**  Percutaneous aspiration, spinal cord cyst or syrinx

(For radiological supervision and interpretation, see 76942, 77002, 77012)

**62269**  Biopsy of spinal cord, percutaneous needle

(For radiological supervision and interpretation, see 76942, 77002, 77012)

(For fine needle aspiration, see 10021, 10022)

(For evaluation of fine needle aspirate, see 88172, 88173)

**62270**  Spinal puncture, lumbar, diagnostic

**62272**  Spinal puncture, therapeutic, for drainage of cerebrospinal fluid (by needle or catheter)

**62273**  Injection, epidural, of blood or clot patch

(For injection of diagnostic or therapeutic substance(s), see 62310, 62311, 62318, 62319)

**62280**  Injection/infusion of neurolytic substance (eg, alcohol, phenol, iced saline solutions), with or without other therapeutic substance; subarachnoid

**62281**  epidural, cervical or thoracic

**62282**  epidural, lumbar, sacral (caudal)

**62284**  Injection procedure for myelography and/or computed tomography, spinal (other than C1-C2 and posterior fossa)

(For injection procedure at C1-C2, use 61055)

(For radiological supervision and interpretation, see **Radiology**)

**Nervous**

**62287** Decompression procedure, percutaneous, of nucleus pulposus of intervertebral disc, any method utilizing needle based technique to remove disc material under fluoroscopic imaging or other form of indirect visualization, with the use of an endoscope, with discography and/or epidural injection(s) at the treated level(s), when performed, single or multiple levels, lumbar

(This includes endoscopic approach)

(Do not report 62287 in conjunction with 62267, 62290, 62311,77003, 77012, 72295, when performed at same level)

(For non-needle based technique for percutaneous decompression of nucleus pulposus of intervertebral disc, see 0274T, 0275T)

**62290** Injection procedure for discography, each level; lumbar

**62291** cervical or thoracic

(For radiological supervision and interpretation, see 72285, 72295)

**62292** Injection procedure for chemonucleolysis, including discography, intervertebral disc, single or multiple levels, lumbar

**62294** Injection procedure, arterial, for occlusion of arteriovenous malformation, spinal

**62310** Injection(s), of diagnostic or therapeutic substance(s) (including anesthetic, antispasmodic, opioid, steroid, other solution), not including neurolytic substances, including needle or catheter placement, includes contrast for localization when performed, epidural or subarachnoid; cervical or thoracic

**62311** lumbar or sacral (caudal)

**62318** Injection(s), including indwelling catheter placement, continuous infusion or intermittent bolus, of diagnostic or therapeutic substance(s) (including anesthetic, antispasmodic, opioid, steroid, other solution), not including neurolytic substances, includes contrast for localization when performed, epidural or subarachnoid, cervical or thoracic

**62319** lumbar or sacral (caudal)

(For transforaminal epidural injection, see 64479-64484)

(Report 01996 for daily hospital management of continuous epidural or subarachnoid drug administration performed in conjunction with 62318-62319)

## Catheter Implantation

(For percutaneous placement of intrathecal or epidural catheter, see codes 62270-62273, 62280-62284, 62310-62319)

**62350** Implantation, revision or repositioning of tunneled intrathecal or epidural catheter, for long-term medication administration via an external pump or implantable reservoir/infusion pump; without laminectomy

**62351** with laminectomy

(For refilling and maintenance of an implantable infusion pump for spinal or brain drug therapy, see 95990, 95991)

**62355** Removal of previously implanted intrathecal or epidural catheter

## Reservoir/Pump Implantation

**62360** Implantation or replacement of device for intrathecal or epidural drug infusion; subcutaneous reservoir

**62361** nonprogrammable pump

**62362** programmable pump, including preparation of pump, with or without programming

**62365** Removal of subcutaneous reservoir or pump, previously implanted for intrathecal or epidural infusion

**62367** Electronic analysis of programmable, implanted pump for intrathecal or epidural drug infusion (includes evaluation of reservoir status, alarm status, drug prescription status); without reprogramming or refill

**62368** with reprogramming

(For refilling and maintenance of an implantable infusion pump for spinal or brain drug therapy, see 95990-95991)

**62369** with reprogramming and refill

**62370** with reprogramming and refill (requiring skill of a physician or other qualified health care professional)

(Do not report 62367-62370 in conjunction with 95990, 95991. For refilling and maintenance of a reservoir or an implantable infusion pump for spinal or brain drug delivery without reprogramming, see 95990, 95991)

## Posterior Extradural Laminotomy or Laminectomy for Exploration/ Decompression of Neural Elements or Excision of Herniated Intervertebral Discs

Endoscopically assisted laminotomy (hemilaminectomy) requires open and direct visualization. When visualization is only endoscopic and/or image guidance, the procedure is percutaneous and reported using 0274T, 0275T.

(When 63001-63048 are followed by arthrodesis, see 22590-22614)

**63001** Laminectomy with exploration and/or decompression of spinal cord and/or cauda equina, without facetectomy, foraminotomy or discectomy (eg, spinal stenosis), 1 or 2 vertebral segments; cervical

**63003** thoracic

**63005** lumbar, except for spondylolisthesis

**63011** sacral

Nervous

**63012**   Laminectomy with removal of abnormal facets and/or pars inter-articularis with decompression of cauda equina and nerve roots for spondylolisthesis, lumbar (Gill type procedure)

**63015**   Laminectomy with exploration and/or decompression of spinal cord and/or cauda equina, without facetectomy, foraminotomy or discectomy (eg, spinal stenosis), more than 2 vertebral segments; cervical

**63016**       thoracic

**63017**       lumbar

**63020**   Laminotomy (hemilaminectomy), with decompression of nerve root(s), including partial facetectomy, foraminotomy and/or excision of herniated intervertebral disc; 1 interspace, cervical

(For bilateral procedure, report 63020 with modifier 50)

**63030**       1 interspace, lumbar

(For bilateral procedure, report 63030 with modifier 50)

**+ 63035**       each additional interspace, cervical or lumbar (List separately in addition to code for primary procedure)

(Use 63035 in conjunction with 63020-63030)

(For bilateral procedure, report 63035 with modifier 50)

(For percutaneous endoscopic approach, see 0274T, 0275T)

**63040**   Laminotomy (hemilaminectomy), with decompression of nerve root(s), including partial facetectomy, foraminotomy and/or excision of herniated intervertebral disc, reexploration, single interspace; cervical

(For bilateral procedure, report 63040 with modifier 50)

**63042**       lumbar

(For bilateral procedure, report 63042 with modifier 50)

**+ 63043**       each additional cervical interspace (List separately in addition to code for primary procedure)

(Use 63043 in conjunction with 63040)

(For bilateral procedure, report 63043 with modifier 50)

**+ 63044**       each additional lumbar interspace (List separately in addition to code for primary procedure)

(Use 63044 in conjunction with 63042)

(For bilateral procedure, report 63044 with modifier 50)

**63045**   Laminectomy, facetectomy and foraminotomy (unilateral or bilateral with decompression of spinal cord, cauda equina and/or nerve root[s], [eg, spinal or lateral recess stenosis]), single vertebral segment; cervical

**63046**       thoracic

**63047**       lumbar

**+ 63048**       each additional segment, cervical, thoracic, or lumbar (List separately in addition to code for primary procedure)

(Use 63048 in conjunction with 63045-63047)

**63050**   Laminoplasty, cervical, with decompression of the spinal cord, 2 or more vertebral segments;

**63051**       with reconstruction of the posterior bony elements (including the application of bridging bone graft and non-segmental fixation devices [eg, wire, suture, mini-plates], when performed)

(Do not report 63050 or 63051 in conjunction with 22600, 22614, 22840-22842, 63001, 63015, 63045, 63048, 63295 for the same vertebral segment(s))

## Transpedicular or Costovertebral Approach for Posterolateral Extradural Exploration/Decompression

**63055**   Transpedicular approach with decompression of spinal cord, equina and/or nerve root(s) (eg, herniated intervertebral disc), single segment; thoracic

**63056**       lumbar (including transfacet, or lateral extraforaminal approach) (eg, far lateral herniated intervertebral disc)

**+ 63057**       each additional segment, thoracic or lumbar (List separately in addition to code for primary procedure)

(Use 63057 in conjunction with 63055, 63056)

**63064**   Costovertebral approach with decompression of spinal cord or nerve root(s) (eg, herniated intervertebral disc), thoracic; single segment

**+ 63066**       each additional segment (List separately in addition to code for primary procedure)

(Use 63066 in conjunction with 63064)

(For excision of thoracic intraspinal lesions by laminectomy, see 63266, 63271, 63276, 63281, 63286)

## Anterior or Anterolateral Approach for Extradural Exploration/Decompression

For the following codes, when two surgeons work together as primary surgeons performing distinct part(s) of spinal cord exploration/decompression operation, each surgeon should report his/her distinct operative work by appending modifier 62 to the procedure code (and any associated add-on codes for that procedure code as long as both surgeons continue to work together as primary surgeons). In this situation, modifier 62 may be appended to the definitive procedure code(s) 63075, 63077, 63081, 63085, 63087, 63090 and, as appropriate, to associated additional interspace add-on code(s) 63076, 63078 or additional segment add-on code(s) 63082, 63086, 63088, 63091 as long as both surgeons continue to work together as primary surgeons.

**Nervous**

**63075** Discectomy, anterior, with decompression of spinal cord and/or nerve root(s), including osteophytectomy; cervical, single interspace

(Do not report 63075 in conjunction with 22554, even if performed by separate individuals. To report anterior cervical discectomy and interbody fusion at the same level during the same session, use 22551)

**+ 63076** cervical, each additional interspace (List separately in addition to code for primary procedure)

(Do not report 63076 in conjunction with 22554, even if performed by separate individuals. To report anterior cervical discectomy and interbody fusion at the same level during the same session, use 22552)

(Use 63076 in conjunction with 63075)

**63077** thoracic, single interspace

**+ 63078** thoracic, each additional interspace (List separately in addition to code for primary procedure)

(Use 63078 in conjunction with 63077)

(Do not report code 69990 in addition to codes 63075-63078)

**63081** Vertebral corpectomy (vertebral body resection), partial or complete, anterior approach with decompression of spinal cord and/or nerve root(s); cervical, single segment

**+ 63082** cervical, each additional segment (List separately in addition to code for primary procedure)

(Use 63082 in conjunction with 63081)

(For transoral approach, see 61575, 61576)

**63085** Vertebral corpectomy (vertebral body resection), partial or complete, transthoracic approach with decompression of spinal cord and/or nerve root(s); thoracic, single segment

**+ 63086** thoracic, each additional segment (List separately in addition to code for primary procedure)

(Use 63086 in conjunction with 63085)

**63087** Vertebral corpectomy (vertebral body resection), partial or complete, combined thoracolumbar approach with decompression of spinal cord, cauda equina or nerve root(s), lower thoracic or lumbar; single segment

**+ 63088** each additional segment (List separately in addition to code for primary procedure)

(Use 63088 in conjunction with 63087)

**63090** Vertebral corpectomy (vertebral body resection), partial or complete, transperitoneal or retroperitoneal approach with decompression of spinal cord, cauda equina or nerve root(s), lower thoracic, lumbar, or sacral; single segment

**+ 63091** each additional segment (List separately in addition to code for primary procedure)

(Use 63091 in conjunction with 63090)

(Procedures 63081-63091 include discectomy above and/or below vertebral segment)

(If followed by arthrodesis, see 22548-22812)

(For reconstruction of spine, use appropriate vertebral corpectomy codes 63081-63091, bone graft codes 20930-20938, arthrodesis codes 22548-22812, and spinal instrumentation codes 22840-22855)

## Lateral Extracavitary Approach for Extradural Exploration/Decompression

**63101** Vertebral corpectomy (vertebral body resection), partial or complete, lateral extracavitary approach with decompression of spinal cord and/or nerve root(s) (eg, for tumor or retropulsed bone fragments); thoracic, single segment

**63102** lumbar, single segment

**+ 63103** thoracic or lumbar, each additional segment (List separately in addition to code for primary procedure)

(Use 63103 in conjunction with 63101 and 63102)

## Incision

**63170** Laminectomy with myelotomy (eg, Bischof or DREZ type), cervical, thoracic, or thoracolumbar

**63172** Laminectomy with drainage of intramedullary cyst/syrinx; to subarachnoid space

**63173** to peritoneal or pleural space

**63180** Laminectomy and section of dentate ligaments, with or without dural graft, cervical; 1 or 2 segments

**63182** more than 2 segments

**63185** Laminectomy with rhizotomy; 1 or 2 segments

**63190** more than 2 segments

**63191** Laminectomy with section of spinal accessory nerve

(For bilateral procedure, report 63191 with modifier 50)

(For resection of sternocleidomastoid muscle, use 21720)

**63194** Laminectomy with cordotomy, with section of 1 spinothalamic tract, 1 stage; cervical

**63195** thoracic

**63196** Laminectomy with cordotomy, with section of both spinothalamic tracts, 1 stage; cervical

**63197** thoracic

**63198** Laminectomy with cordotomy with section of both spinothalamic tracts, 2 stages within 14 days; cervical

**63199** thoracic

Nervous

**63200**   Laminectomy, with release of tethered spinal cord, lumbar

## Excision by Laminectomy of Lesion Other Than Herniated Disc

**63250**   Laminectomy for excision or occlusion of arteriovenous malformation of spinal cord; cervical

**63251**        thoracic

**63252**        thoracolumbar

**63265**   Laminectomy for excision or evacuation of intraspinal lesion other than neoplasm, extradural; cervical

**63266**        thoracic

**63267**        lumbar

**63268**        sacral

**63270**   Laminectomy for excision of intraspinal lesion other than neoplasm, intradural; cervical

**63271**        thoracic

**63272**        lumbar

**63273**        sacral

**63275**   Laminectomy for biopsy/excision of intraspinal neoplasm; extradural, cervical

**63276**        extradural, thoracic

**63277**        extradural, lumbar

**63278**        extradural, sacral

**63280**        intradural, extramedullary, cervical

**63281**        intradural, extramedullary, thoracic

**63282**        intradural, extramedullary, lumbar

**63283**        intradural, sacral

**63285**        intradural, intramedullary, cervical

**63286**        intradural, intramedullary, thoracic

**63287**        intradural, intramedullary, thoracolumbar

**63290**        combined extradural-intradural lesion, any level

(For drainage of intramedullary cyst/syrinx, use 63172, 63173)

**+ 63295**   Osteoplastic reconstruction of dorsal spinal elements, following primary intraspinal procedure (List separately in addition to code for primary procedure)

(Use 63295 in conjunction with 63172, 63173, 63185, 63190, 63200-63290)

(Do not report 63295 in conjunction with 22590-22614, 22840-22844, 63050, 63051 for the same vertebral segment(s))

## Excision, Anterior or Anterolateral Approach, Intraspinal Lesion

For the following codes, when two surgeons work together as primary surgeons performing distinct part(s) of an anterior approach for an intraspinal excision, each surgeon should report his/her distinct operative work by appending modifier 62 to the single definitive procedure code. In this situation, modifier 62 may be appended to the definitive procedure code(s) 63300-63307 and, as appropriate, to the associated additional segment add-on code 63308 as long as both surgeons continue to work together as primary surgeons.

(For arthrodesis, see 22548-22585)

(For reconstruction of spine, see 20930-20938)

**63300**   Vertebral corpectomy (vertebral body resection), partial or complete, for excision of intraspinal lesion, single segment; extradural, cervical

**63301**        extradural, thoracic by transthoracic approach

**63302**        extradural, thoracic by thoracolumbar approach

**63303**        extradural, lumbar or sacral by transperitoneal or retroperitoneal approach

**63304**        intradural, cervical

**63305**        intradural, thoracic by transthoracic approach

**63306**        intradural, thoracic by thoracolumbar approach

**63307**        intradural, lumbar or sacral by transperitoneal or retroperitoneal approach

**+ 63308**        each additional segment (List separately in addition to codes for single segment)

(Use 63308 in conjunction with 63300-63307)

## Stereotaxis

**63600**   Creation of lesion of spinal cord by stereotactic method, percutaneous, any modality (including stimulation and/or recording)

**63610**   Stereotactic stimulation of spinal cord, percutaneous, separate procedure not followed by other surgery

**63615**   Stereotactic biopsy, aspiration, or excision of lesion, spinal cord

## Stereotactic Radiosurgery (Spinal)

Spinal stereotactic radiosurgery is a distinct procedure that utilizes externally generated ionizing radiation to inactivate or eradicate defined target(s) in the spine without the need to make an incision. The target is defined by and the treatment is delivered using high-resolution stereotactic imaging. These codes are reported by the surgeon. The radiation oncologist reports the

**Nervous**

appropriate code(s) for clinical treatment planning, physics and dosimetry, treatment delivery and management from the **Radiation Oncology** section (77261-77790). Any necessary planning, dosimetry, targeting, positioning, or blocking by the neurosurgeon is included in the stereotactic radiation surgery services. The same individual should not report stereotactic radiosurgery services with radiation treatment management codes (77427-77432).

Spinal stereotactic radiosurgery is typically performed in a single planning and treatment session using a stereotactic image-guidance system, but can be performed with a planning session and in a limited number of treatment sessions, up to a maximum of five sessions. Do not report stereotactic radiosurgery more than once per lesion per course of treatment when the treatment requires greater than one session.

Stereotactic spinal surgery is only used when the tumor being treated affects spinal neural tissue or abuts the dura mater. Arteriovenous malformations must be subdural. For other radiation services of the spine, see **Radiation Oncology** services.

Codes 63620, 63621 include computer-assisted planning. Do not report 63620, 63621 in conjunction with 61781-61783.

> (For intensity modulated beam delivery plan and treatment, see 77301, 77418. For stereotactic body radiation therapy, see 77373, 77435)

**63620**    Stereotactic radiosurgery (particle beam, gamma ray, or linear accelerator); 1 spinal lesion

> (Do not report 63620 more than once per course of treatment)

**+ 63621**    each additional spinal lesion (List separately in addition to code for primary procedure)

> (Report 63621 in conjunction with 63620)

> (For each course of treatment, 63621 may be reported no more than once per lesion. Do not report 63621 more than 2 times for entire course of treatment regardless of number of lesions treated)

## Neurostimulators (Spinal)

Codes 63650-63688 apply to both simple and complex neurostimulators. For initial or subsequent electronic analysis and programming of neurostimulator pulse generators, see codes 95970-95975.

Codes 63650, 63655, and 63661-63664 describe the operative placement, revision, replacement, or removal of the spinal neurostimulator system components to provide spinal electrical stimulation. A neurostimulator system includes an implanted neurostimulator, external controller, extension, and collection of contacts. Multiple contacts or electrodes (4 or more) provide the actual electrical stimulation in the epidural space.

For percutaneously placed neurostimulator systems (63650, 63661, 63663), the contacts are on a catheter-like lead. An array defines the collection of contacts that are on one catheter.

For systems placed via an open surgical exposure (63655, 63662, 63664), the contacts are on a plate or paddle-shaped surface.

Do not report 63661 or 63663 when removing or replacing a temporary percutaneously placed array for an external generator.

**63650**    Percutaneous implantation of neurostimulator electrode array, epidural

**63655**    Laminectomy for implantation of neurostimulator electrodes, plate/paddle, epidural

> (63660 has been deleted. To report, see 63661-63664)

**63661**    Removal of spinal neurostimulator electrode percutaneous array(s), including fluoroscopy, when performed

**63662**    Removal of spinal neurostimulator electrode plate/paddle(s) placed via laminotomy or laminectomy, including fluoroscopy, when performed

**63663**    Revision including replacement, when performed, of spinal neurostimulator electrode percutaneous array(s), including fluoroscopy, when performed

> (Do not report 63663 in conjunction with 63661, 63662 for the same spinal level)

**63664**    Revision including replacement, when performed, of spinal neurostimulator electrode plate/paddle(s) placed via laminotomy or laminectomy, including fluoroscopy, when performed

> (Do not report 63664 in conjunction with 63661, 63662 for the same spinal level)

**63685**    Insertion or replacement of spinal neurostimulator pulse generator or receiver, direct or inductive coupling

> (Do not report 63685 in conjunction with 63688 for the same pulse generator or receiver)

**63688**    Revision or removal of implanted spinal neurostimulator pulse generator or receiver

> (For electronic analysis of implanted neurostimulator pulse generator system, see 95970-95975)

## Repair

**63700**    Repair of meningocele; less than 5 cm diameter

**63702**    larger than 5 cm diameter

> (Do not use modifier 63 in conjunction with 63700, 63702)

**63704**    Repair of myelomeningocele; less than 5 cm diameter

**Nervous**

**63706**        larger than 5 cm diameter

(Do not use modifier 63 in conjunction with 63704, 63706)

(For complex skin closure, see **Integumentary System**)

**63707**    Repair of dural/cerebrospinal fluid leak, not requiring laminectomy

**63709**    Repair of dural/cerebrospinal fluid leak or pseudomeningocele, with laminectomy

**63710**    Dural graft, spinal

(For laminectomy and section of dentate ligaments, with or without dural graft, cervical, see 63180, 63182)

## Shunt, Spinal CSF

**63740**    Creation of shunt, lumbar, subarachnoid-peritoneal, -pleural, or other; including laminectomy

**63741**        percutaneous, not requiring laminectomy

**63744**    Replacement, irrigation or revision of lumbosubarachnoid shunt

**63746**    Removal of entire lumbosubarachnoid shunt system without replacement

(For insertion of subarachnoid catheter with reservoir and/or pump for intermittent or continuous infusion of drug including laminectomy, see 62351 and 62360, 62361 or 62362)

(For insertion or replacement of subarachnoid or epidural catheter, with reservoir and/or pump for drug infusion without laminectomy, see 62350 and 62360, 62361 or 62362)

# Extracranial Nerves, Peripheral Nerves, and Autonomic Nervous System

(For intracranial surgery on cranial nerves, see 61450, 61460, 61790)

## Introduction/Injection of Anesthetic Agent (Nerve Block), Diagnostic or Therapeutic

(For destruction by neurolytic agent or chemodenervation, see 62280-62282, 64600-64681)

(For epidural or subarachnoid injection, see 62310-62319)

(64479-64495 are unilateral procedures. For bilateral procedures, use modifier 50)

### Somatic Nerves

**64400**    Injection, anesthetic agent; trigeminal nerve, any division or branch

**64402**        facial nerve

**64405**        greater occipital nerve

**64408**        vagus nerve

**64410**        phrenic nerve

**64412**        spinal accessory nerve

**64413**        cervical plexus

**64415**        brachial plexus, single

**64416**        brachial plexus, continuous infusion by catheter (including catheter placement)

(Do not report 64416 in conjunction with 01996)

**64417**        axillary nerve

**64418**        suprascapular nerve

**64420**        intercostal nerve, single

**64421**        intercostal nerves, multiple, regional block

**64425**        ilioinguinal, iliohypogastric nerves

**64430**        pudendal nerve

**64435**        paracervical (uterine) nerve

**64445**        sciatic nerve, single

**64446**        sciatic nerve, continuous infusion by catheter (including catheter placement)

(Do not report 64446 in conjunction with 01996)

**64447**        femoral nerve, single

(Do not report 64447 in conjunction with 01996)

**64448**        femoral nerve, continuous infusion by catheter (including catheter placement)

(Do not report 64448 in conjunction with 01996)

**64449**        lumbar plexus, posterior approach, continuous infusion by catheter (including catheter placement)

(Do not report 64449 in conjunction with 01996)

**64450**        other peripheral nerve or branch

**64455**    Injection(s), anesthetic agent and/or steroid, plantar common digital nerve(s) (eg, Morton's neuroma)

(Do not report 64455 in conjunction with 64632)

(Imaging guidance [fluoroscopy or CT] and any injection of contrast are inclusive components of 64479-64484. Imaging guidance and localization are required for the performance of 64479-64484)

(64470-64476 have been deleted. To report, see 64490-64495)

**64479**    Injection(s), anesthetic agent and/or steroid, transforaminal epidural, with imaging guidance (fluoroscopy or CT); cervical or thoracic, single level

(For transforaminal epidural injection under ultrasound guidance, use 0228T)

**Nervous**

**+ 64480**      cervical or thoracic, each additional level (List separately in addition to code for primary procedure)

(Use 64480 in conjunction with 64479)

(For transforaminal epidural injection under ultrasound guidance, use 0229T)

(For transforaminal epidural injection at the T12-L1 level, use 64479)

**64483**      lumbar or sacral, single level

(For transforaminal epidural injection under ultrasound guidance, use 0230T)

**+ 64484**      lumbar or sacral, each additional level (List separately in addition to code for primary procedure)

(Use 64484 in conjunction with 64483)

(For transforaminal epidural injection under ultrasound guidance, use 0231T)

(64479-64484 are unilateral procedures. For bilateral procedures, use modifier 50)

## Paravertebral Spinal Nerves and Branches

(Image guidance [fluoroscopy or CT] and any injection of contrast are inclusive components of 64490-64495. Imaging guidance and localization are required for the performance of paravertebral facet joint injections described by codes 64490-64495. If imaging is not used, report 20552-20553. If ultrasound guidance is used, report 0213T-0218T)

(For bilateral paravertebral facet injection procedures, use modifier 50)

(For paravertebral facet injection of the T12-L1 joint, or nerves innervating that joint, use 64490)

**64490**      Injection(s), diagnostic or therapeutic agent, paravertebral facet (zygapophyseal) joint (or nerves innervating that joint) with image guidance (fluoroscopy or CT), cervical or thoracic; single level

**+ 64491**      second level (List separately in addition to code for primary procedure)

**+ 64492**      third and any additional level(s) (List separately in addition to code for primary procedure)

(Do not report 64492 more than once per day)

(Use 64491, 64492 in conjunction with 64490)

**64493**      Injection(s), diagnostic or therapeutic agent, paravertebral facet (zygapophyseal) joint (or nerves innervating that joint) with image guidance (fluoroscopy or CT), lumbar or sacral; single level

**+ 64494**      second level (List separately in addition to code for primary procedure)

**+ 64495**      third and any additional level(s) (List separately in addition to code for primary procedure)

(Do not report 64495 more than once per day)

(Use 64494, 64495 in conjunction with 64493)

## Autonomic Nerves

**64505**   Injection, anesthetic agent; sphenopalatine ganglion

**64508**      carotid sinus (separate procedure)

**64510**      stellate ganglion (cervical sympathetic)

**64517**      superior hypogastric plexus

**64520**      lumbar or thoracic (paravertebral sympathetic)

**64530**      celiac plexus, with or without radiologic monitoring

▶(For transendoscopic ultrasound-guided transmural injection, anesthetic, celiac plexus, use 43253)◀

# Neurostimulators (Peripheral Nerve)

Codes 64553-64595 apply to both simple and complex neurostimulators. For initial or subsequent electronic analysis and programming of neurostimulator pulse generators, see codes 95970-95975. An electrode array is a catheter or other device with more than one contact. The function of each contact may be capable of being adjusted during programming services.

(For implantation of trial or permanent electrode arrays or pulse generators for peripheral subcutaneous field stimulation, see 0282T-0284T)

**64550**   Application of surface (transcutaneous) neurostimulator

**64553**   Percutaneous implantation of neurostimulator electrode array; cranial nerve

(For open placement of cranial nerve (eg, vagus, trigeminal) neurostimulator pulse generator or receiver, see 61885, 61886, as appropriate)

**64555**      peripheral nerve (excludes sacral nerve)

(Do not report 64555 in conjunction with 64566)

(64560 has been deleted)

**64561**      sacral nerve (transforaminal placement) including image guidance, if performed

**64565**      neuromuscular

**64566**   Posterior tibial neurostimulation, percutaneous needle electrode, single treatment, includes programming

(Do not report 64566 in conjunction with 64555, 95970-95972)

**64568**   Incision for implantation of cranial nerve (eg, vagus nerve) neurostimulator electrode array and pulse generator

(Do not report 64568 in conjunction with 61885, 61886, 64570)

**64569**   Revision or replacement of cranial nerve (eg, vagus nerve) neurostimulator electrode array, including connection to existing pulse generator

(Do not report 64569 in conjunction with 64570 or 61888)

(For replacement of pulse generator, use 61885)

**64570**   Removal of cranial nerve (eg, vagus nerve) neurostimulator electrode array and pulse generator

(Do not report 64570 in conjunction with 61888)

(For laparoscopic implantation, revision, replacement, or removal of vagus nerve blocking neurostimulator electrode array and/or pulse generator at the esophagogastric junction, see 0312T-0317T)

(64573 has been deleted)

**64575**   Incision for implantation of neurostimulator electrode array; peripheral nerve (excludes sacral nerve)

(64577 has been deleted)

**64580**       neuromuscular

**64581**       sacral nerve (transforaminal placement)

**64585**   Revision or removal of peripheral neurostimulator electrode array

**64590**   Insertion or replacement of peripheral or gastric neurostimulator pulse generator or receiver, direct or inductive coupling

(Do not report 64590 in conjunction with 64595)

**64595**   Revision or removal of peripheral or gastric neurostimulator pulse generator or receiver

# Destruction by Neurolytic Agent (eg, Chemical, Thermal, Electrical or Radiofrequency), Chemodenervation

Codes 64600-64681 include the injection of other therapeutic agents (eg, corticosteroids). Do not report diagnostic/therapeutic injections separately. Do not report a code labeled as destruction when using therapies that are not destructive of the target nerve (eg, pulsed radiofrequency), use 64999. For codes labeled as chemodenervation, the supply of the chemodenervation agent is reported separately.

(For chemodenervation of internal anal sphincter, use 46505)

(For chemodenervation of the bladder, use 52287)

(For chemodenervation for strabismus involving the extraocular muscles, use 67345)

(For chemodenervation guided by needle electromyography or muscle electrical stimulation, see 95873, 95874)

## Somatic Nerves

**64600**   Destruction by neurolytic agent, trigeminal nerve; supraorbital, infraorbital, mental, or inferior alveolar branch

**64605**       second and third division branches at foramen ovale

**64610**       second and third division branches at foramen ovale under radiologic monitoring

**64611**   Chemodenervation of parotid and submandibular salivary glands, bilateral

(Report 64611 with modifier 52 if fewer than four salivary glands are injected)

**64612**   Chemodenervation of muscle(s); muscle(s) innervated by facial nerve, unilateral (eg, for blepharospasm, hemifacial spasm)

(For bilateral procedure, report 64612 with modifier 50)

▶(64613 has been deleted. To report, use 64616)◀

▶(64614 has been deleted. To report, see 64642, 64643, 64644, 64645, 64646, 64647)◀

**64615**       muscle(s) innervated by facial, trigeminal, cervical spinal and accessory nerves, bilateral (eg, for chronic migraine)

(Report 64615 only once per session)

▶(Do not report 64615 in conjunction with 64612, 64616, 64617, 64642, 64643, 64644, 64645, 64646, 64647)◀

▶(For guidance see 95873, 95874. Do not report more than one guidance code for 64615)◀

● **64616**       neck muscle(s), excluding muscles of the larynx, unilateral (eg, for cervical dystonia, spasmodic torticollis)

▶(For bilateral procedure, report 64616 with modifier 50)◀

▶(For chemodenervation guided by needle electromyography or muscle electrical stimulation, see 95873, 95874. Do not report more than one guidance code for any unit of 64616)◀

● **64617**       larynx, unilateral, percutaneous (eg, for spasmodic dysphonia), includes guidance by needle electromyography, when performed

▶(For bilateral procedure, report 64617 with modifier 50)◀

▶(Do not report 64617 in conjunction with 95873, 95874)◀

▶(For diagnostic needle electromyography of the larynx, use 95865)◀

▶(For chemodenervation of the larynx performed with direct laryngoscopy, see 31570, 31571)◀

**Nervous**

---

**64620** Destruction by neurolytic agent, intercostal nerve

(64622-64627 have been deleted. For image-guided neurolysis of facet joint nerve(s), see 64633-64636)

(Imaging guidance [fluoroscopy or CT] are inclusive components of 64333-64636)

(Image guidance [fluoroscopy or CT] and any injection of contrast are inclusive components of 64633-64636. Image guidance and localization are required for the performance of paravertebral facet joint nerve destruction by neurolytic agent described by 64633-64636. If CT or fluoroscopic imaging is not used, report 64999)

(For paravertebral facet destruction by neurolysis of the T12-L1 joint, or nerves innervating that joint, use 64633)

**# 64633** Destruction by neurolytic agent, paravertebral facet joint nerve(s), with imaging guidance (fluoroscopy or CT); cervical or thoracic, single facet joint

(For bilateral procedure, report 64633 with modifier 50)

**#✚ 64634** cervical or thoracic, each additional facet joint (List separately in addition to code for primary procedure)

(Use 64634 in conjunction with 64633)

(For bilateral procedure, report 64634 with modifier 50)

**# 64635** lumbar or sacral, single facet joint

(For bilateral procedure, report 64635 with modifier 50)

**#✚ 64636** lumbar or sacral, each additional facet joint (List separately in addition to code for primary procedure)

(Use 64636 in conjunction with 64635)

(For bilateral procedure, report 64636 with modifier 50)

(Do not report 64633-64636 in conjunction with 77003, 77012)

**64630** Destruction by neurolytic agent; pudendal nerve

**64632** plantar common digital nerve

(Do not report 64632 in conjunction with 64455)

**64633** Code is out of numerical sequence. See 64600-64640

**64634** Code is out of numerical sequence. See 64600-64640

**64635** Code is out of numerical sequence. See 64600-64640

**64636** Code is out of numerical sequence. See 64600-64640

**64640** other peripheral nerve or branch

▶Report 64642, 64643, 64644, 64645 once per extremity. Codes 64642, 64643, 64644, 64645 can be reported together up to a combined total of four units of service per patient when all four extremities are injected. Report only one base code (64642 or 64644) per session. Report one or more units of additional extremity code(s) (64643 or 64645) for each additional extremity injected.

Report 64646 or 64647 for chemodenervation of muscles of the trunk.

Trunk muscles include the erector spinae and paraspinal muscles, rectus abdominus and obliques. All other somatic muscles are extremity muscles, head muscles, or neck muscles.◀

▶(For chemodenervation guided by needle electromyography or muscle electrical stimulation, see 95873, 95874. Do not report more than one guidance code for each corresponding chemodenervation of extremity or trunk code)◀

▶(Do not report modifier 50 in conjunction with 64642, 64643, 64644, 64645, 64646, 64647)◀

**⊙ 64642** Chemodenervation of one extremity; 1-4 muscle(s)

**✚⊙ 64643** each additional extremity, 1-4 muscle(s) (List separately in addition to code for primary procedure)

▶(Use 64643 in conjunction with 64642, 64644)◀

**⊙ 64644** Chemodenervation of one extremity; 5 or more muscle(s)

**✚⊙ 64645** each additional extremity, 5 or more muscle(s) (List separately in addition to code for primary procedure)

▶(Use 64645 in conjunction with 64644)◀

**⊙ 64646** Chemodenervation of trunk muscle(s); 1-5 muscle(s)

**⊙ 64647** 6 or more muscle(s)

▶(Report either 64646 or 64647 only once per session)◀

## Sympathetic Nerves

**64650** Chemodenervation of eccrine glands; both axillae

**64653** other area(s) (eg, scalp, face, neck), per day

(Report the specific service in conjunction with code(s) for the specific substance(s) or drug(s) provided)

(For chemodenervation of extremities (eg, hands or feet), use 64999)

(For chemodenervation of bladder, use 52287)

**64680** Destruction by neurolytic agent, with or without radiologic monitoring; celiac plexus

▶(For transendoscopic ultrasound-guided transmural injection, neurolytic agent, celiac plexus, use 43253)◀

**64681** superior hypogastric plexus

## Neuroplasty (Exploration, Neurolysis or Nerve Decompression)

Neuroplasty is the surgical decompression or freeing of intact nerve from scar tissue, including external neurolysis and/or transposition to repair or restore the nerve.

(For percutaneous neurolysis, see 62263, 62264, 62280-62282)

(For internal neurolysis requiring use of operating microscope, use 64727)

(For facial nerve decompression, use 69720)

(For neuroplasty with nerve wrapping, see 64702-64727, 64999)

**64702** Neuroplasty; digital, 1 or both, same digit

**64704** nerve of hand or foot

**64708** Neuroplasty, major peripheral nerve, arm or leg, open; other than specified

**64712** sciatic nerve

**64713** brachial plexus

**64714** lumbar plexus

**64716** Neuroplasty and/or transposition; cranial nerve (specify)

**64718** ulnar nerve at elbow

**64719** ulnar nerve at wrist

**64721** median nerve at carpal tunnel

(For arthroscopic procedure, use 29848)

**64722** Decompression; unspecified nerve(s) (specify)

**64726** plantar digital nerve

**+ 64727** Internal neurolysis, requiring use of operating microscope (List separately in addition to code for neuroplasty) (Neuroplasty includes external neurolysis)

(Do not report code 69990 in addition to code 64727)

## Transection or Avulsion

(For stereotactic lesion of gasserian ganglion, use 61790)

**64732** Transection or avulsion of; supraorbital nerve

**64734** infraorbital nerve

**64736** mental nerve

**64738** inferior alveolar nerve by osteotomy

**64740** lingual nerve

**64742** facial nerve, differential or complete

**64744** greater occipital nerve

**64746** phrenic nerve

(For section of recurrent laryngeal nerve, use 31595)

**64752** vagus nerve (vagotomy), transthoracic

**64755** vagus nerves limited to proximal stomach (selective proximal vagotomy, proximal gastric vagotomy, parietal cell vagotomy, supra- or highly selective vagotomy)

(For laparoscopic approach, use 43652)

**64760** vagus nerve (vagotomy), abdominal

(For laparoscopic approach, use 43651)

**64761** pudendal nerve

(For bilateral procedure, report 64761 with modifier 50)

**64763** Transection or avulsion of obturator nerve, extrapelvic, with or without adductor tenotomy

(For bilateral procedure, report 64763 with modifier 50)

**64766** Transection or avulsion of obturator nerve, intrapelvic, with or without adductor tenotomy

(For bilateral procedure, report 64766 with modifier 50)

**64771** Transection or avulsion of other cranial nerve, extradural

**64772** Transection or avulsion of other spinal nerve, extradural

(For excision of tender scar, skin and subcutaneous tissue, with or without tiny neuroma, see 11400-11446, 13100-13153)

## Excision

### Somatic Nerves

(For Morton neurectomy, use 28080)

**64774** Excision of neuroma; cutaneous nerve, surgically identifiable

**64776** digital nerve, 1 or both, same digit

**+ 64778** digital nerve, each additional digit (List separately in addition to code for primary procedure)

(Use 64778 in conjunction with 64776)

**64782** hand or foot, except digital nerve

**+ 64783** hand or foot, each additional nerve, except same digit (List separately in addition to code for primary procedure)

(Use 64783 in conjunction with 64782)

**64784** major peripheral nerve, except sciatic

**64786** sciatic nerve

**+ 64787** Implantation of nerve end into bone or muscle (List separately in addition to neuroma excision)

(Use 64787 in conjunction with 64774-64786)

**64788** Excision of neurofibroma or neurolemmoma; cutaneous nerve

**64790** major peripheral nerve

**64792** extensive (including malignant type)

**64795** Biopsy of nerve

### Sympathetic Nerves

**64802** Sympathectomy, cervical

(For bilateral procedure, report 64802 with modifier 50)

**64804** Sympathectomy, cervicothoracic

(For bilateral procedure, report 64804 with modifier 50)

**64809** Sympathectomy, thoracolumbar

(For bilateral procedure, report 64809 with modifier 50)

**Nervous**

**64818** Sympathectomy, lumbar

(For bilateral procedure, report 64818 with modifier 50)

**64820** Sympathectomy; digital arteries, each digit

(Do not report 69990 in addition to code 64820)

**64821** radial artery

(Do not report 69990 in addition to code 64821)

**64822** ulnar artery

(Do not report 69990 in addition to code 64822)

**64823** superficial palmar arch

(Do not report 69990 in addition to code 64823)

## Neurorrhaphy

**64831** Suture of digital nerve, hand or foot; 1 nerve

**+ 64832** each additional digital nerve (List separately in addition to code for primary procedure)

(Use 64832 in conjunction with 64831)

**64834** Suture of 1 nerve; hand or foot, common sensory nerve

**64835** median motor thenar

**64836** ulnar motor

**+ 64837** Suture of each additional nerve, hand or foot (List separately in addition to code for primary procedure)

(Use 64837 in conjunction with 64834-64836)

**64840** Suture of posterior tibial nerve

**64856** Suture of major peripheral nerve, arm or leg, except sciatic; including transposition

**64857** without transposition

**64858** Suture of sciatic nerve

**+ 64859** Suture of each additional major peripheral nerve (List separately in addition to code for primary procedure)

(Use 64859 in conjunction with 64856, 64857)

**64861** Suture of; brachial plexus

**64862** lumbar plexus

**64864** Suture of facial nerve; extracranial

**64865** infratemporal, with or without grafting

**64866** Anastomosis; facial-spinal accessory

**64868** facial-hypoglossal

**64870** facial-phrenic

**+ 64872** Suture of nerve; requiring secondary or delayed suture (List separately in addition to code for primary neurorrhaphy)

(Use 64872 in conjunction with 64831-64865)

**+ 64874** requiring extensive mobilization, or transposition of nerve (List separately in addition to code for nerve suture)

(Use 64874 in conjunction with 64831-64865)

**+ 64876** requiring shortening of bone of extremity (List separately in addition to code for nerve suture)

(Use 64876 in conjunction with 64831-64865)

## Neurorrhaphy With Nerve Graft, Vein Graft, or Conduit

**64885** Nerve graft (includes obtaining graft), head or neck; up to 4 cm in length

**64886** more than 4 cm length

**64890** Nerve graft (includes obtaining graft), single strand, hand or foot; up to 4 cm length

**64891** more than 4 cm length

**64892** Nerve graft (includes obtaining graft), single strand, arm or leg; up to 4 cm length

**64893** more than 4 cm length

**64895** Nerve graft (includes obtaining graft), multiple strands (cable), hand or foot; up to 4 cm length

**64896** more than 4 cm length

**64897** Nerve graft (includes obtaining graft), multiple strands (cable), arm or leg; up to 4 cm length

**64898** more than 4 cm length

**+ 64901** Nerve graft, each additional nerve; single strand (List separately in addition to code for primary procedure)

(Use 64901 in conjunction with 64885-64893)

**+ 64902** multiple strands (cable) (List separately in addition to code for primary procedure)

(Use 64902 in conjunction with 64885, 64886, 64895-64898)

**64905** Nerve pedicle transfer; first stage

**64907** second stage

**64910** Nerve repair; with synthetic conduit or vein allograft (eg, nerve tube), each nerve

**64911** with autogenous vein graft (includes harvest of vein graft), each nerve

(Do not report 69990 in addition to 64910, 64911)

## Other Procedures

**64999** Unlisted procedure, nervous system

⊙=Moderate sedation ✚=Add-on code ✗=FDA approval pending #=Resequenced code ○=Recycled/reinstated code

Nervous

# Eye and Ocular Adnexa

(For diagnostic and treatment ophthalmological services, see **Medicine, Ophthalmology,** and 92002 et seq)

(Do not report code 69990 in addition to codes 65091-68850)

## Eyeball

### Removal of Eye

**65091** Evisceration of ocular contents; without implant

**65093** with implant

**65101** Enucleation of eye; without implant

**65103** with implant, muscles not attached to implant

**65105** with implant, muscles attached to implant

(For conjunctivoplasty after enucleation, see 68320 et seq)

**65110** Exenteration of orbit (does not include skin graft), removal of orbital contents; only

**65112** with therapeutic removal of bone

**65114** with muscle or myocutaneous flap

(For skin graft to orbit (split skin), see 15120, 15121; free, full thickness, see 15260, 15261)

(For eyelid repair involving more than skin, see 67930 et seq)

### Secondary Implant(s) Procedures

An ocular implant is an implant inside muscular cone; an orbital implant is an implant outside muscular cone.

**65125** Modification of ocular implant with placement or replacement of pegs (eg, drilling receptacle for prosthesis appendage) (separate procedure)

**65130** Insertion of ocular implant secondary; after evisceration, in scleral shell

**65135** after enucleation, muscles not attached to implant

**65140** after enucleation, muscles attached to implant

**65150** Reinsertion of ocular implant; with or without conjunctival graft

**65155** with use of foreign material for reinforcement and/or attachment of muscles to implant

**65175** Removal of ocular implant

(For orbital implant (implant outside muscle cone) insertion, use 67550; removal, use 67560)

## Removal of Foreign Body

(For removal of implanted material: ocular implant, use 65175; anterior segment implant, use 65920; posterior segment implant, use 67120; orbital implant, use 67560)

(For diagnostic x-ray for foreign body, use 70030)

(For diagnostic echography for foreign body, use 76529)

(For removal of foreign body from orbit: frontal approach, use 67413; lateral approach, use 67430; transcranial approach, use 61334)

(For removal of foreign body from eyelid, embedded, use 67938)

(For removal of foreign body from lacrimal system, use 68530)

**65205** Removal of foreign body, external eye; conjunctival superficial

**65210** conjunctival embedded (includes concretions), subconjunctival, or scleral nonperforating

**65220** corneal, without slit lamp

**65222** corneal, with slit lamp

(For repair of corneal laceration with foreign body, use 65275)

**65235** Removal of foreign body, intraocular; from anterior chamber of eye or lens

(For removal of implanted material from anterior segment, use 65920)

**65260** from posterior segment, magnetic extraction, anterior or posterior route

**65265** from posterior segment, nonmagnetic extraction

(For removal of implanted material from posterior segment, use 67120)

## Repair of Laceration

(For fracture of orbit, see 21385 et seq)

▶(For repair of wound of eyelid, skin, linear, simple, see 12011-12018; intermediate, layered closure, see 12051-12057; linear, complex, see 13151-13160; other, see 67930, 67935)◀

(For repair of wound of lacrimal system, use 68700)

(For repair of operative wound, use 66250)

**65270** Repair of laceration; conjunctiva, with or without nonperforating laceration sclera, direct closure

**65272** conjunctiva, by mobilization and rearrangement, without hospitalization

**65273** conjunctiva, by mobilization and rearrangement, with hospitalization

**65275** cornea, nonperforating, with or without removal foreign body

Eye/Ocular Adnexa

---

65280     cornea and/or sclera, perforating, not involving uveal tissue

65285     cornea and/or sclera, perforating, with reposition or resection of uveal tissue

(65280 and 65285 are not used for repair of a surgical wound)

65286     application of tissue glue, wounds of cornea and/or sclera

(Repair of laceration includes use of conjunctival flap and restoration of anterior chamber, by air or saline injection when indicated)

(For repair of iris or ciliary body, use 66680)

65290     Repair of wound, extraocular muscle, tendon and/or Tenon's capsule

# Anterior Segment

## Cornea

### Excision

65400     Excision of lesion, cornea (keratectomy, lamellar, partial), except pterygium

65410     Biopsy of cornea

65420     Excision or transposition of pterygium; without graft

65426       with graft

### Removal or Destruction

65430     Scraping of cornea, diagnostic, for smear and/or culture

65435     Removal of corneal epithelium; with or without chemocauterization (abrasion, curettage)

65436       with application of chelating agent (eg, EDTA)

65450     Destruction of lesion of cornea by cryotherapy, photocoagulation or thermocauterization

65600     Multiple punctures of anterior cornea (eg, for corneal erosion, tattoo)

### Keratoplasty

Corneal transplant includes use of fresh or preserved grafts. The preparation of donor material is included for penetrating or anterior lamellar keratoplasty, but reported separately for endothelial keratoplasty. Do not report 65710-65757 in conjunction with 92025.

(Keratoplasty excludes refractive keratoplasty procedures, 65760, 65765, and 65767)

65710     Keratoplasty (corneal transplant); anterior lamellar

65730       penetrating (except in aphakia or pseudophakia)

65750       penetrating (in aphakia)

65755       penetrating (in pseudophakia)

65756       endothelial

+ 65757     Backbench preparation of corneal endothelial allograft prior to transplantation (List separately in addition to code for primary procedure)

(Use 65757 in conjunction with 65756)

### Other Procedures

Do not report 65760-65771 in conjunction with 92025.

65760     Keratomileusis

65765     Keratophakia

65767     Epikeratoplasty

65770     Keratoprosthesis

65771     Radial keratotomy

65772     Corneal relaxing incision for correction of surgically induced astigmatism

65775     Corneal wedge resection for correction of surgically induced astigmatism

(For fitting of contact lens for treatment of disease, see 92071, 92072)

(For unlisted procedures on cornea, use 66999)

▲ 65778     Placement of amniotic membrane on the ocular surface; without sutures

▲ 65779       single layer, sutured

(Do not report 65778, 65779 in conjunction with 65430, 65435, 65780)

(For placement of amniotic membrane using tissue glue, use 66999)

65780     Ocular surface reconstruction; amniotic membrane transplantation, multiple layers

▶(For placement of amniotic membrane without reconstruction using no sutures or single layer suture technique, see 65778, 65779)◀

65781       limbal stem cell allograft (eg, cadaveric or living donor)

65782       limbal conjunctival autograft (includes obtaining graft)

(For harvesting conjunctival allograft, living donor, use 68371)

## Anterior Chamber

### Incision

65800     Paracentesis of anterior chamber of eye (separate procedure); with removal of aqueous

(65805 has been deleted. To report, use 65800)

Eye/Ocular Adnexa

| | |
|---|---|
| **65810** | with removal of vitreous and/or discission of anterior hyaloid membrane, with or without air injection |
| **65815** | with removal of blood, with or without irrigation and/or air injection |

(For injection, see 66020-66030)

(For removal of blood clot, use 65930)

**65820** Goniotomy

(Do not report modifier 63 in conjunction with 65820)

(For use of ophthalmic endoscope with 65820, use 66990)

**65850** Trabeculotomy ab externo

**65855** Trabeculoplasty by laser surgery, 1 or more sessions (defined treatment series)

(If re-treatment is necessary after several months because of disease progression, a new treatment or treatment series should be reported with a modifier, if necessary, to indicate lesser or greater complexity)

(For trabeculectomy, use 66170)

**65860** Severing adhesions of anterior segment, laser technique (separate procedure)

**65865** Severing adhesions of anterior segment of eye, incisional technique (with or without injection of air or liquid) (separate procedure); goniosynechiae

(For trabeculoplasty by laser surgery, use 65855)

**65870** anterior synechiae, except goniosynechiae

**65875** posterior synechiae

(For use of ophthalmic endoscope with 65875, use 66990)

**65880** corneovitreal adhesions

(For laser surgery, use 66821)

## Removal

**65900** Removal of epithelial downgrowth, anterior chamber of eye

**65920** Removal of implanted material, anterior segment of eye

(For use of ophthalmic endoscope with 65920, use 66990)

**65930** Removal of blood clot, anterior segment of eye

## Introduction

**66020** Injection, anterior chamber of eye (separate procedure); air or liquid

**66030** medication

(For unlisted procedures on anterior segment, use 66999)

# Anterior Sclera

## Excision

(For removal of intraocular foreign body, use 65235)

(For operations on posterior sclera, use 67250, 67255)

**66130** Excision of lesion, sclera

**66150** Fistulization of sclera for glaucoma; trephination with iridectomy

**66155** thermocauterization with iridectomy

**66160** sclerectomy with punch or scissors, with iridectomy

**66165** iridencleisis or iridotasis

**66170** trabeculectomy ab externo in absence of previous surgery

(For trabeculotomy ab externo, use 65850)

(For repair of operative wound, use 66250)

**66172** trabeculectomy ab externo with scarring from previous ocular surgery or trauma (includes injection of antifibrotic agents)

**66174** Transluminal dilation of aqueous outflow canal; without retention of device or stent

**66175** with retention of device or stent

## Aqueous Shunt

**66180** Aqueous shunt to extraocular reservoir (eg, Molteno, Schocket, Denver-Krupin)

● **66183** Insertion of anterior segment aqueous drainage device, without extraocular reservoir, external approach

**66185** Revision of aqueous shunt to extraocular reservoir

(For removal of implanted shunt, use 67120)

## Repair or Revision

(For scleral procedures in retinal surgery, see 67101 et seq)

**66220** Repair of scleral staphyloma; without graft

**66225** with graft

(For scleral reinforcement, see 67250, 67255)

**66250** Revision or repair of operative wound of anterior segment, any type, early or late, major or minor procedure

(For unlisted procedures on anterior sclera, use 66999)

**Eye/Ocular Adnexa**

# Iris, Ciliary Body

## Incision

**66500** Iridotomy by stab incision (separate procedure); except transfixion

**66505**      with transfixion as for iris bombe

(For iridotomy by photocoagulation, use 66761)

## Excision

**66600** Iridectomy, with corneoscleral or corneal section; for removal of lesion

**66605**      with cyclectomy

**66625**      peripheral for glaucoma (separate procedure)

**66630**      sector for glaucoma (separate procedure)

**66635**      optical (separate procedure)

(For coreoplasty by photocoagulation, use 66762)

## Repair

**66680** Repair of iris, ciliary body (as for iridodialysis)

(For reposition or resection of uveal tissue with perforating wound of cornea or sclera, use 65285)

**66682** Suture of iris, ciliary body (separate procedure) with retrieval of suture through small incision (eg, McCannel suture)

## Destruction

**66700** Ciliary body destruction; diathermy

**66710**      cyclophotocoagulation, transscleral

**66711**      cyclophotocoagulation, endoscopic

(Do not report 66711 in conjunction with 66990)

⊙ **66720**      cryotherapy

**66740**      cyclodialysis

**66761** Iridotomy/iridectomy by laser surgery (eg, for glaucoma) (per session)

**66762** Iridoplasty by photocoagulation (1 or more sessions) (eg, for improvement of vision, for widening of anterior chamber angle)

**66770** Destruction of cyst or lesion iris or ciliary body (nonexcisional procedure)

(For excision lesion iris, ciliary body, see 66600, 66605; for removal of epithelial downgrowth, use 65900)

(For unlisted procedures on iris, ciliary body, use 66999)

# Lens

## Incision

**66820** Discission of secondary membranous cataract (opacified posterior lens capsule and/or anterior hyaloid); stab incision technique (Ziegler or Wheeler knife)

**66821**      laser surgery (eg, YAG laser) (1 or more stages)

**66825** Repositioning of intraocular lens prosthesis, requiring an incision (separate procedure)

## Removal

Lateral canthotomy, iridectomy, iridotomy, anterior capsulotomy, posterior capsulotomy, the use of viscoelastic agents, enzymatic zonulysis, use of other pharmacologic agents, and subconjunctival or sub-tenon injections are included as part of the code for the extraction of lens.

**66830** Removal of secondary membranous cataract (opacified posterior lens capsule and/or anterior hyaloid) with corneo-scleral section, with or without iridectomy (iridocapsulotomy, iridocapsulectomy)

**66840** Removal of lens material; aspiration technique, 1 or more stages

**66850**      phacofragmentation technique (mechanical or ultrasonic) (eg, phacoemulsification), with aspiration

**66852**      pars plana approach, with or without vitrectomy

**66920**      intracapsular

**66930**      intracapsular, for dislocated lens

**66940**      extracapsular (other than 66840, 66850, 66852)

(For removal of intralenticular foreign body without lens extraction, use 65235)

(For repair of operative wound, use 66250)

## Intraocular Lens Procedures

**66982** Extracapsular cataract removal with insertion of intraocular lens prosthesis (1-stage procedure), manual or mechanical technique (eg, irrigation and aspiration or phacoemulsification), complex, requiring devices or techniques not generally used in routine cataract surgery (eg, iris expansion device, suture support for intraocular lens, or primary posterior capsulorrhexis) or performed on patients in the amblyogenic developmental stage

(For insertion of ocular telescope prosthesis including removal of crystalline lens, use 0308T)

**66983** Intracapsular cataract extraction with insertion of intraocular lens prosthesis (1 stage procedure)

(Do not report 66983 in conjunction with 0308T)

**66984**    Extracapsular cataract removal with insertion of intraocular lens prosthesis (1 stage procedure), manual or mechanical technique (eg, irrigation and aspiration or phacoemulsification)

(For complex extracapsular cataract removal, use 66982)

(For insertion of ocular telescope prosthesis including removal of crystalline lens, use 0308T)

**66985**    Insertion of intraocular lens prosthesis (secondary implant), not associated with concurrent cataract removal

(To code implant at time of concurrent cataract surgery, see 66982, 66983, 66984)

(To report supply of intraocular lens prosthesis, use 99070)

(For ultrasonic determination of intraocular lens power, use 76519)

(For removal of implanted material from anterior segment, use 65920)

(For secondary fixation (separate procedure), use 66682)

(For use of ophthalmic endoscope with 66985, use 66990)

**66986**    Exchange of intraocular lens

(For use of ophthalmic endoscope with 66986, use 66990)

## Other Procedures

+ **66990**    Use of ophthalmic endoscope (List separately in addition to code for primary procedure)

(66990 may be used only with codes 65820, 65875, 65920, 66985, 66986, 67036, 67039, 67040, 67041, 67042, 67043, 67112, 67113)

**66999**    Unlisted procedure, anterior segment of eye

# Posterior Segment

## Vitreous

**67005**    Removal of vitreous, anterior approach (open sky technique or limbal incision); partial removal

**67010**        subtotal removal with mechanical vitrectomy

(For removal of vitreous by paracentesis of anterior chamber, use 65810)

(For removal of corneovitreal adhesions, use 65880)

**67015**    Aspiration or release of vitreous, subretinal or choroidal fluid, pars plana approach (posterior sclerotomy)

**67025**    Injection of vitreous substitute, pars plana or limbal approach (fluid-gas exchange), with or without aspiration (separate procedure)

**67027**    Implantation of intravitreal drug delivery system (eg, ganciclovir implant), includes concomitant removal of vitreous

(For removal, use 67121)

**67028**    Intravitreal injection of a pharmacologic agent (separate procedure)

**67030**    Discission of vitreous strands (without removal), pars plana approach

**67031**    Severing of vitreous strands, vitreous face adhesions, sheets, membranes or opacities, laser surgery (1 or more stages)

**67036**    Vitrectomy, mechanical, pars plana approach;

(For application of intraocular epiretinal radiation with 67036, use 0190T)

**67039**        with focal endolaser photocoagulation

**67040**        with endolaser panretinal photocoagulation

**67041**        with removal of preretinal cellular membrane (eg, macular pucker)

**67042**        with removal of internal limiting membrane of retina (eg, for repair of macular hole, diabetic macular edema), includes, if performed, intraocular tamponade (ie, air, gas or silicone oil)

**67043**        with removal of subretinal membrane (eg, choroidal neovascularization), includes, if performed, intraocular tamponade (ie, air, gas or silicone oil) and laser photocoagulation

(For use of ophthalmic endoscope with 67036, 67039, 67040-67043, use 66990)

(For associated lensectomy, use 66850)

(For use of vitrectomy in retinal detachment surgery, see 67108, 67113)

(For associated removal of foreign body, see 65260, 65265)

(For unlisted procedures on vitreous, use 67299)

## Retina or Choroid

### Repair

(If diathermy, cryotherapy and/or photocoagulation are combined, report under principal modality used)

**67101**    Repair of retinal detachment, 1 or more sessions; cryotherapy or diathermy, with or without drainage of subretinal fluid

**67105**        photocoagulation, with or without drainage of subretinal fluid

**67107**    Repair of retinal detachment; scleral buckling (such as lamellar scleral dissection, imbrication or encircling procedure), with or without implant, with or without cryotherapy, photocoagulation, and drainage of subretinal fluid

Eye/Ocular Adnexa

**67108**   with vitrectomy, any method, with or without air or gas tamponade, focal endolaser photocoagulation, cryotherapy, drainage of subretinal fluid, scleral buckling, and/or removal of lens by same technique

**67110**   by injection of air or other gas (eg, pneumatic retinopexy)

**67112**   by scleral buckling or vitrectomy, on patient having previous ipsilateral retinal detachment repair(s) using scleral buckling or vitrectomy techniques

(For aspiration or drainage of subretinal or subchoroidal fluid, use 67015)

(For use of ophthalmic endoscope with 67112, use 66990)

**67113**   Repair of complex retinal detachment (eg, proliferative vitreoretinopathy, stage C-1 or greater, diabetic traction retinal detachment, retinopathy of prematurity, retinal tear of greater than 90 degrees), with vitrectomy and membrane peeling, may include air, gas, or silicone oil tamponade, cryotherapy, endolaser photocoagulation, drainage of subretinal fluid, scleral buckling, and/or removal of lens

(To report vitrectomy, pars plana approach, other than in retinal detachment surgery, see 67036-67043)

(For use of ophthalmic endoscope with 67113, use 66990)

**67115**   Release of encircling material (posterior segment)

**67120**   Removal of implanted material, posterior segment; extraocular

**67121**      intraocular

(For removal from anterior segment, use 65920)

(For removal of foreign body, see 65260, 65265)

### Prophylaxis

Codes 67141, 67145 include treatment at one or more sessions that may occur at different encounters. These codes should be reported once during a defined treatment period.

Repetitive services. The services listed below are often performed in multiple sessions or groups of sessions. The methods of reporting vary.

The following descriptors are intended to include all sessions in a defined treatment period.

**67141**   Prophylaxis of retinal detachment (eg, retinal break, lattice degeneration) without drainage, 1 or more sessions; cryotherapy, diathermy

**67145**      photocoagulation (laser or xenon arc)

### Destruction

Codes 67208, 67210, 67218, 67220, 67227, 67228, 67229 include treatment at one or more sessions that may occur at different encounters. These codes should be reported once during a defined treatment period.

**67208**   Destruction of localized lesion of retina (eg, macular edema, tumors), 1 or more sessions; cryotherapy, diathermy

**67210**      photocoagulation

**67218**      radiation by implantation of source (includes removal of source)

**67220**   Destruction of localized lesion of choroid (eg, choroidal neovascularization); photocoagulation (eg, laser), 1 or more sessions

**67221**      photodynamic therapy (includes intravenous infusion)

**+ 67225**    photodynamic therapy, second eye, at single session (List separately in addition to code for primary eye treatment)

(Use 67225 in conjunction with 67221)

**67227**   Destruction of extensive or progressive retinopathy (eg, diabetic retinopathy), 1 or more sessions, cryotherapy, diathermy

**67228**   Treatment of extensive or progressive retinopathy, 1 or more sessions; (eg, diabetic retinopathy), photocoagulation

**67229**      preterm infant (less than 37 weeks gestation at birth), performed from birth up to 1 year of age (eg, retinopathy of prematurity), photocoagulation or cryotherapy

(For bilateral procedure, use modifier 50)

(For unlisted procedures on retina, use 67299)

## Posterior Sclera

### Repair

(For excision lesion sclera, use 66130)

**67250**   Scleral reinforcement (separate procedure); without graft

**67255**      with graft

(For repair scleral staphyloma, see 66220, 66225)

## Other Procedures

**67299**   Unlisted procedure, posterior segment

## Ocular Adnexa

### Extraocular Muscles

**67311**   Strabismus surgery, recession or resection procedure; 1 horizontal muscle

**67312**      2 horizontal muscles

**67314**      1 vertical muscle (excluding superior oblique)

Eye/Ocular Adnexa

**67316**   2 or more vertical muscles (excluding superior oblique)

(For adjustable sutures, use 67335 in addition to codes 67311-67334 for primary procedure reflecting number of muscles operated on)

**67318**   Strabismus surgery, any procedure, superior oblique muscle

**+ 67320**   Transposition procedure (eg, for paretic extraocular muscle), any extraocular muscle (specify) (List separately in addition to code for primary procedure)

(Use 67320 in conjunction with 67311-67318)

**+ 67331**   Strabismus surgery on patient with previous eye surgery or injury that did not involve the extraocular muscles (List separately in addition to code for primary procedure)

(Use 67331 in conjunction with 67311-67318)

**+ 67332**   Strabismus surgery on patient with scarring of extraocular muscles (eg, prior ocular injury, strabismus or retinal detachment surgery) or restrictive myopathy (eg, dysthyroid ophthalmopathy) (List separately in addition to code for primary procedure)

(Use 67332 in conjunction with 67311-67318)

**+ 67334**   Strabismus surgery by posterior fixation suture technique, with or without muscle recession (List separately in addition to code for primary procedure)

(Use 67334 in conjunction with 67311-67318)

**+ 67335**   Placement of adjustable suture(s) during strabismus surgery, including postoperative adjustment(s) of suture(s) (List separately in addition to code for specific strabismus surgery)

(Use 67335 in conjunction with 67311-67334)

**+ 67340**   Strabismus surgery involving exploration and/or repair of detached extraocular muscle(s) (List separately in addition to code for primary procedure)

(Use 67340 in conjunction with 67311-67334)

**67343**   Release of extensive scar tissue without detaching extraocular muscle (separate procedure)

(Use 67343 in conjunction with 67311-67340, when such procedures are performed other than on the affected muscle)

**67345**   Chemodenervation of extraocular muscle

►(For chemodenervation for blepharospasm and other neurological disorders, see 64612 and 64616)◄

**67346**   Biopsy of extraocular muscle

(For repair of wound, extraocular muscle, tendon or Tenon's capsule, use 65290)

## Other Procedures

**67399**   Unlisted procedure, ocular muscle

# Orbit

## Exploration, Excision, Decompression

**67400**   Orbitotomy without bone flap (frontal or transconjunctival approach); for exploration, with or without biopsy

**67405**      with drainage only

**67412**      with removal of lesion

**67413**      with removal of foreign body

**67414**      with removal of bone for decompression

**67415**   Fine needle aspiration of orbital contents

(For exenteration, enucleation, and repair, see 65101 et seq; for optic nerve decompression, use 67570)

**67420**   Orbitotomy with bone flap or window, lateral approach (eg, Kroenlein); with removal of lesion

**67430**      with removal of foreign body

**67440**      with drainage

**67445**      with removal of bone for decompression

(For optic nerve sheath decompression, use 67570)

**67450**      for exploration, with or without biopsy

(For orbitotomy, transcranial approach, see 61330-61334)

(For orbital implant, see 67550, 67560)

(For removal of eyeball or for repair after removal, see 65091-65175)

## Other Procedures

**67500**   Retrobulbar injection; medication (separate procedure, does not include supply of medication)

**67505**      alcohol

**67515**   Injection of medication or other substance into Tenon's capsule

(For subconjunctival injection, use 68200)

**67550**   Orbital implant (implant outside muscle cone); insertion

**67560**      removal or revision

(For ocular implant (implant inside muscle cone), see 65093-65105, 65130-65175)

(For treatment of fractures of malar area, orbit, see 21355 et seq)

**67570**   Optic nerve decompression (eg, incision or fenestration of optic nerve sheath)

**67599**   Unlisted procedure, orbit

**Eye/Ocular Adnexa**

# Eyelids

## Incision

**67700** Blepharotomy, drainage of abscess, eyelid

**67710** Severing of tarsorrhaphy

**67715** Canthotomy (separate procedure)

(For canthoplasty, use 67950)

(For division of symblepharon, use 68340)

**# 67810** Incisional biopsy of eyelid skin including lid margin

(For biopsy of skin of the eyelid, see 11100, 11101, 11310-11313)

## Excision, Destruction

Codes for removal of lesion include more than skin (ie, involving lid margin, tarsus, and/or palpebral conjunctiva).

(For removal of lesion, involving mainly skin of eyelid, see 11310-11313; 11440-11446, 11640-11646; 17000-17004)

(For repair of wounds, blepharoplasty, grafts, reconstructive surgery, see 67930-67975)

**67800** Excision of chalazion; single

**67801** multiple, same lid

**67805** multiple, different lids

**67808** under general anesthesia and/or requiring hospitalization, single or multiple

**67810** Code is out of numerical sequence. See 67700-67810

**67820** Correction of trichiasis; epilation, by forceps only

**67825** epilation by other than forceps (eg, by electrosurgery, cryotherapy, laser surgery)

**67830** incision of lid margin

**67835** incision of lid margin, with free mucous membrane graft

**67840** Excision of lesion of eyelid (except chalazion) without closure or with simple direct closure

(For excision and repair of eyelid by reconstructive surgery, see 67961, 67966)

**67850** Destruction of lesion of lid margin (up to 1 cm)

(For Mohs micrographic surgery, see 17311-17315)

(For initiation or follow-up care of topical chemotherapy (eg, 5-FU or similar agents), see appropriate office visits)

## Tarsorrhaphy

**67875** Temporary closure of eyelids by suture (eg, Frost suture)

**67880** Construction of intermarginal adhesions, median tarsorrhaphy, or canthorrhaphy;

**67882** with transposition of tarsal plate

(For severing of tarsorrhaphy, use 67710)

(For canthoplasty, reconstruction canthus, use 67950)

(For canthotomy, use 67715)

## Repair (Brow Ptosis, Blepharoptosis, Lid Retraction, Ectropion, Entropion)

**67900** Repair of brow ptosis (supraciliary, mid-forehead or coronal approach)

(For forehead rhytidectomy, use 15824)

**67901** Repair of blepharoptosis; frontalis muscle technique with suture or other material (eg, banked fascia)

**67902** frontalis muscle technique with autologous fascial sling (includes obtaining fascia)

**67903** (tarso) levator resection or advancement, internal approach

**67904** (tarso) levator resection or advancement, external approach

**67906** superior rectus technique with fascial sling (includes obtaining fascia)

**67908** conjunctivo-tarso-Muller's muscle-levator resection (eg, Fasanella-Servat type)

**67909** Reduction of overcorrection of ptosis

**67911** Correction of lid retraction

(For obtaining autogenous graft materials, see 20920, 20922 or 20926)

(For correction of trichiasis by mucous membrane graft, use 67835)

**67912** Correction of lagophthalmos, with implantation of upper eyelid lid load (eg, gold weight)

**67914** Repair of ectropion; suture

**67915** thermocauterization

**67916** excision tarsal wedge

**67917** extensive (eg, tarsal strip operations)

(For correction of everted punctum, use 68705)

**67921** Repair of entropion; suture

**67922** thermocauterization

**67923** excision tarsal wedge

**67924** extensive (eg, tarsal strip or capsulopalpebral fascia repairs operation)

(For repair of cicatricial ectropion or entropion requiring scar excision or skin graft, see also 67961 et seq)

⊙=Moderate sedation ✚=Add-on code ✔=FDA approval pending #=Resequenced code O=Recycled/reinstated code

**Eye/Ocular Adnexa**

### Reconstruction

Codes for blepharoplasty involve more than skin (ie, involving lid margin, tarsus, and/or palpebral conjunctiva).

**67930**  Suture of recent wound, eyelid, involving lid margin, tarsus, and/or palpebral conjunctiva direct closure; partial thickness

**67935**      full thickness

**67938**  Removal of embedded foreign body, eyelid

▶(For repair of skin of eyelid, see 12011-12018, 12051-12057, 13151-13153)◀

(For tarsorrhaphy, canthorrhaphy, see 67880, 67882)

(For repair of blepharoptosis and lid retraction, see 67901-67911)

(For blepharoplasty for entropion, ectropion, see 67916, 67917, 67923, 67924)

(For correction of blepharochalasis (blepharorhytidectomy), see 15820-15823)

(For repair of skin of eyelid, adjacent tissue transfer, see 14060, 14061; preparation for graft, use 15004; free graft, see 15120, 15121, 15260, 15261)

(For excision of lesion of eyelid, use 67800 et seq)

(For repair of lacrimal canaliculi, use 68700)

**67950**  Canthoplasty (reconstruction of canthus)

**67961**  Excision and repair of eyelid, involving lid margin, tarsus, conjunctiva, canthus, or full thickness, may include preparation for skin graft or pedicle flap with adjacent tissue transfer or rearrangement; up to one-fourth of lid margin

**67966**      over one-fourth of lid margin

(For canthoplasty, use 67950)

(For free skin grafts, see 15120, 15121, 15260, 15261)

(For tubed pedicle flap preparation, use 15576; for delay, use 15630; for attachment, use 15650)

**67971**  Reconstruction of eyelid, full thickness by transfer of tarsoconjunctival flap from opposing eyelid; up to two-thirds of eyelid, 1 stage or first stage

**67973**      total eyelid, lower, 1 stage or first stage

**67974**      total eyelid, upper, 1 stage or first stage

**67975**      second stage

### Other Procedures

**67999**  Unlisted procedure, eyelids

# Conjunctiva

(For removal of foreign body, see 65205 et seq)

### Incision and Drainage

**68020**  Incision of conjunctiva, drainage of cyst

**68040**  Expression of conjunctival follicles (eg, for trachoma)

▶(To report automated evacuation of Meibomian glands, use 0207T)◀

### Excision and/or Destruction

**68100**  Biopsy of conjunctiva

**68110**  Excision of lesion, conjunctiva; up to 1 cm

**68115**      over 1 cm

**68130**      with adjacent sclera

**68135**  Destruction of lesion, conjunctiva

### Injection

(For injection into Tenon's capsule or retrobulbar injection, see 67500-67515)

**68200**  Subconjunctival injection

### Conjunctivoplasty

(For wound repair, see 65270-65273)

**68320**  Conjunctivoplasty; with conjunctival graft or extensive rearrangement

**68325**      with buccal mucous membrane graft (includes obtaining graft)

**68326**  Conjunctivoplasty, reconstruction cul-de-sac; with conjunctival graft or extensive rearrangement

**68328**      with buccal mucous membrane graft (includes obtaining graft)

**68330**  Repair of symblepharon; conjunctivoplasty, without graft

**68335**      with free graft conjunctiva or buccal mucous membrane (includes obtaining graft)

**68340**      division of symblepharon, with or without insertion of conformer or contact lens

### Other Procedures

**68360**  Conjunctival flap; bridge or partial (separate procedure)

**68362**      total (such as Gunderson thin flap or purse string flap)

(For conjunctival flap for perforating injury, see 65280, 65285)

(For repair of operative wound, use 66250)

(For removal of conjunctival foreign body, see 65205, 65210)

**68371**  Harvesting conjunctival allograft, living donor

**68399**  Unlisted procedure, conjunctiva

**Eye/Ocular Adnexa**

---

# Lacrimal System

## Incision

**68400** Incision, drainage of lacrimal gland

**68420** Incision, drainage of lacrimal sac (dacryocystotomy or dacryocystostomy)

**68440** Snip incision of lacrimal punctum

## Excision

**68500** Excision of lacrimal gland (dacryoadenectomy), except for tumor; total

**68505** partial

**68510** Biopsy of lacrimal gland

**68520** Excision of lacrimal sac (dacryocystectomy)

**68525** Biopsy of lacrimal sac

**68530** Removal of foreign body or dacryolith, lacrimal passages

**68540** Excision of lacrimal gland tumor; frontal approach

**68550** involving osteotomy

## Repair

**68700** Plastic repair of canaliculi

**68705** Correction of everted punctum, cautery

**68720** Dacryocystorhinostomy (fistulization of lacrimal sac to nasal cavity)

**68745** Conjunctivorhinostomy (fistulization of conjunctiva to nasal cavity); without tube

**68750** with insertion of tube or stent

**68760** Closure of the lacrimal punctum; by thermocauterization, ligation, or laser surgery

**68761** by plug, each

**68770** Closure of lacrimal fistula (separate procedure)

## Probing and/or Related Procedures

**68801** Dilation of lacrimal punctum, with or without irrigation

(To report a bilateral procedure, use 68801 with modifier 50)

**68810** Probing of nasolacrimal duct, with or without irrigation;

(For bilateral procedure, report 68810 with modifier 50)

**68811** requiring general anesthesia

(For bilateral procedure, report 68811 with modifier 50)

**68815** with insertion of tube or stent

(See also 92018)

(For bilateral procedure, report 68815 with modifier 50)

**68816** with transluminal balloon catheter dilation

(Do not report 68816 in conjunction with 68810, 68811, 68815)

(For bilateral procedure, report 68816 with modifier 50)

**68840** Probing of lacrimal canaliculi, with or without irrigation

**68850** Injection of contrast medium for dacryocystography

(For radiological supervision and interpretation, see 70170, 78660)

## Other Procedures

**68899** Unlisted procedure, lacrimal system

# Auditory System

(For diagnostic services (eg, audiometry, vestibular tests), see 92502 et seq)

## External Ear

### Incision

**69000**  Drainage external ear, abscess or hematoma; simple

**69005**  complicated

**69020**  Drainage external auditory canal, abscess

**69090**  Ear piercing

### Excision

**69100**  Biopsy external ear

**69105**  Biopsy external auditory canal

**69110**  Excision external ear; partial, simple repair

**69120**  complete amputation

(For reconstruction of ear, see 15120 et seq)

**69140**  Excision exostosis(es), external auditory canal

**69145**  Excision soft tissue lesion, external auditory canal

**69150**  Radical excision external auditory canal lesion; without neck dissection

**69155**  with neck dissection

(For resection of temporal bone, use 69535)

(For skin grafting, see 15004-15261)

### Removal

**69200**  Removal foreign body from external auditory canal; without general anesthesia

**69205**  with general anesthesia

▲ **69210**  Removal impacted cerumen requiring instrumentation, unilateral

▶(For bilateral procedure, report 69210 with modifier 50)◀

▶(For cerumen removal that is not impacted or does not require instrumentation, eg, by irrigation only, see E/M service code, which may include new or established patient office or other outpatient services [99201-99215], hospital observation services [99217-99220, 99224-99226], hospital care [99221-99223, 99231-99233], consultations [99241-99255], emergency department services [99281-99285], nursing facility services [99304-99318], domiciliary, rest home, or custodial care services [99324-99337], home services [99341-99350])◀

**69220**  Debridement, mastoidectomy cavity, simple (eg, routine cleaning)

(For bilateral procedure, report 69220 with modifier 50)

**69222**  Debridement, mastoidectomy cavity, complex (eg, with anesthesia or more than routine cleaning)

(For bilateral procedure, report 69222 with modifier 50)

## Repair

(For suture of wound or injury of external ear, see 12011-14302)

⊙ **69300**  Otoplasty, protruding ear, with or without size reduction

(For bilateral procedure, report 69300 with modifier 50)

**69310**  Reconstruction of external auditory canal (meatoplasty) (eg, for stenosis due to injury, infection) (separate procedure)

**69320**  Reconstruction external auditory canal for congenital atresia, single stage

(For combination with middle ear reconstruction, see 69631, 69641)

▶(For other reconstructive procedures with grafts (eg, skin, cartilage, bone), see 13151-15760, 21230-21235)◀

## Other Procedures

(For otoscopy under general anesthesia, use 92502)

**69399**  Unlisted procedure, external ear

## Middle Ear

### Introduction

**69400**  Eustachian tube inflation, transnasal; with catheterization

**69401**  without catheterization

**69405**  Eustachian tube catheterization, transtympanic

### Incision

**69420**  Myringotomy including aspiration and/or eustachian tube inflation

**69421**  Myringotomy including aspiration and/or eustachian tube inflation requiring general anesthesia

**69424**  Ventilating tube removal requiring general anesthesia

(For bilateral procedure, report 69424 with modifier 50)

(Do not report code 69424 in conjunction with 69205, 69210, 69420, 69421, 69433-69676, 69710-69745, 69801-69930)

**69433**  Tympanostomy (requiring insertion of ventilating tube), local or topical anesthesia

(For bilateral procedure, report 69433 with modifier 50)

**69436**  Tympanostomy (requiring insertion of ventilating tube), general anesthesia

(For bilateral procedure, report 69436 with modifier 50)

**Auditory**

**69440**   Middle ear exploration through postauricular or ear canal incision

(For atticotomy, see 69601 et seq)

**69450**   Tympanolysis, transcanal

## Excision

**69501**   Transmastoid antrotomy (simple mastoidectomy)

**69502**   Mastoidectomy; complete

**69505**       modified radical

**69511**       radical

(For skin graft, see 15004 et seq)

(For mastoidectomy cavity debridement, see 69220, 69222)

**69530**   Petrous apicectomy including radical mastoidectomy

**69535**   Resection temporal bone, external approach

(For middle fossa approach, see 69950-69970)

**69540**   Excision aural polyp

**69550**   Excision aural glomus tumor; transcanal

**69552**       transmastoid

**69554**       extended (extratemporal)

## Repair

**69601**   Revision mastoidectomy; resulting in complete mastoidectomy

**69602**       resulting in modified radical mastoidectomy

**69603**       resulting in radical mastoidectomy

**69604**       resulting in tympanoplasty

(For planned secondary tympanoplasty after mastoidectomy, see 69631, 69632)

**69605**       with apicectomy

(For skin graft, see 15120, 15121, 15260, 15261)

**69610**   Tympanic membrane repair, with or without site preparation of perforation for closure, with or without patch

**69620**   Myringoplasty (surgery confined to drumhead and donor area)

**69631**   Tympanoplasty without mastoidectomy (including canalplasty, atticotomy and/or middle ear surgery), initial or revision; without ossicular chain reconstruction

**69632**       with ossicular chain reconstruction (eg, postfenestration)

**69633**       with ossicular chain reconstruction and synthetic prosthesis (eg, partial ossicular replacement prosthesis [PORP], total ossicular replacement prosthesis [TORP])

**69635**   Tympanoplasty with antrotomy or mastoidotomy (including canalplasty, atticotomy, middle ear surgery, and/or tympanic membrane repair); without ossicular chain reconstruction

**69636**       with ossicular chain reconstruction

**69637**       with ossicular chain reconstruction and synthetic prosthesis (eg, partial ossicular replacement prosthesis [PORP], total ossicular replacement prosthesis [TORP])

**69641**   Tympanoplasty with mastoidectomy (including canalplasty, middle ear surgery, tympanic membrane repair); without ossicular chain reconstruction

**69642**       with ossicular chain reconstruction

**69643**       with intact or reconstructed wall, without ossicular chain reconstruction

**69644**       with intact or reconstructed canal wall, with ossicular chain reconstruction

**69645**       radical or complete, without ossicular chain reconstruction

**69646**       radical or complete, with ossicular chain reconstruction

**69650**   Stapes mobilization

**69660**   Stapedectomy or stapedotomy with reestablishment of ossicular continuity, with or without use of foreign material;

**69661**       with footplate drill out

**69662**   Revision of stapedectomy or stapedotomy

**69666**   Repair oval window fistula

**69667**   Repair round window fistula

**69670**   Mastoid obliteration (separate procedure)

**69676**   Tympanic neurectomy

(For bilateral procedure, report 69676 with modifier 50)

## Other Procedures

**69700**   Closure postauricular fistula, mastoid (separate procedure)

**69710**   Implantation or replacement of electromagnetic bone conduction hearing device in temporal bone

(Replacement procedure includes removal of old device)

**69711**   Removal or repair of electromagnetic bone conduction hearing device in temporal bone

**69714**   Implantation, osseointegrated implant, temporal bone, with percutaneous attachment to external speech processor/cochlear stimulator; without mastoidectomy

**69715**       with mastoidectomy

**69717**   Replacement (including removal of existing device), osseointegrated implant, temporal bone, with percutaneous attachment to external speech processor/ cochlear stimulator; without mastoidectomy

| | |
|---|---|
| **69718** | with mastoidectomy |
| **69720** | Decompression facial nerve, intratemporal; lateral to geniculate ganglion |
| **69725** | including medial to geniculate ganglion |
| **69740** | Suture facial nerve, intratemporal, with or without graft or decompression; lateral to geniculate ganglion |
| **69745** | including medial to geniculate ganglion |
| | (For extracranial suture of facial nerve, use 64864) |
| **69799** | Unlisted procedure, middle ear |

## Inner Ear

### Incision and/or Destruction

| | |
|---|---|
| **69801** | Labyrinthotomy, with perfusion of vestibuloactive drug(s); transcanal |
| | (Do not report 69801 more than once per day) |
| | (Do not report 69801 in conjunction with 69420, 69421, 69433, 69436 when performed on the same ear) |
| | (69802 has been deleted) |
| **69805** | Endolymphatic sac operation; without shunt |
| **69806** | with shunt |
| **69820** | Fenestration semicircular canal |
| **69840** | Revision fenestration operation |

### Excision

| | |
|---|---|
| **69905** | Labyrinthectomy; transcanal |
| **69910** | with mastoidectomy |
| **69915** | Vestibular nerve section, translabyrinthine approach |
| | (For transcranial approach, use 69950) |

### Introduction

| | |
|---|---|
| **69930** | Cochlear device implantation, with or without mastoidectomy |

### Other Procedures

| | |
|---|---|
| **69949** | Unlisted procedure, inner ear |

## Temporal Bone, Middle Fossa Approach

| | |
|---|---|
| | (For external approach, use 69535) |
| **69950** | Vestibular nerve section, transcranial approach |

| | |
|---|---|
| **69955** | Total facial nerve decompression and/or repair (may include graft) |
| **69960** | Decompression internal auditory canal |
| **69970** | Removal of tumor, temporal bone |

### Other Procedures

| | |
|---|---|
| **69979** | Unlisted procedure, temporal bone, middle fossa approach |

# Operating Microscope

The surgical microscope is employed when the surgical services are performed using the techniques of microsurgery. Code 69990 should be reported (without modifier 51 appended) in addition to the code for the primary procedure performed. Do not use 69990 for visualization with magnifying loupes or corrected vision. Do not report 69990 in addition to procedures where use of the operating microscope is an inclusive component (15756-15758, 15842, 19364, 19368, 20955-20962, 20969-20973, 22551, 22552, 22856-22861, 26551-26554, 26556, 31526, 31531, 31536, 31541, 31545, 31546, 31561, 31571, 43116, 43496, 49906, 61548, 63075-63078, 64727, 64820-64823, 65091-68850, 0184T, 0226T, 0227T, 0308T).

| | |
|---|---|
| **+ 69990** | Microsurgical techniques, requiring use of operating microscope (List separately in addition to code for primary procedure) |

**Auditory**

# Notes

Auditory

# Radiology Guidelines (Including Nuclear Medicine and Diagnostic Ultrasound)

Guidelines to direct general reporting of services are presented in the **Introduction.** Some of the commonalities are repeated here for the convenience of those referring to this section on **Radiology (Including Nuclear Medicine and Diagnostic Ultrasound).** Other definitions and items unique to Radiology are also listed.

## Subject Listings

Subject listings apply when radiological services are performed by or under the responsible supervision of a physician or other qualified health care professional.

## Separate Procedures

Some of the procedures or services listed in the CPT codebook that are commonly carried out as an integral component of a total service or procedure have been identified by the inclusion of the term "separate procedure." The codes designated as "separate procedure" should not be reported in addition to the code for the total procedure or service of which it is considered an integral component.

However, when a procedure or service that is designated as a "separate procedure" is carried out independently or considered to be unrelated or distinct from other procedures/services provided at that time, it may be reported by itself, or in addition to other procedures/ services by appending modifier 59 to the specific "separate procedure" code to indicate that the procedure is not considered to be a component of another procedure, but is a distinct, independent procedure. This may represent a different session or patient encounter, different procedure or surgery, different site or organ system, separate incision/excision, separate lesion, separate injury, or area of injury in extensive injuries.

## Unlisted Service or Procedure

A service or procedure may be provided that is not listed in this edition of the CPT codebook. When reporting such a service, the appropriate "Unlisted Procedure" code may be used to indicate the service, identifying it by "Special Report" as discussed below. The "Unlisted Procedures" and accompanying codes for **Radiology (Including Nuclear Medicine and Diagnostic Ultrasound)** are as follows:

**76496**    Unlisted fluoroscopic procedure (eg, diagnostic, interventional)

**76497**    Unlisted computed tomography procedure (eg, diagnostic, interventional)

**76498**    Unlisted magnetic resonance procedure (eg, diagnostic, interventional)

**76499**    Unlisted diagnostic radiographic procedure

**76999**    Unlisted ultrasound procedure (eg, diagnostic, interventional)

**77299**    Unlisted procedure, therapeutic radiology clinical treatment planning

**77399**    Unlisted procedure, medical radiation physics, dosimetry and treatment devices, and special services

**77499**    Unlisted procedure, therapeutic radiology treatment management

**77799**    Unlisted procedure, clinical brachytherapy

**78099**    Unlisted endocrine procedure, diagnostic nuclear medicine

**78199**    Unlisted hematopoietic, reticuloendothelial and lymphatic procedure, diagnostic nuclear medicine

**78299**    Unlisted gastrointestinal procedure, diagnostic nuclear medicine

**78399**    Unlisted musculoskeletal procedure, diagnostic nuclear medicine

**78499**    Unlisted cardiovascular procedure, diagnostic nuclear medicine

**78599**    Unlisted respiratory procedure, diagnostic nuclear medicine

**Radiology**

| | |
|---|---|
| **78699** | Unlisted nervous system procedure, diagnostic nuclear medicine |
| **78799** | Unlisted genitourinary procedure, diagnostic nuclear medicine |
| **78999** | Unlisted miscellaneous procedure, diagnostic nuclear medicine |
| **79999** | Radiopharmaceutical therapy, unlisted procedure |

## Special Report

A service that is rarely provided, unusual, variable, or new may require a special report. Pertinent information should include an adequate definition or description of the nature, extent, and need for the procedure; and the time, effort, and equipment necessary to provide the service.

## Supervision and Interpretation

Imaging may be required during the performance of certain procedures or certain imaging procedures may require surgical procedures to access the imaged area. Many services include image guidance, which is not separately reportable and is so stated in the descriptor or guidelines. When imaging is not included in a surgical procedure or procedure from the **Medicine** section, image guidance codes or codes labeled "radiological supervision and interpretation" may be reported for the portion of the service that requires imaging. Both services require image documentation and radiological supervision, interpretation, and report services require a separate interpretation.

(The Radiological Supervision and Interpretation codes are not applicable to the Radiation Oncology subsection.)

## Administration of Contrast Material(s)

The phrase "with contrast" used in the codes for procedures performed using contrast for imaging enhancement represents contrast material administered intravascularly, intra-articularly, or intrathecally.

For intra-articular injection, use the appropriate joint injection code. If radiographic arthrography is performed, also use the arthrography supervision and interpretation code for the appropriate joint (which includes fluoroscopy). If computed tomography (CT) or magnetic resonance (MR) arthrography are performed without radiographic arthrography, use the appropriate joint injection code, the appropriate CT or MR code ("with contrast" or "without followed by contrast"), and the appropriate imaging guidance code for needle placement for contrast injection.

For spine examinations using computed tomography, magnetic resonance imaging, magnetic resonance angiography, "with contrast" includes intrathecal or intravascular injection. For intrathecal injection, use also 61055 or 62284.

Injection of intravascular contrast material is part of the "with contrast" CT, computed tomographic angiography (CTA), magnetic resonance imaging (MRI), and magnetic resonance angiography (MRA) procedures.

Oral and/or rectal contrast administration alone does not qualify as a study "with contrast."

## Written Report(s)

A written report signed by the interpreting individual should be considered an integral part of a radiologic procedure or interpretation.

# Radiology

## Diagnostic Radiology (Diagnostic Imaging)

### Head and Neck

**70010** Myelography, posterior fossa, radiological supervision and interpretation

**70015** Cisternography, positive contrast, radiological supervision and interpretation

**70030** Radiologic examination, eye, for detection of foreign body

**70100** Radiologic examination, mandible; partial, less than 4 views

**70110**      complete, minimum of 4 views

**70120** Radiologic examination, mastoids; less than 3 views per side

**70130**      complete, minimum of 3 views per side

**70134** Radiologic examination, internal auditory meati, complete

**70140** Radiologic examination, facial bones; less than 3 views

**70150**      complete, minimum of 3 views

**70160** Radiologic examination, nasal bones, complete, minimum of 3 views

**70170** Dacryocystography, nasolacrimal duct, radiological supervision and interpretation

**70190** Radiologic examination; optic foramina

**70200**      orbits, complete, minimum of 4 views

**70210** Radiologic examination, sinuses, paranasal, less than 3 views

**70220** Radiologic examination, sinuses, paranasal, complete, minimum of 3 views

**70240** Radiologic examination, sella turcica

**70250** Radiologic examination, skull; less than 4 views

**70260**      complete, minimum of 4 views

**70300** Radiologic examination, teeth; single view

**70310**      partial examination, less than full mouth

**70320**      complete, full mouth

**70328** Radiologic examination, temporomandibular joint, open and closed mouth; unilateral

**70330**      bilateral

**70332** Temporomandibular joint arthrography, radiological supervision and interpretation

     (Do not report 70332 in conjunction with 77002)

**70336** Magnetic resonance (eg, proton) imaging, temporomandibular joint(s)

**70350** Cephalogram, orthodontic

**70355** Orthopantogram (eg, panoramic x-ray)

**70360** Radiologic examination; neck, soft tissue

**70370**      pharynx or larynx, including fluoroscopy and/or magnification technique

**70371** Complex dynamic pharyngeal and speech evaluation by cine or video recording

**70373** Laryngography, contrast, radiological supervision and interpretation

**70380** Radiologic examination, salivary gland for calculus

**70390** Sialography, radiological supervision and interpretation

**70450** Computed tomography, head or brain; without contrast material

**70460**      with contrast material(s)

**70470**      without contrast material, followed by contrast material(s) and further sections

     (To report 3D rendering, see 76376, 76377)

**70480** Computed tomography, orbit, sella, or posterior fossa or outer, middle, or inner ear; without contrast material

**70481**      with contrast material(s)

**70482**      without contrast material, followed by contrast material(s) and further sections

     (To report 3D rendering, see 76376, 76377)

**70486** Computed tomography, maxillofacial area; without contrast material

**70487**      with contrast material(s)

**70488**      without contrast material, followed by contrast material(s) and further sections

     (To report 3D rendering, see 76376, 76377)

**70490** Computed tomography, soft tissue neck; without contrast material

**70491**      with contrast material(s)

**70492**      without contrast material followed by contrast material(s) and further sections

     (To report 3D rendering, see 76376, 76377)

     (For cervical spine, see 72125, 72126)

**70496** Computed tomographic angiography, head, with contrast material(s), including noncontrast images, if performed, and image postprocessing

**70498** Computed tomographic angiography, neck, with contrast material(s), including noncontrast images, if performed, and image postprocessing

**Radiology**

---

**70540**  Magnetic resonance (eg, proton) imaging, orbit, face, and/or neck; without contrast material(s)

(For head or neck magnetic resonance angiography studies, see 70544-70546, 70547-70549)

**70542**      with contrast material(s)

**70543**      without contrast material(s), followed by contrast material(s) and further sequences

(Report 70540-70543 once per imaging session)

**70544**  Magnetic resonance angiography, head; without contrast material(s)

**70545**      with contrast material(s)

**70546**      without contrast material(s), followed by contrast material(s) and further sequences

**70547**  Magnetic resonance angiography, neck; without contrast material(s)

**70548**      with contrast material(s)

**70549**      without contrast material(s), followed by contrast material(s) and further sequences

**70551**  Magnetic resonance (eg, proton) imaging, brain (including brain stem); without contrast material

**70552**      with contrast material(s)

**70553**      without contrast material, followed by contrast material(s) and further sequences

(For magnetic spectroscopy, use 76390)

Functional MRI involves identification and mapping of stimulation of brain function. When neurofunctional tests are administered by a technologist or other non-physician or non-psychologist, use 70554. When neurofunctional tests are entirely administered by a physician or psychologist, use 70555.

**70554**  Magnetic resonance imaging, brain, functional MRI; including test selection and administration of repetitive body part movement and/or visual stimulation, not requiring physician or psychologist administration

(Do not report 70554 in conjunction with 96020)

**70555**      requiring physician or psychologist administration of entire neurofunctional testing

(Do not report 70555 unless 96020 is performed)

(Do not report 70554, 70555 in conjunction with 70551-70553 unless a separate diagnostic MRI is performed)

**70557**  Magnetic resonance (eg, proton) imaging, brain (including brain stem and skull base), during open intracranial procedure (eg, to assess for residual tumor or residual vascular malformation); without contrast material

**70558**      with contrast material(s)

**70559**      without contrast material(s), followed by contrast material(s) and further sequences

(For stereotactic biopsy of intracranial lesion with magnetic resonance guidance, use 61751.70557, 70558, or 70559 may be reported only if a separate report is generated. Report only 1 of the above codes once per operative session. Do not use these codes in conjunction with 61751, 77021, 77022)

# Chest

(For fluoroscopic or ultrasonic guidance for needle placement procedures (eg, biopsy, aspiration, injection, localization device) of the thorax, see 76942, 77002)

**71010**  Radiologic examination, chest; single view, frontal

**71015**      stereo, frontal

**71020**  Radiologic examination, chest, 2 views, frontal and lateral;

**71021**      with apical lordotic procedure

**71022**      with oblique projections

**71023**      with fluoroscopy

**71030**  Radiologic examination, chest, complete, minimum of 4 views;

(For concurrent computer-aided detection [CAD] performed in addition to codes 71010, 71020, 71021, 71022, and 71030, use 0174T. Do not report 71010, 71020, 71021, 71022, and 71030 in conjunction with 0175T for CAD performed remotely from the primary interpretation)

**71034**      with fluoroscopy

(For separate chest fluoroscopy, use 76000)

**71035**  Radiologic examination, chest, special views (eg, lateral decubitus, Bucky studies)

(71040, 71060 have been deleted. To report, use 76499)

(71090 has been deleted. To report pacemaker or pacing cardioverter-defibrillator lead insertion, replacement, or revision procedures with fluoroscopic guidance, see 33206-33249. To report fluoroscopic guidance for diagnostic lead evaluation without lead insertion, replacement, or revision procedures, use 76000)

**71100**  Radiologic examination, ribs, unilateral; 2 views

**71101**      including posteroanterior chest, minimum of 3 views

**71110**  Radiologic examination, ribs, bilateral; 3 views

**71111**      including posteroanterior chest, minimum of 4 views

**71120**  Radiologic examination; sternum, minimum of 2 views

**71130**      sternoclavicular joint or joints, minimum of 3 views

**71250**  Computed tomography, thorax; without contrast material

**71260**      with contrast material(s)

**71270**    without contrast material, followed by contrast material(s) and further sections

(For cardiac computed tomography of the heart, see 75571-75574)

(To report 3D rendering, see 76376, 76377)

**71275**    Computed tomographic angiography, chest (noncoronary), with contrast material(s), including noncontrast images, if performed, and image postprocessing

(For coronary artery computed tomographic angiography including calcification score and/or cardiac morphology, use 75574)

**71550**    Magnetic resonance (eg, proton) imaging, chest (eg, for evaluation of hilar and mediastinal lymphadenopathy); without contrast material(s)

**71551**    with contrast material(s)

**71552**    without contrast material(s), followed by contrast material(s) and further sequences

(For breast MRI, see 77058, 77059)

**71555**    Magnetic resonance angiography, chest (excluding myocardium), with or without contrast material(s)

# Spine and Pelvis

**72010**    Radiologic examination, spine, entire, survey study, anteroposterior and lateral

**72020**    Radiologic examination, spine, single view, specify level

▲ **72040**    Radiologic examination, spine, cervical; 2 or 3 views

**72050**    4 or 5 views

**72052**    6 or more views

**72069**    Radiologic examination, spine, thoracolumbar, standing (scoliosis)

**72070**    Radiologic examination, spine; thoracic, 2 views

**72072**    thoracic, 3 views

**72074**    thoracic, minimum of 4 views

**72080**    thoracolumbar, 2 views

**72090**    scoliosis study, including supine and erect studies

**72100**    Radiologic examination, spine, lumbosacral; 2 or 3 views

**72110**    minimum of 4 views

**72114**    complete, including bending views, minimum of 6 views

**72120**    bending views only, 2 or 3 views

(Contrast material in CT of spine is either by intrathecal or intravenous injection. For intrathecal injection, use also 61055 or 62284. IV injection of contrast material is part of the CT procedure)

**72125**    Computed tomography, cervical spine; without contrast material

**72126**    with contrast material

**72127**    without contrast material, followed by contrast material(s) and further sections

(For intrathecal injection procedure, see 61055, 62284)

**72128**    Computed tomography, thoracic spine; without contrast material

**72129**    with contrast material

(For intrathecal injection procedure, see 61055, 62284)

**72130**    without contrast material, followed by contrast material(s) and further sections

(For intrathecal injection procedure, see 61055, 62284)

**72131**    Computed tomography, lumbar spine; without contrast material

**72132**    with contrast material

**72133**    without contrast material, followed by contrast material(s) and further sections

(For intrathecal injection procedure, see 61055, 62284)

(To report 3D rendering, see 76376, 76377)

**72141**    Magnetic resonance (eg, proton) imaging, spinal canal and contents, cervical; without contrast material

**72142**    with contrast material(s)

(For cervical spinal canal imaging without contrast material followed by contrast material, use 72156)

**72146**    Magnetic resonance (eg, proton) imaging, spinal canal and contents, thoracic; without contrast material

**72147**    with contrast material(s)

(For thoracic spinal canal imaging without contrast material followed by contrast material, use 72157)

**72148**    Magnetic resonance (eg, proton) imaging, spinal canal and contents, lumbar; without contrast material

**72149**    with contrast material(s)

(For lumbar spinal canal imaging without contrast material followed by contrast material, use 72158)

**72156**    Magnetic resonance (eg, proton) imaging, spinal canal and contents, without contrast material, followed by contrast material(s) and further sequences; cervical

**72157**    thoracic

**72158**    lumbar

**72159**    Magnetic resonance angiography, spinal canal and contents, with or without contrast material(s)

**72170**    Radiologic examination, pelvis; 1 or 2 views

**72190**    complete, minimum of 3 views

(For pelvimetry, use 74710)

(For a combined computed tomography [CT] or computed tomographic angiography abdomen and pelvis study, see 74174, 74176-74178)

Radiology

**72191**  Computed tomographic angiography, pelvis, with contrast material(s), including noncontrast images, if performed, and image postprocessing

(Do not report 72191 in conjunction with 73706 or 75635. For CTA aorto-iliofemoral runoff, use 75635)

(Do not report 72191 in conjunction with 74175. For a combined computed tomographic angiography abdomen and pelvis study, use 74174)

**72192**  Computed tomography, pelvis; without contrast material

**72193**  with contrast material(s)

**72194**  without contrast material, followed by contrast material(s) and further sections

(For a combined CT abdomen and pelvis study, see 74176-74178)

(To report 3D rendering, see 76376, 76377)

(For computed tomographic colonography, diagnostic, see 74261-74262. For computed tomographic colonography, screening, use 74263)

(Do not report 72192-72194 in conjunction with 74261-74263)

**72195**  Magnetic resonance (eg, proton) imaging, pelvis; without contrast material(s)

**72196**  with contrast material(s)

**72197**  without contrast material(s), followed by contrast material(s) and further sequences

**72198**  Magnetic resonance angiography, pelvis, with or without contrast material(s)

**72200**  Radiologic examination, sacroiliac joints; less than 3 views

**72202**  3 or more views

**72220**  Radiologic examination, sacrum and coccyx, minimum of 2 views

**72240**  Myelography, cervical, radiological supervision and interpretation

(For complete cervical myelography, see 61055, 62284, 72240)

**72255**  Myelography, thoracic, radiological supervision and interpretation

(For complete thoracic myelography, see 61055, 62284, 72255)

**72265**  Myelography, lumbosacral, radiological supervision and interpretation

(For complete lumbosacral myelography, see 61055, 62284, 72265)

**72270**  Myelography, 2 or more regions (eg, lumbar/thoracic, cervical/thoracic, lumbar/cervical, lumbar/thoracic/cervical), radiological supervision and interpretation

(For complete myelography of entire spinal canal, see 61055, 62284, 72270)

**72275**  Epidurography, radiological supervision and interpretation

(72275 includes 77003)

(For injection procedure, see 62280-62282, 62310-62319, 64479-64484)

(Use 72275 only when an epidurogram is performed, images documented, and a formal radiologic report is issued)

(Do not report 72275 in conjunction with 22586, 0195T, 0196T, 0309T)

**72285**  Discography, cervical or thoracic, radiological supervision and interpretation

**72291**  Radiological supervision and interpretation, percutaneous vertebroplasty, vertebral augmentation, or sacral augmentation (sacroplasty), including cavity creation, per vertebral body or sacrum; under fluoroscopic guidance

**72292**  under CT guidance

(For procedure, see 22520-22525, 0200T, 0201T)

**72295**  Discography, lumbar, radiological supervision and interpretation

# Upper Extremities

(For stress views, any joint, use 77071)

**73000**  Radiologic examination; clavicle, complete

**73010**  scapula, complete

**73020**  Radiologic examination, shoulder; 1 view

**73030**  complete, minimum of 2 views

**73040**  Radiologic examination, shoulder, arthrography, radiological supervision and interpretation

(Do not report 77002 in conjunction with 73040)

**73050**  Radiologic examination; acromioclavicular joints, bilateral, with or without weighted distraction

**73060**  humerus, minimum of 2 views

**73070**  Radiologic examination, elbow; 2 views

**73080**  complete, minimum of 3 views

**73085**  Radiologic examination, elbow, arthrography, radiological supervision and interpretation

(Do not report 77002 in conjunction with 73085)

**73090**  Radiologic examination; forearm, 2 views

**73092**  upper extremity, infant, minimum of 2 views

**73100**  Radiologic examination, wrist; 2 views

**73110**  complete, minimum of 3 views

**73115**  Radiologic examination, wrist, arthrography, radiological supervision and interpretation

(Do not report 77002 in conjunction with 73115)

**73120**  Radiologic examination, hand; 2 views

**73130**  minimum of 3 views

**73140** Radiologic examination, finger(s), minimum of 2 views

**73200** Computed tomography, upper extremity; without contrast material

**73201**      with contrast material(s)

**73202**      without contrast material, followed by contrast material(s) and further sections

     (To report 3D rendering, see 76376, 76377)

**73206** Computed tomographic angiography, upper extremity, with contrast material(s), including noncontrast images, if performed, and image postprocessing

**73218** Magnetic resonance (eg, proton) imaging, upper extremity, other than joint; without contrast material(s)

**73219**      with contrast material(s)

**73220**      without contrast material(s), followed by contrast material(s) and further sequences

**73221** Magnetic resonance (eg, proton) imaging, any joint of upper extremity; without contrast material(s)

**73222**      with contrast material(s)

**73223**      without contrast material(s), followed by contrast material(s) and further sequences

**73225** Magnetic resonance angiography, upper extremity, with or without contrast material(s)

# Lower Extremities

     (For stress views, any joint, use 77071)

**73500** Radiologic examination, hip, unilateral; 1 view

**73510**      complete, minimum of 2 views

**73520** Radiologic examination, hips, bilateral, minimum of 2 views of each hip, including anteroposterior view of pelvis

**73525** Radiologic examination, hip, arthrography, radiological supervision and interpretation

     (Do not report 73525 in conjunction with 77002)

**73530** Radiologic examination, hip, during operative procedure

**73540** Radiologic examination, pelvis and hips, infant or child, minimum of 2 views

     (73542 has been deleted, for arthrography use 27096)

**73550** Radiologic examination, femur, 2 views

**73560** Radiologic examination, knee; 1 or 2 views

**73562**      3 views

**73564**      complete, 4 or more views

**73565**      both knees, standing, anteroposterior

**73580** Radiologic examination, knee, arthrography, radiological supervision and interpretation

     (Do not report 73580 in conjunction with 77002)

**73590** Radiologic examination; tibia and fibula, 2 views

**73592**      lower extremity, infant, minimum of 2 views

**73600** Radiologic examination, ankle; 2 views

**73610**      complete, minimum of 3 views

**73615** Radiologic examination, ankle, arthrography, radiological supervision and interpretation

     (Do not report 73615 in conjunction with 77002)

**73620** Radiologic examination, foot; 2 views

**73630**      complete, minimum of 3 views

**73650** Radiologic examination; calcaneus, minimum of 2 views

**73660**      toe(s), minimum of 2 views

**73700** Computed tomography, lower extremity; without contrast material

**73701**      with contrast material(s)

**73702**      without contrast material, followed by contrast material(s) and further sections

     (To report 3D rendering, see 76376, 76377)

**73706** Computed tomographic angiography, lower extremity, with contrast material(s), including noncontrast images, if performed, and image postprocessing

     (For CTA aorto-iliofemoral runoff, use 75635)

**73718** Magnetic resonance (eg, proton) imaging, lower extremity other than joint; without contrast material(s)

**73719**      with contrast material(s)

**73720**      without contrast material(s), followed by contrast material(s) and further sequences

**73721** Magnetic resonance (eg, proton) imaging, any joint of lower extremity; without contrast material

**73722**      with contrast material(s)

**73723**      without contrast material(s), followed by contrast material(s) and further sequences

**73725** Magnetic resonance angiography, lower extremity, with or without contrast material(s)

# Abdomen

**74000** Radiologic examination, abdomen; single anteroposterior view

**74010**      anteroposterior and additional oblique and cone views

**74020**      complete, including decubitus and/or erect views

**74022**      complete acute abdomen series, including supine, erect, and/or decubitus views, single view chest

**74150** Computed tomography, abdomen; without contrast material

**74160**      with contrast material(s)

**Radiology**

**74170** without contrast material, followed by contrast material(s) and further sections

(For a combined CT abdomen and pelvis study, see 74176-74178)

(To report 3D rendering, see 76376, 76377)

(For computed tomographic colonography, diagnostic, see 74261-74262. For computed tomographic colonography, screening, use 74263)

(Do not report 74150-74170 in conjunction with 74261-74263)

**74174** Computed tomographic angiography, abdomen and pelvis, with contrast material(s), including noncontrast images, if performed, and image postprocessing

(Do not report 74174 in conjunction with 72191, 73706, 74175, 75635, 76376, 76377)

(For CTA aorto-iliofemoral runoff, use 75635)

**74175** Computed tomographic angiography, abdomen, with contrast material(s), including noncontrast images, if performed, and image postprocessing

(Do not report 74175 in conjunction with 73706 or 75635. For CTA aorto-iliofemoral runoff, use 75635)

(Do not report 74175 in conjunction with 72191. For a combined computed tomographic angiography abdomen and pelvis study, use 74174)

For combinations of CT of the abdomen with CT of the pelvis performed at the same session, use the following table. Do not report more than one CT of the abdomen or CT of the pelvis for any session.

| Stand Alone Code | 74150 CT Abdomen WO Contrast | 74160 CT Abdomen W Contrast | 74170 CT Abdomen WO/W Contrast |
|---|---|---|---|
| 72192 CT Pelvis WO Contrast | 74176 | 74178 | 74178 |
| 72193 CT Pelvis W Contrast | 74178 | 74177 | 74178 |
| 72194 CT Pelvis WO/W Contrast | 74178 | 74178 | 74178 |

**74176** Computed tomography, abdomen and pelvis; without contrast material

**74177** with contrast material(s)

**74178** without contrast material in one or both body regions, followed by contrast material(s) and further sections in one or both body regions

(Do not report 74176-74178 in conjunction with 72192-72194, 74150-74170)

(Report 74176, 74177, or 74178 only once per CT abdomen and pelvis examination)

**74181** Magnetic resonance (eg, proton) imaging, abdomen; without contrast material(s)

**74182** with contrast material(s)

**74183** without contrast material(s), followed by with contrast material(s) and further sequences

**74185** Magnetic resonance angiography, abdomen, with or without contrast material(s)

**74190** Peritoneogram (eg, after injection of air or contrast), radiological supervision and interpretation

(For procedure, use 49400)

(For computed tomography, see 72192 or 74150)

## Gastrointestinal Tract

(For percutaneous placement of gastrostomy tube, use 43246)

**74210** Radiologic examination; pharynx and/or cervical esophagus

**74220** esophagus

**74230** Swallowing function, with cineradiography/videoradiography

**74235** Removal of foreign body(s), esophageal, with use of balloon catheter, radiological supervision and interpretation

▶(For procedure, see 43194, 43215, 43247)◀

**74240** Radiologic examination, gastrointestinal tract, upper; with or without delayed films, without KUB

**74241** with or without delayed films, with KUB

**74245** with small intestine, includes multiple serial films

**74246** Radiological examination, gastrointestinal tract, upper, air contrast, with specific high density barium, effervescent agent, with or without glucagon; with or without delayed films, without KUB

**74247** with or without delayed films, with KUB

**74249** with small intestine follow-through

**74250** Radiologic examination, small intestine, includes multiple serial films;

**74251** via enteroclysis tube

**74260** Duodenography, hypotonic

**74261** Computed tomographic (CT) colonography, diagnostic, including image postprocessing; without contrast material

**74262** with contrast material(s) including non-contrast images, if performed

(Do not report 74261, 74262 in conjunction with 72192-72194, 74150-74170, 74263, 76376, 76377)

Radiology

**74263**   Computed tomographic (CT) colonography, screening, including image postprocessing

(Do not report 74263 in conjunction with 72192-72194, 74150-74170, 74261, 74262, 76376, 76377)

**74270**   Radiologic examination, colon; contrast (eg, barium) enema, with or without KUB

**74280**   air contrast with specific high density barium, with or without glucagon

**74283**   Therapeutic enema, contrast or air, for reduction of intussusception or other intraluminal obstruction (eg, meconium ileus)

**74290**   Cholecystography, oral contrast;

**74291**   additional or repeat examination or multiple day examination

**74300**   Cholangiography and/or pancreatography; intraoperative, radiological supervision and interpretation

**+ 74301**   additional set intraoperative, radiological supervision and interpretation (List separately in addition to code for primary procedure)

(Use 74301 in conjunction with 74300)

**74305**   through existing catheter, radiological supervision and interpretation

(For procedure, see 47505, 48400, 47560-47561, 47563)

(For biliary duct stone extraction, percutaneous, see 47630, 74327)

**74320**   Cholangiography, percutaneous, transhepatic, radiological supervision and interpretation

**74327**   Postoperative biliary duct calculus removal, percutaneous via T-tube tract, basket, or snare (eg, Burhenne technique), radiological supervision and interpretation

(For procedure, use 47630)

**74328**   Endoscopic catheterization of the biliary ductal system, radiological supervision and interpretation

►(For procedure, see 43260-43278 as appropriate)◄

**74329**   Endoscopic catheterization of the pancreatic ductal system, radiological supervision and interpretation

►(For procedure, see 43260-43278 as appropriate)◄

**74330**   Combined endoscopic catheterization of the biliary and pancreatic ductal systems, radiological supervision and interpretation

►(For procedure, see 43260-43278 as appropriate)◄

**74340**   Introduction of long gastrointestinal tube (eg, Miller-Abbott), including multiple fluoroscopies and films, radiological supervision and interpretation

(For tube placement, use 44500)

**74355**   Percutaneous placement of enteroclysis tube, radiological supervision and interpretation

**74360**   Intraluminal dilation of strictures and/or obstructions (eg, esophagus), radiological supervision and interpretation

►(For procedure, see 43195, 43196, 43220, 43226, 43453)◄

►(Do not report 74360 in conjunction with 43213, 43214, 43233)◄

**74363**   Percutaneous transhepatic dilation of biliary duct stricture with or without placement of stent, radiological supervision and interpretation

(For procedure, see 47510, 47511, 47555, 47556)

## Urinary Tract

**74400**   Urography (pyelography), intravenous, with or without KUB, with or without tomography

**74410**   Urography, infusion, drip technique and/or bolus technique;

**74415**   with nephrotomography

**74420**   Urography, retrograde, with or without KUB

**74425**   Urography, antegrade (pyelostogram, nephrostogram, loopogram), radiological supervision and interpretation

**74430**   Cystography, minimum of 3 views, radiological supervision and interpretation

**74440**   Vasography, vesiculography, or epididymography, radiological supervision and interpretation

**74445**   Corpora cavernosography, radiological supervision and interpretation

**74450**   Urethrocystography, retrograde, radiological supervision and interpretation

**74455**   Urethrocystography, voiding, radiological supervision and interpretation

**74470**   Radiologic examination, renal cyst study, translumbar, contrast visualization, radiological supervision and interpretation

**74475**   Introduction of intracatheter or catheter into renal pelvis for drainage and/or injection, percutaneous, radiological supervision and interpretation

**74480**   Introduction of ureteral catheter or stent into ureter through renal pelvis for drainage and/or injection, percutaneous, radiological supervision and interpretation

►(For transurethral surgery [ureter and pelvis], see 52320-52356)◄

**74485**   Dilation of nephrostomy, ureters, or urethra, radiological supervision and interpretation

(For dilation of ureter without radiologic guidance, use 52341, 52344)

(For change of nephrostomy or pyelostomy tube, use 50398)

**Radiology**

# Gynecological and Obstetrical

(For abdomen and pelvis, see 72170-72190, 74000-74170)

**74710**  Pelvimetry, with or without placental localization

**74740**  Hysterosalpingography, radiological supervision and interpretation

(For introduction of saline or contrast for hysterosalpingography, see 58340)

**74742**  Transcervical catheterization of fallopian tube, radiological supervision and interpretation

(For procedure, use 58345)

**74775**  Perineogram (eg, vaginogram, for sex determination or extent of anomalies)

# Heart

Cardiac magnetic imaging differs from traditional magnetic resonance imaging (MRI) in its ability to provide a physiologic evaluation of cardiac function. Traditional MRI relies on static images to obtain clinical diagnoses based upon anatomic information. Improvement in spatial and temporal resolution has expanded the application from an anatomic test and includes physiologic evaluation of cardiac function. Flow and velocity assessment for valves and intracardiac shunts is performed in addition to a function and morphologic evaluation. Use 75559 with 75565 to report flow with pharmacologic wall motion stress evaluation without contrast. Use 75563 with 75565 to report flow with pharmacologic perfusion stress with contrast.

Cardiac MRI for velocity flow mapping can be reported in conjunction with 75557, 75559, 75561, or 75563.

Listed procedures may be performed independently or in the course of overall medical care. If the individual providing these services is also responsible for diagnostic workup and/or follow-up care of the patient, also see appropriate sections. Only one procedure in the series 75557-75563 is appropriately reported per session. Only one add-on code for flow velocity can be reported per session.

Cardiac MRI studies may be performed at rest and/or during pharmacologic stress. Therefore, the appropriate stress testing code from the 93015-93018 series should be reported in addition to 75559 or 75563.

Cardiac computed tomography (CT) and coronary computed tomographic angiography (CTA) include the axial source images of the pre-contrast, arterial phase sequence, and venous phase sequence (if performed), as well as the two-dimensional and three-dimensional reformatted images resulting from the study, including cine review. Contrast enhanced cardiac CT and coronary CTA codes 75571-75574 include any quantitative assessment when performed as part of the same encounter. Report only one computed tomography heart service per encounter.

(For separate injection procedures for vascular radiology, see **Surgery** section, 36000-36299)

(For cardiac catheterization procedures, see 93451-93572)

(75552-75556 have been deleted. To report, see 75557, 75559, 75561, 75563, 75565)

**75557**  Cardiac magnetic resonance imaging for morphology and function without contrast material;

**75559**       with stress imaging

**75561**  Cardiac magnetic resonance imaging for morphology and function without contrast material(s), followed by contrast material(s) and further sequences;

**75563**       with stress imaging

(75558, 75560, 75562, 75564 have been deleted. To report flow velocity, use 75565)

**+ 75565**  Cardiac magnetic resonance imaging for velocity flow mapping (List separately in addition to code for primary procedure)

(Use 75565 in conjunction with 75557, 75559, 75561, 75563)

(Do not report 75557, 75559, 75561, 75563, 75565 in conjunction with 76376, 76377)

**75571**  Computed tomography, heart, without contrast material, with quantitative evaluation of coronary calcium

**75572**  Computed tomography, heart, with contrast material, for evaluation of cardiac structure and morphology (including 3D image postprocessing, assessment of cardiac function, and evaluation of venous structures, if performed)

**75573**  Computed tomography, heart, with contrast material, for evaluation of cardiac structure and morphology in the setting of congenital heart disease (including 3D image postprocessing, assessment of LV cardiac function, RV structure and function and evaluation of venous structures, if performed)

**75574**  Computed tomographic angiography, heart, coronary arteries and bypass grafts (when present), with contrast material, including 3D image postprocessing (including evaluation of cardiac structure and morphology, assessment of cardiac function, and evaluation of venous structures, if performed)

# Vascular Procedures

## Aorta and Arteries

Selective vascular catheterizations should be coded to include introduction and all lesser order selective catheterizations used in the approach (eg, the description for a selective right middle cerebral artery catheterization includes the introduction and placement catheterization of the right common and internal carotid arteries).

Radiology

Additional second and/or third order arterial catheterizations within the same family of arteries supplied by a single first order artery should be expressed by 36218 or 36248. Additional first order or higher catheterizations in vascular families supplied by a first order vessel different from a previously selected and coded family should be separately coded using the conventions described above.

The lower extremity endovascular revascularization codes describing services performed for occlusive disease (37220-37235) include catheterization (36200, 36140, 36245-36248) in the work described by the codes. Catheterization codes are not additionally reported for diagnostic lower extremity angiography when performed through the same access site as the therapy (37220-37235) performed in the same session. However, catheterization for the diagnostic lower extremity angiogram may be reported separately if a different arterial puncture site is necessary.

For angiography performed in conjunction with therapeutic transcatheter radiological supervision and interpretation services, see the **Radiology Transcatheter Procedures** guidelines.

Diagnostic angiography (radiological supervision and interpretation) codes should NOT be used with interventional procedures for:

1. Contrast injections, angiography, roadmapping, and/or fluoroscopic guidance for the intervention,

2. Vessel measurement, and

3. Post-angioplasty/stent/atherectomy angiography, as this work is captured in the radiological supervision and interpretation code(s). In those therapeutic codes that include radiological supervision and interpretation, this work is captured in the therapeutic code.

Diagnostic angiography performed at the time of an interventional procedure is separately reportable if:

1. No prior catheter-based angiographic study is available and a full diagnostic study is performed, and the decision to intervene is based on the diagnostic study, OR

2. A prior study is available, but as documented in the medical record:

   a. The patient's condition with respect to the clinical indication has changed since the prior study, OR

   b. There is inadequate visualization of the anatomy and/or pathology, OR

   c. There is a clinical change during the procedure that requires new evaluation outside the target area of intervention.

Diagnostic angiography performed at a separate sessions from an interventional procedure is separately reported.

If diagnostic angiography is necessary, is performed at the same session as the interventional procedure and meets the above criteria, modifier 59 must be appended to the diagnostic radiological supervision and interpretation code(s) to denote that diagnostic work has been done following these guidelines.

Diagnostic angiography performed at the time of an interventional procedure is NOT separately reportable if it is specifically included in the interventional code descriptor.

(For intravenous procedure, see 36000, 36005-36015, and for intra-arterial procedure, see 36100-36248)

(For radiological supervision and interpretation, see 75600-75893)

**75600**   Aortography, thoracic, without serialography, radiological supervision and interpretation

(For supravalvular aortography performed at the time of cardiac catheterization, use 93567, which includes imaging supervision, interpretation, and report)

**75605**   Aortography, thoracic, by serialography, radiological supervision and interpretation

(For supravalvular aortography performed at the time of cardiac catheterization, use 93567, which includes imaging supervision, interpretation, and report)

**75625**   Aortography, abdominal, by serialography, radiological supervision and interpretation

**75630**   Aortography, abdominal plus bilateral iliofemoral lower extremity, catheter, by serialography, radiological supervision and interpretation

**75635**   Computed tomographic angiography, abdominal aorta and bilateral iliofemoral lower extremity runoff, with contrast material(s), including noncontrast images, if performed, and image postprocessing

(Do not report 75635 in conjunction with 72191, 73706, 74174 or 74175)

(75650 has been deleted. To report, see 36221-36226)

**75658**   Angiography, brachial, retrograde, radiological supervision and interpretation

(75660 has been deleted. To report, use 36227)

(75662 has been deleted. To report, use 36227 and append modifier 50)

(75665 has been deleted. To report, see 36223, 36224)

(75671 has been deleted. To report, see 36223 and 36224 and append modifier 50 as appropriate)

(75676 has been deleted. To report, see 36222-36224)

(75680 has been deleted. To report, see 36222-36224 and append modifier 50 as appropriate)

(75685 has been deleted. To report, see 36225, 36226)

**75705**   Angiography, spinal, selective, radiological supervision and interpretation

**Radiology**

**75710** Angiography, extremity, unilateral, radiological supervision and interpretation

**75716** Angiography, extremity, bilateral, radiological supervision and interpretation

(75722 has been deleted. To report, see 36251, 36253)

(75724 has been deleted. To report, see 36252, 36254)

**75726** Angiography, visceral, selective or supraselective (with or without flush aortogram), radiological supervision and interpretation

(For selective angiography, each additional visceral vessel studied after basic examination, use 75774)

**75731** Angiography, adrenal, unilateral, selective, radiological supervision and interpretation

**75733** Angiography, adrenal, bilateral, selective, radiological supervision and interpretation

**75736** Angiography, pelvic, selective or supraselective, radiological supervision and interpretation

**75741** Angiography, pulmonary, unilateral, selective, radiological supervision and interpretation

**75743** Angiography, pulmonary, bilateral, selective, radiological supervision and interpretation

**75746** Angiography, pulmonary, by nonselective catheter or venous injection, radiological supervision and interpretation

(For pulmonary angiography by nonselective catheter or venous injection performed at the time of cardiac catheterization, use 93568, which includes imaging supervision, interpretation, and report)

**75756** Angiography, internal mammary, radiological supervision and interpretation

(For internal mammary angiography performed at the time of cardiac catheterization, see 93455, 93457, 93459, 93461, 93564, which include imaging supervision, interpretation, and report)

+ **75774** Angiography, selective, each additional vessel studied after basic examination, radiological supervision and interpretation (List separately in addition to code for primary procedure)

(Use 75774 in addition to code for specific initial vessel studied)

(Do not report 75774 as part of diagnostic angiography of the extracranial and intracranial cervicocerebral vessels. It may be appropriate to report 75774 for diagnostic angiography of upper extremities and other vascular beds performed in the same session)

(For angiography, see 36147, 75600-75756, 75791)

(For catheterizations, see codes 36215-36248)

(For cardiac catheterization procedures, see 93452-93462, 93531-93533, 93563-93568)

(75790 has been deleted. To report, see 36147, 75791)

**75791** Angiography, arteriovenous shunt (eg, dialysis patient fistula/graft), complete evaluation of dialysis access, including fluoroscopy, image documentation and report (includes injections of contrast and all necessary imaging from the arterial anastomosis and adjacent artery through entire venous outflow including the inferior or superior vena cava), radiological supervision and interpretation

(Do not report 75791 in conjunction with 36147, 36148)

(For introduction of catheter, if necessary, see 36140, 36215-36217, 36245-36247)

(Use 75791 only if radiological evaluation is performed through an already existing access into the shunt or from an access that is not a direct puncture of the shunt)

(For radiological evaluation with needle/catheter introduction, AV dialysis shunt, complete procedure, use 36147)

## Veins and Lymphatics

For venography performed in conjunction with therapeutic transcatheter radiological supervision and interpretation services, see the **Radiology Transcatheter Procedures** guidelines.

Diagnostic venography (radiological supervision and interpretation) codes should NOT be used with interventional procedures for:

1. Contrast injections, venography, roadmapping, and/or fluoroscopic guidance for the intervention,

2. Vessel measurement, and

3. Post-angioplasty/stent venography, as this work is captured in the radiological supervision and intrepretation code(s).

Diagnostic venography performed at the time of an interventional procedure is separately reportable if:

1. No prior catheter-based venographic study is available and a full diagnostic study is performed, and decision to intervene is based on the diagnostic study, OR

2. A prior study is available, but as documented in the medical record:

   a. The patient's condition with respect to the clinical indication has changed since the prior study, OR

   b. There is inadequate visualization of the anatomy and/or pathology, OR

   c. There is a clinical change during the procedure that requires new evaluation outside the target area of intervention.

Diagnostic venography performed at a separate setting from an interventional procedure is separately reported.

Diagnostic venography performed at the time of an interventional procedure is NOT separately reportable if it is specifically included in the interventional code descriptor.

(For injection procedure for venous system, see 36000-36015, 36400-36510)

(For injection procedure for lymphatic system, use 38790)

**75801**    Lymphangiography, extremity only, unilateral, radiological supervision and interpretation

**75803**    Lymphangiography, extremity only, bilateral, radiological supervision and interpretation

**75805**    Lymphangiography, pelvic/abdominal, unilateral, radiological supervision and interpretation

**75807**    Lymphangiography, pelvic/abdominal, bilateral, radiological supervision and interpretation

**75809**    Shuntogram for investigation of previously placed indwelling nonvascular shunt (eg, LeVeen shunt, ventriculoperitoneal shunt, indwelling infusion pump), radiological supervision and interpretation

(For procedure, see 49427 or 61070)

**75810**    Splenoportography, radiological supervision and interpretation

**75820**    Venography, extremity, unilateral, radiological supervision and interpretation

**75822**    Venography, extremity, bilateral, radiological supervision and interpretation

**75825**    Venography, caval, inferior, with serialography, radiological supervision and interpretation

**75827**    Venography, caval, superior, with serialography, radiological supervision and interpretation

**75831**    Venography, renal, unilateral, selective, radiological supervision and interpretation

**75833**    Venography, renal, bilateral, selective, radiological supervision and interpretation

**75840**    Venography, adrenal, unilateral, selective, radiological supervision and interpretation

**75842**    Venography, adrenal, bilateral, selective, radiological supervision and interpretation

**75860**    Venography, venous sinus (eg, petrosal and inferior sagittal) or jugular, catheter, radiological supervision and interpretation

**75870**    Venography, superior sagittal sinus, radiological supervision and interpretation

**75872**    Venography, epidural, radiological supervision and interpretation

**75880**    Venography, orbital, radiological supervision and interpretation

**75885**    Percutaneous transhepatic portography with hemodynamic evaluation, radiological supervision and interpretation

**75887**    Percutaneous transhepatic portography without hemodynamic evaluation, radiological supervision and interpretation

**75889**    Hepatic venography, wedged or free, with hemodynamic evaluation, radiological supervision and interpretation

**75891**    Hepatic venography, wedged or free, without hemodynamic evaluation, radiological supervision and interpretation

**75893**    Venous sampling through catheter, with or without angiography (eg, for parathyroid hormone, renin), radiological supervision and interpretation

(For procedure, use 36500)

## Transcatheter Procedures

Therapeutic transcatheter radiological supervision and interpretation code(s) include the following services associated with that intervention:

1. Contrast injections, angiography/venography, roadmapping, and fluoroscopic guidance for the intervention,

2. Vessel measurement, and

3. Completion angiography/venography (except for those uses permitted by 75898).

Unless specifically included in the code descriptor, diagnostic angiography/venography performed at the time of transcatheter therapeutic radiological and interpretation service(s) is separately reportable (eg, no prior catheter-based diagnostic angiography/venography study of the target vessel is available, prior diagnostic study is inadequate, patient's condition with respect to the clinical indication has changed since the prior study or during the intervention). See 75600-75893.

Codes 75956 and 75957 include all angiography of the thoracic aorta and its branches for diagnostic imaging prior to deployment of the primary endovascular devices (including all routine components of modular devices), fluoroscopic guidance in the delivery of the endovascular components, and intraprocedural arterial angiography (eg, confirm position, detect endoleak, evaluate runoff).

Code 75958 includes the analogous services for placement of each proximal thoracic endovascular extension. Code 75959 includes the analogous services for placement of a distal thoracic endovascular extension(s) placed during a procedure after the primary repair.

**75894**    Transcatheter therapy, embolization, any method, radiological supervision and interpretation

▶(Do not report 75894 in conjunction with 36475, 36476, 36478, 36479, 37241-37244)◀

**Radiology**

**75896**  Transcatheter therapy, infusion, other than for thrombolysis, radiological supervision and interpretation

(For radiological supervision and interpretation for thrombolysis other than coronary, see 37211-37214)

(Do not report 75896 in conjunction with 37211-37214)

(For infusion for coronary disease, see 92975, 92977)

**75898**  Angiography through existing catheter for follow-up study for transcatheter therapy, embolization or infusion, other than for thrombolysis

(For thrombolysis infusion management other than coronary, see 37211-37214)

▶(Do not report 75898 in conjunction with 37211-37214, 37241-37244)◀

(75900 has been deleted. For exchange of a previously placed intravascular catheter during thrombolytic therapy with contrast monitoring, radiological supervision and interpretation, see 37211-37214)

**75901**  Mechanical removal of pericatheter obstructive material (eg, fibrin sheath) from central venous device via separate venous access, radiologic supervision and interpretation

(For procedure, use 36595)

(For venous catheterization, see 36010-36012)

**75902**  Mechanical removal of intraluminal (intracatheter) obstructive material from central venous device through device lumen, radiologic supervision and interpretation

(For procedure, use 36596)

(For venous catheterization, see 36010-36012)

(75940 has been deleted. To report, use 37191)

**75945**  Intravascular ultrasound (non-coronary vessel), radiological supervision and interpretation; initial vessel

**+ 75946**  each additional non-coronary vessel (List separately in addition to code for primary procedure)

(Use 75946 in conjunction with 75945)

(For catheterizations, see codes 36215-36248)

▶(For transcatheter therapies, see codes 37200, 37202, 37236-37239, 37241-37244, 61624, 61626)◀

(For procedure, see 37250, 37251)

**75952**  Endovascular repair of infrarenal abdominal aortic aneurysm or dissection, radiological supervision and interpretation

(For implantation of endovascular grafts, see 34800-34805)

▶(For radiologic supervision and interpretation of fenestrated endovascular repair of the visceral aorta with or without concomitant infrarenal abdominal aorta and common iliac artery[s], see 34841-34848)◀

▶(Do not report 75952 in conjunction with 34841-34848)◀

**75953**  Placement of proximal or distal extension prosthesis for endovascular repair of infrarenal aortic or iliac artery aneurysm, pseudoaneurysm, or dissection, radiological supervision and interpretation

(For implantation of endovascular extension prostheses, see 34825, 34826)

**75954**  Endovascular repair of iliac artery aneurysm, pseudoaneurysm, arteriovenous malformation, or trauma, using ilio-iliac tube endoprosthesis, radiological supervision and interpretation

(For implantation of endovascular graft, see 34900)

(For endovascular repair of iliac artery bifurcation [eg, aneurysm, pseudoaneurysm, arteriovenous malformation, trauma] using bifurcated endoprosthesis, radiological supervision and interpretation, use 0255T)

**75956**  Endovascular repair of descending thoracic aorta (eg, aneurysm, pseudoaneurysm, dissection, penetrating ulcer, intramural hematoma, or traumatic disruption); involving coverage of left subclavian artery origin, initial endoprosthesis plus descending thoracic aortic extension(s), if required, to level of celiac artery origin, radiological supervision and interpretation

(For implantation of endovascular graft, use 33880)

**75957**  not involving coverage of left subclavian artery origin, initial endoprosthesis plus descending thoracic aortic extension(s), if required, to level of celiac artery origin, radiological supervision and interpretation

(For implantation of endovascular graft, use 33881)

**75958**  Placement of proximal extension prosthesis for endovascular repair of descending thoracic aorta (eg, aneurysm, pseudoaneurysm, dissection, penetrating ulcer, intramural hematoma, or traumatic disruption), radiological supervision and interpretation

(Report 75958 for each proximal extension)

(For implantation of proximal endovascular extension, see 33883, 33884)

**75959**  Placement of distal extension prosthesis(s) (delayed) after endovascular repair of descending thoracic aorta, as needed, to level of celiac origin, radiological supervision and interpretation

(Do not report 75959 in conjunction with 75956, 75957)

(Report 75959 once, regardless of number of modules deployed)

(For implantation of distal endovascular extension, use 33886)

▶(75960 has been deleted)◀

▶(Radiologic supervision for transcatheter placement of stent[s] is included in the therapeutic service codes)◀

(75961 has been deleted. To report, use 37197)

(For removal of a vena cava filter, use 37193)

⊙=Moderate sedation  ✚=Add-on code  ✔=FDA approval pending  #=Resequenced code  ○=Recycled/reinstated code

Radiology

**75962** Transluminal balloon angioplasty, peripheral artery other than renal, or other visceral artery, iliac or lower extremity, radiological supervision and interpretation

(For radiological supervision and interpretation for transluminal balloon angioplasty in iliac, femoral, popliteal, and tibial/peroneal arteries, see 37220-37235)

(For procedure, see 35458, 35475)

▶(Do not report 75962 in conjunction with 37217 for ipsilateral services)◀

**+ 75964** Transluminal balloon angioplasty, each additional peripheral artery other than renal or other visceral artery, iliac or lower extremity, radiological supervision and interpretation (List separately in addition to code for primary procedure)

(Use 75964 in conjunction with 75962)

**75966** Transluminal balloon angioplasty, renal or other visceral artery, radiological supervision and interpretation

**+ 75968** Transluminal balloon angioplasty, each additional visceral artery, radiological supervision and interpretation (List separately in addition to code for primary procedure)

(Use 75968 in conjunction with 75966)

(For percutaneous transluminal coronary angioplasty, see 92920-92944)

**75970** Transcatheter biopsy, radiological supervision and interpretation

(For injection procedure only for transcatheter therapy or biopsy, see 36100-36299)

(For transcatheter renal and ureteral biopsy, use 52007)

(For percutaneous needle biopsy of pancreas, use 48102; of retroperitoneal lymph node or mass, use 49180)

**75978** Transluminal balloon angioplasty, venous (eg, subclavian stenosis), radiological supervision and interpretation

**75980** Percutaneous transhepatic biliary drainage with contrast monitoring, radiological supervision and interpretation

**75982** Percutaneous placement of drainage catheter for combined internal and external biliary drainage or of a drainage stent for internal biliary drainage in patients with an inoperable mechanical biliary obstruction, radiological supervision and interpretation

**75984** Change of percutaneous tube or drainage catheter with contrast monitoring (eg, genitourinary system, abscess), radiological supervision and interpretation

(For percutaneous replacement of gastrostomy, duodenostomy, jejunostomy, gastro-jejunostomy, or cecostomy [or other colonic] tube including fluoroscopic imaging guidance, see 49450-49452)

(For change of nephrostomy or pyelostomy tube only, use 50398)

(For introduction procedure only for percutaneous biliary drainage, see 47510, 47511)

(For percutaneous cholecystostomy, use 47490)

(For change of percutaneous biliary drainage catheter only, use 47525)

(For percutaneous nephrostolithotomy or pyelostolithotomy, see 50080, 50081)

(For removal and/or replacement of an internally dwelling ureteral stent via a transurethral approach, see 50385-50386)

**75989** Radiological guidance (ie, fluoroscopy, ultrasound, or computed tomography), for percutaneous drainage (eg, abscess, specimen collection), with placement of catheter, radiological supervision and interpretation

▶(Do not report 75989 in conjunction with 10030, 32554, 32555, 32556, 32557, 47490, 49405, 49406, 49407)◀

(75992 has been deleted. To report, see 37225, 37227, 37229, 37231, 0238T)

(75993 has been deleted. To report, see 37233, 37235, 0238T)

(75994 has been deleted. To report, use 0234T)

(75995 has been deleted. To report, use 0235T)

(75996 has been deleted. To report, use 0235T)

# Other Procedures

(For computed tomography cerebral perfusion analysis, see Category III code 0042T)

(For arthrography of shoulder, use 73040; elbow, use 73085; wrist, use 73115; hip, use 73525; knee, use 73580; ankle, use 73615)

**76000** Fluoroscopy (separate procedure), up to 1 hour physician or other qualified health care professional time, other than 71023 or 71034 (eg, cardiac fluoroscopy)

**76001** Fluoroscopy, physician or other qualified health care professional time more than 1 hour, assisting a nonradiologic physician or other qualified health care professional (eg, nephrostolithotomy, ERCP, bronchoscopy, transbronchial biopsy)

**76010** Radiologic examination from nose to rectum for foreign body, single view, child

**76080** Radiologic examination, abscess, fistula or sinus tract study, radiological supervision and interpretation

(For contrast injection[s] and radiological assessment of gastrostomy, duodenostomy, jejunostomy, gastro-jejunostomy, or cecostomy [or other colonic] tube including fluoroscopic imaging guidance, use 49465)

**76098** Radiological examination, surgical specimen

▶(Do not report 76098 in conjunction with 19081-19086)◀

**76100** Radiologic examination, single plane body section (eg, tomography), other than with urography

**76101** Radiologic examination, complex motion (ie, hypercycloidal) body section (eg, mastoid polytomography), other than with urography; unilateral

**Radiology**

---

**76102** bilateral

(Do not report 76101, 76102 more than once per day)

(For panoramic X-ray, use 70355)

(For nephrotomography, use 74415)

**76120** Cineradiography/videoradiography, except where specifically included

**+ 76125** Cineradiography/videoradiography to complement routine examination (List separately in addition to code for primary procedure)

**76140** Consultation on X-ray examination made elsewhere, written report

(76150 has been deleted)

(76350 has been deleted)

(2D reformatting is no longer separately reported. To report 3D rendering, see 76376, 76377)

**76376** 3D rendering with interpretation and reporting of computed tomography, magnetic resonance imaging, ultrasound, or other tomographic modality with image postprocessing under concurrent supervision; not requiring image postprocessing on an independent workstation

(Use 76376 in conjunction with code[s] for base imaging procedure[s])

(Do not report 76376 in conjunction with 31627, 70496, 70498, 70544-70549, 71275, 71555, 72159, 72191, 72198, 73206, 73225, 73706, 73725, 74174, 74175,74185, 74261-74263, 75557, 75559, 75561, 75563, 75565, 75571-75574, 75635, 76377, 78012-78999, 0159T)

**76377** requiring image postprocessing on an independent workstation

(Use 76377 in conjunction with code[s] for base imaging procedure[s])

(Do not report 76377 in conjunction with 70496, 70498, 70544-70549, 71275, 71555, 72159, 72191, 72198, 73206, 73225, 73706, 73725, 74174, 74175, 74185, 74261-74263, 75557, 75559, 75561, 75563, 75565, 75571-75574, 75635, 76376, 78012-78999, 0159T)

(To report computer-aided detection, including computer algorithm analysis of MRI data for lesion detection/characterization, pharmacokinetic analysis, breast MRI, use Category III code 0159T)

(76376, 76377 require concurrent supervision of image postprocessing 3D manipulation of volumetric data set and image rendering)

**76380** Computed tomography, limited or localized follow-up study

**76390** Magnetic resonance spectroscopy

(For magnetic resonance imaging, use appropriate MRI body site code)

**76496** Unlisted fluoroscopic procedure (eg, diagnostic, interventional)

**76497** Unlisted computed tomography procedure (eg, diagnostic, interventional)

**76498** Unlisted magnetic resonance procedure (eg, diagnostic, interventional)

**76499** Unlisted diagnostic radiographic procedure

# Diagnostic Ultrasound

All diagnostic ultrasound examinations require permanently recorded images with measurements, when such measurements are clinically indicated. For those codes whose sole diagnostic goal is a biometric measure (ie, 76514, 76516, and 76519), permanently recorded images are not required. A final, written report should be issued for inclusion in the patient's medical record. The prescription form for the intraocular lens satisfies the written report requirement for 76519. For those anatomic regions that have "complete" and "limited" ultrasound codes, note the elements that comprise a "complete" exam. The report should contain a description of these elements or the reason that an element could not be visualized (eg, obscured by bowel gas, surgically absent).

If less than the required elements for a "complete" exam are reported (eg, limited number of organs or limited portion of region evaluated), the "limited" code for that anatomic region should be used once per patient exam session. A "limited" exam of an anatomic region should not be reported for the same exam session as a "complete" exam of that same region.

Evaluation of vascular structures using both color and spectral Doppler is separately reportable. To report, see **Noninvasive Vascular Diagnostic Studies** (93880-93990). However, color Doppler alone, when performed for anatomic structure identification in conjunction with a real-time ultrasound examination, is not reported separately.

Ultrasound guidance procedures also require permanently recorded images of the site to be localized, as well as a documented description of the localization process, either separately or within the report of the procedure for which the guidance is utilized.

Use of ultrasound, without thorough evaluation of organ(s) or anatomic region, image documentation, and final, written report, is not separately reportable.

### Definitions

*A-mode* implies a one-dimensional ultrasonic measurement procedure.

*M-mode* implies a one-dimensional ultrasonic measurement procedure with movement of the trace to record amplitude and velocity of moving echo-producing structures.

*B-scan* implies a two-dimensional ultrasonic scanning procedure with a two-dimensional display.

Radiology

*Real-time scan* implies a two-dimensional ultrasonic scanning procedure with display of both two-dimensional structure and motion with time.

(To report diagnostic vascular ultrasound studies, see 93880-93990)

(For focused ultrasound ablation treatment of uterine leiomyomata, see Category III codes 0071T, 0072T)

## Head and Neck

**76506**   Echoencephalography, real time with image documentation (gray scale) (for determination of ventricular size, delineation of cerebral contents, and detection of fluid masses or other intracranial abnormalities), including A-mode encephalography as secondary component where indicated

**76510**   Ophthalmic ultrasound, diagnostic; B-scan and quantitative A-scan performed during the same patient encounter

**76511**       quantitative A-scan only

**76512**       B-scan (with or without superimposed non-quantitative A-scan)

**76513**       anterior segment ultrasound, immersion (water bath) B-scan or high resolution biomicroscopy

(For scanning computerized ophthalmic diagnostic imaging of the anterior and posterior segments using technology other than ultrasound, see 92132, 92133, 92134)

**76514**       corneal pachymetry, unilateral or bilateral (determination of corneal thickness)

**76516**   Ophthalmic biometry by ultrasound echography, A-scan;

**76519**       with intraocular lens power calculation

(For partial coherence interferometry, use 92136)

**76529**   Ophthalmic ultrasonic foreign body localization

**76536**   Ultrasound, soft tissues of head and neck (eg, thyroid, parathyroid, parotid); real time with image documentation

## Chest

**76604**   Ultrasound, chest (includes mediastinum), real time with image documentation

**76645**   Ultrasound, breast(s) (unilateral or bilateral), real time with image documentation

(Do not report 76645 in conjunction with 0301T)

## Abdomen and Retroperitoneum

A complete ultrasound examination of the abdomen (76700) consists of real time scans of the liver, gall bladder, common bile duct, pancreas, spleen, kidneys, and the upper abdominal aorta and inferior vena cava including any demonstrated abdominal abnormality.

A complete ultrasound examination of the retroperitoneum (76770) consists of real time scans of the kidneys, abdominal aorta, common iliac artery origins, and inferior vena cava, including any demonstrated retroperitoneal abnormality. Alternatively, if clinical history suggests urinary tract pathology, complete evaluation of the kidneys and urinary bladder also comprises a complete retroperitoneal ultrasound.

Use of ultrasound, without thorough evaluation of organ(s) or anatomic region, image documentation and final, written report, is not separately reportable.

**76700**   Ultrasound, abdominal, real time with image documentation; complete

**76705**       limited (eg, single organ, quadrant, follow-up)

**76770**   Ultrasound, retroperitoneal (eg, renal, aorta, nodes), real time with image documentation; complete

**76775**       limited

**76776**   Ultrasound, transplanted kidney, real time and duplex Doppler with image documentation

(For ultrasound of transplanted kidney without duplex Doppler, use 76775)

(For ultrasound and duplex Doppler of a transplanted kidney, do not report 76776 in conjunction with 93975, 93976)

## Spinal Canal

**76800**   Ultrasound, spinal canal and contents

## Pelvis

### Obstetrical

Codes 76801 and 76802 include determination of the number of gestational sacs and fetuses, gestational sac/fetal measurements appropriate for gestation (younger than 14 weeks 0 days), survey of visible fetal and placental anatomic structure, qualitative assessment of amniotic fluid volume/gestational sac shape and examination of the maternal uterus and adnexa.

Codes 76805 and 76810 include determination of number of fetuses and amniotic/chorionic sacs, measurements appropriate for gestational age (older than or equal to 14 weeks 0 days), survey of intracranial/spinal/abdominal anatomy, 4 chambered heart, umbilical cord insertion site, placenta location and amniotic fluid assessment and, when visible, examination of maternal adnexa.

Codes 76811 and 76812 include all elements of codes 76805 and 76810 plus detailed anatomic evaluation of the fetal brain/ventricles, face, heart/outflow tracts and chest anatomy, abdominal organ specific anatomy, number/length/architecture of limbs and detailed evaluation of the umbilical cord and placenta and other fetal anatomy as clinically indicated.

**Radiology**

Report should document the results of the evaluation of each element described above or the reason for non-visualization.

Code 76815 represents a focused "quick look" exam limited to the assessment of one or more of the elements listed in code 76815.

Code 76816 describes an examination designed to reassess fetal size and interval growth or reevaluate one or more anatomic abnormalities of a fetus previously demonstrated on ultrasound, and should be coded once for each fetus requiring reevaluation using modifier 59 for each fetus after the first.

Code 76817 describes a transvaginal obstetric ultrasound performed separately or in addition to one of the transabdominal examinations described above. For transvaginal examinations performed for non-obstetrical purposes, use code 76830.

**76801** Ultrasound, pregnant uterus, real time with image documentation, fetal and maternal evaluation, first trimester (< 14 weeks 0 days), transabdominal approach; single or first gestation

(To report first trimester fetal nuchal translucency measurement, use 76813)

**+ 76802** each additional gestation (List separately in addition to code for primary procedure)

(Use 76802 in conjunction with 76801)

(To report first trimester fetal nuchal translucency measurement, use 76814)

**76805** Ultrasound, pregnant uterus, real time with image documentation, fetal and maternal evaluation, after first trimester (> or = 14 weeks 0 days), transabdominal approach; single or first gestation

**+ 76810** each additional gestation (List separately in addition to code for primary procedure)

(Use 76810 in conjunction with 76805)

**76811** Ultrasound, pregnant uterus, real time with image documentation, fetal and maternal evaluation plus detailed fetal anatomic examination, transabdominal approach; single or first gestation

**+ 76812** each additional gestation (List separately in addition to code for primary procedure)

(Use 76812 in conjunction with 76811)

**76813** Ultrasound, pregnant uterus, real time with image documentation, first trimester fetal nuchal translucency measurement, transabdominal or transvaginal approach; single or first gestation

**+ 76814** each additional gestation (List separately in addition to code for primary procedure)

(Use 76814 in conjunction with 76813)

**76815** Ultrasound, pregnant uterus, real time with image documentation, limited (eg, fetal heart beat, placental location, fetal position and/or qualitative amniotic fluid volume), 1 or more fetuses

(Use 76815 only once per exam and not per element)

(To report first trimester fetal nuchal translucency measurement, see 76813, 76814)

**76816** Ultrasound, pregnant uterus, real time with image documentation, follow-up (eg, re-evaluation of fetal size by measuring standard growth parameters and amniotic fluid volume, re-evaluation of organ system(s) suspected or confirmed to be abnormal on a previous scan), transabdominal approach, per fetus

(Report 76816 with modifier 59 for each additional fetus examined in a multiple pregnancy)

**76817** Ultrasound, pregnant uterus, real time with image documentation, transvaginal

(For non-obstetrical transvaginal ultrasound, use 76830)

(If transvaginal examination is done in addition to transabdominal obstetrical ultrasound exam, use 76817 in addition to appropriate transabdominal exam code)

**76818** Fetal biophysical profile; with non-stress testing

**76819** without non-stress testing

(Fetal biophysical profile assessments for the second and any additional fetuses, should be reported separately by code 76818 or 76819 with the modifier 59 appended)

(For amniotic fluid index without non-stress test, use 76815)

**76820** Doppler velocimetry, fetal; umbilical artery

**76821** middle cerebral artery

**76825** Echocardiography, fetal, cardiovascular system, real time with image documentation (2D), with or without M-mode recording;

**76826** follow-up or repeat study

**76827** Doppler echocardiography, fetal, pulsed wave and/or continuous wave with spectral display; complete

**76828** follow-up or repeat study

(To report the use of color mapping, use 93325)

# Nonobstetrical

Code 76856 includes the complete evaluation of the female pelvic anatomy. Elements of this examination include a description and measurements of the uterus and adnexal structures, measurement of the endometrium, measurement of the bladder (when applicable), and a description of any pelvic pathology (eg, ovarian cysts, uterine leiomyomata, free pelvic fluid).

Code 76856 is also applicable to a complete evaluation of the male pelvis. Elements of the examination include evaluation and measurement (when applicable) of the

Radiology

urinary bladder, evaluation of the prostate and seminal vesicles to the extent that they are visualized transabdominally, and any pelvic pathology (eg, bladder tumor, enlarged prostate, free pelvic fluid, pelvic abscess).

Code 76857 represents a focused examination limited to the assessment of one or more elements listed in code 76856 and/or the reevaluation of one or more pelvic abnormalities previously demonstrated on ultrasound. Code 76857, rather than 76770, should be utilized if the urinary bladder alone (ie, not including the kidneys) is imaged, whereas code 51798 should be utilized if a bladder volume or post-void residual measurement is obtained without imaging the bladder.

Use of ultrasound, without thorough evaluation of organ(s) or anatomic region, image documentation, and final, written report, is not separately reportable.

**76830**   Ultrasound, transvaginal

(For obstetrical transvaginal ultrasound, use 76817)

(If transvaginal examination is done in addition to transabdominal non-obstetrical ultrasound exam, use 76830 in addition to appropriate transabdominal exam code)

**76831**   Saline infusion sonohysterography (SIS), including color flow Doppler, when performed

(For introduction of saline for saline infusion sonohysterography, use 58340)

**76856**   Ultrasound, pelvic (nonobstetric), real time with image documentation; complete

**76857**        limited or follow-up (eg, for follicles)

## Genitalia

**76870**   Ultrasound, scrotum and contents

**76872**   Ultrasound, transrectal;

(Do not report 76872 in conjunction with 0249T)

**76873**        prostate volume study for brachytherapy treatment planning (separate procedure)

## Extremities

A complete ultrasound examination of an extremity (76881) consists of real time scans of a specific joint that includes examination of the muscles, tendons, joint, other soft tissue structures, and any identifiable abnormality.

Code 76882 refers to an examination of an extremity that would be performed primarily for evaluation of muscles, tendons, joints, and/or soft tissues. This is a limited examination of the extremity where a specific anatomic structure such as a tendon or muscle is assessed. In addition, the code would be used to evaluate a soft-tissue mass that may be present in an extremity where knowledge of its cystic or solid characteristics is needed.

For spectral and color Doppler evaluation of the extremities, use 93925, 93926, 93930, 93931, 93970, or 93971 as appropriate.

(76880 has been deleted. To report ultrasound examination of an extremity, see 76881, 76882)

**76881**   Ultrasound, extremity, nonvascular, real-time with image documentation; complete

**76882**        limited, anatomic specific

**76885**   Ultrasound, infant hips, real time with imaging documentation; dynamic (requiring physician or other qualified health care professional manipulation)

**76886**        limited, static (not requiring physician or other qualified health care professional manipulation)

## Ultrasonic Guidance Procedures

**76930**   Ultrasonic guidance for pericardiocentesis, imaging supervision and interpretation

**76932**   Ultrasonic guidance for endomyocardial biopsy, imaging supervision and interpretation

**76936**   Ultrasound guided compression repair of arterial pseudoaneurysm or arteriovenous fistulae (includes diagnostic ultrasound evaluation, compression of lesion and imaging)

**+ 76937**   Ultrasound guidance for vascular access requiring ultrasound evaluation of potential access sites, documentation of selected vessel patency, concurrent realtime ultrasound visualization of vascular needle entry, with permanent recording and reporting (List separately in addition to code for primary procedure)

(Do not report 76937 in conjunction with 37191, 37192, 37193, 37760, 37761, 76942)

(If extremity venous non-invasive vascular diagnostic study is performed separate from venous access guidance, use 93965, 93970 or 93971)

**76940**   Ultrasound guidance for, and monitoring of, parenchymal tissue ablation

(Do not report 76940 in conjunction with 50250, 50542, 76942, 76998)

(For ablation, see 32998, 47370-47382, 50592, 50593)

**76941**   Ultrasonic guidance for intrauterine fetal transfusion or cordocentesis, imaging supervision and interpretation

(For procedure, see 36460, 59012)

**76942**   Ultrasonic guidance for needle placement (eg, biopsy, aspiration, injection, localization device), imaging supervision and interpretation

▶(Do not report 76942 in conjunction with 10030, 19083, 19285, 27096, 32554, 32555, 32556, 32557, 37760, 37761, 43232, 43237, 43242, 45341, 45342, 64479-64484, 64490-64495, 76975, 0213T-0218T, 0228T-0231T, 0232T, 0249T, 0301T)◀

(For injection(s) of platelet rich plasma, use 0232T)

**Radiology**

**76945**   Ultrasonic guidance for chorionic villus sampling, imaging supervision and interpretation

(For procedure, use 59015)

**76946**   Ultrasonic guidance for amniocentesis, imaging supervision and interpretation

**76948**   Ultrasonic guidance for aspiration of ova, imaging supervision and interpretation

**76950**   Ultrasonic guidance for placement of radiation therapy fields

(For placement of interstitial device[s] for radiation therapy guidance, see 31627, 32553, 49411, 55876)

**76965**   Ultrasonic guidance for interstitial radioelement application

## Other Procedures

**76970**   Ultrasound study follow-up (specify)

**76975**   Gastrointestinal endoscopic ultrasound, supervision and interpretation

(Do not report 76975 in conjunction with 43231, 43232, 43237, 43238, 43242, 43259, 45341, 45342, or 76942)

**76977**   Ultrasound bone density measurement and interpretation, peripheral site(s), any method

**76998**   Ultrasonic guidance, intraoperative

►(Do not report 76998 in conjunction with 36475,36479, 37760, 37761, 47370-47382, 0249T, 0301T)◄

(For ultrasound guidance for open and laparoscopic radiofrequency tissue ablation, use 76940)

**76999**   Unlisted ultrasound procedure (eg, diagnostic, interventional)

# Radiologic Guidance

## Fluoroscopic Guidance

(Do not report guidance codes 77001, 77002, 77003 for services in which fluoroscopic guidance is included in the descriptor)

**+ 77001**   Fluoroscopic guidance for central venous access device placement, replacement (catheter only or complete), or removal (includes fluoroscopic guidance for vascular access and catheter manipulation, any necessary contrast injections through access site or catheter with related venography radiologic supervision and interpretation, and radiographic documentation of final catheter position) (List separately in addition to code for primary procedure)

(Do not use 77001 in conjunction with 77002)

(If formal extremity venography is performed from separate venous access and separately interpreted, use 36005 and 75820, 75822, 75825, or 75827)

**77002**   Fluoroscopic guidance for needle placement (eg, biopsy, aspiration, injection, localization device)

(See appropriate surgical code for procedure and anatomic location)

►(77002 is included in all arthrography radiological supervision and interpretation codes. See **Administration of Contrast Material[s]** introductory guidelines for reporting of arthrography procedures)◄

►(Do not report 77002 in conjunction with 10030, 19081-19086, 19281-19288, 32554, 32555, 32556, 32557, 70332, 73040, 73085, 73115, 73525, 73580, 73615, 0232T)◄

(For injection(s) of platelet rich plasma, use 0232T)

(77002 is included in the organ/anatomic specific radiological supervision and interpretation procedures 49440, 74320, 74355, 74445, 74470, 74475, 75809, 75810, 75885, 75887, 75980, 75982, 75989)

**77003**   Fluoroscopic guidance and localization of needle or catheter tip for spine or paraspinous diagnostic or therapeutic injection procedures (epidural or subarachnoid)

(Injection of contrast during fluoroscopic guidance and localization [77003] is included in 22526, 22527, 27096, 62263, 62264, 62267, 62270-62282, 62310-62319)

(Fluoroscopic guidance for subarachnoid puncture for diagnostic radiographic myelography is included in supervision and interpretation codes 72240-72270)

(For epidural or subarachnoid needle or catheter placement and injection, see 62270-62282, 62310-62319)

(For sacroiliac joint arthrography, see 27096)

(For paravertebral facet joint injection, see 64490-64495. For paravertebral facet joint nerve destruction by neurolysis, see 64633-64636. For transforaminal epidural needle placement and injection, see 64479-64484)

►(Do not report 77002, 77003 in conjunction with 10030, 22586, 27096, 64479–64484, 64490-64495, 64633-64636,0195T, 0196T, 0309T)◄

(For percutaneous or endoscopic lysis of epidural adhesions, 62263, 62264 include fluoroscopic guidance and localization)

## Computed Tomography Guidance

**77011**   Computed tomography guidance for stereotactic localization

**77012**   Computed tomography guidance for needle placement (eg, biopsy, aspiration, injection, localization device), radiological supervision and interpretation

(Do not report 77011, 77012 in conjunction with 22586, 0195T, 0196T, 0309T)

►(Do not report 77012 in conjunction with 10030, 27096, 32554, 32555, 32556, 32557, 64479-64484, 64490-64495, 64633-64636, 0232T)◄

(For injection(s) of platelet rich plasma, use 0232T)

Radiology

**77013**   Computed tomography guidance for, and monitoring of, parenchymal tissue ablation

(Do not report 77013 in conjunction with 20982)

(For percutaneous ablation, see 32998, 47382, 50592, 50593)

**77014**   Computed tomography guidance for placement of radiation therapy fields

(For placement of interstitial device[s] for radiation therapy guidance, see 31627, 32553, 49411, 55876)

# Magnetic Resonance Guidance

**77021**   Magnetic resonance guidance for needle placement (eg, for biopsy, needle aspiration, injection, or placement of localization device) radiological supervision and interpretation

(For procedure, see appropriate organ or site)

▶(Do not report 77021 in conjunction with 10030, 19085, 19287, 32554, 32555, 32556, 32557, 0232T)◀

(For injection(s) of platelet rich plasma, use 0232T)

**77022**   Magnetic resonance guidance for, and monitoring of, parenchymal tissue ablation

(For percutaneous ablation, see 32998, 47382, 50592, 50593)

(For focused ultrasound ablation treatment of uterine leiomyomata, see Category III codes 0071T, 0072T)

▶(Do not report 77022 in conjunction with 0071T, 0072T)◀

▶(77031 has been deleted)◀

▶(To report stereotactic localization guidance for breast biopsy or for placement of breast localization device[s], see 19081, 19283)◀

▶(77032 has been deleted)◀

▶(To report mammographic guidance for placement of breast localization device[s], use 19281)◀

# Breast, Mammography

**+ 77051**   Computer-aided detection (computer algorithm analysis of digital image data for lesion detection) with further review for interpretation, with or without digitization of film radiographic images; diagnostic mammography (List separately in addition to code for primary procedure)

(Use 77051 in conjunction with 77055, 77056)

**+ 77052**     screening mammography (List separately in addition to code for primary procedure)

(Use 77052 in conjunction with 77057)

**77053**   Mammary ductogram or galactogram, single duct, radiological supervision and interpretation

(For mammary ductogram or galactogram injection, use 19030)

**77054**   Mammary ductogram or galactogram, multiple ducts, radiological supervision and interpretation

**77055**   Mammography; unilateral

**77056**     bilateral

(Use 77055, 77056 in conjunction with 77051 for computer-aided detection applied to a diagnostic mammogram)

**77057**   Screening mammography, bilateral (2-view film study of each breast)

(Use 77057 in conjunction with 77052 for computer-aided detection applied to a screening mammogram)

(For electrical impedance breast scan, use 76499)

**77058**   Magnetic resonance imaging, breast, without and/or with contrast material(s); unilateral

**77059**     bilateral

# Bone/Joint Studies

**77071**   Manual application of stress performed by physician or other qualified health care professional for joint radiography, including contralateral joint if indicated

(For radiographic interpretation of stressed images, see appropriate anatomic site and number of views)

**77072**   Bone age studies

**77073**   Bone length studies (orthoroentgenogram, scanogram)

**77074**   Radiologic examination, osseous survey; limited (eg, for metastases)

**77075**     complete (axial and appendicular skeleton)

**77076**   Radiologic examination, osseous survey, infant

**77077**   Joint survey, single view, 2 or more joints (specify)

**77078**   Computed tomography, bone mineral density study, 1 or more sites; axial skeleton (eg, hips, pelvis, spine)

(77079 has been deleted)

**77080**   Dual-energy X-ray absorptiometry (DXA), bone density study, 1 or more sites; axial skeleton (eg, hips, pelvis, spine)

**77081**     appendicular skeleton (peripheral) (eg, radius, wrist, heel)

**77082**     vertebral fracture assessment

(For dual energy x-ray absorptiometry [DXA] body composition study, use 76499)

(77083 has been deleted)

**77084**   Magnetic resonance (eg, proton) imaging, bone marrow blood supply

**Radiology**

# Radiation Oncology

Listings for Radiation Oncology provide for teletherapy and brachytherapy to include initial consultation, clinical treatment planning, simulation, medical radiation physics, dosimetry, treatment devices, special services, and clinical treatment management procedures. They include normal follow-up care during course of treatment and for three months following its completion.

When a service or procedure is provided that is not listed in this edition of the CPT codebook it should be identified by a Special Report (see page 266) and one of the following unlisted procedure codes:

77299 Unlisted procedure, therapeutic radiology clinical treatment planning

77399 Unlisted procedure, medical radiation physics, dosimetry and treatment devices, and special services

77499 Unlisted procedure, therapeutic radiology treatment management

77799 Unlisted procedure, clinical brachytherapy

**For treatment by injectable or ingestible isotopes, see subsection Nuclear Medicine.**

## Consultation: Clinical Management

Preliminary consultation, evaluation of patient prior to decision to treat, or full medical care (in addition to treatment management) when provided by the therapeutic radiologist may be identified by the appropriate procedure codes from **Evaluation and Management, Medicine,** or **Surgery** sections.

## Clinical Treatment Planning (External and Internal Sources)

The clinical treatment planning process is a complex service including interpretation of special testing, tumor localization, treatment volume determination, treatment time/dosage determination, choice of treatment modality, determination of number and size of treatment ports, selection of appropriate treatment devices, and other procedures.

**Definitions**

*Simple* planning requires a single treatment area of interest encompassed in a single port or simple parallel opposed ports with simple or no blocking.

*Intermediate* planning requires 3 or more converging ports, 2 separate treatment areas, multiple blocks, or special time dose constraints.

*Complex* planning requires highly complex blocking, custom shielding blocks, tangential ports, special wedges or compensators, three or more separate treatment areas, rotational or special beam considerations, combination of therapeutic modalities.

| | |
|---|---|
| 77261 | Therapeutic radiology treatment planning; simple |
| 77262 | intermediate |
| 77263 | complex |

▶Simulation is the process of defining relevant normal and abnormal target anatomy, and acquiring the images and data necessary to develop the optimal radiation treatment process for the patient. A simulation is defined as complex if any of these criteria are met: particle, rotation or arc therapy, complex or custom blocking, brachytherapy simulation, hyperthermia probe verification, or any use of contrast material. If a simulation does not meet any of these criteria, the complexity is defined by the number of treatment areas: one treatment area is simple, two treatment areas are intermediate, and three or more treatment areas are complex.

A treatment area is a contiguous anatomic location that will be treated with radiation therapy. Generally, this includes the primary tumor organ or the resection bed and the draining lymph node chains, if indicated. An example is a breast cancer patient for whom a single treatment area could be the breast alone or the breast, adjacent supraclavicular fossa, and internal mammary nodes. In some cases, a patient might receive radiation therapy to more than one discontinuous anatomic location. An example would be a patient with multiple bone metastases in separate sites (eg, femur and cervical spine); in this case, each distinct and separate anatomic site to be irradiated is a separate treatment area.◀

**Definitions**

▶*Simple:* simulation of a single treatment area.

*Intermediate:* two separate treatment areas.

*Complex:* three or more treatment areas, or any number of treatment areas if any of the following are involved: particle, rotation or arc therapy, complex blocking, custom shielding blocks, brachytherapy simulation, hyperthermia probe verification, any use of contrast materials.◀

| | |
|---|---|
| 77280 | Therapeutic radiology simulation-aided field setting; simple |
| 77285 | intermediate |
| 77290 | complex |
| +● 77293 | Respiratory motion management simulation (List separately in addition to code for primary procedure) |
| | ▶(Use 77293 in conjunction with 77295, 77301)◀ |
| 77295 | Code is out of numerical sequence. See 77295-77370 |
| 77299 | Unlisted procedure, therapeutic radiology clinical treatment planning |

Radiology

# Medical Radiation Physics, Dosimetry, Treatment Devices, and Special Services

#▲ **77295**  3-dimensional radiotherapy plan, including dose-volume histograms

**77300**  Basic radiation dosimetry calculation, central axis depth dose calculation, TDF, NSD, gap calculation, off axis factor, tissue inhomogeneity factors, calculation of non-ionizing radiation surface and depth dose, as required during course of treatment, only when prescribed by the treating physician

**77301**  Intensity modulated radiotherapy plan, including dose-volume histograms for target and critical structure partial tolerance specifications

(Dose plan is optimized using inverse or forward planning technique for modulated beam delivery [eg, binary, dynamic MLC] to create highly conformal dose distribution. Computer plan distribution must be verified for positional accuracy based on dosimetric verification of the intensity map with verification of treatment set-up and interpretation of verification methodology)

**77305**  Teletherapy, isodose plan (whether hand or computer calculated); simple (1 or 2 parallel opposed unmodified ports directed to a single area of interest)

**77310**  intermediate (3 or more treatment ports directed to a single area of interest)

**77315**  complex (mantle or inverted Y, tangential ports, the use of wedges, compensators, complex blocking, rotational beam, or special beam considerations)

(Only 1 teletherapy isodose plan may be reported for a given course of therapy to a specific treatment area)

**77321**  Special teletherapy port plan, particles, hemibody, total body

**77326**  Brachytherapy isodose plan; simple (calculation made from single plane, 1 to 4 sources/ribbon application, remote afterloading brachytherapy, 1 to 8 sources)

(For definition of source/ribbon, see page 289)

**77327**  intermediate (multiplane dosage calculations, application involving 5 to 10 sources/ribbons, remote afterloading brachytherapy, 9 to 12 sources)

**77328**  complex (multiplane isodose plan, volume implant calculations, over 10 sources/ribbons used, special spatial reconstruction, remote afterloading brachytherapy, over 12 sources)

**77331**  Special dosimetry (eg, TLD, microdosimetry) (specify), only when prescribed by the treating physician

**77332**  Treatment devices, design and construction; simple (simple block, simple bolus)

**77333**  intermediate (multiple blocks, stents, bite blocks, special bolus)

**77334**  complex (irregular blocks, special shields, compensators, wedges, molds or casts)

**77336**  Continuing medical physics consultation, including assessment of treatment parameters, quality assurance of dose delivery, and review of patient treatment documentation in support of the radiation oncologist, reported per week of therapy

**77338**  Multi-leaf collimator (MLC) device(s) for intensity modulated radiation therapy (IMRT), design and construction per IMRT plan

(Do not report 77338 more than once per IMRT plan)

(For immobilization in IMRT treatment, see 77332-77334)

(Do not report 77338 in conjunction with 0073T, compensator based IMRT)

**77370**  Special medical radiation physics consultation

## Stereotactic Radiation Treatment Delivery

⊙ **77371**  Radiation treatment delivery, stereotactic radiosurgery (SRS), complete course of treatment of cranial lesion(s) consisting of 1 session; multi-source Cobalt 60 based

**77372**  linear accelerator based

(For radiation treatment management, use 77432)

**77373**  Stereotactic body radiation therapy, treatment delivery, per fraction to 1 or more lesions, including image guidance, entire course not to exceed 5 fractions

(Do not report 77373 in conjunction with 77401-77416, 77418)

(For single fraction cranial lesion[s], see 77371, 77372)

## Other Procedures

**77399**  Unlisted procedure, medical radiation physics, dosimetry and treatment devices, and special services

## Radiation Treatment Delivery

(Radiation treatment delivery [77401-77416] recognizes the technical component and the various energy levels)

(For intra-fraction localization and tracking of target, use 0197T)

**77401**  Radiation treatment delivery, superficial and/or ortho voltage

**77402**  Radiation treatment delivery, single treatment area, single port or parallel opposed ports, simple blocks or no blocks; up to 5 MeV

**77403**  6-10 MeV

**77404**  11-19 MeV

**77406**  20 MeV or greater

**77407**  Radiation treatment delivery, 2 separate treatment areas, 3 or more ports on a single treatment area, use of multiple blocks; up to 5 MeV

**77408**  6-10 MeV

Radiology

**77409**   11-19 MeV

**77411**   20 MeV or greater

**77412**   Radiation treatment delivery, 3 or more separate treatment areas, custom blocking, tangential ports, wedges, rotational beam, compensators, electron beam; up to 5 MeV

**77413**   6-10 MeV

**77414**   11-19 MeV

**77416**   20 MeV or greater

**77417**   Therapeutic radiology port film(s)

**77418**   Intensity modulated treatment delivery, single or multiple fields/arcs, via narrow spatially and temporally modulated beams, binary, dynamic MLC, per treatment session

(For intensity modulated treatment planning, use 77301)

(For compensator-based beam modulation treatment delivery, use Category III code 0073T)

**77421**   Stereoscopic X-ray guidance for localization of target volume for the delivery of radiation therapy

(Do not report 77421 in conjunction with 77432, 77435)

(Do not report 77421 more than once per treatment delivery session)

(For placement of interstitial device[s] for radiation therapy guidance, see 31627, 32553, 49411, 55876)

# **77424**   Intraoperative radiation treatment delivery, x-ray, single treatment session

# **77425**   Intraoperative radiation treatment delivery, electrons, single treatment session

## Neutron Beam Treatment Delivery

**77422**   High energy neutron radiation treatment delivery; single treatment area using a single port or parallel-opposed ports with no blocks or simple blocking

**77423**   1 or more isocenter(s) with coplanar or non-coplanar geometry with blocking and/or wedge, and/or compensator(s)

**77424**   Code is out of numerical sequence. See 77401-77425

**77425**   Code is out of numerical sequence. See 77401-77425

## Radiation Treatment Management

Radiation treatment management is reported in units of five fractions or treatment sessions, regardless of the actual time period in which the services are furnished. The services need not be furnished on consecutive days. Multiple fractions representing two or more treatment sessions furnished on the same day may be counted separately as long as there has been a distinct break in therapy sessions, and the fractions are of the character usually furnished on different days. Code 77427 is also reported if there are three or four fractions beyond a

multiple of five at the end of a course of treatment; one or two fractions beyond a multiple of five at the end of a course of treatment are not reported separately.

Radiation treatment management requires **and includes** a minimum of one examination of the patient by the physician for medical evaluation and management (eg, assessment of the patient's response to treatment, coordination of care and treatment, review of imaging and/or lab test results with documentation) for each reporting of the radiation treatment management service. Code 77469 represents only the intraoperative session management and does not include medical evaluation and management outside of that session. The professional services furnished during treatment management typically include:

■ Review of port films;

■ Review of dosimetry, dose delivery, and treatment parameters;

■ Review of patient treatment set-up.

**77427**   Radiation treatment management, 5 treatments

**77431**   Radiation therapy management with complete course of therapy consisting of 1 or 2 fractions only

(77431 is not to be used to fill in the last week of a long course of therapy)

**77432**   Stereotactic radiation treatment management of cranial lesion(s) (complete course of treatment consisting of 1 session)

(The same physician should not report both stereotactic radiosurgery services [61796-61800] and radiation treatment management [77432 or 77435] for cranial lesions)

(For stereotactic body radiation therapy treatment, use 77435)

**77435**   Stereotactic body radiation therapy, treatment management, per treatment course, to 1 or more lesions, including image guidance, entire course not to exceed 5 fractions

(Do not report 77435 in conjunction with 77427-77432)

(The same physician should not report both stereotactic radiosurgery services [32701, 63620, 63621] and radiation treatment management [77435])

**77469**   Intraoperative radiation treatment management

**77470**   Special treatment procedure (eg, total body irradiation, hemibody radiation, per oral or endocavitary irradiation)

(77470 assumes that the procedure is performed 1 or more times during the course of therapy, in addition to daily or weekly patient management)

(For intraoperative radiation treatment delivery and management, see 77424, 77425, 77469)

**77499**   Unlisted procedure, therapeutic radiology treatment management

# Proton Beam Treatment Delivery

### Definitions

*Simple* proton treatment delivery to a single treatment area utilizing a single non-tangential/oblique port, custom block with compensation (77522) and without compensation (77520).

*Intermediate* proton treatment delivery to one or more treatment areas utilizing two or more ports or one or more tangential/oblique ports, with custom blocks and compensators.

*Complex* proton treatment delivery to one or more treatment areas utilizing two or more ports per treatment area with matching or patching fields and/or multiple isocenters, with custom blocks and compensators.

**77520**   Proton treatment delivery; simple, without compensation

**77522**       simple, with compensation

**77523**       intermediate

**77525**       complex

# Hyperthermia

Hyperthermia treatments as listed in this section include external (superficial and deep), interstitial, and intracavitary.

Radiation therapy when given concurrently is listed separately.

Hyperthermia is used only as an adjunct to radiation therapy or chemotherapy. It may be induced by a variety of sources (eg, microwave, ultrasound, low energy radio-frequency conduction, or by probes).

The listed treatments include management during the course of therapy and follow-up care for three months after completion.

Preliminary consultation is not included (see **Evaluation and Management** 99241-99255).

Physics planning and interstitial insertion of temperature sensors, and use of external or interstitial heat generating sources are included.

The following descriptors are included in the treatment schedule:

⊙ **77600**   Hyperthermia, externally generated; superficial (ie, heating to a depth of 4 cm or less)

⊙ **77605**       deep (ie, heating to depths greater than 4 cm)

(For focused microwave thermotherapy of the breast, use 0301T)

⊙ **77610**   Hyperthermia generated by interstitial probe(s); 5 or fewer interstitial applicators

⊙ **77615**       more than 5 interstitial applicators

# Clinical Intracavitary Hyperthermia

**77620**   Hyperthermia generated by intracavitary probe(s)

# Clinical Brachytherapy

Clinical brachytherapy requires the use of either natural or man-made radioelements applied into or around a treatment field of interest. The supervision of radioelements and dose interpretation are performed solely by the therapeutic radiologist.

Services 77750-77799 include admission to the hospital and daily visits.

For insertion of ovoids and tandems, use 57155.

For insertion of Heyman capsules, use 58346.

### Definitions

(Sources refer to intracavitary placement or permanent interstitial placement; ribbons refer to temporary interstitial placement)

*A simple* application has one to four sources/ribbons.

*An intermediate* application has five to 10 sources/ribbons.

*A complex* application has greater than 10 sources/ribbons.

(For high dose rate electronic brachytherapy, per fraction, use Category III code 0182T)

**77750**   Infusion or instillation of radioelement solution (includes 3-month follow-up care)

(For administration of radiolabeled monoclonal antibodies, use 79403)

(For non-antibody radiopharmaceutical therapy by intravenous administration only, not including 3-month follow-up care, use 79101)

**77761**   Intracavitary radiation source application; simple

**77762**       intermediate

**77763**       complex

(Do not report 77761-77763 in conjunction with Category III code 0182T)

**77776**   Interstitial radiation source application; simple

**77777**       intermediate

**77778**       complex

(Do not report 77776-77778 in conjunction with Category III code 0182T)

(77781 has been deleted. To report, see 77785, 77786)

(77782-77784 have been deleted. To report, see 77785-77787)

**77785**   Remote afterloading high dose rate radionuclide brachytherapy; 1 channel

**77786**       2-12 channels

**Radiology**

---

**77787** over 12 channels

(Do not report 77785-77787 in conjunction with Category III code 0182T)

**77789** Surface application of radiation source

(Do not report 77789 in conjunction with Category III code 0182T)

**77790** Supervision, handling, loading of radiation source

**77799** Unlisted procedure, clinical brachytherapy

# Nuclear Medicine

Listed procedures may be performed independently or in the course of overall medical care. If the individual providing these services is also responsible for diagnostic workup and/or follow-up care of patient, see appropriate sections also.

Radioimmunoassay tests are found in the **Clinical Pathology** section (codes 82000-84999). These codes can be appropriately used by any specialist performing such tests in a laboratory licensed and/or certified for radioimmunoassays. The reporting of these tests is not confined to clinical pathology laboratories alone.

The services listed do not include the radiopharmaceutical or drug. To separately report supply of diagnostic and therapeutic radiopharmaceuticals and drugs, use the appropriate supply code(s), in addition to the procedure code.

## Diagnostic

### Endocrine System

(78000-78011 have been deleted. To report, see 78012-78014)

**78012** Thyroid uptake, single or multiple quantitative measurement(s) (including stimulation, suppression, or discharge, when performed)

**78013** Thyroid imaging (including vascular flow, when performed);

**78014** with single or multiple uptake(s) quantitative measurement(s) (including stimulation, suppression, or discharge, when performed)

**78015** Thyroid carcinoma metastases imaging; limited area (eg, neck and chest only)

**78016** with additional studies (eg, urinary recovery)

**78018** whole body

**+ 78020** Thyroid carcinoma metastases uptake (List separately in addition to code for primary procedure)

(Use 78020 in conjunction with 78018 only)

**78070** Parathyroid planar imaging (including subtraction, when performed);

**78071** with tomographic (SPECT)

**78072** with tomographic (SPECT), and concurrently acquired computed tomography (CT) for anatomical localization

**78075** Adrenal imaging, cortex and/or medulla

**78099** Unlisted endocrine procedure, diagnostic nuclear medicine

(For chemical analysis, see **Chemistry** section)

## Hematopoietic, Reticuloendothelial and Lymphatic System

**78102** Bone marrow imaging; limited area

**78103** multiple areas

**78104** whole body

**78110** Plasma volume, radiopharmaceutical volume-dilution technique (separate procedure); single sampling

**78111** multiple samplings

**78120** Red cell volume determination (separate procedure); single sampling

**78121** multiple samplings

**78122** Whole blood volume determination, including separate measurement of plasma volume and red cell volume (radiopharmaceutical volume-dilution technique)

**78130** Red cell survival study;

**78135** differential organ/tissue kinetics (eg, splenic and/or hepatic sequestration)

**78140** Labeled red cell sequestration, differential organ/tissue (eg, splenic and/or hepatic)

**78185** Spleen imaging only, with or without vascular flow

(If combined with liver study, use procedures 78215 and 78216)

**78190** Kinetics, study of platelet survival, with or without differential organ/tissue localization

**78191** Platelet survival study

**78195** Lymphatics and lymph nodes imaging

(For sentinel node identification without scintigraphy imaging, use 38792)

(For sentinel node excision, see 38500-38542)

**78199** Unlisted hematopoietic, reticuloendothelial and lymphatic procedure, diagnostic nuclear medicine

(For chemical analysis, see **Chemistry** section)

## Gastrointestinal System

**78201** Liver imaging; static only

**78202** with vascular flow

(For spleen imaging only, use 78185)

**78205** Liver imaging (SPECT);

Radiology

| 78206 | with vascular flow |
|---|---|
| 78215 | Liver and spleen imaging; static only |
| 78216 | with vascular flow |

(78220 has been deleted)

(78223 has been deleted. To report hepatobiliary system imaging, see 78226, 78227)

| 78226 | Hepatobiliary system imaging, including gallbladder when present; |
|---|---|
| 78227 | with pharmacologic intervention, including quantitative measurement(s) when performed |
| 78230 | Salivary gland imaging; |
| 78231 | with serial images |
| 78232 | Salivary gland function study |
| 78258 | Esophageal motility |
| 78261 | Gastric mucosa imaging |
| 78262 | Gastroesophageal reflux study |
| 78264 | Gastric emptying study |
| 78267 | Urea breath test, C-14 (isotopic); acquisition for analysis |
| 78268 | analysis |

►(For breath hydrogen or methane testing and analysis, use 91065)◄

| 78270 | Vitamin B-12 absorption study (eg, Schilling test); without intrinsic factor |
|---|---|
| 78271 | with intrinsic factor |
| 78272 | Vitamin B-12 absorption studies combined, with and without intrinsic factor |
| 78278 | Acute gastrointestinal blood loss imaging |
| 78282 | Gastrointestinal protein loss |
| 78290 | Intestine imaging (eg, ectopic gastric mucosa, Meckel's localization, volvulus) |
| 78291 | Peritoneal-venous shunt patency test (eg, for LeVeen, Denver shunt) |

(For injection procedure, use 49427)

| 78299 | Unlisted gastrointestinal procedure, diagnostic nuclear medicine |
|---|---|

## Musculoskeletal System

Bone and joint imaging can be used in the diagnosis of a variety of inflammatory processes (eg, osteomyelitis), as well as for localization of primary and/or metastatic neoplasms.

| 78300 | Bone and/or joint imaging; limited area |
|---|---|
| 78305 | multiple areas |
| 78306 | whole body |
| 78315 | 3 phase study |

| 78320 | tomographic (SPECT) |
|---|---|
| 78350 | Bone density (bone mineral content) study, 1 or more sites; single photon absorptiometry |
| 78351 | dual photon absorptiometry, 1 or more sites |
| 78399 | Unlisted musculoskeletal procedure, diagnostic nuclear medicine |

## Cardiovascular System

Myocardial perfusion and cardiac blood pool imaging studies may be performed at rest and/or during stress. When performed during exercise and/or pharmacologic stress, the appropriate stress testing code from the 93015-93018 series should be reported in addition to 78451-78454, 78472-78492.

| 78414 | Determination of central c-v hemodynamics (non-imaging) (eg, ejection fraction with probe technique) with or without pharmacologic intervention or exercise, single or multiple determinations |
|---|---|
| 78428 | Cardiac shunt detection |
| 78445 | Non-cardiac vascular flow imaging (ie, angiography, venography) |
| 78451 | Myocardial perfusion imaging, tomographic (SPECT) (including attenuation correction, qualitative or quantitative wall motion, ejection fraction by first pass or gated technique, additional quantification, when performed); single study, at rest or stress (exercise or pharmacologic) |
| 78452 | multiple studies, at rest and/or stress (exercise or pharmacologic) and/or redistribution and/or rest reinjection |
| 78453 | Myocardial perfusion imaging, planar (including qualitative or quantitative wall motion, ejection fraction by first pass or gated technique, additional quantification, when performed); single study, at rest or stress (exercise or pharmacologic) |
| 78454 | multiple studies, at rest and/or stress (exercise or pharmacologic) and/or redistribution and/or rest reinjection |
| 78456 | Acute venous thrombosis imaging, peptide |
| 78457 | Venous thrombosis imaging, venogram; unilateral |
| 78458 | bilateral |
| 78459 | Myocardial imaging, positron emission tomography (PET), metabolic evaluation |

(For myocardial perfusion study, see 78491-78492)

(78460-78465 have been deleted. To report, see 78451-78454)

| 78466 | Myocardial imaging, infarct avid, planar; qualitative or quantitative |
|---|---|
| 78468 | with ejection fraction by first pass technique |

**Radiology**

**78469**      tomographic SPECT with or without quantification

▶(For myocardial sympathetic innervation imaging, see 0331T, 0332T)◄

**78472**   Cardiac blood pool imaging, gated equilibrium; planar, single study at rest or stress (exercise and/or pharmacologic), wall motion study plus ejection fraction, with or without additional quantitative processing

(For assessment of right ventricular ejection fraction by first pass technique, use 78496)

**78473**      multiple studies, wall motion study plus ejection fraction, at rest and stress (exercise and/or pharmacologic), with or without additional quantification

(Do not report 78472, 78473 in conjunction with 78451-78454, 78481, 78483, 78494)

(78478, 78480 have been deleted. To report, see 78451-78454)

**78481**   Cardiac blood pool imaging (planar), first pass technique; single study, at rest or with stress (exercise and/or pharmacologic), wall motion study plus ejection fraction, with or without quantification

**78483**      multiple studies, at rest and with stress (exercise and/or pharmacologic), wall motion study plus ejection fraction, with or without quantification

(For cerebral blood flow study, use 78610)

(Do not report 78481-78483 in conjunction with 78451-78454)

**78491**   Myocardial imaging, positron emission tomography (PET), perfusion; single study at rest or stress

**78492**      multiple studies at rest and/or stress

**78494**   Cardiac blood pool imaging, gated equilibrium, SPECT, at rest, wall motion study plus ejection fraction, with or without quantitative processing

+ **78496**   Cardiac blood pool imaging, gated equilibrium, single study, at rest, with right ventricular ejection fraction by first pass technique (List separately in addition to code for primary procedure)

(Use 70406 in conjunction with 78472)

**78499**   Unlisted cardiovascular procedure, diagnostic nuclear medicine

## Respiratory System

**78579**   Pulmonary ventilation imaging (eg, aerosol or gas)

**78580**   Pulmonary perfusion imaging (eg, particulate)

**78582**   Pulmonary ventilation (eg, aerosol or gas) and perfusion imaging

**78597**   Quantitative differential pulmonary perfusion, including imaging when performed

**78598**   Quantitative differential pulmonary perfusion and ventilation (eg, aerosol or gas), including imaging when performed

(Report 78579, 78580, 78582-78598 only once per imaging session)

(Do not report 78580, 78582-78598 in conjunction with 78451-78454)

(78584-78596 have been deleted. To report, see 78579, 78582-78598)

**78599**   Unlisted respiratory procedure, diagnostic nuclear medicine

## Nervous System

**78600**   Brain imaging, less than 4 static views;

**78601**      with vascular flow

**78605**   Brain imaging, minimum 4 static views;

**78606**      with vascular flow

**78607**   Brain imaging, tomographic (SPECT)

**78608**   Brain imaging, positron emission tomography (PET); metabolic evaluation

**78609**      perfusion evaluation

**78610**   Brain imaging, vascular flow only

**78630**   Cerebrospinal fluid flow, imaging (not including introduction of material); cisternography

(For injection procedure, see 61000-61070, 62270-62319)

**78635**      ventriculography

(For injection procedure, see 61000-61070, 62270-62294)

**78645**      shunt evaluation

(For injection procedure, see 61000-61070, 62270-62294)

**78647**      tomographic (SPECT)

**78650**   Cerebrospinal fluid leakage detection and localization

(For injection procedure, see 61000-61070, 62270-62294)

**78660**   Radiopharmaceutical dacryocystography

**78699**   Unlisted nervous system procedure, diagnostic nuclear medicine

## Genitourinary System

**78700**   Kidney imaging morphology;

**78701**      with vascular flow

**78707**      with vascular flow and function, single study without pharmacological intervention

**78708**      with vascular flow and function, single study, with pharmacological intervention (eg, angiotensin converting enzyme inhibitor and/or diuretic)

**78709**    with vascular flow and function, multiple studies, with and without pharmacological intervention (eg, angiotensin converting enzyme inhibitor and/or diuretic)

(For introduction of radioactive substance in association with renal endoscopy, see 77776-77778)

**78710**    tomographic (SPECT)

**78725**    Kidney function study, non-imaging radioisotopic study

**+ 78730**    Urinary bladder residual study (List separately in addition to code for primary procedure)

(Use 78730 in conjunction with 78740)

(For measurement of postvoid residual urine and/or bladder capacity by ultrasound, nonimaging, use 51798)

(For ultrasound imaging of the bladder only, with measurement of postvoid residual urine when performed, use 76857)

**78740**    Ureteral reflux study (radiopharmaceutical voiding cystogram)

(Use 78740 in conjunction with 78730 for urinary bladder residual study)

(For catheterization, see 51701, 51702, 51703)

**78761**    Testicular imaging with vascular flow

**78799**    Unlisted genitourinary procedure, diagnostic nuclear medicine

(For chemical analysis, see **Chemistry** section)

## Other Procedures

(For specific organ, see appropriate heading)

(For radiophosphorus tumor identification, ocular, see 78800)

**78800**    Radiopharmaceutical localization of tumor or distribution of radiopharmaceutical agent(s); limited area

(For specific organ, see appropriate heading)

**78801**    multiple areas

**78802**    whole body, single day imaging

**78803**    tomographic (SPECT)

**78804**    whole body, requiring 2 or more days imaging

**78805**    Radiopharmaceutical localization of inflammatory process; limited area

**78806**    whole body

**78807**    tomographic (SPECT)

(For imaging bone infectious or inflammatory disease with a bone imaging radiopharmaceutical, see 78300, 78305, 78306)

**78808**    Injection procedure for radiopharmaceutical localization by non-imaging probe study, intravenous (eg, parathyroid adenoma)

(For sentinel lymph node identification, use 38792)

(For PET of brain, see 78608, 78609)

(For PET myocardial imaging, see 78459, 78491, 78492)

**78811**    Positron emission tomography (PET) imaging; limited area (eg, chest, head/neck)

**78812**    skull base to mid-thigh

**78813**    whole body

**78814**    Positron emission tomography (PET) with concurrently acquired computed tomography (CT) for attenuation correction and anatomical localization imaging; limited area (eg, chest, head/neck)

**78815**    skull base to mid-thigh

**78816**    whole body

(Report 78811-78816 only once per imaging session)

(Computed tomography [CT] performed for other than attenuation correction and anatomical localization is reported using the appropriate site specific CT code with modifier 59)

(78890, 78891 have been deleted)

**78999**    Unlisted miscellaneous procedure, diagnostic nuclear medicine

## Therapeutic

The oral and intravenous administration codes in this section are inclusive of the mode of administration. For intra-arterial, intra-cavitary, and intra-articular administration, also use the appropriate injection and/or procedure codes, as well as imaging guidance and radiological supervision and interpretation codes, when appropriate.

**79005**    Radiopharmaceutical therapy, by oral administration

(For monoclonal antibody therapy, use 79403)

**79101**    Radiopharmaceutical therapy, by intravenous administration

(Do not report 79101 in conjunction with 36400, 36410, 79403, 96360, 96374 or 96375, 96409)

(For radiolabeled monoclonal antibody by intravenous infusion, use 79403)

(For infusion or instillation of non-antibody radioelement solution that includes 3 months follow-up care, use 77750)

**79200**    Radiopharmaceutical therapy, by intracavitary administration

**Radiology**

**79300**  Radiopharmaceutical therapy, by interstitial radioactive colloid administration

**79403**  Radiopharmaceutical therapy, radiolabeled monoclonal antibody by intravenous infusion

(For pre-treatment imaging, see 78802, 78804)

(Do not report 79403 in conjunction with 79101)

**79440**  Radiopharmaceutical therapy, by intra-articular administration

**79445**  Radiopharmaceutical therapy, by intra-arterial particulate administration

(Do not report 79445 in conjunction with 96373, 96420)

(Use appropriate procedural and radiological supervision and interpretation codes for the angiographic and interventional procedures provided prerequisite to intra-arterial radiopharmaceutical therapy)

**79999**  Radiopharmaceutical therapy, unlisted procedure

⊙=Moderate sedation  ✚=Add-on code  ✔=FDA approval pending  #=Resequenced code  ○=Recycled/reinstated code

# Pathology and Laboratory Guidelines

Guidelines to direct general reporting of services are presented in the **Introduction.** Some of the commonalities are repeated here for the convenience of those referring to this section on **Pathology and Laboratory.** Other definitions and items unique to Pathology and Laboratory are also listed.

## Services in Pathology and Laboratory

Services in Pathology and Laboratory are provided by a physician or by technologists under responsible supervision of a physician.

## Separate or Multiple Procedures

It is appropriate to designate multiple procedures that are rendered on the same date by separate entries.

## Unlisted Service or Procedure

A service or procedure may be provided that is not listed in this edition of the CPT codebook. When reporting such a service, the appropriate "Unlisted Procedure" code may be used to indicate the service, identifying it by "Special Report" as discussed below. The "Unlisted Procedures" and accompanying codes for **Pathology and Laboratory** are as follows:

| | |
|---|---|
| 81099 | Unlisted urinalysis procedure |
| 81479 | Unlisted molecular pathology procedure |
| 81599 | Unlisted multianalyte assay with algorithmic analysis |
| 84999 | Unlisted chemistry procedure |
| 85999 | Unlisted hematology and coagulation procedure |
| 86486 | unlisted antigen, each |
| 86849 | Unlisted immunology procedure |
| 86999 | Unlisted transfusion medicine procedure |
| 87999 | Unlisted microbiology procedure |
| 88099 | Unlisted necropsy (autopsy) procedure |
| 88199 | Unlisted cytopathology procedure |
| 88299 | Unlisted cytogenetic study |
| 88399 | Unlisted surgical pathology procedure |
| 88749 | Unlisted in vivo (eg, transcutaneous) laboratory service |
| 89240 | Unlisted miscellaneous pathology test |
| 89398 | Unlisted reproductive medicine laboratory procedure |

## Special Report

A service that is rarely provided, unusual, variable, or new may require a special report. Pertinent information should include an adequate definition or description of the nature, extent, and need for the procedure; and the time, effort, and equipment necessary to provide the service.

Pathology and Laboratory

# Pathology and Laboratory

## Organ or Disease-Oriented Panels

These panels were developed for coding purposes only and should not be interpreted as clinical parameters. The tests listed with each panel identify the defined components of that panel.

These panel components are not intended to limit the performance of other tests. If one performs tests in addition to those specifically indicated for a particular panel, those tests should be reported separately in addition to the panel code.

Do not report two or more panel codes that include any of the same constituent tests performed from the same patient collection. If a group of tests overlaps two or more panels, report the panel that incorporates the greater number of tests to fulfill the code definition and report the remaining tests using individual test codes (eg, do not report 80047 in conjunction with 80053).

**80047**   Basic metabolic panel (Calcium, ionized)

This panel must include the following:

Calcium, ionized (82330)

Carbon dioxide (bicarbonate) (82374)

Chloride (82435)

Creatinine (82565)

Glucose (82947)

Potassium (84132)

Sodium (84295)

Urea Nitrogen (BUN) (84520)

**80048**   Basic metabolic panel (Calcium, total)

This panel must include the following:

Calcium, total (82310)

Carbon dioxide (bicarbonate) (82374)

Chloride (82435)

Creatinine (82565)

Glucose (82947)

Potassium (84132)

Sodium (84295)

Urea nitrogen (BUN) (84520)

**80050**   General health panel

This panel must include the following:

Comprehensive metabolic panel (80053)

Blood count, complete (CBC), automated and automated differential WBC count (85025 or 85027 and 85004)

OR

Blood count, complete (CBC), automated (85027) and appropriate manual differential WBC count (85007 or 85009)

Thyroid stimulating hormone (TSH) (84443)

**80051**   Electrolyte panel

This panel must include the following:

Carbon dioxide (bicarbonate) (82374)

Chloride (82435)

Potassium (84132)

Sodium (84295)

**80053**   Comprehensive metabolic panel

This panel must include the following:

Albumin (82040)

Bilirubin, total (82247)

Calcium, total (82310)

Carbon dioxide (bicarbonate) (82374)

Chloride (82435)

Creatinine (82565)

Glucose (82947)

Phosphatase, alkaline (84075)

Potassium (84132)

Protein, total (84155)

Sodium (84295)

Transferase, alanine amino (ALT) (SGPT) (84460)

Transferase, aspartate amino (AST) (SGOT) (84450)

Urea nitrogen (BUN) (84520)

**80055**   Obstetric panel

This panel must include the following:

Blood count, complete (CBC), automated and automated differential WBC count (85025 or 85027 and 85004)

OR

Blood count, complete (CBC), automated (85027) and appropriate manual differential WBC count (85007 or 85009)

Hepatitis B surface antigen (HBsAg) (87340)

Antibody, rubella (86762)

Pathology and Laboratory

Syphilis test, non-treponemal antibody; qualitative (eg, VDRL, RPR, ART) (86592)

Antibody screen, RBC, each serum technique (86850)

Blood typing, ABO (86900) AND

Blood typing, Rh (D) (86901)

(When syphilis screening is performed using a treponemal antibody approach [86780], do not use 80055. Use the individual codes for the tests performed in the obstetric panel)

**80061**    Lipid panel

This panel must include the following:

Cholesterol, serum, total (82465)

Lipoprotein, direct measurement, high density cholesterol (HDL cholesterol) (83718)

Triglycerides (84478)

**80069**    Renal function panel

This panel must include the following:

Albumin (82040)

Calcium, total (82310)

Carbon dioxide (bicarbonate) (82374)

Chloride (82435)

Creatinine (82565)

Glucose (82947)

Phosphorus inorganic (phosphate) (84100)

Potassium (84132)

Sodium (84295)

Urea nitrogen (BUN) (84520)

**80074**    Acute hepatitis panel

This panel must include the following:

Hepatitis A antibody (HAAb), IgM antibody (86709)

Hepatitis B core antibody (HBcAb), IgM antibody (86705)

Hepatitis B surface antigen (HBsAg) (87340)

Hepatitis C antibody (86803)

**80076**    Hepatic function panel

This panel must include the following:

Albumin (82040)

Bilirubin, total (82247)

Bilirubin, direct (82248)

Phosphatase, alkaline (84075)

Protein, total (84155)

Transferase, alanine amino (ALT) (SGPT) (84460)

Transferase, aspartate amino (AST) (SGOT) (84450)

# Drug Testing

The following list contains examples of drugs or classes of drugs that are commonly assayed by qualitative screen, followed by confirmation with a second method:

- Alcohols
- Amphetamines
- Barbiturates
- Benzodiazepines
- Cocaine and metabolites
- Methadones
- Methaqualones
- Opiates
- Phencyclidines
- Phenothiazines
- Propoxyphenes
- Tetrahydrocannabinoïds
- Tricyclic antidepressants

Confirmed drugs may also be quantitated.

Use 80100 for each multiple drug class chromatographic procedure. Use 80102 for each procedure necessary for confirmation. For chromatography, each combination of stationary and mobile phase is to be counted as one procedure. For example, if detection of three drugs by chromatography requires one stationary phase with three mobile phases, use 80100 three times. However, if multiple drugs can be detected using a single analysis (eg, one stationary phase with one mobile phase), use 80100 only once.

For quantitation of drugs screened, use appropriate code in **Chemistry** section (82000-84999) or **Therapeutic Drug Assay** section (80150-80299).

**80100**    Drug screen, qualitative; multiple drug classes chromatographic method, each procedure

**80101**         single drug class method (eg, immunoassay, enzyme assay), each drug class

(For qualitative analysis by multiplexed screening kit for multiple drugs or drug classes, use 80104)

# **80104**         multiple drug classes other than chromatographic method, each procedure

**80102**    Drug confirmation, each procedure

**80103**    Tissue preparation for drug analysis

**80104**    Code is out of numerical sequence. See 80100-80103

**Pathology and Laboratory**

# Therapeutic Drug Assays

The material for examination may be from any source. Examination is quantitative. For nonquantitative testing, see Drug Testing (80100-80104).

| | |
|---|---|
| 80150 | Amikacin |
| 80152 | Amitriptyline |
| 80154 | Benzodiazepines |
| ● 80155 | Caffeine |
| 80156 | Carbamazepine; total |
| 80157 | free |
| 80158 | Cyclosporine |
| ● 80159 | Clozapine |
| 80160 | Desipramine |
| 80162 | Digoxin |
| 80164 | Dipropylacetic acid (valproic acid) |
| 80166 | Doxepin |
| 80168 | Ethosuximide |
| ● 80169 | Everolimus |
| 80170 | Gentamicin |
| ● 80171 | Gabapentin |
| 80172 | Gold |
| 80173 | Haloperidol |
| 80174 | Imipramine |
| ● 80175 | Lamotrigine |
| 80176 | Lidocaine |
| ● 80177 | Levetiracetam |
| 80178 | Lithium |
| ● 80180 | Mycophenolate (mycophenolic acid) |
| 80182 | Nortriptyline |
| ● 80183 | Oxcarbazepine |
| 80184 | Phenobarbital |
| 80185 | Phenytoin; total |
| 80186 | free |
| 80188 | Primidone |
| 80190 | Procainamide; |
| 80192 | with metabolites (eg, n-acetyl procainamide) |
| 80194 | Quinidine |
| 80195 | Sirolimus |
| 80196 | Salicylate |
| 80197 | Tacrolimus |
| 80198 | Theophylline |

| | |
|---|---|
| ● 80199 | Tiagabine |
| 80200 | Tobramycin |
| 80201 | Topiramate |
| 80202 | Vancomycin |
| ● 80203 | Zonisamide |
| 80299 | Quantitation of drug, not elsewhere specified |

# Evocative/Suppression Testing

The following test panels involve the administration of evocative or suppressive agents, and the baseline and subsequent measurement of their effects on chemical constituents. These codes are to be used for the reporting of the laboratory component of the overall testing protocol. For the administration of the evocative or suppressive agents, see Hydration, Therapeutic, Prophylactic, Diagnostic Injections and Infusions, and Chemotherapy and Other Highly Complex Drug or Highly Complex Biologic Agent Administration (eg,96365, 96366, 96367, 96368, 96372, 96374, 96375, 96376). In the code descriptors where reference is made to a particular analyte (eg, Cortisol: 82533 x 2) the "x 2" refers to the number of times the test for that particular analyte is performed.

| | |
|---|---|
| 80400 | ACTH stimulation panel; for adrenal insufficiency |
| | This panel must include the following: |
| | Cortisol (82533 x 2) |
| 80402 | for 21 hydroxylase deficiency |
| | This panel must include the following: |
| | Cortisol (82533 x 2) |
| | 17 hydroxyprogesterone (83498 x 2) |
| 80406 | for 3 beta-hydroxydehydrogenase deficiency |
| | This panel must include the following: |
| | Cortisol (82533 x 2) |
| | 17 hydroxypregnenolone (84143 x 2) |
| 80408 | Aldosterone suppression evaluation panel (eg, saline infusion) |
| | This panel must include the following: |
| | Aldosterone (82088 x 2) |
| | Renin (84244 x 2) |
| 80410 | Calcitonin stimulation panel (eg, calcium, pentagastrin) |
| | This panel must include the following: |
| | Calcitonin (82308 x 3) |
| 80412 | Corticotropic releasing hormone (CRH) stimulation panel |
| | This panel must include the following: |
| | Cortisol (82533 x 6) |
| | Adrenocorticotropic hormone (ACTH) (82024 x 6) |

**80414**   Chorionic gonadotropin stimulation panel; testosterone response

This panel must include the following:

Testosterone (84403 x 2 on 3 pooled blood samples)

**80415**     estradiol response

This panel must include the following:

Estradiol (82670 x 2 on 3 pooled blood samples)

**80416**   Renal vein renin stimulation panel (eg, captopril)

This panel must include the following:

Renin (84244 x 6)

**80417**   Peripheral vein renin stimulation panel (eg, captopril)

This panel must include the following:

Renin (84244 x 2)

**80418**   Combined rapid anterior pituitary evaluation panel

This panel must include the following:

Adrenocorticotropic hormone (ACTH) (82024 x 4)

Luteinizing hormone (LH) (83002 x 4)

Follicle stimulating hormone (FSH) (83001 x 4)

Prolactin (84146 x 4)

Human growth hormone (HGH) (83003 x 4)

Cortisol (82533 x 4)

Thyroid stimulating hormone (TSH) (84443 x 4)

**80420**   Dexamethasone suppression panel, 48 hour

This panel must include the following:

Free cortisol, urine (82530 x 2)

Cortisol (82533 x 2)

Volume measurement for timed collection (81050 x 2)

(For single dose dexamethasone, use 82533)

**80422**   Glucagon tolerance panel; for insulinoma

This panel must include the following:

Glucose (82947 x 3)

Insulin (83525 x 3)

**80424**     for pheochromocytoma

This panel must include the following:

Catecholamines, fractionated (82384 x 2)

**80426**   Gonadotropin releasing hormone stimulation panel

This panel must include the following:

Follicle stimulating hormone (FSH) (83001 x 4)

Luteinizing hormone (LH) (83002 x 4)

**80428**   Growth hormone stimulation panel (eg, arginine infusion, l-dopa administration)

This panel must include the following:

Human growth hormone (HGH) (83003 x 4)

**80430**   Growth hormone suppression panel (glucose administration)

This panel must include the following:

Glucose (82947 x 3)

Human growth hormone (HGH) (83003 x 4)

**80432**   Insulin-induced C-peptide suppression panel

This panel must include the following:

Insulin (83525)

C-peptide (84681 x 5)

Glucose (82947 x 5)

**80434**   Insulin tolerance panel; for ACTH insufficiency

This panel must include the following:

Cortisol (82533 x 5)

Glucose (82947 x 5)

**80435**     for growth hormone deficiency

This panel must include the following:

Glucose (82947 x 5)

Human growth hormone (HGH) (83003 x 5)

**80436**   Metyrapone panel

This panel must include the following:

Cortisol (82533 x 2)

11 deoxycortisol (82634 x 2)

**80438**   Thyrotropin releasing hormone (TRH) stimulation panel; 1 hour

This panel must include the following:

Thyroid stimulating hormone (TSH) (84443 x 3)

**80439**     2 hour

This panel must include the following:

Thyroid stimulating hormone (TSH) (84443 x 4)

**80440**     for hyperprolactinemia

This panel must include the following:

Prolactin (84146 x 3)

# Consultations (Clinical Pathology)

A clinical pathology consultation is a service, including a written report, rendered by the pathologist in response to a request from a physician or qualified health care

**Pathology and Laboratory**

professional in relation to a test result(s) requiring additional medical interpretive judgment.

Reporting of a test result(s) without medical interpretive judgment is not considered a clinical pathology consultation.

**80500**   Clinical pathology consultation; limited, without review of patient's history and medical records

**80502**       comprehensive, for a complex diagnostic problem, with review of patient's history and medical records

(These codes may also be used for pharmacokinetic consultations)

(For consultations involving the examination and evaluation of the patient, see 99241-99255)

# Urinalysis

For specific analyses, see appropriate section.

**81000**   Urinalysis, by dip stick or tablet reagent for bilirubin, glucose, hemoglobin, ketones, leukocytes, nitrite, pH, protein, specific gravity, urobilinogen, any number of these constituents; non-automated, with microscopy

**81001**       automated, with microscopy

**81002**       non-automated, without microscopy

**81003**       automated, without microscopy

**81005**   Urinalysis; qualitative or semiquantitative, except immunoassays

(For non-immunoassay reagent strip urinalysis, see 81000, 81002)

(For immunoassay, qualitative or semiquantitative, use 83518)

(For microalbumin, see 82043, 82044)

**81007**       bacteriuria screen, except by culture or dipstick

(For culture, see 87086-87088)

(For dipstick, use 81000 or 81002)

**81015**       microscopic only

(For sperm evaluation for retrograde ejaculation, use 89331)

**81020**       2 or 3 glass test

**81025**   Urine pregnancy test, by visual color comparison methods

**81050**   Volume measurement for timed collection, each

**81099**   Unlisted urinalysis procedure

# Molecular Pathology

Molecular pathology procedures are medical laboratory procedures involving the analyses of nucleic acid to detect variants in genes that may be indicative of germline (eg, constitutional disorders) or somatic (eg, neoplasia)

conditions, or to test for histocompatibility antigens (eg, HLA). Code selection is typically based on the specific gene(s) that is being analyzed. Genes are described using Human Genome Organization (HUGO) approved gene names and are italicized in the code descriptors. Gene names were taken from tables of the HUGO Gene Nomenclature Committee (HGNC) at the time the CPT codes were developed. For the most part, Human Genome Variation Society (HGVS) recommendations were followed for the names of specific molecular variants. The familiar name is used for some variants because defined criteria were not in place when the variant was first described or because HGVS recommendations were changed over time (eg, intronic variants, processed proteins). When the gene name is represented by an abbreviation, the abbreviation is listed first, followed by the full gene name italicized in parentheses (eg, "F5 *[coagulation Factor V]*"), except for the HLA series of codes. Proteins or diseases commonly associated with the genes are listed as examples in the code descriptors. The examples do not represent all conditions in which testing of the gene may be indicated.

Codes that describe tests to assess for the presence of gene variants (see definitions) use common gene variant names. Typically, all of the listed variants would be tested. However, these lists are not exclusive. If other variants are also tested in the analysis, they would be included in the procedure and not reported separately. Full gene sequencing should not be reported using codes that assess for the presence of gene variants unless specifically stated in the code descriptor.

The molecular pathology codes include all analytical services performed in the test (eg, cell lysis, nucleic acid stabilization, extraction, digestion, amplification, and detection). Any procedures required prior to cell lysis (eg, microdissection, codes 88380 and 88381) should be reported separately.

The results of the procedure may require interpretation by a physician or other qualified health care professional. When only the interpretation and report are performed, modifier 26 may be appended to the specific molecular pathology code.

All analyses are qualitative unless otherwise noted.

For microbial identification, see 87149-87153 and 87470-87801, and 87900-87904. For in situ hybridization analyses, see 88271-88275 and 88365-88368.

Molecular pathology procedures that are not specified in 81161, 81200-81383 should be reported using either the appropriate Tier 2 code (81400-81408) or the unlisted molecular pathology procedure code, 81479.

**Definitions**

For purposes of CPT reporting, the following definitions apply:

**Abnormal allele:** an alternative form of a gene that contains a disease-related variation from the normal sequence.

**Breakpoint:** the region at which a chromosome breaks during a translocation (defined elsewhere). These regions are often consistent for a given translocation.

**Codon:** a discrete unit of three nucleotides of a DNA or mRNA sequence that encodes a specific amino acid within, or signals the termination of, a polypeptide.

**Common variants:** variants (as defined elsewhere) that are associated with compromised gene function and are interrogated in a single round of laboratory testing (in a single, typically multiplex, assay format or using more than one assay to encompass all variants to be tested). These variants typically fit the definition of a "mutation," and are usually the predominant ones causing disease. Testing for additional uncommon variants may provide additional limited value in assessment of a patient. Often there are professional society recommendations or guidelines for which variants are most appropriate to test (eg, American College of Medical Genetics/American College of Obstetrics and Gynecology guidelines for variants used in population screening for cystic fibrosis).

**Constitutional:** synonymous with germline, often used in reference to the genetic code that is present at birth.

**Cytogenomic:** chromosome analysis using molecular techniques.

**Duplication/Deletion (Dup/Del):** terms that are usually used together with the "/" to refer to molecular testing, which assesses the dosage of a particular genomic region. The region tested is typically of modest to substantial size - from several dozen to several million or more nucleotides. Normal gene dosage is two copies per cell, except for the sex chromosomes (X and Y). Thus, zero or one copy represents a deletion, and three (or more) copies represent a duplication.

**Dynamic mutation:** polynucleotide (eg, trinucleotide) repeats that are in or associated with genes that can undergo disease-producing increases or decreases in the numbers of repeats within tissues and across generations.

**Exon:** typically, one of multiple nucleic acid sequences used to encode information for a gene product (polypeptide or protein). Exons are separated from each other by non-protein-coding sequences known as introns. Exons at the respective ends of a gene also contain nucleic acid sequence that does not code for the gene's protein product.

**Gene:** a nucleic acid sequence that typically contains information for coding a protein as well as for the regulated expression of that protein. Human genes usually contain multiple protein coding regions (exons) separated by non-protein coding regions (introns). See also *exon*, *intron*, and *polypeptide*.

**Intron:** a nucleic acid sequence found between exons in human genes. An intron contains essential sequences for its proper removal (by a process known as *splicing*) to join exons together and thus facilitate production of a functional protein from a gene. An intron is sometimes referred to as an intervening sequence (IVS).

**Inversion:** A defect in a chromosome in which a segment breaks and reinserts in the same place but in the opposite orientation.

**Loss of heterozygosity (LOH, allelic imbalance):** An event that can occur in dividing cells that are heterozygous for one or more alleles, in which a daughter cell becomes hemizygous or homozygous for the allele(s) through mitotic recombination, deletion, or other chromosomal event.

**Microarray:** surface(s) on which multiple specific nucleic acid sequences are attached in a known arrangement. Sometimes referred to as a "gene chip". Examples of uses of microarrays include evaluation of a patient specimen for gains or losses of DNA sequences (copy number variants, CNVs), identification of the presence of specific nucleotide sequence variants (also known as single nucleotide polymorphisms, SNPs), mRNA expression levels, or DNA sequence analysis.

**Mutations:** typically are variants associated with altered gene function that lead to functional deficits or disease (pathogenic).

**Mutation scanning:** a technique (eg, single strand conformation polymorphism, temperature gradient gel electrophoresis, etc.) typically employed on multiple PCR amplicons to indicate the presence of DNA sequence variants by differences in physical properties compared to normal. Variants are then further characterized by DNA sequence analysis only in amplicons which demonstrate differences.

**Polymorphisms:** typically are variants that do not compromise gene function or produce disease (benign).

**Polypeptide:** a sequence of amino acids covalently linked in a specified order. Polypeptides alone or in combination with other polypeptide subunits are the building blocks of proteins.

**Short Tandem Repeat (STR):** a region of DNA where a pattern of two or more nucleotides are repeated. The number of repeating segments can be used as genetic markers for human identity testing.

**Single-nucleotide polymorphism (SNP):** a DNA sequence variation existing at a significant frequency in the population, in which a single nucleotide (A, T, C, or G) differs between individuals and/or within an individual"s paired chromosomes,

**Somatic:** synonymous with acquired, referring to genetic code alterations that develop after birth (eg, occurring in neoplastic cells)

**Translocation:** an abnormality resulting from the breakage of a chromosome and the relocation of a portion of that chromosome's DNA sequence to the same or another chromosome. Most common translocations involve a reciprocal exchange of DNA sequences between two differently numbered (ie, non-homologous) chromosomes, with or without a clinically significant loss of DNA.

***Uniparental disomy (UPD):*** Abnormal inheritance of both members of a chromosome pair from one parent, with absence of the other parent's chromosome for the pair.

***Variant:*** a nucleotide sequence difference from the "normal" (predominant) sequence for a given region. Variants are typically of two types: substitutions of one nucleotide for another, and deletions or insertions of nucleotides. Occasionally, variants reflect several nucleotide sequence changes in reasonably close proximity on the same chromosomal strand of DNA (a haplotype). These nucleotide sequence variants often result in amino acid changes in the protein made by the gene. The term *variant* does not itself carry a functional implication for those protein changes.

Variants in introns are typically described in one of two ways. The altered nucleotide(s) within a defined intervening sequence (eg, IVS3-2A>G) of a gene is listed with a "+" or "-" sign, which indicates the position relative to the first or last nucleotide of the intron. Or, the variant position is indicated relative to the last nucleotide of the preceding exon or first nucleotide of the following exon (eg, c.171+1G>A c.172-1G>T are single nucleotide changes at the first and last nucleotide of a given intron for a specific gene).

The majority of the variants described here are listed by the amino acid change using the single letter amino acid code for the original amino acid followed by the numerical position in the protein product and the amino acid substitution, eg, for *ASPA* E285A, Glutamic acid (E) at position 285 is replaced with an alanine (A). A few of the variants are described by the DNA change using the numerical position followed by the original nucleotide, a greater than sign (>) and the new nucleotide, eg, *MTHFR.* 677C>T.

A known familial variant is a specific mutation that has previously been identified within a patient's family.

# Tier 1 Molecular Pathology Procedures

The following codes represent gene-specific and genomic procedures:

**81161** Code is out of numerical sequence. See 81200-81383

**81200** *ASPA (aspartoacylase)* (eg, Canavan disease) gene analysis, common variants (eg, E285A, Y231X)

**81201** *APC (adenomatous polyposis coli)* (eg, familial adenomatosis polyposis [FAP], attenuated FAP) gene analysis; full gene sequence

**81202** known familial variants

**81203** duplication/deletion variants

**81205** *BCKDHB (branched-chain keto acid dehydrogenase E1, beta polypeptide)* (eg, maple syrup urine disease) gene analysis, common variants (eg, R183P, G278S, E422X)

**81206** *BCR/ABL1 (t(9;22))* (eg, chronic myelogenous leukemia) translocation analysis; major breakpoint, qualitative or quantitative

**81207** minor breakpoint, qualitative or quantitative

**81208** other breakpoint, qualitative or quantitative

**81209** *BLM (Bloom syndrome, RecQ helicase-like)* (eg, Bloom syndrome) gene analysis, 2281del6ins7 variant

**81210** *BRAF (v-raf murine sarcoma viral oncogene homolog B1)* (eg, colon cancer), gene analysis, V600E variant

**81211** *BRCA1, BRCA2 (breast cancer 1 and 2)* (eg, hereditary breast and ovarian cancer) gene analysis; full sequence analysis and common duplication/deletion variants in BRCA1 (ie, exon 13 del 3.835kb, exon 13 dup 6kb, exon 14-20 del 26kb, exon 22 del 510bp, exon 8-9 del 7.1kb)

**81212** 185delAG, 5385insC, 6174delT variants

**81213** uncommon duplication/deletion variants

**81214** *BRCA1 (breast cancer 1)* (eg, hereditary breast and ovarian cancer) gene analysis; full sequence analysis and common duplication/deletion variants (ie, exon 13 del 3.835kb, exon 13 dup 6kb, exon 14-20 del 26kb, exon 22 del 510bp, exon 8-9 del 7.1kb)

(When performing *BRCA1* full sequence analysis with *BRCA2* full sequence analysis, use 81211)

**81215** known familial variant

**81216** *BRCA2 (breast cancer 2)* (eg, hereditary breast and ovarian cancer) gene analysis; full sequence analysis

(When performing *BRCA2* full sequence analysis with *BRCA1* full sequence analysis, use 81211)

**81217** known familial variant

**81220** *CFTR (cystic fibrosis transmembrane conductance regulator)* (eg, cystic fibrosis) gene analysis; common variants (eg, ACMG/ACOG guidelines)

(When Intron 8 poly-T analysis is performed in conjunction with 81220 in a R117H positive patient, do not report 81224)

**81221** known familial variants

**81222** duplication/deletion variants

**81223** full gene sequence

**81224** intron 8 poly-T analysis (eg, male infertility)

**81225** *CYP2C19 (cytochrome P450, family 2, subfamily C, polypeptide 19)* (eg, drug metabolism), gene analysis, common variants (eg, *2, *3, *4, *8, *17)

**81226** *CYP2D6 (cytochrome P450, family 2, subfamily D, polypeptide 6)* (eg, drug metabolism), gene analysis, common variants (eg, *2, *3, *4, *5, *6, *9, *10, *17, *19, *29, *35, *41, *1XN, *2XN, *4XN)

**81227**    *CYP2C9 (cytochrome P450, family 2, subfamily C, polypeptide 9)* (eg, drug metabolism), gene analysis, common variants (eg, *2, *3, *5, *6)

**81228**    Cytogenomic constitutional (genome-wide) microarray analysis; interrogation of genomic regions for copy number variants (eg, bacterial artificial chromosome [BAC] or oligo-based comparative genomic hybridization [CGH] microarray analysis)

**81229**      interrogation of genomic regions for copy number and single nucleotide polymorphism (SNP) variants for chromosomal abnormalities

(Do not report 81228 in conjunction with 81229)

►(When performing cytogenomic constitutional microarray analysis that is not genome-wide [ie, regionally targeted], report the specific code for the targeted analysis if available [eg, 81405] or the unlisted molecular pathology code [81479])◄

►(Do not report analyte-specific molecular pathology procedures separately in conjunction with 81228, 81229 when the specific analytes are included as part of the microarray analysis)◄

►(Do not report 88271 when performing cytogenomic microarray analysis)◄

**# 81161**    *DMD (dystrophin)* (eg, Duchenne/Becker muscular dystrophy) deletion analysis, and duplication analysis, if performed

**81235**    *EGFR (epidermal growth factor receptor)* (eg, non-small cell lung cancer) gene analysis, common variants (eg, exon 19 LREA deletion, L858R, T790M, G719A, G719S, L861Q)

**81240**    *F2 (prothrombin, coagulation factor II)* (eg, hereditary hypercoagulability) gene analysis, 20210G>A variant

**81241**    *F5 (coagulation factor V)* (eg, hereditary hypercoagulability) gene analysis, Leiden variant

**81242**    *FANCC (Fanconi anemia, complementation group C)* (eg, Fanconi anemia, type C) gene analysis, common variant (eg, IVS4+4A>T)

**81243**    *FMR1 (fragile X mental retardation 1)* (eg, fragile X mental retardation) gene analysis; evaluation to detect abnormal (eg, expanded) alleles

(For evaluation to detect and characterize abnormal alleles, see 81243, 81244)

(For evaluation to detect and characterize abnormal alleles using a single assay [eg, PCR], use 81243)

**81244**      characterization of alleles (eg, expanded size and methylation status)

**81245**    *FLT3 (fms-related tyrosine kinase 3)* (eg, acute myeloid leukemia), gene analysis, internal tandem duplication (ITD) variants (ie, exons 14, 15)

**81250**    *G6PC (glucose-6-phosphatase, catalytic subunit)* (eg, Glycogen storage disease, type 1a, von Gierke disease) gene analysis, common variants (eg, R83C, Q347X)

**81251**    *GBA (glucosidase, beta, acid)* (eg, Gaucher disease) gene analysis, common variants (eg, N370S, 84GG, L444P, IVS2+1G>A)

**81252**    *GJB2 (gap junction protein, beta 2, 26kDa, connexin 26)* (eg, nonsyndromic hearing loss) gene analysis; full gene sequence

**81253**      known familial variants

**81254**    *GJB6 (gap junction protein, beta 6, 30kDa, connexin 30)* (eg, nonsyndromic hearing loss) gene analysis, common variants (eg, 309kb [del(GJB6-D13S1830)] and 232kb [del(GJB6-D13S1854)])

**81255**    *HEXA (hexosaminidase A [alpha polypeptide])* (eg, Tay-Sachs disease) gene analysis, common variants (eg, 1278insTATC, 1421+1G>C, G269S)

**81256**    *HFE (hemochromatosis)* (eg, hereditary hemochromatosis) gene analysis, common variants (eg, C282Y, H63D)

**81257**    *HBA1/HBA2 (alpha globin 1 and alpha globin 2)* (eg, alpha thalassemia, Hb Bart hydrops fetalis syndrome, HbH disease), gene analysis, for common deletions or variant (eg, Southeast Asian, Thai, Filipino, Mediterranean, alpha3.7, alpha4.2, alpha20.5, and Constant Spring)

**81260**    *IKBKAP (inhibitor of kappa light polypeptide gene enhancer in B-cells, kinase complex-associated protein)* (eg, familial dysautonomia) gene analysis, common variants (eg, 2507+6T>C, R696P)

**81261**    *IGH@ (Immunoglobulin heavy chain locus)* (eg, leukemias and lymphomas, B-cell), gene rearrangement analysis to detect abnormal clonal population(s); amplified methodology (eg, polymerase chain reaction)

**81262**      direct probe methodology (eg, Southern blot)

**81263**    *IGH@ (Immunoglobulin heavy chain locus)* (eg, leukemia and lymphoma, B-cell), variable region somatic mutation analysis

**81264**    *IGK@ (Immunoglobulin kappa light chain locus)* (eg, leukemia and lymphoma, B-cell), gene rearrangement analysis, evaluation to detect abnormal clonal population(s)

(For immunoglobulin lambda gene *[IGL@]* rearrangement or immunoglobulin kappa deleting element, *[IGKDEL]* analysis, use 81479)

**81265**    Comparative analysis using Short Tandem Repeat (STR) markers; patient and comparative specimen (eg, pre-transplant recipient and donor germline testing, post-transplant non-hematopoietic recipient germline [eg, buccal swab or other germline tissue sample] and donor testing, twin zygosity testing, or maternal cell contamination of fetal cells)

**+ 81266**      each additional specimen (eg, additional cord blood donor, additional fetal samples from different cultures, or additional zygosity in multiple birth pregnancies) (List separately in addition to code for primary procedure)

(Use 81266 in conjunction with 81265)

---

Pathology and Laboratory

**81267**   Chimerism (engraftment) analysis, post transplantation specimen (eg, hematopoietic stem cell), includes comparison to previously performed baseline analyses; without cell selection

**81268**   with cell selection (eg, CD3, CD33), each cell type

(If comparative STR analysis of recipient [using buccal swab or other germline tissue sample] and donor are performed after hematopoietic stem cell transplantation, report 81265, 81266 in conjunction with 81267, 81268 for chimerism testing)

**81270**   JAK2 (Janus kinase 2) (eg, myeloproliferative disorder) gene analysis, p.Val617Phe (V617F) variant

**81275**   KRAS (v-Ki-ras2 Kirsten rat sarcoma viral oncogene) (eg, carcinoma) gene analysis, variants in codons 12 and 13

**81280**   Long QT syndrome gene analyses (eg, KCNQ1, KCNH2, SCN5A, KCNE1, KCNE2, KCNJ2, CACNA1C, CAV3, SCN4B, AKAP, SNTA1, and ANK2); full sequence analysis

**81281**   known familial sequence variant

**81282**   duplication/deletion variants

**81287**   Code is out of numerical sequence. See 81200-81383

**81290**   MCOLN1 (mucolipin 1) (eg, Mucolipidosis, type IV) gene analysis, common variants (eg, IVS3-2A>G, del6.4kb)

#● **81287**   MGMT (O-6-methylguanine-DNA methyltransferase) (eg, glioblastoma multiforme), methylation analysis

**81291**   MTHFR (5,10-methylenetetrahydrofolate reductase) (eg, hereditary hypercoagulability) gene analysis, common variants (eg, 677T, 1298C)

**81292**   MLH1 (mutL homolog 1, colon cancer, nonpolyposis type 2) (eg, hereditary non-polyposis colorectal cancer, Lynch syndrome) gene analysis; full sequence analysis

**81293**   known familial variants

**81294**   duplication/deletion variants

**81295**   MSH2 (mutS homolog 2, colon cancer, nonpolyposis type 1) (eg, hereditary non-polyposis colorectal cancer, Lynch syndrome) gene analysis; full sequence analysis

**81296**   known familial variants

**81297**   duplication/deletion variants

**81298**   MSH6 (mutS homolog 6 [E. coli]) (eg, hereditary non-polyposis colorectal cancer, Lynch syndrome) gene analysis; full sequence analysis

**81299**   known familial variants

**81300**   duplication/deletion variants

**81301**   Microsatellite instability analysis (eg, hereditary non-polyposis colorectal cancer, Lynch syndrome) of markers for mismatch repair deficiency (eg, BAT25, BAT26), includes comparison of neoplastic and normal tissue, if performed

**81302**   MECP2 (methyl CpG binding protein 2) (eg, Rett syndrome) gene analysis; full sequence analysis

**81303**   known familial variant

**81304**   duplication/deletion variants

**81310**   NPM1 (nucleophosmin) (eg, acute myeloid leukemia) gene analysis, exon 12 variants

**81315**   PML/RARalpha, (t(15;17)), (promyelocytic leukemia/retinoic acid receptor alpha) (eg, promyelocytic leukemia) translocation analysis; common breakpoints (eg, intron 3 and intron 6), qualitative or quantitative

**81316**   single breakpoint (eg, intron 3, intron 6 or exon 6), qualitative or quantitative

(For intron 3 and intron 6 [including exon 6 if performed] analysis, use 81315)

(If both intron 6 and exon 6 are analyzed, without intron 3, use one unit of 81316)

**81317**   PMS2 (postmeiotic segregation increased 2 [S. cerevisiae]) (eg, hereditary non-polyposis colorectal cancer, Lynch syndrome) gene analysis; full sequence analysis

**81318**   known familial variants

**81319**   duplication/deletion variants

**81321**   PTEN (phosphatase and tensin homolog) (eg, Cowden syndrome, PTEN hamartoma tumor syndrome) gene analysis; full sequence analysis

**81322**   known familial variant

**81323**   duplication/deletion variant

**81324**   PMP22 (peripheral myelin protein 22) (eg, Charcot-Marie-Tooth, hereditary neuropathy with liability to pressure palsies) gene analysis; duplication/deletion analysis

**81325**   full sequence analysis

**81326**   known familial variant

**81330**   SMPD1 (sphingomyelin phosphodiesterase 1, acid lysosomal) (eg, Niemann-Pick disease, Type A) gene analysis, common variants (eg, R496L, L302P, fsP330)

**81331**   SNRPN/UBE3A (small nuclear ribonucleoprotein polypeptide N and ubiquitin protein ligase E3A) (eg, Prader-Willi syndrome and/or Angelman syndrome), methylation analysis

**81332**   SERPINA1 (serpin peptidase inhibitor, clade A, alpha-1 antiproteinase, antitrypsin, member 1) (eg, alpha-1-antitrypsin deficiency), gene analysis, common variants (eg, *S and *Z)

**81340**   TRB@ (T cell antigen receptor, beta) (eg, leukemia and lymphoma), gene rearrangement analysis to detect abnormal clonal population(s); using amplification methodology (eg, polymerase chain reaction)

**81341**   using direct probe methodology (eg, Southern blot)

**81342**   TRG@ (T cell antigen receptor, gamma) (eg, leukemia and lymphoma), gene rearrangement analysis, evaluation to detect abnormal clonal population(s)

(For T cell antigen alpha [TRA@] gene rearrangement analysis, use 81479)

(For T cell antigen delta [*TRD@*] gene rearrangement analysis, use 81402)

**81350**   *UGT1A1 (UDP glucuronosyltransferase 1 family, polypeptide A1)* (eg, irinotecan metabolism), gene analysis, common variants (eg, *28, *36, *37)

**81355**   *VKORC1 (vitamin K epoxide reductase complex, subunit 1)* (eg, warfarin metabolism), gene analysis, common variants (eg, -1639/3673)

Human Leukocyte Antigen (HLA) typing is performed to assess compatibility of recipients and potential donors as a part of solid organ and hematopoietic stem cell pretransplant testing. HLA testing is also performed to identify HLA alleles and allele groups (antigen equivalents) associated with specific diseases and individualized responses to drug therapy (eg, HLA-B*27 and ankylosing spondylitis and HLA-B*57:01 and abacavir hypersensitivity), as well as other clinical uses. One or more HLA genes may be tested in specific clinical situations (eg, HLA-DQB1 for narcolepsy and HLA-A, -B, -C, -DRB1, and -DQB1 for kidney transplantation). Each HLA gene typically has multiple variant alleles or allele groups that can be identified by typing. For HLA result reporting, a low resolution HLA type is denoted by a two digit HLA name (eg, A*02) and intermediate resolution typing by a string of alleles or an NMDP (National Marrow Donor Program) code (eg, B*14:01/07N/08/12/14, B*39CKGN). Both low and intermediate resolution are considered low resolution for code assignment. High resolution typing resolves the common well defined (CWD) alleles and is usually denoted by at least 4 digits (eg, A*02:02, *03:01:01:01, A*26:01:01G, and C*03:04P), however, high resolution typing may include some ambiguities for rare alleles, which may be reported as a string of alleles or an NMDP code.

If additional testing is required to resolve ambiguous allele combinations for high resolution typing, this is included in the base HLA typing codes below. The gene names have been italicized similar to the other molecular pathology codes.

(For HLA antigen typing by non-molecular pathology techniques, see 86812-86822)

**81370**   HLA Class I and II typing, low resolution (eg, antigen equivalents); *HLA-A, -B, -C, -DRB1/3/4/5*, and *-DQB1*

▲ **81371**       *HLA-A, -B,* and *-DRB1* (eg, verification typing)

►(When HLA typing includes a determination of the presence or absence of the DRB3/4/5 genes, that service is included in the typing and is not separately reported)◄

**81372**   HLA Class I typing, low resolution (eg, antigen equivalents); complete *(ie, HLA-A, -B,* and *-C)*

(When performing both Class I and II low resolution *HLA typing for HLA-A,-B,-C, -DRB1/3/4/5*, and *-DQB1*, use 81370)

**81373**       one locus *(eg, HLA-A, -B,* or *-C)*, each

(When performing a complete Class I *[HLA-A,-B,* and *-C]* low resolution HLA typing, use 81372)

(When the presence or absence of a single antigen equivalent is reported using low resolution testing, use 81374)

**81374**       one antigen equivalent (eg, *B*27*), each

(When testing for presence or absence of more than 2 antigen equivalents at a locus, use 81373 for each locus tested)

**81375**   HLA Class II typing, low resolution (eg, antigen equivalents); *HLA-DRB1/3/4/5* and *-DQB1*

(When performing both Class I and II low resolution HLA typing *for HLA-A,-B,-C, -DRB1/3/4/5*, and *-DQB1*, use 81370)

▲ **81376**       one locus *(eg, HLA-DRB1, -DRB3/4/5, -DQB1, -DQA1, -DPB1,* or *-DPA1)*, each

(When low resolution typing is performed for *HLA-DRB1/3/4/5* and *-DQB1*, use 81375)

►(When HLA typing includes a determination of the presence or absence of the DRB3/4/5 genes, that service is included in the typing and is not separately reported. When low or intermediate resolution typing of any or all of the DRB3/4/5 genes is performed, treat as one locus)◄

**81377**       one antigen equivalent, each

(When testing for presence or absence of more than 2 antigen equivalents at a locus, use 81376 for each locus)

**81378**   HLA Class I and II typing, high resolution (ie, alleles or allele groups), *HLA-A, -B, -C,* and *-DRB1*

**81379**   HLA Class I typing, high resolution (ie, alleles or allele groups); complete (ie, *HLA-A, -B,* and *-C)*

**81380**       one locus (eg, *HLA-A, -B,* or *-C)*, each

(When a complete Class I high resolution typing for *HLA-A,-B,* and *-C* is performed, use 81379)

(When the presence or absence of a single allele or allele group is reported using high resolution testing, use 81381)

**81381**       one allele or allele group (eg, *B*57:01P)*, each

(When testing for the presence or absence of more than 2 alleles or allele groups at a locus, use 81380 for each locus)

▲ **81382**   HLA Class II typing, high resolution (ie, alleles or allele groups); one locus (eg, *HLA-DRB1, -DRB3/4/5, -DQB1, -DQA1, -DPB1,* or *-DPA1)*, each

(When only the presence or absence of a single allele or allele group is reported using high resolution testing, use 81383)

►(When high resolution typing of any or all of the DRB3/4/5 genes is performed, treat as one locus)◄

---

▲=Revised code   ●=New code   ► ◄=Contains new or revised text   ⦸=Modifier 51 exempt

**81383**    one allele or allele group (eg, *HLA-DQB1\*06:02P*), each

(When testing for the presence or absence of more than 2 alleles or allele groups at a locus, use 81382 for each locus)

# Tier 2 Molecular Pathology Procedures

The following molecular pathology procedure (Tier 2) codes are used to report procedures not listed in the Tier 1 molecular pathology codes (81161, 81200-81383). They represent medically useful procedures that are generally performed in lower volumes than Tier 1 procedures (eg, the incidence of the disease being tested is rare). They are arranged by level of technical resources and interpretive work by the physician or other qualified health care professional. The individual analyses listed under each code (ie, level of procedure) utilize the definitions and coding principles as described in the introduction preceding the Tier 1 molecular pathology codes. The parenthetical examples of methodologies presented near the beginning of each code provide general guidelines used to group procedures for a given level and are not all-inclusive.

Use the appropriate molecular pathology procedure level code that includes the specific analyte listed after the code descriptor. If the analyte tested is not listed under one of the Tier 2 codes or is not represented by a Tier 1 code, use the unlisted molecular pathology procedure code, 81479.

▲ **81400**    Molecular pathology procedure, Level 1 (eg, identification of single germline variant [eg, SNP] by techniques such as restriction enzyme digestion or melt curve analysis)

*ACADM (acyl-CoA dehydrogenase, C-4 to C-12 straight chain, MCAD)* (eg, medium chain acyl dehydrogenase deficiency), K304E variant

*ACE (angiotensin converting enzyme)* (eg, hereditary blood pressure regulation), insertion/deletion variant

*AGTR1 (angiotensin II receptor, type 1)* (eg, essential hypertension), 1166A>C variant

▶*BCKDHA (branched chain keto acid dehydrogenase E1, alpha polypeptide)* (eg, maple syrup urine disease, type 1A), Y438N variant◀

*CCR5 (chemokine C-C motif receptor 5)* (eg, HIV resistance), 32-bp deletion mutation/794 825del32 deletion

*CLRN1 (clarin 1)* (eg, Usher syndrome, type 3), N48K variant

*DPYD (dihydropyrimidine dehydrogenase)* (eg, 5-fluorouracil/5-FU and capecitabine drug metabolism), IVS14+1G>A variant

*F2 (coagulation factor 2)* (eg, hereditary hypercoagulability), 1199G>A variant

*F5 (coagulation factor V)* (eg, hereditary hypercoagulability), HR2 variant

*F7 (coagulation factor VII [serum prothrombin conversion accelerator])* (eg, hereditary hypercoagulability), R353Q variant

*F13B (coagulation factor XIII, B polypeptide)* (eg, hereditary hypercoagulability), V34L variant

*FGB (fibrinogen beta chain)* (eg, hereditary ischemic heart disease), -455G>A variant

▶*FGFR1 (fibroblast growth factor receptor 1)* (eg, Pfeiffer syndrome type 1, craniosynostosis), P252R variant◀

*FGFR3 (fibroblast growth factor receptor 3)* (eg, Muenke syndrome), P250R variant

▶*FKTN (fukutin)* (eg, Fukuyama congenital muscular dystrophy), retrotransposon insertion variant

*GNE (glucosamine [UDP-N-acetyl]-2-epimerase/N-acetylmannosamine kinase)* (eg, inclusion body myopathy 2 [IBM2], Nonaka myopathy), M712T variant◀

*Human Platelet Antigen 1 genotyping (HPA-1), ITGB3 (integrin, beta 3 [platelet glycoprotein IIIa], antigen CD61 [GPIIIa])* (eg, neonatal alloimmune thrombocytopenia [NAIT], post-transfusion purpura), HPA-1a/b (L33P)

*Human Platelet Antigen 2 genotyping (HPA-2), GP1BA (glycoprotein Ib [platelet], alpha polypeptide [GPIbα])* (eg, neonatal alloimmune thrombocytopenia [NAIT], post-transfusion purpura), HPA-2a/b (T145M)

*Human Platelet Antigen 3 genotyping (HPA-3), ITGA2B (integrin, alpha 2b [platelet glycoprotein IIb of IIb/IIIa complex], antigen CD41 [GPIIb])* (eg, neonatal alloimmune thrombocytopenia [NAIT], post-transfusion purpura), HPA-3a/b (I843S)

*Human Platelet Antigen 4 genotyping (HPA-4), ITGB3 (integrin, beta 3 [platelet glycoprotein IIIa], antigen CD61 [GPIIIa])* (eg, neonatal alloimmune thrombocytopenia [NAIT], post-transfusion purpura), HPA-4a/b (R143Q)

*Human Platelet Antigen 5 genotyping (HPA-5), ITGA2 (integrin, alpha 2 [CD49B, alpha 2 subunit of VLA-2 receptor] [GPIa])* (eg, neonatal alloimmune thrombocytopenia [NAIT], post-transfusion purpura), HPA-5a/b (K505E)

*Human Platelet Antigen 6 genotyping (HPA-6w), ITGB3 (integrin, beta 3 [platelet glycoprotein IIIa, antigen CD61] [GPIIIa])* (eg, neonatal alloimmune thrombocytopenia [NAIT], post-transfusion purpura), HPA-6a/b (R489Q)

*Human Platelet Antigen 9 genotyping (HPA-9w), ITGA2B (integrin, alpha 2b [platelet glycoprotein IIb of IIb/IIIa complex, antigen CD41] [GPIIb])* (eg, neonatal alloimmune thrombocytopenia [NAIT], post-transfusion purpura), HPA-9a/b (V837M)

*Human Platelet Antigen 15 genotyping (HPA-15), CD109 (CD109 molecule)* (eg, neonatal alloimmune thrombocytopenia [NAIT], post-transfusion purpura), HPA-15a/b (S682Y)

---

►*IL28B (interleukin 28B [interferon, lambda 3])* (eg, drug response), rs12979860 variant◄

*IVD (isovaleryl-CoA dehydrogenase)* (eg, isovaleric acidemia), A282V variant

►*LCT (lactase-phlorizin hydrolase)* (eg, lactose intolerance), 13910 C>T variant

*NEB (nebulin)* (eg, nemaline myopathy 2), exon 55 deletion variant

*PCDH15 (protocadherin-related 15)* (eg, Usher syndrome type 1F), R245X variant◄

*SERPINE1 (serpine peptidase inhibitor clade E, member 1, plasminogen activator inhibitor -1, PAI-1)* (eg, thrombophilia), 4G variant

*SHOC2 (soc-2 suppressor of clear homolog)* (eg, Noonan-like syndrome with loose anagen hair), S2G variant

►*SLCO1B1 (solute carrier organic anion transporter family, member 1B1)* (eg, adverse drug reaction), V174A variant◄

*SMN1 (survival of motor neuron 1, telomeric)* (eg, spinal muscular atrophy), exon 7 deletion

*SRY (sex determining region Y)* (eg, 46,XX testicular disorder of sex development, gonadal dysgenesis), gene analysis

*TOR1A (torsin family 1, member A [torsin A])* (eg, early-onset primary dystonia [DYT1]), 907_909delGAG (904_906delGAG) variant

▲ **81401**　Molecular pathology procedure, Level 2 (eg, 2-10 SNPs, 1 methylated variant, or 1 somatic variant [typically using nonsequencing target variant analysis], or detection of a dynamic mutation disorder/triplet repeat)

►*ABCC8 (ATP-binding cassette, sub-family C [CFTR/MRP], member 8)* (eg, familial hyperinsulinism), common variants (eg, c.3898-9G>A [c.3992-9G>A], F1388del)◄

*ABL (c-abl oncogene 1, receptor tyrosine kinase)* (eg, acquired imatinib resistance), T315I variant

*ACADM (acyl-CoA dehydrogenase, C-4 to C-12 straight chain, MCAD)* (eg, medium chain acyl dehydrogenase deficiency), commons variants (eg, K304E, Y42H)

*ADRB2 (adrenergic beta-2 receptor surface)* (eg, drug metabolism), common variants (eg, G16R, Q27E)

►*AFF2 (AF4/FMR2 family, member 2 [FMR2])* (eg, fragile X mental retardation 2 [FRAXE]), evaluation to detect abnormal (eg, expanded) alleles◄

APOB (apolipoprotein B) (eg, familial hypercholesterolemia type B), common variants (eg, R3500Q, R3500W)

*APOE (apolipoprotein E)* (eg, hyperlipoproteinemia type III, cardiovascular disease, Alzheimer disease), common variants (eg, *2, *3, *4)

*AR (androgen receptor)* (eg, spinal and bulbar muscular atrophy, Kennedy disease, X chromosome inactivation), characterization of alleles (eg, expanded size or methylation status)

*ATN1 (atrophin 1)* (eg, dentatorubral-pallidoluysian atrophy), evaluation to detect abnormal (eg, expanded) alleles

►*ATXN1 (ataxin 1)* (eg, spinocerebellar ataxia), evaluation to detect abnormal (eg, expanded) alleles

*ATXN2 (ataxin 2)* (eg, spinocerebellar ataxia), evaluation to detect abnormal (eg, expanded) alleles

*ATXN3 (ataxin 3)* (eg, spinocerebellar ataxia, Machado-Joseph disease), evaluation to detect abnormal (eg, expanded) alleles

*ATXN7 (ataxin 7)* (eg, spinocerebellar ataxia), evaluation to detect abnormal (eg, expanded) alleles

*ATXN8OS (ATXN8 opposite strand [non-protein coding])* (eg, spinocerebellar ataxia), evaluation to detect abnormal (eg, expanded) alleles

*ATXN10 (ataxin 10)* (eg, spinocerebellar ataxia), evaluation to detect abnormal (eg, expanded) alleles

*CACNA1A (calcium channel, voltage-dependent, P/Q type, alpha 1A subunit)* (eg, spinocerebellar ataxia), evaluation to detect abnormal (eg, expanded) alleles◄

*CBFB/MYH11 (inv(16))* (eg, acute myeloid leukemia), qualitative, and quantitative, if performed

*CBS (cystathionine-beta-synthase)* (eg, homocystinuria, cystathionine beta-synthase deficiency), common variants (eg, I278T, G307S)

*CCND1/IGH (BCL1/IgH, t(11;14))* (eg, mantle cell lymphoma) translocation analysis, major breakpoint, qualitative, and quantitative, if performed

*CFH/ARMS2 (complement factor H/age-related maculopathy susceptibility 2)* (eg, macular degeneration), common variants (eg, Y402H [CFH], A69S [ARMS2])

►*CNBP (CCHC-type zinc finger, nucleic acid binding protein)* (eg, myotonic dystrophy type 2), evaluation to detect abnormal (eg, expanded) alleles

*CSTB (cystatin B [stefin B])* (eg, Unverricht-Lundborg disease), evaluation to detect abnormal (eg, expanded) alleles◄

*CYP3A4 (cytochrome P450, family 3, subfamily A, polypeptide 4)* (eg, drug metabolism), common variants (eg, *2, *3, *4, *5, *6)

*CYP3A5 (cytochrome P450, family 3, subfamily A, polypeptide 5)* (eg, drug metabolism), common variants (eg, *2, *3, *4, *5, *6)

*DMPK (dystrophia myotonica-protein kinase)* (eg, myotonic dystrophy, type 1), evaluation to detect abnormal (eg, expanded) alleles

**Pathology and Laboratory**

*E2A/PBX1 (t(1;19))* (eg, acute lymphocytic leukemia), translocation analysis, qualitative, and quantitative, if performed

*EML4/ALK (inv(2))* (eg, non-small cell lung cancer), translocation or inversion analysis

▶*ETV6/NTRK3 (t(12;15))* (eg, congenital/infantile fibrosarcoma), translocation analysis, qualitative, and quantitative, if performed◀

*ETV6/RUNX1 (t(12;21))* (eg, acute lymphocytic leukemia), translocation analysis, qualitative, and quantitative, if performed

▶*EWSR1/ATF1 (t(12;22))* (eg, clear cell sarcoma), translocation analysis, qualitative, and quantitative, if performed◀

*EWSR1/ERG (t(21;22))* (eg, Ewing sarcoma/peripheral neuroectodermal tumor), translocation analysis, qualitative, and quantitative, if performed

*EWSR1/FLI1 (t(11;22))* (eg, Ewing sarcoma/peripheral neuroectodermal tumor), translocation analysis, qualitative, and quantitative, if performed

▶*EWSR1/WT1 (t(11;22))* (eg, desmoplastic small round cell tumor), translocation analysis, qualitative, and quantitative, if performed◀

*F11 (coagulation factor XI)* (eg, coagulation disorder), common variants (eg, E117X [Type II], F283L [Type III], IVS14del14, and IVS14+1G>A [Type I])

*FGFR3 (fibroblast growth factor receptor 3)* (eg, achondroplasia, hypochondroplasia), common variants (eg, 1138G>A, 1138G>C, 1620C>A, 1620C>G)

*FIP1L1/PDGFRA (del[4q12])* (eg, imatinib-sensitive chronic eosinophilic leukemia), qualitative, and quantitative, if performed

▶*FLG (filaggrin)* (eg, icthyosis vulgaris), common variants (eg, R501X, 2282del4, R2447X, S3247X, 3702delG)

*FOXO1/PAX3 (t(2;13))* (eg, alveolar rhabdomyosarcoma), translocation analysis, qualitative, and quantitative, if performed

*FOXO1/PAX7 (t(1;13))* (eg, alveolar rhabdomyosarcoma), translocation analysis, qualitative, and quantitative, if performed

*FUS/DDIT3 (t(12;16))* (eg, myxoid liposarcoma), translocation analysis, qualitative, and quantitative, if performed◀

*FXN (frataxin)* (eg, Friedreich ataxia), evaluation to detect abnormal (expanded) alleles

▶*GALC (galactosylceramidase)* (eg, Krabbe disease), common variants (eg, c.857G>A, 30-kb deletion)◀

*GALT (galactose-1-phosphate uridylyltransferase)* (eg, galactosemia), common variants (eg, Q188R, S135L, K285N, T138M, L195P, Y209C, IVS2-2A>G, P171S, del5kb, N314D, L218L/N314D)

*H19 (imprinted maternally expressed transcript [non-protein coding])* (eg, Beckwith-Wiedemann syndrome), methylation analysis

*HBB (hemoglobin, beta)* (eg, sickle cell anemia, hemoglobin C, hemoglobin E), common variants (eg, HbS, HbC, HbE)

*HTT (huntingtin)* (eg, Huntington disease), evaluation to detect abnormal (eg, expanded) alleles

*KCNQ1OT1 (KCNQ1 overlapping transcript 1 [non-protein coding])* (eg, Beckwith-Wiedemann syndrome), methylation analysis

▶*LRRK2 (leucine-rich repeat kinase 2)* (eg, Parkinson disease), common variants (eg, R1441G, G2019S, I2020T)

*MED12 (mediator complex subunit 12)* (eg, FG syndrome type 1, Lujan syndrome), common variants (eg, R961W, N1007S)◀

*MEG3/DLK1 (maternally expressed 3 [non-protein coding]/delta-like 1 homolog [Drosophila])* (eg, intrauterine growth retardation), methylation analysis

*MLL/AFF1 (t(4;11))* (eg, acute lymphoblastic leukemia), translocation analysis, qualitative, and quantitative, if performed

*MLL/MLLT3 (t(9;11))* (eg, acute myeloid leukemia), translocation analysis, qualitative, and quantitative, if performed

*MT-RNR1 (mitochondrially encoded 12S RNA)* (eg, nonsyndromic hearing loss), common variants (eg, m.1555A>G, m.1494C>T)

*MUTYH (mutY homolog [E. coli])* (eg, MYH-associated polyposis), common variants (eg, Y165C, G382D)

*MT-ATP6 (mitochondrially encoded ATP synthase 6)* (eg, neuropathy with ataxia and retinitis pigmentosa [NARP], Leigh syndrome), common variants (eg, m.8993T>G, m.8993T>C)

*MT-ND4, MT-ND6 (mitochondrially encoded NADH dehydrogenase 4, mitochondrially encoded NADH dehydrogenase 6)* (eg, Leber hereditary optic neuropathy [LHON]), common variants (eg, m.11778G>A, m.3460G>A, m.14484T>C)

*MT-TK (mitochondrially encoded tRNA lysine)* (eg, myoclonic epilepsy with ragged-red fibers [MERRF]), common variants (eg, m.8344A>G, m.8356T>C)

*MT-TL1 (mitochondrially encoded tRNA leucine 1 [UUA/G])* (eg, diabetes and hearing loss), common variants (eg, m.3243A>G, m.14709 T>C) MT-TL1

*MT-ND5 (mitochondrially encoded tRNA leucine 1 [UUA/G], mitochondrially encoded NADH dehydrogenase 5)* (eg, mitochondrial encephalopathy with lactic acidosis and stroke-like episodes [MELAS]), common variants (eg, m.3243A>G, m.3271T>C, m.3252A>G, m.13513G>A)

*MT-TS1, MT-RNR1 (mitochondrially encoded tRNA serine 1 [UCN], mitochondrially encoded 12S RNA)* (eg, nonsyndromic sensorineural deafness [including aminoglycoside-induced nonsyndromic deafness]), common variants (eg, m.7445A>G, m.1555A>G)

▶*NOD2 (nucleotide-binding oligomerization domain containing 2)* (eg, Crohn's disease, Blau syndrome), common variants (eg, SNP 8, SNP 12, SNP 13)◀

*NPM1/ALK (t(2;5))* (eg, anaplastic large cell lymphoma), translocation analysis

▶*PABPN1 (poly[A] binding protein, nuclear 1)* (eg, oculopharyngeal muscular dystrophy), evaluation to detect abnormal (eg, expanded) alleles◀

*PAX8/PPARG (t(2;3) (q13;p25))* (eg, follicular thyroid carcinoma), translocation analysis

▶*PPP2R2B (protein phosphatase 2, regulatory subunit B, beta)* (eg, spinocerebellar ataxia), evaluation to detect abnormal (eg, expanded) alleles◀

*PRSS1 (protease, serine, 1 [trypsin 1])* (eg, hereditary pancreatitis), common variants (eg, N29I, A16V, R122H)

*PYGM (phosphorylase, glycogen, muscle)* (eg, glycogen storage disease type V, McArdle disease), common variants (eg, R50X, G205S)

*RUNX1/RUNX1T1 (t(8;21))* (eg, acute myeloid leukemia) translocation analysis, qualitative, and quantitative, if performed

*SEPT9 (septin 9)* (eg, colon cancer), methylation analysis

*SMN1/SMN2 (survival of motor neuron 1, telomeric/ survival of motor neuron 2, centromeric)* (eg, spinal muscular atrophy), dosage analysis (eg, carrier testing)

▶(For duplication/deletion analysis of SMN1/SMN2, use 81401)

*SS18/SSX1 (t(X;18))* (eg, synovial sarcoma), translocation analysis, qualitative, and quantitative, if performed

*SS18/SSX2 (t(X;18))* (eg, synovial sarcoma), translocation analysis, qualitative, and quantitative, if performed

*TBP (TATA box binding protein)* (eg, spinocerebellar ataxia), evaluation to detect abnormal (eg, expanded) alleles◀

*TPMT (thiopurine S-methyltransferase)* (eg, drug metabolism), common variants (eg, *2, *3)

*TYMS (thymidylate synthetase)* (eg, 5-fluorouracil/5-FU drug metabolism), tandem repeat variant

*VWF (von Willebrand factor)* (eg, von Willebrand disease type 2N), common variants (eg, T791M, R816W, R854Q)

▲ **81402**   Molecular pathology procedure, Level 3 (eg, >10 SNPs, 2-10 methylated variants, or 2-10 somatic variants [typically using non-sequencing target variant analysis], immunoglobulin and T-cell receptor gene rearrangements, duplication/deletion variants of 1 exon, loss of heterozygosity [LOH], uniparental disomy [UPD])

Chromosome 18q- (eg, D18S55, D18S58, D18S61, D18S64, and D18S69) (eg, colon cancer), allelic imbalance assessment (ie, loss of heterozygosity)

▶*COL1A1/PDGFB (t(17;22))* (eg, dermatofibrosarcoma protuberans), translocation analysis, multiple breakpoints, qualitative, and quantitative, if performed◀

*CYP21A2 (cytochrome P450, family 21, subfamily A, polypeptide 2)* (eg, congenital adrenal hyperplasia, 21-hydroxylase deficiency), common variants (eg, IVS2-13G, P30L, I172N, exon 6 mutation cluster [I235N, V236E, M238K], V281L, L307FfsX6, Q318X, R356W, P453S, G110VfsX21, 30-kb deletion variant)

*ESR1/PGR (receptor 1/progesterone receptor)* ratio (eg, breast cancer)

*IGH@/BCL2 (t(14;18))* (eg, follicular lymphoma), translocation analysis; major breakpoint region (MBR) and minor cluster region (mcr) breakpoints, qualitative or quantitative

*KIT (v-kit Hardy-Zuckerman 4 feline sarcoma viral oncogene homolog)* (eg, mastocytosis), common variants (eg, D816V, D816Y, D816F)

*MEFV (Mediterranean fever)* (eg, familial Mediterranean fever), common variants (eg, E148Q, P369S, F479L, M680I, I692del, M694V, M694I, K695R, V726A, A744S, R761H)

*MPL (myeloproliferative leukemia virus oncogene, thrombopoietin receptor, TPOR)* (eg, myeloproliferative disorder), common variants (eg, W515A, W515K, W515L, W515R)

*TRD@ (T cell antigen receptor, delta)* (eg, leukemia and lymphoma), gene rearrangement analysis, evaluation to detect abnormal clonal population

Uniparental disomy (UPD) (eg, Russell-Silver syndrome, Prader-Willi/Angelman syndrome), short tandem repeat (STR) analysis

▲ **81403**   Molecular pathology procedure, Level 4 (eg, analysis of single exon by DNA sequence analysis, analysis of >10 amplicons using multiplex PCR in 2 or more independent reactions, mutation scanning or duplication/deletion variants of 2-5 exons)

*ABL1 (c-abl oncogene 1, receptor tyrosine kinase)* (eg, acquired imatinib tyrosine kinase inhibitor resistance), variants in the kinase domain

*ANG (angiogenin, ribonuclease, RNase A family, 5)* (eg, amyotrophic lateral sclerosis), full gene sequence

▶*ARX (aristaless-related homeobox)* (eg, X-linked lissencephaly with ambiguous genitalia, X-linked mental retardation), duplication/deletion analysis◀

*CEBPA (CCAAT/enhancer binding protein [C/EBP], alpha)* (eg, acute myeloid leukemia), full gene sequence

*CEL (carboxyl ester lipase [bile salt-stimulated lipase])* (eg, maturity-onset diabetes of the young [MODY]), targeted sequence analysis of exon 11 (eg, c.1785delC, c.1686delT)

**Pathology and Laboratory**

►*CTNNB1 (catenin [cadherin-associated protein], beta 1, 88kDa)* (eg, desmoid tumors), targeted sequence analysis (eg, exon 3)◄

*DAZ/SRY (deleted in azoospermia and sex determining region Y)* (eg, male infertility), common deletions (eg, AZFa, AZFb, AZFc, AZFd)

►*DNMT3A (DNA [cytosine-5-]-methyltransferase 3 alpha)* (eg, acute myeloid leukemia), targeted sequence analysis (eg, exon 23)

*EPCAM (epithelial cell adhesion molecule)* (eg, Lynch syndrome), duplication/deletion analysis◄

*F8 (coagulation factor VIII)* (eg, hemophilia A), inversion analysis, intron 1 and intron 22A

►*F12 (coagulation factor XII [Hageman factor])* (eg, angioedema, hereditary, type III; factor XII deficiency), targeted sequence analysis of exon 9◄

*FGFR3 (fibroblast growth factor receptor 3)* (eg, isolated craniosynostosis), targeted sequence analysis (eg, exon 7)

(For targeted sequence analysis of multiple FGFR3 exons, use 81404)

*GJB1 (gap junction protein, beta 1)* (eg, Charcot-Marie-Tooth X-linked), full gene sequence

►*GNAQ (guanine nucleotide-binding protein G[q] subunit alpha)* (eg, uveal melanoma), common variants (eg, R183, Q209)◄

*HBB (hemoglobin, beta, beta-globin)* (eg, beta thalassemia), duplication/deletion analysis

*HRAS (v-Ha-ras Harvey rat sarcoma viral oncogene homolog)* (eg, Costello syndrome), exon 2 sequence

*IDH1 (isocitrate dehydrogenase 1 [NADP+], soluble)* (eg, glioma), common exon 4 variants (eg, R132H, R132C)

*IDH2 (isocitrate dehydrogenase 2 [NADP+], mitochondrial)* (eg, glioma), common exon 4 variants (eg, R140W, R172M)

*JAK2 (Janus kinase 2)* (eg, myeloproliferative disorder), exon 12 sequence and exon 13 sequence, if performed

►Killer cell immunoglobulin-like receptor (KIR) gene family (eg, hematopoietic stem cell transplantation), genotyping of KIR family genes◄

Known familial variant not otherwise specified, for gene listed in Tier 1 or Tier 2, DNA sequence analysis, each variant exon

(For a known familial variant that is considered a common variant, use specific common variant Tier 1 or Tier 2 code)

►*KCNC3 (potassium voltage-gated channel, Shaw-related subfamily, member 3)* (eg, spinocerebellar ataxia), targeted sequence analysis (eg, exon 2)

*KCNJ2 (potassium inwardly-rectifying channel, subfamily J, member 2)* (eg, Andersen-Tawil syndrome), full gene sequence

*KCNJ11 (potassium inwardly-rectifying channel, subfamily J, member 11)* (eg, familial hyperinsulinism), full gene sequence◄

*KRAS (v-Ki-ras2 Kirsten rat sarcoma viral oncogene)* (eg, carcinoma), gene analysis, variant(s) in exon 3 (eg, codon 61)

►*MC4R (melanocortin 4 receptor)* (eg, obesity), full gene sequence

*MICA (MHC class I polypeptide-related sequence A)* (eg, solid organ transplantation), common variants (eg, *001, *002)◄

*MPL (myeloproliferative leukemia virus oncogene, thrombopoietin receptor, TPOR)* (eg, myeloproliferative disorder), exon 10 sequence

*MT-RNR1 (mitochondrially encoded 12S RNA)* (eg, nonsyndromic hearing loss), full gene sequence

*MT-TS1 (mitochondrially encoded tRNA serine 1)* (eg, nonsyndromic hearing loss), full gene sequence

►*NDP (Norrie disease [pseudoglioma])* (eg, Norrie disease), duplication/deletion analysis

*NHLRC1 (NHL repeat containing 1)* (eg, progressive myoclonus epilepsy), full gene sequence

*PHOX2B (paired-like homeobox 2b)* (eg, congenital central hypoventilation syndrome), duplication/deletion analysis

*PLN (phospholamban)* (eg, dilated cardiomyopathy, hypertrophic cardiomyopathy), full gene sequence

*SH2D1A (SH2 domain containing 1A)* (eg, X-linked lymphoproliferative syndrome), duplication/deletion analysis◄

*SMN1 (survival of motor neuron 1, telomeric)* (eg, spinal muscular atrophy), known familial sequence variant(s)

►*TWIST1 (twist homolog 1 [Drosophila])* (eg, Saethre-Chotzen syndrome), duplication/deletion analysis

*UBA1 (ubiquitin-like modifier activating enzyme 1)* (eg, spinal muscular atrophy, X-linked), targeted sequence analysis (eg, exon 15)◄

*VHL (von Hippel-Lindau tumor suppressor)* (eg, von Hippel-Lindau familial cancer syndrome), deletion/duplication analysis

*VWF (von Willebrand factor)* (eg, von Willebrand disease types 2A, 2B, 2M), targeted sequence analysis (eg, exon 28)

▲ **81404** Molecular pathology procedure, Level 5 (eg, analysis of 2-5 exons by DNA sequence analysis, mutation scanning or duplication/deletion variants of 6-10 exons, or characterization of a dynamic mutation disorder/triplet repeat by Southern blot analysis)

*ACADS (acyl-CoA dehydrogenase, C-2 to C-3 short chain)* (eg, short chain acyl-CoA dehydrogenase deficiency), targeted sequence analysis (eg, exons 5 and 6)

►AFF2 (AF4/FMR2 family, member 2 [FMR2]) (eg, fragile X mental retardation 2 [FRAXE]), characterization of alleles (eg, expanded size and methylation status)◄

AQP2 (aquaporin 2 [collecting duct]) (eg, nephrogenic diabetes insipidus), full gene sequence

ARX (aristaless related homeobox) (eg, X-linked lissencephaly with ambiguous genitalia, X-linked mental retardation), full gene sequence

►AVPR2 (arginine vasopressin receptor 2) (eg, nephrogenic diabetes insipidus), full gene sequence

BBS10 (Bardet-Biedl syndrome 10) (eg, Bardet-Biedl syndrome), full gene sequence◄

BTD (biotinidase) (eg, biotinidase deficiency), full gene sequence

►C10orf2 (chromosome 10 open reading frame 2) (eg, mitochondrial DNA depletion syndrome), full gene sequence◄

CAV3 (caveolin 3) (eg, CAV3-related distal myopathy, limb-girdle muscular dystrophy type 1C), full gene sequence

►CD40LG (CD40 ligand) (eg, X-linked hyper IgM syndrome), full gene sequence◄

CDKN2A (cyclin-dependent kinase inhibitor 2A) (eg, CDKN2A-related cutaneous malignant melanoma, familial atypical mole-malignant melanoma syndrome), full gene sequence

CLRN1 (clarin 1) (eg, Usher syndrome, type 3), full gene sequence

►COX6B1 (cytochrome c oxidase subunit VIb polypeptide 1) (eg, mitochondrial respiratory chain complex IV deficiency), full gene sequence◄

CPT2 (carnitine palmitoyltransferase 2) (eg, carnitine palmitoyltransferase II deficiency), full gene sequence

►CRX (cone-rod homeobox) (eg, cone-rod dystrophy 2, Leber congenital amaurosis), full gene sequence

CSTB (cystatin B [stefin B]) (eg, Unverricht-Lundborg disease), full gene sequence◄

CYP1B1 (cytochrome P450, family 1, subfamily B, polypeptide 1) (eg, primary congenital glaucoma), full gene sequence

DMPK (dystrophia myotonica-protein kinase) (eg, myotonic dystrophy type 1), characterization of abnormal (eg, expanded) alleles

EGR2 (early growth response 2) (eg, Charcot-Marie-Tooth), full gene sequence

►EMD (emerin) (eg, Emery-Dreifuss muscular dystrophy), duplication/deletion analysis

EPM2A (epilepsy, progressive myoclonus type 2A, Lafora disease [laforin]) (eg, progressive myoclonus epilepsy), full gene sequence

FGF23 (fibroblast growth factor 23) (eg, hypophosphatemic rickets), full gene sequence◄

FGFR2 (fibroblast growth factor receptor 2) (eg, craniosynostosis, Apert syndrome, Crouzon syndrome), targeted sequence analysis (eg, exons 8, 10)

FGFR3 (fibroblast growth factor receptor 3) (eg, achondroplasia, hypochondroplasia), targeted sequence analysis (eg, exons 8, 11, 12, 13)

►FHL1 (four and a half LIM domains 1) (eg, Emery-Dreifuss muscular dystrophy), full gene sequence◄

FKRP (fukutin related protein) (eg, congenital muscular dystrophy type 1C [MDC1C], limb-girdle muscular dystrophy [LGMD] type 2I), full gene sequence

FOXG1 (forkhead box G1) (eg, Rett syndrome), full gene sequence

FSHMD1A (facioscapulohumeral muscular dystrophy 1A) (eg, facioscapulohumeral muscular dystrophy), evaluation to detect abnormal (eg, deleted) alleles

FSHMD1A (facioscapulohumeral muscular dystrophy 1A) (eg, facioscapulohumeral muscular dystrophy), characterization of haplotype(s) (ie, chromosome 4A and 4B haplotypes)

FXN (frataxin) (eg, Friedreich ataxia), full gene sequence

►GH1 (growth hormone 1) (eg, growth hormone deficiency), full gene sequence

GP1BB (glycoprotein Ib [platelet], beta polypeptide) (eg, Bernard-Soulier syndrome type B), full gene sequence◄

HBA1/HBA2 (alpha globin 1 and alpha globin 2) (eg, alpha thalassemia), duplication/deletion analysis

(For common deletion variants of alpha globin 1 and alpha globin 2 genes, use 81257)

HBB (hemoglobin, beta, Beta-Globin) (eg, thalassemia), full gene sequence

HNF1B (HNF1 homeobox B) (eg, maturity-onset diabetes of the young [MODY]), duplication/deletion analysis

HRAS (v-Ha-ras Harvey rat sarcoma viral oncogene homolog) (eg, Costello syndrome), full gene sequence

►HSD3B2 (hydroxy-delta-5-steroid dehydrogenase, 3 beta- and steroid delta-isomerase 2) (eg, 3-beta-hydroxysteroid dehydrogenase type II deficiency), full gene sequence

HSD11B2 (hydroxysteroid [11-beta] dehydrogenase 2) (eg, mineralocorticoid excess syndrome), full gene sequence

HSPB1 (heat shock 27kDa protein 1) (eg, Charcot-Marie-Tooth disease), full gene sequence

INS (insulin) (eg, diabetes mellitus), full gene sequence

KCNJ1 (potassium inwardly-rectifying channel, subfamily J, member 1) (eg, Bartter syndrome), full gene sequence◄

*KCNJ10 (potassium inwardly-rectifying channel, subfamily J, member 10)* (eg, SeSAME syndrome, EAST syndrome, sensorineural hearing loss), full gene sequence

*KIT (C-kit) (v-kit Hardy-Zuckerman 4 feline sarcoma viral oncogene homolog)* (eg, GIST, acute myeloid leukemia, melanoma), targeted gene analysis (eg, exons 8, 11, 13, 17, 18)

*LITAF (lipopolysaccharide-induced TNF factor)* (eg, Charcot-Marie-Tooth), full gene sequence

*MEFV (Mediterranean fever)* (eg, familial Mediterranean fever), full gene sequence

*MEN1 (multiple endocrine neoplasia I)* (eg, multiple endocrine neoplasia type 1, Wermer syndrome), duplication/deletion analysis

▶*MMACHC (methylmalonic aciduria [cobalamin deficiency] cblC type, with homocystinuria)* (eg, methylmalonic acidemia and homocystinuria), full gene sequence

*NDP (Norrie disease [pseudoglioma])* (eg, Norrie disease), full gene sequence

*NDUFA1 (NADH dehydrogenase [ubiquinone] 1 alpha subcomplex, 1, 7.5kDa)* (eg, Leigh syndrome, mitochondrial complex I deficiency), full gene sequence

*NDUFAF2 (NADH dehydrogenase [ubiquinone] 1 alpha subcomplex, assembly factor 2)* (eg, Leigh syndrome, mitochondrial complex I deficiency), full gene sequence

*NDUFS4 (NADH dehydrogenase [ubiquinone] Fe-S protein 4, 18kDa [NADH-coenzyme Q reductase])* (eg, Leigh syndrome, mitochondrial complex I deficiency), full gene sequence

*NIPA1 (non-imprinted in Prader-Willi/Angelman syndrome 1)* (eg, spastic paraplegia), full gene sequence

*NLGN4X (neuroligin 4, X-linked)* (eg, autism spectrum disorders), duplication/deletion analysis

*NPC2 (Niemann-Pick disease, type C2 [epididymal secretory protein E1])* (eg, Niemann-Pick disease type C2), full gene sequence

*NR0B1 (nuclear receptor subfamily 0, group B, member 1)* (eg, congenital adrenal hypoplasia), full gene sequence◀

*NRAS (neuroblastoma RAS viral oncogene homolog)* (eg, colorectal carcinoma), exon 1 and exon 2 sequences

*PDGFRA (platelet-derived growth factor receptor alpha polypeptide)* (eg, gastrointestinal stromal tumor), targeted sequence analysis (eg, exons 12, 18)

*PDX1 (pancreatic and duodenal homeobox 1)* (eg, maturity-onset diabetes of the young [MODY]), full gene sequence

▶*PHOX2B (paired-like homeobox 2b)* (eg, congenital central hypoventilation syndrome), full gene sequence

*PLP1 (proteolipid protein 1)* (eg, Pelizaeus-Merzbacher disease, spastic paraplegia), duplication/deletion analysis

*PQBP1 (polyglutamine binding protein 1)* (eg, Renpenning syndrome), duplication/deletion analysis◀

*PRNP (prion protein)* (eg, genetic prion disease), full gene sequence

▶*PROP1 (PROP paired-like homeobox 1)* (eg, combined pituitary hormone deficiency), full gene sequence

*PRPH2 (peripherin 2 [retinal degeneration, slow])* (eg, retinitis pigmentosa), full gene sequence◀

*PRSS1 (protease, serine, 1 [trypsin 1])* (eg, hereditary pancreatitis), full gene sequence

*RAF1 (v-raf-1 murine leukemia viral oncogene homolog 1)* (eg, LEOPARD syndrome), targeted sequence analysis (eg, exons 7, 12, 14, 17)

*RET (ret proto-oncogene)* (eg, multiple endocrine neoplasia, type 2B and familial medullary thyroid carcinoma), common variants (eg, M918T, 2647_2648delinsTT, A883F)

▶*RHO (rhodopsin)* (eg, retinitis pigmentosa), full gene sequence

*RP1 (retinitis pigmentosa 1)* (eg, retinitis pigmentosa), full gene sequence

*SCN1B (sodium channel, voltage-gated, type I, beta)* (eg, Brugada syndrome), full gene sequence

*SCO2 (SCO cytochrome oxidase deficient homolog 2 [SCO1L])* (eg, mitochondrial respiratory chain complex IV deficiency), full gene sequence

*SDHC (succinate dehydrogenase complex, subunit C, integral membrane protein, 15kDa)* (eg, hereditary paraganglioma-pheochromocytoma syndrome), duplication/deletion analysis◀

*SDHD (succinate dehydrogenase complex, subunit D, integral membrane protein)* (eg, hereditary paraganglioma), full gene sequence

▶*SGCG (sarcoglycan, gamma [35kDa dystrophin-associated glycoprotein])* (eg, limb-girdle muscular dystrophy), duplication/deletion analysis

*SH2D1A (SH2 domain containing 1A)* (eg, X-linked lymphoproliferative syndrome), full gene sequence

*SLC16A2 (solute carrier family 16, member 2 [thyroid hormone transporter])* (eg, specific thyroid hormone cell transporter deficiency, Allan-Herndon-Dudley syndrome), duplication/deletion analysis

*SLC25A20 (solute carrier family 25 [carnitine/acylcarnitine translocase], member 20)* (eg, carnitine-acylcarnitine translocase deficiency), duplication/deletion analysis◀

⊙=Moderate sedation ✚=Add-on code ✗=FDA approval pending #=Resequenced code ○=Recycled/reinstated code

SLC25A4 *(solute carrier family 25 [mitochondrial carrier; adenine nucleotide translocator], member 4)* (eg, progressive external ophthalmoplegia), full gene sequence

► SOD1 *(superoxide dismutase 1, soluble)* (eg, amyotrophic lateral sclerosis), full gene sequence

SPINK1 *(serine peptidase inhibitor, Kazal type 1)* (eg, hereditary pancreatitis), full gene sequence

STK11 *(serine/threonine kinase 11)* (eg, Peutz-Jeghers syndrome), duplication/deletion analysis

TACO1 *(translational activator of mitochondrial encoded cytochrome c oxidase I)* (eg, mitochondrial respiratory chain complex IV deficiency), full gene sequence

THAP1 *(THAP domain containing, apoptosis associated protein 1)* (eg, torsion dystonia), full gene sequence

TOR1A *(torsin family 1, member A [torsin A])* (eg, torsion dystonia), full gene sequence◄

TP53 *(tumor protein 53)* (eg, tumor samples), targeted sequence analysis of 2-5 exons

► TTPA *(tocopherol [alpha] transfer protein)* (eg, ataxia), full gene sequence◄

TTR *(transthyretin)* (eg, familial transthyretin amyloidosis), full gene sequence

► TWIST1 *(twist homolog 1 [Drosophila])* (eg, Saethre-Chotzen syndrome), full gene sequence◄

TYR *(tyrosinase [oculocutaneous albinism IA])* (eg, oculocutaneous albinism IA), full gene sequence

USH1G *(Usher syndrome 1G [autosomal recessive])* (eg, Usher syndrome, type 1), full gene sequence

VHL *(von Hippel-Lindau tumor suppressor)* (eg, von Hippel-Lindau familial cancer syndrome), full gene sequence

VWF *(von Willebrand factor)* (eg, von Willebrand disease type 1C), targeted sequence analysis (eg, exons 26, 27, 37)

► ZEB2 *(zinc finger E-box binding homeobox 2)* (eg, Mowat-Wilson syndrome), duplication/deletion analysis

ZNF41 *(zinc finger protein 41)* (eg, X-linked mental retardation 89), full gene sequence

▲ **81405**    Molecular pathology procedure, Level 6 (eg, analysis of 6-10 exons by DNA sequence analysis, mutation scanning or duplication/deletion variants of 11-25 exons), regionally targeted cytogenomic array analysis◄

ABCD1 *(ATP-binding cassette, sub-family D [ALD], member 1)* (eg, adrenoleukodystrophy), full gene sequence

ACADS *(acyl-CoA dehydrogenase, C-2 to C-3 short chain)* (eg, short chain acyl-CoA dehydrogenase deficiency), full gene sequence

► ACTA2 *(actin, alpha 2, smooth muscle, aorta)* (eg, thoracic aortic aneurysms and aortic dissections), full gene sequence◄

ACTC1 *(actin, alpha, cardiac muscle 1)* (eg, familial hypertrophic cardiomyopathy), full gene sequence

► ANKRD1 *(ankyrin repeat domain 1)* (eg, dilated cardiomyopathy), full gene sequence◄

APTX *(aprataxin)* (eg, ataxia with oculomotor apraxia 1), full gene sequence

AR *(androgen receptor)* (eg, androgen insensitivity syndrome), full gene sequence

► ARSA *(arylsulfatase A)* (eg, arylsulfatase A deficiency), full gene sequence

BCKDHA *(branched chain keto acid dehydrogenase E1, alpha polypeptide)* (eg, maple syrup urine disease, type 1A), full gene sequence

BCS1L *(BCS1-like [S. cerevisiae])* (eg, Leigh syndrome, mitochondrial complex III deficiency, GRACILE syndrome), full gene sequence

BMPR2 *(bone morphogenetic protein receptor, type II [serine/threonine kinase])* (eg, heritable pulmonary arterial hypertension), duplication/deletion analysis

CASQ2 *(calsequestrin 2 [cardiac muscle])* (eg, catecholaminergic polymorphic ventricular tachycardia), full gene sequence

CASR *(calcium-sensing receptor)* (eg, hypocalcemia), full gene sequence

CDKL5 *(cyclin-dependent kinase-like 5)* (eg, early infantile epileptic encephalopathy), duplication/deletion analysis◄

CHRNA4 *(cholinergic receptor, nicotinic, alpha 4)* (eg, nocturnal frontal lobe epilepsy), full gene sequence

CHRNB2 *(cholinergic receptor, nicotinic, beta 2 [neuronal])* (eg, nocturnal frontal lobe epilepsy), full gene sequence

► COX10 *(COX10 homolog, cytochrome c oxidase assembly protein)* (eg, mitochondrial respiratory chain complex IV deficiency), full gene sequence

COX15 *(COX15 homolog, cytochrome c oxidase assembly protein)* (eg, mitochondrial respiratory chain complex IV deficiency), full gene sequence

CYP11B1 *(cytochrome P450, family 11, subfamily B, polypeptide 1)* (eg, congenital adrenal hyperplasia), full gene sequence

CYP17A1 *(cytochrome P450, family 17, subfamily A, polypeptide 1)* (eg, congenital adrenal hyperplasia), full gene sequence◄

CYP21A2 *(cytochrome P450, family 21, subfamily A, polypeptide2)* (eg, steroid 21-hydroxylase isoform, congenital adrenal hyperplasia), full gene sequence

**Pathology and Laboratory**

▶Cytogenomic constitutional targeted microarray analysis of the X chromosome by interrogation of genomic regions for copy number and single nucleotide polymorphism (SNP) variants for chromosomal abnormalities

(When performing genome-wide cytogenomic constitutional microarray analysis, see 81228, 81229)

(Do not report analyte-specific molecular pathology procedures separately when the specific analytes are included as part of the microarray analysis of the X chromosome)

(Do not report 88271 when performing cytogenomic microarray analysis)

Cytogenomic constitutional targeted microarray analysis of chromosome 22q13 by interrogation of genomic regions for copy number and single nucleotide polymorphism (SNP) variants for chromosomal abnormalities

(When performing genome-wide cytogenomic constitutional microarray analysis, see 81228, 81229)

(Do not report analyte-specific molecular pathology procedures separately when the specific analytes are included as part of the microarray analysis of chromosome 22q13)

(Do not report 88271 when performing cytogenomic microarray analysis)

*DBT (dihydrolipoamide branched chain transacylase E2)* (eg, maple syrup urine disease, type 2), duplication/deletion analysis

*DCX (doublecortin)* (eg, X-linked lissencephaly), full gene sequence

*DES (desmin)* (eg, myofibrillar myopathy), full gene sequence◀

*DFNB59 (deafness, autosomal recessive 59)* (eg, autosomal recessive nonsyndromic hearing impairment), full gene sequence

▶*DGUOK (deoxyguanosine kinase)* (eg, hepatocerebral mitochondrial DNA depletion syndrome), full gene sequence◀

*DHCR7 (7-dehydrocholesterol reductase)* (eg, Smith Lemli-Opitz syndrome), full gene sequence

▶*EIF2B2 (eukaryotic translation initiation factor 2B, subunit 2 beta, 39kDa)* (eg, leukoencephalopathy with vanishing white matter), full gene sequence

*EMD (emerin)* (eg, Emery-Dreifuss muscular dystrophy), full gene sequence

*ENG (endoglin)* (eg, hereditary hemorrhagic telangiectasia, type 1), duplication/deletion analysis◀

*EYA1 (eyes absent homolog 1 [Drosophila])* (eg, branchio-oto-renal [BOR] spectrum disorders), duplication/deletion analysis

*F9 (coagulation factor IX)* (eg, hemophilia B), full gene sequence

▶*FGFR1 (fibroblast growth factor receptor 1)* (eg, Kallmann syndrome 2), full gene sequence◀

*FH (fumarate hydratase)* (eg, fumarate hydratase deficiency, hereditary leiomyomatosis with renal cell cancer), full gene sequence

*FKTN (fukutin)* (eg, limb-girdle muscular dystrophy [LGMD] type 2M or 2L), full gene sequence

▶*FTSJ1 (FtsJ RNA methyltransferase homolog 1 [E. coli])* (eg, X-linked mental retardation 9), duplication/deletion analysis

*GABRG2 (gamma-aminobutyric acid [GABA] A receptor, gamma 2)* (eg, generalized epilepsy with febrile seizures), full gene sequence

*GCH1 (GTP cyclohydrolase 1)* (eg, autosomal dominant dopa-responsive dystonia), full gene sequence

*GDAP1 (ganglioside-induced differentiation-associated protein 1)* (eg, Charcot-Marie-Tooth disease), full gene sequence◀

*GFAP (glial fibrillary acidic protein)* (eg, Alexander disease), full gene sequence

▶*GHR (growth hormone receptor)* (eg, Laron syndrome), full gene sequence

*GHRHR (growth hormone releasing hormone receptor)* (eg, growth hormone deficiency), full gene sequence◀

*GLA (galactosidase, alpha)* (eg, Fabry disease), full gene sequence

*HBA1/HBA2 (alpha globin 1 and alpha globin 2)* (eg, thalassemia), full gene sequence

*HNF1A (HNF1 homeobox A)* (eg, maturity-onset diabetes of the young [MODY]), full gene sequence

*HNF1B (HNF1 homeobox B)* (eg, maturity-onset diabetes of the young [MODY]), full gene sequence

▶*HTRA1 (HtrA serine peptidase 1)* (eg, macular degeneration), full gene sequence

*IDS (iduronate 2-sulfatase)* (eg, mucopolysacchridosis, type II), full gene sequence

*IL2RG (interleukin 2 receptor, gamma)* (eg, X-linked severe combined immunodeficiency), full gene sequence

*ISPD (isoprenoid synthase domain containing)* (eg, muscle-eye-brain disease, Walker-Warburg syndrome), full gene sequence◀

*KRAS (v-Ki-ras2 Kirsten rat sarcoma viral oncogene homolog)* (eg, Noonan syndrome), full gene sequence

*LAMP2 (lysosomal-associated membrane protein 2)* (eg, Danon disease), full gene sequence

▶*LDLR (low density lipoprotein receptor)* (eg, familial hypercholesterolemia), duplication/deletion analysis◀

⊙=Moderate sedation  ✚=Add-on code  ✗=FDA approval pending  #=Resequenced code  ○=Recycled/reinstated code

*MEN1 (multiple endocrine neoplasia I)* (eg, multiple endocrine neoplasia type 1, Wermer syndrome), full gene sequence

▶Mitochondrial genome deletions (eg, Kearns-Sayre syndrome [KSS], chronic progressive external ophthalmoplegia [CPEO], Pearson syndrome), deletion analysis, and duplication analysis, if performed

*MMAA (methylmalonic aciduria [cobalamine deficiency] type A)* (eg, MMAA-related methylmalonic acidemia), full gene sequence

*MMAB (methylmalonic aciduria [cobalamine deficiency] type B)* (eg, MMAA-related methylmalonic acidemia), full gene sequence

*MPI (mannose phosphate isomerase)* (eg, congenital disorder of glycosylation 1b), full gene sequence

*MPV17 (MpV17 mitochondrial inner membrane protein)* (eg, mitochondrial DNA depletion syndrome), full gene sequence◀

*MPZ (myelin protein zero)* (eg, Charcot-Marie-Tooth), full gene sequence

▶MTM1 (myotubularin 1) (eg, X-linked centronuclear myopathy), duplication/deletion analysis◀

*MYL2 (myosin, light chain 2, regulatory, cardiac, slow)* (eg, familial hypertrophic cardiomyopathy), full gene sequence

*MYL3 (myosin, light chain 3, alkali, ventricular, skeletal, slow)* (eg, familial hypertrophic cardiomyopathy), full gene sequence

*MYOT (myotilin)* (eg, limb-girdle muscular dystrophy), full gene sequence

▶*NDUFS7 (NADH dehydrogenase [ubiquinone] Fe-S protein 7, 20kDa [NADH-coenzyme Q reductase])* (eg, Leigh syndrome, mitochondrial complex I deficiency), full gene sequence

*NDUFS8 (NADH dehydrogenase [ubiquinone] Fe-S protein 8, 23kDa [NADH-coenzyme Q reductase])* (eg, Leigh syndrome, mitochondrial complex I deficiency), full gene sequence

*NDUFV1 (NADH dehydrogenase [ubiquinone] flavoprotein 1, 51kDa)* (eg, Leigh syndrome, mitochondrial complex I deficiency), full gene sequence◀

*NEFL (neurofilament, light polypeptide)* (eg, Charcot-Marie-Tooth), full gene sequence

*NF2 (neurofibromin 2 [merlin])* (eg, neurofibromatosis, type 2), duplication/deletion analysis

▶NLGN3 (neuroligin 3) (eg, autism spectrum disorders), full gene sequence

*NLGN4X (neuroligin 4, X-linked)* (eg, autism spectrum disorders), full gene sequence

*NPHP1 (nephronophthisis 1 [juvenile])* (eg, Joubert syndrome), deletion analysis, and duplication analysis, if performed

*NPHS2 (nephrosis 2, idiopathic, steroid-resistant [podocin])* (eg, steroid-resistant nephrotic syndrome), full gene sequence◀

*NSD1 (nuclear receptor binding SET domain protein 1)* (eg, Sotos syndrome), duplication/deletion analysis

*OTC (ornithine carbamoyltransferase)* (eg, ornithine transcarbamylase deficiency), full gene sequence

▶*PAFAH1B1 (platelet-activating factor acetylhydrolase 1b, regulatory subunit 1 [45kDa])* (eg, lissencephaly, Miller-Dieker syndrome), duplication/deletion analysis

*PARK2 (Parkinson protein 2, E3 ubiquitin protein ligase [parkin])* (eg, Parkinson disease), duplication/deletion analysis

*PCCA (propionyl CoA carboxylase, alpha polypeptide)* (eg, propionic acidemia, type 1), duplication/deletion analysis

*PCDH19 (protocadherin 19)* (eg, epileptic encephalopathy), full gene sequence

*PDHA1 (pyruvate dehydrogenase [lipoamide] alpha 1)* (eg, lactic acidosis), duplication/deletion analysis◀

*PDHB (pyruvate dehydrogenase [lipoamide] beta)* (eg, lactic acidosis), full gene sequence

▶*PINK1 (PTEN induced putative kinase 1)* (eg, Parkinson disease), full gene sequence

*PLP1 (proteolipid protein 1)* (eg, Pelizaeus-Merzbacher disease, spastic paraplegia), full gene sequence

*POU1F1 (POU class 1 homeobox 1)* (eg, combined pituitary hormone deficiency), full gene sequence

*PRX (periaxin)* (eg, Charcot-Marie-Tooth disease), full gene sequence

*PQBP1 (polyglutamine binding protein 1)* (eg, Renpenning syndrome), full gene sequence◀

*PSEN1 (presenilin 1)* (eg, Alzheimer disease), full gene sequence

▶*RAB7A (RAB7A, member RAS oncogene family)* (eg, Charcot-Marie-Tooth disease), full gene sequence

*RAI1 (retinoic acid induced 1)* (eg, Smith-Magenis syndrome), full gene sequence

*REEP1 (receptor accessory protein 1)* (eg, spastic paraplegia), full gene sequence◀

*RET (ret proto-oncogene)* (eg, multiple endocrine neoplasia, type 2A and familial medullary thyroid carcinoma), targeted sequence analysis (eg, exons 10, 11, 13-16)

▶*RPS19 (ribosomal protein S19)* (eg, Diamond-Blackfan anemia), full gene sequence

*RRM2B (ribonucleotide reductase M2 B [TP53 inducible])* (eg, mitochondrial DNA depletion), full gene sequence

*SCO1 (SCO cytochrome oxidase deficient homolog 1)* (eg, mitochondrial respiratory chain complex IV deficiency), full gene sequence◀

*Pathology and Laboratory*

*SDHB (succinate dehydrogenase complex, subunit B, iron sulfur)* (eg, hereditary paraganglioma), full gene sequence

*SDHC (succinate dehydrogenase complex, subunit C, integral membrane protein, 15kDa)* (eg, hereditary paraganglioma-pheochromocytoma syndrome), full gene sequence

*SGCA (sarcoglycan, alpha [50kDa dystrophin-associated glycoprotein])* (eg, limb-girdle muscular dystrophy), full gene sequence

*SGCB (sarcoglycan, beta [43kDa dystrophin-associated glycoprotein])* (eg, limb-girdle muscular dystrophy), full gene sequence

*SGCD (sarcoglycan, delta [35kDa dystrophin-associated glycoprotein])* (eg, limb-girdle muscular dystrophy), full gene sequence

► *SGCE (sarcoglycan, epsilon)* (eg, myoclonic dystonia), duplication/deletion analysis ◄

*SGCG (sarcoglycan, gamma [35kDa dystrophin-associated glycoprotein])* (eg, limb-girdle muscular dystrophy), full gene sequence

*SHOC2 (soc-2 suppressor of clear homolog)* (eg, Noonan-like syndrome with loose anagen hair), full gene sequence

► *SHOX (short stature homeobox)* (eg, Langer mesomelic dysplasia), full gene sequence

*SIL1 (SIL1 homolog, endoplasmic reticulum chaperone [S. cerevisiae])* (eg, ataxia), full gene sequence

*SLC2A1 (solute carrier family 2 [facilitated glucose transporter], member 1)* (eg, glucose transporter type 1 [GLUT 1] deficiency syndrome), full gene sequence

*SLC16A2 (solute carrier family 16, member 2 [thyroid hormone transporter])* (eg, specific thyroid hormone cell transporter deficiency, Allan-Herndon-Dudley syndrome), full gene sequence

*SLC22A5 (solute carrier family 22 [organic cation/carnitine transporter], member 5)* (eg, systemic primary carnitine deficiency), full gene sequence

*SLC25A20 (solute carrier family 25 [carnitine/acylcarnitine translocase], member 20)* (eg, carnitine-acylcarnitine translocase deficiency), full gene sequence

*SMAD4 (SMAD family member 4)* (eg, hemorrhagic telangiectasia syndrome, juvenile polyposis), duplication/deletion analysis ◄

*SMN1 (survival of motor neuron 1, telomeric)* (eg, spinal muscular atrophy), full gene sequence

► *SPAST (spastin)* (eg, spastic paraplegia), duplication/deletion analysis

*SPG7 (spastic paraplegia 7 [pure and complicated autosomal recessive])* (eg, spastic paraplegia), duplication/deletion analysis ◄

*SPRED1 (sprouty-related, EVH1 domain containing 1)* (eg, Legius syndrome), full gene sequence

► *STAT3 (signal transducer and activator of transcription 3 [acute-phase response factor])* (eg, autosomal dominant hyper-IgE syndrome), targeted sequence analysis (eg, exons 12, 13, 14, 16, 17, 20, 21)

*STK11 (serine/threonine kinase 11)* (eg, Peutz-Jeghers syndrome), full gene sequence

*SURF1 (surfeit 1)* (eg, mitochondrial respiratory chain complex IV deficiency), full gene sequence

*TARDBP (TAR DNA binding protein)* (eg, amyotrophic lateral sclerosis), full gene sequence

*TBX5 (T-box 5)* (eg, Holt-Oram syndrome), full gene sequence

*TCF4 (transcription factor 4)* (eg, Pitt-Hopkins syndrome), duplication/deletion analysis ◄

*TGFBR1 (transforming growth factor, beta receptor 1)* (eg, Marfan syndrome), full gene sequence

*TGFBR2 (transforming growth factor, beta receptor 2)* (eg, Marfan syndrome), full gene sequence

*THRB (thyroid hormone receptor, beta)* (eg, thyroid hormone resistance, thyroid hormone beta receptor deficiency), full gene sequence or targeted sequence analysis of >5 exons

► *TK2 (thymidine kinase 2, mitochondrial)* (eg, mitochondrial DNA depletion syndrome), full gene sequence

*TNNC1 (troponin C type 1 [slow])* (eg, hypertrophic cardiomyopathy or dilated cardiomyopathy), full gene sequence ◄

*TNNI3 (troponin I, type 3 [cardiac])* (eg, familial hypertrophic cardiomyopathy), full gene sequence

*TP53 (tumor protein 53)* (eg, Li-Fraumeni syndrome, tumor samples), full gene sequence or targeted sequence analysis of >5 exons

*TPM1 (tropomyosin 1 [alpha])* (eg, familial hypertrophic cardiomyopathy), full gene sequence

*TSC1 (tuberous sclerosis 1)* (eg, tuberous sclerosis), duplication/deletion analysis

► *TYMP (thymidine phosphorylase)* (eg, mitochondrial DNA depletion syndrome), full gene sequence ◄

*VWF (von Willebrand factor)* (eg, von Willebrand disease type 2N), targeted sequence analysis (eg, exons 18-20, 23-25)

► *WT1 (Wilms tumor 1)* (eg, Denys-Drash syndrome, familial Wilms tumor), full gene sequence

*ZEB2 (zinc finger E-box binding homeobox 2)* (eg, Mowat-Wilson syndrome), full gene sequence ◄

▲ **81406** Molecular pathology procedure, Level 7 (eg, analysis of 11-25 exons by DNA sequence analysis, mutation scanning or duplication/deletion variants of 26-50 exons, cytogenomic array analysis for neoplasia)

⊙=Moderate sedation   ✚=Add-on code   ✗=FDA approval pending   #=Resequenced code   ○=Recycled/reinstated code

**Pathology and Laboratory**

*ACADVL (acyl-CoA dehydrogenase, very long chain)* (eg, very long chain acyl-coenzyme A dehydrogenase deficiency), full gene sequence

*ACTN4 (actinin, alpha 4)* (eg, focal segmental glomerulosclerosis), full gene sequence

▶*AFG3L2 (AFG3 ATPase family gene 3-like 2 [S. cerevisiae])* (eg, spinocerebellar ataxia), full gene sequence

*AIRE (autoimmune regulator)* (eg, autoimmune polyendocrinopathy syndrome type 1), full gene sequence

*ALDH7A1 (aldehyde dehydrogenase 7 family, member A1)* (eg, pyridoxine-dependent epilepsy), full gene sequence◀

*ANO5 (anoctamin 5)* (eg, limb-girdle muscular dystrophy), full gene sequence

*APP (amyloid beta [A4] precursor protein)* (eg, Alzheimer disease), full gene sequence

▶*ASS1 (argininosuccinate synthase 1)* (eg, citrullinemia type I), full gene sequence

*ATL1 (atlastin GTPase 1)* (eg, spastic paraplegia), full gene sequence

*ATP1A2 (ATPase, Na+/K+ transporting, alpha 2 polypeptide)* (eg, familial hemiplegic migraine), full gene sequence◀

*ATP7B (ATPase, Cu++ transporting, beta polypeptide)* (eg, Wilson disease), full gene sequence

▶*BBS1 (Bardet-Biedl syndrome 1)* (eg, Bardet-Biedl syndrome), full gene sequence

*BBS2 (Bardet-Biedl syndrome 2)* (eg, Bardet-Biedl syndrome), full gene sequence

*BCKDHB (branched-chain keto acid dehydrogenase E1, beta polypeptide)* (eg, maple syrup urine disease, type 1B), full gene sequence

*BEST1 (bestrophin 1)* (eg, vitelliform macular dystrophy), full gene sequence

*BMPR2 (bone morphogenetic protein receptor, type II [serine/threonine kinase])* (eg, heritable pulmonary arterial hypertension), full gene sequence◀

*BRAF (v-raf murine sarcoma viral oncogene homolog B1)* (eg, Noonan syndrome), full gene sequence

▶*BSCL2 (Berardinelli-Seip congenital lipodystrophy 2 [seipin])* (eg, Berardinelli-Seip congenital lipodystrophy), full gene sequence

*BTK (Bruton agammaglobulinemia tyrosine kinase)* (eg, X-linked agammaglobulinemia), full gene sequence

*CACNB2 (calcium channel, voltage-dependent, beta 2 subunit)* (eg, Brugada syndrome), full gene sequence◀

*CAPN3 (calpain 3)* (eg, limb-girdle muscular dystrophy [LGMD] type 2A, calpainopathy), full gene sequence

*CBS (cystathionine-beta-synthase)* (eg, homocystinuria, cystathionine beta-synthase deficiency), full gene sequence

*CDH1 (cadherin 1, type 1, E-cadherin [epithelial])* (eg, hereditary diffuse gastric cancer), full gene sequence

*CDKL5 (cyclin-dependent kinase-like 5)* (eg, early infantile epileptic encephalopathy), full gene sequence

▶*CLCN1 (chloride channel 1, skeletal muscle)* (eg, myotonia congenita), full gene sequence

*CLCNKB (chloride channel, voltage-sensitive Kb)* (eg, Bartter syndrome 3 and 4b), full gene sequence

*CNTNAP2 (contactin-associated protein-like 2)* (eg, Pitt-Hopkins-like syndrome 1), full gene sequence

*COL6A2 (collagen, type VI, alpha 2)* (eg, collagen type VI-related disorders), duplication/deletion analysis

*CPT1A (carnitine palmitoyltransferase 1A [liver])* (eg, carnitine palmitoyltransferase 1A [CPT1A] deficiency), full gene sequence

*CRB1 (crumbs homolog 1 [Drosophila])* (eg, Leber congenital amaurosis), full gene sequence

*CREBBP (CREB binding protein)* (eg, Rubinstein-Taybi syndrome), duplication/deletion analysis◀

Cytogenomic microarray analysis, neoplasia (eg, interrogation of copy number, and loss-of-heterozygosity via single nucleotide polymorphism [SNP]-based comparative genomic hybridization [CGH] microarray analysis)

▶(Do not report analyte-specific molecular pathology procedures separately when the specific analytes are included as part of the cytogenomic microarray analysis for neoplasia)

(Do not report 88271 when performing cytogenomic microarray analysis)

*DBT (dihydrolipoamide branched chain transacylase E2)* (eg, maple syrup urine disease, type 2), full gene sequence◀

*DLAT (dihydrolipoamide S-acetyltransferase)* (eg, pyruvate dehydrogenase E2 deficiency), full gene sequence

*DLD (dihydrolipoamide dehydrogenase)* (eg, maple syrup urine disease, type III), full gene sequence

▶*DSC2 (desmocollin)* (eg, arrhythmogenic right ventricular dysplasia/cardiomyopathy 11), full gene sequence

*DSG2 (desmoglein 2)* (eg, arrhythmogenic right ventricular dysplasia/cardiomyopathy 10), full gene sequence

*DSP (desmoplakin)* (eg, arrhythmogenic right ventricular dysplasia/cardiomyopathy 8), full gene sequence

*EFHC1 (EF-hand domain [C-terminal] containing 1)* (eg, juvenile myoclonic epilepsy), full gene sequence

**Pathology and Laboratory**

*EIF2B3 (eukaryotic translation initiation factor 2B, subunit 3 gamma, 58kDa)* (eg, leukoencephalopathy with vanishing white matter), full gene sequence

*EIF2B4 (eukaryotic translation initiation factor 2B, subunit 4 delta, 67kDa)* (eg, leukoencephalopathy with vanishing white matter), full gene sequence

*EIF2B5 (eukaryotic translation initiation factor 2B, subunit 5 epsilon, 82kDa)* (eg, childhood ataxia with central nervous system hypomyelination/vanishing white matter), full gene sequence

*ENG (endoglin)* (eg, hereditary hemorrhagic telangiectasia, type 1), full gene sequence◄

*EYA1 (eyes absent homolog 1 [Drosophila])* (eg, branchio-oto-renal [BOR] spectrum disorders), full gene sequence

*F8 (coagulation factor VIII)* (eg, hemophilia A), duplication/deletion analysis

►*FAH (fumarylacetoacetate hydrolase [fumarylacetoacetase])* (eg, tyrosinemia, type 1), full gene sequence

*FASTKD2 (FAST kinase domains 2)* (eg, mitochondrial respiratory chain complex IV deficiency), full gene sequence

*FIG4 (FIG4 homolog, SAC1 lipid phosphatase domain containing [S. cerevisiae])* (eg, Charcot-Marie-Tooth disease), full gene sequence

*FTSJ1 (FtsJ RNA methyltransferase homolog 1 [E. coli])* (eg, X-linked mental retardation 9), full gene sequence

*FUS (fused in sarcoma)* (eg, amyotrophic lateral sclerosis), full gene sequence◄

*GAA (glucosidase, alpha; acid)* (eg, glycogen storage disease type II [Pompe disease]), full gene sequence

►*GALC (galactosylceramidase)* (eg, Krabbe disease), full gene sequence◄

*GALT (galactose-1-phosphate uridylyltransferase)* (eg, galactosemia), full gene sequence

►*GARS (glycyl-tRNA synthetase)* (eg, Charcot-Marie-Tooth disease), full gene sequence◄

*GCDH (glutaryl-CoA dehydrogenase)* (eg, glutaricacidemia type 1), full gene sequence

*GCK (glucokinase [hexokinase 4])* (eg, maturity-onset diabetes of the young [MODY]), full gene sequence

►*GLUD1 (glutamate dehydrogenase 1)* (eg, familial hyperinsulinism), full gene sequence

*GNE (glucosamine [UDP-N-acetyl]-2-epimerase/N-acetylmannosamine kinase)* (eg, inclusion body myopathy 2 [IBM2], Nonaka myopathy), full gene sequence

*GRN (granulin)* (eg, frontotemporal dementia), full gene sequence◄

*HADHA (hydroxyacyl-CoA dehydrogenase/3-ketoacyl-CoA thiolase/enoyl-CoA hydratase [trifunctional protein] alpha subunit)* (eg, long chain acyl-coenzyme A dehydrogenase deficiency), full gene sequence

►*HADHB (hydroxyacyl-CoA dehydrogenase/3-ketoacyl-CoA thiolase/enoyl-CoA hydratase [trifunctional protein], beta subunit)* (eg, trifunctional protein deficiency), full gene sequence◄

*HEXA (hexosaminidase A, alpha polypeptide)* (eg, Tay-Sachs disease), full gene sequence

►*HLCS (HLCS holocarboxylase synthetase)* (eg, holocarboxylase synthetase deficiency), full gene sequence◄

*HNF4A (hepatocyte nuclear factor 4, alpha)* (eg, maturity-onset diabetes of the young [MODY]), full gene sequence

►*IDUA (iduronidase, alpha-L-)* (eg, mucopolysaccharidosis type I), full gene sequence

*INF2 (inverted formin, FH2 and WH2 domain containing)* (eg, focal segmental glomerulosclerosis), full gene sequence◄

*IVD (isovaleryl-CoA dehydrogenase)* (eg, isovaleric acidemia), full gene sequence

*JAG1 (jagged 1)* (eg, Alagille syndrome), duplication/deletion analysis

►*JUP (junction plakoglobin)* (eg, arrhythmogenic right ventricular dysplasia/cardiomyopathy 11), full gene sequence

*KAL1 (Kallmann syndrome 1 sequence)* (eg, Kallmann syndrome), full gene sequence

*KCNH2 (potassium voltage-gated channel, subfamily H [eag-related], member 2)* (eg, short QT syndrome, long QT syndrome), full gene sequence

(Do not report 81406 for KCNH2 full gene sequence in conjunction with 81280)

*KCNQ1 (potassium voltage-gated channel, KQT-like subfamily, member 1)* (eg, short QT syndrome, long QT syndrome), full gene sequence

(Do not report 81406 for KCNQ1 full gene sequence with 81280)

*KCNQ2 (potassium voltage-gated channel, KQT-like subfamily, member 2)* (eg, epileptic encephalopathy), full gene sequence◄

*LDB3 (LIM domain binding 3)* (eg, familial dilated cardiomyopathy, myofibrillar myopathy), full gene sequence

►*LDLR (low density lipoprotein receptor)* (eg, familial hypercholesterolemia), full gene sequence

*LEPR (leptin receptor)* (eg, obesity with hypogonadism), full gene sequence

*LHCGR (luteinizing hormone/choriogonadotropin receptor)* (eg, precocious male puberty), full gene sequence◄

*LMNA (lamin A/C)* (eg, Emery-Dreifuss muscular dystrophy [EDMD1, 2 and 3] limb-girdle muscular dystrophy [LGMD] type 1B, dilated cardiomyopathy [CMD1A], familial partial lipodystrophy [FPLD2]), full gene sequence

▶*LRP5 (low density lipoprotein receptor-related protein 5)* (eg, osteopetrosis), full gene sequence◀

*MAP2K1 (mitogen-activated protein kinase 1)* (eg, cardiofaciocutaneous syndrome), full gene sequence

*MAP2K2 (mitogen-activated protein kinase 2)* (eg, cardiofaciocutaneous syndrome), full gene sequence

▶*MAPT (microtubule-associated protein tau)* (eg, frontotemporal dementia), full gene sequence

*MCCC1 (methylcrotonoyl-CoA carboxylase 1 [alpha])* (eg, 3-methylcrotonyl-CoA carboxylase deficiency), full gene sequence◀

*MCCC2 (methylcrotonoyl-CoA carboxylase 2 [beta])* (eg, 3-methylcrotonyl carboxylase deficiency), full gene sequence

▶*MFN2 (mitofusin 2)* (eg, Charcot-Marie-Tooth disease), full gene sequence

*MTM1 (myotubularin 1)* (eg, X-linked centronuclear myopathy), full gene sequence

*MUT (methylmalonyl CoA mutase)* (eg, methylmalonic acidemia), full gene sequence◀

*MUTYH (mutY homolog [E. coli])* (eg, MYH-associated polyposis), full gene sequence

▶*NDUFS1 (NADH dehydrogenase [ubiquinone] Fe-S protein 1, 75kDa [NADH-coenzyme Q reductase])* (eg, Leigh syndrome, mitochondrial complex I deficiency), full gene sequence◀

*NF2 (neurofibromin 2 [merlin])* (eg, neurofibromatosis, type 2), full gene sequence

*NOTCH3 (notch 3)* (eg, cerebral autosomal dominant arteriopathy with subcortical infarcts and leukoencephalopathy [CADASIL]), targeted sequence analysis (eg, exons 1-23)

▶*NPC1 (Niemann-Pick disease, type C1)* (eg, Niemann-Pick disease), full gene sequence

*NPHP1 (nephronophthisis 1 [juvenile])* (eg, Joubert syndrome), full gene sequence◀

*NSD1 (nuclear receptor binding SET domain protein 1)* (eg, Sotos syndrome), full gene sequence

*OPA1 (optic atrophy 1)* (eg, optic atrophy), duplication/deletion analysis

▶*OPTN (optineurin)* (eg, amyotrophic lateral sclerosis), full gene sequence

*PAFAH1B1 (platelet-activating factor acetylhydrolase 1b, regulatory subunit 1 [45kDa])* (eg, lissencephaly, Miller-Dieker syndrome), full gene sequence◀

*PAH (phenylalanine hydroxylase)* (eg, phenylketonuria), full gene sequence

*PALB2 (partner and localizer of BRCA2)* (eg, breast and pancreatic cancer), full gene sequence

▶*PARK2 (Parkinson protein 2, E3 ubiquitin protein ligase [parkin])* (eg, Parkinson disease), full gene sequence◀

*PAX2 (paired box 2)* (eg, renal coloboma syndrome), full gene sequence

*PC (pyruvate carboxylase)* (eg, pyruvate carboxylase deficiency), full gene sequence

▶*PCCA (propionyl CoA carboxylase, alpha polypeptide)* (eg, propionic acidemia, type 1), full gene sequence◀

*PCCB (propionyl CoA carboxylase, beta polypeptide)* (eg, propionic acidemia), full gene sequence

▶*PCDH15 (protocadherin-related 15)* (eg, Usher syndrome type 1F), duplication/deletion analysis◀

*PDHA1 (pyruvate dehydrogenase [lipoamide] alpha 1)* (eg, lactic acidosis), full gene sequence

*PDHX (pyruvate dehydrogenase complex, component X)* (eg, lactic acidosis), full gene sequence

▶*PHEX (phosphate-regulating endopeptidase homolog, X-linked)* (eg, hypophosphatemic rickets), full gene sequence

*PKD2 (polycystic kidney disease 2 [autosomal dominant])* (eg, polycystic kidney disease), full gene sequence

*PKP2 (plakophilin 2)* (eg, arrhythmogenic right ventricular dysplasia/cardiomyopathy 9), full gene sequence

*PNKD (eg, paroxysmal nonkinesigenic dyskinesia)* (eg, paroxysmal nonkinesigenic dyskinesia), full gene sequence◀

*POLG (polymerase [DNA directed], gamma)* (eg, Alpers-Huttenlocher syndrome, autosomal dominant progressive external ophthalmoplegia), full gene sequence

*POMGNT1 (protein O-linked mannose beta1,2-N acetylglucosaminyltransferase)* (eg, muscle-eye-brain disease, Walker-Warburg syndrome), full gene sequence

*POMT1 (protein-O-mannosyltransferase 1)* (eg, limb-girdle muscular dystrophy [LGMD] type 2K, Walker-Warburg syndrome), full gene sequence

*POMT2 (protein-O-mannosyltransferase 2)* (eg, limb-girdle muscular dystrophy [LGMD] type 2N, Walker-Warburg syndrome), full gene sequence

*PRKAG2 (protein kinase, AMP-activated, gamma 2 non-catalytic subunit)* (eg, familial hypertrophic cardiomyopathy with Wolff-Parkinson-White syndrome, lethal congenital glycogen storage disease of heart), full gene sequence

▶*PRKCG (protein kinase C, gamma)* (eg, spinocerebellar ataxia), full gene sequence◀

*PSEN2 (presenilin 2 [Alzheimer disease 4])* (eg, Alzheimer disease), full gene sequence

▲=Revised code   ●=New code   ▶ ◀=Contains new or revised text   ⊘=Modifier 51 exempt

*PTPN11 (protein tyrosine phosphatase, non-receptor type 11)* (eg, Noonan syndrome, LEOPARD syndrome), full gene sequence

*PYGM (phosphorylase, glycogen, muscle)* (eg, glycogen storage disease type V, McArdle disease), full gene sequence

*RAF1 (v-raf-1 murine leukemia viral oncogene homolog 1)* (eg, LEOPARD syndrome), full gene sequence

*RET (ret proto-oncogene)* (eg, Hirschsprung disease), full gene sequence

▶*RPE65 (retinal pigment epithelium-specific protein 65kDa)* (eg, retinitis pigmentosa, Leber congenital amaurosis), full gene sequence◀

*RYR1 (ryanodine receptor 1, skeletal)* (eg, malignant hyperthermia), targeted sequence analysis of exons with functionally-confirmed mutations

▶*SCN4A (sodium channel, voltage-gated, type IV, alpha subunit)* (eg, hyperkalemic periodic paralysis), full gene sequence

*SCNN1A (sodium channel, nonvoltage-gated 1 alpha)* (eg, pseudohypoaldosteronism), full gene sequence

*SCNN1B (sodium channel, nonvoltage-gated 1, beta)* (eg, Liddle syndrome, pseudohypoaldosteronism), full gene sequence

*SCNN1G (sodium channel, nonvoltage-gated 1, gamma)* (eg, Liddle syndrome, pseudohypoaldosteronism), full gene sequence

*SDHA (succinate dehydrogenase complex, subunit A, flavoprotein [Fp])* (eg, Leigh syndrome, mitochondrial complex II deficiency), full gene sequence

*SETX (senataxin)* (eg, ataxia), full gene sequence

*SGCE (sarcoglycan, epsilon)* (eg, myoclonic dystonia), full gene sequence

*SH3TC2 (SH3 domain and tetratricopeptide repeats 2)* (eg, Charcot-Marie-Tooth disease), full gene sequence◀

*SLC9A6 (solute carrier family 9 [sodium/hydrogen exchanger], member 6)* (eg, Christianson syndrome), full gene sequence

*SLC26A4 (solute carrier family 26, member 4)* (eg, Pendred syndrome), full gene sequence

▶*SLC37A4 (solute carrier family 37 [glucose-6-phosphate transporter], member 4)* (eg, glycogen storage disease type Ib), full gene sequence

*SMAD4 (SMAD family member 4)* (eg, hemorrhagic telangiectasia syndrome, juvenile polyposis), full gene sequence◀

*SOS1 (son of sevenless homolog 1)* (eg, Noonan syndrome, gingival fibromatosis), full gene sequence

▶*SPAST (spastin)* (eg, spastic paraplegia), full gene sequence

*SPG7 (spastic paraplegia 7 [pure and complicated autosomal recessive])* (eg, spastic paraplegia), full gene sequence

*STXBP1 (syntaxin-binding protein 1)* (eg, epileptic encephalopathy), full gene sequence◀

*TAZ (tafazzin)* (eg, methylglutaconic aciduria type 2, Barth syndrome), full gene sequence

▶*TCF4 (transcription factor 4)* (eg, Pitt-Hopkins syndrome), full gene sequence

*TH (tyrosine hydroxylase)* (eg, Segawa syndrome), full gene sequence

*TMEM43 (transmembrane protein 43)* (eg, arrhythmogenic right ventricular cardiomyopathy), full gene sequence◀

*TNNT2 (troponin T, type 2 [cardiac])* (eg, familial hypertrophic cardiomyopathy), full gene sequence

▶*TRPC6 (transient receptor potential cation channel, subfamily C, member 6)* (eg, focal segmental glomerulosclerosis), full gene sequence◀

*TSC1 (tuberous sclerosis 1)* (eg, tuberous sclerosis), full gene sequence

*TSC2 (tuberous sclerosis 2)* (eg, tuberous sclerosis), duplication/deletion analysis

*UBE3A (ubiquitin protein ligase E3A)* (eg, Angelman syndrome), full gene sequence

▶*UMOD (uromodulin)* (eg, glomerulocystic kidney disease with hyperuricemia and isosthenuria), full gene sequence◀

*VWF (von Willebrand factor)* (von Willebrand disease type 2A), extended targeted sequence analysis (eg, exons 11-16, 24-26, 51, 52)

▶*WAS (Wiskott-Aldrich syndrome [eczema-thrombocytopenia])* (eg, Wiskott-Aldrich syndrome), full gene sequence◀

▲ 81407  Molecular pathology procedure, Level 8 (eg, analysis of 26-50 exons by DNA sequence analysis, mutation scanning or duplication/deletion variants of >50 exons, sequence analysis of multiple genes on one platform)

*ABCC8 (ATP-binding cassette, sub-family C [CFTR/MRP], member 8)* (eg, familial hyperinsulinism), full gene sequence

▶*AGL (amylo-alpha-1, 6-glucosidase, 4-alpha-glucanotransferase)* (eg, glycogen storage disease type III), full gene sequence

*AHI1 (Abelson helper integration site 1)* (eg, Joubert syndrome), full gene sequence

*ASPM (asp [abnormal spindle] homolog, microcephaly associated [Drosophila])* (eg, primary microcephaly), full gene sequence

*CACNA1A (calcium channel, voltage-dependent, P/Q type, alpha 1A subunit)* (eg, familial hemiplegic migraine), full gene sequence◀

*CHD7 (chromodomain helicase DNA binding protein 7)* (eg, CHARGE syndrome), full gene sequence

►*COL4A4 (collagen, type IV, alpha 4)* (eg, Alport syndrome), full gene sequence

*COL4A5 (collagen, type IV, alpha 5)* (eg, Alport syndrome), duplication/deletion analysis

*COL6A1 (collagen, type VI, alpha 1)* (eg, collagen type VI-related disorders), full gene sequence

*COL6A2 (collagen, type VI, alpha 2)* (eg, collagen type VI-related disorders), full gene sequence

*COL6A3 (collagen, type VI, alpha 3)* (eg, collagen type VI-related disorders), full gene sequence

*CREBBP (CREB binding protein)* (eg, Rubinstein-Taybi syndrome), full gene sequence◄

*F8 (coagulation factor VIII)* (eg, hemophilia A), full gene sequence

*JAG1 (jagged 1)* (eg, Alagille syndrome), full gene sequence

►*KDM5C (lysine [K]-specific demethylase 5C)* (eg, X-linked mental retardation), full gene sequence

*KIAA0196 (KIAA0196)* (eg, spastic paraplegia), full gene sequence

*L1CAM (L1 cell adhesion molecule)* (eg, MASA syndrome, X-linked hydrocephaly), full gene sequence

*LAMB2 (laminin, beta 2 [laminin S])* (eg, Pierson syndrome), full gene sequence◄

*MYBPC3 (myosin binding protein C, cardiac)* (eg, familial hypertrophic cardiomyopathy), full gene sequence

*MYH6 (myosin, heavy chain 6, cardiac muscle, alpha)* (eg, familial dilated cardiomyopathy), full gene sequence

*MYH7 (myosin, heavy chain 7, cardiac muscle, beta)* (eg, familial hypertrophic cardiomyopathy, Liang distal myopathy), full gene sequence

*MYO7A (myosin VIIA)* (eg, Usher syndrome, type 1), full gene sequence

*NOTCH1 (notch 1)* (eg, aortic valve disease), full gene sequence

►*NPHS1 (nephrosis 1, congenital, Finnish type [nephrin])* (eg, congenital Finnish nephrosis), full gene sequence◄

*OPA1 (optic atrophy 1)* (eg, optic atrophy), full gene sequence

*PCDH15 (protocadherin-related 15)* (eg, Usher syndrome, type 1), full gene sequence

►*PKD1 (polycystic kidney disease 1 [autosomal dominant])* (eg, polycystic kidney disease), full gene sequence

*PLCE1 (phospholipase C, epsilon 1)* (eg, nephrotic syndrome type 3), full gene sequence◄

*SCN1A (sodium channel, voltage-gated, type 1, alpha subunit)* (eg, generalized epilepsy with febrile seizures), full gene sequence

*SCN5A (sodium channel, voltage-gated, type V, alpha subunit)* (eg, familial dilated cardiomyopathy), full gene sequence

►*SLC12A1 (solute carrier family 12 [sodium/potassium/chloride transporters], member 1)* (eg, Bartter syndrome), full gene sequence

*SLC12A3 (solute carrier family 12 [sodium/chloride transporters], member 3)* (eg, Gitelman syndrome), full gene sequence

*SPG11 (spastic paraplegia 11 [autosomal recessive])* (eg, spastic paraplegia), full gene sequence

*SPTBN2 (spectrin, beta, non-erythrocytic 2)* (eg, spinocerebellar ataxia), full gene sequence

*TMEM67 (transmembrane protein 67)* (eg, Joubert syndrome), full gene sequence◄

*TSC2 (tuberous sclerosis 2)* (eg, tuberous sclerosis), full gene sequence

*USH1C (Usher syndrome 1C [autosomal recessive, severe])* (eg, Usher syndrome, type 1), full gene sequence

►*VPS13B (vacuolar protein sorting 13 homolog B [yeast])* (eg, Cohen syndrome), duplication/deletion analysis

*WDR62 (WD repeat domain 62)* (eg, primary autosomal recessive microcephaly), full gene sequence◄

▲ **81408**   Molecular pathology procedure, Level 9 (eg, analysis of >50 exons in a single gene by DNA sequence analysis)

►*ABCA4 (ATP-binding cassette, sub-family A [ABC1], member 4)* (eg, Stargardt disease, age-related macular degeneration), full gene sequence◄

*ATM (ataxia telangiectasia mutated)* (eg, ataxia telangiectasia), full gene sequence

*CDH23 (cadherin-related 23)* (eg, Usher syndrome, type 1), full gene sequence

►*CEP290 (centrosomal protein 290kDa)* (eg, Joubert syndrome), full gene sequence◄

*COL1A1 (collagen, type I, alpha 1)* (eg, osteogenesis imperfecta, type I), full gene sequence

*COL1A2 (collagen, type I, alpha 2)* (eg, osteogenesis imperfecta, type I), full gene sequence

►*COL4A1 (collagen, type IV, alpha 1)* (eg, brain small-vessel disease with hemorrhage), full gene sequence

*COL4A3 (collagen, type IV, alpha 3 [Goodpasture antigen])* (eg, Alport syndrome), full gene sequence

*COL4A5 (collagen, type IV, alpha 5)* (eg, Alport syndrome), full gene sequence

*DMD (dystrophin)* (eg, Duchenne/Becker muscular dystrophy), full gene sequence◄

**Pathology and Laboratory**

*DYSF (dysferlin, limb girdle muscular dystrophy 2B [autosomal recessive])* (eg, limb-girdle muscular dystrophy), full gene sequence

*FBN1 (fibrillin 1)* (eg, Marfan syndrome), full gene sequence

▶*ITPR1 (inositol 1,4,5-trisphosphate receptor, type 1)* (eg, spinocerebellar ataxia), full gene sequence

*LAMA2 (laminin, alpha 2)* (eg, congenital muscular dystrophy), full gene sequence

*LRRK2 (leucine-rich repeat kinase 2)* (eg, Parkinson disease), full gene sequence

*MYH11 (myosin, heavy chain 11, smooth muscle)* (eg, thoracic aortic aneurysms and aortic dissections), full gene sequence

*NEB (nebulin)* (eg, nemaline myopathy 2), full gene sequence◀

*NF1 (neurofibromin 1)* (eg, neurofibromatosis, type 1), full gene sequence

▶*PKHD1 (polycystic kidney and hepatic disease 1)* (eg, autosomal recessive polycystic kidney disease), full gene sequence◀

*RYR1 (ryanodine receptor 1, skeletal)* (eg, malignant hyperthermia), full gene sequence

▶*RYR2 (ryanodine receptor 2 [cardiac])* (eg, catecholaminergic polymorphic ventricular tachycardia, arrhythmogenic right ventricular dysplasia), full gene sequence or targeted sequence analysis of > 50 exons◀

*USH2A (Usher syndrome 2A [autosomal recessive, mild])* (eg, Usher syndrome, type 2), full gene sequence

▶*VPS13B (vacuolar protein sorting 13 homolog B [yeast])* (eg, Cohen syndrome), full gene sequence◀

*VWF (von Willebrand factor)* (eg, von Willebrand disease types 1 and 3), full gene sequence

**81479**     Unlisted molecular pathology procedure

# Multianalyte Assays with Algorithmic Analyses

Multianalyte Assays with Algorithmic Analyses (MAAAs) are procedures that utilize multiple results derived from assays of various types, including molecular pathology assays, fluorescent in situ hybridization assays and non-nucleic acid based assays (eg, proteins, polypeptides, lipids, carbohydrates). Algorithmic analysis using the results of these assays as well as other patient information (if used) is then performed, and reported typically as a numeric score(s) or as a probability. MAAAs are typically unique to a single clinical laboratory or manufacturer. The results of individual component procedure(s) that are inputs to the MAAAs may be provided on the associated laboratory report, however these assays are not reported separately using additional codes.

The format for the code descriptors of MAAAs usually include (in order):

• Disease type (eg, oncology, autoimmune, tissue rejection),

• Material(s) analyzed (eg, DNA, RNA, protein, antibody),

• Number of markers (eg, number of genes, number of proteins),

• Methodology(ies) (eg, microarray, real-time [RT]-PCR, in situ hybridization [ISH], enzyme linked immunosorbent assays [ELISA]),

• Number of functional domains (if indicated),

• Specimen type (eg, blood, fresh tissue, formalin-fixed paraffin embedded),

• Algorithm result type (eg, prognostic, diagnostic),

• Report (eg, probability index, risk score)

MAAAs, including those that do not have a Category I code, may be found in Appendix O. MAAAs that do not have a Category I code are identified in Appendix O by a four-digit number followed by the letter "M." The Category I MAAA codes that are included in this subsection are also included in Appendix O. All MAAA codes are listed in Appendix O along with the procedure's proprietary name.

When a specific MAAA procedure is not listed below or in Appendix O, the procedure must be reported using the Category I MAAA unlisted code (81599).

These codes encompass all analytical services required (eg, cell lysis, nucleic acid stabilization, extraction, digestion, amplification, hybridization, and detection) in addition to the algorithmic analysis itself. Procedures that are required prior to cell lysis (eg, microdissection, codes 88380 and 88381) should be reported separately.

**81500**     Oncology (ovarian), biochemical assays of two proteins (CA-125 and HE4), utilizing serum, with menopausal status, algorithm reported as a risk score

(Do not report 81500 in conjunction with 86304, 86305)

**81503**     Oncology (ovarian), biochemical assays of five proteins (CA-125, apolipoprotein A1, beta-2 microglobulin, transferrin, and pre-albumin), utilizing serum, algorithm reported as a risk score

(Do not report 81503 in conjunction with 82172, 82232, 83695, 83700, 84134, 84466, 86304)

● **81504**     Oncology (tissue of origin), microarray gene expression profiling of > 2000 genes, utilizing formalin-fixed paraffin-embedded tissue, algorithm reported as tissue similarity scores

**81506**     Endocrinology (type 2 diabetes), biochemical assays of seven analytes (glucose, HbA1c, insulin, hs-CRP, adiponectin, ferritin, interleukin 2-receptor alpha), utilizing serum or plasma, algorithm reporting a risk score

(Do not report 81506 in conjunction with constituent components [ie, 82728, 82947, 83036, 83525, 86141], 84999 [for adopectin], and 83520 [for interleukin 2-receptor alpha])

● 81507    Fetal aneuploidy (trisomy 21, 18, and 13) DNA sequence analysis of selected regions using maternal plasma, algorithm reported as a risk score for each trisomy

81508    Fetal congenital abnormalities, biochemical assays of two proteins (PAPP-A, hCG [any form]), utilizing maternal serum, algorithm reported as a risk score

(Do not report 81508 in conjunction with 84163, 84702)

81509    Fetal congenital abnormalities, biochemical assays of three proteins (PAPP-A, hCG [any form], DIA), utilizing maternal serum, algorithm reported as a risk score

(Do not report 81509 in conjunction with 84163, 84702, 86336)

81510    Fetal congenital abnormalities, biochemical assays of three analytes (AFP, uE3, hCG [any form]), utilizing maternal serum, algorithm reported as a risk score

(Do not report 81510 in conjunction with 82105, 82677, 84702)

81511    Fetal congenital abnormalities, biochemical assays of four analytes (AFP, uE3, hCG [any form], DIA) utilizing maternal serum, algorithm reported as a risk score (may include additional results from previous biochemical testing)

(Do not report 81511 in conjunction with 82105, 82677, 84702, 86336)

81512    Fetal congenital abnormalities, biochemical assays of five analytes (AFP, uE3, total hCG, hyperglycosylated hCG, DIA) utilizing maternal serum, algorithm reported as a risk score

(Do not report 81512 in conjunction with 82105, 82677, 84702, 86336

81599    Unlisted multianalyte assay with algorithmic analysis

(Do not use 81599 for multianalyte assays with algorithmic analyses listed in Appendix O)

# Chemistry

The material for examination may be from any source unless otherwise specified in the code descriptor. When an analyte is measured in multiple specimens from different sources, or in specimens that are obtained at different times, the analyte is reported separately for each source and for each specimen. The examination is quantitative unless specified. To report an organ or disease oriented panel, see codes 80048-80076.

When a code describes a method where measurement of multiple analytes may require one or several procedures, each procedure is coded separately (eg, 82491-82492, 82541-82544). For example, if two analytes are measured using column chromatography using a single stationary

or mobile phase, use 82492. If the same two analytes are measured using different stationary or mobile phase conditions, 82491 would be used twice. If a total of four analytes are measured where two analytes are measured with a single stationary and mobile phase, and the other two analytes are measured using a different stationary and mobile phase, use 82492 twice. If a total of three analytes are measured where two analytes are measured using a single stationary or mobile phase condition, and the third analyte is measured separately using a different stationary or mobile phase procedure, use 82492 once for the two analytes measured under the same condition, and use 82491 once for the third analyte measured separately.

Clinical information or mathematically calculated values, which are not specifically requested by the ordering physician and are derived from the results of other ordered or performed laboratory tests, are considered part of the ordered test procedure(s) and therefore are not separately reportable service(s).

When the requested analyte result is derived using a calculation that requires values from non-requested laboratory analyses, only the requested analyte code should be reported.

When the calculated analyte determination requires values derived from other requested and nonrequested laboratory analyses, the requested analyte codes (including those calculated) should be reported.

An exception to the above is when an analyte (eg, urinary creatinine) is performed to compensate for variations in urine concentration (eg, microalbumin, thromboxane metabolites) in random urine samples; the appropriate CPT code is reported for both the ordered analyte and the additional required analyte. When the calculated result(s) represent an algorithmically derived numeric score or probability, see the appropriate multianalyte assay with algorithmic analyses (MAAA) code or the MAAA unlisted code (81599).

| | |
|---|---|
| 82000 | Acetaldehyde, blood |
| 82003 | Acetaminophen |
| 82009 | Ketone body(s) (eg, acetone, acetoacetic acid, beta-hydroxybutyrate); qualitative |
| 82010 | quantitative |
| 82013 | Acetylcholinesterase |
| | (For gastric acid analysis, use 82930) |
| | (Acid phosphatase, see 84060-84066) |
| 82016 | Acylcarnitines; qualitative, each specimen |
| 82017 | quantitative, each specimen |
| | (For carnitine, use 82379) |
| 82024 | Adrenocorticotropic hormone (ACTH) |
| 82030 | Adenosine, 5-monophosphate, cyclic (cyclic AMP) |
| 82040 | Albumin; serum, plasma or whole blood |

**Pathology and Laboratory**

| | |
|---|---|
| 82042 | urine or other source, quantitative, each specimen |
| 82043 | urine, microalbumin, quantitative |
| 82044 | urine, microalbumin, semiquantitative (eg, reagent strip assay) |
| | (For prealbumin, use 84134) |
| 82045 | ischemia modified |
| 82055 | Alcohol (ethanol); any specimen except breath |
| | (For other volatiles, alcohol, use 84600) |
| 82075 | breath |
| 82085 | Aldolase |
| 82088 | Aldosterone |
| | (Alkaline phosphatase, see 84075, 84080) |
| 82101 | Alkaloids, urine, quantitative |
| | (Alphaketoglutarate, see 82009, 82010) |
| | (Alpha tocopherol [Vitamin E], use 84446) |
| 82103 | Alpha-1-antitrypsin; total |
| 82104 | phenotype |
| 82105 | Alpha-fetoprotein (AFP); serum |
| 82106 | amniotic fluid |
| 82107 | AFP-L3 fraction isoform and total AFP (including ratio) |
| 82108 | Aluminum |
| 82120 | Amines, vaginal fluid, qualitative |
| | (For combined pH and amines test for vaginitis, use 82120 and 83986) |
| 82127 | Amino acids; single, qualitative; each specimen |
| 82128 | multiple, qualitative, each specimen |
| 82131 | single, quantitative, each specimen |
| 82135 | Aminolevulinic acid, delta (ALA) |
| 82136 | Amino acids, 2 to 5 amino acids, quantitative, each specimen |
| 82139 | Amino acids, 6 or more amino acids, quantitative, each specimen |
| 82140 | Ammonia |
| 82143 | Amniotic fluid scan (spectrophotometric) |
| | (For L/S ratio, use 83661) |
| | (Amobarbital, see 80100-80103 for qualitative analysis, 82205 for quantitative analysis) |
| 82145 | Amphetamine or methamphetamine |
| | (For qualitative analysis, see 80100-80103) |
| 82150 | Amylase |
| 82154 | Androstanediol glucuronide |
| 82157 | Androstenedione |
| 82160 | Androsterone |

| | |
|---|---|
| 82163 | Angiotensin II |
| 82164 | Angiotensin I - converting enzyme (ACE) |
| | (Antidiuretic hormone (ADH), use 84588) |
| | (Antimony, use 83015) |
| | (Antitrypsin, alpha-1-, see 82103, 82104) |
| 82172 | Apolipoprotein, each |
| 82175 | Arsenic |
| | (For heavy metal screening, use 83015) |
| 82180 | Ascorbic acid (Vitamin C), blood |
| | (Aspirin, see acetylsalicylic acid, 80196) |
| | (Atherogenic index, blood, ultracentrifugation, quantitative, use 83701) |
| 82190 | Atomic absorption spectroscopy, each analyte |
| 82205 | Barbiturates, not elsewhere specified |
| | (For qualitative analysis, see 80100-80103) |
| | (For B-Natriuretic peptide, use 83880) |
| 82232 | Beta-2 microglobulin |
| | (Bicarbonate, use 82374) |
| 82239 | Bile acids; total |
| 82240 | cholylglycine |
| | (For bile pigments, urine, see 81000-81005) |
| 82247 | Bilirubin; total |
| 82248 | direct |
| 82252 | feces, qualitative |
| 82261 | Biotinidase, each specimen |
| 82270 | Blood, occult, by peroxidase activity (eg, guaiac), qualitative; feces, consecutive collected specimens with single determination, for colorectal neoplasm screening (ie, patient was provided 3 cards or single triple card for consecutive collection) |
| 82271 | other sources |
| 82272 | Blood, occult, by peroxidase activity (eg, guaiac), qualitative, feces, 1-3 simultaneous determinations, performed for other than colorectal neoplasm screening |
| | (Blood urea nitrogen [BUN], see 84520, 84525) |
| 82274 | Blood, occult, by fecal hemoglobin determination by immunoassay, qualitative, feces, 1-3 simultaneous determinations |
| 82286 | Bradykinin |
| 82300 | Cadmium |
| 82306 | Vitamin D; 25 hydroxy, includes fraction(s), if performed |
| # 82652 | 1, 25 dihydroxy, includes fraction(s), if performed |
| | (82307 has been deleted. For 25 hydroxy vitamin D, use 82306) |

| | |
|---|---|
| **82308** | Calcitonin |
| **82310** | Calcium; total |
| **82330** | ionized |
| **82331** | after calcium infusion test |
| **82340** | urine quantitative, timed specimen |
| **82355** | Calculus; qualitative analysis |
| **82360** | quantitative analysis, chemical |
| **82365** | infrared spectroscopy |
| **82370** | X-ray diffraction |

(Carbamates, see individual listings)

| | |
|---|---|
| **82373** | Carbohydrate deficient transferrin |
| **82374** | Carbon dioxide (bicarbonate) |

(See also 82803)

| | |
|---|---|
| **82375** | Carboxyhemoglobin; quantitative |
| **82376** | qualitative |

(For transcutaneous measurement of carboxyhemoglobin, use 88740)

| | |
|---|---|
| **82378** | Carcinoembryonic antigen (CEA) |
| **82379** | Carnitine (total and free), quantitative, each specimen |

(For acylcarnitine, see 82016, 82017)

| | |
|---|---|
| **82380** | Carotene |
| **82382** | Catecholamines; total urine |
| **82383** | blood |
| **82384** | fractionated |

(For urine metabolites, see 83835, 84585)

| | |
|---|---|
| **82387** | Cathepsin-D |
| **82390** | Ceruloplasmin |
| **82397** | Chemiluminescent assay |
| **82415** | Chloramphenicol |
| **82435** | Chloride; blood |
| **82436** | urine |
| **82438** | other source |

(For sweat collection by iontophoresis, use 89230)

| | |
|---|---|
| **82441** | Chlorinated hydrocarbons, screen |

(Chlorpromazine, use 84022)

(Cholecalciferol [Vitamin D], use 82306)

| | |
|---|---|
| **82465** | Cholesterol, serum or whole blood, total |

(For high density lipoprotein [HDL], use 83718)

| | |
|---|---|
| **82480** | Cholinesterase; serum |
| **82482** | RBC |
| **82485** | Chondroitin B sulfate, quantitative |

(Chorionic gonadotropin, see gonadotropin, 84702, 84703)

| | |
|---|---|
| **82486** | Chromatography, qualitative; column (eg, gas liquid or HPLC), analyte not elsewhere specified |
| **82487** | paper, 1-dimensional, analyte not elsewhere specified |
| **82488** | paper, 2-dimensional, analyte not elsewhere specified |
| **82489** | thin layer, analyte not elsewhere specified |
| **82491** | Chromatography, quantitative, column (eg, gas liquid or HPLC); single analyte not elsewhere specified, single stationary and mobile phase |
| **82492** | multiple analytes, single stationary and mobile phase |
| **82495** | Chromium |
| **82507** | Citrate |
| **82520** | Cocaine or metabolite |

(Cocaine, qualitative analysis, see 80100-80103)

(Codeine, qualitative analysis, see 80100-80103)

(Codeine, quantitative analysis, see 82101)

(Complement, see 86160-86162)

| | |
|---|---|
| **82523** | Collagen cross links, any method |
| **82525** | Copper |

(Coproporphyrin, see 84119, 84120)

(Corticosteroids, use 83491)

| | |
|---|---|
| **82528** | Corticosterone |
| **82530** | Cortisol; free |
| **82533** | total |

(C-peptide, use 84681)

| | |
|---|---|
| **82540** | Creatine |
| **82541** | Column chromatography/mass spectrometry (eg, GC/MS, or HPLC/MS), analyte not elsewhere specified; qualitative, single stationary and mobile phase |
| **82542** | quantitative, single stationary and mobile phase |
| **82543** | stable isotope dilution, single analyte, quantitative, single stationary and mobile phase |
| **82544** | stable isotope dilution, multiple analytes, quantitative, single stationary and mobile phase |
| **82550** | Creatine kinase (CK), (CPK); total |
| **82552** | isoenzymes |
| **82553** | MB fraction only |
| **82554** | isoforms |
| **82565** | Creatinine; blood |
| **82570** | other source |
| **82575** | clearance |
| **82585** | Cryofibrinogen |

**Pathology and Laboratory**

82595    Cryoglobulin, qualitative or semi-quantitative (eg, cryocrit)

(For quantitative, cryoglobulin, see 82784, 82785)

(Crystals, pyrophosphate vs urate, use 89060)

82600    Cyanide

82607    Cyanocobalamin (Vitamin B-12);

82608        unsaturated binding capacity

(Cyclic AMP, use 82030)

(Cyclic GMP, use 83008)

(Cyclosporine, use 80158)

82610    Cystatin C

82615    Cystine and homocystine, urine, qualitative

82626    Dehydroepiandrosterone (DHEA)

82627    Dehydroepiandrosterone-sulfate (DHEA-S)

(Delta-aminolevulinic acid (ALA), use 82135)

82633    Desoxycorticosterone, 11-

82634    Deoxycortisol, 11-

(Dexamethasone suppression test, use 80420)

(Diastase, urine, use 82150)

82638    Dibucaine number

(Dichloroethane, use 84600)

(Dichloromethane, use 84600)

(Diethylether, use 84600)

82646    Dihydrocodeinone

(For qualitative analysis, see 80100-80103)

82649    Dihydromorphinone

(For qualitative analysis, see 80100-80103)

82651    Dihydrotestosterone (DHT)

82652    Code is out of numerical sequence. See 82000-84999

82654    Dimethadione

(For qualitative analysis, see 80100-80103)

(Diphenylhydantoin, use 80185)

(Dipropylacetic acid, use 80164)

(Dopamine, see 82382-82384)

(Duodenal contents, see individual enzymes; for intubation and collection, see 43756, 43757)

82656    Elastase, pancreatic (EL-1), fecal, qualitative or semi-quantitative

82657    Enzyme activity in blood cells, cultured cells, or tissue, not elsewhere specified; nonradioactive substrate, each specimen

82658        radioactive substrate, each specimen

82664    Electrophoretic technique, not elsewhere specified

(Endocrine receptor assays, see 84233-84235)

82666    Epiandrosterone

(Epinephrine, see 82382-82384)

82668    Erythropoietin

82670    Estradiol

82671    Estrogens; fractionated

82672        total

(Estrogen receptor assay, use 84233)

82677    Estriol

82679    Estrone

(Ethanol, see 82055 and 82075)

82690    Ethchlorvynol

(Ethyl alcohol, see 82055 and 82075)

82693    Ethylene glycol

82696    Etiocholanolone

(For fractionation of ketosteroids, use 83593)

82705    Fat or lipids, feces; qualitative

82710        quantitative

82715    Fat differential, feces, quantitative

82725    Fatty acids, nonesterified

82726    Very long chain fatty acids

(For long-chain [C20-22] omega-3 fatty acids in red blood cell [RBC] membranes, use Category III code 0111T)

82728    Ferritin

(Fetal hemoglobin, see hemoglobin 83030, 83033, and 85460)

(Fetoprotein, alpha-1, see 82105, 82106)

82731    Fetal fibronectin, cervicovaginal secretions, semi-quantitative

82735    Fluoride

82742    Flurazepam

(For qualitative analysis, see 80100-80103)

(Foam stability test, use 83662)

82746    Folic acid; serum

82747        RBC

(Follicle stimulating hormone [FSH], use 83001)

82757    Fructose, semen

(Fructosamine, use 82985)

(Fructose, TLC screen, use 84375)

82759    Galactokinase, RBC

82760    Galactose

82775    Galactose-1-phosphate uridyl transferase; quantitative

⊙=Moderate sedation    ✚=Add-on code    ✗=FDA approval pending    #=Resequenced code    ○=Recycled/reinstated code

| | |
|---|---|
| **82776** | screen |
| **82777** | Galectin-3 |
| **82784** | Gammaglobulin (immunoglobulin); IgA, IgD, IgG, IgM, each |
| **82785** | IgE |
| | (For allergen specific IgE, see 86003, 86005) |
| **82787** | immunoglobulin subclasses (eg, IgG1, 2, 3, or 4), each |
| | (Gamma-glutamyltransferase [GGT], use 82977) |
| **82800** | Gases, blood, pH only |
| **82803** | Gases, blood, any combination of pH, pCO2, pO2, CO2, HCO3 (including calculated O2 saturation); |
| | (Use 82803 for 2 or more of the above listed analytes) |
| **82805** | with O2 saturation, by direct measurement, except pulse oximetry |
| **82810** | Gases, blood, O2 saturation only, by direct measurement, except pulse oximetry |
| | (For pulse oximetry, use 94760) |
| **82820** | Hemoglobin-oxygen affinity (pO2 for 50% hemoglobin saturation with oxygen) |
| | (82926, 82928 have been deleted) |
| | (For gastric acid analysis, use 82930) |
| **82930** | Gastric acid analysis, includes pH if performed, each specimen |
| **82938** | Gastrin after secretin stimulation |
| **82941** | Gastrin |
| | (Gentamicin, use 80170) |
| | (GGT, use 82977) |
| | (GLC, gas liquid chromatography, use 82486) |
| **82943** | Glucagon |
| **82945** | Glucose, body fluid, other than blood |
| **82946** | Glucagon tolerance test |
| **82947** | Glucose; quantitative, blood (except reagent strip) |
| **82948** | blood, reagent strip |
| **82950** | post glucose dose (includes glucose) |
| **82951** | tolerance test (GTT), 3 specimens (includes glucose) |
| **+ 82952** | tolerance test, each additional beyond 3 specimens (List separately in addition to code for primary procedure) |
| | (Use 82952 in conjunction with 82951) |
| **82953** | tolbutamide tolerance test |
| | (For insulin tolerance test, see 80434, 80435) |
| | (For leucine tolerance test, use 80428) |
| | (For semiquantitative urine glucose, see 81000, 81002, 81005, 81099) |

| | |
|---|---|
| **82955** | Glucose-6-phosphate dehydrogenase (G6PD); quantitative |
| **82960** | screen |
| | (For glucose tolerance test with medication, use 96374 in addition) |
| **82962** | Glucose, blood by glucose monitoring device(s) cleared by the FDA specifically for home use |
| **82963** | Glucosidase, beta |
| **82965** | Glutamate dehydrogenase |
| **82975** | Glutamine (glutamic acid amide) |
| **82977** | Glutamyltransferase, gamma (GGT) |
| **82978** | Glutathione |
| **82979** | Glutathione reductase, RBC |
| **82980** | Glutethimide |
| | (Glycohemoglobin, use 83036) |
| **82985** | Glycated protein |
| | (Gonadotropin, chorionic, see 84702, 84703) |
| **83001** | Gonadotropin; follicle stimulating hormone (FSH) |
| **83002** | luteinizing hormone (LH) |
| | (For luteinizing releasing factor [LRH], use 83727) |
| **83003** | Growth hormone, human (HGH) (somatotropin) |
| | (For antibody to human growth hormone, use 86277) |
| **83008** | Guanosine monophosphate (GMP), cyclic |
| **83009** | Helicobacter pylori, blood test analysis for urease activity, non-radioactive isotope (eg, C-13) |
| | (For H. pylori, breath test analysis for urease activity, see 83013, 83014) |
| **83010** | Haptoglobin; quantitative |
| **83012** | phenotypes |
| **83013** | Helicobacter pylori; breath test analysis for urease activity, non-radioactive isotope (eg, C-13) |
| **83014** | drug administration |
| | (For H. pylori, stool, use 87338. For H. pylori, liquid scintillation counter, see 78267, 78268. For H. pylori, enzyme immunoassay, use 87339) |
| | (For H. pylori, blood test analysis for urease activity, use 83009) |
| **83015** | Heavy metal (eg, arsenic, barium, beryllium, bismuth, antimony, mercury); screen |
| **83018** | quantitative, each |
| **83020** | Hemoglobin fractionation and quantitation; electrophoresis (eg, A2, S, C, and/or F) |
| **83021** | chromatography (eg, A2, S, C, and/or F) |
| | (For glycosylated [A1c] hemoglobin analysis, by chromatography, in the absence of an identified hemoglobin variant, use 83036) |

**Pathology and Laboratory**

| | | |
|---|---|---|
| 83026 | Hemoglobin; by copper sulfate method, non-automated | |
| 83030 | F (fetal), chemical | |
| 83033 | F (fetal), qualitative | |
| 83036 | glycosylated (A1C) | |

(For glycosylated [A1C] hemoglobin analysis, by chromatography, in the setting of an identified hemoglobin variant, use 83021)

(For fecal hemoglobin detection by immunoassay, use 82274)

| | |
|---|---|
| 83037 | glycosylated (A1C) by device cleared by FDA for home use |
| 83045 | methemoglobin, qualitative |
| 83050 | methemoglobin, quantitative |

(For transcutaneous quantitative methemoglobin determination, use 88741)

| | |
|---|---|
| 83051 | plasma |
| 83055 | sulfhemoglobin, qualitative |
| 83060 | sulfhemoglobin, quantitative |
| 83065 | thermolabile |
| 83068 | unstable, screen |
| 83069 | urine |
| 83070 | Hemosiderin; qualitative |
| 83071 | quantitative |

(Heroin, see 80100-80103)

(HIAA, use 83497)

(High performance liquid chromatography [HPLC], use 82486)

| | |
|---|---|
| 83080 | b-Hexosaminidase, each assay |
| 83088 | Histamine |

(Hollander test, see 43754, 43755)

| | |
|---|---|
| 83090 | Homocysteine |
| 83150 | Homovanillic acid (HVA) |

(Hormones, see individual alphabetic listings in **Chemistry** section)

►(For hydrogen/methane breath test, use 91065)◄

| | |
|---|---|
| 83491 | Hydroxycorticosteroids, 17- (17-OHCS) |

(For cortisol, see 82530, 82533. For deoxycortisol, use 82634)

| | |
|---|---|
| 83497 | Hydroxyindolacetic acid, 5-(HIAA) |

(For urine qualitative test, use 81005)

(5-Hydroxytryptamine, use 84260)

| | |
|---|---|
| 83498 | Hydroxyprogesterone, 17-d |
| 83499 | Hydroxyprogesterone, 20- |

| | |
|---|---|
| 83500 | Hydroxyproline; free |
| 83505 | total |
| 83516 | Immunoassay for analyte other than infectious agent antibody or infectious agent antigen; qualitative or semiquantitative, multiple step method |
| 83518 | qualitative or semiquantitative, single step method (eg, reagent strip) |
| 83519 | quantitative, by radioimmunoassay (eg, RIA) |
| 83520 | quantitative, not otherwise specified |

(For immunoassays for antibodies to infectious agent antigens, see analyte and method specific codes in the **Immunology** section)

(For immunoassay of tumor antigen not elsewhere specified, use 86316)

(Immunoglobulins, see 82784, 82785)

| | |
|---|---|
| 83525 | Insulin; total |

(For proinsulin, use 84206)

| | |
|---|---|
| 83527 | free |
| 83528 | Intrinsic factor |

(For intrinsic factor antibodies, use 86340)

| | |
|---|---|
| 83540 | Iron |
| 83550 | Iron binding capacity |
| 83570 | Isocitric dehydrogenase (IDH) |

(Isonicotinic acid hydrazide, INH, see code for specific method)

(Isopropyl alcohol, use 84600)

| | |
|---|---|
| 83582 | Ketogenic steroids, fractionation |

(Ketone bodies, for serum, see 82009, 82010; for urine, see 81000-81003)

| | |
|---|---|
| 83586 | Ketosteroids, 17- (17-KS); total |
| 83593 | fractionation |
| 83605 | Lactate (lactic acid) |
| 83615 | Lactate dehydrogenase (LD), (LDH); |
| 83625 | isoenzymes, separation and quantitation |
| 83630 | Lactoferrin, fecal; qualitative |
| 83631 | quantitative |
| 83632 | Lactogen, human placental (HPL) human chorionic somatomammotropin |
| 83633 | Lactose, urine; qualitative |
| 83634 | quantitative |

(For tolerance, see 82951, 82952)

►(For breath hydrogen/methane test for lactase deficiency, use 91065)◄

| | |
|---|---|
| 83655 | Lead |

**83661**    Fetal lung maturity assessment; lecithin sphingomyelin (L/S) ratio

**83662**        foam stability test

**83663**        fluorescence polarization

**83664**        lamellar body density

        (For phosphatidylglycerol, use 84081)

**83670**    Leucine aminopeptidase (LAP)

**83690**    Lipase

**83695**    Lipoprotein (a)

**83698**    Lipoprotein-associated phospholipase A2 (Lp-PLA2)

**83700**    Lipoprotein, blood; electrophoretic separation and quantitation

**83701**        high resolution fractionation and quantitation of lipoproteins including lipoprotein subclasses when performed (eg, electrophoresis, ultracentrifugation)

**83704**        quantitation of lipoprotein particle numbers and lipoprotein particle subclasses (eg, by nuclear magnetic resonance spectroscopy)

**83718**    Lipoprotein, direct measurement; high density cholesterol (HDL cholesterol)

**83719**        VLDL cholesterol

**83721**        LDL cholesterol

        (For fractionation by high resolution electrophoresis or ultracentrifugation, use 83701)

        (For lipoprotein particle numbers and subclasses analysis by nuclear magnetic resonance spectroscopy, use 83704)

**83727**    Luteinizing releasing factor (LRH)

        (Luteinizing hormone [LH], use 83002)

        (For qualitative analysis, see 80100-80103)

        (Macroglobulins, alpha-2, use 86329)

**83735**    Magnesium

**83775**    Malate dehydrogenase

        (Maltose tolerance, see 82951, 82952)

        (Mammotropin, use 84146)

**83785**    Manganese

        (Marijuana, see 80100-80103)

**83788**    Mass spectrometry and tandem mass spectrometry (MS, MS/MS), analyte not elsewhere specified; qualitative, each specimen

**83789**        quantitative, each specimen

**83805**    Meprobamate

        (For qualitative analysis, see 80100-80103)

**83825**    Mercury, quantitative

        (Mercury screen, use 83015)

**83835**    Metanephrines

        (For catecholamines, see 82382-82384)

**83840**    Methadone

        (For methadone qualitative analysis, see 80100-80103)

        (Methamphetamine, see 80100-80103, 82145)

        ▶(Methane breath test, use 91065)◀

        (Methanol, use 84600)

**83857**    Methemalbumin

        (Methemoglobin, see hemoglobin 83045, 83050)

**83858**    Methsuximide

        (Methyl alcohol, use 84600)

        (Microalbumin, see 82043 for quantitative, see 82044 for semiquantitative)

**83861**    Microfluidic analysis utilizing an integrated collection and analysis device, tear osmolarity

        (Microglobulin, beta-2, use 82232)

        (For microfluidic tear osmolarity of both eyes, report 83861 twice)

**83864**    Mucopolysaccharides, acid; quantitative

**83866**        screen

**83872**    Mucin, synovial fluid (Ropes test)

**83873**    Myelin basic protein, cerebrospinal fluid

        (For oligoclonal bands, use 83916)

**83874**    Myoglobin

        (Nalorphine, use 83925)

**83876**    Myeloperoxidase (MPO)

**83880**    Natriuretic peptide

**83883**    Nephelometry, each analyte not elsewhere specified

**83885**    Nickel

**83887**    Nicotine

        (83890-83914 have been deleted. To report, see 81161, 81200-81479)

**83915**    Nucleotidase 5'-

**83916**    Oligoclonal immune (oligoclonal bands)

**83918**    Organic acids; total, quantitative, each specimen

**83919**        qualitative, each specimen

**83921**    Organic acid, single, quantitative

**83925**    Opiate(s), drug and metabolites, each procedure

**83930**    Osmolality; blood

**83935**        urine

        (For tear osmolarity using microfluidic analysis, use 83861)

**83937**    Osteocalcin (bone g1a protein)

**Pathology and Laboratory**

| | |
|---|---|
| 83945 | Oxalate |
| 83950 | Oncoprotein; HER-2/neu |
| | ▶(For tissue, see 88342, 88343, 88365)◀ |
| 83951 | des-gamma-carboxy-prothrombin (DCP) |
| 83970 | Parathormone (parathyroid hormone) |
| | (Pesticide, quantitative, see code for specific method. For screen for chlorinated hydrocarbons, use 82441) |
| 83986 | pH; body fluid, not otherwise specified |
| 83987 | exhaled breath condensate |
| | (For blood pH, see 82800, 82803) |
| 83992 | Phencyclidine (PCP) |
| | (For qualitative analysis, see 80100-80103) |
| | (Phenobarbital, use 80184) |
| 83993 | Calprotectin, fecal |
| 84022 | Phenothiazine |
| | (For qualitative analysis, see 80100, 80101) |
| 84030 | Phenylalanine (PKU), blood |
| | (Phenylalanine-tyrosine ratio, see 84030, 84510) |
| 84035 | Phenylketones, qualitative |
| 84060 | Phosphatase, acid; total |
| 84061 | forensic examination |
| 84066 | prostatic |
| 84075 | Phosphatase, alkaline; |
| 84078 | heat stable (total not included) |
| 84080 | isoenzymes |
| 84081 | Phosphatidylglycerol |
| | (Phosphates inorganic, use 84100) |
| | (Phosphates, organic, see code for specific method. For cholinesterase, see 82480, 82482) |
| 84085 | Phosphogluconate, 6-, dehydrogenase, RBC |
| 84087 | Phosphohexose isomerase |
| 84100 | Phosphorus inorganic (phosphate); |
| 84105 | urine |
| | (Pituitary gonadotropins, see 83001-83002) |
| | (PKU, see 84030, 84035) |
| 84106 | Porphobilinogen, urine; qualitative |
| 84110 | quantitative |
| ▲ 84112 | Evaluation of cervicovaginal fluid for specific amniotic fluid protein(s) (eg, placental alpha microglobulin-1 [PAMG-1], placental protein 12 [PP12], alpha-fetoprotein), qualitative, each specimen |
| 84119 | Porphyrins, urine; qualitative |
| 84120 | quantitation and fractionation |

| | |
|---|---|
| 84126 | Porphyrins, feces; quantitative |
| 84127 | qualitative |
| | (Porphyrin precursors, see 82135, 84106, 84110) |
| | (For protoporphyrin, RBC, see 84202, 84203) |
| 84132 | Potassium; serum, plasma or whole blood |
| 84133 | urine |
| 84134 | Prealbumin |
| | (For microalbumin, see 82043, 82044) |
| 84135 | Pregnanediol |
| 84138 | Pregnanetriol |
| 84140 | Pregnenolone |
| 84143 | 17-hydroxypregnenolone |
| 84144 | Progesterone |
| | (Progesterone receptor assay, use 84234) |
| | (For proinsulin, use 84206) |
| 84145 | Procalcitonin (PCT) |
| 84146 | Prolactin |
| 84150 | Prostaglandin, each |
| 84152 | Prostate specific antigen (PSA); complexed (direct measurement) |
| 84153 | total |
| 84154 | free |
| 84155 | Protein, total, except by refractometry; serum, plasma or whole blood |
| 84156 | urine |
| 84157 | other source (eg, synovial fluid, cerebrospinal fluid) |
| 84160 | Protein, total, by refractometry, any source |
| | (For urine total protein by dipstick method, use 81000-81003) |
| 84163 | Pregnancy-associated plasma protein-A (PAPP-A) |
| 84165 | Protein; electrophoretic fractionation and quantitation, serum |
| 84166 | electrophoretic fractionation and quantitation, other fluids with concentration (eg, urine, CSF) |
| 84181 | Western Blot, with interpretation and report, blood or other body fluid |
| 84182 | Western Blot, with interpretation and report, blood or other body fluid, immunological probe for band identification, each |
| | (For Western Blot tissue analysis, use 88371) |
| 84202 | Protoporphyrin, RBC; quantitative |
| 84203 | screen |
| 84206 | Proinsulin |
| | (Pseudocholinesterase, use 82480) |

Pathology and Laboratory

| | |
|---|---|
| **84207** | Pyridoxal phosphate (Vitamin B-6) |
| **84210** | Pyruvate |
| **84220** | Pyruvate kinase |
| **84228** | Quinine |
| **84233** | Receptor assay; estrogen |
| **84234** | progesterone |
| **84235** | endocrine, other than estrogen or progesterone (specify hormone) |
| **84238** | non-endocrine (specify receptor) |
| **84244** | Renin |
| **84252** | Riboflavin (Vitamin B-2) |

(Salicylates, use 80196)

(Secretin test, see 99070, 43756, 43757 and appropriate analyses)

| | |
|---|---|
| **84255** | Selenium |
| **84260** | Serotonin |

(For urine metabolites (HIAA), use 83497)

| | |
|---|---|
| **84270** | Sex hormone binding globulin (SHBG) |
| **84275** | Sialic acid |

(Sickle hemoglobin, use 85660)

| | |
|---|---|
| **84285** | Silica |
| **84295** | Sodium; serum, plasma or whole blood |
| **84300** | urine |
| **84302** | other source |

(Somatomammotropin, use 83632)

(Somatotropin, use 83003)

| | |
|---|---|
| **84305** | Somatomedin |
| **84307** | Somatostatin |
| **84311** | Spectrophotometry, analyte not elsewhere specified |
| **84315** | Specific gravity (except urine) |

(For specific gravity, urine, see 81000-81003)

(Stone analysis, see 82355-82370)

| | |
|---|---|
| **84375** | Sugars, chromatographic, TLC or paper chromatography |
| **84376** | Sugars (mono-, di-, and oligosaccharides); single qualitative, each specimen |
| **84377** | multiple qualitative, each specimen |
| **84378** | single quantitative, each specimen |
| **84379** | multiple quantitative, each specimen |
| **84392** | Sulfate, urine |

(Sulfhemoglobin, see hemoglobin, 83055, 83060)

(T-3, see 84479-84481)

(T-4, see 84436-84439)

| | |
|---|---|
| **84402** | Testosterone; free |
| **84403** | total |
| **84425** | Thiamine (Vitamin B-1) |
| **84430** | Thiocyanate |
| **84431** | Thromboxane metabolite(s), including thromboxane if performed, urine |

(For concurrent urine creatinine determination, use 84431 in conjunction with 82570)

| | |
|---|---|
| **84432** | Thyroglobulin |

(Thyroglobulin, antibody, use 86800)

(Thyrotropin releasing hormone [TRH] test, see 80438, 80439)

| | |
|---|---|
| **84436** | Thyroxine; total |
| **84437** | requiring elution (eg, neonatal) |
| **84439** | free |
| **84442** | Thyroxine binding globulin (TBG) |
| **84443** | Thyroid stimulating hormone (TSH) |
| **84445** | Thyroid stimulating immune globulins (TSI) |

(Tobramycin, use 80200)

| | |
|---|---|
| **84446** | Tocopherol alpha (Vitamin E) |

(Tolbutamide tolerance, use 82953)

| | |
|---|---|
| **84449** | Transcortin (cortisol binding globulin) |
| **84450** | Transferase; aspartate amino (AST) (SGOT) |
| **84460** | alanine amino (ALT) (SGPT) |
| **84466** | Transferrin |

(Iron binding capacity, use 83550)

| | |
|---|---|
| **84478** | Triglycerides |
| **84479** | Thyroid hormone (T3 or T4) uptake or thyroid hormone binding ratio (THBR) |
| **84480** | Triiodothyronine T3; total (TT-3) |
| **84481** | free |
| **84482** | reverse |
| **84484** | Troponin, quantitative |

(For troponin, qualitative assay, use 84512)

| | |
|---|---|
| **84485** | Trypsin; duodenal fluid |
| **84488** | feces, qualitative |
| **84490** | feces, quantitative, 24-hour collection |
| **84510** | Tyrosine |

(Urate crystal identification, use 89060)

| | |
|---|---|
| **84512** | Troponin, qualitative |

(For troponin, quantitative assay, use 84484)

| | |
|---|---|
| **84520** | Urea nitrogen; quantitative |
| **84525** | semiquantitative (eg, reagent strip test) |

**Pathology and Laboratory**

---

| | |
|---|---|
| 84540 | Urea nitrogen, urine |
| 84545 | Urea nitrogen, clearance |
| 84550 | Uric acid; blood |
| 84560 | other source |
| 84577 | Urobilinogen, feces, quantitative |
| 84578 | Urobilinogen, urine; qualitative |
| 84580 | quantitative, timed specimen |
| 84583 | semiquantitative |

(Uroporphyrins, use 84120)

(Valproic acid [dipropylacetic acid], use 80164)

| | |
|---|---|
| 84585 | Vanillylmandelic acid (VMA), urine |
| 84586 | Vasoactive intestinal peptide (VIP) |
| 84588 | Vasopressin (antidiuretic hormone, ADH) |
| 84590 | Vitamin A |

(Vitamin B-1, use 84425)

(Vitamin B-2, use 84252)

(Vitamin B-6, use 84207)

(Vitamin B-12, use 82607)

(Vitamin B-12, absorption (Schilling), see 78270, 78271)

(Vitamin C, use 82180)

(Vitamin D, see 82306, 82652)

(Vitamin E, use 84446)

| | |
|---|---|
| 84591 | Vitamin, not otherwise specified |
| 84597 | Vitamin K |

(VMA, use 84585)

| | |
|---|---|
| 84600 | Volatiles (eg, acetic anhydride, carbon tetrachloride, dichloroethane, dichloromethane, diethylether, isopropyl alcohol, methanol) |

(For acetaldehyde, use 82000)

(Volume, blood, RISA or Cr-51, see 78110, 78111)

| | |
|---|---|
| 84620 | Xylose absorption test, blood and/or urine |

(For administration, use 99070)

| | |
|---|---|
| 84630 | Zinc |
| 84681 | C-peptide |
| 84702 | Gonadotropin, chorionic (hCG); quantitative |
| 84703 | qualitative |

(For urine pregnancy test by visual color comparison, use 81025)

| | |
|---|---|
| 84704 | free beta chain |
| 84830 | Ovulation tests, by visual color comparison methods for human luteinizing hormone |
| 84999 | Unlisted chemistry procedure |

# Hematology and Coagulation

(For blood banking procedures, see **Transfusion Medicine**)

(Agglutinins, see **Immunology**)

(Antiplasmin, use 85410)

(Antithrombin III, see 85300, 85301)

| | |
|---|---|
| 85002 | Bleeding time |
| 85004 | Blood count; automated differential WBC count |
| 85007 | blood smear, microscopic examination with manual differential WBC count |
| 85008 | blood smear, microscopic examination without manual differential WBC count |

(For other fluids [eg, CSF], see 89050, 89051)

| | |
|---|---|
| 85009 | manual differential WBC count, buffy coat |

(Eosinophils, nasal smear, use 89190)

| | |
|---|---|
| 85013 | spun microhematocrit |
| 85014 | hematocrit (Hct) |
| 85018 | hemoglobin (Hgb) |

(For other hemoglobin determination, see 83020-83069)

(For immunoassay, hemoglobin, fecal, use 82274)

(For transcutaneous hemoglobin measurement, use 88738)

| | |
|---|---|
| 85025 | complete (CBC), automated (Hgb, Hct, RBC, WBC and platelet count) and automated differential WBC count |
| 85027 | complete (CBC), automated (Hgb, Hct, RBC, WBC and platelet count) |
| 85032 | manual cell count (erythrocyte, leukocyte, or platelet) each |
| 85041 | red blood cell (RBC), automated |

(Do not report code 85041 in conjunction with 85025 or 85027)

| | |
|---|---|
| 85044 | reticulocyte, manual |
| 85045 | reticulocyte, automated |
| 85046 | reticulocytes, automated, including 1 or more cellular parameters (eg, reticulocyte hemoglobin content [CHr], immature reticulocyte fraction [IRF], reticulocyte volume [MRV], RNA content), direct measurement |
| 85048 | leukocyte (WBC), automated |
| 85049 | platelet, automated |
| 85055 | Reticulated platelet assay |
| 85060 | Blood smear, peripheral, interpretation by physician with written report |

---

**85097** Bone marrow, smear interpretation

(For special stains, see 88312, 88313)

(For bone biopsy, see 20220, 20225, 20240, 20245, 20250, 20251)

**85130** Chromogenic substrate assay

(Circulating anti-coagulant screen [mixing studies], see 85611, 85732)

**85170** Clot retraction

**85175** Clot lysis time, whole blood dilution

(Clotting factor I [fibrinogen], see 85384, 85385)

**85210** Clotting; factor II, prothrombin, specific

(See also 85610-85613)

**85220**      factor V (AcG or proaccelerin), labile factor

**85230**      factor VII (proconvertin, stable factor)

**85240**      factor VIII (AHG), 1-stage

**85244**      factor VIII related antigen

**85245**      factor VIII, VW factor, ristocetin cofactor

**85246**      factor VIII, VW factor antigen

**85247**      factor VIII, von Willebrand factor, multimetric analysis

**85250**      factor IX (PTC or Christmas)

**85260**      factor X (Stuart-Prower)

**85270**      factor XI (PTA)

**85280**      factor XII (Hageman)

**85290**      factor XIII (fibrin stabilizing)

**85291**      factor XIII (fibrin stabilizing), screen solubility

**85292**      prekallikrein assay (Fletcher factor assay)

**85293**      high molecular weight kininogen assay (Fitzgerald factor assay)

**85300** Clotting inhibitors or anticoagulants; antithrombin III, activity

**85301**      antithrombin III, antigen assay

**85302**      protein C, antigen

**85303**      protein C, activity

**85305**      protein S, total

**85306**      protein S, free

**85307** Activated Protein C (APC) resistance assay

**85335** Factor inhibitor test

**85337** Thrombomodulin

(For mixing studies for inhibitors, use 85732)

**85345** Coagulation time; Lee and White

**85347**      activated

**85348**      other methods

(Differential count, see 85007 et seq)

(Duke bleeding time, use 85002)

(Eosinophils, nasal smear, use 89190)

**85360** Euglobulin lysis

(Fetal hemoglobin, see 83030, 83033, 85460)

**85362** Fibrin(ogen) degradation (split) products (FDP) (FSP); agglutination slide, semiquantitative

(Immunoelectrophoresis, use 86320)

**85366**      paracoagulation

**85370**      quantitative

**85378** Fibrin degradation products, D-dimer; qualitative or semiquantitative

**85379**      quantitative

(For ultrasensitive and standard sensitivity quantitative D-dimer, use 85379)

**85380**      ultrasensitive (eg, for evaluation for venous thromboembolism), qualitative or semiquantitative

**85384** Fibrinogen; activity

**85385**      antigen

**85390** Fibrinolysins or coagulopathy screen, interpretation and report

**85396** Coagulation/fibrinolysis assay, whole blood (eg, viscoelastic clot assessment), including use of any pharmacologic additive(s), as indicated, including interpretation and written report, per day

**85397** Coagulation and fibrinolysis, functional activity, not otherwise specified (eg, ADAMTS-13), each analyte

**85400** Fibrinolytic factors and inhibitors; plasmin

**85410**      alpha-2 antiplasmin

**85415**      plasminogen activator

**85420**      plasminogen, except antigenic assay

**85421**      plasminogen, antigenic assay

(Fragility, red blood cell, see 85547, 85555-85557)

**85441** Heinz bodies; direct

**85445**      induced, acetyl phenylhydrazine

(Hematocrit [PCV], see 85014, 85025, 85027)

(Hemoglobin, see 83020-83068, 85018, 85025, 85027)

**85460** Hemoglobin or RBCs, fetal, for fetomaternal hemorrhage; differential lysis (Kleihauer-Betke)

(See also 83030, 83033)

(Hemolysins, see 86940, 86941)

**85461**      rosette

**85475** Hemolysin, acid

(See also 86940, 86941)

Pathology and Laboratory

| | |
|---|---|
| 85520 | Heparin assay |
| 85525 | Heparin neutralization |
| 85530 | Heparin-protamine tolerance test |
| 85536 | Iron stain, peripheral blood |

(For iron stains on bone marrow or other tissues with physician evaluation, use 88313)

| | |
|---|---|
| 85540 | Leukocyte alkaline phosphatase with count |
| 85547 | Mechanical fragility, RBC |
| 85549 | Muramidase |

(Nitroblue tetrazolium dye test, use 86384)

| | |
|---|---|
| 85555 | Osmotic fragility, RBC; unincubated |
| 85557 | incubated |

(Packed cell volume, use 85013)

(Partial thromboplastin time, see 85730, 85732)

(Parasites, blood [eg, malaria smears], use 87207)

(Plasmin, use 85400)

(Plasminogen, use 85420)

(Plasminogen activator, use 85415)

| | |
|---|---|
| 85576 | Platelet, aggregation (in vitro), each agent |

(For thromboxane metabolite[s], including thromboxane, if performed, measurement[s] in urine, use 84431)

| | |
|---|---|
| 85597 | Phospholipid neutralization; platelet |
| 85598 | hexagonal phospholipid |
| 85610 | Prothrombin time; |
| 85611 | substitution, plasma fractions, each |
| 85612 | Russell viper venom time (includes venom); undiluted |
| 85613 | diluted |

(Red blood cell count, see 85025, 85027, 85041)

| | |
|---|---|
| 85635 | Reptilase test |

(Reticulocyte count, see 85044, 85045)

| | |
|---|---|
| 85651 | Sedimentation rate, erythrocyte; non-automated |
| 85652 | automated |
| 85660 | Sickling of RBC, reduction |

(Hemoglobin electrophoresis, use 83020)

(Smears [eg, for parasites, malaria], use 87207)

| | |
|---|---|
| 85670 | Thrombin time; plasma |
| 85675 | titer |
| 85705 | Thromboplastin inhibition, tissue |

(For individual clotting factors, see 85245-85247)

| | |
|---|---|
| 85730 | Thromboplastin time, partial (PTT); plasma or whole blood |
| 85732 | substitution, plasma fractions, each |

| | |
|---|---|
| 85810 | Viscosity |

(von Willebrand factor assay, see 85245-85247)

(WBC count, see 85025, 85027, 85048, 89050)

| | |
|---|---|
| 85999 | Unlisted hematology and coagulation procedure |

# Immunology

(Acetylcholine receptor antibody, see 83519, 86255, 86256)

(Actinomyces, antibodies to, use 86602)

(Adrenal cortex antibodies, see 86255, 86256)

| | |
|---|---|
| 86000 | Agglutinins, febrile (eg, Brucella, Francisella, Murine typhus, Q fever, Rocky Mountain spotted fever, scrub typhus), each antigen |

(For antibodies to infectious agents, see 86602-86804)

| | |
|---|---|
| 86001 | Allergen specific IgG quantitative or semiquantitative, each allergen |

(Agglutinins and autohemolysins, see 86940, 86941)

| | |
|---|---|
| 86003 | Allergen specific IgE; quantitative or semiquantitative, each allergen |

(For total quantitative IgE, use 82785)

| | |
|---|---|
| 86005 | qualitative, multiallergen screen (dipstick, paddle, or disk) |

(For total qualitative IgE, use 83518)

(Alpha-1 antitrypsin, see 82103, 82104)

(Alpha-1 feto-protein, see 82105, 82106)

(Anti-AChR [acetylcholine receptor] antibody titer, see 86255, 86256)

(Anticardiolipin antibody, use 86147)

(Anti-DNA, use 86225)

(Anti-deoxyribonuclease titer, use 86215)

| | |
|---|---|
| 86021 | Antibody identification; leukocyte antibodies |
| 86022 | platelet antibodies |
| 86023 | platelet associated immunoglobulin assay |
| 86038 | Antinuclear antibodies (ANA); |
| 86039 | titer |

(Antistreptococcal antibody, ie, anti-DNAse, use 86215)

(Antistreptokinase titer, use 86590)

| | |
|---|---|
| 86060 | Antistreptolysin O; titer |

(For antibodies to infectious agents, see 86602-86804)

| | |
|---|---|
| 86063 | screen |

(For antibodies to infectious agents, see 86602-86804)

(Blastomyces, antibodies to, use 86612)

**86077** Blood bank physician services; difficult cross match and/or evaluation of irregular antibody(s), interpretation and written report

**86078** investigation of transfusion reaction including suspicion of transmissible disease, interpretation and written report

**86079** authorization for deviation from standard blood banking procedures (eg, use of outdated blood, transfusion of Rh incompatible units), with written report

(Brucella, antibodies to, use 86622)

(Candida, antibodies to, use 86628. For skin testing, use 86485)

**86140** C-reactive protein;

(Candidiasis, use 86628)

**86141** high sensitivity (hsCRP)

**86146** Beta 2 Glycoprotein I antibody, each

**86147** Cardiolipin (phospholipid) antibody, each Ig class

**# 86152** Cell enumeration using immunologic selection and identification in fluid specimen (eg, circulating tumor cells in blood);

(For physician interpretation and report, use 86153. For cell enumeration with interpretation and report, use 86152 and 86153)

**# 86153** physician interpretation and report, when required

(For cell enumeration, use 86152. For cell enumeration with interpretation and report, use 86152 and 86153)

(For flow cytometric immunophenotyping, see 88184-88189)

(For flow cytometric quantitation, see 86355, 86356, 86357, 86359, 86360, 86361, 86367)

**86148** Anti-phosphatidylserine (phospholipid) antibody

(To report antiprothrombin [phospholipid cofactor] antibody, use 86849)

**86152** Code is out of numerical sequence. See 86000-86804

**86153** Code is out of numerical sequence. See 86000-86804

**86155** Chemotaxis assay, specify method

(Clostridium difficile toxin, use 87230)

(Coccidioides, antibodies to, see 86635. For skin testing, use 86490)

**86156** Cold agglutinin; screen

**86157** titer

**86160** Complement; antigen, each component

**86161** functional activity, each component

**86162** total hemolytic (CH50)

**86171** Complement fixation tests, each antigen

(Coombs test, see 86880-86886)

**86185** Counterimmunoelectrophoresis, each antigen

(Cryptococcus, antibodies to, use 86641)

**86200** Cyclic citrullinated peptide (CCP), antibody

**86215** Deoxyribonuclease, antibody

**86225** Deoxyribonucleic acid (DNA) antibody; native or double stranded

(Echinococcus, antibodies to, see code for specific method)

(For HIV antibody tests, see 86701-86703)

**86226** single stranded

(Anti D.S., DNA, IFA, eg, using C.Lucilae, see 86255 and 86256)

**86235** Extractable nuclear antigen, antibody to, any method (eg, nRNP, SS-A, SS-B, Sm, RNP, Sc170, J01), each antibody

**86243** Fc receptor

(Filaria, antibodies to, see code for specific method)

**86255** Fluorescent noninfectious agent antibody; screen, each antibody

**86256** titer, each antibody

(Fluorescent technique for antigen identification in tissue, use 88346; for indirect fluorescence, use 88347)

(FTA, use 86780)

(Gel [agar] diffusion tests, use 86331)

**86277** Growth hormone, human (HGH), antibody

**86280** Hemagglutination inhibition test (HAI)

(For rubella, use 86762)

(For antibodies to infectious agents, see 86602-86804)

**86294** Immunoassay for tumor antigen, qualitative or semiquantitative (eg, bladder tumor antigen)

(For qualitative NMP22 protein, use 86386)

**86300** Immunoassay for tumor antigen, quantitative; CA 15-3 (27.29)

**86301** CA 19-9

**86304** CA 125

(For measurement of serum HER-2/neu oncoprotein, see 83950)

(For hepatitis delta agent, antibody, use 86692)

**86305** Human epididymis protein 4 (HE4)

**86308** Heterophile antibodies; screening

(For antibodies to infectious agents, see 86602-86804)

**86309** titer

(For antibodies to infectious agents, see 86602-86804)

Pathology and Laboratory

86310    titers after absorption with beef cells and guinea pig kidney

(Histoplasma, antibodies to, use 86698. For skin testing, use 86510)

(For antibodies to infectious agents, see 86602-86804)

(Human growth hormone antibody, use 86277)

86316    Immunoassay for tumor antigen, other antigen, quantitative (eg, CA 50, 72-4, 549), each

86317    Immunoassay for infectious agent antibody, quantitative, not otherwise specified

(For immunoassay techniques for antigens, see 83516, 83518, 83519, 83520, 87301-87450, 87810-87899)

(For particle agglutination procedures, use 86403)

86318    Immunoassay for infectious agent antibody, qualitative or semiquantitative, single step method (eg, reagent strip)

86320    Immunoelectrophoresis; serum

86325    other fluids (eg, urine, cerebrospinal fluid) with concentration

86327    crossed (2-dimensional assay)

86329    Immunodiffusion; not elsewhere specified

86331    gel diffusion, qualitative (Ouchterlony), each antigen or antibody

86332    Immune complex assay

86334    Immunofixation electrophoresis; serum

86335    other fluids with concentration (eg, urine, CSF)

86336    Inhibin A

86337    Insulin antibodies

86340    Intrinsic factor antibodies

(Leptospira, antibodies to, use 86720)

(Leukoagglutinins, use 86021)

86341    Islet cell antibody

86343    Leukocyte histamine release test (LHR)

86344    Leukocyte phagocytosis

86352    Cellular function assay involving stimulation (eg, mitogen or antigen) and detection of biomarker (eg, ATP)

86353    Lymphocyte transformation, mitogen (phytomitogen) or antigen induced blastogenesis

(Malaria antibodies, use 86750)

(For cellular function assay involving stimulation and detection of biomarker, use 86352)

86355    B cells, total count

86356    Mononuclear cell antigen, quantitative (eg, flow cytometry), not otherwise specified, each antigen

(Do not report 88187-88189 for interpretation of 86355, 86356, 86357, 86359, 86360, 86361, 86367)

86357    Natural killer (NK) cells, total count

86359    T cells; total count

86360    absolute CD4 and CD8 count, including ratio

86361    absolute CD4 count

86367    Stem cells (ie, CD34), total count

(For flow cytometric immunophenotyping for the assessment of potential hematolymphoid neoplasia, see 88184-88189)

86376    Microsomal antibodies (eg, thyroid or liver-kidney), each

86378    Migration inhibitory factor test (MIF)

(Mitochondrial antibody, liver, see 86255, 86256)

(Mononucleosis, see 86308-86310)

86382    Neutralization test, viral

86384    Nitroblue tetrazolium dye test (NTD)

86386    Nuclear Matrix Protein 22 (NMP22), qualitative

(Ouchterlony diffusion, use 86331)

(Platelet antibodies, see 86022, 86023)

86403    Particle agglutination; screen, each antibody

86406    titer, each antibody

(Pregnancy test, see 84702, 84703)

(Rapid plasma reagin test (RPR), see 86592, 86593)

86430    Rheumatoid factor; qualitative

86431    quantitative

(Serologic test for syphilis, see 86592, 86593)

86480    Tuberculosis test, cell mediated immunity antigen response measurement; gamma interferon

86481    enumeration of gamma interferon-producing T-cells in cell suspension

86485    Skin test; candida

(For antibody, candida, use 86628)

86486    unlisted antigen, each

86490    coccidioidomycosis

86510    histoplasmosis

(For histoplasma, antibody, use 86698)

86580    tuberculosis, intradermal

(For tuberculosis test, cell mediated immunity measurement of gamma interferon antigen response, use 86480)

(For skin tests for allergy, see 95012-95199)

(Smooth muscle antibody, see 86255, 86256)

(Sporothrix, antibodies to, see code for specific method)

(For skin testing, unlisted antigen, use 86486. For flow cytometry, quantitative, not otherwise specified, use 86356)

| 86590 | Streptokinase, antibody |
|---|---|

(For antibodies to infectious agents, see 86602-86804)

(Streptolysin O antibody, see antistreptolysin O, 86060, 86063)

| 86592 | Syphilis test, non-treponemal antibody; qualitative (eg, VDRL, RPR, ART) |
|---|---|

(For antibodies to infectious agents, see 86602-86804)

| 86593 | quantitative |
|---|---|

(For antibodies to infectious agents, see 86602-86804)

(Tetanus antibody, use 86774)

(Thyroglobulin antibody, use 86800)

(Thyroglobulin, use 84432)

(Thyroid microsomal antibody, use 86376)

(For toxoplasma antibody, see 86777-86778)

The following codes (86602-86804) are qualitative or semiquantitative immunoassays performed by multiple-step methods for the detection of antibodies to infectious agents. For immunoassays by single-step method (eg, reagent strips), use code 86318. Procedures for the identification of antibodies should be coded as precisely as possible. For example, an antibody to a virus could be coded with increasing specificity for virus, family, genus, species, or type. In some cases, further precision may be added to codes by specifying the class of immunoglobulin being detected. When multiple tests are done to detect antibodies to organisms classified more precisely than the specificity allowed by available codes, it is appropriate to code each as a separate service. For example, a test for antibody to an enterovirus is coded as 86658. Coxsackie viruses are enteroviruses, but there are no codes for the individual species of enterovirus. If assays are performed for antibodies to coxsackie A and B species, each assay should be separately coded. Similarly, if multiple assays are performed for antibodies of different immunoglobulin classes, each assay should be coded separately. When a coding option exists for reporting IgM specific antibodies (eg, 86632), the corresponding nonspecific code (eg, 86631) may be reported for performance of either an antibody analysis not specific for a particular immunoglobulin class or for an IgG analysis.

(For the detection of antibodies other than those to infectious agents, see specific antibody [eg, 86021-86023, 86376, 86800, 86850-86870] or specific method [eg, 83516, 86255, 86256]).

(For infectious agent/antigen detection, see 87260-87899)

| 86602 | Antibody; actinomyces |
|---|---|
| 86603 | adenovirus |
| 86606 | Aspergillus |
| 86609 | bacterium, not elsewhere specified |
| 86611 | Bartonella |
| 86612 | Blastomyces |
| 86615 | Bordetella |
| 86617 | Borrelia burgdorferi (Lyme disease) confirmatory test (eg, Western Blot or immunoblot) |
| 86618 | Borrelia burgdorferi (Lyme disease) |
| 86619 | Borrelia (relapsing fever) |
| 86622 | Brucella |
| 86625 | Campylobacter |
| 86628 | Candida |

(For skin test, candida, use 86485)

| 86631 | Chlamydia |
|---|---|
| 86632 | Chlamydia, IgM |

(For chlamydia antigen, see 87270, 87320. For fluorescent antibody technique, see 86255, 86256)

| 86635 | Coccidioides |
|---|---|
| 86638 | Coxiella burnetii (Q fever) |
| 86641 | Cryptococcus |
| 86644 | cytomegalovirus (CMV) |
| 86645 | cytomegalovirus (CMV), IgM |
| 86648 | Diphtheria |
| 86651 | encephalitis, California (La Crosse) |
| 86652 | encephalitis, Eastern equine |
| 86653 | encephalitis, St. Louis |
| 86654 | encephalitis, Western equine |
| 86658 | enterovirus (eg, coxsackie, echo, polio) |

(Trichinella, antibodies to, use 86784)

(Trypanosoma, antibodies to, see code for specific method)

(Tuberculosis, use 86580 for skin testing)

(Viral antibodies, see code for specific method)

| 86663 | Epstein-Barr (EB) virus, early antigen (EA) |
|---|---|
| 86664 | Epstein-Barr (EB) virus, nuclear antigen (EBNA) |
| 86665 | Epstein-Barr (EB) virus, viral capsid (VCA) |
| 86666 | Ehrlichia |
| 86668 | Francisella tularensis |
| 86671 | fungus, not elsewhere specified |
| 86674 | Giardia lamblia |
| 86677 | Helicobacter pylori |
| 86682 | helminth, not elsewhere specified |
| 86684 | Haemophilus influenza |
| 86687 | HTLV-I |
| 86688 | HTLV-II |

**Pathology and Laboratory**

| 86689 | HTLV or HIV antibody, confirmatory test (eg, Western Blot) |
|---|---|
| 86692 | hepatitis, delta agent |

(For hepatitis delta agent, antigen, use 87380)

| 86694 | herpes simplex, non-specific type test |
|---|---|
| 86695 | herpes simplex, type 1 |
| 86696 | herpes simplex, type 2 |
| 86698 | histoplasma |
| 86701 | HIV-1 |
| 86702 | HIV-2 |
| 86703 | HIV-1 and HIV-2, single result |

(For HIV-1 antigen(s) with HIV-1 and HIV-2 antibodies, single result, use 87389)

(When HIV immunoassay [HIV testing 86701-86703 or 87389] is performed using a kit or transportable instrument that wholly or in part consists of a single use, disposable analytical chamber, the service may be identified by adding modifier 92 to the usual code)

(For HIV-1 antigen, use 87390)

(For HIV-2 antigen, use 87391)

(For confirmatory test for HIV antibody (eg, Western Blot), use 86689)

| 86704 | Hepatitis B core antibody (HBcAb); total |
|---|---|
| 86705 | IgM antibody |
| 86706 | Hepatitis B surface antibody (HBsAb) |
| 86707 | Hepatitis Be antibody (HBeAb) |
| 86708 | Hepatitis A antibody (HAAb); total |
| 86709 | IgM antibody |
| 86710 | Antibody; influenza virus |
| 86711 | JC (John Cunningham) virus |
| 86713 | Legionella |
| 86717 | Leishmania |
| 86720 | Leptospira |
| 86723 | Listeria monocytogenes |
| 86727 | lymphocytic choriomeningitis |
| 86729 | lymphogranuloma venereum |
| 86732 | mucormycosis |
| 86735 | mumps |
| 86738 | mycoplasma |
| 86741 | Neisseria meningitidis |
| 86744 | Nocardia |
| 86747 | parvovirus |
| 86750 | Plasmodium (malaria) |

| 86753 | protozoa, not elsewhere specified |
|---|---|
| 86756 | respiratory syncytial virus |
| 86757 | Rickettsia |
| 86759 | rotavirus |
| 86762 | rubella |
| 86765 | rubeola |
| 86768 | Salmonella |
| 86771 | Shigella |
| 86774 | tetanus |
| 86777 | Toxoplasma |
| 86778 | Toxoplasma, IgM |
| 86780 | Treponema pallidum |

(86781 has been deleted)

(For syphilis testing by non-treponemal antibody analysis, see 86592-86593)

| 86784 | Trichinella |
|---|---|
| 86787 | varicella-zoster |
| 86788 | West Nile virus, IgM |
| 86789 | West Nile virus |
| 86790 | virus, not elsewhere specified |
| 86793 | Yersinia |
| 86800 | Thyroglobulin antibody |

(For thyroglobulin, use 84432)

| 86803 | Hepatitis C antibody; |
|---|---|
| 86804 | confirmatory test (eg, immunoblot) |

# Tissue Typing

| 86805 | Lymphocytotoxicity assay, visual crossmatch; with titration |
|---|---|
| 86806 | without titration |
| 86807 | Serum screening for cytotoxic percent reactive antibody (PRA); standard method |
| 86808 | quick method |
| 86812 | HLA typing; A, B, or C (eg, A10, B7, B27), single antigen |
| 86813 | A, B, or C, multiple antigens |
| 86816 | DR/DQ, single antigen |
| 86817 | DR/DQ, multiple antigens |
| 86821 | lymphocyte culture, mixed (MLC) |
| 86822 | lymphocyte culture, primed (PLC) |

(For HLA typing by molecular pathology techniques, see 81370-81383)

| 86825 | Human leukocyte antigen (HLA) crossmatch, non cytotoxic (eg, using flow cytometry); first serum sample or dilution |
|---|---|

**+ 86826**    each additional serum sample or sample dilution (List separately in addition to primary procedure)

(Use 86826 in conjunction with 86825)

(Do not report 86825, 86826 in conjunction with 86355, 86359, 88184-88189 for antibody surface markers integral to crossmatch testing)

(For autologous HLA crossmatch, see 86825, 86826)

(For lymphocytotoxicity visual crossmatch, see 86805, 86806)

**86828**    Antibody to human leukocyte antigens (HLA), solid phase assays (eg, microspheres or beads, ELISA, flow cytometry); qualitative assessment of the presence or absence of antibody(ies) to HLA Class I and Class II HLA antigens

**86829**    qualitative assessment of the presence or absence of antibody(ies) to HLA Class I or Class II HLA antigens

(If solid phase testing is performed to assess presence or absence of antibody to both HLA classes, use 86828)

**86830**    antibody identification by qualitative panel using complete HLA phenotypes, HLA Class I

**86831**    antibody identification by qualitative panel using complete HLA phenotypes, HLA Class II

**86832**    high definition qualitative panel for identification of antibody specificities (eg, individual antigen per bead methodology), HLA Class I

**86833**    high definition qualitative panel for identification of antibody specificities (eg, individual antigen per bead methodology), HLA Class II

(If solid phase testing is performed to test for HLA Class I or II antibody after treatment [eg, to remove IgM antibodies or other interfering substances], report 86828-86833 once for each panel with the untreated serum and once for each panel with the treated serum)

**86834**    semi-quantitative panel (eg, titer), HLA Class I

**86835**    semi-quantitative panel (eg, titer), HLA Class II

**86849**    Unlisted immunology procedure

# Transfusion Medicine

(For apheresis, use 36511, 36512)

(For therapeutic phlebotomy, use 99195)

**86850**    Antibody screen, RBC, each serum technique

**86860**    Antibody elution (RBC), each elution

**86870**    Antibody identification, RBC antibodies, each panel for each serum technique

**86880**    Antihuman globulin test (Coombs test); direct, each antiserum

**86885**    indirect, qualitative, each reagent red cell

**86886**    indirect, each antibody titer

(For indirect antihuman globulin [Coombs] test for RBC antibody screening, use 86850)

(For indirect antihuman globulin [Coombs] test for RBC antibody identification using reagent red cell panels, use 86870)

**86890**    Autologous blood or component, collection processing and storage; predeposited

**86891**    intra- or postoperative salvage

**86900**    Blood typing; ABO

**86901**    Rh (D)

**86902**    antigen testing of donor blood using reagent serum, each antigen test

(If multiple blood units are tested for the same antigen, 86902 should be reported once for each antigen for each unit tested)

(86903 has been deleted. To report, use 86902)

**86904**    antigen screening for compatible unit using patient serum, per unit screened

**86905**    RBC antigens, other than ABO or Rh (D), each

**86906**    Rh phenotyping, complete

**86910**    Blood typing, for paternity testing, per individual; ABO, Rh and MN

**86911**    each additional antigen system

**86920**    Compatibility test each unit; immediate spin technique

**86921**    incubation technique

**86922**    antiglobulin technique

**86923**    electronic

(Do not use 86923 in conjunction with 86920-86922 for same unit crossmatch)

**86927**    Fresh frozen plasma, thawing, each unit

**86930**    Frozen blood, each unit; freezing (includes preparation)

**86931**    thawing

**86932**    freezing (includes preparation) and thawing

**86940**    Hemolysins and agglutinins; auto, screen, each

**86941**    incubated

**86945**    Irradiation of blood product, each unit

**86950**    Leukocyte transfusion

(For allogeneic lymphocyte infusion, use 38242)

(For leukapheresis, use 36511)

**86960**    Volume reduction of blood or blood product (eg, red blood cells or platelets), each unit

**86965**    Pooling of platelets or other blood products

(For injection(s) of platelet rich plasma, use 0232T)

**86970**  Pretreatment of RBCs for use in RBC antibody detection, identification, and/or compatibility testing; incubation with chemical agents or drugs, each

**86971**  incubation with enzymes, each

**86972**  by density gradient separation

**86975**  Pretreatment of serum for use in RBC antibody identification; incubation with drugs, each

**86976**  by dilution

**86977**  incubation with inhibitors, each

**86978**  by differential red cell absorption using patient RBCs or RBCs of known phenotype, each absorption

**86985**  Splitting of blood or blood products, each unit

**86999**  Unlisted transfusion medicine procedure

# Microbiology

Includes bacteriology, mycology, parasitology, and virology.

Presumptive identification of microorganisms is defined as identification by colony morphology, growth on selective media, Gram stains, or up to three tests (eg, catalase, oxidase, indole, urease). Definitive identification of microorganisms is defined as an identification to the genus or species level that requires additional tests (eg, biochemical panels, slide cultures). If additional studies involve molecular probes, nucleic acid sequencing, chromatography, or immunologic techniques, these should be separately coded using 87140-87158, in addition to definitive identification codes. The molecular diagnostic codes (eg, 81161, 81200-81408) are not to be used in combination with or instead of the procedures represented by 87140-87158. For multiple specimens/sites use modifier 59. For repeat laboratory tests performed on the same day, use modifier 91.

**87001**  Animal inoculation, small animal; with observation

**87003**  with observation and dissection

**87015**  Concentration (any type), for infectious agents

(Do not report 87015 in conjunction with 87177)

**87040**  Culture, bacterial; blood, aerobic, with isolation and presumptive identification of isolates (includes anaerobic culture, if appropriate)

**87045**  stool, aerobic, with isolation and preliminary examination (eg, KIA, LIA), Salmonella and Shigella species

**87046**  stool, aerobic, additional pathogens, isolation and presumptive identification of isolates, each plate

**87070**  any other source except urine, blood or stool, aerobic, with isolation and presumptive identification of isolates

(For urine, use 87088)

**87071**  quantitative, aerobic with isolation and presumptive identification of isolates, any source except urine, blood or stool

(For urine, use 87088)

**87073**  quantitative, anaerobic with isolation and presumptive identification of isolates, any source except urine, blood or stool

(For definitive identification of isolates, use 87076 or 87077. For typing of isolates see 87140-87158)

**87075**  any source, except blood, anaerobic with isolation and presumptive identification of isolates

**87076**  anaerobic isolate, additional methods required for definitive identification, each isolate

**87077**  aerobic isolate, additional methods required for definitive identification, each isolate

**87081**  Culture, presumptive, pathogenic organisms, screening only;

**87084**  with colony estimation from density chart

**87086**  Culture, bacterial; quantitative colony count, urine

**87088**  with isolation and presumptive identification of each isolate, urine

**87101**  Culture, fungi (mold or yeast) isolation, with presumptive identification of isolates; skin, hair, or nail

**87102**  other source (except blood)

**87103**  blood

**87106**  Culture, fungi, definitive identification, each organism; yeast

**87107**  mold

**87109**  Culture, mycoplasma, any source

**87110**  Culture, chlamydia, any source

(For immunofluorescence staining of shell vials, use 87140)

**87116**  Culture, tubercle or other acid-fast bacilli (eg, TB, AFB, mycobacteria) any source, with isolation and presumptive identification of isolates

(For concentration, use 87015)

**87118**  Culture, mycobacterial, definitive identification, each isolate

**87140**  Culture, typing; immunofluorescent method, each antiserum

**87143**  gas liquid chromatography (GLC) or high pressure liquid chromatography (HPLC) method

**87147**  immunologic method, other than immunofluorescence (eg, agglutination grouping), per antiserum

**87149**  identification by nucleic acid (DNA or RNA) probe, direct probe technique, per culture or isolate, each organism probed

(Do not report 87149 in conjunction with 81161, 81200-81408)

⊙=Moderate sedation   ✚=Add-on code   ⊮=FDA approval pending   #=Resequenced code   ○=Recycled/reinstated code

**87150**    identification by nucleic acid (DNA or RNA) probe, amplified probe technique, per culture or isolate, each organism probed

(Do not report 87150 in conjunction with 81161, 81200-81408)

**87152**    identification by pulse field gel typing

(Do not report 87152 in conjunction with 81161, 81200-81408)

**87153**    identification by nucleic acid sequencing method, each isolate (eg, sequencing of the 16S rRNA gene)

**87158**    other methods

**87164**    Dark field examination, any source (eg, penile, vaginal, oral, skin); includes specimen collection

**87166**    without collection

**87168**    Macroscopic examination; arthropod

**87169**    parasite

**87172**    Pinworm exam (eg, cellophane tape prep)

**87176**    Homogenization, tissue, for culture

**87177**    Ova and parasites, direct smears, concentration and identification

(Do not report 87177 in conjunction with 87015)

(For direct smears from a primary source, use 87207)

(For coccidia or microsporidia exam, use 87207)

(For complex special stain (trichrome, iron hematoxylin), use 87209)

(For nucleic acid probes in cytologic material, use 88365)

**87181**    Susceptibility studies, antimicrobial agent; agar dilution method, per agent (eg, antibiotic gradient strip)

**87184**    disk method, per plate (12 or fewer agents)

**87185**    enzyme detection (eg, beta lactamase), per enzyme

**87186**    microdilution or agar dilution (minimum inhibitory concentration [MIC] or breakpoint), each multi-antimicrobial, per plate

+ **87187**    microdilution or agar dilution, minimum lethal concentration (MLC), each plate (List separately in addition to code for primary procedure)

(Use 87187 in conjunction with 87186 or 87188)

**87188**    macrobroth dilution method, each agent

**87190**    mycobacteria, proportion method, each agent

(For other mycobacterial susceptibility studies, see 87181, 87184, 87186, or 87188)

**87197**    Serum bactericidal titer (Schlicter test)

**87205**    Smear, primary source with interpretation; Gram or Giemsa stain for bacteria, fungi, or cell types

**87206**    fluorescent and/or acid fast stain for bacteria, fungi, parasites, viruses or cell types

**87207**    special stain for inclusion bodies or parasites (eg, malaria, coccidia, microsporidia, trypanosomes, herpes viruses)

(For direct smears with concentration and identification, use 87177)

(For thick smear preparation, use 87015)

(For fat, meat, fibers, nasal eosinophils, and starch, see miscellaneous section)

**87209**    complex special stain (eg, trichrome, iron hemotoxylin) for ova and parasites

**87210**    wet mount for infectious agents (eg, saline, India ink, KOH preps)

(For KOH examination of skin, hair or nails, see 87220)

**87220**    Tissue examination by KOH slide of samples from skin, hair, or nails for fungi or ectoparasite ova or mites (eg, scabies)

**87230**    Toxin or antitoxin assay, tissue culture (eg, Clostridium difficile toxin)

**87250**    Virus isolation; inoculation of embryonated eggs, or small animal, includes observation and dissection

**87252**    tissue culture inoculation, observation, and presumptive identification by cytopathic effect

**87253**    tissue culture, additional studies or definitive identification (eg, hemabsorption, neutralization, immunofluoresence stain), each isolate

(Electron microscopy, use 88348)

(Inclusion bodies in tissue sections, see 88304-88309; in smears, see 87207-87210; in fluids, use 88106)

**87254**    centrifuge enhanced (shell vial) technique, includes identification with immunofluorescence stain, each virus

(Report 87254 in addition to 87252 as appropriate)

**87255**    including identification by non-immunologic method, other than by cytopathic effect (eg, virus specific enzymatic activity)

These codes are intended for primary source only. For similar studies on culture material, refer to codes 87140-87158. Infectious agents by antigen detection, immunofluorescence microscopy, or nucleic acid probe techniques should be reported as precisely as possible. The molecular pathology procedures codes (81161, 81200-81408) are not to be used in combination with or instead of the procedures represented by 87470-87801. The most specific code possible should be reported. If there is no specific agent code, the general methodology code (eg, 87299, 87449, 87450, 87797, 87798, 87799, 87899) should be used. For identification of antibodies to many of the listed infectious agents, see 86602-86804. When separate results are reported for different species or

**Pathology and Laboratory**

strain of organisms, each result should be coded separately. Use modifier 59 when separate results are reported for different species or strains that are described by the same code.

| | |
|---|---|
| 87260 | Infectious agent antigen detection by immunofluorescent technique; adenovirus |
| 87265 | Bordetella pertussis/parapertussis |
| 87267 | Enterovirus, direct fluorescent antibody (DFA) |
| 87269 | giardia |
| 87270 | Chlamydia trachomatis |
| 87271 | Cytomegalovirus, direct fluorescent antibody (DFA) |
| 87272 | cryptosporidium |
| 87273 | Herpes simplex virus type 2 |
| 87274 | Herpes simplex virus type 1 |
| 87275 | influenza B virus |
| 87276 | influenza A virus |
| 87277 | Legionella micdadei |
| 87278 | Legionella pneumophila |
| 87279 | Parainfluenza virus, each type |
| 87280 | respiratory syncytial virus |
| 87281 | Pneumocystis carinii |
| 87283 | Rubeola |
| 87285 | Treponema pallidum |
| 87290 | Varicella zoster virus |
| 87299 | not otherwise specified, each organism |
| 87300 | Infectious agent antigen detection by immunofluorescent technique, polyvalent for multiple organisms, each polyvalent antiserum |

(For physician evaluation of infectious disease agents by immunofluorescence, use 88346)

| | |
|---|---|
| 87301 | Infectious agent antigen detection by enzyme immunoassay technique, qualitative or semiquantitative, multiple-step method; adenovirus enteric types 40/41 |
| 87305 | Aspergillus |
| 87320 | Chlamydia trachomatis |
| 87324 | Clostridium difficile toxin(s) |
| 87327 | Cryptococcus neoformans |

(For Cryptococcus latex agglutination, use 86403)

| | |
|---|---|
| 87328 | cryptosporidium |
| 87329 | giardia |
| 87332 | cytomegalovirus |
| 87335 | Escherichia coli 0157 |

(For giardia antigen, use 87329)

| | |
|---|---|
| 87336 | Entamoeba histolytica dispar group |
| 87337 | Entamoeba histolytica group |
| 87338 | Helicobacter pylori, stool |
| 87339 | Helicobacter pylori |

(For H. pylori, stool, use 87338. For H. pylori, breath and blood by mass spectrometry, see 83013, 83014. For H. pylori, liquid scintillation counter, see 78267, 78268)

| | |
|---|---|
| 87340 | hepatitis B surface antigen (HBsAg) |
| 87341 | hepatitis B surface antigen (HBsAg) neutralization |
| 87350 | hepatitis Be antigen (HBeAg) |
| 87380 | hepatitis, delta agent |
| 87385 | Histoplasma capsulatum |
| 87389 | HIV-1 antigen(s), with HIV-1 and HIV-2 antibodies, single result |
| 87390 | HIV-1 |
| 87391 | HIV-2 |
| 87400 | Influenza, A or B, each |
| 87420 | respiratory syncytial virus |
| 87425 | rotavirus |
| 87427 | Shiga-like toxin |
| 87430 | Streptococcus, group A |
| 87449 | Infectious agent antigen detection by enzyme immunoassay technique qualitative or semiquantitative; multiple step method, not otherwise specified, each organism |
| 87450 | single step method, not otherwise specified, each organism |
| 87451 | multiple step method, polyvalent for multiple organisms, each polyvalent antiserum |
| 87470 | Infectious agent detection by nucleic acid (DNA or RNA); Bartonella henselae and Bartonella quintana, direct probe technique |
| 87471 | Bartonella henselae and Bartonella quintana, amplified probe technique |
| 87472 | Bartonella henselae and Bartonella quintana, quantification |
| 87475 | Borrelia burgdorferi, direct probe technique |
| 87476 | Borrelia burgdorferi, amplified probe technique |
| 87477 | Borrelia burgdorferi, quantification |
| 87480 | Candida species, direct probe technique |
| 87481 | Candida species, amplified probe technique |
| 87482 | Candida species, quantification |
| 87485 | Chlamydia pneumoniae, direct probe technique |
| 87486 | Chlamydia pneumoniae, amplified probe technique |
| 87487 | Chlamydia pneumoniae, quantification |
| 87490 | Chlamydia trachomatis, direct probe technique |

| | | | | |
|---|---|---|---|---|
| 87491 | Chlamydia trachomatis, amplified probe technique | | ▲ 87535 | HIV-1, amplified probe technique, includes reverse transcription when performed |
| 87492 | Chlamydia trachomatis, quantification | | ▲ 87536 | HIV-1, quantification, includes reverse transcription when performed |
| 87493 | Clostridium difficile, toxin gene(s), amplified probe technique | | 87537 | HIV-2, direct probe technique |

87491 Chlamydia trachomatis, amplified probe technique

87492 Chlamydia trachomatis, quantification

87493 Clostridium difficile, toxin gene(s), amplified probe technique

87495 cytomegalovirus, direct probe technique

87496 cytomegalovirus, amplified probe technique

87497 cytomegalovirus, quantification

▲ 87498 enterovirus, amplified probe technique, includes reverse transcription when performed

87500 vancomycin resistance (eg, enterococcus species van A, van B), amplified probe technique

87501 influenza virus, reverse transcription and amplified probe technique, each type or subtype

87502 influenza virus, for multiple types or sub-types, multiplex reverse transcription and amplified probe technique, first 2 types or sub-types

+ 87503 influenza virus, for multiple types or sub-types, multiplex reverse transcription and amplified probe technique, each additional influenza virus type or sub-type beyond 2 (List separately in addition to code for primary procedure)

(Use 87503 in conjunction with 87502)

87510 Gardnerella vaginalis, direct probe technique

87511 Gardnerella vaginalis, amplified probe technique

87512 Gardnerella vaginalis, quantification

87515 hepatitis B virus, direct probe technique

87516 hepatitis B virus, amplified probe technique

87517 hepatitis B virus, quantification

87520 hepatitis C, direct probe technique

▲ 87521 hepatitis C, amplified probe technique, includes reverse transcription when performed

▲ 87522 hepatitis C, quantification, includes reverse transcription when performed

87525 hepatitis G, direct probe technique

87526 hepatitis G, amplified probe technique

87527 hepatitis G, quantification

87528 Herpes simplex virus, direct probe technique

87529 Herpes simplex virus; amplified probe technique

87530 Herpes simplex virus, quantification

87531 Herpes virus-6, direct probe technique

87532 Herpes virus-6, amplified probe technique

87533 Herpes virus-6, quantification

87534 HIV-1, direct probe technique

▲ 87535 HIV-1, amplified probe technique, includes reverse transcription when performed

▲ 87536 HIV-1, quantification, includes reverse transcription when performed

87537 HIV-2, direct probe technique

▲ 87538 HIV-2, amplified probe technique, includes reverse transcription when performed

▲ 87539 HIV-2, quantification, includes reverse transcription when performed

87540 Legionella pneumophila, direct probe technique

87541 Legionella pneumophila, amplified probe technique

87542 Legionella pneumophila, quantification

87550 Mycobacteria species, direct probe technique

87551 Mycobacteria species, amplified probe technique

87552 Mycobacteria species, quantification

87555 Mycobacteria tuberculosis, direct probe technique

87556 Mycobacteria tuberculosis, amplified probe technique

87557 Mycobacteria tuberculosis, quantification

87560 Mycobacteria avium-intracellulare, direct probe technique

87561 Mycobacteria avium-intracellulare, amplified probe technique

87562 Mycobacteria avium-intracellulare, quantification

87580 Mycoplasma pneumoniae, direct probe technique

87581 Mycoplasma pneumoniae, amplified probe technique

87582 Mycoplasma pneumoniae, quantification

87590 Neisseria gonorrhoeae, direct probe technique

87591 Neisseria gonorrhoeae, amplified probe technique

87592 Neisseria gonorrhoeae, quantification

87620 papillomavirus, human, direct probe technique

87621 papillomavirus, human, amplified probe technique

87622 papillomavirus, human, quantification

87631 respiratory virus (eg, adenovirus, influenza virus, coronavirus, metapneumovirus, parainfluenza virus, respiratory syncytial virus, rhinovirus), multiplex reverse transcription and amplified probe technique, multiple types or subtypes, 3-5 targets

87632 respiratory virus (eg, adenovirus, influenza virus, coronavirus, metapneumovirus, parainfluenza virus, respiratory syncytial virus, rhinovirus), multiplex reverse transcription and amplified probe technique, multiple types or subtypes, 6-11 targets

87633    respiratory virus (eg, adenovirus, influenza virus, coronavirus, metapneumovirus, parainfluenza virus, respiratory syncytial virus, rhinovirus), multiplex reverse transcription and amplified probe technique, multiple types or subtypes, 12-25 targets

(Use 87631-87633 for nucleic acid assays which detect multiple respiratory viruses in a multiplex reaction [ie, single procedure with multiple results])

(For assays that are used to type or subtype influenza viruses only, see 87501-87503)

(For assays that include influenza viruses with additional respiratory viruses, see 87631-87633)

(For detection of multiple infectious agents not otherwise specified which report a single result, see 87800, 87801)

87640    Staphylococcus aureus, amplified probe technique

87641    Staphylococcus aureus, methicillin resistant, amplified probe technique

(For assays that detect methicillin resistance and identify Staphylococcus aureus using a single nucleic acid sequence, use 87641)

87650    Streptococcus, group A, direct probe technique

87651    Streptococcus, group A, amplified probe technique

87652    Streptococcus, group A, quantification

87653    Streptococcus, group B, amplified probe technique

87660    Trichomonas vaginalis, direct probe technique

● 87661    Trichomonas vaginalis, amplified probe technique

87797    Infectious agent detection by nucleic acid (DNA or RNA), not otherwise specified; direct probe technique, each organism

87798    amplified probe technique, each organism

87799    quantification, each organism

87800    Infectious agent detection by nucleic acid (DNA or RNA), multiple organisms; direct probe(s) technique

87801    amplified probe(s) technique

(For each specific organism nucleic acid detection from a primary source, see 87470-87660. For detection of specific infectious agents not otherwise specified, see 87797, 87798, or 87799 1 time for each agent)

(For detection of multiple infectious agents not otherwise specified which report a single result, see 87800, 87801)

(Do not use 87801 for nucleic acid assays that detect multiple respiratory viruses in a multiplex reaction [ie, single procedure with multiple results], see 87631-87633)

87802    Infectious agent antigen detection by immunoassay with direct optical observation; Streptococcus, group B

87803    Clostridium difficile toxin A

87804    Influenza

87807    respiratory syncytial virus

87808    Trichomonas vaginalis

87809    adenovirus

87810    Chlamydia trachomatis

87850    Neisseria gonorrhoeae

87880    Streptococcus, group A

87899    not otherwise specified

87900    Infectious agent drug susceptibility phenotype prediction using regularly updated genotypic bioinformatics

# 87910    Infectious agent genotype analysis by nucleic acid (DNA or RNA); cytomegalovirus

87901    HIV-1, reverse transcriptase and protease regions

# 87906    HIV-1, other region (eg, integrase, fusion)

(For infectious agent drug susceptibility phenotype prediction for HIV-1, use 87900)

# 87912    Hepatitis B virus

87902    Hepatitis C virus

87903    Infectious agent phenotype analysis by nucleic acid (DNA or RNA) with drug resistance tissue culture analysis, HIV 1; first through 10 drugs tested

+ 87904    each additional drug tested (List separately in addition to code for primary procedure)

(Use 87904 in conjunction with 87903)

87905    Infectious agent enzymatic activity other than virus (eg, sialidase activity in vaginal fluid)

(For virus isolation including identification by non-immunologic method, other than by cytopathic effect, use 87255)

87906    Code is out of numerical sequence. See 87001-87999

87910    Code is out of numerical sequence. See 87001-87999

87912    Code is out of numerical sequence. See 87001-87999

87999    Unlisted microbiology procedure

# Anatomic Pathology

## Postmortem Examination

Procedures 88000 through 88099 represent physician services only. Use modifier 90 for outside laboratory services.

88000    Necropsy (autopsy), gross examination only; without CNS

88005    with brain

88007    with brain and spinal cord

88012    infant with brain

88014    stillborn or newborn with brain

88016    macerated stillborn

88020    Necropsy (autopsy), gross and microscopic; without CNS

| | |
|---|---|
| **88025** | with brain |
| **88027** | with brain and spinal cord |
| **88028** | infant with brain |
| **88029** | stillborn or newborn with brain |
| **88036** | Necropsy (autopsy), limited, gross and/or microscopic; regional |
| **88037** | single organ |
| **88040** | Necropsy (autopsy); forensic examination |
| **88045** | coroner's call |
| **88099** | Unlisted necropsy (autopsy) procedure |

# Cytopathology

| | |
|---|---|
| **88104** | Cytopathology, fluids, washings or brushings, except cervical or vaginal; smears with interpretation |
| **88106** | simple filter method with interpretation |

(Do not report 88106 in conjunction with 88104)

(88107 has been deleted. To report smears and simple filter preparation, see 88104, 88106)

(For nongynecological selective cellular enhancement including filter transfer techniques, use 88112)

| | |
|---|---|
| **88108** | Cytopathology, concentration technique, smears and interpretation (eg, Saccomanno technique) |

(For cervical or vaginal smears, see 88150-88155)

(For gastric intubation with lavage, see 43754, 43755)

(For x-ray localization, use 74340)

| | |
|---|---|
| **88112** | Cytopathology, selective cellular enhancement technique with interpretation (eg, liquid based slide preparation method), except cervical or vaginal |

(Do not report 88112 with 88108)

| | |
|---|---|
| **88120** | Cytopathology, in situ hybridization (eg, FISH), urinary tract specimen with morphometric analysis, 3-5 molecular probes, each specimen; manual |
| **88121** | using computer-assisted technology |

(For morphometric in situ hybridization on cytologic specimens other than urinary tract, see 88367, 88368)

(For more than 5 probes, use 88399)

| | |
|---|---|
| **88125** | Cytopathology, forensic (eg, sperm) |
| **88130** | Sex chromatin identification; Barr bodies |
| **88140** | peripheral blood smear, polymorphonuclear drumsticks |

(For Guard stain, use 88313)

Codes 88141-88155, 88164-88167, 88174-88175 are used to report cervical or vaginal screening by various methods and to report physician interpretation services. Use codes 88150-88154 to report conventional Pap smears that are examined using non-Bethesda reporting. Use codes 88164-88167 to report conventional Pap smears that are examined using the Bethesda System of reporting. Use codes 88142-88143 to report liquid-based specimens processed as thin-layer preparations that are examined using any system of reporting (Bethesda or non-Bethesda). Use codes 88174-88175 to report automated screening of liquid-based specimens that are examined using any system of reporting (Bethesda or non-Bethesda). Within each of these three code families choose the one code that describes the screening method(s) used. Codes 88141 and 88155 should be reported in addition to the screening code chosen when the additional services are provided. Manual rescreening requires a complete visual reassessment of the entire slide initially screened by either an automated or manual process. Manual review represents an assessment of selected cells or regions of a slide identified by initial automated review.

| | |
|---|---|
| **88141** | Cytopathology, cervical or vaginal (any reporting system), requiring interpretation by physician |

(Use 88141 in conjunction with 88142-88154, 88164-88167, 88174-88175)

| | |
|---|---|
| **88142** | Cytopathology, cervical or vaginal (any reporting system), collected in preservative fluid, automated thin layer preparation; manual screening under physician supervision |
| **88143** | with manual screening and rescreening under physician supervision |

(For automated screening of automated thin layer preparation, see 88174, 88175)

| | |
|---|---|
| **88147** | Cytopathology smears, cervical or vaginal; screening by automated system under physician supervision |
| **88148** | screening by automated system with manual rescreening under physician supervision |
| **88150** | Cytopathology, slides, cervical or vaginal; manual screening under physician supervision |
| **88152** | with manual screening and computer-assisted rescreening under physician supervision |
| **88153** | with manual screening and rescreening under physician supervision |
| **88154** | with manual screening and computer-assisted rescreening using cell selection and review under physician supervision |
| **+ 88155** | Cytopathology, slides, cervical or vaginal, definitive hormonal evaluation (eg, maturation index, karyopyknotic index, estrogenic index) (List separately in addition to code[s] for other technical and interpretation services) |

(Use 88155 in conjunction with 88142-88154, 88164-88167, 88174-88175)

| | |
|---|---|
| **88160** | Cytopathology, smears, any other source; screening and interpretation |
| **88161** | preparation, screening and interpretation |

**Pathology and Laboratory**

**88162**         extended study involving over 5 slides and/or multiple stains

(For aerosol collection of sputum, use 89220)

(For special stains, see 88312-88314)

**88164**   Cytopathology, slides, cervical or vaginal (the Bethesda System); manual screening under physician supervision

**88165**         with manual screening and rescreening under physician supervision

**88166**         with manual screening and computer-assisted rescreening under physician supervision

**88167**         with manual screening and computer-assisted rescreening using cell selection and review under physician supervision

(To report collection of specimen via fine needle aspiration, see 10021, 10022)

**88172**   Cytopathology, evaluation of fine needle aspirate; immediate cytohistologic study to determine adequacy for diagnosis, first evaluation episode, each site

(The evaluation episode represents a complete set of cytologic material submitted for evaluation and is independent of the number of needle passes or slides prepared. A separate evaluation episode occurs if the proceduralist provider obtains additional material from the same site, based on the prior immediate adequacy assessment, or a separate lesion is aspirated)

**88173**         interpretation and report

(Report one unit of 88173 for the interpretation and report from each anatomic site, regardless of the number of passes or evaluation episodes performed during the aspiration procedure)

(For fine needle aspirate, see 10021, 10022)

(Do not report 88172, 88173 in conjunction with 88333 and 88334 for the same specimen)

**#+ 88177**      immediate cytohistologic study to determine adequacy for diagnosis, each separate additional evaluation episode, same site (List separately in addition to code for primary procedure)

(When repeat immediate evaluation episode(s) is required on subsequent cytologic material from the same site, eg, following determination the prior sampling that was not adequate for diagnosis, use 1 unit of 88177 for each additional evaluation episode)

(Use 88177 in conjunction with 88172)

**88174**   Cytopathology, cervical or vaginal (any reporting system), collected in preservative fluid, automated thin layer preparation; screening by automated system, under physician supervision

**88175**         with screening by automated system and manual rescreening or review, under physician supervision

(For manual screening, see 88142, 88143)

**88177**   Code is out of numerical sequence. See 88104-88199

**88182**   Flow cytometry, cell cycle or DNA analysis

(For DNA ploidy analysis by morphometric technique, use 88358)

**88184**   Flow cytometry, cell surface, cytoplasmic, or nuclear marker, technical component only; first marker

**+ 88185**       each additional marker (List separately in addition to code for first marker)

(Report 88185 in conjunction with 88184)

**88187**   Flow cytometry, interpretation; 2 to 8 markers

**88188**         9 to 15 markers

**88189**         16 or more markers

(Do not report 88187-88189 for interpretation of 86355, 86356, 86357, 86359, 86360, 86361, 86367)

(For assessment of circulating antibodies by flow cytometric techniques, see analyte and method-specific codes in the Chemistry section [83516-83520] or Immunology section [86000-86849])

(For cell enumeration using immunologic selection and identification in fluid specimen [eg, circulating tumor cells in blood], see 86152, 86153)

**88199**   Unlisted cytopathology procedure

(For electron microscopy, see 88348, 88349)

# Cytogenetic Studies

Molecular pathology procedures should be reported using either the appropriate Tier 1 (81161, 81200-81383), Tier 2 (81400-81408) or the unlisted molecular pathology procedure code 81479.

(For acetylcholinesterase, use 82013)

(For alpha-fetoprotein, serum or amniotic fluid, see 82105, 82106)

(For laser microdissection of cells from tissue sample, see 88380)

**88230**   Tissue culture for non-neoplastic disorders; lymphocyte

**88233**         skin or other solid tissue biopsy

**88235**         amniotic fluid or chorionic villus cells

**88237**   Tissue culture for neoplastic disorders; bone marrow, blood cells

**88239**         solid tumor

**88240**   Cryopreservation, freezing and storage of cells, each cell line

(For therapeutic cryopreservation and storage, use 38207)

**88241**   Thawing and expansion of frozen cells, each aliquot

(For therapeutic thawing of previous harvest, use 38208)

**88245**   Chromosome analysis for breakage syndromes; baseline Sister Chromatid Exchange (SCE), 20-25 cells

---

| | |
|---|---|
| 88248 | baseline breakage, score 50-100 cells, count 20 cells, 2 karyotypes (eg, for ataxia telangiectasia, Fanconi anemia, fragile X) |
| 88249 | score 100 cells, clastogen stress (eg, diepoxybutane, mitomycin C, ionizing radiation, UV radiation) |
| 88261 | Chromosome analysis; count 5 cells, 1 karyotype, with banding |
| 88262 | count 15-20 cells, 2 karyotypes, with banding |
| 88263 | count 45 cells for mosaicism, 2 karyotypes, with banding |
| 88264 | analyze 20-25 cells |
| 88267 | Chromosome analysis, amniotic fluid or chorionic villus, count 15 cells, 1 karyotype, with banding |
| 88269 | Chromosome analysis, in situ for amniotic fluid cells, count cells from 6-12 colonies, 1 karyotype, with banding |
| 88271 | Molecular cytogenetics; DNA probe, each (eg, FISH) |

▶(For cytogenomic microarray analysis, see 81228, 81229, 81405, 81406, 81479)◀

| | |
|---|---|
| 88272 | chromosomal in situ hybridization, analyze 3-5 cells (eg, for derivatives and markers) |
| 88273 | chromosomal in situ hybridization, analyze 10-30 cells (eg, for microdeletions) |
| 88274 | interphase in situ hybridization, analyze 25-99 cells |
| 88275 | interphase in situ hybridization, analyze 100-300 cells |
| 88280 | Chromosome analysis; additional karyotypes, each study |
| 88283 | additional specialized banding technique (eg, NOR, C-banding) |
| 88285 | additional cells counted, each study |
| 88289 | additional high resolution study |
| 88291 | Cytogenetics and molecular cytogenetics, interpretation and report |
| 88299 | Unlisted cytogenetic study |

# Surgical Pathology

Services 88300 through 88309 include accession, examination, and reporting. They do not include the services designated in codes 88311 through 88365 and 88399, which are coded in addition when provided.

The unit of service for codes 88300 through 88309 is the specimen.

A specimen is defined as tissue or tissues that is (are) submitted for individual and separate attention, requiring individual examination and pathologic diagnosis. Two or more such specimens from the same patient (eg, separately identified endoscopic biopsies, skin lesions) are each appropriately assigned an individual code reflective of its proper level of service.

Service code 88300 is used for any specimen that in the opinion of the examining pathologist can be accurately diagnosed without microscopic examination. Service code 88302 is used when gross and microscopic examination is performed on a specimen to confirm identification and the absence of disease. Service codes 88304 through 88309 describe all other specimens requiring gross and microscopic examination, and represent additional ascending levels of physician work. Levels 88302 through 88309 are specifically defined by the assigned specimens.

Any unlisted specimen should be assigned to the code which most closely reflects the physician work involved when compared to other specimens assigned to that code.

(Do not report 88302-88309 on the same specimen as part of Mohs surgery)

| | |
|---|---|
| 88300 | **Level I** - Surgical pathology, gross examination only |
| 88302 | **Level II** - Surgical pathology, gross and microscopic examination |

Appendix, incidental

Fallopian tube, sterilization

Fingers/toes, amputation, traumatic

Foreskin, newborn

Hernia sac, any location

Hydrocele sac

Nerve

Skin, plastic repair

Sympathetic ganglion

Testis, castration

Vaginal mucosa, incidental

Vas deferens, sterilization

| | |
|---|---|
| 88304 | **Level III** - Surgical pathology, gross and microscopic examination |

Abortion, induced

Abscess

Aneurysm - arterial/ventricular

Anus, tag

Appendix, other than incidental

Artery, atheromatous plaque

Bartholin's gland cyst

Bone fragment(s), other than pathologic fracture

Bursa/synovial cyst

Carpal tunnel tissue

Cartilage, shavings

Cholesteatoma

Colon, colostomy stoma

Conjunctiva - biopsy/pterygium

Cornea

Diverticulum - esophagus/small intestine

Dupuytren's contracture tissue

Femoral head, other than fracture

Fissure/fistula

Foreskin, other than newborn

Gallbladder

Ganglion cyst

Hematoma

Hemorrhoids

Hydatid of Morgagni

Intervertebral disc

Joint, loose body

Meniscus

Mucocele, salivary

Neuroma - Morton's/traumatic

Pilonidal cyst/sinus

Polyps, inflammatory - nasal/sinusoidal

Skin - cyst/tag/debridement

Soft tissue, debridement

Soft tissue, lipoma

Spermatocele

Tendon/tendon sheath

Testicular appendage

Thrombus or embolus

Tonsil and/or adenoids

Varicocele

Vas deferens, other than sterilization

Vein, varicosity

**88305    Level IV** - Surgical pathology, gross and microscopic examination

Abortion - spontaneous/missed

Artery, biopsy

Bone marrow, biopsy

Bone exostosis

Brain/meninges, other than for tumor resection

Breast, biopsy, not requiring microscopic evaluation of surgical margins

Breast, reduction mammoplasty

Bronchus, biopsy

Cell block, any source

Cervix, biopsy

Colon, biopsy

Duodenum, biopsy

Endocervix, curettings/biopsy

Endometrium, curettings/biopsy

Esophagus, biopsy

Extremity, amputation, traumatic

Fallopian tube, biopsy

Fallopian tube, ectopic pregnancy

Femoral head, fracture

Fingers/toes, amputation, non-traumatic

Gingiva/oral mucosa, biopsy

Heart valve

Joint, resection

Kidney, biopsy

Larynx, biopsy

Leiomyoma(s), uterine myomectomy - without uterus

Lip, biopsy/wedge resection

Lung, transbronchial biopsy

Lymph node, biopsy

Muscle, biopsy

Nasal mucosa, biopsy

Nasopharynx/oropharynx, biopsy

Nerve, biopsy

Odontogenic/dental cyst

Omentum, biopsy

Ovary with or without tube, non-neoplastic

Ovary, biopsy/wedge resection

Parathyroid gland

Peritoneum, biopsy

Pituitary tumor

Placenta, other than third trimester

Pleura/pericardium - biopsy/tissue

Polyp, cervical/endometrial

Polyp, colorectal

Polyp, stomach/small intestine

Prostate, needle biopsy

Prostate, TUR

Salivary gland, biopsy

Sinus, paranasal biopsy

Skin, other than cyst/tag/debridement/plastic repair

Small intestine, biopsy

Soft tissue, other than tumor/mass/lipoma/debridement

Spleen

Stomach, biopsy

Synovium

Testis, other than tumor/biopsy/castration

Thyroglossal duct/brachial cleft cyst

Tongue, biopsy

Tonsil, biopsy

Trachea, biopsy

Ureter, biopsy

Urethra, biopsy

Urinary bladder, biopsy

Uterus, with or without tubes and ovaries, for prolapse

Vagina, biopsy

Vulva/labia, biopsy

**88307    Level V** - Surgical pathology, gross and microscopic examination

Adrenal, resection

Bone - biopsy/curettings

Bone fragment(s), pathologic fracture

Brain, biopsy

Brain/meninges, tumor resection

Breast, excision of lesion, requiring microscopic evaluation of surgical margins

Breast, mastectomy - partial/simple

Cervix, conization

Colon, segmental resection, other than for tumor

Extremity, amputation, non-traumatic

Eye, enucleation

Kidney, partial/total nephrectomy

Larynx, partial/total resection

Liver, biopsy - needle/wedge

Liver, partial resection

Lung, wedge biopsy

Lymph nodes, regional resection

Mediastinum, mass

Myocardium, biopsy

Odontogenic tumor

Ovary with or without tube, neoplastic

Pancreas, biopsy

Placenta, third trimester

Prostate, except radical resection

Salivary gland

Sentinel lymph node

Small intestine, resection, other than for tumor

Soft tissue mass (except lipoma) - biopsy/simple excision

Stomach - subtotal/total resection, other than for tumor

Testis, biopsy

Thymus, tumor

Thyroid, total/lobe

Ureter, resection

Urinary bladder, TUR

Uterus, with or without tubes and ovaries, other than neoplastic/prolapse

**88309    Level VI** - Surgical pathology, gross and microscopic examination

Bone resection

Breast, mastectomy - with regional lymph nodes

Colon, segmental resection for tumor

Colon, total resection

Esophagus, partial/total resection

Extremity, disarticulation

Fetus, with dissection

Larynx, partial/total resection - with regional lymph nodes

Lung - total/lobe/segment resection

Pancreas, total/subtotal resection

Prostate, radical resection

Small intestine, resection for tumor

Soft tissue tumor, extensive resection

Stomach - subtotal/total resection for tumor

Testis, tumor

Tongue/tonsil -resection for tumor

Urinary bladder, partial/total resection

Uterus, with or without tubes and ovaries, neoplastic

Vulva, total/subtotal resection

(For fine needle aspiration, see 10021, 10022)

(For evaluation of fine needle aspirate, see 88172-88173)

(Do not report 88302-88309 on the same specimen as part of Mohs surgery)

**+ 88311**   Decalcification procedure (List separately in addition to code for surgical pathology examination)

Pathology and Laboratory

**88312**   Special stain including interpretation and report; Group I for microorganisms (eg, acid fast, methenamine silver)

(Report one unit of 88312 for each special stain, on each surgical pathology block, cytologic specimen, or hematologic smear)

**88313**   Group II, all other (eg, iron, trichrome), except stain for microorganisms, stains for enzyme constituents, or immunocytochemistry and immunohistochemistry

(Report one unit of 88313 for each special stain, on each surgical pathology block, cytologic specimen, or hematologic smear)

▶(For immunocytochemistry and immunohistochemistry, see 88342, 88343)◀

**+ 88314**   histochemical stain on frozen tissue block (List separately in addition to code for primary procedure)

(Use 88314 in conjunction with 17311-17315, 88302-88309, 88331, 88332)

(Do not report 88314 with 17311-17315 for routine frozen section stain [eg, hematoxylin and eosin, toluidine blue], performed during Mohs surgery. When a nonroutine histochemical stain on frozen tissue during Mohs surgery is utilized, report 88314 with modifier 59)

(Report one unit of 88314 for each special stain on each frozen surgical pathology block)

(For a special stain performed on frozen tissue section material to identify enzyme constituents, use 88319)

(88318 has been deleted)

(For determinative histochemistry to identify chemical components, use 88313)

**88319**   Group III, for enzyme constituents

(For each stain on each surgical pathology block, cytologic specimen, or hematologic smear, use one unit of 88319)

▶(For detection of enzyme constituents by immunohistochemical or immunocytochemical technique, see 88342, 88343)◀

**88321**   Consultation and report on referred slides prepared elsewhere

**88323**   Consultation and report on referred material requiring preparation of slides

**88325**   Consultation, comprehensive, with review of records and specimens, with report on referred material

**88329**   Pathology consultation during surgery;

**88331**   first tissue block, with frozen section(s), single specimen

**+ 88332**   each additional tissue block with frozen section(s) (List separately in addition to code for primary procedure)

(Use 88332 in conjunction with 88331)

**88333**   cytologic examination (eg, touch prep, squash prep), initial site

**+ 88334**   cytologic examination (eg, touch prep, squash prep), each additional site (List separately in addition to code for primary procedure)

(Use 88334 in conjunction with 88331, 88333)

(For intraoperative consultation on a specimen requiring both frozen section and cytologic evaluation, use 88331 and 88334)

(For percutaneous needle biopsy requiring intraprocedural cytologic examination, use 88333)

(Do not report 88333 and 88334 for non-intraoperative cytologic examination, see 88160-88162)

(Do not report 88333 and 88334 for intraprocedural cytologic evaluation of fine needle aspirate, see 88172)

**▲ 88342**   Immunohistochemistry or immunocytochemistry, each separately identifiable antibody per block, cytologic preparation, or hematologic smear; first separately identifiable antibody per slide

(Do not report 88342 in conjunction with 88360 or 88361 for the same antibody)

(For quantitative or semiquantitative immunohistochemistry, see 88360, 88361)

**+● 88343**   each additional separately identifiable antibody per slide (List separately in addition to code for primary procedure)

▶(Use 88343 in conjunction with 88342)◀

▶(When multiple antibodies are applied to the same slide, use one unit of 88342 for the first separately identifiable antibody and one unit of 88343 for each additional separately identifiable antibody)◀

**88346**   Immunofluorescent study, each antibody; direct method

**88347**   indirect method

**88348**   Electron microscopy; diagnostic

**88349**   scanning

**88355**   Morphometric analysis; skeletal muscle

**88356**   nerve

**88358**   tumor (eg, DNA ploidy)

(Do not report 88358 with 88313 unless each procedure is for a different special stain)

**88360**   Morphometric analysis, tumor immunohistochemistry (eg, Her-2/neu, estrogen receptor/progesterone receptor), quantitative or semiquantitative, each antibody; manual

**88361**   using computer-assisted technology

(Do not report 88360, 88361 with 88342 unless each procedure is for a different antibody)

(For morphometric analysis using in situ hybridization techniques, see 88367, 88368)

(When semi-thin plastic-embedded sections are performed in conjunction with morphometric analysis, only the morphometric analysis should be reported; if performed as an independent procedure, see codes 88300-88309 for surgical pathology.)

**88362**    Nerve teasing preparations

**88363**    Examination and selection of retrieved archival (ie, previously diagnosed) tissue(s) for molecular analysis (eg, KRAS mutational analysis)

**88365**    In situ hybridization (eg, FISH), each probe

(Do not report 88365 in conjunction with 88367, 88368 for the same probe)

**88367**    Morphometric analysis, in situ hybridization (quantitative or semi-quantitative) each probe; using computer-assisted technology

**88368**        manual

(For morphometric in situ hybridization evaluation of urinary tract cytologic specimens, see 88120, 88121)

**88371**    Protein analysis of tissue by Western Blot, with interpretation and report;

**88372**        immunological probe for band identification, each

**88375**    Optical endomicroscopic image(s), interpretation and report, real-time or referred, each endoscopic session

(Do not report 88375 in conjunction with 43206 or 43252)

**88380**    Microdissection (ie, sample preparation of microscopically identified target); laser capture

**88381**        manual

(Do not report 88380 in conjunction with 88381)

(88384-88386 have been deleted. To report, see 81161, 81200-81479)

**88387**    Macroscopic examination, dissection, and preparation of tissue for non-microscopic analytical studies (eg, nucleic acid-based molecular studies); each tissue preparation (eg, a single lymph node)

(Do not report 88387 for tissue preparation for microbiologic cultures or flow cytometric studies)

(Do not report 88387 in conjunction with 88388, 88329-88334)

**+ 88388**        in conjunction with a touch imprint, intraoperative consultation, or frozen section, each tissue preparation (eg, a single lymph node) (List separately in addition to code for primary procedure)

(Use 88388 in conjunction with 88329-88334)

(Do not report 88387 or 88388 for tissue preparation for microbiologic cultures or flow cytometric studies)

**88399**    Unlisted surgical pathology procedure

(88400 has been deleted. To report, use 88720)

# In Vivo (eg, Transcutaneous) Laboratory Procedures

(For all in vivo measurements not specifically listed, use 88749)

(For wavelength fluorescent spectroscopy of advanced glycation end products (skin), use 0233T)

(For transcutaneous oxyhemoglobin measurement in a lower extremity wound by near infrared spectroscopy, use 0286T)

**88720**    Bilirubin, total, transcutaneous

(For transdermal oxygen saturation, see 94760-94762)

**88738**    Hemoglobin (Hgb), quantitative, transcutaneous

(For in vitro hemoglobin measurement, use 85018)

**88740**    Hemoglobin, quantitative, transcutaneous, per day; carboxyhemoglobin

(For in vitro carboxyhemoglobin measurement, use 82375)

**88741**        methemoglobin

(For in vitro quantitative methemoglobin determination, use 83050)

**88749**    Unlisted in vivo (eg, transcutaneous) laboratory service

# Other Procedures

**89049**    Caffeine halothane contracture test (CHCT) for malignant hyperthermia susceptibility, including interpretation and report

**89050**    Cell count, miscellaneous body fluids (eg, cerebrospinal fluid, joint fluid), except blood;

**89051**        with differential count

**89055**    Leukocyte assessment, fecal, qualitative or semiquantitative

**89060**    Crystal identification by light microscopy with or without polarizing lens analysis, tissue or any body fluid (except urine)

(Do not report 89060 for crystal identification on paraffin-embedded tissue)

(89100, 89105 have been deleted. To report, see 43756, 43757)

**89125**    Fat stain, feces, urine, or respiratory secretions

(89130-89141 have been deleted. To report, see 43754, 43755)

**89160**    Meat fibers, feces

**89190**    Nasal smear for eosinophils

(Occult blood, feces, use 82270)

(Paternity tests, use 86910)

**Pathology and Laboratory**

**89220** Sputum, obtaining specimen, aerosol induced technique (separate procedure)

(89225 has been deleted)

**89230** Sweat collection by iontophoresis

(89235 has been deleted)

**89240** Unlisted miscellaneous pathology test

# Reproductive Medicine Procedures

**89250** Culture of oocyte(s)/embryo(s), less than 4 days;

**89251** with co-culture of oocyte(s)/embryos

(For extended culture of oocyte[s]/embryo[s], see 89272)

**89253** Assisted embryo hatching, microtechniques (any method)

**89254** Oocyte identification from follicular fluid

**89255** Preparation of embryo for transfer (any method)

**89257** Sperm identification from aspiration (other than seminal fluid)

(For semen analysis, see 89300-89320)

(For sperm identification from testis tissue, use 89264)

**89258** Cryopreservation; embryo(s)

**89259** sperm

(For cryopreservation of reproductive tissue, testicular, use 89335)

**89260** Sperm isolation; simple prep (eg, sperm wash and swim-up) for insemination or diagnosis with semen analysis

**89261** complex prep (eg, Percoll gradient, albumin gradient) for insemination or diagnosis with semen analysis

(For semen analysis without sperm wash or swim-up, use 89320)

**89264** Sperm identification from testis tissue, fresh or cryopreserved

(For biopsy of testis, see 54500, 54505)

(For sperm identification from aspiration, use 89257)

(For semen analysis, see 89300-89320)

**89268** Insemination of oocytes

**89272** Extended culture of oocyte(s)/embryo(s), 4-7 days

**89280** Assisted oocyte fertilization, microtechnique; less than or equal to 10 oocytes

**89281** greater than 10 oocytes

**89290** Biopsy, oocyte polar body or embryo blastomere, microtechnique (for pre-implantation genetic diagnosis); less than or equal to 5 embryos

**89291** greater than 5 embryos

**89300** Semen analysis; presence and/or motility of sperm including Huhner test (post coital)

**89310** motility and count (not including Huhner test)

**89320** volume, count, motility, and differential

(Skin tests, see 86485-86580 and 95012-95199)

**89321** sperm presence and motility of sperm, if performed

(To report Hyaluronan binding assay [HBA], use 89398)

**89322** volume, count, motility, and differential using strict morphologic criteria (eg, Kruger)

**89325** Sperm antibodies

(For medicolegal identification of sperm, use 88125)

**89329** Sperm evaluation; hamster penetration test

**89330** cervical mucus penetration test, with or without spinnbarkeit test

**89331** Sperm evaluation, for retrograde ejaculation, urine (sperm concentration, motility, and morphology, as indicated)

(For semen analysis on concurrent semen specimen, see 89300-89322 in conjunction with 89331)

(For detection of sperm in urine, use 81015)

**89335** Cryopreservation, reproductive tissue, testicular

(For cryopreservation of embryo[s], use 89258. For cryopreservation of sperm, use 89259)

(For cryopreservation, ovarian reproductive tissue, oocytes, use 89240)

**89342** Storage (per year); embryo(s)

**89343** sperm/semen

**89344** reproductive tissue, testicular/ovarian

**89346** oocyte(s)

**89352** Thawing of cryopreserved; embryo(s)

**89353** sperm/semen, each aliquot

**89354** reproductive tissue, testicular/ovarian

**89356** oocytes, each aliquot

**89398** Unlisted reproductive medicine laboratory procedure

⊙=Moderate sedation ✚=Add-on code ⧸=FDA approval pending #=Resequenced code ○=Recycled/reinstated code

# Medicine Guidelines

In addition to the definitions and commonly used terms presented in the **Introduction**, several other items unique to this section on **Medicine** are defined or identified here.

## Add-on Codes

Some of the listed procedures are commonly carried out in addition to the primary procedure performed. All add-on codes found in the CPT codebook are exempt from the multiple procedure concept. They are exempt from the use of modifier 51, as these procedures are not reported as stand-alone codes. These additional or supplemental procedures are designated as "add-on" codes. Add-on codes in the CPT codebook can be readily identified by specific descriptor nomenclature which includes phrases such as "each additional" or "(List separately in addition to primary procedure)."

## Separate Procedures

Some of the procedures or services listed in the CPT codebook that are commonly carried out as an integral component of a total service or procedure have been identified by the inclusion of the term "separate procedure." The codes designated as "separate procedure" should not be reported in addition to the code for the total procedure or service of which it is considered an integral component.

However, when a procedure or service that is designated as a "separate procedure" is carried out independently or considered to be unrelated or distinct from other procedures/services provided at that time, it may be reported by itself, or in addition to other procedures/services by appending modifier 59 to the specific "separate procedure" code to indicate that the procedure is not considered to be a component of another procedure, but is a distinct, independent procedure. This may represent a different session or patient encounter, different procedure or surgery, different site or organ system, separate incision/excision, separate lesion, or separate injury (or area of injury in extensive injuries).

## Unlisted Service or Procedure

A service or procedure may be provided that is not listed in this edition of the CPT codebook. When reporting such a service, the appropriate "Unlisted Procedure" code may be used to indicate the service, identifying it by "Special Report" as discussed on the next page. The "Unlisted Procedures" and accompanying codes for **Medicine** are as follows:

| Code | Description |
|------|-------------|
| 90399 | Unlisted immune globulin |
| 90749 | Unlisted vaccine/toxoid |
| 90899 | Unlisted psychiatric service or procedure |
| 90999 | Unlisted dialysis procedure, inpatient or outpatient |
| 91299 | Unlisted diagnostic gastroenterology procedure |
| 92499 | Unlisted ophthalmological service or procedure |
| 92700 | Unlisted otorhinolaryngological service or procedure |
| 93799 | Unlisted cardiovascular service or procedure |
| 93998 | Unlisted noninvasive vascular diagnostic study |
| 94799 | Unlisted pulmonary service or procedure |
| 95199 | Unlisted allergy/clinical immunologic service or procedure |
| 95999 | Unlisted neurological or neuromuscular diagnostic procedure |
| 96379 | Unlisted therapeutic, prophylactic, or diagnostic intravenous or intra-arterial injection or infusion |
| 96549 | Unlisted chemotherapy procedure |
| 96999 | Unlisted special dermatological service or procedure |
| 97039 | Unlisted modality (specify type and time if constant attendance) |
| 97139 | Unlisted therapeutic procedure (specify) |
| 97799 | Unlisted physical medicine/rehabilitation service or procedure |
| 99199 | Unlisted special service, procedure or report |
| 99600 | Unlisted home visit service or procedure |

Medicine

# Special Report

A service that is rarely provided, unusual, variable, or new may require a special report. Pertinent information should include an adequate definition or description of the nature, extent, and need for the procedure; and the time, effort, and equipment necessary to provide the service.

# Supplied Materials

Supplies and materials (eg, trays, drug supplies, and materials) over and above those usually included with the procedure(s) rendered are reported separately using code 99070 or a specific supply code.

# Medicine

## Immune Globulins, Serum or Recombinant Products

Codes 90281-90399 identify the serum globulins, extracted from human blood; or recombinant immune globulin products created in a laboratory through genetic modification of human and/or animal proteins. Both are reported in addition to the administration codes 96365-96368, 96372, 96374, 96375 as appropriate. Modifier 51 should not be reported with this section of products codes when performed with another procedure. The serum or recombinant globulin products listed here include broad-spectrum anti-infective immune globulins, antitoxins, various isoantibodies, and monoclonal antibodies.

| | |
|---|---|
| **90281** | Immune globulin (Ig), human, for intramuscular use |
| **90283** | Immune globulin (IgIV), human, for intravenous use |
| **90284** | Immune globulin (SCIg), human, for use in subcutaneous infusions, 100 mg, each |
| **90287** | Botulinum antitoxin, equine, any route |
| **90288** | Botulism immune globulin, human, for intravenous use |
| **90291** | Cytomegalovirus immune globulin (CMV-IgIV), human, for intravenous use |
| **90296** | Diphtheria antitoxin, equine, any route |
| **90371** | Hepatitis B immune globulin (HBIg), human, for intramuscular use |
| **90375** | Rabies immune globulin (RIg), human, for intramuscular and/or subcutaneous use |
| **90376** | Rabies immune globulin, heat-treated (RIg-HT), human, for intramuscular and/or subcutaneous use |
| **90378** | Respiratory syncytial virus, monoclonal antibody, recombinant, for intramuscular use, 50 mg, each |
| | (90379 has been deleted) |
| **90384** | Rho(D) immune globulin (RhIg), human, full-dose, for intramuscular use |
| **90385** | Rho(D) immune globulin (RhIg), human, mini-dose, for intramuscular use |
| **90386** | Rho(D) immune globulin (RhIgIV), human, for intravenous use |
| **90389** | Tetanus immune globulin (TIg), human, for intramuscular use |
| **90393** | Vaccinia immune globulin, human, for intramuscular use |
| **90396** | Varicella-zoster immune globulin, human, for intramuscular use |
| **90399** | Unlisted immune globulin |

## Immunization Administration for Vaccines/Toxoids

Report vaccine immunization administration codes 90460, 90461, 90471-90474 in addition to the vaccine and toxoid code(s) 90476-90749.

Report codes 90460 and 90461 only when the physician or qualified health care professional provides face-to-face counseling of the patient/family during the administration of a vaccine. For immunization administration of any vaccine that is not accompanied by face-to-face physician or qualified health care professional counseling to the patient/family or for administration of vaccines to patients over 18 years of age, report codes 90471-90474. (See also Instructions for Use of the CPT Codebook for definition of reporting qualifications.)

If a significant separately identifiable Evaluation and Management service (eg, new or established patient office or other outpatient services [99201-99215], office or other outpatient consultations [99241-99245], emergency department services [99281-99285], preventive medicine services [99381-99429]) is performed, the appropriate E/M service code should be reported in addition to the vaccine and toxoid administration codes.

A component refers to all antigens in a vaccine that prevent disease(s) caused by one organism (90460 and 90461). Multi-valent antigens or multiple serotypes of antigens against a single organism are considered a single component of vaccines. Combination vaccines are those vaccines that contain multiple vaccine components. Conjugates or adjuvants contained in vaccines are not considered to be component parts of the vaccine as defined above.

> (For allergy testing, see 95004 et seq)
>
> (For skin testing of bacterial, viral, fungal extracts, see 86485-86580)
>
> (For therapeutic or diagnostic injections, see 96372-96379)

| | |
|---|---|
| **90460** | Immunization administration through 18 years of age via any route of administration, with counseling by physician or other qualified health care professional; first or only component of each vaccine or toxoid administered |

**Medicine**

---

+ **90461**      each additional vaccine or toxoid component administered (List separately in addition to code for primary procedure)

(Use 90460 for each vaccine administered. For vaccines with multiple components [combination vaccines], report 90460 in conjunction with 90461 for each additional component in a given vaccine)

(90465-90468 have been deleted. To report, see 90460, 90461, 90471-90474)

(90470 has been deleted)

**90471**      Immunization administration (includes percutaneous, intradermal, subcutaneous, or intramuscular injections); 1 vaccine (single or combination vaccine/toxoid)

(Do not report 90471 in conjunction with 90473)

+ **90472**      each additional vaccine (single or combination vaccine/toxoid) (List separately in addition to code for primary procedure)

(Use 90472 in conjunction with 90460, 90471, 90473)

(For administration of immune globulins, see 90281-90399, 96360, 96361, 96365-96368, 96374)

(For intravesical administration of BCG vaccine, see 51720, 90586)

**90473**      Immunization administration by intranasal or oral route; 1 vaccine (single or combination vaccine/toxoid)

(Do not report 90473 in conjunction with 90471)

+ **90474**      each additional vaccine (single or combination vaccine/toxoid) (List separately in addition to code for primary procedure)

(Use 90474 in conjunction with 90460, 90471, 90473)

# Vaccines, Toxoids

To assist users to report the most recent new or revised vaccine product codes, the American Medical Association (AMA) currently uses the CPT Website, which features updates of CPT Editorial Panel actions regarding these products. Once approved by the CPT Editorial Panel, these codes will be made available for release on a semi-annual (twice a year: July 1 and January 1) basis. As part of the electronic distribution, there is a six-month implementation period from the initial release date (ie, codes released on January 1 are eligible for use on July 1 and codes released on July 1 are eligible for use January 1).

The CPT Editorial Panel, in recognition of the public health interest in vaccine products, has chosen to publish new vaccine product codes prior to approval by the U. S. Food and Drug Administration (FDA). These codes are indicated with the ✗ symbol and will be tracked by the AMA to monitor FDA approval status. Once the FDA status changes to approval, the ✗ symbol will be removed. CPT users should refer to the AMA Internet

site (www.ama-assn.org/ama/pub/category/10902.html) for the most up-to-date information on codes with the ✗ symbol.

Codes 90476-90748 identify the vaccine product **only.** To report the administration of a vaccine/toxoid, the vaccine/toxoid product codes 90476-90749 must be used in addition to an immunization administration code(s) 90460-90474. Modifier 51 should not be reported for the vaccines, toxoids when performed with these administration procedures.

If a significantly separately identifiable Evaluation and Management (E/M) service (eg, office or other outpatient services, preventive medicine services) is performed, the appropriate E/M service code should be reported in addition to the vaccine and toxoid administration codes.

To meet the reporting requirements of immunization registries, vaccine distribution programs, and reporting systems (eg, Vaccine Adverse Event Reporting System) the exact vaccine product administered needs to be reported. Multiple codes for a particular vaccine are provided in the CPT codebook when the schedule (number of doses or timing) differs for two or more products of the same vaccine type (eg, hepatitis A, Hib) or the vaccine product is available in more than one chemical formulation, dosage, or route of administration.

The "when administered to" age descriptions included in CPT vaccine codes are not intended to identify a product's licensed age indication. The term "preservative free" includes use for vaccines that contain no preservative and vaccines that contain trace amounts of preservative agents that are not present in a sufficient concentration for the purpose of preserving the final vaccine formulation. The absence of a designation regarding a preservative does not necessarily indicate the presence or absence of preservative in the vaccine. Refer to the product's prescribing information (PI) for the licensed age indication before administering vaccine to a patient.

Separate codes are available for combination vaccines (eg, DTP-Hib, DtaP-Hib, HepB-Hib). It is inappropriate to code each component of a combination vaccine separately. If a specific vaccine code is not available, the unlisted procedure code should be reported, until a new code becomes available.

(For immune globulins, see codes 90281-90399, 96365-96368, 96372-96375 for administration of immune globulins)

**90476**      Adenovirus vaccine, type 4, live, for oral use

**90477**      Adenovirus vaccine, type 7, live, for oral use

**90581**      Anthrax vaccine, for subcutaneous or intramuscular use

**90585**      Bacillus Calmette-Guerin vaccine (BCG) for tuberculosis, live, for percutaneous use

**90586**      Bacillus Calmette-Guerin vaccine (BCG) for bladder cancer, live, for intravesical use

**90632**      Hepatitis A vaccine, adult dosage, for intramuscular use

90633    Hepatitis A vaccine, pediatric/adolescent dosage-2 dose schedule, for intramuscular use

90634    Hepatitis A vaccine, pediatric/adolescent dosage-3 dose schedule, for intramuscular use

90636    Hepatitis A and hepatitis B vaccine (HepA-HepB), adult dosage, for intramuscular use

90644    Meningococcal conjugate vaccine, serogroups C & Y and Hemophilus influenza B vaccine (Hib-MenCY), 4 dose schedule, when administered to children 2-15 months of age, for intramuscular use

90645    Hemophilus influenza b vaccine (Hib), HbOC conjugate (4 dose schedule), for intramuscular use

90646    Hemophilus influenza b vaccine (Hib), PRP-D conjugate, for booster use only, intramuscular use

90647    Hemophilus influenza b vaccine (Hib), PRP-OMP conjugate (3 dose schedule), for intramuscular use

90648    Hemophilus influenza b vaccine (Hib), PRP-T conjugate (4 dose schedule), for intramuscular use

90649    Human Papilloma virus (HPV) vaccine, types 6, 11, 16, 18 (quadrivalent), 3 dose schedule, for intramuscular use

90650    Human Papilloma virus (HPV) vaccine, types 16, 18, bivalent, 3 dose schedule, for intramuscular use

✗ 90653    Influenza vaccine, inactivated, subunit, adjuvanted, for intramuscular use

90654    Influenza virus vaccine, split virus, preservative-free, for intradermal use

90655    Influenza virus vaccine, trivalent, split virus, preservative free, when administered to children 6-35 months of age, for intramuscular use

90656    Influenza virus vaccine, trivalent, split virus, preservative free, when administered to individuals 3 years and older, for intramuscular use

90657    Influenza virus vaccine, trivalent, split virus, when administered to children 6-35 months of age, for intramuscular use

90658    Influenza virus vaccine, trivalent, split virus, when administered to individuals 3 years of age and older, for intramuscular use

90660    Influenza virus vaccine, trivalent, live, for intranasal use

\# 90672    Influenza virus vaccine, quadrivalent, live, for intranasal use

90661    Influenza virus vaccine, derived from cell cultures, subunit, preservative and antibiotic free, for intramuscular use

\#● 90673    Influenza virus vaccine, trivalent, derived from recombinant DNA (RIV3), hemagglutinin (HA) protein only, preservative and antibiotic free, for intramuscular use

90662    Influenza virus vaccine, split virus, preservative free, enhanced immunogenicity via increased antigen content, for intramuscular use

(90663 has been deleted)

90664    Influenza virus vaccine, pandemic formulation, live, for intranasal use

(90665 has been deleted)

✗ 90666    Influenza virus vaccine, pandemic formulation, split virus, preservative free, for intramuscular use

✗ 90667    Influenza virus vaccine, pandemic formulation, split virus, adjuvanted, for intramuscular use

✗ 90668    Influenza virus vaccine, pandemic formulation, split virus, for intramuscular use

90669    Pneumococcal conjugate vaccine, 7 valent, for intramuscular use

90670    Pneumococcal conjugate vaccine, 13 valent, for intramuscular use

90672    Code is out of numerical sequence. See 90476-90749

90673    Code is out of numerical sequence. See 90476-90749

90675    Rabies vaccine, for intramuscular use

90676    Rabies vaccine, for intradermal use

90680    Rotavirus vaccine, pentavalent, 3 dose schedule, live, for oral use

90681    Rotavirus vaccine, human, attenuated, 2 dose schedule, live, for oral use

● 90685    Influenza virus vaccine, quadrivalent, split virus, preservative free, when administered to children 6-35 months of age, for intramuscular use

● 90686    Influenza virus vaccine, quadrivalent, split virus, preservative free, when administered to individuals 3 years of age and older, for intramuscular use

✗● 90687    Influenza virus vaccine, quadrivalent, split virus, when administered to children 6-35 months of age, for intramuscular use

✗● 90688    Influenza virus vaccine, quadrivalent, split virus, when administered to individuals 3 years of age and older, for intramuscular use

90690    Typhoid vaccine, live, oral

90691    Typhoid vaccine, Vi capsular polysaccharide (ViCPs), for intramuscular use

90692    Typhoid vaccine, heat- and phenol-inactivated (H-P), for subcutaneous or intradermal use

90693    Typhoid vaccine, acetone-killed, dried (AKD), for subcutaneous use (U.S. military)

90696    Diphtheria, tetanus toxoids, acellular pertussis vaccine and poliovirus vaccine, inactivated (DTaP-IPV), when administered to children 4 through 6 years of age, for intramuscular use

90698    Diphtheria, tetanus toxoids, acellular pertussis vaccine, haemophilus influenza Type B, and poliovirus vaccine, inactivated (DTaP - Hib - IPV), for intramuscular use

**Medicine**

---

▲=Revised code    ●=New code    ►◄=Contains new or revised text    ⊘=Modifier 51 exempt

**90700**  Diphtheria, tetanus toxoids, and acellular pertussis vaccine (DTaP), when administered to individuals younger than 7 years, for intramuscular use

(90701 has been deleted)

**90702**  Diphtheria and tetanus toxoids (DT) adsorbed when administered to individuals younger than 7 years, for intramuscular use

**90703**  Tetanus toxoid adsorbed, for intramuscular use

**90704**  Mumps virus vaccine, live, for subcutaneous use

**90705**  Measles virus vaccine, live, for subcutaneous use

**90706**  Rubella virus vaccine, live, for subcutaneous use

**90707**  Measles, mumps and rubella virus vaccine (MMR), live, for subcutaneous use

**90708**  Measles and rubella virus vaccine, live, for subcutaneous use

**90710**  Measles, mumps, rubella, and varicella vaccine (MMRV), live, for subcutaneous use

**90712**  Poliovirus vaccine, (any type[s]) (OPV), live, for oral use

**90713**  Poliovirus vaccine, inactivated (IPV), for subcutaneous or intramuscular use

**90714**  Tetanus and diphtheria toxoids (Td) adsorbed, preservative free, when administered to individuals 7 years or older, for intramuscular use

**90715**  Tetanus, diphtheria toxoids and acellular pertussis vaccine (Tdap), when administered to individuals 7 years or older, for intramuscular use

**90716**  Varicella virus vaccine, live, for subcutaneous use

**90717**  Yellow fever vaccine, live, for subcutaneous use

(90718 has been deleted)

**90719**  Diphtheria toxoid, for intramuscular use

**90720**  Diphtheria, tetanus toxoids, and whole cell pertussis vaccine and Hemophilus influenza B vaccine (DTP-Hib) for intramuscular use

**90721**  Diphtheria, tetanus toxoids, and acellular pertussis vaccine and Hemophilus influenza B vaccine (DtaP-Hib), for intramuscular use

**90723**  Diphtheria, tetanus toxoids, acellular pertussis vaccine, Hepatitis B, and poliovirus vaccine, inactivated (DtaP-HepB-IPV), for intramuscular use

**90725**  Cholera vaccine for injectable use

**90727**  Plague vaccine, for intramuscular use

**90732**  Pneumococcal polysaccharide vaccine, 23-valent, adult or immunosuppressed patient dosage, when administered to individuals 2 years or older, for subcutaneous or intramuscular use

**90733**  Meningococcal polysaccharide vaccine (any group(s)), for subcutaneous use

**90734**  Meningococcal conjugate vaccine, serogroups A, C, Y and W-135 (tetravalent), for intramuscular use

**90735**  Japanese encephalitis virus vaccine, for subcutaneous use

**90736**  Zoster (shingles) vaccine, live, for subcutaneous injection

**90738**  Japanese encephalitis virus vaccine, inactivated, for intramuscular use

✗ **90739**  Hepatitis B vaccine, adult dosage (2 dose schedule), for intramuscular use

**90740**  Hepatitis B vaccine, dialysis or immunosuppressed patient dosage (3 dose schedule), for intramuscular use

**90743**  Hepatitis B vaccine, adolescent (2 dose schedule), for intramuscular use

**90744**  Hepatitis B vaccine, pediatric/adolescent dosage (3 dose schedule), for intramuscular use

**90746**  Hepatitis B vaccine, adult dosage (3 dose schedule), for intramuscular use

**90747**  Hepatitis B vaccine, dialysis or immunosuppressed patient dosage (4 dose schedule), for intramuscular use

**90748**  Hepatitis B and Hemophilus influenza b vaccine (HepB-Hib), for intramuscular use

**90749**  Unlisted vaccine/toxoid

# Psychiatry

Psychiatry services include diagnostic services, psychotherapy, and other services to an individual, family, or group. Patient condition, characteristics, or situational factors may require services described as being with interactive complexity. Services may be provided to a patient in crisis. Services are provided in all settings of care and psychiatry services codes are reported without regard to setting. Services may be provided by a physician or other qualified health care professional. Some psychiatry services may be reported with **Evaluation and Management Services** (99201-99255, 99281-99285, 99304-99337, 99341-99350) or other services when performed. **Evaluation and Management Services** (99201-99285, 99304-99337, 99341-99350) may be reported for treatment of psychiatric conditions, rather than using **Psychiatry Services** codes, when appropriate.

Hospital care in treating a psychiatric inpatient or partial hospitalization may be initial or subsequent in nature (see 99221-99233).

Some patients receive hospital evaluation and management services only and others receive hospital evaluation and management services and other procedures. If other procedures such as electroconvulsive therapy or psychotherapy are rendered in addition to hospital evaluation and management services, these may be listed separately (eg, hospital care services [99221-99223, 99231-99233] plus electroconvulsive therapy [90870]), or when psychotherapy is done, with appropriate code(s) defining psychotherapy services.

Medicine

Consultation for psychiatric evaluation of a patient includes examination of a patient and exchange of information with the primary physician and other informants such as nurses or family members, and preparation of a report. These services may be reported using consultation codes (see **Consultations**).

## Interactive Complexity

Code 90785 is an add-on code for interactive complexity to be reported in conjunction with codes for diagnostic psychiatric evaluation (90791, 90792), psychotherapy (90832, 90834, 90837), psychotherapy when performed with an evaluation and management service (90833, 90836, 90838, 99201-99255, 99304-99337, 99341-99350), and group psychotherapy (90853).

Interactive complexity refers to specific communication factors that complicate the delivery of a psychiatric procedure. Common factors include more difficult communication with discordant or emotional family members and engagement of young and verbally undeveloped or impaired patients. Typical patients are those who have third parties, such as parents, guardians, other family members, interpreters, language translators, agencies, court officers, or schools involved in their psychiatric care.

These factors are typically present with patients who:

- Have other individuals legally responsible for their care, such as minors or adults with guardians, or

- Request others to be involved in their care during the visit, such as adults accompanied by one or more participating family members or interpreter or language translator, or

- Require the involvement of other third parties, such as child welfare agencies, parole or probation officers, or schools.

Psychiatric procedures may be reported "with interactive complexity" when at least one of the following is present:

1. The need to manage maladaptive communication (related to, eg, high anxiety, high reactivity, repeated questions, or disagreement) among participants that complicates delivery of care.

2. Caregiver emotions or behavior that interferes with the caregiver's understanding and ability to assist in the implementation of the treatment plan.

3. Evidence or disclosure of a sentinel event and mandated report to third party (eg, abuse or neglect with report to state agency) with initiation of discussion of the sentinel event and/or report with patient and other visit participants.

4. Use of play equipment, other physical devices, interpreter, or translator to communicate with the patient to overcome barriers to therapeutic or diagnostic interaction between the physician or other qualified health care professional and a patient who:

- Is not fluent in the same language as the physician or other qualified health care professional, or

- Has not developed, or has lost, either the expressive language communication skills to explain his/her symptoms and response to treatment, or the receptive communication skills to understand the physician or other qualified health care professional if he/she were to use typical language for communication.

When provided in conjunction with the psychotherapy services (90832-90838), the amount of time spent by a physician or other qualified health care professional providing interactive complexity services should be reflected in the timed service code for psychotherapy (90832, 90834, 90837) or the psychotherapy add-on code performed with an evaluation and management service (90833, 90836, 90838) and must relate to the psychotherapy service only. Interactive complexity is not a factor for evaluation and management services selection (99201-99255, 99281-99285, 99304-99337, 99341-99350), except as it directly affects key components as defined in the Evaluation and Management Services Guidelines (ie, history, examination, and medical decision making).

+ **90785**    Interactive complexity (List separately in addition to the code for primary procedure)

(Use 90785 in conjunction with codes for diagnostic psychiatric evaluation [90791, 90792], psychotherapy [90832, 90834, 90837], psychotherapy when performed with an evaluation and management service [90833, 90836, 90838, 99201-99255, 99304-99337, 99341-99350], and group psychotherapy [90853])

(Do not report 90785 in conjunction with 90839, 90840, or in conjunction with E/M services when no psychotherapy service is also reported)

## Psychiatric Diagnostic Procedures

Psychiatric diagnostic evaluation is an integrated biopsychosocial assessment, including history, mental status, and recommendations. The evaluation may include communication with family or other sources and review and ordering of diagnostic studies.

Psychiatric diagnostic evaluation with medical services is an integrated biopsychosocial and medical assessment, including history, mental status, other physical examination elements as indicated, and recommendations. The evaluation may include communication with family or other sources, prescription of medications, and review and ordering of laboratory or other diagnostic studies.

In certain circumstances one or more other informants (family members, guardians, or significant others) may be seen in lieu of the patient. Codes 90791, 90792 may be reported more than once for the patient when separate diagnostic evaluations are conducted with the patient and other informants. Report services as being provided to the patient and not the informant or other party in such circumstances. Codes 90791, 90792 may be reported once per day and not on the same day as an evaluation and management service performed by the same individual for the same patient.

The psychiatric diagnostic evaluation may include interactive complexity services when factors exist that complicate the delivery of the psychiatric procedure. These services should be reported with add-on code 90785 used in conjunction with the diagnostic psychiatric evaluation codes 90791, 90792.

Codes 90791, 90792 are used for the diagnostic assessment(s) or reassessment(s), if required, and do not include psychotherapeutic services. Psychotherapy services, including for crisis, may not be reported on the same day.

**90791**   Psychiatric diagnostic evaluation

**90792**   Psychiatric diagnostic evaluation with medical services

(Do not report 90791 or 90792 in conjunction with 99201-99337, 99341-99350, 99366-99368, 99401-99444)

(Use 90785 in conjunction with 90791, 90792 when the diagnostic evaluation includes interactive complexity services)

(90801 and 90802 have been deleted. To report diagnostic evaluations, see 90791, 90792)

(90804, 90805, 90806, 90807, 90808, 90809 have been deleted. To report, see psychotherapy codes 90832, 90834, 90837 or psychotherapy add-on codes when performed with an evaluation and management service [90833, 90836, 90838, 99201-99255, 99304-99337, 99341-99350])

(90810, 90811, 90812, 90813, 90814, 90815 have been deleted. To report interactive psychotherapy, report 90785 in conjunction with psychotherapy codes 90832, 90834, 90837 or psychotherapy add-on codes when performed with an evaluation and management service [90833, 90836, 90838, 99201-99255, 99304-99337, 99341-99350])

(90816, 90817, 90818, 90819, 90821, 90822 have been deleted. To report, see psychotherapy codes 90832, 90834, 90837 or psychotherapy add-on codes when performed with an evaluation and management service [90833, 90836, 90838, 99201-99255, 99304-99337, 99341-99350])

(90823, 90824, 90826, 90827, 90828, 90829 have been deleted. To report interactive psychotherapy, report 90785 in conjunction with psychotherapy codes 90832, 90834, 90837 or psychotherapy add-on codes when performed with an evaluation and management service [90833, 90836, 90838, 99201-99255, 99304-99337, 99341-99350])

# Psychotherapy

Psychotherapy is the treatment of mental illness and behavioral disturbances in which the physician or other qualified health care professional, through definitive therapeutic communication, attempts to alleviate the emotional disturbances, reverse or change maladaptive patterns of behavior, and encourage personality growth and development.

The psychotherapy service codes 90832-90838 include ongoing assessment and adjustment of psychotherapeutic interventions, and may include involvement of family member(s) or others in the treatment process.

Psychotherapy times are for face-to-face services with patient and/or family member. The patient must be present for all or some of the service. For family psychotherapy without the patient present, use 90846. In reporting, choose the code closest to the actual time (ie, 16-37 minutes for 90832 and 90833, 38-52 minutes for 90834 and 90836, and 53 or more minutes for 90837 and 90838). Do not report psychotherapy of less than 16 minutes duration. (See instructions for the usage of time in the Introduction of the CPT code set.)

Psychotherapy provided to a patient in a crisis state is reported with codes 90839 and 90840 and cannot be reported in addition to the psychotherapy codes 90832-90838. For psychotherapy for crisis, see "Other Psychotherapy."

Code 90785 is an add-on code to report interactive complexity services when provided in conjunction with the psychotherapy codes 90832-90838. The amount of time spent by a physician or other qualified health care professional providing interactive complexity services should be reflected in the timed service code for psychotherapy (90832, 90834, 90837) or the psychotherapy add-on code performed with an evaluation and management service (90833, 90836, 90838).

Some psychiatric patients receive a medical evaluation and management (E/M) service on the same day as a psychotherapy service by the same physician or other qualified health care professional. To report both E/M and psychotherapy, the two services must be significant and separately identifiable. These services are reported by using codes specific for psychotherapy when performed with evaluation and management services (90833, 90836, 90838) as add-on codes to the evaluation and management service.

Medical symptoms and disorders inform treatment choices of psychotherapeutic interventions, and data from therapeutic communication are used to evaluate the presence, type, and severity of medical symptoms and disorders. For the purposes of reporting, the medical and psychotherapeutic components of the service may be separately identified as follows:

Medicine

1. The type and level of E/M service is selected first based upon the key components of history, examination, and medical decision-making.

2. Time associated with activities used to meet criteria for the E/M service is not included in the time used for reporting the psychotherapy service (ie, time spent on history, examination and medical decision making **when used for the E/M service** is not psychotherapy time). Time may not be used as the basis of E/M code selection and Prolonged Services may not be reported when psychotherapy with E/M (90833, 90836, 90838) are reported.

3. A separate diagnosis is not required for the reporting of E/M and psychotherapy on the same date of service.

**90832**    Psychotherapy, 30 minutes with patient and/or family member

**+ 90833**    Psychotherapy, 30 minutes with patient and/or family member when performed with an evaluation and management service (List separately in addition to the code for primary procedure)

(Use 90833 in conjunction with 99201-99255, 99304-99337, 99341-99350)

**90834**    Psychotherapy, 45 minutes with patient and/or family member

**+ 90836**    Psychotherapy, 45 minutes with patient and/or family member when performed with an evaluation and management service (List separately in addition to the code for primary procedure)

(Use 90836 in conjunction with 99201-99255, 99304-99337, 99341-99350)

**90837**    Psychotherapy, 60 minutes with patient and/or family member

▶(Use the appropriate prolonged services code [99354, 99355, 99356, 99357] for psychotherapy services not performed with an E/M service of 90 minutes or longer face-to-face with the patient)◀

**+ 90838**    Psychotherapy, 60 minutes with patient and/or family member when performed with an evaluation and management service (List separately in addition to the code for primary procedure)

(Use 90838 in conjunction with 99201-99255, 99304-99337, 99341-99350)

(Use 90785 in conjunction with 90832, 90833, 90834, 90836, 90837, 90838 when psychotherapy includes interactive complexity services)

## Other Psychotherapy

### Psychotherapy for Crisis

Psychotherapy for crisis is an urgent assessment and history of a crisis state, a mental status exam, and a

disposition. The treatment includes psychotherapy, mobilization of resources to defuse the crisis and restore safety, and implementation of psychotherapeutic interventions to minimize the potential for psychological trauma. The presenting problem is typically life threatening or complex and requires immediate attention to a patient in high distress.

Codes 90839, 90840 are used to report the total duration of time face-to-face with the patient and/or family spent by the physician or other qualified health care professional providing psychotherapy for crisis, even if the time spent on that date is not continuous. For any given period of time spent providing psychotherapy for crisis state, the physician or other qualified health care professional must devote his or her full attention to the patient and, therefore, cannot provide services to any other patient during the same time period. The patient must be present for all or some of the service. Do not report with 90791 or 90792.

Code 90839 is used to report the first 30-74 minutes of psychotherapy for crisis on a given date. It should be used only once per date even if the time spent by the physician or other health care professional is not continuous on that date. Psychotherapy for crisis of less than 30 minutes total duration on a given date should be reported with 90832 or 90833 (when provided with evaluation and management services).

Code 90840 is used to report additional block(s) of time, of up to 30 minutes each beyond the first 74 minutes.

**90839**    Psychotherapy for crisis; first 60 minutes

**+ 90840**      each additional 30 minutes (List separately in addition to code for primary service)

(Use 90840 in conjunction with 90839)

(Do not report 90839, 90840 in conjunction with 90791, 90792, psychotherapy codes 90832-90838 or other psychiatric services, or 90785-90899)

**90845**    Psychoanalysis

**90846**    Family psychotherapy (without the patient present)

**90847**    Family psychotherapy (conjoint psychotherapy) (with patient present)

**90849**    Multiple-family group psychotherapy

**90853**    Group psychotherapy (other than of a multiple-family group)

(Use 90853 in conjunction with 90785 for the specified patient when group psychotherapy includes interactive complexity)

(90857 has been deleted. To report, use 90785 in conjunction with 90853)

**Medicine**

## Other Psychiatric Services or Procedures

(For analysis/programming of neurostimulators used for vagus nerve stimulation therapy, see 95970, 95974, 95975)

(90862 has been deleted. To report, see 90863 or Evaluation and Management services codes 99201-99255, 99281-99285, 99304-99337, 99341-99350)

**+ 90863** Pharmacologic management, including prescription and review of medication, when performed with psychotherapy services (List separately in addition to the code for primary procedure)

(Use 90863 in conjunction with 90832, 90834, 90837)

(For pharmacologic management with psychotherapy services performed by a physician or other qualified health care professional who may report evaluation and management codes, use the appropriate evaluation and management codes 99201-99255, 99281-99285, 99304-99337, 99341-99350 and the appropriate psychotherapy with evaluation and management service 90833, 90836, 90838)

(Do not count time spent on providing pharmacologic management services in the time used for selection of the psychotherapy service)

**90865** Narcosynthesis for psychiatric diagnostic and therapeutic purposes (eg, sodium amobarbital (Amytal) interview)

**90867** Therapeutic repetitive transcranial magnetic stimulation (TMS) treatment; initial, including cortical mapping, motor threshold determination, delivery and management

(Report only once per course of treatment)

(Do not report 90867 in conjunction with 90868, 90869, 95860, 95870, 95928, 95929, 95939)

**90868** subsequent delivery and management, per session

**90869** subsequent motor threshold re-determination with delivery and management

(Do not report 90869 in conjunction with 90867, 90868, 95860-95870, 95928, 95929, 95939)

(If a significant, separately identifiable evaluation and management, medication management, or psychotherapy service is performed, the appropriate E/M or psychotherapy code may be reported in addition to 90867-90869. Evaluation and management activities directly related to cortical mapping, motor threshold determination, delivery and management of TMS are not separately reported)

(For transcranial magnetic stimulation motor function mapping for therapeutic planning other than for repetitive transcranial magnetic stimulation, use 0310T)

(Do not count time spent on providing pharmacologic management services in the time used for selection of the psychotherapy service)

**90870** Electroconvulsive therapy (includes necessary monitoring)

**90875** Individual psychophysiological therapy incorporating biofeedback training by any modality (face-to-face with the patient), with psychotherapy (eg, insight oriented, behavior modifying or supportive psychotherapy); 30 minutes

**90876** 45 minutes

**90880** Hypnotherapy

**90882** Environmental intervention for medical management purposes on a psychiatric patient's behalf with agencies, employers, or institutions

**90885** Psychiatric evaluation of hospital records, other psychiatric reports, psychometric and/or projective tests, and other accumulated data for medical diagnostic purposes

**90887** Interpretation or explanation of results of psychiatric, other medical examinations and procedures, or other accumulated data to family or other responsible persons, or advising them how to assist patient

**90889** Preparation of report of patient's psychiatric status, history, treatment, or progress (other than for legal or consultative purposes) for other individuals, agencies, or insurance carriers

**90899** Unlisted psychiatric service or procedure

# Biofeedback

(For psychophysiological therapy incorporating biofeedback training, see 90875, 90876)

**90901** Biofeedback training by any modality

**90911** Biofeedback training, perineal muscles, anorectal or urethral sphincter, including EMG and/or manometry

(For testing of rectal sensation, tone and compliance, use 91120)

(For incontinence treatment by pulsed magnetic neuromodulation, use 53899)

# Dialysis

(90918, 90922 have been deleted. To report ESRD-related services for patients younger than 2 years of age, see 90951-90953, 90963, 90967)

(90919, 90923 have been deleted. To report ESRD-related services for patients between 2 and 11 years of age, see 90954-90956, 90964, 90968)

(90920, 90924 have been deleted. To report ESRD-related services for patients between 12 and 19 years of age, see 90957-90959, 90965, 90969)

(90921, 90925 have been deleted. To report ESRD-related services for patients 20 years of age and older, see 90960-90962, 90966, 90970)

Medicine

# Hemodialysis

Codes 90935, 90937 are reported to describe the hemodialysis procedure with all evaluation and management services related to the patient's renal disease on the day of the hemodialysis procedure. These codes are used for inpatient ESRD and non-ESRD procedures or for outpatient non-ESRD dialysis services. Code 90935 is reported if only one evaluation of the patient is required related to that hemodialysis procedure. Code 90937 is reported when patient re-evaluation(s) is required during a hemodialysis procedure. Use modifier 25 with evaluation and management codes including new or established patient office or other outpatient services (99201-99215), office or other outpatient consultations (99241-99245), observation care (99217-99220, 99224-99226), observation or inpatient care including admission and discharge (99234-99236), initial hospital care (99221-99226, 99231-99239), new or established patient emergency department services (99281-99285), critical care services (99291, 99292), inpatient neonatal intensive care services and pediatric and neonatal critical care services (99466-99480), nursing facility services (99304-99318), domiciliary, rest home services, or custodial care (99324-99337), and home services (99341-99350), for separately identifiable services unrelated to the dialysis procedure or renal failure which cannot be rendered during the dialysis session.

> (For home visit hemodialysis services performed by a non-physician health care professional, use 99512)

> (For cannula declotting, see 36831, 36833, 36860, 36861)

> (For declotting of implanted vascular access device or catheter by thrombolytic agent, use 36593)

> (For collection of blood specimen from a partially or completely implantable venous access device, use 36591)

> (For prolonged attendance by a physician or other qualified health care professional, see 99354-99360)

**90935**   Hemodialysis procedure with single evaluation by a physician or other qualified health care professional

**90937**   Hemodialysis procedure requiring repeated evaluation(s) with or without substantial revision of dialysis prescription

**90940**   Hemodialysis access flow study to determine blood flow in grafts and arteriovenous fistulae by an indicator method

> (For duplex scan of hemodialysis access, use 93990)

# Miscellaneous Dialysis Procedures

Codes 90945, 90947 describe dialysis procedures other than hemodialysis (eg, peritoneal dialysis, hemofiltration or continuous renal replacement therapies), and all evaluation and management services related to the patient's renal disease on the day of the procedure. Code 90945 is reported if only one evaluation of the patient is required related to that procedure. Code 90947 is

reported when patient re-evaluation(s) is required during a procedure. Use modifier 25 with Evaluation and Management codes including office or other outpatient services (99201-99215), office or other outpatient consultations (99241-99245), observation care (99217-99220, 99224-99226), observation or inpatient care including admission and discharge (99234-99239), hospital care (99221-99226, 99231-99239), new or established patient emergency department services (99281-99285), critical care services (99291, 99292), inpatient neonatal intensive care services and pediatric and neonatal critical care services (99466-99480), nursing facility services (99304-99318), domiciliary, rest home, or custodial care services (99324-99337), and home services (99341-99350) for separately identifiable services unrelated to the procedure or the renal failure which cannot be rendered during the dialysis session.

> (For percutaneous insertion of intraperitoneal tunneled catheter, use 49418. For open insertion of tunneled intraperitoneal catheter, use 49421)

> (For prolonged attendance by a physician or other qualified health care professional, see 99354-99360)

**90945**   Dialysis procedure other than hemodialysis (eg, peritoneal dialysis, hemofiltration, or other continuous renal replacement therapies), with single evaluation by a physician or other qualified health care professional

> (For home infusion of peritoneal dialysis, use 99601, 99602)

**90947**   Dialysis procedure other than hemodialysis (eg, peritoneal dialysis, hemofiltration, or other continuous renal replacement therapies) requiring repeated evaluations by a physician or other qualified health care professional, with or without substantial revision of dialysis prescription

# End-Stage Renal Disease Services

Codes 90951-90962 are reported **once** per month to distinguish age-specific services related to the patient's end-stage renal disease (ESRD) performed in an outpatient setting with three levels of service based on the number of face-to-face visits. ESRD-related services by a physician or other qualified health care professional include establishment of a dialyzing cycle, outpatient evaluation and management of the dialysis visits, telephone calls, and patient management during the dialysis provided during a full month. In the circumstances in which the patient has had a complete assessment visit during the month and services are provided over a period of less than a month, 90951-90962 may be used according to the number of visits performed.

Codes 90963-90966 are reported once per month for a full month of service to distinguish age-specific services for end-stage renal disease (ESRD) services for home dialysis patients.

**Medicine**

For ESRD and non-ESRD dialysis services performed in an inpatient setting, and for non-ESRD dialysis services performed in an outpatient setting, see 90935-90937 and 90945-90947.

Evaluation and management services unrelated to ESRD services that cannot be performed during the dialysis session may be reported separately.

Codes 90967-90970 are reported to distinguish age-specific services for end-stage renal disease (ESRD) services for less than a full month of service, per day, for services provided under the following circumstances: home dialysis patients less than a full month, transient patients, partial month where there was one or more face-to-face visits without the complete assessment, the patient was hospitalized before a complete assessment was furnished, dialysis was stopped due to recovery or death, or the patient received a kidney transplant. For reporting purposes, each month is considered 30 days.

### Examples:

ESRD-related services:

ESRD-related services are initiated on July 1 for a 57-year-old male. On July 11, he is admitted to the hospital as an inpatient and is discharged on July 27. He has had a complete assessment and the physician or other qualified health care professional has performed two face-to-face visits prior to admission. Another face-to-face visit occurs after discharge during the month.

In this example, 90961 is reported for the three face-to-face outpatient visits. Report inpatient E/M services as appropriate. Dialysis procedures rendered during the hospitalization (July 11-27) should be reported as appropriate (90935-90937, 90945-90947).

If the patient did not have a complete assessment during the month or was a transient or dialysis was stopped due to recovery or death, 90970 would be used to report each day outside the inpatient hospitalization as described in the home dialysis example below.

ESRD-related services for the home dialysis patient:

Home ESRD-related services are initiated on July 1 for a 57-year-old male. On July 11, he is admitted to the hospital as an inpatient and is discharged on July 27.

In this example, 90970 should be reported for each day outside of the inpatient hospitalization (30 days/month less 17 days/hospitalization = 13 days). Report inpatient E/M services as appropriate. Dialysis procedures rendered during the hospitalization (July 11-27) should be reported as appropriate (90935-90937, 90945-90947).

> (Do not report 90951-90970 during the same month in conjunction with 99487-99489)

> (Do not report 90951-90970 during the service time of 99495-99496)

**90951** End-stage renal disease (ESRD) related services monthly, for patients younger than 2 years of age to include monitoring for the adequacy of nutrition, assessment of growth and development, and counseling of parents; with 4 or more face-to-face visits by a physician or other qualified health care professional per month

**90952** with 2-3 face-to-face visits by a physician or other qualified health care professional per month

**90953** with 1 face-to-face visit by a physician or other qualified health care professional per month

**90954** End-stage renal disease (ESRD) related services monthly, for patients 2-11 years of age to include monitoring for the adequacy of nutrition, assessment of growth and development, and counseling of parents; with 4 or more face-to-face visits by a physician or other qualified health care professional per month

**90955** with 2-3 face-to-face visits by a physician or other qualified health care professional per month

**90956** with 1 face-to-face visit by a physician or other qualified health care professional per month

**90957** End-stage renal disease (ESRD) related services monthly, for patients 12-19 years of age to include monitoring for the adequacy of nutrition, assessment of growth and development, and counseling of parents; with 4 or more face-to-face visits by a physician or other qualified health care professional per month

**90958** with 2-3 face-to-face visits by a physician or other qualified health care professional per month

**90959** with 1 face-to-face visit by a physician or other qualified health care professional per month

**90960** End-stage renal disease (ESRD) related services monthly, for patients 20 years of age and older; with 4 or more face-to-face visits by a physician or other qualified health care professional per month

**90961** with 2-3 face-to-face visits by a physician or other qualified health care professional per month

**90962** with 1 face-to-face visit by a physician or other qualified health care professional per month

**90963** End-stage renal disease (ESRD) related services for home dialysis per full month, for patients younger than 2 years of age to include monitoring for the adequacy of nutrition, assessment of growth and development, and counseling of parents

**90964** End-stage renal disease (ESRD) related services for home dialysis per full month, for patients 2-11 years of age to include monitoring for the adequacy of nutrition, assessment of growth and development, and counseling of parents

**90965** End-stage renal disease (ESRD) related services for home dialysis per full month, for patients 12-19 years of age to include monitoring for the adequacy of nutrition, assessment of growth and development, and counseling of parents

Medicine

**90966**    End-stage renal disease (ESRD) related services for home dialysis per full month, for patients 20 years of age and older

**90967**    End-stage renal disease (ESRD) related services for dialysis less than a full month of service, per day; for patients younger than 2 years of age

**90968**        for patients 2-11 years of age

**90969**        for patients 12-19 years of age

**90970**        for patients 20 years of age and older

## Other Dialysis Procedures

**90989**    Dialysis training, patient, including helper where applicable, any mode, completed course

**90993**    Dialysis training, patient, including helper where applicable, any mode, course not completed, per training session

**90997**    Hemoperfusion (eg, with activated charcoal or resin)

**90999**    Unlisted dialysis procedure, inpatient or outpatient

# Gastroenterology

(91000 has been deleted)

**91010**    Esophageal motility (manometric study of the esophagus and/or gastroesophageal junction) study with interpretation and report;

(91011, 91012 have been deleted. To report esophageal motility studies with stimulant or perfusion, use 91013 in conjunction with 91010)

**+ 91013**        with stimulation or perfusion (eg, stimulant, acid or alkali perfusion) (List separately in addition to code for primary procedure)

(Use 91013 in conjunction with 91010)

(Do not report 91013 more than once per session)

(To report esophageal motility studies with high resolution esophageal pressure topography, use 0240T and with stimulant or perfusion, use 0241T)

**91020**    Gastric motility (manometric) studies

**91022**    Duodenal motility (manometric) study

(If gastrointestinal endoscopy is performed, use 43235)

(If fluoroscopy is performed, use 76000)

(If gastric motility study is performed, use 91020)

(Do not report 91020, 91022 in conjunction with 91112)

**91030**    Esophagus, acid perfusion (Bernstein) test for esophagitis

**91034**    Esophagus, gastroesophageal reflux test; with nasal catheter pH electrode(s) placement, recording, analysis and interpretation

**91035**        with mucosal attached telemetry pH electrode placement, recording, analysis and interpretation

**91037**    Esophageal function test, gastroesophageal reflux test with nasal catheter intraluminal impedance electrode(s) placement, recording, analysis and interpretation;

**91038**        prolonged (greater than 1 hour, up to 24 hours)

**91040**    Esophageal balloon distension provocation study

(91052, 91055 have been deleted. To report, see 43754, 43755)

▲ **91065**    Breath hydrogen or methane test (eg, for detection of lactase deficiency, fructose intolerance, bacterial overgrowth, or oro-cecal gastrointestinal transit)

►(Report 91065 once for each administered challenge)◄

(For H. pylori breath test analysis, use 83013 for non-radioactive (C-13) isotope or 78268 for radioactive (C-14) isotope)

(91100 has been deleted)

(To report placement of an esophageal tamponade tube for management of variceal bleeding, use 43460. To report placement of a long intestinal Miller-Abbott tube, use 44500)

(91105 has been deleted. To report, use 43753)

(For cholangiography, see 47500, 74320)

(For abdominal paracentesis, see 49082, 49083, 49084; with instillation of medication, see 96440, 96446)

(For peritoneoscopy, use 49320; with biopsy, use 49321)

(For peritoneoscopy and guided transhepatic cholangiography, use 47560; with biopsy, use 47561)

(For splenoportography, see 38200, 75810)

**91110**    Gastrointestinal tract imaging, intraluminal (eg, capsule endoscopy), esophagus through ileum, with interpretation and report

(Visualization of the colon is not reported separately)

(Append modifier 52 if the ileum is not visualized)

**91111**    Gastrointestinal tract imaging, intraluminal (eg, capsule endoscopy), esophagus with interpretation and report

(Do not report 91111 in conjunction with 91110)

(For measurement of gastrointestinal tract transit times or pressure using wireless capsule, use 91112)

**91112**    Gastrointestinal transit and pressure measurement, stomach through colon, wireless capsule, with interpretation and report

(Do not report 91112 in conjunction with 83986, 91020, 91022, 91117)

**91117**    Colon motility (manometric) study, minimum 6 hours continuous recording (including provocation tests, eg, meal, intracolonic balloon distension, pharmacologic agents, if performed), with interpretation and report

(For wireless capsule pressure measurements, use 91112)

(Do not report 91117 in conjunction with 91120, 91122)

**Medicine**

**91120**  Rectal sensation, tone, and compliance test (ie, response to graded balloon distention)

(For biofeedback training, use 90911)

(For anorectal manometry, use 91122)

**91122**  Anorectal manometry

(Do not report 91120, 91122 in conjunction with 91117)

(91123 has been deleted)

## Gastric Physiology

**91132**  Electrogastrography, diagnostic, transcutaneous;

**91133**  with provocative testing

## Other Procedures

**91299**  Unlisted diagnostic gastroenterology procedure

# Ophthalmology

(For surgical procedures, see **Surgery,** Eye and Ocular Adnexa, 65091 et seq)

### Definitions

*Intermediate ophthalmological services* describes an evaluation of a new or existing condition complicated with a new diagnostic or management problem not necessarily relating to the primary diagnosis, including history, general medical observation, external ocular and adnexal examination and other diagnostic procedures as indicated; may include the use of mydriasis for ophthalmoscopy.

*For example:*

a. Review of history, external examination, ophthalmoscopy, biomicroscopy for an acute complicated condition (eg, iritis) not requiring comprehensive ophthalmological services.

b. Review of interval history, external examination, ophthalmoscopy, biomicroscopy and tonometry in established patient with known cataract not requiring comprehensive ophthalmological services.

*Comprehensive ophthalmological services* describes a general evaluation of the complete visual system. The comprehensive services constitute a single service entity but need not be performed at one session. The service includes history, general medical observation, external and ophthalmoscopic examinations, gross visual fields and basic sensorimotor examination. It often includes, as indicated: biomicroscopy, examination with cycloplegia or mydriasis and tonometry. It always includes initiation of diagnostic and treatment programs.

Intermediate and comprehensive ophthalmological services constitute integrated services in which medical decision making cannot be separated from the examining techniques used. Itemization of service components, such as slit lamp examination, keratometry, routine ophthalmoscopy, retinoscopy, tonometry, or motor evaluation is not applicable.

*For example:*

The comprehensive services required for diagnosis and treatment of a patient with symptoms indicating possible disease of the visual system, such as glaucoma, cataract or retinal disease, or to rule out disease of the visual system, new or established patient.

*Initiation of diagnostic and treatment program* includes the prescription of medication, and arranging for special ophthalmological diagnostic or treatment services, consultations, laboratory procedures and radiological services.

*Special ophthalmological services* describes services in which a special evaluation of part of the visual system is made, which goes beyond the services included under general ophthalmological services, or in which special treatment is given. Special ophthalmological services may be reported in addition to the general ophthalmological services or evaluation and management services.

*For example:*

Fluorescein angioscopy, quantitative visual field examination, refraction or extended color vision examination (such as Nagel's anomaloscope) should be separately reported.

Prescription of lenses, when required, is included in 92015. It includes specification of lens type (monofocal, bifocal, other), lens power, axis, prism, absorptive factor, impact resistance, and other factors.

Interpretation and report by the physician or other qualified health care professional is an integral part of special ophthalmological services where indicated. Technical procedures (which may or may not be performed personally) are often part of the service, but should not be mistaken to constitute the service itself.

## General Ophthalmological Services

### New Patient

(For distinguishing between new and established patients, see **Evaluation and Management** guidelines)

**92002**  Ophthalmological services: medical examination and evaluation with initiation of diagnostic and treatment program; intermediate, new patient

**92004**  comprehensive, new patient, 1 or more visits

Medicine

## Established Patient

(For distinguishing between new and established patients, see **Evaluation and Management** guidelines)

**92012** Ophthalmological services: medical examination and evaluation, with initiation or continuation of diagnostic and treatment program; intermediate, established patient

**92014** comprehensive, established patient, 1 or more visits

(For surgical procedures, see **Surgery,** Eye and Ocular Adnexa, 65091 et seq)

# Special Ophthalmological Services

**92015** Determination of refractive state

(For instrument based ocular screening, use 99174)

**92018** Ophthalmological examination and evaluation, under general anesthesia, with or without manipulation of globe for passive range of motion or other manipulation to facilitate diagnostic examination; complete

**92019** limited

**92020** Gonioscopy (separate procedure)

(For gonioscopy under general anesthesia, use 92018)

**92025** Computerized corneal topography, unilateral or bilateral, with interpretation and report

(Do not report 92025 in conjunction with 65710-65771)

(92025 is not used for manual keratoscopy, which is part of a single system Evaluation and Management or ophthalmological service)

**92060** Sensorimotor examination with multiple measurements of ocular deviation (eg, restrictive or paretic muscle with diplopia) with interpretation and report (separate procedure)

**92065** Orthoptic and/or pleoptic training, with continuing medical direction and evaluation

(92070 has been deleted. To report, see 92071, 92072)

**92071** Fitting of contact lens for treatment of ocular surface disease

(Do not report 92071 in conjunction with 92072)

(Report supply of lens separately with 99070 or appropriate supply code)

**92072** Fitting of contact lens for management of keratoconus, initial fitting

(For subsequent fittings, report using evaluation and management services or general ophthalmological services)

(Do not report 92072 in conjunction with 92071)

(Report supply of lens separately with 99070 or appropriate supply code)

**92081** Visual field examination, unilateral or bilateral, with interpretation and report; limited examination (eg, tangent screen, Autoplot, arc perimeter, or single stimulus level automated test, such as Octopus 3 or 7 equivalent)

**92082** intermediate examination (eg, at least 2 isopters on Goldmann perimeter, or semiquantitative, automated suprathreshold screening program, Humphrey suprathreshold automatic diagnostic test, Octopus program 33)

**92083** extended examination (eg, Goldmann visual fields with at least 3 isopters plotted and static determination within the central 30°, or quantitative, automated threshold perimetry, Octopus program G-1, 32 or 42, Humphrey visual field analyzer full threshold programs 30-2, 24-2, or 30/60-2)

(Gross visual field testing (eg, confrontation testing) is a part of general ophthalmological services and is not reported separately)

**92100** Serial tonometry (separate procedure) with multiple measurements of intraocular pressure over an extended time period with interpretation and report, same day (eg, diurnal curve or medical treatment of acute elevation of intraocular pressure)

▶(For monitoring of intraocular pressure for 24 hours or longer, use 0329T)◀

(92120, 92130 have been deleted)

(Ocular blood flow measurements are reported with 0198T. Single-episode tonometry is a component of general ophthalmological service or E/M service)

**92132** Scanning computerized ophthalmic diagnostic imaging, anterior segment, with interpretation and report, unilateral or bilateral

(For specular microscopy and endothelial cell analysis, use 92286)

▶(For tear film imaging, use 0330T)◀

**92133** Scanning computerized ophthalmic diagnostic imaging, posterior segment, with interpretation and report, unilateral or bilateral; optic nerve

**92134** retina

(Do not report 92133 and 92134 at the same patient encounter)

(92135 has been deleted)

(For scanning computerized ophthalmic diagnostic imaging of the optic nerve and retina, see 92133, 92134)

**92136** Ophthalmic biometry by partial coherence interferometry with intraocular lens power calculation

▶(For tear film imaging, use 0330T)◀

**92140** Provocative tests for glaucoma, with interpretation and report, without tonography

**Medicine**

## Ophthalmoscopy

Routine ophthalmoscopy is part of general and special ophthalmologic services whenever indicated. It is a non-itemized service and is not reported separately.

92225 Ophthalmoscopy, extended, with retinal drawing (eg, for retinal detachment, melanoma), with interpretation and report; initial

92226       subsequent

92227 Remote imaging for detection of retinal disease (eg, retinopathy in a patient with diabetes) with analysis and report under physician supervision, unilateral or bilateral

(Do not report 92227 in conjunction with 92002-92014, 92133, 92134, 92250, 92228 or with the evaluation and management of the single organ system, the eye, 99201-99350)

92228 Remote imaging for monitoring and management of active retinal disease (eg, diabetic retinopathy) with physician review, interpretation and report, unilateral or bilateral

(Do not report 92228 in conjunction with 92002-92014, 92133, 92134, 92250, 92227 or with the evaluation and management of the single organ system, the eye, 99201-99350)

92230 Fluorescein angioscopy with interpretation and report

92235 Fluorescein angiography (includes multiframe imaging) with interpretation and report

92240 Indocyanine-green angiography (includes multiframe imaging) with interpretation and report

92250 Fundus photography with interpretation and report

92260 Ophthalmodynamometry

(For ophthalmoscopy under general anesthesia, use 92018)

## Other Specialized Services

For prescription, fitting, and/or medical supervision of ocular prosthetic (artificial eye) adaptation by a physician, see evaluation and management services including office or other outpatient services (99201-99215), office or other outpatient consultations (99241-99245) or general ophthalmological service codes 92002-92014.

92265 Needle oculoelectromyography, 1 or more extraocular muscles, 1 or both eyes, with interpretation and report

92270 Electro-oculography with interpretation and report

92275 Electroretinography with interpretation and report

(For electronystagmography for vestibular function studies, see 92541 et seq)

(For ophthalmic echography (diagnostic ultrasound), see 76511-76529)

92283 Color vision examination, extended, eg, anomaloscope or equivalent

(Color vision testing with pseudoisochromatic plates [such as HRR or Ishihara] is not reported separately. It is included in the appropriate general or ophthalmological service, or 99172)

92284 Dark adaptation examination with interpretation and report

92285 External ocular photography with interpretation and report for documentation of medical progress (eg, close-up photography, slit lamp photography, goniophotography, stereo-photography)

►(For tear film imaging, use 0330T)◄

92286 Anterior segment imaging with interpretation and report; with specular microscopy and endothelial cell analysis

92287       with fluorescein angiography

## Contact Lens Services

The prescription of contact lens includes specification of optical and physical characteristics (such as power, size, curvature, flexibility, gas-permeability). It is **not** a part of the general ophthalmological services.

The fitting of contact lens includes instruction and training of the wearer and incidental revision of the lens during the training period.

Follow-up of successfully fitted extended wear lenses is reported as part of a general ophthalmological service (92012 et seq).

The supply of contact lenses may be reported as part of the service of fitting. It may also be reported separately by using the appropriate supply codes.

(For therapeutic or surgical use of contact lens, see 68340, 92071, 92072)

92310 Prescription of optical and physical characteristics of and fitting of contact lens, with medical supervision of adaptation; corneal lens, both eyes, except for aphakia

(For prescription and fitting of 1 eye, add modifier 52)

92311       corneal lens for aphakia, 1 eye

92312       corneal lens for aphakia, both eyes

92313       corneoscleral lens

92314 Prescription of optical and physical characteristics of contact lens, with medical supervision of adaptation and direction of fitting by independent technician; corneal lens, both eyes except for aphakia

(For prescription and fitting of 1 eye, add modifier 52)

92315       corneal lens for aphakia, 1 eye

92316       corneal lens for aphakia, both eyes

92317       corneoscleral lens

Medicine

**92325**    Modification of contact lens (separate procedure), with medical supervision of adaptation

**92326**    Replacement of contact lens

# Spectacle Services (Including Prosthesis for Aphakia)

Prescription of lenses, when required, is included in 92015 Determination of refractive state. It includes specification of lens type (monofocal, bifocal, other), lens power, axis, prism, absorptive factor, impact resistance, and other factors.

When provided, fitting of spectacles is a separate service and is reported as indicated by 92340-92371.

Fitting includes measurement of anatomical facial characteristics, the writing of laboratory specifications, and the final adjustment of the spectacles to the visual axes and anatomical topography. Presence of the physician or other qualified health care professional is not required.

Supply of materials is a separate service component; it is not part of the service of fitting spectacles.

**92340**    Fitting of spectacles, except for aphakia; monofocal

**92341**        bifocal

**92342**        multifocal, other than bifocal

**92352**    Fitting of spectacle prosthesis for aphakia; monofocal

**92353**        multifocal

**92354**    Fitting of spectacle mounted low vision aid; single element system

**92355**        telescopic or other compound lens system

**92358**    Prosthesis service for aphakia, temporary (disposable or loan, including materials)

**92370**    Repair and refitting spectacles; except for aphakia

**92371**        spectacle prosthesis for aphakia

## Other Procedures

**92499**    Unlisted ophthalmological service or procedure

# Special Otorhinolaryngologic Services

Diagnostic or treatment procedures that are reported as evaluation and management services (eg, otoscopy, anterior rhinoscopy, tuning fork test, removal of non-impacted cerumen) are not reported separately.

Special otorhinolaryngologic services are those diagnostic and treatment services not included in an evaluation and management service, including office or other outpatient services (99201-99215), or office or other outpatient consultations (99241-99245).

►Codes 92521, 92522, 92523, and 92524 are used to report evaluation of speech production, receptive language, and expressive language abilities. Tests may examine speech sound production, articulatory movements of oral musculature, the patient's ability to understand the meaning and intent of written and verbal expressions, and the appropriate formulation and utterance of expressive thought. In contrast, 92626 and 92627 are reported for an evaluation of auditory rehabilitation status determining the patient's ability to use residual hearing in order to identify the acoustic characteristics of sounds associated with speech communication.◄

(For laryngoscopy with stroboscopy, use 31579)

**92502**    Otolaryngologic examination under general anesthesia

**92504**    Binocular microscopy (separate diagnostic procedure)

►(92506 has been deleted. To report, see 92521, 92522, 92523, 92524)◄

**92507**    Treatment of speech, language, voice, communication, and/or auditory processing disorder; individual

**92508**        group, 2 or more individuals

(For auditory rehabilitation, prelingual hearing loss, use 92630)

(For auditory rehabilitation, postlingual hearing loss, use 92633)

(For cochlear implant programming, see 92601-92604)

**92511**    Nasopharyngoscopy with endoscope (separate procedure)

**92512**    Nasal function studies (eg, rhinomanometry)

**92516**    Facial nerve function studies (eg, electroneuronography)

**92520**    Laryngeal function studies (ie, aerodynamic testing and acoustic testing)

(For performance of a single test, use modifier 52)

(To report flexible fiberoptic laryngeal evaluation of swallowing and laryngeal sensory testing, see 92611-92617)

(To report other testing of laryngeal function (eg, electroglottography), use 92700)

● **92521**    Evaluation of speech fluency (eg, stuttering, cluttering)

● **92522**    Evaluation of speech sound production (eg, articulation, phonological process, apraxia, dysarthria)

● **92523**        with evaluation of language comprehension and expression (eg, receptive and expressive language)

● **92524**    Behavioral and qualitative analysis of voice and resonance

**92526**    Treatment of swallowing dysfunction and/or oral function for feeding

**Medicine**

# Vestibular Function Tests, Without Electrical Recording

**92531**   Spontaneous nystagmus, including gaze

**92532**   Positional nystagmus test

(Do not report 92531, 92532 with evaluation and management services including office or other outpatient services [99201-99215], observation care [99218-99220, 99224-99226], observation or inpatient care including admission and discharge [99234-99236], hospital care [99221-99223, 99231-99233], office or other outpatient consultations [99241-99245], nursing facility services [99304-99318], and domiciliary, rest home, or custodial care services [99324-99337])

**92533**   Caloric vestibular test, each irrigation (binaural, bithermal stimulation constitutes 4 tests)

**92534**   Optokinetic nystagmus test

# Vestibular Function Tests, With Recording (eg, ENG)

**92540**   Basic vestibular evaluation, includes spontaneous nystagmus test with eccentric gaze fixation nystagmus, with recording, positional nystagmus test, minimum of 4 positions, with recording, optokinetic nystagmus test, bidirectional foveal and peripheral stimulation, with recording, and oscillating tracking test, with recording

(Do not report 92540 in conjunction with 92541, 92542, 92544, or 92545)

**92541**   Spontaneous nystagmus test, including gaze and fixation nystagmus, with recording

(Do not report 92541 in conjunction with 92540 or the set of 92542, 92544, 92545)

**92542**   Positional nystagmus test, minimum of 4 positions, with recording

(Do not report 92542 in conjunction with 92540 or the set of 92541, 92544, and 92545)

**92543**   Caloric vestibular test, each irrigation (binaural, bithermal stimulation constitutes 4 tests), with recording

**92544**   Optokinetic nystagmus test, bidirectional, foveal or peripheral stimulation, with recording

(Do not report 92544 in conjunction with 92540 or the set of 92541, 92542, and 92545)

**92545**   Oscillating tracking test, with recording

(Do not report 92545 in conjunction with 92540 or the set of 92541, 92542, and 92544)

**92546**   Sinusoidal vertical axis rotational testing

**+ 92547**   Use of vertical electrodes (List separately in addition to code for primary procedure)

(Use 92547 in conjunction with 92540-92546)

(For unlisted vestibular tests, use 92700)

**92548**   Computerized dynamic posturography

# Audiologic Function Tests

The audiometric tests listed below require the use of calibrated electronic equipment, recording of results and a report with interpretation. Hearing tests (such as whispered voice, tuning fork) that are otorhinolaryngologic Evaluation and Management services are not reported separately. All services include testing of both ears. Use modifier 52 if a test is applied to one ear instead of two ears. All codes (except 92559) apply to testing of individuals. For testing of groups, use 92559 and specify test(s) used.

►(For evaluation of speech, language, and/or hearing problems through observation and assessment of performance, see 92521, 92522, 92523, 92524)◄

**92550**   Tympanometry and reflex threshold measurements

(Do not report 92550 in conjunction with 92567, 92568)

**92551**   Screening test, pure tone, air only

**92552**   Pure tone audiometry (threshold); air only

**92553**       air and bone

**92555**   Speech audiometry threshold;

**92556**       with speech recognition

**92557**   Comprehensive audiometry threshold evaluation and speech recognition (92553 and 92556 combined)

(For hearing aid evaluation and selection, see 92590-92595)

(For automated audiometry, see 0208T-0212T)

**92558**   Code is out of numerical sequence. See 92550-92597

**92559**   Audiometric testing of groups

**92560**   Bekesy audiometry; screening

**92561**       diagnostic

**92562**   Loudness balance test, alternate binaural or monaural

**92563**   Tone decay test

**92564**   Short increment sensitivity index (SISI)

**92565**   Stenger test, pure tone

**92567**   Tympanometry (impedance testing)

**92568**   Acoustic reflex testing, threshold

(92569 has been deleted. For acoustic reflex decay testing performed in conjunction with tympanometry, use 92570)

**92570**   Acoustic immittance testing, includes tympanometry (impedance testing), acoustic reflex threshold testing, and acoustic reflex decay testing

(Do not report 92570 in conjunction with 92567, 92568)

**92571**   Filtered speech test

**92572**   Staggered spondaic word test

Medicine

92575   Sensorineural acuity level test

92576   Synthetic sentence identification test

92577   Stenger test, speech

92579   Visual reinforcement audiometry (VRA)

92582   Conditioning play audiometry

92583   Select picture audiometry

92584   Electrocochleography

92585   Auditory evoked potentials for evoked response audiometry and/or testing of the central nervous system; comprehensive

92586       limited

# 92558  Evoked otoacoustic emissions, screening (qualitative measurement of distortion product or transient evoked otoacoustic emissions), automated analysis

92587   Distortion product evoked otoacoustic emissions; limited evaluation (to confirm the presence or absence of hearing disorder, 3-6 frequencies) or transient evoked otoacoustic emissions, with interpretation and report

92588       comprehensive diagnostic evaluation (quantitative analysis of outer hair cell function by cochlear mapping, minimum of 12 frequencies), with interpretation and report

        (For central auditory function evaluation, see 92620, 92621)

92590   Hearing aid examination and selection; monaural

92591       binaural

92592   Hearing aid check; monaural

92593       binaural

92594   Electroacoustic evaluation for hearing aid; monaural

92595       binaural

92596   Ear protector attenuation measurements

92597   Evaluation for use and/or fitting of voice prosthetic device to supplement oral speech

        (To report augmentative and alternative communication device services, see 92605, 92607, 92608)

# Evaluative and Therapeutic Services

Codes 92601 and 92603 describe post-operative analysis and fitting of previously placed external devices, connection to the cochlear implant, and programming of the stimulator. Codes 92602 and 92604 describe subsequent sessions for measurements and adjustment of the external transmitter and re-programming of the internal stimulator.

        (For placement of cochlear implant, use 69930)

92601   Diagnostic analysis of cochlear implant, patient younger than 7 years of age; with programming

92602       subsequent reprogramming

        (Do not report 92602 in addition to 92601)

        (For aural rehabilitation services following cochlear implant, including evaluation of rehabilitation status, see 92626-92627, 92630-92633)

92603   Diagnostic analysis of cochlear implant, age 7 years or older; with programming

92604       subsequent reprogramming

        (Do not report 92604 in addition to 92603)

92605   Evaluation for prescription of non-speech-generating augmentative and alternative communication device, face-to-face with the patient; first hour

#+ 92618     each additional 30 minutes (List separately in addition to code for primary procedure)

        (Use 92618 in conjunction with 92605)

92606   Therapeutic service(s) for the use of non-speech-generating device, including programming and modification

92607   Evaluation for prescription for speech-generating augmentative and alternative communication device, face-to-face with the patient; first hour

        (For evaluation for prescription of a non-speech-generating device, use 92605)

+ 92608     each additional 30 minutes (List separately in addition to code for primary procedure)

        (Use 92608 in conjunction with 92607)

92609   Therapeutic services for the use of speech-generating device, including programming and modification

        (For therapeutic service(s) for the use of a non-speech-generating device, use 92606)

92610   Evaluation of oral and pharyngeal swallowing function

        (For motion fluoroscopic evaluation of swallowing function, use 92611)

        (For flexible endoscopic examination, use 92612-92617)

92611   Motion fluoroscopic evaluation of swallowing function by cine or video recording

        (For radiological supervision and interpretation, use 74230)

        (For evaluation of oral and pharyngeal swallowing function, use 92610)

        (For flexible fiberoptic diagnostic laryngoscopy, use 31575. Do not report 31575 in conjunction with 92612-92617)

92612   Flexible fiberoptic endoscopic evaluation of swallowing by cine or video recording;

        (If flexible fiberoptic or endoscopic evaluation of swallowing is performed without cine or video recording, use 92700)

**Medicine**

**92613**     interpretation and report only

(To report an evaluation of oral and pharyngeal swallowing function, use 92610)

(To report motion fluoroscopic evaluation of swallowing function, use 92611)

**92614** Flexible fiberoptic endoscopic evaluation, laryngeal sensory testing by cine or video recording;

(If flexible fiberoptic or endoscopic evaluation of swallowing is performed without cine or video recording, use 92700)

**92615**     interpretation and report only

**92616** Flexible fiberoptic endoscopic evaluation of swallowing and laryngeal sensory testing by cine or video recording;

(If flexible fiberoptic or endoscopic evaluation of swallowing is performed without cine or video recording, use 92700)

**92617**     interpretation and report only

**92618** Code is out of numerical sequence. See 92601-92633

**92620** Evaluation of central auditory function, with report; initial 60 minutes

**+ 92621**     each additional 15 minutes (List separately in addition to code for primary procedure)

(Use 92621 in conjunction with 92620)

▶(Do not report 92620, 92621 in conjunction with 92521, 92522, 92523, 92524)◀

**92625** Assessment of tinnitus (includes pitch, loudness matching, and masking)

(Do not report 92625 in conjunction with 92562)

(For unilateral assessment, use modifier 52)

**92626** Evaluation of auditory rehabilitation status; first hour

**+ 92627**     each additional 15 minutes (List separately in addition to code for primary procedure)

(Use 92627 in conjunction with 92626)

(When reporting 92626, 92627, use the face-to-face time with the patient or family)

**92630** Auditory rehabilitation; prelingual hearing loss

**92633**     postlingual hearing loss

## Special Diagnostic Procedures

**92640** Diagnostic analysis with programming of auditory brainstem implant, per hour

(Report nonprogramming services separately [eg, cardiac monitoring])

## Other Procedures

**92700** Unlisted otorhinolaryngological service or procedure

# Cardiovascular

## Therapeutic Services and Procedures

**92920** Code is out of numerical sequence. See 92998-93000

**92921** Code is out of numerical sequence. See 92998-93000

**92924** Code is out of numerical sequence. See 92998-93000

**92925** Code is out of numerical sequence. See 92998-93000

**92928** Code is out of numerical sequence. See 92998-93000

**92929** Code is out of numerical sequence. See 92998-93000

**92933** Code is out of numerical sequence. See 92998-93000

**92934** Code is out of numerical sequence. See 92998-93000

**92937** Code is out of numerical sequence. See 92998-93000

**92938** Code is out of numerical sequence. See 92998-93000

**92941** Code is out of numerical sequence. See 92998-93000

**92943** Code is out of numerical sequence. See 92998-93000

**92944** Code is out of numerical sequence. See 92998-93000

## Other Therapeutic Services and Procedures

**92950** Cardiopulmonary resuscitation (eg, in cardiac arrest)

(See also critical care services, 99291, 99292)

⊙ **92953** Temporary transcutaneous pacing

(For direction of ambulance or rescue personnel outside the hospital by a physician or other qualified health care professional, use 99288)

⊙ **92960** Cardioversion, elective, electrical conversion of arrhythmia; external

⊙ **92961**     internal (separate procedure)

(Do not report 92961 in conjunction with 93282-93284, 93287, 93289, 93295, 93296, 93618-93624, 93631, 93640-93642, 93650, 93653-93657, 93662)

**92970** Cardioassist-method of circulatory assist; internal

**92971**     external

(For balloon atrial-septostomy, use 92992)

(For placement of catheters for use in circulatory assist devices such as intra-aortic balloon pump, use 33970)

**92973** Code is out of numerical sequence. See 92998-93000

**92974** Code is out of numerical sequence. See 92998-93000

**92975** Code is out of numerical sequence. See 92998-93000

**92977** Code is out of numerical sequence. See 92998-93000

**92978** Code is out of numerical sequence. See 92998-93000

Medicine

| | |
|---|---|
| **92979** | Code is out of numerical sequence. See 92998-93000 |
| | (92980, 92981, 92982, 92984 have been deleted. To report, see 92920-92944) |
| ⊙ **92986** | Percutaneous balloon valvuloplasty; aortic valve |
| ⊙ **92987** | mitral valve |
| **92990** | pulmonary valve |
| **92992** | Atrial septectomy or septostomy; transvenous method, balloon (eg, Rashkind type) (includes cardiac catheterization) |
| **92993** | blade method (Park septostomy) (includes cardiac catheterization) |
| | (92995, 92996 have been deleted. To report, see 92924, 92925, 92933-92944) |
| **92997** | Percutaneous transluminal pulmonary artery balloon angioplasty; single vessel |
| **+ 92998** | each additional vessel (List separately in addition to code for primary procedure) |
| | (Use 92998 in conjunction with 92997) |

# Coronary Therapeutic Services and Procedures

Codes 92920-92944 describe percutaneous revascularization services performed for occlusive disease of the coronary vessels (major coronary arteries, coronary artery branches, or coronary artery bypass grafts). These percutaneous coronary intervention (PCI) codes are built on progressive hierarchies with more intensive services inclusive of lesser intensive services. These PCI codes all include the work of accessing and selectively catheterizing the vessel, traversing the lesion, radiological supervision and interpretation directly related to the intervention(s) performed, closure of the arteriotomy when performed through the access sheath, and imaging performed to document completion of the intervention in addition to the intervention(s) performed. These codes include angioplasty (eg, balloon, cutting balloon, wired balloons, cryoplasty), atherectomy (eg, directional, rotational, laser), and stenting (eg, balloon expandable, self-expanding, bare metal, drug eluting, covered). Each code in this family includes balloon angioplasty, when performed. Diagnostic coronary angiography may be reported separately under specific circumstances.

Diagnostic coronary angiography codes (93454-93461) and injection procedure codes (93563-93564) should not be used with percutaneous coronary revascularization services (92920-92944) to report:

1. Contrast injections, angiography, roadmapping, and/or fluoroscopic guidance for the coronary intervention,

2. Vessel measurement for the coronary intervention, or

3. Post-coronary angioplasty/stent/atherectomy angiography, as this work is captured in the percutaneous coronary revascularization services codes (92920-92944).

Diagnostic angiography performed at the time of a coronary interventional procedure may be separately reportable if:

1. No prior catheter-based coronary angiography study is available, and a full diagnostic study is performed, and a decision to intervene is based on the diagnostic angiography, **or**

2. A prior study is available, but as documented in the medical record:

   a. The patient's condition with respect to the clinical indication has changed since the prior study, **or**

   b. There is inadequate visualization of the anatomy and/or pathology, **or**

   c. There is a clinical change during the procedure that requires new evaluation outside the target area of intervention.

Diagnostic coronary angiography performed at a separate session from an interventional procedure is separately reportable.

*Major coronary arteries:* The major coronary arteries are the left main, left anterior descending, left circumflex, right, and ramus intermedius arteries. All PCI procedures performed in all segments (proximal, mid, distal) of a single major coronary artery through the native coronary circulation are reported with one code. When one segment of a major coronary artery is treated through the native circulation and treatment of another segment of the same artery requires access through a coronary artery bypass graft, the intervention through the bypass graft is reported separately.

*Coronary artery branches:* Up to two coronary artery branches of the left anterior descending (diagonals), left circumflex (marginals), and right (posterior descending, posterolaterals) coronary arteries are recognized. The left main and ramus intermedius coronary arteries do not have recognized branches for reporting purposes. All PCI(s) performed in any segment (proximal, mid, distal) of a coronary artery branch is reported with one code. PCI is reported for up to two branches of a major coronary artery. Additional PCI in a third branch of the same major coronary artery is not separately reportable.

*Coronary artery bypass grafts:* Each coronary artery bypass graft represents a coronary vessel. A sequential bypass graft with more than one distal anastomosis represents only one graft. A branching bypass graft (eg, Y graft) represents a coronary vessel for the main graft, and each branch off the main graft constitutes an additional coronary vessel. PCI performed on major coronary arteries or coronary artery branches by access through a bypass graft is reported using the bypass graft PCI codes.

All bypass graft PCI codes include the use of coronary artery embolic protection devices when performed.

Only one base code from this family may be reported for revascularization of a major coronary artery and its recognized branches. Only one base code should be reported for revascularization of a coronary artery bypass graft, its subtended coronary artery, and recognized branches of the subtended coronary artery. If one segment of a major coronary artery and its recognized branches is treated through the native circulation, and treatment of another segment of the same vessel requires access through a coronary artery bypass graft, an additional base code is reported to describe the intervention performed through the bypass graft. The PCI base codes are 92920, 92924, 92928, 92933, 92937, 92941, and 92943. The PCI base code that includes the most intensive service provided for the target vessel should be reported. The hierarchy of these services is built on an intensity of service ranked from highest to lowest as 92943 = 92941 = 92933 > 92924 > 92937 = 92928 > 92920.

PCI performed during the same session in additional recognized branches of the target vessel should be reported using the applicable add-on code(s). The add-on codes are 92921, 92925, 92928, 92934, 92938, and 92944 and follow the same principle in regard to reporting the most intensive service provided. The intensity of service is ranked from highest to lowest as 92944 = 92938 > 92934 > 92925 > 92929 > 92921.

PCI performed during the same session in additional major coronary or in additional coronary artery bypass grafts should be reported using the applicable additional base code(s). PCI performed during the same session in additional coronary artery branches should be reported using the applicable additional add-on code(s).

If a single lesion extends from one target vessel (major coronary artery, coronary artery bypass graft, or coronary artery branch) into another target vessel, but can be revascularized with a single intervention bridging the two vessels, this PCI should be reported with a single code despite treating more than one vessel. For example, if a left main coronary lesion extends into the proximal left circumflex coronary artery and a single stent is placed to treat the entire lesion, this PCI should be reported as a single vessel stent (92928). In this example, a code for additional vessel treatment (92929) would not be additionally reported.

When bifurcation lesions are treated, PCI is reported for both vessels treated. For example, when a bifurcation lesion involving the left anterior descending artery and the first diagonal artery is treated by stenting both vessels, 92928 and 92929 are both reported.

Target vessel PCI for acute myocardial infarction is inclusive of all balloon angioplasty, atherectomy, stenting, manual aspiration thrombectomy, distal protection, and intracoronary rheolytic agent administration performed. Mechanical thrombectomy is reported separately.

Chronic total occlusion of a coronary vessel is present when there is no antegrade flow through the true lumen, accompanied by suggestive angiographic and clinical criteria (eg, antegrade "bridging" collaterals present, calcification at the occlusion site, no current presentation with ST elevation or Q wave acute myocardial infarction attributable to the occluded target lesion). Current presentation with ST elevation or Q wave acute myocardial infarction attributable to the occluded target lesion, subtotal occlusion, and occlusion with dye staining at the site consistent with fresh thrombus are not considered chronic total occlusion.

Codes 92973 (percutaneous transluminal coronary thrombectomy, mechanical), 92974 (coronary brachytherapy), 92978 and 92979 (intravascular ultrasound), and 93571 and 93572 (intravascular Doppler velocity and/or pressure [fractional flow reserve (FFR) or coronary flow reserve (CFR)]) are add-on codes for reporting procedures performed in addition to coronary and bypass graft diagnostic and interventional services, unless included in the base code. Non-mechanical, aspiration thrombectomy is not reported with 92973, and is included in the PCI code for acute myocardial infarction (92941), when performed.

(To report transcatheter placement of radiation delivery device for coronary intravascular brachytherapy, use 92974)

(For intravascular radioelement application, see 77785-77787)

(For nonsurgical septal reduction therapy [eg, alcohol ablation], use 93799)

#⊙ **92920**    Percutaneous transluminal coronary angioplasty; single major coronary artery or branch

#⊙+ **92921**        each additional branch of a major coronary artery (List separately in addition to code for primary procedure)

(Use 92921 in conjunction with 92920, 92924, 92928, 92933, 92937, 92941, 92943)

#⊙ **92924**    Percutaneous transluminal coronary atherectomy, with coronary angioplasty when performed; single major coronary artery or branch

#⊙+ **92925**        each additional branch of a major coronary artery (List separately in addition to code for primary procedure)

(Use 92925 in conjunction with 92924, 92928, 92933, 92937, 92941, 92943)

#⊙ **92928**    Percutaneous transcatheter placement of intracoronary stent(s), with coronary angioplasty when performed; single major coronary artery or branch

#⊙+ **92929**        each additional branch of a major coronary artery (List separately in addition to code for primary procedure)

(Use 92929 in conjunction with 92928, 92933, 92937, 92941, 92943)

#⊙ **92933**    Percutaneous transluminal coronary atherectomy, with intracoronary stent, with coronary angioplasty when performed; single major coronary artery or branch

#⊙+ **92934**   each additional branch of a major coronary artery (List separately in addition to code for primary procedure)

(Use 92934 in conjunction with 92933, 92937, 92941, 92943)

#⊙ **92937**   Percutaneous transluminal revascularization of or through coronary artery bypass graft (internal mammary, free arterial, venous), any combination of intracoronary stent, atherectomy and angioplasty, including distal protection when performed; single vessel

#⊙+ **92938**   each additional branch subtended by the bypass graft (List separately in addition to code for primary procedure)

(Use 92938 in conjunction with 92937)

#⊙ **92941**   Percutaneous transluminal revascularization of acute total/subtotal occlusion during acute myocardial infarction, coronary artery or coronary artery bypass graft, any combination of intracoronary stent, atherectomy and angioplasty, including aspiration thrombectomy when performed, single vessel

(For additional vessels treated, see 92920-92938, 92943, 92944)

#⊙ **92943**   Percutaneous transluminal revascularization of chronic total occlusion, coronary artery, coronary artery branch, or coronary artery bypass graft, any combination of intracoronary stent, atherectomy and angioplasty; single vessel

#⊙+ **92944**   each additional coronary artery, coronary artery branch, or bypass graft (List separately in addition to code for primary procedure)

(Use 92944 in conjunction with 92924, 92928, 92933, 92937, 92941, 92943)

(To report transcatheter placement of radiation delivery device for coronary intravascular brachytherapy, use 92974)

(For intravascular radioelement application, see 77785-77787)

#⊙+ **92973**   Percutaneous transluminal coronary thrombectomy mechanical (List separately in addition to code for primary procedure)

(Use 92973 in conjunction with 92920, 92924, 92928, 92933, 92937, 92941, 92943, 92975, 93454-93461, 93563, 93564)

(Do not report 92973 for aspiration thrombectomy)

#⊙+ **92974**   Transcatheter placement of radiation delivery device for subsequent coronary intravascular brachytherapy (List separately in addition to code for primary procedure)

(Use 92974 in conjunction with 92920, 92924, 92928, 92933, 92937, 92941, 92943, 93454-93461)

(For intravascular radioelement application, see 77785-77787)

#⊙ **92975**   Thrombolysis, coronary; by intracoronary infusion, including selective coronary angiography

# **92977**   by intravenous infusion

(For thrombolysis of vessels other than coronary, see 37211-37214)

(For cerebral thrombolysis, use 37195)

#⊙+ **92978**   Intravascular ultrasound (coronary vessel or graft) during diagnostic evaluation and/or therapeutic intervention including imaging supervision, interpretation and report; initial vessel (List separately in addition to code for primary procedure)

(Use 92978 in conjunction with 92975, 92920, 92924, 92928, 92933, 92937, 92941, 92943, 93454-93461, 93563, 93564)

#⊙+ **92979**   each additional vessel (List separately in addition to code for primary procedure)

(Use 92979 in conjunction with 92978)

(Intravascular ultrasound services include all transducer manipulations and repositioning within the specific vessel being examined, both before and after therapeutic intervention [eg, stent placement])

(For intravascular spectroscopy, use 0205T)

(For intravascular optical coherence tomography, see 0291T, 0292T)

# Cardiography

Codes 93040-93042 are appropriate when an order for the test is triggered by an event, the rhythm strip is used to help diagnose the presence or absence of an arrhythmia, and a report is generated. There must be a specific order for an electrocardiogram or rhythm strip followed by a separate, signed, written, and retrievable report. It is not appropriate to use these codes for reviewing the telemetry monitor strips taken from a monitoring system. The need for an electrocardiogram or rhythm strip should be supported by documentation in the patient medical record.

(For echocardiography, see 93303-93350)

(For electrocardiogram, 64 leads or greater, with graphic presentation and analysis, use 93799)

(For acoustic cardiography services, see 0223T-0225T)

**93000**   Electrocardiogram, routine ECG with at least 12 leads; with interpretation and report

**93005**   tracing only, without interpretation and report

**93010**   interpretation and report only

(For ECG monitoring, see 99354-99360)

(93012, 93014 have been deleted. To report telephonic transmission of post-symptom electrocardiogram rhythm strips, see 93268-93272)

**93015**   Cardiovascular stress test using maximal or submaximal treadmill or bicycle exercise, continuous electrocardiographic monitoring, and/or pharmacological stress; with supervision, interpretation and report

| | |
|---|---|
| **93016** | supervision only, without interpretation and report |
| **93017** | tracing only, without interpretation and report |
| **93018** | interpretation and report only |
| **93024** | Ergonovine provocation test |
| **93025** | Microvolt T-wave alternans for assessment of ventricular arrhythmias |
| **93040** | Rhythm ECG, 1-3 leads; with interpretation and report |
| **93041** | tracing only without interpretation and report |
| **93042** | interpretation and report only |

## Cardiovascular Monitoring Services

Cardiovascular monitoring services are diagnostic medical procedures using in-person and remote technology to assess cardiovascular rhythm (ECG) data. Holter monitors (93224-93227) include up to 48 hours of continuous recording. Mobile cardiac telemetry monitors (93228, 93229) have the capability of transmitting a tracing at any time, always have internal ECG analysis algorithms designed to detect major arrhythmias, and transmit to an attended surveillance center. Event monitors (93268-93272) record segments of ECGs with recording initiation triggered either by patient activation or by an internal automatic, pre-programmed detection algorithm (or both) and transmit the recorded electrocardiographic data when requested (but cannot transmit immediately based upon the patient or algorithmic activation rhythm) and require attended surveillance.

*Attended surveillance:* is the immediate availability of a remote technician to respond to rhythm or device alert transmissions from a patient, either from an implanted or wearable monitoring or therapy device, as they are generated and transmitted to the remote surveillance location or center.

*Electrocardiographic rhythm derived elements:* elements derived from recordings of the electrical activation of the heart including, but not limited to heart rhythm, rate, ST analysis, heart rate variability, T-wave alternans.

*Mobile cardiovascular telemetry (MCT):* continuously records the electrocardiographic rhythm from external electrodes placed on the patient's body. Segments of the ECG data are automatically (without patient intervention) transmitted to a remote surveillance location by cellular or landline telephone signal. The segments of the rhythm, selected for transmission, are triggered automatically (MCT device algorithm) by rapid and slow heart rates or by the patient during a symptomatic episode. There is continuous real time data analysis by preprogrammed algorithms in the device and attended surveillance of the transmitted rhythm segments by a surveillance center technician to evaluate any arrhythmias and to determine signal quality. The surveillance center technician reviews the data and

notifies the physician or other qualified health care professional depending on the prescribed criteria.

ECG rhythm derived elements are distinct from physiologic data, even when the same device is capable of producing both. Implantable cardiovascular monitor (ICM) device services are always separately reported from implantable cardioverter-defibrillator (ICD) service.

| | |
|---|---|
| **93224** | External electrocardiographic recording up to 48 hours by continuous rhythm recording and storage; includes recording, scanning analysis with report, review and interpretation by a physician or other qualified health care professional |
| **93225** | recording (includes connection, recording, and disconnection) |
| **93226** | scanning analysis with report |
| **93227** | review and interpretation by a physician or other qualified health care professional |

(For less than 12 hours of continuous recording, use modifier 52)

(For greater than 48 hours of monitoring, see Category III codes 0295T-0298T)

| | |
|---|---|
| **93228** | External mobile cardiovascular telemetry with electrocardiographic recording, concurrent computerized real time data analysis and greater than 24 hours of accessible ECG data storage (retrievable with query) with ECG triggered and patient selected events transmitted to a remote attended surveillance center for up to 30 days; review and interpretation with report by a physician or other qualified health care professional |

(Report 93228 only once per 30 days)

(Do not report 93228 in conjunction with 93224, 93227)

| | |
|---|---|
| **93229** | technical support for connection and patient instructions for use, attended surveillance, analysis and transmission of daily and emergent data reports as prescribed by a physician or other qualified health care professional |

(Report 93229 only once per 30 days)

(Do not report 93229 in conjunction with 93224, 93226)

(For external cardiovascular monitors that do not perform automatic ECG triggered transmissions to an attended surveillance center, see 93224-93227, 93268-93272)

(93230-93237 have been deleted. To report external electrocardiographic rhythm derived monitoring for up to 48 hours, see 93224-93227)

| | |
|---|---|
| **93268** | External patient and, when performed, auto activated electrocardiographic rhythm derived event recording with symptom-related memory loop with remote download capability up to 30 days, 24-hour attended monitoring; includes transmission, review and interpretation by a physician or other qualified health care professional |
| **93270** | recording (includes connection, recording, and disconnection) |

Medicine

**93271**         transmission and analysis

**93272**         review and interpretation by a physician or other qualified health care professional

(For implanted patient activated cardiac event recording, see 33282, 93285, 93291, 93298)

**93278**         Signal-averaged electrocardiography (SAECG), with or without ECG

(For interpretation and report only, use 93278 with modifier 26)

(For unlisted cardiographic procedure, use 93799)

## Implantable and Wearable Cardiac Device Evaluations

►(For subcutaneous implantable defibrillator device evaluation, see 0327T, 0328T)◄

Cardiac device evaluation services are diagnostic medical procedures using in-person and remote technology to assess device therapy and cardiovascular physiologic data. Codes 93279-93299 describe this technology and technical/professional and service center practice. Codes 93279-93292 are reported per procedure. Codes 93293-93296 are reported no more than **once** every 90 days. Do not report 93293-93296 if the monitoring period is less than 30 days. Codes 93297, 93298 are reported no more than **once** up to every 30 days. Do not report 93297-93299 if the monitoring period is less than 10 days.

A service center may report 93296 or 93299 during a period in which a physician or other qualified health care professional performs an in-person interrogation device evaluation. The same individual may not report an in-person and remote interrogation of the same device during the same period. Report only remote services when an in-person interrogation device evaluation is performed during a period of remote interrogation device evaluation. A period is established by the initiation of the remote monitoring or the 91st day of a pacemaker or implantable cardioverter-defibrillator (ICD) monitoring or the 31st day of an implantable loop recorder (ILR) or implantable cardiovascular monitor (ICM) monitoring and extends for the subsequent 90 or 30 days, respectively, for which remote monitoring is occurring. Programming device evaluations and in-person interrogation device evaluations may not be reported on the same date by the same individual. Programming device evaluations and remote interrogation device evaluations may both be reported during the remote interrogation device evaluation period.

For monitoring by wearable devices, see 93224-93272.

ECG rhythm derived elements are distinct from physiologic data, even when the same device is capable of producing both. ICM device services are always separately reported from ICD services. When ILR data is derived from an ICD or pacemaker, do not report ILR services with pacemaker or ICD services.

Do not report 93268-93272 when performing 93279-93289, 93291-93296 or 93298-93299. Do not report 93040-93042 when performing 93279-93289, 93291-93296, or 93298-93299.

The pacemaker and ICD interrogation device evaluations, peri-procedural device evaluations and programming, and programming device evaluations may not be reported in conjunction with pacemaker or ICD device and/or lead insertion or revision services by the same individual.

The following definitions and instructions apply to codes 93279-93299:

*Attended surveillance:* the immediate availability of a remote technician to respond to rhythm or device alert transmissions from a patient, either from an implanted or wearable monitoring or therapy device, as they are generated and transmitted to the remote surveillance location or center.

*Device, single lead:* a pacemaker or implantable cardioverter-defibrillator with pacing and sensing function in only one chamber of the heart.

*Device, dual lead:* a pacemaker or implantable cardioverter-defibrillator with pacing and sensing function in only two chambers of the heart.

*Device, multiple lead:* a pacemaker or implantable cardioverter-defibrillator with pacing and sensing function in three or more chambers of the heart.

*Electrocardiographic rhythm derived elements:* elements derived from recordings of the electrical activation of the heart including, but not limited to heart rhythm, rate, ST analysis, heart rate variability, T-wave alternans.

*Implantable cardiovascular monitor (ICM):* an implantable cardiovascular device used to assist the physician in the management of non-rhythm related cardiac conditions such as heart failure. The device collects longitudinal physiologic cardiovascular data elements from one or more internal sensors (such as right ventricular pressure, left atrial pressure or an index of lung water) and/or external sensors (such as blood pressure or body weight) for patient assessment and management. The data are stored and transmitted by either local telemetry or remotely to an Internet-based file server or surveillance technician. The function of the ICM may be an additional function of an implantable cardiac device (eg, implantable cardioverter-defibrillator) or a function of a stand-alone device. When ICM functionality is included in an ICD device or pacemaker, the ICM data and the ICD or pacemaker, heart rhythm data such as sensing, pacing, and tachycardia detection therapy are distinct and therefore, the monitoring processes are distinct.

*Implantable cardioverter-defibrillator (ICD):* an implantable device that provides high-energy and low-energy stimulation to one or more chambers of the heart

*Medicine*

---

to terminate rapid heart rhythms called tachycardia or fibrillation. ICDs also have pacemaker functions to treat slow heart rhythms called bradycardia. In addition to the tachycardia and bradycardia functions, the ICD may or may not include the functionality of an implantable cardiovascular monitor or an implantable loop recorder.

*Implantable loop recorder (ILR):* an implantable device that continuously records the electrocardiographic rhythm triggered automatically by rapid and slow heart rates or by the patient during a symptomatic episode. The ILR function may be the only function of the device or it may be part of a pacemaker or implantable cardioverter-defibrillator device. The data are stored and transmitted by either local telemetry or remotely to an Internet-based file server or surveillance technician. Extraction of data and compilation or report for physician or qualified health care professional interpretation is usually performed in the office setting.

*Interrogation device evaluation:* an evaluation of an implantable device such as a cardiac pacemaker, implantable cardioverter-defibrillator, implantable cardiovascular monitor, or implantable loop recorder. Using an office, hospital, or emergency room instrument or via a remote interrogation system, stored and measured information about the lead(s) when present, sensor(s) when present, battery and the implanted device function, as well as data collected about the patient's heart rhythm and heart rate is retrieved. The retrieved information is evaluated to determine the current programming of the device and to evaluate certain aspects of the device function such as battery voltage, lead impedance, tachycardia detection settings, and rhythm treatment settings.

The components that must be evaluated for the various types of implantable cardiac devices are listed below. (The required components for both remote and in-person interrogations are the same.)

*Pacemaker:* Programmed parameters, lead(s), battery, capture and sensing function and heart rhythm.

*Implantable cardioverter-defibrillator:* Programmed parameters, lead(s), battery, capture and sensing function, presence or absence of therapy for ventricular tachyarrhythmias and underlying heart rhythm.

*Implantable cardiovascular monitor:* Programmed parameters and analysis of at least one recorded physiologic cardiovascular data element from either internal or external sensors.

*Implantable loop recorder:* Programmed parameters and the heart rate and rhythm during recorded episodes from both patient initiated and device algorithm detected events, when present.

*Interrogation device evaluation (remote):* a procedure performed for patients with pacemakers, implantable cardioverter-defibrillators or implantable loop recorders using data obtained remotely. All device functions, including the programmed parameters, lead(s), battery,

capture and sensing function, presence or absence of therapy for ventricular tachyarrhythmias (for ICDs) and underlying heart rhythm are evaluated.

The components that must be evaluated for the various types of implantable cardiac devices are listed below. (The required components for both remote and in person interrogations are the same.)

*Pacemaker:* Programmed parameters, lead(s), battery, capture and sensing function, and heart rhythm.

*Implantable cardioverter-defibrillator:* Programmed parameters, lead(s), battery, capture and sensing function, presence or absence of therapy for ventricular tachyarrhythmias, and underlying heart rhythm.

*Implantable cardiovascular monitor:* Programmed parameters and analysis of at least one recorded physiologic cardiovascular data element from either internal or external sensors.

*Implantable loop recorder:* Programmed parameters and the heart rate and rhythm during recorded episodes from both patient-initiated and device algorithm detected events, when present.

*Pacemaker:* an implantable device that provides low energy localized stimulation to one or more chambers of the heart to initiate contraction in that chamber.

*Peri-procedural device evaluation and programming:* an evaluation of an implantable device system (either a pacemaker or implantable cardioverter defibrillator) to adjust the device to settings appropriate for the patient prior to a surgery, procedure, or test. The device system data are interrogated to evaluate the lead(s), sensor(s), and battery in addition to review of stored information, including patient and system measurements. The device is programmed to settings appropriate for the surgery, procedure, or test, as required. A second evaluation and programming are performed after the surgery, procedure, or test to provide settings appropriate to the post procedural situation, as required. If one performs both the pre- and post-evaluation and programming service, the appropriate code, either 93286 or 93287, would be reported two times. If one performs the pre-surgical service and a separate individual performs the post-surgical service, each reports either 93286 or 93287 only one time.

*Physiologic cardiovascular data elements:* data elements from one or more internal sensors (such as right ventricular pressure, left atrial pressure or an index of lung water) and/or external sensors (such as blood pressure or body weight) for patient assessement and management. It does not include ECG rhythm derived data elements.

*Programming device evaluation (in person):* a procedure performed for patients with a pacemaker, implantable cardioverter-defibrillator, or implantable loop recorder. All device functions, including the battery, programmable settings and lead(s), when present, are evaluated. To assess capture thresholds, iterative adjustments (eg, progressive changes in pacing output of a pacing lead) of the programmable parameters are conducted. The iterative adjustments provide information that permits the operator to assess and select the most appropriate final program parameters to provide for consistent delivery of the appropriate therapy and to verify the function of the device. The final program parameters may or may not change after evaluation.

The programming device evaluation includes all of the components of the interrogation device evaluation (remote) or the interrogation device evaluation (in person), and it includes the selection of patient specific programmed parameters depending on the type of device.

The components that must be evaluated for the various types of programming device evaluations are listed below. (See also required interrogation device evaluation [remote and in person] components above.)

*Pacemaker:* Programmed parameters, lead(s), battery, capture and sensing function, and heart rhythm. Often, but not always, the sensor rate response, lower and upper heart rates, AV intervals, pacing voltage and pulse duration, sensing value, and diagnostics will be adjusted during a programming evaluation.

*Implantable cardioverter-defibrillator:* Programmed parameters, lead(s), battery, capture and sensing function, presence or absence of therapy for ventricular tachyarrhythmias and underlying heart rhythm. Often, but not always, the sensor rate response, lower and upper heart rates, AV intervals, pacing voltage and pulse duration, sensing value, and diagnostics will be adjusted during a programming evaluation. In addition, ventricular tachycardia detection and therapies are sometimes altered depending on the interrogated data, patient's rhythm, symptoms, and condition.

*Implantable loop recorder:* Programmed parameters and the heart rhythm during recorded episodes from both patient initiated and device algorithm detected events. Often, but not always, the tachycardia and bradycardia detection criteria will be adjusted during a programming evaluation.

*Transtelephonic rhythm strip pacemaker evaluation:* service of transmission of an electrocardiographic rhythm strip over the telephone by the patient using a transmitter and recorded by a receiving location using a receiver/recorder (also commonly known as transtelephonic pacemaker monitoring). The electrocardiographic rhythm strip is recorded both with and without a magnet applied over the pacemaker. The rhythm strip is evaluated for heart rate and rhythm, atrial and ventricular capture (if observed) and atrial and ventricular sensing (if observed). In addition, the battery status of the pacemaker is determined by measurement of the paced rate on the electrocardiographic rhythm strip recorded with the magnet applied.

**93279**  Programming device evaluation (in person) with iterative adjustment of the implantable device to test the function of the device and select optimal permanent programmed values with analysis, review and report by a physician or other qualified health care professional; single lead pacemaker system

(Do not report 93279 in conjunction with 93286, 93288)

**93280**      dual lead pacemaker system

(Do not report 93280 in conjunction with 93286, 93288)

**93281**      multiple lead pacemaker system

(Do not report 93281 in conjunction with 93286, 93288)

**93282**      single lead implantable cardioverter-defibrillator system

(Do not report 93282 in conjunction with 93287, 93289, 93745)

**93283**      dual lead implantable cardioverter-defibrillator system

(Do not report 93283 in conjunction with 93287, 93289)

**93284**      multiple lead implantable cardioverter-defibrillator system

(Do not report 93284 in conjunction with 93287, 93289)

**93285**      implantable loop recorder system

(Do not report 93285 in conjunction with 33282, 93279-93284, 93291)

**93286**  Peri-procedural device evaluation (in person) and programming of device system parameters before or after a surgery, procedure, or test with analysis, review and report by a physician or other qualified health care professional; single, dual, or multiple lead pacemaker system

(Report 93286 once before and once after surgery, procedure, or test, when device evaluation and programming is performed before and after surgery, procedure, or test)

(Do not report 93286 in conjunction with 93279-93281, 93288)

**93287**      single, dual, or multiple lead implantable cardioverter-defibrillator system

(Report 93287 once before and once after surgery, procedure, or test, when device evaluation and programming is performed before and after surgery, procedure, or test)

(Do not report 93287 in conjunction with 93282-93284, 93289)

►(For peri-procedural device evaluation and programming of a subcutaneous implantable defibrillator, see 0327T, 0328T)◄

Medicine

**93288**    Interrogation device evaluation (in person) with analysis, review and report by a physician or other qualified health care professional, includes connection, recording and disconnection per patient encounter; single, dual, or multiple lead pacemaker system

(Do not report 93288 in conjunction with 93279-93281, 93286, 93294, 93296)

**93289**    single, dual, or multiple lead implantable cardioverter-defibrillator system, including analysis of heart rhythm derived data elements

(For monitoring physiologic cardiovascular data elements derived from an ICD, use 93290)

(Do not report 93289 in conjunction with 93282-93284, 93287, 93295, 93296)

**93290**    implantable cardiovascular monitor system, including analysis of 1 or more recorded physiologic cardiovascular data elements from all internal and external sensors

(For heart rhythm derived data elements, use 93289)

(Do not report 93290 in conjunction with 93297, 93299)

**93291**    implantable loop recorder system, including heart rhythm derived data analysis

(Do not report 93291 in conjunction with 33282, 93288-93290, 93298, 93299)

**93292**    wearable defibrillator system

(Do not report 93292 in conjunction with 93745)

**93293**    Transtelephonic rhythm strip pacemaker evaluation(s) single, dual, or multiple lead pacemaker system, includes recording with and without magnet application with analysis, review and report(s) by a physician or other qualified health care professional, up to 90 days

(Do not report 93293 in conjunction with 93294)

(For in person evaluation, see 93040, 93041, 93042)

(Report 93293 only once per 90 days)

**93294**    Interrogation device evaluation(s) (remote), up to 90 days; single, dual, or multiple lead pacemaker system with interim analysis, review(s) and report(s) by a physician or other qualified health care professional

(Do not report 93294 in conjunction with 93288, 93293)

(Report 93294 only once per 90 days)

**93295**    single, dual, or multiple lead implantable cardioverter-defibrillator system with interim analysis, review(s) and report(s) by a physician or other qualified health care professional

(For remote monitoring of physiologic cardiovascular data elements derived from an ICD, use 93297)

(Do not report 93295 in conjunction with 93289)

(Report 93295 only once per 90 days)

**93296**    single, dual, or multiple lead pacemaker system or implantable cardioverter-defibrillator system, remote data acquisition(s), receipt of transmissions and technician review, technical support and distribution of results

(Do not report 93296 in conjunction with 93288, 93289, 93299)

(Report 93296 only once per 90 days)

**93297**    Interrogation device evaluation(s), (remote) up to 30 days; implantable cardiovascular monitor system, including analysis of 1 or more recorded physiologic cardiovascular data elements from all internal and external sensors, analysis, review(s) and report(s) by a physician or other qualified health care professional

(For heart rhythm derived data elements, use 93295)

(Do not report 93297 in conjunction with 93290, 93298)

(Report 93297 only once per 30 days)

**93298**    implantable loop recorder system, including analysis of recorded heart rhythm data, analysis, review(s) and report(s) by a physician or other qualified health care professional

(Do not report 93298 in conjunction with 33282, 93291, 93297)

(Report 93298 only once per 30 days)

**93299**    implantable cardiovascular monitor system or implantable loop recorder system, remote data acquisition(s), receipt of transmissions and technician review, technical support and distribution of results

(Do not report 93299 in conjunction with 93290, 93291, 93296)

(Report 93299 only once per 30 days)

# Echocardiography

Echocardiography includes obtaining ultrasonic signals from the heart and great vessels, with real time image and/or Doppler ultrasonic signal documentation, with interpretation and report. When interpretation is performed separately, use modifier 26.

A complete transthoracic echocardiogram without spectral or color flow Doppler (93307) is a comprehensive procedure that includes 2-dimensional and, when performed, selected M-mode examination of the left and right atria, left and right ventricles, the aortic, mitral, and tricuspid valves, the pericardium, and adjacent portions of the aorta. Multiple views are required to obtain a complete functional and anatomic evaluation, and appropriate measurements are obtained and recorded. Despite significant effort, identification and measurement of some structures may not always be possible. In such instances, the reason that an element could not be visualized must be documented. Additional structures that may be visualized (eg, pulmonary veins, pulmonary

Medicine

artery, pulmonic valve, inferior vena cava) would be included as part of the service.

A complete transthoracic echocardiogram with spectral and color flow Doppler (93306) is a comprehensive procedure that includes spectral Doppler and color flow Doppler in addition to the 2-dimensional and selected M-mode examinations, when performed. Spectral Doppler (93320, 93321) and color flow Doppler (93325) provide information regarding intracardiac blood flow and hemodynamics.

A follow-up or limited echocardiographic study (93308) is an examination that does not evaluate or document the attempt to evaluate all the structures that comprise the complete echocardiographic exam. This is typically limited to, or performed in follow-up of a focused clinical concern.

In stress echocardiography, echocardiographic images are recorded from multiple cardiac windows before, after, and in some protocols, during stress. The stress is achieved by (1) walking on a treadmill; (2) using a bicycle (supine or upright); or (3) the administration of pharmacological agents that either simulate exercise (by increasing heart rate, blood pressure, or myocardial contractility) or alter coronary flow (vasodilation). The patient's ECG, heart rate, and blood pressure are monitored at baseline, throughout the procedure and during recovery. Reports are prepared to evaluate (1) the duration of stress, the reason for stopping, and the hemodynamic response to stress; (2) the electrocardiographic response to stress; and (3) the echocardiographic response to stress.

When a stress echocardiogram is performed with a complete cardiovascular stress test(continuous electrocardiographic monitoring, supervision, interpretation and report by a physician or other qualified health care professional), use 93351. When only the professional components of a complete stress test and a stress echocardiogram are provided (eg, in a facility setting) by the same physician, use 93351 with modifier 26. When all professional services of a stress test are not performed by the same physician performing the stress echocardiogram, use 93350 in conjunction with the appropriate codes (93016-93018) for the components of the cardiovascular stress test that are provided.

When left ventricular endocardial borders cannot be adequately identified by standard echocardiographic imaging, echocardiographic contrast may be infused intravenously both at rest and with stress to achieve that purpose. Code 93352 is used to report the administration of echocardiographic contrast agent in conjunction with the stress echocardiography codes (93350 or 93351). Supply of contrast agent and/or drugs used for pharmacological stress is reported separately in addition to the procedure code.

Report of an echocardiographic study, whether complete or limited, includes an interpretation of all obtained information, documentation of all clinically relevant findings including quantitative measurements obtained, plus a description of any recognized abnormalities. Pertinent images, videotape, and/or digital data are archived for permanent storage and are available for subsequent review. Use of echocardiography not meeting these criteria is not separately reportable.

Use of ultrasound, without thorough evaluation of organ(s) or anatomic region, image documentation and final, written report, is not separately reportable.

(For fetal echocardiography, see 76825-76828)

**93303** Transthoracic echocardiography for congenital cardiac anomalies; complete

**93304**       follow-up or limited study

**93306** Echocardiography, transthoracic, real-time with image documentation (2D), includes M-mode recording, when performed, complete, with spectral Doppler echocardiography, and with color flow Doppler echocardiography

(For transthoracic echocardiography without spectral and color Doppler, use 93307)

**93307** Echocardiography, transthoracic, real-time with image documentation (2D), includes M-mode recording, when performed, complete, without spectral or color Doppler echocardiography

(Do not report 93307 in conjunction with 93320, 93321, 93325)

**93308** Echocardiography, transthoracic, real-time with image documentation (2D), includes M-mode recording, when performed, follow-up or limited study

⊙ **93312** Echocardiography, transesophageal, real-time with image documentation (2D) (with or without M-mode recording); including probe placement, image acquisition, interpretation and report

⊙ **93313**       placement of transesophageal probe only

⊙ **93314**       image acquisition, interpretation and report only

⊙ **93315** Transesophageal echocardiography for congenital cardiac anomalies; including probe placement, image acquisition, interpretation and report

⊙ **93316**       placement of transesophageal probe only

⊙ **93317**       image acquisition, interpretation and report only

⊙ **93318** Echocardiography, transesophageal (TEE) for monitoring purposes, including probe placement, real time 2-dimensional image acquisition and interpretation leading to ongoing (continuous) assessment of (dynamically changing) cardiac pumping function and to therapeutic measures on an immediate time basis

✛ **93320** Doppler echocardiography, pulsed wave and/or continuous wave with spectral display (List separately in addition to codes for echocardiographic imaging); complete

(Use 93320 in conjunction with 93303, 93304, 93312, 93314, 93315, 93317, 93350, 93351)

Medicine

**+ 93321**    follow-up or limited study (List separately in addition to codes for echocardiographic imaging)

(Use 93321 in conjunction with 93303, 93304, 93308, 93312, 93314, 93315, 93317, 93350, 93351)

**+ 93325**    Doppler echocardiography color flow velocity mapping (List separately in addition to codes for echocardiography)

(Use 93325 in conjunction with 76825, 76826, 76827, 76828, 93303, 93304, 93308, 93312, 93314, 93315, 93317, 93350, 93351)

**93350**    Echocardiography, transthoracic, real-time with image documentation (2D), includes M-mode recording, when performed, during rest and cardiovascular stress test using treadmill, bicycle exercise and/or pharmacologically induced stress, with interpretation and report;

(Stress testing codes 93016-93018 should be reported, when appropriate, in conjunction with 93350 to capture the cardiovascular stress portion of the study)

(Do not report 93350 in conjunction with 93015)

**93351**    including performance of continuous electrocardiographic monitoring, with supervision by a physician or other qualified health care professional

(Do not report 93351 in conjunction with 93015-93018, 93350. Do not report 93351-26 in conjunction with 93016, 93018, 93350-26)

**+ 93352**    Use of echocardiographic contrast agent during stress echocardiography (List separately in addition to code for primary procedure)

(Do not report 93352 more than once per stress echocardiogram)

(Use 93352 in conjunction with 93350, 93351)

# Cardiac Catheterization

Cardiac catheterization is a diagnostic medical procedure which includes introduction, positioning and repositioning, when necessary, of catheter(s), within the vascular system, recording of intracardiac and/or intravascular pressure(s), and final evaluation and report of procedure. There are two code families for cardiac catheterization: one for congenital heart disease and one for all other conditions. Anomalous coronary arteries, patent foramen ovale, mitral valve prolapse, and bicuspid aortic valve are to be reported with 93451-93464, 93566-93568.

Right heart catheterization includes catheter placement in one or more right-sided cardiac chamber(s) or structures (ie, the right atrium, right ventricle, pulmonary artery, pulmonary wedge), obtaining blood samples for measurement of blood gases, and cardiac output measurements (Fick or other method), when performed. Left heart catheterization involves catheter placement in a left-sided (systemic) cardiac chamber(s) (left ventricle or left atrium) and includes left ventricular injection(s) when performed. Do not report 93503 in conjunction with other diagnostic cardiac catheterization codes. When right heart catheterization is performed in conjunction with other cardiac catheterization services, report 93453, 93456, 93457, 93460, or 93461. For placement of a flow directed catheter (eg, Swan-Ganz) performed for hemodynamic monitoring purposes not in conjunction with other catheterization services, use 93503. Right heart catheterization does not include right ventricular or right atrial angiography (93566). When left heart catheterization is performed using either transapical puncture of the left ventricle or transseptal puncture of an intact septum, report 93462 in conjunction with 93452, 93453, 93458-93461, 93653, 93654. Catheter placement(s) in coronary artery(ies) involves selective engagement of the origins of the native coronary artery(ies) for the purpose of coronary angiography. Catheter placement(s) in bypass graft(s) (venous, internal mammary, free arterial graft[s]) involve selective engagement of the origins of the graft(s) for the purpose of bypass angiography. It is typically performed only in conjunction with coronary angiography of native vessels.

The cardiac catheterization codes (93452-93461), other than those for congenital heart disease, include contrast injection(s), imaging supervision, interpretation, and report for imaging typically performed. Codes for left heart catheterization (93452, 93453, 93458-93461), other than those for congenital heart disease, include intraprocedural injection(s) for left ventricular/left atrial angiography, imaging supervision, and interpretation, when performed. Codes for coronary catheter placement(s) (93454-93461), other than those for congenital heart disease, include intraprocedural injection(s) for coronary angiography, imaging supervision, and interpretation. Codes for catheter placement(s) in bypass graft(s) (93455, 93457, 93459, 93461), other than those for congenital heart disease, include intraprocedural injection(s) for bypass graft angiography, imaging supervision, and interpretation. Do not report 93563-93565 in conjunction with 93452-93461.

For cardiac catheterization for congenital cardiac anomalies, see 93530-93533. When contrast injection(s) are performed in conjunction with cardiac catheterization for congenital anomalies, see 93563-93568.

Cardiac catheterization (93451-93461) includes all roadmapping angiography in order to place the catheters, including any injections and imaging supervision, interpretation, and report. It does not include contrast injection(s) and imaging supervision, interpretation, and report for imaging that is separately identified by specific procedure code(s). For right ventricular or right atrial angiography performed in conjunction with cardiac catheterization for congenital or noncongenital heart disease (93451-93461, 93530-93533), use 93566. For aortography, use 93567. For pulmonary angiography, use 93568. For angiography of noncoronary arteries and veins, performed as a distinct service, use appropriate

Medicine

codes from the Radiology section and the Vascular Injection Procedures section.

When cardiac catheterization is combined with pharmacologic agent administration with the specific purpose of repeating hemodynamic measurements to evaluate hemodynamic response, use 93463 in conjunction with 93451-93453 and 93456-93461. Do not report 93463 for intracoronary administration of pharmacologic agents during percutaneous coronary interventional procedures, during intracoronary assessment of coronary pressure, flow or resistance, or during intracoronary imaging procedures. Do not report 93463 in conjunction with 92920-92944, 92975, 92977.

When cardiac catheterization is combined with exercise (eg, walking or arm or leg ergometry protocol) with the specific purpose of repeating hemodynamic measurements to evaluate hemodynamic response, report 93464 in conjunction with 93451-93453, 93456-93461, and 93530-93533.

Contrast injection to image the access site(s) for the specific purpose of placing a closure device is inherent to the catheterization procedure and not separately reportable. Closure device placement at the vascular access site is inherent to the catheterization procedure and not separately reportable.

Modifier 51 should not be appended to 93451, 93456, 93503.

Please see the cardiac catheterization table located following 93567.

⊙⦸ **93451**   Right heart catheterization including measurement(s) of oxygen saturation and cardiac output, when performed

(Do not report 93451 in conjunction with 93453, 93456, 93457, 93460, 93461)

⊙ **93452**   Left heart catheterization including intraprocedural injection(s) for left ventriculography, imaging supervision and interpretation, when performed

(Do not report 93452 in conjunction with 93453, 93458-93461)

⊙ **93453**   Combined right and left heart catheterization including intraprocedural injection(s) for left ventriculography, imaging supervision and interpretation, when performed

(Do not report 93453 in conjunction with 93451, 93452, 93456-93461)

⊙ **93454**   Catheter placement in coronary artery(s) for coronary angiography, including intraprocedural injection(s) for coronary angiography, imaging supervision and interpretation;

⊙ **93455**   with catheter placement(s) in bypass graft(s) (internal mammary, free arterial, venous grafts) including intraprocedural injection(s) for bypass graft angiography

⊙⦸ **93456**   with right heart catheterization

⊙ **93457**   with catheter placement(s) in bypass graft(s) (internal mammary, free arterial, venous grafts) including intraprocedural injection(s) for bypass graft angiography and right heart catheterization

⊙ **93458**   with left heart catheterization including intraprocedural injection(s) for left ventriculography, when performed

⊙ **93459**   with left heart catheterization including intraprocedural injection(s) for left ventriculography, when performed, catheter placement(s) in bypass graft(s) (internal mammary, free arterial, venous grafts) with bypass graft angiography

⊙ **93460**   with right and left heart catheterization including intraprocedural injection(s) for left ventriculography, when performed

⊙ **93461**   with right and left heart catheterization including intraprocedural injection(s) for left ventriculography, when performed, catheter placement(s) in bypass graft(s) (internal mammary, free arterial, venous grafts) with bypass graft angiography

⊙+ **93462**   Left heart catheterization by transseptal puncture through intact septum or by transapical puncture (List separately in addition to code for primary procedure)

▶(Use 93462 in conjunction with 93452, 93453, 93458, 93459, 93460, 93461, 93582, 93653, 93654)◀

(Do not report 93462 in conjunction with 93656)

⊙+ **93463**   Pharmacologic agent administration (eg, inhaled nitric oxide, intravenous infusion of nitroprusside, dobutamine, milrinone, or other agent) including assessing hemodynamic measurements before, during, after and repeat pharmacologic agent administration, when performed (List separately in addition to code for primary procedure)

(Use 93463 in conjunction with 93451-93453, 93456-93461, 93563, 93564, 93580, 93581)

(Report 93463 only once per catheterization procedure)

(Do not report 93463 for pharmacologic agent administration in conjunction with coronary interventional procedure codes 92920-92944, 92975, 92977)

⊙+ **93464**   Physiologic exercise study (eg, bicycle or arm ergometry) including assessing hemodynamic measurements before and after (List separately in addition to code for primary procedure)

(Use 93464 in conjunction with 93451-93453, 93456-93461, 93530-93533)

(Report 93464 only once per catheterization procedure)

(For pharmacologic agent administration, use 93463)

(For bundle of His recording, use 93600)

⦸ **93503**   Insertion and placement of flow directed catheter (eg, Swan-Ganz) for monitoring purposes

(For subsequent monitoring, see 99356-99357)

---

▲=Revised code    ●=New code    ▶◀=Contains new or revised text    ⦸=Modifier 51 exempt

Medicine

⊙ **93505**   Endomyocardial biopsy

(To report transcatheter placement of radiation delivery device for coronary intravascular brachytherapy, use 92974)

(For intravascular radioelement application, see 77785-77787)

(93501, 93508-93529 have been deleted. To report, see 93451-93461)

⊙ **93530**   Right heart catheterization, for congenital cardiac anomalies

**93531**   Combined right heart catheterization and retrograde left heart catheterization, for congenital cardiac anomalies

**93532**   Combined right heart catheterization and transseptal left heart catheterization through intact septum with or without retrograde left heart catheterization, for congenital cardiac anomalies

**93533**   Combined right heart catheterization and transseptal left heart catheterization through existing septal opening, with or without retrograde left heart catheterization, for congenital cardiac anomalies

## Injection Procedures

All injection codes include radiological supervision, interpretation, and report. Cardiac catheterization codes (93452-93461), other than those for congenital heart disease, include contrast injection(s) for imaging typically performed during these procedures (see Cardiac Catheterization above). Do not report 93563-93565 in conjunction with 93452-93461. When injection procedures for right ventricular, right atrial, aortic, or pulmonary angiography are performed in conjunction with cardiac catheterization, these services are reported separately (93566-93568). When right ventricular or right atrial angiography is performed at the time of heart catheterization, use 93566 with the appropriate catheterization code (93451, 93453, 93456, 93457, 93460, or 93461). Use 93567 when supravalvular ascending aortography is performed at the time of heart catheterization. Use 93568 with the appropriate right heart catheterization code when pulmonary angiography is performed. Separately reported injection procedures do not include introduction of catheters but do include repositioning of catheters when necessary and use of automatic power injectors, when performed.

When contrast injection(s) are performed in conjunction with cardiac catheterization for congenital cardiac anomalies (93530-93533), see 93563-93568. Injection procedure codes 93563-93568 include imaging supervision, interpretation, and report.

Injection procedures 93563-93568 represent separate identifiable services and may be coded in conjunction with one another when appropriate. The technical details

of angiography, supervision of filming and processing, interpretation, and report are included.

(93539-93545 have been deleted. To report, see 93451-93461, 93563-93568)

(93555, 93556 have been deleted. See introductory guidelines for Cardiac Catheterization and Injection Procedures)

⊙ **93561**   Indicator dilution studies such as dye or thermodilution, including arterial and/or venous catheterization; with cardiac output measurement (separate procedure)

⊙ **93562**      subsequent measurement of cardiac output

▶(Do not report 93561, 93562 in conjunction with 93451-93462, 93582)◀

(For radioisotope method of cardiac output, see 78472, 78473, or 78481)

⊙✚ **93563**   Injection procedure during cardiac catheterization including imaging supervision, interpretation, and report; for selective coronary angiography during congenital heart catheterization (List separately in addition to code for primary procedure)

⊙✚ **93564**      for selective opacification of aortocoronary venous or arterial bypass graft(s) (eg, aortocoronary saphenous vein, free radial artery, or free mammary artery graft) to one or more coronary arteries and in situ arterial conduits (eg, internal mammary), whether native or used for bypass to one or more coronary arteries during congenital heart catheterization, when performed (List separately in addition to code for primary procedure)

⊙✚ **93565**      for selective left ventricular or left atrial angiography (List separately in addition to code for primary procedure)

(Do not report 93563-93565 in conjunction with 93452-93461)

(Use 93563-93565 in conjunction with 93530-93533)

⊙✚ **93566**      for selective right ventricular or right atrial angiography (List separately in addition to code for primary procedure)

(Use 93566 in conjunction with 93451, 93453, 93456, 93457, 93460, 93461, 93530-93533)

⊙✚ **93567**      for supravalvular aortography (List separately in addition to code for primary procedure)

(Use 93567 in conjunction with 93451-93461, 93530-93533)

(For non-supravalvular thoracic aortography or abdominal aortography performed at the time of cardiac catheterization, use the appropriate radiological supervision and interpretation codes [36221, 75600-75630])

## Cardiac Catheterization Codes

| CPT Code | Code Descriptor | Catheter Placement Type — RHC | LHC | Coronary Artery Placement | Bypass Graft(s) | With Transseptal or Transapical Puncture 93462 | Add-on Procedures (Can Be Reported Separately) — With Pharmacological Study 93463 | With Exercise Study 93464 | Injection Procedure for Selective Right Ventricular or Right Atrial Angiography 93566 | Injection Procedure for Supravalvular Aortography 93567 | Injection Procedure for Pulmonary Angiography 93568 |
|---|---|---|---|---|---|---|---|---|---|---|---|
| 93451 | Right heart catheterization including measurement(s) of oxygen saturation and cardiac output, when performed | X | | | | | X | X | X | | X |
| 93452 | Left heart catheterization including intraprocedural injection(s) for left ventriculography, imaging supervision and interpretation, when performed | | X | | | X | X | X | | X | |
| 93453 | Combined right and left heart catheterization including intraprocedural injection(s) for left ventriculography, imaging supervision and interpretation, when performed | X | X | | | X | X | X | X | X | |
| 93454 | Catheter placement in coronary artery(s) for coronary angiography, including intraprocedural injection(s) for coronary angiography, imaging supervision and interpretation; | | | X | | | | | | X | |
| 93455 | Catheter placement in coronary artery(s) for coronary angiography, including intraprocedural injection(s) for coronary angiography, imaging supervision and interpretation; with catheter placement(s) in bypass graft(s) (internal mammary, free arterial, venous grafts) including intraprocedural injection(s) for bypass graft angiography | | | X | X | | | | | X | |

Medicine

## Cardiac Catheterization Codes, *continued*

| CPT Code | Code Descriptor | Catheter Placement Type | | | | Add-on Procedures (Can Be Reported Separately) | | | | | |
|---|---|---|---|---|---|---|---|---|---|---|---|
| | | RHC | LHC | Coronary Artery Placement | Bypass Graft(s) | With Transseptal or Transapical Puncture 93462 | With Pharmacological Study 93463 | With Exercise Study 93464 | Injection Procedure for Selective Right Ventricular or Right Atrial Angiography 93566 | Injection Procedure for Supravalvular Aortography 93567 | Injection Procedure for Pulmonary Angiography 93568 |
| 93456 | Catheter placement in coronary artery(s) for coronary angiography, including intraprocedural injection(s) for coronary angiography, imaging supervision and interpretation; **with right heart catheterization** | X | | X | | | X | X | X | X | X |
| 93457 | Catheter placement in coronary artery(s) for coronary angiography, including intraprocedural injection(s) for coronary angiography, imaging supervision and interpretation; **with catheter placement(s) in bypass graft(s) (internal mammary, free arterial, venous grafts) including intraprocedural injection(s) for bypass graft angiography and right heart catheterization** | X | | X | X | | X | X | X | X | X |
| 93458 | Catheter placement in coronary artery(s) for coronary angiography, including intraprocedural injection(s) for coronary angiography, imaging supervision and interpretation; **with left heart catheterization including intraprocedural injection(s) for left ventriculography, when performed** | | X | X | | X | X | X | | X | |

**Medicine**

⊙=Moderate sedation ✚=Add-on code ✗=FDA approval pending #=Resequenced code ○=Recycled/reinstated code

**Cardiac Catheterization Codes,** *continued*

| CPT Code | Code Descriptor | Catheter Placement Type | | | | Add-on Procedures (Can Be Reported Separately) | | | | | |
|---|---|---|---|---|---|---|---|---|---|---|---|
| | | RHC | LHC | Coronary Artery Placement | Bypass Graft(s) | With Transseptal or Transapical Puncture 93462 | With Pharmacological Study 93463 | With Exercise Study 93464 | Injection Procedure for Selective Right Ventricular or Right Atrial Angiography 93566 | Injection Procedure for Supravalvular Aortography 93567 | Injection Procedure for Pulmonary Angiography 93568 |
| 93459 | Catheter placement in coronary artery(s) for coronary angiography, including intraprocedural injection(s) for coronary angiography, imaging supervision and interpretation; **with left heart catheterization including intraprocedural injection(s) for left ventriculography, when performed, catheter placement(s) in bypass graft(s) (internal mammary, free arterial, venous grafts) with bypass graft angiography** | | X | X | X | X | X | X | | X | |
| 93460 | Catheter placement in coronary artery(s) for coronary angiography, including intraprocedural injection(s) for coronary angiography, imaging supervision and interpretation; **with right and left heart catheterization including intraprocedural injection(s) for left ventriculography, when performed** | X | X | X | | X | X | X | X | X | X |
| 93461 | Catheter placement in coronary artery(s) for coronary angiography, including intraprocedural injection(s) for coronary angiography, imaging supervision and interpretation; **with right and left heart catheterization including intraprocedural injection(s) for left ventriculography, when performed, catheter placement(s) in bypass graft(s) (internal mammary, free arterial, venous grafts) with bypass graft angiography** | X | X | X | X | X | X | X | X | X | X |

**Medicine**

⊙+ **93568**      for pulmonary angiography (List separately in addition to code for primary procedure)

(Use 93568 in conjunction with 93451, 93453, 93456, 93457, 93460, 93461, 93530-93533)

⊙+ **93571**      Intravascular Doppler velocity and/or pressure derived coronary flow reserve measurement (coronary vessel or graft) during coronary angiography including pharmacologically induced stress; initial vessel (List separately in addition to code for primary procedure)

(Use 93571 in conjunction with 92920, 92924, 92928, 92933, 92937, 92941, 92943, 92975, 93454-93461, 93563, 93564)

⊙+ **93572**      each additional vessel (List separately in addition to code for primary procedure)

(Use 93572 in conjunction with 93571)

(Intravascular distal coronary blood flow velocity measurements include all Doppler transducer manipulations and repositioning within the specific vessel being examined, during coronary angiography or therapeutic intervention [eg, angioplasty])

(For unlisted cardiac catheterization procedure, use 93799)

## ▶Repair of Structural Heart Defect◀

**93580**      Percutaneous transcatheter closure of congenital interatrial communication (ie, Fontan fenestration, atrial septal defect) with implant

(Percutaneous transcatheter closure of atrial septal defect includes a right heart catheterization procedure. Code 93580 includes injection of contrast for atrial and ventricular angiograms. Codes 93451-93453, 93455-93461, 93530-93533, 93564-93566 should not be reported separately in addition to code 93580)

**93581**      Percutaneous transcatheter closure of a congenital ventricular septal defect with implant

(Percutaneous transcatheter closure of ventricular septal defect includes a right heart catheterization procedure. Code 93581 includes injection of contrast for atrial and ventricular angiograms. Codes 93451-93453, 93455-93461, 93530-93533, 93564-93566 should not be reported separately in addition to code 93581)

(For echocardiographic services performed in addition to 93580, 93581, see 93303-93317, 93662 as appropriate)

⊙● **93582**      Percutaneous transcatheter closure of patent ductus arteriosus

▶(93582 includes congenital right and left heart catheterization, catheter placement in the aorta, and aortic arch angiography, when performed)◀

▶(Do not report 93582 in conjunction with 36013, 36014, 36200, 75600, 75605, 93451-93461, 93530, 93531, 93532, 93533, 93567)◀

▶(For other cardiac angiographic procedures performed at the time of transcatheter PDA closure, see 93563, 93564, 93565, 93566, 93568 as appropriate)◀

▶(For left heart catheterization by transseptal puncture through intact septum or by transapical puncture performed at the time of transcatheter PDA closure, use 93462)◀

▶(For repair of patent ductus arteriosus by ligation, see 33820, 33822, 33824)◀

▶(For intracardiac echocardiographic services performed at the time of transcatheter PDA closure, use 93662. Other echocardiographic services provided by a separate physician are reported using the appropriate echocardiography service codes, 93315, 93316, 93317)◀

⊙● **93583**      Percutaneous transcatheter septal reduction therapy (eg, alcohol septal ablation) including temporary pacemaker insertion when performed

▶(93583 includes insertion of temporary pacemaker, when performed, and left heart catheterization)◀

▶(Do not report 93583 in conjunction with 33210, 93452, 93453, 93458, 93459, 93460, 93461, 93531, 93532, 93533, 93565)◀

▶(93583 includes left anterior descending coronary angiography for the purpose of roadmapping to guide the intervention. Do not report 93454, 93455, 93456, 93457, 93458, 93459, 93460, 93461, 93563 for coronary angiography performed during alcohol septal ablation for the purpose of roadmapping, guidance of the intervention, vessel measurement, and completion angiography)◀

▶(Diagnostic cardiac catheterization procedures may be separately reportable when no prior catheter-based diagnostic study of the treatment zone is available, the prior diagnostic study is inadequate, or the patient's condition with respect to the clinical indication has changed since the prior study or during the intervention. Use the appropriate codes from 93451, 93454, 93455, 93456, 93457, 93530, 93563, 93564, 93566, 93567, 93568)◀

▶(Do not report 93583 in conjunction with 33210, 33211)◀

▶(Do not report 93463 for the injection of alcohol for this procedure)◀

▶(For intracardiac echocardiographic services performed at the time of alcohol septal ablation, use 93662)◀

▶(Other echocardiographic services provided by a separate physician are reported using the appropriate echocardiography services codes, 93312, 93313, 93314, 93315, 93316, 93317)◀

▶(For surgical ventriculomyotomy [-myectomy] for idiopathic hypertrophic subaortic stenosis, use 33416)◀

**Medicine**

# Intracardiac Electrophysiological Procedures/Studies

Intracardiac electrophysiologic studies (EPS) are invasive diagnostic medical procedures which include the insertion and repositioning of electrode catheters, recording of electrograms before and during pacing, programmed stimulation of multiple locations in the heart, analysis of recorded information, and report of the procedure. In many circumstances, patients with arrhythmias are evaluated and treated at the same encounter. In this situation, a diagnostic *electrophysiologic study* is performed, induced tachycardia(s) are *mapped*, and on the basis of the diagnostic and mapping information, the tissue is *ablated*.

## Definitions

*Arrhythmia Induction*: In most electrophysiologic studies, an attempt is made to induce arrhythmia(s) from single or multiple sites within the heart. Arrhythmia induction may be achieved by multiple techniques, eg, by performing pacing at different rates or programmed stimulation (introduction of critically timed electrical impulses). Because arrhythmia induction occurs via the same catheter(s) inserted for the electrophysiologic study(ies), catheter insertion and temporary pacemaker codes are not additionally reported. Codes 93600-93603, 93610, 93612, and 93618 are used to describe unusual situations where there may be recording, pacing, or an attempt at arrhythmia induction from only one site in the heart. Code 93619 describes only evaluation of the sinus node, atrioventricular node, and His-Purkinje conduction system, without arrhythmia induction. Codes 93620-93624, 93640-93642, 93653, 93654, and 93656 all include recording, pacing, and attempted arrhythmia induction from one or more site(s) in the heart.

*Mapping*: When a tachycardia is induced, the site of tachycardia origination or its electrical path through the heart is often defined by mapping. Mapping creates a multidimensional depiction of a tachycardia by recording multiple electrograms obtained sequentially or simultaneously from multiple catheter sites in the heart. Depending upon the technique, certain types of mapping catheters may be repositioned from point-to-point within the heart, allowing sequential recording from the various sites to construct maps. Other types of mapping catheters allow mapping without a point-to-point technique by allowing simultaneous recording from many electrodes on the same catheter and computer-assisted three-dimensional reconstruction of the tachycardia activation sequence.

Mapping is a distinct procedure performed in addition to a diagnostic electrophysiologic study or ablation procedure and may be separately reported using 93609 or 93613. Do not report standard mapping (93609) in addition to 3-dimensional mapping (93613).

▶*Ablation*: Once the part of the heart involved in the tachycardia is localized, the tachycardia may be treated by ablation (the delivery of a radiofrequency or cryo-energy to the area to selectively destroy cardiac tissue). Ablation procedures (93653-93657) are performed at the same session as electrophysiology studies and therefore represent a combined code description. When reporting ablation therapy codes (93653-93657), the single site electrophysiology studies (93600-93603, 93610, 93612, 93618) and the comprehensive electrophysiology studies (93619, 93620) may not be reported separately. Code 93622 may be reported separately with 93653 and 93656. Code 93623 may be reported separately with 93653, 93654, and 93656. However, 93621 for left atrial pacing and recording from coronary sinus or left atrium should not be reported in conjunction with 93656, as this procedure is a component of 93656. Codes 93653 and 93654 include right ventricular pacing and recording and His bundle recording when clinically indicated. When performance of one or more components is not possible or indicated, document the reason for not performing. Code 93656 includes each of left atrial pacing/recording, right ventricular pacing/recording, and His bundle recording when clinically indicated. When performance of one or more components is not possible or indicated, document the reason for not performing.◀

The differences in the techniques involved for ablation of supraventricular arrhythmias, ventricular arrhythmias, and atrial fibrillation are reflected within the descriptions for 93653-93657. Code 93653 is a primary code for catheter ablation for treatment of supraventricular tachycardia caused by dual atrioventricular nodal pathways, accessory atrioventricular connections, or other atrial foci. Code 93654 describes catheter ablation for treatment of ventricular tachycardia or focus of ventricular ectopy. Code 93656 is a primary code for reporting treatment of atrial fibrillation by ablation to achieve complete pulmonary vein electrical isolation. Codes 93653, 93654, and 93656 are distinct primary procedure codes and may not be reported together.

Codes 93655 and 93657 are add-on codes listed in addition to the primary ablation code to report ablation of sites distinct from the primary ablation site. After ablation of the primary target site, post-ablation electrophysiologic evaluation is performed as part of those ablation services (93653, 93654, 93656) and additional mechanisms of tachycardia may be identified. For example, if the primary tachycardia ablated was atrioventricular nodal reentrant tachycardia and during post-ablation testing an atrial tachycardia, atrial flutter, or accessory pathway with orthodromic reentry tachycardia was identified, this would be considered a separate mechanism of tachycardia. Pacing maneuvers are performed to define the mechanism(s) of the new tachycardia(s). Catheter ablation of this distinct mechanism of tachycardia is then performed at the newly discovered atrial or ventricular origin. Appropriate post-ablation attempts at re-induction and observation are again performed. Code 93655 is listed in conjunction with 93653 when repeat ablation is for treatment of an

**Medicine**

additional supraventricular tachycardia mechanism and with 93654 when the repeat ablation is for treatment of an additional ventricular tachycardia mechanism. Code 93655 may be reported with 93656 when an additional non-atrial fibrillation tachycardia is separately diagnosed after pulmonary vein isolation. Code 93657 is reported in conjunction with 93656 when successful pulmonary vein isolation is achieved, attempts at re-induction of atrial fibrillation identify an additional left or right atrial focus for atrial fibrillation, and further ablation of this new focus is performed.

In certain circumstances, depending on the chamber of origin, a catheter or catheters may be maneuvered into the left ventricle to facilitate arrhythmia diagnosis. This may be accomplished via a retrograde aortic approach by means of the arterial access or through a transseptal puncture. For ablation treatment of supraventricular tachycardia (93653) and ventricular tachycardia (93654), the left heart catheterization by transseptal puncture through intact septum (93462) may be reported separately as an add-on code. However, for ablation treatment of atrial fibrillation (93656), the transseptal puncture (93462) is a standard component of the procedure and may not be reported separately. Do not report 93462 in conjunction with 93656.

Modifier 51 should not be appended to 93600-93603, 93610, 93612, 93615-93618, 93631.

⊘ **93600**   Bundle of His recording

  ▶(Do not report 93600 in conjunction with 93619, 93620, 93653, 93654, 93656)◀

⊘ **93602**   Intra-atrial recording

  ▶(Do not report 93602 in conjunction with 93619, 93620, 93653, 93654, 93656)◀

⊘ **93603**   Right ventricular recording

  ▶(Do not report 93603 in conjunction with 93619, 93620, 93653, 93654, 93656)◀

⊙+ **93609**   Intraventricular and/or intra-atrial mapping of tachycardia site(s) with catheter manipulation to record from multiple sites to identify origin of tachycardia (List separately in addition to code for primary procedure)

  ▶(Use 93609 in conjunction with 93620, 93653, 93656)◀

  (Do not report 93609 in conjunction with 93613, 93654)

⊘ **93610**   Intra-atrial pacing

  ▶(Do not report 93610 in conjunction with 93619, 93620, 93653, 93654, 93656)◀

⊘ **93612**   Intraventricular pacing

  ▶(Do not report 93612 in conjunction with 93619, 93620, 93621, 93622, 93653, 93654, 93656)◀

⊙+ **93613**   Intracardiac electrophysiologic 3-dimensional mapping (List separately in addition to code for primary procedure)

  ▶(Use 93613 in conjunction with 93620, 93653, 93656)◀

  (Do not report 93613 in conjunction with 93609, 93654)

⊙⊘ **93615**   Esophageal recording of atrial electrogram with or without ventricular electrogram(s);

⊙⊘ **93616**       with pacing

⊙⊘ **93618**   Induction of arrhythmia by electrical pacing

  ▶(Do not report 93618 in conjunction with 93619, 93620, 93621, 93622, 93653, 93654, 93656)◀

  (For intracardiac phonocardiogram, use 93799)

⊙ **93619**   Comprehensive electrophysiologic evaluation with right atrial pacing and recording, right ventricular pacing and recording, His bundle recording, including insertion and repositioning of multiple electrode catheters, without induction or attempted induction of arrhythmia

  ▶(Do not report 93619 in conjunction with 93600, 93602, 93603, 93610, 93612, 93618, 93620, 93621, 93622, 93653, 93654, 93655, 93656, 93657)◀

⊙ **93620**   Comprehensive electrophysiologic evaluation including insertion and repositioning of multiple electrode catheters with induction or attempted induction of arrhythmia; with right atrial pacing and recording, right ventricular pacing and recording, His bundle recording

  ▶(Do not report 93620 in conjunction with 93600, 93602, 93603, 93610, 93612, 93618, 93619, 93653, 93654, 93655, 93656, 93657)◀

⊙+ **93621**       with left atrial pacing and recording from coronary sinus or left atrium (List separately in addition to code for primary procedure)

  ▶(Use 93621 in conjunction with 93620, 93653, 93654)◀

  (Do not report 93621 in conjunction with 93656)

⊙+ **93622**       with left ventricular pacing and recording (List separately in addition to code for primary procedure)

  ▶(Use 93622 in conjunction with 93620, 93653, 93656)◀

  ▶(Do not report 93622 in conjunction with 93654)◀

+ **93623**   Programmed stimulation and pacing after intravenous drug infusion (List separately in addition to code for primary procedure)

  ▶(Use 93623 in conjunction with 93610, 93612, 93619, 93620, 93653, 93654, 93656)◀

⊙ **93624**   Electrophysiologic follow-up study with pacing and recording to test effectiveness of therapy, including induction or attempted induction of arrhythmia

⊘ **93631**   Intra-operative epicardial and endocardial pacing and mapping to localize the site of tachycardia or zone of slow conduction for surgical correction

  (For operative ablation of an arrhythmogenic focus or pathway by a separate individual, see 33250-33261)

⊙ **93640**   Electrophysiologic evaluation of single or dual chamber pacing cardioverter-defibrillator leads including defibrillation threshold evaluation (induction of arrhythmia, evaluation of sensing and pacing for arrhythmia termination) at time of initial implantation or replacement;

⊙ **93641**   with testing of single or dual chamber pacing cardioverter-defibrillator pulse generator

(For subsequent or periodic electronic analysis and/or reprogramming of single or dual chamber pacing cardioverter-defibrillators, see 93282, 93283, 93289, 93292, 93295, 93642)

►(For electrophysiologic evaluation of a subcutaneous implantable defibrillator device evaluation, use 0326T)◄

⊙ **93642**   Electrophysiologic evaluation of single or dual chamber pacing cardioverter-defibrillator (includes defibrillation threshold evaluation, induction of arrhythmia, evaluation of sensing and pacing for arrhythmia termination, and programming or reprogramming of sensing or therapeutic parameters)

⊙ **93650**   Intracardiac catheter ablation of atrioventricular node function, atrioventricular conduction for creation of complete heart block, with or without temporary pacemaker placement

(93651, 93652 have been deleted. To report, see 93653-93657)

⊙▲ **93653**   Comprehensive electrophysiologic evaluation including insertion and repositioning of multiple electrode catheters with induction or attempted induction of an arrhythmia with right atrial pacing and recording, right ventricular pacing and recording (when necessary), and His bundle recording (when necessary) with intracardiac catheter ablation of arrhythmogenic focus; with treatment of supraventricular tachycardia by ablation of fast or slow atrioventricular pathway, accessory atrioventricular connection, cavo-tricuspid isthmus or other single atrial focus or source of atrial re-entry

►(Do not report 93653 in conjunction with 93600-93603, 93610, 93612, 93618-93620, 93642, 93654, 93656)◄

⊙▲ **93654**   with treatment of ventricular tachycardia or focus of ventricular ectopy including intracardiac electrophysiologic 3D mapping, when performed, and left ventricular pacing and recording, when performed

►(Do not report 93654 in conjunction with 93279-93284, 93286-93289, 93600-93603, 93609, 93610, 93612, 93613, 93618-93620, 93622, 93642, 93653, 93656)◄

⊙+ **93655**   Intracardiac catheter ablation of a discrete mechanism of arrhythmia which is distinct from the primary ablated mechanism, including repeat diagnostic maneuvers, to treat a spontaneous or induced arrhythmia (List separately in addition to code for primary procedure)

(Use 93655 in conjunction with 93653, 93654, 93656)

⊙▲ **93656**   Comprehensive electrophysiologic evaluation including transseptal catheterizations, insertion and repositioning of multiple electrode catheters with induction or attempted induction of an arrhythmia including left or right atrial pacing/recording when necessary, right ventricular pacing/recording when necessary, and His bundle recording when necessary with intracardiac catheter ablation of atrial fibrillation by pulmonary vein isolation

(Do not report 93656 in conjunction with 93279-93284, 93286-93289, 93462, 93600, 93602, 93603, 93610, 93612, 93618, 93619, 93620, 93621, 93653, 93654)

⊙+ **93657**   Additional linear or focal intracardiac catheter ablation of the left or right atrium for treatment of atrial fibrillation remaining after completion of pulmonary vein isolation (List separately in addition to code for primary procedure)

(Use 93657 in conjunction with 93656)

**93660**   Evaluation of cardiovascular function with tilt table evaluation, with continuous ECG monitoring and intermittent blood pressure monitoring, with or without pharmacological intervention

(For testing of autonomic nervous system function, see 95921, 95924, 95943)

+ **93662**   Intracardiac echocardiography during therapeutic/diagnostic intervention, including imaging supervision and interpretation (List separately in addition to code for primary procedure)

►(Use 93662 in conjunction with 92987, 93453, 93460-93462, 93532, 93580, 93581, 93620, 93621, 93622, 93653, 93654, 93656 as appropriate)◄

(Do not report 92961 in addition to 93662)

# Peripheral Arterial Disease Rehabilitation

Peripheral arterial disease (PAD) rehabilitative physical exercise consists of a series of sessions, lasting 45-60 minutes per session, involving use of either a motorized treadmill or a track to permit each patient to achieve symptom-limited claudication. Each session is supervised by an exercise physiologist or nurse. The supervising provider monitors the individual patient's claudication threshold and other cardiovascular limitations for adjustment of workload. During this supervised rehabilitation program, the development of new arrhythmias, symptoms that might suggest angina or the continued inability of the patient to progress to an adequate level of exercise may require review and examination of the patient by a physician or other qualified health care professional. These services would be separately reported with an appropriate level E/M service code including office or other outpatient services (99201-99215), initial hospital care (99221-99223), subsequent hospital care (99231-99233), critical care services (99291-99292).

**Medicine**

**93668**  Peripheral arterial disease (PAD) rehabilitation, per session

# Noninvasive Physiologic Studies and Procedures

(For arterial cannulization and recording of direct arterial pressure, use 36620)

(For radiographic injection procedures, see 36000-36299)

(For vascular cannulization for hemodialysis, see 36800-36821)

(For chemotherapy for malignant disease, see 96409-96549)

(For penile plethysmography, use 54240)

**93701**  Bioimpedance-derived physiologic cardiovascular analysis

(For left ventricular filling pressure indirect measurement by computerized calibration of the arterial waveform response to Valsalva, use 93799)

(93720-93722 have been deleted. To report, use 94726)

**93724**  Electronic analysis of antitachycardia pacemaker system (includes electrocardiographic recording, programming of device, induction and termination of tachycardia via implanted pacemaker, and interpretation of recordings)

(93727 has been deleted. For programming of implantable loop recorder, use 93285. For interrogation of implantable loop recorder, see 93291, 93298)

(93731, 93732 have been deleted. For interrogation of dual lead pacemaker, see 93288, 93294. For programming of dual chamber pacemaker, use 93280)

(93733 has been deleted. For transtelephonic rhythm strip pacemaker, single and dual, or multiple lead pacemaker evaluation, use 93293)

(93734, 93735 have been deleted. For interrogation of single lead pacemaker, see 93288, 93294. For programming of single lead pacemaker, use 93279)

(93736 has been deleted. For transtelephonic rhythm strip pacemaker, single and dual, or multiple lead pacemaker evaluation, use 93293)

**93740**  Temperature gradient studies

(93741, 93742 have been deleted. For interrogation of single implantable cardioverter-defibrillator [ICD], see 93289, 93295. For programming of single ICD, use 93282. For interrogation of wearable cardioverter-defibrillator, use 93292)

(93743, 93744 have been deleted. For interrogation of dual implantable cardioverter-defibrillator [ICD], see 93289, 93295. For programming of dual ICD, use 93283)

**93745**  Initial set-up and programming by a physician or other qualified health care professional of wearable cardioverter-defibrillator includes initial programming of system, establishing baseline electronic ECG, transmission of data to data repository, patient instruction in wearing system and patient reporting of problems or events

(Do not report 93745 in conjunction with 93282, 93292)

**93750**  Interrogation of ventricular assist device (VAD), in person, with physician or other qualified health care professional analysis of device parameters (eg, drivelines, alarms, power surges), review of device function (eg, flow and volume status, septum status, recovery), with programming, if performed, and report

(Do not report 93750 in conjunction with 33975, 33976, 33979, 33981-33983)

(93760, 93762 have been deleted)

**93770**  Determination of venous pressure

(For central venous cannulization see 36555-36556, 36500)

**93784**  Ambulatory blood pressure monitoring, utilizing a system such as magnetic tape and/or computer disk, for 24 hours or longer; including recording, scanning analysis, interpretation and report

**93786**  recording only

**93788**  scanning analysis with report

**93790**  review with interpretation and report

# Other Procedures

**93797**  Physician or other qualified health care professional services for outpatient cardiac rehabilitation; without continuous ECG monitoring (per session)

**93798**  with continuous ECG monitoring (per session)

**93799**  Unlisted cardiovascular service or procedure

# Noninvasive Vascular Diagnostic Studies

Vascular studies include patient care required to perform the studies, supervision of the studies and interpretation of study results with copies for patient records of hard copy output with analysis of all data, including bidirectional vascular flow or imaging when provided.

The use of a simple hand-held or other Doppler device that does not produce hard copy output, or that produces a record that does not permit analysis of bidirectional vascular flow, is considered to be part of the physical examination of the vascular system and is not separately reported. The Ankle-Brachial Index (or ABI) is reportable with 93922 or 93923 as long as simultaneous Doppler recording and analysis of bidirectional blood flow, volume

Medicine

plethysmography, or transcutaneous oxygen tension measurements are also performed.

***Duplex scan*** (eg, 93880, 93882) describes an ultrasonic scanning procedure for characterizing the pattern and direction of blood flow in arteries or veins with the production of real-time images integrating B-mode two-dimensional vascular structure, Doppler spectral analysis, and color flow Doppler imaging.

***Physiologic studies*** Noninvasive physiologic studies are performed using equipment separate and distinct from the duplex ultrasound imager. Codes 93922, 93923, 93924, and 93965 describe the evaluation of non-imaging physiologic recordings of pressures with Doppler analysis of bi-directional blood flow, plethysmography, and/or oxygen tension measurements appropriate for the anatomic area studied.

Limited studies for lower extremity require either:

(1) ankle/brachial indices at distal posterior tibial and anterior tibial/dorsalis pedis arteries plus bidirectional Doppler waveform recording and analysis at 1-2 levels; or (2) ankle/brachial indices at distal posterior tibial and anterior tibial/dorsalis pedis arteries plus volume plethysmography at 1-2 levels; or (3) ankle/brachial indices at distal posterior tibial and anterior tibial/dorsalis pedis arteries with transcutaneous oxygen tension measurements at 1-2 levels. Potential levels include high thigh, low thigh, calf, ankle, metatarsal and toes.

Limited studies for upper extremity require either:

(1) Doppler-determined systolic pressures and bidirectional Doppler waveform recording and analysis at 1-2 levels; or (2) Doppler-determined systolic pressures and volume plethysmography at 1-2 levels; or (3) Doppler-determined systolic pressures and transcutaneous oxygen tension measurements at 1-2 levels. Potential levels include arm, forearm, wrist, and digits.

Complete studies for lower extremity require either:

(1) ankle/brachial indices at distal posterior tibial and anterior tibial/dorsalis pedis arteries plus bidirectional Doppler waveform recording and analysis at 3 or more levels; or (2) ankle/brachial indices at distal posterior tibial and anterior tibial/dorsalis pedis arteries plus volume plethysmography at 3 or more levels; or (3) ankle/brachial indices at distal posterior tibial and anterior tibial/dorsalis pedis arteries with transcutaneous oxygen tension measurements at 3 or more levels. Alternatively, a complete study may be reported with measurements at a single level if provocative functional maneuvers (eg, measurements with postural provocative tests, or measurements with reactive hyperemia) are performed.

Complete studies for upper extremity require either:

(1) Doppler-determined systolic pressures and bidirectional Doppler waveform recording and analysis at 3 or more levels; or (2) Doppler-determined systolic pressures and volume plethysmography at 3 or more

levels; or (3) Doppler-determined systolic pressures and transcutaneous oxygen tension measurements at 3 or more levels. Potential levels include arm, forearm, wrist, and digits. Alternatively, a complete study may be reported with measurements at a single level if provocative functional maneuvers (eg, measurements with postural provocative tests, or measurements with cold stress) are performed.

## Cerebrovascular Arterial Studies

A complete transcranial Doppler (TCD) study (93886) includes ultrasound evaluation of the right and left anterior circulation territories and the posterior circulation territory (to include vertebral arteries and basilar artery). In a limited TCD study (93888) there is ultrasound evaluation of two or fewer of these territories. For TCD, ultrasound evaluation is a reasonable and concerted attempt to identify arterial signals through an acoustic window.

(93875 has been deleted)

93880   Duplex scan of extracranial arteries; complete bilateral study

93882        unilateral or limited study

(To report common carotid intima-media thickness (IMT) study for evaluation of atherosclerotic burden or coronary heart disease risk factor assessment, use Category III code 0126T)

93886   Transcranial Doppler study of the intracranial arteries; complete study

93888        limited study

93890        vasoreactivity study

93892        emboli detection without intravenous microbubble injection

93893        emboli detection with intravenous microbubble injection

(Do not report 93890-93893 in conjunction with 93888)

## Extremity Arterial Studies (Including Digits)

93922   Limited bilateral noninvasive physiologic studies of upper or lower extremity arteries, (eg, for lower extremity: ankle/brachial indices at distal posterior tibial and anterior tibial/dorsalis pedis arteries plus bidirectional, Doppler waveform recording and analysis at 1-2 levels, or ankle/brachial indices at distal posterior tibial and anterior tibial/dorsalis pedis arteries plus volume plethysmography at 1-2 levels, or ankle/brachial indices at distal posterior tibial and anterior tibial/dorsalis pedis arteries with, transcutaneous oxygen tension measurement at 1-2 levels)

**Medicine**

(When only 1 arm or leg is available for study, report 93922 with modifier 52 for a unilateral study when recording 1-2 levels. Report 93922 when recording 3 or more levels or performing provocative functional maneuvers)

(Report 93922 only once in the upper extremity(s) and/or once in the lower extremity(s). When both the upper and lower extremities are evaluated in the same setting, 93922 may be reported twice by adding modifier 59 to the second procedure)

(For transcutaneous oxyhemoglobin measurement in a lower extremity wound by near infrared spectroscopy, use 0286T)

►(Do not report 93922 in conjunction with 0337T)◄

**93923** Complete bilateral noninvasive physiologic studies of upper or lower extremity arteries, 3 or more levels (eg, for lower extremity: ankle/brachial indices at distal posterior tibial and anterior tibial/dorsalis pedis arteries plus segmental blood pressure measurements with bidirectional Doppler waveform recording and analysis, at 3 or more levels, or ankle/brachial indices at distal posterior tibial and anterior tibial/dorsalis pedis arteries plus segmental volume plethysmography at 3 or more levels, or ankle/brachial indices at distal posterior tibial and anterior tibial/dorsalis pedis arteries plus segmental transcutaneous oxygen tension measurements at 3 or more levels), or single level study with provocative functional maneuvers (eg, measurements with postural provocative tests, or measurements with reactive hyperemia)

(When only 1 arm or leg is available for study, report 93922 for a unilateral study when recording 3 or more levels or when performing provocative functional maneuvers)

(Report 93923 only once in the upper extremity(s) and/or once in the lower extremity(s). When both the upper and lower extremities are evaluated in the same setting, 93923 may be reported twice by adding modifier 59 to the second procedure)

(For transcutaneous oxyhemoglobin measurement in a lower extremity wound by near infrared spectroscopy, use 0286T)

►(Do not report 93923 in conjunction with 0337T)◄

**93924** Noninvasive physiologic studies of lower extremity arteries, at rest and following treadmill stress testing, (ie, bidirectional Doppler waveform or volume plethysmography recording and analysis at rest with ankle/brachial indices immediately after and at timed intervals following performance of a standardized protocol on a motorized treadmill plus recording of time of onset of claudication or other symptoms, maximal walking time, and time to recovery) complete bilateral study

(Do not report 93924 in conjunction with 93922, 93923)

**93925** Duplex scan of lower extremity arteries or arterial bypass grafts; complete bilateral study

**93926** unilateral or limited study

**93930** Duplex scan of upper extremity arteries or arterial bypass grafts; complete bilateral study

**93931** unilateral or limited study

# Extremity Venous Studies (Including Digits)

**93965** Noninvasive physiologic studies of extremity veins, complete bilateral study (eg, Doppler waveform analysis with responses to compression and other maneuvers, phleborheography, impedance plethysmography)

**93970** Duplex scan of extremity veins including responses to compression and other maneuvers; complete bilateral study

**93971** unilateral or limited study

►(Do not report 93970, 93971 in conjunction with 36475, 36476, 36478, 36479)◄

# Visceral and Penile Vascular Studies

**93975** Duplex scan of arterial inflow and venous outflow of abdominal, pelvic, scrotal contents and/or retroperitoneal organs; complete study

**93976** limited study

**93978** Duplex scan of aorta, inferior vena cava, iliac vasculature, or bypass grafts; complete study

**93979** unilateral or limited study

**93980** Duplex scan of arterial inflow and venous outflow of penile vessels; complete study

**93981** follow-up or limited study

**93982** Noninvasive physiologic study of implanted wireless pressure sensor in aneurysmal sac following endovascular repair, complete study including recording, analysis of pressure and waveform tracings, interpretation and report

(Do not report 93982 in conjunction with 34806)

# Extremity Arterial-Venous Studies

**93990** Duplex scan of hemodialysis access (including arterial inflow, body of access and venous outflow)

(For measurement of hemodialysis access flow using indicator dilution methods, use 90940)

# Other Noninvasive Vascular Diagnostic Studies

**93998** Unlisted noninvasive vascular diagnostic study

# Pulmonary

## Ventilator Management

**94002**   Ventilation assist and management, initiation of pressure or volume preset ventilators for assisted or controlled breathing; hospital inpatient/observation, initial day

**94003**      hospital inpatient/observation, each subsequent day

**94004**      nursing facility, per day

(Do not report 94002-94004 in conjunction with Evaluation and Management services 99201-99499)

**94005**   Home ventilator management care plan oversight of a patient (patient not present) in home, domiciliary or rest home (eg, assisted living) requiring review of status, review of laboratories and other studies and revision of orders and respiratory care plan (as appropriate), within a calendar month, 30 minutes or more

(Do not report 94005 in conjunction with 99339, 99340, 99374-99378)

(Ventilator management care plan oversight is reported separately from home or domiciliary, rest home [eg, assisted living] services. A physician or other qualified health care professional may report 94005, when performed, including when a different individual reports 99339, 99340, 99374-99378 for the same 30 days)

## Pulmonary Diagnostic Testing and Therapies

Codes 94010-94799 include laboratory procedure(s) and interpretation of test results. If a separate identifiable evaluation and management service is performed, the appropriate E/M service code including new or established patient office or other outpatient services (99201-99215), office or other outpatient consultations (99241-99245), emergency department services (99281-99285), nursing facility services (99304-99318), domiciliary, rest home, or custodial care services (99324-99337), and home services (99341-99350) may be reported in addition to 94010-94799.

Spirometry (94010) measures expiratory airflow and volumes and forms the basis of most pulmonary function testing. When spirometry is performed before and after administration of a bronchodilator, report 94060. Measurement of vital capacity (94150) is a component of spirometry and is only reported when performed alone. The flow-volume loop (94375) is used to identify patterns of inspiratory and/or expiratory obstruction in central or peripheral airways. Spirometry (94010, 94060) includes maximal breathing capacity (94200) and flow-volume loop (94375), when performed.

Measurement of lung volumes may be performed using plethysmography, helium dilution or nitrogen washout. Plethysmography (94726) is utilized to determine total lung capacity, residual volume, functional residual capacity, and airway resistance. Nitrogen washout or helium dilution (94727) may be used to measure lung volumes, distribution of ventilation and closing volume. Impulse oscillometry (94728) assesses airway resistance and may be reported in addition to gas dilution techniques. Spirometry (94010, 94060) and bronchial provocation (94070) are not included in 94726 and 94727 and may be reported separately.

Diffusing capacity (94729) is most commonly performed in conjunction with lung volumes or spirometry and is an add-on code to 94726-94728, 94010, 94060, 94070, and 94375.

Pulmonary function tests (94011-94013) are reported for measurements in infants and young children through 2 years of age.

Pulmonary function testing measurements are reported as actual values and as a percent of predicted values by age, gender, height, and race.

►Chest wall manipulation for the mobilization of secretions and improvement in lung function can be performed using manual (94667, 94668) or mechanical (94669) methods. Manual techniques include cupping, percussing, and use of a hand-held vibration device. A mechanical technique is the application of an external vest or wrap that delivers mechanical oscillation.◄

**94010**   Spirometry, including graphic record, total and timed vital capacity, expiratory flow rate measurement(s), with or without maximal voluntary ventilation

(Do not report 94010 in conjunction with 94150, 94200, 94375, 94728)

⊙ **94011**   Measurement of spirometric forced expiratory flows in an infant or child through 2 years of age

⊙ **94012**   Measurement of spirometric forced expiratory flows, before and after bronchodilator, in an infant or child through 2 years of age

⊙ **94013**   Measurement of lung volumes (ie, functional residual capacity [FRC], forced vital capacity [FVC], and expiratory reserve volume [ERV]) in an infant or child through 2 years of age

**94014**   Patient-initiated spirometric recording per 30-day period of time; includes reinforced education, transmission of spirometric tracing, data capture, analysis of transmitted data, periodic recalibration and review and interpretation by a physician or other qualified health care professional

**94015**      recording (includes hook-up, reinforced education, data transmission, data capture, trend analysis, and periodic recalibration)

**94016**      review and interpretation only by a physician or other qualified health care professional

**94060**   Bronchodilation responsiveness, spirometry as in 94010, pre- and post-bronchodilator administration

(Do not report 94060 in conjunction with 94150, 94200, 94375, 94728)

Medicine

(Report bronchodilator supply separately with 99070 or appropriate supply code)

(For prolonged exercise test for bronchospasm with pre- and post-spirometry, use 94620)

**94070** Bronchospasm provocation evaluation, multiple spirometric determinations as in 94010, with administered agents (eg, antigen[s], cold air, methacholine)

(Report antigen[s] administration separately with 99070 or appropriate supply code)

**94150** Vital capacity, total (separate procedure)

(Do not report 94150 in conjunction with 94010, 94060, 94728. To report thoracic gas volumes, see 94726, 94727)

**94200** Maximum breathing capacity, maximal voluntary ventilation

(Do not report 94200 in conjunction with 94010, 94060)

(94240 has been deleted. To report thoracic gas volumes, see 94726, 94727)

**94250** Expired gas collection, quantitative, single procedure (separate procedure)

(94260 has been deleted. To report thoracic gas volumes, see 94726, 94727)

(94350 has been deleted. To report, use 94727)

(94360 has been deleted. To report, see 94726, 94728)

(94370 has been deleted. To report, see 94726, 94727)

**94375** Respiratory flow volume loop

(Do not report 94375 in conjunction with 94010, 94060, 94728)

**94400** Breathing response to $CO_2$ ($CO_2$ response curve)

**94450** Breathing response to hypoxia (hypoxia response curve)

(For high altitude simulation test [HAST], see 94452, 94453)

**94452** High altitude simulation test (HAST), with interpretation and report by a physician or other qualified health care professional;

(For obtaining arterial blood gases, use 36600)

(Do not report 94452 in conjunction with 94453, 94760, 94761)

**94453**     with supplemental oxygen titration

(For obtaining arterial blood gases, use 36600)

(Do not report 94453 in conjunction with 94452, 94760, 94761)

⊘ **94610** Intrapulmonary surfactant administration by a physician or other qualified health care professional through endotracheal tube

(Do not report 94610 in conjunction with 99468-99472)

(For endotracheal intubation, use 31500)

(Report 94610 once per dosing episode)

**94620** Pulmonary stress testing; simple (eg, 6-minute walk test, prolonged exercise test for bronchospasm with pre- and post-spirometry and oximetry)

**94621**     complex (including measurements of $CO_2$ production, $O_2$ uptake, and electrocardiographic recordings)

**94640** Pressurized or nonpressurized inhalation treatment for acute airway obstruction or for sputum induction for diagnostic purposes (eg, with an aerosol generator, nebulizer, metered dose inhaler or intermittent positive pressure breathing [IPPB] device)

(For more than 1 inhalation treatment performed on the same date, append modifier 76)

(For continuous inhalation treatment of 1 hour or more, see 94644, 94645)

**94642** Aerosol inhalation of pentamidine for pneumocystis carinii pneumonia treatment or prophylaxis

**94644** Continuous inhalation treatment with aerosol medication for acute airway obstruction; first hour

(For services of less than 1 hour, use 94640)

+ **94645**     each additional hour (List separately in addition to code for primary procedure)

(Use 94645 in conjunction with 94644)

**94660** Continuous positive airway pressure ventilation (CPAP), initiation and management

**94662** Continuous negative pressure ventilation (CNP), initiation and management

**94664** Demonstration and/or evaluation of patient utilization of an aerosol generator, nebulizer, metered dose inhaler or IPPB device

(94664 can be reported 1 time only per day of service)

**94667** Manipulation chest wall, such as cupping, percussing, and vibration to facilitate lung function; initial demonstration and/or evaluation

**94668**     subsequent

● **94669** Mechanical chest wall oscillation to facilitate lung function, per session

**94680** Oxygen uptake, expired gas analysis; rest and exercise, direct, simple

**94681**     including $CO_2$ output, percentage oxygen extracted

**94690**     rest, indirect (separate procedure)

(For single arterial puncture, use 36600)

(94720, 94725 have been deleted. To report, see 94729)

**94726** Plethysmography for determination of lung volumes and, when performed, airway resistance

(Do not report 94726 in conjunction with 94727, 94728)

**94727** Gas dilution or washout for determination of lung volumes and, when performed, distribution of ventilation and closing volumes

(Do not report 94727 in conjunction with 94726)

**Medicine**

**94728**    Airway resistance by impulse oscillometry

(Do not report 94728 in conjunction with 94010, 94060, 94070, 94375, 94726)

**+ 94729**    Diffusing capacity (eg, carbon monoxide, membrane) (List separately in addition to code for primary procedure)

(Report 94729 in conjunction with 94010, 94060, 94070, 94375, 94726-94728)

**94750**    Pulmonary compliance study (eg, plethysmography, volume and pressure measurements)

**94760**    Noninvasive ear or pulse oximetry for oxygen saturation; single determination

(For blood gases, see 82803-82810)

**94761**    multiple determinations (eg, during exercise)

**94762**    by continuous overnight monitoring (separate procedure)

(For other in vivo laboratory procedures, see 88720-88741)

**94770**    Carbon dioxide, expired gas determination by infrared analyzer

(For bronchoscopy, see 31622-31646)

(For placement of flow directed catheter, use 93503)

(For venipuncture, use 36410)

(For central venous catheter placement, see 36555-36556)

(For arterial puncture, use 36600)

(For arterial catheterization, use 36620)

(For thoracentesis, use 32554, 32555)

(For phlebotomy, therapeutic, use 99195)

(For lung biopsy, needle, use 32405)

(For intubation, orotracheal or nasotracheal, use 31500)

**94772**    Circadian respiratory pattern recording (pediatric pneumogram), 12-24 hour continuous recording, infant

(Separate procedure codes for electromyograms, EEG, ECG, and recordings of respiration are excluded when 94772 is reported)

**94774**    Pediatric home apnea monitoring event recording including respiratory rate, pattern and heart rate per 30-day period of time; includes monitor attachment, download of data, review, interpretation, and preparation of a report by a physician or other qualified health care professional

(Do not report 94774 in conjunction with 94775-94777 during the same reporting period)

**94775**    monitor attachment only (includes hook-up, initiation of recording and disconnection)

**94776**    monitoring, download of information, receipt of transmission(s) and analyses by computer only

**94777**    review, interpretation and preparation of report only by a physician or other qualified health care professional

(When oxygen saturation monitoring is used in addition to heart rate and respiratory monitoring, it is not reported separately)

(Do not report 94774-94777 in conjunction with 93224-93272)

(Do not report apnea recording device separately)

(For sleep study, see 95805-95811)

**94780**    Car seat/bed testing for airway integrity, neonate, with continual nursing observation and continuous recording of pulse oximetry, heart rate and respiratory rate, with interpretation and report; 60 minutes

(Do not report 94780 for less than 60 minutes)

(Do not report 94780 in conjunction with 93040-93042, 94760, 94761, 99468-99472, 99477-99480)

**+ 94781**    each additional full 30 minutes (List separately in addition to code for primary procedure)

(Use 94781 in conjunction with 94780)

**94799**    Unlisted pulmonary service or procedure

# Allergy and Clinical Immunology

### Definitions

***Immunotherapy (desensitization, hyposensitization):*** is the parenteral administration of allergenic extracts as antigens at periodic intervals, usually on an increasing dosage scale to a dosage which is maintained as maintenance therapy. Indications for immunotherapy are determined by appropriate diagnostic procedures coordinated with clinical judgment and knowledge of the natural history of allergic diseases.

***Other therapy:*** for medical conferences on the use of mechanical and electronic devices (precipitators, air conditioners, air filters, humidifiers, dehumidifiers), climatotherapy, physical therapy, occupational and recreational therapy, see **Evaluation and Management** services.

Do not report Evaluation and Management (E/M) services for test interpretation and report. If a significant separately identifiable E/M service is performed, the appropriate E/M service code, which may include new or established patient office or other outpatient services (99201-99215), hospital observation services (99217-99220, 99224-99226), hospital care (99221-99223, 99231-99233), consultations (99241-99255), emergency department services (99281-99285), nursing facility services (99304-99318), domiciliary, rest home, or custodial care services (99324-99337), home services

(99341-99350), or preventive medicine services (99381-99429), should be reported using modifier 25.

## Allergy Testing

(For allergy laboratory tests, see 86000-86999)

(For administration of medications [eg, epinephrine, steroidal agents, antihistamines] for therapy for severe or intractable allergic reaction, use 96372)

**95004** Percutaneous tests (scratch, puncture, prick) with allergenic extracts, immediate type reaction, including test interpretation and report, specify number of tests

**95012** Nitric oxide expired gas determination

(95010 and 95015 have been deleted. To report, see 95017 and 95018)

**95017** Allergy testing, any combination of percutaneous (scratch, puncture, prick) and intracutaneous (intradermal), sequential and incremental, with venoms, immediate type reaction, including test interpretation and report, specify number of tests

**95018** Allergy testing, any combination of percutaneous (scratch, puncture, prick) and intracutaneous (intradermal), sequential and incremental, with drugs or biologicals, immediate type reaction, including test interpretation and report, specify number of tests

**95024** Intracutaneous (intradermal) tests with allergenic extracts, immediate type reaction, including test interpretation and report, specify number of tests

**95027** Intracutaneous (intradermal) tests, sequential and incremental, with allergenic extracts for airborne allergens, immediate type reaction, including test interpretation and report, specify number of tests

**95028** Intracutaneous (intradermal) tests with allergenic extracts, delayed type reaction, including reading, specify number of tests

**95044** Patch or application test(s) (specify number of tests)

**95052** Photo patch test(s) (specify number of tests)

**95056** Photo tests

**95060** Ophthalmic mucous membrane tests

**95065** Direct nasal mucous membrane test

**95070** Inhalation bronchial challenge testing (not including necessary pulmonary function tests); with histamine, methacholine, or similar compounds

**95071** with antigens or gases, specify

(For pulmonary function tests, see 94060, 94070)

(95075 has been deleted. For ingestion challenge testing, see 95076, 95079)

## Ingestion Challenge Testing

Codes 95076 and 95079 are used to report ingestion challenge testing. Report 95076 for initial 120 minutes of testing time (ie, not physician face-to-face time). Report 95079 for each additional 60 minutes of testing time (ie, not physician face-to-face time). For total testing time less than 61 minutes (eg, positive challenge resulting in cessation of testing), report an evaluation and management service, if appropriate. Patient assessment/monitoring activities for allergic reaction (eg, blood pressure testing, peak flow meter testing) are not separately reported. Intervention therapy (eg, injection of steroid or epinephrine) may be reported separately as appropriate.

For purposes of reporting testing times, if an evaluation and management service is required, then testing time ends.

**95076** Ingestion challenge test (sequential and incremental ingestion of test items, eg, food, drug or other substance); initial 120 minutes of testing

**+ 95079** each additional 60 minutes of testing (List separately in addition to code for primary procedure)

(Use 95079 in conjunction with 95076)

## Allergen Immunotherapy

Codes 95115-95199 include the professional services necessary for allergen immunotherapy. Office visit codes may be used in addition to allergen immunotherapy if other identifiable services are provided at that time.

**95115** Professional services for allergen immunotherapy not including provision of allergenic extracts; single injection

**95117** 2 or more injections

**95120** Professional services for allergen immunotherapy in the office or institution of the prescribing physician or other qualified health care professional, including provision of allergenic extract; single injection

**95125** 2 or more injections

**95130** single stinging insect venom

**95131** 2 stinging insect venoms

**95132** 3 stinging insect venoms

**95133** 4 stinging insect venoms

**95134** 5 stinging insect venoms

**95144** Professional services for the supervision of preparation and provision of antigens for allergen immunotherapy, single dose vial(s) (specify number of vials)

(A single dose vial contains a single dose of antigen administered in 1 injection)

**95145** Professional services for the supervision of preparation and provision of antigens for allergen immunotherapy (specify number of doses); single stinging insect venom

**95146** 2 single stinging insect venoms

**95147** 3 single stinging insect venoms

**95148** 4 single stinging insect venoms

**95149**     5 single stinging insect venoms

**95165**     Professional services for the supervision of preparation and provision of antigens for allergen immunotherapy; single or multiple antigens (specify number of doses)

**95170**     whole body extract of biting insect or other arthropod (specify number of doses)

(For allergy immunotherapy reporting, a dose is the amount of antigen[s] administered in a single injection from a multiple dose vial)

**95180**     Rapid desensitization procedure, each hour (eg, insulin, penicillin, equine serum)

**95199**     Unlisted allergy/clinical immunologic service or procedure

(For skin testing of bacterial, viral, fungal extracts, see 86485-86580, 95028)

(For special reports on allergy patients, use 99080)

(For testing procedures such as radioallergosorbent testing [RAST], rat mast cell technique [RMCT], mast cell degranulation test [MCDT], lymphocytic transformation test [LTT], leukocyte histamine release [LHR], migration inhibitory factor test [MIF], transfer factor test [TFT], nitroblue tetrazolium dye test [NTD], see Immunology section in **Pathology** or use 95199)

# Endocrinology

**95250**     Ambulatory continuous glucose monitoring of interstitial tissue fluid via a subcutaneous sensor for a minimum of 72 hours; sensor placement, hook-up, calibration of monitor, patient training, removal of sensor, and printout of recording

(Do not report 95250 more than once per month)

(Do not report 95250 in conjunction with 99091)

**95251**     interpretation and report

(Do not report 95251 more than once per month)

(Do not report 95251 in conjunction with 99091)

# Neurology and Neuromuscular Procedures

Neurologic services are typically consultative, and any of the levels of consultation (99241-99255) may be appropriate.

In addition, services and skills outlined under **Evaluation and Management** levels of service appropriate to neurologic illnesses should be reported similarly.

The EEG, autonomic function, evoked potential, reflex tests, EMG, NCV, and MEG services (95812-95829 and 95860-95967) include recording, interpretation, and report by a physician or other qualified health care professional. For interpretation only, use modifier 26. For EMG guidance, see 95873, 95874.

Codes 95812-95822, 95950-95953 and 95956 use recording time as a basis for code use. Recording time is when the recording is underway and data is being collected. Recording time excludes set up and take down time. Codes 95961-95962 use physician or other qualified health care professional attendance time as a basis for code use.

(Do not report codes 95860-95875 in addition to 96000-96004)

## Sleep Medicine Testing

Sleep medicine services include procedures that evaluate adult and pediatric patients for a variety of sleep disorders. Sleep medicine testing services are diagnostic procedures using in-laboratory and portable technology to assess physiologic data and therapy.

All sleep services (95800-95811) include recording, interpretation, and report. (Report with modifier 52 if less than 6 hours of recording for 95800, 95801 and 95806, 95807, 95810, 95811; if less than 7 hours of recording for 95782, 95783, or if less than four nap opportunities are recorded for 95805).

**Definitions**

For purposes of CPT reporting of sleep medicine testing services, the following definitions apply:

*Actigraphy:* the use of a portable, non-invasive, device that continuously records gross motor movement over an extended period of time. The periods of activity and rest are indirect parameters for estimates of the periods of wakefulness and sleep of an individual.

*Attended:* a technologist or qualified health care professional is physically present (ie, sufficient proximity such that the qualified health care professional can physically respond to emergencies, to other appropriate patient needs or to technical problems at the bedside) throughout the recording session.

*Electrooculogram (EOG):* a recording of electrical activity indicative of eye movement.

*Maintenance of wakefulness test (MWT):* a standardized objective test used to determine a person's ability to stay awake. MWT requires sleep staging of the trials that are performed at defined intervals and is attended by a qualified health care professional.

*Multiple sleep latency test (MSLT):* a standardized objective test of the tendency to fall asleep. MSLT requires sleep staging of the nap opportunities that are performed at defined intervals and is attended by a technologist or qualified health care professional.

*Peripheral arterial tonometry (PAT):* a plethysmography technique that continuously measures pulsatile volume changes in a digit. This reflects the relative change of blood volume as an indirect measure of

**Medicine**

sympathetic nervous system activity which is used in respiratory analysis.

*Physiological measurements of sleep as used in 95805:* the parameters measured are a frontal, central and occipital lead of EEG (3 leads), submental EMG lead and a left and right EOG. These parameters are used together for staging sleep.

*Polysomnography:* a sleep test involving the continuous, simultaneous, recording of physiological parameters for a period of at least 6 hours that is performed in a sleep laboratory and attended by a technologist or qualified health care professional. The parameters measured are a frontal, central and occipital lead of EEG (3 leads), submental EMG lead and a left and right EOG, (from which sleep is staged), plus four or more additional parameters. The additional parameters typically required in polysomnography are listed below:

   a. Electrocardiogram (ECG)

   b. Nasal and/or oral airflow

   c. Respiratory effort

   d. Oxyhemoglobin saturation, SpO2

   e. Bilateral anterior tibialis EMG

*Positive airway pressure (PAP):* a device used to treat sleep-related breathing disorders with the use of non-invasive delivery of positive pressure to the airway. Examples include but are not limited to: CPAP (continuous positive airway pressure), bilevel PAP, AutoPAP (autotitrating or adjusting PAP), ASV (adaptive-servo ventilation).

*Remote:* the site of service is distant from the monitoring center. Neither a technologist nor a qualified health care professional is physically present at the testing site.

*Respiratory airflow (ventilation):* the movement of air during inhaled and exhaled breaths. This is typically assessed using thermistor and nasal pressure sensors.

*Respiratory analysis:* generation of derived parameters that describe components of respiration obtained by using direct or indirect parameters, eg, by airflow or peripheral arterial tone.

*Respiratory effort:* contraction of the diaphragmatic and/or intercostal muscles to cause (or attempt to cause) respiratory airflow. This is typically measured using transducers that estimate motion of the thorax and abdomen such as respiratory inductive plethysmography, transducers that estimate pressures generated by breathing muscles such as esophageal monometry, or by contraction of breathing muscles, such as diaphragmatic/intercostal EMG.

*Respiratory (thoracoabdominal) movement:* movement of the chest and abdomen during respiratory effort.

*Sleep latency:* the length of time it takes to transition from wakefulness to sleep. In the sleep laboratory it is the time from "lights out" to the first epoch scored as any stage of sleep.

*Sleep staging:* the delineation of the distinct sleep levels through the simultaneous evaluation of physiologic measures including a frontal, central and occipital lead of EEG (3 leads), submental EMG lead and a left and right EOG.

*Sleep testing (or sleep study):* the continuous, simultaneous monitoring of physiological parameters during sleep (eg, polysomnography, EEG).

*Total sleep time:* a derived parameter obtained by sleep staging or may be estimated indirectly using actigraphy or other methods.

*Unattended:* a technologist or qualified health care professional is not physically present with the patient during the recording session.

   (Report with modifier 52 if less than 6 hours of recording or in other cases of reduced services as appropriate)

   (For unattended sleep study, use 95806)

**95782**   Code is out of numerical sequence. See 95803-95783

**95783**   Code is out of numerical sequence. See 95803-95783

**95800**   Code is out of numerical sequence. See 95803-95811

**95801**   Code is out of numerical sequence. See 95800-95811

**95803**   Actigraphy testing, recording, analysis, interpretation, and report (minimum of 72 hours to 14 consecutive days of recording)

   (Do not report 95803 more than once in any 14 day period)

   (Do not report 95803 in conjunction with 95806-95811)

**95805**   Multiple sleep latency or maintenance of wakefulness testing, recording, analysis and interpretation of physiological measurements of sleep during multiple trials to assess sleepiness

**95806**   Sleep study, unattended, simultaneous recording of, heart rate, oxygen saturation, respiratory airflow, and respiratory effort (eg, thoracoabdominal movement)

   (Do not report 95806 in conjunction with 93041-93227, 93228, 93229, 93268-93272, 95800, 95801)

   (For unattended sleep study that measures heart rate, oxygen saturation, respiratory analysis, and sleep time, use 95800)

   (For unattended sleep study that measures a minimum heart rate, oxygen saturation, and respiratory analysis, use 95801)

**# 95800**   Sleep study, unattended, simultaneous recording; heart rate, oxygen saturation, respiratory analysis (eg, by airflow or peripheral arterial tone), and sleep time

   (Do not report 95800 in conjunction with 93041-93227, 93228, 93229, 93268-93272, 95801, 95803, 95806)

   (For unattended sleep study that measures a minimum of heart rate, oxygen saturation, and respiratory analysis, use 95801)

Medicine

**# 95801**    minimum of heart rate, oxygen saturation, and respiratory analysis (eg, by airflow or peripheral arterial tone)

(Do not report 95801 in conjunction with 93041-93227, 93228, 93229, 93268-93272, 95800, 95806)

(For unattended sleep study that measures heart rate, oxygen saturation, respiratory analysis and sleep time, use 95800)

**95807**    Sleep study, simultaneous recording of ventilation, respiratory effort, ECG or heart rate, and oxygen saturation, attended by a technologist

**95808**    Polysomnography; any age, sleep staging with 1-3 additional parameters of sleep, attended by a technologist

**95810**    age 6 years or older, sleep staging with 4 or more additional parameters of sleep, attended by a technologist

**95811**    age 6 years or older, sleep staging with 4 or more additional parameters of sleep, with initiation of continuous positive airway pressure therapy or bilevel ventilation, attended by a technologist

**# 95782**    younger than 6 years, sleep staging with 4 or more additional parameters of sleep, attended by a technologist

**# 95783**    younger than 6 years, sleep staging with 4 or more additional parameters of sleep, with initiation of continuous positive airway pressure therapy or bi-level ventilation, attended by a technologist

## Routine Electroencephalography (EEG)

EEG codes 95812-95822 include hyperventilation and/ or photic stimulation when appropriate. Routine EEG codes 95816-95822 include 20 to 40 minutes of recording. Extended EEG codes 95812-95813 include reporting times longer than 40 minutes.

**95812**    Electroencephalogram (EEG) extended monitoring; 41-60 minutes

**95813**    greater than 1 hour

**95816**    Electroencephalogram (EEG); including recording awake and drowsy

**95819**    including recording awake and asleep

**95822**    recording in coma or sleep only

**95824**    cerebral death evaluation only

**95827**    all night recording

(For 24-hour EEG monitoring, see 95950-95953 or 95956)

(For EEG during nonintracranial surgery, use 95955)

(For Wada test, use 95958)

(For digital analysis of EEG, use 95957)

**95829**    Electrocorticogram at surgery (separate procedure)

**95830**    Insertion by physician or other qualified health care professional of sphenoidal electrodes for electroencephalographic (EEG) recording

## Muscle and Range of Motion Testing

**95831**    Muscle testing, manual (separate procedure) with report; extremity (excluding hand) or trunk

**95832**    hand, with or without comparison with normal side

**95833**    total evaluation of body, excluding hands

**95834**    total evaluation of body, including hands

**95851**    Range of motion measurements and report (separate procedure); each extremity (excluding hand) or each trunk section (spine)

**95852**    hand, with or without comparison with normal side

**95857**    Cholinesterase inhibitor challenge test for myasthenia gravis

## Electromyography

Needle electromyographic (EMG) procedures include the interpretation of electrical waveforms measured by equipment that produces both visible and audible components of electrical signals recorded from the muscle(s) studied by the needle electrode.

Use 95870 or 95885 when four or fewer muscles are tested in an extremity. Use 95860-95864 or 95886 when five or more muscles are tested in an extremity.

Use EMG codes (95860-95864 and 95867-95870) when no nerve conduction studies (95907-95913) are performed on that day. Use 95885, 95886, and 95887 for EMG services when nerve conduction studies (95907-95913) are performed in conjunction with EMG on the same day.

Report either 95885 or 95886 once per extremity. Codes 95885 and 95886 can be reported together up to a combined total of four units of service per patient when all four extremities are tested.

**95860**    Needle electromyography; 1 extremity with or without related paraspinal areas

**95861**    2 extremities with or without related paraspinal areas

(For dynamic electromyography performed during motion analysis studies, see 96002-96003)

**95863**    3 extremities with or without related paraspinal areas

**95864**    4 extremities with or without related paraspinal areas

**95865**    larynx

(Do not report modifier 50 in conjunction with 95865)

(For unilateral procedure, report modifier 52 in conjunction with 95865)

**95866**    hemidiaphragm

**95867**    cranial nerve supplied muscle(s), unilateral

**Medicine**

**95868**  cranial nerve supplied muscles, bilateral

**95869**  thoracic paraspinal muscles (excluding T1 or T12)

**95870**  limited study of muscles in 1 extremity or non-limb (axial) muscles (unilateral or bilateral), other than thoracic paraspinal, cranial nerve supplied muscles, or sphincters

(To report a complete study of the extremities, see 95860-95864)

(For anal or urethral sphincter, detrusor, urethra, perineum musculature, see 51785-51792)

(For eye muscles, use 92265)

**95872**  Needle electromyography using single fiber electrode, with quantitative measurement of jitter, blocking and/or fiber density, any/all sites of each muscle studied

**#+ 95885**  Needle electromyography, each extremity, with related paraspinal areas, when performed, done with nerve conduction, amplitude and latency/velocity study; limited (List separately in addition to code for primary procedure)

**#+ 95886**  complete, five or more muscles studied, innervated by three or more nerves or four or more spinal levels (List separately in addition to code for primary procedure)

(Use 95885, 95886 in conjunction with 95907-95913)

(Do not report 95885, 95886 in conjunction with 95860-95864, 95870, 95905)

**#+ 95887**  Needle electromyography, non-extremity (cranial nerve supplied or axial) muscle(s) done with nerve conduction, amplitude and latency/velocity study (List separately in addition to code for primary procedure)

(Use 95887 in conjunction with 95907-95913)

(Do not report 95887 in conjunction with 95867-95870, 95905)

## Guidance for Chemodenervation and Ischemic Muscle Testing

**+ 95873**  Electrical stimulation for guidance in conjunction with chemodenervation (List separately in addition to code for primary procedure)

▶(Do not report 95873 in conjunction with 64617, 95860-95870, 95874)◀

**+ 95874**  Needle electromyography for guidance in conjunction with chemodenervation (List separately in addition to code for primary procedure)

▶(Use 95873, 95874 in conjunction with 64612, 64615, 64616, 64642, 64643, 64644, 64645, 64646, 64647)◀

▶(Do not report more than one guidance code for each corresponding chemodenervation code)◀

▶(Do not report 95874 in conjunction with 64617, 95860-95870, 95873)◀

**95875**  Ischemic limb exercise test with serial specimen(s) acquisition for muscle(s) metabolite(s)

(For listing of nerves considered for separate study, see **Appendix J**)

**95885**  Code is out of numerical sequence. See 95860-95887

**95886**  Code is out of numerical sequence. See 95860-95887

**95887**  Code is out of numerical sequence. See 95860-95887

## Nerve Conduction Tests

The following applies to nerve conduction tests (95907-95913): Codes 95907-95913 describe nerve conduction tests when performed with individually placed stimulating, recording, and ground electrodes. The stimulating, recording, and ground electrode placement and the test design must be individualized to the patient's unique anatomy. Nerves tested must be limited to the specific nerves and conduction studies needed for the particular clinical question being investigated. The stimulating electrode must be placed directly over the nerve to be tested, and stimulation parameters properly adjusted to avoid stimulating other nerves or nerve branches. In most motor nerve conduction studies, and in some sensory and mixed nerve conduction studies, both proximal and distal stimulation will be used. Motor nerve conduction study recordings must be made from electrodes placed directly over the motor point of the specific muscle to be tested. Sensory nerve conduction study recordings must be made from electrodes placed directly over the specific nerve to be tested. Waveforms must be reviewed on site in real time, and the technique (stimulus site, recording site, ground site, filter settings) must be adjusted, as appropriate, as the test proceeds in order to minimize artifact, and to minimize the chances of unintended stimulation of adjacent nerves and the unintended recording from adjacent muscles or nerves. Reports must be prepared on site by the examiner, and consist of the work product of the interpretation of numerous test results, using well-established techniques to assess the amplitude, latency, and configuration of waveforms elicited by stimulation at each site of each nerve tested. This includes the calculation of nerve conduction velocities, sometimes including specialized F-wave indices, along with comparison to normal values, summarization of clinical and electrodiagnostic data, and physician or other qualified health care professional interpretation. Codes 95907-95913 describe one or more nerve conduction studies. For the purposes of coding, a single conduction study is defined as a sensory conduction test, a motor conduction test with or without an F wave test, or an H-reflex test. Each type of study (sensory, motor with or without F wave, H-reflex) for each nerve includes all orthodromic and antidromic impulses associated with that nerve and constitutes a distinct study when determining the number of studies in each grouping (eg, 1-2 or 3-4 nerve conduction studies). Each type of nerve conduction study is counted only once when multiple sites on the same nerve are stimulated or recorded. The numbers of these separate tests should be added to determine which code to use. For a list of nerves, see Appendix J. Use 95885-95887 in conjunction with 95907-95913 when performing electromyography with nerve conduction studies.

Code 95905 describes nerve conduction tests when performed with preconfigured electrodes customized to a specific anatomic site.

> (95900, 95903, 95904 have been deleted. For nerve conduction studies, see 95907-95913)

⊘ **95905**    Motor and/or sensory nerve conduction, using preconfigured electrode array(s), amplitude and latency/velocity study, each limb, includes F-wave study when performed, with interpretation and report;

> (Report 95905 only once per limb studied)

> (Do not report 95905 in conjunction with 95885, 95886, 95907-95913)

**95907**    Nerve conduction studies; 1-2 studies

**95908**        3-4 studies

**95909**        5-6 studies

**95910**        7-8 studies

**95911**        9-10 studies

**95912**        11-12 studies

**95913**        13 or more studies

# Intraoperative Neurophysiology

Codes 95940, 95941 describe ongoing neurophysiologic monitoring, testing, and data interpretation distinct from performance of specific type(s) of baseline neurophysiologic study(s) performed during surgical procedures. When the service is performed by the surgeon or anesthesiologist, the professional services are included in the surgeon's or anesthesiologist's primary service code(s) for the procedure and are not reported separately. Do not report these codes for automated monitoring devices that do not require continuous attendance by a professional qualified to interpret the testing and monitoring.

Recording and testing are performed either personally or by a technologist who is physically present with the patient during the service. Supervision is performed either in the operating room or by real time connection outside the operating room. The monitoring professional must be solely dedicated to performing the intraoperative neurophysiologic monitoring and must be available to intervene at all times during the service as necessary, for the reported time period(s). For any given period of time spent providing these services, the service takes full attention and, therefore, other clinical activities beyond providing and interpreting of monitoring cannot be provided during the same period of time.

Throughout the monitoring, there must be provisions for continuous and immediate communication directly with the operating room team in the surgical suite. One or more simultaneous cases may be reported (95941). When monitoring more than one procedure, there must be the immediate ability to transfer patient monitoring to another monitoring professional during the surgical procedure should that individual's exclusive attention be required for another procedure. Report 95941 for all remote or non-one-on-one monitoring time connected to each case regardless of overlap with other cases.

►Codes 95940, 95941 include only the ongoing neurophysiologic monitoring time distinct from performance of specific type(s) of baseline neurophysiologic study(s), or other services such as intraoperative functional cortical or subcortical mapping. Codes 95940 and 95941 are reported based upon the time spent monitoring only, and not the number of baseline tests performed or parameters monitored. The time spent performing or interpreting the baseline neurophysiologic study(ies) should not be counted as intraoperative monitoring, but represents separately reportable procedures. When reporting 95940 and 95941, the same neurophysiologic study(ies) performed at baseline should be reported not more than once per operative session. Baseline study reporting is based upon the total unique studies performed. For example, if during the course of baseline testing and one-on-one monitoring, two separate nerves have motor testing performed in conjunction with limited single extremity EMG, then 95885 and 95907 would be reported in addition to 95940. Time spent monitoring (95940, 95941) excludes time to set up, record, and interpret the baseline studies, and to remove electrodes at the end of the procedure. To report time spent waiting on standby for a case to start, use 99360. For procedures that last beyond midnight, report services using the day on which the monitoring began and using the total time monitored.

Code 95940 is reported per 15 minutes of service. Code 95940 requires reporting only the portion of time the monitoring professional was physically present in the operating room providing one-on-one patient monitoring, and no other cases may be monitored at the same time. Time spent in the operating room is cumulative. To determine units of service of 95940, use the total minutes monitoring in the operating room one-on-one. Monitoring may begin prior to incision (eg, when positioning on the table is a time of risk). Report continuous intraoperative neurophysiologic monitoring in the operating room (95940) in addition to the services related to monitoring from outside the operating room (95941).◄

Code 95941 should be used once per hour even if multiple methods of neurophysiologic monitoring are used during the time. Code 95941 requires the monitoring of neurophysiological data that is collected from the operating room continuously on-line in real time via a secure data link. When reporting 95941, real-time ability must be available through sufficient data bandwidth transfer rates to view and interrogate the neurophysiologic data contemporaneously.

Report 95941 for all cases in which there was no physical presence by the monitoring professional in the operating room during the monitoring time or when monitoring more than one case in an operating room. It is also used to report the time of monitoring physically performed outside of the operating room in those cases where monitoring occurred both within and outside the operating room. Do not report 95941 if the monitoring lasts 30 minutes or less.

Intraoperative neurophysiology monitoring codes 95940 and 95941 are each used to report the total duration of respective time spent providing each service, even if that time is not in a single continuous block.

> (95920 has been deleted. To report, see 95940, 95941)

**#✚ 95940**  Continuous intraoperative neurophysiology monitoring in the operating room, one on one monitoring requiring personal attendance, each 15 minutes (List separately in addition to code for primary procedure)

> (Use 95940 in conjunction with the study performed, 92585, 95822, 95860-95870, 95907-95913, 95925, 95926, 95927, 95928, 95929, 95930-95937, 95938, 95939)

**#✚ 95941**  Continuous intraoperative neurophysiology monitoring, from outside the operating room (remote or nearby) or for monitoring of more than one case while in the operating room, per hour (List separately in addition to code for primary procedure)

> (Use 95941 in conjunction with the study performed, 92585, 95822, 95860-95870, 95907-95913, 95925, 95926, 95927, 95928, 95929, 95930-95937, 95938, 95939)

> (For time spent waiting on standby before monitoring, use 99360)

> (For electrocorticography, use 95829)

> (For intraoperative EEG during nonintracranial surgery, use 95955)

> (For intraoperative functional cortical or subcortical mapping, see 95961-95962)

> (For intraoperative neurostimulator programming and analysis, see 95970-95975)

## Autonomic Function Tests

The purpose of autonomic nervous system function testing is to determine the presence of autonomic dysfunction, the site of autonomic dysfunction, and the various autonomic subsystems that may be disordered.

Code 95921 should be reported only when electrocardiographic monitoring of heart rate derived from the time elapsing between two consecutive R waves in the electrocardiogram, or the R-R interval, is displayed on a monitor and stored for subsequent analysis of

waveforms. Testing is typically performed in the prone position. A tilt table may be used, but is not required equipment for testing of the parasympathetic function. At least two of the following components need to be included in testing:

1. Heart rate response to deep breathing derived from a visual quantitative analysis of recordings with subject breathing at a rate of 5-6 breaths per minute.

2. Valsalva ratio determined by dividing the maximum heart rate by the lowest heart rate. The initial heart rate responses to sustained oral pressure (blowing into a tube with an open glottis) consist of tachycardia followed by a bradycardia at 15-45 seconds after the Valsalva pressure has been released. A minimum of two Valsalva maneuvers are to be performed. The initial cardioacceleration is an exercise reflex while the subsequent tachycardia and bradycardia are baroreflex-mediated.

3. A 30:15 ratio (R-R interval at beat 30)/(R-R interval at beat 15) used as an index of cardiovascular function.

Code 95922 should be reported only when all of the following components are included in testing:

1. Continuous recording of beat-to-beat BP and heart rate. The heart rate needs to be derived from an electrocardiogram (ECG) unit such that an accurate quantitative graphical measurement of the R-R interval is obtained.

2. A period of supine rest of at least 20 minutes prior to testing.

3. The performance and recording of beat-to-beat blood pressure and heart rate during a minimum of two (2) Valsalva maneuvers.

4. The performance of passive head-up tilt with continuous recording of beat-to-beat blood pressure and heart rate for a minimum of five minutes, followed by passive tilt-back to the supine position. This must be performed using a tilt table.

Code 95924 should be reported only when both the parasympathetic function and the adrenergic function are tested together with the use of a tilt table.

> (To report autonomic function testing that does not include beat-to-beat recording or for testing without use of a tilt table, use 95943)

**95921**  Testing of autonomic nervous system function; cardiovagal innervation (parasympathetic function), including 2 or more of the following: heart rate response to deep breathing with recorded R-R interval, Valsalva ratio, and 30:15 ratio

**95922**  vasomotor adrenergic innervation (sympathetic adrenergic function), including beat-to-beat blood pressure and R-R interval changes during Valsalva maneuver and at least 5 minutes of passive tilt

> (Do not report 95922 in conjunction with 95921)

**95923**       sudomotor, including 1 or more of the following: quantitative sudomotor axon reflex test (QSART), silastic sweat imprint, thermoregulatory sweat test, and changes in sympathetic skin potential

**95924**       combined parasympathetic and sympathetic adrenergic function testing with at least 5 minutes of passive tilt

(Do not report 95924 in conjunction with 95921 or 95922)

**# 95943**       Simultaneous, independent, quantitative measures of both parasympathetic function and sympathetic function, based on time-frequency analysis of heart rate variability concurrent with time-frequency analysis of continuous respiratory activity, with mean heart rate and blood pressure measures, during rest, paced (deep) breathing, Valsalva maneuvers, and head-up postural change

(Do not report 95943 in conjunction with 93040, 95921, 95922, 95924)

## Evoked Potentials and Reflex Tests

**95925**       Short-latency somatosensory evoked potential study, stimulation of any/all peripheral nerves or skin sites, recording from the central nervous system; in upper limbs

(Do not report 95925 in conjunction with 95926)

**95926**       in lower limbs

(Do not report 95926 in conjunction with 95925)

**# 95938**       in upper and lower limbs

(Do not report 95938 in conjunction with 95925, 95926)

**95927**       in the trunk or head

(To report a unilateral study, use modifier 52)

(For auditory evoked potentials, use 92585)

**95928**       Central motor evoked potential study (transcranial motor stimulation); upper limbs

(Do not report 95928 in conjunction with 95929)

**95929**       lower limbs

(Do not report 95929 in conjunction with 95928)

**# 95939**       in upper and lower limbs

(Do not report 95939 in conjunction with 95928, 95929)

**95930**       Visual evoked potential (VEP) testing central nervous system, checkerboard or flash

▶(For screening of visual acuity using automated visual evoked potential devices, use 0333T)◀

**95933**       Orbicularis oculi (blink) reflex, by electrodiagnostic testing

(95934, 95936 have been deleted. To report H-reflex testing, see 95907-95913)

**95937**       Neuromuscular junction testing (repetitive stimulation, paired stimuli), each nerve, any 1 method

**95938**       Code is out of numerical sequence. See 95925-95939

**95939**       Code is out of numerical sequence. See 95925-95939

**95940**       Code is out of numerical sequence. See 95921-95943

**95941**       Code is out of numerical sequence. See 95921-95943

**95943**       Code is out of numerical sequence. See 95921-95943

## Special EEG Tests

Codes 95950-95953 and 95956 are used per 24 hours of recording. For recording more than 12 hours, do not use modifier 52. For recording 12 hours or less, use modifier 52. Codes 95951 and 95956 are used for recordings in which interpretations can be made throughout the recording time, with interventions to alter or end the recording or to alter the patient care during the recordings as needed.

Codes 95961 and 95962 use physician or other qualified health care professional time as a basis for unit of service. Report 95961 for the first hour of attendance. Use modifier 52 with 95961 for 30 minutes or less. Report 95962 for each additional hour of attendance.

**95950**       Monitoring for identification and lateralization of cerebral seizure focus, electroencephalographic (eg, 8 channel EEG) recording and interpretation, each 24 hours

**95951**       Monitoring for localization of cerebral seizure focus by cable or radio, 16 or more channel telemetry, combined electroencephalographic (EEG) and video recording and interpretation (eg, for presurgical localization), each 24 hours

**95953**       Monitoring for localization of cerebral seizure focus by computerized portable 16 or more channel EEG, electroencephalographic (EEG) recording and interpretation, each 24 hours, unattended

**95954**       Pharmacological or physical activation requiring physician or other qualified health care professional attendance during EEG recording of activation phase (eg, thiopental activation test)

**95955**       Electroencephalogram (EEG) during nonintracranial surgery (eg, carotid surgery)

**95956**       Monitoring for localization of cerebral seizure focus by cable or radio, 16 or more channel telemetry, electroencephalographic (EEG) recording and interpretation, each 24 hours, attended by a technologist or nurse

**95957**       Digital analysis of electroencephalogram (EEG) (eg, for epileptic spike analysis)

**95958**       Wada activation test for hemispheric function, including electroencephalographic (EEG) monitoring

**95961**       Functional cortical and subcortical mapping by stimulation and/or recording of electrodes on brain surface, or of depth electrodes, to provoke seizures or identify vital brain structures; initial hour of attendance by a physician or other qualified health care professional

**Medicine**

---

**+ 95962** each additional hour of attendance by a physician or other qualified health care professional (List separately in addition to code for primary procedure)

(Use 95962 in conjunction with 95961)

**95965** Magnetoencephalography (MEG), recording and analysis; for spontaneous brain magnetic activity (eg, epileptic cerebral cortex localization)

**95966** for evoked magnetic fields, single modality (eg, sensory, motor, language, or visual cortex localization)

**+ 95967** for evoked magnetic fields, each additional modality (eg, sensory, motor, language, or visual cortex localization) (List separately in addition to code for primary procedure)

(Use 95967 in conjunction with 95966)

(For electroencephalography performed in addition to magnetoencephalography, see 95812-95827)

(For somatosensory evoked potentials, auditory evoked potentials, and visual evoked potentials performed in addition to magnetic evoked field responses, see 92585, 95925, 95926, and/or 95930)

(For computerized tomography performed in addition to magnetoencephalography, see 70450-70470, 70496)

(For magnetic resonance imaging performed in addition to magnetoencephalography, see 70551-70553)

# Neurostimulators, Analysis-Programming

Simple intraoperative or subsequent programming of the neurostimulator pulse generator/transmitter (95971) includes changes to three or fewer of the following parameters: rate, pulse amplitude, pulse duration, pulse frequency, eight or more electrode contacts, cycling, stimulation train duration, train spacing, number of programs, number of channels, alternating electrode polarities, dose time (stimulation parameters changing in time periods of minutes including dose lockout times), more than one clinical feature (eg, rigidity, dyskinesia, tremor). Complex intraoperative or subsequent programming (95972-95979) includes changes to more than three of the above.

Code 95970 describes subsequent electronic analysis of a previously-implanted simple or complex brain, spinal cord, or peripheral neurostimulator pulse generator system, without reprogramming. Code 95971 describes intraoperative or subsequent electronic analysis of an implanted simple spinal cord, or peripheral (ie, peripheral nerve, autonomic nerve, neuromuscular) neurostimulator pulse generator system, with programming. Codes 95972 and 95973 describe intraoperative (at initial insertion/revision) or subsequent electronic analysis of an implanted complex spinal cord or peripheral (except cranial nerve) neurostimulator pulse generator system, with programming. Codes 95974 and 95975 describe intraoperative (at initial insertion/revision) or subsequent

electronic analysis of an implanted complex cranial nerve neurostimulator pulse generator system, with programming. Codes 95978 and 95979 describe initial or subsequent electronic analysis of an implanted brain neurostimulator pulse generator system, with programming.

Code 95980 describes intraoperative electronic analysis of an implanted gastric neurostimulator pulse generator system, with programming; code 95981 describes subsequent analysis of the device; code 95982 describes subsequent analysis and reprogramming. For electronic analysis and reprogramming of gastric neurostimulator, lesser curvature, see 95980-95982.

For 95972, 95974, and 95978, use modifier 52 if less than 31 minutes in duration.

(For electronic analysis and reprogramming of a peripheral subcutaneous field stimulation pulse generator, use 0285T)

(For insertion of neurostimulator pulse generator, see 61885, 63685, 64590)

(For revision or removal of neurostimulator pulse generator or receiver, see 61888, 63688, 64595)

(For implantation of neurostimulator electrodes, see 43647, 43881, 61850-61875, 63650-63655, 64553-64580. For revision or removal of neurostimulator electrodes, see 43648, 43882, 61880, 63661-63664, 64585)

**95970** Electronic analysis of implanted neurostimulator pulse generator system (eg, rate, pulse amplitude, pulse duration, configuration of wave form, battery status, electrode selectability, output modulation, cycling, impedance and patient compliance measurements); simple or complex brain, spinal cord, or peripheral (ie, cranial nerve, peripheral nerve, sacral nerve, neuromuscular) neurostimulator pulse generator/transmitter, without reprogramming

**95971** simple spinal cord, or peripheral (ie, peripheral nerve, sacral nerve, neuromuscular) neurostimulator pulse generator/transmitter, with intraoperative or subsequent programming

**95972** complex spinal cord, or peripheral (ie, peripheral nerve, sacral nerve, neuromuscular) (except cranial nerve) neurostimulator pulse generator/transmitter, with intraoperative or subsequent programming, first hour

**+ 95973** complex spinal cord, or peripheral (ie, peripheral nerve, sacral nerve, neuromuscular) (except cranial nerve) neurostimulator pulse generator/transmitter, with intraoperative or subsequent programming, each additional 30 minutes after first hour (List separately in addition to code for primary procedure)

(Use 95973 in conjunction with 95972)

**95974** complex cranial nerve neurostimulator pulse generator/transmitter, with intraoperative or subsequent programming, with or without nerve interface testing, first hour

Medicine

**+ 95975**    complex cranial nerve neurostimulator pulse generator/transmitter, with intraoperative or subsequent programming, each additional 30 minutes after first hour (List separately in addition to code for primary procedure)

    (Use 95975 in conjunction with 95974)

**95978**    Electronic analysis of implanted neurostimulator pulse generator system (eg, rate, pulse amplitude and duration, battery status, electrode selectability and polarity, impedance and patient compliance measurements), complex deep brain neurostimulator pulse generator/transmitter, with initial or subsequent programming; first hour

**+ 95979**    each additional 30 minutes after first hour (List separately in addition to code for primary procedure)

    (Use 95979 in conjunction with 95978)

**95980**    Electronic analysis of implanted neurostimulator pulse generator system (eg, rate, pulse amplitude and duration, configuration of wave form, battery status, electrode selectability, output modulation, cycling, impedance and patient measurements) gastric neurostimulator pulse generator/transmitter; intraoperative, with programming

**95981**    subsequent, without reprogramming

**95982**    subsequent, with reprogramming

    (For intraoperative or subsequent analysis, with programming, when performed, of vagus nerve trunk stimulator used for blocking therapy [morbid obesity], see 0312T, 0317T)

## Other Procedures

**95990**    Refilling and maintenance of implantable pump or reservoir for drug delivery, spinal (intrathecal, epidural) or brain (intraventricular), includes electronic analysis of pump, when performed;

**95991**    requiring skill of a physician or other qualified health care professional

    (Do not report 95990, 95991 in conjunction with 62367-62370. For analysis and/or reprogramming of implantable infusion pump, see 62367-62370)

    (For refill and maintenance of implanted infusion pump or reservoir for systemic drug therapy [eg, chemotherapy], use 96522)

⊘ **95992**    Canalith repositioning procedure(s) (eg, Epley maneuver, Semont maneuver), per day

    (Do not report 95992 in conjunction with 92531, 92532)

**95999**    Unlisted neurological or neuromuscular diagnostic procedure

## Motion Analysis

Codes 96000-96004 describe services performed as part of a major therapeutic or diagnostic decision making process. Motion analysis is performed in a dedicated motion analysis laboratory (ie, a facility capable of performing videotaping from the front, back and both sides, computerized 3D kinematics, 3D kinetics, and dynamic electromyography). Code 96000 may include 3D kinetics and stride characteristics. Codes 96002-96003 describe dynamic electromyography.

Code 96004 should only be reported once regardless of the number of study(ies) reviewed/interpreted.

    (For performance of needle electromyography procedures, see 95860-95870, 95872, 95885-95887)

    (For gait training, use 97116)

**96000**    Comprehensive computer-based motion analysis by video-taping and 3D kinematics;

**96001**    with dynamic plantar pressure measurements during walking

**96002**    Dynamic surface electromyography, during walking or other functional activities, 1-12 muscles

**96003**    Dynamic fine wire electromyography, during walking or other functional activities, 1 muscle

    (Do not report 96002, 96003 in conjunction with 95860-95866, 95869-95872, 95885-95887)

**96004**    Review and interpretation by physician or other qualified health care professional of comprehensive computer-based motion analysis, dynamic plantar pressure measurements, dynamic surface electromyography during walking or other functional activities, and dynamic fine wire electromyography, with written report

## Functional Brain Mapping

Code 96020 includes selection and administration of testing of language, memory, cognition, movement, sensation, and other neurological functions when conducted in association with functional neuroimaging, monitoring of performance of this testing, and determination of validity of neurofunctional testing relative to separately interpreted functional magnetic resonance images.

**96020**    Neurofunctional testing selection and administration during noninvasive imaging functional brain mapping, with test administered entirely by a physician or other qualified health care professional (ie, psychologist), with review of test results and report

    (For functional magnetic resonance imaging [fMRI], brain, use 70555)

    (Do not report 96020 in conjunction with 96101-96103, 96116-96120)

    (Do not report 96020 in conjunction with 70554)

    (Evaluation and Management services codes should not be reported on the same day as 96020)

**Medicine**

---

# Medical Genetics and Genetic Counseling Services

These services are provided by trained genetic counselors and may include obtaining a structured family genetic history, pedigree construction, analysis for genetic risk assessment, and counseling of the patient and family. These activities may be provided during one or more sessions and may include review of medical data and family information, face-to-face interviews, and counseling services.

Code 96040 is reported for each 30-minute increment of face-to-face time. Do not report 96040 for 15 minutes or less of face-to-face time. Report 96040 once for 16 to 30 minutes of face-to-face time.

**96040**   Medical genetics and genetic counseling services, each 30 minutes face-to-face with patient/family

(For genetic counseling and education provided to an individual by a physician or other qualified health care professional who may report evaluation and management services, see the appropriate Evaluation and Management codes)

(For genetic counseling and education to a group by a physician or other qualified health care professional, use 99078)

(For education regarding genetic risks by a nonphysician to a group, see 98961, 98962)

(For genetic counseling and/or risk factor reduction intervention provided to patient(s) without symptoms or established disease, by a physician or other qualified health care professional who may report evaluation and management services, see 99401-99412)

# Central Nervous System Assessments/Tests (eg, Neuro-Cognitive, Mental Status, Speech Testing)

The following codes are used to report the services provided during testing of the cognitive function of the central nervous system. The testing of cognitive processes, visual motor responses, and abstractive abilities is accomplished by the combination of several types of testing procedures. It is expected that the administration of these tests will generate material that will be formulated into a report. A minimum of 31 minutes must be provided to report any per hour code. Services 96101, 96116, 96118 and 96125 report time as face-to-face time with the patient and the time spent interpreting and preparing the report.

(For development of cognitive skills, see 97532, 97533)

(For mini-mental status examination performed by a physician, see **Evaluation and Management** services codes)

**96101**   Psychological testing (includes psychodiagnostic assessment of emotionality, intellectual abilities, personality and psychopathology, eg, MMPI, Rorschach, WAIS), per hour of the psychologist's or physician's time, both face-to-face time administering tests to the patient and time interpreting these test results and preparing the report

(96101 is also used in those circumstances when additional time is necessary to integrate other sources of clinical data, including previously completed and reported technician- and computer-administered tests)

(Do not report 96101 for the interpretation and report of 96102, 96103)

**96102**   Psychological testing (includes psychodiagnostic assessment of emotionality, intellectual abilities, personality and psychopathology, eg, MMPI and WAIS), with qualified health care professional interpretation and report, administered by technician, per hour of technician time, face-to-face

**96103**   Psychological testing (includes psychodiagnostic assessment of emotionality, intellectual abilities, personality and psychopathology, eg, MMPI), administered by a computer, with qualified health care professional interpretation and report

**96105**   Assessment of aphasia (includes assessment of expressive and receptive speech and language function, language comprehension, speech production ability, reading, spelling, writing, eg, by Boston Diagnostic Aphasia Examination) with interpretation and report, per hour

**96110**   Developmental screening, with interpretation and report, per standardized instrument form

**96111**   Developmental testing, (includes assessment of motor, language, social, adaptive, and/or cognitive functioning by standardized developmental instruments) with interpretation and report

**96116**   Neurobehavioral status exam (clinical assessment of thinking, reasoning and judgment, eg, acquired knowledge, attention, language, memory, planning and problem solving, and visual spatial abilities), per hour of the psychologist's or physician's time, both face-to-face time with the patient and time interpreting test results and preparing the report

Medicine

**96118**  Neuropsychological testing (eg, Halstead-Reitan Neuropsychological Battery, Wechsler Memory Scales and Wisconsin Card Sorting Test), per hour of the psychologist's or physician's time, both face-to-face time administering tests to the patient and time interpreting these test results and preparing the report

(96118 is also used in those circumstances when additional time is necessary to integrate other sources of clinical data, including previously completed and reported technician- and computer-administered tests)

(Do not report 96118 for the interpretation and report of 96119 or 96120)

**96119**  Neuropsychological testing (eg, Halstead-Reitan Neuropsychological Battery, Wechsler Memory Scales and Wisconsin Card Sorting Test), with qualified health care professional interpretation and report, administered by technician, per hour of technician time, face-to-face

**96120**  Neuropsychological testing (eg, Wisconsin Card Sorting Test), administered by a computer, with qualified health care professional interpretation and report

**96125**  Standardized cognitive performance testing (eg, Ross Information Processing Assessment) per hour of a qualified health care professional's time, both face-to-face time administering tests to the patient and time interpreting these test results and preparing the report

(For psychological and neuropsychological testing by a physician or psychologist, see 96101-96103, 96118-96120)

# Health and Behavior Assessment/Intervention

Health and behavior assessment procedures are used to identify the psychological, behavioral, emotional, cognitive, and social factors important to the prevention, treatment, or management of physical health problems.

The focus of the assessment is not on mental health but on the biopsychosocial factors important to physical health problems and treatments. The focus of the intervention is to improve the patient's health and well-being utilizing cognitive, behavioral, social, and/or psychophysiological procedures designed to ameliorate specific disease-related problems.

Codes 96150-96155 describe services offered to patients who present with primary physical illnesses, diagnoses, or symptoms and may benefit from assessments and interventions that focus on the biopsychosocial factors related to the patient's health status. These services do not represent preventive medicine counseling and risk factor reduction interventions.

For patients that require psychiatric services (90785-90899) as well as health and behavior assessment/intervention (96150-96155), report the predominant

service performed. Do not report 96150-96155 in conjunction with 90785-90899 on the same date.

Evaluation and Management services codes (including Counseling Risk Factor Reduction and Behavior Change Intervention [99401-99412]), should not be reported on the same day.

(For health and behavior assessment and/or intervention performed by a physician or other qualified health care professional who may report evaluation and management services, see **Evaluation and Management** or **Preventive Medicine** services codes)

**96150**  Health and behavior assessment (eg, health-focused clinical interview, behavioral observations, psychophysiological monitoring, health-oriented questionnaires), each 15 minutes face-to-face with the patient; initial assessment

**96151**      re-assessment

**96152**  Health and behavior intervention, each 15 minutes, face-to-face; individual

**96153**      group (2 or more patients)

**96154**      family (with the patient present)

**96155**      family (without the patient present)

# Hydration, Therapeutic, Prophylactic, Diagnostic Injections and Infusions, and Chemotherapy and Other Highly Complex Drug or Highly Complex Biologic Agent Administration

Physician or other qualified health care professional work related to hydration, injection, and infusion services predominantly involves affirmation of treatment plan and direct supervision of staff.

Codes 96360-96379, 96401, 96402, 96409-96425, 96521-96523 are not intended to be reported by the physician in the facility setting. If a significant, separately identifiable office or other outpatient Evaluation and Management service is performed, the appropriate E/M service (99201-99215, 99241-99245, 99354-99355) should be reported using modifier 25 in addition to 96360-96549. For same day E/M service, a different diagnosis is not required.

If performed to facilitate the infusion or injection, the following services are included and are not reported separately:

a. Use of local anesthesia

b. IV start

**Medicine**

c. Access to indwelling IV, subcutaneous catheter or port

d. Flush at conclusion of infusion

e. Standard tubing, syringes, and supplies

(For declotting a catheter or port, use 36593)

When multiple drugs are administered, report the service(s) and the specific materials or drugs for each.

When administering multiple infusions, injections or combinations, only one "initial" service code should be reported for a given date, unless protocol requires that two separate IV sites must be used. Do not report a second initial service on the same date due to an intravenous line requiring a re-start, an IV rate not being able to be reached without two lines, or for accessing a port of a multi-lumen catheter. If an injection or infusion is of a subsequent or concurrent nature, even if it is the first such service within that group of services, then a subsequent or concurrent code from the appropriate section should be reported (eg, the first IV push given subsequent to an initial one-hour infusion is reported using a subsequent IV push code).

**Initial infusion:** For physician or other qualified health care professional reporting, an initial infusion is the *key or primary reason for the encounter* reported irrespective of the temporal order in which the infusion(s) or injection(s) are administered. For facility reporting, an initial infusion is based using the hierarchy. For both physician or other qualified health care professional and facility reporting, only one *initial* service code (eg, 96365) should be reported unless the protocol or patient condition requires that two separate IV sites must be utilized. The difference in time and effort in providing this second IV site access is also reported using the *initial* service code with modifier 59 appended (eg, 96365, 96365-59).

**Sequential infusion:** A sequential infusion is an infusion or IV push of a new substance or drug following a primary or initial service. All sequential services require that there be a new substance or drug, except that facilities may report a sequential intravenous push of the same drug using 96376.

**Concurrent infusion:** A concurrent infusion is an infusion of a new substance or drug infused at the same time as another substance or drug. A concurrent infusion service is not time based and is only reported once per day regardless of whether an additional new drug or substance is administered concurrently. Hydration may not be reported concurrently with any other service. A separate subsequent concurrent administration of another new drug or substance (the third substance or drug) is not reported.

In order to determine which service should be reported as the initial service when there is more than one type of service, hierarchies have been created. These vary by whether the physician or other qualified health care professional or a facility is reporting. The order of

selection for reporting is based upon the physician's or other qualified health care professional's knowledge of the clinical condition(s) and treatment(s). The hierarchy that facilities are to use is based upon a structural algorithm. When these codes are reported by the physician or other qualified health care professional, the "initial" code that best describes the key or primary reason for the encounter should always be reported irrespective of the order in which the infusions or injections occur.

When these codes are reported *by the facility*, the following instructions apply. The initial code should be selected using a hierarchy whereby chemotherapy services are primary to therapeutic, prophylactic, and diagnostic services which are primary to hydration services. Infusions are primary to pushes, which are primary to injections. This hierarchy is to be followed by facilities and supersedes parenthetical instructions for add-on codes that suggest an add-on of a higher hierarchical position may be reported in conjunction with a base code of a lower position. (For example, the hierarchy would not permit reporting 96376 with 96360, as 96376 is a higher order code. IV push is primary to hydration.)

When reporting multiple infusions of the same drug/substance on the same date of service, the initial code should be selected. The second and subsequent infusion(s) should be reported based on the individual time(s) of each additional infusion(s) of the same drug/substance using the appropriate add-on code.

**Example:** In the outpatient observation setting, a patient receives one-hour intravenous infusions of the same antibiotic every 8 hours on the same date of service through the same IV access. The hierarchy for facility reporting permits the reporting of code 96365 for the first one-hour dose administered. Add-on 96366 would be reported twice (once for the second and third one-hour infusions of the same drug).

▶When reporting codes for which infusion time is a factor, use the actual time over which the infusion is administered. Intravenous or intra-arterial push is defined as: (a) an injection in which the individual who administers the drug/substance is continuously present to administer the injection and observe the patient, or (b) an infusion of 15 minutes or less. If intravenous hydration (96360, 96361) is given from 11 PM to 2 AM, 96360 would be reported once and 96361 twice. For continuous services that last beyond midnight, use the date in which the service began and report the total units of time provided continuously. However, if instead of a continuous infusion, a medication was given by intravenous push at 10 PM and 2 AM, as the service was not continuous, the two administrations would be reported as an initial service (96374) and sequential (96376) as: (1) no other infusion services were performed; and (2) the push of the same drug was performed more than 30 minutes beyond the initial administration. A "keep open" infusion of any type is not separately reported.◀

# Hydration

Codes 96360-96361 are intended to report a hydration IV infusion to consist of a pre-packaged fluid and electrolytes (eg, normal saline, D5-1/2 normal saline+30mEq KCl/liter), but are not used to report infusion of drugs or other substances. Hydration IV infusions typically require direct supervision for purposes of consent, safety oversight, or intraservice supervision of staff. Typically such infusions require little special handling to prepare or dispose of, and staff that administer these do not typically require advanced practice training. After initial set-up, infusion typically entails little patient risk and thus little monitoring. These codes are not intended to be reported by the physician or other qualified health care professional in the facility setting.

Some chemotherapeutic agents and other therapeutic agents require pre- and/or post-hydration to be given in order to avoid specific toxicities. A minimum time duration of 31 minutes of hydration infusion is required to report the service. However, the hydration codes 96360 or 96361 are not used when the purpose of the intravenous fluid is to "keep open" an IV line prior or subsequent to a therapeutic infusion, or as a free-flowing IV during chemotherapy or other therapeutic infusion.

**96360**     Intravenous infusion, hydration; initial, 31 minutes to 1 hour

(Do not report 96360 if performed as a concurrent infusion service)

(Do not report intravenous infusion for hydration of 30 minutes or less)

**+ 96361**     each additional hour (List separately in addition to code for primary procedure)

(Use 96361 in conjunction with 96360)

(Report 96361 for hydration infusion intervals of greater than 30 minutes beyond 1 hour increments)

(Report 96361 to identify hydration if provided as a secondary or subsequent service after a different initial service [96360, 96365, 96374, 96409, 96413] is administered through the same IV access)

# Therapeutic, Prophylactic, and Diagnostic Injections and Infusions (Excludes Chemotherapy and Other Highly Complex Drug or Highly Complex Biologic Agent Administration)

A therapeutic, prophylactic, or diagnostic IV infusion or injection (other than hydration) is for the administration of substances/drugs. When fluids are used to administer the drug(s), the administration of the fluid is considered incidental hydration and is not separately reportable.

These services typically require direct supervision for any or all purposes of patient assessment, provision of consent, safety oversight, and intra-service supervision of staff. Typically, such infusions require special consideration to prepare, dose or dispose of, require practice training and competency for staff who administer the infusions, and require periodic patient assessment with vital sign monitoring during the infusion. These codes are not intended to be reported by the physician or other qualified health care professional in the facility setting.

See codes 96401-96549 for the administration of chemotherapy or other highly complex drug or highly complex biologic agent services. These highly complex services require advanced practice training and competency for staff who provide these services; special considerations for preparation, dosage or disposal; and commonly, these services entail significant patient risk and frequent monitoring. Examples are frequent changes in the infusion rate, prolonged presence of nurse administering the solution for patient monitoring and infusion adjustments, and frequent conferring with the physician or other qualified health care professional about these issues.

(Do not report 96365-96379 with codes for which IV push or infusion is an inherent part of the procedure [eg, administration of contrast material for a diagnostic imaging study])

**96365**     Intravenous infusion, for therapy, prophylaxis, or diagnosis (specify substance or drug); initial, up to 1 hour

**+ 96366**     each additional hour (List separately in addition to code for primary procedure)

(Report 96366 in conjunction with 96365, 96367)

(Report 96366 for additional hour[s] of sequential infusion)

(Report 96366 for infusion intervals of greater than 30 minutes beyond 1 hour increments)

(Report 96366 in conjunction with 96365 to identify each second and subsequent infusions of the same drug/substance)

**+ 96367**     additional sequential infusion of a new drug/substance, up to 1 hour (List separately in addition to code for primary procedure)

(Report 96367 in conjunction with 96365, 96374, 96409, 96413 to identify the infusion of a new drug/substance provided as a secondary or subsequent service after a different initial service is administered through the same IV access. Report 96367 only once per sequential infusion of same infusate mix)

**+ 96368**     concurrent infusion (List separately in addition to code for primary procedure)

(Report 96368 only once per date of service)

(Report 96368 in conjunction with 96365, 96366, 96413, 96415, 96416)

**Medicine**

96369     Subcutaneous infusion for therapy or prophylaxis (specify substance or drug); initial, up to 1 hour, including pump set-up and establishment of subcutaneous infusion site(s)

(For infusions of 15 minutes or less, use 96372)

**+ 96370**     each additional hour (List separately in addition to code for primary procedure)

(Use 96370 in conjunction with 96369)

(Use 96370 for infusion intervals of greater than 30 minutes beyond 1 hour increments)

**+ 96371**     additional pump set-up with establishment of new subcutaneous infusion site(s) (List separately in addition to code for primary procedure)

(Use 96371 in conjunction with 96369)

(Use 96369, 96371 only once per encounter)

96372     Therapeutic, prophylactic, or diagnostic injection (specify substance or drug); subcutaneous or intramuscular

(For administration of vaccines/toxoids, see 90471, 90472, 96365, 96366)

(Report 96372 for non-antineoplastic hormonal therapy injections)

(Report 96401 for anti-neoplastic nonhormonal injection therapy)

(Report 96402 for anti-neoplastic hormonal injection therapy)

(Do not report 96372 for injections given without direct physician or other qualified health care professional supervision. To report, use 99211. Hospitals may report 96372 when the physician or other qualified health care professional is not present)

(96372 does not include injections for allergen immunotherapy. For allergen immunotherapy injections, see 95115-95117)

96373     intra-arterial

96374     intravenous push, single or initial substance/drug

**+ 96375**     each additional sequential intravenous push of a new substance/drug (List separately in addition to code for primary procedure)

(Use 96375 in conjunction with 96365, 96374, 96409, 96413)

(Report 96375 to identify intravenous push of a new substance/drug if provided as a secondary or subsequent service after a different initial service is administered through the same IV access)

**+ 96376**     each additional sequential intravenous push of the same substance/drug provided in a facility (List separately in addition to code for primary procedure)

(Do not report 96376 for a push performed within 30 minutes of a reported push of the same substance or drug)

(96376 may be reported by facilities only)

(Report 96376 in conjunction with 96365, 96374, 96409, 96413)

96379     Unlisted therapeutic, prophylactic, or diagnostic intravenous or intra-arterial injection or infusion

(For allergy immunology, see 95004 et seq)

# Chemotherapy and Other Highly Complex Drug or Highly Complex Biologic Agent Administration

Chemotherapy administration codes 96401-96549 apply to parenteral administration of non-radionuclide anti-neoplastic drugs; and also to anti-neoplastic agents provided for treatment of noncancer diagnoses (eg, cyclophosphamide for auto-immune conditions) or to substances such as certain monoclonal antibody agents, and other biologic response modifiers. The highly complex infusion of chemotherapy or other drug or biologic agents requires physician or other qualified health care professional work and/or clinical staff monitoring well beyond that of therapeutic drug agents (96360-96379) because the incidence of severe adverse patient reactions are typically greater. These services can be provided by any physician or other qualified health care professional. Chemotherapy services are typically highly complex and require direct supervision for any or all purposes of patient assessment, provision of consent, safety oversight, and intraservice supervision of staff. Typically, such chemotherapy services require advanced practice training and competency for staff who provide these services; special considerations for preparation, dosage, or disposal; and commonly, these services entail significant patient risk and frequent monitoring. Examples are frequent changes in the infusion rate, prolonged presence of the nurse administering the solution for patient monitoring and infusion adjustments, and frequent conferring with the physician or other qualified health care professional about these issues. When performed to facilitate the infusion of injection, preparation of chemotherapy agent(s), highly complex agent(s), or other highly complex drugs is included and is not reported separately. To report infusions that do not require this level of complexity, see 96360-96379. Codes 96401-96402, 96409-96425, 96521-96523 are not intended to be reported by the individual physician or other qualified health care professional in the facility setting.

The term "chemotherapy" in 96401-96549 includes other highly complex drugs or highly complex biologic agents.

Report separate codes for each parenteral method of administration employed when chemotherapy is administered by different techniques. The administration of medications (eg, antibiotics, steroidal agents, antiemetics, narcotics, analgesics) administered independently or sequentially as supportive management of chemotherapy administration, should be separately reported using 96360, 96361, 96365, 96379 as appropriate.

Report both the specific service as well as code(s) for the specific substance(s) or drug(s) provided. The fluid used to administer the drug(s) is considered incidental hydration and is not separately reportable.

Regional (isolation) chemotherapy perfusion should be reported using the codes for arterial infusion (96420-96425). Placement of the intra-arterial catheter should be reported using the appropriate code from the **Cardiovascular Surgery** section. Placement of arterial and venous cannula(s) for extracorporeal circulation via a membrane oxygenator perfusion pump should be reported using 36823. Code 36823 includes dose calculation and administration of the chemotherapy agent by injection into the perfusate. Do not report 96409-96425 in conjunction with 36823.

(For home infusion services, see 99601-99602)

## Injection and Intravenous Infusion Chemotherapy and Other Highly Complex Drug or Highly Complex Biologic Agent Administration

Intravenous or intra-arterial push is defined as: (a) an injection in which the healthcare professional who administers the substance/drug is continuously present to administer the injection and observe the patient, or (b) an infusion of 15 minutes or less.

**96401**    Chemotherapy administration, subcutaneous or intramuscular; non-hormonal anti-neoplastic

**96402**    hormonal anti-neoplastic

**96405**    Chemotherapy administration; intralesional, up to and including 7 lesions

**96406**    intralesional, more than 7 lesions

**96409**    intravenous, push technique, single or initial substance/drug

**+ 96411**    intravenous, push technique, each additional substance/drug (List separately in addition to code for primary procedure)

(Use 96411 in conjunction with 96409, 96413)

**96413**    Chemotherapy administration, intravenous infusion technique; up to 1 hour, single or initial substance/drug

(Report 96361 to identify hydration if administered as a secondary or subsequent service in association with 96413 through the same IV access)

(Report 96366, 96367, 96375 to identify therapeutic, prophylactic, or diagnostic drug infusion or injection, if administered as a secondary or subsequent service in association with 96413 through the same IV access)

**+ 96415**    each additional hour (List separately in addition to code for primary procedure)

(Use 96415 in conjunction with 96413)

(Report 96415 for infusion intervals of greater than 30 minutes beyond 1-hour increments)

**96416**    initiation of prolonged chemotherapy infusion (more than 8 hours), requiring use of a portable or implantable pump

(For refilling and maintenance of a portable pump or an implantable infusion pump or reservoir for drug delivery, see 96521-96523)

**+ 96417**    each additional sequential infusion (different substance/drug), up to 1 hour (List separately in addition to code for primary procedure)

(Use 96417 in conjunction with 96413)

(Report only once per sequential infusion. Report 96415 for additional hour(s) of sequential infusion)

## Intra-Arterial Chemotherapy and Other Highly Complex Drug or Highly Complex Biologic Agent Administration

**96420**    Chemotherapy administration, intra-arterial; push technique

**96422**    infusion technique, up to 1 hour

**+ 96423**    infusion technique, each additional hour (List separately in addition to code for primary procedure)

(Use 96423 in conjunction with 96422)

(Report 96423 for infusion intervals of greater than 30 minutes beyond 1-hour increments)

(For regional chemotherapy perfusion via membrane oxygenator perfusion pump to an extremity, use 36823)

**96425**    infusion technique, initiation of prolonged infusion (more than 8 hours), requiring the use of a portable or implantable pump

(For refilling and maintenance of a portable pump or an implantable infusion pump or reservoir for drug delivery, see 96521-96523)

## Other Injection and Infusion Services

Code 96523 does not require direct supervision. Codes 96521-96523 may be reported when these devices are used for therapeutic drugs other than chemotherapy.

(For collection of blood specimen from a completely implantable venous access device, use 36591)

**96440**    Chemotherapy administration into pleural cavity, requiring and including thoracentesis

(96445 has been deleted. To report intraperitoneal chemotherapy administration, use 96446)

Medicine

**96446** Chemotherapy administration into the peritoneal cavity via indwelling port or catheter

**96450** Chemotherapy administration, into CNS (eg, intrathecal), requiring and including spinal puncture

(For intravesical (bladder) chemotherapy administration, use 51720)

(For insertion of subarachnoid catheter and reservoir for infusion of drug, see 62350, 62351, 62360-62362; for insertion of intraventricular catheter and reservoir, see 61210, 61215)

**96521** Refilling and maintenance of portable pump

**96522** Refilling and maintenance of implantable pump or reservoir for drug delivery, systemic (eg, intravenous, intra-arterial)

(For refilling and maintenance of an implantable infusion pump for spinal or brain drug infusion, use 95990-95991)

**96523** Irrigation of implanted venous access device for drug delivery systems

(Do not report 96523 in conjunction with other services. To report collection of blood specimen, use 36591)

**96542** Chemotherapy injection, subarachnoid or intraventricular via subcutaneous reservoir, single or multiple agents

(For radioactive isotope therapy, use 79005)

**96549** Unlisted chemotherapy procedure

# Photodynamic Therapy

(To report ocular photodynamic therapy, use 67221)

**96567** Photodynamic therapy by external application of light to destroy premalignant and/or malignant lesions of the skin and adjacent mucosa (eg, lip) by activation of photosensitive drug(s), each phototherapy exposure session

**✛ 96570** Photodynamic therapy by endoscopic application of light to ablate abnormal tissue via activation of photosensitive drug(s); first 30 minutes (List separately in addition to code for endoscopy or bronchoscopy procedures of lung and gastrointestinal tract)

(Report 96570 with modifier 52 for service of less than 23 minutes with report)

**✛ 96571** each additional 15 minutes (List separately in addition to code for endoscopy or bronchoscopy procedures of lung and gastrointestinal tract)

(For 23-37 minutes of service, use 96570. For 38-52 minutes of service, use 96570 in conjunction with 96571)

(96570, 96571 are to be used in addition to bronchoscopy, endoscopy codes)

▶(Use 96570, 96571 in conjunction with 31641, 43229 as appropriate)◀

# Special Dermatological Procedures

See the **Evaluation and Management coding guidelines** for further instructions on reporting that is appropriate for management of dermatologic illnesses.

(For intralesional injections, see 11900, 11901)

(For Tzanck smear, see 88160-88161)

**96900** Actinotherapy (ultraviolet light)

(For rhinophototherapy, intranasal application of ultraviolet and visible light, use 30999)

**96902** Microscopic examination of hairs plucked or clipped by the examiner (excluding hair collected by the patient) to determine telogen and anagen counts, or structural hair shaft abnormality

**96904** Whole body integumentary photography, for monitoring of high risk patients with dysplastic nevus syndrome or a history of dysplastic nevi, or patients with a personal or familial history of melanoma

**96910** Photochemotherapy; tar and ultraviolet B (Goeckerman treatment) or petrolatum and ultraviolet B

**96912** psoralens and ultraviolet A (PUVA)

**96913** Photochemotherapy (Goeckerman and/or PUVA) for severe photoresponsive dermatoses requiring at least 4-8 hours of care under direct supervision of the physician (includes application of medication and dressings)

**96920** Laser treatment for inflammatory skin disease (psoriasis); total area less than 250 sq cm

**96921** 250 sq cm to 500 sq cm

**96922** over 500 sq cm

(For laser destruction of premalignant lesions, see 17000-17004)

(For laser destruction of cutaneous vascular proliferative lesions, see 17106-17108)

(For laser destruction of benign lesions, see 17110-17111)

(For laser destruction of malignant lesions, see 17260-17286)

**96999** Unlisted special dermatological service or procedure

# Physical Medicine and Rehabilitation

Codes 97001-97755 should be used to report each distinct procedure performed. Do not append modifier 51 to 97001-97755.

The work of the physician or other qualified health care professional consists of face-to-face time with the patient (and caregiver, if applicable) delivering skilled services.

Medicine

For the purpose of determining the total time of a service, incremental intervals of treatment at the same visit may be accumulated.

(For muscle testing, range of joint motion, electromyography, see 95831 et seq)

(For biofeedback training by EMG, use 90901)

(For transcutaneous nerve stimulation (TNS), use 64550)

**97001**　Physical therapy evaluation

**97002**　Physical therapy re-evaluation

**97003**　Occupational therapy evaluation

**97004**　Occupational therapy re-evaluation

**97005**　Athletic training evaluation

**97006**　Athletic training re-evaluation

# Modalities

Any physical agent applied to produce therapeutic changes to biologic tissue; includes but not limited to thermal, acoustic, light, mechanical, or electric energy.

## Supervised

The application of a modality that does not require direct (one-on-one) patient contact.

**97010**　Application of a modality to 1 or more areas; hot or cold packs

**97012**　traction, mechanical

**97014**　electrical stimulation (unattended)

(For acupuncture with electrical stimulation, see 97813, 97814)

**97016**　vasopneumatic devices

**97018**　paraffin bath

**97022**　whirlpool

**97024**　diathermy (eg, microwave)

**97026**　infrared

**97028**　ultraviolet

## Constant Attendance

The application of a modality that requires direct (one-on-one) patient contact.

**97032**　Application of a modality to 1 or more areas; electrical stimulation (manual), each 15 minutes

(For transcutaneous electrical modulation pain reprocessing [TEMPR/scrambler therapy], use 0278T)

**97033**　iontophoresis, each 15 minutes

**97034**　contrast baths, each 15 minutes

**97035**　ultrasound, each 15 minutes

**97036**　Hubbard tank, each 15 minutes

**97039**　Unlisted modality (specify type and time if constant attendance)

# Therapeutic Procedures

A manner of effecting change through the application of clinical skills and/or services that attempt to improve function.

Physician or other qualified health care professional (ie, therapist) required to have direct (one-on-one) patient contact.

**97110**　Therapeutic procedure, 1 or more areas, each 15 minutes; therapeutic exercises to develop strength and endurance, range of motion and flexibility

**97112**　neuromuscular reeducation of movement, balance, coordination, kinesthetic sense, posture, and/or proprioception for sitting and/or standing activities

**97113**　aquatic therapy with therapeutic exercises

**97116**　gait training (includes stair climbing)

(Use 96000-96003 to report comprehensive gait and motion analysis procedures)

**97124**　massage, including effleurage, petrissage and/or tapotement (stroking, compression, percussion)

(For myofascial release, use 97140)

**97139**　Unlisted therapeutic procedure (specify)

**97140**　Manual therapy techniques (eg, mobilization/manipulation, manual lymphatic drainage, manual traction), 1 or more regions, each 15 minutes

(Do not report 97140 in conjunction with 29581-29584)

**97150**　Therapeutic procedure(s), group (2 or more individuals)

(Report 97150 for each member of group)

(Group therapy procedures involve constant attendance of the physician or other qualified health care professional [ie, therapist], but by definition do not require one-on-one patient contact by the same physician or other qualified health care professional)

(For manipulation under general anesthesia, see appropriate anatomic section in **Musculoskeletal System**)

(For osteopathic manipulative treatment [OMT], see 98925-98929)

**97530**　Therapeutic activities, direct (one-on-one) patient contact (use of dynamic activities to improve functional performance), each 15 minutes

**97532**　Development of cognitive skills to improve attention, memory, problem solving (includes compensatory training), direct (one-on-one) patient contact, each 15 minutes

**97533**　Sensory integrative techniques to enhance sensory processing and promote adaptive responses to environmental demands, direct (one-on-one) patient contact, each 15 minutes

**Medicine**

**97535** Self-care/home management training (eg, activities of daily living (ADL) and compensatory training, meal preparation, safety procedures, and instructions in use of assistive technology devices/adaptive equipment) direct one-on-one contact, each 15 minutes

**97537** Community/work reintegration training (eg, shopping, transportation, money management, avocational activities and/or work environment/modification analysis, work task analysis, use of assistive technology device/adaptive equipment), direct one-on-one contact, each 15 minutes

(For wheelchair management/propulsion training, use 97542)

**97542** Wheelchair management (eg, assessment, fitting, training), each 15 minutes

**97545** Work hardening/conditioning; initial 2 hours

**+ 97546** each additional hour (List separately in addition to code for primary procedure)

(Use 97546 in conjunction with 97545)

## Active Wound Care Management

Active wound care procedures are performed to remove devitalized and/or necrotic tissue and promote healing. Services require direct (one-on-one) contact with the patient.

(Do not report 97597-97602 in conjunction with 11042-11047 for the same wound)

(For debridement of burn wounds, see 16020-16030)

**97597** Debridement (eg, high pressure waterjet with/without suction, sharp selective debridement with scissors, scalpel and forceps), open wound, (eg, fibrin, devitalized epidermis and/or dermis, exudate, debris, biofilm), including topical application(s), wound assessment, use of a whirlpool, when performed and instruction(s) for ongoing care, per session, total wound(s) surface area; first 20 sq cm or less

**+ 97598** each additional 20 sq cm, or part thereof (List separately in addition to code for primary procedure)

(Use 97598 in conjunction with 97597)

**97602** Removal of devitalized tissue from wound(s), non-selective debridement, without anesthesia (eg, wet-to-moist dressings, enzymatic, abrasion), including topical application(s), wound assessment, and instruction(s) for ongoing care, per session

**97605** Negative pressure wound therapy (eg, vacuum assisted drainage collection), including topical application(s), wound assessment, and instruction(s) for ongoing care, per session; total wound(s) surface area less than or equal to 50 square centimeters

**97606** total wound(s) surface area greater than 50 square centimeters

**● 97610** Low frequency, non-contact, non-thermal ultrasound, including topical application(s), when performed, wound assessment, and instruction(s) for ongoing care, per day

## Tests and Measurements

Requires direct one-on-one patient contact.

(For muscle testing, manual or electrical, joint range of motion, electromyography, or nerve velocity determination, see 95831-95857, 95860-95872, 95885-95887, 95907-95913)

**97750** Physical performance test or measurement (eg, musculoskeletal, functional capacity), with written report, each 15 minutes

**97755** Assistive technology assessment (eg, to restore, augment or compensate for existing function, optimize functional tasks and/or maximize environmental accessibility), direct one-on-one contact, with written report, each 15 minutes

(To report augmentative and alternative communication devices, see 92605, 92607)

## Orthotic Management and Prosthetic Management

**97760** Orthotic(s) management and training (including assessment and fitting when not otherwise reported), upper extremity(s), lower extremity(s) and/or trunk, each 15 minutes

(Code 97760 should not be reported with 97116 for the same extremity)

**97761** Prosthetic training, upper and/or lower extremity(s), each 15 minutes

**97762** Checkout for orthotic/prosthetic use, established patient, each 15 minutes

## Other Procedures

(For extracorporeal shock wave musculoskeletal therapy, see Category III codes 0019T, 0101T, 0102T)

**97799** Unlisted physical medicine/rehabilitation service or procedure

## Medical Nutrition Therapy

**97802** Medical nutrition therapy; initial assessment and intervention, individual, face-to-face with the patient, each 15 minutes

**97803** re-assessment and intervention, individual, face-to-face with the patient, each 15 minutes

**97804** group (2 or more individual(s)), each 30 minutes

(Physicians and other qualified health care professionals who may report evaluation and management services should use the appropriate evaluation and management codes)

Medicine

# Acupuncture

Acupuncture is reported based on 15-minute increments of personal (face-to-face) contact with the patient, not the duration of acupuncture needle(s) placement.

If no electrical stimulation is used during a 15-minute increment, use 97810, 97811. If electrical stimulation of any needle is used during a 15-minute increment, use 97813, 97814.

Only one code may be reported for each 15-minute increment. Use either 97810 or 97813 for the initial 15-minute increment. Only one initial code is reported per day.

Evaluation and management services may be reported in addition to acupuncture procedures when performed by physicians or other health care professionals, who may report evaluation and management services, including new or established patient office or other outpatient services (99201-99215), hospital observation care (99217-99220, 99224-99226), hospital care (99221-99223, 99231-99233), office or other outpatient consultations (99241-99245), inpatient consultations (99251-99255), critical care services (99291, 99292), inpatient neonatal intensive care services and pediatric and neonatal critical care services (99466-99480), emergency department services (99281-99285), nursing facility services (99304-99318), domiciliary, rest home, or custodial care services (99324-99337), and home services (99341-99350) may be reported separately using modifier 25 if the patient's condition requires a significant, separately identifiable E/M service above and beyond the usual preservice and postservice work associated with the acupuncture services. The time of the E/M service is not included in the time of the acupuncture service.

**97810**   Acupuncture, 1 or more needles; without electrical stimulation, initial 15 minutes of personal one-on-one contact with the patient

(Do not report 97810 in conjunction with 97813)

**+ 97811**   without electrical stimulation, each additional 15 minutes of personal one-on-one contact with the patient, with re-insertion of needle(s) (List separately in addition to code for primary procedure)

(Use 97811 in conjunction with 97810, 97813)

**97813**   with electrical stimulation, initial 15 minutes of personal one-on-one contact with the patient

(Do not report 97813 in conjunction with 97810)

**+ 97814**   with electrical stimulation, each additional 15 minutes of personal one-on-one contact with the patient, with re-insertion of needle(s) (List separately in addition to code for primary procedure)

(Use 97814 in conjunction with 97810, 97813)

# Osteopathic Manipulative Treatment

Osteopathic manipulative treatment (OMT) is a form of manual treatment applied by a physician or other qualified health care professional to eliminate or alleviate somatic dysfunction and related disorders. This treatment may be accomplished by a variety of techniques.

Evaluation and Management services including new or established patient office or other outpatient services (99201-99215), hospital observation care (99217-99220, 99224-99226), hospital care (99221-99223, 99231-99233), critical care services (99291, 99292), observation or inpatient care services (99234-99236), office or other outpatient consultations (99241-99245), emergency department services (99281-99285), nursing facility services (99304-99318), domiciliary, rest home, or custodial care services (99324-99337), and home services (99341-99350) may be reported separately using modifier 25 if the patient's condition requires a significant, separately identifiable E/M service above and beyond the usual preservice and postservice work associated with the procedure. The E/M service may be caused or prompted by the same symptoms or condition for which the OMT service was provided. As such, different diagnoses are not required for the reporting of the OMT and E/M service on the same date.

Body regions referred to are: head region; cervical region; thoracic region; lumbar region; sacral region; pelvic region; lower extremities; upper extremities; rib cage region; abdomen and viscera region.

**98925**   Osteopathic manipulative treatment (OMT); 1-2 body regions involved

**98926**   3-4 body regions involved

**98927**   5-6 body regions involved

**98928**   7-8 body regions involved

**98929**   9-10 body regions involved

# Chiropractic Manipulative Treatment

Chiropractic manipulative treatment (CMT) is a form of manual treatment to influence joint and neurophysiological function. This treatment may be accomplished using a variety of techniques.

The chiropractic manipulative treatment codes include a pre-manipulation patient assessment. Additional evaluation and management services including office or other outpatient services (99201-99215), subsequent observation care (99224-99226), subsequent hospital care (99231-99233), office or other outpatient consultations (99241-99245), subsequent nursing facility services (99307-99310), domiciliary, rest home, or custodial care

**Medicine**

services (99324-99337), and home services (99341-99350) may be reported separately using modifier 25 if the patient's condition requires a significant, separately identifiable E/M service above and beyond the usual preservice and postservice work associated with the procedure. The E/M service may be caused or prompted by the same symptoms or condition for which the CMT service was provided. As such, different diagnoses are not required for the reporting of the CMT and E/M service on the same date.

For purposes of CMT, the five spinal regions referred to are: cervical region (includes atlanto-occipital joint); thoracic region (includes costovertebral and costotransverse joints); lumbar region; sacral region; and pelvic (sacro-iliac joint) region. The five extraspinal regions referred to are: head (including temporomandibular joint, excluding atlanto-occipital) region; lower extremities; upper extremities; rib cage (excluding costotransverse and costovertebral joints) and abdomen.

**98940**    Chiropractic manipulative treatment (CMT); spinal, 1-2 regions

**98941**        spinal, 3-4 regions

**98942**        spinal, 5 regions

**98943**        extraspinal, 1 or more regions

# Education and Training for Patient Self-Management

The following codes are used to report educational and training services prescribed by a physician or other qualified health care professional and provided by a qualified, nonphysician health care professional using a standardized curriculum to an individual or a group of patients for the treatment of established illness(s)/disease(s) or to delay comorbidity(s). Education and training for patient self-management may be reported with these codes only when using a standardized curriculum as described below. This curriculum may be modified as necessary for the clinical needs, cultural norms and health literacy of the individual patient(s).

The purpose of the educational and training services is to teach the patient (may include caregiver[s]) how to effectively self-manage the patient's illness(s)/disease(s) or delay disease comorbidity(s) in conjunction with the patient's professional healthcare team. Education and training related to subsequent reinforcement or due to changes in the patient's condition or treatment plan are reported in the same manner as the original education and training. The type of education and training provided for the patient's clinical condition will be identified by the appropriate diagnosis code(s) reported.

The qualifications of the nonphysician healthcare professionals and the content of the educational and

training program must be consistent with guidelines or standards established or recognized by a physician society, nonphysician healthcare professional society/association, or other appropriate source.

(For counseling and education provided by a physician to an individual, see the appropriate evaluation and management codes including office or other outpatient services [99201-99215], hospital observation care [99217-99220, 99224-99226], hospital care [99221-99223, 99231-99233], new or established patient office or other outpatient consultations [99241-99245], inpatient consultations [99251-99255], emergency department services [99281-99285], nursing facility services [99304-99318], domiciliary, rest home, or custodial care services [99324-99337], home services [99341-99350], and counseling risk factor reduction and behavior change intervention [99401-99429]. See also **Instructions for Use of the CPT Codebook** for definition of reporting qualifications)

(For counseling and education provided by a physician to a group, use 99078)

(For counseling and/or risk factor reduction intervention provided by a physician to patient[s] without symptoms or established disease, see 99401-99412)

(For medical nutrition therapy, see 97802-97804)

(For health and behavior assessment/intervention that is not part of a standardized curriculum, see 96150-96155)

(For education provided as genetic counseling services, use 96040. For education to a group regarding genetic risks, see 98961, 98962)

**98960**    Education and training for patient self-management by a qualified, nonphysician health care professional using a standardized curriculum, face-to-face with the patient (could include caregiver/family) each 30 minutes; individual patient

**98961**        2-4 patients

**98962**        5-8 patients

# Non-Face-to-Face Nonphysician Services

## Telephone Services

Telephone services are non-face-to-face assessment and management services provided by a qualified health care professional to a patient using the telephone. These codes are used to report episodes of care by the qualified health care professional initiated by an established patient or guardian of an established patient. If the telephone service ends with a decision to see the patient within 24 hours or the next available urgent visit appointment, the code is not reported; rather the encounter is considered part of the preservice work of the subsequent assessment and management service, procedure, and visit. Likewise,

Medicine

if the telephone call refers to a service performed and reported by the qualified health care professional within the previous seven days (either qualified health care professional requested or unsolicited patient follow-up) or within the postoperative period of the previously completed procedure, then the service(s) are considered part of that previous service or procedure. (Do not report 98966-98969 if reporting 98966-98969 performed in the previous seven days.)

> (For telephone services provided by a physician, see 99441-99443)

**98966**    Telephone assessment and management service provided by a qualified nonphysician health care professional to an established patient, parent, or guardian not originating from a related assessment and management service provided within the previous 7 days nor leading to an assessment and management service or procedure within the next 24 hours or soonest available appointment; 5-10 minutes of medical discussion

**98967**      11-20 minutes of medical discussion

**98968**      21-30 minutes of medical discussion

> (Do not report 98966-98968 during the same month with 99487-99489)

> (Do not report 98966-98968 when performed during the service time of codes 99495, 99496)

## On-line Medical Evaluation

An on-line electronic medical evaluation is a non-face-to-face assessment and management service by a qualified health care professional to a patient using Internet resources in response to a patient's on-line inquiry. Reportable services involve the qualified health care professional's personal timely response to the patient's inquiry and must involve permanent storage (electronic or hard copy) of the encounter. This service is reported only once for the same episode of care during a seven-day period, although multiple qualified health care professionals could report their exchange with the same patient. If the on-line medical evaluation refers to an assessment and management service previously performed and reported by the qualified health care professional within the previous seven days (either qualified health care professional requested or unsolicited patient follow-up) or within the postoperative period of the previously completed procedure, then the service(s) are considered covered by the previous assessment and management office service or procedure. A reportable service encompasses the sum of communication (eg, related telephone calls, prescription provision, laboratory orders) pertaining to the on-line patient encounter.

> (For an on-line medical evaluation provided by a physician, use 99444)

**98969**    Online assessment and management service provided by a qualified nonphysician health care professional to an established patient or guardian, not originating from a related assessment and management service provided within the previous 7 days, using the Internet or similar electronic communications network

> (Do not report 98969 when using 99339-99340, 99374-99380 for the same communication[s])

> (Do not report 98969 for anticoagulation management when reporting 99363, 99364)

> (Do not report 98969 during the same month with 99487-99489)

> (Do not report 98969 when performed during the service time of codes 99495, 99496)

## Special Services, Procedures and Reports

The procedures with code numbers 99000 through 99091 provide the reporting physician or other qualified health care professional with the means of identifying the completion of special reports and services that are an adjunct to the basic services rendered. The specific number assigned indicates the special circumstances under which a basic procedure is performed.

Code 99091 should be reported no more than once in a 30-day period to include the physician or other qualified health care professional time involved with data accession, review and interpretation, modification of care plan as necessary (including communication to patient and/or caregiver), and associated documentation.

If the services described by 99091 are provided on the same day the patient presents for an E/M service, these services should be considered part of the E/M service and not separately reported.

Do not report 99091 if it occurs within 30 days of care plan oversight services 99374-99380. Do not report 99091 if other more specific CPT codes exist (eg,93227,93272 for cardiographic services; 95250 for continuous glucose monitoring). Do not report 99091 for transfer and interpretation of data from hospital or clinical laboratory computers.

Codes 99050-99060 are reported in addition to an associated basic service. Do not append modifier 51 to 99050-99060. Typically only a single adjunct code from among 99050-99060 would be reported per patient encounter. However, there may be circumstances in which reporting multiple adjunct codes per patient encounter may be appropriate.

**Medicine**

## Miscellaneous Services

**99000**   Handling and/or conveyance of specimen for transfer from the office to a laboratory

**99001**   Handling and/or conveyance of specimen for transfer from the patient in other than an office to a laboratory (distance may be indicated)

**99002**   Handling, conveyance, and/or any other service in connection with the implementation of an order involving devices (eg, designing, fitting, packaging, handling, delivery or mailing) when devices such as orthotics, protectives, prosthetics are fabricated by an outside laboratory or shop but which items have been designed, and are to be fitted and adjusted by the attending physician or other qualified health care professional

(For routine collection of venous blood, use 36415)

**99024**   Postoperative follow-up visit, normally included in the surgical package, to indicate that an evaluation and management service was performed during a postoperative period for a reason(s) related to the original procedure

(As a component of a surgical "package," see **Surgery Guidelines**)

**99026**   Hospital mandated on call service; in-hospital, each hour

**99027**       out-of-hospital, each hour

(For standby services requiring prolonged attendance, use 99360, as appropriate. Time spent performing separately reportable procedure(s) or service(s) should not be included in the time reported as mandated on-call service)

**99050**   Services provided in the office at times other than regularly scheduled office hours, or days when the office is normally closed (eg, holidays, Saturday or Sunday), in addition to basic service

**99051**   Service(s) provided in the office during regularly scheduled evening, weekend, or holiday office hours, in addition to basic service

**99053**   Service(s) provided between 10:00 PM and 8:00 AM at 24-hour facility, in addition to basic service

**99056**   Service(s) typically provided in the office, provided out of the office at request of patient, in addition to basic service

**99058**   Service(s) provided on an emergency basis in the office, which disrupts other scheduled office services, in addition to basic service

**99060**   Service(s) provided on an emergency basis, out of the office, which disrupts other scheduled office services, in addition to basic service

**99070**   Supplies and materials (except spectacles), provided by the physician or other qualified health care professional over and above those usually included with the office visit or other services rendered (list drugs, trays, supplies, or materials provided)

(For supply of spectacles, use the appropriate supply codes)

**99071**   Educational supplies, such as books, tapes, and pamphlets, for the patient's education at cost to physician or other qualified health care professional

**99075**   Medical testimony

**99078**   Physician or other qualified health care professional qualified by education, training, licensure/regulation (when applicable) educational services rendered to patients in a group setting (eg, prenatal, obesity, or diabetic instructions)

**99080**   Special reports such as insurance forms, more than the information conveyed in the usual medical communications or standard reporting form

(Do not report 99080 in conjunction with 99455, 99456 for the completion of Workmen's Compensation forms)

**99082**   Unusual travel (eg, transportation and escort of patient)

**99090**   Analysis of clinical data stored in computers (eg, ECGs, blood pressures, hematologic data)

(For physician/or other qualified health care professional qualified by education, training, licensure/regulation [when applicable] collection and interpretation of physiologic data stored/transmitted by patient/caregiver, see 99091)

(Do not report 99090 if other more specific CPT codes exist, eg, 93227, 93272, 0206T for cardiographic services; 95250 for continuous glucose monitoring; 97750 for musculoskeletal function testing)

**99091**   Collection and interpretation of physiologic data (eg, ECG, blood pressure, glucose monitoring) digitally stored and/or transmitted by the patient and/or caregiver to the physician or other qualified health care professional, qualified by education, training, licensure/regulation (when applicable) requiring a minimum of 30 minutes of time

# Qualifying Circumstances for Anesthesia

(For explanation of these services, see **Anesthesia Guidelines**)

**✚ 99100**   Anesthesia for patient of extreme age, younger than 1 year and older than 70 (List separately in addition to code for primary anesthesia procedure)

(For procedure performed on infants younger than 1 year of age at time of surgery, see 00326, 00561, 00834, 00836)

Medicine

+ **99116**    Anesthesia complicated by utilization of total body hypothermia (List separately in addition to code for primary anesthesia procedure)

+ **99135**    Anesthesia complicated by utilization of controlled hypotension (List separately in addition to code for primary anesthesia procedure)

+ **99140**    Anesthesia complicated by emergency conditions (specify) (List separately in addition to code for primary anesthesia procedure)

              (An emergency is defined as existing when delay in treatment of the patient would lead to a significant increase in the threat to life or body part)

# Moderate (Conscious) Sedation

Moderate (conscious) sedation is a drug induced depression of consciousness during which patients respond purposefully to verbal commands, either alone or accompanied by light tactile stimulation. No interventions are required to maintain a patent airway, and spontaneous ventilation is adequate. Cardiovascular function is usually maintained.

Moderate sedation does not include minimal sedation (anxiolysis), deep sedation or monitored anesthesia care (00100-01999).

When providing moderate sedation, the following services are included and **not** reported separately:

■ Assessment of the patient (not included in intraservice time);

■ Establishment of IV access and fluids to maintain patency, when performed;

■ Administration of agent(s);

■ Maintenance of sedation;

■ Monitoring of oxygen saturation, heart rate and blood pressure; and

■ Recovery (not included in intraservice time).

Intraservice time starts with the administration of the sedation agent(s), requires continuous face-to-face attendance, and ends at the conclusion of personal contact by the physician providing the sedation.

Do not report 99143-99150 in conjunction with 94760-94762.

Do not report 99143-99145 in conjunction with codes listed in Appendix G. Do not report 99148-99150 in conjunction with codes listed in Appendix G when performed in the nonfacility setting.

When a second physician or other qualified health care professional other than the health care professional performing the diagnostic or therapeutic services provides moderate sedation in the facility setting (eg, hospital, outpatient hospital/ambulatory surgery center, skilled nursing facility) for the procedures listed in Appendix G, the second physician or other qualified health care professional reports 99148-99150. However, for the circumstance in which these services are performed by the second physician or other qualified health care professional in the nonfacility setting (eg, office, freestanding imaging center), codes 99148-99150 are not reported. See also **Instructions for Use of the CPT Codebook** for definition of reporting qualifications.

⊘ **99143**    Moderate sedation services (other than those services described by codes 00100-01999) provided by the same physician or other qualified health care professional performing the diagnostic or therapeutic service that the sedation supports, requiring the presence of an independent trained observer to assist in the monitoring of the patient's level of consciousness and physiological status; younger than 5 years of age, first 30 minutes intra-service time

⊘ **99144**        age 5 years or older, first 30 minutes intra-service time

+ **99145**        each additional 15 minutes intra-service time (List separately in addition to code for primary service)

              (Use 99145 in conjunction with 99143, 99144)

  **99148**    Moderate sedation services (other than those services described by codes 00100-01999), provided by a physician or other qualified health care professional other than the health care professional performing the diagnostic or therapeutic service that the sedation supports; younger than 5 years of age, first 30 minutes intra-service time

  **99149**        age 5 years or older, first 30 minutes intra-service time

+ **99150**        each additional 15 minutes intra-service time (List separately in addition to code for primary service)

              (Use 99150 in conjunction with 99148, 99149)

# Other Services and Procedures

▲ **99170**    Anogenital examination, magnified, in childhood for suspected trauma, including image recording when performed

              ►(For moderate sedation, use 99143-99150)◄

**Medicine**

**99172**  Visual function screening, automated or semi-automated bilateral quantitative determination of visual acuity, ocular alignment, color vision by pseudoisochromatic plates, and field of vision (may include all or some screening of the determination[s] for contrast sensitivity, vision under glare)

(This service must employ graduated visual acuity stimuli that allow a quantitative determination of visual acuity [eg, Snellen chart]. This service may not be used in addition to a general ophthalmological service or an E/M service)

(Do not report 99172 in conjunction with 99173)

**99173**  Screening test of visual acuity, quantitative, bilateral

(The screening test used must employ graduated visual acuity stimuli that allow a quantitative estimate of visual acuity [eg, Snellen chart]. Other identifiable services unrelated to this screening test provided at the same time may be reported separately [eg, preventive medicine services]. When acuity is measured as part of a general ophthalmological service or of an E/M service of the eye, it is a diagnostic examination and not a screening test.)

(Do not report 99173 in conjunction with 99172)

**99174**  Instrument-based ocular screening (eg, photoscreening, automated-refraction), bilateral

(Do not report 99174 in conjunction with 92002-92014, 99172, 99173)

**99175**  Ipecac or similar administration for individual emesis and continued observation until stomach adequately emptied of poison

(For diagnostic intubation, see 43754, 43755)

(For gastric lavage for diagnostic purposes, see 43754, 43755)

**99183**  Physician or other qualified health care professional attendance and supervision of hyperbaric oxygen therapy, per session

(Evaluation and Management services and/or procedures [eg, wound debridement] provided in a hyperbaric oxygen treatment facility in conjunction with a hyperbaric oxygen therapy session should be reported separately)

(99185, 99186 have been deleted)

**99190**  Assembly and operation of pump with oxygenator or heat exchanger (with or without ECG and/or pressure monitoring); each hour

**99191**      45 minutes

**99192**      30 minutes

**99195**  Phlebotomy, therapeutic (separate procedure)

**99199**  Unlisted special service, procedure or report

# Home Health Procedures/ Services

These codes are used by non-physician health care professionals. Physicians should utilize the home visit codes 99341-99350 and utilize CPT codes other than 99500-99600 for any additional procedure/service provided to a patient living in a residence.

The following codes are used to report services provided in a patient's residence (including assisted living apartments, group homes, nontraditional private homes, custodial care facilities, or schools).

Health care professionals who are authorized to use Evaluation and Management (E/M) Home Visit codes (99341-99350) may report 99500-99600 in addition to 99341-99350 if both services are performed. E/M services may be reported separately, using modifier 25, if the patient's condition requires a significant separately identifiable E/M service, above and beyond the home health service(s)/procedure(s) codes 99500-99600.

**99500**  Home visit for prenatal monitoring and assessment to include fetal heart rate, non-stress test, uterine monitoring, and gestational diabetes monitoring

**99501**  Home visit for postnatal assessment and follow-up care

**99502**  Home visit for newborn care and assessment

**99503**  Home visit for respiratory therapy care (eg, bronchodilator, oxygen therapy, respiratory assessment, apnea evaluation)

**99504**  Home visit for mechanical ventilation care

**99505**  Home visit for stoma care and maintenance including colostomy and cystostomy

**99506**  Home visit for intramuscular injections

**99507**  Home visit for care and maintenance of catheter(s) (eg, urinary, drainage, and enteral)

**99509**  Home visit for assistance with activities of daily living and personal care

(To report self-care/home management training, see 97535)

(To report home medical nutrition assessment and intervention services, see 97802-97804)

(To report home speech therapy services, see 92507-92508)

**99510**  Home visit for individual, family, or marriage counseling

**99511**  Home visit for fecal impaction management and enema administration

**99512**  Home visit for hemodialysis

(For home infusion of peritoneal dialysis, use 99601, 99602)

**99600**  Unlisted home visit service or procedure

Medicine

## Home Infusion Procedures/Services

**99601**    Home infusion/specialty drug administration, per visit (up to 2 hours);

**+ 99602**        each additional hour (List separately in addition to code for primary procedure)

        (Use 99602 in conjunction with 99601)

# Medication Therapy Management Services

Medication therapy management service(s) (MTMS) describe face-to-face patient assessment and intervention as appropriate, by a pharmacist, upon request. MTMS is provided to optimize the response to medications or to manage treatment-related medication interactions or complications.

MTMS includes the following documented elements: review of the pertinent patient history, medication profile (prescription and nonprescription), and recommendations for improving health outcomes and treatment compliance. These codes are not to be used to describe the provision of product-specific information at the point of dispensing or any other routine dispensing-related activities.

**99605**    Medication therapy management service(s) provided by a pharmacist, individual, face-to-face with patient, with assessment and intervention if provided; initial 15 minutes, new patient

**99606**        initial 15 minutes, established patient

**+ 99607**        each additional 15 minutes (List separately in addition to code for primary service)

        (Use 99607 in conjunction with 99605, 99606)

**Medicine**

# Notes

⊙=Moderate sedation ✚=Add-on code ✎=FDA approval pending #=Resequenced code ○=Recycled/reinstated code

# Category II Codes

The following section of *Current Procedural Terminology* (CPT) contains a set of supplemental tracking codes that can be used for performance measurement. It is anticipated that the use of Category II codes for performance measurement will decrease the need for record abstraction and chart review, and thereby minimize administrative burden on physicians, other health care professionals, hospitals, and entities seeking to measure the quality of patient care. These codes are intended to facilitate data collection about the quality of care rendered by coding certain services and test results that support nationally established performance measures and that have an evidence base as contributing to quality patient care.

The use of these codes is optional. The codes are not required for correct coding and may not be used as a substitute for Category I codes.

These codes describe clinical components that may be typically included in evaluation and management services or clinical services and, therefore, do not have a relative value associated with them. Category II codes may also describe results from clinical laboratory or radiology tests and other procedures, identified processes intended to address patient safety practices, or services reflecting compliance with state or federal law.

Category II codes described in this section make use of alphabetical characters as the 5th character in the string (ie, 4 digits followed by the letter **F**). These digits are not intended to reflect the placement of the code in the regular (Category I) part of the CPT code set. To promote understanding of these codes and their associated measures, users are referred to the Alphabetical Clinical Topics Listing, which contains information about performance measurement exclusion modifiers, measures, and the measure's source.

Cross-references to the measures associated with each Category II code and their source are included for reference in the Alphabetical Clinical Topics Listing. In addition, acronyms for the related diseases or clinical condition(s) have been added at the end of each code descriptor to identify the topic or clinical category in which that code is included. A complete listing of the diseases/clinical conditions, and their acronyms are provided in alphabetical order in the Alphabetical Clinical Topics Listing. The Alphabetical Clinical Topics Listing can be accessed on the Web site at www.ama-assn.org, under the Category II link. Users should review the complete measure(s) associated with each code prior to implementation.

Category II codes are reviewed by the Performance Measures Advisory Group (PMAG), an advisory body to the CPT Editorial Panel and the CPT/HCPAC Advisory Committee. The PMAG is comprised of performance measurement experts representing the Agency for Healthcare Research and Quality (AHRQ), the American Medical Association (AMA), the Centers for Medicare and Medicaid Services (CMS), The Joint Commission (TJC), and the Physician Consortium for Performance Improvement® (PCPI). The PMAG may seek additional expertise and/or input from other national health care organizations, as necessary, for the development of tracking codes. These may include national medical specialty societies, other national health care professional associations, accrediting bodies, and federal regulatory agencies.

The most current listing of Category II codes, including guidelines, Code Change Proposal forms, and release and implementation dates for Category II codes may be accessed at www.ama-assn.org/go/cpt.

> (For blood pressure measured, use 2000F)
>
> (For tobacco use cessation intervention, pharmacologic therapy, use 4001F)

The superscripted numbers included at the end of each code descriptor direct users to the footnotes. The following information identifies the name and web address of the measure developers that are associated with these footnotes:

**Footnotes**

[1]Physician Consortium for Performance Improvement®(PCPI), www.physicianconsortium.org.

[2]National Committee on Quality Assurance (NCQA), Health Employer Data Information Set (HEDIS®), www.ncqa.org.

[3]The Joint Commission (TJC), ORYX Initiative Performance Measures, www.jointcommission.org/performancemeasurement/aspx.

[4]National Diabetes Quality Improvement Alliance (NDQIA),www.nationaldiabetesalliance.org.

[5]Joint measure from The Physician Consortium for Performance Improvement, www.physicianconsortium.org and National Committee on Quality Assurance (NCQA), www.ncqa.org.

[6]The Society of Thoracic Surgeons at www.sts.org and National Quality Forum, www.qualityforum.org.

[7]Ingenix, www.ingenix.com.

[8]American Academy of Neurology, www.aan.com/go/practice/quality/measurements or quality@aan.com.

[9]College of American Pathologists (CAP), www.cap.org/apps/docs/advocacy/pathology performance measurement.pdf.

[10]American Gastroenterological Association (AGA), www.gastro.org/quality.

►[11]American Society of Anesthesiologists (ASA), www.asahq.org.◄

Category II

# Modifiers

The following performance measurement modifiers may be used for Category II codes to indicate that a service specified in the associated measure(s) was considered but, due to either medical, patient, or system circumstance(s) documented in the medical record, the service was not provided. These modifiers serve as denominator exclusions from the performance measure. The user should note that not all listed measures provide for exclusions (see Alphabetical Clinical Topics Listing for more discussion regarding exclusion criteria).

Category II modifiers should only be reported with Category II codes—they should not be reported with Category I or Category III codes. In addition, the modifiers in the Category II section should only be used where specified in the guidelines, reporting instructions, parenthetic notes, or code descriptor language listed in the Category II section (code listing and the Alphabetical Clinical Topics Listing).

**1P** Performance Measure Exclusion Modifier due to Medical Reasons

Reasons include:

- Not indicated (absence of organ/limb, already received/performed, other)

- Contraindicated (patient allergic history, potential adverse drug interaction, other)

- Other medical reasons

**2P** Performance Measure Exclusion Modifier due to Patient Reasons

Reasons include:

- Patient declined

- Economic, social, or religious reasons

- Other patient reasons

**3P** Performance Measure Exclusion Modifier due to System Reasons

Reasons include:

- Resources to perform the services not available

- Insurance coverage/payor-related limitations

- Other reasons attributable to health care delivery system

Modifier 8P is intended to be used as a "reporting modifier" to allow the reporting of circumstances when an action described in a measure's numerator is not performed and the reason is not otherwise specified.

**8P** Performance measure reporting modifier–action not performed, reason not otherwise specified

# Composite Codes

Composite codes combine several measures grouped within a single code descriptor to facilitate reporting for a clinical condition when all components are met. If only some of the components are met or if services are provided in addition to those included in the composite code, they may be reported individually using the corresponding CPT Category II codes for those services.

**0001F** Heart failure assessed (includes assessment of all the following components) (CAD)[1]:

Blood pressure measured (2000F)[1]

Level of activity assessed (1003F)[1]

Clinical symptoms of volume overload (excess) assessed (1004F)[1]

Weight, recorded (2001F)[1]

Clinical signs of volume overload (excess) assessed (2002F)[1]

(To report blood pressure measured, use 2000F)

**0005F** Osteoarthritis assessed (OA)[1]

Includes assessment of all the following components:

Osteoarthritis symptoms and functional status assessed (1006F)[1]

Use of anti-inflammatory or over-the-counter (OTC) analgesic medications assessed (1007F)[1]

Initial examination of the involved joint(s) (includes visual inspection, palpation, range of motion) (2004F)[1]

(To report tobacco use cessation intervention, use 4001F)

**0012F** Community-acquired bacterial pneumonia assessment (includes all of the following components) (CAP)[1]:

Co-morbid conditions assessed (1026F)[1]

Vital signs recorded (2010F)[1]

Mental status assessed (2014F)[1]

Hydration status assessed (2018F)[1]

**0014F** Comprehensive preoperative assessment performed for cataract surgery with intraocular lens (IOL) placement (includes assessment of all of the following components) (EC)[5]:

Dilated fundus evaluation performed within 12 months prior to cataract surgery (2020F)[5]

Pre-surgical (cataract) axial length, corneal power measurement and method of intraocular lens power calculation documented (must be performed within 12 months prior to surgery) (3073F)[5]

Preoperative assessment of functional or medical indication(s) for surgery prior to the cataract surgery with intraocular lens placement (must be performed within 12 months prior to cataract surgery) (3325F)[5]

**0015F**   Melanoma follow up completed (includes assessment of all of the following components) (ML)[5]:

    History obtained regarding new or changing moles (1050F)[5]

    Complete physical skin exam performed (2029F)[5]

    Patient counseled to perform a monthly self skin examination (5005F)[5]

# Patient Management

Patient management codes describe utilization measures or measures of patient care provided for specific clinical purposes (eg, prenatal care, pre- and post-surgical care).

**0500F**   Initial prenatal care visit (report at first prenatal encounter with health care professional providing obstetrical care. Report also date of visit and, in a separate field, the date of the last menstrual period [LMP]) (Prenatal)[2]

**0501F**   Prenatal flow sheet documented in medical record by first prenatal visit (documentation includes at minimum blood pressure, weight, urine protein, uterine size, fetal heart tones, and estimated date of delivery). Report also: date of visit and, in a separate field, the date of the last menstrual period [LMP] (Note: If reporting 0501F Prenatal flow sheet, it is not necessary to report 0500F Initial prenatal care visit) (Prenatal)[1]

**0502F**   Subsequent prenatal care visit (Prenatal)[2]

    [Excludes: patients who are seen for a condition unrelated to pregnancy or prenatal care (eg, an upper respiratory infection; patients seen for consultation only, not for continuing care)]

**0503F**   Postpartum care visit (Prenatal)[2]

**0505F**   Hemodialysis plan of care documented (ESRD, P-ESRD)[1]

**0507F**   Peritoneal dialysis plan of care documented (ESRD)[1]

**0509F**   Urinary incontinence plan of care documented (GER)[5]

**0513F**   Elevated blood pressure plan of care documented (CKD)[1]

**0514F**   Plan of care for elevated hemoglobin level documented for patient receiving Erythropoiesis-Stimulating Agent therapy (ESA) (CKD)[1]

**0516F**   Anemia plan of care documented (ESRD)[1]

**0517F**   Glaucoma plan of care documented (EC)[5]

**0518F**   Falls plan of care documented (GER)[5]

**0519F**   Planned chemotherapy regimen, including at a minimum: drug(s) prescribed, dose, and duration, documented prior to initiation of a new treatment regimen (ONC)[1]

**0520F**   Radiation dose limits to normal tissues established prior to the initiation of a course of 3D conformal radiation for a minimum of 2 tissue/organ (ONC)[1]

**0521F**   Plan of care to address pain documented (COA)[2] (ONC)[1]

**0525F**   Initial visit for episode (BkP)[2]

**0526F**   Subsequent visit for episode (BkP)[2]

**0528F**   Recommended follow-up interval for repeat colonoscopy of at least 10 years documented in colonoscopy report (End/Polyp)[5]

**0529F**   Interval of 3 or more years since patient's last colonoscopy, documented (End/Polyp)[5]

**0535F**   Dyspnea management plan of care, documented (Pall Cr)[5]

**0540F**   Glucorticoid Management Plan Documented (RA)[5]

**0545F**   Plan for follow-up care for major depressive disorder, documented (MDD ADOL)[11]

**0550F**   Cytopathology report on routine nongynecologic specimen finalized within two working days of accession date (PATH)[9]

**0551F**   Cytopathology report on nongynecologic specimen with documentation that the specimen was non-routine (PATH)[9]

**0555F**   Symptom management plan of care documented (HF)[1]

**0556F**   Plan of care to achieve lipid control documented (CAD)[1]

**0557F**   Plan of care to manage anginal symptoms documented (CAD)[1]

**0575F**   HIV RNA control plan of care, documented (HIV)[5]

● **0580F**   Multidisciplinary care plan developed or updated (ALS)[8]

● **0581F**   Patient transferred directly from anesthetizing location to critical care unit (Peri2)[11]

● **0582F**   Patient not transferred directly from anesthetizing location to critical care unit (Peri)[11]

● **0583F**   Transfer of care checklist used (Peri2)[11]

● **0584F**   Transfer of care checklist not used (Peri2)[11]

# Patient History

Patient history codes describe measures for select aspects of patient history or review of systems.

**1000F**   Tobacco use assessed (CAD, CAP, COPD, PV)[1] (DM)[4]

**1002F**   Anginal symptoms and level of activity assessed (NMA - No Measure Associated)

**1003F**   Level of activity assessed (NMA - No Measure Associated)

**1004F**   Clinical symptoms of volume overload (excess) assessed (NMA - No Measure Associated)

**1005F**   Asthma symptoms evaluated (includes documentation of numeric frequency of symptoms or patient completion of an asthma assessment tool/survey/questionnaire) (NMA - No Measure Associated)

Category II

**1006F** Osteoarthritis symptoms and functional status assessed (may include the use of a standardized scale or the completion of an assessment questionnaire, such as the SF-36, AAOS Hip & Knee Questionnaire) (OA)[1]

[Instructions: Report when osteoarthritis is addressed during the patient encounter]

**1007F** Use of anti-inflammatory or analgesic over-the-counter (OTC) medications for symptom relief assessed (OA)[1]

**1008F** Gastrointestinal and renal risk factors assessed for patients on prescribed or OTC non-steroidal anti-inflammatory drug (NSAID) (OA)[1]

**1010F** Severity of angina assessed by level of activity (CAD)[1]

**1011F** Angina present (CAD)[1]

**1012F** Angina absent (CAD)[1]

**1015F** Chronic obstructive pulmonary disease (COPD) symptoms assessed (Includes assessment of at least 1 of the following: dyspnea, cough/sputum, wheezing), or respiratory symptom assessment tool completed (COPD)[1]

**1018F** Dyspnea assessed, not present (COPD)[1]

**1019F** Dyspnea assessed, present (COPD)[1]

**1022F** Pneumococcus immunization status assessed (CAP, COPD)[1]

**1026F** Co-morbid conditions assessed (eg, includes assessment for presence or absence of: malignancy, liver disease, congestive heart failure, cerebrovascular disease, renal disease, chronic obstructive pulmonary disease, asthma, diabetes, other co-morbid conditions) (CAP)[1]

**1030F** Influenza immunization status assessed (CAP)[1]

**1031F** Smoking status and exposure to second hand smoke in the home assessed (Asthma)[1]

**1032F** Current tobacco smoker **or** currently exposed to secondhand smoke (Asthma)[1]

**1033F** Current tobacco non-smoker **and** not currently exposed to secondhand smoke (Asthma)[1]

**1034F** Current tobacco smoker (CAD, CAP, COPD, PV)[1] (DM)[4]

**1035F** Current smokeless tobacco user (eg, chew, snuff) (PV)[1]

**1036F** Current tobacco non-user (CAD, CAP, COPD, PV)[1] (DM)[4] (IBD)[10]

**1038F** Persistent asthma (mild, moderate or severe) (Asthma)[1]

**1039F** Intermittent asthma (Asthma)[1]

▲ **1040F** DSM-V™ criteria for major depressive disorder documented at the initial evaluation (MDD, MDD ADOL)[1]

**1050F** History obtained regarding new or changing moles (ML)[5]

**1052F** Type, anatomic location, and activity all assessed (IBD)[10]

**1055F** Visual functional status assessed (EC)[5]

**1060F** Documentation of permanent **or** persistent **or** paroxysmal atrial fibrillation (STR)[5]

**1061F** Documentation of absence of permanent **and** persistent **and** paroxysmal atrial fibrillation (STR)[5]

**1065F** Ischemic stroke symptom onset of less than 3 hours prior to arrival (STR)[5]

**1066F** Ischemic stroke symptom onset greater than or equal to 3 hours prior to arrival (STR)[5]

**1070F** Alarm symptoms (involuntary weight loss, dysphagia, or gastrointestinal bleeding) assessed; none present (GERD)[5]

**1071F** 1 or more present (GERD)[5]

(1080F has been deleted. To report Surrogate decision maker or advance care plan documented in the medical record, report code 1123F or 1124F.)

**1090F** Presence or absence of urinary incontinence assessed (GER)[5]

**1091F** Urinary incontinence characterized (eg, frequency, volume, timing, type of symptoms, how bothersome) (GER)[5]

**1100F** Patient screened for future fall risk; documentation of 2 or more falls in the past year or any fall with injury in the past year (GER)[5]

**1101F** documentation of no falls in the past year or only 1 fall without injury in the past year (GER)[5]

**1110F** Patient discharged from an inpatient facility (eg, hospital, skilled nursing facility, or rehabilitation facility) within the last 60 days (GER)[5]

**1111F** Discharge medications reconciled with the current medication list in outpatient medical record (COA)[2] (GER)[5]

**1116F** Auricular or periauricular pain assessed (AOE)[1]

**1118F** GERD symptoms assessed after 12 months of therapy (GERD)[5]

**1119F** Initial evaluation for condition (HEP C)[1](EPI, DSP)[8]

**1121F** Subsequent evaluation for condition (HEP C)[1](EPI)[8]

**1123F** Advance Care Planning discussed and documented advance care plan or surrogate decision maker documented in the medical record (DEM)[1] (GER, Pall Cr)[5]

**1124F** Advance Care Planning discussed and documented in the medical record, patient did not wish or was not able to name a surrogate decision maker or provide an advance care plan (DEM)[1] (GER, Pall Cr)[5]

**1125F** Pain severity quantified; pain present (COA)[2] (ONC)[1]

**1126F** no pain present (COA)[2] (ONC)[1]

**1127F** New episode for condition (NMA-No Measure Associated)

**1128F** Subsequent episode for condition (NMA-No Measure Associated)

**1130F** Back pain and function assessed, including all of the following: Pain assessment **and** functional status **and** patient history, including notation of presence or absence of "red flags" (warning signs) **and** assessment of prior treatment and response, **and** employment status (BkP)[2]

**1134F** Episode of back pain lasting 6 weeks or less (BkP)[2]

---

⊙=Moderate sedation   ✚=Add-on code   ✗=FDA approval pending   #=Resequenced code   ○=Recycled/reinstated code

**1135F** Episode of back pain lasting longer than 6 weeks (BkP)[2]

**1136F** Episode of back pain lasting 12 weeks or less (BkP)[2]

**1137F** Episode of back pain lasting longer than 12 weeks (BkP)[2]

**1150F** Documentation that a patient has a substantial risk of death within 1 year (Pall Cr)[5]

**1151F** Documentation that a patient does not have a substantial risk of death within one year (Pall Cr)[5]

**1152F** Documentation of advanced disease diagnosis, goals of care prioritize comfort (Pall Cr)[5]

**1153F** Documentation of advanced disease diagnosis, goals of care do not prioritize comfort (Pall Cr)[5]

**1157F** Advance care plan or similar legal document present in the medical record (COA)[2]

**1158F** Advance care planning discussion documented in the medical record (COA)[2]

**1159F** Medication list documented in medical record (COA)[2]

**1160F** Review of all medications by a prescribing practitioner or clinical pharmacist (such as, prescriptions, OTCs, herbal therapies and supplements) documented in the medical record (COA)[2]

**1170F** Functional status assessed (COA)[2] (RA)[5]

**1175F** Functional status for dementia assessed and results reviewed (DEM)[1]

**1180F** All specified thromboembolic risk factors assessed (AFIB)[1]

**1181F** Neuropsychiatric symptoms assessed and results reviewed (DEM)[1]

**1182F** Neuropsychiatric symptoms, one or more present (DEM)[1]

**1183F** Neuropsychiatric symptoms, absent (DEM)[1]

**1200F** Seizure type(s) and current seizure frequency(ies) documented (EPI)[8]

**1205F** Etiology of epilepsy or epilepsy syndrome(s) reviewed and documented (EPI)[8]

**1220F** Patient screened for depression (SUD)[5]

**1400F** Parkinson's disease diagnosis reviewed (Prkns)[8]

**1450F** Symptoms improved or remained consistent with treatment goals since last assessment (HF)[1]

**1451F** Symptoms demonstrated clinically important deterioration since last assessment (HF)[1]

**1460F** Qualifying cardiac event/diagnosis in previous 12 months (CAD)[1]

**1461F** No qualifying cardiac event/diagnosis in previous 12 months (CAD)[1]

**1490F** Dementia severity classified, mild (DEM)[1]

**1491F** Dementia severity classified, moderate (DEM)

**1493F** Dementia severity classified, severe (DEM)[1]

**1494F** Cognition assessed and reviewed (DEM)[1]

● **1500F** Symptoms and signs of distal symmetric polyneuropathy reviewed and documented (DSP)[8]

● **1501F** Not initial evaluation for condition (DSP)[8]

● **1502F** Patient queried about pain and pain interference with function using a valid and reliable instrument (DSP)[8]

● **1503F** Patient queried about symptoms of respiratory insufficiency (ALS)[8]

● **1504F** Patient has respiratory insufficiency (ALS)[8]

● **1505F** Patient does not have respiratory insufficiency (ALS)[8]

# Physical Examination

Physical examination codes describe aspects of physical examination or clinical assessment.

**2000F** Blood pressure measured (CKD)[1](DM)[2,4]

**2001F** Weight recorded (PAG)[1]

**2002F** Clinical signs of volume overload (excess) assessed (NMA – No Measure Associated)

**2004F** Initial examination of the involved joint(s) (includes visual inspection, palpation, range of motion) (OA)[1]

[Instructions: Report only for initial osteoarthritis visit or for visits for new joint involvement]

**2010F** Vital signs (temperature, pulse, respiratory rate, and blood pressure) documented and reviewed (CAP)[1] (EM)[5]

**2014F** Mental status assessed (CAP)[1] (EM)[5]

**2015F** Asthma impairment assessed (Asthma)[1]

**2016F** Asthma risk assessed (Asthma)[1]

**2018F** Hydration status assessed (normal/mildly dehydrated/severely dehydrated) (CAP)[1]

**2019F** Dilated macular exam performed, including documentation of the presence or absence of macular thickening or hemorrhage **and** the level of macular degeneration severity (EC)[5]

**2020F** Dilated fundus evaluation performed within 12 months prior to cataract surgery (EC)[5]

**2021F** Dilated macular or fundus exam performed, including documentation of the presence or absence of macular edema **and** level of severity of retinopathy (EC)[5]

**2022F** Dilated retinal eye exam with interpretation by an ophthalmologist or optometrist documented and reviewed (DM)[2,4]

**2024F** 7 standard field stereoscopic photos with interpretation by an ophthalmologist or optometrist documented and reviewed (DM)[2,4]

**2026F** Eye imaging validated to match diagnosis from 7 standard field stereoscopic photos results documented and reviewed (DM)[2,4]

**2027F** Optic nerve head evaluation performed (EC)[5]

**2028F** Foot examination performed (includes examination through visual inspection, sensory exam with monofilament, and pulse exam – report when any of the 3 components are completed) (DM)[4]

**2029F** Complete physical skin exam performed (ML)[5]

**2030F** Hydration status documented, normally hydrated (PAG)[1]

**2031F** Hydration status documented, dehydrated (PAG)[1]

**2035F** Tympanic membrane mobility assessed with pneumatic otoscopy or tympanometry (OME)[1]

**2040F** Physical examination on the date of the initial visit for low back pain performed, in accordance with specifications (BkP)[2]

**2044F** Documentation of mental health assessment prior to intervention (back surgery or epidural steroid injection) or for back pain episode lasting longer than 6 weeks (BkP)[2]

**2050F** Wound characteristics including size **and** nature of wound base tissue **and** amount of drainage prior to debridement documented (CWC)[5]

**2060F** Patient interviewed directly on or before date of diagnosis of major depressive disorder (MDD ADOL)[1]

# Diagnostic/Screening Processes or Results

Diagnostic/screening processes or results codes describe results of tests ordered (clinical laboratory tests, radiological or other procedural examinations, and conclusions of medical decision-making).

> (To report blood pressure use the corresponding systolic codes [3074F, 3075F, 3077F] and diastolic codes [3078F, 3079F, 3080F])

**3006F** Chest X-ray results documented and reviewed (CAP)[1]

**3008F** Body Mass Index (BMI), documented (PV)[1]

**3011F** Lipid panel results documented and reviewed (must include total cholesterol, HDL-C, triglycerides and calculated LDL-C) (CAD)[1]

**3014F** Screening mammography results documented and reviewed (PV)[1,2]

**3015F** Cervical cancer screening results documented and reviewed (PV)[1]

**3016F** Patient screened for unhealthy alcohol use using a systematic screening method (PV)[1] (DSP)[8]

**3017F** Colorectal cancer screening results documented and reviewed (PV)[12]

**3018F** Pre-procedure risk assessment **and** depth of insertion **and** quality of the bowel prep **and** complete description of polyp(s) found, including location of each polyp, size, number and gross morphology **and** recommendations for follow-up in final colonoscopy report documented (End/Polyp)[5]

**3019F** Left ventricular ejection fraction (LVEF) assessment planned post discharge (HF)[1]

**3020F** Left ventricular function (LVF) assessment (eg, echocardiography, nuclear test, or ventriculography) documented in the medical record (Includes quantitative or qualitative assessment results) (NMA – No Measure Associated)

**3021F** Left ventricular ejection fraction (LVEF) less than 40% or documentation of moderately or severely depressed left ventricular systolic function (CAD, HF)[1]

**3022F** Left ventricular ejection fraction (LVEF) greater than or equal to 40% or documentation as normal or mildly depressed left ventricular systolic function (CAD, HF)[1]

**3023F** Spirometry results documented and reviewed (COPD)[1]

**3025F** Spirometry test results demonstrate FEV1/FVC less than 70% with COPD symptoms (eg, dyspnea, cough/sputum, wheezing) (CAP, COPD)[1]

**3027F** Spirometry test results demonstrate FEV1/FVC greater than or equal to 70% or patient does not have COPD symptoms (COPD)[1]

**3028F** Oxygen saturation results documented and reviewed (includes assessment through pulse oximetry or arterial blood gas measurement) (CAP, COPD)[1] (EM)[5]

**3035F** Oxygen saturation less than or equal to 88% or a $PaO_2$ less than or equal to 55 mm Hg (COPD)[1]

**3037F** Oxygen saturation greater than 88% or $PaO_2$ greater than 55 mm Hg (COPD)[1]

**3038F** Pulmonary function test performed within 12 months prior to surgery (Lung/Esop Cx)[6]

**3040F** Functional expiratory volume (FEV1) less than 40% of predicted value (COPD)[1]

**3042F** Functional expiratory volume (FEV1) greater than or equal to 40% of predicted value (COPD)[1]

**3044F** Most recent hemoglobin A1c (HbA1c) level less than 7.0% (DM)[2,4]

**3045F** Most recent hemoglobin A1c (HbA1c) level 7.0–9.0% (DM)[2,4]

**3046F** Most recent hemoglobin A1c level greater than 9.0% (DM)[4]

> (To report most recent hemoglobin A1c level less than or equal to 9.0%, see codes 3044F-3045F)

**3048F** Most recent LDL-C less than 100 mg/dL (CAD)[1] (DM)[4]

**3049F** Most recent LDL-C 100-129 mg/dL (CAD)[1] (DM)[4]

**3050F** Most recent LDL-C greater than or equal to 130 mg/dL (CAD)[1] (DM)[4]

**3055F** Left ventricular ejection fraction (LVEF) less than or equal to 35% (HF)[1]

**3056F** Left ventricular ejection fraction (LVEF) greater than 35% or no LVEF result available (HF)[1]

Category II

**3060F**    Positive microalbuminuria test result documented and reviewed (DM)[2,4]

**3061F**    Negative microalbuminuria test result documented and reviewed (DM)[2,4]

**3062F**    Positive macroalbuminuria test result documented and reviewed (DM)[2,4]

**3066F**    Documentation of treatment for nephropathy (eg, patient receiving dialysis, patient being treated for ESRD, CRF, ARF, or renal insufficiency, any visit to a nephrologist) (DM)[2,4]

**3072F**    Low risk for retinopathy (no evidence of retinopathy in the prior year) (DM)[2,4]

**3073F**    Pre-surgical (cataract) axial length, corneal power measurement and method of intraocular lens power calculation documented within 12 months prior to surgery (EC)[5]

**3074F**    Most recent systolic blood pressure less than 130 mm Hg (DM)[2,4] (HTN, CKD, CAD)[1]

**3075F**    Most recent systolic blood pressure 130 - 139 mm Hg (DM)[2,4] (HTN, CKD, CAD)[1]

(To report most recent systolic blood pressure less than 140 mm Hg, see codes 3074F-3075F)

**3077F**    Most recent systolic blood pressure greater than or equal to 140 mm Hg (HTN, CKD, CAD)[1] (DM)[2,4]

**3078F**    Most recent diastolic blood pressure less than 80 mm Hg (HTN, CKD, CAD)[1] (DM)[2,4]

**3079F**    Most recent diastolic blood pressure 80-89 mm Hg (HTN, CKD, CAD)[1] (DM)[2,4]

**3080F**    Most recent diastolic blood pressure greater than or equal to 90 mm Hg (HTN, CKD, CAD)[1] (DM)[2,4]

**3082F**    Kt/V less than 1.2 (Clearance of urea [Kt]/volume [V]) (ESRD, P-ESRD)[1]

**3083F**    Kt/V equal to or greater than 1.2 and less than 1.7 (Clearance of urea [Kt]/volume [V]) (ESRD, P-ESRD)[1]

**3084F**    Kt/V greater than or equal to 1.7 (Clearance of urea [Kt]/volume [V]) (ESRD, P-ESRD)[1]

**3085F**    Suicide risk assessed (MDD, MDD ADOL)[1]

**3088F**    Major depressive disorder, mild (MDD)[1]

**3089F**    Major depressive disorder, moderate (MDD)[1]

**3090F**    Major depressive disorder, severe without psychotic features (MDD)[1]

**3091F**    Major depressive disorder, severe with psychotic features (MDD)[1]

**3092F**    Major depressive disorder, in remission (MDD)[1]

**3093F**    Documentation of new diagnosis of initial or recurrent episode of major depressive disorder (MDD)[1]

**3095F**    Central dual-energy X-ray absorptiometry (DXA) results documented (OP)[5](IBD)[10]

**3096F**    Central dual-energy X-ray absorptiometry (DXA) ordered (OP)[5](IBD)[10]

**3100F**    Carotid imaging study report (includes direct or indirect reference to measurements of distal internal carotid diameter as the denominator for stenosis measurement) (STR, RAD)[5]

**3110F**    Documentation in final CT or MRI report of presence or absence of hemorrhage and mass lesion and acute infarction (STR)[5]

**3111F**    CT or MRI of the brain performed in the hospital within 24 hours of arrival **or** performed in an outpatient imaging center, to confirm initial diagnosis of stroke, TIA or intracranial hemorrhage (STR)[5]

**3112F**    CT or MRI of the brain performed greater than 24 hours after arrival to the hospital **or** performed in an outpatient imaging center for purpose other than confirmation of initial diagnosis of stroke, TIA, or intracranial hemorrhage (STR)[5]

**3115F**    Quantitative results of an evaluation of current level of activity and clinical symptoms (HF)[1]

**3117F**    Heart failure disease specific structured assessment tool completed (HF)[1]

**3118F**    New York Heart Association (NYHA) Class documented (HF)[1]

**3119F**    No evaluation of level of activity or clinical symptoms (HF)[1]

**3120F**    12-Lead ECG Performed (EM)[5]

**3125F**    Esophageal biopsy report with statement about dysplasia (present, absent, or indefinite) (PATH)[9]

**3130F**    Upper gastrointestinal endoscopy performed (GERD)[5]

**3132F**    Documentation of referral for upper gastrointestinal endoscopy (GERD)[5]

**3140F**    Upper gastrointestinal endoscopy report indicates suspicion of Barrett's esophagus (GERD)[5]

**3141F**    Upper gastrointestinal endoscopy report indicates no suspicion of Barrett's esophagus (GERD)[5]

**3142F**    Barium swallow test ordered (GERD)[1]

(To report documentation of barium swallow study, use code 3142F)

**3150F**    Forceps esophageal biopsy performed (GERD)[5]

**3155F**    Cytogenetic testing performed on bone marrow at time of diagnosis or prior to initiating treatment (HEM)[1]

**3160F**    Documentation of iron stores prior to initiating erythropoietin therapy (HEM)[1]

**3170F**    Flow cytometry studies performed at time of diagnosis or prior to initiating treatment (HEM)[1]

**3200F**    Barium swallow test not ordered (GERD)[5]

**3210F**    Group A Strep Test Performed (PHAR)[2]

**3215F** Patient has documented immunity to Hepatitis A (HEP-C)[1]

**3216F** Patient has documented immunity to Hepatitis B (HEP-C)[1](IBD)[10]

(3217F has been deleted)

**3218F** RNA testing for Hepatitis C documented as performed within 6 months prior to initiation of antiviral treatment for Hepatitis C (HEP-C)[1]

(3219F has been deleted)

**3220F** Hepatitis C quantitative RNA testing documented as performed at 12 weeks from initiation of antiviral treatment (HEP-C)[1]

**3230F** Documentation that hearing test was performed within 6 months prior to tympanostomy tube insertion (OME)[1]

**3250F** Specimen site other than anatomic location of primary tumor (PATH)[1]

**3260F** pT category (primary tumor), pN category (regional lymph nodes), and histologic grade documented in pathology report (PATH)[1]

**3265F** Ribonucleic acid (RNA) testing for Hepatitis C viremia ordered or results documented (HEP C)[1]

**3266F** Hepatitis C genotype testing documented as performed prior to initiation of antiviral treatment for Hepatitis C (HEP C)[1]

**3267F** Pathology report includes pT category, pN category, Gleason score, and statement about margin status (PATH)[9]

**3268F** Prostate-specific antigen (PSA), **and** primary tumor (T) stage, **and** Gleason score documented prior to initiation of treatment (PRCA)[1]

**3269F** Bone scan performed prior to initiation of treatment or at any time since diagnosis of prostate cancer (PRCA)[1]

**3270F** Bone scan not performed prior to initiation of treatment nor at any time since diagnosis of prostate cancer (PRCA)[1]

**3271F** Low risk of recurrence, prostate cancer (PRCA)[1]

**3272F** Intermediate risk of recurrence, prostate cancer (PRCA)[1]

**3273F** High risk of recurrence, prostate cancer (PRCA)[1]

**3274F** Prostate cancer risk of recurrence not determined or neither low, intermediate nor high (PRCA)[1]

**3278F** Serum levels of calcium, phosphorus, intact Parathyroid Hormone (PTH) and lipid profile ordered (CKD)[1]

**3279F** Hemoglobin level greater than or equal to 13 g/dL (CKD, ESRD)[1]

**3280F** Hemoglobin level 11 g/dL to 12.9 g/dL (CKD, ESRD)[1]

**3281F** Hemoglobin level less than 11 g/dL (CKD, ESRD)[1]

**3284F** Intraocular pressure (IOP) reduced by a value of greater than or equal to 15% from the pre-intervention level (EC)[5]

**3285F** Intraocular pressure (IOP) reduced by a value less than 15% from the pre-intervention level (EC)[5]

**3288F** Falls risk assessment documented (GER)[5]

**3290F** Patient is D (Rh) negative and unsensitized (Pre-Cr)[1]

**3291F** Patient is D (Rh) positive or sensitized (Pre-Cr)[1]

**3292F** HIV testing ordered or documented and reviewed during the first or second prenatal visit (Pre-Cr)[1]

**3293F** ABO and Rh blood typing documented as performed (Pre-Cr)[7]

**3294F** Group B Streptococcus (GBS) screening documented as performed during week 35-37 gestation (Pre-Cr)[7]

**3300F** American Joint Committee on Cancer (AJCC) stage documented and reviewed (ONC)[1]

**3301F** Cancer stage documented in medical record as metastatic and reviewed (ONC)[1]

(Codes 3302F-3312F have been deleted)

(To report measures for cancer staging, see 3321F-3390F)

**3315F** Estrogen receptor (ER) or progesterone receptor (PR) positive breast cancer (ONC)[1]

**3316F** Estrogen receptor (ER) and progesterone receptor (PR) negative breast cancer (ONC)[1]

**3317F** Pathology report confirming malignancy documented in the medical record and reviewed prior to the initiation of chemotherapy (ONC)[1]

**3318F** Pathology report confirming malignancy documented in the medical record and reviewed prior to the initiation of radiation therapy (ONC)[1]

**3319F** 1 of the following diagnostic imaging studies ordered: chest x-ray, CT, Ultrasound, MRI, PET, or nuclear medicine scans (ML)[5]

**3320F** None of the following diagnostic imaging studies ordered: chest X-ray, CT, Ultrasound, MRI, PET, or nuclear medicine scans (ML)[5]

**3321F** AJCC Cancer Stage 0 or IA Melanoma, documented (ML)[5]

**3322F** Melanoma greater than AJCC Stage 0 or IA (ML)[5]

**3323F** Clinical tumor, node and metastases (TNM) staging documented and reviewed prior to surgery (Lung/Esop Cx)[6]

**3324F** MRI or CT scan ordered, reviewed or requested (EPI)[8]

**3325F** Preoperative assessment of functional or medical indication(s) for surgery prior to the cataract surgery with intraocular lens placement (must be performed within 12 months prior to cataract surgery) (EC)[5]

**3328F** Performance status documented and reviewed within 2 weeks prior to surgery (Lung/Esop Cx)[6]

**3330F** Imaging study ordered (BkP)[2]

**3331F** Imaging study not ordered (BkP)[2]

**3340F** Mammogram assessment category of "incomplete: need additional imaging evaluation" documented (RAD)[5]

**3341F** Mammogram assessment category of "negative," documented (RAD)[5]

---

⊙=Moderate sedation ✚=Add-on code ✗=FDA approval pending #=Resequenced code ○=Recycled/reinstated code

**3342F**   Mammogram assessment category of "benign," documented (RAD)[5]

**3343F**   Mammogram assessment category of "probably benign," documented (RAD)[5]

**3344F**   Mammogram assessment category of "suspicious," documented (RAD)[5]

**3345F**   Mammogram assessment category of "highly suggestive of malignancy," documented (RAD)[5]

**3350F**   Mammogram assessment category of "known biopsy proven malignancy," documented (RAD)[5]

**3351F**   Negative screen for depressive symptoms as categorized by using a standardized depression screening/assessment tool (MDD)[2]

**3352F**   No significant depressive symptoms as categorized by using a standardized depression assessment tool (MDD)[2]

**3353F**   Mild to moderate depressive symptoms as categorized by using a standardized depression screening/assessment tool (MDD)[2]

**3354F**   Clinically significant depressive symptoms as categorized by using a standardized depression screening/assessment tool (MDD)[2]

**3370F**   AJCC Breast Cancer Stage 0 documented (ONC)[1]

**3372F**   AJCC Breast Cancer Stage I: T1mic, T1a or T1b (tumor size ≤ 1 cm) documented (ONC)[1]

**3374F**   AJCC Breast Cancer Stage I: T1c (tumor size > 1 cm to 2 cm) documented (ONC)[1]

**3376F**   AJCC Breast Cancer Stage II documented (ONC)[1]

**3378F**   AJCC Breast Cancer Stage III documented (ONC)[1]

**3380F**   AJCC Breast Cancer Stage IV documented (ONC)[1]

**3382F**   AJCC colon cancer, Stage 0 documented (ONC)[1]

**3384F**   AJCC colon cancer, Stage I documented (ONC)[1]

**3386F**   AJCC colon cancer, Stage II documented (ONC)[1]

**3388F**   AJCC colon cancer, Stage III documented (ONC)[1]

**3390F**   AJCC colon cancer, Stage IV documented (ONC)[1]

**3394F**   Quantitative HER2 immunohistochemistry (IHC) evaluation of breast cancer consistent with the scoring system defined in the ASCO/CAP guidelines (PATH)[9]

**3395F**   Quantitative non-HER2 immunohistochemistry (IHC) evaluation of breast cancer (eg, testing for estrogen or progesterone receptors [ER/PR]) performed (PATH)[9]

**3450F**   Dyspnea screened, no dyspnea or mild dyspnea (Pall Cr)[5]

**3451F**   Dyspnea screened, moderate or severe dyspnea (Pall Cr)[5]

**3452F**   Dyspnea not screened (Pall Cr)[5]

**3455F**   TB screening performed and results interpreted within six months prior to initiation of first-time biologic disease modifying anti-rheumatic drug therapy for RA (RA)[5]

**3470F**   Rheumatoid arthritis (RA) disease activity, low (RA)[5]

**3471F**   Rheumatoid arthritis (RA) disease activity, moderate (RA)[5]

**3472F**   Rheumatoid arthritis (RA) disease activity, high (RA)[5]

**3475F**   Disease prognosis for rheumatoid arthritis assessed, poor prognosis documented (RA)[5]

**3476F**   Disease prognosis for rheumatoid arthritis assessed, good prognosis documented (RA)[5]

**3490F**   History of AIDS-defining condition (HIV)[5]

**3491F**   HIV indeterminate (infants of undetermined HIV status born of HIV-infected mothers) (HIV)[5]

**3492F**   History of nadir CD4+ cell count <350 cells/mm$^3$ (HIV)[5]

**3493F**   No history of nadir CD4+ cell count <350 cells/mm$^3$ **and** no history of AIDS-defining condition (HIV)[5]

**3494F**   CD4+ cell count <200 cells/mm3 (HIV)[5]

**3495F**   CD4+ cell count 200 – 499 cells/mm3 (HIV)[5]

**3496F**   CD4+ cell count ≥500 cells/mm3 (HIV)[5]

**3497F**   CD4+ cell percentage <15% (HIV)[5]

**3498F**   CD4+ cell percentage ≥15% (HIV)[5]

**3500F**   CD4+ cell count or CD4+ cell percentage documented as performed (HIV)[5]

**3502F**   HIV RNA viral load below limits of quantification (HIV)[5]

**3503F**   HIV RNA viral load not below limits of quantification (HIV)[5]

**3510F**   Documentation that tuberculosis (TB) screening test performed and results interpreted (HIV)[5] (IBD)[10]

**3511F**   Chlamydia and gonorrhea screenings documented as performed (HIV)[5]

**3512F**   Syphilis screening documented as performed (HIV)[5]

**3513F**   Hepatitis B screening documented as performed (HIV)[5]

**3514F**   Hepatitis C screening documented as performed (HIV)[5]

**3515F**   Patient has documented immunity to Hepatitis C (HIV)[5]

**3517F**   Hepatitis B Virus (HBV) status assessed and results interpreted within one year prior to receiving a first course of anti-TNF (tumor necrosis factor) therapy (IBD)[10]

**3520F**   Clostridium difficile testing performed (IBD)[10]

**3550F**   Low risk for thromboembolism (AFIB)[1]

**3551F**   Intermediate risk for thromboembolism (AFIB)[1]

**3552F**   High risk for thromboembolism (AFIB)[1]

**3555F**   Patient had International Normalized Ratio (INR) measurement performed (AFIB)[1]

**3570F**   Final report for bone scintigraphy study includes correlation with existing relevant imaging studies (eg, x-ray, MRI, CT) corresponding to the same anatomical region in question (NUC_MED)[1]

**3572F**   Patient considered to be potentially at risk for fracture in a weight-bearing site (NUC_MED)[1]

**3573F**   Patient not considered to be potentially at risk for fracture in a weight-bearing site (NUC_MED)[1]

---

▲=Revised code    ●=New code    ▶ ◀=Contains new or revised text    ⊘=Modifier 51 exempt

**Category II**

**3650F** Electroencephalogram (EEG) ordered, reviewed or requested (EPI)[8]

**3700F** Psychiatric disorders or disturbances assessed (Prkns)[8]

**3720F** Cognitive impairment or dysfunction assessed (Prkns)[8]

**3725F** Screening for depression performed (DEM)[1]

**3750F** Patient not receiving dose of corticosteroids greater than or equal to 10mg/day for 60 or greater consecutive days (IBD)[10]

● **3751F** Electrodiagnostic studies for distal symmetric polyneuropathy conducted (or requested), documented, and reviewed within 6 months of initial evaluation for condition (DSP)[8]

● **3752F** Electrodiagnostic studies for distal symmetric polyneuropathy **not** conducted (or requested), documented, or reviewed within 6 months of initial evaluation for condition (DSP)[8]

● **3753F** Patient has clear clinical symptoms and signs that are highly suggestive of neuropathy AND cannot be attributed to another condition, AND has an obvious cause for the neuropathy (DSP)[8]

● **3754F** Screening tests for diabetes mellitus reviewed, requested, or ordered (DSP)[8]

● **3755F** Cognitive and behavioral impairment screening performed (ALS)[8]

● **3756F** Patient has pseudobulbar affect, sialorrhea, or ALS-related symptoms (ALS)[8]

● **3757F** Patient does not have pseudobulbar affect, sialorrhea, or ALS-related symptoms (ALS)[8]

● **3758F** Patient referred for pulmonary function testing or peak cough expiratory flow (ALS)[8]

● **3759F** Patient screened for dysphagia, weight loss, and impaired nutrition, and results documented (ALS)[8]

● **3760F** Patient exhibits dysphagia, weight loss, or impaired nutrition (ALS)[8]

● **3761F** Patient does not exhibit dysphagia, weight loss, or impaired nutrition (ALS)[8]

● **3762F** Patient is dysarthric (ALS)[8]

● **3763F** Patient is not dysarthric (ALS)[8]

# Therapeutic, Preventive, or Other Interventions

Therapeutic, preventive, or other interventions codes describe pharmacologic, procedural, or behavioral therapies, including preventive services such as patient education and counseling.

**4000F** Tobacco use cessation intervention, counseling (COPD, CAP, CAD, Asthma)[1] (DM)[4] (PV)[2]

**4001F** Tobacco use cessation intervention, pharmacologic therapy (COPD, CAD, CAP, PV, Asthma)[1] (DM)[4] (PV)[2]

(4002F has been deleted. To report statin therapy, use 4013F)

**4003F** Patient education, written/oral, appropriate for patients with heart failure, performed (NMA – No measure Associated)[1]

**4004F** Patient screened for tobacco use **and** received tobacco cessation intervention (counseling, pharmacotherapy, or both), if identified as a tobacco user (PV, CAD)[1]

**4005F** Pharmacologic therapy (other than minerals/vitamins) for osteoporosis prescribed (OP)[5] (IBD)[10]

(4006F has been deleted. To report beta blocker therapy, use 4008F.)

(4007F has been deleted. To report age related eye disease study (AREDS) formulation prescribed or recommended, use code 4177F)

**4008F** Beta-blocker therapy prescribed or currently being taken (CAD,HF)[1]

(4009F has been deleted. To report Angiotensin converting enzyme [ACE] inhibitor or angiotensin receptor blocker [ARB] therapy, use 4010F)

**4010F** Angiotensin Converting Enzyme (ACE) Inhibitor or Angiotensin Receptor Blocker (ARB) therapy prescribed or currently being taken (CAD, CKD, HF)[1] (DM)[2]

**4011F** Oral antiplatelet therapy prescribed (CAD)[1]

**4012F** Warfarin therapy prescribed (NMA-No Measure Associated)

**4013F** Statin therapy prescribed or currently being taken (CAD)[1]

**4014F** Written discharge instructions provided to heart failure patients discharged home (Instructions include all of the following components: activity level, diet, discharge medications, follow-up appointment, weight monitoring, what to do if symptoms worsen) (NMA-No Measure Associated)

**4015F** Persistent asthma, preferred long term control medication or an acceptable alternative treatment, prescribed (NMA–No Measure Associated)

(Note: There are no medical exclusion criteria)

(Do not report modifier 1P with 4015F)

(To report patient reasons for not prescribing, use modifier 2P)

**4016F** Anti-inflammatory/analgesic agent prescribed (OA)[1]

(Use for prescribed or continued medication[s], including over-the-counter medication[s])

**4017F** Gastrointestinal prophylaxis for NSAID use prescribed (OA)[1]

**4018F** Therapeutic exercise for the involved joint(s) instructed or physical or occupational therapy prescribed (OA)[1]

**4019F**  Documentation of receipt of counseling on exercise **and** either both calcium and vitamin D use or counseling regarding both calcium and vitamin D use (OP)[5]

**4025F**  Inhaled bronchodilator prescribed (COPD)[1]

**4030F**  Long-term oxygen therapy prescribed (more than 15 hours per day) (COPD)[1]

**4033F**  Pulmonary rehabilitation exercise training recommended (COPD)[1]

(Report 4033F with 1019F)

**4035F**  Influenza immunization recommended (COPD)[1] (IBD)[10]

**4037F**  Influenza immunization ordered or administered (COPD, PV, CKD, ESRD)[1](IBD)[10]

**4040F**  Pneumococcal vaccine administered or previously received (COPD)[1] (PV)[1,2] (IBD)[10]

**4041F**  Documentation of order for cefazolin OR cefuroxime for antimicrobial prophylaxis (PERI 2)[5]

**4042F**  Documentation that prophylactic antibiotics were neither given within 4 hours prior to surgical incision nor given intraoperatively (PERI 2)[5]

**4043F**  Documentation that an order was given to discontinue prophylactic antibiotics within 48 hours of surgical end time, cardiac procedures (PERI 2)[5]

**4044F**  Documentation that an order was given for venous thromboembolism (VTE) prophylaxis to be given within 24 hours prior to incision time or 24 hours after surgery end time (PERI 2)[5]

**4045F**  Appropriate empiric antibiotic prescribed (CAP)[1], (EM)[5]

**4046F**  Documentation that prophylactic antibiotics were given within 4 hours prior to surgical incision or given intraoperatively (PERI 2)[5]

**4047F**  Documentation of order for prophylactic parenteral antibiotics to be given within 1 hour (if fluoroquinolone or vancomycin, 2 hours) prior to surgical incision (or start of procedure when no incision is required) (PERI 2)[5]

**4048F**  Documentation that administration of prophylactic parenteral antibiotic was initiated within 1 hour (if fluoroquinolone or vancomycin, 2 hours) prior to surgical incision (or start of procedure when no incision is required) as ordered (PERI 2)[5]

**4049F**  Documentation that order was given to discontinue prophylactic antibiotics within 24 hours of surgical end time, non-cardiac procedure (PERI 2)[5]

**4050F**  Hypertension plan of care documented as appropriate (NMA - No Measure Associated)[1]

**4051F**  Referred for an arteriovenous (AV) fistula (ESRD, CKD)[1]

**4052F**  Hemodialysis via functioning arteriovenous (AV) fistula (ESRD)[1]

**4053F**  Hemodialysis via functioning arteriovenous (AV) graft (ESRD)[1]

**4054F**  Hemodialysis via catheter (ESRD)[1]

**4055F**  Patient receiving peritoneal dialysis (ESRD)[1]

**4056F**  Appropriate oral rehydration solution recommended (PAG)[1]

**4058F**  Pediatric gastroenteritis education provided to caregiver (PAG)[1]

**4060F**  Psychotherapy services provided (MDD, MDD ADOL)[1]

**4062F**  Patient referral for psychotherapy documented (MDD, MDD ADOL)[1]

**4063F**  Antidepressant pharmacotherapy considered and not prescribed (MDD ADOL)[1]

**4064F**  Antidepressant pharmacotherapy prescribed (MDD, MDD ADOL)[1]

**4065F**  Antipsychotic pharmacotherapy prescribed (MDD)[1]

**4066F**  Electroconvulsive therapy (ECT) provided (MDD)[1]

**4067F**  Patient referral for electroconvulsive therapy (ECT) documented (MDD)[1]

**4069F**  Venous thromboembolism (VTE) prophylaxis received (IBD)[10]

**4070F**  Deep vein thrombosis (DVT) prophylaxis received by end of hospital day 2 (STR)[5]

**4073F**  Oral antiplatelet therapy prescribed at discharge (STR)[5]

**4075F**  Anticoagulant therapy prescribed at discharge (STR)[5]

**4077F**  Documentation that tissue plasminogen activator (t-PA) administration was considered (STR)[5]

**4079F**  Documentation that rehabilitation services were considered (STR)[5]

**4084F**  Aspirin received within 24 hours before emergency department arrival or during emergency department stay (EM)[5]

**4086F**  Aspirin or clopidogrel prescribed or currently being taken (CAD)[1]

**4090F**  Patient receiving erythropoietin therapy (HEM)[1]

**4095F**  Patient not receiving erythropoietin therapy (HEM)[1]

**4100F**  Bisphosphonate therapy, intravenous, ordered or received (HEM)[1]

**4110F**  Internal mammary artery graft performed for primary, isolated coronary artery bypass graft procedure (CABG)[6]

**4115F**  Beta blocker administered within 24 hours prior to surgical incision (CABG)[6]

**4120F**  Antibiotic prescribed or dispensed (URI, PHAR)[2], (A-BRONCH)[2]

**4124F**  Antibiotic neither prescribed nor dispensed (URI, PHAR)[2], (A-BRONCH)[2]

**4130F**  Topical preparations (including OTC) prescribed for acute otitis externa (AOE)[1]

**4131F**  Systemic antimicrobial therapy prescribed (AOE)[1]

**4132F**  Systemic antimicrobial therapy not prescribed (AOE)[1]

**4133F** Antihistamines or decongestants prescribed or recommended (OME)[1]

**4134F** Antihistamines or decongestants neither prescribed nor recommended (OME)[1]

**4135F** Systemic corticosteroids prescribed (OME)[1]

**4136F** Systemic corticosteroids not prescribed (OME)[1]

**4140F** Inhaled corticosteroids prescribed (Asthma)[1]

**4142F** Corticosteroid sparing therapy prescribed (IBD)[10]

**4144F** Alternative long-term control medication prescribed (Asthma)[1]

**4145F** Two or more anti-hypertensive agents prescribed or currently being taken (CAD, HTN)

**4148F** Hepatitis A vaccine injection administered or previously received (HEP-C)[1]

**4149F** Hepatitis B vaccine injection administered or previously received (HEP-C, HIV)[1] (IBD)[10]

**4150F** Patient receiving antiviral treatment for Hepatitis C (HEP-C)[1]

**4151F** Patient not receiving antiviral treatment for Hepatitis C (HEP-C)[1]

(Code 4152F has been deleted.)

**4153F** Combination peginterferon and ribavirin therapy prescribed (HEP-C)[1]

(Code 4154F has been deleted.)

**4155F** Hepatitis A vaccine series previously received (HEP-C)[1]

(Code 4156F has been deleted.)

**4157F** Hepatitis B vaccine series previously received (HEP-C)[1]

**4158F** Patient counseled about risks of alcohol use (HEP-C)[1]

**4159F** Counseling regarding contraception received prior to initiation of antiviral treatment (HEP-C)[1]

**4163F** Patient counseling at a minimum on all of the following treatment options for clinically localized prostate cancer: active surveillance, **and** interstitial prostate brachytherapy, **and** external beam radiotherapy, **and** radical prostatectomy, provided prior to initiation of treatment (PRCA)[1]

**4164F** Adjuvant (ie, in combination with external beam radiotherapy to the prostate for prostate cancer) hormonal therapy (gonadotropin-releasing hormone [GnRH] agonist or antagonist) prescribed/administered (PRCA)[1]

**4165F** 3-dimensional conformal radiotherapy (3D-CRT) or intensity modulated radiation therapy (IMRT) received (PRCA)[1]

**4167F** Head of bed elevation (30-45 degrees) on first ventilator day ordered (CRIT)[1]

**4168F** Patient receiving care in the intensive care unit (ICU) and receiving mechanical ventilation, 24 hours or less (CRIT)[1]

**4169F** Patient either not receiving care in the intensive care unit (ICU) OR not receiving mechanical ventilation OR receiving mechanical ventilation greater than 24 hours (CRIT)[1]

**4171F** Patient receiving erythropoiesis-stimulating agents (ESA) therapy (CKD)[1]

**4172F** Patient not receiving erythropoiesis-stimulating agents (ESA) therapy (CKD)[1]

**4174F** Counseling about the potential impact of glaucoma on visual functioning and quality of life, and importance of treatment adherence provided to patient and/or caregiver(s) (EC)[5]

**4175F** Best-corrected visual acuity of 20/40 or better (distance or near) achieved within the 90 days following cataract surgery (EC)[5]

**4176F** Counseling about value of protection from UV light and lack of proven efficacy of nutritional supplements in prevention or progression of cataract development provided to patient and/or caregiver(s) (NMA No Measure Associated)

**4177F** Counseling about the benefits and/or risks of the Age-Related Eye Disease Study (AREDS) formulation for preventing progression of age-related macular degeneration (AMD) provided to patient and/or caregiver(s) (EC)[5]

**4178F** Anti-D immune globulin received between 26 and 30 weeks gestation (Pre-Cr)[1]

**4179F** Tamoxifen or aromatase inhibitor (AI) prescribed (ONC)[1]

**4180F** Adjuvant chemotherapy referred, prescribed, or previously received for Stage III colon cancer (ONC)[1]

**4181F** Conformal radiation therapy received (NMA-No Measure Assoc.)

**4182F** Conformal radiation therapy not received (NMA-No Measure Assoc.)

**4185F** Continuous (12-months) therapy with proton pump inhibitor (PPI) or histamine H2 receptor antagonist (H2RA) received (GERD)[5]

**4186F** No continuous (12-months) therapy with either proton pump inhibitor (PPI) or histamine H2 receptor antagonist (H2RA) received (GERD)[5]

**4187F** Disease modifying anti-rheumatic drug therapy prescribed or dispensed (RA)[2]

**4188F** Appropriate angiotensin converting enzyme (ACE)/ angiotensin receptor blockers (ARB) therapeutic monitoring test ordered or performed (AM)[2]

**4189F** Appropriate digoxin therapeutic monitoring test ordered or performed (AM)[2]

**4190F** Appropriate diuretic therapeutic monitoring test ordered or performed (AM)[2]

**4191F** Appropriate anticonvulsant therapeutic monitoring test ordered or performed (AM)[2]

**4192F** Patient not receiving glucocorticoid therapy (RA)[5]

Category II

**4193F**   Patient receiving <10 mg daily prednisone (or equivalent), or RA activity is worsening, or glucocorticoid use is for less than 6 months (RA)[5]

**4194F**   Patient receiving ≥10 mg daily prednisone (or equivalent) for longer than 6 months, and improvement or no change in disease activity (RA)[5]

**4195F**   Patient receiving first-time biologic disease modifying anti-rheumatic drug therapy for rheumatoid arthritis (RA)[5]

**4196F**   Patient not receiving first-time biologic disease modifying anti-rheumatic drug therapy for rheumatoid arthritis (RA)[5]

**4200F**   External beam radiotherapy as primary therapy to prostate with or without nodal irradiation (PRCA)[1]

**4201F**   External beam radiotherapy with or without nodal irradiation as adjuvant or salvage therapy for prostate cancer patient (PRCA)[1]

**4210F**   Angiotensin converting enzyme (ACE) or angiotensin receptor blockers (ARB) medication therapy for 6 months or more (MM)[2]

**4220F**   Digoxin medication therapy for 6 months or more (MM)[2]

**4221F**   Diuretic medication therapy for 6 months or more (MM)[2]

**4230F**   Anticonvulsant medication therapy for 6 months or more (MM)[2]

**4240F**   Instruction in therapeutic exercise with follow-up provided to patients during episode of back pain lasting longer than 12 weeks (BkP)[2]

**4242F**   Counseling for supervised exercise program provided to patients during episode of back pain lasting longer than 12 weeks (BkP)[2]

**4245F**   Patient counseled during the initial visit to maintain or resume normal activities (BkP)[2]

**4248F**   Patient counseled during the initial visit for an episode of back pain against bed rest lasting 4 days or longer (BkP)[2]

**4250F**   Active warming used intraoperatively for the purpose of maintaining normothermia, **or** at least 1 body temperature equal to or greater than 36 degrees Centigrade (or 96.8 degrees Fahrenheit) recorded within the 30 minutes immediately before or the 15 minutes immediately after anesthesia end time (CRIT)[1]

**4255F**   Duration of general or neuraxial anesthesia 60 minutes or longer, as documented in the anesthesia record (CRIT)[5] (Peri2)[11]

**4256F**   Duration of general or neuraxial anesthesia less than 60 minutes, as documented in the anesthesia record (CRIT)[5] (Peri)[11]

**4260F**   Wound surface culture technique used (CWC)[5]

**4261F**   Technique other than surface culture of the wound exudate used (eg, Levine/deep swab technique, semi-quantitative or quantitative swab technique) **or** wound surface culture technique not used (CWC)[5]

**4265F**   Use of wet to dry dressings prescribed or recommended (CWC)[5]

**4266F**   Use of wet to dry dressings neither prescribed nor recommended (CWC)[5]

**4267F**   Compression therapy prescribed (CWC)[5]

**4268F**   Patient education regarding the need for long term compression therapy including interval replacement of compression stockings received (CWC)[5]

**4269F**   Appropriate method of offloading (pressure relief) prescribed (CWC)[5]

**4270F**   Patient receiving potent antiretroviral therapy for 6 months or longer (HIV)[5]

**4271F**   Patient receiving potent antiretroviral therapy for less than 6 months or not receiving potent antiretroviral therapy (HIV)[5]

**4274F**   Influenza immunization administered or previously received (HIV)[5] (P-ESRD)[1]

     (4275F has been deleted. To report Hepatitis B vaccine injection administered or previously received, use 4149F)

**4276F**   Potent antiretroviral therapy prescribed (HIV)[5]

**4279F**   Pneumocystis jiroveci pneumonia prophylaxis prescribed (HIV)[5]

**4280F**   Pneumocystis jiroveci pneumonia prophylaxis prescribed within 3 months of low CD4+ cell count or percentage (HIV)[5]

**4290F**   Patient screened for injection drug use (HIV)[5]

**4293F**   Patient screened for high-risk sexual behavior (HIV)[5]

**4300F**   Patient receiving warfarin therapy for nonvalvular atrial fibrillation or atrial flutter (AFIB)[1]

**4301F**   Patient not receiving warfarin therapy for nonvalvular atrial fibrillation or atrial flutter (AFIB)[1]

**4305F**   Patient education regarding appropriate foot care **and** daily inspection of the feet received (CWC)[5]

**4306F**   Patient counseled regarding psychosocial **and** pharmacologic treatment options for opioid addiction (SUD)[1]

**4320F**   Patient counseled regarding psychosocial **and** pharmacologic treatment options for alcohol dependence (SUD)[5]

**4322F**   Caregiver provided with education and referred to additional resources for support (DEM)[1]

**4324F**   Patient (or caregiver) queried about Parkinson's disease medication related motor complications (Prkns)[8]

**4325F**   Medical and surgical treatment options reviewed with patient (or caregiver) (Prkns)[8]

**4326F**   Patient (or caregiver) queried about symptoms of autonomic dysfunction (Prkns)[8]

**4328F**   Patient (or caregiver) queried about sleep disturbances (Prkns)[8]

**4330F** Counseling about epilepsy specific safety issues provided to patient (or caregiver(s)) (EPI)[8]

**4340F** Counseling for women of childbearing potential with epilepsy (EPI)[8]

**4350F** Counseling provided on symptom management, end of life decisions, and palliation (DEM)[1]

**4400F** Rehabilitative therapy options discussed with patient (or caregiver) (Prkns)[8]

**4450F** Self-care education provided to patient (HF)[1]

**4470F** Implantable cardioverter-defibrillator (ICD) counseling provided (HF)[1]

**4480F** Patient receiving ACE inhibitor/ARB therapy and beta-blocker therapy for 3 months or longer (HF)[1]

**4481F** Patient receiving ACE inhibitor/ARB therapy and beta-blocker therapy for less than 3 months or patient not receiving ACE inhibitor/ARB therapy and beta-blocker therapy (HF)[1]

**4500F** Referred to an outpatient cardiac rehabilitation program (CAD)[1]

**4510F** Previous cardiac rehabilitation for qualifying cardiac event completed (CAD)[1]

**4525F** Neuropsychiatric intervention ordered (DEM)[1]

**4526F** Neuropsychiatric intervention received (DEM)[1]

● **4540F** Disease modifying pharmacotherapy discussed (ALS)[8]

● **4541F** Patient offered treatment for pseudobulbar affect, sialorrhea, or ALS-related symptoms (ALS)[8]

● **4550F** Options for noninvasive respiratory support discussed with patient (ALS)[8]

● **4551F** Nutritional support offered (ALS)[8]

● **4552F** Patient offered referral to a speech language pathologist (ALS)[8]

● **4553F** Patient offered assistance in planning for end of life issues (ALS)[8]

● **4554F** Patient received inhalational anesthetic agent (Peri2)[11]

● **4555F** Patient did not receive inhalational anesthetic agent (Peri2)[11]

● **4556F** Patient exhibits 3 or more risk factors for post-operative nausea and vomiting (Peri2)[11]

● **4557F** Patient does not exhibit 3 or more risk factors for post-operative nausea and vomiting (Peri2)[11]

● **4558F** Patient received at least 2 prophylactic pharmacologic anti-emetic agents of different classes preoperatively and intraoperatively (Peri2)[11]

● **4559F** At least 1 body temperature measurement equal to or greater than 35.5 degrees Celsius (or 95.9 degrees Fahrenheit) recorded within the 30 minutes immediately before or the 15 minutes immediately after anesthesia end time (Peri2)[11]

● **4560F** Anesthesia technique did not involve general or neuraxial anesthesia (Peri2)[11]

● **4561F** Patient has a coronary artery stent (Peri2)[11]

● **4562F** Patient does not have a coronary artery stent (Peri2)[11]

● **4563F** Patient received aspirin within 24 hours prior to anesthesia start time (Peri2)[11]

# Follow-up or Other Outcomes

Follow-up or other outcomes codes describe review and communication of test results to patients, patient satisfaction or experience with care, patient functional status, and patient morbidity and mortality.

**5005F** Patient counseled on self-examination for new or changing moles (ML)[5]

**5010F** Findings of dilated macular or fundus exam communicated to the physician or other qualified health care professional managing the diabetes care (EC)[5]

**5015F** Documentation of communication that a fracture occurred and that the patient was or should be tested or treated for osteoporosis (OP)[5]

**5020F** Treatment summary report communicated to physician(s) or other qualified health care professional(s) managing continuing care and to the patient within 1 month of completing treatment (ONC)[1]

**5050F** Treatment plan communicated to provider(s) managing continuing care within 1 month of diagnosis (ML)[5]

**5060F** Findings from diagnostic mammogram communicated to practice managing patient's on-going care within 3 business days of exam interpretation (RAD)[5]

**5062F** Findings from diagnostic mammogram communicated to the patient within 5 days of exam interpretation (RAD)[5]

**5100F** Potential risk for fracture communicated to the referring physician or other qualified health care professional within 24 hours of completion of the imaging study (NUC_MED)[1]

**5200F** Consideration of referral for a neurological evaluation of appropriateness for surgical therapy for intractable epilepsy within the past 3 years (EPI)[8]

**5250F** Asthma discharge plan provided to patient (Asthma)[1]

# Patient Safety

Patient safety codes that describe patient safety practices.

**6005F** Rationale (eg, severity of illness and safety) for level of care (eg, home, hospital) documented (CAP)[1]

**6010F** Dysphagia screening conducted prior to order for or receipt of any foods, fluids, or medication by mouth (STR)[5]

**6015F**   Patient receiving or eligible to receive foods, fluids, or medication by mouth (STR)[5]

**6020F**   NPO (nothing by mouth) ordered (STR)[5]

**6030F**   All elements of maximal sterile barrier technique followed including: cap **and** mask **and** sterile gown **and** sterile gloves **and** a large sterile sheet **and** hand hygiene **and** 2% chlorhexidine for cutaneous antisepsis (or acceptable alternative antiseptics, per current guideline) (CRIT)[1]

**6040F**   Use of appropriate radiation dose reduction devices OR manual techniques for appropriate moderation of exposure, documented (RAD)[5]

**6045F**   Radiation exposure or exposure time in final report for procedure using fluoroscopy, documented (RAD)[5]

**6070F**   Patient queried and counseled about anti-epileptic drug (AED) side effects (EPI)[8]

**6080F**   Patient (or caregiver) queried about falls (Prkns, DSP)[8]

**6090F**   Patient (or caregiver) counseled about safety issues appropriate to patient's stage of disease (Prkns)[8]

**6100F**   Timeout to verify correct patient, correct site, and correct procedure, documented (PATH)[9]

**6101F**   Safety counseling for dementia provided (DEM)[1]

**6102F**   Safety counseling for dementia ordered (DEM)[1]

**6110F**   Counseling provided regarding risks of driving and the alternatives to driving (DEM)[1]

**6150F**   Patient not receiving a first course of anti-TNF (tumor necrosis factor) therapy (IBD)[10]

# Structural Measures

Structural measures codes are used to identify measures that address the setting or system of the delivered care. These codes also address aspects of the capabilities of the organization or health care professional providing the care.

**7010F**   Patient information entered into a recall system that includes: target date for the next exam specified **and** a process to follow up with patients regarding missed or unscheduled appointments (ML)[5]

**7020F**   Mammogram assessment category (eg, Mammography Quality Standards Act [MQSA], Breast Imaging Reporting and Data System [BI-RADS®], or FDA approved equivalent categories) entered into an internal database to allow for analysis of abnormal interpretation (recall) rate (RAD)[5]

**7025F**   Patient information entered into a reminder system with a target due date for the next mammogram (RAD)[5]

# ►Nonmeasure Code Listing◄

►The following codes are included for reporting of certain aspects of care. These factors are not represented by measures developed by existing measures organizations or recognized measures-development processes at the time they are placed in the CPT code set, but may ultimately be associated with measures approved by an appropriate quality improvement organization.◄

● **9001F**   Aortic aneurysm less than 5.0 cm maximum diameter on centerline formatted CT or minor diameter on axial formatted CT (NMA – No Measure Associated)

● **9002F**   Aortic aneurysm 5.0 - 5.4 cm maximum diameter on centerline formatted CT or minor diameter on axial formatted CT (NMA – No Measure Associated)

● **9003F**   Aortic aneurysm 5.5 - 5.9 cm maximum diameter on centerline formatted CT or minor diameter on axial formatted CT (NMA – No Measure Associated)

● **9004F**   Aortic aneurysm 6.0 cm or greater maximum diameter on centerline formatted CT or minor diameter on axial formatted CT (NMA – No Measure Associated)

● **9005F**   Asymptomatic carotid stenosis: No history of any transient ischemic attack or stroke in any carotid or vertebrobasilar territory (NMA – No Measure Associated)

● **9006F**   Symptomatic carotid stenosis: Ipsilateral carotid territory TIA or stroke less than 120 days prior to procedure (NMA – No Measure Associated)

● **9007F**   Other carotid stenosis: Ipsilateral TIA or stroke 120 days or greater prior to procedure or any prior contralateral carotid territory or vertebrobasilar TIA or stroke (NMA – No Measure Associated)

Category II

# Notes

⊙=Moderate sedation ✦=Add-on code ✗=FDA approval pending #=Resequenced code ○=Recycled/reinstated code

# Category III Codes

The following section contains a set of temporary codes for emerging technology, services, and procedures. Category III codes allow data collection for these services/procedures. Use of unlisted codes does not offer the opportunity for the collection of specific data. If a Category III code is available, this code must be reported instead of a Category I unlisted code. This is an activity that is critically important in the evaluation of health care delivery and the formation of public and private policy. The use of the codes in this section allow physicians and other qualified health care professionals, insurers, health services researchers, and health policy experts to identify emerging technology, services, and procedures for clinical efficacy, utilization and outcomes.

The inclusion of a service or procedure in this section neither implies nor endorses clinical efficacy, safety, or the applicability to clinical practice. The codes in this section may not conform to the usual requirements for CPT Category I codes established by the Editorial Panel. For Category I codes, the Panel requires that the service/procedure be performed by many health care professionals in clinical practice in multiple locations and that FDA approval, as appropriate, has already been received. The nature of emerging technology, services, and procedures is such that these requirements may not be met. For these reasons, temporary codes for emerging technology, services, and procedures have been placed in a separate section of the CPT code set and the codes are differentiated from Category I CPT codes by the use of alphanumeric characters.

►Services and procedures described in this section make use of alphanumeric characters. These codes have an alpha character as the 5th character in the string (ie, four digits followed by the letter T). The digits are not intended to reflect the placement of the code in the Category I section of CPT nomenclature. Codes in this section may or may not eventually receive a Category I CPT code. In either case, in general, a given Category III code will be archived five years from the date of initial publication or extension unless a modification of the archival date is specifically noted at the time of a revision or change to a code (eg, addition of parenthetical instructions, reinstatement). Services and procedures described by Category III codes which have been archived after five years, without conversion, must be reported using the Category I unlisted code unless another specific cross-reference is established at the time of archiving. New codes or revised codes in this section are released semi-annually via the AMA CPT Internet site, to expedite dissemination for reporting. The full set of temporary codes for emerging technology, services, and procedures are published annually in the CPT code set. Go to www.ama-assn.org/go/cpt for the most current listing.◄

(0016T, 0017T have been deleted)

(For destruction of localized lesion of choroid by transpupillary thermotherapy, use 67299)

(For destruction of macular drusen, photocoagulation, use 67299)

**0019T**  Extracorporeal shock wave involving musculoskeletal system, not otherwise specified, low energy
Sunset January 2017

(For application of high energy extracorporeal shock wave involving musculoskeletal system not otherwise specified, use 0101T)

(For application of high energy extracorporeal shock wave involving lateral humeral epicondyle, use 0102T)

(0024T has been deleted)

(For non-surgical septal reduction therapy, use 93799)

(0026T has been deleted)

(For lipoprotein, direct measurement, intermediate density lipoproteins [IDL] [remnant lipoprotein], use 84999)

(0027T has been deleted)

(For endoscopic lysis of epidural adhesions with direct visualization using mechnical means or solution injection [eg, normal saline], use 64999)

(0028T has been deleted)

(For dual energy x-ray absorptiometry [DXA] body composition study, use 76499)

(0029T has been deleted)

(For pulsed magnetic neuromodulation incontinence treatment, use 53899)

(0030T has been deleted)

(To report antiprothrombin [phospholipid cofactor] antibody, use 86849)

(0031T, 0032T have been deleted)

(For speculoscopy, including sampling, use 58999)

(0041T has been deleted)

(For urinalysis infectious agent detection, semi-quantitative analysis of volatile compounds, use 81099)

**Category III**

**0042T** Cerebral perfusion analysis using computed tomography with contrast administration, including post-processing of parametric maps with determination of cerebral blood flow, cerebral blood volume, and mean transit time
Sunset January 2019

(0043T has been deleted)

(For carbon monoxide, expired gas analysis [eg, ETCO$_c$/hemolysis breath test], use 84999)

(0046T, 0047T have been deleted)

(For mammary duct[s] catheter lavage, use 19499)

(0048T has been deleted. To report, use 33991)

(0049T has been deleted)

(0050T has been deleted. To report, see 33990-33993)

**0051T** Implantation of a total replacement heart system (artificial heart) with recipient cardiectomy
Sunset January 2019

(For implantation of heart assist or ventricular assist device, see 33975, 33976)

**0052T** Replacement or repair of thoracic unit of a total replacement heart system (artificial heart)
Sunset January 2019

(For replacement or repair of other implantable components in a total replacement heart system (artificial heart), use 0053T)

**0053T** Replacement or repair of implantable component or components of total replacement heart system (artificial heart), excluding thoracic unit
Sunset January 2019

(For replacement or repair of a thoracic unit of a total replacement heart system (artificial heart), use 0052T)

**+ 0054T** Computer-assisted musculoskeletal surgical navigational orthopedic procedure, with image-guidance based on fluoroscopic images (List separately in addition to code for primary procedure)
Sunset January 2019

**+ 0055T** Computer-assisted musculoskeletal surgical navigational orthopedic procedure, with image-guidance based on CT/MRI images (List separately in addition to code for primary procedure)
Sunset January 2019

(When CT and MRI are both performed, report 0055T only once)

(0056T has been deleted. To report, use 20985)

**0058T** Cryopreservation; reproductive tissue, ovarian
Sunset January 2016

**0059T** oocyte(s)
Sunset January 2016

(For cryopreservation of embryo(s), sperm and testicular reproductive tissue, see 89258, 89259, 89335)

(0060T has been deleted)

(For electrical impedance breast scan, use 76499)

(0061T has been deleted)

(For destruction/reduction of malignant breast tumor, microwave phased array thermotherapy, use 19499)

(0062T, 0063T have been deleted)

(For percutaneous intradiscal annuloplasty, any method other than electrothermal, use 22899)

(For intradiscal electrothermal annuloplasty, see 22526, 22527)

(0064T has been deleted. To report, use 94799)

(0066T has been deleted)

(To report CT colon, screening, use 74263)

(0067T has been deleted)

(To report CT colon, diagnostic, see 74261-74262)

(0068T-0070T have been deleted)

(For acoustic heart sound recording and computer analysis, use 93799)

**0071T** Focused ultrasound ablation of uterine leiomyomata, including MR guidance; total leiomyomata volume less than 200 cc of tissue
Sunset January 2015

**0072T** total leiomyomata volume greater or equal to 200 cc of tissue
Sunset January 2015

(Do not report 0071T, 0072T in conjunction with 51702 or 77022)

**0073T** Compensator-based beam modulation treatment delivery of inverse planned treatment using 3 or more high resolution (milled or cast) compensator convergent beam modulated fields, per treatment session
Sunset January 2015

(For treatment planning, use 77301)

(Do not report 0073T in conjunction with 77401-77416, 77418)

**0075T** Transcatheter placement of extracranial vertebral or intrathoracic carotid artery stent(s), including radiologic supervision and interpretation, percutaneous; initial vessel
Sunset January 2015

+ **0076T**    each additional vessel (List separately in addition to code for primary procedure)
Sunset January 2015

(Use 0076T in conjunction with 0075T)

(When the ipsilateral extracranial vertebral or intrathoracic carotid arteriogram (including imaging and selective catheterization) confirms the need for stenting, then 0075T and 0076T include all ipsilateral extracranial vertebral or intrathoracic selective carotid catheterization, all diagnostic imaging for ipsilateral extracranial vertebral or intrathoracic carotid artery stenting, and all related radiologic supervision and interpretation. If stenting is not indicated, then the appropriate codes for selective catheterization and imaging should be reported in lieu of code 0075T or 0076T.)

(0077T has been deleted. To report, see 61107, 61210)

►(0078T-0081T have been deleted. To report, see 34841-34848)◄

(0084T has been deleted. To report, use 53855)

**0085T**    Breath test for heart transplant rejection
Sunset January 2016

(0086T has been deleted. To report use, 93799)

(0087T has been deleted. To report, use 89398)

(0088T has been deleted. To report, use 41530)

(0089T has been deleted. For actigraphy testing, use 95803)

(0090T has been deleted. To report total disc cervical arthroplasty, use 22856)

(To report total disc lumbar arthroplasty, use 22857)

+ **0092T**    Total disc arthroplasty (artificial disc), anterior approach, including discectomy with end plate preparation (includes osteophytectomy for nerve root or spinal cord decompression and microdissection), each additional interspace, cervical (List separately in addition to code for primary procedure)
Sunset January 2019

(Use 0092T in conjunction with 22856)

(Do not report 0092T in conjunction with 22851 when performed at the same level)

(0093T has been deleted. To report removal of total disc cervical arthroplasty, use 22864)

(To report removal of total disc lumbar arthroplasty, use 22865)

+ **0095T**    Removal of total disc arthroplasty (artificial disc), anterior approach, each additional interspace, cervical (List separately in addition to code for primary procedure)
Sunset January 2019

(Use 0095T in conjunction with 22864)

(0096T has been deleted. To report revision of total disc cervical arthroplasty, use 22861)

(To report revision of total disc lumbar arthroplasty, use 22862)

+ **0098T**    Revision including replacement of total disc arthroplasty (artificial disc), anterior approach, each additional interspace, cervical (List separately in addition to code for primary procedure)
Sunset January 2019

(Use 0098T in conjunction with 22861)

(Do not report 0098T in conjunction with 0095T)

(Do not report 0098T in conjunction with 22851 when performed at the same level)

(For decompression, see 63001-63048)

**0099T**    Implantation of intrastromal corneal ring segments
Sunset January 2016

**0100T**    Placement of a subconjunctival retinal prosthesis receiver and pulse generator, and implantation of intra-ocular retinal electrode array, with vitrectomy
Sunset January 2016

**0101T**    Extracorporeal shock wave involving musculoskeletal system, not otherwise specified, high energy
Sunset January 2016

(For application of low energy musculoskeletal system extracorporeal shock wave, use 0019T)

(For extracorporeal shock wave therapy involving integumentary system not otherwise specified, see 0299T, 0300T)

(Do not report 0101T in conjunction with 0299T, 0300T when treating same area)

**0102T**    Extracorporeal shock wave, high energy, performed by a physician, requiring anesthesia other than local, involving lateral humeral epicondyle
Sunset January 2016

(For application of low energy musculoskeletal system extracorporeal shock wave, use 0019T)

**0103T**    Holotranscobalamin, quantitative
Sunset January 2016

(0104T, 0105T have been deleted)

(For inert gas rebreathing for cardiac output measurement during rest, use 93799)

(For inert gas rebreathing for cardiac output measurement during exercise, use 93799)

**Category III**

**0106T**    Quantitative sensory testing (QST), testing and interpretation per extremity; using touch pressure stimuli to assess large diameter sensation
Sunset January 2016

**0107T**    using vibration stimuli to assess large diameter fiber sensation
Sunset January 2016

**0108T**    using cooling stimuli to assess small nerve fiber sensation and hyperalgesia
Sunset January 2016

**0109T**    using heat-pain stimuli to assess small nerve fiber sensation and hyperalgesia
Sunset January 2016

**0110T**    using other stimuli to assess sensation
Sunset January 2016

**0111T**    Long-chain (C20-22) omega-3 fatty acids in red blood cell (RBC) membranes
Sunset January 2016

(For very long chain fatty acids, use 82726)

**0123T**    Fistulization of sclera for glaucoma, through ciliary body
Sunset January 2016

▶(0124T has been deleted)◀

▶(For conjunctival incision with posterior extrascleral placement of pharmacological agent, use 68399)◀

**0126T**    Common carotid intima-media thickness (IMT) study for evaluation of atherosclerotic burden or coronary heart disease risk factor assessment
Sunset January 2016

(0130T has been deleted)

(For validated, statistically reliable, randomized, controlled, single-patient clinical investigation of FDA approved chronic care drugs, provided by a pharmacist, interpretation and report to the prescribing health care professional, use 99199)

(0137T has been deleted. For transperineal stereotactic template guided saturation prostate biopsies, use 55706)

(0140T has been deleted. To report, use 83987)

(0141T-0143T have been deleted)

(To report pancreatic islet cell transplantation, use 48999)

(0144T-0151T have been deleted. To report, see 75571-75574)

(0155T, 0156T have been deleted)

(For laparoscopic implantation, replacement, revision, or removal of gastric stimulation electrodes, lesser curvature, use 43659)

(0157T, 0158T have been deleted)

(For open implantation, replacement, revision, or removal of gastric stimulation electrodes, lesser curvature, use 43999)

**+ 0159T**    Computer-aided detection, including computer algorithm analysis of MRI image data for lesion detection/characterization, pharmacokinetic analysis, with further physician review for interpretation, breast MRI (List separately in addition to code for primary procedure)
Sunset January 2017

(Use 0159T in conjunction with 77058, 77059)

(Do not report 0159T in conjunction with 76376, 76377)

(0160T, 0161T have been deleted. To report, see 90867, 90869)

(0162T has been deleted. To report, see 95980-95982)

**+ 0163T**    Total disc arthroplasty (artificial disc), anterior approach, including discectomy to prepare interspace (other than for decompression), each additional interspace, lumbar (List separately in addition to code for primary procedure)
Sunset January 2019

(Use 0163T in conjunction with 22857)

**+ 0164T**    Removal of total disc arthroplasty, (artificial disc), anterior approach, each additional interspace, lumbar (List separately in addition to code for primary procedure)
Sunset January 2019

(Use 0164T in conjunction with 22865)

**+ 0165T**    Revision including replacement of total disc arthroplasty (artificial disc), anterior approach, each additional interspace, lumbar (List separately in addition to code for primary procedure)
Sunset January 2019

(Use 0165T in conjunction with 22862)

(Do not report 0163T-0165T in conjunction with 22851, 49010, when performed at the same level)

(For decompression, see 63001-63048)

(0166T, 0167T have been deleted)

(For transmyocardial transcatheter closure of ventricular septal defect, with implant, including cardiopulmonary bypass if performed, use 33999)

(0168T has been deleted)

(For rhinophototherapy, intranasal application of ultraviolet and visible light, use 30999)

**0169T**    Stereotactic placement of infusion catheter(s) in the brain for delivery of therapeutic agent(s), including computerized stereotactic planning and burr hole(s)
Sunset January 2017

(Do not report code 0169T in conjunction with 20660, 61107, 61781, 61782, 61783)

(0170T has been deleted. To report, use 46707)

**0171T**    Insertion of posterior spinous process distraction device (including necessary removal of bone or ligament for insertion and imaging guidance), lumbar; single level
Sunset December 2017

**+ 0172T**        each additional level (List separately in addition to code for primary procedure)
Sunset December 2017

(Use 0172T in conjunction with 0171T)

(0173T has been deleted)

**+ 0174T**    Computer-aided detection (CAD) (computer algorithm analysis of digital image data for lesion detection) with further physician review for interpretation and report, with or without digitization of film radiographic images, chest radiograph(s), performed concurrent with primary interpretation (List separately in addition to code for primary procedure)
Sunset December 2017

(Use 0174T in conjunction with 71010, 71020, 71021, 71022, 71030)

**0175T**    Computer-aided detection (CAD) (computer algorithm analysis of digital image data for lesion detection) with further physician review for interpretation and report, with or without digitization of film radiographic images, chest radiograph(s), performed remote from primary interpretation
Sunset December 2017

(Do not report 0175T in conjunction with 71010, 71020, 71021, 71022, 71030)

(0176T, 0177T have been deleted. To report, see 66174, 66175)

**0178T**    Electrocardiogram, 64 leads or greater, with graphic presentation and analysis; with interpretation and report
Sunset January 2018

**0179T**        tracing and graphics only, without interpretation and report
Sunset January 2018

**0180T**        interpretation and report only
Sunset January 2018

(For electrocardiogram routine, with at least 12 leads separately performed, see 93000-93010)

**0181T**    Corneal hysteresis determination, by air impulse stimulation, bilateral, with interpretation and report
Sunset January 2018

**0182T**    High dose rate electronic brachytherapy, per fraction
Sunset January 2018

(Do not report 0182T in conjunction with 77761-77763, 77776-77778, 77785-77787, 77789)

►(0183T has been deleted. To report, use 97610)◄

**0184T**    Excision of rectal tumor, transanal endoscopic microsurgical approach (ie, TEMS), including muscularis propria (ie, full thickness)
Sunset January 2019

(For non-endoscopic excision of rectal tumor, see 45160, 45171, 45172)

(Do not report 0184T in conjunction with 45300-45327, 69990)

►(0185T has been deleted)◄

►(For multivariate analysis of patient-specific findings with quantifiable computer probability assessment, including report, use 99199)◄

►(0186T has been deleted)◄

►(For suprachoroidal delivery of pharmacologic agent, use 67299)◄

(0187T has been deleted. To report, use 92132)

## Remote Real-Time Interactive Video-conferenced Critical Care Services

Remote real-time interactive video-conferenced critical care is the direct delivery by a physician(s) or other qualified health care professional(s) of medical care for a critically ill or critically injured patient from an off-site location. Remote real-time interactive video-conferenced critical care is intended to supplement on-site critical care services at times when a critically ill or injured patient requires additional critical care resources than are available on-site. (For definitions of critical illness or injury and critical care services, see **Critical Care Services** section.)

In order to report remote real-time interactive video-conferenced critical care, the physician(s) or other qualified health care professional(s) in the remote location must have real-time access to the patient's medical record including progress notes, nursing notes, current medications, vital signs, clinical laboratory test results, other diagnostic test results, and radiographic images. The remote physician or other qualified health care professional must have real-time capability to enter electronic orders; document the remote care services provided in the hospital medical record; video conference with the on-site health care team in the patient room; assess patients in their individual rooms, using high fidelity audio and video capabilities, including clear observation of the patient, monitors, ventilators, and infusion pumps; and speak to patients and family members.

Category III

The review and/or interpretation of all diagnostic information is included in reporting remote real-time interactive video-conferenced critical care when performed during the critical period by the individual(s) providing remote real-time interactive video-conferenced critical care and should not be reported separately.

The remote real-time interactive video-conferenced critical care codes 0188T and 0189T are used to report the total duration of time spent by the individual providing remote real-time interactive video-conferenced critical care services to a critically ill or critically injured patient, even if the time spent by the individual on that date is not continuous. For any given period of time spent providing remote real-time interactive video-conferenced critical care services, the physician or other qualified health care professional must devote his or her full attention to the patient and, therefore, cannot provide services to any other patient during the same period of time.

Time spent with the individual patient should be recorded in the patient's record. The time that can be reported as remote real-time interactive video-conferenced critical care is the time spent engaged in work directly related to the individual patient's care. For example, time spent reviewing test results or imaging studies, discussing the critically ill patient's care with other medical staff or documenting remote real-time interactive video-conferenced critical care services in the medical record would be reported as remote real-time interactive video-conferenced critical care, even though it does not occur at the bedside. Also, when the patient is unable or lacks capacity to participate in discussions, time spent from the remote site with family members or surrogate decision makers obtaining a medical history, reviewing the patient's condition or prognosis, or discussing treatment or limitation(s) of treatment may be reported as remote real-time interactive video-conferenced critical care, provided that the conversation bears directly on the management of the patient.

Time spent in activities that occur away from the bedside when the individual does not have the real-time capabilities described above may not be reported as remote real-time interactive video-conferenced critical care because the individual is not immediately available to the patient. Time spent in activities that do not directly contribute to the treatment of the patient may not be reported as remote real-time interactive video-conferenced critical care, even if they are performed in the remote site (eg, participation in administrative meetings or telephone calls to discuss other patients). Only one physician or other qualified health care professional may report either critical care services (99291, 99292) or remote real-time interactive video-conferenced critical care for the same period of time. Do not report remote real-time interactive video-conferenced critical care if another individual reports pediatric or neonatal critical care or intensive care services (99468-99476).

Code 0188T is used to report the first 30 to 74 minutes of remote real-time interactive video-conferenced, critical care on a given date. It should be used only once per date even if the time spent by the physician or other qualified health care professional is not continuous on that date. Remote real-time interactive video-conferenced, critical care of less than 30 minutes total duration on a given date should not be reported.

Code 0189T is used to report additional block(s) of time, of up to 30 minutes each, beyond the first 74 minutes (see table below).

The following examples illustrate the correct reporting of remote critical care services:

| Total Duration of Critical Care | Codes |
|---|---|
| less than 30 minutes (less than 1/2 hour) | do not report |
| 30-74 minutes (1/2 hr. - 1 hr. 14 min.) | 0188T X 1 |
| 75-104 minutes (1 hr. 15 min. - 1 hr. 44 min.) | 0188T X 1 AND 0189T X 1 |
| 105-134 minutes (1 hr. 45 min. - 2 hr. 14 min.) | 0188T X 1 AND 0189T X 2 |

**0188T**   Remote real-time interactive video-conferenced critical care, evaluation and management of the critically ill or critically injured patient; first 30-74 minutes
Sunset January 2019

**+ 0189T**   each additional 30 minutes (List separately in addition to code for primary service)
Sunset January 2019

(Use 0189T in conjunction with 0188T)

**+ 0190T**   Placement of intraocular radiation source applicator (List separately in addition to primary procedure)
Sunset January 2019

(Use 0190T in conjunction with 67036)

(For application of the source by radiation oncologist, see Clinical Brachytherapy section)

**0191T**   Insertion of anterior segment aqueous drainage device, without extraocular reservoir; internal approach, into the trabecular meshwork
Sunset January 2019

**# 0253T**   internal approach, into the suprachoroidal space
Sunset January 2019

►(0192T has been deleted)◄

►(To report insertion of drainage device by external approach, use 66183)◄

(0193T has been deleted. To report, use 53860)

(0194T has been deleted. To report procalcitonin, use 84145)

**0195T**   Arthrodesis, pre-sacral interbody technique, disc space preparation, discectomy, without instrumentation, with image guidance, includes bone graft when performed; L5-S1 interspace
Sunset January 2014

**+ 0196T**   L4-L5 interspace (List separately in addition to code for primary procedure)
Sunset January 2014

(Use 0196T in conjunction with 0195T)

(Do not report 0195T, 0196T in conjunction with 20930-20938, 22558, 22840,22845, 22848, 22851, 72275, 76000, 76380, 76496, 76497, 77002, 77003, 77011, 77012)

**0197T**   Intra-fraction localization and tracking of target or patient motion during delivery of radiation therapy (eg, 3D positional tracking, gating, 3D surface tracking), each fraction of treatment
Sunset January 2015

**0198T**   Measurement of ocular blood flow by repetitive intraocular pressure sampling, with interpretation and report
Sunset January 2015

**0199T**   Physiologic recording of tremor using accelerometer(s) and/or gyroscope(s) (including frequency and amplitude), including interpretation and report
Sunset January 2015

⊙ **0200T**   Percutaneous sacral augmentation (sacroplasty), unilateral injection(s), including the use of a balloon or mechanical device, when used, 1 or more needles
Sunset January 2015

⊙ **0201T**   Percutaneous sacral augmentation (sacroplasty), bilateral injections, including the use of a balloon or mechanical device, when used, 2 or more needles
Sunset January 2015

(For radiological supervision and interpretation, see 72291, 72292)

(If bone biopsy is performed, see 20220, 20225)

**0202T**   Posterior vertebral joint(s) arthroplasty (eg, facet joint[s] replacement), including facetectomy, laminectomy, foraminotomy, and vertebral column fixation, injection of bone cement, when performed, including fluoroscopy, single level, lumbar spine
Sunset January 2015

(Do not report 0202T in conjunction with 22521, 22524, 22840, 22851, 22857, 63005, 63012, 63017, 63030, 63042, 63047, 63056 at the same level)

(0203T has been deleted. To report, use 95800)

(0204T has been deleted. To report, use 95801)

**+ 0205T**   Intravascular catheter-based coronary vessel or graft spectroscopy (eg, infrared) during diagnostic evaluation and/or therapeutic intervention including imaging supervision, interpretation, and report, each vessel (List separately in addition to code for primary procedure)
Sunset January 2015

(Use 0205T in conjunction with 92920, 92924, 92928, 92933, 92937, 92941, 92943, 92975, 93454-93461, 93563, 93564)

**0206T**   Computerized database analysis of multiple cycles of digitized cardiac electrical data from two or more ECG leads, including transmission to a remote center, application of multiple nonlinear mathematical transformations, with coronary artery obstruction severity assessment
Sunset January 2015

(When a 12-lead ECG is performed, 93000-93010 may be reported, as appropriate)

**0207T**   Evacuation of meibomian glands, automated, using heat and intermittent pressure, unilateral
Sunset January 2015

**0208T**   Pure tone audiometry (threshold), automated; air only
Sunset January 2016

**0209T**   air and bone
Sunset January 2016

**0210T**   Speech audiometry threshold, automated;
Sunset January 2016

**0211T**   with speech recognition
Sunset January 2016

**0212T**   Comprehensive audiometry threshold evaluation and speech recognition (0209T, 0211T combined), automated
Sunset January 2016

(For audiometric testing using audiometers performed manually by a qualified health care professional, see 92551-92557)

**0213T**   Injection(s), diagnostic or therapeutic agent, paravertebral facet (zygapophyseal) joint (or nerves innervating that joint) with ultrasound guidance, cervical or thoracic; single level
Sunset January 2016

(To report bilateral procedure, use 0213T with modifier 50)

**+ 0214T**   second level (List separately in addition to code for primary procedure)
Sunset January 2016

(To report bilateral procedure, use 0214T with modifier 50)

**Category III**

**+ 0215T**    third and any additional level(s) (List separately in addition to code for primary procedure)
Sunset January 2016

(Do not report 0215T more than once per day)

(Use 0214T, 0215T in conjunction with 0213T)

(To report bilateral procedure, use 0215T with modifier 50)

**0216T**    Injection(s), diagnostic or therapeutic agent, paravertebral facet (zygapophyseal) joint (or nerves innervating that joint) with ultrasound guidance, lumbar or sacral; single level
Sunset January 2016

(To report bilateral procedure, use 0216T with modifier 50)

**+ 0217T**    second level (List separately in addition to code for primary procedure)
Sunset January 2016

(To report bilateral procedure, use 0217T with modifier 50)

**+ 0218T**    third and any additional level(s) (List separately in addition to code for primary procedure)
Sunset January 2016

(Do not report 0218T more than once per day)

(Use 0217T, 0218T in conjunction with 0216T)

(If injection(s) are performed using fluoroscopy or CT, see 64490-64495)

(To report bilateral procedure, use 0218T with modifier 50)

**0219T**    Placement of a posterior intrafacet implant(s), unilateral or bilateral, including imaging and placement of bone graft(s) or synthetic device(s), single level; cervical
Sunset January 2016

**0220T**    thoracic
Sunset January 2016

**0221T**    lumbar
Sunset January 2016

(Do not report 0219T-0221T in conjunction with any radiological service)

(Do not report 0219T-0221T in conjunction with 20930, 20931, 22600-22614, 22840, 22851 at the same level)

**+ 0222T**    each additional vertebral segment (List separately in addition to code for primary procedure)
Sunset January 2016

(Use 0222T in conjunction with 0219T-0221T)

(For posterior or posterolateral arthrodesis technique, see 22600-22614)

Acoustic cardiography codes 0223T-0225T describe the evaluation and optimization of physiologic data including systolic and diastolic heart sounds and their temporal relationships to the electrocardiogram (ECG).

Codes 0224T and 0225T also include interrogation and limited reprogramming of a cardiac pacing device to ensure hemodynamic optimization (heart rate parameter and/or automated timing modes, including explicit changes of AV/VV intervals) and facilitate device parameter optimization. Do not report 0224T or 0225T in conjunction with 93288 or 93289.

Acoustic cardiography services include a rhythm strip ECG. Do not report 93040-93042 in conjunction with 0223T-0225T.

For complete programming services as a separate procedure, see 93280, 93281, 93283, and 93284.

**0223T**    Acoustic cardiography, including automated analysis of combined acoustic and electrical intervals; single, with interpretation and report
Sunset January 2016

**0224T**    multiple, including serial trended analysis and limited reprogramming of device parameter, AV or VV delays only, with interpretation and report
Sunset January 2016

**0225T**    multiple, including serial trended analysis and limited reprogramming of device parameter, AV and VV delays, with interpretation and report
Sunset January 2016

**0226T**    Anoscopy, high resolution (HRA) (with magnification and chemical agent enhancement); diagnostic, including collection of specimen(s) by brushing or washing when performed
Sunset January 2016

**0227T**    with biopsy(ies)
Sunset January 2016

**0228T**    Injection(s), anesthetic agent and/or steroid, transforaminal epidural, with ultrasound guidance, cervical or thoracic; single level
Sunset January 2016

**+ 0229T**    each additional level (List separately in addition to code for primary procedure)
Sunset January 2016

(Use 0229T in conjunction with 0228T)

**0230T**    Injection(s), anesthetic agent and/or steroid, transforaminal epidural, with ultrasound guidance, lumbar or sacral; single level
Sunset January 2016

**Category III** (side tab)

**+ 0231T**   each additional level (List separately in addition to code for primary procedure)
Sunset January 2016

(Use 0231T in conjunction with 0230T)

(For transforaminal epidural injections performed under fluoroscopy or CT, see 64479–64484)

(Do not report 0228T-0231T in conjunction with 76942, 76998, 76999)

**0232T**   Injection(s), platelet rich plasma, any site, including image guidance, harvesting and preparation when performed
Sunset January 2016

(Do not report 0232T in conjunction with 20550, 20551, 20600-20610, 20926, 76942, 77002, 77012, 77021, 86965)

(Do not report 38220-38230 for bone marrow aspiration for platelet rich stem cell injection. For bone marrow aspiration for platelet rich stem cell injection, use 0232T)

**0233T**   Skin advanced glycation endproducts (AGE) measurement by multi-wavelength fluorescent spectroscopy
Sunset January 2016

## Atherectomy (Open or Percutaneous) for Supra-Inguinal Arteries

Codes 0234T-0238T describe atherectomy performed by any method (eg, directional, rotational, laser) in arteries above the inguinal ligaments. These codes are structured differently than the codes describing atherectomy performed below the inguinal ligaments (37225, 37227, 37229, 37231, 37233, 37235).

These supra-inguinal atherectomy codes all include the surgical work of performing the atherectomy plus the radiological supervision and interpretation of the atherectomy. Unlike the atherectomy codes for infra-inguinal arteries, this set of Category III codes does not include accessing and selectively catheterizing the vessel, traversing the lesion, embolic protection if used, other intervention used to treat the same or other vessels, or closure of the arteriotomy by any method. These codes describe endovascular procedures performed percutaneously and/or through an open surgical exposure.

**0234T**   Transluminal peripheral atherectomy, open or percutaneous, including radiological supervision and interpretation; renal artery
Sunset January 2016

**0235T**   visceral artery (except renal), each vessel
Sunset January 2016

**0236T**   abdominal aorta
Sunset January 2016

**0237T**   brachiocephalic trunk and branches, each vessel
Sunset January 2016

**0238T**   iliac artery, each vessel
Sunset January 2016

**0239T**   Bioimpedance spectroscopy (BIS), measuring 100 frequencies or greater, direct measurement of extracellular fluid differences between the limbs
Sunset January 2016

**0240T**   Esophageal motility (manometric study of the esophagus and/or gastroesophageal junction) study with interpretation and report; with high resolution esophageal pressure topography
Sunset January 2016

(Do not report 0240T in conjunction with 91010 or 91013)

**+ 0241T**   with stimulation or perfusion during high resolution esophageal pressure topography study (eg, stimulant, acid or alkali perfusion) (List separately in addition to code for primary procedure)
Sunset January 2016

(Use 0241T in conjunction with 0240T)

(Do not report 0241T in conjunction with 91010 or 91013)

(Do not report 0241T more than once per session)

(To report esophageal motility studies without high resolution esophageal pressure topography, use 91010 and with stimulant or perfusion, use 91013)

(0242T has been deleted. To report, use 91112)

**0243T**   Intermittent measurement of wheeze rate for bronchodilator or bronchial-challenge diagnostic evaluation(s), with interpretation and report
Sunset January 2016

(Use 0243T once per 24 hour period)

(Do not report 0243T in conjunction with 0244T for the same 24 hour period)

**0244T**   Continuous measurement of wheeze rate during treatment assessment or during sleep for documentation of nocturnal wheeze and cough for diagnostic evaluation 3 to 24 hours, with interpretation and report
Sunset January 2016

**0245T**   Open treatment of rib fracture requiring internal fixation, unilateral; 1-2 ribs
Sunset January 2016

**0246T**   3-4 ribs
Sunset January 2016

**0247T**   5-6 ribs
Sunset January 2016

**0248T**   7 or more ribs
Sunset January 2016

**Category III**

**0249T** Ligation, hemorrhoidal vascular bundle(s), including ultrasound guidance
Sunset January 2016

(Do not report 0249T in conjunction with 46020, 46221, 46250-46262, 46600, 46945, 46946, 76872, 76942, 76998)

(0250T-0252T have been deleted. For airway sizing and insertion and removal of bronchial valve[s], see 31647-31649)

**0253T** Code is out of numerical sequence. See 0188T-0254T

**0254T** Endovascular repair of iliac artery bifurcation (eg, aneurysm, pseudoaneurysm, arteriovenous malformation, trauma) using bifurcated endoprosthesis from the common iliac artery into both the external and internal iliac artery, unilateral;
Sunset January 2016

**0255T** radiological supervision and interpretation
Sunset January 2016

▶(0256T has been deleted. To report, see 33361, 33362, 33363, 33364)◀

▶(0257T has been deleted. To report, see 33365, 33366)◀

▶(0258T has been deleted. To report, see 33365, 33366)◀

▶(0259T has been deleted. To report, see 33365, 33367, 33368, 33369)◀

▶(0260T, 0261T have been deleted. To report, see 99481, 99482)◀

**0262T** Implantation of catheter-delivered prosthetic pulmonary valve, endovascular approach
Sunset January 2017

(0262T includes all congenital cardiac catheterization[s], intraprocedural contrast injection[s], fluoroscopic radiological supervision and interpretation, and imaging guidance performed to complete the pulmonary valve procedure. Do not report 0262T in conjunction with 76000, 76001, 93530, 93563, 93566-93568)

(0262T includes percutaneous balloon angioplasty/valvuloplasty of the pulmonary valve/conduit. Do not report 0262T in conjunction with 92990)

▶(0262T includes stent deployment within the pulmonary conduit. Do not report 37236-37239 for stent placement within the pulmonary conduit. Report 37236-37239, 92928-92944 separately when cardiovascular stent placement is performed at a site separate from the prosthetic valve delivery site. Report 92997, 92998 separately when pulmonary artery angioplasty is performed at a site separate from the prosthetic valve delivery site, unless stenting also performed at that site.)◀

**0263T** Intramuscular autologous bone marrow cell therapy, with preparation of harvested cells, multiple injections, one leg, including ultrasound guidance, if performed; complete procedure including unilateral or bilateral bone marrow harvest
Sunset January 2017

(Do not report 0263T in conjunction with 38204-38242, 76942, 93925, 93926)

**0264T** complete procedure excluding bone marrow harvest
Sunset January 2017

(Do not report 0264T in conjunction with 38204-38242, 76942, 93925, 93926, 0265T)

**0265T** unilateral or bilateral bone marrow harvest only for intramuscular autologous bone marrow cell therapy
Sunset January 2017

(Do not report 0265T in conjunction with 38204-38242, 0264T. For complete procedure, use 0263T)

**0266T** Implantation or replacement of carotid sinus baroreflex activation device; total system (includes generator placement, unilateral or bilateral lead placement, intra-operative interrogation, programming, and repositioning, when performed)
Sunset January 2017

**0267T** lead only, unilateral (includes intra-operative interrogation, programming, and repositioning, when performed)
Sunset January 2017

(For bilateral lead implantation or replacement, use 0267T with modifier 50)

**0268T** pulse generator only (includes intra-operative interrogation, programming, and repositioning, when performed)
Sunset January 2017

(Do not report 0267T, 0268T in conjunction with 0266T, 0269T-0273T)

**0269T** Revision or removal of carotid sinus baroreflex activation device; total system (includes generator placement, unilateral or bilateral lead placement, intra-operative interrogation, programming, and repositioning, when performed)
Sunset January 2017

(Do not report 0269T in conjunction with 0266T-0268T, 0270T-0273T)

**0270T** lead only, unilateral (includes intra-operative interrogation, programming, and repositioning, when performed)
Sunset January 2017

(Do not report 0270T in conjunction with 0266T-0269T, 0271T-0273T)

(For bilateral lead removal, use 0270T with modifier 50)

(For removal of total carotid sinus baroreflex activation device, use 0269T)

⊙=Moderate sedation  ✚=Add-on code  ✗=FDA approval pending  #=Resequenced code  ○=Recycled/reinstated code

**0271T**     pulse generator only (includes intra-operative interrogation, programming, and repositioning, when performed)
Sunset January 2017

(Do not report 0271T in conjunction with 0266T-0270T, 0272T, 0273T)

(For removal and replacement, see 0266T, 0267T, 0268T)

**0272T**  Interrogation device evaluation (in person), carotid sinus baroreflex activation system, including telemetric iterative communication with the implantable device to monitor device diagnostics and programmed therapy values, with interpretation and report (eg, battery status, lead impedance, pulse amplitude, pulse width, therapy frequency, pathway mode, burst mode, therapy start/stop times each day);
Sunset January 2017

(Do not report 0272T in conjunction with 0266T-0271T, 0273T)

**0273T**     with programming
Sunset January 2017

(Do not report 0273T in conjunction with 0266T-0272T)

**0274T**  Percutaneous laminotomy/laminectomy (interlaminar approach) for decompression of neural elements, (with or without ligamentous resection, discectomy, facetectomy and/or foraminotomy), any method, under indirect image guidance (eg, fluoroscopic, CT), with or without the use of an endoscope, single or multiple levels, unilateral or bilateral; cervical or thoracic
Sunset January 2017

**0275T**     lumbar
Sunset January 2017

(For laminotomy/hemilaminectomy performed using an open and endoscopically-assisted approach, see 63020-63035)

(For percutaneous decompression of the nucleus pulposus of intervertebral disc utilizing needle based technique, use 62287)

(0276T, 0277T have been deleted. To report, see 31660, 31661)

**0278T**  Transcutaneous electrical modulation pain reprocessing (eg, scrambler therapy), each treatment session (includes placement of electrodes)
Sunset January 2017

(0279T, 0280T have been deleted. To report, see 86152, 86153)

**0281T**  Percutaneous transcatheter closure of the left atrial appendage with implant, including fluoroscopy, transseptal puncture, catheter placement(s), left atrial angiography, left atrial appendage angiography, radiological supervision and interpretation
Sunset January 2017

(Do not report 0281T in conjunction with 93462 [left heart catheterization by transseptal puncture])

(Report cardiac catheterization procedures [93451-93461, 93530-93533] separately for indications distinct from the left atrial appendage closure procedure)

(For left ventriculography performed by transseptal approach for indications distinct from the left atrial appendage closure procedure, use 93565)

(Do not report 0281T in conjunction with 93452, 93453, 93458-93461, 93531-93533 unless catheterization of the left ventricle is performed by a non-transseptal approach for indications distinct from the left atrial appendage closure procedure)

(Do not report 0281T in conjunction with 93451, 93453, 93456, 93460, 93461, 93530-93533 unless complete right heart catheterization is performed for indications distinct from the left atrial appendage closure procedure)

⊙ **0282T**  Percutaneous or open implantation of neurostimulator electrode array(s), subcutaneous (peripheral subcutaneous field stimulation), including imaging guidance, when performed, cervical, thoracic or lumbar; for trial, including removal at the conclusion of trial period
Sunset January 2017

⊙ **0283T**     permanent, with implantation of a pulse generator
Sunset January 2017

⊙ **0284T**  Revision or removal of pulse generator or electrodes, including imaging guidance, when performed, including addition of new electrodes, when performed
Sunset January 2017

**0285T**  Electronic analysis of implanted peripheral subcutaneous field stimulation pulse generator, with reprogramming when performed
Sunset January 2017

(Do not report 0282T-0285T in conjunction with 64550-64595, 77002, 77003, 95970-95973)

**0286T**  Near-infrared spectroscopy studies of lower extremity wounds (eg, for oxyhemoglobin measurement)
Sunset January 2017

**0287T**  Near-infrared guidance for vascular access requiring real-time digital visualization of subcutaneous vasculature for evaluation of potential access sites and vessel patency
Sunset January 2017

Category III

**0288T** Anoscopy, with delivery of thermal energy to the muscle of the anal canal (eg, for fecal incontinence)
Sunset January 2017

(Do not report 0288T in conjunction with 46600-46615)

**+ 0289T** Corneal incisions in the donor cornea created using a laser, in preparation for penetrating or lamellar keratoplasty (List separately in addition to code for primary procedure)
Sunset January 2017

(Use 0289T in conjunction with 65710, 65730, 65750, 65755)

**+ 0290T** Corneal incisions in the recipient cornea created using a laser, in preparation for penetrating or lamellar keratoplasty (List separately in addition to code for primary procedure)
Sunset January 2017

(Use 0290T in conjunction with 65710, 65730, 65750, 65755)

**⊙+ 0291T** Intravascular optical coherence tomography (coronary native vessel or graft) during diagnostic evaluation and/ or therapeutic intervention, including imaging supervision, interpretation, and report; initial vessel (List separately in addition to primary procedure)
Sunset January 2018

(Use 0291T in conjunction with cardiac catheterization codes 92920, 92924, 92928, 92933, 92937, 92941, 92943, 92975, 93454-93461, 93563, 93564)

(Intravascular optical coherence tomography services include all transducer manipulations and repositioning within the specific vessel being examined, both before and after therapeutic intervention [eg, stent placement])

**⊙+ 0292T** each additional vessel (List separately in addition to primary procedure)
Sunset January 2018

(Use 0292T in conjunction with 0291T)

(For intravascular spectroscopy, use 0205T)

**⊙ 0293T** Insertion of left atrial hemodynamic monitor; complete system, includes implanted communication module and pressure sensor lead in left atrium including transseptal access, radiological supervision and interpretation, and associated injection procedures, when performed
Sunset January 2018

(Do not report 0293T in conjunction with 93462, 93662)

**⊙+ 0294T** pressure sensor lead at time of insertion of pacing cardioverter-defibrillator pulse generator including radiological supervision and interpretation and associated injection procedures, when performed (List separately in addition to code for primary procedure)
Sunset January 2018

(Use 0294T in conjunction with 33230, 33231, 33240, 33262-33264, 33249)

(Do not report 0294T in conjunction with 93462, 93662)

(Do not report 0293T or 0294T in conjunction with 33202-33249, 93451-93453 unless performed for separate and distinct clinical indication other than for placement or calibration of left atrial hemodynamic monitoring system)

**0295T** External electrocardiographic recording for more than 48 hours up to 21 days by continuous rhythm recording and storage; includes recording, scanning analysis with report, review and interpretation
Sunset January 2018

**0296T** recording (includes connection and initial recording)
Sunset January 2018

**0297T** scanning analysis with report
Sunset January 2018

**0298T** review and interpretation
Sunset January 2018

(Do not report 0295T-0298T in conjunction with 93224-93272 for same monitoring period)

**0299T** Extracorporeal shock wave for integumentary wound healing, high energy, including topical application and dressing care; initial wound
Sunset January 2018

**+ 0300T** each additional wound (List separately in addition to code for primary procedure)
Sunset January 2018

(Use 0300T in conjunction with 0299T)

(Do not report 0300T in conjunction with 28890, 0101T, 0102T when treating same area)

**⊙ 0301T** Destruction/reduction of malignant breast tumor with externally applied focused microwave, including interstitial placement of disposable catheter with combined temperature monitoring probe and microwave focusing sensocatheter under ultrasound thermotherapy guidance
Sunset January 2018

(Do not report 0301T in conjunction with 76645, 76942, 76998, 77600-77615)

**⊙ 0302T** Insertion or removal and replacement of intracardiac ischemia monitoring system including imaging supervision and interpretation when performed and intra-operative interrogation and programming when performed; complete system (includes device and electrode)
Sunset January 2018

Category III

⊙ **0303T**     electrode only
Sunset January 2018

⊙ **0304T**     device only
Sunset January 2018

(Do not report 0302T-0304T in conjunction with 93000-93010)

**0305T**     Programming device evaluation (in person) of intracardiac ischemia monitoring system with iterative adjustment of programmed values, with analysis, review, and report
Sunset January 2018

(Do not report 0305T in conjunction with 93000-93010, 0302T-0304T, 0306T)

**0306T**     Interrogation device evaluation (in person) of intracardiac ischemia monitoring system with analysis, review, and report
Sunset January 2018

(Do not report 0306T in conjunction with 93000-93010, 0302T-0305T)

⊙ **0307T**     Removal of intracardiac ischemia monitoring device
Sunset January 2018

⊙ **0308T**     Insertion of ocular telescope prosthesis including removal of crystalline lens
Sunset January 2018

(Do not report 0308T in conjunction with 65800-65815, 66020, 66030, 66600-66635, 66761, 66825, 66982-66986, 69990)

✚ **0309T**     Arthrodesis, pre-sacral interbody technique, including disc space preparation, discectomy, with posterior instrumentation, with image guidance, includes bone graft, when performed, lumbar, L4-L5 interspace (List separately in addition to code for primary procedure)
Sunset January 2018

(Use 0309T in conjunction with 22586)

(Do not report 0309T in conjunction with 20930-20938, 22840, 22848, 72275, 77002, 77003, 77011, 77012)

**0310T**     Motor function mapping using non-invasive navigated transcranial magnetic stimulation (nTMS) for therapeutic treatment planning, upper and lower extremity
Sunset January 2018

(Do not report 0310T in conjunction with 95860-95870, 95928, 95929, 95939)

**0311T**     Non-invasive calculation and analysis of central arterial pressure waveforms with interpretation and report
Sunset January 2018

**0312T**     Vagus nerve blocking therapy (morbid obesity); laparoscopic implantation of neurostimulator electrode array, anterior and posterior vagal trunks adjacent to esophagogastric junction (EGJ), with implantation of pulse generator, includes programming
Sunset January 2018

**0313T**     laparoscopic revision or replacement of vagal trunk neurostimulator electrode array, including connection to existing pulse generator
Sunset January 2018

**0314T**     laparoscopic removal of vagal trunk neurostimulator electrode array and pulse generator
Sunset January 2018

**0315T**     removal of pulse generator
Sunset January 2018

**0316T**     replacement of pulse generator
Sunset January 2018

(Do not report 0315T in conjunction with 0316T)

**0317T**     neurostimulator pulse generator electronic analysis, includes reprogramming when performed
Sunset January 2018

(For implantation, revision, replacement, and/or removal of vagus [cranial] nerve neurostimulator electrode array and/or pulse generator for vagus nerve stimulation performed other than at the EGJ [eg, epilepsy], see 64568-64570)

(For analysis and/or [re]programming for vagus nerve stimulator, see 95970, 95974, 95975)

▶(0318T has been deleted. To report, use 33366)◀

## ▶Subcutaneous Implantable Defibrillator System◀

▶A subcutaneous implantable defibrillator system is an implantable technology that uses a subcutaneous pulse generator attached to a single subcutaneous electrode to treat ventricular tachyarrhythmias.

Use 0319T for insertion or replacement of a subcutaneous implantable defibrillator system, including pulse generator and lead. This code includes intraoperative interrogation, programming, skin pocket revision, and repositioning, when performed.

When the pulse generator or battery requires replacement, the existing pulse generator is removed and a new pulse generator is placed. For removal of pulse generator only without replacement, use 0322T. For removal of pulse generator with insertion of a new subcutaneous implantable defibrillator pulse generator without any replacement or insertion of a lead, use 0323T. For insertion of a new pulse generator when existing electrode (lead) is already in place and when no existing pulse generator is removed, use 0321T. When a pulse generator insertion or replacement involves the insertion or replacement of an electrode (lead), use system code 0319T. Removal of existing pulse generator (0322T) or removal of subcutaneous electrode (0324T) should be reported separately, when performed.

**Category III**

When electrode and/or pulse generator repositioning is performed intraoperatively during insertion or replacement of a pulse generator or electrode, 0325T is included. Do not report 0325T in conjunction with 0319T, 0320T, 0321T, 0322T, 0323T, 0324T.

Revision of skin pocket for subcutaneous implantable defibrillator when performed intraoperatively during insertion, replacement or repositioning of pulse generator and/or lead is included in 0319T, 0320T, 0321T, 0322T, 0323T, 0324T, and 0325T.

The subcutaneous implantable defibrillator device evaluation codes 0327T and 0328T may not be reported in conjunction with pulse generator and lead insertion or repositioning codes 0319T, 0320T, 0321T, 0322T, 0323T, 0324T, and 0325T.

Radiological supervision and interpretation related to the subcutaneous implantable defibrillator procedure is included in 0319T, 0320T, 0321T, 0322T, 0323T, 0324T, and 0325T. To report fluoroscopic guidance for diagnostic lead evaluation without lead insertion, replacement, or repositioning procedures, use 76000.◄

● **0319T** Insertion or replacement of subcutaneous implantable defibrillator system with subcutaneous electrode
Sunset January 2019

►(For removal and replacement of subcutaneous defibrillator system [pulse generator and electrode], report 0319T in conjunction with 0322T, 0324T)◄

● **0320T** Insertion of subcutaneous defibrillator electrode
Sunset January 2019

►(Do not report 0320T in conjunction with 0319T)◄

● **0321T** Insertion of subcutaneous implantable defibrillator pulse generator only with existing subcutaneous electrode
Sunset January 2019

►(Do not report 0321T in conjunction with 0322T, 0323T for removal and replacement of the subcutaneous defibrillator pulse generator)◄

►(For removal of pulse generator with insertion of a new subcutaneous implantable defibrillator pulse generator without any replacement or insertion of a lead, use 0323T)◄

● **0322T** Removal of subcutaneous implantable defibrillator pulse generator only
Sunset January 2019

►(Do not report 0322T in conjunction with 0321T, 0323T for removal and replacement of the subcutaneous defibrillator pulse generator)◄

►(For removal and replacement of subcutaneous defibrillator system [pulse generator and electrode], report 0322T in conjunction with 0319T, 0324T)◄

● **0323T** Removal of subcutaneous implantable defibrillator pulse generator with replacement of subcutaneous implantable defibrillator pulse generator only
Sunset January 2019

►(Do not report 0323T in conjunction with 0322T)◄

►(For removal of electrode[s] in conjunction with pulse generator removal or replacement, use 0324T in conjunction with 0322T, 0323T)◄

● **0324T** Removal of subcutaneous defibrillator electrode
Sunset January 2019

►(For removal and replacement of subcutaneous defibrillator system [pulse generator and electrode], report 0324T in conjunction with 0319T, 0322T)◄

● **0325T** Repositioning of subcutaneous implantable defibrillator electrode and/or pulse generator
Sunset January 2019

►(Do not report 0325T in conjunction with 0319T, 0320T, 0321T, 0322T, 0323T, 0324T)◄

● **0326T** Electrophysiologic evaluation of subcutaneous implantable defibrillator (includes defibrillation threshold evaluation, induction of arrhythmia, evaluation of sensing for arrhythmia termination, and programming or reprogramming of sensing or therapeutic parameters)
Sunset January 2019

►(Report 0326T separately during device insertion, replacement, or for follow-up device testing, when performed)◄

● **0327T** Interrogation device evaluation (in person) with analysis, review and report, includes connection, recording and disconnection per patient encounter, implantable subcutaneous lead defibrillator system
Sunset January 2019

►(Do not report 0327T in conjunction with pulse generator and lead insertion or repositioning codes 0319T, 0320T, 0321T, 0322T, 0323T, 0324T, 0325T, 0326T, 0328T)◄

►(For peri-procedural device evaluation and programming for evaluation of the implantable defibrillator to adjust device to settings appropriate for the patient prior to or after a surgery, procedure, or test, see 0327T, 0328T)◄

● **0328T** Programming device evaluation (in person) with iterative adjustment of the implantable device to test the function of the device and select optimal permanent programmed values with analysis, implantable subcutaneous lead defibrillator system
Sunset January 2019

►(Do not report 0328T in conjunction with pulse generator and lead insertion or repositioning codes 0319T, 0320T, 0321T, 0322T, 0323T, 0324T, 0325T, 0326T, 0327T)◄

● **0329T**    Monitoring of intraocular pressure for 24 hours or longer, unilateral or bilateral, with interpretation and report
Sunset January 2019

● **0330T**    Tear film imaging, unilateral or bilateral, with interpretation and report
Sunset January 2019

● **0331T**    Myocardial sympathetic innervation imaging, planar qualitative and quantitative assessment
Sunset January 2019

● **0332T**        with tomographic SPECT
Sunset January 2019

▶(For myocardial infarct avid imaging, see 78466, 78468, 78469)◀

● **0333T**    Visual evoked potential, screening of visual acuity, automated
Sunset January 2019

● **0334T**    Sacroiliac joint stabilization for arthrodesis, percutaneous or minimally invasive (indirect visualization), includes obtaining and applying autograft or allograft (structural or morselized), when performed, includes image guidance when performed (eg, CT or fluoroscopic)
Sunset January 2019

▶(For bilateral procedure, report 0334T with modifier 50)◀

⊙● **0335T**    Extra-osseous subtalar joint implant for talotarsal stabilization
Sunset January 2019

● **0336T**    Laparoscopy, surgical, ablation of uterine fibroid(s), including intraoperative ultrasound guidance and monitoring, radiofrequency
Sunset January 2019

▶(Do not report 0336T in conjunction with 76998, 0071T)◀

● **0337T**    Endothelial function assessment, using peripheral vascular response to reactive hyperemia, non-invasive (eg, brachial artery ultrasound, peripheral artery tonometry), unilateral or bilateral
Sunset January 2019

▶(Do not report 0337T in conjunction with 93922, 93923)◀

● **0338T**    Transcatheter renal sympathetic denervation, percutaneous approach including arterial puncture, selective catheter placement(s) renal artery(ies), fluoroscopy, contrast injection(s), intraprocedural roadmapping and radiological supervision and interpretation, including pressure gradient measurements, flush aortogram and diagnostic renal angiography when performed; unilateral
Sunset January 2019

● **0339T**        bilateral
Sunset January 2019

▶(Do not report 0338T, 0339T in conjunction with 36251, 36252, 36253, 36254)◀

---

▲=Revised code    ●=New code    ▶◀=Contains new or revised text    ⊘=Modifier 51 exempt                    American Medical Association    **455**

# Notes

⊙=Moderate sedation ✚=Add-on code ⚡=FDA approval pending #=Resequenced code ⊙=Recycled/reinstated code

Category III

# Appendix A

## Modifiers

This list includes all of the modifiers applicable to *CPT 2014* codes.

A modifier provides the means to report or indicate that a service or procedure that has been performed has been altered by some specific circumstance but not changed in its definition or code. Modifiers also enable health care professionals to effectively respond to payment policy requirements established by other entities.

**22** **Increased Procedural Services:** When the work required to provide a service is substantially greater than typically required, it may be identified by adding modifier 22 to the usual procedure code. Documentation must support the substantial additional work and the reason for the additional work (ie, increased intensity, time, technical difficulty of procedure, severity of patient's condition, physical and mental effort required). **Note:** This modifier should not be appended to an E/M service.

**23** **Unusual Anesthesia:** Occasionally, a procedure, which usually requires either no anesthesia or local anesthesia, because of unusual circumstances must be done under general anesthesia. This circumstance may be reported by adding modifier 23 to the procedure code of the basic service.

**24** **Unrelated Evaluation and Management Service by the Same Physician or Other Qualified Health Care Professional During a Postoperative Period:** The physician or other qualified health care professional may need to indicate that an evaluation and management service was performed during a postoperative period for a reason(s) unrelated to the original procedure. This circumstance may be reported by adding modifier 24 to the appropriate level of E/M service.

**25** **Significant, Separately Identifiable Evaluation and Management Service by the Same Physician or Other Qualified Health Care Professional on the Same Day of the Procedure or Other Service:** It may be necessary to indicate that on the day a procedure or service identified by a CPT code was performed, the patient's condition required a significant, separately identifiable E/M service above and beyond the other service provided or beyond the usual preoperative and postoperative care associated with the procedure that was performed. A significant, separately identifiable E/M service is defined or substantiated by documentation that satisfies the relevant criteria for the respective E/M service to be reported (see **Evaluation and Management Services Guidelines** for instructions on determining level of E/M service). The E/M service may be prompted by the symptom or condition for which the procedure and/or service was provided. As such, different diagnoses are not required for reporting of the E/M services

on the same date. This circumstance may be reported by adding modifier 25 to the appropriate level of E/M service. **Note:** This modifier is not used to report an E/M service that resulted in a decision to perform surgery. See modifier 57. For significant, separately identifiable non-E/M services, see modifier 59.

**26** **Professional Component:** Certain procedures are a combination of a physician or other qualified health care professional component and a technical component. When the physician or other qualified health care professional component is reported separately, the service may be identified by adding modifier 26 to the usual procedure number.

**32** **Mandated Services:** Services related to *mandated* consultation and/or related services (eg, third party payer, governmental, legislative or regulatory requirement) may be identified by adding modifier 32 to the basic procedure.

**33** **Preventive Services:** When the primary purpose of the service is the delivery of an evidence based service in accordance with a US Preventive Services Task Force A or B rating in effect and other preventive services identified in preventive services mandates (legislative or regulatory), the service may be identified by adding 33 to the procedure. For separately reported services specifically identified as preventive, the modifier should not be used.

**47** **Anesthesia by Surgeon:** Regional or general anesthesia provided by the surgeon may be reported by adding modifier 47 to the basic service. (This does not include local anesthesia.) **Note:** Modifier 47 would not be used as a modifier for the anesthesia procedures.

**50** **Bilateral Procedure:** Unless otherwise identified in the listings, bilateral procedures that are performed at the same session, should be identified by adding modifier 50 to the appropriate 5 digit code.

**51** **Multiple Procedures:** When multiple procedures, other than E/M services, Physical Medicine and Rehabilitation services or provision of supplies (eg, vaccines), are performed at the same session by the same individual, the primary procedure or service may be reported as listed. The additional procedure(s) or service(s) may be identified by appending modifier 51 to the additional procedure or service code(s). **Note:** This modifier should not be appended to designated "add-on" codes (see Appendix D).

**52** **Reduced Services:** Under certain circumstances a service or procedure is partially reduced or eliminated at the discretion of the physician or other qualified health care professional. Under these circumstances the service provided can be identified by its usual procedure number and the addition of modifier 52, signifying that the service is reduced. This provides a means of reporting reduced services without disturbing the identification of the basic service. **Note:** For hospital outpatient reporting of a

**Appendix A**

previously scheduled procedure/service that is partially reduced or cancelled as a result of extenuating circumstances or those that threaten the well-being of the patient prior to or after administration of anesthesia, see modifiers 73 and 74 (see modifiers approved for ASC hospital outpatient use).

**53** **Discontinued Procedure:** Under certain circumstances, the physician or other qualified health care professional may elect to terminate a surgical or diagnostic procedure. Due to extenuating circumstances or those that threaten the well being of the patient, it may be necessary to indicate that a surgical or diagnostic procedure was started but discontinued. This circumstance may be reported by adding modifier 53 to the code reported by the individual for the discontinued procedure. **Note:** This modifier is not used to report the elective cancellation of a procedure prior to the patient's anesthesia induction and/or surgical preparation in the operating suite. For outpatient hospital/ambulatory surgery center (ASC) reporting of a previously scheduled procedure/service that is partially reduced or cancelled as a result of extenuating circumstances or those that threaten the well being of the patient prior to or after administration of anesthesia, see modifiers 73 and 74 (see modifiers approved for ASC hospital outpatient use).

**54** **Surgical Care Only:** When 1 physician or other qualified health care professional performs a surgical procedure and another provides preoperative and/or postoperative management, surgical services may be identified by adding modifier 54 to the usual procedure number.

**55** **Postoperative Management Only:** When 1 physician or other qualified health care professional performed the postoperative management and another performed the surgical procedure, the postoperative component may be identified by adding modifier 55 to the usual procedure number.

**56** **Preoperative Management Only:** When 1 physician or other qualified health care professional performed the preoperative care and evaluation and another performed the surgical procedure, the preoperative component may be identified by adding modifier 56 to the usual procedure number.

**57** **Decision for Surgery:** An evaluation and management service that resulted in the initial decision to perform the surgery may be identified by adding modifier 57 to the appropriate level of E/M service.

**58** **Staged or Related Procedure or Service by the Same Physician or Other Qualified Health Care Professional During the Postoperative Period:** It may be necessary to indicate that the performance of a procedure or service during the postoperative period was: (a) planned or anticipated (staged); (b) more extensive than the original procedure; or (c) for therapy following a surgical procedure. This circumstance may be reported by adding modifier 58 to the staged or related procedure. **Note:** For treatment of a problem that requires a return to the operating/procedure room (eg, unanticipated clinical condition), see modifier 78.

**59** **Distinct Procedural Service:** Under certain circumstances, it may be necessary to indicate that a procedure or service was distinct or independent from other non-E/M services performed on the same day. Modifier 59 is used to identify procedures/services, other than E/M services, that are not normally reported together, but are appropriate under the circumstances. Documentation must support a different session, different procedure or surgery, different site or organ system, separate incision/excision, separate lesion, or separate injury (or area of injury in extensive injuries) not ordinarily encountered or performed on the same day by the same individual. However, when another already established modifier is appropriate it should be used rather than modifier 59. Only if no more descriptive modifier is available, and the use of modifier 59 best explains the circumstances, should modifier 59 be used. **Note:** Modifier 59 should not be appended to an E/M service. To report a separate and distinct E/M service with a non-E/M service performed on the same date, see modifier 25.

**62** **Two Surgeons:** When 2 surgeons work together as primary surgeons performing distinct part(s) of a procedure, each surgeon should report his/her distinct operative work by adding modifier 62 to the procedure code and any associated add-on code(s) for that procedure as long as both surgeons continue to work together as primary surgeons. Each surgeon should report the co-surgery once using the same procedure code. If additional procedure(s) (including add-on procedure(s) are performed during the same surgical session, separate code(s) may also be reported with modifier 62 added. **Note:** If a co-surgeon acts as an assistant in the performance of additional procedure(s), other than those reported with the modifier 62, during the same surgical session, those services may be reported using separate procedure code(s) with modifier 80 or modifier 82 added, as appropriate.

**63** **Procedure Performed on Infants less than 4 kg:** Procedures performed on neonates and infants up to a present body weight of 4 kg may involve significantly increased complexity and physician or other qualified health care professional work commonly associated with these patients. This circumstance may be reported by adding modifier 63 to the procedure number. **Note:** Unless otherwise designated, this modifier may only be appended to procedures/services listed in the 20005-69990 code series. Modifier 63 should not be appended to any CPT codes listed in the **Evaluation and Management Services, Anesthesia, Radiology, Pathology/Laboratory, or Medicine** sections.

**66** **Surgical Team:** Under some circumstances, highly complex procedures (requiring the concomitant services of several physicians or other qualified health care professionals, often of different specialties, plus other highly skilled, specially trained personnel, various types of complex equipment) are carried out under the "surgical team" concept. Such circumstances may be identified by each participating individual with the addition of modifier 66 to the basic procedure number used for reporting services.

**76    Repeat Procedure or Service by Same Physician or Other Qualified Health Care Professional:** It may be necessary to indicate that a procedure or service was repeated by the same physician or other qualified health care professional subsequent to the original procedure or service. This circumstance may be reported by adding modifier 76 to the repeated procedure or service. **Note:** This modifier should not be appended to an E/M service.

**77    Repeat Procedure by Another Physician or Other Qualified Health Care Professional:** It may be necessary to indicate that a basic procedure or service was repeated by another physician or other qualified health care professional subsequent to the original procedure or service. This circumstance may be reported by adding modifier 77 to the repeated procedure or service. **Note:** This modifier should not be appended to an E/M service.

**78    Unplanned Return to the Operating/Procedure Room by the Same Physician or Other Qualified Health Care Professional Following Initial Procedure for a Related Procedure During the Postoperative Period:** It may be necessary to indicate that another procedure was performed during the postoperative period of the initial procedure (unplanned procedure following initial procedure). When this procedure is related to the first, and requires the use of an operating/procedure room, it may be reported by adding modifier 78 to the related procedure. (For repeat procedures, see modifier 76.)

**79    Unrelated Procedure or Service by the Same Physician or Other Qualified Health Care Professional During the Postoperative Period:** The individual may need to indicate that the performance of a procedure or service during the postoperative period was unrelated to the original procedure. This circumstance may be reported by using modifier 79. (For repeat procedures on the same day, see modifier 76.)

**80    Assistant Surgeon:** Surgical assistant services may be identified by adding modifier 80 to the usual procedure number(s).

**81    Minimum Assistant Surgeon:** Minimum surgical assistant services are identified by adding modifier 81 to the usual procedure number.

**82    Assistant Surgeon (when qualified resident surgeon not available):** The unavailability of a qualified resident surgeon is a prerequisite for use of modifier 82 appended to the usual procedure code number(s).

**90    Reference (Outside) Laboratory:** When laboratory procedures are performed by a party other than the treating or reporting physician or other qualified health care professional, the procedure may be identified by adding modifier 90 to the usual procedure number.

**91    Repeat Clinical Diagnostic Laboratory Test:** In the course of treatment of the patient, it may be necessary to repeat the same laboratory test on the same day to obtain subsequent (multiple) test results. Under these circumstances, the laboratory test performed can be identified by its usual procedure number and the addition of modifier 91. **Note:** This modifier may not be used when tests are rerun to confirm initial results; due to testing problems with specimens or equipment; or for any other reason when a normal, one-time, reportable result is all that is required. This modifier may not be used when other code(s) describe a series of test results (eg, glucose tolerance tests, evocative/suppression testing). This modifier may only be used for laboratory test(s) performed more than once on the same day on the same patient.

**92    Alternative Laboratory Platform Testing:** When laboratory testing is being performed using a kit or transportable instrument that wholly or in part consists of a single use, disposable analytical chamber, the service may be identified by adding modifier 92 to the usual laboratory procedure code (HIV testing 86701-86703, and 87389). The test does not require permanent dedicated space, hence by its design may be hand carried or transported to the vicinity of the patient for immediate testing at that site, although location of the testing is not in itself determinative of the use of this modifier.

**99    Multiple Modifiers:** Under certain circumstances 2 or more modifiers may be necessary to completely delineate a service. In such situations modifier 99 should be added to the basic procedure, and other applicable modifiers may be listed as part of the description of the service.

# Anesthesia Physical Status Modifiers

The Physical Status modifiers are consistent with the American Society of Anesthesiologists ranking of patient physical status, and distinguishing various levels of complexity of the anesthesia service provided. All anesthesia services are reported by use of the anesthesia five-digit procedure code (00100-01999) with the appropriate physical status modifier appended.

Example: 00100-P1

Under certain circumstances, when another established modifier(s) is appropriate, it should be used in addition to the physical status modifier.

Example: 00100-P4-53

**Physical Status Modifier P1:** A normal healthy patient

**Physical Status Modifier P2:** A patient with mild systemic disease

**Physical Status Modifier P3:** A patient with severe systemic disease

**Physical Status Modifier P4:** A patient with severe systemic disease that is a constant threat to life

**Physical Status Modifier P5:** A moribund patient who is not expected to survive without the operation

**Physical Status Modifier P6:** A declared brain-dead patient whose organs are being removed for donor purposes

# Modifiers Approved for Ambulatory Surgery Center (ASC) Hospital Outpatient Use

## CPT Level I Modifiers

**25 Significant, Separately Identifiable Evaluation and Management Service by the Same Physician or Other Qualified Health Care Professional on the Same Day of the Procedure or Other Service:** It may be necessary to indicate that on the day a procedure or service identified by a CPT code was performed, the patient's condition required a significant, separately identifiable E/M service above and beyond the other service provided or beyond the usual preoperative and postoperative care associated with the procedure that was performed. A significant, separately identifiable E/M service is defined or substantiated by documentation that satisfies the relevant criteria for the respective E/M service to be reported (see **Evaluation and Management Services Guidelines** for instructions on determining level of E/M service). The E/M service may be prompted by the symptom or condition for which the procedure and/or service was provided. As such, different diagnoses are not required for reporting of the E/M services on the same date. This circumstance may be reported by adding modifier 25 to the appropriate level of E/M service. **Note:** This modifier is not used to report an E/M service that resulted in a decision to perform surgery. See modifier 57. For significant, separately identifiable non-E/M services, see modifier 59.

**27 Multiple Outpatient Hospital E/M Encounters on the Same Date:** For hospital outpatient reporting purposes, utilization of hospital resources related to separate and distinct E/M encounters performed in multiple outpatient hospital settings on the same date may be reported by adding modifier 27 to each appropriate level outpatient and/or emergency department E/M code(s). This modifier provides a means of reporting circumstances involving evaluation and management services provided by physician(s) in more than one (multiple) outpatient hospital setting(s) (eg, hospital emergency department, clinic). **Note:** This modifier is not to be used for physician reporting of multiple E/M services performed by the same physician on the same date. For physician reporting of all outpatient evaluation and management services provided by the same physician on the same date and performed in multiple outpatient setting(s) (eg, hospital emergency department, clinic), see **Evaluation and Management, Emergency Department, or Preventive Medicine Services** codes.

**50 Bilateral Procedure:** Unless otherwise identified in the listings, bilateral procedures that are performed at the same session, should be identified by adding modifier 50 to the appropriate 5 digit code.

**52 Reduced Services:** Under certain circumstances a service or procedure is partially reduced or eliminated at the discretion of the physician or other qualified health care professional. Under these circumstances the service provided can be identified by its usual procedure number and the addition of modifier 52, signifying that the service is reduced. This provides a means of reporting reduced services without disturbing the identification of the basic service. **Note:** For hospital outpatient reporting of a previously scheduled procedure/service that is partially reduced or cancelled as a result of extenuating circumstances or those that threaten the well-being of the patient prior to or after administration of anesthesia, see modifiers 73 and 74 (see modifiers approved for ASC hospital outpatient use).

**58 Staged or Related Procedure or Service by the Same Physician or Other Qualified Health Care Professional During the Postoperative Period:** It may be necessary to indicate that the performance of a procedure or service during the postoperative period was: (a) planned or anticipated (staged); (b) more extensive than the original procedure; or (c) for therapy following a surgical procedure. This circumstance may be reported by adding modifier 58 to the staged or related procedure. **Note:** For treatment of a problem that requires a return to the operating/procedure room (eg, unanticipated clinical condition), see modifier 78.

**59 Distinct Procedural Service:** Under certain circumstances, it may be necessary to indicate that a procedure or service was distinct or independent from other non-E/M services performed on the same day. Modifier 59 is used to identify procedures/services, other than E/M services, that are not normally reported together, but are appropriate under the circumstances. Documentation must support a different session, different procedure or surgery, different site or organ system, separate incision/excision, separate lesion, or separate injury (or area of injury in extensive injuries) not ordinarily encountered or performed on the same day by the same individual. However, when another already established modifier is appropriate it should be used rather than modifier 59. Only if no more descriptive modifier is available, and the use of modifier 59 best explains the circumstances, should modifier 59 be used. **Note:** Modifier 59 should not be appended to an E/M service. To report a separate and distinct E/M service with a non-E/M service performed on the same date, see modifier 25.

**73 Discontinued Out-Patient Hospital/Ambulatory Surgery Center (ASC) Procedure Prior to the Administration of Anesthesia:** Due to extenuating circumstances or those that threaten the well being of the patient, the physician may cancel a surgical or diagnostic procedure subsequent to the patient's surgical preparation (including sedation when provided, and being taken to the room where the procedure is to be performed), but prior to the administration of anesthesia (local, regional block(s) or general). Under these circumstances, the intended service that is prepared for but cancelled can be reported by its usual procedure number and the addition of modifier 73. **Note:** The elective cancellation of a service prior to the administration of anesthesia and/or surgical preparation of the patient should not be reported. For physician reporting of a discontinued procedure, see modifier 53.

**74**  **Discontinued Out-Patient Hospital/Ambulatory Surgery Center (ASC) Procedure After Administration of Anesthesia:** Due to extenuating circumstances or those that threaten the well being of the patient, the physician may terminate a surgical or diagnostic procedure after the administration of anesthesia (local, regional block(s), general) or after the procedure was started (incision made, intubation started, scope inserted, etc). Under these circumstances, the procedure started but terminated can be reported by its usual procedure number and the addition of modifier 74. **Note:** The elective cancellation of a service prior to the administration of anesthesia and/or surgical preparation of the patient should not be reported. For physician reporting of a discontinued procedure, see modifier 53.

**76**  **Repeat Procedure or Service by Same Physician or Other Qualified Health Care Professional:** It may be necessary to indicate that a procedure or service was repeated by the same physician or other qualified health care professional subsequent to the original procedure or service. This circumstance may be reported by adding modifier 76 to the repeated procedure or service. **Note:** This modifier should not be appended to an E/M service.

**77**  **Repeat Procedure by Another Physician or Other Qualified Health Care Professional:** It may be necessary to indicate that a basic procedure or service was repeated by another physician or other qualified health care professional subsequent to the original procedure or service. This circumstance may be reported by adding modifier 77 to the repeated procedure or service. **Note:** This modifier should not be appended to an E/M service.

**78**  **Unplanned Return to the Operating/Procedure Room by the Same Physician or Other Qualified Health Care Professional Following Initial Procedure for a Related Procedure During the Postoperative Period:** It may be necessary to indicate that another procedure was performed during the postoperative period of the initial procedure (unplanned procedure following initial procedure). When this procedure is related to the first, and requires the use of an operating/procedure room, it may be reported by adding modifier 78 to the related procedure. (For repeat procedures, see modifier 76.)

**79**  **Unrelated Procedure or Service by the Same Physician or Other Qualified Health Care Professional During the Postoperative Period:** The individual may need to indicate that the performance of a procedure or service during the postoperative period was unrelated to the original procedure. This circumstance may be reported by using modifier 79. (For repeat procedures on the same day, see modifier 76.)

**91**  **Repeat Clinical Diagnostic Laboratory Test:** In the course of treatment of the patient, it may be necessary to repeat the same laboratory test on the same day to obtain subsequent (multiple) test results. Under these circumstances, the laboratory test performed can be identified by its usual procedure number and the addition of modifier 91. **Note:** This modifier may not be used when tests are rerun to confirm initial results; due to testing problems with specimens or equipment; or for any other reason when a normal, one-time, reportable result is all that is required. This modifier may not be used when other code(s) describe a series of test results (eg, glucose tolerance tests, evocative/suppression testing). This modifier may only be used for laboratory test(s) performed more than once on the same day on the same patient.

## Level II (HCPCS/National) Modifiers

**E1**  **Upper left, eyelid**

**E2**  **Lower left, eyelid**

**E3**  **Upper right, eyelid**

**E4**  **Lower right, eyelid**

**F1**  **Left hand, second digit**

**F2**  **Left hand, third digit**

**F3**  **Left hand, fourth digit**

**F4**  **Left hand, fifth digit**

**F5**  **Right hand, thumb**

**F6**  **Right hand, second digit**

**F7**  **Right hand, third digit**

**F8**  **Right hand, fourth digit**

**F9**  **Right hand, fifth digit**

**FA**  **Left hand, thumb**

**Appendix A**

**GG** Performance and payment of a screening mammogram and diagnostic mammogram on the same patient, same day

**GH** Diagnostic mammogram converted from screening mammogram on same day

**LC** Left circumflex coronary artery

**LD** Left anterior descending coronary artery

**LM** Left main coronary artery

**LT** Left side (used to identify procedures performed on the left side of the body)

**QM** Ambulance service provided under arrangement by a provider of services

**QN** Ambulance service furnished directly by a provider of services

**RC** Right coronary artery

**RI** Ramus intermedius coronary artery

**RT** Right side (used to identify procedures performed on the right side of the body)

**T1** Left foot, second digit

**T2** Left foot, third digit

**T3** Left foot, fourth digit

**T4** Left foot, fifth digit

**T5** Right foot, great toe

**T6** Right foot, second digit

**T7** Right foot, third digit

**T8** Right foot, fourth digit

**T9** Right foot, fifth digit

**TA** Left foot, great toe

# Appendix B

## Summary of Additions, Deletions, and Revisions

Appendix B shows the actual changes that were made to the code descriptors. New codes appear with a bullet ( ● ) and are indicated as "Code Added." Revised codes are preceded with a triangle ( ▲ ). Within revised codes, the deleted language appears with a ~~strikethrough~~, while new text appears <u>underlined</u>. Codes with which moderate sedation would not be separately reported when performed at the same session by the same individual are denoted with the bullseye ( ⊙ ). The symbol ⁄ is used to identify codes for vaccines that are pending FDA approval (see **Appendix K**). The symbol # is used to identify codes that have been resequenced (see **Appendix N**). CPT add-on codes are annotated by the symbol ✚ (see **Appendix D**). The symbol ⊘ is used to identify codes that are exempt from the use of modifier 51 (see **Appendix E**).

### Evaluation and Management (E/M) Services Guidelines

#### Evaluation and Management

| | | |
|---|---|---|
| ● | **99446** | Code added |
| ● | **99447** | Code added |
| ● | **99448** | Code added |
| ● | **99449** | Code added |
| #✚● | **99481** | Code added |
| #✚● | **99482** | Code added |

### Surgery

| | | |
|---|---|---|
| ⊙● | **10030** | Code added |
| | ~~13150~~ | ~~Repair, complex, eyelids, nose, ears and/or lips; 1.0 cm or less~~ |
| ▲ | **13151** | Repair, complex, eyelids, nose, ears and/or lips; 1.1 cm to 2.5 cm |
| ▲ | **13152** | 2.6 cm to 7.5 cm |
| ✚▲ | **13153** | each additional 5 cm or less (List separately in addition to code for primary procedure) |
| ✚▲ | **15777** | Implantation of biologic implant (eg, acellular dermal matrix) for soft tissue reinforcement (~~egie~~, breast, trunk) (List separately in addition to code for primary procedure); |
| ● | **19081** | Code added |
| ✚● | **19082** | Code added |
| ● | **19083** | Code added |
| ✚● | **19084** | Code added |
| ● | **19085** | Code added |
| ✚● | **19086** | Code added |
| | ~~19102~~ | ~~percutaneous, needle core, using imaging guidance~~ |
| | ~~19103~~ | ~~percutaneous, automated vacuum assisted or rotating biopsy device, using imaging guidance~~ |
| ● | **19281** | Code added |
| ✚● | **19282** | Code added |
| ● | **19283** | Code added |
| ✚● | **19284** | Code added |
| ● | **19285** | Code added |
| ✚● | **19286** | Code added |
| ● | **19287** | Code added |
| ✚● | **19288** | Code added |
| | ~~19290~~ | ~~Preoperative placement of needle localization wire, breast;~~ |
| | ~~19291~~ | ~~each additional lesion (List separately in addition to code for primary procedure)~~ |
| | ~~19295~~ | ~~Image guided placement, metallic localization clip, percutaneous, during breast biopsy/aspiration (List separately in addition to code for primary procedure);~~ |
| ▲ | **21015** | Radical resection of tumor (eg, ~~malignant neoplasm~~<u>sarcoma</u>), soft tissue of face or scalp; less than 2 cm |
| ▲ | **21016** | 2 cm or greater |
| ▲ | **21557** | Radical resection of tumor (eg, ~~malignant neoplasm~~<u>sarcoma</u>), soft tissue of neck or anterior thorax; less than 5 cm |
| ▲ | **21558** | 5 cm or greater |
| ▲ | **21935** | Radical resection of tumor (eg, ~~malignant neoplasm~~<u>sarcoma</u>), soft tissue of back or flank; less than 5 cm |
| ▲ | **21936** | 5 cm or greater |
| ▲ | **22904** | Radical resection of tumor (eg, ~~malignant neoplasm~~<u>sarcoma</u>), soft tissue of abdominal wall; less than 5 cm |
| ▲ | **22905** | 5 cm or greater |
| ▲ | **23077** | Radical resection of tumor (eg, ~~malignant neoplasm~~<u>sarcoma</u>), soft tissue of shoulder area; less than 5 cm |
| ▲ | **23078** | 5 cm or greater |
| | ~~23331~~ | ~~deep (eg, Neer hemiarthroplasty removal)~~ |
| | ~~23332~~ | ~~complicated (eg, total shoulder)~~ |
| ● | **23333** | Code added |
| ● | **23334** | Code added |
| ● | **23335** | Code added |
| ▲ | **24077** | Radical resection of tumor (eg, ~~malignant neoplasm~~<u>sarcoma</u>), soft tissue of upper arm or elbow area; less than 5 cm |
| ▲ | **24079** | 5 cm or greater |
| ▲ | **24160** | ~~Implant removal~~<u>Removal of prosthesis, includes debridement and synovectomy when performed</u>; ~~elbow joint~~<u>humeral **and** ulnar components</u> |
| ▲ | **24164** | radial head |
| ▲ | **25077** | Radical resection of tumor (eg, ~~malignant neoplasm~~<u>sarcoma</u>), soft tissue of forearm and/or wrist area; less than 3 cm |
| ▲ | **25078** | 3 cm or greater |
| ▲ | **26117** | Radical resection of tumor (eg, ~~malignant neoplasm~~<u>sarcoma</u>), soft tissue of hand or finger; less than 3 cm |

▲ 26118    3 cm or greater

▲ 27049    Radical resection of tumor (eg, ~~malignant neoplasm~~sarcoma), soft tissue of pelvis and hip area; less than 5 cm

#▲ 27059    5 cm or greater

#▲ 27329    Radical resection of tumor (eg, ~~malignant neoplasm~~sarcoma), soft tissue of thigh or knee area; less than 5 cm

▲ 27364    5 cm or greater

▲ 27615    Radical resection of tumor (eg, ~~malignant neoplasm~~sarcoma), soft tissue of leg or ankle area; less than 5 cm

▲ 27616    5 cm or greater

▲ 28046    Radical resection of tumor (eg, ~~malignant neoplasm~~sarcoma), soft tissue of foot or toe; less than 3 cm

▲ 28047    3 cm or greater

~~32201~~    ~~with percutaneous drainage of abscess or cyst~~

⊙▲ 33222    ~~Revision or relocation~~Relocation of skin pocket for pacemaker;

⊙▲ 33223    ~~Revision~~Relocation of skin pocket for cardioverter-defibrillator;

⊙▲ 33282    Implantation of patient-activated cardiac event recorder

⊙▲ 33284    Removal of an implantable, patient-activated cardiac event recorder

● 33366    Code added

● 34841    Code added

● 34842    Code added

● 34843    Code added

● 34844    Code added

● 34845    Code added

● 34846    Code added

● 34847    Code added

● 34848    Code added

~~37204~~    ~~Transcatheter occlusion or embolization (eg, for tumor destruction, to achieve hemostasis, to occlude a vascular malformation), percutaneous, any method, non-central nervous system, non-head or neck;~~

~~37205~~    ~~Transcatheter placement of an intravascular stent(s) (except coronary, carotid, vertebral, iliac, and lower extremity arteries), percutaneous; initial vessel~~

~~37206~~    ~~each additional vessel (List separately in addition to code for primary procedure)~~

~~37207~~    ~~Transcatheter placement of an intravascular stent(s) (except coronary, carotid, vertebral, iliac and lower extremity arteries), open; initial vessel~~

~~37208~~    ~~Transcatheter placement of an intravascular stent(s) (except coronary, carotid, vertebral, iliac and lower extremity arteries), open; each additional vessel (List separately in addition to code for primary procedure)~~

~~37210~~    ~~Uterine fibroid embolization (UFE, embolization of the uterine arteries to treat uterine fibroids, leiomyomata), percutaneous approach inclusive of vascular access, vessel selection, embolization, and all radiological supervision and interpretation, intraprocedural roadmapping, and imaging guidance necessary to complete the procedure;~~

● 37217    Code added

⊙● 37236    Code added

⊙+● 37237    Code added

⊙● 37238    Code added

⊙+● 37239    Code added

⊙● 37241    Code added

⊙● 37242    Code added

⊙● 37243    Code added

⊙● 37244    Code added

~~42802~~    ~~hypopharynx~~

● 43191    Code added

● 43192    Code added

● 43193    Code added

● 43194    Code added

● 43195    Code added

● 43196    Code added

● 43197    Code added

● 43198    Code added

⊙▲ 43200    Esophagoscopy, ~~rigid or~~ flexible, transoral; diagnostic, ~~with or without~~including collection of specimen(s) by brushing or washing, when performed (separate procedure)

⊙▲ 43201    with directed submucosal injection(s), any substance

⊙▲ 43202    with biopsy, single or multiple

⊙▲ 43204    with injection sclerosis of esophageal varices

⊙▲ 43205    with band ligation of esophageal varices

⊙▲ 43206    with optical endomicroscopy

⊙▲ 43215    with removal of foreign body

⊙▲ 43216    with removal of tumor(s), polyp(s), or other lesion(s) by hot biopsy forceps or bipolar cautery

⊙▲ 43217    with removal of tumor(s), polyp(s), or other lesion(s) by snare technique

#⊙● 43211    Code added

~~43219~~    ~~with insertion of plastic tube or stent~~

#⊙● 43212    Code added

⊙▲ 43220    with transendoscopic balloon dilation (less than 30 mm diameter)

#⊙● 43213    Code added

#⊙● 43214    Code added

⊙▲ 43226    with insertion of guide wire followed by ~~dilation~~passage of dilator(s) over guide wire

⊙▲ 43227    with control of bleeding ~~(eg, injection, bipolar cautery, unipolar cautery, laser, heater probe, stapler, plasma coagulator)~~ any method

~~43228~~    ~~with ablation of tumor(s), polyp(s), or other lesion(s), not amenable to removal by hot biopsy forceps, bipolar cautery or snare technique~~

⊙● 43229    Code added

⊙▲ 43231    with endoscopic ultrasound examination

⊙▲ 43232    with transendoscopic ultrasound-guided intramural or transmural fine needle aspiration/biopsy(s)

⊙▲ **43235** ~~Upper gastrointestinal endoscopy including esophagus~~Esophagogastroduodenoscopy, ~~stomach~~flexible, ~~and either the duodenum and/or jejunum as appropriate~~transoral; diagnostic, ~~with or without~~including collection of specimen(s) by brushing or washing, when performed (separate procedure)

⊙▲ **43236** with directed submucosal injection(s), any substance

⊙▲ **43237** with endoscopic ultrasound examination limited to the esophagus, stomach or duodenum, and adjacent structures

⊙▲ **43238** with transendoscopic ultrasound-guided intramural or transmural fine needle aspiration/biopsy(s), esophagus (includes endoscopic ultrasound examination limited to the esophagus, stomach or duodenum, and adjacent structures)

⊙▲ **43239** with biopsy, single or multiple

⊙▲ **43240** with transmural drainage of pseudocyst (includes placement of transmural drainage catheter[s]/stent[s], when performed, and endoscopic ultrasound, when performed)

⊙▲ **43241** with ~~transendoscopic~~insertion of intraluminal tube or catheter ~~placement~~

⊙▲ **43242** with transendoscopic ultrasound-guided intramural or transmural fine needle aspiration/biopsy(s) (includes endoscopic ultrasound examination of the esophagus, stomach, and either the duodenum ~~and/or~~ a surgically altered stomach where the jejunum ~~as appropriate~~is examined distal to the anastomosis)

⊙▲ **43243** with injection sclerosis of esophageal ~~and/or~~ gastric varices

⊙▲ **43244** with band ligation of esophageal ~~and/or~~ gastric varices

⊙▲ **43245** with dilation of gastric ~~outlet for obstruction~~/duodenal stricture(s) (eg, balloon, ~~guide wire~~, bougie)

⊙▲ **43246** with directed placement of percutaneous gastrostomy tube

⊙▲ **43247** with removal of foreign body

⊙▲ **43248** with insertion of guide wire followed by ~~dilation~~passage of dilator(s) through esophagus over guide wire

⊙▲ **43249** with transendoscopic balloon dilation of esophagus (less than 30 mm diameter)

#⊙● **43233** Code added

⊙▲ **43250** with removal of tumor(s), polyp(s), or other lesion(s) by hot biopsy forceps or bipolar cautery

⊙▲ **43251** with removal of tumor(s), polyp(s), or other lesion(s) by snare technique

⊙▲ **43252** with optical endomicroscopy

⊙● **43253** Code added

⊙● **43254** Code added

⊙▲ **43255** with control of bleeding, any method

**43256** ~~with transendoscopic stent placement (includes predilation)~~

#⊙● **43266** Code added

⊙▲ **43257** with delivery of thermal energy to the muscle of lower esophageal sphincter and/or gastric cardia, for treatment of gastroesophageal reflux disease

**43258** ~~with ablation of tumor(s), polyp(s), or other lesion(s) not amenable to removal by hot biopsy forceps, bipolar cautery or snare technique~~

#⊙● **43270** Code added

⊙▲ **43259** with endoscopic ultrasound examination, including the esophagus, stomach, and either the duodenum ~~and/or~~ a surgically altered stomach where the jejunum ~~as appropriate~~is examined distal to the anastomosis

⊙▲ **43260** Endoscopic retrograde cholangiopancreatography (ERCP); diagnostic, ~~with or without~~including collection of specimen(s) by brushing or washing, when performed (separate procedure)

⊙▲ **43263** with pressure measurement of sphincter of Oddi ~~(pancreatic duct or common bile duct)~~

⊙▲ **43264** with ~~endoscopic retrograde~~removal of ~~calculus~~calculi/~~calculi~~debris from biliary ~~and/or~~pancreatic duct(s)

⊙▲ **43265** with ~~endoscopic retrograde~~destruction, ~~lithotripsy~~ of calculus/calculi, any method (eg, mechanical, electrohydraulic, lithotripsy)

**43267** ~~with endoscopic retrograde insertion of nasobiliary or nasopancreatic drainage tube~~

**43268** ~~with endoscopic retrograde insertion of tube or stent into bile or pancreatic duct~~

#⊙● **43274** Code added

**43269** ~~with endoscopic retrograde removal of foreign body and/or change of tube or stent~~

**43271** ~~with endoscopic retrograde balloon dilation of ampulla, biliary and/or pancreatic duct(s)~~

**43272** ~~with ablation of tumor(s), polyp(s), or other lesion(s) not amenable to removal by hot biopsy forceps, bipolar cautery or snare technique~~

#⊙● **43275** Code added

#⊙● **43276** Code added

#⊙● **43277** Code added

#⊙● **43278** Code added

⊙+▲ **43273** Endoscopic cannulation of papilla with direct visualization of pancreatic/common bile ~~duct(s) and/or pancreatic~~duct(s) (List separately in addition to code(s) for primary procedure)

**43456** ~~Dilation of esophagus, by balloon or dilator, retrograde;~~

**43458** ~~Dilation of esophagus with balloon (30 mm diameter or larger) for achalasia;~~

**44901** ~~percutaneous~~

**47011** ~~for percutaneous drainage of abscess or cyst, 1 or 2 stages~~

▲ **47552** Biliary endoscopy, percutaneous via T-tube or other tract; diagnostic, with ~~or without~~collection of specimen(s) by brushing and/or washing, when performed (separate procedure)

**48511** ~~percutaneous~~

**49021** ~~percutaneous~~

**49041** ~~percutaneous~~

**49061** ~~percutaneous~~

⊙● **49405** Code added

⊙● **49406** Code added

⊙● **49407** Code added

**50021** ~~percutaneous~~

#● **52356** Code added

**58823** ~~Drainage of pelvic abscess, transvaginal or transrectal approach, percutaneous (eg, ovarian, pericolic);~~

**64613** ~~neck muscle(s) (eg, for spasmodic torticollis, spasmodic dysphonia)~~

**64614** ~~extremity and/or trunk muscle(s) (eg, for dystonia, cerebral palsy, multiple sclerosis)~~

● 64616    Code added

● 64617    Code added

● 64642    Code added

+● 64643    Code added

● 64644    Code added

+● 64645    Code added

● 64646    Code added

● 64647    Code added

▲ 65778    Placement of amniotic membrane on the ocular surface ~~for wound healing; self-retaining~~without sutures

▲ 65779    single layer, sutured

● 66183    Code added

▲ 69210    Removal impacted cerumen ~~(separate procedure)~~requiring instrumentation, ~~1 or both ears~~unilateral

## Radiology

▲ 72040    Radiologic examination, spine, cervical; 2 or 3 views ~~or less~~

75960    ~~Transcatheter introduction of intravascular stent(s) (except coronary, carotid, vertebral, iliac, and lower extremity artery), percutaneous and/or open, radiological supervision and interpretation, each vessel;~~

77031    ~~Stereotactic localization guidance for breast biopsy or needle placement (eg, for wire localization or for injection), each lesion, radiological supervision and interpretation;~~

77032    ~~Mammographic guidance for needle placement, breast (eg, for wire localization or for injection), each lesion, radiological supervision and interpretation;~~

+● 77293    Code added

#▲ 77295    ~~Therapeutic radiology simulation~~3-dimensional radiotherapy plan, including dose ~~aided field setting~~volume histograms; ~~3-dimensional~~

## Pathology and Laboratory

● 80155    Code added

● 80159    Code added

● 80169    Code added

● 80171    Code added

● 80175    Code added

● 80177    Code added

● 80180    Code added

● 80183    Code added

● 80199    Code added

● 80203    Code added

#● 81287    Code added

▲ 81371    HLA-A, -B, and -DRB1~~/3/4/5~~ (eg, verification typing)

▲ 81376    one locus (eg, ~~HLA-DRB1/3/4/5, -DQB1, -DQA1, -DPB1, or -DPA1),~~(eg, HLA-DRB1, -DRB3/4/5, -DQB1, -DQA1, -DPB1, or -DPA1), each

▲ 81382    HLA Class II typing, high resolution (ie, alleles or allele groups); one locus (eg, HLA-DRB1, -DRB3, ~~-DRB4, -DRB5~~/4/5, -DQB1, -DQA1, -DPB1, or -DPA1), each

▲ 81400    Molecular pathology procedure, Level 1 (eg, identification of single germline variant [eg, SNP] by techniques such as restriction enzyme digestion or melt curve analysis)

*~~ABCC8 (ATP-binding cassette, sub-family C [CFTR/MRP], member 8)~~(eg, familial hyperinsulinism), F1388del variant*

*ACADM (acyl-CoA dehydrogenase, C-4 to C-12 straight chain, MCAD)(eg, medium chain acyl dehydrogenase deficiency), K304E variant*

*ACE (angiotensin converting enzyme)(eg, hereditary blood pressure regulation), insertion/deletion variant*

*AGTR1 (angiotensin II receptor, type 1)(eg, essential hypertension), 1166A>C variant*

*BCKDHA (branched chain keto acid dehydrogenase E1, alpha polypeptide)(eg, maple syrup urine disease, type 1A), Y438N variant*

*CCR5 (chemokine C-C motif receptor 5)(eg, HIV resistance), 32-bp deletion mutation/794 825del32 deletion*

*CLRN1 (clarin 1)(eg, Usher syndrome, type 3), N48K variant*

*DPYD (dihydropyrimidine dehydrogenase)(eg, 5-fluorouracil/5-FU and capecitabine drug metabolism), IVS14+1G>A variant*

*F2 (coagulation factor 2)(eg, hereditary hypercoagulability), 1199G>A variant*

*F5 (coagulation factor V)(eg, hereditary hypercoagulability), HR2 variant*

*F7 (coagulation factor VII [serum prothrombin conversion accelerator])(eg, hereditary hypercoagulability), R353Q variant*

*F13B (coagulation factor XIII, B polypeptide)(eg, hereditary hypercoagulability), V34L variant*

*FGB (fibrinogen beta chain)(eg, hereditary ischemic heart disease), -455G>A variant*

*FGFR1 (fibroblast growth factor receptor 1)(eg, Pfeiffer syndrome type 1, craniosynostosis), P252R variant*

*FGFR3 (fibroblast growth factor receptor 3)(eg, Muenke syndrome), P250R variant*

*FKTN (fukutin)(eg, Fukuyama congenital muscular dystrophy), retrotransposon insertion variant*

*GNE (glucosamine [UDP-N-acetyl]-2-epimerase/N-acetylmannosamine kinase)(eg, inclusion body myopathy 2 [IBM2], Nonaka myopathy), M712T variant*

*Human Platelet Antigen 1 genotyping (HPA-1), ITGB3 (integrin, beta 3 [platelet glycoprotein IIIa], antigen CD61 [GPIIIa])(eg, neonatal alloimmune thrombocytopenia [NAIT], post-transfusion purpura), HPA-1a/b (L33P)*

*Human Platelet Antigen 2 genotyping (HPA-2), GP1BA (glycoprotein Ib [platelet], alpha polypeptide [GPIba])(eg, neonatal alloimmune thrombocytopenia [NAIT], post-transfusion purpura), HPA-2a/b (T145M)*

*Human Platelet Antigen 3 genotyping (HPA-3), ITGA2B (integrin, alpha 2b [platelet glycoprotein IIb of IIb/IIIa complex], antigen CD41 [GPIIb])(eg, neonatal alloimmune thrombocytopenia [NAIT], post-transfusion purpura), HPA-3a/b (I843S)*

*Human Platelet Antigen 4 genotyping (HPA-4), ITGB3 (integrin, beta 3 [platelet glycoprotein IIIa], antigen CD61 [GPIIIa])(eg, neonatal alloimmune thrombocytopenia [NAIT], post-transfusion purpura), HPA 4a/b (R143Q)*

*Human Platelet Antigen 5 genotyping (HPA-5), ITGA2 (integrin, alpha 2 [CD49B, alpha 2 subunit of VLA-2 receptor] [GPIa])* (eg, neonatal alloimmune thrombocytopenia [NAIT], post-transfusion purpura), HPA-5a/b (K505E)

*Human Platelet Antigen 6 genotyping (HPA-6w), ITGB3 (integrin, beta 3 [platelet glycoprotein IIIa, antigen CD61] [GPIIIa])* (eg, neonatal alloimmune thrombocytopenia [NAIT], post-transfusion purpura), HPA-6a/b (R489Q)

*Human Platelet Antigen 9 genotyping (HPA-9w), ITGA2B (integrin, alpha 2b [platelet glycoprotein IIb of IIb/IIIa complex, antigen CD41] [GPIIb])* (eg, neonatal alloimmune thrombocytopenia [NAIT], post-transfusion purpura), HPA-9a/b (V837M)

*Human Platelet Antigen 15 genotyping (HPA-15), CD109 (CD109 molecule)* (eg, neonatal alloimmune thrombocytopenia [NAIT], post-transfusion purpura), HPA-15a/b (S682Y)

*IL28B (interleukin 28B [interferon, lambda 3])* (eg, drug response), rs12979860 variant

*IVD (isovaleryl-CoA dehydrogenase)* (eg, isovaleric acidemia), A282V variant

*LCT (lactase-phlorizin hydrolase)* (eg, lactose intolerance), 13910 C>T variant

*NEB (nebulin)* (eg, nemaline myopathy 2), exon 55 deletion variant

*PCDH15 (protocadherin-related 15)* (eg, Usher syndrome type 1F), R245X variant

*SERPINE1 (serpine peptidase inhibitor clade E, member 1, plasminogen activator inhibitor -1, PAI-1)* (eg, thrombophilia), 4G variant

*SHOC2 (soc-2 suppressor of clear homolog)* (eg, Noonan-like syndrome with loose anagen hair), S2G variant

*SLCO1B1 (solute carrier organic anion transporter family, member 1B1)* (eg, adverse drug reaction), V174A variant

*SMN1 (survival of motor neuron 1, telomeric)* (eg, spinal muscular atrophy), exon 7 deletion

*SRY (sex determining region Y)* (eg, 46,XX testicular disorder of sex development, gonadal dysgenesis), gene analysis

*TOR1A (torsin family 1, member A [torsin A])* (eg, early-onset primary dystonia [DYT1]), 907_909delGAG (904_906delGAG) variant

▲ 81401 Molecular pathology procedure, Level 2 (eg, 2-10 SNPs, 1 methylated variant, or 1 somatic variant [typically using nonsequencing target variant analysis], or detection of a dynamic mutation disorder/triplet repeat)

*ABCC8 (ATP-binding cassette, sub-family C [CFTR/MRP], member 8)* (eg, familial hyperinsulinism), common variants (eg, c.3898-9G>A [c.3992-9G>A], F1388del)

*ABL (c-abl oncogene 1, receptor tyrosine kinase)* (eg, acquired imatinib resistance), T315I variant

*ACADM (acyl-CoA dehydrogenase, C-4 to C-12 straight chain, MCAD)* (eg, medium chain acyl dehydrogenase deficiency), commons variants (eg, K304E, Y42H)

*ADRB2 (adrenergic beta-2 receptor surface)* (eg, drug metabolism), common variants (eg, G16R, Q27E)

*AFF2 (AF4/FMR2 family, member 2 [FMR2])* (eg, fragile X mental retardation 2 [FRAXE]), evaluation to detect abnormal (eg, expanded) alleles

APOB (apolipoprotein B) (eg, familial hypercholesterolemia type B), common variants (eg, R3500Q, R3500W)

*APOE (apolipoprotein E)* (eg, hyperlipoproteinemia type III, cardiovascular disease, Alzheimer disease), common variants (eg, *2, *3, *4)

*AR (androgen receptor)* (eg, spinal and bulbar muscular atrophy, Kennedy disease, X chromosome inactivation), characterization of alleles (eg, expanded size or methylation status)

*ATN1 (atrophin 1)* (eg, dentatorubral-pallidoluysian atrophy), evaluation to detect abnormal (eg, expanded) alleles

*ATXN1 (ataxin 1)* (eg, spinocerebellar ataxia), evaluation to detect abnormal (eg, expanded) alleles

*ATXN2 (ataxin 2)* (eg, spinocerebellar ataxia), evaluation to detect abnormal (eg, expanded) alleles

*ATXN3 (ataxin 3)* (eg, spinocerebellar ataxia, Machado-Joseph disease), evaluation to detect abnormal (eg, expanded) alleles

*ATXN7 (ataxin 7)* (eg, spinocerebellar ataxia), evaluation to detect abnormal (eg, expanded) alleles

*ATXN8OS (ATXN8 opposite strand [non-protein coding])* (eg, spinocerebellar ataxia), evaluation to detect abnormal (eg, expanded) alleles

*ATXN10 (ataxin 10)* (eg, spinocerebellar ataxia), evaluation to detect abnormal (eg, expanded) alleles

*CACNA1A (calcium channel, voltage-dependent, P/Q type, alpha 1A subunit)* (eg, spinocerebellar ataxia), evaluation to detect abnormal (eg, expanded) alleles

*CBFB/MYH11 (inv(16))* (eg, acute myeloid leukemia), qualitative, and quantitative, if performed

*CBS (cystathionine-beta-synthase)* (eg, homocystinuria, cystathionine beta-synthase deficiency), common variants (eg, I278T, G307S)

*CCND1/IGH (BCL1/IgH, t(11;14))* (eg, mantle cell lymphoma) translocation analysis, major breakpoint, qualitative, and quantitative, if performed

*CFH/ARMS2 (complement factor H/age-related maculopathy susceptibility 2)* (eg, macular degeneration), common variants (eg, Y402H [CFH], A69S [ARMS2])

*CNBP (CCHC-type zinc finger, nucleic acid binding protein)* (eg, myotonic dystrophy type 2), evaluation to detect abnormal (eg, expanded) alleles

*CSTB (cystatin B [stefin B])* (eg, Unverricht-Lundborg disease), evaluation to detect abnormal (eg, expanded) alleles

*CYP3A4 (cytochrome P450, family 3, subfamily A, polypeptide 4)* (eg, drug metabolism), common variants (eg, *2, *3, *4, *5, *6)

*CYP3A5 (cytochrome P450, family 3, subfamily A, polypeptide 5)* (eg, drug metabolism), common variants (eg, *2, *3, *4, *5, *6)

*DMPK (dystrophia myotonica-protein kinase)* (eg, myotonic dystrophy, type 1), evaluation to detect abnormal (eg, expanded) alleles

*E2A/PBX1 (t(1;19))* (eg, acute lymphocytic leukemia), translocation analysis, qualitative, and quantitative, if performed

*EML4/ALK (inv(2))* (eg, non-small cell lung cancer), translocation or inversion analysis

*ETV6/NTRK3 (t(12;15))* (eg, congenital/infantile fibrosarcoma), translocation analysis, qualitative, and quantitative, if performed

*ETV6/RUNX1 (t(12;21))* (eg, acute lymphocytic leukemia), translocation analysis, qualitative, and quantitative, if performed

*EWSR1/ATF1 (t(12;22))* (eg, clear cell sarcoma), translocation analysis, qualitative, and quantitative, if performed

**Appendix B**

*EWSR1/ERG (t(21;22))* (eg, Ewing sarcoma/peripheral neuroectodermal tumor), translocation analysis, qualitative, and quantitative, if performed

*EWSR1/FLI1 (t(11;22))* (eg, Ewing sarcoma/peripheral neuroectodermal tumor), translocation analysis, qualitative, and quantitative, if performed

*EWSR1/WT1 (t(11;22))* (eg, ~~Ewing sarcoma/peripheral neuroectodermal~~desmoplastic small round cell tumor), translocation analysis, qualitative, and quantitative, if performed

*F11 (coagulation factor XI)* (eg, coagulation disorder), common variants (eg, E117X [Type II], F283L [Type III], IVS14del14, and IVS14+1G>A [Type I])

*FGFR3 (fibroblast growth factor receptor 3)* (eg, achondroplasia, hypochondroplasia), common variants (eg, 1138G>A, 1138G>C, 1620C>A, 1620C>G)

*FIP1L1/PDGFRA (del[4q12])* (eg, imatinib-sensitive chronic eosinophilic leukemia), qualitative, and quantitative, if performed

*FLG (filaggrin)* (eg, icthyosis vulgaris), common variants (eg, R501X, 2282del4, R2447X, S3247X, 3702delG)

*FOXO1/PAX3 ~~(t(1;13))~~(t(2;13))* (eg, ~~Ewing sarcoma/peripheral neuroectodermal tumor~~alveolar rhabdomyosarcoma), translocation analysis, qualitative, and quantitative, if performed

*FOXO1/PAX7 ~~(t(2;13))~~(t(1;13))* (eg, alveolar rhabdomyosarcoma), translocation analysis, qualitative, and quantitative, ~~Ewing sarcoma/peripheral neuroectodermal tumor), translocation analysis, qualitative, and quantitative, if performed~~

*FUS/DDIT3 (t(12;16))* (eg, myxoid liposarcoma), translocation analysis, qualitative, and quantitative, if performed

*FXN (frataxin)* (eg, Friedreich ataxia), evaluation to detect abnormal (expanded) alleles

*GALC (galactosylceramidase)* (eg, Krabbe disease), common variants (eg, c.857G>A, 30-kb deletion)

*GALT (galactose-1-phosphate uridylyltransferase)* (eg, galactosemia), common variants (eg, Q188R, S135L, K285N, T138M, L195P, Y209C, IVS2-2A>G, P171S, del5kb, N314D, L218L/N314D)

*H19 (imprinted maternally expressed transcript [non-protein coding])* (eg, Beckwith-Wiedemann syndrome), methylation analysis

*HBB (hemoglobin, beta)* (eg, sickle cell anemia, hemoglobin C, hemoglobin E), common variants (eg, HbS, HbC, HbE)

*HTT (huntingtin)* (eg, Huntington disease), evaluation to detect abnormal (eg, expanded) alleles

*KCNQ1OT1 (KCNQ1 overlapping transcript 1 [non-protein coding])* (eg, Beckwith-Wiedemann syndrome), methylation analysis

*LRRK2 (leucine-rich repeat kinase 2)* (eg, Parkinson disease), common variants (eg, R1441G, G2019S, I2020T)

*MED12 (mediator complex subunit 12)* (eg, FG syndrome type 1, Lujan syndrome), common variants (eg, R961W, N1007S)

*MEG3/DLK1 (maternally expressed 3 [non-protein coding]/delta-like 1 homolog [Drosophila])* (eg, intrauterine growth retardation), methylation analysis

*MLL/AFF1 (t(4;11))* (eg, acute lymphoblastic leukemia), translocation analysis, qualitative, and quantitative, if performed

*MLL/MLLT3 (t(9;11))* (eg, acute myeloid leukemia), translocation analysis, qualitative, and quantitative, if performed

*MT-RNR1 (mitochondrially encoded 12S RNA)* (eg, nonsyndromic hearing loss), common variants (eg, m.1555A>G, m.1494C>T)

*MUTYH (mutY homolog [E. coli])* (eg, MYH-associated polyposis), common variants (eg, Y165C, G382D)

*MT-ATP6 (mitochondrially encoded ATP synthase 6)* (eg, neuropathy with ataxia and retinitis pigmentosa [NARP], Leigh syndrome), common variants (eg, m.8993T>G, m.8993T>C)

*MT-ND4, MT-ND6 (mitochondrially encoded NADH dehydrogenase 4, mitochondrially encoded NADH dehydrogenase 6)* (eg, Leber hereditary optic neuropathy [LHON]), common variants (eg, m.11778G>A, m.3460G>A, m.14484T>C)

*MT-TK (mitochondrially encoded tRNA lysine)* (eg, myoclonic epilepsy with ragged-red fibers [MERRF]), common variants (eg, m.8344A>G, m.8356T>C)

*MT-TL1 (mitochondrially encoded tRNA leucine 1 [UUA/G])* (eg, diabetes and hearing loss), common variants (eg, m.3243A>G, m.14709 T>C) MT-TL1

*MT-ND5 (mitochondrially encoded tRNA leucine 1 [UUA/G], mitochondrially encoded NADH dehydrogenase 5)* (eg, mitochondrial encephalopathy with lactic acidosis and stroke-like episodes [MELAS]), common variants (eg, m.3243A>G, m.3271T>C, m.3252A>G, m.13513G>A)

*MT-TS1, MT-RNR1 (mitochondrially encoded tRNA serine 1 [UCN], mitochondrially encoded 12S RNA)* (eg, nonsyndromic sensorineural deafness [including aminoglycoside-induced nonsyndromic deafness]), common variants (eg, m.7445A>G, m.1555A>G)

*NOD2 (nucleotide-binding oligomerization domain containing 2)* (eg, Crohn's disease, Blau syndrome), common variants (eg, SNP 8, SNP 12, SNP 13)

*NPM1/ALK (t(2;5))* (eg, anaplastic large cell lymphoma), translocation analysis

*PABPN1 (poly[A] binding protein, nuclear 1)* (eg, oculopharyngeal muscular dystrophy), evaluation to detect abnormal (eg, expanded) alleles

*PAX8/PPARG (t(2;3) (q13;p25))* (eg, follicular thyroid carcinoma), translocation analysis

*PPP2R2B (protein phosphatase 2, regulatory subunit B, beta)* (eg, spinocerebellar ataxia), evaluation to detect abnormal (eg, expanded) alleles

*PRSS1 (protease, serine, 1 [trypsin 1])* (eg, hereditary pancreatitis), common variants (eg, N29I, A16V, R122H)

*PYGM (phosphorylase, glycogen, muscle)* (eg, glycogen storage disease type V, McArdle disease), common variants (eg, R50X, G205S)

*RUNX1/RUNX1T1 (t(8;21))* (eg, acute myeloid leukemia) translocation analysis, qualitative, and quantitative, if performed

*SEPT9 (septin 9)* (eg, colon cancer), methylation analysis

*SMN1/SMN2 (survival of motor neuron 1, telomeric/survival of motor neuron 2, centromeric)* (eg, spinal muscular atrophy), dosage analysis (eg, carrier testing)

(For duplication/deletion analysis of SMN1/SMN2, use 81401)

*SS18/SSX1 (t(X;18))* (eg, synovial sarcoma), translocation analysis, qualitative, and quantitative, if performed

*SS18/SSX2 (t(X;18))* (eg, synovial sarcoma), translocation analysis, qualitative, and quantitative, if performed

*TRP (TATA box binding protein)* (eg, spinocerebellar ataxia), evaluation to detect abnormal (eg, expanded) alleles

*TPMT (thiopurine S-methyltransferase)* (eg, drug metabolism), common variants (eg, *2, *3)

*TYMS (thymidylate synthetase)* (eg, 5-fluorouracil/5-FU drug metabolism), tandem repeat variant

*VWF (von Willebrand factor)* (eg, von Willebrand disease type 2N), common variants (eg, T791M, R816W, R854Q)

▲ 81402    Molecular pathology procedure, Level 3 (eg, >10 SNPs, 2-10 methylated variants, or 2-10 somatic variants [typically using non-sequencing target variant analysis], immunoglobulin and T-cell receptor gene rearrangements, duplication/deletion variants of 1 exon, loss of heterozygosity [LOH], uniparental disomy [UPD])

Chromosome 18q- (eg, D18S55, D18S58, D18S61, D18S64, and D18S69) (eg, colon cancer), allelic imbalance assessment (ie, loss of heterozygosity)

*COL1A1/PDGFB (t(17;22))* (eg, dermatofibrosarcoma protuberans), translocation analysis, multiple breakpoints, qualitative, and quantitative, if performed

*CYP21A2 (cytochrome P450, family 21, subfamily A, polypeptide 2)* (eg, congenital adrenal hyperplasia, 21-hydroxylase deficiency), common variants (eg, IVS2-13G, P30L, I172N, exon 6 mutation cluster [I235N, V236E, M238K], V281L, L307FfsX6, Q318X, R356W, P453S, G110VfsX21, 30-kb deletion variant)

*ESR1/PGR (receptor 1/progesterone receptor)* ratio (eg, breast cancer)

*IGH@/BCL2 (t(14;18))* (eg, follicular lymphoma), translocation analysis; major breakpoint region (MBR) and minor cluster region (mcr) breakpoints, qualitative or quantitative

*KIT (v-kit Hardy-Zuckerman 4 feline sarcoma viral oncogene homolog)* (eg, mastocytosis), common variants (eg, D816V, D816Y, D816F)

*MEFV (Mediterranean fever)* (eg, familial Mediterranean fever), common variants (eg, E148Q, P369S, F479L, M680I, I692del, M694V, M694I, K695R, V726A, A744S, R761H)

*MPL (myeloproliferative leukemia virus oncogene, thrombopoietin receptor, TPOR)* (eg, myeloproliferative disorder), common variants (eg, W515A, W515K, W515L, W515R)

*TRD@ (T cell antigen receptor, delta)* (eg, leukemia and lymphoma), gene rearrangement analysis, evaluation to detect abnormal clonal population

Uniparental disomy (UPD) (eg, Russell-Silver syndrome, Prader-Willi/Angelman syndrome), short tandem repeat (STR) analysis

▲ 81403    Molecular pathology procedure, Level 4 (eg, analysis of single exon by DNA sequence analysis, analysis of >10 amplicons using multiplex PCR in 2 or more independent reactions, mutation scanning or duplication/deletion variants of 2-5 exons)

*ABL1 (c-abl oncogene 1, receptor tyrosine kinase)* (eg, acquired imatinib tyrosine kinase inhibitor resistance), variants in the kinase domain

*ANG (angiogenin, ribonuclease, RNase A family, 5)* (eg, amyotrophic lateral sclerosis), full gene sequence

*ARX (aristaless-related homeobox)* (eg, X-linked lissencephaly with ambiguous genitalia, X-linked mental retardation), duplication/deletion analysis

*CEBPA (CCAAT/enhancer binding protein [C/EBP], alpha)* (eg, acute myeloid leukemia), full gene sequence

*CEL (carboxyl ester lipase [bile salt-stimulated lipase])* (eg, maturity-onset diabetes of the young [MODY]), targeted sequence analysis of exon 11 (eg, c.1785delC, c.1686delT)

*CTNNB1 (catenin [cadherin-associated protein], beta 1, 88kDa)* (eg, desmoid tumors), targeted sequence analysis (eg, exon 3)

*DAZ/SRY (deleted in azoospermia and sex determining region Y)* (eg, male infertility), common deletions (eg, AZFa, AZFb, AZFc, AZFd)

*DNMT3A (DNA [cytosine-5-]-methyltransferase 3 alpha)* (eg, acute myeloid leukemia), targeted sequence analysis (eg, exon 23)

*EPCAM (epithelial cell adhesion molecule)* (eg, Lynch syndrome), duplication/deletion analysis

*F8 (coagulation factor VIII)* (eg, hemophilia A), inversion analysis, intron 1 and intron 22A

*F12 (coagulation factor XII [Hageman factor])* (eg, angioedema, hereditary, type III; factor XII deficiency), targeted sequence analysis of exon 9

*FGFR3 (fibroblast growth factor receptor 3)* (eg, isolated craniosynostosis), targeted sequence analysis (eg, exon 7)

(For targeted sequence analysis of multiple FGFR3 exons, use 81404)

*GJB1 (gap junction protein, beta 1)* (eg, Charcot-Marie-Tooth X-linked), full gene sequence

*GNAQ (guanine nucleotide-binding protein G[q] subunit alpha)* (eg, uveal melanoma), common variants (eg, R183, Q209)

*HBB (hemoglobin, beta, beta-globin)* (eg, beta thalassemia), duplication/deletion analysis

*HRAS (v-Ha-ras Harvey rat sarcoma viral oncogene homolog)* (eg, Costello syndrome), exon 2 sequence

*IDH1 (isocitrate dehydrogenase 1 [NADP+], soluble)* (eg, glioma), common exon 4 variants (eg, R132H, R132C)

*IDH2 (isocitrate dehydrogenase 2 [NADP+], mitochondrial)* (eg, glioma), common exon 4 variants (eg, R140W, R172M)

*JAK2 (Janus kinase 2)* (eg, myeloproliferative disorder), exon 12 sequence and exon 13 sequence, if performed

Killer cell immunoglobulin-like receptor (KIR) gene family (eg, hematopoietic stem cell transplantation), genotyping of KIR family genes

Known familial variant not otherwise specified, for gene listed in Tier 1 or Tier 2, DNA sequence analysis, each variant exon

(For a known familial variant that is considered a common variant, use specific common variant Tier 1 or Tier 2 code)

*KCNC3 (potassium voltage-gated channel, Shaw-related subfamily, member 3)* (eg, spinocerebellar ataxia), targeted sequence analysis (eg, exon 2)

*KCNJ2 (potassium inwardly-rectifying channel, subfamily J, member 2)* (eg, Andersen-Tawil syndrome), full gene sequence

*KCNJ11 (potassium inwardly-rectifying channel, subfamily J, member 11)* (eg, familial hyperinsulinism), full gene sequence

*KRAS (v-Ki-ras2 Kirsten rat sarcoma viral oncogene)* (eg, carcinoma), gene analysis, variant(s) in exon 3 (eg, codon 61)

*MC4R (melanocortin 4 receptor)* (eg, obesity), full gene sequence

*MICA (MHC class I polypeptide-related sequence A)* (eg, solid organ transplantation), common variants (eg, *001, *002)

*MPL (myeloproliferative leukemia virus oncogene, thrombopoietin receptor, TPOR)* (eg, myeloproliferative disorder), exon 10 sequence

*MT-RNR1 (mitochondrially encoded 12S RNA)* (eg, nonsyndromic hearing loss), full gene sequence

*MT-TS1 (mitochondrially encoded tRNA serine 1)* (eg, nonsyndromic hearing loss), full gene sequence

_NDP (Norrie disease [pseudoglioma])_ (eg, Norrie disease), duplication/deletion analysis

_NHLRC1 (NHL repeat containing 1)_ (eg, progressive myoclonus epilepsy), full gene sequence

_PHOX2B (paired-like homeobox 2b)_ (eg, congenital central hypoventilation syndrome), duplication/deletion analysis

_PLN (phospholamban)_ (eg, dilated cardiomyopathy, hypertrophic cardiomyopathy), full gene sequence

_SH2D1A (SH2 domain containing 1A)_ (eg, X-linked lymphoproliferative syndrome), duplication/deletion analysis

SMN1 (survival of motor neuron 1, telomeric) (eg, spinal muscular atrophy), known familial sequence variant(s)

_TWIST1 (twist homolog 1 [Drosophila])_ (eg, Saethre-Chotzen syndrome), duplication/deletion analysis

_UBA1 (ubiquitin-like modifier activating enzyme 1)_ (eg, spinal muscular atrophy, X-linked), targeted sequence analysis (eg, exon 15)

VHL (von Hippel-Lindau tumor suppressor) (eg, von Hippel-Lindau familial cancer syndrome), deletion/duplication analysis

VWF (von Willebrand factor) (eg, von Willebrand disease types 2A, 2B, 2M), targeted sequence analysis (eg, exon 28)

▲ 81404    Molecular pathology procedure, Level 5 (eg, analysis of 2-5 exons by DNA sequence analysis, mutation scanning or duplication/deletion variants of 6-10 exons, or characterization of a dynamic mutation disorder/triplet repeat by Southern blot analysis)

ACADS (acyl-CoA dehydrogenase, C-2 to C-3 short chain) (eg, short chain acyl-CoA dehydrogenase deficiency), targeted sequence analysis (eg, exons 5 and 6)

_AFF2 (AF4/FMR2 family, member 2 [FMR2])_ (eg, fragile X mental retardation 2 [FRAXE]), characterization of alleles (eg, expanded size and methylation status)

AQP2 (aquaporin 2 [collecting duct]) (eg, nephrogenic diabetes insipidus), full gene sequence

ARX (aristaless related homeobox) (eg, X-linked lissencephaly with ambiguous genitalia, X-linked mental retardation), full gene sequence

_AVPR2 (arginine vasopressin receptor 2)_ (eg, nephrogenic diabetes insipidus), full gene sequence

_BBS10 (Bardet-Biedl syndrome 10)_ (eg, Bardet-Biedl syndrome), full gene sequence

BTD (biotinidase) (eg, biotinidase deficiency), full gene sequence

_C10orf2 (chromosome 10 open reading frame 2)_ (eg, mitochondrial DNA depletion syndrome), full gene sequence

CAV3 (caveolin 3) (eg, CAV3-related distal myopathy, limb-girdle muscular dystrophy type 1C), full gene sequence

_CD40LG (CD40 ligand)_ (eg, X-linked hyper IgM syndrome), full gene sequence

CDKN2A (cyclin-dependent kinase inhibitor 2A) (eg, CDKN2A-related cutaneous malignant melanoma, familial atypical mole-malignant melanoma syndrome), full gene sequence

CLRN1 (clarin 1) (eg, Usher syndrome, type 3), full gene sequence

_COX6B1 (cytochrome c oxidase subunit VIb polypeptide 1)_ (eg, mitochondrial respiratory chain complex IV deficiency), full gene sequence

CPT2 (carnitine palmitoyltransferase 2) (eg, carnitine palmitoyltransferase II deficiency), full gene sequence

_CRX (cone-rod homeobox)_ (eg, cone-rod dystrophy 2, Leber congenital amaurosis), full gene sequence

_CSTB (cystatin B [stefin B])_ (eg, Unverricht-Lundborg disease), full gene sequence

CYP1B1 (cytochrome P450, family 1, subfamily B, polypeptide 1) (eg, primary congenital glaucoma), full gene sequence

DMPK (dystrophia myotonica-protein kinase) (eg, myotonic dystrophy type 1), characterization of abnormal (eg, expanded) alleles

EGR2 (early growth response 2) (eg, Charcot-Marie-Tooth), full gene sequence

_EMD (emerin)_ (eg, Emery-Dreifuss muscular dystrophy), duplication/deletion analysis

_EPM2A (epilepsy, progressive myoclonus type 2A, Lafora disease [laforin])_ (eg, progressive myoclonus epilepsy), full gene sequence

_FGF23 (fibroblast growth factor 23)_ (eg, hypophosphatemic rickets), full gene sequence

FGFR2 (fibroblast growth factor receptor 2) (eg, craniosynostosis, Apert syndrome, Crouzon syndrome), targeted sequence analysis (eg, exons 8, 10)

FGFR3 (fibroblast growth factor receptor 3) (eg, achondroplasia, hypochondroplasia), targeted sequence analysis (eg, exons 8, 11, 12, 13)

_FHL1 (four and a half LIM domains 1)_ (eg, Emery-Dreifuss muscular dystrophy), full gene sequence

FKRP (fukutin related protein) (eg, congenital muscular dystrophy type 1C [MDC1C], limb-girdle muscular dystrophy [LGMD] type 2I), full gene sequence

FOXG1 (forkhead box G1) (eg, Rett syndrome), full gene sequence

FSHMD1A (facioscapulohumeral muscular dystrophy 1A) (eg, facioscapulohumeral muscular dystrophy), evaluation to detect abnormal (eg, deleted) alleles

FSHMD1A (facioscapulohumeral muscular dystrophy 1A) (eg, facioscapulohumeral muscular dystrophy), characterization of haplotype(s) (ie, chromosome 4A and 4B haplotypes)

FXN (frataxin) (eg, Friedreich ataxia), full gene sequence

_GH1 (growth hormone 1)_ (eg, growth hormone deficiency), full gene sequence

_GP1BB (glycoprotein Ib [platelet], beta polypeptide)_ (eg, Bernard-Soulier syndrome type B), full gene sequence

HBA1/HBA2 (alpha globin 1 and alpha globin 2) (eg, alpha thalassemia), duplication/deletion analysis

(For common deletion variants of alpha globin 1 and alpha globin 2 genes, use 81257)

HBB (hemoglobin, beta, Beta-Globin) (eg, thalassemia), full gene sequence

HNF1B (HNF1 homeobox B) (eg, maturity-onset diabetes of the young [MODY]), duplication/deletion analysis

HRAS (v-Ha-ras Harvey rat sarcoma viral oncogene homolog) (eg, Costello syndrome), full gene sequence

_HSD3B2 (hydroxy-delta-5-steroid dehydrogenase, 3 beta- and steroid delta-isomerase 2)_ (eg, 3-beta-hydroxysteroid dehydrogenase type II deficiency), full gene sequence

_HSD11B2 (hydroxysteroid [11-beta] dehydrogenase 2)_ (eg, mineralocorticoid excess syndrome), full gene sequence

HSPB1 (heat shock 27kDa protein 1) (eg, Charcot-Marie-Tooth disease), full gene sequence

INS (insulin) (eg, diabetes mellitus), full gene sequence

KCNJ1 (potassium inwardly-rectifying channel, subfamily J, member 1) (eg, Bartter syndrome), full gene sequence

KCNJ10 (potassium inwardly-rectifying channel, subfamily J, member 10) (eg, SeSAME syndrome, EAST syndrome, sensorineural hearing loss), full gene sequence

KIT (C-kit) (v-kit Hardy-Zuckerman 4 feline sarcoma viral oncogene homolog) (eg, GIST, acute myeloid leukemia, melanoma), targeted gene analysis (eg, exons 8, 11, 13, 17, 18)

LITAF (lipopolysaccharide-induced TNF factor) (eg, Charcot-Marie-Tooth), full gene sequence

MEFV (Mediterranean fever) (eg, familial Mediterranean fever), full gene sequence

MEN1 (multiple endocrine neoplasia I) (eg, multiple endocrine neoplasia type 1, Wermer syndromeanalysis deletion/duplication ,)

MMACHC (methylmalonic aciduria [cobalamin deficiency] cblC type, with homocystinuria) (eg, methylmalonic acidemia and homocystinuria), full gene sequence

NDP (Norrie disease [pseudoglioma]) (eg, Norrie disease), full gene sequence

NDUFA1 (NADH dehydrogenase [ubiquinone] 1 alpha subcomplex, 1, 7.5kDa) (eg, Leigh syndrome, mitochondrial complex I deficiency), full gene sequence

NDUFAF2 (NADH dehydrogenase [ubiquinone] 1 alpha subcomplex, assembly factor 2) (eg, Leigh syndrome, mitochondrial complex I deficiency), full gene sequence

NDUFS4 (NADH dehydrogenase [ubiquinone] Fe-S protein 4, 18kDa [NADH-coenzyme Q reductase]) (eg, Leigh syndrome, mitochondrial complex I deficiency), full gene sequence

NIPA1 (non-imprinted in Prader-Willi/Angelman syndrome 1) (eg, spastic paraplegia), full gene sequence

NLGN4X (neuroligin 4, X-linked) (eg, autism spectrum disorders), duplication/deletion analysis

NPC2 (Niemann-Pick disease, type C2 [epididymal secretory protein E1]) (eg, Niemann-Pick disease type C2), full gene sequence

NR0B1 (nuclear receptor subfamily 0, group B, member 1) (eg, congenital adrenal hypoplasia), full gene sequence

NRAS (neuroblastoma RAS viral oncogene homolog) (eg, colorectal carcinoma), exon 1 and exon 2 sequences

PDGFRA (platelet-derived growth factor receptor alpha polypeptide) (eg, gastrointestinal stromal tumor), targeted sequence analysis (eg, exons 12, 18)

PDX1 (pancreatic and duodenal homeobox 1) (eg, maturity-onset diabetes of the young [MODY]), full gene sequence

PHOX2B (paired-like homeobox 2b) (eg, congenital central hypoventilation syndrome), full gene sequence

PLP1 (proteolipid protein 1) (eg, Pelizaeus-Merzbacher disease, spastic paraplegia), duplication/deletion analysis

PQBP1 (polyglutamine binding protein 1) (eg, Renpenning syndrome), duplication/deletion analysis

PRNP (prion protein) (eg, genetic prion disease), full gene sequence

PROP1 (PROP paired-like homeobox 1) (eg, combined pituitary hormone deficiency), full gene sequence

PRPH2 (peripherin 2 [retinal degeneration, slow]) (eg, retinitis pigmentosa), full gene sequence

PRSS1 (protease, serine, 1 [trypsin 1]) (eg, hereditary pancreatitis), full gene sequence

RAF1 (v-raf-1 murine leukemia viral oncogene homolog 1) (eg, LEOPARD syndrome), targeted sequence analysis (eg, exons 7, 12, 14, 17)

RET (ret proto-oncogene) (eg, multiple endocrine neoplasia, type 2B and familial medullary thyroid carcinoma), common variants (eg, M918T, 2647_2648delinsTT, A883F)

RHO (rhodopsin) (eg, retinitis pigmentosa), full gene sequence

RP1 (retinitis pigmentosa 1) (eg, retinitis pigmentosa), full gene sequence

SCN1B (sodium channel, voltage-gated, type I, beta) (eg, Brugada syndrome), full gene sequence

SCO2 (SCO cytochrome oxidase deficient homolog 2 [SCO1L]) (eg, mitochondrial respiratory chain complex IV deficiency), full gene sequence

SDHC (succinate dehydrogenase complex, subunit C, integral membrane protein, 15kDa) (eg, hereditary paraganglioma-pheochromocytoma syndrome), duplication/deletion analysis

SDHD (succinate dehydrogenase complex, subunit D, integral membrane protein) (eg, hereditary paraganglioma), full gene sequence

SGCG (sarcoglycan, gamma [35kDa dystrophin-associated glycoprotein]) (eg, limb-girdle muscular dystrophy), duplication/deletion analysis

SH2D1A (SH2 domain containing 1A) (eg, X-linked lymphoproliferative syndrome), full gene sequence

SLC16A2 (solute carrier family 16, member 2 [thyroid hormone transporter]) (eg, specific thyroid hormone cell transporter deficiency, Allan-Herndon-Dudley syndrome), duplication/deletion analysis

SLC25A20 (solute carrier family 25 [carnitine/acylcarnitine translocase], member 20) (eg, carnitine-acylcarnitine translocase deficiency), duplication/deletion analysis

SLC25A4 (solute carrier family 25 [mitochondrial carrier; adenine nucleotide translocator], member 4) (eg, progressive external ophthalmoplegia), full gene sequence

SOD1 (superoxide dismutase 1, soluble) (eg, amyotrophic lateral sclerosis), full gene sequence

SPINK1 (serine peptidase inhibitor, Kazal type 1) (eg, hereditary pancreatitis), full gene sequence

STK11 (serine/threonine kinase 11) (eg, Peutz-Jeghers syndrome), duplication/deletion analysis

TACO1 (translational activator of mitochondrial encoded cytochrome c oxidase I) (eg, mitochondrial respiratory chain complex IV deficiency), full gene sequence

THAP1 (THAP domain containing, apoptosis associated protein 1) (eg, torsion dystonia), full gene sequence

TOR1A (torsin family 1, member A [torsin A]) (eg, torsion dystonia), full gene sequence

TP53 (tumor protein 53) (eg, tumor samples), targeted sequence analysis of 2-5 exons

TTPA (tocopherol [alpha] transfer protein) (eg, ataxia), full gene sequence

*TTR (transthyretin)* (eg, familial transthyretin amyloidosis), full gene sequence

*TWIST1 (twist homolog 1 [Drosophila])* (eg, Saethre-Chotzen syndrome), full gene sequence

*TYR (tyrosinase [oculocutaneous albinism IA])* (eg, oculocutaneous albinism IA), full gene sequence

*USH1G (Usher syndrome 1G [autosomal recessive])* (eg, Usher syndrome, type 1), full gene sequence

*VHL (von Hippel-Lindau tumor suppressor)* (eg, von Hippel-Lindau familial cancer syndrome), full gene sequence

*VWF (von Willebrand factor)* (eg, von Willebrand disease type 1C), targeted sequence analysis (eg, exons 26, 27, 37)

*ZEB2 (zinc finger E-box binding homeobox 2)* (eg, Mowat-Wilson syndrome), duplication/deletion analysis

*ZNF41 (zinc finger protein 41)* (eg, X-linked mental retardation 89), full gene sequence

▲ 81405 ~~Molecular pathology procedure, Level 6~~Molecular pathology procedure, Level 6 (eg, analysis of 6-10 exons by DNA sequence analysis, mutation scanning or duplication/deletion variants of 11-25 exons), regionally targeted cytogenomic array analysis

*ABCD1 (ATP-binding cassette, sub-family D [ALD], member 1)* (eg, adrenoleukodystrophy), full gene sequence

*ACADS (acyl-CoA dehydrogenase, C-2 to C-3 short chain)* (eg, short chain acyl-CoA dehydrogenase deficiency), full gene sequence

*ACTA2 (actin, alpha 2, smooth muscle, aorta)* (eg, thoracic aortic aneurysms and aortic dissections), full gene sequence

*ACTC1 (actin, alpha, cardiac muscle 1)* (eg, familial hypertrophic cardiomyopathy), full gene sequence

*ANKRD1 (ankyrin repeat domain 1)* (eg, dilated cardiomyopathy), full gene sequence

*APTX (aprataxin)* (eg, ataxia with oculomotor apraxia 1), full gene sequence

*AR (androgen receptor)* (eg, androgen insensitivity syndrome), full gene sequence

*ARSA (arylsulfatase A)* (eg, arylsulfatase A deficiency), full gene sequence

*BCKDHA (branched chain keto acid dehydrogenase E1, alpha polypeptide)* (eg, maple syrup urine disease, type 1A), full gene sequence

*BCS1L (BCS1-like [S. cerevisiae])* (eg, Leigh syndrome, mitochondrial complex III deficiency, GRACILE syndrome), full gene sequence

*BMPR2 (bone morphogenetic protein receptor, type II [serine/threonine kinase])* (eg, heritable pulmonary arterial hypertension), duplication/deletion analysis

*CASQ2 (calsequestrin 2 [cardiac muscle])* (eg, catecholaminergic polymorphic ventricular tachycardia), full gene sequence

*CASR (calcium-sensing receptor)* (eg, hypocalcemia), full gene sequence

*CDKL5 (cyclin-dependent kinase-like 5)* (eg, early infantile epileptic encephalopathy), duplication/deletion analysis

*CHRNA4 (cholinergic receptor, nicotinic, alpha 4)* (eg, nocturnal frontal lobe epilepsy), full gene sequence

*CHRNB2 (cholinergic receptor, nicotinic, beta 2 [neuronal])* (eg, nocturnal frontal lobe epilepsy), full gene sequence

*COX10 (COX10 homolog, cytochrome c oxidase assembly protein)* (eg, mitochondrial respiratory chain complex IV deficiency), full gene sequence

*COX15 (COX15 homolog, cytochrome c oxidase assembly protein)* (eg, mitochondrial respiratory chain complex IV deficiency), full gene sequence

*CYP11B1 (cytochrome P450, family 11, subfamily B, polypeptide 1)* (eg, congenital adrenal hyperplasia), full gene sequence

*CYP17A1 (cytochrome P450, family 17, subfamily A, polypeptide 1)* (eg, congenital adrenal hyperplasia), full gene sequence

*CYP21A2 (cytochrome P450, family 21, subfamily A, polypeptide 2)* (eg, steroid 21-hydroxylase isoform, congenital adrenal hyperplasia), full gene sequence

Cytogenomic constitutional targeted microarray analysis of the X chromosome by interrogation of genomic regions for copy number and single nucleotide polymorphism (SNP) variants for chromosomal abnormalities

(When performing genome-wide cytogenomic constitutional microarray analysis, see 81228, 81229)

(Do not report analyte-specific molecular pathology procedures separately when the specific analytes are included as part of the microarray analysis of the X chromosome)

(Do not report 88271 when performing cytogenomic microarray analysis)

Cytogenomic constitutional targeted microarray analysis of chromosome 22q13 by interrogation of genomic regions for copy number and single nucleotide polymorphism (SNP) variants for chromosomal abnormalities

(When performing genome-wide cytogenomic constitutional microarray analysis, see 81228, 81229)

(Do not report analyte-specific molecular pathology procedures separately when the specific analytes are included as part of the microarray analysis of chromosome 22q13)

(Do not report 88271 when performing cytogenomic microarray analysis)

*DBT (dihydrolipoamide branched chain transacylase E2)* (eg, maple syrup urine disease, type 2), duplication/deletion analysis

*DCX (doublecortin)* (eg, X-linked lissencephaly), full gene sequence

*DES (desmin)* (eg, myofibrillar myopathy), full gene sequence

*DFNB59 (deafness, autosomal recessive 59)* (eg, autosomal recessive nonsyndromic hearing impairment), full gene sequence

*DGUOK (deoxyguanosine kinase)* (eg, hepatocerebral mitochondrial DNA depletion syndrome), full gene sequence

*DHCR7 (7-dehydrocholesterol reductase)* (eg, Smith-Lemli-Opitz syndrome), full gene sequence

*EIF2B2 (eukaryotic translation initiation factor 2B, subunit 2 beta, 39kDa)* (eg, leukoencephalopathy with vanishing white matter), full gene sequence

*EMD (emerin)* (eg, Emery-Dreifuss muscular dystrophy), full gene sequence

*ENG (endoglin)* (eg, hereditary hemorrhagic telangiectasia, type 1), duplication/deletion analysis

*EYA1 (eyes absent homolog 1 [Drosophila])* (eg, branchio-oto-renal [BOR] spectrum disorders), duplication/deletion analysis

*F9 (coagulation factor IX)* (eg, hemophilia B), full gene sequence

*FGFR1 (fibroblast growth factor receptor 1)* (eg, Kallmann syndrome 2), full gene sequence

*FH (fumarate hydratase)* (eg, fumarate hydratase deficiency, hereditary leiomyomatosis with renal cell cancer), full gene sequence

*FKTN (fukutin)* (eg, limb-girdle muscular dystrophy [LGMD] type 2M or 2L), full gene sequence

*FTSJ1 (FtsJ RNA methyltransferase homolog 1 [E. coli])* (eg, X-linked mental retardation 9), duplication/deletion analysis

*GABRG2 (gamma-aminobutyric acid [GABA] A receptor, gamma 2)* (eg, generalized epilepsy with febrile seizures), full gene sequence

*GCH1 (GTP cyclohydrolase 1)* (eg, autosomal dominant dopa-responsive dystonia), full gene sequence

*GDAP1 (ganglioside-induced differentiation-associated protein 1)* (eg, Charcot-Marie-Tooth disease), full gene sequence

*GFAP (glial fibrillary acidic protein)* (eg, Alexander disease), full gene sequence

*GHR (growth hormone receptor)* (eg, Laron syndrome), full gene sequence

*GHRHR (growth hormone releasing hormone receptor)* (eg, growth hormone deficiency), full gene sequence

*GLA (galactosidase, alpha)* (eg, Fabry disease), full gene sequence

*HBA1/HBA2 (alpha globin 1 and alpha globin 2)* (eg, thalassemia), full gene sequence

*HNF1A (HNF1 homeobox A)* (eg, maturity-onset diabetes of the young [MODY]), full gene sequence

*HNF1B (HNF1 homeobox B)* (eg, maturity-onset diabetes of the young [MODY]), full gene sequence

*HTRA1 (HtrA serine peptidase 1)* (eg, macular degeneration), full gene sequence

*IDS (iduronate 2-sulfatase)* (eg, mucopolysaccridosis, type II), full gene sequence

*IL2RG (interleukin 2 receptor, gamma)* (eg, X-linked severe combined immunodeficiency), full gene sequence

*ISPD (isoprenoid synthase domain containing)* (eg, muscle-eye-brain disease, Walker-Warburg syndrome), full gene sequence

*KRAS (v-Ki-ras2 Kirsten rat sarcoma viral oncogene homolog)* (eg, Noonan syndrome), full gene sequence

*LAMP2 (lysosomal-associated membrane protein 2)* (eg, Danon disease), full gene sequence

*LDLR (low density lipoprotein receptor)* (eg, familial hypercholesterolemia), duplication/deletion analysis

*MEN1 (multiple endocrine neoplasia I)* (eg, multiple endocrine neoplasia type 1, Wermer syndrome), full gene sequence

Mitochondrial genome deletions (eg, Kearns-Sayre syndrome [KSS], chronic progressive external ophthalmoplegia [CPEO], Pearson syndrome), deletion analysis, and duplication analysis, if performed

*MMAA (methylmalonic aciduria [cobalamine deficiency] type A)* (eg, MMAA-related methylmalonic acidemia), full gene sequence

*MMAB (methylmalonic aciduria [cobalamine deficiency] type B)* (eg, MMAA-related methylmalonic acidemia), full gene sequence

*MPI (mannose phosphate isomerase)* (eg, congenital disorder of glycosylation 1b), full gene sequence

*MPV17 (MpV17 mitochondrial inner membrane protein)* (eg, mitochondrial DNA depletion syndrome), full gene sequence

*MPZ (myelin protein zero)* (eg, Charcot-Marie-Tooth), full gene sequence

*MTM1 (myotubularin 1)* (eg, X-linked centronuclear myopathy), duplication/deletion analysis

*MYL2 (myosin, light chain 2, regulatory, cardiac, slow)* (eg, familial hypertrophic cardiomyopathy), full gene sequence

*MYL3 (myosin, light chain 3, alkali, ventricular, skeletal, slow)* (eg, familial hypertrophic cardiomyopathy), full gene sequence

*MYOT (myotilin)* (eg, limb-girdle muscular dystrophy), full gene sequence

*NDUFS7 (NADH dehydrogenase [ubiquinone] Fe-S protein 7, 20kDa [NADH-coenzyme Q reductase])* (eg, Leigh syndrome, mitochondrial complex I deficiency), full gene sequence

*NDUFS8 (NADH dehydrogenase [ubiquinone] Fe-S protein 8, 23kDa [NADH-coenzyme Q reductase])* (eg, Leigh syndrome, mitochondrial complex I deficiency), full gene sequence

*NDUFV1 (NADH dehydrogenase [ubiquinone] flavoprotein 1, 51kDa)* (eg, Leigh syndrome, mitochondrial complex I deficiency), full gene sequence

*NEFL (neurofilament, light polypeptide)* (eg, Charcot-Marie-Tooth), full gene sequence

*NF2 (neurofibromin 2 [merlin])* (eg, neurofibromatosis, type 2), duplication/deletionanalysis

*NLGN3 (neuroligin 3)* (eg, autism spectrum disorders), full gene sequence

*NLGN4X (neuroligin 4, X-linked)* (eg, autism spectrum disorders), full gene sequence

*NPHP1 (nephronophthisis 1 [juvenile])* (eg, Joubert syndrome), deletion analysis, and duplication analysis, if performed

*NPHS2 (nephrosis 2, idiopathic, steroid-resistant [podocin])* (eg, steroid-resistant nephrotic syndrome), full gene sequence

*NSD1 (nuclear receptor binding SET domain protein 1)* (eg, Sotos syndrome), duplication/deletion analysis

*OTC (ornithine carbamoyltransferase)* (eg, ornithine transcarbamylase deficiency), full gene sequence

*PAFAH1B1 (platelet-activating factor acetylhydrolase 1b, regulatory subunit 1 [45kDa])* (eg, lissencephaly, Miller-Dieker syndrome), duplication/deletion analysis

*PARK2 (Parkinson protein 2, E3 ubiquitin protein ligase [parkin])* (eg, Parkinson disease), duplication/deletion analysis

*PCCA (propionyl CoA carboxylase, alpha polypeptide)* (eg, propionic acidemia, type 1), duplication/deletion analysis

*PCDH19 (protocadherin 19)* (eg, epileptic encephalopathy), full gene sequence

*PDHA1 (pyruvate dehydrogenase [lipoamide] alpha 1)* (eg, lactic acidosis), duplication/deletion analysis

*PDHB (pyruvate dehydrogenase [lipoamide] beta)* (eg, lactic acidosis), full gene sequence

*PINK1 (PTEN induced putative kinase 1)* (eg, Parkinson disease), full gene sequence

*PLP1 (proteolipid protein 1)* (eg, Pelizaeus-Merzbacher disease, spastic paraplegia), full gene sequence

*POU1F1 (POU class 1 homeobox 1)* (eg, combined pituitary hormone deficiency), full gene sequence

*PRX (periaxin)* (eg, Charcot-Marie-Tooth disease), full gene sequence

*PQBP1 (polyglutamine binding protein 1)* (eg, Renpenning syndrome), full gene sequence

PSEN1 *(presenilin 1)* (eg, Alzheimer disease), full gene sequence

*RAB7A (RAB7A, member RAS oncogene family)* (eg, Charcot-Marie-Tooth disease), full gene sequence

*RAI1 (retinoic acid induced 1)* (eg, Smith-Magenis syndrome), full gene sequence

*REEP1 (receptor accessory protein 1)* (eg, spastic paraplegia), full gene sequence

RET *(ret proto-oncogene)* (eg, multiple endocrine neoplasia, type 2A and familial medullary thyroid carcinoma), targeted sequence analysis (eg, exons 10, 11, 13-16)

*RPS19 (ribosomal protein S19)* (eg, Diamond-Blackfan anemia), full gene sequence

*RRM2B (ribonucleotide reductase M2 B [TP53 inducible])* (eg, mitochondrial DNA depletion), full gene sequence

*SCO1 (SCO cytochrome oxidase deficient homolog 1)* (eg, mitochondrial respiratory chain complex IV deficiency), full gene sequence

SDHB *(succinate dehydrogenase complex, subunit B, iron sulfur)* (eg, hereditary paraganglioma), full gene sequence

SDHC *(succinate dehydrogenase complex, subunit C, integral membrane protein, 15kDa)* (eg, hereditary paraganglioma-pheochromocytoma syndrome), full gene sequence

SGCA *(sarcoglycan, alpha [50kDa dystrophin-associated glycoprotein])* (eg, limb-girdle muscular dystrophy), full gene sequence

SGCB *(sarcoglycan, beta [43kDa dystrophin-associated glycoprotein])* (eg, limb-girdle muscular dystrophy), full gene sequence

SGCD *(sarcoglycan, delta [35kDa dystrophin-associated glycoprotein])* (eg, limb-girdle muscular dystrophy), full gene sequence

*SGCE (sarcoglycan, epsilon)* (eg, myoclonic dystonia), duplication/deletion analysis

SGCG *(sarcoglycan, gamma [35kDa dystrophin-associated glycoprotein])* (eg, limb-girdle muscular dystrophy), full gene sequence

SHOC2 *(soc-2 suppressor of clear homolog)* (eg, Noonan-like syndrome with loose anagen hair), full gene sequence

*SHOX (short stature homeobox)* (eg, Langer mesomelic dysplasia), full gene sequence

*SIL1 (SIL1 homolog, endoplasmic reticulum chaperone [S. cerevisiae])* (eg, ataxia), full gene sequence

*SLC2A1 (solute carrier family 2 [facilitated glucose transporter], member 1)* (eg, glucose transporter type 1 [GLUT 1] deficiency syndrome), full gene sequence

*SLC16A2 (solute carrier family 16, member 2 [thyroid hormone transporter])* (eg, specific thyroid hormone cell transporter deficiency, Allan-Herndon-Dudley syndrome), full gene sequence

*SLC22A5 (solute carrier family 22 [organic cation/carnitine transporter], member 5)* (eg, systemic primary carnitine deficiency), full gene sequence

*SLC25A20 (solute carrier family 25 [carnitine/acylcarnitine translocase], member 20)* (eg, carnitine-acylcarnitine translocase deficiency), full gene sequence

*SMAD4 (SMAD family member 4)* (eg, hemorrhagic telangiectasia syndrome, juvenile polyposis), duplication/deletion analysis

SMN1 *(survival of motor neuron 1, telomeric)* (eg, spinal muscular atrophy), full gene sequence

*SPAST (spastin)* (eg, spastic paraplegia), duplication/deletion analysis

*SPG7 (spastic paraplegia 7 [pure and complicated autosomal recessive])* (eg, spastic paraplegia), duplication/deletion analysis

SPRED1 *(sprouty-related, EVH1 domain containing 1)* (eg, Legius syndrome), full gene sequence

*STAT3 (signal transducer and activator of transcription 3 [acute-phase response factor])* (eg, autosomal dominant hyper-IgE syndrome), targeted sequence analysis (eg, exons 12, 13, 14, 16, 17, 20, 21)

*STK11 (serine/threonine kinase 11)* (eg, Peutz-Jeghers syndrome), full gene sequence

*SURF1 (surfeit 1)* (eg, mitochondrial respiratory chain complex IV deficiency), full gene sequence

*TARDBP (TAR DNA binding protein)* (eg, amyotrophic lateral sclerosis), full gene sequence

*TBX5 (T-box 5)* (eg, Holt-Oram syndrome), full gene sequence

*TCF4 (transcription factor 4)* (eg, Pitt-Hopkins syndrome), duplication/deletion analysis

TGFBR1 *(transforming growth factor, beta receptor 1)* (eg, Marfan syndrome), full gene sequence

TGFBR2 *(transforming growth factor, beta receptor 2)* (eg, Marfan syndrome), full gene sequence

THRB *(thyroid hormone receptor, beta)* (eg, thyroid hormone resistance, thyroid hormone beta receptor deficiency), full gene sequence or targeted sequence analysis of >5 exons

*TK2 (thymidine kinase 2, mitochondrial)* (eg, mitochondrial DNA depletion syndrome), full gene sequence

*TNNC1 (troponin C type 1 [slow])* (eg, hypertrophic cardiomyopathy or dilated cardiomyopathy), full gene sequence

TNNI3 *(troponin I, type 3 [cardiac])* (eg, familial hypertrophic cardiomyopathy), full gene sequence

TP53 *(tumor protein 53)* (eg, Li-Fraumeni syndrome, tumor samples), full gene sequence or targeted sequence analysis of >5 exons

TPM1 *(tropomyosin 1 [alpha])* (eg, familial hypertrophic cardiomyopathy), full gene sequence

TSC1 *(tuberous sclerosis 1)* (eg, tuberous sclerosis), duplication/deletion analysis

*TYMP (thymidine phosphorylase)* (eg, mitochondrial DNA depletion syndrome), full gene sequence

VWF *(von Willebrand factor)* (eg, von Willebrand disease type 2N), targeted sequence analysis (eg, exons 18-20, 23-25)

*WT1 (Wilms tumor 1)* (eg, Denys-Drash syndrome, familial Wilms tumor), full gene sequence

*ZEB2 (zinc finger E-box binding homeobox 2)* (eg, Mowat-Wilson syndrome), full gene sequence

▲ 81406    Molecular pathology procedure, Level 7 (eg, analysis of 11-25 exons by DNA sequence analysis, mutation scanning or duplication/deletion variants of 26-50 exons, cytogenomic array analysis for neoplasia)

*ACADVL (acyl-CoA dehydrogenase, very long chain)* (eg, very long chain acyl-coenzyme A dehydrogenase deficiency), full gene sequence

*ACTN4 (actinin, alpha 4)* (eg, focal segmental glomerulosclerosis), full gene sequence

*AFG3L2 (AFG3 ATPase family gene 3-like 2 [S. cerevisiae])* (eg, spinocerebellar ataxia), full gene sequence

*AIRE (autoimmune regulator)* (eg, autoimmune polyendocrinopathy syndrome type 1), full gene sequence

*ALDH7A1 (aldehyde dehydrogenase 7 family, member A1)* (eg, pyridoxine-dependent epilepsy), full gene sequence

*ANO5 (anoctamin 5)* (eg, limb-girdle muscular dystrophy), full gene sequence

*APP (amyloid beta [A4] precursor protein)* (eg, Alzheimer disease), full gene sequence

*ASS1 (argininosuccinate synthase 1)* (eg, citrullinemia type I), full gene sequence

*ATL1 (atlastin GTPase 1)* (eg, spastic paraplegia), full gene sequence

*ATP1A2 (ATPase, Na+/K+ transporting, alpha 2 polypeptide)* (eg, familial hemiplegic migraine), full gene sequence

*ATP7B (ATPase, Cu++ transporting, beta polypeptide)* (eg, Wilson disease), full gene sequence

*BBS1 (Bardet-Biedl syndrome 1)* (eg, Bardet-Biedl syndrome), full gene sequence

*BBS2 (Bardet-Biedl syndrome 2)* (eg, Bardet-Biedl syndrome), full gene sequence

*BCKDHB (branched-chain keto acid dehydrogenase E1, beta polypeptide)* (eg, maple syrup urine disease, type 1B), full gene sequence

*BEST1 (bestrophin 1)* (eg, vitelliform macular dystrophy), full gene sequence

*BMPR2 (bone morphogenetic protein receptor, type II [serine/ threonine kinase])* (eg, heritable pulmonary arterial hypertension), full gene sequence

*BRAF (v-raf murine sarcoma viral oncogene homolog B1)* (eg, Noonan syndrome), full gene sequence

*BSCL2 (Berardinelli-Seip congenital lipodystrophy 2 [seipin])* (eg, Berardinelli-Seip congenital lipodystrophy), full gene sequence

*BTK (Bruton agammaglobulinemia tyrosine kinase)* (eg, X-linked agammaglobulinemia), full gene sequence

*CACNB2 (calcium channel, voltage-dependent, beta 2 subunit)* (eg, Brugada syndrome), full gene sequence

*CAPN3 (~~Calpain~~calpain 3)* (eg, limb-girdle muscular dystrophy [LGMD] type 2A, calpainopathy), full gene sequence

*CBS (cystathionine-beta-synthase)* (eg, homocystinuria, cystathionine beta-synthase deficiency), full gene sequence

*CDH1 (cadherin 1, type 1, E-cadherin [epithelial])* (eg, hereditary diffuse gastric cancer), full gene sequence

*CDKL5 (cyclin-dependent kinase-like 5)* (eg, early infantile epileptic encephalopathy), full gene sequence

*CLCN1 (chloride channel 1, skeletal muscle)* (eg, myotonia congenita), full gene sequence

*CLCNKB (chloride channel, voltage-sensitive Kb)* (eg, Bartter syndrome 3 and 4b), full gene sequence

*CNTNAP2 (contactin-associated protein-like 2)* (eg, Pitt-Hopkins-like syndrome 1), full gene sequence

*COL6A2 (collagen, type VI, alpha 2)* (eg, collagen type VI-related disorders), duplication/deletion analysis

*CPT1A (carnitine palmitoyltransferase 1A [liver])* (eg, carnitine palmitoyltransferase 1A [CPT1A] deficiency), full gene sequence

*CRB1 (crumbs homolog 1 [Drosophila])* (eg, Leber congenital amaurosis), full gene sequence

*CREBBP (CREB binding protein)* (eg, Rubinstein-Taybi syndrome), duplication/deletion analysis

Cytogenomic microarray analysis, neoplasia (eg, interrogation of copy number, and loss-of-heterozygosity via single nucleotide polymorphism [SNP]-based comparative genomic hybridization [CGH] microarray)analysis

(Do not report analyte-specific molecular pathology procedures separately when the specific analytes are included as part of the cytogenomic microarray analysis for neoplasia)

(Do not report 88271 when performing cytogenomic microarray analysis)

*DBT (dihydrolipoamide branched chain transacylase E2)* (eg, maple syrup urine disease, type 2), full gene sequence

*DLAT (dihydrolipoamide S-acetyltransferase)* (eg, pyruvate dehydrogenase E2 deficiency), full gene sequence

*DLD (dihydrolipoamide dehydrogenase)* (eg, maple syrup urine disease, type III), full gene sequence

*DSC2 (desmocollin)* (eg, arrhythmogenic right ventricular dysplasia/cardiomyopathy 11), full gene sequence

*DSG2 (desmoglein 2)* (eg, arrhythmogenic right ventricular dysplasia/cardiomyopathy 10), full gene sequence

*DSP (desmoplakin)* (eg, arrhythmogenic right ventricular dysplasia/cardiomyopathy 8), full gene sequence

*EFHC1 (EF-hand domain [C-terminal] containing 1)* (eg, juvenile myoclonic epilepsy), full gene sequence

*EIF2B3 (eukaryotic translation initiation factor 2B, subunit 3 gamma, 58kDa)* (eg, leukoencephalopathy with vanishing white matter), full gene sequence

*EIF2B4 (eukaryotic translation initiation factor 2B, subunit 4 delta, 67kDa)* (eg, leukoencephalopathy with vanishing white matter), full gene sequence

*EIF2B5 (eukaryotic translation initiation factor 2B, subunit 5 epsilon, 82kDa)* (eg, childhood ataxia with central nervous system hypomyelination/vanishing white matter), full gene sequence

*ENG (endoglin)* (eg, hereditary hemorrhagic telangiectasia, type 1), full gene sequence

*EYA1 (eyes absent homolog 1 [Drosophila])* (eg, branchio-oto-renal [BOR] spectrum disorders), full gene sequence

*F8 (coagulation factor VIII)* (eg, hemophilia A), duplication/ deletion analysis

*FAH (fumarylacetoacetate hydrolase [fumarylacetoacetase])* (eg, tyrosinemia, type 1), full gene sequence

*FASTKD2 (FAST kinase domains 2)* (eg, mitochondrial respiratory chain complex IV deficiency), full gene sequence

FIG4 (FIG4 homolog, SAC1 lipid phosphatase domain containing [S. cerevisiae]) (eg, Charcot-Marie-Tooth disease), full gene sequence

FTSJ1 (FtsJ RNA methyltransferase homolog 1 [E. coli]) (eg, X-linked mental retardation 9), full gene sequence

FUS (fused in sarcoma) (eg, amyotrophic lateral sclerosis), full gene sequence

GAA (glucosidase, alpha; acid) (eg, glycogen storage disease type II [Pompe disease]), full gene sequence

GALC (galactosylceramidase) (eg, Krabbe disease), full gene sequence

GALT (galactose-1-phosphate uridylyltransferase) (eg, galactosemia), full gene sequence

GARS (glycyl-tRNA synthetase) (eg, Charcot-Marie-Tooth disease), full gene sequence

GCDH (glutaryl-CoA dehydrogenase) (eg, glutaricacidemia type 1), full gene sequence

GCK (glucokinase [hexokinase 4]) (eg, maturity-onset diabetes of the young [MODY]), full gene sequence

GLUD1 (glutamate dehydrogenase 1) (eg, familial hyperinsulinism), full gene sequence

GNE (glucosamine [UDP-N-acetyl]-2-epimerase/N-acetylmannosamine kinase) (eg, inclusion body myopathy 2 [IBM2], Nonaka myopathy), full gene sequence

GRN (granulin) (eg, frontotemporal dementia), full gene sequence

HADHA (hydroxyacyl-CoA dehydrogenase/3-ketoacyl-CoA thiolase/enoyl-CoA hydratase [trifunctional protein] alpha subunit) (eg, long chain acyl-coenzyme A dehydrogenase deficiency), full gene sequence

HADHB (hydroxyacyl-CoA dehydrogenase/3-ketoacyl-CoA thiolase/enoyl-CoA hydratase [trifunctional protein], beta subunit) (eg, trifunctional protein deficiency), full gene sequence

HEXA (hexosaminidase A, alpha polypeptide) (eg, Tay-Sachs disease), full gene sequence

HLCS (HLCS holocarboxylase synthetase) (eg, holocarboxylase synthetase deficiency), full gene sequence

HNF4A (hepatocyte nuclear factor 4, alpha) (eg, maturity-onset diabetes of the young [MODY]), full gene sequence

IDUA (iduronidase, alpha-L-) (eg, mucopolysaccharidosis type I), full gene sequence

INF2 (inverted formin, FH2 and WH2 domain containing) (eg, focal segmental glomerulosclerosis), full gene sequence

IVD (isovaleryl-CoA dehydrogenase) (eg, isovaleric acidemia), full gene sequence

JAG1 (jagged 1) (eg, Alagille syndrome), duplication/deletion analysis

JUP (junction plakoglobin) (eg, arrhythmogenic right ventricular dysplasia/cardiomyopathy 11), full gene sequence

KAL1 (Kallmann syndrome 1 sequence) (eg, Kallmann syndrome), full gene sequence

KCNH2 (potassium voltage-gated channel, subfamily H [eag-related], member 2) (eg, short QT syndrome, long QT syndrome), full gene sequence

(Do not report 81406 for KCNH2 full gene sequence in conjunction with 81280)

KCNQ1 (potassium voltage-gated channel, KQT-like subfamily, member 1) (eg, short QT syndrome, long QT syndrome), full gene sequence

(Do not report 81406 for KCNQ1 full gene sequence with 81280)

KCNQ2 (potassium voltage-gated channel, KQT-like subfamily, member 2) (eg, epileptic encephalopathy), full gene sequence

LDB3 (LIM domain binding 3) (eg, familial dilated cardiomyopathy, myofibrillar myopathy), full gene sequence

LDLR (low density lipoprotein receptor) (eg, familial hypercholesterolemia), full gene sequence

LEPR (leptin receptor) (eg, obesity with hypogonadism), full gene sequence

LHCGR (luteinizing hormone/choriogonadotropin receptor) (eg, precocious male puberty), full gene sequence

LMNA (lamin A/C) (eg, Emery-Dreifuss muscular dystrophy [EDMD1, 2 and 3] limb-girdle muscular dystrophy [LGMD] type 1B, dilated cardiomyopathy [CMD1A], familial partial lipodystrophy [FPLD2]), full gene sequence

LRP5 (low density lipoprotein receptor-related protein 5) (eg, osteopetrosis), full gene sequence

MAP2K1 (mitogen-activated protein kinase 1) (eg, cardiofaciocutaneous syndrome), full gene sequence

MAP2K2 (mitogen-activated protein kinase 2) (eg, cardiofaciocutaneous syndrome), full gene sequence

MAPT (microtubule-associated protein tau) (eg, frontotemporal dementia), full gene sequence

MCCC1 (methylcrotonoyl-CoA carboxylase 1 [alpha]) (eg, 3-methylcrotonyl-CoA carboxylase deficiency), full gene sequence

MCCC2 (methylcrotonoyl-CoA carboxylase 2 [beta]) (eg, 3-methylcrotonyl carboxylase deficiency), full gene sequence

MFN2 (mitofusin 2) (eg, Charcot-Marie-Tooth disease), full gene sequence

MTM1 (myotubularin 1) (eg, X-linked centronuclear myopathy), full gene sequence

MUT (methylmalonyl CoA mutase) (eg, methylmalonic acidemia), full gene sequence

MUTYH (mutY homolog [E. coli]) (eg, MYH-associated polyposis), full gene sequence

NDUFS1 (NADH dehydrogenase [ubiquinone] Fe-S protein 1, 75kDa [NADH-coenzyme Q reductase]) (eg, Leigh syndrome, mitochondrial complex I deficiency), full gene sequence

NF2 (neurofibromin 2 [merlin]) (eg, neurofibromatosis, type 2), full gene sequence

NOTCH3 (notch 3) (eg, cerebral autosomal dominant arteriopathy with subcortical infarcts and leukoencephalopathy [CADASIL]), targeted sequence analysis (eg, exons 1-23)

NPC1 (Niemann-Pick disease, type C1) (eg, Niemann-Pick disease), full gene sequence

NPHP1 (nephronophthisis 1 [juvenile]) (eg, Joubert syndrome), full gene sequence

NSD1 (nuclear receptor binding SET domain protein 1) (eg, Sotos syndrome), full gene sequence

OPA1 (optic atrophy 1) (eg, optic atrophy), duplication/deletion analysis

OPTN (optineurin) (eg, amyotrophic lateral sclerosis), full gene sequence

PAFAH1B1 (platelet-activating factor acetylhydrolase 1b, regulatory subunit 1 [45kDa]) (eg, lissencephaly, Miller-Dieker syndrome), full gene sequence

PAH (phenylalanine hydroxylase) (eg, phenylketonuria), full gene sequence

PALB2 (partner and localizer of BRCA2) (eg, breast and pancreatic cancer), full gene sequence

PARK2 (Parkinson protein 2, E3 ubiquitin protein ligase [parkin]) (eg, Parkinson disease), full gene sequence

PAX2 (paired box 2) (eg, renal coloboma syndrome), full gene sequence

PC (pyruvate carboxylase) (eg, pyruvate carboxylase deficiency), full gene sequence

PCCA (propionyl CoA carboxylase, alpha polypeptide) (eg, propionic acidemia, type 1), full gene sequence

PCCB (propionyl CoA carboxylase, beta polypeptide) (eg, propionic acidemia), full gene sequence

PCDH15 (protocadherin-related 15) (eg, Usher syndrome type 1F), duplication/deletion analysis

PDHA1 (pyruvate dehydrogenase [lipoamide] alpha 1) (eg, lactic acidosis), full gene sequence

PDHX (pyruvate dehydrogenase complex, component X) (eg, lactic acidosis), full gene sequence

PHEX (phosphate-regulating endopeptidase homolog, X-linked) (eg, hypophosphatemic rickets), full gene sequence

PKD2 (polycystic kidney disease 2 [autosomal dominant]) (eg, polycystic kidney disease), full gene sequence

PKP2 (plakophilin 2) (eg, arrhythmogenic right ventricular dysplasia/cardiomyopathy 9), full gene sequence

PNKD (eg, paroxysmal nonkinesigenic dyskinesia) (eg, paroxysmal nonkinesigenic dyskinesia), full gene sequence

POLG (polymerase [DNA directed], gamma) (eg, Alpers-Huttenlocher syndrome, autosomal dominant progressive external ophthalmoplegia), full gene sequence

POMGNT1 (protein O-linked mannose beta1,2-N acetylglucosaminyltransferase) (eg, muscle-eye-brain disease, Walker-Warburg syndrome), full gene sequence

POMT1 (protein-O-mannosyltransferase 1) (eg, limb-girdle muscular dystrophy [LGMD] type 2K, Walker-Warburg syndrome), full gene sequence

POMT2 (protein-O-mannosyltransferase 2) (eg, limb-girdle muscular dystrophy [LGMD] type 2N, Walker-Warburg syndrome), full gene sequence

PRKAG2 (protein kinase, AMP-activated, gamma 2 non-catalytic subunit) (eg, familial hypertrophic cardiomyopathy with Wolff-Parkinson-White syndrome, lethal congenital glycogen storage disease of heart), full gene sequence

PRKCG (protein kinase C, gamma) (eg, spinocerebellar ataxia), full gene sequence

PSEN2 (presenilin 2 [Alzheimer disease 4]) (eg, Alzheimer disease), full gene sequence

PTPN11 (protein tyrosine phosphatase, non-receptor type 11) (eg, Noonan syndrome, LEOPARD syndrome), full gene sequence

PYGM (phosphorylase, glycogen, muscle) (eg, glycogen storage disease type V, McArdle disease), full gene sequence

RAF1 (v-raf-1 murine leukemia viral oncogene homolog 1) (eg, LEOPARD syndrome), full gene sequence

RET (ret proto-oncogene) (eg, Hirschsprung disease), full gene sequence

RPE65 (retinal pigment epithelium-specific protein 65kDa) (eg, retinitis pigmentosa, Leber congenital amaurosis), full gene sequence

RYR1 (ryanodine receptor 1, skeletal) (eg, malignant hyperthermia), targeted sequence analysis of exons with functionally-confirmed mutations

SCN4A (sodium channel, voltage-gated, type IV, alpha subunit) (eg, hyperkalemic periodic paralysis), full gene sequence

SCNN1A (sodium channel, nonvoltage-gated 1 alpha) (eg, pseudohypoaldosteronism), full gene sequence

SCNN1B (sodium channel, nonvoltage-gated 1, beta) (eg, Liddle syndrome, pseudohypoaldosteronism), full gene sequence

SCNN1G (sodium channel, nonvoltage-gated 1, gamma) (eg, Liddle syndrome, pseudohypoaldosteronism), full gene sequence

SDHA (succinate dehydrogenase complex, subunit A, flavoprotein [Fp]) (eg, Leigh syndrome, mitochondrial complex II deficiency), full gene sequence

SETX (senataxin) (eg, ataxia), full gene sequence

SGCE (sarcoglycan, epsilon) (eg, myoclonic dystonia), full gene sequence

SH3TC2 (SH3 domain and tetratricopeptide repeats 2) (eg, Charcot-Marie-Tooth disease), full gene sequence

SLC9A6 (solute carrier family 9 [sodium/hydrogen exchanger], member 6) (eg, Christianson syndrome), full gene sequence

SLC26A4 (solute carrier family 26, member 4) (eg, Pendred syndrome), full gene sequence

SLC37A4 (solute carrier family 37 [glucose-6-phosphate transporter], member 4) (eg, glycogen storage disease type Ib), full gene sequence

SMAD4 (SMAD family member 4) (eg, hemorrhagic telangiectasia syndrome, juvenile polyposis), full gene sequence

SOS1 (son of sevenless homolog 1) (eg, Noonan syndrome, gingival fibromatosis), full gene sequence

SPAST (spastin) (eg, spastic paraplegia), full gene sequence

SPG7 (spastic paraplegia 7 [pure and complicated autosomal recessive]) (eg, spastic paraplegia), full gene sequence

STXBP1 (syntaxin-binding protein 1) (eg, epileptic encephalopathy), full gene sequence

TAZ (tafazzin) (eg, methylglutaconic aciduria type 2, Barth syndrome), full gene sequence

TCF4 (transcription factor 4) (eg, Pitt-Hopkins syndrome), full gene sequence

TH (tyrosine hydroxylase) (eg, Segawa syndrome), full gene sequence

TMEM43 (transmembrane protein 43) (eg, arrhythmogenic right ventricular cardiomyopathy), full gene sequence

TNNT2 (troponin T, type 2 [cardiac]) (eg, familial hypertrophic cardiomyopathy), full gene sequence

TRPC6 (transient receptor potential cation channel, subfamily C, member 6) (eg, focal segmental glomerulosclerosis), full gene sequence

TSC1 (tuberous sclerosis 1) (eg, tuberous sclerosis), full gene sequence

TSC2 (tuberous sclerosis 2) (eg, tuberous sclerosis), duplication/deletion analysis

UBE3A (ubiquitin protein ligase E3A) (eg, Angelman syndrome), full gene sequence

UMOD (uromodulin) (eg, glomerulocystic kidney disease with hyperuricemia and isosthenuria), full gene sequence

VWF (von Willebrand factor) (von Willebrand disease type 2A), extended targeted sequence analysis (eg, exons 11-16, 24-26, 51, 52)

WAS (Wiskott-Aldrich syndrome [eczema-thrombocytopenia]) (eg, Wiskott-Aldrich syndrome), full gene sequence

▲ 81407   Molecular pathology procedure, Level 8 (eg, analysis of 26-50 exons by DNA sequence analysis, mutation scanning or duplication/deletion variants of >50 exons, sequence analysis of multiple genes on one platform)

ABCC8 (ATP-binding cassette, sub-family C [CFTR/MRP], member 8) (eg, familial hyperinsulinism), full gene sequence

AGL (amylo-alpha-1, 6-glucosidase, 4-alpha-glucanotransferase) (eg, glycogen storage disease type III), full gene sequence

AHI1 (Abelson helper integration site 1) (eg, Joubert syndrome), full gene sequence

ASPM (asp [abnormal spindle] homolog, microcephaly associated [Drosophila]) (eg, primary microcephaly), full gene sequence

CACNA1A (calcium channel, voltage-dependent, P/Q type, alpha 1A subunit) (eg, familial hemiplegic migraine), full gene sequence

CHD7 (chromodomain helicase DNA binding protein 7) (eg, CHARGE syndrome), full gene sequence

COL4A4 (collagen, type IV, alpha 4) (eg, Alport syndrome), full gene sequence

COL4A5 (collagen, type IV, alpha 5) (eg, Alport syndrome), duplication/deletion analysis

COL6A1 (collagen, type VI, alpha 1) (eg, collagen type VI-related disorders), full gene sequence

COL6A2 (collagen, type VI, alpha 2) (eg, collagen type VI-related disorders), full gene sequence

COL6A3 (collagen, type VI, alpha 3) (eg, collagen type VI-related disorders), full gene sequence

CREBBP (CREB binding protein) (eg, Rubinstein-Taybi syndrome), full gene sequence

F8 (coagulation factor VIII) (eg, hemophilia A), full gene sequence

JAG1 (jagged 1) (eg, Alagille syndrome), full gene sequence

KDM5C (lysine [K]-specific demethylase 5C) (eg, X-linked mental retardation), full gene sequence

KIAA0196 (KIAA0196) (eg, spastic paraplegia), full gene sequence

L1CAM (L1 cell adhesion molecule) (eg, MASA syndrome, X-linked hydrocephaly), full gene sequence

LAMB2 (laminin, beta 2 [laminin S]) (eg, Pierson syndrome), full gene sequence

MYBPC3 (myosin binding protein C, cardiac) (eg, familial hypertrophic cardiomyopathy), full gene sequence

MYH6 (myosin, heavy chain 6, cardiac muscle, alpha) (eg, familial dilated cardiomyopathy), full gene sequence

MYH7 (myosin, heavy chain 7, cardiac muscle, beta) (eg, familial hypertrophic cardiomyopathy, Liang distal myopathy), full gene sequence

MYO7A (myosin VIIA) (eg, Usher syndrome, type 1), full gene sequence

NOTCH1 (notch 1) (eg, aortic valve disease), full gene sequence

NPHS1 (nephrosis 1, congenital, Finnish type [nephrin]) (eg, congenital Finnish nephrosis), full gene sequence

OPA1 (optic atrophy 1) (eg, optic atrophy), full gene sequence

PCDH15 (protocadherin-related 15) (eg, Usher syndrome, type 1), full gene sequence

PKD1 (polycystic kidney disease 1 [autosomal dominant]) (eg, polycystic kidney disease), full gene sequence

PLCE1 (phospholipase C, epsilon 1) (eg, nephrotic syndrome type 3), full gene sequence

SCN1A (sodium channel, voltage-gated, type 1, alpha subunit) (eg, generalized epilepsy with febrile seizures), full gene sequence

SCN5A (sodium channel, voltage-gated, type V, alpha subunit) (eg, familial dilated cardiomyopathy), full gene sequence

SLC12A1 (solute carrier family 12 [sodium/potassium/chloride transporters], member 1) (eg, Bartter syndrome), full gene sequence

SLC12A3 (solute carrier family 12 [sodium/chloride transporters], member 3) (eg, Gitelman syndrome), full gene sequence

SPG11 (spastic paraplegia 11 [autosomal recessive]) (eg, spastic paraplegia), full gene sequence

SPTBN2 (spectrin, beta, non-erythrocytic 2) (eg, spinocerebellar ataxia), full gene sequence

TMEM67 (transmembrane protein 67) (eg, Joubert syndrome), full gene sequence

TSC2 (tuberous sclerosis 2) (eg, tuberous sclerosis), full gene sequence

USH1C (Usher syndrome 1C [autosomal recessive, severe]) (eg, Usher syndrome, type 1), full gene sequence

VPS13B (vacuolar protein sorting 13 homolog B [yeast]) (eg, Cohen syndrome), duplication/deletion analysis

WDR62 (WD repeat domain 62) (eg, primary autosomal recessive microcephaly), full gene sequence

▲ 81408   Molecular pathology procedure, Level 9 (eg, analysis of >50 exons in a single gene by DNA sequence analysis)

ABCA4 (ATP-binding cassette, sub-family A [ABC1], member 4) (eg, Stargardt disease, age-related macular degeneration), full gene sequence

ATM (ataxia telangiectasia mutated) (eg, ataxia telangiectasia), full gene sequence

CDH23 (cadherin-related 23) (eg, Usher syndrome, type 1), full gene sequence

CEP290 (centrosomal protein 290kDa) (eg, Joubert syndrome), full gene sequence

COL1A1 (collagen, type I, alpha 1) (eg, osteogenesis imperfecta, type I), full gene sequence

COL1A2 (collagen, type I, alpha 2) (eg, osteogenesis imperfecta, type I), full gene sequence

COL4A1 (collagen, type IV, alpha 1) (eg, brain small-vessel disease with hemorrhage), full gene sequence

COL4A3 (collagen, type IV, alpha 3 [Goodpasture antigen]) (eg, Alport syndrome), full gene sequence

*COL4A5 (collagen, type IV, alpha 5)* (eg, Alport syndrome), full gene sequence

*DMD (dystrophin)* (eg, Duchenne/Becker muscular dystrophy), full gene sequence

*DYSF (dysferlin, limb girdle muscular dystrophy 2B [autosomal recessive])* (eg, limb-girdle muscular dystrophy), full gene sequence

*FBN1 (fibrillin 1)* (eg, Marfan syndrome), full gene sequence

*ITPR1 (inositol 1,4,5-trisphosphate receptor, type 1)* (eg, spinocerebellar ataxia), full gene sequence

*LAMA2 (laminin, alpha 2)* (eg, congenital muscular dystrophy), full gene sequence

*LRRK2 (leucine-rich repeat kinase 2)* (eg, Parkinson disease), full gene sequence

*MYH11 (myosin, heavy chain 11, smooth muscle)* (eg, thoracic aortic aneurysms and aortic dissections), full gene sequence

*NEB (nebulin)* (eg, nemaline myopathy 2), full gene sequence

*NF1 (neurofibromin 1)* (eg, neurofibromatosis, type 1), full gene sequence

*PKHD1 (polycystic kidney and hepatic disease 1)* (eg, autosomal recessive polycystic kidney disease), full gene sequence

*RYR1 (ryanodine receptor 1, skeletal)* (eg, malignant hyperthermia), full gene sequence

*RYR2 (ryanodine receptor 2 [cardiac])* (eg, catecholaminergic polymorphic ventricular tachycardia, arrhythmogenic right ventricular dysplasia), full gene sequence or targeted sequence analysis of > 50 exons

*USH2A (Usher syndrome 2A [autosomal recessive, mild])* (eg, Usher syndrome, type 2), full gene sequence

*VPS13B (vacuolar protein sorting 13 homolog B [yeast])* (eg, Cohen syndrome), full gene sequence

*VWF (von Willebrand factor)* (eg, von Willebrand disease types 1 and 3), full gene sequence

● 81504    Code added

● 81507    Code added

▲ 84112    ~~Placental~~Evaluation of cervicovaginal fluid for specific amniotic fluid protein(s) (eg, placental alpha microglobulin-1 ~~(PAMG-1)~~ [PAMG-1], ~~cervicovaginal secretion~~placental protein 12 [PP12], alpha-fetoprotein), qualitative, each specimen;

▲ 87498    enterovirus, amplified probe technique, includes reverse transcription ~~and amplified probe technique~~when performed

▲ 87521    hepatitis C, amplified probe technique, includes reverse transcription ~~and amplified probe technique~~when performed

▲ 87522    hepatitis C, quantification, includes reverse transcription ~~and quantification~~when performed

▲ 87535    HIV-1, amplified probe technique, includes reverse transcription ~~and amplified probe technique~~when performed

▲ 87536    HIV-1, quantification, includes reverse transcription ~~and quantification~~when performed

▲ 87538    HIV-2, amplified probe technique, includes reverse transcription ~~and amplified probe technique~~when performed

▲ 87539    HIV-2, quantification, includes reverse transcription ~~and quantification~~when performed

● 87661    Code added

▲ 88342    Immunohistochemistry ~~(including tissue immunoperoxidase)~~or immunocytochemistry, each separately identifiable antibody per block, cytologic preparation, or hematologic smear; first separately identifiable antibody per slide

✛● 88343    Code added

## Medicine

#● 90673    Code added

● 90685    Code added

● 90686    Code added

∥● 90687    Code added

∥● 90688    Code added

▲ 91065    Breath hydrogen or methane test (eg, for detection of lactase deficiency, fructose intolerance, bacterial overgrowth, or oro-cecal gastrointestinal transit);

92506    ~~Evaluation of speech, language, voice, communication, and/or auditory processing;~~

● 92521    Code added

● 92522    Code added

● 92523    Code added

● 92524    Code added

⊙● 93582    Code added

⊙● 93583    Code added

⊙▲ 93653    Comprehensive electrophysiologic evaluation including insertion and repositioning of multiple electrode catheters with induction or attempted induction of an arrhythmia with right atrial pacing and recording, right ventricular pacing and recording (when necessary), and His bundle recording (when necessary) with intracardiac catheter ablation of arrhythmogenic focus; with treatment of supraventricular tachycardia by ablation of fast or slow atrioventricular pathway, accessory atrioventricular connection, cavo-tricuspid isthmus or other single atrial focus or source of atrial re-entry

⊙▲ 93654    with treatment of ventricular tachycardia or focus of ventricular ectopy including intracardiac electrophysiologic 3D mapping, when performed, and left ventricular pacing and recording, when performed

⊙▲ 93656    Comprehensive electrophysiologic evaluation including transseptal catheterizations, insertion and repositioning of multiple electrode catheters with induction or attempted induction of an arrhythmia ~~with atrial recording and~~including left or right atrial pacing,/recording when ~~possible~~necessary, right ventricular pacing/recording when necessary and ~~recording, His~~ bundle recording when necessary with intracardiac catheter ablation ~~of arrhythmogenic focus, with treatment~~of atrial fibrillation ~~by ablation~~by pulmonary vein isolation;

● 94669    Code added

● 97610    Code added

▲ 99170    Anogenital examination ~~with colposcopic magnification,~~ magnified, in childhood for suspected trauma, including image recording when performed;

## Category II Codes

● **0580F**    Code added

● **0581F**    Code added

● **0582F**    Code added

● **0583F**    Code added

● **0584F**    Code added

▲ **1040F**    DSM-~~IV~~ V™ criteria for major depressive disorder documented at the initial evaluation (MDD, MDD ADOL)[1]

● **1500F**    Code added

● **1501F**    Code added

● **1502F**    Code added

● **1503F**    Code added

● **1504F**    Code added

● **1505F**    Code added

● **3751F**    Code added

● **3752F**    Code added

● **3753F**    Code added

● **3754F**    Code added

● **3755F**    Code added

● **3756F**    Code added

● **3757F**    Code added

● **3758F**    Code added

● **3759F**    Code added

● **3760F**    Code added

● **3761F**    Code added

● **3762F**    Code added

● **3763F**    Code added

● **4540F**    Code added

● **4541F**    Code added

● **4550F**    Code added

● **4551F**    Code added

● **4552F**    Code added

● **4553F**    Code added

● **4554F**    Code added

● **4555F**    Code added

● **4556F**    Code added

● **4557F**    Code added

● **4558F**    Code added

● **4559F**    Code added

● **4560F**    Code added

● **4561F**    Code added

● **4562F**    Code added

● **4563F**    Code added

● **9001F**    Code added

● **9002F**    Code added

● **9003F**    Code added

● **9004F**    Code added

● **9005F**    Code added

● **9006F**    Code added

● **9007F**    Code added

## Category III Codes

**0078T**    ~~Endovascular repair using prosthesis of abdominal aortic aneurysm, pseudoaneurysm or dissection, abdominal aorta involving visceral branches (superior mesenteric, celiac and/or renal artery[s]);~~

**0079T**    ~~Placement of visceral extension prosthesis for endovascular repair of abdominal aortic aneurysm involving visceral vessels, each visceral branch (List separately in addition to code for primary procedure);~~

**0080T**    ~~Endovascular repair using prosthesis of abdominal aortic aneurysm, pseudoaneurysm or dissection, abdominal aorta involving visceral vessels (superior mesenteric, celiac and/or renal artery[s]), radiological supervision and interpretation;~~

**0081T**    ~~Placement of visceral extension prosthesis for endovascular repair of abdominal aortic aneurysm involving visceral vessels, each visceral branch, radiological supervision and interpretation (List separately in addition to code for primary procedure);~~

**0124T**    ~~Conjunctival incision with posterior extrascleral placement of pharmacological agent (does not include supply of medication);~~

**0183T**    ~~Low frequency, non-contact, non-thermal ultrasound, including topical application(s), when performed, wound assessment, and instruction(s) for ongoing care, per day;~~

**0185T**    ~~Multivariate analysis of patient-specific findings with quantifiable computer probability assessment, including report;~~

**0186T**    ~~Suprachoroidal delivery of pharmacologic agent (does not include supply of medication);~~

**0192T**    ~~external approach~~

**0260T**    ~~Total body systemic hypothermia, per day, in the neonate 28 days of age or younger;~~

**0261T**    ~~Selective head hypothermia, per day, in the neonate 28 days of age or younger;~~

**0318T**    ~~Implantation of catheter-delivered prosthetic aortic heart valve, open thoracic approach, (eg, transapical, other than transaortic);~~

● **0319T**    Code added

- ● 0320T    Code added
- ● 0321T    Code added
- ● 0322T    Code added
- ● 0323T    Code added
- ● 0324T    Code added
- ● 0325T    Code added
- ● 0326T    Code added
- ● 0327T    Code added
- ● 0328T    Code added
- ● 0329T    Code added
- ● 0330T    Code added
- ● 0331T    Code added
- ● 0332T    Code added
- ● 0333T    Code added
- ● 0334T    Code added
- ⊙● 0335T    Code added
- ● 0336T    Code added
- ● 0337T    Code added
- ● 0338T    Code added
- ● 0339T    Code added

# Appendix C

## Clinical Examples

▶As described in the CPT 2014 code set, clinical examples of the CPT codes for Evaluation and Management (E/M) services are intended to be an important element of the coding system. The clinical examples, when used with the E/M descriptors contained in the full text of the CPT code set, provide a useful tool and guidance for individuals to report the services provided to their patients. Clinical examples of the codes for E/M services are provided to assist physicians in understanding the meaning of the descriptors and selecting the correct code. Each example was developed by physicians in the specialties shown.

The same problem, when seen by physicians in different specialties, may involve different amounts of work. Therefore, the appropriate level of encounter should be reported using the descriptors rather than the examples.

The American Medical Association is pleased to provide you with these clinical examples for the CPT 2014 code set. The clinical examples that are provided in this supplement are limited to Office or Other Outpatient Services, Hospital Inpatient Services, Consultations, Critical Care, Prolonged Services, and Care Plan Oversight.

These clinical examples are used to describe presenting problems that are frequently encountered in a given specialty. Typical patients with such problems may commonly require the listed Evaluation and Management (E/M) service. Therefore, these examples are **not** appropriately used for any review of correct coding or estimating physician or qualified health care professional work. These clinical examples do not encompass the entire scope of medical practice. Inclusion or exclusion of any particular specialty group does not infer any judgment of importance or lack thereof; nor does it limit the applicability of the example to any particular specialty. We present these examples to provide additional educational context when used in conjunction with the E/M descriptors and guidelines.

Of utmost importance is that these clinical examples are just that: examples. A particular patient encounter, depending on the specific circumstances, must be judged by the services provided by the physician or other qualified health care professional for that particular patient. Simply because the patient's complaints, symptoms, or diagnoses match those of a particular clinical example does not automatically assign that patient encounter to that particular level of service. Moreover, simply because the patient's complaints, symptoms, or diagnoses **do not** match those of a particular clinical example does not automatically **exclude** that patient encounter from a particular level of service. The three components (history, examination, and medical decision making) must be met, consistent with the Nature of Presenting Problem, and documented in the medical record to report a particular level of service.◀

## Office or Other Outpatient Service

### New Patient

**99201**    Initial office visit for a 50-year-old male from out-of-town who needs a prescription refill for a nonsteroidal anti-inflammatory drug. (Anesthesiology)

Initial office visit for a 40-year-old female, new patient, requesting information about local pain clinics. (Anesthesiology/Pain Medicine)

Initial office visit for a 10-year-old female for determination of visual acuity as part of a summer camp physical (does not include determination of refractive error). (Ophthalmology)

Initial office visit for an out-of-town patient requiring topical refill.

Initial office visit for a 65-year-old male for reassurance about an isolated seborrheic keratosis on upper back. (Dermatology)

Initial office visit for an out-of-state visitor who needs refill of topical steroid to treat lichen planus. (Dermatology)

Initial office visit for an 86-year-old male, out-of-town visitor, who needs prescription refilled for an anal skin preparation that he forgot. (Colon & Rectal Surgery)

Initial office visit for a patient following surgery in another OMS practice. Timing and symptoms suggest diagnosis of alveolar osteitis for which packing will be indicated. (Oral & Maxillofacial Surgery)

Initial office visit for a patient with a pedunculated lesion of the neck which is unsightly. (Dermatology)

Initial office visit for a 10-year-old male, for limited subungual hematoma not requiring drainage. (Internal Medicine/Podiatry Surgery)

Initial office visit with a 9-month-old female with diaper rash. (Pediatrics)

Initial office visit with a 5-year-old female to remove sutures from simple wound placed by another physician. (Dermatology)

Initial office visit for a patient with a small area of sunburn requiring first aid. (Dermatology)

Initial office visit for the evaluation and management of a contusion of a finger. (Orthopaedic Surgery)

Initial office visit for a 22-year-old male with a small area of sunburn requiring first aid. (Family Medicine/Internal Medicine)

Initial office visit for a 25-year-old female, presents with complaints of skin tags on her neck. (Plastic Surgery)

Initial office visit for an 86-year-old male with a 2 cm lipoma on back that he is concerned is infected. (General Surgery)

Initial office visit with a 5-year-old female who had absorbable sutures, in for a wound check with no complications. (Plastic Surgery)

Initial office visit for an 85-year-old patient with a history of cigarette smoking now with an asymmetrical neck mass, referred by primary care physician for fine-needle aspiration. (Pathology)

Initial office visit for a 25-year-old patient with brief history of cigarette smoking now with a symmetrical neck enlargement, referred by primary care physician for fine-needle aspiration. (Pathology)

Initial office visit for a 55-year-old male, out-of-town visitor, with treated sleep apnea who requests a prescription for a replacement CPAP interface. (Sleep Medicine)

**99202** Initial office visit for a 13-year-old patient with comedopapular acne of the face unresponsive to over-the-counter medications. (Family Medicine)

Initial office visit for a patient with a clinically benign lesion or nodule of the lower leg that has been present for many years. (Dermatology)

Initial office visit for a patient with a circumscribed patch of dermatitis of the leg. (Dermatology)

Initial office visit for a patient with papulosquamous eruption of elbows. (Dermatology)

Initial office visit for a 9-year-old patient with erythematous grouped, vesicular eruption of the lip of three days' duration. (Pediatrics)

Initial office visit for an 18-year-old male referred by an orthodontist for advice regarding removal of four wisdom teeth. (Oral & Maxillofacial Surgery)

Initial office visit for a 14-year-old male, who was referred by his orthodontist, for advice on the exposure of impacted maxillary cuspids. (Oral & Maxillofacial Surgery)

Initial office visit for a patient presenting with itching patches on the wrists and ankles. (Dermatology)

Initial office visit for a 30-year-old male with a two-week-old burn of the hand, now healed but patient concerned with redness and swelling. (Plastic Surgery)

Initial evaluation and management of recurrent urinary infection in female. (Internal Medicine)

Initial office visit with a 10-year-old female with history of chronic otitis media and a draining ear. (Pediatrics)

Initial office visit for a 10-year-old female with acute maxillary sinusitis. (Family Medicine)

Initial office visit for a patient with papulopustular and comedonal acne. (Dermatology)

Initial office visit for a patient with recurring episodes of herpes simplex who has developed a clustering of vesicles on the upper lip. (Internal Medicine)

Initial office visit with a 10-year-old male with severe rash and itching for the past 24 hours, positive history for contact with poison oak 48 hours prior to the visit. (Family Medicine)

Initial office visit for a 65-year-old female with low hemoglobin level, no evidence of clinical bleeding, who was referred by her internist for possible bone marrow aspiration. (Pathology)

Initial office visit for a 55-year-old patient with a history of cigarette smoking now with an asymmetrical neck mass, referred by primary care physician for fine-needle aspiration. (Pathology)

Initial office visit for a 45-year-old male with known sleep apnea and an inability to tolerate CPAP due to dry mouth. (Sleep Medicine)

Initial office visit for an 18-year-old male with cellulitis around a superficial puncture wound of the skin. (General Surgery)

Initial office visit for a 61-year-old male with a macerated, itching rash between the toes that has been present for three weeks. (Podiatric Surgery)

Initial office visit for a healthy 16-year-old male with an ingrown nail with paronychia. (Podiatric Surgery)

**99203** Initial office visit of a 76-year-old male with a stasis ulcer of three months' duration. (Dermatology)

Initial office visit for a 30-year-old female with pain in the lateral aspect of the forearm. (Physical Medicine & Rehabilitation)

Initial office visit for a patient with cystic acne of the face, chest, and back. Discussion of use of systemic medication. (Dermatology)

Initial office visit for a patient with a patchy, scaly erythematous eruption of the extremities. (Dermatology)

Initial office visit for a 57-year-old female who complains of painful parotid swelling of one week's duration. (Oral & Maxillofacial Surgery)

Initial office visit for a diffusely photodamaged patient with multiple crusted lesions. (Dermatology)

Initial office visit for a patient with dermatitis of the antecubital and popliteal fossae. (Dermatology)

Initial office visit for a 22-year-old female with irregular menses. (Family Medicine)

**Appendix C**

Initial office visit for a 50-year-old female with dyspepsia and nausea. (Family Medicine)

Initial office visit for a 53-year-old laborer with degenerative joint disease of the knee with no prior treatment. (Orthopaedic Surgery)

Initial office visit for a 60-year-old male with Dupuytren's contracture of one hand with multiple digit involvement. (Orthopaedic Surgery)

Initial office visit for a 33-year-old male with painless gross hematuria without cystoscopy. (Internal Medicine)

Initial office visit for a 55-year-old female with chronic blepharitis. There is a history of use of many medications. (Ophthalmology)

Initial office visit for an 18-year-old female with a two-day history of acute conjunctivitis. Extensive history of possible exposures, prior normal ocular history, and medication use is obtained. (Ophthalmology)

Initial office visit for a 14-year-old male with unilateral anterior knee pain. (Physical Medicine & Rehabilitation)

Initial office visit of an adult who presents with symtoms of an upper-respiratory infection that has progressed to unilateral purulent nasal discharge and discomfort in the right maxillary teeth. (Otolaryngology/Head & Neck Surgery)

Initial office visit of a 65-year-old with long-standing nasal stuffiness on multiple medications and continuous positive airway pressure (CPAP) for obstructive sleep apnea syndrome (OSAS). (Otolaryngology/Head & Neck Surgery)

Initial office visit for a 35-year-old female with postprandial right upper quadrant abdominal pain. (General Surgery)

Initial office visit with couple for counseling concerning voluntary vasectomy for sterility. Spent 30 minutes discussing procedure, risks and benefits, and answering questions. (Urology)

Initial office visit for evaluation, diagnosis, and management of painless gross hematuria in a new patient, without cystoscopy. (Internal Medicine)

Initial office visit for evaluation of a 13-year-old female with progressive scoliosis. (Physical Medicine & Rehabilitation)

Initial office visit for a 21-year-old female desiring counseling and evaluation of initiation of contraception. (Family Practice/Internal Medicine/Obstetrics & Gynecology)

Initial office visit for a 49-year-old male presenting with painless blood per rectum associated with bowel movement. (Colon & Rectal Surgery)

Initial office visit for a 19-year-old football player with three-day-old acute knee injury; now with swelling and pain. (Orthopaedic Surgery)

Initial office visit of a 49-year-old male with nasal obstruction. Detailed exam with topical anesthesia. (Plastic Surgery)

Initial office evaluation for gradual symmetric hearing loss, without other otologic symptoms or history, 58-year-old male, history and physical examination, with interpretation of complete audiogram, air bone, etc. (Otolaryngology)

25-year-old male with back pain of six weeks' duration. (Neurology)

Initial office visit for a 61-year-old female whose husband reports loud disruptive snoring that interferes with his sleep. (Sleep Medicine)

Initial office evaluation of a 58-year-old male, gradual symmetric hearing loss, without other otologic symptoms or history. (Otolaryngology)

Initial office visit for a 45-year-old hypertensive female with a two-month history of plantar heel pain. (Podiatry Surgery)

Initial office visit for a 12-year-old male athlete with retrocalcaneal pain and swelling with no prior treatment. (Podiatry Surgery)

**99204** Initial office visit for a 13-year-old female with progressive scoliosis. (Orthopaedic Surgery)

Initial office visit for a 34-year-old female with primary infertility for evaluation and counseling. (Obstetrics & Gynecology)

Initial office visit for a patient with a personal history of multiple non-melanoma skin cancers who presents with a rapidly enlarging 2 cm nodule located on the left temple along with associated tingling in the area and fullness of the subcutaneous tissue in the left prearuricular region. (Dermatology)

Initial office visit for an adolescent who was referred by school counselor because of repeated skipping school and declining grades. (Psychiatry)

Initial office visit for a 50-year-old machinist with a generalized eruption. (Dermatology)

Initial office visit for a 45-year-old female who has been abstinent from alcohol and benzodiazepines for three months but complains of headaches, insomnia, and anxiety. (Psychiatry)

Initial office visit for a 60-year-old male with recent change in bowel habits, weight loss, and abdominal pain. (Abdominal Surgery/Colon & Rectal Surgery)

Initial office visit for a 50-year-old male with an aortic aneurysm who is considering surgery. (General Surgery)

Initial office visit for a 17-year-old female with depression. (Internal Medicine)

Initial office visit of a 40-year-old with chronic draining ear, progressive hearing loss and imbalance, with findings consistent with chronic otitis media and cholesteatoma. (Otolaryngology/Head & Neck Surgery)

Initial office visit for initial evaluation of a 63-year-old male with chest pain on exertion. (Cardiology/Internal Medicine)

Initial office visit for evaluation of a 70-year-old patient with recent onset of episodic confusion. (Internal Medicine)

Initial office visit for a 7-year-old female with juvenile diabetes mellitus, new to area, past history of hospitalization times three. (Pediatrics)

Initial office visit of a 50-year-old female with progressive solid food dysphagia. (Gastroenterology)

Initial office visit for a 34-year-old patient with primary infertility, including counseling. (Obstetrics & Gynecology)

Initial office visit for evaluation of a 70-year-old female with polyarthralgia. (Rheumatology)

Initial office visit for a patient with papulosquamous eruption involving 60 percent of the cutaneous surface with joint pain. Combinations of topical and systemic treatments discussed. (Dermatology)

Initial office visit of a 40-year-old female with symptoms of atopic allergies including eye and sinus congestion, often associated with infections. She would like to be tested for allergies. (Otolaryngology/Head & Neck Surgery)

An 8-year-old healthy male with attention problems in school. (Neurology)

Initial office visit for a 67-year-old male with nocturnal choking, witnessed apneas, and excessive daytime sleepiness. (Sleep Medicine)

Initial office visit for a 42-year-old female with Charcot-Marie-Tooth disease, pes cavus, and worsening painful hammer toes. (Podiatry Surgery)

Initial office visit for a 55-year-old-male with progressive rheumatoid arthritis and deformity of the ankle secondary to previous injury. (Podiatry Surgery)

**99205** Initial office visit for a patient with disseminated lupus erythematosus with kidney disease, edema, purpura, and scarring lesions on the extremities plus cardiac symptoms. (Dermatology/Internal Medicine)

Initial office visit for a 25-year-old female with systemic lupus erythematosus, fever, seizures, and profound thrombocytopenia. (Rheumatology)

Initial office visit for an adult with multiple cutaneous blisters, denuded secondarily infected ulcerations, oral lesions, weight loss, and increasing weakness refractory to high dose corticosteroid. Initiation of new immunosuppressive therapy. (Dermatology)

Initial office visit for a 28-year-old male with systemic vasculitis and compromised circulation to the limbs. (Rheumatology)

Initial office visit for a 41-year-old female new to the area requesting rheumatologic care, on disability due to scleroderma and recent hospitalization for malignant hypertension. (Rheumatology)

Initial office visit for a 52-year-old female with acute four extimity weakness and shortness of breath one week post-flu vaccination. (Physical Medicine & Rehabilitation)

Initial office visit for a 60-year-old male with previous back surgery; now presents with back and pelvic pain, two-month history of bilateral progressive calf and thigh tightness and weakness when walking, causing several falls. (Orthopaedic Surgery)

Initial office visit for an adolescent referred from emergency department after taking a near-lethal overdose that required hospitalization. (Psychiatry)

Initial office visit for a 49-year-old female with a history of headaches and dependence on opioids. She reports weight loss, progressive headache, and depression. (Psychiatry)

Initial office visit for a 34-year-old uremic Type I diabetic patient referred for ESRD modality assessment and planning. (Nephrology)

Initial office visit for a 75-year-old female with neck and bilateral shoulder pain, brisk deep tendon reflexes, and stress incontinence. (Physical Medicine & Rehabilitation)

Initial office visit for an 8-year-old male with cerebral palsy and spastic quadriparesis. (Physical Medicine & Rehabilitation)

Initial office visit for a 73-year-old male with known prostate malignancy, who presents with severe back pain and a recent onset of lower extremity weakness. (Physical Medicine & Rehabilitation)

Initial office visit for a 38-year-old male with paranoid delusions and a history of alcohol abuse. (Psychiatry)

Initial office visit for a 12-week-old with bilateral hip dislocations and bilateral club feet. (Orthopaedic Surgery)

Initial office visit for a 29-year-old female with acute orbital congestion, eyelid retraction, and bilateral visual loss from optic neuropathy. (Ophthalmology)

Initial office visit for a 70-year-old diabetic patient with progressive visual field loss, advanced optic disc cupping, and neovascularization of retina. (Ophthalmology)

Initial office visit for a newly diagnosed Type I diabetic patient. (Endocrinology)

Initial office evaluation of a 65-year-old female with exertional chest pain, intermittent claudication, syncope, and a murmur of aortic stenosis. (Cardiology)

Initial office visit for a 73-year-old male with an unexplained 20 lb weight loss. (Hematology/Oncology)

Initial office evaluaton and management of patient with systemic vasculitis and compromised circulation to the limbs. (Rheumatology)

Initial office visit for a 24-year-old with risk factors for HIV infection who has a fever, cough, and shortness of breath. (Infectious Disease)

Initial outpatient evaluation of a 69-year-old male with severe chronic obstructive pulmonary disease, congestive heart failure, and hypertension. (Family Medicine)

Initial office visit for a 17-year-old female who is having school problems and has told a friend that she is considering suicide. She has recently cut herself. The patient and her family are consulted in regard to treatment options. (Psychiatry)

Initial office visit for a female with severe hirsutism, amenorrhea, weight loss, and a desire to have children. (Obstetrics & Gynecology)

Initial office visit for a 42-year-old male on hypertensive medication, newly arrived to the area, with diastolic blood pressure of 110, history of recurrent calculi, episodic headaches, intermittent chest pain, and orthopnea. (Internal Medicine)

Initial office visit for 70-year-old female with hypertension, diabetes, morbid obesity, and recurrent incisional hernia that has become increasingly painful. (General Surgery)

57-year-old man with new-onset dementia. (Neurology)

Initial office visit for a 25-year-old female with a history of depression who presents with complaints of difficulty maintaining sleep, excessive daytime somnolence, and fatigue. She also complains of episodes of muscle weakness. (Sleep Medicine)

Initial office visit for a 75-year-old febrile female with an infected posterior heel ulceration penetrating to bone with comorbidities of diabetes and peripheral vascular disease. (Podiatric Surgery)

Initial office visit for a 36-year-old hypertensive laborer with inability to bear weight due to multiple metatarsal fractures and forefoot compartment syndrome stemming from a crush injury suffered two days prior. (Podiatric Surgery)

Initial office visit for a child with a long history of bipolar disorder, ADHD, anxiety, and school problems, relatively stable and recently moved from another state. (Psychiatry)

Initial office visit for 61-year-old male with depression and a history of diabetes mellitus, arthritis, hypertension, and coronary artery disease. (Psychiatry)

Initial office visit of a 40-year-old with chronic draining ear, progressive hearing loss, and imbalance, with findings consistent with chronic otitis media and cholesteatoma. (Head & Neck Surgery/Otolaryngology)

## Established Patient

**99211** Office visit for an 82-year-old female, established patient, for a monthly B12 injection with documented Vitamin B12 deficiency. (Geriatrics/Internal Medicine/Family Medicine)

Office visit for a 50-year-old male, established patient, for removal of uncomplicated facial sutures. (Plastic Surgery)

Office visit for an established patient who lost prescription for lichen planus. Returned for new copy. (Dermatology)

Office visit for an established patient undergoing orthodontics who complains of a wire and is irritating his/her cheek and asks you to check it. (Oral & Maxillofacial Surgery)

Office visit for a 50-year-old female, established patient, seen for her gold injection by the nurse. (Rheumatology)

Office visit for a 73-year-old female, established patient, with pernicious anemia for weekly B12 injection. (Gastroenterology)

Office visit for an established patient for dressing change on a skin biopsy. (Dermatology/Podiatric Surgery)

Office visit for a 19-year-old, established patient, three days postirrigation and drainage of an infected sebaceous cyst, for removal of packing. (Plastic Surgery)

Office visit of a 20-year-old female, established patient, who receives an allergy vaccine injection and is observed for a reaction by the nurse. (Otolaryngology/Head & Neck Surgery)

Office visit for a 45-year-old male, established patient, with chronic renal failure for the administration of erythropoietin. (Nephrology)

Office visit for an established patient, a Peace Corps enlistee, who requests documentation that third molars have been removed. (Oral & Maxillofacial Surgery)

Office visit for a 45-year-old female, established patient, three weeks post simple repair of scalp laceration, noted a retained suture in healed wound, removed by nurse. (Plastic Surgery)

Office visit for a 9-year-old, established patient, successfully treated for impetigo, requiring release to return to school. (Dermatology/Pediatrics)

Office visit for an established patient requesting a return-to-work certificate for resolving contact dermatitis. (Dermatology)

Office visit for an established patient who is performing glucose monitoring and wants to check accuracy of machine with lab blood glucose by technician who checks accuracy and function of patient machine. (Endocrinology)

Follow-up office visit for a 65-year-old female with a chronic indwelling percutaneous nephrostomy catheter seen for routine pericatheter skin care and dressing change. (Interventional Radiology)

Outpatient visit with 19-year-old male, established patient, for supervised drug screen. (Addiction Medicine)

Office visit with 12-year-old male, established patient, for cursory check of hematoma one day after venipuncture. (Internal Medicine)

Office visit with 31-year-old female, established patient, for return to work certificate. (Anesthesiology)

Office visit for 14-year-old, established patient, to re-dress an abrasion. (Orthopaedic Surgery)

Office visit for a 45-year-old female, established patient, for a blood pressure check. (Obstetrics & Gynecology)

Office visit for prescription refill for a 35-year-old female, established patient, with schizophrenia who is stable but has run out of neuroleptic and is scheduled to be seen in a week. (Psychiatry)

Office visit with a nurse for a 6-year-old asthmatic patient who brings his nebulizer to learn how to use it with the new medicine he was prescribed. (Allergy & Immunology)

Office visit for a 38-year-old male, established patient, for evaluation of resolving nasal erythema from use of CPAP interface. (Sleep Medicine)

Office visit for a 58-year-old male presenting for nursing examination of wound. Patient had incsion and drainage of abscess in ER. (General Surgery)

Office visit for a patient treated four months ago. He presents as scheduled for examination of final healing of an intraoral incision at a bone graft site. (Oral & Maxillofacial Surgery)

**99212** Office visit for an 11-year-old, established patient, seen in follow-up for mild comedonal acne of the cheeks on topical desquamating agents. (Dermatology/Family Medicine/Pediatrics)

Office visit for a 10-year-old female, established patient, who has been swimming in a lake, now presents with a one-day history of left ear pain with purulent drainage. (Family Medicine)

Office visit for an established patient seen in follow-up of clearing patch of localized contact dermatitis. (Family Medicine/Dermatology)

Office visit for an established patient returning for evaluation of response to treatment of lichen planus on wrists and ankles. (Dermatology)

Office visit for an established patient with tinea pedis being treated with topical therapy. (Dermatology)

Office visit for an established patient with localized erythematous plaque of psoriasis with topical hydration. (Dermatology)

Office visit for a 23-year-old healthy female fully recovered from Bell's palsy, seen one week after onset and initial visit. (Neurology)

Office visit for an established patient with recurring episodes of herpes simplex who has developed a clustering of vesicles on the upper lip. (Oral & Maxillofacial Surgery)

Evaluation of a 50-year-old male, established patient, who has experienced a recurrence of knee pain after he discontinued NSAID. (Anesthesiology/Pain Medicine)

Office visit for an established patient with an irritated skin tag for reassurance. (Dermatology)

Office visit for a 33-year-old, established patient, for contusion and abrasion of lower extremity. (Orthopaedic Surgery)

Office visit for a 22-year-old male, established patient, one month after incision and drainage of sebacious cyst. (Plastic Surgery)

Office visit for a 21-year-old, established patient, who is seen in follow-up after antibiotic therapy for acute bacterial tonsillitis with resolution of symptoms. (Otolaryngology/Head & Neck Surgery)

Office visit, established patient, 6-year-old with sore throat and headache. (Family Medicine/Pediatrics)

Office evaluation for possible purulent bacterial conjunctivitis with one- to two-day history of redness and discharge, 16-year-old female, established patient. (Pediatrics/Internal Medicine/Family Medicine)

Office visit for a 65-year-old female, established patient, returns for three-week follow-up for resolving severe ankle sprain. (Orthopaedic Surgery)

Office visit, sore throat, fever, and fatigue in a 19-year-old college student, established patient. (Internal Medicine)

Office visit for 66-year-old male, with sebaceous cyst on shoulder. (General Surgery)

Office visit with a 36-year-old male, established patient, for follow-up on effectiveness of medicine management of oral candidiasis. (Oral & Maxillofacial Surgery)

Office visit for a 27-year-old female, established patient, with complaints of vaginal itching. (Obstetrics & Gynecology)

Office visit with a 36-year-old male, established patient, for follow-up on effectiveness of medicine management of oral candidiasis, with improvement in symptoms. (Oral & Maxillofacial Surgery)

Office visit for a 32-year-old patient who has allergic rhinitis that is controlled with intranasal steroids but now is having eye symptoms. (Allergy & Immunology)

Office visit for a 45-year-old asthmatic patient who is seen for renewal of inhaler prescription. She is noted to have wheezing on exam and the dose of medication is increased. (Allergy & Immunology)

Office visit for a 65-year-old, established patient, for CPAP compliance data review. (Sleep Medicine)

Office visit for 66-year-old male with sebaceous cyst on shoulder. (General Surgery)

Office visit for an established patient returning for evaluation of response to medication prescribed for plantar warts. (Podiatric Surgery)

Office visit for an established patient with tinea pedis being treated with topical therapy. (Dermatology)

Office visit for a 65-year-old female, established patient, returns for three-week follow-up for resolving severe ankle sprain. (Orthopedic Surgery)

**99213** Office visit for a child, established patient, with chronic secretory otitis media history and physical exam, with interpretation of audiogram. (Otolaryngology/Head & Neck Surgery)

Office visit, established patient, for evaluation and treatment of an acutely draining ear in a 5-year-old with tympanotomy tubes. (Otolaryngology/Head & Neck Surgery)

Office visit for an established patient with new lesions of lichen planus in spite of topical therapies. (Dermatology)

Office visit for a 13-year-old, established patient, with comedopapular acne of the face that has shown poor response to topical medication. Discussion of use of systemic medication. (Dermatology)

Office visit for a 62-year-old female, established patient, for follow-up for stable cirrhosis of the liver. (Internal Medicine/Family Medicine)

Office visit for an 80-year-old female, established patient, to evaluate medical management of osteoarthritis of the temporomandibular joint. (Rheumatology)

Office visit for a healthy 45-year-old female, established patient. Presents with suspicious lesion on the back. (Plastic Surgery)

Office visit for a 68-year-old female, established patient, with polymyalgia rheumatic, maintained on chronic low-dose corticosteroid, with no new complaints. (Rheumatology)

Office visit for a 3-year-old female, established patient, for earache and dyshidrosis of feet. (Pediatrics/Family Medicine)

Office visit for an established patient for 18-months post-operative follow-up of TMJ repair. (Oral & Maxillofacial Surgery)

Office visit for a 45-year-old male, established patient, being re-evaluated for recurrent acute prostatitis. (Urology)

Office visit for a 43-year-old male, established patient, with known reflex sympathetic dystrophy. (Anesthesiology)

Office visit for an established patient with an evenly pigmented superficial nodule of leg that is symptomatic. (Dermatology)

Office visit for an established patient with psoriasis involvement of the elbows, pitting of the nails, and itchy scalp. (Dermatology)

Office visit for a 27-year-old male, established patient, with deep follicular and perifollicular inflammation unable to tolerate systemic antibiotics due to GI upset, requires change of systemic medication. (Dermatology)

Office visit for a 60-year-old, established patient, with chronic essential hypertension on multiple drug regimen, for blood pressure check. (Family Medicine)

Office visit for a 20-year-old male, established patient, for removal of sutures in hand. (Family Medicine)

Office visit for a 58-year-old female, established patient, with unilateral painful bunion. (Orthopaedic Surgery)

Office visit for a 45-year-old female, established patient, with known osteoarthritis and painful swollen knees. (Rheumatology)

Office visit for a 25-year-old female, established patient, complaining of bleeding and heavy menses. (Obstetrics & Gynecology)

Office visit for a 55-year-old male, established patient, with hypertension managed by a beta blocker/thiazide regime; now experiencing mild fatigue. (Nephrology)

Office visit for a 65-year-old female, established patient, with primary glaucoma for interval determination of intraocular pressure and possible adjustment of medication. (Ophthalmology)

Office visit for a 56-year-old male, established patient, with stable exertional angina who complains of new onset of calf pain while walking. (Cardiology)

Office visit for a 63-year-old female, established patient, with rheumatoid arthritis on auranofin and ibuprofen, seen for routine follow-up visit. (Rheumatology)

Office visit for an established patient with Graves' disease, three months post I-131 therapy, who presents with lassitude and malaise. (Endocrinology)

Office visit for the quarterly follow-up of a 63-year-old male, established patient, with chronic myofascial pain syndrome, effectively managed by doxepin, who presents with new onset urinary hesitancy. (Pain Medicine)

Office visit for the biannual follow-up of an established patient with migraine variant having infrequent, intermittent, moderate to severe headaches with nausea and vomiting, which are sometimes effectively managed by ergotamine tartrate and an antiemetic, but occasionally requiring visits to an emergency department. (Pain Medicine)

Office visit for an established patient after discharge from a pain rehabilitation program to review and adjust medication dosage. (Pain Medicine)

Office visit with 55-year-old male, established patient, for management of hypertension, mild fatigue, on beta blocker/thiazide regimen. (Family Medicine/Internal Medicine)

Outpatient visit for a 35-year-old female who had plastic surgery in Mexico two weeks before, presents for wound evaluation and suture removal. (General Surgery)

Office visit for a 70-year-old diabetic hypertensive established patient with recent change in insulin requirement. (Internal Medicine/Nephrology)

Office visit with 80-year-old female, established patient, for follow-up osteoporosis, status-post compression fractures. (Rheumatology)

Office visit for an established patient with stable cirrhosis of the liver. (Gastroenterology)

Routine, follow-up office evaluation at a three-month interval for a 77-year-old female, established patient, with nodular small cleaved-cell lymphoma. (Hematology/Oncology)

Quarterly follow-up office visit for a 45-year-old male, established patient, with stable chronic asthma, on steroid and bronchodilator therapy. (Pulmonary Medicine)

Office visit for a 50-year-old female, established patient, with insulin-dependent diabetes mellitus and stable coronary artery disease, for monitoring. (Family Medicine/Internal Medicine)

Office visit for a patient followed for a diagnosis of allergic rhinitis who recently acquired a cat. Oral nasal medicines are no longer controlling symptoms. Head congestion and yellow drainage are constant. (Allergy & Immunology)

Office visit for a 60-year-old asthmatic who recently developed high blood pressure and is now on BP medicine is seen for worsening asthma and found to have reduced pulmonary function tests compared to last year. (Allergy & Immunology)

Office visit for a 40-year-old female with well-controlled migraine who desires to remain on the same medication. (Neurology)

Office visit for a 25-year-old male, established patient, for periodic follow-up of narcolepsy, stable on stimulant medication. (Sleep Medicine)

Office visit for an established patient with photodamage and a new onset of a bleeding papulonodule on the leg. (Dermatology)

Quarterly follow-up office visit for a 45-year-old male, established patient, with stable chronic asthma, on steroid and bronchodilator therapy. (Pulmonary Medicine)

Office visit for an established diabetic patient, reevaluation of a worsening plantar fasciitis requiring a change in therapy. (Podiatry Surgery)

Office visit for a 58-year-old female, established patient, with unilateral painful bunion. (Orthopaedic Surgery/Podiatry Surgery)

Office visit for a 9-year-old male, established patient, with ADHD. Mild symptoms and minimal medication side effects. (Psychiatry)

Office visit for a 27-year-old female, established patient, with stable depression and anxiety. Intermittent moderate stress. (Psychiatry)

Office visit for a 16-year-old female, established patient, with intermittent moderate depression. (Psychiatry)

**99214** Office visit, established patient, presenting with a new onset of a generalized pruritic to painful eruption and mouth sores. (Dermatology)

Office visit for a 32-year-old female, established patient, with new onset right lower quadrant pain. (Family Medicine)

Office visit for reassessment and reassurance/counseling of a 40-year-old female, established patient, who is experiencing increased symptoms while on a pain management treatment program. (Pain Medicine)

Office visit for a 30-year-old, established patient, under management for intractable low back pain, who now presents with new onset right posterior thigh pain. (Pain Medicine)

Office visit for an established patient with frequent intermittent, moderate to severe headaches requiring beta blocker or tricyclic antidepressant prophylaxis, as well as four symptomatic treatments, but who is still experiencing headaches at a frequency of several times a month that are unresponsive to treatment. (Pain Medicine)

Office visit for an established patient with psoriasis with extensive involvement of scalp, trunk, palms, and soles with joint pain. Combinations of topical and systemic treatments discussed and instituted. (Dermatology)

Office visit for a 55-year-old male, established patient, with increasing night pain, limp, and progressive varus of both knees. (Orthopaedic Surgery)

Follow-up visit for a 15-year-old withdrawn patient with four-year history of papulocystic acne of the face, chest, and back with early scarring and poor response to past treatment. Discussion of use of systemic medication. (Dermatology)

Office visit for a 28-year-old male, established patient, with regional enteritis, diarrhea, and low-grade fever. (Internal Medicine)

Office visit for a 25-year-old female, established patient, following recent arthrogram and MR imaging for TMJ pain. (Oral & Maxillofacial Surgery)

Office visit for a 32-year-old female, established patient, with large obstructing stone in left mid-ureter, to discuss management options including urethroscopy with extraction or ESWL. (Urology)

Evaluation for a 28-year-old male, established patient, with new onset of low back pain. (Anesthesiology/Pain Medicine)

Office visit for a 28-year-old female, established patient, with right lower quadrant abdominal pain, fever, and anorexia. (Internal Medicine/Family Medicine)

Office visit for a 45-year-old male, established patient, four months follow-up of L4-5 diskectomy, with persistent incapacitating low back and leg pain. (Orthopaedic Surgery)

Outpatient visit for a 77-year-old male, established patient, with hypertension, presenting with a three-month history of episodic substernal chest pain on exertion. (Cardiology)

Office visit for a 25-year-old female, established patient, for evaluation of progressive saddle nose deformity of unknown etiology. (Plastic Surgery)

Office visit for a 65-year-old male, established patient, with BPH and severe bladder outlet obstruction, to discuss management options such as TURP. (Urology)

Office visit for an established patient with lichen planus and 60% of the cutaneous surface involved, not responsive to systemic steroids, as well as developing symptoms of progressive heartburn and paranoid ideation. (Dermatology)

Office visit for a 52-year-old male, established patient, with a 12-year history of bipolar disorder responding to lithium carbonate and brief psychotherapy. Psychotherapy and prescription provided. (Psychiatry)

Office visit for a 63-year-old female, established patient, with a history of familial polyposis, status post-colectomy with sphincter sparing procedure, who now presents with rectal bleeding and increase in stooling frequency. (General Surgery)

Office visit for a 68-year-old male, established patient, with the sudden onset of multiple flashes and floaters in the right eye due to a posterior vitreous detachment. (Ophthalmology)

Office visit for a 55-year-old female, established patient, on cyclosporin for treatment of resistant, small vessel vasculitis. (Rheumatology)

Follow-up office visit for a 55-year-old male, two months after iliac angioplasty with new onset of contralateral extremity claudication. (Interventional Radiology)

Office visit for a 68-year-old male, established patient, with stable angina, two months post myocardial infarction, who is not tolerating one of his medications. (Cardiology)

Weekly office visit for 5FU therapy for an ambulatory established patient with metastatic colon cancer and increasing shortness of breath. (Hematology/Oncology)

Office visit for a 65-year-old male with Parkinson disease, on medication with sleep disturbance after medication increase. (Neurology)

Office visit for a 32-year-old female with obesity and diabetes. presents with new onset right lower quadrant pain. (Urology/General Surgery/Internal Medicine/Family Medicine)

Office evaluation of 28-year-old, established patient, with regional enteritis, diarrhea, and low-grade fever. (Family Medicine/Internal Medicine)

Office visit with 50-year-old female, established patient, diabetic, blood sugar controlled by diet. She now complains of frequency of urination and weight loss, blood sugar of 320 and negative ketones on dipstick. (Internal Medicine)

Follow-up office visit for a 45-year-old, established patient, with rheumatoid arthritis on gold, methotrexate, or immunosuppressive therapy. (Rheumatology)

Office visit for a 60-year-old male, established patient, two years post-removal of intracranial meningioma, now with new headaches and visual disturbance. (Neurosurgery)

Office visit for a 68-year-old female, established patient, for routine review and follow-up of non-insulin dependent diabetes, obesity, hypertension, and congestive heart failure. Complains of vision difficulties and admits dietary noncompliance. Patient is counseled concerning diet and current medications adjusted. (Family Medicine)

Office visit for an established patient who presents with severe dysphagia, oynophagia, and trismus and is found on physical exam to have a peritonsilar abscess. (Otolaryngology/Head & Neck Surgery)

Office visit for a 65-year-old male with hypertension, BPH, and allergic rhinitis seen because he cannot sleep due to nasal congestion. He was told by his PCP not to use decongestant pills so he uses a nasal decongestant spray regularly to breathe. He has been using the spray daily for the past six months. (Allergy & Immunology)

Office visit for an asthmatic patient who has missed three days of work due to asthma exacerbation and is found to have acute maxillary sinusitis and nocturnal asthma requiring treatment of both the sinusitis and altering the medication regimen. (Allergy & Immunology)

Office visit for an established diabetic patient with peripheral vascular disease with a new noninfected deep plantar ulceration. (Podiatry Surgery)

Office visit for a 48-year-old male, established patient, with bipolar disorder, marital problems, chronic insomnia, and several medical conditions. Mild psychiatric symptoms and minimal medication side effects. (Psychiatry)

Office visit for 7-year-old female, established patient, with ADHD. The patient has been disruptive in school, resulting in daily phone calls to parents over the last two weeks. Low appetite from the medication has been improving. (Psychiatry)

Office visit for a 13-year-old male, established patient, with depression, anxiety, and anger outbursts. (Psychiatry)

Office visit for a 22-year-old female, established patient, with bipolar disorder and obesity. The patient wants to stop the medication because of resulting weight gain. (Psychiatry)

Office visit for a 70-year-old male, established patient, with stable depression and recent mild forgetfulness. (Psychiatry)

Quarterly follow-up office visit for a 45-year-old male, established patient, with chronic asthma, on steroid and bronchodilator therapy. (Pulmonary Medicine)

Office visit for a 70-year-old female, established patient with sleep apnea and diabetes, who continues to have difficulty staying awake during the day despite treatment. (Sleep Medicine)

**99215** Office visit for an adult diabetic established patient with a past history of recurrent sinusitis who presents with a one-week history of double vision and CT scan consistent with periorbital abscess. (Otolaryngology/Head & Neck Surgery)

Office visit for an established patient with disseminated lupus erythematosus, extensive edema of extremities, kidney disease, and weakness requiring monitored course on azathioprene and corticosteroid and complicated by acute depression. (Internal Medicine/Rheumatology)

Office visit for a patient with history of metastatic melanoma presenting with clinical lymphadenopathy distant to the primary tumor and subcutaneous nodules requiring a detailed discussion of treatment alternatives. (Dermatology)

Office visit for an established male patient with dermatomyositis, accelerated weakness, recent onset of fever, diffuse skin rash, nasal speech, and dysphagia with burning retrosternal pain. (Dermatology)

Office visit for an established adolescent patient with history of bipolar disorder treated with lithium; seen on urgent basis at family's request because of severe depressive symptoms. (Psychiatry)

Office visit for an established patient having acute migraine with new onset neurological symptoms and whose headaches are unresponsive to previous attempts at management with a combination of preventive and abortive medication. (Pain Medicine)

Office visit for an established patient with exfoliative lichen planus with daily fever spikes, disorientation, and shortness of breath. (Dermatology)

Office visit for a 25-year-old, established patient, two years post-burn with bilateral ectropion, hypertrophic facial burn scars, near absence of left breast, and burn syndactyly of both hands. Discussion of treatment options following examination. (Plastic Surgery)

Office visit for a 36-year-old, established patient, three-month status post-transplant, with new onset of peripheral edema, increased blood pressure, and progressive fatigue. (Nephrology)

Office visit for a 27-year-old female, established patient, with bipolar disorder who was stable on lithium carbonate and monthly supportive psychotherapy but now has developed symptoms of hypomania. (Psychiatry)

Office visit for a 25-year-old male, established patient with a history of schizophrenia who has been seen bi-monthly but is complaining of auditory hallucinations. (Psychiatry)

Office visit for a 62-year-old male, established patient, three years postoperative abdominal perineal resection, now with a rising carcinoembryonic antigen, weight loss, and pelvic pain. (Abdominal Surgery)

Office visit for a 42-year-old male, established patient, nine months postoperative emergency vena cava shunt for variceal bleeding, now presents with complaints of one episode of "dark" bowel movement, weight gain, tightness in abdomen, whites of eyes seem yellow, and occasional drowsiness after eating hamburgers. (Abdominal Surgery)

Office visit for a 68-year-old male with biopsy-proven rectal carcinoma, for evaluation and discussion of treatment options. (General Surgery)

Office visit for a 60-year-old, established patient, with diabetic nephropathy with increasing edema and dyspnea. (Endocrinology)

Office visit with 30-year-old male, established patient for three-month history of fatigue, weight loss, intermittent fever, and presenting with diffuse adenopathy and splenomegaly. (Family Medicine)

Office visit for restaging of an established patient with new lymphadenopathy one year post-therapy for lymphoma. (Hematology/Oncology)

Office visit for evaluation of recent onset syncopal attacks in a 70-year-old female, established patient. (Internal Medicine)

Follow-up visit, 40-year-old female mother of three, established patient, with acute rheumatoid arthritis, anatomical Stage 3, ARA function Class 3 rheumatoid arthritis, and deteriorating function. (Rheumatology)

Follow-up office visit for a 65-year-old male with a fever of recent onset while on outpatient antibiotic therapy for endocarditis. (Infectious Disease)

Office visit for a healthy 16-year-old male who suffered a concussion a week ago, now fully recovered, needing an evaluation to return to playing football. (Neurology)

Office visit for a 70-year-old female, established patient, with diabetes mellitus and hypertension, presenting with a two-month history of increasing confusion, agitation, and short-term memory loss. (Family Medicine/Internal Medicine)

Office visit for a 28-year-old female, established patient, who is abstinent from previous cocaine dependence but reports progressive panic attacks and chest pains. (Psychiatry)

Office visit for a 10-year-old asthmatic who has been to the emergency room for severe persistent asthma and is on combination therapy and oral steroids but has not stopped wheezing or coughing at night. (Allergy & Immunology)

Office visit, established patient, female with systemic lupus erythematosus and renal disease requiring combination systemic immunosuppressive therapy presents with a new onset of peripheral edema, diffuse skin rash, weakness, and acute depression. (Dermatology)

Office visit for a 53-year-old female, established patient, with sleep apnea and new-onset heart failure, who presents with a recent weight gain as well as recurrence of symptoms of daytime sleepiness and frequent nocturnal awakenings. (Sleep Medicine)

Office visit for an established diabetic patient with a cellulitic deep plantar abscess and history of previous forefoot amputation on the contralateral side. (Podiatry Surgery)

# Hospital Inpatient Services

## Initial Hospital Care

### New or Established Patient

**99221**  Initial hospital visit following admission for a 42-year-old male for observation following institution of IV antibiotics for a cellulitis of the forearm. (Plastic Surgery/Oral & Maxillofacial Surgery)

Initial hospital visit for a 40-year-old patient with a thrombosed synthetic arteriovenous conduit. (Nephrology)

Initial hospital visit for a healthy 24-year-old male with an acute onset of low back pain following a lifting injury. (Internal Medicine/Anesthesiology/Pain Medicine)

Initial hospital visit for a 69-year-old female with controlled hypertension, scheduled for surgery. (Internal Medicine/Cardiology)

Initial hospital visit for a 24-year-old healthy female with benign tumor of palate. (Oral & Maxillofacial Surgery)

Initial hospital visit for a 14-year-old female with infectious mononucleosis and dehydration. (Internal Medicine)

Initial hospital visit for a 62-year-old female with stable rheumatoid arthritis, admitted for total joint replacement. (Rheumatology)

Initial hospital visit for a 6-month-old infant admitted for observation for apnea after craniofacial CT scan with sedation. (Plastic Surgery)

Initial hospital visit for a 69-year-old female with controlled hypertension, scheduled for surgery. (Cardiology)

Hospital admission, examination, and initiation of treatment program for a 67-year-old male with uncomplicated pneumonia who requires IV antibiotic therapy. (Internal Medicine)

Hospital admission for a 12-year-old with a laceration of the upper eyelid involving the lid margin admitted prior to surgery for IV antibiotic therapy. (Ophthalmology)

Hospital admission for a 32-year-old female with severe flank pain, hematuria, and presumed diagnosis of ureteral calculus as determined by Emergency Department physician. (Urology)

Initial hospital visit for a patient with several large venous stasis ulcers not responding to outpatient therapy. (Dermatology)

Initial hospital visit for 21-year-old pregnant patient (nine-weeks gestation) with hyperemesis gravidarum. (Obstetrics & Gynecology)

Initial hospital visit for a 73-year-old female with acute pyelonephritis who is otherwise generally healthy. (Geriatrics)

Initial hospital visit for 62-year-old patient with cellulitis of the foot requiring bedrest and intravenous antibiotics. (Orthopaedic Surgery)

Initial hospital visit for a 55-year-old female admitted to the hospital with nausea and vomiting, has a benign exam and a nonspecific bowel gas pattern on X ray. (General Surgery)

**99222**  Hospital admission for an 18-month-old with 10% dehydration. (Pediatrics)

Initial hospital visit for a 65-year-old female with right upper quadrant pain, mild jaundice, and gallstones. (General Surgery/Abdominal Surgery/Colon & Rectal Surgery)

Initial hospital visit for airway management, due to a benign laryngeal mass. (Otolaryngology/Head & Neck Surgery)

Initial hospital visit for a 66-year-old female with an L-2 vertebral compression fracture with acute onset of paralytic ileus; seen in the office two days previously. (Orthopaedic Surgery)

Initial hospital visit and evaluation of a 15-year-old male admitted with peritonsillar abscess or cellulitis requiring intravenous antibiotic therapy. (Otolaryngology/Head & Neck Surgery)

Initial hospital visit for a 42-year-old male with vertebral compression fracture following a motor vehicle accident. (Orthopaedic Surgery)

Initial hospital evaluation of a patient with a diffuse erythematous maculopapular eruption of new onset. Patient has multiple medical problems requiring various medications. (Dermatology)

Initial hospital visit for a 3-year-old patient with high temperature, limp, and painful hip motion of 18 hours' duration. (Pediatrics/Orthopaedic Surgery)

Initial hospital visit for an 18-year-old male who has suppurative sialoadenitis and dehydration. (Oral & Maxillofacial Surgery)

Initial hospital visit for a 65-year-old female for acute onset of thrombotic cerebrovascular accident with contralateral paralysis and aphasia. (Neurology)

Initial hospital visit for a 50-year-old male chronic paraplegic patient with pain and spasm below the lesion. (Anesthesiology)

Partial hospital admission for an adolescent patient from chaotic blended family, transferred from inpatient setting, for continued treatment to maintain symptomatic control of hostility and depression. (Psychiatry)

Initial hospital visit for a 61-year-old male with history of previous myocardial infarction, who now complains of chest pain. (Internal Medicine)

Initial hospital visit of a 15-year-old on medications for a sore throat over the last two weeks. The sore throat has worsened and patient now has dysphagia. The exam shows large necrotic tonsils with an adequate airway and small palpable nodes. The initial mono test was negative. (Otolaryngology/Head & Neck Surgery)

Initial hospital evaluation of a 23-year-old allergy patient admitted with eyelid edema and pain on fifth day of oral antibiotic therapy. (Otolaryngology/Head & Neck Surgery)

Hospital admission for a 30-year-old female with epilepsy, not compliant with medication, admitted after three seizures. (Neurology)

Hospital admission, examination, and initiation of treatment program for a 66-year-old chronic hemodialysis patient with fever. (Nephrology)

Hospital admission for a 40-year-old male with submaxillary cellulitis and trismus from infected lower molar. (Oral & Maxillofacial Surgery)

Initial hospital visit following admission for a 42-year-old male for observation following an uncomplicated mandible fracture. (Oral & Maxillofacial Surgery)

Initial hospital visit for a 24-year-old healthy female with benign tumor of palate. (Oral & Maxillofacial Surgery)

Initial hospital visit for a 15-year-old male with acute status asthmaticus, unresponsive to outpatient therapy. (Internal Medicine)

**99223**  Hospital admission of a 62-year-old smoker, established patient, with bronchitis in acute respiratory distress. (Internal Medicine/Pulmonary Medicine)

Initial hospital visit for a 45-year-old female, who has a history of rheumatic fever as a child and now has anemia, fever, and congestive heart failure. (Cardiology)

Initial hospital visit for a 50-year-old male with acute chest pain and diagnostic electrocardiographic changes of an acute anterior myocardial infarction. (Cardiology/Family Medicine/Internal Medicine)

Initial hospital visit of a 75-year-old with progressive stridor and dysphagia with history of cancer of the larynx treated by radiation therapy in the past. Exam shows a large recurrent tumor of the glottis with a mass in the neck. (Otolaryngology/Head & Neck Surgery)

Initial hospital visit for a 70-year-old male admitted with chest pain, complete heart block, and congestive heart failure. (Cardiology)

Initial hospital visit for an 82-year-old male who presents with syncope, chest pain, and ventricular arrhythmias. (Cardiology)

Initial hospital visit for a 75-year-old male with history of arteriosclerotic coronary vascular disease, who is severely dehydrated, disoriented, and confused. (Psychiatry)

Initial hospital visit for a 70-year-old male with alcohol and sedative-hypnotic dependence, admitted by family for severe withdrawal, hypertension, and diabetes mellitus. (Psychiatry)

Initial hospital visit for a persistently suicidal latency-aged child whose parents have requested admission to provide safety but are anxious about separation from her. (Psychiatry)

Initial psychiatric visit for an adolescent patient without previous psychiatric history, who was transferred from the medical ICU after an overdose. (Psychiatry)

Initial hospital visit for a 35-year-old female with severe systemic lupus erythematosus on corticosteroid and cyclophosphamide, with new onset of fever, chills, rash, and chest pain. (Rheumatology)

Initial hospital visit for a 52-year-old male with known rheumatic heart disease who presents with anasarca, hypertension, and history of alcohol abuse. (Cardiology)

Initial hospital visit for a 55-year-old female with a history of congenital heart disease; now presents with cyanosis. (Cardiology)

Initial hospital visit for a psychotic, hostile, violently combative adolescent, involuntarily committed for his and others' safety. (Psychiatry)

Initial hospital visit for a now subdued and sullen teenage male with six-month history of declining school performance, increasing self-endangerment, and resistance of parental expectations, including running away past weekend after physical fight with father. (Psychiatry)

Initial partial hospital admission for a 17-year-old female with history of borderline mental retardation who has developed auditory hallucinations. Parents are known to abuse alcohol, and Child Protective Services is investigating allegations of sexual abuse of a younger sibling. (Psychiatry)

Initial hospital visit of a 67-year-old male admitted with a large neck mass, dysphagia, and history of myocardial infarction three months before. (Otolaryngology/Head & Neck Surgery)

Initial hospital visit for a patient with suspected cerebrospinal fluid rhinorrhea that developed two weeks after head injury. (Otolaryngology/Head & Neck Surgery)

Initial hospital visit for a 25-year-old female with history of poly-substance abuse and psychiatric disorder. The patient appears to be psychotic with markedly elevated vital signs. (Psychiatry)

Initial hospital visit for a 70-year-old male with cutaneous T-cell lymphoma who has developed fever and lymphadenopathy. (Internal Medicine)

Initial hospital visit for a 62-year-old female with known coronary artery disease, for evaluation of increasing edema, dyspnea on exertion, confusion, and sudden onset of fever with productive cough. (Internal Medicine)

Initial hospital visit for a 3-year-old female with 36-hour history of sore throat and high fever; now with sudden onset of lethargy, irritability, photophobia, and nuchal rigidity. (Pediatrics)

Initial hospital visit for a 26-year-old female for evaluation of severe facial fractures (LeFort's II/III). (Plastic Surgery)

Initial hospital visit for a 55-year-old female for bilateral mandibular fractures resulting in flail mandible and airway obstruction. (Plastic Surgery)

Initial hospital visit for a 71-year-old patient with a red painful eye four days following uncomplicated cataract surgery due to endophthalmitis. (Ophthalmology)

Initial hospital visit for a 45-year-old patient involved in a motor vehicle accident who suffered a perforating corneoscleral laceration with loss of vision. (Ophthalmology)

Initial hospital visit for a 58-year-old male who has Ludwig's angina and progressive airway compromise. (Oral & Maxillofacial Surgery)

Initial hospital visit for an adult with multiple cutaneous blisters, denuded secondarily infected ulcerations, oral lesions, weight loss, and increasing weakness refactory to high-dose corticosteroid. Initiation of new immunosuppressive therapy . (Dermatology)

Initial hospital visit for an 82-year-old male who presents with syncope, chest pain, and ventricular arrhythmias. (Cardiology)

Initial hospital visit for a 62-year-old male with history of previous myocardial infarction, comes in with recurrent, sustained ventricular tachycardia. (Cardiology)

Initial hospital visit for a chronic dialysis patient with infected PTFE fistula, septicemia, and shock. (Nephrology)

Initial hospital visit for a 1-year-old male, victim of child abuse, with central nervous system depression, skull fracture, and retinal hemorrhage. (Neurology)

Initial hospital visit for a 25-year-old female with recent C4-C5 quadriplegia, admitted for rehabilitation. (Physical Medicine & Rehabilitation)

Initial hospital visit for an 18-year-old male, post-traumatic brain injury with multiple impairment. (Physical Medicine & Rehabilitation)

Initial partial hospital admission for 16-year-old male, sullen and subdued, with six-month history of declining school performance, increasing self-endangerment, and resistance to parental expectations. (Psychiatry)

Initial hospital visit for a 16-year-old primigravida at 32 weeks gestation with severe hypertension (200/110), thrombocytopenia, and headache. (Obstetrics & Gynecology)

Initial hospital visit for a 49-year-old male with cirrhosis of liver with hematemesis, hepatic encephalopathy, and fever. (Gastroenterology)

Initial hospital visit for a 55-year-old female in chronic pain who has attempted suicide. (Psychiatry)

Initial hospital visit for a 70-year-old male, with multiple organ system disease, admitted with history of being aneuric and septic for 24 hours prior to admission. (Urology)

Initial hospital visit for a 3-year-old female with 36-hour history of sore throat and high fever, now with sudden onset of lethargy, irritability, photophobia, and nuchal rigidity. (Pediatrics/Critical Care)

Initial hospital visit for a 78-year-old male, transfers from nursing home with dysuria and pyuria, increasing confusion, and high fever. (Internal Medicine)

Initial hospital visit for a 1-day-old male with cyanosis, respiratory distress, and tachypnea. (Cardiology)

Initial hospital visit for a 3-year-old female with recurrent tachycardia and syncope. (Cardiology)

Initial hospital visit for a thyrotoxic patient who presents with fever, atrial fibrillation, and delirium. (Endocrinology)

Initial hospital visit for a 50-year-old Type I diabetic who presents with diabetic ketoacidosis with fever and obtundation. (Endocrinology)

Initial hospital visit for a 40-year-old female with anatomical stage 3, ARA functional class 3 rheumatoid arthritis on methotrexate, corticosteroid, and nonsteroidal anti-inflammatory drugs. Patient presents with severe arthritis flare, new oral ulcers, abdominal pain, and leukopenia. (Rheumatology)

Initial hospital exam of a pediatric patient with high fever and proptosis. (Otolaryngology/Head & Neck Surgery)

Initial hospital visit for a 25-year-old patient admitted for the first time to the rehab unit, with recent C4-C5 quadriplegia. (Physical Medicine & Rehabilitation)

Hospital admission, examination, and initiation of treatment program for a previously unknown 58-year-old male who presents with acute chest pain. (Cardiology)

Hospital admission, examination, and initiation of induction chemotherapy for a 42-year-old patient with newly diagnosed acute myelogenous leukemia. (Hematology/Oncology)

Hospital admission following a motor vehicle accident of a 24-year-old male with fracture dislocation of C5-C6; neurologically intact. (Neurosurgery)

Hospital admission for a 78-year-old female with left lower lobe pneumonia and a history of coronary artery disease, congestive heart failure, osteoarthritis, and gout. (Family Medicine)

Hospital admission, examination, and initiation of treatment program for a 65-year-old immunosuppressed male with confusion, fever, and a headache. (Infectious Disease)

Hospital admission for a 9-year-old with vomiting, dehydration, fever, tachypnea, and an admitting diagnosis of diabetic ketoacidosis. (Pediatrics)

Initial hospital visit for a 65-year-old male who presents with acute myocardial infarction, oliguria, hypotension, and altered state of consciousness. (Cardiology)

Initial hospital visit for a 15-year-old male with acute status asthmaticus, unresponsive to outpatient therapy. (Internal Medicine/Pulmonary Medicine/Pediatrics)

Initial hospital visit for a hostile/resistant adolescent patient who is severely depressed and involved in poly-substance abuse. Patient is experiencing significant conflict in his chaotic family situation and was suspended from school following an attack on a teacher with a baseball bat. (Psychiatry)

Initial hospital visit for 89-year-old female with fulminant hepatic failure and encephalopathy. (Gastroenterology)

Initial hospital visit for a patient with congestive heart failure, type 1 diabetes mellitus, and renal failure who has developed an acute onset of fever and a generalized bullous erythematous and purpuric eruption. (Dermatology)

Hospital admission for a 50-year-old male with new-onset left hemiparesis (Neurology)

Hospital admission for an 18-year-old male admitted to the trauma service following a motor vehicle accident for treatment of a closed head injury, liver laceration, and long bone fractures. (General Surgery)

First hour of critical care of a 15-year-old with acute respiratory failure from asthma. (Pulmonary Medicine)

Hospital admission of a 62-year-old smoker, established patient, with bronchitis in acute respiratory distress. (Pulmonary Medicine/Critical Care)

Initial hospital visit for a 15-year-old male with acute status asthmaticus, unresponsive to outpatient therapy. (Cardiology/Family Practice/General Surgery/Pulmonary Medicine/Critical Care)

Initial hospital visit for a 42-year-old female with rapidly progressing scleroderma, malignant hypertension, digital infarcts, and oligurea. (Rheumatology/Cardiology/Family Practice/General Surgery/Pulmonary Medicine/Critical Care)

# Subsequent Hospital Care

**99231**  Subsequent hospital visit for a 65-year-old female, post-open reduction and internal fixation of a fracture. (Physical Medicine & Rehabilitation)

Subsequent hospital visit for a 33-year-old patient with pelvic pain who is responding to pain medication and observation. (Obstetrics & Gynecology)

Subsequent hospital visit for a 21-year-old female with hyperemesis who has responded well to intravenous fluids. (Obstetrics & Gynecology)

Subsequent hospital visit to re-evaluate postoperative pain and titrate patient-controlled analgesia for a 27-year-old female. (Anesthesiology)

Follow-up hospital visit for a 35-year-old female, status post-epidural analgesia. (Anesthesiology/Pain Medicine)

Subsequent hospital visit for a 56-year-old male, post-gastrectomy, for maintenance of analgesia using an intravenous dilaudid infusion. (Anesthesiology)

Subsequent hospital visit for a male with improving venous stasis ulcers. (Dermatology)

Subsequent hospital visit for a 24-year-old female with otitis externa, seen two days before in consultation, now to have otic wick removal. (Otolaryngology/Head & Neck Surgery)

Subsequent hospital visit for a 62-year-old patient with resolving cellulitis of the foot. (Orthopaedic Surgery)

Subsequent hospital visit for a 25-year-old male admitted for supra-ventricular tachycardia and converted on medical therapy. (Cardiology)

Subsequent hospital visit for a 27-year-old male with nasal fracture who was intoxicated and uncooperative on admission exam. Patient confirms no difficulty breathing and no change in nasal appearance, exam normal other than mild tenderness. (Plastic Surgery)

Subsequent hospital visit for a 76-year-old male with venous stasis ulcers. (Geriatrics)

Subsequent hospital visit for a 67-year-old female admitted three days ago with bleeding gastric ulcer; now stable. (Gastroenterology)

Subsequent hospital visit for stable 33-year-old male following a motor vehicle accident who is stable with bruised ribs and improving dyspnea. (General Surgery/Gastroenterology)

Subsequent hospital visit for a 29-year-old male with effort thrombosis of left upper extremity. (General Surgery)

Subsequent hospital visit for a 14-year-old female in middle phase of residential or day treatment who is now behaviorally stable and making satisfactory progress in treatment. (Psychiatry)

Subsequent hospital visit for a 55-year-old male with rheumatoid arthritis, two days following an uncomplicated total joint replacement. (Rheumatology)

Subsequent hospital visit for a 60-year-old dialysis patient with an access infection, now afebrile on antibiotic. (Nephrology)

Subsequent hospital visit for a 23-year-old female admitted for cellulitis following dog bite to hand, redness, pain, and swelling resolving. (Plastic Surgery)

Subsequent hospital visit for a 66-year-old female with L-2 vertebral compression fracture with resolving ileus. (Orthopaedic Surgery)

Subsequent hospital visit for an 18-year-old female responding to intravenous antibiotic therapy for ear or sinus infection. (Otolaryngology/Head & Neck Surgery)

Subsequent hospital visit for a 70-year-old male admitted with congestive heart failure who has responded to therapy. (Cardiology)

Follow-up hospital visit for a 32-year-old female with left ureteral calculus; being followed in anticipation of spontaneous passage. (Urology)

Subsequent hospital visit for a 42-year-old female, admitted for acute gastroenteritis and dehydration, requiring IV hydration; now stable but refusing oral intake. (Family Medicine/Pediatrics)

Subsequent hospital visit for a 50-year-old Type II diabetic who is clinically stable and without complications requiring regulation of a single dose of insulin daily. (Endocrinology)

Subsequent hospital visit to reassesses the status of a 65-year-old patient post-open reduction and internal fixation of hip fracture, on the rehab unit. (Physical Medicine & Rehabilitation)

Subsequent hospital visit for a 78-year-old male with cholangiocarcinoma managed by biliary drainage. (Interventional Radiology)

Subsequent hospital visit for a 50-year-old male with uncomplicated myocardial infarction who is clinically stable and without chest pain. (Family Medicine/Cardiology/Internal Medicine)

Subsequent hospital visit for a stable 72-year-old lung cancer patient undergoing a five-day course of infusion chemotherapy. (Hematology/Oncology)

Subsequent hospital visit, two days post admission for a 65-year-old male with a CVA (cerebral vascular accident) and left hemiparesis, who is clinically stable. (Neurology/Physical Medicine & Rehabilitation)

Subsequent hospital visit for now stable, 33-year-old male, status post lower gastrointestinal bleeding. (General Surgery)

Subsequent hospital visit for a 3-year-old patient in traction for a congenital dislocation of the hip. (Orthopaedic Surgery)

Subsequent hospital visit for a 4-year-old female, admitted for acute gastroenteritis and dehydration, requiring IV hydration; now stable. (Family Medicine/Internal Medicine)

Subsequent hospital visit for 50-year-old female with resolving uncomplicated acute pancreatitis. (Gastroenterology)

Subsequent hospital visit for a 30-day-old male admitted for sepsis evaluation and IV antibiotics due to fever; afebrile now with cultures pending. (Family Medicine/Pediatrics)

Subsequent hospital visit for a 10-year-old male admitted for lobar pneumonia with vomiting and dehydration; is becoming afebrile and tolerating oral fluids. (Pulmonary Medicine)

Subsequent visit on third day of hospitalization for a 60-year-old female recovering from an uncomplicated lower extremity cellulitis. (Infectious Disease/Internal Medicine/Pulmonary Medicine)

Subsequent visit for a 75-year-old female, now three days after onset of left hemiparesis, awaiting placement in a rehabilitation unit. (Neurology)

**99232**  Subsequent visit on third day of hospitalization for a 60-year-old female recovering from an uncomplicated pneumonia. (Infectious Disease/Internal Medicine/Pulmonary Medicine)

Subsequent hospital visit for a patient with peritonsillar cellulitis, with slow response to antibiotic therapy, with consideration for additional testing and changes in treatment plan. (Otolaryngology/Head & Neck Surgery)

Subsequent hospital visit for a 27-year-old with acute vertigo, with review of laboaratory and imaging studies. (Otolaryngology/Head & Neck Surgery)

Subsequent hospital visit for a patient with venous stasis ulcers who developed fever and red streaks adjacent to the ulcer. (Dermatology/Internal Medicine/Family Medicine)

Subsequent hospital visit for a 45-year-old male admitted for IV antibiotics for cellulitis post dog bite to hand. Increased redness and fluctuance found. (Plastic Surgery)

Subsequent hospital visit for a 54-year-old female admitted for myocardial infarction, but who is now having frequent premature ventricular contractions. (Internal Medicine)

Subsequent hospital visit for an 80-year-old patient with a pelvic rim fracture, inability to walk, and severe pain; now 36 hours post-injury, experiencing urinary retention. (Orthopaedic Surgery)

Subsequent hospital visit for a 17-year-old female with fever, pharyngitis, and airway obstruction, who after 48 hours develops a maculopapular rash. (Pediatrics/Family Medicine)

Follow-up visit for a 67-year-old male with congestive heart failure who has responded to antibiotics and diuretics and has now developed a monoarthropathy. (Internal Medicine)

Follow-up hospital visit for a 58-year-old male receiving continuous opioids who is experiencing severe nausea and vomiting. (Pain Medicine)

Subsequent hospital visit for a patient after an auto accident who is slow to respond to ambulation training. (Physical Medicine & Rehabilitation)

Subsequent hospital visit for a 50-year-old diabetic, hypertensive male with back pain not responding to conservative inpatient management with continued radiation of pain to the lower left extremity. (Orthopaedic Surgery)

Subsequent hospital visit for a 37-year-old female on day five of antibiotics for bacterial endocarditis, who still has low-grade fever. (Cardiology)

Subsequent hospital visit for a 54-year-old patient, post MI (myocardial infarction), who is out of the CCU (coronary care unit) but is now having frequent premature ventricular contractions on telemetry. (Cardiology/Internal Medicine)

Subsequent hospital visit for a patient with neutropenia, a fever responding to antibiotics, and continued slow gastrointestinal bleeding on platelet support. (Hematology/Oncology)

Subsequent hospital visit for a 50-year-old male admitted two days ago for sub-acute renal allograft rejection. (Nephrology)

Subsequent hospital visit for a 35-year-old drug addict, not responding to initial antibiotic therapy for pyelonephritis. (Urology)

Subsequent hospital visit for a 79-year-old male with worsening jaundice and a pancreatic mass. (General Surgery)

Subsequent hospital care for a 62-year-old female with congestive heart failure, who remains dyspneic and febrile. (Internal Medicine)

Subsequent hospital visit for a 73-year-old female with recently diagnosed lung cancer, who complains of unsteady gait. (Pulmonary Medicine)

Subsequent hospital visit for a 20-month-old male with bacterial meningitis treated one week with antibiotic therapy; has now developed a temperature of 101 degrees. (Pediatrics)

Subsequent hospital visit for 13-year-old male admitted with left lower quadrant abdominal pain and fever, not responding to therapy. (General Surgery)

Subsequent hospital visit for a 65-year-old male with hemiplegia and painful paretic shoulder. (Physical Medicine & Rehabilitation)

Subsequent hospital visit for a patient admitted for treatment of congestive heart failure, on multiple medications, whose previous pale, diffuse rash has now generalized, brightened, and is intensely pruritic. (Dermatology)

Subsequent hospital visit for a 41-year-old female whose altered mental status improved. (General Surgery)

Subsequent hospital visit for adolescent female who continues to struggle with suicidal thoughts and has multiple questions about her antidepressant medication. (Psychiatry)

Subsequent partial hospital visit for a child with depression and severe anxiety. (Psychiatry)

Subsequent hospital visit for 59-year-old male with depression, anxiety, and medication side effects. (Psychiatry)

Subsequent partial hospital visit for a 25-year-old female with body image ruminations and high anxiety about following the prescribed meal plan. (Psychiatry)

**99233** Subsequent hospital visit for a 38-year-old male, quadriplegic with acute autonomic hyperreflexia, who is not responsive to initial care. (Physical Medicine & Rehabilitation)

Follow-up hospital visit for a teenage female who continues to experience severely disruptive, violent, and life-threatening symptoms in a complicated multi-system illness. Family/social circumstances also a contributing factor. (Psychiatry)

Subsequent hospital visit for a 42-year-old female with progressive systemic sclerosis (scleroderma), renal failure on dialysis, congestive heart failure, cardiac arrhythmias, and digital ulcers. (Allergy & Immunology)

Subsequent hospital visit for a 50-year-old diabetic, hypertensive male with nonresponding back pain and radiating pain to the lower left extremity, who develops chest pain, cough, and bloody sputum. (Orthopaedic Surgery)

Subsequent hospital visit for a 64-year-old female, status post-abdominal aortic aneurysm resection, with non-responsive coagulopathy, who has now developed lower GI bleeding. (Abdominal Surgery/Colon & Rectal Surgery/General Surgery)

Follow-up hospital care of a patient with pansinusitis infection complicated by a brain abscess and asthma; no response to current treatment. (Otolaryngology/Head & Neck Surgery)

Subsequent hospital visit for a patient with a laryngeal neoplasm who develops airway compromise, suspected metastasis. (Otolaryngology/Head & Neck Surgery)

Subsequent hospital visit for a 49-year-old male with significant rectal bleeding, etiology undetermined, not responding to treatment. (Abdominal Surgery/General Surgery/Colon & Rectal Surgery)

Subsequent hospital visit for a 50-year-old male, post-aortocoronary bypass surgery; now develops hypotension and oliguria. (Cardiology)

Subsequent hospital visit for an adolescent patient who is violent, unsafe, and noncompliant, with multiple expectations for participation in treatment plan and behavior on the treatment unit. (Psychiatry)

Subsequent hospital visit for an 18-year-old male being treated for presumed PCP-induced psychosis. Patient still has moderate auditory hallucinations and is insisting on signing out against medical advice. (Psychiatry)

Subsequent hospital visit for an 8-year-old female with caustic ingestion, who now has fever, dyspnea, and dropping hemoglobin. (Gastroenterology)

Subsequent hospital visit for a 44-year-old patient with electrical burns to the left arm with ascending infection. (Orthopaedic Surgery)

Subsequent hospital visit for a type 1 diabetes mellitus patient with a new onset of fever, change in mental status, and a diffuse petechial, purpuric eruption. (Internal Medicine)

Subsequent hospital visit for a 65-year-old female, status postoperative resection of abdominal aortic aneurysm, with suspected ischemic bowel. (General Surgery)

Subsequent hospital visit for a 50-year-old male, post-aortocoronary bypass surgery, now develops hypotension and oliguria. (Cardiology)

Subsequent hospital visit for a 65-year-old male, following an acute myocardial infarction, who complains of shortness of breath and new chest pain. (Cardiology)

Subsequent hospital visit for a 65-year-old female with rheumatoid arthritis (stage 3, class 3) admitted for urosepsis. On the third hospital day, chest pain, dyspnea, and fever develop. (Rheumatology)

Follow-up hospital care of a pediatric case with stridor, laryngomalacia, established tracheostomy, complicated by multiple medical problems in PICU. (Otolaryngology/Head & Neck Surgery)

Subsequent hospital visit for a 60-year-old female, four days post uncomplicated inferior myocardial infarction who has developed severe chest pain, dyspnea, diaphoresis, and nausea. (Family Medicine)

Subsequent hospital visit for a patient with AML (acute myelogenous leukemia), fever, elevated white count and uric acid undergoing induction chemotherapy. (Hematology/Oncology)

Subsequent hospital visit for a 38-year-old quadriplegic male with acute autonomic hyperreflexia, who is not responsive to initial care. (Physical Medicine & Rehabilitation)

Subsequent hospital visit for a 65-year-old female postoperative resection of abdominal aortic aneurysm, with suspected ischemic bowel. (General Surgery)

Subsequent hospital visit for a 60-year-old female with persistent leukocytosis, fever, abdominal pain, and hypotension seven days after a sigmoid colon resection for carcinoma. (Infectious Disease)

Subsequent hospital visit for a chronic renal failure patient on dialysis, who develops chest pain, shortness of breath. (Nephrology)

Subsequent hospital visit for a 65-year-old male with acute myocardial infarction who now demonstrates complete heart block and congestive heart failure. (Cardiology)

Subsequent hospital visit for a 55-year-old male with severe chronic obstructive pulmonary disease and bronchospasm; initially admitted for acute respiratory distress requiring ventilatory support in the ICU. The patient was stabilized, extubated, and transferred to the floor but has now developed acute fever, dyspnea, left lower lobe rhonchi, and laboratory evidence of carbon dioxide retention and hypoxemia. (Family Medicine/Internal Medicine)

Subsequent hospital visit for 46-year-old female, known liver cirrhosis patient, with recent upper gastrointestinal hemorrhage from varices; now with worsening ascites and encephalopathy. (Gastroenterology)

Subsequent hospital visit for 62-year-old female admitted with acute subarachnoid hemorrhage, negative cerebral arteriogram, increased lethargy, and hemiparesis with fever. (Neurosurgery)

Subsequent partial hospital visit for an adolescent female who cut herself over the weekend following an intense family argument. (Psychiatry)

Subsequent hospital visit for an adolescent patient who is actively suicidal and experiencing significant medication side effects. (Psychiatry)

Subsequent hospital visit for a 70-year-old male with depression who had a syncopal episode on the unit. (Psychiatry)

Subsequent hospital visit for a 43-year-old male with new onset foot drop after removing a cast from his leg. (Neurology)

# Consultations

## Office or Other Outpatient Consultations

### New or Established Patient

**99241** Initial office consultation for a 40-year-old female in pain from blister on lip following a cold. (Oral & Maxillofacial Surgery)

Initial office consultation for a 62-year-old construction worker with olecranon bursitis. (Orthopaedic Surgery)

Office consultation with 25-year-old postpartum female with suspected hemorrhoids. (General Surgery)

Office consultation with 58-year-old male, referred for follow-up of creatinine level and evaluation of obstructive uropathy, relieved two months ago. (Nephrology)

Office consultation for 30-year-old female tennis player with sprain or contusion of the forearm. (Orthopaedic Surgery)

Office consultation for a 45-year-old male, requested by his internist, with asymptomatic torus palatinus requiring no further treatment. (Oral & Maxillofacial Surgery)

**99242** Initial office consultation for a 29-year-old soccer player with painful proximal thigh/groin injury. (Orthopaedic Surgery)

Initial office consultation for an 8-year-old female with a five-day-old second-degree scald burn of the foot. (Plastic Surgery)

Initial office consultation for a patient with a history of discoid lupus erythematosus who has developed a new erythematous nodule on a cheek. (Dermatology)

Office consultation for management of systolic hypertension in a 70-year-old male scheduled for elective prostate resection. (Geriatrics)

Office consultation with 27-year-old female, with old amputation, for evaluation of existing above-knee prosthesis. (Physical Medicine & Rehabilitation)

Office consultation with 66-year-old female with wrist and hand pain, and finger numbness, secondary to suspected carpal tunnel syndrome. (Orthopaedic Surgery)

Office consultation for 61-year-old female, recently on antibiotic therapy, now with diarrhea and leukocytosis. (Abdominal Surgery)

Office consultation for a patient with papulosquamous eruption of elbow with pitting of nails and itchy scalp. (Dermatology)

Office consultation for a 25-year-old female seen in consultation for complaints of breast pain, with no nipple discharge, mass, or family history of breast cancer. (General Surgery)

Initial office consultation for a 60-year-old female with ptosis, muscle weakness, and thymic tumor who was referred by her neurologist for possible therapeutic plasmapheresis. (Pathology)

**99252** Inpatient consultation for a 28-year-old female with thrombocytopenia and neurologic symptoms who was referred by her hematologist for possible therapeutic plasmapheresis for thrombotic thrombocytopenic purpura. (Pathology)

**99243** Initial office consultation for a 60-year-old male with avascular necrosis of the left femoral head with increasing pain. (Orthopaedic Surgery)

Office consultation for a 31-year-old female complaining of palpitations and chest pains. Her internist had described a mild systolic click. (Cardiology)

Office consultation for a 65-year-old female with recurrent upper extremity cellulitis following axillary lymph node dissection for breast carcinoma. (Infectious Disease)

Office consultation for a 65-year-old male with chronic low-back pain radiating to the leg. (Neurosurgery)

Office consultation for 23-year-old female with Crohn's disease not responding to therapy. (Abdominal Surgery/Colon & Rectal Surgery)

Office consultation for 25-year-old patient with symptomatic knee pain and swelling, with torn anterior cruciate ligament and/or torn meniscus. (Orthopaedic Surgery)

Office consultation for a 67-year-old patient with osteoporosis and mandibular atrophy with regard to reconstructive alternatives. (Oral & Maxillofacial Surgery)

Office consultation for 39-year-old patient referred at a perimenopausal age for irregular menses and menopausal symptoms. (Obstetrics & Gynecology)

Office consultation for a patient with a papulosquamous eruption of the elbows, pitting of the nails, an itchy, scaly scalp, and localized joint pains. (Dermatology)

Initial office consultation for a 40-year-old female in pain from blister on lip following a cold. (Oral & Maxillofacial Surgery)

Office consultation for a 45-year-old male, requested by his internist, with asymptomatic torus palatinus requiring no further treatment. (Oral & Maxillofacial Surgery)

Office consultation for a 16-year-old male who suffered a concussion a week ago, now fully recovered, needing an evaluation to return to playing football. (Neurology)

**99244** Initial office consultation for a 28-year-old male, HIV+, with a recent change in visual acuity. (Ophthalmology)

Initial office consultation for a 15-year-old male with failing grades, suspected drug abuse. (Pediatrics)

Initial office consultation for a 36-year-old factory worker, status four months post-occupational low back injury and requires management of intractable low back pain. (Pain Medicine)

Initial office consultation for a 45-year-old female with a history of chronic arthralgia of TMJ and associated myalgia and sudden progressive symptomatology over last two to three months. (Oral & Maxillofacial Surgery)

Initial office consultation for a 23-year-old female with developmental facial skeletal anomaly and subsequent abnormal relationship of jaw(s) to cranial base. (Oral & Maxillofacial Surgery)

Initial office consultation for a 45-year-old myopic patient with a one-week history of floaters and a partial retinal detachment. (Ophthalmology)

Initial office consultation for a 65-year-old female with moderate dementia, mild unsteadiness, back pain fatigue on ambulation, intermittent urinary incontinence. (Neurosurgery)

Initial office consultation for a 33-year-old female referred by endocrinologist with amenorrhea and galactorrhea, for evaluation of pituitary tumor. (Neurosurgery)

Initial office consultation for a 34-year-old male with new onset nephrotic syndrome. (Nephrology)

Initial office consultation for a patient with multiple giant tumors of jaws. (Oral & Maxillofacial Surgery)

Initial office consultation for a patient with a failed total hip replacement with loosening and pain upon walking. (Orthopaedic Surgery)

Initial office consultation for a 60-year-old female with three-year history of intermittent tic-like unilateral facial pain; now constant pain for six weeks without relief by adequate carbamazepine dosage. (Neurosurgery)

Initial office consultation for a 45-year-old male heavy construction worker with prior lumbar disk surgery two years earlier; now gradually recurring low back and unilateral leg pain for three months, unable to work for two weeks. (Neurosurgery)

Office consultation with 38-year-old female with inflammatory bowel disease, complaints of pain in the right lower quadrant, and suspected intra-abdominal abscess. (General Surgery/Colon & Rectal Surgery)

Office consultation with 72-year-old male with esophageal carcinoma, symptoms of dysphagia and reflux. (Thoracic Surgery)

Office consultation for discussion of treatment options for a 40-year-old female with a 2 cm adenocarcinoma of the breast. (Radiation Oncology)

Office consultation for 66-year-old female, history of colon resection for adenocarcinoma six years earlier, now with severe mid-back pain; X-rays showing osteoporosis and multiple vertebral compression fractures. (Neurosurgery)

Office consultation for a patient with chronic pelvic inflammatory disease who now has left lower quadrant pain with a palpable pelvic mass. (Obstetrics & Gynecology)

Office consultation for a patient with long-standing psoriasis with acute onset of erythroderma, pustular lesions, chills, and fever. Combinations of topical and systemic treatments discussed and instituted. (Dermatology)

Office consultation for a 39-year-old female with persistent migraines failing medications prescribed by her primary care provider. (Neurology)

**99245**  Office consultation for young patient referred by pediatrician because of patient's short attention span, easy distractibility, and hyperactivity after a failed stimulant trial. (Psychiatry)

Initial office consultation for evaluation of a 70-year-old male with multiple medical problems and recent unexplained appetite loss and diminished energy. (Psychiatry)

Initial office consultation for an elementary school-aged patient, referred by pediatrician, with multiple somatic complaints and recent onset of behavioral discontrol. (Psychiatry)

Initial office consultation of a patient who presents with a 30-year history of smoking, hypertension, chronic obstructive pulmonary disease, and a hard, fixed right neck mass. Patient on other meds for conditions. Patient presents with CT ordered by PCP. (Otolaryngology/Head & Neck Surgery)

Initial office consultation for a 35-year-old multiple-trauma male patient with complex pelvic fractures, for evaluation and formulation of management plan. (Orthopaedic Surgery)

Initial emergency room consultation for 10-year-old male in status epilepticus, recent closed head injury, information about medication not available. (Neurosurgery)

Initial emergency room consultation for a 23-year-old patient with severe abdominal pain, guarding, febrile, and unstable vital signs. (Obstetrics & Gynecology)

Office consultation for a 67-year-old female longstanding uncontrolled diabetic who presents with retinopathy, nephropathy, and a foot ulcer. (Endocrinology)

Office consultation for a 37-year-old male for initial evaluation and management of Cushing's disease. (Endocrinology)

Office consultation for a 60-year-old male who presents with thyrotoxicosis, exophthalmos, frequent premature ventricular contractions, and congestive heart failure. (Endocrinology)

Initial office consultation for a 36-year-old patient, one year status post occupational herniated cervical disk treated by laminectomy, requiring management of multiple sites of intractable pain, depression, and narcotic dependence. (Pain Medicine)

Office consultation for a 58-year-old male with a history of MI and CHF who complains of the recent onset of rest angina and shortness of breath. The patient has a systolic blood pressure of 90 mmHG and is in Class IV heart failure. (Cardiology)

Emergency room consultation for a 1-year-old with a three-day history of fever with increasing respiratory distress who is thought to have cardiac tamponade by the ER physician. (Cardiology)

Office consultation in the emergency room for a 25-year-old male with severe, acute, closed head injury. (Neurosurgery)

Office consultation for a 53-year-old female with advanced head and neck cancer. (Radiation Oncology)

Office consultation for a 27-year-old juvenile diabetic patient with severe diabetic retinopathy, gastric atony, nephrotic syndrome, and progressive renal failure, now with a serum creatinine of 2.7, and a blood pressure of 170/114. (Nephrology)

Office consultation for independent medical evaluation of a patient with a history of complicated low back and neck problems with previous multiple failed back surgeries. (Orthopaedic Surgery)

Office consultation for an adolescent referred by pediatrician PCP for recent onset of violent and self-injurious behavior. (Psychiatry)

Office consultation for a 6-year-old male for evaluation of severe muscle and joint pain and a diffuse rash. Patient well until 4-6 weeks earlier, when he developed arthralgia, myalgias, and a fever of 102 degrees for one week. (Rheumatology)

Office consultation for a 70-year-old male with COPD, congestive heart failure, and diabetes who presents with rectal bleeding and pain and worsening constipation. The patient has a fixed, partially obstructing rectal mass. (General Surgery)

Office consultation for a 57-year-old male with recent onset of three events of left arm weakness lasting 30 minutes each. (Neurology)

Initial office consultation of a patient who presents with a 30 year history of smoking and hard, fixed right neck mass, HTN, COPD fo which he is on other meds and/or a suspicious epiglottic lesion on indirect laryngoscopy. He brings a CT ordered by his PCP. (Otolaryngology)

# Inpatient Consultations

## New or Established Patient

**99251**   Initial hospital consultation for a 27-year-old female with fractured incisor post-intubation. (Oral & Maxillofacial Surgery)

Initial hospital consultation for an orthopaedic patient on IV antibiotics who has developed an apparent candida infection of the oral cavity. (Oral & Maxillofacial Surgery)

Initial inpatient consultation for a 30-year-old female complaining of vaginal itching, post orthopaedic surgery. (Obstetrics & Gynecology)

Initial inpatient consultation for a 36-year-old male on orthopaedic service with complaint of localized dental pain. (Oral & Maxillofacial Surgery)

Initial hospital consultation for a 20-year-old male following a motor vehicle accident who developed cellulitis around a laceration that was sutured in the emergency room. (General Surgery)

Initial inpatient consultation for a 64-year-old bedridden male with skin irritation and pain in posterior heel. (Podiatric Surgery)

**99252**   Initial hospital consultation for a 45-year-old male, previously abstinent alcoholic, who relapsed and was admitted for management of gastritis. The patient readily accepts the need for further treatment. (Addiction Medicine)

Initial hospital consultation for a 35-year-old dialysis patient with episodic oral ulcerations. (Oral & Maxillofacial Surgery)

Initial inpatient preoperative consultation for a 43-year-old female with cholecystitis and well-controlled hypertension. (Cardiology)

Initial inpatient consultation for recommendation of antibiotic prophylaxis for a patient with a synthetic heart valve who will undergo urologic surgery. (Internal Medicine)

Initial inpatient consultation for possible drug induced skin eruption in 50-year-old male. (Dermatology)

Preoperative inpatient consultation for evaluation of hypertension in a 60-year-old male who will undergo a cholecystectomy. Patient had a normal annual check-up in your office four months ago. (Internal Medicine)

Initial inpatient consultation for 66-year-old patient with wrist and hand pain and finger numbness, secondary to carpal tunnel syndrome. (Orthopaedic Surgery/Plastic Surgery)

Initial inpatient consultation for a 66-year-old male smoker referred for pain management immediately status post-biliary tract surgery done via sub-costal incision. (Anesthesiology/Pain Medicine)

Initial inpatient consultation for an asymptomatic patient with an established diagnosis of allergic rhinitis, who has gone six weeks since last allergy injection and needs a dose adjustment before the next dose is given. (Allergy & Immunology)

Initial office visit for an 86-year old male with a 2 cm lipoma on back that he is concerned is infected. (General Surgery)

Initial inpatient consultation for a 70-year-old female who has had no bowel sounds for two days following an orthopedic operation. (General Surgery)

Initial hospital consultation for a 56-year-old stroke patient with ankle venous stasis ulcerations. (Podiatric Surgery)

Initial consultation for 66-year-old patient with a grade 1 sacral decubitus following a six-hour abdominal surgical procedure. (Orthopaedic Surgery/Plastic Surgery)

**99253** Initial hospital consultation for a 50-year-old female with incapacitating knee pain due to generalized rheumatoid arthritis. (Orthopaedic Surgery)

Initial hospital consultation for a 60-year-old male with avascular necrosis of the left femoral heel with increasing pain. (Orthopaedic Surgery)

Initial hospital consultation for a 45-year-old female with compound mandibular fracture and concurrent head, abdominal, and/or orthopaedic injuries. (Oral & Maxillofacial Surgery)

Initial hospital consultation for a 22-year-old female, paraplegic, to evaluate wrist and hand pain. (Orthopaedic Surgery)

Initial hospital consultation for a 40-year-old male with 10-day history of incapacitating unilateral sciatica, unable to walk now, not improved by bed rest. (Neurosurgery)

Initial hospital consultation, requested by pediatrician, for treatment recommendations for a patient admitted with persistent inability to walk following soft tissue injury to ankle. (Physiatry)

Initial hospital consultation for a 27-year-old previously healthy male who vomited during IV sedation and may have aspirated gastric contents. (Anesthesiology)

Initial hospital consultation for a 33-year-old female, post-abdominal surgery, who now has a fever. (Internal Medicine)

Initial inpatient consultation for a 57-year-old male admitted for severe abdominal pain and fever two days post lower endoscopy. (General Surgery)

Initial inpatient consultation for rehabilitation of a 73-year-old female one week after surgical management of a hip fracture. (Physical Medicine & Rehabilitation)

Initial inpatient consultation for diagnosis/management of fever following abdominal surgery. (Internal Medicine)

Initial inpatient consultation for a 42-year-old non-diabetic patient, postoperative cholecystectomy, now with an acute urinary tract infection. (Nephrology)

Initial inpatient consultation for 53-year-old female with moderate uncomplicated pancreatitis. (Gastroenterology)

Initial inpatient consultation for 45-year-old patient with chronic neck pain with radicular pain of the left arm. (Orthopaedic Surgery)

Initial inpatient consultation for a 43-year-old male with new onset foot drop after removing a cast from his leg. (Neurology)

Initial hospital consultation for an orthopaedic patient on IV antibiotics who has developed an apparent candida infection of the oral cavity. (Oral & Maxillofacial Surgery)

Initial inpatient consultation for a 36-year-old male on orthopaedic service with complaint of localized dental pain. (Oral & Maxillofacial Surgery)

Initial hospital consultation for a 35-year-old dialysis patient with episodic oral ulcerations. (Oral & Maxillofacial Surgery)

Initial hospital consultation for a 55-year-old diabetic patient on dialysis with infected ingrown toenail. (Podiatric Surgery)

**99254** Initial inpatient consultation for a 35-year-old female with a fever and pulmonary infiltrate following cesarean section. (Pulmonary Medicine)

Initial hospital consultation for a 15-year-old patient with painless swelling of proximal humerus with lytic lesion by X-ray. (Orthopaedic Surgery)

Initial hospital consultation for evaluation of a 29-year-old female with a diffusely positive medical review of systems and history of multiple surgeries. (Psychiatry)

Initial hospital consultation for a 70-year-old diabetic female with gangrene of the foot. (Orthopaedic Surgery)

Initial inpatient consultation for a 47-year-old female with progressive pulmonary infiltrate, hypoxemia, and diminished urine output. (Anesthesiology)

Initial hospital consultation for a patient with failed total hip replacement with loosening and pain upon walking. (Orthopaedic Surgery)

Initial hospital consultation for a 62-year-old female with metastatic breast cancer to the femoral neck and thoracic vertebra. (Orthopaedic Surgery)

Initial hospital consultation for a 39-year-old female with nephrolithiasis requiring extensive opioid analgesics, whose vital signs are now elevated. She initially denied any drug use but today gives history of multiple substance abuse, including opioids and prior treatment for a personality disorder. (Psychiatry)

Initial inpatient consultation for evaluation of a 63-year-old in the ICU with diabetes and chronic renal failure who develops acute respiratory distress syndrome 36 hours after a mitral valve replacement. (Anesthesiology)

Initial inpatient consultation for a 66-year-old female with enlarged supraclavicular lymph nodes, found on biopsy to be malignant. (Hematology/Oncology)

Initial inpatient consultation for a 43-year-old female for evaluation of sudden painful visual loss, optic neuritis, and episodic paresthesia. (Ophthalmology)

Initial inpatient consultation for evaluation of a 71-year-old male with hyponatremia (serum sodium 114) who was admitted to the hospital with pneumonia. (Nephrology)

Initial inpatient consultation for a 72-year-old male with emergency admission for possible bowel obstruction. (Internal Medicine/General Surgery)

Initial inpatient consultation for a 35-year-old female with fever, swollen joints, and rash of one-week duration. (Rheumatology)

Initial hospital consultation for a 45-year-old female with compound mandibular fracture and concurrent head, abdominal, and/or orthopaedic injuries. (Oral & Maxillofacial Surgery)

Initial hospital consultation for a 70-year-old diabetic female with gangrene of the foot. (Podiatric Surgery)

Initial hospital consultation for a 39-year-old female with myasthenia admitted for a thymectomy surgery tomorrow. (Neurology)

**99255** Initial hospital consultation for a 70-year-old female without previous psychiatric history who is now experiencing nocturnal confusion and visual hallucinations following hip replacement surgery. (Psychiatry)

Initial inpatient consultation for a 76-year-old female with massive, life-threatening gastrointestinal hemorrhage and chest pain. (Gastroenterology)

Initial inpatient consultation for a 75-year-old female, admitted to intensive care with acute respiratory distress syndrome, who is hypersensitive, and has a moderate metabolic acidosis, and a rising serum creatinine. (Nephrology)

Initial hospital consultation for patient with a history of complicated low back pain and neck problems with previous multiple failed back surgeries. (Orthopaedic Surgery/Neurosurgery)

Initial hospital consultation for a 66-year-old female, two days post-abdominal aneurysm repair, with oliguria and hypertension of one-day duration. (Nephrology/Internal Medicine)

Initial hospital consultation for a patient with shotgun wound to face with massive facial trauma and airway obstruction. (Oral & Maxillofacial Surgery)

Initial hospital consultation for patient with severe pancreatitis complicated by respiratory insufficiency, acute renal failure, and abscess formation. (General Surgery/Colon & Rectal Surgery)

Initial hospital consultation for a 35-year-old multiple-trauma male patient with complex pelvic fractures to evaluate and formulate management plan. (Orthopaedic Surgery)

Initial inpatient consultation for adolescent patient with fractured femur and pelvis who pulled out IVs and disconnected traction in attempt to elope from hospital. (Psychiatry)

Initial hospital consultation for a 16-year-old primigravida at 32-weeks gestation requested by a family practitioner for evaluation of severe hypertension, thrombocytopenia, and headache. (Obstetrics & Gynecology)

Initial hospital consultation for a 58-year-old insulin-dependent diabetic with multiple antibiotic allergies, now with multiple fascial plane abscesses and airway obstruction. (Oral & Maxillofacial Surgery)

Initial inpatient consultation for a 55-year-old male with known cirrhosis and ascites, now with jaundice, encephalopathy, and massive hematemesis. (Gastroenterology)

Initial hospital consultation for a 25-year-old male, seen in emergency room with severe, closed head injury. (Neurosurgery)

Initial hospital consultation for a 2-day-old male with single ventricle physiology and subaortic obstruction. Family counseling following evaluation for multiple, staged surgical procedures. (Thoracic Surgery)

Initial hospital consultation for a 45-year-old male admitted with subarachnoid hemorrhage and intracranial aneurysm on angiogram. (Neurosurgery)

Initial inpatient consultation for myxedematous patient who is hypoventilating and obtunded. (Endocrinology)

Initial hospital consultation for a 45-year-old patient with widely metastatic lung carcinoma, intractable back pain, and a history that includes substance dependence, NSAID allergy, and two prior laminectomies with fusion for low back pain. (Pain Medicine)

Initial hospital consultation for evaluation of treatment options in a 50-year-old patient with cirrhosis, known peptic ulcer disease, hypotension, encephalopathy, and massive acute upper gastrointestinal bleeding that cannot be localized by endoscopy. (Interventional Radiology)

Initial inpatient consultation in the ICU for a 70-year-old male who experienced a cardiac arrest during surgery and was resuscitated. (Cardiology)

Initial inpatient consultation for a patient with severe pancreatitis complicated by respiratory insufficiency, acute renal failure, and abscess formation. (Gastroenterology)

Initial inpatient consultation for a 70-year-old cirrhotic male admitted with ascites, jaundice, encephalopathy, and massive hematemesis. (Gastroenterology)

Initial inpatient consultation in the ICU for a 51-year-old patient who has a fever, respiratory failure requiring mechanical ventilation, and bilateral pulmonary infiltrates on chest radiograph two weeks after a renal transplantation. (Infectious Disease)

Initial inpatient consultation for evaluation and formulation of plan for management of multiple-trauma patient with complex pelvic fracture, 35-year-old male. (General Surgery/Orthopaedic Surgery)

Initial inpatient consultation for a 50-year-old male with a history of previous myocardial infarction, now with acute pulmonary edema and hypotension. (Cardiology)

Initial inpatient consultation for 45-year-old male with recent, acute subarachnoid hemorrhage, hesitant speech, mildly confused, drowsy. High risk group for HIV+ status. (Neurosurgery)

Initial inpatient consultation for 36-year-old female referred by her internist to evaluate a patient being followed for abdominal pain and fever. The patient has developed diffuse abdominal pain, guarding, rigidity, and increased fever. (Obstetrics & Gynecology)

Initial inpatient consultation for adolescent patient with fractured femur and pelvis who expressed feeling hopeless and suicidal. (Psychiatry)

Initial inpatient consultation for a 35-year-old male with closed head injury, pulmonary contusion, liver laceration, and complex pelvic fracture. (General Surgery)

Initial hospital consultation for a 35-year-old male patient with acute partial traumatic amputation of the forefoot for evaluation and formulation of a management plan. (Podiatric Surgery)

Initial hospital consultation for a 57-year-old male with new-onset right hemiparesis and aphasia. (Neurology)

# Emergency Department Services

## New or Established Patient

**99281**  Emergency department visit for a patient for removal of sutures from a well-healed, uncomplicated laceration. (Emergency Medicine)

Emergency department visit for a patient for tetanus toxoid immunization. (Emergency Medicine)

Emergency department visit for a patient with several uncomplicated insect bites. (Pediatrics)

**99282**  Emergency department visit for a 20-year-old student who presents with a painful sunburn with blister formation on the back. (Emergency Medicine)

Emergency department visit for a child presenting with impetigo localized to the face. (Emergency Medicine)

Emergency department visit for a patient with a minor traumatic injury of an extremity with localized pain, swelling, and bruising. (Emergency Medicine)

Emergency department visit for an otherwise healthy patient whose chief complaint is a red, swollen cystic lesion on his/her back. (Emergency Medicine)

Emergency department visit for a patient presenting with a rash on both legs after exposure to poison ivy. (Emergency Medicine)

Emergency department visit for a child presenting with impetigo localized to the face with use of topical OTC treatment. (Pediatrics)

Emergency department visit for a patient with a minor traumatic injury of an extremity with localized pain, swelling, and bruising (no imaging done). (Pediatrics)

**99283**  Emergency department visit for a sexually active female complaining of vaginal discharge who is afebrile and denies experiencing abdominal or back pain. (Emergency Medicine)

Emergency department visit for a well-appearing 8-year-old who has a fever, diarrhea, and abdominal cramps; is tolerating oral fluids and is not vomiting. (Pediatrics)

Emergency department visit for a patient with an inversion ankle injury, who is unable to bear weight on the injured foot and ankle. (Emergency Medicine)

Emergency department visit for a patient who has a complaint of acute pain associated with a suspected foreign body in the painful eye. (Emergency Medicine)

Emergency department visit for a healthy, young adult patient who sustained a blunt head injury with local swelling and bruising without subsequent confusion, loss of consciousness, or memory deficit. (Emergency Medicine)

**99284**  Emergency department visit for a 4-year-old who fell off a bike sustaining a head injury with brief loss of consciousness. (Emergency Medicine)

Emergency department visit for a patient with flank pain and hematuria. (Emergency Medicine)

Emergency department visit for a female presenting with lower abdominal pain and a vaginal discharge. (Emergency Medicine)

**99285**  Emergency department visit for a patient with a complicated overdose requiring aggressive management to prevent side effects from the ingested materials. (Emergency Medicine)

Emergency department visit for a patient exhibiting active, upper gastrointestinal bleeding. (Emergency Medicine)

Emergency department visit for a previously healthy young adult patient who is injured in an automobile accident and is brought to the emergency department immobilized and has symptoms compatible with intra-abdominal injuries or multiple extremity injuries. (Emergency Medicine)

Emergency department visit for a patient with an acute onset of chest pain compatible with symptoms of cardiac ischemia and/or pulmonary embolus. (Emergency Medicine)

Emergency department visit for a patient who presents with a sudden onset of "the worst headache of her life," and complains of a stiff neck, nausea, and inability to concentrate. (Emergency Medicine)

Emergency department visit for a patient with a new onset of a cerebral vascular accident. (Emergency Medicine)

Emergency department visit for acute febrile illness in an adult, associated with shortness of breath and an altered level of alertness. (Emergency Medicine)

# Critical Care Services

**99291** First hour of critical care of a 65-year-old male with septic shock following relief of ureteral obstruction caused by a stone. (Cardiology/Emergency Medicine/Family Practice/General Surgery/Internal Medicine/Pulmonary Medicine)

First hour of critical care of a 15-year-old with acute respiratory failure from asthma. (Cardiology/Emergency Medicine/Family Practice/General Surgery/Internal Medicine/Pulmonary Medicine)

First hour of critical care of a 45-year-old who sustained a liver laceration, cerebral hematoma, flailed chest, and pulmonary contusion after being struck by an automobile. (Cardiology/Emergency Medicine/Family Practice/General Surgery/Internal Medicine/Pulmonary Medicine)

First hour of critical care of a 65-year-old female who, following a hysterectomy, suffered a cardiac arrest associated with a pulmonary embolus. (Cardiology/Emergency Medicine/Family Practice/General Surgery/Internal Medicine/Pulmonary Medicine)

First hour of critical care of a 6-month-old with hypovolemic shock secondary to diarrhea and dehydration. (Cardiology/Emergency Medicine/Family Practice/General Surgery/Internal Medicine/Pulmonary Medicine/Critical Care)

First hour of critical care of a 3-year-old with respiratory failure secondary to pneumocystis carinii pneumonia. (Cardiology/Emergency Medicine/Family Practice/General Surgery/Internal Medicine/Pulmonary Medicine/Critical Care)

First hour of critical care of a 13-year-old with hypovolemic shock secondary to diarrhea and dehydration. (Cardiology/Emergency Medicine/Family Practice/General Surgery/Internal Medicine/Pulmonary Medicine/Critical Care)

First hour of critical care of a 13-year-old with respiratory failure secondary to pneumocystis carinii pneumonia (Pediatrics)

Subsequent hospital visit for a 55-year-old male with severe chronic obstructive pulmonary disease and bronchospasm; initially admitted for acute respiratory distress requiring ventilatory support in the ICU. The patient was stabilized, extubated, and transferred to the floor but has now developed acute fever, dyspnea, left lower lobe rhonchi, and laboratory evidence of carbon dioxide retention and hypoxemia. (Family Medicine)

Initial hospital visit for a 15-year-old male with acute status asthmaticus, unresponsive to outpatient therapy. (Pulmonary Medicine)

Initial hospital visit for a 62-year-old male with history of previous myocardial infarction, comes in with recurrent, sustained ventricular tachycardia. (Cardiology)

# Prolonged Services

## Prolonged Service With Direct Patient Contact

### Office or Other Outpatient

**99354** A 20-year-old female with history of asthma presents with acute bronchospasm and moderate respiratory distress. Initial evaluation shows respiratory rate 30, labored breathing and wheezing heard in all lung fields. Office treatment is initiated which includes intermittent bronchial dilation and subcutaneous epinephrine. Requires intermittent time with patient over a period of 2-3 hours. (Family Medicine/Internal Medicine)

**99355** A 20-year-old female with history of asthma presents with acute bronchospasm and moderate respiratory distress. Initial evaluation shows respiratory rate 30, labored breathing, and wheezing heard in all lung fields. Office treatment is initiated that includes intermittent bronchial dilation and subcutaneous epinephrine. Requires intermittent time with patient over a period of 2-3 hours. (Family Medicine/Internal Medicine/Pulmonary Medicine)

### Inpatient

**99356** A 34-year-old primigravida female presents to hospital in early labor. Admission history and physical reveals severe preeclampsia. Physician supervises management of preeclampsia, IV magnesium initiation and maintenance, labor augmentation with pitocin, and close maternal-fetal monitoring. Involvement includes 40 minutes of continuous bedside care until the patient is stable, then is intermittent over several hours until the delivery. (Family Medicine/Internal Medicine/Obstetrics & Gynecology)

## Prolonged Service Without Direct Patient Contact

**99358** An 85-year-old new patient with multiple complicated medical problems has moved to the area to live closer to her daughter. She is brought to the primary care office by her daughter and has been seen and examined by the physician. The physician indicated that past medical records would be obtained from the patient's prior physicians' and that he will communicate further with the daughter upon review of them.

**99359** An 85-year-old new patient with multiple complicated medical problems has moved to the area to live closer to her daughter. She is brought to the primary care office by her daughter and has been seen and examined by the physician. The physician indicated that past medical records would be obtained from the patient's prior physicians' and that he will communicate further with the daughter upon review of them.

## Physician Standby Services

**99360** A 24-year-old patient is admitted to OB unit attempting VBAC. Fetal monitoring shows increasing fetal distress. Patient's blood pressure is rising and labor progressing slowly. A primary care physician is requested by the OB/GYN to standby in the unit for possible cesarean delivery and neonatal resuscitation. (Family Medicine/Internal Medicine)

## Care Plan Oversight Services

**99375** First month of care plan oversight for terminal care of a 58-year-old female with advanced intraabdominal ovarian cancer. Care plan includes home oxygen, diuretics IV for edema and ascites control and pain control management involving IV morphine infusion when progressive ileus occurred. Physician phone contacts with nurse, family, and MSW. Discussion with MSW concerning plans to withdraw supportive measures per patient wishes. Documentation includes review and modification of care plan and certifications from nursing, MSW, pharmacy, and DME. (Family Medicine/Internal Medicine)

## Inpatient Neonatal Intensive Care Service and Pediatric and Neonatal Critical Care Services

**99477** Initial hospital visit for a 1-day-old male with cyanosis, respiratory distress, and tachypnea. (Cardiology)

# Appendix D

## Summary of CPT Add-on Codes

This listing is a summary of CPT add-on codes for *CPT 2014*. The codes listed below are identified in *CPT 2014* with a + symbol.

| | | | | | | | |
|---|---|---|---|---|---|---|---|
| 01953 | 15241 | 22116 | 31627 | 33924 | 38900 | 61797 | 64872 |
| 01968 | 15261 | 22208 | 31632 | 34806 | 43273 | 61799 | 64874 |
| 01969 | 15272 | 22216 | 31633 | 34808 | 43283 | 61800 | 64876 |
| 11001 | 15274 | 22226 | 31637 | 34813 | 43338 | 61864 | 64901 |
| 11008 | 15276 | 22328 | 31649 | 34826 | 43635 | 61868 | 64902 |
| 11045 | 15278 | 22522 | 31651 | 35306 | 44015 | 62148 | 65757 |
| 11046 | 15777 | 22525 | 32501 | 35390 | 44121 | 62160 | 66990 |
| 11047 | 15787 | 22527 | 32506 | 35400 | 44128 | 63035 | 67225 |
| 11101 | 15847 | 22534 | 32507 | 35500 | 44139 | 63043 | 67320 |
| 11201 | 16036 | 22552 | 32667 | 35572 | 44203 | 63044 | 67331 |
| 11732 | 17003 | 22585 | 32668 | 35600 | 44213 | 63048 | 67332 |
| 11922 | 17312 | 22614 | 32674 | 35681 | 44701 | 63057 | 67334 |
| 13102 | 17314 | 22632 | 33141 | 35682 | 44955 | 63066 | 67335 |
| 13122 | 17315 | 22634 | 33225 | 35683 | 47001 | 63076 | 67340 |
| 13133 | 19001 | 22840 | 33257 | 35685 | 47550 | 63078 | 69990 |
| 13153 | 19082 | 22841 | 33258 | 35686 | 48400 | 63082 | 74301 |
| 14302 | 19084 | 22842 | 33259 | 35697 | 49326 | 63086 | 75565 |
| 15003 | 19086 | 22843 | 33367 | 35700 | 49327 | 63088 | 75774 |
| 15005 | 19126 | 22844 | 33368 | 36148 | 49412 | 63091 | 75946 |
| 15101 | 19282 | 22845 | 33369 | 36218 | 49435 | 63103 | 75964 |
| 15111 | 19284 | 22846 | 33508 | 36227 | 49568 | 63295 | 75968 |
| 15116 | 19286 | 22847 | 33517 | 36228 | 49905 | 63308 | 76125 |
| 15121 | 19288 | 22848 | 33518 | 36248 | 51797 | 63621 | 76802 |
| 15131 | 19297 | 22851 | 33519 | 36476 | 56606 | 64480 | 76810 |
| 15136 | 20930 | 26125 | 33521 | 36479 | 57267 | 64484 | 76812 |
| 15151 | 20931 | 26861 | 33522 | 37185 | 58110 | 64491 | 76814 |
| 15152 | 20936 | 26863 | 33523 | 37186 | 58611 | 64492 | 76937 |
| 15156 | 20937 | 27358 | 33530 | 37222 | 59525 | 64494 | 77001 |
| 15157 | 20938 | 27692 | 33572 | 37223 | 60512 | 64495 | 77051 |
| 15201 | 20985 | 29826 | 33768 | 37232 | 61316 | 64634 | 77052 |
| 15221 | 22103 | 31620 | 33884 | 37233 | 61517 | 64636 | 77293 |
| | | | | 37234 | 61609 | 64643 | 78020 |
| | | | | 37235 | 61610 | 64645 | 78496 |
| | | | | 37237 | 61611 | 64727 | 78730 |
| | | | | 37239 | 61612 | 64778 | 81266 |
| | | | | 37250 | 61641 | 64783 | 82952 |
| | | | | 37251 | 61642 | 64787 | 86826 |
| | | | | 38102 | 61781 | 64832 | 87187 |
| | | | | 38746 | 61782 | 64837 | 87503 |
| | | | | 38747 | 61783 | 64859 | 87904 |

| | | | |
|---|---|---|---|
| 88155 | 93463 | 96375 | 0165T |
| 88177 | 93464 | 96376 | 0172T |
| 88185 | 93563 | 96411 | 0174T |
| 88311 | 93564 | 96415 | 0189T |
| 88314 | 93565 | 96417 | 0190T |
| 88332 | 93566 | 96423 | 0196T |
| 88334 | 93567 | 96570 | 0205T |
| 88343 | 93568 | 96571 | 0214T |
| 88388 | 93571 | 97546 | 0215T |
| 90461 | 93572 | 97598 | 0217T |
| 90472 | 93609 | 97811 | 0218T |
| 90474 | 93613 | 97814 | 0222T |
| 90785 | 93621 | 99100 | 0229T |
| 90833 | 93622 | 99116 | 0231T |
| 90836 | 93623 | 99135 | 0241T |
| 90838 | 93655 | 99140 | 0289T |
| 90840 | 93657 | 99145 | 0290T |
| 90863 | 93662 | 99150 | 0291T |
| 91013 | 94645 | 99292 | 0292T |
| 92547 | 94729 | 99354 | 0294T |
| 92608 | 94781 | 99355 | 0300T |
| 92618 | 95079 | 99356 | 0309T |
| 92621 | 95873 | 99357 | |
| 92627 | 95874 | 99359 | |
| 92921 | 95885 | 99467 | |
| 92925 | 95886 | 99481 | |
| 92929 | 95887 | 99482 | |
| 92934 | 95940 | 99486 | |
| 92938 | 95941 | 99489 | |
| 92944 | 95962 | 99602 | |
| 92973 | 95967 | 99607 | |
| 92974 | 95973 | 0054T | |
| 92978 | 95975 | 0055T | |
| 92979 | 95979 | 0076T | |
| 92998 | 96361 | 0092T | |
| 93320 | 96366 | 0095T | |
| 93321 | 96367 | 0098T | |
| 93325 | 96368 | 0159T | |
| 93352 | 96370 | 0163T | |
| 93462 | 96371 | 0164T | |

# Appendix E

## Summary of CPT Codes Exempt from Modifier 51

This listing is a summary of CPT codes that are exempt from the use of modifier 51. Procedures on this list are typically performed with another procedure but may be a stand alone procedure and not always be performed with other specified procedures. For add-on codes see Appendix D. This is not an exhaustive list of procedures that are typically exempt from multiple procedure reductions. The codes listed below are identified in *CPT 2014* with a ⊘ symbol.

| | | |
|---|---|---|
| 17004 | 93451 | 93616 |
| 20697 | 93456 | 93618 |
| 20974 | 93503 | 93631 |
| 20975 | 93600 | 94610 |
| 31500 | 93602 | 95905 |
| 33961 | 93603 | 95992 |
| 36620 | 93610 | 99143 |
| 44500 | 93612 | 99144 |
| 61107 | 93615 | |

# Appendix F

## Summary of CPT Codes Exempt from Modifier 63

The listing is a summary of CPT codes that are exempt from the use of modifier 63. The codes listed below are additionally identified in *CPT 2014* with the parenthetical instruction "(Do not report modifier 63 in conjunction with…)"

| | | |
|---|---|---|
| 30540 | 36415 | 49496 |
| 30545 | 36420 | 49600 |
| 31520 | 36450 | 49605 |
| 33401 | 36460 | 49606 |
| 33403 | 36510 | 49610 |
| 33470 | 36660 | 49611 |
| 33472 | 39503 | 53025 |
| 33502 | 43313 | 54000 |
| 33503 | 43314 | 54150 |
| 33505 | 43520 | 54160 |
| 33506 | 43831 | 63700 |
| 33610 | 44055 | 63702 |
| 33611 | 44126 | 63704 |
| 33619 | 44127 | 63706 |
| 33647 | 44128 | 65820 |
| 33670 | 46070 | |
| 33690 | 46705 | |
| 33694 | 46715 | |
| 33730 | 46716 | |
| 33732 | 46730 | |
| 33735 | 46735 | |
| 33736 | 46740 | |
| 33750 | 46742 | |
| 33755 | 46744 | |
| 33762 | 47700 | |
| 33778 | 47701 | |
| 33786 | 49215 | |
| 33922 | 49491 | |
| 33960 | 49492 | |
| 33961 | 49495 | |

# Appendix G

## Summary of CPT Codes That Include Moderate (Conscious) Sedation

The following list of procedures includes conscious sedation as an inherent part of providing the procedure. These codes are identified in the CPT code set with a symbol.

Since these services include moderate sedation, it is not appropriate for the same physician or other qualified health care professional to report both the service and the sedation codes 99143-99145. It is expected that if conscious sedation is provided to the patient as part of one of these services, it is provided by the same physician or other qualified health care professional who is providing the service.

In the unusual event when a second physician or other qualified health care professional other than the health care professional performing the diagnostic or therapeutic services provides moderate sedation in the facility setting (eg, hospital, outpatient hospital/ambulatory surgery center, skilled nursing facility) for the procedures listed in Appendix G, the second individual can report 99148-99150. However, for the circumstance in which these services are performed by the second individual in the nonfacility setting (eg, office, freestanding imaging center), codes 99148-99150 would not be reported. Moderate sedation does not include minimal sedation (anxiolysis), deep sedation, or monitored anesthesia care (00100-01999).

The inclusion of a procedure on this list does not prevent separate reporting of an associated anesthesia procedure/service (CPT codes 00100-01999) when performed by a physician or other qualified health care professional other than the health care professional performing the diagnostic or therapeutic procedure. In such cases, the person providing anesthesia services shall be present for the purpose of continuously monitoring the patient and shall not act as a surgical assistant. When clinical conditions of the patient require such anesthesia services or in the circumstances when the patient does not require sedation, the operating physician or other qualified health care professional is not required to report the procedure as a reduced service using modifier 52.

| | | | | | | |
|---|---|---|---|---|---|---|
| | | | | 31628 | 33235 | 36557 |
| | | | | 31629 | 33240 | 36558 |
| | | | | 31634 | 33241 | 36560 |
| | | | | 31635 | 33244 | 36561 |
| | | | | 31645 | 33249 | 36563 |
| | | | | 31646 | 33262 | 36565 |
| | | | | 31647 | 33263 | 36566 |
| | | | | 31648 | 33264 | 36568 |
| | | | | 31649 | 33282 | 36570 |
| | | | | 31651 | 33284 | 36571 |
| | | | | 31660 | 33990 | 36576 |
| | | | | 31661 | 33991 | 36578 |
| | | | | 31725 | 33992 | 36581 |
| | | | | 32405 | 33993 | 36582 |
| | | | | 32550 | 35471 | 36583 |
| | | | | 32551 | 35472 | 36585 |
| | | | | 32553 | 35475 | 36590 |
| | | | | 33010 | 35476 | 36870 |
| | | | | 33011 | 36010 | 37183 |
| | | | | 33206 | 36140 | 37184 |
| | | | | 33207 | 36147 | 37185 |
| | | | | 33208 | 36148 | 37186 |
| | | | | 33210 | 36200 | 37187 |
| | | | | 33211 | 36221 | 37188 |
| | | | | 33212 | 36222 | 37191 |
| | | | | 33213 | 36223 | 37192 |
| | | | | 33214 | 36224 | 37193 |
| | | | | 33216 | 36225 | 37197 |
| | | | | 33217 | 36226 | 37211 |
| | | | | 33218 | 36227 | 37212 |
| | | | | 33220 | 36228 | 37213 |
| | | | | 33221 | 36245 | 37214 |
| | | | | 33222 | 36246 | 37215 |
| | | | | 33223 | 36247 | 37216 |
| | | | | 33227 | 36248 | 37220 |
| | | | | 33228 | 36251 | 37221 |
| | | | | 33229 | 36252 | 37222 |
| 10030 | 22521 | 31615 | 31624 | 33230 | 36253 | 37223 |
| 19298 | 22522 | 31620 | 31625 | 33231 | 36254 | 37224 |
| 20982 | 22526 | 31622 | 31626 | 33233 | 36481 | 37225 |
| 22520 | 22527 | 31623 | 31627 | 33234 | 36555 | 37226 |

| | | | | | | |
|---|---|---|---|---|---|---|
| 37227 | 43238 | 44366 | 45340 | 77371 | 93456 | 93656 |
| 37228 | 43239 | 44369 | 45341 | 77600 | 93457 | 93657 |
| 37229 | 43240 | 44370 | 45342 | 77605 | 93458 | 94011 |
| 37230 | 43241 | 44372 | 45345 | 77610 | 93459 | 94012 |
| 37231 | 43242 | 44373 | 45355 | 77615 | 93460 | 94013 |
| 37232 | 43243 | 44376 | 45378 | 92920 | 93461 | 0200T |
| 37233 | 43244 | 44377 | 45379 | 92921 | 93462 | 0201T |
| 37234 | 43245 | 44378 | 45380 | 92924 | 93463 | 0282T |
| 37235 | 43246 | 44379 | 45381 | 92925 | 93464 | 0283T |
| 37236 | 43247 | 44380 | 45382 | 92928 | 93505 | 0284T |
| 37237 | 43248 | 44382 | 45383 | 92929 | 93530 | 0291T |
| 37238 | 43249 | 44383 | 45384 | 92933 | 93561 | 0292T |
| 37239 | 43250 | 44385 | 45385 | 92934 | 93562 | 0293T |
| 37241 | 43251 | 44386 | 45386 | 92937 | 93563 | 0294T |
| 37242 | 43252 | 44388 | 45387 | 92938 | 93564 | 0301T |
| 37243 | 43253 | 44389 | 45391 | 92941 | 93565 | 0302T |
| 37244 | 43254 | 44390 | 45392 | 92943 | 93566 | 0303T |
| 43200 | 43255 | 44391 | 47000 | 92944 | 93567 | 0304T |
| 43201 | 43257 | 44392 | 47382 | 92953 | 93568 | 0307T |
| 43202 | 43259 | 44393 | 47525 | 92960 | 93571 | 0308T |
| 43204 | 43260 | 44394 | 49405 | 92961 | 93572 | 0335T |
| 43205 | 43261 | 44397 | 49406 | 92973 | 93582 | |
| 43206 | 43262 | 44500 | 49407 | 92974 | 93583 | |
| 43211 | 43263 | 45303 | 49411 | 92975 | 93609 | |
| 43212 | 43264 | 45305 | 49418 | 92978 | 93613 | |
| 43213 | 43265 | 45307 | 49440 | 92979 | 93615 | |
| 43214 | 43266 | 45308 | 49441 | 92986 | 93616 | |
| 43215 | 43270 | 45309 | 49442 | 92987 | 93618 | |
| 43216 | 43273 | 45315 | 49446 | 93312 | 93619 | |
| 43217 | 43274 | 45317 | 50200 | 93313 | 93620 | |
| 43220 | 43275 | 45320 | 50382 | 93314 | 93621 | |
| 43226 | 43276 | 45321 | 50384 | 93315 | 93622 | |
| 43227 | 43277 | 45327 | 50385 | 93316 | 93624 | |
| 43229 | 43278 | 45332 | 50386 | 93317 | 93640 | |
| 43231 | 43453 | 45333 | 50387 | 93318 | 93641 | |
| 43232 | 44360 | 45334 | 50592 | 93451 | 93642 | |
| 43233 | 44361 | 45335 | 50593 | 93452 | 93650 | |
| 43235 | 44363 | 45337 | 57155 | 93453 | 93653 | |
| 43236 | 44364 | 45338 | 66720 | 93454 | 93654 | |
| 43237 | 44365 | 45339 | 69300 | 93455 | 93655 | |

# Appendix H

## Alphabetical Clinical Topics Listing (AKA – Alphabetical Listing)

The **Alphabetical Clinical Topics Listing** (formerly Appendix H) has been removed from the CPT codebook. Since this document is a dynamic and rapidly expanding source of information to link CPT Category II codes, clinical conditions, and measure abstracts, the Alphabetical Listing is now solely accessed on the AMA Web site at www.ama-assn.org/go/cpt.

In addition, new codes for the publication cycle (ie, the **Update to the List of Category II Codes**) will continue to be located on the AMA Web site prior to publication in the next edition of the CPT codebook (subsequent to its listing to the Web).

# Appendix I

## Genetic Testing Code Modifiers

The **Genetic Testing Code Modifiers** (formerly Appendix I) has been removed from the CPT code set.

The addition of more than 100 molecular pathology codes to the 2012 code set and still more codes to the 2013 CPT code set resulted in the deletion of the stacking codes (83890–83914). The genetic testing code modifiers formerly described in Appendix I applied to those stacking codes, and therefore, the Appendix and modifiers have been removed from the code set.

For the most up-to-date information on future updates for molecular pathology coding in the CPT code set, see www.ama-assn.org/ama/pub/physician-resources/solutions-managing-your-practice/coding-billing-insurance/cpt/about-cpt/mopath-codes.page.

# Appendix J

## Electrodiagnostic Medicine Listing of Sensory, Motor, and Mixed Nerves

This summary assigns each sensory, motor, and mixed nerve with its appropriate nerve conduction study code in order to enhance accurate reporting of codes 95907-95913. Each nerve constitutes one unit of service.

### Motor Nerves Assigned to Codes 95900 and 95907-95913

I. Upper extremity, cervical plexus, and brachial plexus motor nerves
   A. Axillary motor nerve to the deltoid
   B. Long thoracic motor nerve to the serratus anterior
   C. Median nerve
      1. Median motor nerve to the abductor pollicis brevis
      2. Median motor nerve, anterior interosseous branch, to the flexor pollicis longus
      3. Median motor nerve, anterior interosseous branch, to the pronator quadratus
      4. Median motor nerve to the first lumbrical
      5. Median motor nerve to the second lumbrical
   D. Musculocutaneous motor nerve to the biceps brachii
   E. Radial nerve
      1. Radial motor nerve to the extensor carpi ulnaris
      2. Radial motor nerve to the extensor digitorum communis
      3. Radial motor nerve to the extensor indicis proprius
      4. Radial motor nerve to the brachioradialis
   F. Suprascapular nerve
      1. Suprascapular motor nerve to the supraspinatus
      2. Suprascapular motor nerve to the infraspinatus
   G. Thoracodorsal motor nerve to the latissimus dorsi

H. Ulnar nerve
   1. Ulnar motor nerve to the abductor digiti minimi
   2. Ulnar motor nerve to the palmar interosseous
   3. Ulnar motor nerve to the first dorsal interosseous
   4. Ulnar motor nerve to the flexor carpi ulnaris
I. Other
II. Lower extremity motor nerves
   A. Femoral motor nerve to the quadriceps
      1. Femoral motor nerve to vastus medialis
      2. Femoral motor nerve to vastus lateralis
      3. Femoral motor nerve to vastus intermedialis
      4. Femoral motor nerve to rectus femoris
   B. Ilioinguinal motor nerve
   C. Peroneal (fibular) nerve
      1. Peroneal motor nerve to the extensor digitorum brevis
      2. Peroneal motor nerve to the peroneus brevis
      3. Peroneal motor nerve to the peroneus longus
      4. Peroneal motor nerve to the tibialis anterior
   D. Plantar motor nerve
   E. Sciatic nerve
   F. Tibial nerve
      1. Tibial motor nerve, inferior calcaneal branch, to the abductor digiti minimi
      2. Tibial motor nerve, medial plantar branch, to the abductor hallucis
      3. Tibial motor nerve, lateral plantar branch, to the flexor digiti minimi brevis
   G. Other
III. Cranial nerves and trunk
   A. Cranial nerve VII (facial motor nerve)
      1. Facial nerve to the frontalis
      2. Facial nerve to the nasalis
      3. Facial nerve to the orbicularis oculi
      4. Facial nerve to the orbicularis oris
   B. Cranial nerve XI (spinal accessory motor nerve)
   C. Cranial nerve XII (hypoglossal motor nerve)
   D. Intercostal motor nerve
   E. Phrenic motor nerve to the diaphragm
   F. Recurrent laryngeal nerve
   G. Other
IV. Nerve Roots
   A. Cervical nerve root stimulation
      1. Cervical level 5 (CT)
      2. Cervical level 6 (C6)
      3. Cervical level 7 (C7)
      4. Cervical level 8 (C8)

B. Thoracic nerve root stimulation
1. Thoracic level 1 (T1)
2. Thoracic level 2 (T2)
3. Thoracic level 3 (T3)
4. Thoracic level 4 (T4)
5. Thoracic level 5 (T5)
6. Thoracic level 6 (T6)
7. Thoracic level 7 (T7)
8. Thoracic level 8 (T8)
9. Thoracic level 9 (T9)
10. Thoracic level 10 (T10)
11. Thoracic level 11 (T11)
12. Thoracic level 12 (T12)
C. Lumbar nerve root stimulation
1. Lumbar level 1 (L1)
2. Lumbar level 2 (L2)
3. Lumbar level 3 (L3)
4. Lumbar level 4 (L4)
5. Lumbar level 5 (L5)
D. Sacral nerve root stimulation
1. Sacral level 1 (S1)
2. Sacral level 2 (S2)
3. Sacral level 3 (S3)
4. Sacral level 4 (S4)

## Sensory and Mixed Nerves Assigned to Codes 95907-95913

I. Upper extremity sensory and mixed nerves
A. Lateral antebrachial cutaneous sensory nerve
B. Medial antebrachial cutaneous sensory nerve
C. Medial brachial cutaneous sensory nerve
D. Median nerve
1. Median sensory nerve to the first digit
2. Median sensory nerve to the second digit
3. Median sensory nerve to the third digit
4. Median sensory nerve to the fourth digit
5. Median palmar cutaneous sensory nerve
6. Median palmar mixed nerve
E. Posterior antebrachial cutaneous sensory nerve
F. Radial sensory nerve
1. Radial sensory nerve to the base of the thumb
2. Radial sensory nerve to digit 1
G. Ulnar nerve
1. Ulnar dorsal cutaneous sensory nerve
2. Ulnar sensory nerve to the fourth digit
3. Ulnar sensory nerve to the fifth digit
4. Ulnar palmar mixed nerve
H. Intercostal sensory nerve
I. Other

II. Lower extremity sensory and mixed nerves
A. Lateral femoral cutaneous sensory nerve
B. Medial calcaneal sensory nerve
C. Medial femoral cutaneous sensory nerve
D. Peroneal nerve
1. Deep peroneal sensory nerve
2. Superficial peroneal sensory nerve, medial dorsal cutaneous branch
3. Superficial peroneal sensory nerve, intermediate dorsal cutaneous branch
E. Posterior femoral cutaneous sensory nerve
F. Saphenous nerve
1. Saphenous sensory nerve (distal technique)
2. Saphenous sensory nerve (proximal technique)
G. Sural nerve
1. Sural sensory nerve, lateral dorsal cutaneous branch
2. Sural sensory nerve
H. Tibial sensory nerve (digital nerve to toe 1)
I. Tibial sensory nerve (medial plantar nerve)
J. Tibial sensory nerve (lateral plantar nerve)
K. Other
III. Head and trunk sensory nerves
A. Dorsal nerve of the penis
B. Greater auricular nerve
C. Ophthalmic branch of the trigeminal nerve
D. Pudendal sensory nerve
E. Suprascapular sensory nerves
F. Other

The following table provides a reasonable maximum number of studies performed per diagnostic category necessary for a physician to arrive at a diagnosis in 90% of patients with that final diagnosis. The numbers in each column represent the number of studies recommended. The appropriate number of studies to be performed is based upon the physician's discretion.

| Type of Study/Maximum Number of Studies | | | |
|---|---|---|---|
| **Indication** | **Limbs Studied by Needle EMG (95860-95864, 95867-95870, 95885-95887)** | **Nerve Conduction Studies (Total nerves studied, 95907-95913)** | **Neuromuscular Junction Testing (Repetitive Stimulation, 95937)** |
| Carpal Tunnel (Unilateral) | 1 | 7 | — |
| Carpal Tunnel (Bilateral) | 2 | 10 | — |
| Radiculopathy | 2 | 7 | — |
| Mononeuropathy | 1 | 8 | — |
| Polyneuropathy/Mononeuropathy Multiplex | 3 | 10 | — |
| Myopathy | 2 | 4 | 2 |
| Motor Neuronopathy (eg, ALS) | 4 | 6 | 2 |
| Plexopathy | 2 | 12 | — |
| Neuromuscular Junction | 2 | 4 | 3 |
| Tarsal Tunnel Syndrome (Unilateral) | 1 | 8 | — |
| Tarsal Tunnel Syndrome (Bilateral) | 2 | 11 | — |
| Weakness, Fatigue, Cramps, or Twitching (Focal) | 2 | 7 | 2 |
| Weakness, Fatigue, Cramps, or Twitching (General) | 4 | 8 | 2 |
| Pain, Numbness, or Tingling (Unilateral) | 1 | 9 | — |
| Pain, Numbness, or Tingling (Bilateral) | 2 | 12 | — |

Appendix K

# Appendix K

## Product Pending FDA Approval

Some vaccine products have been assigned a CPT Category I code in anticipation of future approval from the Food and Drug Administration (FDA). Following is a list of the vaccine product codes pending FDA approval status that are identified in the CPT code set with the ( ⚡ ) symbol. Upon revision of the approval status by the FDA, notation of this revision will be provided via the AMA CPT "Category I Vaccine Codes" Internet listing (www.ama-assn.org/ama/pub/category/10902.html) and in subsequent publications of the CPT code set.

90653

90666

90667

90668

90687

90688

90739

# Appendix L

## Vascular Families

Assignment of branches to first, second, and third order in this table makes the assumption that the starting point is catheterization of the aorta. This categorization would not be accurate, for instance, if a femoral or carotid artery were catheterized directly in an antegrade direction. Arteries highlighted in bold are those more commonly reported during arteriographic procedures.

| First Order | Second Order Branch | Third Order Branch | Beyond Third Order Branches |
|---|---|---|---|
| **Innominate** | **R. common carotid** | **R. internal carotid** | R. ophthalmic<br>R. p. communicating<br>R. middle cerebral<br>R. a. cerebral |
| | | **R. external carotid** | R. superior thyroid<br>R. ascending pharyngeal<br>R. facial<br>R. lingual<br>R. occipital<br>R. p. auricular<br>R. superficial temporal<br>R. internal maxillary<br>R. middle meningeal |
| | **R. subclavian & axillary** | **R. vertebral** | Basilar |
| | | R. internal thoracic (internal mammary) | |
| | | R. thyrocervical trunk | R. inferior thyroid<br>R. suprascapular<br>R. transverse cervical |
| | | R. costocervical trunk | R. highest intercostal<br>R. deep cervical |
| | | R. lateral thoracic<br>R. thoracoacromial<br>R. humeral circumflex (A/P) | |
| | | R. subscapular | R. circumflex scapular |
| | | **R. brachial** | |
| | | R. deep brachial | R. ulnar<br>R. radial<br>R. interosseous<br>R. deep palmar arch<br>R. superficial palmar arch<br>R. metacarpals and digitals |
| **L. common carotid** | **L. internal carotid** | L. ophthalmic<br>L. p. communicating<br>L. middle cerebral<br>L. a. cerebral | |
| | **L. external carotid** | L. superior thyroid<br>L. ascending pharyngeal<br>L. facial<br>L. lingual<br>L. occipital<br>L. p. auricular<br>L. superficial temporal | |
| | | L. internal maxillary | L. middle meningeal |

R = right, L = left, A = anterior, P = posterior

**Appendix L**

| First Order | Second Order Branch | Third Order Branch | Beyond Third Order Branches |
|---|---|---|---|

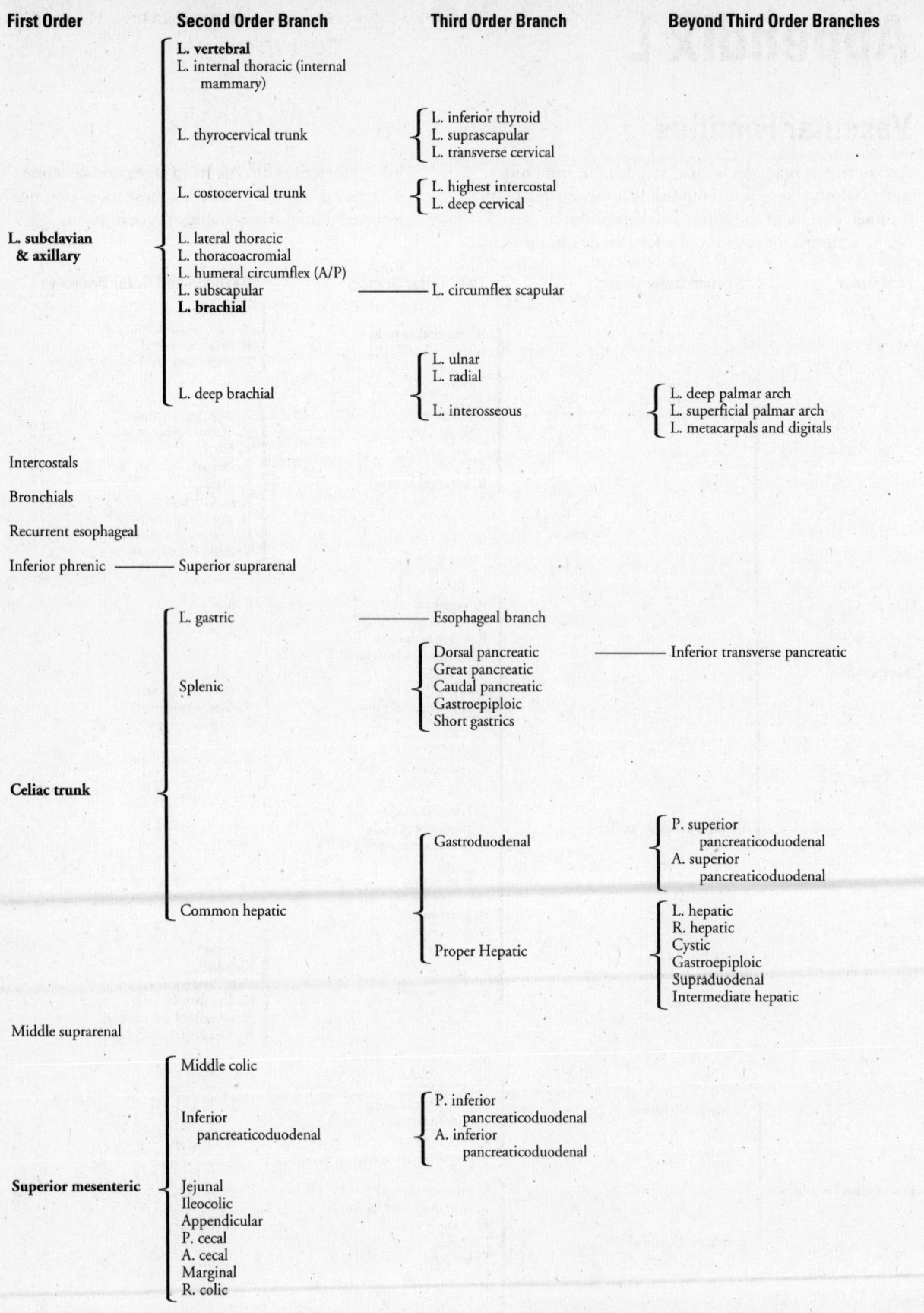

**L. subclavian & axillary**

**L. vertebral**
L. internal thoracic (internal mammary)

L. thyrocervical trunk
- L. inferior thyroid
- L. suprascapular
- L. transverse cervical

L. costocervical trunk
- L. highest intercostal
- L. deep cervical

L. lateral thoracic
L. thoracoacromial
L. humeral circumflex (A/P)
L. subscapular —— L. circumflex scapular
**L. brachial**

L. deep brachial
- L. ulnar
- L. radial
- L. interosseous
  - L. deep palmar arch
  - L. superficial palmar arch
  - L. metacarpals and digitals

Intercostals

Bronchials

Recurrent esophageal

Inferior phrenic —— Superior suprarenal

**Celiac trunk**

L. gastric —— Esophageal branch

Splenic
- Dorsal pancreatic —— Inferior transverse pancreatic
- Great pancreatic
- Caudal pancreatic
- Gastroepiploic
- Short gastrics

Common hepatic
- Gastroduodenal
  - P. superior pancreaticoduodenal
  - A. superior pancreaticoduodenal
- Proper Hepatic
  - L. hepatic
  - R. hepatic
  - Cystic
  - Gastroepiploic
  - Supraduodenal
  - Intermediate hepatic

Middle suprarenal

**Superior mesenteric**

Middle colic

Inferior pancreaticoduodenal
- P. inferior pancreaticoduodenal
- A. inferior pancreaticoduodenal

Jejunal
Ileocolic
Appendicular
P. cecal
A. cecal
Marginal
R. colic

R = right, L = left, A = anterior, P = posterior

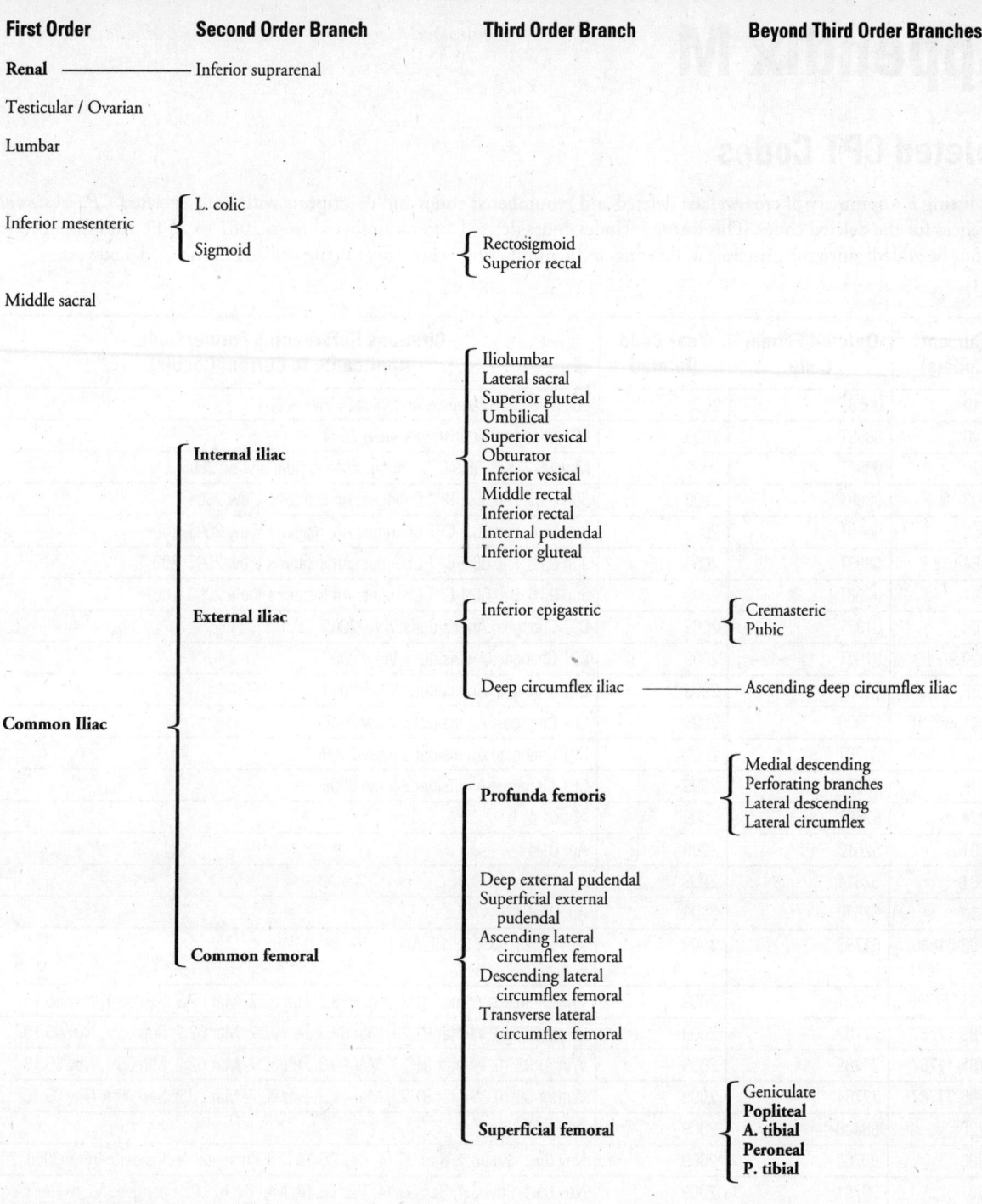

| First Order | Second Order Branch | Third Order Branch | Beyond Third Order Branches |
|---|---|---|---|
| **Renal** | Inferior suprarenal | | |
| Testicular / Ovarian | | | |
| Lumbar | | | |
| Inferior mesenteric | L. colic | | |
| | Sigmoid | Rectosigmoid | |
| | | Superior rectal | |
| Middle sacral | | | |
| **Common Iliac** | **Internal iliac** | Iliolumbar | |
| | | Lateral sacral | |
| | | Superior gluteal | |
| | | Umbilical | |
| | | Superior vesical | |
| | | Obturator | |
| | | Inferior vesical | |
| | | Middle rectal | |
| | | Inferior rectal | |
| | | Internal pudendal | |
| | | Inferior gluteal | |
| | **External iliac** | Inferior epigastric | Cremasteric |
| | | | Pubic |
| | | Deep circumflex iliac | Ascending deep circumflex iliac |
| | **Common femoral** | **Profunda femoris** | Medial descending |
| | | | Perforating branches |
| | | | Lateral descending |
| | | | Lateral circumflex |
| | | Deep external pudendal | |
| | | Superficial external pudendal | |
| | | Ascending lateral circumflex femoral | |
| | | Descending lateral circumflex femoral | |
| | | Transverse lateral circumflex femoral | |
| | | **Superficial femoral** | Geniculate |
| | | | **Popliteal** |
| | | | **A. tibial** |
| | | | **Peroneal** |
| | | | **P. tibial** |

**R. & L. main pulmonary arteries**
**(venous selective)**

*Reference:* Kadir S. *Atlas of Normal and Variant Angiographic Anatomy.* Philadephia, Pa: WB Saunders Co; 1991.
R = right, L = left, A = anterior, P = posterior

# Appendix M

## Deleted CPT Codes

This listing is a summary of crosswalked deleted and renumbered codes and descriptors with the associated *CPT Assistant* references for the deleted codes. This listing includes codes deleted and renumbered from 2007 to 2009. Additional codes will not be added, since the principle of deleting and renumbering is no longer being utilized in the CPT code set.

| Current Code(s) | Deleted/Former Code | Year Code Deleted | Citations Referencing Former Code— Applicable to Current Code(s) |
|---|---|---|---|
| 89240 | 0058T | 2009 | Jun 04:8 CPT Changes: An Insider's View 2004 |
| 89240 | 0059T | 2009 | CPT Changes: An Insider's View 2004 |
| 41530 | 0088T | 2009 | May 05:7, Sep 05:9 CPT Changes: An Insider's View 2005 |
| 95803 | 0089T | 2009 | Jun 05:6, Feb 06:1 CPT Changes: An Insider's View 2006 |
| 22856 | 0090T | 2009 | Jun 05:6, Feb 06:1 CPT Changes: An Insider's View 2006, 2007 |
| 22864 | 0093T | 2009 | Jun 05:6, Feb 06:1 CPT Changes: An Insider's View 2006, 2007 |
| 22861 | 0096T | 2009 | Jun 05:6, Feb 06:1 CPT Changes: An Insider's View 2006, 2007 |
| 55706 | 0137T | 2009 | CPT Changes: An Insider's View 2006 |
| 95980-95982 | 0162T | 2009 | CPT Changes: An Insider's View 2007 |
| 1123F, 1124F | 1080F | 2009 | CPT Changes: An Insider's View 2008 |
| 0054T, 0055T | 20986 | 2009 | CPT Changes: An Insider's View 2008 |
| 0054T, 0055T | 20987 | 2009 | CPT Changes: An Insider's View 2008 |
| 4177F | 4007F | 2009 | CPT Changes: An Insider's View 2008 |
| 52214 | 52606 | 2009 | Apr 01:4 |
| 52601 | 52612 | 2009 | Apr 01:4 |
| 52601 | 52614 | 2009 | Apr 01:4 |
| 52630 | 52620 | 2009 | Apr 01:4 |
| 61796-61800, 63620, 63621 | 61793 | 2009 | Nov 97:23, May 03:19, Apr 04:15, Jan 06:46 |
| 77785, 77786 | 77781 | 2009 | Winter 90:10, Winter 91:23, Mar 99:3, Feb 02:7, Mar 02:2, Sep 05:1, Nov 05:15 |
| 77785-77787 | 77782 | 2009 | Winter 90:10, Winter 91:23, Mar 99:3, Feb 02:7, Mar 02:2, Sep 05:1, Nov 05:15 |
| 77785-77787 | 77783 | 2009 | Winter 90:10, Winter 91:23, Mar 99:3, Feb 02:7, Mar 02:2, Sep 05:1, Nov 05:15 |
| 77785-77787 | 77784 | 2009 | Winter 90:10, Winter 91:23, Mar 99:3, Feb 02:7, Mar 02:2, Sep 05:1, Nov 05:15 |
| 88720 | 88400 | 2009 | Aug 05:9 |
| 96360 | 90760 | 2009 | Nov 05:1, Jul 06:4, Sep 06:14, Dec 06:14 CPT Changes: An Insider's View 2006, 2008 |
| 96361 | 90761 | 2009 | Nov 05:1, Jul 06:4, Sep 06:14, Dec 06:14, Mar 07:10 CPT Changes: An Insider's View 2006, 2007 |
| 96365 | 90765 | 2009 | Nov 05:1, Sep 06:14, Nov 06:22, Dec 06:14 CPT Changes: An Insider's View 2006 |
| 96366 | 90766 | 2009 | Nov 05:1, Sep 06:14, Dec 06:14, Mar 07:10 CPT Changes: An Insider's View 2006, 2007 |
| 96367 | 90767 | 2009 | Nov 05:1, Sep 06:14, Nov 06:22, Dec 06:14 CPT Changes: An Insider's View 2006 |
| 96368 | 90768 | 2009 | Nov 05:1, Aug 06:11, Sep 06:14, Nov 06:22, Dec 06:14 CPT Changes: An Insider's View 2006 |
| 96369 | 90769 | 2009 | CPT Changes: An Insider's View 2008 |
| 96370 | 90770 | 2009 | CPT Changes: An Insider's View 2008 |
| 96371 | 90771 | 2009 | CPT Changes: An Insider's View 2008 |
| 96372 | 90772 | 2009 | Nov 05:1, Sep 06:14, Dec 06:14 CPT Changes: An Insider's View 2006 |
| 96373 | 90773 | 2009 | Nov 05:1, Sep 06:14, Dec 06:14 CPT Changes: An Insider's View 2006 |

| Current Code(s) | Deleted/Former Code | Year Code Deleted | Citations Referencing Former Code—Applicable to Current Code(s) |
|---|---|---|---|
| 96374 | 90774 | 2009 | Nov 05:1, Sep 06:14, Dec 06:14 CPT Changes: An Insider's View 2006 |
| 96375 | 90775 | 2009 | Nov 05:1, Sep 06:14, Dec 06:14 CPT Changes: An Insider's View 2006 |
| 96376 | 90776 | 2009 | CPT Changes: An Insider's View 2008 |
| 96379 | 90779 | 2009 | Nov 05:1, Sep 06:14, Dec 06:14 CPT Changes: An Insider's View 2006 |
| 90951-90953, 90963, 90967 | 90918 | 2009 | Fall 93:5, May 96:4, May 02:17, Jan 03:22 |
| 90954-90956, 90964, 90968 | 90919 | 2009 | Fall 93:5, May 96:5, May 02:17, Jan 03:22 |
| 90957-90959, 90965, 90969 | 90920 | 2009 | Fall 93:5, May 96:5, May 02:17, Jan 03:22 |
| 90960-90962, 90966, 90970 | 90921 | 2009 | Fall 93:5, May 96:5, May 02:17, Jan 03:22 |
| 90951-90953, 90963, 90967 | 90922 | 2009 | Fall 93:5, May 96:5, May 02:17, Jan 03:22 |
| 90954-90956, 90964, 90968 | 90923 | 2009 | May 96:5, May 02:17, Jan 03:22 |
| 90957-90959, 90965, 90969 | 90924 | 2009 | May 96:5, May 02:17, Jan 03:22 |
| 90960-90962, 90966, 90970 | 90925 | 2009 | May 96:5, May 02:17, Jan 03:22 |
| 93285, 93291, 93298 | 93727 | 2009 | Nov 99:50, Jul 00:5, CPT Changes: An Insider's View 2000 |
| 93280, 93288, 93294 | 93731 | 2009 | Summer 94:23, Feb 98:11 |
| 93280, 93288, 93294 | 93732 | 2009 | Summer 94:23, Feb 98:11, Mar 00:10 |
| 93293 | 93733 | 2009 | Summer 94:23 |
| 93279, 93288, 93294 | 93734 | 2009 | Summer 94:23, Feb 98:11 |
| 93279, 93288, 93294 | 93735 | 2009 | Summer 94:23, Feb 98:11 |
| 93293 | 93736 | 2009 | Summer 94:23 |
| 93282, 93289, 93292, 93295 | 93741 | 2009 | Nov 99:50-51, Jul 00:5, Nov 00:9, Sep 05:8 CPT Changes: An Insider's View 2000, 2005 |
| 93282, 93289, 93292, 93295 | 93742 | 2009 | Nov 99:50-51, Jul 00:5, Nov 00:9 CPT Changes: An Insider's View 2000, 2005 |
| 93283, 93289, 93295 | 93743 | 2009 | Nov 99:50-51, Jul 00:5, Nov 00:9, Sep 05:8 CPT Changes: An Insider's View 2000 |
| 93283, 93289, 93295 | 93744 | 2009 | Nov 99:50-51, Jul 00:5, Nov 00:9 CPT Changes: An Insider's View 2000 |
| 99466 | 99289 | 2009 | May 05:1, Jul 06:4 CPT Changes: An Insider's View 2002, 2003 |
| 99467 | 99290 | 2009 | CPT Changes: An Insider's View 2002 |
| 99471 | 99293 | 2009 | Feb 03:15, Oct 03:2, Aug 04:7, 10, May 05:1, Nov 05:10, Jul 06:4, Apr 07:3 CPT Changes: An Insider's View 2003, 2004, 2005 |
| 99472 | 99294 | 2009 | Feb 03:15, Oct 03:2, Aug 04:7, Nov 05:10, Jul 06:4, Apr 07:3 CPT Changes: An Insider's View 2003, 2004, 2005 |
| 99468 | 99295 | 2009 | Summer 93:1, Nov 97:4-5, Mar 98:11, Nov 99:5-6, Dec 00:14, Feb 03:15, Oct 03:1, May 05:1, Nov 05:10, CPT Changes: An Insider's View 2000, 2003, 2004, 2005 |
| 99469 | 99296 | 2009 | Summer 93:1, Nov 97:4-5, Mar 98:11, Nov 99:5-6, Dec 00:14, Feb 03:15, Oct 03:1, Nov 05:10, CPT Changes: An Insider's View 2000, 2003, 2004, 2005, 2008 |

| Current Code(s) | Deleted/Former Code | Year Code Deleted | Citations Referencing Former Code— Applicable to Current Code(s) |
|---|---|---|---|
| 99478 | 99298 | 2009 | Nov 98:2-3, Nov 99: 5-6, Aug 00:4, Dec 00:15, Oct 03:2, May 05:1, Nov 05:10; CPT Changes: An Insider's View 2000, 2003 |
| 99479 | 99299 | 2009 | Oct 03:2, Nov 05:10; CPT Changes: An Insider's View 2003 |
| 99480 | 99300 | 2009 | CPT Changes: An Insider's View 2006 |
| 99460 | 99431 | 2009 | Apr 97:10, Nov 97:9, Sep 98:5, Apr 04:14, May 05:1 |
| 99461 | 99432 | 2009 | Sep 98:5, May 99:11, Apr 04:14 |
| 99462 | 99433 | 2009 | Sep 98:5, Apr 03:27 |
| 99463 | 99435 | 2009 | Sep 98:5, Apr 04:14 |
| 99464 | 99436 | 2009 | Nov 97:9-10, Sep 98:5, Nov 99:5-6, Aug 00:3, Aug 04:9, Nov 05:15 |
| 99465 | 99440 | 2009 | Summer 93:3, Mar 96:10, Nov 97:9, Sep 98:5, Nov 99:5-6, Aug 00:3, Oct 03:3, Aug 04:9, Apr 07:3 |
| 20985-20987 | 0054T | 2008 | May 04:14, Jun 04:8 CPT Changes: An Insider's View 2004 |
| 20985-20987 | 0055T | 2008 | May 04:14, Jun 04:8 CPT Changes: An Insider's View 2004, 2005 |
| 20985-20987 | 0056T | 2008 | May 04:14, Jun 04:8 CPT Changes: An Insider's View 2004 |
| 99174 | 0065T | 2008 | Mar 05:1, 3-4 CPT Changes: An Insider's View 2005 |
| 99444 | 0074T | 2008 | May 05:7, Sep 05:6 CPT Changes: An Insider's View 2005 |
| 99605-99607 | 0115T | 2008 | CPT Changes: An Insider's View 2006 |
| 99605-99607 | 0116T | 2008 | CPT Changes: An Insider's View 2006 |
| 99605-99607 | 0117T | 2008 | CPT Changes: An Insider's View 2006 |
| 50593 | 0135T | 2008 | CPT Changes: An Insider's View 2006, Clinical Examples in Radiology Winter 06:18 |
| 34806 | 0153T | 2008 | CPT Changes: An Insider's View 2007, Clinical Examples in Radiology Winter 06:19 |
| 93982 | 0154T | 2008 | CPT Changes: An Insider's View 2007, Clinical Examples in Radiology Winter 06:19 |
| 01935, 01936 | 01905 | 2008 | Mar 06:15 CPT Changes: An Insider's View 2002 |
| 24357-24359 | 24350 | 2008 | |
| 24357-24359 | 24351 | 2008 | |
| 24357-24359 | 24352 | 2008 | |
| 24357-24359 | 24354 | 2008 | |
| 24357-24359 | 24356 | 2008 | |
| 3044F-3045F | 3047F | 2008 | CPT Changes: An Insider's View 2007 |
| 3074F-3075F | 3076F | 2008 | CPT Changes: An Insider's View 2007 |
| 32421 | 32000 | 2008 | Spring 91:4, Winter 92:20 |
| 32422 | 32002 | 2008 | Nov 03:14 |
| 32560 | 32005 | 2008 | |
| 32550 | 32019 | 2008 | CPT Changes: An Insider's View 2005 |
| 32551 | 32020 | 2008 | Fall 92:13, Nov 03:14 |
| 36591 | 36540 | 2008 | Jan 02:11, Nov 02:3, Apr 03:26, Nov 05:1 CPT Changes; An Insider's View 2001, 2003 |
| 36593 | 36550 | 2008 | Nov 99:20, Nov 05:1 CPT Changes: An Insider's View 2000 |
| 49203-49205, 58957, 58958 | 49200 | 2008 | CPT Changes: An Insider's View 2003 |
| 49203-49205, 58957, 58958 | 49201 | 2008 | |
| 51100 | 51000 | 2008 | Nov 99:32-33, Aug 00:3, Oct 03:2 |
| 51101 | 51005 | 2008 | |
| 51102 | 51010 | 2008 | |
| 60300 | 60001 | 2008 | |
| 67041, 67042, 67043 | 67038 | 2008 | Aug 03:15, Sep 05:12 |

| Current Code(s) | Deleted/Former Code | Year Code Deleted | Citations Referencing Former Code— Applicable to Current Code(s) |
|---|---|---|---|
| 75557-75564 | 75552 | 2008 | Fall 95:2 |
| 75557-75564 | 75553 | 2008 | Fall 95:2 |
| 75557-75564 | 75554 | 2008 | Fall 95:2 |
| 75557-75564 | 75555 | 2008 | Fall 95:2 |
| 75557-75564 | 75556 | 2008 | Fall 95:2 |
| 78610 | 78615 | 2008 | CPT Changes: An Insider's View 2002 |
| 86356, 86486 | 86586 | 2008 | Jul 98:11 |
| 99366-99368 | 99361 | 2008 | May 05:1 |
| 99366-99368 | 99362 | 2008 | |
| 99441-99443 | 99371 | 2008 | Spring 94:34, May 00:11, May 05:1, Nov 05:10 |
| 99441-99443 | 99372 | 2008 | Spring 94:34, May 00:11, Nov 05:10 |
| 99441-99443 | 99373 | 2008 | Spring 94:34, May 00:11, Nov 05:10 |
| 0160T, 0161T | 0018T | 2007 | CPT Changes: An Insider's View 2002 |
| 96904 | 0044T | 2007 | CPT Changes: An Insider's View 2003, 2004 |
| 96904 | 0045T | 2007 | Jul 04:7 CPT Changes: An Insider's View 2004 |
| 77371-77373 | 0082T | 2007 | CPT Changes: An Insider's View 2005 |
| 77371-77373 | 0083T | 2007 | CPT Changes: An Insider's View 2005 |
| 22857 | 0091T | 2007 | CPT Changes: An Insider's View 2006 |
| 22865 | 0094T | 2007 | CPT Changes: An Insider's View 2006 |
| 22862 | 0097T | 2007 | CPT Changes: An Insider's View 2006 |
| 19105 | 0120T | 2007 | CPT Changes: An Insider's View 2006 |
| 15002, 15004 | 15000 | 2007 | Fall 93:7, Apr 97:4, Aug 97:6, Sep 97:2, Nov 98:5, Jan 99:4, Apr 99:10, May 99:10, Nov 02:7, Aug 03:14 CPT Changes: An Insider's View 2001, 2006 |
| 15003, 15005 | 15001 | 2007 | Nov 98:5-6, Jan 99:4, May 99:10, Aug 03:14 |
| 15830, 15847, 17999 | 15831 | 2007 | May 01:11 CPT Changes: An Insider's View 2007 |
| 17311 | 17304 | 2007 | Winter 94:19, Mar 99:11, Jun 99:10, Nov 02:7, Nov 03:15, Feb 04:11, Jul 04:2 CPT Changes: An Insider's View 2003 |
| 17312, 17314 | 17305 | 2007 | Winter 94:19, Mar 99:11, Jun 99:10, Nov 02:7, Feb 04:11, Jul 04:3 |
| 17312, 17314 | 17306 | 2007 | Winter 94:19, Mar 99:11, Jun 99:10, Nov 02:7, Feb 04:11, Jul 04:4 |
| 17312, 17314 | 17307 | 2007 | Winter 94:19, Mar 99:11, Jun 99:10, Nov 02:7, Nov 03:15, Feb 04:11, Jul 04:4 |
| 17315 | 17310 | 2007 | Winter 94:19, Mar 99:11, Jun 99:10, Nov 02:7, Feb 04:11, May 04:14, Jul 04:4 CPT Changes: An Insider's View 2003 |
| 19300 | 19140 | 2007 | Feb 96:9, Apr 05:13 |
| 19301 | 19160 | 2007 | Apr 05:7 CPT Changes: An Insider's View 2005 |
| 19302 | 19162 | 2007 | Jun 00:11, Apr 05:7 |
| 19303 | 19180 | 2007 | Apr 05:7 |
| 19304 | 19182 | 2007 | Apr 05:7 |
| 19305 | 19200 | 2007 | Apr 05:7 |
| 19306 | 19220 | 2007 | Apr 05:7 |
| 19307 | 19240 | 2007 | Apr 05:7 |
| 25606 | 25611 | 2007 | Fall 93:23, Oct 99:5 |
| 25607-25609 | 25620 | 2007 | |
| 26390 | 26504 | 2007 | |
| 27325 | 27315 | 2007 | |
| 27326 | 27320 | 2007 | |

| Current Code(s) | Deleted/Former Code | Year Code Deleted | Citations Referencing Former Code— Applicable to Current Code(s) |
|---|---|---|---|
| 28055 | 28030 | 2007 | |
| 33254-33256 | 33253 | 2007 | |
| 35302-35306 | 35381 | 2007 | |
| 35506 | 35507 | 2007 | |
| 35537, 35538 | 35541 | 2007 | |
| 35539, 35540 | 35546 | 2007 | |
| 35637, 35638 | 35641 | 2007 | Dec 01:7 |
| 44799 | 44152 | 2007 | |
| 44799 | 44153 | 2007 | |
| 47719 | 47716 | 2007 | |
| 48105 | 48005 | 2007 | |
| 48548 | 48180 | 2007 | |
| 49402 | 49085 | 2007 | |
| 54150 | 54152 | 2007 | Sep 96:11, Dec 96:10, May 98:11, Apr 03:27 CPT Changes: An Insider's View 2007 |
| 54865 | 54820 | 2007 | Oct 01:8 |
| 55875 | 55859 | 2007 | Apr 04:6 |
| 56442 | 56720 | 2007 | |
| 57558 | 57820 | 2007 | |
| 67346 | 67350 | 2007 | |
| 77001 | 75998 | 2007 | Dec 04:12-13 CPT Changes: An Insider's View 2004 Clinical Examples in Radiology Inaugural 04:1-2, Winter 05:9 |
| 77002 | 76003 | 2007 | Fall 93:14, Jul 01:7 CPT Changes: An Insider's View 2001 Clinical Examples in Radiology Spring 05:5-6 |
| 77003 | 76005 | 2007 | Nov 99:32, 34, 41, Jan 00:2, Feb 00:6, Aug 00:8, Sep 02:11, Sep 04:5 CPT Changes: An Insider's View 2000 |
| 77071 | 76006 | 2007 | Nov 98:21 CPT Changes: An Insider's View 2003 |
| 72291 | 76012 | 2007 | Mar 01:2 CPT Changes: An Insider's View 2001, 2006 |
| 72292 | 76013 | 2007 | Mar 01:2 CPT Changes: An Insider's View 2001 |
| 77072 | 76020 | 2007 | |
| 77073 | 76040 | 2007 | |
| 77074 | 76061 | 2007 | |
| 77075 | 76062 | 2007 | |
| 77076 | 76065 | 2007 | |
| 77077 | 76066 | 2007 | CPT Changes: An Insider's View 2002 |
| 77078 | 76070 | 2007 | Nov 97:24 CPT Changes: An Insider's View 2002, 2003 |
| 77079 | 76071 | 2007 | CPT Changes: An Insider's View 2003 |
| 77080 | 76075 | 2007 | Nov 97:24, Jun 03:11 CPT Changes: An Insider's View 2005 |
| 77081 | 76076 | 2007 | Nov 97:24 |
| 77082 | 76077 | 2007 | CPT Changes: An Insider's View 2005 |
| 77083 | 76078 | 2007 | Nov 97:24 CPT Changes: An Insider's View 2002 |
| 77051 | 76082 | 2007 | CPT Changes: An Insider's View 2004 |
| 77052 | 76083 | 2007 | CPT Changes: An Insider's View 2004 |
| 77053 | 76086 | 2007 | |
| 77054 | 76088 | 2007 | |
| 77055 | 76090 | 2007 | Jul 96:6, Jun 99:10 CPT Changes: An Insider's View 2004 |
| 77056 | 76091 | 2007 | Jul 96:6 CPT Changes: An Insider's View 2004 |

| Current Code(s) | Deleted/Former Code | Year Code Deleted | Citations Referencing Former Code— Applicable to Current Code(s) |
|---|---|---|---|
| 77057 | 76092 | 2007 | Jul 96:6; Jun 99:10 CPT Changes: An Insider's View 2004 |
| 77058 | 76093 | 2007 | |
| 77059 | 76094 | 2007 | |
| 77031 | 76095 | 2007 | Apr 96:9, Nov 97:24, Jan 01:9 CPT Changes: An Insider's View 2001 |
| 77032 | 76096 | 2007 | Jan 01:10 CPT Changes: An Insider's View 2001 |
| 77011 | 76355 | 2007 | CPT Changes: An Insider's View 2002, 2003 |
| 77012 | 76360 | 2007 | Fall 93:12, Fall 94:2, Jan 01:9-10, Mar 05:2 CPT Changes: An Insider's View 2001, 2002, 2003 |
| 77013 | 76362 | 2007 | Oct 02:4 CPT Changes: An Insider's View 2002, 2004 |
| 77014 | 76370 | 2007 | Fall 91:12 CPT Changes: An Insider's View 2002, 2003 |
| 77021 | 76393 | 2007 | Jan 01:10, Mar 05:2 CPT Changes: An Insider's View 2001, 2002 |
| 77022 | 76394 | 2007 | Oct 02:4, Mar 05:5 CPT Changes: An Insider's View 2002, 2004 |
| 77084 | 76400 | 2007 | |
| 76775, 76776 | 76778 | 2007 | CPT Changes: An Insider's View 2002 |
| 76998 | 76986 | 2007 | CPT Changes: An Insider's View 2001 |
| 78707-78709 | 78704 | 2007 | |
| 78701-78709 | 78715 | 2007 | |
| 78761 | 78760 | 2007 | |
| 92700 | 92573 | 2007 | |
| 94002, 94004 | 94656 | 2007 | Fall 92:30, Spring 95:4, Summer 95:4, Feb 96:9, Aug 00:2, Oct 03:2 |
| 94003, 94004 | 94657 | 2007 | Fall 92:30, Spring 95:4, Summer 95:4, Feb 96:9, Aug 00:2, Oct 03:2 |

**Appendix M**

# Appendix N

## Summary of Resequenced CPT Codes

This is a summary of CPT codes that do not apear in numeric sequence in the listing of CPT codes. Rather than deleting and renumbering, resequencing allows existing codes to be relocated to an appropriate location for the code concept, regardless of the numeric sequence. The codes listed below are identified in the CPT 2014 code set with a # symbol for location of the resequenced number within the family of related concepts. Numerically placed references (eg, **Code is out of numerical sequence. See...**) are used as navigational alerts to direct the user to the location of out-of-sequence code.

| | | | |
|---|---|---|---|
| 11045 | 33221 | 46220 | 90673 |
| 11046 | 33227 | 46320 | 92558 |
| 21552 | 33228 | 46945 | 92618 |
| 21554 | 33229 | 46946 | 92920 |
| 23071 | 33230 | 46947 | 92921 |
| 23073 | 33231 | 51797 | 92924 |
| 24071 | 33262 | 52356 | 92925 |
| 24073 | 33263 | 64633 | 92928 |
| 25071 | 33264 | 64634 | 92929 |
| 25073 | 37211 | 64635 | 92933 |
| 26111 | 37212 | 64636 | 92934 |
| 26113 | 37213 | 67810 | 92937 |
| 27043 | 37214 | 77295 | 92938 |
| 27045 | 38243 | 77424 | 92941 |
| 27059 | 43211 | 77425 | 92943 |
| 27329 | 43212 | 80104 | 92944 |
| 27337 | 43213 | 81161 | 92973 |
| 27339 | 43214 | 81287 | 92974 |
| 27632 | 43233 | 82652 | 92975 |
| 27634 | 43266 | 86152 | 92977 |
| 28039 | 43270 | 86153 | 92978 |
| 28041 | 43274 | 87906 | 92979 |
| 29914 | 43275 | 87910 | 95782 |
| 29915 | 43276 | 87912 | 95783 |
| 29916 | 43277 | 88177 | 95800 |
| 31651 | 43278 | 90672 | 95801 |

| |
|---|
| 95885 |
| 95886 |
| 95887 |
| 95938 |
| 95939 |
| 95940 |
| 95941 |
| 95943 |
| 99224 |
| 99225 |
| 99226 |
| 99481 |
| 99482 |
| 99485 |
| 99486 |
| 0253T |

# Appendix O

## Multianalyte Assays with Algorithmic Analyses

The following list includes a set of administrative codes for Multianalyte Assays with Algorithmic Analyses (MAAA) procedures that by their nature are typically unique to a single clinical laboratory or manufacturer.

Multianalyte Assays with Algorithmic Analyses (MAAAs) are procedures that utilize multiple results derived from assays of various types, including molecular pathology assays, fluorescent in situ hybridization assays and non-nucleic acid based assays (eg, proteins, polypeptides, lipids, carbohydrates). Algorithmic analysis using the results of these assays as well as other patient information (if used) is then performed and reported typically as a numeric score(s) or as a probability. MAAAs are typically unique to a single clinical laboratory or manufacturer. The results of individual component procedure(s) that are inputs to the MAAAs may be provided on the associated laboratory report, however these assays are not reported separately using additional codes.

The list includes a proprietary name and clinical laboratory or manufacturer in the first column, an alpha-numeric code in the second column and code descriptor in the third column. The format for the code descriptor usually includes (in order):

- Disease type (eg, oncology, autoimmune, tissue rejection),
- Chemical(s) analyzed (eg, DNA, RNA, protein, antibody),
- Number of markers (eg, number of genes, number of proteins),
- Methodology(s) (eg, microarray, real-time [RT]-PCR, in situ hybridization [ISH], enzyme linked immunosorbent assays [ELISA]),
- Number of functional domains (if indicated),
- Specimen type (eg, blood, fresh tissue, formalin-fixed paraffin embedded),
- Algorithm result type (eg, prognostic, diagnostic),
- Report (eg, probability index, risk score).

MAAA procedures that have been assigned a Category I code are noted in the list below and additionally listed in the Category I MAAA section (81500-81599). The Category I MAAA section introductory language and associated parenthetical instruction(s) should be used to govern the appropriate use for Category I MAAA codes. If a specific MAAA procedure has not been assigned a Category I code, it is indicated as a four-digit number followed by the letter M.

When a specific MAAA procedure is not included in either the list below or in the Category I MAAA section, report the analysis using the Category I MAAA unlisted code (81599). The codes below are specific to the assays identified in Appendix O by proprietary name. When an analysis is performed that may potentially fall within a specific descriptor, however the proprietary name is not included in the list below, the MAAA unlisted code (81599) should be used.

Additions in this section may be released tri-annually via the AMA/CPT Internet site to expedite dissemination for reporting. The list will be published annually in the CPT codebook. Go to www.ama-assn.org/go/cpt for the most current listing.

These administrative codes encompass all analytical services required for the algorithmic analysis (eg, cell lysis, nucleic acid stabilization, extraction, digestion, amplification, hybridization and detection) in addition to the algorithmic analysis itself. Procedures that are required prior to cell lysis (eg, microdissection, codes 88380 and 88381) should be reported separately.

The codes in this list are provided as an administrative coding set to facilitate accurate reporting of MAAA services. The minimum standard for inclusion in this list is that an analysis is generally available for patient care. The AMA has not reviewed procedures in the administrative coding set for clinical utility. The list is not a complete list of all MAAA procedures.

| Proprietary Name and Clinical Laboratory or Manufacturer | Alpha-Numeric Code | Code Descriptor |
|---|---|---|
| **Administrative Codes for Multianalyte Assays with Algorithmic Analyses (MAAA)** | | |
| HCV FibroSURE™, LabCorp | 0001M | Infectious disease, HCV, six biochemical assays (ALT, A2-macroglobulin, apolipoprotein A-1, total bilirubin, GGT, and haptoglobin) utilizing serum, prognostic algorithm reported as scores for fibrosis and necroinflammatory activity in liver |
| ASH FibroSURE™, LabCorp | 0002M | Liver disease, ten biochemical assays (ALT, A2-macroglobulin, apolipoprotein A-1, total bilirubin, GGT, haptoglobin, AST, glucose, total cholesterol and triglycerides) utilizing serum, prognostic algorithm reported as quantitative scores for fibrosis, steatosis and alcoholic steatohepatitis (ASH) |
| NASH FibroSURE™, LabCorp | 0003M | Liver disease, ten biochemical assays (ALT, A2-macroglobulin, apolipoprotein A-1, total bilirubin, GGT, haptoglobin, AST, glucose, total cholesterol and triglycerides) utilizing serum, prognostic algorithm reported as quantitative scores for fibrosis, steatosis and nonalcoholic steatohepatitis (NASH) |
| ScoliScore™ Transgenomic | ● 0004M | Scoliosis, DNA analysis of 53 single nucleotide polymorphisms (SNPs), using saliva, prognostic algorithm reported as a risk score |
| | ▶(0005M has been deleted, use 81507)◀ | — |
| **Category I Codes for Multianalyte Assays with Algorithmic Analyses (MAAA)** | | |
| Risk of Ovarian Malignacy Algorithm (ROMA)™, Fujirebio Diagnostics | 81500 | Oncology (ovarian), biochemical assays of two proteins (CA-125 and HE4), utilizing serum, with menopausal status, algorithm reported as a risk score |
| OVA1™, Vermillion, Inc. | 81503 | Oncology (ovarian), biochemical assays of five proteins (CA-125, apoliproprotein A1, beta-2 microglobulin, transferrin, and pre-albumin), utilizing serum, algorithm reported as a risk score |
| Pathwork® Tissue of Origin Test, Pathwork Diagnostics | ● 81504 | Oncology (tissue of origin), microarray gene expression profiling of >2000 genes, utilizing formalin-fixed paraffin embedded tissue, algorithm reported as tissue similarity scores |
| PreDx Diabetes Risk Score™, Tethys Clinical Laboratory | 81506 | Endocrinology (type 2 diabetes), biochemical assays of seven analytes (glucose, HbA1c, insulin, hs-CRP, adoponectin, ferritin, interleukin 2-receptor alpha), utilizing serum or plasma, algorithm reporting a risk score |

| | | |
|---|---|---|
| Harmony™ Prenatal Test, Ariosa Diagnostics | ● 81507 | Fetal aneuploidy (trisomy 21, 18, and 13) DNA sequence analysis of selected regions using maternal plasma, algorithm reported as a risk score for each trisomy |
| **No proprietary name and clinical laboratory or manufacturer.**<br><br>Maternal serum screening procedures are well established procedures and are performed by many labs throughout the country. The concept of prenatal screens has existed and evolved for over ten years and is not exclusive to any one facility. | 81508 | Fetal congenital abnormalities, biochemical assays of two proteins (PAPP-A, hCG [any form]), utilizing maternal serum, algorithm reported as a risk score |
| | 81509 | Fetal congenital abnormalities, biochemical assays of three proteins (PAPP-A, hCG [any form], DIA), utilizing maternal serum, algorithm reported as a risk score |
| | 81510 | Fetal congenital abnormalities, biochemical assays of three analytes (AFP, uE3, hCG (any form)), utilizing maternal serum, algorithm reported as a risk score |
| | 81511 | Fetal congenital abnormalities, biochemical assays of four analytes (AFP, uE3, hCG (any form), DIA) utilizing maternal serum, algorithm reported as a risk score (may include additional results from previous biochemical testing) |
| | 81512 | Fetal congenital abnormalities, biochemical assays of five analytes (AFP, uE3, total hCG, hyperglycosylated hCG, DIA) utilizing maternal serum, algorithm reported as a risk score |
| | 81599 | Unlisted multianalyte assay with algorithmic analysis |

**Appendix O**

# Notes

# Index

## Instructions for the Use of the CPT Index

The alphabetic index is **not** a substitute for the main text of the CPT codebook. Even if only one code is present, the user must refer to the main text to ensure that the code selected accurately identifies the service performed.

## Main Terms

The index is organized by main terms. Each main term can stand alone, or be followed by up to three modifying terms. There are four primary classes of main entries:

1. Procedure or service.
   For example: Endoscopy; Anastomosis; Splint

2. Organ or other anatomic site.
   For example: Tibia; Colon; Salivary Gland

3. Condition.
   For example: Abscess; Entropion; Tetralogy of Fallot

4. Synonyms, Eponyms, and Abbreviations.
   For example: EEG; Bricker Operation; Clagett Procedure

The Anesthesia-section codes are indexed under the Anesthesia main entry and are not double-entered under the anatomical sites. Only specific codes within the Surgery, Medicine, Category II, and Category III sections that reference the service of anesthesia are indexed under the anatomical sites.

## Modifying Terms

A main term may be followed by up to three indented terms that modify the terms they follow. For example, the main term Endoscopy is subdivided by the anatomical sites in which it is used, and within these anatomical sites, the specific purpose of the procedure is identified. In the following example, the code for an endoscopic removal of calculus from the urethra could be located:

Urethra
  Removal
    Calculus . . . . . 52352

Note that in this entry, the inclusion of a subentry under "Removal" implies the reading "Removal [of]" the term that follows it. If no subheads followed "Removal," the procedure would relate to the subhead that preceded it, as in this entry for the endoscopic removal of the spleen:

Spleen
  Removal . . . . . 38120

When modifying terms appear, one should review the list, as these subterms further qualify the selection of the appropriate code for the procedure.

## Code Ranges

Whenever more than one code applies to a given index entry, a code range is listed. If several nonsequential codes apply, they will be separated by a comma. In the following example, three nonsequential codes apply:

Esophagus
  Reconstruction . . . . . . . . . 43300, 43310, 43313

If two or more sequential codes apply, they will be separated by a hyphen. If more than one code range applies, the code ranges will be separated by a comma as in the following example:

Monitoring
  Electroencephalogram . . . . . 95812-95813, 95950-95953

## Conventions

As a space-saving convention, certain terms carry meaning inferred from the context. This convention is primarily used when a procedure or service is listed as a subterm. For example:

Knee
  Exploration [of] . . . . . 27310, 27331

In this example, the bracketed qualifier "[of ]" does not appear in the index; "of" is understood in the context of the term "Exploration." As another example:

Pelvis
  Halo [Application of ] . . . . . 20662

In this example, as there is no such entity as "pelvis halo," the bracketed words are inferred.

## Pathology and Laboratory

The Pathology and Laboratory listing in the index presents the headings, subheadings, procedures, and analytes in the Pathology and Laboratory section of the CPT codebook. Analytes are either listed alphabetically (for example, the Chemistry analytes) or cross-referenced to the index main heads where they are alphabetically listed (for example, to reference infectious agent analytes, the entry will indicate "See Infectious Agents").

# A

## A Vitamin
*See* Vitamin, A

## A-II
*See* Angiotensin II

## Abbe-Estlander Procedure
Lip Reconstruction . . . . . . . . . . . . . . 40527, 40761
*See* Reconstruction; Repair, Cleft Lip

## Abdomen
Abdominal Aorta
   Angiography. . . . . . . . . . . . . . . . . . . . . . 75635
Abdominal Wall
  Debridement
    Infected. . . . . . . . . . . . . . . . . . 11005-11006
  Removal
    Mesh. . . . . . . . . . . . . . . . . . . . . . . . . . 11008
    Prosthesis. . . . . . . . . . . . . . . . . . . . . . 11008
  Repair
    Hernia. . . . . . . . . . . . . 49491-49496, 49501,
             49507, 49521, 49590
  Tumor
    Excision. . . . . . . . . . . . . . . . . 22900-22903
    Radical Resection. . . . . . . . . . 22904-22905
Abscess
  Incision and Drainage
    Open . . . . . . . . . . . . . . . . . . 49020, 49040
Anesthesia
  *See* Anesthesia, Abdomen
Angiography . . . . . . . . 74174-74175, 74185, 75635
Aorta
  *See* Abdomen, Abdominal Aorta; Aorta,
  Abdominal
Aortic Aneurysm
  *See* Aorta, Abdominal, Aneurysm
Artery
    Ligation . . . . . . . . . . . . . . . . . . . . . . 37617
Biopsy . . . . . . . . . . . . . . . . . . . . . . . . . . . 49000
Bypass Graft
    Excision . . . . . . . . . . . . . . . . . . . . . . 35907
Catheter
    Removal. . . . . . . . . . . . . . . . . . . . . . . 49422
Celiotomy
  *See* Laparotomy
    for Staging . . . . . . . . . . . . . . . . . . . . 49220
CT Scan. . . . . . . . . . . . . 74150, 74160, 74170,
            74174-74178, 75635
Cyst
    Destruction/Excision . . . . . . . . . 49203-49205
Deliveries
  *See* Caesarean Delivery
Drainage
    Fluid . . . . . . . . . . . . . . . . . . . 49082-49083
Ectopic Pregnancy. . . . . . . . . . . . . . . . . . 59130
Endometrioma
    Destruction/Excision . . . . . . . . . 49203-49205
Exploration . . . . . . . . . . . . . . . . . 49000, 49010
    Blood Vessel. . . . . . . . . . . . . . . . . . . 35840
    Staging. . . . . . . . . . . . . . . . . . . . . . . 58960
Hysterectomy
  *See* Hysterectomy, Abdominal
Incision . . . . . . . . . . . . . . . . . . 49000-49084
    Staging. . . . . . . . . . . . . . . . . . . . . . . 58960
Incision and Drainage
    Pancreatitis . . . . . . . . . . . . . . . . . . . 48000
Infraumbilical Panniculectomy . . . . . . . . . . 15830

Injection
  Air. . . . . . . . . . . . . . . . . . . . . . . . . . . . 49400
  Contrast Material. . . . . . . . . . . . . . . . . 49400
Insertion
  Catheter . . . . . . . . 49324, 49418-49419, 49421
  Venous Shunt. . . . . . . . . . . . . . . . . . . . 49425
Intraperitoneal
  Catheter Exit Site. . . . . . . . . . . . . . . . . 49436
  Catheter Insertion . . . . . . 49418-49421, 49435
  Catheter Removal . . . . . . . . . . . . . . . . 49422
  Catheter Revision. . . . . . . . . . . . . . . . . 49325
  Shunt
    Insertion . . . . . . . . . . . . . . . . . . . . . 49425
    Ligation. . . . . . . . . . . . . . . . . . . . . . . 49428
    Removal . . . . . . . . . . . . . . . . . . . . . . 49429
    Revision . . . . . . . . . . . . . . . . . . . . . 49426
Laparoscopy . . . . . . . . . . . . 49320-49327, 49329
Laparotomy
  Reopening . . . . . . . . . . . . . . . . . . . . . . 49002
  Staging. . . . . . . . . . . . . . . . . 49220, 58960
Lymphangiogram
  *See* Lymphangiography, Abdomen
Magnetic Resonance Imaging (MRI). . 74181-74183
Needle Biopsy (Mass). . . . . . . . . . . . . . . . 49180
Paracentesis . . . . . . . . . . . . . . . . 49082-49083
Radical Resection . . . . . . . . . . . . . . . . . . 51597
Radiation Therapy
  Placement of Guidance Devices. . 49411-49412
Radiographies
  *See* Abdomen, X-ray
Removal
  Node(s). . . . . . . . . . . . . . . . . . . . . . . . 49220
Repair
  Blood Vessel. . . . . . . . . . . . . . . . . . . 35221
    with Other Graft . . . . . . . . . . . . . . . 35281
    with Vein Graft . . . . . . . . . . . . . . . . 35251
  Hernia. . . . . . . . . . . . . . . . . 49491-49525,
           49560-49587, 49590
  Suture. . . . . . . . . . . . . . . . . . . . . . . . 49900
Revision
  Venous Shunt. . . . . . . . . . . . . . . . . . . 49426
Suture . . . . . . . . . . . . . . . . . . . . . . . . . 49900
Tumor
  Destruction/Excision . . . . . . . . . 49203-49205
Ultrasound. . . . . . . . . . . . . . . . . 76700-76705
Unlisted Services and Procedures . . . . . . . 49999
Wall
  *See* Abdomen, Abdominal Wall
Wound Exploration
  Penetrating. . . . . . . . . . . . . . . . . . . . 20102
X-ray . . . . . . . . . . . . 74000, 74010, 74020, 74022

## Abdominal
*See* Abdomen
Aorta
  *See* Abdomen, Abdominal Aorta; Aorta,
  Abdominal
Aortic Aneurysm
  *See* Aorta, Abdominal, Aneurysm
Deliveries
  *See* Caesarean Delivery
Hysterectomy
  *See* Hysterectomy, Abdominal
Lymphangiogram
  *See* Lymphangiography, Abdomen
Paracentesis
  *See* Abdomen, Drainage
Radiographies
  *See* Abdomen, X-ray
Wall
  *See* Abdomen, Abdominal Wall

## Abdominohysterectomy
*See* Hysterectomy, Abdominal

## Abdominopelvic Amputation
*See* Amputation, Interpelviabdominal

## Abdominoplasty
*See* Panniculectomy
Excision, Skin and Tissue . . . . . . . . . 15830, 15847
Unlisted Procedure . . . . . . . . . . . . . . . . . . 17999

## Ablation
Anus
  Polyp. . . . . . . . . . . . . . . . . . . . . . . . . 46615
  Tumor. . . . . . . . . . . . . . . . . . . . . . . . . 46615
Bone
  Tumor . . . . . . . . . . . . . . . . . . . . . . . . 20982
Colon
  Polyp. . . . . . . . . . . . . . . . . . . . . . . . . 44393
  Tumor . . . . . . . . . . . . . . . . . . 44393, 45339
Cryosurgical
  Fibroadenoma . . . . . . . . . . . . . . . . . . 19105
  Liver Tumor. . . . . . . . . . . . . . . . . . . . 47381
  Renal Mass . . . . . . . . . . . . . . . . . . . . 50250
  Renal Tumor
    Percutaneous . . . . . . . . . . . . . . . . . 50593
CT Scan Guidance. . . . . . . . . . . . . . . . . . 77013
Endometrial. . . . . . . . . . . 58353, 58356, 58563
  with Ultrasound Guidance. . . . . . . . . . . 58356
Uterine Fibroids
  Laparoscopic . . . . . . . . . . . . . . . . . . 0336T
Heart
  Arrhythmogenic Focus . . . 33250-33251, 33261,
            93653, 93654, 93655
  Atrioventricular . . . . . . . . 93650, 93653, 93654
Liver (Tumor)
  Cryosurgical . . . . . . . . . . . . . . . . . . . 47381
  Laparoscopic . . . . . . . . . . . . . 47370-47371
  Radiofrequency . . . . . . . . . . . . . 47380-47382
Lung
  Tumor
    Radiofrequency. . . . . . . . . . . . . . . . . 32998
Parenchymal Tissue
  CT Scan Guidance . . . . . . . . . . . . . . . 77013
  Magnetic Resonance Guidance. . . . . . . . 77022
  Ultrasound Guidance . . . . . . . . . . . . . . 76940
Prostate . . . . . . . . . . . . . . . . . . . . . . . . . 55873
Pulmonary Tumor . . . . . . . . . . . . . . . . . . 32998
Radiofrequency
  Liver Tumor. . . . . . . . . . . . . . . . . . . . 47382
  Lung Tumor. . . . . . . . . . . . . . . . . . . . 32998
  Renal Tumor . . . . . . . . . . . . . . . . . . . 50592
  Tongue Base . . . . . . . . . . . . . . . . . . . 41530
Rectum
  Polyp. . . . . . . . . . . . . . . . . . . . . . . . . 45339
  Tumor . . . . . . . . . . . . . . . . . . . . . . . . 45339
Renal Cyst . . . . . . . . . . . . . . . . . . . . . . . 50541
Renal Mass. . . . . . . . . . . . . . . . . . . . . . . 50542
Renal Tumor
  Cryotherapy
    Percutaneous . . . . . . . . . . . . . . . . . 50593
  Radiofrequency . . . . . . . . . . . . . . . . . 50592
Tongue Base
  Radiofrequency . . . . . . . . . . . . . . . . . 41530
Turbinate Mucosa . . . . . . . . . . . . . 30801-30802
Uterine Tumor
  Ultrasound, Focused . . . . . . . . . .0071T-0072T
Vein
  Endovenous . . . . . . . . . . . . . . . 36475-36479

## Abortion
*See* Obstetrical Care
Incomplete . . . . . . . . . . . . . . . . . . . . . . . 59812

**Induced**
    by Dilation and Curettage . . . . . . . . . . . 59840
    by Dilation and Evacuation . . . . . . . . . . 59841
    by Saline . . . . . . . . . . . . . . . . . . . 59850-59851
    by Vaginal Suppositories . . . . . . . 59855-59856
    with Hysterotomy. . . . . . . 59100, 59852, 59857
**Missed**
    First Trimester . . . . . . . . . . . . . . . . . . . 59820
    Second Trimester . . . . . . . . . . . . . . . . . . 59821
**Septic** . . . . . . . . . . . . . . . . . . . . . . . . . . 59830
**Spontaneous**
    Complete
        *See* Hospital Services
    Incomplete . . . . . . . . . . . . . . . . . . . . . 59812
**Therapeutic**
    by Saline . . . . . . . . . . . . . . . . . . . . . . 59850
        with Dilation and Curettage . . . . . . . . 59851
        with Hysterotomy . . . . . . . . . . . . . . . 59852

## Abrasion (Skin)

Chemical Peel . . . . . . . 15788-15789, 15792-15793
Dermabrasion . . . . . . . . . . . . . . . . . 15780-15783
Lesion . . . . . . . . . . . . . . . . . . . . . . 15786-15787

## Abscess

**Bone**
    Ankle
        Incision . . . . . . . . . . . . . . . . . . . . . 27607
    Clavicle
        Sequestrectomy . . . . . . . . . . . . . . . 23170
    Elbow
        Incision . . . . . . . . . . . . . . . . 23930, 23935
    Facial
        Excision . . . . . . . . . . . . . . . . . . . . . 21026
    Femur
        Incision . . . . . . . . . . . . . . . . . . . . . 27303
    Finger
        Incision . . . . . . . . . . . . . . . . . . . . . 26034
    Foot
        Incision . . . . . . . . . . . . . . . . . . . . . 28005
    Forearm
        Incision . . . . . . . . . . . . . . . . . . . . . 25035
        Sequestrectomy . . . . . . . . . . . . . . . 25145
    Humeral Head
        Incision . . . . . . . . . . . . . . . . . . . . . 23174
    Humerus
        Excision . . . . . . . . . . . . . . . . . . . . . 24134
        Incision and Drainage . . . . . . . . . . . . 23935
    Knee
        Incision . . . . . . . . . . . . . . . . . . . . . 27303
    Leg, Lower
        Incision . . . . . . . . . . . . . . . . . . . . . 27607
    Olecranon Process . . . . . . . . . . . . . . . 24138
        Sequestrectomy . . . . . . . . . . . . . . . 24136
    Pelvis
    Incision . . . . . . . . . . . . . . . . . . . . . . 26992
    Radius
        Incision, Deep . . . . . . . . . . . . . . . . . 25035
        Sequestrectomy . . . . . . . . . . . . . . . 24136
    Scapula
        Sequestrectomy . . . . . . . . . . . . . . . 23172
    Shoulder
        Incision . . . . . . . . . . . . . . . . . . . . . 23035
    Thorax
        Incision . . . . . . . . . . . . . . . . . . . . . 21510
    Wrist
        Incision . . . . . . . . . . . . . . . . . . . . . 25035
        Sequestrectomy . . . . . . . . . . . . . . . 25145
**Drainage**
    with X-ray . . . . . . . . . . . . . . . . . . . . . 75989
**Localization**
    Nuclear Medicine . . . . . . . . . . . 78806-78807
**Tissue**
    Abdomen . . . . . . . . . . . . . . . . . . . . . . 49040

Incision and Drainage . . . . . . . . . . . . . 49040
**Anus**
    Incision and Drainage . . . . . . . 46045-46060
**Ankle**
    Incision and Drainage . . . . . . . . . . . . 27603
**Appendix**
    Incision and Drainage . . . . . . . . . . . . 44900
**Arm, Lower**
    Incision and Drainage . . . . . . . . . . . . 25028
**Auditory Canal, External**
    Incision and Drainage . . . . . . . . . . . . 69020
**Bartholin's Gland**
    Incision and Drainage . . . . . . . . . . . . 56420
**Bladder**
    Incision and Drainage . . . . . . . . . . . . 51080
**Brain**
    Drainage via Burr Hole . . . . . . . 61150-61151
    Drainage via Craniotomy . . . . . 61320-61321
    Excision . . . . . . . . . . . . . . . . 61514, 61522
**Breast**
    Incision and Drainage . . . . . . . . . . . . 19020
**Ear, External**
    Incision and Drainage . . . . . . . 69000, 69005
**Elbow**
    Incision and Drainage . . . . . . 23930-23931
**Epididymis**
    Incision and Drainage . . . . . . . . . . . . 54700
**Eyelid**
    Incision and Drainage . . . . . . . . . . . . 67700
**Finger**
    Incision and Drainage . . . . . . 26010-26011
**Forearm**
    Incision and Drainage . . . . . . . . . . . . 25028
**Gums**
    Incision and Drainage . . . . . . . . . . . . 41800
**Hand**
    Incision and Drainage . . . . . . . . . . . . 26034
**Hip**
    Incision and Drainage . . . . . . 26990-26992
**Kidney**
    Incision and Drainage . . . . . . . . . . . . 50020
**Knee**
    Incision and Drainage . . . . . . . . . . . . 27301
**Leg, Lower**
    Incision and Drainage . . . . . . . . . . . . 27603
**Liver**
    Drainage
        Open . . . . . . . . . . . . . . . . . . . . . 47010
        Injection . . . . . . . . . . . . . . . . . . . 47015
        Marsupialization . . . . . . . . . . . . . . 47300
**Lung**
    Percutaneous Drainage . . . . . . . . . . . 32200
**Lymph Node**
    Incision and Drainage . . . . . . 38300, 38305
**Lymphocele Drainage** . . . . . . . . . . . . . . . 49062
**Mandible**
    Excision . . . . . . . . . . . . . . . . . . . . . . 21025
**Mouth** . . . . . . . . . . . . . . . . . 41015-41018
    Incision and Drainage
        Dentoalveolar . . . . . . . . . . . . . . . 41800
        Lingual . . . . . . . . . . . . . . . . . . . . 41000
        Masticator Space . . . . . . . . 41009, 41018
        Sublingual . . . . 41005-41006, 41015
        Submandibular . . . . . . . . . 41008, 41017
        Submental . . . . . . . . . . . . . 41007, 41016
        Vestibular . . . . . . . . . . . . . 40800-40801
**Musculoskeletal**
    Incision and Drainage . . . . . . . . . . . . 20005
**Nasal**
    Incision and Drainage . . . . . . 30000, 30020
**Neck**
    Incision and Drainage . . . . . . 21501-21502

**Olecranon Process**
    Excision . . . . . . . . . . . . . . . . . . . . . . 24138
**Ovary**
    Incision and Drainage . . . . . . 58820, 58822
    Abdominal Approach . . . . . . . . . . . . . 58822
    Vaginal Approach . . . . . . . . . . . . . . . 58820
**Palate**
    Incision and Drainage . . . . . . . . . . . . 42000
**Paraurethral Gland**
    Incision and Drainage . . . . . . . . . . . . 53060
**Parotid Gland**
    Drainage . . . . . . . . . . . . . . . 42300, 42305
**Pelvis**
    Incision and Drainage . . 26990-26991, 45000
**Pericolic**
**Perineum**
    Incision and Drainage . . . . . . . . . . . . 56405
**Perirenal or Renal**
    Incision and Drainage . . . . . . . . . . . . 50020
**Peritoneum**
    Incision and Drainage . . . . . . . . . . . . 49020
**Pharynx**
    Incision and Drainage . . . . . . 42720, 42725
**Prostate**
    Incision and Drainage . . . . . . 55720, 55725
    Transurethral Drainage . . . . . . . . . . . 52700
**Rectum**
    Incision and Drainage . . . . . . 45005, 45020,
                           46040, 46060
**Renal**
    Incision and Drainage . . . . . . . . . . . . 50020
**Retroperitoneal**
    Incision and Drainage . . . . . . . . . . . . 49060
**Salivary Gland**
    Drainage . . . . . . . . . . . . . . . 42300-42320
**Scrotum**
    Incision and Drainage . . . . . . 54700, 55100
**Shoulder**
    Incision and Drainage . . . . . . . . . . . . 23030
**Skene's Gland**
    Incision and Drainage . . . . . . . . . . . . 53060
**Skin/Superficial**
    Incision and Drainage . . . . . . 10060-10061
    Puncture Aspiration . . . . . . . . . . . . . 10160
**Spine**
    Incision and Drainage . . . . . . 22010, 22015
**Subdiaphragmatic**
    Drainage . . . . . . . . . . . . . . . . . . . . . 49040
**Sublingual Gland**
    Drainage . . . . . . . . . . . . . . . 42310-42320
**Submaxillary Gland**
    Drainage . . . . . . . . . . . . . . . 42310, 42320
**Subphrenic**
    Drainage . . . . . . . . . . . . . . . . . . . . . 49040
**Testis**
    Incision and Drainage . . . . . . . . . . . . 54700
**Thigh**
    Incision and Drainage . . . . . . . . . . . . 27301
**Thorax**
    Incision and Drainage . . . . . . 21501-21502
**Throat**
    Incision and Drainage . . . . . . 42700-42725
**Tongue**
    Incision and Drainage . . . . . . 41000-41006
**Tonsil**
    Incision and Drainage . . . . . . . . . . . . 42700
**Urethra**
    Incision and Drainage . . . . . . . . . . . . 53040
**Uvula**
    Incision and Drainage . . . . . . . . . . . . 42000
**Vagina**
    Incision and Drainage . . . . . . . . . . . . 57010

Index

Index

**Index**

Respiratory Syncytial Virus . . . . . . . . . . 86756
Rickettsia . . . . . . . . . . . . . . . . . . . . . . . . . 86757
Rotavirus . . . . . . . . . . . . . . . . . . . . . . . . . 86759
Rubella . . . . . . . . . . . . . . . . . . . . . . . . . . . 86762
Rubeola . . . . . . . . . . . . . . . . . . . . . . . . . . 86765
Salmonella . . . . . . . . . . . . . . . . . . . . . . . . 86768
Shigella . . . . . . . . . . . . . . . . . . . . . . . . . . 86771
Sperm . . . . . . . . . . . . . . . . . . . . . . . . . . . . 89325
Streptokinase . . . . . . . . . . . . . . . . . . . . . . 86590
Tetanus . . . . . . . . . . . . . . . . . . . . . . . . . . . 86774
Thyroglobulin . . . . . . . . . . . . . . . . . . . . . . 86800
Toxoplasma . . . . . . . . . . . . . . 86777-86778
Treponema Pallidum . . . . . . . . . . . . . . . 86780
Trichinella . . . . . . . . . . . . . . . . . . . . . . . . 86784
Tuberculosis . . . . . . . . . . . . . . . . . . . . . . . 86580
Varicella-Zoster . . . . . . . . . . . . . . . . . . . 86787
Virus, Other . . . . . . . . . . . . . . . . . . . . . . . 86790
West Nile Virus . . . . . . . . . . . . . 86788-86789
White Blood Cell . . . . . . . . . . . . . . . . . . . 86021
Yersinia . . . . . . . . . . . . . . . . . . . . . . . . . . 86793

**Antibody Identification**
Fluorescent . . . . . . . . . . . . . . . . . . 86255-86256
Immunoassay . . . . . . . . . . 83516, 83518-83520
Immunocytochemistry . . . . . . . . . . . . 88342-88343
Immunoelectrophoresis . . . . 86320, 86325, 86327,
                                           86334-86335
Leukocyte Antibodies . . . . . . . 86021, 86828-86835
Platelet . . . . . . . . . . . . . . . . . . . . 86022-86023
Red Blood Cell . . . . . . . . . . . . 86850, 86860, 86870
  Pretreatment . . . . . 86970-86972, 86975-86978
Solid Phase Assay . . . . . . . . . . . . 86828-86835

**Antibody Neutralization Test**
See Neutralization Test

**Antibody Receptor**
See Fc Receptor

**Antibody Screening**
Fluorescent Noninfectious . . . . . . . . . . . . . . 86255
Cytotoxic Percent Reactive Antibody
(PRA) . . . . . . . . . . . . . . . . . . . . . . 86807-86808

**Anticoagulant**
See Clotting Inhibitors

**Anticoagulant Management**
Outpatient . . . . . . . . . . . . . . . . . . . 99363-99364

**Antidiabetic Hormone**
See Glucagon

**Antidiuretic Hormone**
Measurement
  Vasopressin . . . . . . . . . . . . . . . . . . . . . 84588

**AntiDNA Autoantibody**
See Antinuclear Antibodies (ANA)

**Antigen**
See Antigen Detection
Allergen Immunotherapy . . . . . . . . 95144-95149,
                                           95165, 95170
Carcinoembryonic . . . . . . . . . . . . . . . . . . . 82378
Prostate Specific . . . . . . . . . . . . . . 84152-84153

**Antigen Bronchial Provocation Tests**
See Bronchial Challenge Test

**Antigen Detection**
Direct Fluorescence
  Cytomegalovirus . . . . . . . . . . . . . . . . . 87271
  Enterovirus . . . . . . . . . . . . . . . . . . . . . 87267
Enzyme Immunoassay
  Adenovirus . . . . . . . . . . . . . . . . . . . . . 87301

Aspergillus . . . . . . . . . . . . . . . . . . . . . . . . 87305
Chlamydia Trachomatis . . . . . . . . . . . . . . 87320
Clostridium Difficile . . . . . . . . . . . . . . . . . 87324
Cryptococcus Neoformans . . . . . . . . . . . . 87327
Cryptosporidium . . . . . . . . . . . . . . . . . . . . 87328
Cytomegalovirus . . . . . . . . . . . . . . . . . . . 87332
Entamoeba Histolytica Dispar Group . . . . 87336
Entamoeba Histolytica Group . . . . . . . . . 87337
Escherichia coli 0157 . . . . . . . . . . . . . . . . 87335
Giardia . . . . . . . . . . . . . . . . . . . . . . . . . . 87329
Helicobacter Pylori . . . . . . . . . . . 87338-87339
Hepatitis B Surface Antigen (HBsAg) . . . 87340
  Neutralization . . . . . . . . . . . . . . . . . . . 87341
Hepatitis Be Antigen (HBeAg) . . . . . . . . . 87350
Hepatitis Delta Agent . . . . . . . . . . . . . . . 87380
Histoplasma capsulatum . . . . . . . . . . . . . 87385
HIV-1 . . . . . . . . . . . . . . . . . . . . . 87389-87390
HIV-2 . . . . . . . . . . . . . . . . . . . . . . . . . . . 87391
Infectious Agent, Otherwise . . . . 87449, 87451
Influenza A . . . . . . . . . . . . . . . . . . . . . . . 87400
Influenza B . . . . . . . . . . . . . . . . . . . . . . . 87400
Polyvalent . . . . . . . . . . . . . . . . . . . . . . . . 87451
Respiratory Syncytial Virus . . . . . . . . . . 87420
Rotavirus . . . . . . . . . . . . . . . . . . . . . . . . . 87425
Shiga-like Toxin . . . . . . . . . . . . . . . . . . . 87427
Streptococcus, Group A . . . . . . . . . . . . . . 87430
Immunoassay
  Direct Optical
    Clostridium Difficile Toxin A . . . . . . . . 87803
    Influenza . . . . . . . . . . . . . . . . . . . . . . 87804
    Respiratory Syncytial Virus . . . . . . . . 87807
    Streptococcus, Group B . . . . . . . . . . . 87802
    Trichomonas Vaginalis . . . . . . . . . . . . 87808
Immunofluorescence
  Adenovirus . . . . . . . . . . . . . . . . . . . . . . 87260
  Bordetella Pertussis . . . . . . . . . . . . . . . 87265
  Chlamydia Trachomatis . . . . . . . . . . . . 87270
  Cryptosporidium . . . . . . . . . . . . . . . . . 87272
  Giardia . . . . . . . . . . . . . . . . . . . . . . . . 87269
  Herpes Simplex . . . . . . . . . . . . 87273-87274
  Influenza A . . . . . . . . . . . . . . . . . . . . . 87276
  Influenza B . . . . . . . . . . . . . . . . . . . . . 87275
  Legionella Micdadei . . . . . . . . . . . . . . . 87277
  Legionella Pneumophila . . . . . . . . . . . . 87278
  Organism, Other . . . . . . . . . . . . . . . . . 87299
  Parainfluenza Virus . . . . . . . . . . . . . . . 87279
  Pneumocystis Carinii . . . . . . . . . . . . . . 87281
  Polyvalent . . . . . . . . . . . . . . . . . . . . . . 87300
  Respiratory Syncytial Virus . . . . . . . . . 87280
  Rubeola . . . . . . . . . . . . . . . . . . . . . . . . 87283
  Treponema Pallidum . . . . . . . . . . . . . . 87285
  Varicella Zoster . . . . . . . . . . . . . . . . . . 87290

**Antigen, Australia**
See Hepatitis Antigen, B Surface

**Antigen, CD4**
See CD4

**Antigen, CD8**
See CD8

**Antigens, CD142**
See Thromboplastin

**Antigens, CD143**
See Angiotensin Converting Enzyme (ACE)

**Antigens, E**
See Hepatitis Antigen, Be

**Antigens, Hepatitis**
See Hepatitis Antigen

**Antigens, Hepatitis B**
See Hepatitis Antigen, B

**Antihemophilic Factor B**
See Christmas Factor

**Antihemophilic Factor C**
See Plasma Thromboplastin, Antecedent

**Antihemophilic Globulin (AHG)** . . . . . . . . . . . . . . . . . . . . . . . 85240

**Antihuman Globulin** . . . . . . . 86880-86886

**Antimony** . . . . . . . . . . . . . . . . . . . . . . 83015

**Antinuclear Antibodies (ANA)** . . . . . . . . . . . . . . . . . . . . 86038-86039

**Antiplasmin, Alpha-2** . . . . . . . . . . . 85410

**Antiplatelet Therapy**
See Performance Measures, Interventions

**Antiprotease, Alpha-1**
See Alpha-1 Antitrypsin

**Antistreptococcal Antibody** . . . . 86215

**Antistreptokinase Titer** . . . . . . . . 86590

**Antistreptolysin O** . . . . . . . . 86060-86063

**Antithrombin III** . . . . . . . . . . . 85300-85301

**Antithrombin VI**
See Fibrin Degradation Products

**Antitoxin Assay** . . . . . . . . . . . . . . . . . . 87230

**Antiviral Antibody**
See Viral Antibodies

**Antrostomy**
Sinus
  Maxillary . . . . . . . . . . . . . . . . . 31256, 31267

**Antrotomy**
Sinus
  Maxillary . . . . . . . . . . . 31020, 31030, 31032
Transmastoid . . . . . . . . . . . . . . . . . . . . . . 69501

**Antrum of Highmore**
See Sinus, Maxillary

**Antrum Puncture**
Sinus
  Maxillary . . . . . . . . . . . . . . . . . . . . . . . 31000
  Sphenoid . . . . . . . . . . . . . . . . . . . . . . . 31002

**Anus**
See Hemorrhoids; Rectum
Ablation . . . . . . . . . . . . . . . . . . . . . . . . . . 46615
Abscess
  Incision and Drainage . . . . . . . . . 46045, 46050
Anal Canal
  Delivery of Thermal Energy . . . . . . . . . . 0288T
Anoscopy
  See Anoscopy
Biofeedback . . . . . . . . . . . . . . . . . . . . . . . 90911
Biopsy
  Endoscopy . . . . . . . . . . . . . . . . . . . . . . 46606
Crypt
  Excision . . . . . . . . . . . . . . . . . . . . . . . . 46999
Dilation
  Endoscopy . . . . . . . . . . . . . . . . . . . . . . 46604
Endoscopy
  Biopsy . . . . . . . . . . . . . . . . . . . . . . . . . 46606
  Dilation . . . . . . . . . . . . . . . . . . . . . . . . 46604

Index

Index

## Bladder Voiding Pressure Studies . . . . . . . . . 51728-51729

## Blalock-Hanlon Procedure . . . . . . . . . . . . . 33735-33737
*See* Septostomy, Atrial

## Blalock-Taussig Procedure
Shunt, Great Vessel . . . . . . . . . . . . . . . . . 33750

## Blast Cells
*See* Stem Cell

## Blast Transformation
*See* Blastogenesis

## Blastocyst Implantation
*See* Implantation, Embryo

## Blastocyst Transfer
*See* Embryo Transfer

## Blastogenesis . . . . . . . . . . . . . . . . . . . 86353

## Blastomyces
Antibody . . . . . . . . . . . . . . . . . . . . . . . . 86612

## Blastomycosis, European
*See* Cryptococcus

## Bleeding
*See* Hemorrhage
Disorder
　*See* Coagulopathy
Time . . . . . . . . . . . . . . . . . . . . . . . . . . . 85002
Uterine
　*See* Hemorrhage, Uterus
Vaginal
　*See* Hemorrhage, Vagina

## Blepharoplasty . . . . . . . . . . . . 15820-15823
*See* Canthoplasty
Anesthesia . . . . . . . . . . . . . . . . . . . . . . 00103
Eyelid Reconstruction . . . . . . . . . . . . 15820-15823

## Blepharoptosis
Repair . . . . . . . . . . . . . . . . . . . . 67901-67909
　Frontalis Muscle Technique . . . . . . . . . . 67901
　　with Fascial Sling . . . . . . . . . . . . . . . 67902
　Superior Rectus Technique with
　　Fascial Sling . . . . . . . . . . . . . . . . . . 67906
　Tarso Levator Resection/Advancement
　　External Approach . . . . . . . . . . . . . . 67904
　　Internal Approach . . . . . . . . . . . . . . . 67903

## Blepharorrhaphy
*See* Tarsorrhaphy

## Blepharospasm
Chemodenervation . . . . . . . . . . . . . . . . . 64612

## Blepharotomy
Drainage of Abscess . . . . . . . . . . . . . . . . 67700

## Blister
*See* Bulla

## Blom-Singer Prosthesis . . . . . . . . 31611

## Blood
*See* Blood Cell Count, Complete Blood Count
Banking
　*See* Blood Banking
Bleeding Time . . . . . . . . . . . . . . . . . . . . 85002

Index

## Cauterization

Anus
Control of Bleeding . . . . . . . . . . . . . . . . . 46614
Fissure . . . . . . . . . . . . . . . . . . . 46940, 46942
Hemorrhoid Destruction. . . . . . . . . . . . . 46930
Tumor Removal . . . . . . . . . . 46610, 46612
Cervix . . . . . . . . . . . . . . . . . . . . . . . . . . . . . . 57522
Cryocautery . . . . . . . . . . . . . . . . . . . . . . 57511
Electro or Thermal . . . . . . . . . . . . . . . . 57510
Laser Ablation . . . . . . . . . . . . . . . . . . . 57513
Chemical
Corneal Epithelium. . . . . . . . . . . 65435-65436
Granulation Tissue. . . . . . . . . . . . . . . . . 17250
Colon
Control of Bleeding . . . . . . . . 45334, 45382
Tumor Removal . . . . . . . . . . . 45333, 45384
Cornea. . . . . . . . . . . . . . . . . . . . . . . . . . . . . . 65450
Ectropion Repair . . . . . . . . . . . . . . . . . . . . . 67915
Entropion Repair . . . . . . . . . . . . . . . . . . . . . 67922
Esophagus
Tumor Removal . . . . . . . . . . 43216, 43250
Everted Punctum. . . . . . . . . . . . . . . . . . . . . 68705
Intrarenal Stricture . . . . . . . . . . . . . 52343, 52346
Iris. . . . . . . . . . . . . . . . . . . . . . . . . . . . . . . . . 66155
Lacrimal Punctum Closure . . . . . . . . . . . . . 68760
Nasopharyngeal Hemorrhage. . . . . . . . . . . . 42970
Nose
Hemorrhage . . . . . 30901, 30903, 30905-30906
Prostate Resection . . . . . . . . . . . . . . . . . . . . 52601
Rectum
Control of Bleeding . . . . . . . . . . . . . . . 45317
Tumor Removal . . . . . . . . . . . 45308, 45315
Skin Lesion . . . . . . . . . . 11055-11057, 17000-17004
Skin Tags. . . . . . . . . . . . . . . . . . . . 11200-11201
Small Intestine
Control of Bleeding . . . . . 44366, 44378, 44391
Tumor Removal . . . . . . . . . . . 44365, 44392
Turbinate Mucosa
Electrocautery . . . . . . . . . . . . . . 30801-30802
Ureteral Stricture . . . . . . . . . . . . . . 52341, 52344
Ureteropelvic Junction Stricture. . . . . 52342, 52345
Urethral Caruncle . . . . . . . . . . . . . . . . . . . . 53265

## Cavernitides, Fibrous
*See* Peyronie Disease

## Cavernosography
Corpora . . . . . . . . . . . . . . . . . . . . . . . . . . . . 54230

## Cavernosometry . . . . . . . . . . . . . . . . 54231

## Cavities, Pleural
*See* Pleural Cavity

## Cavus Foot Correction . . . . . . . . . . . 28309

## CBC
*See* Blood Cell Count; Complete Blood Count (CBC)

## CCL4
*See* Carbon Tetrachloride

## CCU Visit
*See* Critical Care Services

## CD142 Antigens
*See* Thromboplastin

## CD143 Antigens
*See* Angiotensin Converting Enzyme (ACE)

## CD4 . . . . . . . . . . . . . . . . . . . . . . . . . . . . 86360

## CD8 . . . . . . . . . . . . . . . . . . . . . . . . . . . . 86360

## CEA
*See* Carcinoembryonic Antigen

## Cecil Repair
*See* Urethroplasty

## Cecostomy
Laparoscopic. . . . . . . . . . . . . . . . . . . . . . . . 44188
Obstructive Material Removal . . . . . . . . . . . 49460
Skin Level . . . . . . . . . . . . . . . . . . . . . . . . . 44320
Tube
Insertion
Open . . . . . . . . . . . . . . . . . . . . . . . . . 44300
Percutaneous . . . . . . . . . . . . . . . . . . 49442
Radiologic Evaluation. . . . . . . . . . . . . 49465
Replacement. . . . . . . . . . . . . . . . . . . 49450
with Colectomy. . . . . . . . . . . . . . . . . . . . . 44141

## Celiac Plexus
Destruction . . . . . . . . . . . . . . . . . . . . . . . . . 64680
Injection
Anesthetic . . . . . . . . . . . . . . . . . . . . . . 64530
Neurolytic. . . . . . . . . . . . . . . . . . . . . . . 64680

## Celiac Trunk Artery
*See* Artery, Celiac

## Celioscopy
*See* Endoscopy, Peritoneum

## Celiotomy . . . . . . . . . . . . . . . . . . . . . . 49000
Abdomen
for Staging . . . . . . . . . . . . . . . . . . . . . 49220

## Cell Count
B Cells. . . . . . . . . . . . . . . . . . . . . . . . . . . . . 86355
Bacterial Colony . . . . . . . . . . . . . . . . . . . . . 87086
CD4 . . . . . . . . . . . . . . . . . . . . . . . . 86360-86361
CD8 . . . . . . . . . . . . . . . . . . . . . . . . . . . . . . 86360
CD34 . . . . . . . . . . . . . . . . . . . . . . . . . . . . . 86367
Chromosome Analysis
*See* Chromosome Analysis
Body Fluid . . . . . . . . . . . . . . . . . . 86152-86153
Other than Blood . . . . . . . . . . . . 89050-89051
Natural Killer (NK). . . . . . . . . . . . . . . . . . . . 86357
Sperm . . . . . . . . . . . . . . . . . 89310, 89320, 89322
Stem . . . . . . . . . . . . . . . . . . . . . . . . . . . . . 86367
T Cells . . . . . . . . . . . . . . . . . . . . . . 86359-86361

## Cell, Blood
*See* Blood Cell

## Cell, Islet
*See* Islet Cell

## Cell, Mother
*See* Stem Cell

## Cell-Stimulating Hormone, Interstitial
*See* Luteinizing Hormone (LH)

## Cellobiase
*See* Beta Glucosidase

## Cellular Inclusion
*See* Inclusion Bodies

## Central Shunt . . . . . . . . . . . . . . . . . . . 33764

## Central Venous Catheter Placement
Insertion
Central
Non-tunneled . . . . . . . . . . . . . 36555-36556
Tunneled without Port or
Pump. . . . . . . . . . . . 36557-36558, 36565
Tunneled with Port . . . . 36560-36561, 36566
Tunneled with Pump. . . . . . . . . . . . . . 36563
Peripheral
with Port . . . . . . . . . . . . . . . . . 36570-36571

without Port or Pump . . . . . . . . 36568-36569
Repair
with Port or Pump . . . . . . . . . . . . . . . . 36576
without Port or Pump. . . . . . . . . . . . . . 36575
Replacement
Catheter Only. . . . . . . . . . . . . . . . . . . . 36578
Complete
Central . . . . . . . . . . . . . . . . . 36580-36583
Peripheral . . . . . . . . . . . . . . . 36584-36585
Repositioning . . . . . . . . . . . . . . . . . . . . . . . 36597

## Central Venous Catheter Removal . . . . . . . . . . . . . 36589

## Cephalic Version
of Fetus
Anesthesia. . . . . . . . . . . . . . . . . . . . . . . 01958
External . . . . . . . . . . . . . . . . . . . . . . . . . 59412

## Cephalocele
*See* Encephalocele

## Cephalogram, Orthodontic
*See* Orthodontic Cephalogram

## Cerclage
Cervix . . . . . . . . . . . . . . . . . . . . . . . . . . . . 57700
Abdominal . . . . . . . . . . . . . . . . . . . . . . 59325
Removal under Anesthesia . . . . . . . . . . 59871
Vaginal . . . . . . . . . . . . . . . . . . . . . . . . . 59320
Femoral Fracture . . . . . . 27244-27245, 27506-27507
Humeral Shaft Fracture. . . . . . . . . . . 24515-24516
Tibial Shaft Fracture . . . . . . . . . . . . . 27758-27759

## Cerebellopontine Angle Tumor
*See* Brain, Tumor, Excision; Brainstem;
Mesencephalon; Skull Base Surgery

## Cerebral Cortex Decortication
*See* Decortication

## Cerebral Death
*See* Brain Death

## Cerebral Hernia
*See* Encephalocele

## Cerebral Perfusion Analysis
CT Scan . . . . . . . . . . . . . . . . . . . . . . . . . . . . 0042T

## Cerebral Ventriculographies
*See* Ventriculography

## Cerebral Vessels
Anastomosis . . . . . . . . . . . . . . . . . . . . . . . . 61711
Aneurysm Surgery
Carotid Artery Occlusion. . 61705, 61708, 61710
Cervical Approach . . . . . . . . . . . . . . . . . 61703
Intracranial Approach . . . . . . . . . 61697-61698,
61700, 61702
Angioplasty. . . . . . . . . . . . . . . . . . . . . . . . . 61630
Arteriovenous Malformation Surgery
Dural. . . . . . . . . . . . . . . . . . . . . 61690, 61692
Fistula. . . . . . . . . . . . . . . . . . . . . . . . . . 61705
Infratentorial . . . . . . . . . . . . . . . 61684, 61686
Supratentorial . . . . . . . . . . . . . . 61680-61682
Dilation
Intracranial Vasospasm . . . . . . . . 61640-61642
Occlusion. . . . . . . . . . . . . . . . . . . . . . . . . . 61623
Placement
Stent
Intravascular . . . . . . . . . . . . . . . . . . . 61635
Thrombolysis. . . . . . . . . . . . . . . . . . . . . . . . 37195

## Cerebrose
*See* Galactose

## Chemical Exfoliation ........... 17360

## Chemical Peel ........... 15788-15793

## Chemiluminescent Assay ....... 82397

## Chemistry Tests
Clinical
　*See* Pathology and Laboratory, specific analyte
　Unlisted Chemistry Procedure ........ 84999

## Chemocauterization
Corneal Epithelium ............... 65435
　with Chelating Agent ............... 65436

## Chemodenervation
Anal Sphincter .................... 46505
Bladder ......................... 52287
Eccrine Glands
　Axillae ....................... 64650
　Other Area ................... 64653
Extraocular Muscle ............... 67345
Extremity Muscle ............... 64642-64645
Facial Muscle ............... 64612, 64615
Guidance
　Electrical Stimulation............... 95873
　Needle Electromyography ...... 64617, 95874
Larynx ......................... 64617
Neck Muscle ............... 64615, 64616
Salivary Glands................... 64611
Trunk Muscle.................. 64646-64647

## Chemonucleolysis ............. 62292

## Chemosurgery
Destruction of Benign Lesions ...... 17110-17111
Skin Lesion ... 17000-17004, 17110-17111, 17270,
　　　　　　　　　　　　　　　　　17280

## Chemotaxis Assay ............. 86155

## Chemotherapy
Bladder Instillation .................... 51720
Brain ......................... 61517
CNS.................... 61517, 96450
Extracorporeal Circulation
　Extremity ................... 36823
Home Infusion Procedures ......... 99601-99602
Intra-Arterial
　Cannulation ................... 36823
　Catheterization.................... 36640
　Infusion ......... 96422-96423, 96425
　Insertion Infusion Pump ........ 36260
　Push .................... 96420
Intralesional .................. 96405-96406
Intramuscular ................. 96401-96402
Intravenous
　Infusion ....... 96413, 96415, 96416, 96417
　Push ............ 96409, 96411
　Infusion Pump ................ 96416
Kidney Instillation.................... 50391
Peritoneal Cavity.................... 96446
　Catheterization.................... 49418
Pleural Cavity .................... 96440
Pump Services
　Implantable ................... 96522
　Maintenance ............ 95990-95991
　Portable ................... 96521
Reservoir Filling ................... 96542
Subcutaneous................. 96401-96402
Unlisted Procedure ................ 96549
Ureteral Instillation.................... 50391
Venous Cannulation ................ 36823

## Chest
*See* Mediastinum; Thorax
Artery
　Ligation ..................... 37616
Diagnostic Imaging
　Angiography....................... 71275
　CT Angiography ................... 71275
　CT Scan ............. 71250, 71260, 71270
　Magnetic Resonance Angiography ..... 71555
　Magnetic Resonance Imaging
　(MRI)................. 71550-71552
　PET Imaging ................. 78811, 78814
　Ultrasound ..................... 76604
　X-ray
　　*See* X-ray, Chest
Exploration
　Postoperative
　　Hemorrhage ................. 35820
　　Infection .................... 35820
　　Thrombosis.................. 35820
　　Penetrating Wound ............... 20101
Exit Site, Intraperitoneal Cannula/Catheter.. 49435
Flail
　Rib Fracture ................... 21810
Repair
　Blood Vessel............... 35211, 35216
　　with Other Graft............ 35271-35276
　　with Vein Graft............. 35241, 35246
Tube
　*See* Thoracostomy
Tumor
　*See* Chest Wall

## Chest Cavity
Bypass Graft ..................... 35905
Thoracoscopy
　*See* Thoracoscopy

## Chest Wall
*See* Pulmonology; Therapeutic
Debridement................... 11044, 11047
Manipulation.................. 94667-94668
Mechanical Oscillation................. 94669
Reconstruction ................... 49904
　with Lung Tumor Resection .......... 32504
　Trauma ..................... 32820
Repair ......................... 32905
　Closure.................... 32810
　Fistula.................... 32906
　Lung Hernia ................... 32800
Resection ..................... 32503
Tumor
　Ablation ................... 32998
　Excision ............. 19260, 19270-19272
Unlisted Services and Procedures ......... 32999

## Chest Wall Fistula
*See* Fistula, Chest Wall

## Chest, Funnel
*See* Pectus Excavatum

## Chevron Procedure ............. 28296

## Chiari Osteotomy of the Pelvis
*See* Osteotomy, Pelvis

## Chicken Pox Vaccine .......... 90716

## Child Procedure
*See* Excision, Pancreas, Partial

## Chimerism ................. 81267-81268

## Chin
Cartilage Graft ..................... 21230
Repair
　Augmentation ................... 21120
　Osteotomy ................. 21121-21123
Rhytidectomy ................... 15828
Skin Graft ................. 15240-15241
Tissue Transfer
　Adjacent.................. 14040-14041
　Flap.................. 15574, 15620
Wound Repair................. 13131-13133

## Chinidin
*See* Quinidine

## Chiropractic Manipulation
*See* Manipulation, Chiropractic

## Chiropractic Treatment
Spinal
　Extraspinal.................. 98940-98943

## Chlamydia
Antibody ..................... 86631-86632
Antigen Detection
　Amplified Nucleic Acid Probe ... 87486, 87491
　Direct Nucleic Acid Probe ...... 87485, 87490
　Direct Optical.................... 87810
　Enzyme Immunoassay ............. 87320
　Immunofluorescence ................ 87270
　Nucleic Acid Quantification.... 87487, 87492
Culture.......................... 87110

## Chloramphenicol ............. 82415

## Chloride
Blood.......................... 82435
Other Source.................... 82438
Panels
Basic Metabolic ............. 80047, 80048
Comprehensive Metabolic ........... 80053
Electrolyte .................... 80051
Renal Function ................. 80069
Spinal Fluid .................... 82438
Urine .......................... 82436

## Chloride, Methylene
*See* Dichloromethane

## Chlorinated Hydrocarbons ...... 82441

## Chlorohydrocarbon
*See* Chlorinated Hydrocarbons

## Chlorpromazine ................. 84022

## Choanal Atresia
Repair ................. 30540-30545

## Cholangiography
Injection ..................... 47500, 47505
Intraoperative ................. 74300-74301
Percutaneous ..................... 74320
　with Laparoscopy............. 47560-47561
Postoperative ..................... 74305
Repair
　with Bile Duct Exploration........... 47700
　with Cholecystectomy ... 47563, 47605, 47620

## Cholangiopancreatography
*See* Bile Duct; Pancreatic Duct
Endoscopic Retrograde (ERCP)
　with Ablation
　　Lesion..................... 43278
　　Polyp..................... 43278
　　Tumor..................... 43278
　with Biopsy ..................... 43261

with Collection of Specimen(s) . . . . . . . 43260
with Exchange
Stent . . . . . . . . . . . . . . . . . . . . . . . . 43276
with Papillotomy . . . . . . . . . . . . . . . . 43262
with Placement
Stent . . . . . . . . . . . . . . . . . . . . . . . . 43274
with Pressure Measurement Sphincter
of Oddi . . . . . . . . . . . . . . . . . . . . . . . 43263
with Removal
Foreign Body . . . . . . . . . . . . . . . . . . 43275
Stent . . . . . . . . . . . . . . . . 43275, 43276
with Removal/Destruction of
Calculus . . . . . . . . . . . . . . . . . 43264-43265
with Sphincterotomy . . . . . . . . 43262, 43274,
43276, 43277
with Transendoscopic Balloon Dilation . . 43277
Intraoperative . . . . . . . . . . . . . . . . 74300-74301
Postoperative . . . . . . . . . . . . . . . . . . . . 74305

### Cholangiostomy
*See* Hepaticostomy

### Cholangiotomy
*See* Hepaticostomy

### Cholecalciferol
*See* Vitamin, D-3

### Cholecystectomy
Any Method
with Cholangiography . . . 47563, 47605, 47620
with Choledochoenterostomy . . . . . . . . 47612
with Exploration Common Duct . . 47564, 47610
Donor Liver . . . . . . . . . . . . . . . . . . . . . 47143
Excision . . . . . . . . . . . . . . . . . . . 47600-47620
Laparoscopic . . . . . . . . . . . . . . . . . 47562-47564

### Cholecystenterostomy
Direct . . . . . . . . . . . . . . . . . . . . . . . . . 47720
with Gastroenterostomy . . . . . . . . . 47721, 47741
Laparoscopic . . . . . . . . . . . . . . . . . . . . 47570
Roux-en-Y . . . . . . . . . . . . . . . . . . . 47740-47741

### Cholecystography . . . 47490, 74290-74291

### Cholecystostomy
Open . . . . . . . . . . . . . . . . . . . . . . . . . 47480
Percutaneous . . . . . . . . . . . . . . . . . . . . 47490
with Peripancreatic Drain Placement . . . . . . 48000

### Cholecystotomy
Open . . . . . . . . . . . . . . . . . . . . . . . . . 47480
with Choledochostomy . . . . . . . . . . . . . 47420
with Choledochotomy . . . . . . . . . . . . . . 47420

### Choledochoplasty
*See* Bile Duct, Repair

### Choledochoscopy
Biliary Endoscopy . . . . . . . . . . . . . . . . . 47550

### Choledochostomy
Biliary Tract . . . . . . . . . . . . . . . . . 47420, 47425

### Choledochotomy
Biliary Tract . . . . . . . . . . . . . . . . . 47420, 47425

### Choledochus, Cyst
*See* Cyst, Choledochal

### Cholera Vaccine
Injectable . . . . . . . . . . . . . . . . . . . . . . 90725

### Cholesterol
Measurement
HDL . . . . . . . . . . . . . . . . . . . . . . . . . 83718
LDL . . . . . . . . . . . . . . . . . . . . . . . . . 83721
Panel

Lipid . . . . . . . . . . . . . . . . . . . . . . . . . 80061
Serum . . . . . . . . . . . . . . . . . . . . . . . . 82465
VLDL . . . . . . . . . . . . . . . . . . . . . . . . . 83719

### Choline Esterase I
*See* Acetylcholinesterase

### Choline Esterase II
*See* Cholinesterase

### Cholinesterase
Blood . . . . . . . . . . . . . . . . . . . . 82480, 82482

### Cholylglycine
Blood . . . . . . . . . . . . . . . . . . . . . . . . . 82240

### Chondroitin Sulfate
Detection . . . . . . . . . . . . . . . . . . . . . . . 82485

### Chondromalacia Patella
Repair . . . . . . . . . . . . . . . . . . . . . . . . . 27418

### Chondropathia Patellae
*See* Chondromalacia Patella

### Chopart Procedure . . . . . . . 28800-28805
*See* Amputation, Foot; Radical Resection;
Replantation

### Chordotomies
*See* Cordotomy

### Choriogonadotropin
*See* Chorionic Gonadotropin

### Choriomeningitides, Lymphocytic
*See* Lymphocytic Choriomeningitis

### Chorionic Gonadotropin . . . . . . 80414,
84702-84703
Stimulation Panel . . . . . . . . . . . . . 80414-80415

### Chorionic Growth Hormone
*See* Lactogen, Human Placental

### Chorionic Tumor
*See* Hydatidiform Mole

### Chorionic Villi
*See* Biopsy, Chorionic Villus

### Chorionic Villus
Biopsy . . . . . . . . . . . . . . . . . . . . . . . . 59015

### Choroid
Aspiration . . . . . . . . . . . . . . . . . . . . . . 67015
Lesion . . . . . . . . . . . . . 67220-67221, 67225
Neovascularization . . . . . . . . . . . . . . . . . 67043

### Choroid Plexus
Excision . . . . . . . . . . . . . . . . . . . . . . . 61544

### Christmas Factor . . . . . . . . . . . . . . 85250

### Chromaffinoma, Medullary
*See* Pheochromocytoma

### Chromatin, Sex
*See* Barr Bodies

### Chromatography
Column . . . . . . . . . . . 82486-82489, 82491-82492
Column/Mass Spectrometry . . . . . . . 82541-82544
Drug Screen . . . . . . . . . . . . . . . . 80100-80102
Gas Liquid or HPLC . . . . . . . . 82486, 82491-82492
Typing . . . . . . . . . . . . . . . . . . . . . . . 87143
Hemoglobin . . . . . . . . . . . . . . . . 83021, 83036
Paper . . . . . . . . . . . . . . . . . . . . 82487-82488
Sugars . . . . . . . . . . . . . . . . . . . . . . . 84375
Thin-Layer . . . . . . . . . . . . . . . . . . . . . 82489

### Chromium . . . . . . . . . . . . . . . . . . . . 82495

### Chromogenic Substrate
Assay . . . . . . . . . . . . . . . . . . . . . . . . 85130

### Chromosome Analysis
*See* Amniocentesis
Added Study . . . . . . . 88280, 88283, 88285, 88289
Amniotic Fluid . . . . . . . . . . . . . . 88267, 88269
Culture . . . . . . . . . . . . . . . . . . . . . . . 88235
Biopsy Culture
Tissue . . . . . . . . . . . . . . . . . . . . . . . 88233
Bone Marrow Culture . . . . . . . . . . . . . . . 88237
Breakage Syndromes . . . . . . . 88245, 88248-88249
Ataxia Telangiectasia . . . . . . . . . . . . . 88248
Clastogen Stress . . . . . . . . . . . . . . . . 88249
Fanconi Anemia . . . . . . . . . . . . . . . . . 88248
Fragile-X . . . . . . . . . . . . . . . . . . . . . 88248
Chorionic Villus . . . . . . . . . . . . . . . . . . 88267
5 Cells . . . . . . . . . . . . . . . . . . . . . . . 88261
15-20 Cells . . . . . . . . . . . . . . . . . . . . 88262
20-25 Cells . . . . . . . . . . . . . . . . . . . . 88264
45 Cells . . . . . . . . . . . . . . . . . . . . . . 88263
Culture . . . . . . . . . . . . . . . . . . . . . . . 88235
Cytogenomic Constitutional
Microarray . . . . . . . . . . . . . . . 81228-81229
In Situ Hybridization . . . . . . . . . . . . . 88272-88273
Lymphocyte Culture . . . . . . . . . . . . . . . 88230
Molecular Pathology, Level 5 . . . . . . . . . . . 81404
Pregnancy Associated Plasma Protein-A . . . . 84163
Tissue Culture
Amniotic Fluid Cells . . . . . . . . . . . . . . . 88325
Blood Cells . . . . . . . . . . . . . . . . . . . . 88237
Bone Marrow Cells . . . . . . . . . . . . . . . 88237
Chorionic Villus Cells . . . . . . . . . . . . . . 88235
Skin . . . . . . . . . . . . . . . . . . . . . . . . 88233
Tumor . . . . . . . . . . . . . . . . . . . . . . . 88239
Unlisted Cytogenic Study . . . . . . . . . . . . . 88299

### Chromotubation
Oviduct . . . . . . . . . . . . . . . . . . . . . . . . 58350

### Chronic Erection
*See* Priapism

### Chronic Interstitial Cystitides
*See* Cystitis, Interstitial

### Ciliary Body
Cyst
Destruction . . . . . . . . . . . . . . . . . . . . 66770
Excision . . . . . . . . . . . . . . . . . 66500, 66505
Destruction
Cryotherapy . . . . . . . . . . . . . . . . . . . 66720
Cyclodialysis . . . . . . . . . . . . . . . . . . 66740
Cyclophotocoagulation . . . . . . . . 66710-66711
Diathermy . . . . . . . . . . . . . . . . . . . . 66700
Endoscopic . . . . . . . . . . . . . . . . . . . 66711
Lesion
Destruction . . . . . . . . . . . . . . . . . . . . 66770
Excision . . . . . . . . . . . . . . . . . 66500, 66505
Repair . . . . . . . . . . . . . . . . . . . . . . . . 66680
Suture . . . . . . . . . . . . . . . . . . . . . . . . 66682

### Cimino Type Procedure . . . . . . . . 36821

### Cinefluorographies
*See* Cineradiography

### Cineplasty
Arm, Lower or Upper . . . . . . . . . . . . . . . . 24940

### Cineradiography
Esophagus . . . . . . . . . . . . . . . . . . . . . . 74230
Pharynx . . . . . . . . . . . . . . . . . . 70371, 74230
Site Unspecified . . . . . . . . . . . . . . 76120, 76125

**Index**

Index

Index

|

Index

Index

Index

Index

## Dexamethasone
Suppression Panel ..................... 80420

## DHA Sulfate
*See* Dehydroepiandrosterone Sulfate

## DHEA
*See* Dehydroepiandrosterone

## DHEA Sulfate
*See* Dehydroepiandrosterone Sulfate

## DHT
*See* Dihydrotestosterone

## Diagnosis, Psychiatric
*See* Psychiatric Diagnosis

## Diagnostic Amniocentesis
*See* Amniocentesis

## Diagnostic Aspiration, Eye
*See* Paracentesis, Eye, Anterior Chamber Fluid
Removal

## Diagnostic Radiologic Examination
*See* Radiology, Diagnostic

## Diagnostic Skin and Sensitization Tests
*See* Allergy Tests

## Diagnostic Ultrasound
*See* Echography

## Diagnostic Ultrasound of Heart
*See* Echocardiography

## Dialyses, Peritoneal
*See* Dialysis, Peritoneal

## Dialysis
Anesthesia ........................... 01844
Arteriovenous Fistula ............. 36831-36833
Arteriovenous Shunt .............. 36147-36148
End Stage Renal Disease
   *See* End Stage Renal Disease
Hemodialysis
   *See* Hemodialysis
Hemoperfusion ........................ 90997
Hepatitis B Vaccine .............. 90740, 90747
Kt/V Level ......................... 3082F-3084F
Nephropathy Treatment Documented ...... 3066F
Patient Training
   Completed Course .................. 90989
   Per Session ...................... 90003
Peritoneal ............. 90945, 90947, 4055F
   Catheter Insertion ...... 49418-49419, 49421
   Catheter Removal .................. 49422
   Home Infusion ............... 99601-99602
   Plan of Care Documented ............ 0507F
Unlisted Services and Procedures ......... 90999

## Dialysis, Extracorporeal
*See* Hemodialysis

## Diaphragm
Assessment ...................... 58943, 58960
Contraception ........................ 57170
Imbrication
   for Eventration .................... 39545
Repair
   Hernia ....................... 39540-39541
     Esophageal Hiatal .... 43280-43282, 43325
     Neonatal ........................ 39503
   Laceration ........................ 39501
Resection ....................... 39560-39561
Unlisted Diaphragm Procedures .......... 39599

## Diaphragm Contraception
*See* Contraception, Diaphragm

## Diaphysectomy
Calcaneus .......................... 28120
Clavicle ........................... 23180
Femur .............................. 27360
Fibula ....................... 27360, 27641
Humerus ...................... 23184, 24140
Metacarpal ......................... 26230
Metatarsal ......................... 28122
Olecranon Process .................. 24147
Phalanges
   Finger ..................... 26235-26236
   Toe .............................. 28124
Radius ....................... 24145, 25151
Scapula ............................ 23182
Talus .............................. 28120
Tarsal ............................. 28122
Tibia ........................ 27360, 27640
Ulna ......................... 24147, 25150

## Diastase
*See* Amylase

## Diastasis
*See* Separation

## Diathermy
*See* Physical Medicine/Therapy/Occupational
Therapy
Destruction
   Ciliary Body ...................... 66700
Lesion
   Retina ..................... 67208, 67227
Retinal Detachment
   Prophylaxis ....................... 67141
   Repair ............................ 67101
Treatment .......................... 97024

## Diathermy, Surgical
*See* Electrocautery

## Dibucaine Number ............. 82638

## Dichloride, Methylene
*See* Dichloromethane

## Dichlorides, Ethylene
*See* Dichloroethane

## Dichloroethane ............... 84600

## Dichloromethane ............. 84600

## Diethylamide, Lysergic Acid
*See* Lysergic Acid Diethylamide

## Diethylether ................. 84600

## Differential Count
*See* White Blood Cell Count

## Differentiation Reversal Factor
*See* Prothrombin

## Diffusion Test, Gel
*See* Immunodiffusion

## Digestive Tract
*See* Gastrointestinal Tract

## Digit
*See* Finger; Toe
Destruction ......................... 64632
Injection ........................... 64455

Replantation .................... 20816-20822

## Digital Artery
Sympathectomy .................... 64820

## Digital Slit-Beam Radiograph
*See* Scanogram

## Digits
*See* Digit

## Digoxin
Assay .............................. 80162

## Dihydrocodeinone
Detection ........................... 82646
Screen ....................... 80100-80103

## Dihydroepitestosterone
*See* Dihydrotestosterone

## Dihydrohydroxycodeinone
*See* Oxycodinone

## Dihydromorphinone ........... 82486
Detection ........................... 82649
Screen ....................... 80100-80103

## Dihydrotestosterone ........... 82651

## Dihydroxyethanes
*See* Ethylene Glycol

## Dihydroxyvitamin D ............ 82652

## Dilatation, Transluminal Arterial
*See* Angioplasty, Transluminal

## Dilation
*See* Dilation and Curettage; Dilation and
Evacuation
Anal
   Endoscopy ........................ 46604
   Sphincter .................. 45905, 46940
Aortic Valve ........................ 33403
Bile Duct
   Endoscopy ........... 43277, 47555-47556
   Stricture ......................... 74363
Bladder
   Cystourethroscopy ........... 52260, 52265
Bronchi
   Endoscopy .................. 31630, 31636
Cerebral Vessels
   Intracranial Vasospasm ........ 61640-61642
Cervix
   Canal ............................ 57800
   Stump ............................ 57558
Colon
   Endoscopy ........................ 45386
Colon-Sigmoid
   Endoscopy ........................ 45340
Esophagus .................... 43450, 43453
   Balloon ... 43195, 43213-43214, 43220, 43233,
                               43249
   Endoscopy ...... 43195-43196, 43212-43213,
           43220, 43226, 43229, 43233, 43453
Gastric/Duodenal Stricture .............. 43245
   Surgical .......................... 43510
Intestines .......................... 44615
   Endoscopy ........................ 44370
   Stent Placement ........ 44379, 44383, 44397
Kidney ................. 50080-50081, 50395
   Intra-Renal Stricture .......... 52343, 52346
Lacrimal Punctum .................... 68801
Larynx
   Endoscopy .................. 31528-31529

Percutaneous Fixation . . . . . . . . . . . . . . . 28636
Patella
　Closed Treatment . . . . . . . . . . . 27560, 27562
　Open Treatment . . . . . . . . . . . . . . . . . . . 27566
　Recurrent . . . . . . . . . . . . . . . 27420, 27424
Pelvic Ring
　Closed Treatment . . . . . . . . . . . 27193-27194
　Open Treatment . . . . . . . . . . . . . 27217-27218
　Percutaneous Fixation . . . . . . . . . . . . . 27216
　without Manipulation . . . . . . . . 27193-27194
Peroneal Tendons . . . . . . . . . . . . . . 27675-27676
Radiocarpal
　Closed Treatment . . . . . . . . . . . . . . . . . 25660
　Open Treatment . . . . . . . . . . . . . . . . . . . 25670
Radioulnar
　Closed Treatment . . . . . . . . . . . . . . . . . 25675
　Open Treatment . . . . . . . . . . . . . . . . . . . 25676
Radioulnar Joint
　Closed Treatment . . . . . . . . . . . . . . . . . 25520
　Galeazzi . . . . . . . . . . 25520, 25525-25526
　Open Treatment . . . . . . . . . . . . . 25525-25526
Radius
　Closed Treatment . . . . . . . . . . . . . . . . . 24640
　with Fracture
　　Closed Treatment . . . . . . . . . . . . . . . 24620
　　Open Treatment . . . . . . . . . . . . . . . . . 24635
Shoulder
　Closed Treatment with Manipulation . . 23650,
　　　　　　　　　　　　　　　　　　23655
　Open Treatment . . . . . . . . . . . . . . . . . . . 23660
　with Greater Tuberosity Fracture
　　Closed Treatment . . . . . . . . . . . . . . . 23665
　　Open Treatment . . . . . . . . . . . . . . . . . 23670
　with Surgical or Anatomical Neck Fracture
　　Closed Treatment . . . . . . . . . . . . . . . 23675
　　Open Treatment . . . . . . . . . . . . . . . . . 23680
Skin
　Debridement . . . . . . . . . . . . . . . 11010-11012
Sternoclavicular Joint
　Closed Treatment
　　with Manipulation . . . . . . . . . . . . . . . 23525
　　without Manipulation . . . . . . . . . . . . . 23520
　Open Treatment . . . . . . . . . . . . 23530, 23532
Talotarsal Joint
　Closed Treatment . . . . . . . . . . . 28570, 28575
　Open Treatment . . . . . . . . . . . . . . . . . . . 28585
　Percutaneous Fixation . . . . . . . . . . . . . 28576
Tarsal
　Closed Treatment . . . . . . . . . . . 28540, 28545
　Open Treatment . . . . . . . . . . . . . . . . . . . 28555
　Percutaneous Fixation . . . . . . . . . . . . . 28546
Tarsometatarsal Joint
　Closed Treatment . . . . . . . . . . . 28600, 28605
　Open Treatment . . . . . . . . . . . . . . . . . . . 28615
　Percutaneous Fixation . . . . . . . . . . . . . 28606
Temporomandibular Joint
　Closed Treatment . . . . . . . . . . . 21480, 21485
　Open Treatment . . . . . . . . . . . . . . . . . . . 21490
Thumb
　Closed Treatment . . . . . . . . . . . 26641, 26645
　Open Treatment . . . . . . . . . . . . . . . . . . . 26665
　Percutaneous Fixation . . . . . . . . . . . . . 26650
　with Fracture . . . . . . . . . . . . . . . . . . . . 26645
　　Open Treatment . . . . . . . . . . . . . . . . . 26665
　　Percutaneous Fixation . . . . . . . . . . . . 26650
　with Manipulation . . . . . . 26641, 26645, 26650
Tibiofibular Joint
　Closed Treatment . . . . . . . . . . . 27830-27831
　Open Treatment . . . . . . . . . . . . . . . . . . . 27832
Toe
　Closed Treatment . . 26770, 26775, 28630-28635
　Open Treatment . . . . . . . . . . . . . . . . . . . 28645
　Percutaneous Fixation . . . . . . . . 26776, 28636

Trans-Scaphoperilunar
　Closed Treatment . . . . . . . . . . . . . . . . . 25680
　Open Treatment . . . . . . . . . . . . . . . . . . . 25685
Vertebra
　Additional Segment
　　Open Treatment . . . . . . . . . . . . . . . . . 22328
　Cervical
　　Open Treatment . . . . . . 22318-22319, 22326
　Closed Treatment
　　with Manipulation, Casting and/or
　　Bracing . . . . . . . . . . . . . . . . . . . . . . 22315
　Lumbar
　　Open Treatment . . . . . . . . . . . . . . . . . 22325
　Thoracic
　　Open Treatment . . . . . . . . . . . . . . . . . 22327
Wrist
　Closed Treatment . . . . . 25660, 25675, 25680
　Intercarpal . . . . . . . . . . . . . . . . . . . . . . 25660
　　Open Treatment . . . . . . . . . . . . . . . . . 25670
　Open Treatment . . . . . . . . . . . 25670, 25685
　Percutaneous Fixation . . . . . . . . . . . . . 25671
　Radiocarpal . . . . . . . . . . . . . . . . . . . . . 25660
　　Open Treatment . . . . . . . . . . . . . . . . . 25670
　Radioulnar
　　Closed Treatment . . . . . . . . . . . . . . . 25675
　　Open Treatment . . . . . . . . . . . . . . . . . 25676
　　Percutaneous Fixation . . . . . . . . . . . . 25671
　with Fracture
　　Closed Treatment . . . . . . . . . . . . . . . 25680
　　Open Treatment . . . . . . . . . . . . . . . . . 25685
　with Manipulation . . . . . . 25660, 25675, 25680

## Dislocation, Radiocarpal Joint
See Radiocarpal Joint, Dislocation

## Disorder
Blood Coagulation
　See Coagulopathy
Penis
　See Penis
Retinal
　See Retina

## Displacement Therapy
Nose . . . . . . . . . . . . . . . . . . . . . . . . . . . . . 30210

## Dissection
Axial Vessel
　for Island Pedicle . . . . . . . . . . . . . . . . . 15740
Cavernous Sinus . . . . . . . . . . . . . . . . . . . . 61613
Cranial Adhesions . . . . . . . . . . . . . . . . . . . 62161
Donor Organ
　Heart . . . . . . . . . . . . . . . . . . . . . . . . . . 33944
　Heart/Lung . . . . . . . . . . . . . . . . . . . . . . 33933
　Kidney . . . . . . . . . . . . . . . . . . 50323, 50325
　Liver . . . . . . . . . . . . . . . . . . . . . . . . . . . 47143
　Lung . . . . . . . . . . . . . . . . . . . . . . . . . . . 32855
　Pancreas . . . . . . . . . . . . . . . . . . . . . . . . 48551
Facial Nerve . . . . . . . . . . . . . . . . . . . . . . . 42420
for Debulking . . . . . . . . . . . . . . . . . 58952-58953
Hygroma, Cystic
　Axillary/Cervical . . . . . . . . . . . . 38550, 38555
Infrarenal Aneurysm . . . . . . . 34825-34826, 34800,
　　　　　　　　　　　34802, 34830-34832
Lymph Nodes . . . . . . . . . . . . . . . . . . . . . . 38542
Mediastinal . . . . . . . . . . . . . . . . . . 60521-60522
Neck
　See Radical Neck Dissection
Neurovascular . . . . . . . . . . . . . . . . . . . . . . 32503
Sclera . . . . . . . . . . . . . . . . . . . . . . . . . . . 67107
Urethra . . . . . . 54328, 54332, 54336, 54348, 54352

## Dissection, Neck, Radical
See Radical Neck Dissection

## Distention
See Dilation

## Diverticula, Meckel's
See Diverticulum, Meckel's

## Diverticulectomy . . . . . . . . . . . . . . . 44800
Esophagus . . . . . . . . . . . . . . . . . . . 43130, 43135

## Diverticulectomy, Meckel's
See Meckel's Diverticulum, Excision

## Diverticulum
Bladder
　See Bladder, Diverticulum
Large Intestine . . . . . . . . . . . . . . . . . 44604-44605
Meckel's
　Excision . . . . . . . . . . . . . . . . . . . . . . . . 44800
　Unlisted Procedure . . . . . . . . . . . . . . . . 44899
Small Intestine . . . . . . . . . . . . . . . 44602-44603
Urethra
　Excision . . . . . . . . . . . . . . . . . . . 53230, 53235
　Marsupialization . . . . . . . . . . . . . . . . . 53240
　Urethroplasty . . . . . . . . . . . . . . . 53400, 53405

## Division
Anal Sphincter . . . . . . . . . . . . . . . . . . . . . 46080
Flap . . . . . . . . . . . . 15600, 15610, 15620, 15630
Intrauterine Septum . . . . . . . . . . . . . . . . . 58560
Muscle
　Foot . . . . . . . . . . . . . . . . . . . . . . . . . . . 28250
　Neck
　　Scalenus Anticus . . . . . . . . . . 21700, 21705
　　Sternocleidomastoid . . . . . . . . 21720, 21725
Plantar Fascia
　Foot . . . . . . . . . . . . . . . . . . . . . . . . . . . 28250
Rectal Stricture . . . . . . . . . . . . . . . . . . . . . 45150
Saphenous Vein . . . . . . . . . . . 37700, 37722, 37735
Symblepharon . . . . . . . . . . . . . . . . . . . . . . 68340

## Division, Isthmus, Horseshoe Kidney
See Symphysiotomy, Horseshoe Kidney

## Division, Scalenus Anticus Muscle
See Division, Scalenus Anticus

## DI-Amphetamine
See Amphetamine

## DMO
See Dimethadione

## DNA
See Deoxyribonucleic Acid (DNA)

## DNA Endonuclease
See DNAse

## DNA Probe
See Cytogenetics Studies; DNA Probe

## DNAse
Antibody . . . . . . . . . . . . . . . . . . . . . . . . . . 86215

## Domiciliary Services
See Nursing Facility Services
Care Plan Oversight . . . . . . . . . . . . . 99339-99340
Discharge Services . . . . . . . . . . . . . . 99315-99316
Established Patient . . . . . . . . . . . . . . 99334-99337
New Patient . . . . . . . . . . . . . . . . . . . 99324-99328
Supervision . . . . . . . . . . . . . . . . . . . 99374-99375

## Donor Procedures
See Harvesting
Bone Harvesting . . . . . . . . . . . . . . . 20900-20902
Bone Marrow Harvesting . . . . . . . . . 38230, 38232

Index

## Drainage Implant, Glaucoma
*See* Aqueous Shunt

## Dressings

## DREZ Procedure
*See* Incision, Spinal Cord; Incision and Drainage

## DRIL
*See* Revascularization, Distal

## Drill Hole

## Drinking Test for Glaucoma
*See* Glaucoma, Provocative Test

## Drug
*See* Specific Drug

## Drug Assay

## Drug Delivery Implant
*See* Infusion Pump

## Drug Instillation
*See* Instillation, Drugs

## Drug Management

## Drug Screen

## Drugs, Anticoagulant
*See* Anticoagulant Management; Clotting Inhibitors

## DST
*See* Dexamethasone, Suppression Test

## DT Shots

## DTaP Immunization

## DTaP-HepB-IPV Immunization

## DTP Immunization

## Dual Photon Absorptiometry
*See* Absorptiometry, Dual Photon

## Dual X-ray Absorptiometry (DXA)

## Duct, Bile
*See* Bile Duct

## Duct, Hepatic
*See* Hepatic Duct

## Duct, Nasolacrimal
*See* Nasolacrimal Duct

## Duct, Omphalomesenteric
*See* Omphalomesenteric Duct

## Duct, Pancreatic
*See* Pancreatic Duct

## Duct, Salivary
*See* Salivary Duct

## Duct, Stensen
*See* Parotid Duct

Index

Index

**Index**

**Index**

Nasoethmoid
   *See* Nasoethmoid Complex
Repair
   Leak, Cerebrospinal Fluid. . . . . . . . . . . 31290
Sinus
   *See* Sinus, Ethmoid

## Ethmoid, Sinus
*See* Sinus, Ethmoid

## Ethmoidectomy
Anterior. . . . . . . . . . . . . . . . . . . . . . . . 31200
Partial . . . . . . . . . . . . . . . . . . . . . . . . . 31254
Total . . . . . . . . . . . . . . . 31201, 31205, 31255
Endoscopic . . . . . . . . . . . . . . . . . . 31254-31255
Skull Base Surgery . . . . . . . . . . . . . . 61580-61581

## Ethosuccimid
*See* Ethosuximide

## Ethosuximide
Assay. . . . . . . . . . . . . . . . . . . . . . . . . . 80168

## Ethyl Alcohol
*See* Ethanol

## Ethylene Dichlorides
*See* Dichloroethane

## Ethylene Glycol . . . . . . . . . . . . . . . . 82693

## Ethylmethylsuccimide
*See* Ethosuximide

## Etiocholanalone Measurement
*See* Etiocholanolone

## Etiocholanolone . . . . . . . . . . . . . . . 82696

## ETOH
*See* Alcohol, Ethyl

## Euglobulin Lysis . . . . . . . . . . . . . . . 85360

## European Blastomycosis
*See* Cryptococcus

## Eustachian Tube
Catheterization . . . . . . . . . . . . . . . . . . . 69405
Inflation
   Myringotomy . . . . . . . . . . . . . . . . . . 69420
      Anesthesia . . . . . . . . . . . . . . . . . 69421
   with Catheterization . . . . . . . . . . . . . 69400
   without Catheterization. . . . . . . . . . . . 69401
Insertion
   Catheter. . . . . . . . . . . . . . . . . . . . . . 69405

## Eutelegenesis
*See* Artificial Insemination

## Evacuation
Clots
   Endoscopic. . . . . . . . . . . . . . . . . . . . 52001
Hematoma
   Brain. . . . . . . . . . 61108, 61154, 61312-61315
      Anesthesia . . . . . . . . . . . . . . . . . 00211
   Subungual . . . . . . . . . . . . . . . . . . . . 11740
Hydatidiform Mole . . . . . . . . . . . . . . . . 59870
Intraspinal Lesion . . . . . . . . . . . . . . . . . 63265
Meibomian Glands . . . . . . . . . . . . . . . . 0207T
Pregnancy
   *See* Dilation and Evacuation
   Cervical . . . . . . . . . . . . . . . . . . . . . . 59140
Stomach . . . . . . . . . . . . . . . . . . . . . . . 43753

## Evaluation
Aneurysm Pressure. . . . . . . . . . . . . . . . 93982
Cine. . . . . . . . . . . . . . . . . . . . . . . . . . . 74230

Electrophysiologic. . . . . . . . . 93653-93654, 93656
   Subcutaneous Cardioverter-
   Defibrillator . . . . . . . . . . . . . . . . . . . 0326T
Implantable Cardioverter-Defibrillator Device
   Interrogation . . . . . . . . . . . . . . . 0327T, 93289
   Programming . . . . . . . . . . 0328T, 93282-93284
Treatment . . . . . . . . . . . . . . . . . . . . . . 92526
Video. . . . . . . . . . . . . . . . . . . . . . . . . . 74230

## Evaluation and Management
Assistive Technology
   Assessment . . . . . . . . . . . . . . . . . . . 97755
Basic Life and/or Disability Evaluation
Services. . . . . . . . . . . . . . . . . . . . . . . . 99450
Care Plan Oversight Services . . . . . . . 99339-99340,
                      99374-99380
   Home Health Agency Care. . . . . . 99374-99375
   Home or Rest Home Care . . . . . . 99339-99340
   Hospice . . . . . . . . . . . . . . . . . 99377-99378
   Nursing Facility . . . . . . . . . . . . 99379-99380
Case Management Services. . . . . . . . 99366-99368
Consultation . . . . . . . . . . . . . . . . 99241-99255
Critical Care . . . . . . . . . . . . . . . . 99291-99292
   Interfacility Pediatric Transport . . 99466-99467,
                      99485-99486
Domiciliary or Rest Home
   Established Patient . . . . . . . . . . 99334-99337
   New Patient. . . . . . . . . . . . . . . 99324-99328
Emergency Department . . . . . . . . . . 99281-99288
Health Behavior
   Assessment . . . . . . . . . . . . . . . . . . . 96150
   Family Intervention . . . . . . . . . . 96154-96155
   Group Intervention. . . . . . . . . . . . . . . 96153
   Individual Intervention . . . . . . . . . . . . 96152
   Re-assessment. . . . . . . . . . . . . . . . . 96151
Home Services . . . . . . . . . . . . . . . 99341-99350
Hospital. . . . . . . . . . . . . . . . . . . . 99221-99233
   Discharge. . . . . . . . . . . . . . . . 99238-99239
Hospital Services
   Observation Care . . . . . . . . . . . 99217-99220,
           99224-99226, 99234-99236
Hyperbaric Oxygen Treatment Facility . . . . . 99183
Insurance Exam. . . . . . . . . . . . . . . 99455-99456
Internet Communication . . . . . . . . . 98969, 99444
Low Birthweight Infant. . . . . . . . . . 99478-99479
Medical Team Conferences . . . . . . . 99366-99368
Neonatal Critical Care . . . . . . . . . . 99468-99469
Newborn Care. . . . . . . . . . . . . . . . 99460-99465
Nursing Facility
   *See* Nursing Facility Services
   Annual Assessment. . . . . . . . . . . . . . 99318
   Discharge. . . . . . . . . . . . . . . . 99315-99316
   Initial Care . . . . . . . . . . . . . . . 99304-99306
   Other . . . . . . . . . . . . . . . . . . . . . . . 99318
   Subsequent Care . . . . . . . . . . . 99307-99310
Occupation Therapy Evaluation . . . . . . . . . 97003
   Re-evaluation. . . . . . . . . . . . . . . . . . 97004
Office and Other Outpatient . . . . . . . 99201-99215
Online Services. . . . . . . . . . . . . . . . 98969, 99444
Pediatric Critical Care. . . . . . . . . . . 99471-99472
Pediatric Interfacility Transport . . . . 99466-99476,
                      99485-99486
Post-discharge Transitional Care . . . . 99495-99496
Preventive Services. . . . . . . . . . . . . 99381-99429
Prolonged Services . . . . . . . . . . . . . 99354-99360
Standby Services . . . . . . . . . . . . . . . . . . 99360
Team Conferences . . . . . . . . . . . . . 99366-99368
Telephone Services. . . 98966-98968, 99441-99443
Unlisted Services and Procedures . . . . . . . 99499
with Psychotherapy. . . . . . . . 90833, 90836, 90838
Work-Related and/or Medical
Disability Evaluation. . . . . . . . . . . . . . . 99455

*See* Drug Screen

## Everolimus
Drug Assay . . . . . . . . . . . . . . . . . . . . . 80169

## Evisceration
Ocular Contents
   with Implant. . . . . . . . . . . . . . . . . . . 65093
   without Implant . . . . . . . . . . . . . . . . . 65091
Suture
   Abdominal Wall . . . . . . . . . . . . . . . . . 49900

## Evisceration, Pelvic
*See* Exenteration, Pelvis

## Evocative/
## Suppression Test . . . . . . . . . . 80400-80440
*See* Pathology and Laboratory, Evocative/
Suppression Testing

## Evoked Potentials
Auditory
   *See* Audiometry
Auditory Brainstem. . . . . . . . . . . . . 92585-92586
Central Nervous System
   Somatosensory Testing . . 95925-95927, 95938
   Transcranial Motor Stimulation. . 95928-95929,
                        95939
   Visual . . . . . . . . . . . . . . . . . . . . . . . 95930
Visual
   Acuity. . . . . . . . . . . . . . . . . . . . . . . 0333T
   Central Nervous System . . . . . . . . . . . 95930

## Evoked Potential, Auditory
*See* Audiometry

## Ewart Procedure
*See* Palate, Reconstruction, Lengthening

## Excavatum, Pectus
*See* Pectus Excavatum

## Exchange
Drainage Catheter
   Under Radiologic Guidance. . . . . . . . . . 49423
Fluid-Gas, Vitreous . . . . . . . . . . . . . . . . 67025
Intraocular Lens . . . . . . . . . . . . . . . . . . 66986
Strut
   External Fixation System. . . . . . . . . . . 20697

## Exchange Transfusion
*See* Blood, Transfusion, Exchange

## Excision
Abdomen
   Tumor. . . . . . . . . . . . . . . . . . 49203-49205
Abdominal Wall
   Tumor. . . . . . . . . . . . . . . . . . 22900-22903
Abscess
   Brain. . . . . . . . . . . . . . . . . 61514, 61522
   Clavicle. . . . . . . . . . . . . . . . . . . . . . 23170
   Facial Bones. . . . . . . . . . . . . . . . . . . 21026
   Femur. . . . . . . . . . . . . 27070-27071, 27360
   Fibula . . . . . . . . . . . . . . . . . . . . . . . 27360
   Forearm . . . . . . . . . . . . . . . . . . . . . 25145
   Ilium. . . . . . . . . . . . . . . . . . . 27070-27071
   Humerus. . . . . . . . . . . . . . . . 24134, 23174
   Mandible . . . . . . . . . . . . . . . . . . . . . 21025
   Olecranon Process. . . . . . . . . . . . . . . 24138
   Pubic Symphysis . . . . . . . . . . . 27070-27071
   Radial Head or Neck . . . . . . . . . . . . . . 24136
   Scapula . . . . . . . . . . . . . . . . . . . . . . 23172
   Tibia . . . . . . . . . . . . . . . . . . . . . . . . 27360
   Wrist . . . . . . . . . . . . . . . . . . . . . . . 25145

Defect
- Osteochondral . . . . . . . . . . . . . . . . . . . 29891
  - Talus . . . . . . . . . . . . . . . . . . . . . . . 29891
  - Tibia . . . . . . . . . . . . . . . . . . . . . . . 29891
- Dentoalveolar Structures
  - Alveolar Mucosa . . . . . . . . . . . . . . . 41828
  - Alveolectomy . . . . . . . . . . . . . . . . . 41830
  - Gingivectomy . . . . . . . . . . . . . . . . . 41820
  - Operculectomy . . . . . . . . . . . . . . . . 41821
  - Tuberosities . . . . . . . . . . . . 41822-41823
  - Tumor . . . . . . . . . . . . . . . . 41825-41827
- Diverticulum
  - Bladder . . . . . . . . . . . . . . . . . . . . . 51525
  - Esophagus . . . . . . . . . . . . . 43130, 43135
  - Hypopharynx . . . . . . . . . . . . 43130, 43135
  - Mesentery (Meckel's) . . . . . . . . . . . 44800
  - Urethra . . . . . . . . . 53230, 53235, 53240
- Ear
  - External . . . . . . . . . . . . . . . 69110, 69120
  - Inner . . . . . . . . . . . . . . . . . 69905, 69910
    - Vestibular Nerve . . . . . . . . . . . . . 69915
  - Ear, Middle
    - Polyp . . . . . . . . . . . . . . . . . . . . . 69540
    - Tumor . . . . . . . . . . . . 69550, 69552, 69554
- Elbow
  - Tumor . . . . . . . . , 24071, 24073, 24075-24076
- Elbow Joint . . . . . . . . . . . . . . . . . . . . . 24155
- Electrode . . . . . . . . . . . . . . . . . . . . . . 57522
- Embolism
  - *See* Embolectomy
- Epididymis . . . . . . . . . . . . . . . 54860-54861
  - Cyst . . . . . . . . . . . . . . . . . . . . . . 54840
  - Lesion . . . . . . . . . . . . . . . . . . . . . 54830
  - Spermatocele . . . . . . . . . . . . . . . . 54840
- Epiglottis . . . . . . . . . . . . . . . . . . . . . 31420
- Epiphyseal Bar . . . . . . . . . . . . . . . . . 20150
- Esophagus
  - *See* Esophagectomy
  - Lesion . . . . . . . . . . . . . . . . 43100-43101
- Eyelid
  - Lesion . . . . 67800, 67801, 67805, 67808, 67840
- Face
  - Bone Tumor . . . . . . . . . . . . . . 21029, 21030,
    21034-21040, 21044-21049
  - Cyst . . . . . . . . . . . . . . . . . . . . . . 21030
  - Soft Tissue Tumor . . . . . . . . . . . 21011-21014
- Fallopian Tube
  - Salpingectomy . . . . . . . . . . . . . . . . 58700
  - Salpingo-Oophorectomy . . . . . . . . . . . 58720
- Fascia
  - *See* Fasciectomy
- Femur . . . . . . . . . . . . 27070-27071, 27360
  - Cyst . . . . . . . . . . . 27065-27067, 27355-27358
  - Tumor . . . . . . . . 27065-27067, 27327-27328,
    27337-27339, 27355-27358
- Fibroadenoma
  - Breast . . . . . . . . . . . . . . . . . 19120-19126
- Fibula . . . . . . . 27360, 27455, 27457, 27641
  - Cyst . . . . . . . : . . . . . . . . . . 27635-27638
  - Tumor . . . . . . . . . . . . 27635, 27637-27638
- Finger
  - Cyst . . . . . . . . . . . . . 26160, 26210, 26215
  - Lesion . . . . . . . . . . . . . . . . . . . . . 26160
  - Tumor . . . . . . . . 26111-26118, 26200, 26205
  - Vascular Malformation . . . . . . . 26111, 26113,
    26115-26116
- Fistula
  - Anal . . . . . 46270, 46275, 46280, 46285, 46288
  - Lactiferous Duct . . . . . . . . . . . . . . . 19112
- Foot
  - Cyst . . . . . . . . . . 28090, 28100-28103, 28108
  - Tumor . . . . . . . . . . . . 28039, 28041, 28043,
    28045, 28100-28103

- Fasciectomy . . . . . . . . . . . . . . . . . . . 28060
  - Radical . . . . . . . . . . . . . . . . 28060-28062
  - Lesion . . . . . . . . . . . . . . . . . . . . . 28090
- Forearm
  - Tumor . . . . . . . . 25071, 25073, 25075-25076
- Gallbladder
  - *See* Cholecystectomy
- Ganglion
  - Finger or Hand . . . . . . . . . . . . . . . . 26160
  - Foot . . . . . . . . . . . . . . . . . . . . . . 28090
  - Toe . . . . . . . . . . . . . . . . . . . . . . . 28092
  - Wrist . . . . . . . . . . . . . . . . 25111-25112
- Gingiva . . . . . . . . . . . . . . . . . . . . . . 41820
- Gums . . . . . . . . . . . . . . . . . . . . . . . 41820
  - Alveolus . . . . . . . . . . . . . . . . . . . . 41830
  - Lesion . . . . . . . . . . . . . . . . 41825-41827
  - Tumor . . . . . . . . . . . . . . . . 41825-41827
  - Operculum . . . . . . . . . . . . . . . . . . 41821
- Hand
  - Cyst . . . . . . . . . . . . . . . . . . . . . . 26160
  - Lesion . . . . . . . . . . . . . . . . . . . . . 26160
  - Tumor . . . . . . . 26111, 26113, 26115-26116
  - Vascular Malformation . . . . . . . 26111, 26113,
    26115-26116
- Heart
  - Donor . . . . . . . . . . . . . . . . . . . . . 33940
  - Tumor . . . . . . . . . . . . . . . 33210, 33130
- Heart/Lung, Donor . . . . . . . . . . . . . . . 33930
- Hemorrhoids
  - *See* Hemorrhoidectomy
- Hip . . . . . . . . . . . . . . . . . . . 27070-27071
  - Bone Cyst . . . . . . . . . . . . . . 27065-27067
  - Bursa . . . . . . . . . . . . . . . . 27060, 27062
  - Tumor . . . . . . . . 27043-27048, 27065-27067
- Hippocampus . . . . . . . . . . . . . . . . . . 61566
- Humerus
  - Cyst . . . . . . . . . . . . . 23150, 23155-23156,
    24110, 24115-24116
  - Diaphysectomy . . . . . . . . . . . 23184, 24140
  - Head . . . . . . . . . . . . . . . . 23174, 23195
  - Sequestrectomy . . . . . . . . . . . . . . . 24134
  - Tumor . . . . . . . . . . . . 23150, 23155-23156,
    24110, 24115-24116
- Hydrocele
  - Spermatic Cord . . . . . . . . . . . . . . . 55500
  - Tunica Vaginalis . . . . . . . . . . 55040-55041
- Hygroma, Cystic . . . . . . . . . . . . 38550-38555
- Hymenal Ring . . . . . . . . . . . . . . . . . . 56700
- Ileum
  - Cyst . . . . . . . . . . . . . . . . . 27065-27067
  - Ileoanal Reservoir . . . . . . . . . . . . . . 45136
  - Partial . . . . . . . . . . . . . . . . 27070-27071
- Ilium
  - Tumor . . . . . . . . . 27065-27067, 27075, 27076
- Innominate
  - Tumor . . . . . . . . . . . . . . . . . . . . . 27077
- Interphalangeal Joint
  - Toe, Proximal End . . . . . . . . . . . . . . 28160
- Intervertebral Disc
  - *See* Discectomy
  - *See* Hemilaminectomy
- Intestines
  - *See* Enterectomy
  - Lesion . . . . . . . . . . . . . . . . 44110-44111
- Iris
  - *See* Iridectomy
- Ischium
  - Tumor . . . . . . . . . . . . 27075-27076, 27078
- Kidney
  - *See* Nephrectomy
  - Cyst . . . . . . . . . . . . . . . . . 50280, 50290

- Knee
  - Cyst . . . . . . . . . . . . . . . . . . . . . . 27345
  - Tumor . . . . . . . . 27327-27328, 27337-27339
  - Kneecap . . . . . . . . . . . . . . . . . . . . 27350
  - Lesion, Meniscus or Capsule . . . . . . . . 27347
- Labyrinth
  - Transcanal . . . . . . . . . . . . . . . . . . 69905
  - with Mastoidectomy . . . . . . . . . . . . . 69910
- Lacrimal Gland
  - *See* Dacryoadenectomy
  - Tumor . . . . . . . . . . . . . . . . 68540, 68550
- Larynx
  - *See* Laryngectomy
  - Tumor . . . . . . . . . . . 31300, 31540-31541
  - with Pharynx
    - *See* Pharyngolaryngectomy
- Leg, Lower
  - Tumor . . . . . . . . 27615-27616, 27618, 27619,
    27632, 27634, 27645, 27646
- Leg, Upper
  - Tumor . . . . . 27327-27329, 27337-27339, 27365
- Lesion
  - Anal . . . . . . . . . . . . . . . 45108, 46922
  - Ankle Tendon Sheath . . . . . . . . . . . . 27630
  - Auditory Canal, External . . . . . . . . . . 69145,
    69150, 69155
    - Exostosis . . . . . . . . . . . . . . . . . . 69140
  - Brain . . . . . . . . 61600-61608, 61615-61616
  - Brainstem . . . . . . . . . . . . . . 61575-61576
  - Breast . . . . . . . . . . . . . . 19120, 19125-19126
  - Colon . . . . . . . . . . . . . . . . 44110-44111
  - Conjunctiva . . . . . . . . . . . . . 68110-68130
  - Cornea . . . . . . . . . . . . . . . . . . . . 65400
  - Ear, Middle . . . . . . . . . . . . . . . . . . 69540
  - Epididymis . . . . . . . . . . . . . . . . . . 54830
  - Esophagus . . . . . . . . . . . . . . 43100-43101
  - Eyelid . . . . 67840, 67800-67801, 67805, 67808
  - Finger Tendon Sheath . . . . . . . . . . . . 26160
  - Foot . . . . . . . . . . . . . . . . 28080, 28090
  - Forearm Tendon Sheath . . . . . . . . . . . 25110
  - Gums . . . . . . . . . . . . . . . . 41825-41827
  - Hand . . . . . . . . . . . . . . . . . . . . . 26160
  - Intestines . . . . . . . . . . . . . . 44110-44111
  - Intraspinal . . . . . . . . . . . . . 63300-63308
    - *See* Laminectomy
  - Knee Meniscus or Capsule . . . . . . . . . . 27347
  - Leg Tendon/Sheath . . . . . . . . . . . . . 27630
  - Mesentery . . . . . . . . . . . . . . . . . . 44820
  - Mouth . . . . . . . . . . 40810-40816, 41116
  - Nerve . . . . . . . . . . . . . . . 64774-64792
  - Neuroma . . . . . . . 28080, 64774, 64776, 64778
  - Nose
    - Intranasal . . . . . . . . . . . . . . 30117-30118
  - Orbit . . . . . . . . . . . 61333, 67412, 67420
  - Palate . . . . . . . . . . . . 42104, 42106-42107
  - Pancreas . . . . . . . . . . . . . . . . . . . 48120
  - Penis . . . . . . . . . . . . . . . . . . . . . 54060
  - Pharynx . . . . . . . . . . . . . . . . . . . . 42808
  - Rectum . . . . . . . . . . . . . . . . . . . . 45108
  - Sclera . . . . . . . . . . . . . . . . . . . . . 66130
  - Skin
    - Benign . . 11400-11404, 11406, 11420-11424,
      11426, 11440-11444, 11446, 11450-11451,
      11462-11464, 11470-11471
    - Malignant . . 11600-11604, 11606, 11620-
      11624, 11626, 11640-11644, 11646
  - Skull . . . . . . . . . . . . 61500, 61615-61616
    - Anterior . . . . . . . . . . . . . . . 61600-61601
    - Base . . . . . . . . . . . . . . . . 61575-61576
    - Middle . . . . . . . . . . . . . . . 61605-61608
    - Posterior . . . . . . . . . . . . . . 61615-61616
  - Spermatic Cord . . . . . . . . . . . . . . . 55520

## Exclusion

## Exenteration

## Exercise Stress Tests

## Exercise Test

## Exercise Therapy

## Exfoliation

## Exocrine, Pancreas

## Exomphalos

## Exostectomy

## Exostosis

## Expander, Skin, Inflatable

## Expired Gas Analysis

## Exploration

**Index**

**Eye Evisceration**
*See* Evisceration, Ocular Contents

**Eye Exam**
Established Patient . . . . . . . . . . . . . . 92012-92014
New Patient . . . . . . . . . . . . . . . . . . . 92002-92004
Radiologic . . . . . . . . . . . . . . . . . . . . . . . . . 70030
with Anesthesia . . . . . . . . . . . . . . . . . 92018-92019

**Eye Exercises**
Training . . . . . . . . . . . . . . . . . . . . . . . . . . . . 92065

**Eye Muscles**
Attached to Implant . . . . . . . . 65105, 65140, 65155
Biopsy . . . . . . . . . . . . . . . . . . . . . . . . . . . . . 67346
Chemodenervation . . . . . . . . . . . . . . . . . . . . 67345
Flap Graft . . . . . . . . . . . . . . . . . . . . . . . . . . . 65114
Repair
  Strabismus
    *See* Strabismus
  Wound . . . . . . . . . . . . . . . . . . . . . . . . 65290
Transposition . . . . . . . . . . . . . . . . . . . . . . . . 67320
Unlisted Services and Procedures . . . . . . . . 67399

**Eye Prosthesis**
*See* Prosthesis

**Eye Socket**
*See* Orbit; Orbital Contents; Orbital Floor;
Periorbital Region

**Eyebrow**
Repair
  Ptosis . . . . . . . . . . . . . . . . . . . . . . . . . . 67900
Osteoplastic Flap Incision . . . . 31080, 31084, 31086

**Eyeglasses**
*See* Spectacle Services

**Eyelashes**
Trichiasis Correction
  Epilation
    by Forceps Only . . . . . . . . . . . . . . . . 67820
    by Other than Forceps . . . . . . . . . . . . 67825
    Incision of Lid Margin . . . . . . . . 67830, 67835
    for Biopsy . . . . . . . . . . . . . . . . . . . . . 67810

**Eyelid**
Abscess
  Incision and Drainage . . . . . . . . . . . . . . 67700
Biopsy
  Incisional . . . . . . . . . . . . . . . . . . . . . . . 67810
Blepharoplasty . . . . . . . . . . . 15820-15823, 67914
Chalazion
  Excision
    Multiple . . . . . . . . . . . . . . . . . 67801, 67805
    Single . . . . . . . . . . . . . . . . . . . . . . . 67800
    with Anesthesia . . . . . . . . . . . . . . . . 67808
Closure by Suture . . . . . . . . . . . . . . . . . . . 67875
Evacuation
  Meibomian Glands . . . . . . . . . . . . . . . . 0207T
Incision
  Canthus . . . . . . . . . . . . . . . . . . . . . . . . 67715
  Severing of Tarsorrhaphy . . . . . . . . . . . 67710
Injection
  Subconjunctival . . . . . . . . . . . . . . . . . . 68200
Lesion
  Destruction . . . . . . . . . . . . . . . . . . . . . . 67850
  Excision . . . . . . . . . . . . . . . . . . . . . . . . 67840
    Skin, Benign . . . . . . . . 11410-11444, 11446
    Skin, Malignant . . . . . . 11640-11644, 11646,
                   17280-17284, 17286
  Shaving
    Dermal/Epidermal . . . . . . . . . 11310-11313
Meibomian Glands
  Evacuation . . . . . . . . . . . . . . . . . . . . . . 0207T

Reconstruction
  Canthus . . . . . . . . . . . . . . . . . . . . . . . . 67950
  Superficial
    Adjacent Tissue Transfer . . . . . 14060-14061
  Total . . . . . . . . . . . . . . . . . . . . . . 67973-67975
  Total Eyelid
    Lower . . . . . . . . . . . . . . . . . . . 67973-67975
    Second Stage . . . . . . . . . . . . . . . . . . 67975
    Upper . . . . . . . . . . . . . . . . . . . . . . . . 67974
  Transfer of Tarsoconjunctival Flap
  from Opposing Eyelid . . . . . . . . . . . . . . 67971
Removal
  Foreign Body . . . . . . . . . . . . . . . . . . . . 67938
Repair . . . . . . . . . . . . . . . . . . . . . . 21280-21282
  Blepharoptosis
    *See* Blepharoptosis
  Ectropion
    Blepharoplasty . . . . . . . 15820-15823, 67914
    Suture . . . . . . . . . . . . . . . . . . . . . . . 67914
  Entropion
    Excision Tarsal Wedge . . . . . . . . . . . . 67923
    Extensive . . . . . . . . . . . . . . . . . . . . . 67924
    Suture . . . . . . . . . . . . . . . . . . . . . . . 67921
    Thermocauterization . . . . . . . . . . . . . 67922
  Excisional . . . . . . . . . . . . . . . . . . . . . . . 67961
    over One-Fourth of Lid Margin . . . . . . . 67966
  Lagophthalmos . . . . . . . . . . . . . . . . . . . 67912
  Lashes
    Epilation, by Forceps Only . . . . . . . . . 67820
    Epilation, by Other than Forceps . . . . . 67825
    Lid Margin . . . . . . . . . . . . . . 67830, 67835
  Lid Retraction . . . . . . . . . . . . . . . . . . . . 67911
  Overcorrection of Ptosis . . . . . . . . . . . . 67909
  Skin
    Complex . . . . . . . . . . . . . . . . 13151-13153
    Intermediate . . . . . . . . . . . . . 12051-12057
  Wound
    Full Thickness . . . . . . . . . . . . . . . . . . 67935
    Partial Thickness . . . . . . . . . . . . . . . . 67930
    Superficial . . . . . . . . . 12011, 12013-12018
Repair with Graft
  Retraction . . . . . . . . . . . . . . . . . . . . . . . 67911
Skin Graft
  Delayed/Sectioned Flap . . . . . . . . . . . . . 15630
  Dermal Autograft . . . . . . . . . . . . 15135-15136
  Epidermal Autograft . . . . . . . . . . 15115-15116
  Full-Thickness . . . . . . . . 15260-15261, 67961
  Pedicle . . . . . . . . . . . . . . . . . . . . . . . . 15576
  Skin Substitute . . . . . . . . . . . . . 15275-15278
  Split-Thickness . . . . . . . . 15120-15121, 67961
  Superficial
    Recipient Site Preparation . . . . 15004-15005
  Tissue-cultured Autograft . . . . . . 15155-15157
Suture
  for Intermarginal Adhesions . . . . . . . . . 67880
  with Transposition of Tarsal Plate . . . . . . 67882
  for Temporary Closure of Eyelids . . . . . . 67875
Tissue Transfer, Adjacent . . . . . . . . . . . . . 67961
Unlisted Services and Procedures . . . . . . . . 67999

**Eyelid Ptoses**
*See* Blepharoptosis

# F

**Face**
CT Scan . . . . . . . . . . . . . . . . . . . . . 70486-70488
Lesion
  Destruction . . . . . . . 17000-17004, 17280-17286

Magnetic Resonance Imaging
(MRI) . . . . . . . . . . . . . . . . . . . . . 70540-70543
Tumor Resection . . . . . . . . . . . . . . . 21011-21016

**Face Lift** . . . . . . . . . . . 15824-15826, 15828

**Facial Asymmetries**
*See* Hemifacial Microsomia

**Facial Bone**
*See* Mandible; Maxilla
Tumor
  Excision . . . . . . . . . . . . . . . . . . . . . . . 21034

**Facial Bones**
Abscess
  Excision . . . . . . . . . . . . . . . . . . . . . . . 21026
Excision . . . . . . . . . . . . . . . . . . . . . . . . . 21026
Reconstruction
  Augmentation . . . . . . . . . . . . . . . . . . . 21208
  Reduction . . . . . . . . . . . . . . . . . . . . . . 21209
  Secondary . . . . . . . . . . . . . . . . . . . . . 21275
Repair . . . . . . . . . . . . . . . . . . . . . 21208-21209
Tumor
  Contouring . . . . . . . . . . . . . . . . . . . . . 21029
  Excision . . . . . . . . . . . . . . . . . . 21029-21030
X-ray . . . . . . . . . . . . . . . . . . . . . 70140-70150

**Facial Nerve**
Anastomosis
  to Hypoglossal . . . . . . . . . . . . . . . . . . 64868
  to Phrenic Nerve . . . . . . . . . . . . . . . . . 64870
  to Spinal Accessory . . . . . . . . . . . . . . . 64866
Avulsion . . . . . . . . . . . . . . . . . . . . . . . . . 64742
Chemodenervation, Muscles . . . . . . . . . . . 64615
Decompression . . . . . . . . . . . . . . 61590, 61596
  Intratemporal
    Lateral to Geniculate
    Ganglion . . . . . . . . . . . . 69720, 69740
    Medial to Geniculate
    Ganglion . . . . . . . . . . . . 69725, 69745
  Total . . . . . . . . . . . . . . . . . . . . . . . . . 69955
Function Study . . . . . . . . . . . . . . . . . . . . 92516
Incision . . . . . . . . . . . . . . . . . . . . . . . . . 64742
Injection
  Anesthetic . . . . . . . . . . . . . . . . . . . . . 64402
Mobilization . . . . . . . . . . . . 61590, 61595-61596
Repair
  Lateral to Geniculate Ganglion . . . . . . . 69740
  Medial to Geniculate Ganglion . . . . . . . 69745
Repair/Suture
  with or without Graft . . . . . . . . . 64864-64865
Suture
  Lateral to Geniculate Ganglion . . . . . . . 69740
  Medial to Geniculate Ganglion . . . . . . . 69745
Transection . . . . . . . . . . . . . . . . . . . . . . 64742

**Facial Nerve Paralysis**
Graft . . . . . . . . . . . . . . . . 15840-15842, 15845
Repair . . . . . . . . . . . . . . . 15840-15842, 15845

**Facial Prosthesis**
Impression . . . . . . . . . . . . . . . . . . . . . . . 21088

**Facial Rhytidectomy**
*See* Face Lift

**Factor, ACTH-Releasing**
*See* Corticotropic Releasing Hormone (CRH)

**Factor, Antinuclear**
*See* Antinuclear Antibodies (ANA)

**Factor, Blood Coagulation**
*See* Clotting Factor

**Index**

Index

## Gene Product
*See* Protein

## Genioplasty

## Genitourinary Sphincter, Artificial
*See* Prosthesis, Urethral Sphincter

## Genotype Analysis

## Gentamicin

**Gentamycin Level**
See Gentamicin

**Gentiobiase**
See Beta Glucosidase

**Genus: Human Cytomegalovirus Group**
See Cytomegalovirus

**GERD**
See Gastroesophageal Reflux Test

**German Measles**
See Rubella

**Gestational Trophoblastic Tumor**
See Hydatidiform Mole

**GGT**
See Gamma Glutamyl Transferase

**GI Tract**
See Gastrointestinal Tract

**Giardia**
Antigen Detection
    Enzyme Immunoassay . . . . . . . . . . . . . 87329
    Immunofluorescence . . . . . . . . . . . . . . 87269

**Giardia Lamblia**
Antibody . . . . . . . . . . . . . . . . . . . . . . . . . 86674

**Gibbons Stent**
Ureteral . . . . . . . . . . . . . . . . . . . . . . . . . . 52332

**GIF**
See Somatostatin

**GIFT**
See Gamete Intrafallopian Transfer

**Gill Operation**
Laminectomy . . . . . . . . . . . . . . . . . . . . . . 63012

**Gillies Approach**
Fracture
    Zygomatic Arch . . . . . . . . . . . . . . . . . 21356

**Gingiva**
See Gums

**Gingiva, Abscess**
Incision and Drainage . . . . . . . . . . . . . . . . 41800

**Gingivectomy**
Each Quadrant . . . . . . . . . . . . . . . . . . . . . 41820

**Gingivoplasty**
Each Quadrant . . . . . . . . . . . . . . . . . . . . . 41872

**Girdlestone Laminectomy**
See Laminectomy

**Girdlestone Procedure**
See Acetabulum, Reconstruction

**Gla Protein (Bone)**
See Osteocalcin

**Gland**
See Specific Gland

**Gland, Adrenal**
See Adrenal Gland

**Gland, Bartholin's**
See Bartholin's Gland

**Gland, Bulbourethral**
See Bulbourethral Gland

**Gland, Lacrimal**
See Lacrimal Gland

**Gland, Mammary**
See Breast

**Gland, Parathyroid**
See Parathyroid Gland

**Gland, Parotid**
See Parotid Gland

**Gland, Pituitary**
See Pituitary Gland

**Gland, Salivary**
See Salivary Glands

**Gland, Sublingual**
See Sublingual Gland

**Gland, Sweat**
See Sweat Glands

**Gland, Thymus**
See Thymus Gland

**Gland, Thyroid**
See Thyroid Gland

**Glasses**
See Spectacle Services

**Glaucoma**
Counseling . . . . . . . . . . . . . . . . . . . . . . 4174F
Cryotherapy . . . . . . . . . . . . . . . . . . . . . . . 66720
Cyclophotocoagulation . . . . . . . . . . . 66710-66711
Diathermy . . . . . . . . . . . . . . . . . . . . . . . 66700
Filtration Implant
    See Aqueous Shunt
Fistulization of Sclera . . . . . . . . . . . . 0123T, 66150
Iridectomy . . . . . . . . . . . . . . 66625, 66630, 66671
Plan of Care . . . . . . . . . . . . . . . . . . . . . . 0517F
Provocative Test . . . . . . . . . . . . . . . . . . . 92140

**Glaucoma Drainage Implant**
See Aqueous Shunt

**Glenn Procedure** . . . . . . . . . . 33766-33767

**Glenohumeral Joint**
Arthrodesis . . . . . . . . . . . . . . . . . 23800, 23802
Arthrotomy . . . . . . . . . . . . . . . . . . . . . . . 23040
    with Biopsy . . . . . . . . . . . . . . . . . . . 23100
    with Drainage . . . . . . . . . . . . . . . . . . 23040
    Foreign Body Removal . . . . . . . . . . . . 23040
    with Exploration . . . . . . . . . . . 23040, 23107
    with Synovectomy . . . . . . . . . . . . . . . 23105
Arthroplasty . . . . . . . . . . 23470, 23472-23474
Capsulorrhaphy . . . . . . . . . . . . . . 23465-23466
Exploration . . . . . . . . . . . . . . . . 23040, 23107
Removal
    Foreign or Loose Body . . . . . . . . 23040, 23107

**Glenoid Fossa**
Allograft . . . . . . . . . . . . . . . . . . 23473, 23474
Arthroplasty . . . . . . . . . . . . . . . . 23473, 23474
Reconstruction . . . . . . . . . . . . . . . . . . . . 21255

**GLN**
See Glutamine

**Globulin**
Antihuman
    Coombs Test
        Direct . . . . . . . . . . . . 86880, 86885-86886
        Indirect . . . . . . . . . . . . . . . . 86850, 86870

Immune
    Administration . . . . . . . . . . . . . . 96365-96368
    Product
        Botulinum Antitoxin . . . . . . . . . . . . . 90288
        Botulism . . . . . . . . . . . . . . . . . . . . . 90288
        Cytomegalovirus (CMV-IgIV) . . . . . . . 90291
        Diphtheria Antitoxin . . . . . . . . . . . . . 90296
        Gammaglobulin . . . . . . . . . . . 82784-82785
        Hepatitis B (HBIg) . . . . . . . . . . . . . . 90371
        Ig . . . . . . . . . . . . . . . . . . . . . . . . . . 90281
        IgIV . . . . . . . . . . . . . . . . . . . . . . . . 90283
        Rabies (RIg/Rig-HT)) . . . . . . . . 90375-90376
        Respiratory Syncytial Virus . . . . . . . . 90378
        Rho(D) (RhIg/RhIgIV) . . . . . . . . 90384-90386
        SCIg . . . . . . . . . . . . . . . . . . . . . . . . 90284
        Tetanus (TIg) . . . . . . . . . . . . . . . . . . 90389
        Unlisted . . . . . . . . . . . . . . . . . . . . . 90399
        Vaccinia . . . . . . . . . . . . . . . . . . . . . 90393
        Varicella-zoster . . . . . . . . . . . . . . . . 90396
Sex Hormone Binding . . . . . . . . . . . . . . . . 84270

**Globulin, Corticosteroid-Binding**
See Transcortin

**Globulin, Rh Immune**
See Immune Globulins, Rho(D)

**Globulin, Thyroxine-Binding**
See Thyroxine Binding Globulin

**Glomerular Procoagulant Activity**
See Thromboplastin

**Glomus Caroticum**
See Carotid Body

**Glossectomy**
Complete . . . . . . . . . . . . . . . . . . . 41140, 41145
Composite . . . . . . . . . . . . . . 41150, 41153, 41155
Partial . . . . . . . . . . . . . . . . . . . . . . . . . . 41135
    Half . . . . . . . . . . . . . . . . . . . . . . . . . 41130
    Less than Half . . . . . . . . . . . . . . . . . . 41120

**Glossopexy**
See Tongue, Fixation

**Glossorrhaphy**
See Suture, Tongue

**Glucagon**
Measurement . . . . . . . . . . . . . . . . . . . . . . 82943
Tolerance Panel . . . . . . . . . . . . . . 80422, 80424
Tolerance Test . . . . . . . . . . . . . . . . . . . . . 82946

**Glucose**
Blood Test . . . . . . . . . . . . 82947-82948, 82950
    Home Test . . . . . . . . . . . . . . . . . . . . . 82962
Body Fluid . . . . . . . . . . . . . . . . . . . . . . . 82945
Interstitial Fluid
    Continuous Monitoring . . . . . . 95250-95251
        Data Interpretation . . . . . . . . . . . . . . 99091
Panel
    Basic Metabolic . . . . . . . . . . . . 80047-80048
    Comprehensive Metabolic . . . . . . . . . . . 80053
    Glucagon Tolerance . . . . . . . . . . . 80422, 80424
    Growth Hormone Suppression . . . . . . . . 80430
    Insulin Tolerance . . . . . . . . . . . . 80434-80435
    Insulin-induced C-peptide Suppression . . 80432
    Renal Function . . . . . . . . . . . . . . . . . . 80069
Tolerance Test . . . . . . . . . . . . . . . 82951-82952
    Intravenous Push . . . . . . . . . . . . . . . . 96374
    with Tolbutamide . . . . . . . . . . . . . . . . 82953
Urinalysis . . . . . . . . . . . . . 81000-81003, 81005

**Glucose Phosphate Isomerase**
See Phosphohexose Isomerase

**Haygroves Procedure** . . . . . . . . . 27120

**HBcAb**
*See* Antibody, Hepatitis

**HBeAb**
*See* Antibody, Hepatitis

**HBeAg**
*See* Hepatitis Antigen, Be

**HBsAb**
*See* Antibody, Hepatitis

**HBsAg (Hepatitis B Surface Antigen)**
*See* Hepatitis Antigen, B Surface

**HCG**
*See* Chorionic Gonadotropin

**HCO3**
*See* Bicarbonate

**HCV Antibodies**
*See* Antibody, Hepatitis C

**HDL**
*See* Lipoprotein

**Head**
Excision
    Bone, Facial . . . . . . . . . . . . . . . 21025-21026
    Tumor, Soft Tissue . . . . . . . . . . . 21011-21016
Fracture and/or Dislocation
    *See* Fracture; Dislocation
Halo Appliance . . . . . . . . . . . . . . . . . . . . . . . 21100
Imaging
    Angiography . . . . . . . . . . . 70496, 70544-70546
    CT Scan . . . . . . . . 70450, 70460, 70470, 70496
    Magnetic Resonance Angiography
    (MRA) . . . . . . . . . . . . . . . . . . . . . 70544-70546
    Positron Emission Tomography
    (PET) . . . . . . . . . . . . . . . . . . . . 78811, 78814
    Ultrasound Exam . . . . . . . . . . . . . 76506, 76536
    X-ray . . . . . . . . . . . . . . . . . . . . . . . . . . . 70350
Prosthesis
    Custom Preparation
        *See* Impression, Maxillofacial
    Introduction or Removal
        *See* anatomical site
    Unlisted Maxillofacial Prosthetic
    Procedure . . . . . . . . . . . . . . . . . . . . . . . 21089
Lipectomy, Suction Assisted . . . . . . . . . . . . 15876
Nerve
    Graft . . . . . . . . . . . . . . . . . . . 64885, 64886
Other Procedures . . . . . . . . . . . . . . 21299, 21499
Repair/Revision and/or Reconstruction
    *See* Cranioplasty; Face; Mandible
Rhytidectomy
    *See* Rhytidectomy
Unlisted Services and Procedures . . . . . . . . 21499

**Head Rings, Stereotactic**
*See* Stereotactic Frame

**Headbrace**
*See* Halo

**Heaf Test**
*See* TB Test

**Health Behavior**
*See* Evaluation and Management, Health Behavior

**Health Risk Assessment Instrument**
*See* Preventive Medicine, Risk Assessment

**Hearing Aid**
Device
    Attenuation Measurements . . . . . . . . . . 92596
    Check . . . . . . . . . . . . . . . . . . . 92592-92593
    Evaluation, Electroacoustic . . . . . 92594-92595
    Examination and Selection . . . . . 92590-92591
Implants
    Bone Conduction
        Implantation . . . . . . . . . . . . . . . . . . . 69710
        Removal . . . . . . . . . . . . . . . . . . . . . . 69711
        Repair . . . . . . . . . . . . . . . . . . . . . . . 69711
        Replacement . . . . . . . . . . . . . . . . . . . 69710
    Brainstem
        Implantation . . . . . . . . . . . 61863, 61867
        Programming . . . . . . . . . . . . . . . . . . 92640
    Cochlear
        Implantation . . . . . . . . . . . . . . . . . . . 69930
        Programming . . . . . . . . . . . 92601-92604
        Rehabilitation . . . . . . . . . . . 92626-92627
    Osseointegrated
        Implantation . . . . . . . . . . . 69714-69715
        Replacement . . . . . . . . . . . . 69717-69718

**Hearing Aid Check** . . . . . . . 92592-92593

**Hearing Aid Services**
Attenuation Measurements
    Ear Protector . . . . . . . . . . . . . . . . . . . 92596
Electroacoustic Test . . . . . . . . . . . . . 92594-92595
Examination . . . . . . . . . . . . . . . . . 92590-92591

**Hearing Tests**
*See* Audiologic Function Tests

**Hearing Therapy**
Evaluation . . . . . . . . . . . . . . . . . . . . 92626-92627
for Hearing Loss
    Postlingual . . . . . . . . . . . . . . . . . . . . . . 92633
    Prelingual . . . . . . . . . . . . . . . . . . . . . . 92630
Individual . . . . . . . . . . . . . . . . . . . . . . . . . 92507
Group . . . . . . . . . . . . . . . . . . . . . . . . . . . 92508
Cochlear Implant
    Analysis and Programming . . . . . 92601-92604
    Rehabilitation . . . . . . . . . . . . . . 92626-92627

**Heart**
Ablation
    Arrhythmogenic Focus . . . 33250-33251, 33261
    Atrial Tissue . . . . . . . . . . . . . . . 33254-33259
        Endoscopic . . . . . . . . . . . . . . 33265-33266
Anomaly
    Repair . . . . . . . . . . . . . . . . . . . . 33615, 33617
Aorta
    *See* Aorta
Arrhythmia
    *See* Tachycardia
Artificial Heart
    Implantation . . . . . . . . . . . . . . . . . . . . 0051T
    Repair . . . . . . . . . . . . . . . . . . . 0052T, 0053T
Atria
    *See* Atria
Balloon Device
    Insertion . . . . . . . . . . . . . . . . . . . . . . . 33973
    Removal . . . . . . . . . . . . . . . . . . . . . . . 33974
Biopsy . . . . . . . . . . . . . . . . . . . . . . . . . . . 93505
    Ultrasonic Guidance . . . . . . . . . . . . . . . 76932
Blood Vessel
    Repair . . . . . . . . . . . . . . . . . . . 33320-33322
Cardiac Output Measurements . . . . . . . . . . 93451,
                            93561-93562
Cardiac Rehabilitation . . . . . . . . . . . 93797-93798
Cardioassist
    Circulation . . . . . . . . . . . . . . . . 92970-92971
Cardiopulmonary Bypass
    with Aortic Aneurysm Repair . . . . . . . . . 33877

with Ascending Aorta Graft . . . . . . . . . 33860,
                          33863-33864
with Atrial Septectomy/Septostomy . . . . 33736
with Chamber Fistula Repair . . . . . . . . . 33500
with Descending Thoracic Aorta Graft . . 33875
with Lung Transplant . . . . . . . . . 32852, 32854
with Operative Ablation . . . . . . 33251, 33256,
                          33259, 33261
with Pericardiectomy . . . . . . . . . . . . . . 33031
with Pulmonary Artery Repair . . 33910, 33916,
                          33922, 33926
with Replacement of Ventricular
    Assist Device . . . . . . . . . . . . . . . . . . . 33983
with Septal Defect Repair
    *See* Septal Defect
with Sinus of Valsalva Repair . . . 33720, 33702
with Transcatheter Aortic Valve
    Replacement (TAVR/TAVI) . . . . . 33367-33369
with Transverse Arch Graft . . . . . . . . . . 33870
with Tumor Excision/Resection . . . . . . . 33120
with Valve Repair
    *See* Aortic Valve; Mitral Valve; Tricuspid
    Valve; Pulmonary Valve
with Wound Repair . . . . . . . . . . . . . . . . 33305
Cardioversion . . . . . . . . . . . . . . . . 92960-92961
Catheterization
    *See* Cardiac Catheterization
Cardiac Event Recorder
    Implantation . . . . . . . . . . . . . . . . . . . . 33282
    Removal . . . . . . . . . . . . . . . . . . . . . . . 33284
Cor Triatriatum
    Repair . . . . . . . . . . . . . . . . . . . . . . . . 33732
Cyst
    Pericardial
        Resection . . . . . . . . . . . . . . . . . . . . 33050
Diagnostic Imaging
    Acoustic Cardiography . . . . . . . . 0223T-0225T
    Angiography
        *See* Angiography, Heart
    Blood Pool . . . . . . . . . . . . . . . 78472-78473,
                78481, 78483, 78496
        SPECT . . . . . . . . . . . . . . . . . . . . . . 78494
    CT Scan . . . . . . . . . . . . . . . . . . 75571-75573
        Angiography . . . . . . . . . . . . . . . . . . 75574
    Magnetic Resonance
        *See* Cardiac Magnetic Resonance Imaging
    Myocardial Imaging
        Infarct Avid . . . . . . . . . 78466, 78468-78469
        Perfusion . . . . . . . . . . . . . . . . 78451-78454
        Perfusion Study . . . . . . . . . . . 78491-78492
        PET Metabolic Evaluation . . . . . . . . . 78459
        SPECT . . . . . . . . 0332T, 78451, 78452, 78469
        Sympathetic Innervation . . . . . 0331T, 0332T
        Shunt Detection . . . . . . . . . . . . . . . . 78428
    Unlisted Cardiovascular Diagnostic
    Nuclear Medicine Procedure . . . . . . . . . 78499
    Ventriculography
        *See* Ventriculography
Electrical Recording
    *See* Electrophysiology Procedure
Electrode
    Insertion . . . . . . . . 33202-33203, 33210-33211,
              33216-33217, 33224-33225
    Removal . . . . . . . . . . . . . . . . . . . . . . . 33238
        Single/Dual Chamber . . . . . . . 33243-33244
Electrophysiologic Study
    *See* Electrophysiology Procedure
Exploration . . . . . . . . . . . . . . . . . 33310-33315
Foreign Body Removal . . . . . . . . . . . . . . . 33310
Great Vessels
    *See* Great Vessels
Heart-Lung Bypass
    *See* Cardiopulmonary Bypass

Heart-Lung Transplantation
See Transplantation, Heart-Lung
Hemodynamic Monitoring
    Noninvasive . . . . . 93880-93883, 93922-93931,
                          93965-93990, 93998
    with Pharmacologic Agent . . . . . . . . . . . 93463
    with Physiologic Exercise Study . . . . . . . 93464
Infundibular Stenosis . . . . . . . . . . . . . 33476-33478
Injection
    Radiologic
        See Cardiac Catheterization, Injection
Intracardiac Ischemia Monitoring System
    Evaluation . . . . . . . . . . . . . . . . . .0305T-0306T
    Insertion
        Complete System . . . . . . . . . . . . . . . .0302T
        Device Only. . . . . . . . . . . . . . . . . . . .0304T
        Electrode Only . . . . . . . . . . . . . . . . .0303T
    Interrogation Device . . . . . . . . . . . . . .0306T
    Programming Device . . . . . . . . . . . . . .0305T
    Removal . . . . . . . . . . . . . . . . . . . . . .0307T
    Removal/Replacement
        Complete System . . . . . . . . . . . . . . . .0302T
        Device Only. . . . . . . . . . . . . . . . . . . .0304T
        Electrode Only . . . . . . . . . . . . . . . . .0303T
Intraoperative Pacing and Mapping . . . . . . . 93631
Ligation
    Fistula. . . . . . . . . . . . . . . . . . . . . . . .37607
Myocardium
    Imaging . . . . . . . . . . . . . . 78466-78469
        SPECT . . . . . . . 0332T, 78451, 78452, 78469
        Sympathetic Innervation . . . . .0331T-0332T
    Infarction
        Revascularization . . . . . 92941, 92943-92944
        Tissue Plasminogen Activator
        (tPA) Therapy . . . . . . . . . . . . . . . . .4077F
    Perfusion Study . . . . . . . . . . . . . 78451-78454
    Revascularization. . . . . . . . . . . . 33140-33141
Open Chest Massage . . . . . . . . . . . . . . . . .32160
Output
    See Cardiac Output
Pacemaker
    See Pacemaker, Heart
Pacing
    Arrhythmia Induction . . . . . . . . . . . . . . . 93618
    Atria . . . . . . . . . . . . . . . . . . . . . . . . . 93610
    Rate Increase
        See Tachycardia
    Transcutaneous
        Temporary. . . . . . . . . . . . . . . . . . . 92953
    Ventricular . . . . . . . . . . . 33224-33226, 93612
Pacing Cardioverter-Defibrillator System
    See Cardioverter-Defibrillator
Pericardium
    Drainage. . . . . . . . . . . . . . . . . . . . . .33025
    Pericardiectomy . . . . . . . . . . . . 33030, 33031
    Pericardiocentesis . . . . . . . . . . 33010-33011
    Tube Pericardiostomy. . . . . . . . . . . . . .33015
        for Removal of Clot. . . . . . . . . . . . .33020
        for Removal of Foreign Body . . . . . . .33020
    Wound . . . . . . . . . . . . . . . . . . . 33300-33305
Resuscitation . . . . . . . . . . . . . . . . . . . .92950
Septal Defect
    See Septal Defect
Sinus of Valsalva
    Repair. . . . . . . . . . . . . . . . . . 33702-33722
Sinus Venosus
    Repair. . . . . . . . . . . . . . . . . . . . . . .33645
Sounds
    See Heart Sounds
Tetralogy of Fallot
    Repair. . . . . . . . . . . . . 33692-33697, 33924
Thrombectomy
    See Thrombectomy

Total Replacement Heart System
    Intracorporeal. . . . . . . . . . . . . . . 0052T, 0053T
    Transplantation . . . . . . . . . . . . . 33935, 33945
        Allograft Preparation . . . . . . . . . 33933, 33944
        Harvest. . . . . . . . . . . . . . . . . . . . . 33940
Tumor
    Cardiac
        Excision. . . . . . . . . . . . . . . . 33120-33130
    Pericardial
        Resection . . . . . . . . . . . . . . . . . . .33050
Unlisted Services and Procedures . . . . . . . . 33999
Valve
    Aortic
        See Aortic Valve
    Bicuspid
        See Mitral Valve
    Mitral
        See Mitral Valve
    Pulmonary
        See Pulmonary Valve
    Tricuspid
        See Tricuspid Valve
Valve Closure
    Atrioventricular . . . . . . . . . . . . . . . . .33600
    Semilunar. . . . . . . . . . . . . . . . . . . . .33602
Vena Cava
    Reconstruction. . . . . . . . . . . . . . . . . .34502
Ventricle
    Commissurotomy
        Right Ventricle . . . . . . . . . . 33476-33478
    Obstruction Removal . . . . . . . . . . . . . .33619
    Pacing. . . . . . . . . . . . 33224-33226, 93612
    Repair. . . . . . . . . . . . . . 33548, 33611-33612
    Ventricular Tunnel Repair. . . . . . . . . . . .33722
    Ventriculomyectomy . . . . . . . . . . . . . . .33416
Ventricular Assist Device (VAD)
    See Ventricular Assist Device (VAD)
Wound
    Repair. . . . . . . . . . . . . . . . . . 33300-33305

## Heart Sounds
Acoustic Cardiography with
Automated Analysis . . . . . . . . . . . . . .0223T-0225T
Acoustic Recording
    with Computer Analysis. . . . . . . . . . . . 93799

## Heart Vessels
See Great Vessels
Angioplasty
    See Angioplasty; Percutaneous Transluminal
    Angioplasty

## Heat Unstable Haemoglobin
See Hemoglobin, Thermolabile

## Heavy Lipoproteins
See Lipoprotein

## Heavy Metal
Screen. . . . . . . . . . . . . . . . . . . . . . . .83015
Measurement . . . . . . . . . . . . . . . . . . . .83018

## Heel
Bone
    See Calcaneus
Dual-energy X-ray Absorptiometry. . . . . . . .77080
Fracture
    See Calcaneus, Fracture
Spur
    Excision . . . . . . . . . . . . . . . . . . . . . 28119
Stick, for Collection of Blood . . . . . . . . . . .36416
X-ray . . . . . . . . . . . . . . . . . . . . . . . . .73650

## Heel Bone
See Calcaneus

## Heel Fracture
See Calcaneus, Fracture

## Heel Spur
Excision. . . . . . . . . . . . . . . . . . . . . . . 28119

## Heine-Medin Disease
See Polio

## Heinz Bodies
Assessment. . . . . . . . . . . . . . . . . . 85441, 85445

## Helicobacter Pylori
Antibody . . . . . . . . . . . . . . . . . . . . . . 86677
Antigen Detection
    Enzyme Immunoassay . . . . . . . . 87338-87339
Blood Test . . . . . . . . . . . . . . . . . . . . . .83009
Breath Test
    Urea, Liquid Scintillation Counter
        Acquisition . . . . . . . . . . . . . . . . . .78267
        Analysis . . . . . . . . . . . . . . . . . . . .78268
        Urease Activity. . . . . . . . . . . . . . . . .83013
        Injection for Breath Test. . . . . . . . . . .83014
Stool . . . . . . . . . . . . . . . . . . . . . . . . .87338
Urease Activity . . . . . . . . . . . 83009, 83013-83014

## Heller Operation
See Heller Procedure

## Heller Procedure
Esophagomyotomy
    Open. . . . . . . . . . . . . . . . . . . 43330, 43331
    Laparoscopic . . . . . . . . . . . . . . . . . . 43279
    Thoracoscopic . . . . . . . . . . . . . . . . . .32665

## Helminth
Antibody . . . . . . . . . . . . . . . . . . . . . .86682

## Hemagglutination Inhibition Test
by Antibody. . . . . . . . . . . . . . . . . . . . .86280

## Hemangioma
See Lesion, Skin; Tumor

## Hemapheresis
See Apheresis

## Hematochezia
See Blood, Feces

## Hematologic Test
See Blood Tests

## Hematology
Unlisted Services and Procedures . . . . . . . . 85999

## Hematoma
Ankle
    Incision and Drainage . . . . . . . . . . . . . .27603
Arm, Lower
    Incision and Drainage . . . . . . . . . . . . . .25028
Arm, Upper
    Incision and Drainage . . . . . . . . . . . . . .23930
Brain
    Aspiration via Burr Hole. . . . . . . . . . . . .61156
    Drainage via Burr Hole. . . 61008, 61154-61156
    Evacuation via Burr Hole . . . . . . . 61108, 61154
    Evacuation via Craniotomy . . . . . . 61312-61315
Chest
    Incision and Drainage . . . . . . . . 21501, 61154
Ear, External
    Incision and Drainage . . . . . . . . 69000, 69005
Elbow
    Incision and Drainage . . . . . . . . . . . . . .23930
Endovascular
    See Endovascular Repair

Index

## Hernia, Cerebral
*See* Encephalocele

## Hernia, Rectovaginal
*See* Rectocele

## Hernia, Umbilical
*See* Omphalocele

## Heroin Screen

## Heroin, Alkaloid Screening

## Herpes Simplex

## Herpes Smear and Stain

## Herpes Virus-4 (Gamma), Human
*See* Epstein-Barr Virus

## Herpes Virus-6

## Herpetic Vesicle

## Heteroantibodies
*See* Antibody, Heterophile

## Heterophile Antibody

## Heterotropia
*See* Strabismus

## Hex B
*See* b-Hexosaminidase

## Hexadecadrol
*See* Dexamethasone

## Hexosephosphate Isomerase
*See* Phosphohexose Isomerase

## Heyman Procedure

## Hg Factor
*See* Glucagon

## HGB
*See* Hemoglobin, Concentration

## HGH
*See* Growth Hormone, Human

## HHV-4
*See* Epstein-Barr Virus

## HIAA
*See* Hydroxyindoleacetic Acid, Urine

## Hib Vaccine

## Hibb Operation

## Hidradenitis
*See* Sweat Gland

## High Altitude Simulation Test

## High Density Lipoprotein
*See* Lipoprotein

## High Molecular Weight Kininogen
*See* Fitzgerald Factor

## Highly Selective Vagotomy
*See* Vagotomy, Highly Selective

## Highmore Antrum
*See* Sinus/Sinuses, Maxillary

## Hill Procedure
*See* Gastroplasty with Esophagogastric Fundoplasty

## Hinton Positive
*See* RPR

## Hip
*See* Femur; Pelvis

## Hip Joint

## Hormones, Adrenal Cortex
*See* Corticosteroids

## Hormones, Antidiuretic
*See* Antidiuretic Hormone

## Hospital Discharge Services
*See* Discharge Services, Hospital

## Hospital Services
Inpatient Services............... 99238-99239
　Complex Chronic Care
　　Coordination............... 99487-99489
　Discharge Services  99238-99239, 1110F-1111F
　Initial Care
　　New or Established Patient ... 99221-99233
　Initial Hospital Care.......... 99221-99223
　Newborn ............ 99460-99462, 99477
　Prolonged Services ........... 99356-99357
　Subsequent Hospital Care...... 99231-99233
Observation
　Discharge Services ........... 99234-99236
　Initial Care ................. 99218-99223
Same Day Admission
　Discharge Services ........... 99234-99236
Subsequent Newborn Care.............. 99462
Post-discharge Transitional Care
Management Services ........... 99495-99496

## Hot Pack Treatment
Application ........................97010

## House Calls
Established Patient............... 99347-99350
New Patient ................... 99341-99345

## HPC
*See* Hematopoietic Progenitor Cells

## HPL
*See* Lactogen, Human Placental

## HTLV-I
Antibody
　Confirmatory Test...................86689
　Detection.......................86687

## HTLV-II
Antibody ........................86688

## HTLV-III
*See* HIV

## HTLV-III Antibodies
*See* Antibody, HIV

## HTLV-IV
*See* HIV-2

## Hubbard Tank Therapy
Each 15 minutes .......................97036

## Hue Test
Color Vision Exam.....................92283

## Huggin Operation
*See* Orchiectomy, Simple

## Huhner Test
Semen Analysis ................. 89300, 89320

## Human Chorionic Gonadotropin
*See* Chorionic Gonadotropin

## Human Chorionic Somatomammotropin
*See* Lactogen, Human Placental

## Human Cytomegalovirus Group
*See* Cytomegalovirus

## Human Epididymis Protein ..... 86305

## Human Growth Hormone (HGH)
Anterior Pituitary Evaluation Panel......... 80418
Antibody ..........................86277
Insulin Tolerance Panel..................80435
Measurement ........................83003
Stimulation Panel .....................80428
Suppression Panel .....................80430

## Human Herpes Virus 4
*See* Epstein-Barr Virus

## Human Immunodeficiency Virus
*See* HIV

## Human Immunodeficiency Virus 1
*See* HIV-1

## Human Immunodeficiency Virus 2
*See* HIV-2

## Human Leukocyte Antigen (HLA)
Antibody Analysis.................86828-86835
Crossmatch..................... 86825, 86826
Molecular Pathology........... 81370-81383
Tissue Typing....... 86812, 86813, 86816, 86817,
　　　　　　　　　　　　　　86821, 86822

## Human Papillomavirus
*See* Vaccine

## Human Papillomavirus Detection
　Amplified Probe....................87621
　Direct Probe......................87620
　Quantification ....................87622

## Human Placental Lactogen
*See* Lactogen, Human Placental

## Human T Cell Leukemia Virus I
*See* HTLV I

## Human T Cell Leukemia Virus I Antibodies
*See* Antibody, HTLV I

## Human T Cell Leukemia Virus II
*See* HTLV-II

## Human T Cell Leukemia Virus II Antibodies
*See* Antibody, HTLV-II

## Humeral Epicondylitises, Lateral
*See* Tennis Elbow

## Humeral Fracture
*See* Fracture, Humerus

## Humerus
*See* Arm, Upper; Shoulder
Abscess
　Incision and Drainage ............... 23935
Craterization....................23184, 24140
Cyst
　Excision ................... 23150, 24110
　　with Allograft.............. 23156, 24116
　　with Autograft ............. 23155, 24115
Diaphysectomy..................23184, 24140
Excision.................. 23174, 23184, 23195,
　　　　　　　　　　　　24134, 24140, 24150

Fracture
　Closed Treatment............. 24500-24505
　　with Manipulation ............... 23605
　　without Manipulation............. 23600
　Condyle
　　Closed Treatment ....... 24576-24577
　　Open Treatment ........... 24579
　　Percutaneous Fixation ............ 24582
　Epicondyle
　　Closed Treatment ....... 24560-24565
　　Open Treatment ........... 24575
　　Skeletal Fixation
　　　Percutaneous ............ 24566
　Greater Tuberosity Fracture
　　Closed Treatment with
　　　Manipulation ................. 23625
　　Closed Treatment without
　　　Manipulation ................. 23620
　　Open Treatment ............. 23630
　Open Treatment ............. 23615-23616
　Shaft........... 24500-24505, 24516
　　Open Treatment ............. 24515
　Supracondylar
　　Closed Treatment .......... 24530-24535
　　Open Treatment .......... 24545-24546
　　Percutaneous Fixation ............ 24538
　Transcondylar
　　Closed Treatment .......... 24530-24535
　　Open Treatment .......... 24545-24546
　　Percutaneous Fixation ............ 24538
　with Dislocation......... 23665-23670
Osteomyelitis ....................... 24134
Pinning, Wiring.................. 23491, 24498
Prophylactic Treatment............. 23491, 24498
Radical Resection................. 23220, 24150
　Radial Head or Neck ............ 24152
Repair ............................. 24430
　Nonunion, Malunion .......... 24430-24435
　Osteoplasty ..................... 24420
　Osteotomy ............. 24400-24410
　with Graft...................... 24435
Resection Head...................... 23195
Saucerization .................. 23184, 24140
Sequestrectomy ................. 23174, 24134
Tumor
　Excision .. 23150, 23220, 24071-24076, 24110
　　with Allograft............. 23156, 24116
　　with Autograft ............. 23155, 24115
X-ray............................... 73060

## Hummelshein Operation
*See* Strabismus, Repair

## Humor Shunt, Aqueous
*See* Aqueous Shunt

## HVA
*See* Homovanillic Acid

## Hybridization Probes, DNA
*See* Nucleic Acid Probe

## Hydatid Disease
*See* Echinococcosis

## Hydatid Mole
*See* Hydatidiform Mole

## Hydatidiform Mole
Evacuation and Curettage................59870
Excision.............................59100

## Hydration
Intravenous..................... 96360-96361
Rehydration Oral Solution........... 4056F
Status ......................2030F-2031F

Index

**Hysterosonography**
See Ultrasound; Sonohysterography

**Hysterotomy**
See Cesarean Delivery
Abdominal..................................59100
with Failed Abortion.............59852, 59857
with Tubal Ligation.....................58611

**Hysterotrachelectomy**
See Amputation, Cervix

# I

**I Antibodies, HTLV**
See Antibody, HTLV-I

**I, Angiotensin**
See Angiotensin I

**I, Coagulation Factor**
See Fibrinogen

**I, Heparin Co-Factor**
See Antithrombin III

**ICCE**
See Extraction, Lens, Intracapsular

**Ichthyosis, Sex Linked**
See Syphilis Test

**ICSH**
See Luteinizing Hormone (LH)

**Identification**
Antibody
    See Antibody Identification
Antigen
    See Antigen Detection
Axial Vessel
    for Island Pedicle...................15740
Crystal, Light Microscopy...............89060
Microbe
    See Infectious Agent; Bacteria Culture; Ova;
    Parasites
Oocyte
    from Follicular Fluid................89254
Sex Chromatin...................88130, 88140
Sperm
    Medicolegal.......................88125
    from Aspiration ....................89257
    from Tissue.......................89264
Urate Crystal.........................89060

**IDH**
See Isocitric Dehydrogenase, Blood

**IG**
See Immune Globulins

**IgA** ..................................82784

**IgD** ..................................82784

**IgE**.......................82785, 86003-86005

**IgG** ....................82784, 82787, 86001

**IgM**.................................82784

**II, Coagulation Factor**
See Prothrombin
See Gene Analysis

**II, Cranial Nerve**
See Optic Nerve

**Ileal Conduit**
Visualization .........................50690

**Ileoscopy**
via Stoma .............. 44380, 44382-44383

**Ileostomy**........................45136
Continent (Kock Procedure)..............44316
Ileoanal Reservoir.....................45136
Laparoscopic.................. 44186-44187
Non-Tube.................. 44310, 44187
Revision..................... 44312-44314

**Iliac Arteries**
See Artery, Iliac

**Iliac Crest**
Microvascular Anastomosis
    Bone Graft .......................20956
    Free Osteocutaneous Flap ...........20970

**Iliohypogastric Nerve**
Injection
    Anesthetic ........................64425

**Ilioinguinal Nerve**
Injection
    Anesthetic ........................64425

**Ilium**
Craterization ........................27070
Cyst
    Excision ................... 27065-27067
Excision..............................27070
Fracture
    Open Treatment ............ 27215, 27218
Saucerization ........................27070
Tumor
    Excision ........ 27065-27067, 27075, 27076

**Ilizarov Procedure**
Monticelli Type.......................20692
    See Application, Bone Fixation Device

**IM Injection**
See Injection, Intramuscular

**Imaging**
See Vascular Studies

**Imaging, Gamma Camera**
See Nuclear Medicine

**Imaging, Magnetic Resonance**
See Magnetic Resonance Imaging (MRI)

**Imaging, Ultrasonic**
See Echography

**Imbrication**
Diaphragm...........................39545

**Imidobenzyle**
See Imipramine

**Imipramine**
Assay.................................80174

**Immune Complex Assay** ........86332

**Immune Globulin Administration**
Intravenous Infusion . . .96365-96368, 96374-96375
Injection ............................96372

**Immune Globulin E**
See IgE

**Immune Globulins**
Antitoxin
    Botulinum.........................90287
    Diphtheria........................90296
Botulism.............................90288
Cytomegalovirus......................90291
Hepatitis B .........................90371
Human.................. 90281, 90283-90284
Rabies................... 90375-90376
Respiratory Syncytial Virus...........90378
Rho(D)................... 90384-90386
Tetanus..............................90389
Unlisted Immune Globulin .............90399
Vaccinia.............................90393
Varicella-Zoster.....................90396

**Immunization Administration**
Each Additional Vaccine/Toxoid ..... 90472, 90474
    with Counseling...................90461
One Vaccine/Toxoid ............90471, 90473
    with Counseling...................90460

**Immunization, Mumps**
See Mumps, Immunization

**Immunoassay**
Amniotic Fluid Protein.................84112
Analyte ................. 83516, 83518-83520
    Calprotectin, Fecal................83993
    Hemoglobin, Fecal.................82274
Cellular Function
    Detection of Biomarker ............86352
Infectious Agent
    See Infectious Agent
Other than Infectious Agent
Antibody/Antigen ......... 83516, 83518-83519
Tumor Antigen
    Qualitative/Semiquantitative ........86294
    Quantitative
        CA-125.......................86304
        CA 15-3......................86300
        CA 19-9......................86301
        Other Antigen................86316
        Human Epididymis Protein 4 (HE4) ..... 86305

**Immunoblotting, Western**
See Western Blot

**Immunochemical, Lysozyme (Muramidase)**
See Lysozyme

**Immunocytochemistry**
Antibody ..................... 88342, 88343

**Immunodeficiency Virus Type 1, Human**
See HIV 1

**Immunodeficiency Virus Type 2, Human**
See HIV 2

**Immunodeficiency Virus, Human**
See HIV

**Immunodiffusion**
Gel Diffusion
    Antibody or Antigen................86331

**Index**

Index

Index

## Injection

*See* Allergen Immunotherapy; Infusion
Abdomen
  Air............................................49400
  Contrast Material....................49400
Anesthetic Agent
  Sacroiliac Joint ......................27096
  Spine
    Cervical.......0228T-0229T, 62310, 62318
    Lumbar ........0230T-0231T, 62311, 62319
    Sacral .........0230T-0231T, 62311, 62319
    Thoracic ......0228T-0229T, 62310, 62318
Angiography
  Pulmonary ...........................75746
Ankle
  Radial...................................27648
Antibiotic
  *See* Antibiotic Administration
Antigen (Allergen)................95115-95125
Aorta (Aortography)
  Radiologic ...........................93567
Aponeurosis ..........................20550
Arthrography
  Sacroiliac Joint .....................27096
Bladder
  for Chemodenervation ..............52287
  Radiologic ....................51600-51610
Brain Canal ............................61070
Bursa ............................20600-20610
Cardiac Catheterization ..........93454-93464,
                                  93563-93568
Carpal Tunnel
  Therapeutic .........................20526
Chemotherapy....... 96401-96542, 96545, 96549
Cistern
  Medication or Other.................61055
Contrast................................49465
  via Catheter .............36598, 49424
Corpora Cavernosa ...................54235
Cyst
  Bone....................................20615
  Kidney .................................50390
  Pelvis .................................50390
  Thyroid.................................60300
Diagnostic
  Additional Sequential, Each Push ......96376
Elbow
  Arthrography
    Radiologic.........................24220
Epidural
  *See* Epidural, Injection
Esophageal Varices
  Endoscopy ..................43204, 43243
Esophagus
  Sclerosing Agent ....................43204
  Submucosal ..........43192, 43201, 43236
Extremity
  Pseudoaneurysm ....................36002
Eye
  Anterior Segment
    Air....................................66020
    Medication ........................66030
  Posterior Segment
    Intravitreal .........................67028
Eyelid
  Subconjunctival .....................68200
Foot
  Nerve...................................64455
Ganglion
  Anesthetic ..................64505, 64510
Ganglion Cyst ........................20612
Gastric Secretion Stimulant .............43755

Gastric Varices
  Endoscopy ...........................43243
Heart Vessels
  Cardiac Catheterization ........93454-93464,
                                  93563-93568
    *See* Catheterization, Cardiac
  Radiologic ...............93454-93461
Hemorrhoids
  Sclerosing Solution ................46500
Hip
  Radiologic ..................27093-27095
Insect Venom ...............95130-95134
Intervertebral Disc
  Chemonucleolysis Agent .............62292
  Radiological .................62290-62291
Intra-Amniotic..........................59852
Intra-Arterial.................96373, 96379
  Thrombolytic ..............37184-37186
Intradermal
  for Tattooing .............11920-11922
Intralesional
  Skin .....................11900-11901
Intramuscular ........................96372
  Therapeutic .............96372, 99506
Intravenous ...........................96379
  Nuclear Diagnostic Localization .......78808
  Thrombolytic ............37187-37188
  Unlisted ..............................96379
  Vascular Flow Check, Graft ..........15860
Intravenous Push....................96374-96376
Joint .............................20600-20610
Kidney
  Drugs .................................50391
  Radiologic ...........................50394
Knee
  Radiologic ...........................27370
Lacrimal Gland
  Radiologic ...........................68850
Left Heart
  Radiologic ...........................93565
Lesion
  Skin .....................11900-11901
Ligament................................20550
Liver.....................................47015
  Radiologic ..................47500-47505
Mammary Ductogram/Galactogram.......19030
Muscle Endplate
  Facial ..................................64612
Nerve
  Anesthetic .......01991-01992, 64400-64530
  Neurolytic Agent ..64600-64640, 64680-64681
Orbit
  Retrobulbar
    Alcohol ..............................67505
    Medication .........................67500
  Tenon's Capsule....................67515
Pancreatography......................48400
Paravertebral Facet Joint/Nerve
  with Image Guidance..........64490-64495
  with Ultrasound Guidance.......0213T-0218T
Penis
  for Erection.........................54235
  Peyronie Disease ...................54200
    with Surgical Exposure of Plaque ....54205
  Radiology............................54230
  Vasoactive Drugs...................54231
Peritoneal Cavity Air
  *See* Pneumoperitoneum
Platelet Rich Plasma....................0232T
Prophylactic
  Additional Sequential, Each Push ....96376
Radiologic
  Breast.................................19030

Rectum
  Sclerosing Solution .................45520
Right Heart
  *See* Cardiac Catheterization, Injection
  Radiologic ...........................93566
Sacroiliac Joint
  for Arthrography......................27096
Salivary Duct...........................42660
Salivary Gland
  Radiologic ...........................42550
Sclerosing Agent
  Esophagus ...........................43204
  Intravenous ................36470-36471
Sentinel Node
  Identification .............38792, 38900
Shoulder
  Arthrography
    Radiologic.........................23350
Shunt
  Peritoneal
    Venous .............................49427
Sinus Tract ...........................20500
  Diagnostic ...........................20501
Spider Veins
  Telangiectasia .............36468-36469
Spinal Artery...........................62294
Spinal Cord
  Anesthetic .................62310-62319
  Blood ..................................62273
  Neurolytic Agent .........62280-62282
  Other ..................62310-62319
  Radiological...........................62284
Steroids
  Spine
    Cervical.......0228T-0229T, 62310, 62318
    Lumbar ........0230T-0231T, 62311, 62319
    Sacral .........0230T-0231T, 62311, 62319
    Thoracic ......0228T-0229T, 62310, 62318
  Urethral Stricture....................52283
Subcutaneous..........................96372
  Silicone ...............11950-11954
  Therapeutic ..............96372, 90782
Temporomandibular Joint
  Arthrography ........................21116
Tendon Origin, Insertion ...............20551
Tendon Sheath ........................20550
Therapeutic
  Additional Sequential, Each Push ......96376
  Extremity Pseudoaneurysm ..........36002
  Lung ..................................32960
  Thyroid................................60300
  Turbinate ............................30200
Thoracic Cavity
  *See* Pleurodesis, Chemical
Trachea .................................31612
  Puncture..............................31612
Trigger Point(s)
  One or Two Muscles ................20552
  Three or More Muscles.............20553
Turbinate................................30200
Ureter
  Drugs .................................50391
  Radiologic ...........................50684
Venography............................36005
Ventricle
  Dye ...................................61120
  Medication or Other.................61026
Vitreous.................................67028
  Fluid Substitute .....................67025
Vocal Cords
  Therapeutic ..........31513, 31570-31571

## Integumentum Commune
*See* Integumentary System

## Intelligence Test

## Intensive Care

## Interbody

## Intercarpal Joint

## Intercostal Nerve

## Interdental Fixation

## Interdental Papilla
*See* Gums

## Interdental Wire Fixation

## Interferometry

## Intermediate Care Facilities (ICFs)
*See* Nursing Facility Services

## Intermittent Positive Pressure Breathing (IPPB)
*See* Continuous Negative Pressure Breathing (CNPB); Continuous Positive Airway Pressure (CPAP)

## Internal Breast Prostheses
*See* Breast, Implants

## Internal Ear
*See* Ear, Inner

## Internal Rigid Fixation

## International Normalized Ratio

## Internet E/M Service

## Interphalangeal Joint

## Interprofessional Telephone Assessment and Management

## Interruption

## Intersex State

## Intersex Surgery

Index

## Intestinovesical Fistula
*See* Fistula, Enterovesical

## Intima-Media Thickness (IMT) Study

## Intimectomy
*See* Endarterectomy

## Intra Arterial Injections
*See* Injection, Intra-Arterial

## Intra-Abdominal Voiding Pressure Studies

## Intra-Osseous Infusion
*See* Infusion, Intraosseous

## Intracapsular Extraction of Lens
*See* Extraction, Lens, Intracapsular

## Intracardiac Echocardiography
*See* Echocardiography, Cardiac

## Intracranial

## Intracranial Arterial Perfusion

## Intracranial Neoplasm, Acoustic Neuroma
*See* Brain, Tumor, Excision

## Intracranial Neoplasm, Craniopharyngioma
*See* Craniopharyngioma

## Intracranial Neoplasm, Meningioma
*See* Meningioma

## Intrafallopian Transfer, Gamete
*See* GIFT

## Intraluminal Angioplasty
*See* Angioplasty

## Intramuscular Injection
*See* Injection, Intramuscular

## Intraocular Lens

## Intratracheal Intubation
*See* Insertion, Endotracheal Tube

## Intrauterine Contraceptive Device
*See* Intrauterine Device (IUD)

## Intrauterine Device (IUD)

## Intrauterine Synechiae
*See* Adhesions, Intrauterine

## Intravascular Foreign Body Removal (Fractured Catheter) . . 37197

## Intravascular Sensor

## Intravascular Stent
Placement
    *See* Transcatheter, Placement, Intravascular Stents

## Intravascular Ultrasound

## Intravenous Infusion

## Intravenous Injection
*See* Injection, Intravenous

## Intravenous Pyelogram
*See* Urography, Intravenous

## Intravenous Therapy

## Intravesical Instillation
*See* Bladder, Instillation

## Intravitreal Injection

## Intrinsic Factor

## Introduction

## Intubation

## Intubation Tube
*See* Endotracheal Tube

## Intussusception

## Invagination, Intestinal
*See* Intussusception

## Inversion, Nipple
*See* Nipples, Inverted

## Iodide Test
*See* Nuclear Medicine, Thyroid, Uptake

## Ionization, Medical
*See* Iontophoresis

Index

## Iontophoreses
*See* Iontophoresis

## Iontophoresis
Application . . . . . . . . . . . . . . . . . . . . . . . . 97033
Sweat Collection. . . . . . . . . . . . . . . . . . . . . 89230

## Ipecac Administration
for Poisoning . . . . . . . . . . . . . . . . . . . . . . . . 99175

## IPPB
Intermittent Positive Pressure
Breathing Device. . . . . . . . . . . . . . . . . . . . . 94640

## Iridectomy
by Laser Surgery . . . . . . . . . . . . . . . . . . . . 66761
for Glaucoma. . . . . . . . . . . . . . 66625, 66630
Optical. . . . . . . . . . . . . . . . . . . . . . . . . . . . 66635
with Cataract Removal . . . . . . . . . . . . . . . 66830
with Corneoscleral or Corneal Section. . . . . 66600
with Sclerectomy . . . . . . . . . . . . . . . . . . . 66160
with Thermocauterization. . . . . . . . . . . . . 66155
with Cyclectomy . . . . . . . . . . . . . . . . . . . . 66605
with Trephination . . . . . . . . . . . . . . . . . . . 66150

## Iridencleisis
with Scleral Fistulization . . . . . . . . . . . . . . 66165

## Iridodialysis
Ciliary Body Repair . . . . . . . . . . . . . . . . . . . 66680

## Iridoplasty
Photocoagulation . . . . . . . . . . . . . . . . . . . 66762

## Iridotasis
with Scleral Fistulization . . . . . . . . . . . . . . 66165

## Iridotomy
by Laser Surgery . . . . . . . . . . . . . . . . . . . . 66761
by Stab Incision. . . . . . . . . . . . . . . . . . . . . 66500
    with Transfixion as for Iris Bombe . . . . . . 66505

## Iris
Cyst
    Destruction. . . . . . . . . . . . . . . . . . . . . . 66770
Excision
    Optical . . . . . . . . . . . . . . . . . . . . . . . . . 66635
    Peripheral. . . . . . . . . . . . . . . . . . . . . . . 66625
    Sector. . . . . . . . . . . . . . . . . . . . . . . . . . 66630
    with Cataract Removal . . . . . . . . . . . . . 66830
    with Corneoscleral or Corneal Section . . 66600
    with Cyclectomy. . . . . . . . . . . . . . . . . . 66605
    with Sclerectomy. . . . . . . . . . . . . . . . . 66160
    with Thermocauterization . . . . . . . . . . 66155
    with Trephination. . . . . . . . . . . . . . . . . 66150
Incision
    by Laser Surgery . . . . . . . . . . . . . . . . . 66761
    Stab . . . . . . . . . . . . . . . . . . . . . . . . . . . 66500
    with Transfixion as for Iris Bombe . . . . . 66505
Lesion
    Destruction. . . . . . . . . . . . . . . . . . . . . . 66770
Repair
    with Ciliary Body . . . . . . . . . . . . . . . . . 66680
    Suture. . . . . . . . . . . . . . . . . . . . . . . . . . 66682
Revision
    Laser Surgery . . . . . . . . . . . . . . . . . . . 66761
    Photocoagulation . . . . . . . . . . . . . . . . 66762
Suture
    with Ciliary Body . . . . . . . . . . . . . . . . . 66682

## Iron
Blood . . . . . . . . . . . . . . . . . . . . . . . . . . . . . 83540

## Iron Binding Capacity
Blood . . . . . . . . . . . . . . . . . . . . . . . . . . . . . 83550

## Iron Hematoxylin Stain
for Microorganisms. . . . . . . . . . . 87209, 88312

## Iron Stain
Blood. . . . . . . . . . . . . . . . . . . . . 85536, 88313

## Irradiation
Blood Products . . . . . . . . . . . . . . . . . . . . . . 86945

## Irrigation
Bladder . . . . . . . . . . . 51700, 52005, 52010, 53448
Bronchus . . . . . . . . . . . . . . . . . . . . . . . . . . 31624
Catheter
    Brain . . . . . . . . . . . . . . . . . . . 62194, 62225
Corpora Cavernosa
    for Priapism . . . . . . . . . . . . . . . . . . . . . 54220
Eye
    Anterior Chamber. . . . . . . . . . . . . . . . . 65815
    Lacrimal Punctum. . . . . . . . . . . . . . . . . 68801
    Nasolacrimal Duct . . . . . . . . . . . . . . . . 68810
    Lung . . . . . . . . . . . . . . . . . . . . . . . . . . 32997
Penis . . . . . . . . . . . . . . . . . . . . . 54411, 54417
    for Priapism . . . . . . . . . . . . . . . . . . . . . 54220
Peritoneal
    *See* Peritoneal Lavage
Shunt
    Cerebrospinal Fluid . . . . . . . . . . . . . . . 61070
    Spinal Cord. . . . . . . . . . . . . . . . . . . . . . 63744
Sinus
    Maxillary . . . . . . . . . . . . . . . . . . . . . . . 31000
    Sphenoid . . . . . . . . . . . . . . . . . . . . . . . 31002
Ureter
    Endoscopic . . . . . . . . . . . . . 50951, 50970
Vagina . . . . . . . . . . . . . . . . . . . . . . . . . . . . 57150
Venous Access Device . . . . . . . . . . . . . . . . 96523
Ventricular Catheter . . . . . . . . . . . . . . . . . . 62225
Wrist
    Arthroscopy . . . . . . . . . . . . . . . . . . . . . 29843

## Irving Sterilization
*See* Ligation, Fallopian Tube, Oviduct

## Ischemic Stroke
History of Onset . . . . . . . . . . . . . . 1065F-1066F
Tissue Plasminogen Activator (tPA)
Administration . . . . . . . . . . . . . . . . . . . . . . 4077F

## Ischium
Biopsy . . . . . . . . . . . . . . . . . . . . . . . . . . . . 20245
Bursa
    Excision . . . . . . . . . . . . . . . . . . . . . . . . 27060
Pressure Ulcer
    Excision . . . . . . . . . 15940-15941, 15944-15946
Tumor
    Radical Resection . . . . . . 27075-27076, 27078

## Ischiectomy
with Pressure Ulcer Excision . . . . . . . . . . . 15941

## Island Pedicle Flaps
Graft . . . . . . . . . . . . . . . . . . . . . . . . . . . . . 15740

## Islands of Langerhans
*See* Islet Cell

## Islet Cell
Antibody . . . . . . . . . . . . . . . . . . . . . . . . . . 86341

## Isocitrate Dehydrogenase
*See* Isocitric Dehydrogenase

## Isocitric Dehydrogenase
Blood. . . . . . . . . . . . . . . . . . . . . . . . . . . . . 83570

## Isolation
Sperm . . . . . . . . . . . . . . . . . . . . . 89260-89261
Virus

## Centrifuge Enhanced . . . . . . . . . . . . . . . . 87254
Inoculation . . . . . . . . . . . . . . . . . 87250, 87252
Non-immunologic Method. . . . . . . . . . . 87255
Tissue Culture . . . . . . . . . . . . . . . . . . . . 87253

## Isomerase, Glucose 6 Phosphate
*See* Phosphohexose Isomerase

## Isopropanol
*See* Isopropyl Alcohol

## Isopropyl Alcohol
Volatiles . . . . . . . . . . . . . . . . . . . . . . . . . . 84600

## Isthmusectomy
Thyroid Gland . . . . . . . 60210, 60212, 60220, 60225

## IUD
*See* Intrauterine Device (IUD)

## IV
*See* Injection, Chemotherapy; Intravenous Therapy

## IV Infusion Therapy
*See* Intravenous Infusion, Therapeutic

## IV Injection
*See* Injection, Intravenous

## IV, Coagulation Factor
*See* Calcium

## IVF
*See* Artificial Insemination; In Vitro Fertilization

## Ivy Bleeding Time
Bleeding Time . . . . . . . . . . . . . . . . . . . . . . 85002

## IX Complex, Factor
*See* Christmas Factor

# J

## Jaboulay Operation
*See* Gastroduodenostomy

## Jaboulay Operation
## Gastroduodenostomy
*See* Gastroduodenostomy

## Jannetta Procedure
*See* Decompression, Cranial Nerve; Section

## Japanese Encephalitis Virus
*See* Vaccine

## Japanese, River Fever
*See* Scrub Typhus

## Jatene Type Procedure . . . 33770-33781

## Jaw Joint
*See* Facial Bones; Mandible; Maxilla

## Jaws
Muscle Reduction . . . . . . . . . . . . . . 21295-21296
Orthopantogram X-ray
    for Orthodontics . . . . . . . . . . . . . . . . . . 70355

## Jejunostomy
Catheterization . . . . . . . . . . . . . . . . . . . . . 44015
Contrast. . . . . . . . . . . . . . . . . . . . . . . . . . 49465
Conversion
    from Gastrostomy Tube . . . . . . . . . . . . 44373

Endoscopic . . . . . . . . . . . . . . . . . . . . . . 44373
Percutaneous . . . . . . . . . . . . . . . . . . . . 49446
Insertion
Catheter . . . . . . . . . . . . . . . . . . . . . . . . 44015
Endoscopic . . . . . . . . . . . . . . . . . . . . . . 44372
Percutaneous . . . . . . . . . . . . . . . . . . . . 49441
Laparoscopic . . . . . . . . . . . . . . . . . . 44186-44187
Non-Tube . . . . . . . . . . . . . . . . . . . 44187, 44310
Obstructive Material Removal . . . . . . . . . . . 49460
Replacement . . . . . . . . . . . . . . . . . . . . . . 49451
with Pancreatic Drain . . . . . . . . . . . . . . . . 48001

### Jejunum
Creation
Stoma
*See* Jejunostomy
Endoscopy
Examination . . . . . . . . . . . . . . . . . . . . . 43242
Needle Aspiration . . . . . . . . . . . . . . . . . . 43242
Needle Biopsy . . . . . . . . . . . . . . . . . . . . 43242
Ultrasound . . . . . . . . . . . . . . . . . . . . . . 43259
Transfer
with Microvascular Anastomosis
Free . . . . . . . . . . . . . . . . . . . . . . . . . . 43496

### Johannsen Procedure
Urethroplasty . . . . . . . . . . . . . . . . . . . . . . 53400

### Joint
*See* Specific Joint
Acromioclavicular
*See* Acromioclavicular Joint
Arthrocentesis
Bursa . . . . . . . . . . . . . . . . . . . . . . . . . 20600
Intermediate Joint . . . . . . . . . . . . . . . . . 20605
Large Joint . . . . . . . . . . . . . . . . . . . . . . 20610
Small Joint . . . . . . . . . . . . . . . . . . . . . . 20600
Aspiration . . . . . . . . . . . . . . 20600, 20605, 20610
Dislocation
*See* Dislocation
Drainage . . . . . . . . . . . . . . . 20600, 20605, 20610
Exploration
Acromioclavicular . . . . . . . . . . . . . . . . . 23044
Ankle . . . . . . . . . . . . . . . . . . . 27610, 27620
Carpometacarpal . . . . . . . . . . . . . . . . . . 26070
Elbow . . . . . . . . . . . . . . . . . . . . . . . . . 24101
Finger . . . . . . . . . . . . . . . . . . . 26075-26080
Glenohumeral . . . . . . . . . . . . . 23040, 23107
Hand . . . . . . . . . . . . . . . . . . . . . . . . . 26070
Hip . . . . . . . . . . . . . . . . . . . . . . . . . . . 27033
Interphalangeal
Finger . . . . . . . . . . . . . . . . . . . . . . . 26080
Toe . . . . . . . . . . . . . . . . . . . . . . . . . 28024
Intertarsal . . . . . . . . . . . . . . . . . . . . . . 28020
Knee . . . . . . . . . . . . . . . . . . . 27310, 27331
Metacarpophalangeal . . . . . . . . . . . . . . . 26070
Metatarsophalangeal . . . . . . . . . . . . . . . 28022
Midcarpal . . . . . . . . . . . . . . . . . . . . . . 25040
Radiocarpal . . . . . . . . . . . . . . . . . . . . . 25040
Sternoclavicular . . . . . . . . . . . . . . . . . . 23044
Tarsometatarsal . . . . . . . . . . . . . . . . . . 28020
Wrist . . . . . . . . . . . . . . . . . . . . . . . . . 25101
Finger
*See* Finger, Joint
Fixation (Surgical)
*See* Arthrodesis
Foot
*See* Talotarsal Joint; Tarsal Joint;
Tarsometatarsal Joint
Hip
*See* Hip Joint
Injection . . . . . . 0213T-0218T, 20600, 20605, 20610
Intertarsal
*See* Intertarsal Joint

Knee
*See* Knee Joint
Ligament
*See* Ligament
Magnetic Resonance Imaging
Extremity, Lower . . . . . . . . . . . . . . . . . . 73721
Extremity, Upper . . . . . . . . . . . . . . . . . . 73221
Metacarpophalangeal
*See* Metacarpophalangeal Joint
Metatarsophalangeal
*See* Metatarsophalangeal Joint
Nuclear Medicine
Imaging . . . . . . . . 78300, 78305-78306, 78315
SPECT . . . . . . . . . . . . . . . . . . . . . . . . . 78320
Radiology
Stress Views . . . . . . . . . . . . . . . . . . . . 77071
Survey Views . . . . . . . . . . . . . . . . . . . . 77077
Replacement
Temporomandibular . . . . . . . . . . . . . . . . 21243
Vertebral . . 0202T. 20931, 20938, 22554, 22556,
22851, 63081, 63085, 63087, 63090
Sacroiliac
*See* Sacroiliac Joint
Shoulder
*See* Glenohumeral Joint
Sternoclavicular
*See* Sternoclavicular Joint
Survey . . . . . . . . . . . . . . . . . . . . . . . . . . 77077
Temporomandibular
*See* Temporomandibular Joint (TMJ)
Arthrography . . . . . . . . . . . . . . . . . . . . 70332
Magnetic Resonance Imaging . . . . . . . . 70336
Radiology . . . . . . . . . . . . . . . . . . . . . . 70328
Dislocation Temporomandibular
*See* Dislocation, Temporomandibular Joint
Implant
*See* Prosthesis, Temporomandibular Joint
Wrist
*See* Radiocarpal Joint

### Joint Syndrome, Temporomandibular
*See* Temporomandibular Joint (TMJ)

### Jones and Cantarow Test
*See* Blood Urea Nitrogen; Urea Nitrogen, Clearance

### Jones Procedure
Arthrodesis . . . . . . . . . . . . . . . . . . . . . . . 28760

### Joplin Procedure
Hallux Vagus Correction . . . . . . . . . . . . . . . 28294

### Jugal Bone
*See* Cheekbone

### Jugular Vein
*See* Vein, Jugular

# K

### K-Wire Fixation
Tongue . . . . . . . . . . . . . . . . . . . . . . . . . . 41500

### Kader Operation
*See* Incision, Stomach, Creation, Stoma; Incision
and Drainage

### Kala Azar Smear . . . . . . . . . . . . . . . 87207

### Kallidin I /Kallidin 9
*See* Bradykinin

### Kallikrein HK3
*See* Antigen, Prostate Specific

### Kallikreinogen
*See* Fletcher Factor

### Kasai Procedure . . . . . . . . . . . . . . . 47701

### Kedani Fever
*See* Scrub Typhus

### Keel
Insertion/Removal
Laryngoplasty . . . . . . . . . . . . . . . . . . . . 31580

### Kelikian Procedure . . . . . . . . . . . . . 28280

### Keller Procedure . . . . . . . . . . . . . . 28292

### Kelly Urethral Plication . . . . . . . . 57220

### Keratectomy
Partial
for Lesion . . . . . . . . . . . . . . . . . . . . . . . 65400

### Keratomileusis . . . . . . . . . . . . . . . . 65760

### Keratophakia . . . . . . . . . . . . . . . . . 65765

### Keratoplasty
Endothelial . . . . . . . . . . . . . . . . . . . . . . . 65756
Allograft Preparation . . . . . . . . . . . . . . . 65757
Lamellar
Anterior . . . . . . . . . . . . . . . . . . . . . . . 65710
Laser Preparation . . . . . . . . . . . . 0289T-0290T
Penetrating . . . . . . . . . . . . . . . . . . . . . . 65730
in Aphakia . . . . . . . . . . . . . . . . . . . . . 65750
Laser Preparation . . . . . . . . . . . . 0289T-0290T
in Pseudophakia . . . . . . . . . . . . . . . . . . 65755

### Keratoprosthesis . . . . . . . . . . . . . . 65770

### Keratotomy
Radial . . . . . . . . . . . . . . . . . . . . . . . . . . 65771

### Ketogenic Steroids . . . . . . . . . . . . 83582

### Ketone Body . . . . . . . . . . . . . 82009-82010

### Ketosteroids . . . . . . . . . . . . . 83586, 83593

### Kidner Procedure . . . . . . . . . . . . . 28238

### Kidney
Abscess
Incision and Drainage . . . . . . . . . . . . . . 50020
Open . . . . . . . . . . . . . . . . . . . . . . . . . 50020
Anesthesia . . . . . . . . . . . . . . . . . . . . . . . 00862
Biopsy . . . . . . . . . . . . . . . . . . 50200, 50205
Endoscopic . . . . . . . . . . 50555, 50557, 52354
Catheterization
Endoscopic . . . . . . . . . . . . . . . . . . . . . 50572
Cyst
Ablation . . . . . . . . . . . . . . . . . . . . . . . 50541
Aspiration . . . . . . . . . . . . . . . . . . . . . . 50390
Excision . . . . . . . . . . . . . . . . . 50280, 50290
Injection . . . . . . . . . . . . . . . . . . . . . . . 50390
X-ray . . . . . . . . . . . . . . . . . . . . . . . . . 74470
Destruction
Calculus . . . . . . . . . . . . . . . . . . . . . . . 50590
Endoscopic . . . . . . . . . . 50557, 50576, 52354
Dilation . . . . . . . . . . . . . . . . . . . . . . . . . 50395
Endoscopy
Biopsy . . . . . . . . . . 50555, 50574-50576, 52354
Catheterization . . . . . . . . . . . . . 50553, 50572
Destruction . . . . . . . . . . 50557, 50576, 52354

# L

Index

Unlisted Services and Procedures
　Abdomen, Peritoneum, and Omentum. . . 49329
　Appendix . . . . . . . . . . . . . . . . . . . . . . . 44979
　Biliary Tract . . . . . . . . . . . . . . . . . . . . . 47579
　Bladder. . . . . . . . . . . . . . . . . . . . . . . . . 51999
　Endocrine System . . . . . . . . . . . . . . . . 60659
　Esophagus . . . . . . . . . . . . . . . . . . . . . . 43289
　Hernioplasty, Herniorrhaphy,
　　Herniotomy. . . . . . . . . . . . . . . . . . . . 49659
　Intestine. . . . . . . . . . . . . . . . . . . . . . . . 44238
　Liver . . . . . . . . . . . . . . . . . . . . . . . . . . 47379
　Lymphatic System . . . . . . . . . . . . . . . . 38589
　Maternity Care and Delivery . . . . 59898-59899
　Oviduct, Ovary . . . . . . . . . . . . . . . . . . . 58679
　Rectum. . . . . . . . . . . . . . . . . . . . . . . . . 45499
　Renal . . . . . . . . . . . . . . . . . . . . . . . . . . 50549
　Spermatic Cord . . . . . . . . . . . . . . . . . . 55559
　Spleen . . . . . . . . . . . . . . . . . . . . . . . . . 38129
　Stomach. . . . . . . . . . . . . . . . . . . . . . . . 43659
　Testis . . . . . . . . . . . . . . . . . . . . . . . . . . 54699
　Ureter. . . . . . . . . . . . . . . . . . . . . . . . . . 50949
　Uterus. . . . . . . . . . . . . . . . . . . 58578-58579
Ureter
　Ureterectomy . . . . . . . . . . . . 50546, 50548
　Ureterolithotomy . . . . . . . . . . . . . . . . . 50945
　Ureteroneocystostomy. . . . . . . . 50947-50948
　Unlisted Procedure. . . . . . . . . . . . . . . . 50949
Urethra
　Incontinence Repair. . . . . . . . . . 51990, 51992
　Urethral Suspension . . . . . . . . . . . . . . . 51990
Uterus
　Biopsy. . . . . . . . . . . . . . . . . . . . . . . . . 57421
　　Endometrium . . . . . . . . . . . . . . . . . . 58558
　Hysteroscopy
　　Diagnostic. . . . . . . . . . . . . . . . . . . . . 58555
　　with Endometrial Ablation . . . . . . . . . 58563
　　with Endometrial Biopsy . . . . . . . . . . 58558
　　with Division/Resection
　　　Intrauterine Septum . . . . . . . . . . . . 58560
　　with Lysis of Intrauterine Adhesions . . 58559
　　with Polypectomy. . . . . . . . . . . . . . . 58558
　　with Removal
　　　Impacted Foreign Body . . . . . . . . . . 58562
　　　Leiomyomata. . . . . . . . . . . . . . . . . 58561
　　Unlisted Hysteroscopy Procedure . . . . 58578
　Hysterectomy. . . . . . . . . . . . . . 58541-58544
　　Radical . . . . . . . . . . . . . . . . . . . . . . 58548
　　Total . . . . . . . . . . . . . . . . . . . 58570-58573
　　Vaginal . . . . . . . . . . . . 58550, 58552-58554
　In Vitro Fertilization . . . . . . . . . . . . . . . 58976
　　Retrieve Oocyte . . . . . . . . . . . . . . . . 58970
　　Transfer Embryo . . . . . . . . . . . . . . . . 58974
　　Transfer Gamete. . . . . . . . . . . . . . . . 58976
　Myomectomy. . . . . . . . . . . . . . 58545-58546
　Placement
　　Fallopian Tube Cannulation . . . . . . . . 58565
　Unlisted Procedure. . . . . . . . . . . . . . . . 58579
Vagina
　Biopsy. . . . . . . . . . . . . . . . . . . . . . . . . 57421
　Colpopexy. . . . . . . . . . . . . . . . . . . . . . 57425
　Colposcopy. . . . . . . . . . . . . . . . . . . . . 57420
　Paravaginal Defect Repair. . . . . . . . . . . 57423
　Prosthetic Graft Revision. . . . . . . . . . . . 57426
　Vaginal Hysterectomy . . . . . . . . 58550-58554
　Vaginal Suspension . . . . . . . . . . . . . . . 57425

## Laparotomy
Abdominal
　Exploration. . . . . . . . . . . . . . . 49000, 49002
Esophagogastric
　Fundoplasty . . . . . . . . . . . . . . . 43327-43328
　Hiatal Hernia Repair . . . . . . . . . 43332-43333

Gastric
　Electrode
　　Implantation. . . . . . . . . . . . . . . . . . . 43881
　　Removal . . . . . . . . . . . . . . . . . . . . . 43882
　　Replacement. . . . . . . . . . . . . . . . . . . 43881
　　Revision . . . . . . . . . . . . . . . . . . . . . 43882
Intestinal
　Reduction
　　Internal Hernia . . . . . . . . . . . . . . . . . 44050
　　Intussusception . . . . . . . . . . . . . . . . 44050
　　Volvulus . . . . . . . . . . . . . . . . . . . . . 44050
Liver
　Aspiration/Injection
　　Parasitic Abscess. . . . . . . . . . . . . . . 47015
　　Parasitic Cyst . . . . . . . . . . . . . . . . . 47015
Staging
　Hodgkin's Disease . . . . . . . . . . . . . . . . 49220
　Lymphoma . . . . . . . . . . . . . . . . . . . . . 49220
　Ovarian Malignancy. . . . . . . . . . . . . . . 58960
　Peritoneal Malignancy. . . . . . . . . . . . . 58960
　Tubal Malignancy. . . . . . . . . . . . . . . . 58960
Stomach
　Biopsy. . . . . . . . . . . . . . . . . . . . . . . . . 43605

## Laparotomy, Exploratory
*See* Abdomen, Exploration

## Lapidus Procedure . . . . . . . . . . . . . 28297

## Large Bowel
*See* Anus; Rectum

## Laroyenne Operation
*See* Vagina, Abscess, Incision and Drainage

## Laryngeal Function Study . . . . . . 92520

## Laryngeal Sensory
**Testing** . . . . . . . . . . . . . . . . . . . . 92614-92617

## Laryngectomy . . . . . . . . . . . . 31360-31382
Partial . . . . . . . . . . . . . . . . . . . . . 31367-31382
Subtotal. . . . . . . . . . . . . . . . . . . . 31367-31368
Total . . . . . . . . . . . . . . . . . . . . . 31360, 31365

## Laryngocele
Removal . . . . . . . . . . . . . . . . . . . . . . . . 31300

## Laryngofissure . . . . . . . . . . . . . . . . . 31300

## Laryngography . . . . . . . . . . . . . . . . . 70373

## Laryngopharyngectomy
*See* Excision, Larynx, with Pharynx

## Laryngopharynx
*See* Hypopharynx

## Laryngoplasty
Burns. . . . . . . . . . . . . . . . . . . . . . . . . . 31588
Cricoid Split. . . . . . . . . . . . . . . . . . . . . 31587
Laryngeal Stenosis . . . . . . . . . . . . . . . . 31582
Laryngeal Web . . . . . . . . . . . . . . . . . . 31580
Unspecified. . . . . . . . . . . . . . . . . . . . . 31588
Open Reduction of Fracture . . . . . . . . . . 31584

## Laryngoscopy
Direct. . . . . . . . . . . . . . . . . . . . . 31515-31571
　Aspiration. . . . . . . . . . . . . . . . . . . . . . 31515
　Biopsy. . . . . . . . . . . . . . . . . . . 31535-31536
　Diagnostic . . . . . . . . . . . . . . . . 31525-31526
　Newborn . . . . . . . . . . . . . . . . . . . . . . 31520
　Dilation. . . . . . . . . . . . . . . . . . 31528-31529
　Exploration. . . . . . . . . . . 31520-31526, 31575
Fiberoptic . . . . . . . . . . . . . . . . . . 31575-31579
　Biopsy. . . . . . . . . . . . . . . . . . . . . . . . 31576
　Diagnostic . . . . . . . . . . . . . . . . . . . . . 31575

Removal
　Foreign Body. . . . . . . . . . . . . . . . . . . . 31577
　Lesion. . . . . . . . . . . . . . . . . . . . . . . . 31578
Injection
　Vocal Cord. . . . . . . . . . . . . . . . 31570-31571
Removal
　Foreign Body. . . . . . . . . . . . . . 31530-31531
　Lesion. . . . . . . . . . . . . . . . . . . 31545-31546
Operative . . . . . . . . . . . . . . . . . . 31530-31561
　Arytenoidectomy . . . . . . . . . . . 31560-31561
　Excision of Tumor . . . . . . . . . . 31540-31541
　Stripping of Vocal Cords. . . . . . 31540-31541
Indirect . . . . . . . . . . . . . . . . . . . 31505-31513
　Biopsy. . . . . . . . . . . . . . . . . . . . . . . . 31510
　Diagnostic . . . . . . . . . . . . . . . . . . . . . 31505
　Exploration. . . . . . . . . . . . . . . . . . . . 31505
　Injection
　　Vocal Cord. . . . . . . . . . . . . . . . . . . . 31513
　Insertion
　　Obturator . . . . . . . . . . . . . . . . . . . . 31527
　Removal
　　Foreign Body. . . . . . . . . . . . . . . . . . 31511
　　Lesion. . . . . . . . . . . . . . . . . . . . . . . 31512
Newborn . . . . . . . . . . . . . . . . . . . . . . . 31520
with Operating Microscope or Telescope. . . 31526,
　　　　　　　　　31531, 31536, 31541,
　　　　　　　31545-31546, 31561, 31571
with Stroboscopy . . . . . . . . . . . . . . . . . 31579

## Laryngotomy . . . . . . . . . . . . . . . . . 31300
Diagnostic. . . . . . . . . . . . . . . . . . . . . . 31320

## Larynx
Aspiration
　Endoscopy . . . . . . . . . . . . . . . . . . . . . 31515
Biopsy
　Endoscopy . . . . . . 31510, 31535-31536, 31576
Dilation
　Endoscopic . . . . . . . . . . . . . . . 31528-31529
Electromyography
　Needle . . . . . . . . . . . . . . . . . . . . . . . 95865
Endoscopy
　Direct . . . . . . . . . . . . . . . . . . . 31515-31571
　Excision . . . . . . . . . . . . . . . . . 31545-31546
　Exploration. . . . . . . 31505, 31520-31526, 31575
　Fiberoptic . . . . . . . . . . . . . . . . 31575-31579
　　with Stroboscopy . . . . . . . . . . . . . . . 31579
　Indirect . . . . . . . . . . . . . . . . . 31505-31513
　Operative . . . . . . . . . . . . . . . . 31530-31561
Excision
　Lesion. . . . . . . . . . . . . . . . . . . 31512, 31578
　　Endoscopic . . . . . . . . . . . . . . 31545-31546
　Partial. . . . . . . . . . . . . . . . . . . 31367-31382
　Total . . . . . . . . . . . . . . . . . . . . 31360-31365
　with Pharynx . . . . . . . . . . . . . . 31390-31395
Exploration
　Endoscopic . . . . . . 31505, 31520-31526, 31575
Fracture. . . . . . . . . . . . . . . . . . . . . . . . 31584
Insertion
　Obturator . . . . . . . . . . . . . . . . . . . . . 31527
Muscle
　Chemodenervation. . . . . . . . . . . . . . . 64617
Nerve
　Section. . . . . . . . . . . . . . . . . . . . . . . 31595
Reconstruction
　Burns . . . . . . . . . . . . . . . . . . . . . . . . 31588
　Cricoid Split . . . . . . . . . . . . . . . . . . . 31587
　Other . . . . . . . . . . . . . . . . . . . . . . . . 31588
　Stenosis. . . . . . . . . . . . . . . . . . . . . . 31582
　Web . . . . . . . . . . . . . . . . . . . . . . . . . 31580
Removal
　Foreign Body
　　Endoscopic . . . . 31511, 31530-31531, 31577

**Leu 2 Antigens**
*See* CD8

**Leucine Aminopeptidase** . . . . . . . 83670

**Leukemia Lymphoma Virus I Antibodies, Human T Cell**
*See* Antibody, HTLV-I

**Leukemia Lymphoma Virus I, Adult T Cell**
*See* HTLV I

**Leukemia Lymphoma Virus II Antibodies, Human T Cell**
*See* Antibody, HTLV-II

**Leukemia Virus II, Hairy Cell Associated, Human T Cell**
*See* HTLV II

**Leukoagglutinins** . . . . . . . . . . . . . . . 86021

**Leukocyte**
*See* White Blood Cell
Alkaline Phosphatase . . . . . . . . . . . . . . . . . 85540
Antibody . . . . . . . . . . . . . . . . . . . . . . . . . 86021
Count . . . . . . . . . . . . . . . 85032, 85048, 89055
Fecal Assessment . . . . . . . . . . . . . . . . . . . 89055
Histamine Release Test . . . . . . . . . . . . . . 86343
Human Leukocyte Antigen (HLA)
  *See* HLA
Phagocytosis . . . . . . . . . . . . . . . . . . . . . . 86344
Transfusion . . . . . . . . . . . . . . . . . . . . . . . 86950
Urinalysis . . . . . . . . . . . . . . . . . . . . . . . . 81000

**Levarterenol**
*See* Noradrenalin

**Levator Muscle Repair**
*See* Blepharoptosis, Repair

**LeVeen Shunt**
Insertion . . . . . . . . . . . . . . . . . . . . . . . . . 49425
Patency Test . . . . . . . . . . . . . . . . . . . . . . 78291
Revision . . . . . . . . . . . . . . . . . . . . . . . . . 49426

**Levetiracetam**
Drug Assay . . . . . . . . . . . . . . . . . . . . . . . 80177

**Levulose**
*See* Fructose

**LGV**
*See* Lymphogranuloma Venereum

**LH**
*See* Luteinizing Hormone (LH)

**LHR**
*See* Leukocyte Histamine Release Test

**Lid Suture**
*See* Blepharoptosis, Repair

**Lidocaine**
Assay . . . . . . . . . . . . . . . . . . . . . . . . . . . 80176

**Lift, Face**
*See* Face Lift

**Ligament**
*See* Specific Site
Ankle
  Collateral Ligament
    Repair . . . . . . . . . . . . 27695-27696, 27298
      Cruciate Ligament Repair . . . . . 29888-29889
Collateral
  Reconstruction
    Elbow . . . . . . . . . . 24344, 24346, 24362
    Interphalangeal Joint . . . . . . . . . . . 26545
    Metacarpophalangeal Joint . . . 26541-26542
  Reduction
    Ulna . . . . . . . . . . . . . . . . . . . . . . . 29902
  Repair
    Ankle . . . . . . . . . . . 27695-27696, 27698
    Elbow . . . . . . . . . . . . . . . 24343, 24345
    Interphalangeal Joint . . . . . . . . . . . . 26540
    Knee . . . . . . . . . . . . . . . 27405, 27409
    Metacarpophalangeal Joint . . . . . . . . 26540
Coracoacromial
  Release . . . . . . . . . . . . 23130, 23415, 29826

## Liver
See Hepatic Duct
Ablation
  Tumor . . . . . . . . . . . . . . . . . . . . 47380-47382
    Laparoscopic . . . . . . . . . . . . . . 47370-47371
Abscess
  Aspiration . . . . . . . . . . . . . . . . . . . . . . . 47015
  Incision and Drainage
    Open . . . . . . . . . . . . . . . . . . . . . . . . 47010
  Injection . . . . . . . . . . . . . . . . . . . . . . . 47015
Aspiration . . . . . . . . . . . . . . . . . . . . . . . . 47015
Biopsy . . . . . . . . . . . . . . . . . . . . . . . . . . . 47700
  Needle . . . . . . . . . . . . . . . . . . 47000-47001
  Wedge . . . . . . . . . . . . . . . . . . . . . . . . 47100
  with Staging Laparotomy . . . . . . . . . . . 49220
Cyst
  Aspiration . . . . . . . . . . . . . . . . . . . . . . . 47015
  Incision and Drainage
    Open . . . . . . . . . . . . . . . . . . . . . . . . 47010
  Injection . . . . . . . . . . . . . . . . . . . . . . . 47015
Drainage . . . . . . . . . . . . . . . . . . . . . . . . . 47400
  Image Guided Fluid Collection . . . . . . . 49405
Excision
  Extensive . . . . . . . . . . . . . . . . . . . . . . . 47122
  Partial . . . . . . . . . . . . . . 47120, 47125-47130
    Donor . . . . . . . . . . . . . . . . . 47140-47142
  Total
    Donor . . . . . . . . . . . . . . . . . . . . . . . 47133
Exploration . . . . . . . . . . . . . . . . . . . . . . . 47400
Hemorrhage . . . . . . . . . . . . . . . . . . 47350-47362
Injection . . . . . . . . . . . . . . . . . . . . . . . . . 47015
  Radiologic . . . . . . . . . . . . . . . . . . . . . . 47505
  X-ray . . . . . . . . . . . . . . . . . . . . . . . . . . 47500
Lobectomy . . . . . . . . . . . . . . . . . . 47125-47130
  Partial . . . . . . . . . . . . . . . . . . . . . . . . . 47120
Needle Biopsy . . . . . . . . . . . . . . . . 47000-47001
Nuclear Medicine
  Imaging . . . . . . . . . . . . . . . . . 78201-78216
  Vascular Flow . . . . . . . . . . . . . . . . . . . . 78206
Removal
  Calculus . . . . . . . . . . . . . . . . . . . . . . . 47400
Repair
  Abscess . . . . . . . . . . . . . . . . . . . . . . . 47300
  Cyst . . . . . . . . . . . . . . . . . . . . . . . . . . 47300
  Wound . . . . . . . . . . . . . . . . . . 47350-47362
Suture
  Wound . . . . . . . . . . . . . . . . . . 47350-47362
Transplantation
  Partial . . . . . . . . . . 47135-47136, 47144-47145
  Whole . . . . . . . . . . . . . . . . . . 47135-47136
  Allograft Preparation . . . . . . . . . 47143-47147
    Lobe Split . . . . . . . . . . . . . . . . . . . . 47145
    Trisegment Split . . . . . . . . . . . . . . . . 47144
Trisegmentectomy . . . . . . . . . . . . . . . . . . 47122
Unlisted Services and Procedures . . . 47379, 47399

## Living Activities, Daily
See Activities of Daily Living

## Lobectomy
Brain . . . . . . . . . . . . . . . . 61323, 61537-61540
  Partial . . . . . . . . . . . . . . . . . . 61539-61540
  Temporal Lobe . . . . . . . . . . . . . . 61537-61538
Contralateral Subtotal
  Thyroid Gland . . . . . . . . . . . . . . 60212, 60225
Liver . . . . . . . . . . . . . . . . . . . . . . 47120-47130
  Donor . . . . . . . . . . . . . . . . . . 47141-47142
Lung . . . . . . . . . . . . . . . . . . . . . . 32480-32482
  Sleeve . . . . . . . . . . . . . . . . . . . . . . . . 32486
  Thoracoscopic . . . . . . . . . . . . . . 32663, 32670
Parotid Gland . . . . . . . . . . . . . . . . 42410-42415
Sleeve . . . . . . . . . . . . . . . . . . . . . . . . . . 32486
Temporal Lobe . . . . . . . . . . . . . . . 61537-61538

Thoracoscopic
  Lung . . . . . . . . . . . . . . . . . . . 32663, 32670
Thyroid Gland
  Partial . . . . . . . . . . . . . . . . . . 60210-60212
  Total . . . . . . . . . . . . . . . . . . . 60220-60225

## Lobotomy
Frontal . . . . . . . . . . . . . . . . . . . . . . . . . . 61490

## Local Excision Mastectomies
See Breast, Excision, Lesion

## Local Excision of Lesion or Tissue of Femur
See Excision, Lesion, Femur

## Localization of Nodule
Breast
  Device Placement
    with Magnetic Resonance
    Guidance . . . . . . 19085, 19086, 19287, 19288
    with Mammographic
    Guidance . . . . . . . . . . . . . . . . 19281, 19282
    with Stereotactic Guidance . . 19081, 19082,
                         19283, 19284
    with Ultrasound Guidance . . . 19083, 19084,
                         19285, 19286

## Log Hydrogen Ion Concentration
See Blood Gases, pH

## Long Acting Thyroid Stimulator
See Thyrotropin Releasing Hormone (TRH)

## Long-Term Care Facility Visits
See Nursing Facility Services

## Longmire Operation
See Anastomosis, Hepatic Duct to Intestines

## Loopogram
See Urography, Antegrade

## Loose Body
Removal
  Ankle Joint . . . . . . . . . . . . . . . . 27620, 29894
  Carpometacarpal Joint . . . . . . . . . . . . . 26070
  Elbow Joint . . . . . . . . . . . . . . . 24101, 29834
  Glenohumeral Joint . . . . . . . . . . . . . . . 23107
  Hip Joint . . . . . . . . . . . . . . . . . . . . . . . 27033
  Interphalangeal Joint . . . . . . . . . . . . . . 28024
  Intertarsal Joint . . . . . . . . . . . . . . . . . . 28020
  Knee Joint . . . . . . . . . . . . . . . . . . . . . . 27331
  Metatarsophalangeal Joint . . . . . . . . . . 28022
  Shoulder Joint . . . . . . . . . . . . . . . . . . . 29819
  Subtalar Joint . . . . . . . . . . . . . . . . . . . 29904
  Tarsometatarsal Joint . . . . . . . . . . . . . . 28020
  Toe . . . . . . . . . . . . . . . . . . . . . . . . . . 28022
  Wrist Joint . . . . . . . . . . . . . . . . . . . . . 25101

## Lord Procedure
See Anal Sphincter, Dilation

## Louis Bar Syndrome
See Ataxia Telangiectasia

## Low Birth Weight Intensive Care Services . . 99478-99480

## Low Density Lipoprotein
See Lipoprotein, LDL

## Low Frequency Ultrasound . . . . 97610

## Low Vision Aids
See Spectacle Services
Fitting . . . . . . . . . . . . . . . . . . . . . 92354-92355

## Lower Extremities
See Extremity, Lower

## Lower GI Series
See Barium Enema

## LRH
See Luteinizing Releasing Factor

## LSD
See Lysergic Acid Diethylamide

## LTH
See Prolactin

## Lumbar
See Spine

## Lumbar Plexus
Decompression . . . . . . . . . . . . . . . . . . . . 64714
Infusion
  Anesthetic . . . . . . . . . . . . . . . . . . . . . 64449
Neuroplasty . . . . . . . . . . . . . . . . . . . . . . 64714
Repair/Suture . . . . . . . . . . . . . . . . . . . . . 64862

## Lumbar Puncture
See Spinal Tap

## Lumbar Spine Fracture
See Fracture, Vertebra, Lumbar

## Lumbar Sympathectomy
See Sympathectomy, Lumbar

## Lumbar Vertebra
See Vertebra, Lumbar

## Lumen Dilation . . . . . . . . . . . . . . 74360

## Lumpectomy . . . . . . . . . . . . . 19301-19302

## Lunate
Arthroplasty
  with Implant . . . . . . . . . . . . . . . . . . . . 25444
Dislocation
  Closed Treatment . . . . . . . . . . . . . . . . . 25690
  Open Treatment . . . . . . . . . . . . . . . . . . 25695

## Lung
Ablation
  Tumor . . . . . . . . . . . . . . . . . . . . . . . . 32998
Abscess
  Incision and Drainage
    Open . . . . . . . . . . . . . . . . . . . . . . . . 32200
Air Leak Assessment . . . . . . . . . . 31647, 31651
Airway Sizing . . . . . . . . . . . . . . . 31647, 31651
Biopsy . . 31628-31629, 31632-31633, 32096-32097
  Thoracoscopic . . . . . . . . . . . . . . 32607-32608
    Infiltrate . . . . . . . . . . . . . . . . . . . . . 32607
    Mass . . . . . . . . . . . . . . . . . . . . . . . 32608
    Nodule . . . . . . . . . . . . . . . . . . . . . . 32608
Bullae
  Resection-Plication
    Thoracoscopic . . . . . . . . . . . . . . . . . 32655
    Thoracotomy . . . . . . . . . . . . . . . . . . 32141
Collapse
  See Lung Collapse Therapy
Cyst
  Incision and Drainage
    Open . . . . . . . . . . . . . . . . . . . . . . . . 32200
  Removal . . . . . . . . . . . . . . . . . . . . . . . 32140
Decortication
  Endoscopic . . . . . . . . . . . . . . . . 32651-32652
  Partial . . . . . . . . . . . . . . . . . . . 32225, 32651
  Total . . . . . . . . . . . . . . . . . . . . 32220, 32652
  with Parietal Pleurectomy . . . . . . . . . . . 32320

Index

# M

Index

Index

Index

with Microvascular
Anastomosis ............. 15756, 42894
Myocutaneous ................. 15732, 15734,
15736, 15738, 61619

**Muscle Grafts**
Free ................ 15841, 25265, 25274

**Muscle Testing**
Dynamometry, Eye ..................... 92260
Electromyography
   *See* Electromyography
Extraocular Multiple Muscles............. 92265
Ischemic Limb........................ 95875
Manual ........................ 95831-95834
Range of Motion
   *See* Range of Motion Test
Reflex
   *See* Reflex Test

**Muscle, Oculomotor**
*See* Eye Muscles

**Muscles**
*See* Muscle

**Musculo-Skeletal System**
*See* Musculoskeletal System

**Musculoplasty**
*See* Muscle, Repair

**Musculoskeletal System**
Computer-Assisted Surgical
Navigation................0054T-0055T, 20985
Unlisted Services and Procedures ........ 20999,
24999, 25999, 26989, 27299, 27599, 27899
Unlisted Services and Procedures, Head .... 21499

**Musculotendinous (Rotator) Cuff**
Repair ....................... 23410-23412

**Mustard Procedure**
*See* Repair, Great Arteries; Revision

**Myasthenia Gravis**
Cholinesterase Inhibitor Challenge Test..... 95857

**Myasthenic, Gravis**
*See* Myasthenia Gravis

**Mycobacteria**
Culture............................. 87116
   Identification ..................... 87118
Detection....................... 87550-87562
Sensitivity Studies .................... 87190

**Mycophenolate (mycophenolic acid)**
Drug Assay ......................... 80180

**Mycoplasma**
Antibody............................ 86738
Culture............................. 87109
Detection...................... 87580-87582

**Mycota**
*See* Fungus

**Myectomy, Anorectal**
*See* Myomectomy, Anorectal

**Myelencephalon**
*See* Medulla

**Myelin Basic Protein**
Cerebrospinal Fluid.................... 83873

**Myelography**
Brain.............................. 70010
Injection Procedure................... 62284
Spine
   Cervical ......................... 72240
   Lumbosacral....................... 72265
   Thoracic ......................... 72255
   Total ............................ 72270

**Myelomeningocele**
Repair ....................... 63704-63706

**Myeloperoxidase (MPO)**........ 83876

**Myelotomy** ...................... 63170

**Myocardial**
Perfusion Imaging................ 78451-78454
   *See* Nuclear Medicine
Positron Emission Tomography (PET) ....... 78459
Resection .......................... 33542
Revascularization ............... 33140-33141

**Myocardial Imaging**
Infarct Avid .................... 78466-78469
Metabolic Evaluation
   PET ............................. 78459
Perfusion Study
   Nuclear Medicine
      Planar ..................... 78453-78454
      PET ...................... 78491-78492
      SPECT .................... 78451-78452
Repair
   Postinfarction..................... 33542
Sympathetic Innervation...........0331T-0332T

**Myocutaneous Flaps** .....15731-15738,
15756

**Myofascial Pain Dysfunction Syndrome**
*See* Temporomandibular Joint (TMJ)

**Myofibroma**
*See* Leiomyomata

**Myoglobin**...................... 83874

**Myomectomy**
Anorectal........................... 45108
Uterus ...................... 58140-58146
   Laparoscopic ................. 58545-58546

**Myoplasty**
*See* Muscle, Repair

**Myotomy**
Esophagus.... 32665, 43130, 43279, 43330-43331
Hyoid.............................. 21685
Pharynx ..................... 43030, 43130
Pylorus............................ 43520

**Myringoplasty** ................. 69620

**Myringostomy**
*See* Myringotomy

**Myringotomy**.............. 69420-69421

**Myxoid Cyst**
*See* Ganglion

# N

**N. Meningitidis**
*See* Neisseria Meningitidis

**Naffziger Operation**
*See* Decompression, Orbit; Section

**Nagel Test**
*See* Color Vision Examination

**Nail Bed**
Reconstruction ...................... 11762
Repair ............................. 11760

**Nail Fold**
Excision
   Wedge ........................... 11765

**Nail Plate Separation**
*See* Nails, Avulsion

**Nails**
Avulsion ..................... 11730-11732
Biopsy............................. 11755
Debridement................... 11720-11721
Drainage ..................... 10060-10061
Evacuation
   Hematoma, Subungual ............. 11740
Excision ..................... 11750-11752
KOH Examination ..................... 87220
Reconstruction ...................... 11762
Removal ...........11730-11732, 11750-11752
Trimming........................... 11719

**Narcosynthesis**
Diagnostic and Therapeutic .............. 90865

**Nasal Abscess**
*See* Nose, Abscess

**Nasal Area**
Bone Graft.......................... 21210

**Nasal Bleeding**
*See* Epistaxis

**Nasal Bone**
Bone Graft.......................... 21210
Fracture
   Closed Treatment............. 21310-21320
   Open Treatment.............. 21325-21335
   with Manipulation ............ 21315-21320
   without Manipulation ................ 21310
Reconstruction
   *See* Rhinoplasty
X-ray.............................. 70160

**Nasal Deformity**
Repair ....................... 40700-40761

**Nasal Function Study** .......... 92512

**Nasal Polyp**
*See* Nose, Polyp

**Nasal Prosthesis**
Impression.......................... 21087

**Nasal Septum**
Abscess
   Incision and Drainage .............. 30020
Fracture
   Closed Treatment.................. 21337
   Open Treatment................... 21336

Index

Index

## Occlusive Disease of Artery
*See* Repair, Artery; Revision

## Occult Blood ............... 82270-82272
by Hemoglobin Immunoassay ............. 82274

## Occupational Therapy
Evaluation ..................... 97003-97004

## Ocular Implant
*See* Orbital Implant
Insertion
   Drainage Device ........ 0191T, 0253T, 66183
   in Scleral Shell .................... 65130
   Muscles, Attached ................ 65140
   Muscles, Not Attached ............. 65135
Modification ....................... 65125
Reinsertion ........................ 65150
   with Foreign Material .............. 65155
Removal ........................... 65175

## Ocular Muscle
*See* Eye Muscles

## Ocular Orbit
*See* Orbit

## Ocular Screening ................ 99174

## Ocular Prostheses
*See* Prosthesis, Ocular

## Oculomotor Muscle
*See* Eye Muscles

## Oddi Sphincter
*See* Sphincter of Oddi

## Odontoid Dislocation
Open Treatment/Reduction ............. 22318
   with Grafting ...................... 22319

## Odontoid Fracture
Open Treatment/Reduction ............. 22318
   with Grafting ...................... 22319

## Odontoid Process
Excision ........................... 22548

## Oesophageal Neoplasm
*See* Tumor, Esophagus

## Oesophageal Varices
*See* Esophageal Varices

## Oesophagus
*See* Esophagus

## Oestradiol
*See* Estradiol

## Office and/or Other Outpatient Services
*See* History and Physical Consultation
Established Patient ............... 99211-99215
New Patient .................... 99201-99205
Normal Newborn .................... 99461
Office Visit
   Established Patient ........... 99211-99215
   New Patient ................ 99201-99205
Outpatient Visit
   Established Patient ........... 99211-99215
   New Patient ................ 99201-99205
   Prolonged Services .......... 99354-99355

## Office Medical Services
After Hours ........................ 99050
Emergency Care ..................... 99058
Extended Hours ..................... 99051

## Office or Other Outpatient Consultations
*See* Consultation, Office and/or Other Outpatient

## Olecranon
*See* Elbow; Humerus; Radius; Ulna
Bursa
   Arthrocentesis ..................... 20605
Cyst
   Excision ..................... 24125-24126
Tumor
   Cyst ............................. 24120
   Excision ..................... 24125-24126

## Olecranon Process
Craterization ...................... 24147
Diaphysectomy ..................... 24147
Excision ........................... 24147
   Abscess .......................... 24138
Fracture
   *See* Elbow; Humerus; Radius
   Closed Treatment ............ 24670-24675
   Open Treatment .................... 24685
Osteomyelitis .............. 24138, 24147
Saucerization ...................... 24147
Sequestrectomy .................... 24138

## Oligoclonal Immunoglobulins . 83916

## Omentectomy ....... 49255, 58950-58958
Laparotomy ........................ 58960
Oophorectomy ..................... 58943
Resection Ovarian Malignancy ...... 58950-58952
Resection Peritoneal Malignancy ... 58950-58958
Resection Tubal Malignancy ........ 58950-58958

## Omentum
Excision ............. 49255, 58950-58958
Flap ........................ 49904-49905
   Free
     with Microvascular Anastomosis ..... 49906
Omentopexy ....................... 49326
Unlisted Services and Procedures ........ 49999

## Omphalectomy ................. 49250

## Omphalocele
Repair ...................... 49600-49611

## Omphalomesenteric Duct
Excision ........................... 44800

## Omphalomesenteric Duct, Persistent
*See* Diverticulum, Meckel's

## Oncoprotein
Des-gamma-carboxyprothrombin (DCP) ..... 83951
HER-2/neu .......................... 83950

## Online Internet Assessment and Management
Nonphysician ...................... 98969
Physician .......................... 99444

## One Stage Prothrombin Time .......... 85610-85611
*See* Prothrombin Time

## Onychectomy
*See* Excision, Nails

## Onychia
Drainage ..................... 10060-10061

## Oocyte
Assisted Fertilization
   Microtechnique .............. 89280-89281
Biopsy ....................... 89290-89291
Culture
   Extended ......................... 89272
   Less than 4 Days ................. 89250
   with Co-Culture .................. 89251
Identification
   Follicular Fluid .................. 89254
Insemination ....................... 89268
Retrieval
   for In Vitro Fertilization .......... 58970
Storage ............................ 89346
Thawing ........................... 89356

## Oophorectomy ............ 58262-58263,
58291-58292, 58552,
58554, 58661, 58940-58943
Ectopic Pregnancy
   Laparoscopic Treatment ............ 59120
   Surgical Treatment ................ 59120

## Oophorectomy, Partial
*See* Excision, Ovary, Partial

## Oophorocystectomy
*See* Cystectomy, Ovarian

## Open Axillary Artery Approach, Transcatheter Aortic Valve Replacement
*See* Artery, Femoral, Approach, Transcatheter Aortic Valve Replacement

## Open Biopsy, Adrenal Gland
*See* Adrenal Gland, Biopsy

## Open Femoral Artery Approach, Transcatheter Aortic Valve Replacement
*See* Artery, Femoral, Approach, Transcatheter Aortic Valve Replacement

## Open Iliac Artery Approach, Transcatheter Aortic Valve Replacement
*See* Artery, Femoral, Approach, Transcatheter Aortic Valve Replacement

## Operating Microscope .......... 69990

## Operation/Procedure
Abbe-Estlander ............ 00102, 40527, 40761
Akin .............................. 28298
Bankart ........................... 23455
Barker ..................... 28120, 28130
Batch-Spittler-McFadden ...... 01404, 27598
Bischof ........................... 63170
Blalock-Hanlon .................. 33735-33737
Blalock-Taussig .................... 33750
Bohler ............................ 28405
Bristow ........................... 23460
Brunschwig operation ............... 58240
Burrow's ................... 14000-14350
Camey Enterocystoplasty ............ 50825
Campbell .......................... 27422
Chambers ......................... 28300
Chevron ........................... 28296
Clagett ............................ 32810
Colles Fracture .................... 25600
Conjunctivo-Tarso-Müller Resection ...... 67908
Coombs Test ....................... 86880
Cotte Operation ............. 58400-58410
Damus-Kaye-Stansel Procedure .......... 33606

## Operation Microscopes
*See* Operating Microscope

## Operculectomy

## Operculum
*See* Gums

## Ophthalmic Mucous Membrane
## Test
*See* Allergy Tests

## Ophthalmology

## Ophthalmology, Diagnostic

## Ophthalmoscopy
*See* Ophthalmology, Diagnostic

## Otomy
*See* Incision

**Otoplasty** . . . . . . . . . . . . . . . . . . . . . 69300

## Otorhinolaryngology
Unlisted Services and Procedures . . . . . . . . 92700

**Ouchterlony Immunodiffusion** . 86331

## Outer Ear
*See* Ear, Outer

## Outpatient Visit
*See* History and Physical; Office and/or Other
Outpatient Services

## Output, Cardiac
*See* Cardiac Output

## Ova
Smear . . . . . . . . . . . . . . . . . . . . . . . . . . . . 87177

## Oval Window
Repair Fistula . . . . . . . . . . . . . . . . . . . . . 69666

## Oval Window Fistula
*See* Fistula, Oval Window

## Ovarian Cyst
*See* Cyst, Ovarian; Ovary, Cyst

## Ovarian Vein Syndrome
Ureterolysis . . . . . . . . . . . . . . . . . . . . . . . 50722

## Ovariectomies
*See* Oophorectomy

**Ovariolysis** . . . . . . . . . . . . . . . . . . . . . 58740

## Ovary
Abscess
    Incision and Drainage . . . . . . . . . 58820-58822
        Abdominal Approach . . . . . . . . . . . . . 58822
Biopsy . . . . . . . . . . . . . . . . . . . . 49321, 58900
Cryopreservation . . . . . . . . . . . . . . . . . . . . 0058T
Cyst
    Excision . . . . . . . . . . . . . . . . . . . . . . 58925
    Incision and Drainage . . . . . . . . 58800-58805
Excision . . . . . . . . . . . . . . . . . . . . 58662, 58720
    Cyst . . . . . . . . . . . . . . . . . . . . . . . . 58925
    Partial
        Oophorectomy . . . . . . . . . . . 58661, 58940,
                          58953-58954
        Ovarian Malignancy . . . . . . . . . . . . . 58943
        Peritoneal Malignancy . . . . . . . . . . . . 58943
        Tubal Malignancy . . . . . . . . . . . . . . 58943
        Wedge Resection . . . . . . . . . . . . . . 58920
    Total . . . . . . . . . . . . . . . . . . . 58940-58943
Laparoscopy . . . . . . . . . . . . . 58660-58662, 58679
Lesion
    Excision . . . . . . . . . . . . . . . . . . . . . 58662
    Fulguration . . . . . . . . . . . . . . . . . . . 58662
Lysis
    Adhesions . . . . . . . . . . . . . . 58660, 58740
Malignancy
    Resection . . . . . . . . 58950-58952, 58957-58958
    Staging Laparotomy . . . . . . . . . . . . . . 58960
Oncology
    Biochemical Assay
        Apolipoprotein A1 . . . . . . . . . . . . . 81503
        Beta-2 Microglobulin . . . . . . . . . . . . 81503
        CA-125 . . . . . . . . . . . . . . . . 81500, 01503
        HE4 . . . . . . . . . . . . . . . . . . . . 81500
        Menopausal Status . . . . . . . . . . . . . 81500
        Pre-albumin . . . . . . . . . . . . . . . . 81503
        Tissue of Origin . . . . . . . . . . . . . . 81505

Transferrin . . . . . . . . . . . . . . . . . . . . . . 81503
Pregnancy
    Surgical Treatment . . . . . . . . . . . 59120-59121
Radical Resection . . . . . . . . . . . . . . . 58950-58952
Removal
    with Pelvic Exenteration . . . . . : . . 45126, 58240
    with Radical Trachelectomy . . . . . . . . . . 57531
    with Hysterectomy
        Abdominal . . . . . . . . . . . . . . 58150, 58152,
                 58180, 58200, 58210
        Laparoscopic . . . 58542, 58544, 58548, 58554,
                 58552, 58571, 58573
        Vaginal . . . . . . . . . 58262-58263, 58291-58292
Transposition . . . . . . . . . . . . . . . . . . . . 58825
Tumor
    Resection . . . . . . . . . . . . . . . . 58950-58958
Unlisted Services and Procedures . . . 58679, 58999
Wedge Resection . . . . . . . . . . . . . . . . . . 58920

## Oviduct
Anastomosis . . . . . . . . . . . . . . . . . . . . . 58750
Chromotubation . . . . . . . . . . . . . . . . . . . 58350
Ectopic Pregnancy . . . . . . . . . . . . . . 59120-59121
Excision . . . . . . . . . . . . . . . . . . . . 58700-58720
Fulguration
    Laparoscopic . . . . . . . . . . . . . . . . . 58670
Hysterosalpingography . . . . . . . . . . . . . . . 74740
Laparoscopy . . . . . . . . . . . . . . . . . . . . . 58679
Ligation . . . . . . . . . . . . . . . . . . . 58600-58611
Lysis
    Adhesions . . . . . . . . . . . . . . . . . . . 58740
Occlusion . . . . . . . . . . . . . . . . . . . . . . 58615
    Laparoscopic . . . . . . . . . . . . . . . . . 58671
Repair . . . . . . . . . . . . . . . . . . . . . . . . 58752
    Anastomosis . . . . . . . . . . . . . . . . . 58750
    Create Stoma . . . . . . . . . . . . . . . . . 58770
Unlisted Services and Procedures . . . 58679, 58999
X-ray with Contrast . . . . . . . . . . . . . . . . . 74740

## Ovocyte
*See* Oocyte

**Ovulation Tests** . . . . . . . . . . . . . . . 84830

## Ovum Implantation
*See* Implantation

## Ovum Transfer Surgery
*See* Gamete Intrafallopian Transfer (GIFT)

**Oxalate** . . . . . . . . . . . . . . . . . . . . . . . 83945

## Oxcarbazepine
Drug Assay . . . . . . . . . . . . . . . . . . . . . . 80183

## Oxidase, Ceruloplasmin
*See* Ceruloplasmin

## Oxidoreductase, Alcohol-Nad+
*See* Antidiuretic Hormone

## Oximetry (Noninvasive)
*See* Pulmonology, Diagnostic
Blood O2 Saturation Determination
    Ear or Pulse . . . . . . . . . . . . . . . 94760-94762
    Pulse, Recording
        Car Seat/Bed Testing . . . . . . . . 94780-94781
        with Pulmonary Stress Testing . . 94620-94621

## Oxoisomerase
*See* Phosphohexose Isomerase

## Oxosteroids
*See* Ketosteroids

**Oxycodinone** . . . . . . . . 80102-80103, 83925

**Oxygen Saturation** . . . . . . . . 82805-82810

## Oxygenation, Extracorporeal Membrane
*See* Extracorporeal Membrane Oxygenation

## Oxyproline
*See* Hydroxyproline

**Oxytocin Stress Test, Fetal** . . . . . 59020

# P

## P&P
*See* Proconvertin

## P B Antibodies
*See* Antibody, Heterophile

## P-Acetamidophenol
*See* Acetaminophen

## Pacemaker, Heart
*See* Cardiology; Defibrillator, Heart;
Electrocardiography
Conversion
    Single to Dual Chamber . . . . . . . . . . . . 33214
Data Analysis . . . . . . . . . . 93288, 93293 93294
Electronic Analysis . . . . . . . . . . . . . . . . . 93288
    Antitachycardia System . . . . . . . . . . . 93724
Evaluation and Programming
    Dual Lead . . . . . . . . . . . . . 93280, 93286, 93288
    In Person . . . . . . 93279-93281, 93286, 93288
    Multiple Lead . . . . . . . . . 93281, 93286, 93288
    Remote . . . . . . . . . . . . 93293-93294, 93296
    Single Lead . . . . . . . . . 93279, 93286, 93288
Insertion . . . . . . . . . . . . . . . . . . . 33206-33208
    Electrode . . . . . . . . . . . . . . . . . 33202-33203,
                 33216-33217, 33224-33225
    Temporary . . . . . . . . . . . 33210-33211, 93583
    Pulse Generator Only . . . . 33212-33213, 33221
Lead
    Placement . . . . . . . . . . . . . 33202-33203
Relocate
    Skin pocket
        for Pacemaker . . . . . . . . . . . . . . 33222
        for Cardioverter-Defibrillator . . . . . . . 33223
Removal
    Pulse Generator Only . . . . . . . . . . . . . 33233
    Transvenous Electrodes . . . . . . . . 33234-33235
    via Thoracotomy . . . . . . . . . . . . 33236-33237
Repair
    Electrode . . . . . . . . . . . . . . . 33218-33220
Replacement
    Catheter . . . . . . . . . . . . . . . . . . . 33210
    Electrode . . . . . . . . . . . . . . . 33210-33211
    Insertion . . . . . . . . . . . . . . . . 33206-33208
    Pulse Generator . . . . . . . . . . . . 33227-33229
Repositioning
    Electrode . . . . . . . . . . . . . . . 33215, 33226
Relocate Pocket
    Chest . . . . . . . . . . . . . . . . . . 33222, 33223
Telephonic Analysis . . . . . . . . . . . . . . . . 93293
Upgrade . . . . . . . . . . . . . . . . . . . . . . . 33214

## Pachymetry
Eye . . . . . . . . . . . . . . . . . . . . . . . . . . 76514

## Packing
Nasal Hemorrhage . . . . . . . . . . . . . 30901-30906

Index

Index

**Index**

## Physical Therapy
*See* Physical Medicine/Therapy/Occupational Therapy

## Physician Services

## Piercing of Ear Lobe . . . . . . . . . . . 69090

## Piles
*See* Hemorrhoids

## Pilonidal Cyst

## Pin
*See* Wire

## Pinch Graft . . . . . . . . . . . . . . . . . . 15050

## Pinna
*See* Ear, External

## Pinworms

## Pirogoff Procedure . . . . . . . . . . . . 27888

## Pituitary Epidermoid Tumor
*See* Craniopharyngioma

## Pituitary Gland

## Pituitary Growth Hormone
*See* Growth Hormone

## Pituitary Lactogenic Hormone
*See* Prolactin

## Pituitectomy
*See* Pituitary Gland, Excision

## PKU
*See* Phenylalanine

## Placement

## Placenta

## Placenta Alpha Microglobulin-1 . . . . . . . . . . . . . . . 84112

## Placental Lactogen
*See* Lactogen, Human Placental

## Placental Villi
*See* Chorionic Villus

## Plagiocephaly . . . . . . . . . . . . . . . . 21175

## Plague Vaccine . . . . . . . . . . . . . . 90727

Index

Index

Index

Index

Index

Index

## Repeat Surgeries

## Replacement

Index

Index

Vagina
   Prosthetic Graft . . . . . . . 57295-57296, 57426
   Sling
      Stress Incontinence . . . . . . . . . . . . . . 57287
   Venous Access Device . . . . . . . . . . . 36576-36578,
                                 36582-36583, 36585
Ventricle
   Ventriculomyectomy . . . . . . . . . . . . . . . 33416
   Ventriculomyotomy . . . . . . . . . . . . . . . . 33416

**Rh (D)**
*See* Blood Typing

**Rh Immune Globulin**
*See* Immune Globulins, Rho (D)

**Rheumatoid Factor** . . . . . . . 86430-86431

**Rhinectomy**
   Partial . . . . . . . . . . . . . . . . . . . . . . . . . . . 30150
   Total . . . . . . . . . . . . . . . . . . . . . . . . . . . . 30160

**Rhinomanometry** . . . . . . . . . . . . . . . . 92512

**Rhinopharynx**
*See* Nasopharynx

**Rhinophyma**
   Repair . . . . . . . . . . . . . . . . . . . . . . . . . . . 30120

**Rhinoplasty**
   Cleft Lip/Cleft Palate . . . . . . . . . . . . 30460-30462
   Primary . . . . . . . . . . . . . . . . . . . . . 30400-30420
   Secondary . . . . . . . . . . . . . . . . . . . . 30430-30450

**Rhinoscopy**
*See* Endoscopy, Nose

**Rhinotomy**
   Lateral . . . . . . . . . . . . . . . . . . . . 30118, 30320

**Rhizotomy** . . . . . . . . . . . . . . . . 63185-63190

**Rho Variant Du** . . . . . . . . . . . . . . . . . 86905

**Rhomboid Flap** . . . . . . . . . . . 14000-14302

**Rhytidectomy** . . . . . . . . . . . . 15824-15829

**Rhytidoplasties**
*See* Face Lift

**Rib**
   Excision . . . . . . . . . . . . . 21600-21616, 32900
   Fracture
      Closed Treatment . . . . . . . . . . . . . . . 21800
      External Fixation . . . . . . . . . . . . . . . . 21810
      Internal Fixation . . . . . . . . . . . 0245T-0248T
      Open Treatment . . . . . . . . 0245T-0248T, 21805
   Graft
      to Face . . . . . . . . . . . . . . . . . . . . . . . 21230
   Resection . . . . . . . . . . . . . . 19260-19272, 32900
   X-ray . . . . . . . . . . . . . . . . . . . . . 71100-71111

**Riboflavin** . . . . . . . . . . . . . . . . . . . . . 84252

**Richardson Operation
Hysterectomy**
*See* Hysterectomy, Abdominal, Total

**Richardson Procedure** . . . . . . . . . 53460

**Rickettsia**
   Antibody . . . . . . . . . . . . . . . . . . . . . . . . . 86757

**Ridell Operation**
*See* Sinusotomy, Frontal

**Ridge, Alveolar**
*See* Alveolar Ridge

**Right Atrioventricular Valve**
*See* Tricuspid Valve

**Right Heart Cardiac Catheterization**
*See* Cardiac Catheterization, Right Heart

**Ripstein Operation** . . . . . . . . 45540-45541
*See* Proctopexy

**Risk Factor Reduction Intervention**
*See* Performance Measures, Preventive Medicine

**Risser Jacket**
   Application . . . . . . . . . . . . . . . . . . 29010-29015
   Removal . . . . . . . . . . . . . . . . . . . . . . . . . 29710

**Rocky Mountain Spotted
Fever** . . . . . . . . . . . . . . . . . . . . . . . . . . 86000

**Roentgen Rays**
*See* X-ray

**Roentgenographic**
*See* X-ray

**Roentgenography**
*See* Radiology, Diagnostic

**Ropes Test** . . . . . . . . . . . . . . . . . . . . . 83872

**Rorschach Test** . . . . . . . . . . . . . . . . . 96101

**Ross Information Processing
Assessment** . . . . . . . . . . . . . . . . . . . 96125

**Ross Procedure** . . . . . . . . . . . . . . . . 33413

**Rotation Flap**
*See* Skin, Adjacent Tissue Transfer

**Rotator Cuff**
   Repair . . . . . . . . . . . . . . . . . . . . . 23410-23420

**Rotavirus**
   Antibody . . . . . . . . . . . . . . . . . . . . . . . . . 86759
   Antigen Detection
      Enzyme Immunoassay . . . . . . . . . . . . . 87425

**Rotavirus Vaccine**
   3 Dose . . . . . . . . . . . . . . . . . . . . . . . . . . 90680
   2 Dose . . . . . . . . . . . . . . . . . . . . . . . . . . 90681

**Round Window**
   Repair Fistula . . . . . . . . . . . . . . . . . . . . . 69667

**Round Window Fistula**
*See* Fistula, Round Window

**Roux-En-Y Procedure** . . . . . . . . . . 43621,
                     43633-43634, 43644, 43846,
                     47740-47741, 47780-47785, 48540

**RPR**
*See* Syphilis Test

**RSV**
*See* Immune Globulins; Respiratory Syncytial Virus

**RT3**
*See* Triiodothyronine, Reverse

**Rubbing Alcohol**
*See* Isopropyl Alcohol

**Rubella**
   Antibody . . . . . . . . . . . . . . . . . . . . . . . . . 86762
   Vaccine . . . . . . . . . . . . . . . . . . . . 90706-90710

**Rubella HI Test**
*See* Hemagglutination Inhibition Test

**Rubella/Mumps**
*See* Vaccines

**Rubeola**
   Antibody . . . . . . . . . . . . . . . . . . . . . . . . . 86765
   Antigen Detection
      Immunofluorescence . . . . . . . . . . . . . . 87283

**Rubeolla**
*See* Rubeola

**Russell Viper Venom
Time** . . . . . . . . . . . . . . . . . . . . . . 85612-85613

# S

**Sac, Endolymphatic**
*See* Endolymphatic Sac

**Saccomanno Technique** . . . . . . . 88108

**Sacral Nerve**
   Implantation
      Electrode Array . . . . . . . . . . . . 64561, 64581

**Sacral, Pre-**
   Arthrodesis
      *See* Arthrodesis, Vertebra, Lumbar

**Sacroiliac Joint**
   Arthrodesis . . . . . . . . . . . . . . . . . . . . . . . 27280
      Joint Stabilization . . . . . . . . . . . . . . . . 0334T
   Arthrotomy . . . . . . . . . . . . . . . . . . . . . . . 27050
   Biopsy . . . . . . . . . . . . . . . . . . . . . . . . . . 27050
   Dislocation
      Open Treatment . . . . . . . . . . . . . . . . . 27218
   Fusion . . . . . . . . . . . . . . . . . . . . . . . . . . 27280
   Injection for Arthrography . . . . . . . . . . . . 27096
   X-ray . . . . . . . . . . . . . . . . . . . . . 72200-72202

**Sacrum**
   Augmentation
      Percutaneous . . . . . . . . . . . . . . 0200T-0201T
         with CT Guidance . . . . . . . . . . . . . . 72292
         with Fluoroscopic Guidance . . . . . . . 72291
   Sacroplasty
      Percutaneous . . . . . . . . . . . . . . 0200T-0201T
   Tumor
      Excision . . . . . . . . . . . . . . . . . . . . . . . 49215
   X-ray . . . . . . . . . . . . . . . . . . . . . . . . . . . 72220

**Sahli Test**
*See* Gastroenterology, Diagnostic, Stomach

**Salicylate**
   Assay . . . . . . . . . . . . . . . . . . . . . . . . . . . 80196

**Saline-Solution Abortion**
*See* Abortion, Induced, by Saline

**Salivary Duct**
   Catheterization . . . . . . . . . . . . . . . . . . . . 42660
   Dilation . . . . . . . . . . . . . . . . . . . 42650-42660
   Diversion . . . . . . . . . . . . . . . . . . 42507-42510
   Ligation . . . . . . . . . . . . . . . . . . . 42665, 42510
   Repair . . . . . . . . . . . . . . . . . . . . 42500-42505
      Fistula . . . . . . . . . . . . . . . . . . . . . . . . 42600

**Salivary Gland Virus**
*See* Cytomegalovirus

## Salivary Glands

Abscess
  Incision and Drainage
    Parotid . . . . . . . . . . . . . . . . . . 42300-42305
    Sublingual. . . . . . . . . . . . . . . . . . . 42310
    Submaxillary. . . . . . . . . . . . . . 42310-42320
Biopsy . . . . . . . . . . . . . . . . . . . . . . . . . . 42405
Calculi (Stone)
  Excision . . . . . . . . . . . . . . . . 42330-42340
Chemodenervation . . . . . . . . . . . . . . . . . 64611
Cyst
  Marsupialization . . . . . . . . . . . . . . . 42409
  Excision . . . . . . . . . . . . . . . . . . . . . 42408
Duct
  *See* Salivary Duct
Excision
  Parotid Gland . . . . . . . . . . . . . . 42410, 42415,
                42420, 42425-42426
  Sublingual Gland . . . . . . . . . . . . . . . 42450
  Submandibular Gland . . . 42440, 42508-42509
Injection
  X-ray. . . . . . . . . . . . . . . . . . . . . . . . 42550
Needle Biopsy. . . . . . . . . . . . . . . . . . . . 42400
Nuclear Medicine
  Function Study . . . . . . . . . . . . . . . . . 78232
  Imaging . . . . . . . . . . . . . . . . . 78230-78231
Tumor
  Parotid
    Excision. . . . . . . . . . . . . . . 42410, 42415,
            42420, 42425-42426
Unlisted Services and Procedures . . . . . . . . 42699
X-ray . . . . . . . . . . . . . . . . . . . . . 70380-70390
  with Contrast . . . . . . . . . . . . . . . . . . 70390

## Salmonella

Antibody . . . . . . . . . . . . . . . . . . . . . . . 86768

## Salpingectomy

Complete or Partial . . . . . . . . . . . . . . . . . 58700
  Laparoscopic . . . . . . . . . . . . . . . . . 58661
for Ectopic Pregnancy . . . . . . . . . . . . . . . 59120
  Laparoscopic . . . . . . . . . . . . . . . . . 59151
with Vaginal Hysterectomy. . . . . . . . 58262-58263,
                58291-58292
  Laparoscopic . . . . . . . . . . . . 58552, 58554
with Oophorectomy. . . . . . . . . . . . . . . . 58943

## Salpingo-Oophorectomy . . . . . . . . 58720

Resection Ovarian Malignancy. . . . . . 58950-58958
Resection Peritoneal Malignancy. . . . 58950-58958
Resection Tubal Malignancy. . . . . . . . 58950-58958

## Salpingohysterostomy

*See* Implantation, Tubouterine

## Salpingolysis . . . . . . . . . . . . . . . 58740

Laparoscopic . . . . . . . . . . . . . . . . . . . 58660

## Salpingoneostomy . . . . . . . . 58673, 58770

## Salpingoplasty

*See* Fallopian Tube, Repair

## Salpingostomy . . . . . . . . . . . 58673, 58770

Laparoscopic. . . . . . . . . . . . . . . . . . . . 58673

## Salter Osteotomy of the Pelvis

*See* Osteotomy, Pelvis

## Sampling

*See* Biopsy; Brush Biopsy; Needle Biopsy

## Sang-Park Procedure . . . . . 33735-33737

## Sao Paulo Typhus

*See* Rocky Mountain Spotted Fever

## Saucerization

Calcaneus . . . . . . . . . . . . . . . . . . . . . 28120
Clavicle . . . . . . . . . . . . . . . . . . . . . . 23180
Femur . . . . . . . . . . . . . . . . . . 27070, 27360
Fibula. . . . . . . . . . . . . . . . . . . 27360, 27641
Hip. . . . . . . . . . . . . . . . . . . . . . . . . 27070
Humerus . . . . . . . . . . . . . . . . 23184, 24140
Ileum . . . . . . . . . . . . . . . . . . . . . . . 27070
Metacarpal . . . . . . . . . . . . . . . . . . . . 26230
Metatarsal . . . . . . . . . . . . . . . . . . . . 28122
Olecranon Process . . . . . . . . . . . . . . . 24147
Phalanges
  Finger . . . . . . . . . . . . . . . . 26235-26236
  Toe . . . . . . . . . . . . . . . . . . . . . . 28124
Pubis . . . . . . . . . . . . . . . . . . . . . . . 27070
Radius . . . . . . . . . . . . . . . . . 24145, 25151
Scapula . . . . . . . . . . . . . . . . . . . . . . 23182
Symphysis Pubis . . . . . . . . . . . . 27070-27071
Talus . . . . . . . . . . . . . . . . . . . . . . . 28120
Tarsal. . . . . . . . . . . . . . . . . . . . . . . 28122
Tibia . . . . . . . . . . . . . . . . . . 27360, 27640
Ulna . . . . . . . . . . . . . . . . . . . . . . . . 25150

## Saundby Test

*See* Blood, Feces

## Scabies

*See* Tissue, Examination for Ectoparasites

## Scalenotomy

*See* Muscle Division, Scalenus Anticus

## Scalenus Anticus

Division . . . . . . . . . . . . . . . . . . 21700-21705

## Scaling

*See* Exfoliation

## Scalp

Skin Graft
  Dermal Autograft. . . . . . . . . . . 15135-15136
  Epidermal Autograft. . . . . . . . . 15115-15116
  Flap. . . . . . . . . . . . . . . . . . . . . . 15610
  Pedicle Formation . . . . . . . . . . . . . . 15572
  Recipient Site Preparation. . . . . . 15004-15005
  Skin Substitute. . . . . . . . . . . . . 15275-15278
  Split-Thickness. . . . . . . . . . . . . 15120-15121
  Tissue-cultured Autograft . . . . . . 15155-15157
Lesion
  Destruction. . . . . . . . . . . 17270-17274, 17276
  Excision
    Benign. . . . . . . . . . 11420-11424, 11426
    Malignant. . . . . . . . . 11620-11624, 11626
  Shaving . . . . . . . . . . . . . . . . 11305-11308
Tissue Transfer
  Adjacent. . . . . . . . . . . . . . . . 14020-14021
Tumor
  Excision . . . . . . . . . . . . . . . . 21011-21014
  Radical Resection . . . . . . . . . . 21015-21016
Venipuncture
  Child. . . . . . . . . . . . . . . . . . . . . . 36405
Wound
  Repair. . . . . . . . . 12001-12002, 12004-12007,
      12031-12032, 12034-12037, 13120-13122

## Scalp Blood Sampling

Fetal . . . . . . . . . . . . . . . . . . . . . . . . 59030

## Scan

*See* Specific Site, Nuclear Medicine
Abdomen
  *See* Abdomen, CT Scan
CT
  *See* CT Scan
MRI
  *See* Magnetic Resonance Imaging

PET
  *See* Positron Emission Tomography
Radionuclide
  *See* Emission Computerized Tomography
SPECT
  *See* SPECT

## Scanning, Radioisotope

*See* Nuclear Medicine

## Scanogram . . . . . . . . . . . . . . . . . . 77073

## Scaphoid

Fracture
  Closed Treatment. . . . . . . . . . . . . . . 25622
  Open Treatment . . . . . . . . . . . . . . . 25628
  with Manipulation . . . . . . . . . . . . . . 25624
Nonunion
  Repair. . . . . . . . . . . . . . . . . . . . . 25440
Replacement. . . . . . . . . . . . . . . . . . . 25443

## Scapula Bone

Craterization . . . . . . . . . . . . . . . . . . . 23182
Cyst
  Excision . . . . . . . . . . . . . . . . . . . 23140
    with Allograft . . . . . . . . . . . . . . . 23146
    with Autograft . . . . . . . . . . . . . . . 23145
Diaphysectomy . . . . . . . . . . . . . . . . . . 23182
Excision
  Partial. . . . . . . . . . . . 23172, 23182, 23190
Fracture
  Closed Treatment
    with Manipulation . . . . . . . . . . . . . 23575
    without Manipulation . . . . . . . . . . . 23570
  Open Treatment . . . . . . . . . . . . . . . 23585
Ostectomy. . . . . . . . . . . . . . . . . . . . 23190
Repair
  Fixation. . . . . . . . . . . . . . . . . . . . 23400
  Scapulopexy. . . . . . . . . . . . . . . . . 23400
Saucerization . . . . . . . . . . . . . . . . . . 23182
Sequestrectomy . . . . . . . . . . . . . . . . . 23172
Tumor
  Excision . . . . . . . . . . . . . . . 23140, 23210
    with Allograft . . . . . . . . . . . . . . . 23146
    with Autograft . . . . . . . . . . . . . . . 23145
  Radical Resection . . . . . . . . . . . . . . 23210
X-ray . . . . . . . . . . . . . . . . . . . . . . . 73010

## Scapulopexy . . . . . . . . . . . . . . . . . 23400

## Scarification

Pleural. . . . . . . . . . . . . . . . . . . . . . . 32215

## Scarification of Pleura

*See* Pleurodesis

## Schanz Operation

*See* Femur, Osteotomy

## Schauta Operation

*See* Hysterectomy, Vaginal, Radical

## Schede Procedure . . . . . . . . 32905-32906

## Scheie Procedure . . . . . . . . . . . . . 66155

## Schilling Test . . . . . . . . . . . . . . . . 78270

*See* Vitamin B-12 Absorption Study

## Schlatter Operation Total
## Gastrectomy . . . . . . . . . . . . . 43620-43622

## Schlicter Test . . . . . . . . . . . . . . . . 87197

*See* Bactericidal Titer, Serum

## Schocket Procedure . . . . . . . . . . 66180

*See* Aqueous Shunt

## Schuchard Procedure
Osteotomy
    Maxilla . . . . . . . . . . . . . . . . . . . . . . . . . 21206

## Schwannoma, Acoustic
*See* Brain, Tumor, Excision

## Sciatic Nerve
Decompression . . . . . . . . . . . . . . . . . . . . . 64712
Administration, Anesthetic
    Infusion . . . . . . . . . . . . . . . . . . . . . . . 64446
    Injection . . . . . . . . . . . . . . . . . 64445-64446
Neuroma
    Excision . . . . . . . . . . . . . . . . . . . . . . . 64786
Neuroplasty . . . . . . . . . . . . . . . . . . . . . . . . 64712
Release . . . . . . . . . . . . . . . . . . . . . . . . . . . 64712
Repair/Suture . . . . . . . . . . . . . . . . . . . . . . 64858

## Scintigraphy
*See* Nuclear Medicine
Computed Tomographic
    *See* Emission Computerized Tomography

## Scissoring
Skin Tags . . . . . . . . . . . . . . . . . . . . . 11200-11201

## Sclera
Aqueous Drainage Device
    to Extraocular Reservoir . . . . . . . . . . . . . 66180
    without Extraocular Reservoir . . . . . . . . 66183
Excision
    Sclerectomy with Punch or Scissors . . . . 66160
Fistulization
    for Glaucoma . . . . . . . . . . . . . . . . . . . . . 0123T
    Iridencleisis or Iridotasis . . . . . . . . . . . . . 66165
    Sclerectomy with Punch or Scissors
      with Iridectomy . . . . . . . . . . . . . . . . . 66160
    Thermocauterization with Iridectomy . . . 66155
    Trabeculectomy ab Externo . . . . . 66170, 66172
    Trephination with Iridectomy . . . . . . . . . . 66150
Lesion
    Excision . . . . . . . . . . . . . . . . . . . . . . . . 66130
Repair
    Reinforcement
      with Graft . . . . . . . . . . . . . . . . . . . . . 67255
      without Graft . . . . . . . . . . . . . . . . . . . 67250
    Staphyloma
      with Graft . . . . . . . . . . . . . . . . . . . . . 66225
      without Graft . . . . . . . . . . . . . . . . . . . 66220
    with Glue . . . . . . . . . . . . . . . . . . . . . . . 65286
    Wound
      Operative . . . . . . . . . . . . . . . . . . . . . 66250
      Tissue Glue . . . . . . . . . . . . . . . . . . . . 65286

## Scleral Buckling Operation
*See* Retina, Repair, Detachment

## Scleral Ectasia
*See* Staphyloma, Sclera

## Sclerectomy . . . . . . . . . . . . . . . . . . . . . 66160

## Sclerotherapy
Esophageal Varices . . . . . . . . . . . . . 43204, 43243
Gastric Varices . . . . . . . . . . . . . . . . . . . . . 43243
Hemorrhoids . . . . . . . . . . . . . . . . . . . . . . . 46500
Perirectal . . . . . . . . . . . . . . . . . . . . . . . . . 45520
Venous . . . . . . . . . . . . . . . . . . . . . 36468-36471

## Sclerotomy
*See* Incision, Sclera

## Screening, Drug
*See* Drug Screen
Alcohol and/or Substance Abuse . . . . 99408-99409

## Scribner Cannulization . . . . . . . . . 36810

## Scrotal Varices
*See* Varicocele

## Scrotoplasty . . . . . . . . . . . . . . . 55175-55180

## Scrotum
Abscess
    Incision and Drainage . . . . . . . . . 54700, 55100
Exploration . . . . . . . . . . . . . . . . . . . . . . . 55110
Hematoma
    Incision and Drainage . . . . . . . . . . . . . . 54700
Removal
    Foreign Body . . . . . . . . . . . . . . . . . . . . 55120
Repair . . . . . . . . . . . . . . . . . . . . . 55175-55180
Resection . . . . . . . . . . . . . . . . . . . . . . . . 55150
Ultrasound . . . . . . . . . . . . . . . . . . . . . . . 76870
Unlisted Services and Procedures . . . . . . . 55899

## Scrub Typhus . . . . . . . . . . . . . . . . . . . 86000

## Second Look Surgery
*See* Reoperation

## Section
*See* Decompression
Cesarean
    *See* Cesarean Delivery
Cranial Nerve . . . . . . . . . . . . . . . . . . . . . 61460
    Spinal Access . . . . . . . . . . . . . . . . . . . . 63191
Dentate Ligament . . . . . . . . . . . . . . 63180-63182
Gasserian Ganglion
    Sensory Root . . . . . . . . . . . . . . . . . . . . 61450
Medullary Tract . . . . . . . . . . . . . . . . . . . . 61470
Mesencephalic Tract . . . . . . . . . . . . . . . . 61480
Nerve Root . . . . . . . . . . . . . . . . . . . 63185-63190
Spinal Accessory Nerve . . . . . . . . . . . . . . 63191
Spinal Cord Tract . . . . . . . . . . . . . . 63194-63199
Tentorium Cerebelli . . . . . . . . . . . . . . . . . 61440
Vestibular Nerve
    Transcranial Approach . . . . . . . . . . . . . . 69950
    Translabyrinthine Approach . . . . . . . . . . 69915

## Sedation
Moderate . . . . . . . . . . . . . . . . . . 99143-99150
    with Independent Observation . . 99143-99145

## Seddon-Brookes Procedure . . . . 24320

## Sedimentation Rate
Blood Cell
    Automated . . . . . . . . . . . . . . . . . . . . . . 85652
    Manual . . . . . . . . . . . . . . . . . . . . . . . . 85651

## Segmentectomy
Breast . . . . . . . . . . . . . . . . . . . . . . 19301-19302
Lung . . . . . . . . . . . . . . . . . . . . . . . . . . . 32484
    Thoracoscopic . . . . . . . . . . . . . . . . . . . 32669

## Seidlitz Powder Test
*See* X-ray, with Contrast

## Selective Catheterization
Arterial
    First Order
      Abdominal . . . . . . . . . . . . . . . . . . . . . 36245
      Brachiocephalic Branch . . . . . . . . . . . 36215
      Lower Extremity . . . . . . . . . . . . . . . . . 36245
      Pelvic . . . . . . . . . . . . . . . . . . . . . . . . 36245
      Renal . . . . . . . . . . . . . . . . . . . 36251-36252
      Thoracic Branch . . . . . . . . . . . . . . . . . 36215
    Second Order
      Abdominal . . . . . . . . . . . . . . . . . . . . . 36246
      Brachiocephalic Branch . . . . . . . . . . . 36216
      Lower Extremity . . . . . . . . . . . . . . . . . 36246
      Pelvic . . . . . . . . . . . . . . . . . . . . . . . . 36246
      Thoracic Branch . . . . . . . . . . . . . . . . . 36216

Superselective
    Abdominal . . . . . . . . . . . . . . . 36247-36248
    Brachiocephalic Branch . . . . . . 36217-36218
    Lower Extremity . . . . . . . . . . . 36247-36248
    Pelvic . . . . . . . . . . . . . . . . . . 36247-36248
    Renal . . . . . . . . . . . . . . . . . . 36253-36254
    Thoracic Branch . . . . . . . . . . . 36217-36218
    Pulmonary . . . . . . . . . . . . . . . 36014-36015
Venous
    First Order Branch . . . . . . . . . . . . . . . . 36011
    Second Order Branch . . . . . . . . . . . . . . 36012
with Angiography
    Carotid Arch . . . . . . . . . . . . . . 36223-36224
    Carotid Artery . . . . . 36222-36224, 36227-36228
    Cervicocerebral Arch . . . . . . . . 36222-36226
    Innominate Artery . . . . . . 36222-36223, 36225
    Subclavian Artery . . . . . . . . . . . . . . . . 36225
    Vertebral Vessels . . . . . . 36225-36226, 36228

## Selective Cellular Enhancement
## Technique . . . . . . . . . . . . . . . . . . . . . 88112

## Selenium . . . . . . . . . . . . . . . . . . . . . . 84255

## Self Care
*See* Physical Medicine/Therapy/Occupational
Therapy
Training . . . . . . . . . . . 97535, 98960-98962, 99509

## Sella Turcica
CT Scan . . . . . . . . . . . . . . . . . . . . 70480-70482
X-ray . . . . . . . . . . . . . . . . . . . . . . . . . . . 70240

## Semen
*See* Sperm

## Semen Analysis . . . . . . . . . . . 89300-89322
Sperm Analysis . . . . . . . . . . . . . . . . . . . . 89331
    Antibodies . . . . . . . . . . . . . . . . . . . . . 89325
with Sperm Isolation . . . . . . . . . . . . 89260-89261

## Semenogelase
*See* Antigen, Prostate Specific

## Semicircular Canal
Fenestration . . . . . . . . . . . . . . . . . . . . . . 69820
    Revised . . . . . . . . . . . . . . . . . . . . . . . . 69840

## Semilunar
Bone
    *See* Lunate
Ganglion
    *See* Gasserian Ganglion

## Seminal Vesicle
Cyst
    Excision . . . . . . . . . . . . . . . . . . . . . . . 55680
Excision . . . . . . . . . . . . . . . . . . . . . . . . . 55650
Incision . . . . . . . . . . . . . . . . . . . . 55600-55605
Mullerian Duct
    Excision . . . . . . . . . . . . . . . . . . . . . . . 55680
Unlisted Services and Procedures . . . . . . . 55899
Vesiculography . . . . . . . . . . . . . . . . . . . . 74440
X-ray with Contrast . . . . . . . . . . . . . . . . . 74440

## Seminin
*See* Antigen, Prostate Specific

## Semiquantitative . . . . . . . . . . . . . . 81005

## Sengstaken Tamponade
Esophagus . . . . . . . . . . . . . . . . . . . . . . . 43460

## Senning Procedure . . . . . . . . 33774-33777
*See* Repair, Great Arteries; Revision

## Senning Type . . . . . . . . . . . . . . 33774-33777

Index

**Index**

## SRS/SBRT (Stereotactic Body Radiation Therapy)
Thoracic
*See* Radiation Therapy, Stereotactic Body, Target Delineation, Thoracic

## Ssabanejew-Frank Operation ................. 43830-43832

## Stabilizing Factor, Fibrin
*See* Fibrin Stabilizing Factor

## Stable Factor ..................... 85230

## Stallard Procedure
*See* Conjunctivorhinostomy

## Stamey Procedure ............... 51845

## Standby Services ................ 99360

## Stanford-Binet Test
*See* Psychiatric Diagnosis, Psychological Testing

## Stapedectomy
Revision ......................... 69662
with Footplate Drill Out ................ 69661
without Foreign Material ............... 69660

## Stapedotomy
Revision ......................... 69662
with Footplate Drill Out ............... 69661
without Foreign Material ............... 69660

## Stapes
Excision
　with Footplate Drill Out .............. 69661
　without Foreign Material ............. 69660
Mobilization ........................ 69650
Release ........................... 69650
Revision ........................... 69662

## Staphyloma
Sclera
　Repair
　　with Graft ...................... 66225
　　without Graft ................... 66220

## Statin Therapy
*See* Performance Measures, Coronary Artery Disease

## Statistics/Biometry
*See* Biometry

## Steindler Stripping ............. 28250

## Stellate Ganglion
Injection
　Anesthetic ...................... 64510

## Stem Cell
Cell Concentration ................... 38215
Count ............................ 86367
Cryopreservation .............. 38207, 88240
Donor Search ...................... 38204
Harvesting .................... 38205-38206
Hematopoietic Progenitor Cells
　*See* Hematopoietic Progenitor Cells
Limbal
　Allograft ....................... 65781
Plasma Depletion .................... 38214
Platelet Depletion ................... 38213
Red Blood Cell Depletion .............. 38212
T-Cell Depletion .................... 38210
Thawing ............... 38208-38209, 88241
Transplantation ............... 38240-38242
Tumor Cell Depletion ................. 38211

Washing ......................... 38209

## Stem, Brain
*See* Brainstem

## Stenger Test ............... 92565, 92577
*See* Audiologic Function Test; Ear, Nose, and Throat

## Stenosis
Aortic
　*See* Aortic Stenosis
Auditory Canal, External
　Reconstruction .................... 69310
Bronchi ...................... , 96570-96571
　Reconstruction ................... 31775
　Relief ......................... 31641
Laryngeal
　Repair ......................... 31582
Nasal
　Repair ......................... 30465
Pulmonary Artery
　Repair .................... 33782, 33917
Pulmonary Vein
　Repair ......................... 33726
Tracheal
　Excision .................... 31780-31781
Urethral
　*See* Urethral Stenosis
Ventricular
　Resection ....................... 33476

## Stensen Duct
*See* Parotid Duct

## Stent
Exchange
　Biliary Duct ...................... 43276
　Pancreatic Duct .................. 43276
for Revascularization
　Intracoronary ............... 92937-92938, 92941, 92943-92944
Indwelling
　Insertion
　　Ureter ....... 50605, 52282, 52356, 53855
Placement
　Bronchial ........... 31631, 31636-31637
　Cardiac ......................... 33621
　Colonoscopy ..................... 45397
　　via Stoma ..................... 44397
　Endoscopy
　　Bile Duct ..................... 43274
　　Gastrointestinal, Upper ........... 43266
　　Intestinal ..................... 44379
　　Pancreatic Duct ................ 43274
　Enteroscopy ..................... 44370
　Esophagoscopy ................... 43212
　Ileoscopy ....................... 44383
　Proctosigmoidoscopy .............. 45327
　Sigmoidoscopy ................... 45345
　Tracheal ....................... 31631
　Transcatheter
　　Intracoronary ............. 92928-92929
　　Intravascular ... 37215-37217, 37236-37239
　　　Extracranial ............. 0075T-0076T
　Ureteroneocystostomy ........ 50947-50948
Removal
　Ureteral .................... 50382-50387
Replacement
　Ureteral .................. 50382, 50387
Revision
　Bronchoscopy ................... 31638
Transcatheter
　Intravascular
　　Intracranial ................... 61635

Transluminal Placement
　Arterial ........ 37221, 37223, 37226-37227, 37230-37231, 37234-37235
Urethra ......................... 52282

## Stent, Intravascular
*See* Transcatheter, Placement, Intravascular Stents

## Stents, Tracheal
*See* Tracheal, Stent

## Stereotactic Body Radiation Therapy (SRS/SBRT)
Thoracic
*See* Radiation Therapy, Stereotactic Body, Target Delineation

## Stereotactic Frame
Application/Removal ................... 20660

## Stereotaxis
Aspiration
　Brain Lesion ..................... 61750
　　with CT Scan and/or MRI .......... 61751
　Spinal Cord ..................... 63615
Biopsy
　Aspiration
　　Brain Lesion ................... 61750
　Brain .......................... 61750
　　with CT Scan and/or MRI .......... 61751
　Breast ............ 19081, 19283, 19284
　Prostate ........................ 55706
　Spinal Cord ..................... 63615
Catheter Placement
　Brain
　　Infusion ...................... 0169T
　　Radiation Source ................ 61770
Computer Assisted
　Cranial Procedure ........... 61781-61782
　Orthopedic Surgery .......... 20985-20987
　Spinal Procedure ................. 61783
Creation Lesion
　Brain
　　Deep .................. 61720-61735
　　Percutaneous .................. 61790
　　Gasserian Ganglion ............. 61790
　　Spinal Cord ................... 63600
　　Trigeminal Tract ............... 61791
CT Scan
　Aspiration ....................... 61751
　Biopsy ......................... 61751
Excision Lesion
　Brain .......................... 61750
　Spinal Cord ..................... 63615
Focus Beam
　Radiosurgery ............... 77371-77373
　Cranial .................. 61796-61799
　Spinal ................... 63620-63621
　Stereotactic Frame
　　Application ............... 20660, 61800
Placement
　Localization Device
　　Breast ........ 19081-19082, 19283-19284
Radiation Therapy .......... 77421, 77432-77435
Stimulation
　Spinal Cord ..................... 63610
Target Volume Guidance ............... 77421

## Sterile Coverings
*See* Dressings

## Sternal Fracture
*See* Fracture, Sternum

Index

Index

Index

Index

**Index**

**Index**

# U

Index

Placement of Lesion Localization Device
   Breast . . . . . . . . 19083-19084, 19285-19286
   Pseudoaneurysm . . . . . . . . . . . . . . . . . . 76936
   Radiation Therapy . . . . . . . . . . . . . . . . . 76950
   Radioelement. . . . . . . . . . . . . . . . . . . . . 76965
   Shunt Placement
      Fetal . . . . . . . . . . . . . . . . . . . . . . . . . 59076
   Thoracentesis. . . . . . . . . . . . . . . . . . . . . 76942
   Tissue Ablation . . . . . . . . . . . . . . . . . . . 76940
   Uterine Fibroid Ablation. . . . . . . . . . . . . 0336T
   Vascular Access. . . . . . . . . . . . . . . . . . . 76937
Head . . . . . . . . . . . . . . . . . . . . . 76506, 76536
Heart
   Fetal . . . . . . . . . . . . . . . . . . . . . . . . . . . 76825
Hips
   Infant . . . . . . . . . . . . . . . . . . 76885-76886
Hysterosonography. . . . . . . . . . . . . . . . . . . 76831
Intraoperative . . . . . . . . . . . . . . . . . . . . . . 76998
Intravascular
   Intraoperative. . . . . . . . . . . . . . 37250-37251
Kidney . . . . . . . . . . . . . . . . . . . . 76770-76776
   Complete . . . . . . . . . . . . . . . . . . . . . . 76881
   Limited . . . . . . . . . . . . . . . . . . . . . . . . 76882
Neck . . . . . . . . . . . . . . . . . . . . . . . . . . . . . 76536
Needle or Catheter Placement . . . . . . . . . . . 20555
Non-Coronary
   Intravascular . . . . . . . . . . . . . . 75945-75946
Pelvis. . . . . . . . . . . . . . . . . . . . . . 76856-76857
Pregnant Uterus . . . . . . . . . . . . . . 76801-76817
Prostate. . . . . . . . . . . . . . . . . . . . 76856, 76873
Rectal . . . . . . . . . . . . . . . . . . . . . 76872-76873
Retroperitoneal. . . . . . . . . . . . . . . 76770-76775
Scrotum. . . . . . . . . . . . . . . . . . . . . . . . . . . 76870
Sonohysterography. . . . . . . . . . . . . . . . . . . 76831
Spine . . . . . . . . . . . . . . . . . . . . . . . . . . . . 76800
Therapy
   to Aid Bone Healing. . . . . . . . . . . . . . . 20979
   to Aid Wound Healing . . . . . . . . . . . . . 97605
Umbilical Artery . . . . . . . . . . . . . . . . . . . . . 76820
Unlisted Services and Procedures . . . . . . . . 76999
Uterus
   Tumor Ablation. . . . . . . . . . . . . . 0071T-0072T
Vagina . . . . . . . . . . . . . . . . . . . . . . . . . . . 76830
Wound Therapy. . . . . . . . . . . . . . . . . . . . . 97610

## Ultraviolet Light Therapy

Dermatology
   Ultraviolet A. . . . . . . . . . . . . . . . . . . . . 96912
   Ultraviolet B. . . . . . . . . . . . . . . . . . . . . 96910
for Dermatology . . . . . . . . . . . . . . . . . . . . 96900
for Physical Medicine . . . . . . . . . . . . . . . . . 97028

## Umbilectomy . . . . . . . . . . . . . . . . . . . . 49250

## Umbilical

Artery Ultrasound . . . . . . . . . . . . . . . . . . . 76820
Hernia
   *See* Omphalocele
Vein Catheterization
   *See* Catheterization, Umbilical Vein

## Umbilical Cord

Occlusion. . . . . . . . . . . . . . . . . . . . . . . . . . 59072

## Umbilicus

Excision. . . . . . . . . . . . . . . . . . . . . . . . . . . 49250
Repair
   Hernia. . . . . . . . . . . . . . . . . . . . 49580-49587
   Omphalocele . . . . . . . . . . . . . . . 49600-49611

## Undescended Testicle

*See* Testis, Undescended

## Unfertilized Egg

*See* Ova

## Unguis

*See* Nails

## Unilateral Simple Mastectomy

*See* Mastectomy

## Unlisted Services and
## Procedures . . . . . . . . . . . . . . . 99499, 99600

Abdomen. . . . . . . . . . . . . . 22999, 49329, 49999
Allergy/Immunology . . . . . . . . . . . . . . . . . . 95199
Anal. . . . . . . . . . . . . . . . . . . . . . . . . . . . . . 46999
Anesthesia . . . . . . . . . . . . . . . . . . . . . . . . 01999
Arm . . . . . . . . . . . . . . . . . . . . . . . . . . . . . . 25999
Arthroscopy. . . . . . . . . . . . . . . . . . . . . . . . 29999
Autopsy. . . . . . . . . . . . . . . . . . . . . . . . . . . 88099
Bile Duct . . . . . . . . . . . . . . . . . . . . . . . . . . 47999
Bladder . . . . . . . . . . . . . . . . . . . . . . . . . . . 51999
Brachytherapy. . . . . . . . . . . . . . . . . . . . . . 77799
Breast . . . . . . . . . . . . . . . . . . . . . . . . . . . . 19499
Bronchi . . . . . . . . . . . . . . . . . . . . . . . . . . . 31899
Cardiac . . . . . . . . . . . . . . . . . . . . . . . . . . . 33999
Cardiovascular Studies. . . . . . . . . . . . . . . . 93799
Casting . . . . . . . . . . . . . . . . . . . . . . . . . . . 29799
Cervix . . . . . . . . . . . . . . . . . . . . . . . . . . . . 58999
Chemistry Procedure. . . . . . . . . . . . . . . . . . 84999
Chemotherapy. . . . . . . . . . . . . . . . . . . . . . 96549
Chest. . . . . . . . . . . . . . . . . . . . . . . . . . . . . 32999
Coagulation. . . . . . . . . . . . . . . . . . . . . . . . 85999
Colon. . . . . . . . . . . . . . . . . . . . . . . . . . . . . 44799
Conjunctiva Surgery . . . . . . . . . . . . . . . . . . 68399
Craniofacial. . . . . . . . . . . . . . . . . . . . . . . . 21299
CT Scan . . . . . . . . . . . . . . . . . . . . . . . . . . . 76497
Cytogenetic Study. . . . . . . . . . . . . . . . . . . . 88299
Cytopathology. . . . . . . . . . . . . . . . . . . . . . 88199
Dermatology . . . . . . . . . . . . . . . . . . . . . . . 96999
Dialysis . . . . . . . . . . . . . . . . . . . . . . . . . . . 90999
Diaphragm. . . . . . . . . . . . . . . . . . . . . . . . . 39599
Ear
   External . . . . . . . . . . . . . . . . . . . . . . . . 69399
   Inner. . . . . . . . . . . . . . . . . . . . . . . . . . . 69949
   Middle . . . . . . . . . . . . . . . . . . . . . . . . . 69799
Endocrine System . . . . . . . . . . . . . . . . . . . 60699
Epididymis. . . . . . . . . . . . . . . . . . . . . . . . . 55899
Esophagus. . . . . . . . . . . . . . . . . 43289, 43499
Evaluation and Management Services. . . . . . 99499
Eye Muscle . . . . . . . . . . . . . . . . . . . . . . . . 67399
Eye Surgery
   Anterior Segment. . . . . . . . . . . . . . . . . 66999
   Posterior Segment . . . . . . . . . . . . . . . . 67299
Eyelid. . . . . . . . . . . . . . . . . . . . . . . . . . . . . 67999
Fluoroscopy. . . . . . . . . . . . . . . . . . . . . . . . 76496
Forearm. . . . . . . . . . . . . . . . . . . . . . . . . . . 25999
Gallbladder . . . . . . . . . . . . . . . . . . . . . . . . 47999
Gastroenterology Test. . . . . . . . . . . . . . . . . 91299
Gum. . . . . . . . . . . . . . . . . . . . . . . . . . . . . . 41899
Hand . . . . . . . . . . . . . . . . . . . . . . . . . . . . . 26989
Hemic System . . . . . . . . . . . . . . . . . . . . . . 38999
Hepatic Duct . . . . . . . . . . . . . . . . . . . . . . . 47999
Hip Joint . . . . . . . . . . . . . . . . . . . . . . . . . . 27299
Home Services . . . . . . . . . . . . . . . . . . . . . . 99600
Hysteroscopy. . . . . . . . . . . . . . . . . . . . . . . 58579
Immunization. . . . . . . . . . . . . . . . . . . . . . . 90749
Immunology. . . . . . . . . . . . . . . . . . . . . . . . 86849
Infusion. . . . . . . . . . . . . . . . . . . . . . . . . . . 96379
Injection . . . . . . . . . . . . . . . . . . . . . . . . . . 96379
Injection of Medication. . . . . . . . . . . . . . . . 96379
Intestine . . . . . . . . . . . . . . . . . . . 44238, 44799
Kidney. . . . . . . . . . . . . . . . . . . . . . . . . . . . 53899
Lacrimal System . . . . . . . . . . . . . . . . . . . . 68899
Laparoscopy . 38129, 38589, 43289, 43659, 44238,
44979, 47379, 47579, 49329, 49659, 50549, 50949,
54699, 55559, 58578, 58679, 59898, 60659
Larynx . . . . . . . . . . . . . . . . . . . . . . . . . . . . 31599
Lip . . . . . . . . . . . . . . . . . . . . . . . . . . . . . . . 40799

Liver. . . . . . . . . . . . . . . . . . . . . . . . 47379, 47399
Lungs. . . . . . . . . . . . . . . . . . . . . . . . . . . . . 32999
Lymphatic System. . . . . . . . . . . . . . . . . . . . 38999
Magnetic Resonance . . . . . . . . . . . . . . . . . 76498
Maxillofacial. . . . . . . . . . . . . . . . . . . . . . . . 21299
Maxillofacial Prosthetics . . . . . . . . . . . . . . . 21089
Meckel's Diverticulum . . . . . . . . . . . . . . . . . 44899
Mediastinum. . . . . . . . . . . . . . . . . . . . . . . . 39499
Mesentery Surgery . . . . . . . . . . . . . . . . . . . 44899
Microbiology. . . . . . . . . . . . . . . . . . . . . . . . 87999
Mouth . . . . . . . . . . . . . . . . . . . . 40899, 41599
Musculoskeletal . . . . . . . . . . . . . 25999, 26989
Musculoskeletal Surgery
   Abdominal Wall . . . . . . . . . . . . . . . . . . 22999
   Neck . . . . . . . . . . . . . . . . . . . . . . . . . . . 21899
   Spine . . . . . . . . . . . . . . . . . . . . . . . . . . 22899
   Thorax . . . . . . . . . . . . . . . . . . . . . . . . . 21899
Musculoskeletal System. . . . . . . . . . . . . . . 20999
   Ankle . . . . . . . . . . . . . . . . . . . . . . . . . . 27899
   Arm, Upper. . . . . . . . . . . . . . . . . . . . . . 24999
   Elbow . . . . . . . . . . . . . . . . . . . . . . . . . . 24999
   Head. . . . . . . . . . . . . . . . . . . . . . . . . . . 21499
   Knee . . . . . . . . . . . . . . . . . . . . . . . . . . . 27599
   Leg, Lower . . . . . . . . . . . . . . . . . . . . . . 27899
   Leg, Upper . . . . . . . . . . . . . . . . . . . . . . 27599
Necropsy. . . . . . . . . . . . . . . . . . . . . . . . . . 88099
Nervous System Surgery . . . . . . . . . . . . . . . 64999
Neurology/Neuromuscular Testing. . . . . . . . . 95999
Noninvasive Vascular Study . . . . . . . . . . . . . 93998
Nose . . . . . . . . . . . . . . . . . . . . . . . . . . . . . 30999
Nuclear Medicine . . . . . . . . . . . . . . . . . . . . 78999
   Blood . . . . . . . . . . . . . . . . . . . . . . . . . . 78199
   Bone . . . . . . . . . . . . . . . . . . . . . . . . . . . 78399
   Endocrine System . . . . . . . . . . . . . . . . . 78099
   Genitourinary System . . . . . . . . . . . . . . 78799
   Heart . . . . . . . . . . . . . . . . . . . . . . . . . . 78499
   Hematopoietic System. . . . . . . . . . . . . . 78199
   Lymphatic System . . . . . . . . . . . . . . . . . 78199
   Musculoskeletal System . . . . . . . . . . . . 78399
   Nervous System. . . . . . . . . . . . . . . . . . . 78699
   Therapeutic . . . . . . . . . . . . . . . . . . . . . 79999
Obstetrical Care . . . . . . . . . . . . . . 59898-59899
Omentum. . . . . . . . . . . . . . . . . . . 49329, 49999
Ophthalmology . . . . . . . . . . . . . . . . . . . . . 92499
Orbit . . . . . . . . . . . . . . . . . . . . . . . . . . . . . 67599
Otorhinolaryngology . . . . . . . . . . . . . . . . . . 92700
Ovary. . . . . . . . . . . . . . . . . . . . . . 58679, 58999
Oviduct . . . . . . . . . . . . . . . . . . . . 58679, 58999
Palate . . . . . . . . . . . . . . . . . . . . . . . . . . . . 42299
Pancreas Surgery . . . . . . . . . . . . . . . . . . . . 48999
Pathology . . . . . . . . . . . . . . . . . . . . . . . . . 89240
Pelvis. . . . . . . . . . . . . . . . . . . . . . . . . . . . . 27299
Penis . . . . . . . . . . . . . . . . . . . . . . . . . . . . . 55899
Peritoneum . . . . . . . . . . . . . . . . . 49329, 49999
Pharynx . . . . . . . . . . . . . . . . . . . . . . . . . . . 42999
Physical Therapy. . . . . . . . . . 97039, 97139, 97799
Pleura . . . . . . . . . . . . . . . . . . . . . . . . . . . . 32999
Pressure Ulcer. . . . . . . . . . . . . . . . . . . . . . . 15999
Preventive Medicine. . . . . . . . . . . . . . . . . . . 99429
Prostate. . . . . . . . . . . . . . . . . . . . . . . . . . . 55899
Psychiatric. . . . . . . . . . . . . . . . . . . . . . . . . 90899
Pulmonology . . . . . . . . . . . . . . . . . . . . . . . 94799
Radiation Physics . . . . . . . . . . . . . . . . . . . . 77399
Radiation Therapy. . . . . . . . . . . . . . . . . . . . 77499
   Planning . . . . . . . . . . . . . . . . . . . . . . . . 77299
Radiology, Diagnostic . . . . . . . . . . . . . . . . . 76499
Radionuclide Therapy . . . . . . . . . . . . . . . . . 79999
Radiopharmaceutical Therapy . . . . . . . . . . . 79999
Rectum . . . . . . . . . . . . . . . . . . . . 45499, 45999
Reproductive Medicine
   Laboratory Procedure. . . . . . . . . . . . . . . 89398
Salivary Gland. . . . . . . . . . . . . . . . . . . . . . . 42699
Scrotum. . . . . . . . . . . . . . . . . . . . . . . . . . . 55899

# V

Index

Index

# X

## X, Coagulation Factor
*See* Stuart-Prower Factor

## X, Cranial Nerve
*See* Vagus Nerve

## X-Linked Ichthyoses
*See* Syphilis Test

## X-ray

## X-ray Tomography, Computed
See CT Scan

## Xa, Coagulation Factor
See Thrombokinase

## Xenoantibodies
See Antibody, Heterophile

## Xenografts, Skin
See Allograft, Skin Substitute

## Xenotransplantation
See Heterograft

## XI, Coagulation Factor
See Plasma Thromboplastin, Antecedent

## XI, Cranial Nerve
See Accessory Nerve

## XII, Coagulation Factor
See Hageman Factor

**XII, Cranial Nerve**
*See* Hypoglossal Nerve

**XIII, Coagulation Factor**
*See* Fibrin Stabilizing Factor

**Xylose Absorption Test**
Blood................................. 84620
Urine................................. 84620

# Y

**Yacoub Procedure**
*See* Ascending Aorta Graft

**Yeast**
Culture................................ 87106

**Yellow Fever Vaccine**........... 90717

**Yersinia**
Antibody.............................. 86793

**YHrium-Aluminum-Garnet (YAG) Laser**
*See* Eye, Incision

# Z

**Ziegler Procedure**
Discission Secondary Membranous
Cataract.............................. 66820

**Zinc**............................... 84630

**Zinc Manganese Leucine Aminopeptidase**
*See* Leucine Aminopeptidase

**Zonisamide**
Drug Assay........................... 80203

**Zygoma**
*See* Cheekbone

**Zygomatic Arch**
Fracture
   Open Treatment.............. 21356-21366
   with Manipulation.................. 21355
Reconstruction........................ 21255